ANALYTICAL CONCORDANCE TO THE GARŠANA ARCHIVES

To Jonathan and Jeannette Rosen
In Gratitude

The publication of this volume was made possible
thanks to generous subventions from
The Abner Rosen Foundation
and
The Joseph Rosen Foundation

Cornell University Studies in
Assyriology and Sumerology
(CUSAS)

Volume 4

Analytical Concordance to the Garšana Archives

by
Alexandra Kleinerman and David I. Owen

CDL Press
Bethesda, Maryland
2009

Library of Congress Cataloging-in-Publication

Alexandra Kleinerman and Owen, David I.
Analytical Concordance to the Garšana archives / by Alexandra Kleinerman and David I. Owen.
p. cm. — (Cornell University studies in Assyriology and Sumerology; v. 4)
With English translation
Includes bibliographical references and index.
ISBN 978-1934309-032
1. Owen, David I. Garšana archives—Concordances. 2. Owen, David I. Garšana archives—Indexes.
3. Sumerian language—Texts—Concordances. 4. Sumerian language—Glossaries, vocabularies, etc.
5. Garšana (Extinct city)—Concordances. I. Owen, David I . II. Title. III. Series.
PJ4054.G37O94 2007 index
499'.95—dc22 2008051194

Cover and title page drawings of Garšana seal 73a by Rudolf Mayr

Preface

The publication of CUSAS 3 with over 1500 texts precluded the inclusion of indexes in the same volume. It was our intention to publish this Concordance together with that volume, but the sheer size and complexity of the Concordance necessitated a longer production time. Nevertheless, we hope that a delay did not result in any inconvenience to the readers.

The publication of texts from the Third Dynasty of Ur has often been characterized by an absence of transliterations and translations but also of comprehensive indexes to the tablets, often published only in hand copies. The lack of up-to-date Sumerian dictionaries as well as adequate studies of the difficult and complex terminology of the economic texts were often the reasons for a reluctance to provide indexes and, even when provided, to accompany them with adequate translations. When translations were offered they were often vague or general and tended to repeat themselves from volume to volume without any critical updating. In addition, context was rarely, if ever, included in the indexing of the volumes.

Much has changed over the past two decades. The application of computer technology to Assyriology has made the study of the vast Ur III archives easier and more efficient. The creation of both the *CDLI* and *BDTNS* projects, respectively in Berlin/Los Angeles and Madrid, now allows for comprehensive searches of data that previously was impossible or too time-consuming. Furthermore, the beginning of the *Pennsylvania Sumerian Dictionary* (*PSD*) and its continuation, the Internet *ePSD*, coupled with the nearly completed *Chicago Assyrian Dictionary* (*CAD*) and numerous lexical studies, have greatly facilitated the study of the Sumerian terminology found in these texts. Wolfgang Heimpel generously put at our disposal his preliminary chapters to his forthcoming commentary on the Garšana texts (CUSAS 5), which includes extensive additions and clarifications to previous understanding of the terminology found in these and other texts. It is safe to say that without his work much of our translations would have been impossible, although he is not responsible for these translations and interpretations that sometime differ from his. The convergence of all these factors encouraged us to undertake the ambitious Concordance published below. We concluded that the discovery, recovery, and publication of the Garšana archives were significant catalysts to warrant this undertaking, particularly at a time when there are serious attempts to suppress the publication of unprovenanced texts and artifacts whose loss would greatly effect the study of the history and culture of Mesopotamia and the ancient Near East.

Alexandra Kleinerman and
David I. Owen
Cornell University, Ithaca
March, 2009

Acknowledgments

What began as a standard index slowly evolved into a massive concordance, whose creation would not have been possible without the support and assistance of several individuals. First and foremost, it could not have been completed without access to the preliminary drafts of Wolfgang Heimpel's, *Workers and Construction Work in Garšana* (CUSAS 5). His extraordinary analysis of these texts and resultant translations proved invaluable. Likewise, Hagan Brunke's 2008, Inaugural-Dissertation zur Erlangung des Doktorgrades der Philosophie an der Ludwig-Maximilians-Universität München, "Essen in Sumer: Metrologie, Herstellung und Terminologie nach Zeugnis der Ur-III-zeitlichen Wirtschaftsurkunden," provided additional restorations and occasionally more specific translations. Both Heimpel and Brunke promptly answered countless queries, enabling a much more complete understanding of the previously unattested or obscure terminology found throughout these archives. Bram Jagersma and Walther Sallaberger provided a number of helpful suggestions. For the terminology of the textile archive, we have benefited from Hartmut Waetzoldt's preliminary remarks on these texts.

Alhena Gadotti, Rosen Foundation Faculty Associate, Department of Near Eastern Studies, Cornell University, was instrumental in preparing this volume for publication. She was responsible for entering hundreds of corrections and proofing multiple drafts. Without her meticulous organization and precision the completion of the concordance would have been much delayed. Lance Allred, Rosen Foundation Faculty Associate, Department of Near Eastern Studies, Cornell University, carefully read numerous drafts of this volume at various stages. His editorial skills in general and his ability to recognize inconsistencies in particular proved to be invaluable. We are very grateful for their help and support. Lisa Kinney-Bajwa, Rosen Foundation Conservator and Photographer, Department of Near Eastern Studies, Cornell University, provided numerous and superb photographs that greatly aided collations.

This research and publication project could not have existed without the unfailing and extraordinary support of Jonathan and Jeannette Rosen to whom this volume is gratefully dedicated.

Alexandra Kleinerman and
David I. Owen
Cornell University, Ithaca
March, 2009

Table of Contents

Introduction

This Concordance began as a standard index of terms. However, it soon became apparent that the Garšana archives were not the usual assemblage of Ur III texts and thus required a new approach. Because the majority of texts contains much new terminology and longer and more complex syntax than is normally found in Ur III economic archives, we decided to provide complete contexts for all lexical and other terms. Furthermore, because of the formulaic nature of many of the texts, the creation of full contextual references enabled us to include numerous and reliable restorations to damaged passages throughout the archives. It was our intention to attempt complete translations in order to facilitate wider access to this rich new body of data than is usually available in traditional Ur III text publications to those not versed in Sumerian. Wolfgang Heimpel's concomitant work on his *Workers and Construction Work in Garšana* (CUSAS 5) provided much needed clarification of the new terminology found throughout the archives and greatly facilitated the completion of this effort. The concordance is designed to provide scholars and students with a unique tool to further research not just in the Garšana archives but also to integrate these archives into the wider world of Ur III and Mesopotamian studies. It should make the interpretation of the Garšana texts easier and result in an improved and expanded understanding of Ur III society and culture. Indeed, these data will provide many new insights into Sumerian and Babylonian civilization of the late third millennium. The unusual variety of these data will have wider applications for archaeologists, anthropologists, and cultural historians.

The Concordance is composed of several parts, each of which is arranged alphabetically. The initial Glossary provides a listing and definition for each of the terms appearing in the archive with the exception of proper names. In some instances, terms are cross-referenced and the reader is directed elsewhere for fuller citations. An example, using the term barag, is presented here:

barag, *bašamu,* "sack; a part of an animal's body," 848:1, 1272:10

^{kuš}a-g̃á-lá **barag**-bi maš-dà, "gazelle skin leather sack" > ^{kuš}**a-g̃á-lá**

^{kuš}a-g̃á-lá-**barag**-bi udu, "sheep-skin leather sack" > ^{kuš}**a-g̃á-lá**

barag-siki-ud$_5$, "goat-hair sack" > **siki**

The entry notes that the term in question occurs on its own in two texts, nos. 848 and 1272. The term also appears with additional qualifiers and in particular contexts elsewhere in the archive. As noted above, in such cases, the reader is directed to the proper location for the full citation and translation of the passages.

The Glossary also includes several alphabetically arranged thematic lists. These include:

Adjectives,
Agricultural Products,
Akkadian Words,
Animals,
Bovines,
Breads and Cakes,
Caprids,
Cereals and Grains,
Deities,
Equids,

Fowl,
Leather Products,
Metals,
Professions,
Reed Products,
Relative Clauses,
Stones,
Orthographically Written Sumerian,
Temples,
Textiles,
Tools,
Toponyms,
Verbs (simple, compound and reduplicated),
Vessels,
Wood Products.

Thus, for example, a reader interested in knowing which metals are attested in the Garšana archives can quickly find such information by looking under Metals.

Following the Glossary are several Analytical Indexes. These consist of thematic groupings of terms arranged so as to provide translations and citations with context. In effect, they serve as a more focused glossary for specific terms that regularly appear in the corpus. Thus, a reader interested in attestations of Inana at Garšana can consult the Analytical Index of Deities to find the various contexts in which the goddess appears and, moreover, can quickly compare her attestations to those of other deities. Similarly, the Analytical Index of Verbs enables a researcher to study the full semantic range of a verb as it appears in the Garšana corpus.

The volume concludes with a general index of the related Umma, G̃irsu, and unprovenanced texts. Improved readings or restorations made after the original publication of the transliterations are provided in a separate list of additions and corrections but have also been integrated into all the relevant passages. As an extra convenience, occasional additions resulting from further study of the texts will be posted on the Cornell University web site, http://cuneiform.library.cornell.edu.

In the transliteration, "(. . .)" indicates the occurrence of text that has not been included in the citation. In the translation, words within "{ }" describe the nature—but are not a translation—of the omitted text indicated by "(. . .)" in the transliteration. Moreover, words within parentheses are used to add to the citation's readability, but do not correspond to any Sumerian term in the transliteration.

Many terms and phrases found in Ur III documents remain obscure and difficult to translate, and the case of the Garšana archives is no exception. What follows, then, should be considered to be only a starting point for the study of the Garšana material. Indeed, in many places the translations offered must be considered provisional at best. Untranslated, tentative or uncertain translations are marked by double asterisks (**). The use of "(?)" in the translation reflects a passage in the Sumerian that cannot be translated. A "?" immediately following a term indicates a tentative translation. No doubt subsequent investigations will improve upon these translations. Finally, many translations in this Concordance are based on the analyses of Heimpel and other contributors to commentaries in preparation. Justification for these translations will be found in CUSAS 5 and 6.

The publication of the Garšana archives represents a major step forward in our understanding of the complex nature of Ur III history, society, and culture. It provides for the first time a detailed and expanded provincial view of an Akkadian community in the Sumerian heartland of the Umma province.[1] This will be followed shortly by an equally important archive from the poorly documented and possibly nearby city of Iri-Sag̃rig/*Āl-Šarrāki*.[2] Together they demonstrate the importance of providing quick and comprehensive publication of unprovenanced texts.

1 Adams, 2008. This ambitious and thought-provoking study will need to be revised substantially in the light of the new Garšana data.

2 Owen 2009.

Glossary

– A –

a, *mû*, "water"

a . . . bal, "to pour water, to irrigate" > *Verb Index*

a . . . g̃ár, "to waterproof" > *Verb Index*

1. **a im še-g̃á**, "rain(-water)"

a-za-bu-um **a im še-g̃á** ba-al, "to bail out rain-water (from) a cistern" > **ba-al**

a-za-bu-um **a im še-g̃á** dù, "to construct a cistern for rain-water" > **dù**

tuš-a šà **a im še-g̃á**, "sitting (idle) because of rain" > **tuš**

u_4 du_8-ḫa **a im še-g̃á-a**, "{workers} released for a day (because of) rain" > **duḫ**

a . . . bal, *dalû*, "to pour or draw water; to irrigate" > *Verb Index*

a . . . g̃ar, "to waterproof" > *Verb Index*

a-ab-ba, *ajabba*, "body of water, sea, lake"

1. **ég a-ab-ba**, "sea dike"

má saḫar **ég a-ab-ba** sè(g_{10}), "to tamp dirt (delivered by) boat at the sea dike" > **sè(g_{10})**

2. **má a-a-ba**, "sea(-going) boat"

sízkur **má a-a-ba**, "(ceremonial) offerings of the sea(-going) boat" > **sízkur**

★★[o.n.n.] še [n sì]la ì-g̃eš [g̃uruš?] SI $^{g̃eš}$sìg-ga pad-dirig [?] g̃ír-su^{ki} **a-a-ba**-[šè? . . .] níg̃-^{d}b[a-ú-šè?], 970:13–16

a-ba, *mannu*, "who"

a-ba šeš-$g̃u_{10}$-gin_7, "who is like my brother?" 1526:7

a-bu-um, "(a festival)"

ezem-***a-bu-um***-*ma*-šè, "for the *Abum* festival" > **ezem**

a-da-ga, "irrigation ditch"

šu+níĝin 3 ⌜da⌝-n[a 240+]120 nindan ús gú i_7-me-kal-kal *simat-é-a* **a-da-ga**-ta ká-^{d}*šu*-^{d}*suen*-šè, "In total: 3 da-na (and) 360 nindan, the length from the bank of the Mekalkal canal of *Simat-Ea* (and its) irrigation ditch to the *Šu-Suen* gate," 1382:14–16

a-ga-mu-um, *agammu*, "marsh"

i_7-***a-ga-mu-um***, "marsh canal" > *Canal Index*

a-gàr, *ugāru*, "meadow"

in-u **a-gàr**-didli-ta lá, "to transport straw from various meadows" > **lá**

1. **a-gàr ĜEŠ.KÚŠU^{ki}**, "the meadow of ĜEŠ.KÚŠU"

10 géme ⌜kíkken⌝ u_4-1-šè a-rá-1-kam 10 géme kíkken u_4-1-šè a-rá-2-kam 12 géme kíkken u_4-1-šè a-rá-3-kam gi-zi **a-gàr ĜEŠ.KÚŠU^{ki}**-ta gar-ša-an-na^{ki}-⌜šè⌝, "10 female millers for 1 day for the 1st time, 10 female millers for 1 day for the 2nd time, 12 female millers for 1 day for the 3rd time, (having brought) fresh reeds from the meadow of ĜEŠ.KÚŠU to Garšana," 295:1–11

a-gi$_4$-um, *agû*, "(a specification of textiles)"

[^{túg}***a?***]***-gi-um***, "*a-gi$_4$-um* textile," 698:12

gada-⌜gen⌝ ***a-gi$_4$-um***, "ordinary *a-gi$_4$-um* linen textile," 573:1

^{túg}*ḫa-um* ***a-gi$_4$-um*** *simat-^{d}ištaran*, "*a-gi$_4$-um ḫa'um* textile of *Simat-Ištaran*," 581:1

^{túg}níĝ-lám 3-kam-ús ***a-gi$_4$-um***, "3rd-quality *a-gi$_4$-um* níĝ-lám textile," 737:2

^{túg}uš-bar ***a-gi$_4$-um***, "*a-gi$_4$-um* uš-bar textile,"566:1

^{kuš}a-ĝá-lá, *naruqqu*, "leather sack," 1240:2, 1376:62, 1525:2

^{kuš}a-ĝá-lá barag-bi maš-dà, "leather sack, its barag of gazelle skin,"[1] 848:3

^{kuš}a-ĝá-lá barag-bi udu, "leather sack, its barag of sheep skin," 848:2

^{kuš}a-ĝá-lá kéše-rá, "(barley) bound in leather sacks" > **kéše**

^{kuš}a-ĝá-lá-máš, "goat skin leather sack," 1272:2

^{kuš}a-ĝá-lá sumun, "old leather sack," 930:2, 933:2

^{kuš}a-ĝá-lá-udu, "sheep skin leather sack," 1272:1

^{kuš}*maš-lí-um* **^{kuš}a-ĝá-lá** ḫi-a, "various leather buckets and leather sacks," 963:1

ninda **^{kuš}a-ĝá-lá** kéše-rá, "bread in bound leather sacks" > **kéše**

---

1 barag is the container itself whereas ^{kuš}a-ĝá-lá includes the additional bindings etc. that make up the whole sack (Sallaberger, personal communication).

a-g̃á-ri$_{(2)}$-na, **a-g̃á-ri-in**, ***a-ga-ri-nu-um***, *agarinnu*, "pit or basin in which mortar or plaster is mixed"[2]

a-g̃á-ri-in ga$_6$(g̃), "to carry (earth) to the *agarinnum*" > **ga$_6$(g̃)**

a-g̃á-ri-in SUḪUR im g̃ar-ra, "(meaning uncertain)," 192:'17, 194:58–59

g̃á-rí-na lu, "to mix earth in the *agarinnum*" > **lu**

im **a-g̃á-ri-na** dù, "to construct (with) earth (mixed) at the *agarinnum*" > **dù**

im **a-g̃á-ri-na** íl, "to lift earth at the *agarinnum*" > **íl**

im **a-g̃á-ri-na** lu, "to mix earth at the *agarinnum*" > **lu**

im **a-g̃á-ri-na** tuš, "to sit (idle) at the *agarinnum*" > **tuš**

14 g̃u[ruš . . . **a-g̃á**]-**ri-na** g[ub-ba], "14 workmen employed [. . .] at the *agarinnum*," 47:41

a-g̃ar gu$_7$(-a), "de-haired (skin)"[3]

dabin kuš **a-g̃ar gu$_7$-a**-šè, "semolina for (processing) de-haired skins," 837:1–2, 895:2:1–2

kuš **a-g̃ar gu$_7$-a**, "de-haired skins," 955:4, 1376:66

kuš **a-g̃ar nu-gu$_7$-a**, "skin that has not been de-haired," 247:2

kuš-udu **a-g̃ar gu$_7$-a**, "de-haired sheep skin," 868:1, 958:1

kuš-udu kuš-sila$_4$ **a-g̃ar gu$_7$**, "de-haired sheep and lamb skins," 840:1–3

kuš-udu-niga **a-g̃ar gu$_7$**, "de-haired skin of a fattened sheep," 1061:1

a-níg̃in, "(a ceremony)"

2? dug dida$_x$-gen **a-níg̃in**-[šè], "2? jugs of ordinary dida beer [for] the a-níg̃in ceremony," 437:1

1 udu-niga 1 udu-ú 0.0.4. zì-KAL ninda gur$_4$-ra-šè 1 dug dida$_x$-sig$_5$ 1 dug dida$_x$-gen **a-níg̃in**-šè (. . .) 1 dug dida$_x$-gen **a-níg̃in**-šè gaba-ri-a ki na-rú-a (. . .) šà zabala$_4^{ki}$ u$_4$-2-kam, "1 fattened sheep, 1 range-fed sheep, 40 liters of KAL-flour for thick bread, 1 jug of fine dida beer (and) 1 jug of ordinary dida beer for the a-níg̃in ceremony, {other "offerings"} (and) 1 (additional) jug of ordinary dida beer for the a-níg̃in ceremony at the meeting at the place of the stele, {authorizing officials}, in Zabala on the 2nd day," 1028:12–17, 40–41, 45

a-rá, *adi*, *alaktu*, "times (with numbers)"

a-rá-1-kam, "for the 1st time," 285:6, 286:6, 295:3, 296:2, 297:3, 306:8, 348:'12, 351:55, 370:23, 1030:12, 1034:'2, 1294:2

---

2 There seem to be two forms in Sumerian, g̃á-rí-na and a-g̃á-ri-na, as in Akkadian texts, where *garinnum* and *agarinnum* are both attested. The variant spellings may reflect a word borrowed from a third language.

3 For a comprehensive treatment of the often obscure terminology in leather accounts, see R. Englund 2003, §15 where the following additional references are provided: M. Sigrist 1981, as well as the indices of V. Crawford 1948, and M. Van de Mieroop 1987. For a-g̃ar see also A. Salonen 1970, 212. *PSD* A/1 76 translates a-g̃ar gu$_7$, "to treat with a-g̃ar," (literally "to make eat a-g̃ar"). a-g̃ar is defined as "a flour-based watery solution used in the process of tanning hides and skins." M. Stol 1980–83, 531 shows that it means to remove the hair from the skin through a process that treats the hides with a solution of meal-pap.

a-rá-2-kam, 8:31, 285:8, 286:8, 295:6, 296:4, 297:5, 306:11, 351:41, 351:67, 550:'19, 1030:19, 1034:'7, 1294:4

a-rá-3-kam, 285:10, 286:10, 295:9, 296:6, 297:7, 1030:26, 1294:6

a-rá-4-kam, 297:9, 1030:32

a-rá-5-kam, 297:11, 1030:38

^{gi}dur-dağal **a-rá**-3-tab-ba gíd 5 nindan, "30-meter 3-ply wide rope" > **^{gi}dur**

^{gi}dur-gazi **a-rá**-2-tab-ba gíd 1½ nindan-ta, "9-meter 2-ply gazi rope" > **^{gi}dur**

^{gi}dur-gazi **a-rá**-3-tab-ba gíd 1½ nindan-ta, "9-meter 3-ply gazi rope" > **^{gi}dur**

gi-guru$_5$ **a-rá**-3-tab-ba, "triple reedwork panel" > **guru$_5$**

1 ma-na gu-gen **a-rá**-11-ta ì-tab-ba(!), "1 mina of ordinary cord of 11 strands each," 836:7–8

a-rá, "(a designation of oil)"

1 sìla ì-ğeš-ğeš-**a-rá**-me, "1 liter a-rá sesame oil," 1004:2

1 sìla ì-nun-ğeš-**a-rá**-me, "1 liter a-rá ghee," 1004:1

a-šà, *eqlu*, "field" > *Garden and Field Index*

a-šà a-gi-li

a-šà *dì-im-bu-na*-àš-gi$_5$

a-šà du$_6$-ba-an-du$_8$-du$_8$

a-šà gar-ša-an-na^{ki}

a-šà karkar^{ki}

a-šà ^{ğeš}kiri$_6$ gar-ša-an-na^{ki} > **a-šà gar-ša-an-na^{ki}**

a-šà lú-maḫ

a-šà mí-mí

a-šà pa$_4$-lugal-ğu$_{10}$

a-šà sum-túl-túl

a-šà *ṣé-ru-um*

a-šà *ši-ḫu-um*

a-ši-um, "(a specification of textiles)"

1 ^{túg}bar-dul$_5$ abzu? ***a-ši-um***, "1 abzu? *a-ši-um* bar-dul$_5$ textile," 571:1

[n ^{túg}]bar-dul$_5$ *šu-kab-tá* ***a-ši-um***, "[n] *a-ši-um* bar-dul$_5$ textile(s) of *Šu-Kabta*," 762:1

a-za-bu-um, *azabu*, "cistern"

a-za-bu-um ba-al, "to dig a cistern" > **ba-al**

a-za-bu-um dù, "to construct a cistern" > **dù**

a-za-bu-um mu-DU, "delivery (of bricks for) the cistern" > **mu-DU**

a-za-bu-um-šè ğar, "to place for the cistern" > **ğar**

GÍN-bal ***a-za-bu-um*** šà é-a, "the GÍN-bal of the cistern in the house" > **é**

A.ZI/ZI(KWU-127).**ÉŠ**, "(a kind of grass or rush used for making ropes)"

níĝ-si-ga **A.ZI/ZI.ÉŠ** aka "to make a panel of rushes" > **aka**

níĝ-ú-ba **A.ZI/ZI.ÉŠ** sur, "to twist rushes (for use as) corner pieces" > **sur**

n sa **A.ZI/ZI(.ÉŠ)** gi-guru$_5$-šè, "n bundle(s) of rushes for reedwork panels" > **guru$_5$**

2 gu-níĝin **A.ZI/ZI(.ÉŠ)**, "2 bales of rushes," 436:12

40 gu-níĝin **ZI/ZI.ÉŠ**, "40 bales of rushes," 1305:3

260 gu-níĝin ^{ú}**ZI/ZI.ŠÈ**, "260 bales of rushes," 1308:4

á, *aḫu*, *idu*, "arm, side; labor; wage"

1. **Arm, Side**

da bàd sè-ga **á** ^{tumu}mer, "(dirt) tamped at the north side of the (enclosure) wall" > **sè(g$_{10}$)**

2. **Labor**

á mu-DU, "delivery of (completed) work" > **mu-DU**

2.1 Flour Production[4]

(. . .) **á** géme àr-ra, "{raw grain}, the labor of female grinders (to mill)" > *Craftswomen Index*

(. . .) **á** géme kíkken-šè, "{raw grain}, for the labor of female millers (to mill)" > *Craftswomen Index*

n zíz gur ba-na zì-KAL n sìla-ta ì-ĝál **á** géme kíkken-šè, "n bushel(s) of emmer wheat, in each ban (=10 liters) of it there are n liter(s) of KAL-flour, for the labor of female millers" > *Craftswomen Index*

2.2 Reed Products

1 ^{gi}*ba-ti-um* (. . .) **á**-bi u$_4$-n-kam, "1 reed container. (Manufacture required:) (. . .) n day(s) of labor" > ^{gi}***ba-ti-um***

1 ^{gi}gida$_x$ ésir šub-ba (. . .) **á**-bi u$_4$-n-kam, "1 (reed object) coated with bitumen. (Manufacture required:) (. . .) n day(s) of labor" > ^{gi}**gida$_x$**

n gi é-KU-^{ĝeš}banšur (. . .) á-bi u$_4$-n-kam, "n (reed object(s) for? a table). (Manufacture required:) (. . .) n day(s) of labor" > ^{ĝeš}**banšur**

n ^{gi}ig (. . .) **á**-bi u$_4$-n-kam, "n reed door(s). (Manufacture required:) (. . .) n day(s) of labor" > ^{gi}**ig**

n ^{gi}kid (. . .) **á**-bi u$_4$-1-⅓-kam, "n reed mat(s). (Manufacture required:) (. . .) n day(s) of labor" > ^{gi}**kid**

(. . .) **á** de$_6$-a ad-kub$_4$ taḫ-ḫe-dam mu-2-kam, "{assorted mats, baskets and other finished reed products}; 'incoming' labor of the reed craftsman, to be added (to) the 2 year (account)," 1381:66–69

[4] For interpretation of this and similar passages as indicating the amount of flour produced in the é-kíkken from the grain delivered see Brunke 2008, 25 (§2.1.5) n. 35.

2.2.1 Object Broken

[x] ½ kùš dag̃al 1 kùš [x gi]-bi 3 sa [. . .]-bi x? 1 [**á**-bi] u$_4$-1½-kam, "[x] ½ kùš in width, 1 kùš [x]. (Manufacture required:) 3 bundles of reed, [. . .] (and) 1½ days [of labor]," 374:'15-'18

[. . .] ùr ésir šub-ba [gi]-bi ½ sa? [peš]-múrgu-[bi] ½ [pa] $^{g̃eš}$nimbar-bi 4 ésir-é-a-bi 0.0.1 [. . .] **á**-bi u$_4$-½-kam, "[n object(s)] coated with bitumen. (Manufacture required:) ½ bundles? of [reeds], ½ date palm spine, 4 date palm fronds, 10 [+n? liters] of house bitumen (and) ½ day of labor," 1381:19–24

[n ^{gi} . . .]-x-ga gíd-3-kùš [dag̃al-n]-kùš gi-bi 3⅓ sa ^{gi}[dur-bi n sa]^{gi}níg̃-si-ga-b[i n sa] peš-múrgu-bi [n . . .]-bi 3 ésir-é-a-bi 1⅔ sìla **á**-bi u$_4$-2½-kam, "[n reed object(s)], 3 kùš in length, [n] kùš [in width]. (Manufacture required:) 3⅓ bundles of reeds, [n] bundle(s) of rope, [n bundle(s)] of panels, [n] date palm spine(s), [. . .], 1⅔ liter of house bitumen (and) 2½ days of labor," 1381:40–48

2.3 Work for Fullers

1 ^{túg}bar-dul$_5$ abzu? *a-ši-um* 1 túg-guz-za 3-kam-ús 8 g̃uruš ^{lú} ázlag **á**-bi u$_4$-1-še, "1 abzu? *a-ši-um* bar-dul$_5$ textile (and) 1 3rd-quality tufted textile, work (for) 8 fullers for 1 day," 571:1–4

2.4 Broken Context

[. . .] x [. . . **á**]-bi u$_4$-2?-[kam], "[. . .], its [labor] is 2? days," 374:'1-'2

3. Wages for Female Brick Haulers

3.1 Sample Text with Full Context

[šu+níg̃in] 16 sar 2½ gín šeg$_{12}$ ús-bi 72 nindan **á** géme 150-šeg$_{12}$-ta géme-bi 77 u$_4$-1-šè še 3-sìla-ta ba-ḫug̃ še-bi 0.3.5.1 sìla [4 gín] mu-DU bàd-šè *simat-é-a* ugula lú-ḫug̃-g̃á g̃iri ^{d}*adad-tillati* šabra ù *puzur*$_4$-^{d}nin-kar-ak dub-sar

"[In total:] 16 sar (and) 2½ gin of bricks, the distance (they were carried) is 72 nindan. The workwomen wages (are) for each 150 bricks (carried); its workwomen (equal) 77 workerdays, (workwomen) hired (for) 3 liters of barley each. Their barley is 231 liters (and) 4 shekels. Delivery (of bricks) for the (enclosure) wall by *Simat-Ea*, overseer of hired workers, under the authority of *Adad-tillati*, the majordomo, and *Puzur-*Ninkarak, the scribe," 308:41–51

3.1.1 Related References

á(-bi) géme n šeg$_{12}$-ta géme-bi n u$_4$-1-šè, "the workwomen wages (are) for each n bricks (carried); its workwomen (equal) n workerdays," 308:43–44, 309:70–71, 310:'14-'15, 311:16–17, 312:30–31, 313:19–20, 316:67–68, 318:'45-'46, 322:'79-'80, 346:122–123, 351:83–84, 351:135–136, 361:'9-'10, 367:'125-'126

3.1.2 Variants

á géme-1-a n šeg$_{12}$-ta géme-bi n u$_4$-1-šè, 317:25–26, 321:'28-'29, 323:119–120, 324:89–90, 325:13–14, 327:77–78, 330:22–23, 334:60–61, 335:36–37, 336:19–20, 336:25–26, 336:38–39, 343:6–7, 347:'12-'13, 369:'23-'24, 373:'7-'8

á géme 90-ta géme-bi n u$_4$-1-šè, 328:9–10, 339:8–9

á n-ta géme-bi n u$_4$-1-šè, 337:25–26, 338:17–18, 340:28–29, 342:72–73, 342:76–77, 344:'20-'2, 353:12–13, 368:'55-'56

[**á** géme-1]-a 120-ta [. . .] 6-ta? [**á**]? u$_4$-[1]-šè, 341:8–9

á-[. . .] géme-bi n u$_4$-1-šè, 345:'11-'12, 362:'15-'16

šu+níĝin 60+20+7 sar 6 gín igi-6-ĝál á 1⅓ [u$_4$]-1-šè **á** 100-ta géme-bi 347½ 7 gín igi-4-ĝál, 346:69–72

á géme-1-a 216 šeg$_{12}$-ta géme-bi 34½ 5 gín, 352:34–35

á géme 150 šeg$_{12}$-[ta . . .], 364:'29

4. Wages for Workmen Delivering Dirt

4.1 Sample Text with Full Context

šu+níĝin 9½ sar 4 gín igi-6-ĝál ús-bi 30 nindan **á** ĝuruš-a 6 gín-ta ĝuruš-bi 95⅔ 1⅔ gín u$_4$-1-šè še 6 sìla-ta ba-ḫuĝ še-bi 1.4.3.4 sìla 10 gín gur saḫar zi-ga tùn-[lá] da bàd sè-ga á ^{tumu}mer mu-DU *ba-zi* ugula lú-ḫuĝ-ĝá ĝìri ^{d}*adad-tillati* šabra ù *puzur$_4$*-^{d}nin-kar-ak dub-sar

"In total: 9½ sar (and) 4 1/6 gín (of earth), the distance (the earth was) carried is 30 nindan. The workmen wages (are for) each 6 gín (of earth carried). Its workmen (equal) 95⅔ (and) 1⅔ gín workerdays, (workmen) hired (for) 6 liters of barley each. Their barley is 1 bushel, 274 liters (and) 10 shekels. (The work consisted of) dirt removed via a tùn-lá device, tamped at the north side of the (enclosure) wall. Delivery (of dirt) by *Bazi*, overseer of hired workers, under the authority of *Adad-tillati*, the majordomo, and *Puzur*-Ninkarak, the scribe," 331:28–38

4.1.1 Related References

á ĝuruš-a n gín-ta ĝuruš-bi n (gín) u$_4$-1-šè, "the workmen wages (are) n shekel(s) each; its workmen (equal) n workerday(s)," 329:9–10, 331:30–31, 333:17–18, 355:3–4, 354:2–3

4.1.2 Variants

1 sar 10 gín saḫar ús-bi 30 nindan **á** ĝuruš-a 6 gín-ta ½ nindan gíd [. . .], "(in total:) 1 sar (and) 10 gín of dirt, the distance (the dirt was carried) is 30 nindan. The workmen wages (are for) each 6 gín (of earth carried). ½ nindan in length [. . .]," 349:5–8

[**á** ĝ]uruš-a 3⅓ [gí]n 15 še-ta saḫar-bi 128⅓ <sar> u$_4$-1-šè [šu+]níĝin 139 ĝuruš u$_4$-1-šè, "workmen [wages] (are for) each 3⅓ gín (and) 15 še (of dirt carried). (The total amount of) dirt (carried) was 128⅓ (units) for 1 day; in total: 139 worker days," 349:'12-'14

[20+2+]3 sar 10+[5 gín] 5 še im-d[u$_8$-a] **á** ĝuruš 3⅔ gín 15 še-ta ĝuruš-bi 404 [u$_4$-1-šè] še 6-sìla-ta ba-[ḫuĝ] im-du$_8$-a ^{ĝeš}[kiri$_6$]-zabala$_4$$^{[ki]}$ mu-[DU] *ib-ni-ilum* ugula [lú-ḫuĝ-ĝá] ĝìri *puzur$_4$*-^{d}ni[n-kar]-ak dub-[sar] ù ^{d}*adad-tillati* P[A.AL], "[25] sar 1[5] gín (and) 5 še (of dirt for) the adobe wall. Workmen wages are for each 3⅔ gín (and) 15 še (of earth carried). Its workmen (equal) 404 workerdays, (workmen) hired (for) 6 liters of barley each. Delivery for the adobe wall of the Zabala garden by *Ibni-ilum*, overseer [of hired workers], under the authority of *Puzur*-Ninkarak, the scribe and *Adad-tillati*, the majordomo," 356:1–9

4.1.3 Wages for Delivering Bricks

šu+níĝin 7.4.0. š[e gur] šà-bi-⌜ta⌝ 124⅔ sar [šeg$_{12}$] NE-gu$_7$-bi í[b-ta-zi] **á** ĝuruš-a ⅓ sa[r-ta] ĝuruš-bi 360+14 [u$_4$-1-šè] še 5 sìla-ta [ba-ḫuĝ še-bi] 6.1.1. [gur š]eg$_{12}$-bi 124⅔ [sar 1].2.5. še gur [*si*]-*ì-tum*, "In total: 7 bushels (and) 240 liters of barley. From among it 124⅔ sar of damaged [bricks] were deducted. Workman wages at ⅓ sar [each], its workmen (equal) 374 workerdays, (workers) [hired (for)] 5 liters of barley each. Their barley is 6 bushels (and) 70 liters. Their bricks are 124⅔ sar. 1 bushel and 170 liters is the remainder," 496:5–16

5. Wages for Various Work Assignments

á níĝ-àr-ra-ra, "wages for (milling) groats," 432:3

á šeg$_{12}$ ga$_6$-ĝá, "wages of (workers) having carried bricks" > **ga$_6$(ĝ)**

še **á** dabin-šè, "barley, wages for (milling) semolina," 475:1–2

n (sìla) še *si-ì-tum* **á** dabin, "n liter(s) of barley, the remainder of wages (for processing) semolina" > ***si-ì-tum***

n (sìla) še *si-ì-tum* **á** šeg$_{12}$ ga$_6$-ĝá á n sìla-ta, "n liter(s) of barley, the remainder of wages of (workers) having carried bricks; wages of n liter(s) each" > ***si-ì-tum***

šeg$_{12}$ du$_8$-dè **á** 5-sìla-ta, "wages of 5 liters each (for workers) to mold bricks" > **du$_8$**

5.1 Wages for Workmen

5.1.1 ĝuruš á-1/n, "workman at 1/nth wages," *passim*

5.1.2 Wages for Agricultural Work

10 gu-níĝin ^{geš}kišig **á** ĝuruš-a 4 gu-níĝin-ta á-bi 2½ u$_4$-1-šè a-šà-karkar^{ki}-šè ^{geš}kišig ku$_5$-rá, "(In total:) 10 bales of shok. The workmen wages were for 4 bales each. Their wages were for 2½ days (for workers) having cut shok at the Karkar field," 235:1–4

5.4.0. še gur **á** al-aka ù gu$_4$-ḫuĝ-ĝá, "5 bushels and 240 liters of barley, wages (for) hoeing and the hired oxen," 1051:1–2

5.1.3 For Craftsmen

ĝuruš **á**-½ ^{lú}ázlag-me-éš, "fullers at ½ wages" > *Craftsmen Index*

ĝuruš **á**-⅔ ^{lú}ázlag-me-éš, "fullers at ⅔ wages" > *Craftsmen Index*

še **á** ad-kub$_4$, "barley, wages of reed craftsmen," 546:1–2, 547:1–2

še **á** ad-kub$_4$ ḫuĝ-ĝá-šè, "barley for wages of hired reed craftsmen," 518:1–2

še **á** ^{lú}ázlag ḫuĝ-ĝá, "barley, wages of hired fullers," 820:1–2

5.1.4 For Hired Workers

še **á** má ḫuĝ-ĝá n-gur-kam ù má-laḫ$_5$-bi á n-ta, "barley, wages of the hired n-bushel boat and its sailors, wages of n liter(s) each" > **ḫuĝ**

še **á** lú-ḫuĝ-ĝá-šè, "barley for the wages of hired workers," 544:1–2

še **á** lú-ḫuĝ-ĝá mu saḫar-šè, "barley, wages of hired workers for (moving?) dirt," 545:1–3

á sar 1-a še 0.0.1.[n sìla] še-bi 125.2.3. gur šeg$_{12}$ du$_8$-[a] lú-ḫuĝ-ĝá-e-⸢ne⸣, "wages of 10[+n liter(s)] of barley. Their barley is 125 bushels (and) 150 liters, (barley for) hired workers having molded bricks," 350:'23-'26

[. . .] **á** ĝuruš-[a . . .] 0.0.1.6 sìla še-bi sa$_{10}$ má-laḫ$_5$-e-ne u$_4$-1-[šè] é-duru$_5$-kab-⸢bí⸣-ta é-duru$_5$-*simat*-^{d}*ištaran*-šè má diri-ga, "[. . .] wages of workmen [. . .], 16 liters of barley is the (hiring) price of the sailors [for] 1 day having floated boats from the Kabbi village to the village of *Simat-Ištaran*," 561:'1-'5

5.1.5 **Retrieving Wages in Nagsu**

1 g̃uruš **á**-ne nag-su$^{⌜ki⌝}$-šè g̃en-a, "1 workman having gone to Nagsu for his wages," 96:'9

2 g̃uruš še **á**-ne nag-su^{ki}-šè g̃en, "2 workmen having gone to Nagsu for their barley wages," 189:30

5.2 **Wages for Workwomen**

5.2.1 **á-diri**, "additional wages"

[n gé]me **á-diri**-ta nam-^{lú}ázlag-šè, "[n] workwomen at additional wages for fulling," 714:1–2

5.2.2 **géme á-⅔**, "workwomen at ⅔ wages"

géme á-⅔ géme gu-me-éš, "spinners at ⅔ wages" > *Craftswomen Index*

géme á-⅔ géme uš-bar-me-éš, "weavers at ⅔ wages" > *Craftswomen Index*

á-ág̃(-g̃á), *wu'uru*, "(issued) order, decree, (given) instruction, command; assignment"[5]

á-ág̃(-g̃á) de_6, "to bring a message (containing instructions for the messenger)" > **de_6**

****á-ág̃-dè** gub, "instructions to follow?" > **gub**

á-ág̃ g̃en, "to go (to bring) a message" > **g̃en**

^{gi}gur še **á-ág̃-g̃á ésir šub-ba > **^{gi}gur**

[. . .] **á-á[g̃** . . .], 173:30

á-an-zú-lum, "date cluster," 1066:3, 1102:4, 1215:6, 1237:6

á-da-bar, *atbaru*, "black basalt," 1372:4, 1372:29

^{na4}kinkin **á-da-bar** šu sè-ga, "'hand-held' black basalt millstone" > **^{na4}kinkin**

á-gú-zi-ga, *šēru*, "dawn"

4 sìla níg̃-àr-ra-[sig_5] u_4-2-[kam] **á-gú-zi-⌜ga⌝**, "4 liters of [fine] groats at dawn of the 2nd day," 551:5–7

^{túg}***á-gu_4-ḫu-um***, *aguḫḫu*, "belt, sash"

^{túg}***á-gu_4-ḫu-um***-PI-lugal, "royal PI-belt," 578:1, 579:1, 591:1

^{túg}***á-[gu_4-ḫu-um***]-ús 3-[kam-ús], "3rd-quality belt," 759:1

á-ki-ti, "(a festival)"

2 g̃uruš ^{lú}ázlag u_4-1-šè zi-ga kaš-dé-a lugal šà **á-<ki->ti** gub-ba, "2 fullers employed for 1 day, expended (for) the royal banquet of the Akiti festival," 221:1–2

---

5 For discussion of this term see W. Sallaberger 2003 611–12, where Sallaberger collects the published third-millennium references, now enhanced substantially by the Garšana texts.

3 g̃uruš ^{lú}ázlag siki é-^{d}*šu*-^{d}*suen*^{ki}-ka-ta nibru^{ki}-šè de_6-a kaskal šu+níg̃in-na-bi u_4-10!-kam u_4-2 kaš-dé-[a] **á-⌜ki⌝-ti** šu-numun, "3 fullers having brought wool from *Bit-Šu-Suen* to Nippur, a trip of 10 days in total, on day 2 of the banquet of the Akiti festival of month 4," 240:1–6

^{kuš}**á-si**, "whip, hinge, strap"

^{kuš}**á-si** g̃ar-ra é-ba-an, "pair of leather covered hinges," 853:4

á-u_4-te-na, *līliātum*, "evening"

1. Provisions in the Evening

0.0.1. kaš-gen ugula àg[a-ús-e-ne] á-[u_4]-te-⌜na⌝ zi-[ga] 0.0.4. ninda ZÌ.[ŠE] 0.0.3.5 sìla kaš-g[en] **á-u_4-te-⌜na⌝** u_4-1?-[kam], "10 liters of ordinary beer (for) the overseer of the gendarmes expended in the evening (and) 40 liters of semolina bread (and) 35 liters of ordinary beer in the evening of the 1st day," 550:'5-'10

0.0.1. kaš-gen ugula àga-ús-e-ne **á-u_4-te-na** u_4-2-kam, "10 liters of ordinary beer (for) the overseer of the gendarmes in the evening of the 2nd day," 550:20'–23'

0.0.5. ninda-kaš **á-u_4-[te-na]** 2 sìla níg̃-àr-[ra-sig_5] šà $zabala_4^{[ki]}$ u_4-1-[kam], "50 liters of beer bread [in] the evening (and) 2 liters of [fine] barley groats in Zabala on the 1st day," 551:1–3

4 sìla níg̃-àr-ra-si[g_5] **á-u_4-te-na** u_4-3-kam, "4 liters of fine groats in evening of the 3rd day," 551:8–10

ab, "roof vent"

ab-ba dag̃al tà(g), "to widen (the opening of) the roof vent" > **tà(g)**

abzu, *apsû*, "(cosmic) underground water; a ritual water container in a temple"

★★1 ^{túg}bar-dul_5 **abzu**? *a-ši-um*, "1 abzu? *a-ši-um* bar-dul_5 textile," 571:1

1 udu **abzu**-šè (. . .) u_4 ezem-gur-$buru_{14}$, "1 sheep for the abzu, (and) {other offerings}, during the harvest festival," 996:1, 4

ad-kub_4, *atkuppu*, "a craftsman making reed objects"

a-ḫu-DU_{10} **ad-kub_4**, "*Aḫu-ṭabu*, the reed craftsman" > *Personal Name Index*

g̃uruš **ad-kub_4**, "reed craftsman" > *Craftsmen Index*

(. . .) á de_6-a **ad-kub_4** taḫ-ḫe-dam mu-2-kam, "{assorted mats, baskets and other finished reed products}; 'incoming' labor of the reed craftsman, to be added (to) the 2 year (account)," 1381:66–69

ádda, *pagru*, "corpse, carcass"

ádda-gu_4, "ox carcass," 1223:1

ádda-udu, "sheep carcass," 399:14, 399:24, 403:5, 442:17, 445:5, 446:4, 459:1, 472:3, 510:5, 511:'104, 521:5, 528:11, 529:6, 535:5, 548:13, 549:5, 557:15, 1025:9, 1025:32, 1025:49, 1025:67, 1025:85, 1025:110, 1194:5, 1223:2

ádda-udu-bi n, "its sheep carcasses are n," 562:'19, 562:'73

n **ádda**-udu-bi, "its sheep carcasses are n," 562:'59

n **ádda**-udu-ta, "n sheep carcass(es) each," 399:3, 399:16, 406:3, 557:4, 562:'8, 562:'43, 562:'63

ádda-udu ^{urudu}šen-šè, "sheep carcass(es) for the (soup) cauldron," 382:1–2, 388:1–2

[ADJECTIVES]

babbar, "(to be) white"
bíl, "(to be) burnt; sour"
dağal, "(to be) wide; width, breadth"
diri(g), "(to be) surplus, additional"
du_8-ši-a, "turquoise green"
$du_{10}(g_3)$, "(to be) good; (to be) sweet; goodness, good (thing)"
$duru_5$, "(to be) soft, (to be) wet, irrigated, fresh, damp"
gal, "(to be) big, great; large"
gen, "(to be) medium, ordinary quality"
gibil, "(to be) new"
gíd, "(to be) long"
gukkal, "(to be) fat-tailed"
gùn, "(to be) speckled, multicolored"
gur_4, "(to be) thick; (to be) big"
guz, "(to be) tufted"
$\tilde{g}e_6$, "(to be) black, dark"
ḫád, "(to be) dried (out), dry"
niga, "(to be) fattened"
$peš_5$, "(to be) plucked"
sal, "(to be) thin"
sig, "(to be) weak, low, thin, narrow"
sig_5, "(to be) fine, high quality"
su_4, "(to be) red, brown"
sumun, "(to be) old"
tur, "(to be) small, young"
ú, "(to be) range fed"
ús, "(to be) 2nd quality"

[AGRICULTURAL PRODUCTS] (see also **ğeš** for fruits, trees and wood products and **gi** for reeds and reed products)

A.ZI/ZI(.ÉŠ), "(a kind of grass or rush used for making ropes)"
á-an-zú-lum, "date cluster"
ar-za-na, "barley-grits, groats"
eša, "fine flour"
gada, "linen, flax"
^{ú}gamun, "cumin"
gazi, "(a condiment, mustard seed or licorice)"

gi, "reed"
gir-ga, "(an agricultural product)"
gú-gal, "beans"
gú-tur, "peas"
ḫa-šu-um, "(a spice plant)"
ḫu-ri-um, "(a spice)"
imĝaĝa$_3$, "emmer"
in-u, "straw"
kà-ma-am-tum, "(a vegetable)"
kàr-šum, "leek"
kib$_x$, "wheat"
mun-gazi, "(a class of agricultural products)"
naĝar, "(a plant)"
níĝ-àr-ra, "groats"
^{ĝeš}nu-úr-ma, "pomegranate"
peš, "date palm heart, leaflet"
peš-múrgu, "date palm spine"
^{ĝeš}pèš, "fig"
sí-mi-tum, "(a plant)"
^{ú}sullim, "fenugreek"
sum-sikil, "onion"
še, "barley"
še-lú, "coriander"
tuḫ, "bran, husk"
ú-ḫáb, "madder (dye)"
u$_4$-ḫi-in, "fresh dates"
ÚR×A.NA, "mulberry"
zà-ḫi-li, "(edible seed used for flavoring)"
^{ĝeš}zé-na, "date palm frond midrib"
zì, "flour"
zíz, "emmer wheat"

àga-ús, *rēdû*, "gendarme, soldier"

di$_4$-di$_4$-la **àga-ús**, "the small child(ren) of the gendarme" > **di$_4$-di$_4$-la**
níĝ-dab$_5$ **àga-ús-e-ne**, "requisitions of gendarmes" > **níĝ-dab$_5$**

1. **àga-ús é-gal-la gub-ba**, "gendarme employed in the palace"

0.0.4. ⅔ sìla [. . . **àga**]**-ús é-gal-la gub-ba** [íb]-gu$_7$ ⌜u$_4$⌝ [m]á *ra-ba-tum* nibru^{ki}-ta gar-ša-an-na^{ki}-šè i[n-g]íd-sa-a, "the gendarme employed at the palace ate 4⅔ liters [. . .], when they towed the boat of *Rabatum* from Nippur to Garšana," 506:22–26

2. **àga-ús lugal**, "royal gendarme"

la-qì-bu-um **àga-ús lugal**, "*Laqibum*, the royal gendarme" > *Personal Name Index*

3. **ugula àga-ús-e-ne**, "the overseer of the gendarmes"

ugula àga-ús-e-ne àga-ús *ri-im-ilum*, "the overseer of the gendarmes: the gendarme of *Rim-ilum*" > *Personal Name Index*

0.0.1. kaš-gen **ugula àg[a-ús-e-ne]** á-[u_4]-te-⸢na⸣ zi-[ga], "10 liters of ordinary beer (for) the overseer of the gendarmes expended in the evening," 550:'5-'6

0.0.1. kaš-gen **ugula àga-ús-e-ne** á-u_4-te-na u_4-2-kam, "10 liters of ordinary beer (for) the overseer of the gendarmes, in the evening of the 2nd day," 550:'22-'23

4. **Provisions for the Gendarmes**

[. . . n sìla níĝ]-àr-ra-s[ig_5] 0.0.4.5 sìla kaš-[gen **àg]a-ús-e-[ne]**, "[. . . n liter(s)] of fine groats (and) 45 liters of [ordinary] beer (for) the gendarmes," 550:'1-'4

[. . . u_4]-2-[kam n sìla] ninda ZÌ.[ŠE 0.0.1.] kaš-gen **[àga]-ús-e-ne-**[šè], "[. . . for] the 2nd [time], [n (liter(s)] of semolina bread (and) [10] liters of ordinary beer [for] the gendarmes," 550:'18-'21

agrig, *abarakku*, "steward, housekeeper"

an-ta-lú **agrig**, "*Antalu*, the steward" > *Personal Name Index*

é-**agrig**, "house of the steward" > *Household Index*

ak(a), *epēšu*, "to do, to make" > *Verb Index*

[AKKADIAN WORDS]

a-ga-mu-um, "marsh"
a-ga-ri-nu-um, "pit or basin in which mortar or plaster is mixed"
a-gi_4-um, "(a specification of textiles)"
a-ši-um, "(a specification of textiles)"
a-za-bu-um, "cistern"
túg*á-gu_4-ḫu-um*, "belt, sash"
ak-lu-um, "overseer"
al-lu-ḫa-ru-um, "(a mineral tanning agent)"
ar-gi_5-núm, "(a kind of food product?)"
gi*ba-ti-um*, "(a reed container)"
ĝeš*be-rum*, "(a wooden object)"
bí-ni-tum, "a crossbeam"
bu-ti-um, "(a specification of textiles)" > **túg**
dì-um, "wattle and daub"
du-ú-um, "cella platform"
ĝeš*dú-ul-bu-um*, "plane tree"
e-bi-a-tum, "thick"
e-pe-eš, "to do, make"
e-ri-um, "frond, leaf of the date palm"
é-gi-na-tum, "barracks"
ḫa-bu-um > *ḫa-um*

ḫa-šu-um, "(a spice plant)"
ḫa-um, "(a fabric, textile)"
ḫa-za-nu-um, "mayor"
^{ĝeš}*ḫu-pu-um*, "wheel rim"
ḫu-ri-um, "(a spice)"
kà-ma-am-tum, "(a vegetable)"
^{ĝeš}*kà-na-at-ḫu-um*, "(a tree or aromatic product from a tree)"
kàr-šum, "leek"
ki-ri-ip, "a (oil) jar"
^{dug}*ku-kur-rú*, "(a vessel)"
^{ĝeš}*la-ri-um*, "branch?"
li-iq-tum (*cf.* *niqdu*), "leftovers?"
ma-ad-li-um, "bucket"
ma-aZ-ḫa-ru-um, "a vessel? a sieve?"
mu-du-lum, "pickled, salted (meat)"
mul-ṭum, "a comb"
^{kuš}*na-aḫ-ba-tum*, "a leather case for precious objects"
níĝ-*lá-lá-rum*, "(a dessert, pastry)"
niqdum > *liqtum*, "leftovers?"
pù-sú-lum, "(a food product?)"
qí-il-pu-um, "skin, peel; bark for tanning?"
ra-ṭum, "drain(-pipe)"
sà-ḫum^{zabar}, "(a bronze drinking vessel / bowl?)"
^{ĝeš}*sé-er-dum*, "olive tree"
sí-mi-tum, "(a kind of plant)"
šit-tum, "remainder"
tá-ki-ru-um, "(a textile)"
tak-ri-ib-tum, "(performance of) an Emesal lament"
ták-s/ši-ru-um, "repair (of architecture)"
tuḫ-ḫu-um > ba-tab *tuḫ-ḫu-um*, "(a specification of textiles)"
u_4*-tuḫ-ḫu-um*, "(meaning uncertain)"
za-rí-in, "coarsely cleaned (wool) material"
zi-ba-tum, "rear part (of certain implements)"
^{ĝeš}*zi-ri-qum*, "shaduf"

ak-lu-um, *aklu*, "overseer"

★★1 ^{kuš}[x]-x-apin? ***ak-lu-um***, 925:'14

^{túg}**aktum**, *ṣapšu*, "(a textile)"

[n] ^{gada}**aktum** 3-kam-ús [*šu-kab-t*]*á*, "[n] 3rd-quality linen aktum textile(s) of *Šu-Kabta*," 698:23
^{túg}**aktum** 3-kam-ús, "3rd-quality aktum textile," 677:2, 698:8, 698:19, 748:5
^{túg}**aktum** 4-kam-ús, "4th-quality aktum textile," 626:2, 637:2

^{túg}**aktum**-AB 3-kam-ús, "3rd-quality aktum-AB textile," 698:18

^{ĝeš}**al**, *allu*, "hoe," 1255:9, 1340:3

še **al** aka, "barley (for) hoeing" > **aka**

al-àr-ra, "milled"

gú-gal **al-àr-ra**, "milled beans" > **gú-gal**

al-bi-ra, "shredded?"

^{túg}bar-dul$_5$ **al-bi-ra**, "shredded? bar-dul$_5$ textile" > ^{túg}**bar-dul$_5$**

al-dar-ra, "separated, split"

ku$_6$ **al-dar-ra**, "split (dried) fish" > **ku$_6$**

al-dúb-ba, "extracted"

^{ĝeš}eme-sig **al-dúb-ba**, "extracted boat plank" > ^{ĝeš}**eme-sig**

al-lu-ḫa-ru-um, *alluḫaru/annuḫaru*, "(a mineral tanning agent)," 828:2, 898:3, 924:2, 943:3, 947:3

2 ma-na ***al-lu-ḫa-ru-um*** *li-iq-tum*, "2 minas of *alluḫarum* leftovers?," 668:1

al-lu-ḫu-ru-um-sig$_5$, "fine *alluḫarum*," 898:2, 924:1, 943:2

al-naĝ$_4$-ĝá, "crushed"

gazi **al-naĝ$_4$-ĝá**, "crushed gazi" > **gazi**

mun **al-naĝ$_4$-ĝá**, "crushed salt" > **mun**

šim **al-naĝ$_4$-ĝá**, "crushed aromatic" > **šim**

al-tar, *altar(r)u*, "construction (work)"

al-tar é-lùnga é-muḫaldim ù é-kíkken, "construction of the brewery-kitchen-mill complex" > *Household Index*

al-tar é-ki-mu-ra, "construction of the textile depository" > *Household Index*

al-tar é-PN, "construction of the house of PN" > *Household Index*

é-*a-bí-a-ti*
é-*ba-ḫa-a*
é-*ì-lí-bi-šu*
é-*pu-ta-nu-um*
é-*zu-zu-tum*

al-tar é-uš-bar-ra, "construction of the textile mill" > *Household Index*

al-tar ki-sá-a é-lùnga é-muḫaldim ù é-kikken, "construction of the foundation terrace of the brewery-kitchen-mill complex" > *Household Index*

al-tar ki-sá-a é-lùnga ù é-kíkken, "construction of the foundation terrace of the brewery and mill" > *Household Index*

1. **al-tar dù-a**, "having done construction work" > **dù**

2. **al-tar gub-ba**, "(workers) employed (for) construction"

2.1 Construction of the Brewery-Kitchen-Mill Complex

*See *Household Index* for the full context of the following passage.

[n g̃uru]š šidim 5 g̃uruš 3 gé[me] **al-tar gub-⸢ba⸣** (. . .) é-lùnga é-muḫaldim ù é-kíkken, "[n] builder(s), 5 workmen (and) 3 workwomen employed (for) construction (. . .), (for) the brewery-kitchen-mill complex," 155:27–31

2.2 Construction of the Textile Mill and Craftsman's House

23 g̃uruš u$_4$-1-⸢šè⸣ **al-tar gub-ba** é-uš-bar ù é-gašam-e-ne, "23 workmen for 1 day employed (for) construction, (for) the textile mill and craftsmen's house," 336:28–30

2.3 Construction of the (Enclosure) Wall

4 g̃uruš šidim 10-lá-1 g̃uruš 10 géme šeg$_{12}$ šu dím-ma su[m-mu-dè] 10 géme im ga$_6$-g̃á-d[è a]**l-tar** bàd **gub-ba**, "4 builders, 9 workmen (and) 10 workwomen [to] hand (up) bricks for building (and) 10 workwomen to carry earth, (workers) employed (for) construction of the (enclosure) wall," 99:13–16

1 g̃uruš šidim um-mi-[a] 2 g̃uruš šidim 10-lá-1 g̃uruš šu dím-ma 20 géme im ga$_6$-g̃á 10 géme šeg$_{12}$ da bàd g̃á-g̃á-dè 2 géme im gíd-dè 1 géme *du-ú-um* ke$_4$-dè **al-tar** bàd **gub-ba**, "1 master builder, 2 builders (and) 9 workmen having built, 20 workwomen having carried earth, 10 workwomen to place bricks at the side of the (enclosure) wall, 2 workwomen to haul earth (and) 1 workwoman to make a *du-ú-um*, (workers) employed (for) construction of the (enclosure) wall," 102:16–23

1 g̃uruš šidim um-mi-a 3 g̃uruš šidim 6 g̃uruš šu dím-ma 20 géme im ga$_6$-g̃á 2 géme im gíd-dè 1 géme *du-ú-um* <ke$_4$-dè> **al-tar** bàd **gub-ba**, "1 master builder, 3 builders (and) 6 workmen having built, 20 workwomen having carried earth, 2 workwomen to haul earth (and) 1 workwoman <to make> a *du-ú-um*, (workers) employed (for) construction of the (enclosure) wall," 103:15–20

3 g̃uruš u$_4$-1-šè **al-tar** bàd **gub-ba**, "3 workmen for 1 day employed (for) construction of the (enclosure) wall," 336:10–11

2.3.1 The Foundation of the (Enclosure) Wall

3 gé[me im *a-ga-ri*]*-nu-um* ga$_6$-g̃á-dè gub-[ba] **al-tar** uš bàd tà-tà-dè **gub-ba**, "3 workwomen employed to carry [earth] to the *agarinnum*, (workers) employed (for) construction to apply stucco to the foundation of the (enclosure) wall," 7:'25-'27

2.3.2 The urua wall

10-lá-1 g̃uruš u$_4$-1-šè **al-tar** ú(!)-ru-a bàd **gub-ba**, "9 workmen for 1 day employed (for) construction of the urua wall," 336:12–14

2.4 Construction Site Unspecified

1 g̃uruš šidim um-mi-a 1 g̃uruš šidim 2 g̃uruš 1 géme šu dím gub-ba 1 g̃uruš im gíd-dè 8 géme im ga$_6$-g̃á-dè 1 g̃uruš im ì-li-de$_9$ **al-tar gub-ba**, "1 master builder, 1 builder, 2 workmen (and) 1 workwoman employed to build, 1 workman to haul earth, 8

workwomen to carry earth (and) 1 workman to lift earth, (workers) employed (for) construction," 58:19–26

1 g̃uruš um-mi-a [n] g̃uruš šidim 27 g̃uruš 10-lá-1 géme šu dím-ma 44 géme i[m g]a$_6$-g̃á iz-zi im sumur aka 2 g̃uruš šidim 12 g̃uruš šu dím 11 géme im ga$_6$-g̃á g̃eš ùr kéše-rá 1 g̃uruš šidim 8 g̃uruš šu dím 1 géme *du-ú-um* aka 1 géme im gíd 20 géme im ga$_6$-g̃á **al-tar gub-ba**, "1 master builder, [n] builder(s), 27 workmen (and) 9 workwomen having built (and) 44 workwomen having carried earth—(workers) having plastered the iz-zi wall—2 builders (and) 12 workmen to build (and) 11 workwomen having carried earth—(workers) having bound roof beams—(and) 1 builder (and) 8 workmen having built, 1 workwoman having made a *du-ú-um*, 1 workwoman having hauled earth (and) 20 workwomen having carried earth, (workers) employed (for) construction," 140:25–36

1 g̃uruš šidim um-mi-a 8 g̃uruš šidim 8 g̃uruš šu dím 24 géme im ga$_6$-g̃á iz-zi im sumur aka 2 g̃uruš šidim 10 g̃uruš 10 gé[me] g̃eš ùr kéše-rá 2 g̃uruš šidim 6 g̃uruš šu dím 23 géme im ga$_6$-g̃[á] **al-[tar] gub-ba**, "1 master builder, 8 builders (and) 8 workmen having built (and) 24 workwomen having carried earth—(workers) having plastered the iz-zi wall—2 builders, 10 workmen (and) 10 workwomen having bound roof beams (and) 2 builders (and) 6 workmen having built (and) 23 workwomen having carried earth, (workers) employed (for) construction," 144:'7-'15

18 g̃uruš u$_4$-1-šè **al-tar gub-ba**, "18 workmen for 1 day employed (for) construction," 336:15–16

šu+níg̃in 14⅔ sar 5 [gín] ús-bi 80[+10 nindan] á géme-1-a [120-šeg$_{12}$-ta] géme-bi 60+[40½ u$_4$-1-šè] šu+níg̃in 60[+20+8+½ u$_4$-1-šè] **al-t[ar gub-ba]**, "In total: 14⅔ sar and 5 [gín] (of bricks). The distance (the bricks were) carried is 90 [nindan]. The workwomen wages (are) for each 120 bricks (carried); its workwomen (equal) 100½ workerdays. In total: 88½ (workwomen) for 1 day [employed] (for) construction," 336:36–41

2.5 Provisions for those Employed for Construction

šu+níg̃in 0.1.0.3 sìla 10 gín kaš-gen šu+níg̃in 0.0.5.3⅔ sìla ninda šu+níg̃in 0.0.3.8 sìla tu$_7$ kaš-ninda ḫa-la-a? **al-t[ar] gub-ba**, "In total: 63 liters (and) 10 shekels of ordinary beer, 53⅔ liters of bread (and) 38 liters of soup, beer (and) bread divided (for workers) employed (for) construction," 379:17–20

2 ádda-udu ^{urudu}šen-šè éren **al-tar** bàd **gub-ba** íb-gu$_7$, "2 sheep carcasses for the (soup) cauldron. The workmen employed (for) construction of the (enclosure) wall ate (the soup)," 382:1–4, 388:1–4

3. al-tar, Broken Context

1 g̃uru[š šidim] um-m[i-a] 10-lá-1 g̃ur[uš . . .] 3 gé[me . . .] 2 g̃uru[š. . .] 20 [. . .] **al-tar** [. . .], 101:14–19

1 g̃uruš šidim um-m[i-a] 2 g̃uruš šidim 6 g̃uruš šu dím-ma 2 géme ⌜*du*⌝-<*ú*->*um* aka 2 géme [im gíd n] géme im ga$_6$-[g̃á-dè] 1 g̃uruš šidim [2 g̃uruš šu dím n] géme im ga$_6$-g̃[á-dè **a]l-tar** [. . .], "1 master builder, 2 builders (and) 6 workmen having built, 2 workwomen having made a *du-ú-um*, 2 workwomen [having hauled earth, n] workwomen [to] carry earth, 1 builder (and) [2 workmen having built], (and) [n] workwomen [to] carry earth (for) construction [. . .]," 106:22–28

4. á al-tar-ra, "wages for construction"

n še *si-ì-tum* **á** šeg$_{12}$ ga$_6$-g̃á ù **al-tar-ra** PN ugula lú-ḫug̃-g̃á in-da-g̃ál, "n liter(s) of barley, the remainder of wages of (workers) having carried bricks and (employed) for construction, are with PN, overseer of hired workers" > *Personal Name Index*

li-la-a
simat-é-a
ša-at-èr-ra

5. kurum$_7$ aka al-tar, "inspection of construction"

5.1 Construction of the Textile Depository

kurum$_7$ aka al-tar (é-)ki-mu-ra gub-ba, "inspection of (the work of workers) employed (for) construction of the textile depository," 72:28, 76:19, 76:19, 77:10, 84:28

5.2 Construction of the (Enclosure) Wall

kurum$_7$ aka al-tar bàd gub-ba, "inspection of (the work of workers) employed (for) construction of the (enclosure) wall," 14:40, 15:41, 17:37, 20:42, 21:'36, 22:'16, 99:16, 102:22

10 [g̃uruš SIG$_4$].ANŠE **ku[rum$_7$ aka a]l-tar** [bàd gub-ba], "inspection (of the work) of 10 [workmen employed] at the brick stack (for) construction of [the (enclosure) wall]," 23:'13

5.3 Construction of the Walls of the Textile Mill

kurum$_7$ aka al-tar bàd ù ki-sá-a é-uš-bar, "inspection of construction of the (enclosure) wall and foundation terrace of the textile mill," 31:51, 35:57

5.4 The Tablet Basket of Inspection Records

bisag̃-dub-ba gaba-ri **kurum$_7$ aka** u$_4$ **al-tar-ra** gub-ba, "a tablet basket of copies of inspection when (workers) were employed for construction," 1314:1–4

6. kurum$_7$ aka éren al-tar gub-ba, "inspection (of the work) of workers employed (for) construction"

6.1 Construction of the (Enclosure) Wall

kurum$_7$ aka éren al-tar bàd gub-ba, "inspection (of the work) of workers employed (for) construction of the (enclosure) wall," 16:35, 24:'38, 30:'20

6.2 Construction of the (Enclosure) Wall and Textile Mill

kurum$_7$ aka éren al-tar bàd ù é-uš-bar gub-ba, "inspection (of the work) of workers employed (for) construction of the (enclosure) wall and textile mill," 32:50, 33:54

7. u$_4$ al-tar-ra, "during construction"

u$_4$ al-tar é-lùnga é-muḫaldim ù é-kíkken, "{commodities disbursed} during construction of the brewery-kitchen-mill complex" > *Household Index*

u$_4$ al-tar ki-sá-a é-lùnga é-muḫaldim ù é-kikken, "{commodities disbursed} during construction of the foundation terrace of the brewery-kitchen-mill complex" > *Household Index*

7.1 Rations during Construction of the Brick Stack

[n.n.n.n sìla] zú-lum ⌜gur⌝ šidim ù lú-ḫug̃-g̃á-e-ne ba-na-ḫa-la **u$_4$ al-tar** SIG$_4$.AN[ŠE], "[n bushel(s) and liter(s)] of dates were divided for the builders and hired workers during construction of the brick stack," 424:1–3

7.2 Rations during Construction of the (Enclosure) Wall

[n] sìla 10 gín [kaš?] árad-é-a ù lú-ḫug̃-g̃á-e-ne ib-gu$_7$(sic!) **u_4 al-tar** bàd gub-ba, "The household servants and hired workers consumed [n] liter(s) (and) 10 shekels of [beer?] when they were employed (for) construction of the (enclosure) wall," 392:1–7

0.0.5.4 sìla kaš árad-é-a ù lú-ḫug̃-g̃á-e-ne **u_4 al-tar** bàd gub-ba, "54 liters of beer (for) the household servants and hired workers when they were employed (for) construction of the (enclosure) wall," 395:1–4

7.3 Requisitions for Boat Towers during Construction in Garšana

(. . .) níg̃-dab$_5$ g̃uruš má gíd-e-ne **u_4 al-tar-ra** gub-ba šà g̃ar-ša-an-na^{ki}, "{assorted commodities}, requisitions of the boat towers when they were employed for construction in Garšana," 442:19–20

al-ur$_x$(BÁḪAR)-ra, "(baked) brick"[6]

gir$_4$ šeg$_{12}$-**al-ur$_x$-ra** dù, "to construct an oven for baking bricks" > **dù**

šeg$_{12}$-**al-ur$_x$-ra** du$_8$, "to mold bricks" > **du$_8$**

šeg$_{12}$-**al-ur$_x$-ra** ga$_6$(g̃), "to carry bricks" > **ga$_6$(g̃)**

šeg$_{12}$-**al-ur$_x$-ra** gub-ba, "employed (to mold) bricks" > **gub**

šeg$_{12}$-**al-ur$_x$-ra** g̃ar, "to place bricks" > **g̃ar**

šeg$_{12}$-**al-ur$_x$-ra** šég̃$_6$, "to bake bricks" > **šég̃$_6$**

šeg$_{12}$-**al-ur$_x$-ra** ú-ru, "to pave (with) bricks" > **ú-ru**

^{ĝeš}ù-šub šeg$_{12}$-**al-ur$_x$-ra**, "brick mold (for) bricks" > **^{ĝeš}ù-šub**

0.1.0. še 2 ma-na siki-gen 2 sìla ì-g̃eš luḫ 60.0.0. gur-kam mu ésir šeg$_{12}$-**al-ur$_x$-ra**-šè, "60 liters of barley, 2 minas of ordinary wool (and) 2 liters of sesame oil – cleaning(?) of 60 bushels – for the bitumen of the bricks," 1296:1–5

1. Broken Context

10 g̃uruš šeg$_{12}$-[**al-u**]**r$_x$**-[**ra**. . .], 138:38

6 g̃uruš 6 géme šeg$_{12}$-**al-u**[**r$_x$-r**]**a** [. . .], 140:42

al-ús-sa "processed"

dabin **al-ús-sa**, "processed semolina" > **dabin**

é-ùr ku$_6$ **al-ús-sa**, "fish-sauce roof house" > *Household Index*

gú-gal **al-ús-sa**, "processed beans" > **gú-gal**

gú-tur **al-ús-sa**, "processed peas" > **gú-tur**

ku$_6$ **al-ús-sa**, "fish sauce" > **ku$_6$**

še-lú **al-ús-sa**, "processed coriander" > **še-lú**

---

6 The syllabic spelling here is unique for the third millennium. Pre-Sargonic šeg$_{12}$-alur$_x$(BÁḪAR)-ra is written regularly in the Ur III and later periods as šeg$_{12}$-al-ur$_5$-ra, šeg$_{12}$-al-ùr-ra, and šeg$_{12}$-al-lu-ra. The spelling here suggests two possible readings, šeg$_{12}$-^{al}alur$_x$(BÁḪAR)-ra or šeg$_{12}$-al-ur$_x$(BÁḪAR)-ra. We have opted for the reading with ur$_x$ although no such syllabic value is so far attested for BÁḪAR. See P. Steinkeller 1978, 74, n. 6; 1987, 59 and 1993, 145.

šim-sig$_5$ **al-ús-sa**, "processed fine aromatics" > **šim**

al-zi-ra, "used"

1. **niĝ al-zi-ra**, "used goods"

(. . .) [**níĝ**] **al-zi-ra** [. . . gir-r]a ba-ab-⌜gu$_7$⌝, "{assorted baskets and containers}, fire consumed the used goods," 1292:'23-'24

(. . .) **níĝ al-**⌜**zi**⌝**-ra**, "{assorted baskets and other reed products}, used goods," 1299:23

^{dug}**alal**, *alallû*, "pipe, conduit" > ^{dug}**ù-lu-lu**

alam, *ṣalmu*, "statue"

alam-lugal, "royal statue" > **lugal**

ama, *ummu*, "mother"

ama *tá-ḫi-iš-a-tal*, "the mother of *Tahiš-atal*" > *Personal Name Index*

ama-gal, "female mourner"[7]

0.0.2. dabin ninda-sal-la-⌜gen⌝ 1 sìla níĝ-àr-ra-sig$_5$ tu$_7$-šè gala ù **ama-gal-e-ne** íb-gu$_7$ u$_4$ *tak-ri-ib-tum* bàd, "the lamentation singers and the female mourners ate ordinary thin bread (made from) 20 liters of semolina (and) soup (made from) 1 liter of fine groats on the occasion of (their performance) of a *takribtum* at? the (enclosure) wall," 1035:'7-'11

amar, *atmu*, "young (animal)"

gu$_4$-**amar**-ga, "suckling calf" > **gu$_4$**
kuš-**amar**, "skin of a young animal" > **kuš**
kuš-**amar**-gu$_4$, "calf skin" > **kuš**
kuš-**amar**-anše, "donkey-foal skin" > **kuš**

[ANIMALS]

anše, "donkey"
^{munus}áš-gàr, "female kid"
gu$_4$, "ox"
kir$_{11}$, "female lamb"
^{anše}kúnga, "equid, probably a donkey-onager cross"
lulim, "stag"
maš-dà, "gazelle"
máš, "goat"
máš-gal, "billy-goat"

---

7 Gabbay, *forthcoming*.

péš-g̃eš-gi, "a type of large, edible (field) mouse"
$sila_4$, "lamb"
šáḫ, "pig"
u_8, "ewe"
ud_5, "female goat"
udu, "sheep"

an-za-qar, *dimtu*, "fortified tower"

an-za-qar-*da-da*, "fortified tower of *Dada*" > *Personal Name Index*

an-za-qar-$^{g̃eš}$kiri$_6$-zabala$_4$^{ki}, "fortified tower of the Zabala garden" > *Garden Index*

1. Tower (unspecified)

(. . .) [u_4]-3-šè [še x] x x x **an-za-qar**-ta kun-zi-da i_7-a-kàr-ús-sa a-šà lú-maḫ-šè íb-ga_6 ù má-a si-ga ⸢ús⸣-bi 36 nindan [ku]n-zi-da **an-za-qar**-ta [GN-šè] má še gíd-[da . . .] ús-bi 290 [nindan], "{workers and boats} for 3 [days], (the boats) carried [barley . . .] from the fortified tower to the weir of the Agar-usa Canal of the Lu-maḫ field and (the workers) having loaded the boats. Its distance is 36 nindan from the weir of the fortified tower [to GN], boats of barley to be towed a distance of 290 [nindan]," 553: 11–20

anše, *imēru*, "donkey"

kuš-**anše**, "donkey skin" > **kuš**

kuš-amar-**anše**, "donkey-foal skin" > **kuš**

$^{\mathbf{g̃eš}}$**apin**, *epinnu*, "(seed) plow"

★★^{kuš}x-x-**apin**? *ak-lu-um*, 925:'14

$^{g̃eš}$*la-ri-um*-$^{\mathbf{g̃eš}}$**apin**, 1255:2

1 apin!(GÍN) UD.K[A.B]AR ki-lá-bi 1 ma-[na] 3 gín, "1 bronze plow, its weight is 1 mina (and) 3 shekels," 1310:1–2

$^{\mathbf{g̃eš}}$**apin**-ig-ù-suḫ$_5$, "frame of pine door," 1333:1

★★[. . .] 1 gíd-[. . .] 12 sar 18 gín ⸢**apin**⸣? šà é-g̃ar 16½ sar 5 gín [*pe*]-*ṣe-ti* NE-gu$_7$-bi, 1397:'1-'8

apin-lá, *errēšu*, "planter, tiller, cultivator, (leased field?)"

10.2.4.5 sìla še gur še **apin-lá**-a, "10 bushels (and) 165 liters of barley, barley of the cultivator (leased field?)," 1089:1–2

41.2.0. še gur še **apin-lá** ki *a-da-làl* in-da-g̃ál, "41 bushels (and) 120 liters of barley, barley of the cultivator (leased field?) are with *Adallal*, at his place" 1158:1–4

[n] g̃uruš ^{lú}ázlag á-½ ⸢u_4⸣-8-šè (. . .) še **apin-lá**-a ⸢káb⸣ dì-de$_4$ ì-im-g̃en-na-a, "[n] fuller(s) at ½ wages for 8 days, {authorizing officials}, went to check on the grain of the cultivator (leased field?)," 271:1–2, 5–7

ar-gi$_5$-núm, *arginnu?*, "(a kind of food product?)"[8]

ki-ri-ip ***ar-gi$_5$-núm***, "(oil) jar of *arginnum*," 511:65, 972:17, 972:88, 975:18, 975:89

ar-za-na, *arsanu*, "barley-grits, groats," 409:2, 416:2, 493:6, 493:15, 494:6, 511:54, 523:8, 972:12, 972:77, 975:13, 975:78, 981:15, 999:9, 1025:5, 1025:28, 1025:47, 1025:64, 1025:82, 1025:103, 1167:6, 1167:16, 1179:12, 1199:9, 1208:11

ar-za-na šà-gal mušen-na, "barley-grits, fodder of birds" > **šà-gal**

àra, *samādu*, "to mill, grind" > *Verb Index*

árad, *wardu*, "servant"

árad-é-a, "servant of the household" > **árad-é-a**

árad-géme sugal$_7$-maḫ, "male and female servants of the sugal-maḫ" > **sugal$_7$-maḫ**

árad g̃ar, "to place (for) the servant" > **g̃ar**

árad *šu-eš$_4$-tár*, "the servant of *Šu-Eštar*" > *Personal Name Index*

géme-**árad** *simat-^{d}ištaran*, "female and male servants of *Simat-Ištaran*" > *Personal Name Index*

géme-**árad**-é-a ḫal, "to divide (for) female and male household servants" > **ḫal**

ì-ba ù níg̃-dab$_5$ géme-**árad**, "oil rations and requisitions of female and male servants" > **ì-ba**, **níg̃-ba**, **níg̃-dab$_5$**

ninda-ba géme-**árad**, "bread rations of female and male servants" > **ninda**

siki-ba géme-**árad**, "wool rations of female and male servants" > **siki**

še-ba géme-**árad**, "barley rations of female and male servants" > **še**

túg-ba géme-**árad**, "textile rations of female and male servants" > **túg**

árad-é-a, "household servant," *passim*

ma-šum **árad-é-a**, "*Mašum*, the household servant" > *Personal Name Index*

árad-é-a ù lú-ḫug̃-g̃á-e-ne ib-gu$_7$, "the household servants and hired workers ate {assorted comestibles}" > **gu$_7$**

1. **Household Builders**

3 g̃uruš **árad-é-a**, "3 workmen, household servants," 82:1

2 g̃uruš šidim **árad-é-a**, "2 builders, household servants," 78:1

3 g̃uruš šidim **árad-é-a(-me-éš)**, "3 builders, household servants," *passim*

2. **Workers Supervised by a Household Servant**

n g̃uruš ugula **árad-é-a**, "3 workmen supervised by a household servant," 25:'12, 26:'21, 28:'25, 29:'31, 31:36, 32:36, 33:39, 35:43, 36:37, 37:28, 38:36, 39:43, 40:37, 43:'41, 44:40, 45:22, 46:'38, 47:52, 48:57, 49:56

---

[8] Brunke 2008, 165 (§3.3.1.5).

[ki]-sá-a é-uš-bar-šè mu-DU **árad-é-a** ugula, "delivery (of bricks) for the foundation terrace of the textile mill by the overseer of the household servants," 322:'83-'84

^{ğeš}ásal(A.TU.GAB+LIŠ), *ṣarbatu*, "poplar"[9]

n sa+níğin ^{ğeš}**ásal**, "n bundle(s) of poplar wood," 1028:8, 1028:32

^{ğeš}**ásal** šeg$_{12}$-al-ur$_{x}$-ra šéğ$_{6}$, "poplar wood for baking bricks" > **šeğ$_{6}$**

^{ğeš}**ásal** šu aka, "processed poplar wood" > **šu ... aka**

^{ğeš}dal-**ásal**, "poplar beams" > **^{ğeš}dal**

^{ğeš}é-da-**ásal**, "poplar joists" > **^{ğeš}é-da**

^{ğeš}éren 1 gú ésir-**ásal**, "yoke of 1 talent of bitumen (coated) poplar" > **^{ğeš}éren**

^{ğeš}gag-**ásal**, "poplar wood peg" > **^{ğeš}gag**

ğeš ùr **ásal**, "poplar roof beams" > **ğeš ùr**

ḫar ^{ğeš}**ásal**-UD n(-ta), "poplar seedling(s), n (units) each," 1256:34–37, 1315:1, 1315:2, 1375:39–42

★★1 ^{ğeš}ĞEŠ/ĞEŠ 1 gú ésir-⌜**ásal**⌝, 1372:29, 1372:86

^{ğeš}*zi-ri-qum*-**ásal**, "poplar shaduf" > **^{ğeš}*zi-ri-qum***

15 x-⌜ka⌝ **ásal** 2-kùš-ta, 1275:3

aslum$_{x}$, *aslu*, *pasillu*, "long-fleeced sheep"[10]

udu-**aslum$_{x}$**, "long-fleeced sheep" > **udu**

^{munus}áš-gàr, *unīqu*, "female kid," 979:7, 1519:2

^{munus}**áš-gàr** niga, "fattened female kid," 984:4, 984:'60

^{munus}**áš-gàr** niga sá-du$_{11}$, "fattened female kid of regular offerings," 984:'59

ašgab, *aškāpu*, "leatherworker"

ğuruš **ašgab**, "leatherworker" > *Craftsmen Index*

1. **PN ašgab**, "PN, the leatherworker" > *Personal Name Index*

a-na-aḫ-ì-lí

nu-úr-^{d}adad

^{lú}ázlag(TÚG), *ašlāku*, "fuller"

ğuruš ^{lú}**ázlag**, "fuller" > *Craftsmen Index*

1. **nam-^{lú}ázlag**, "the craft of the fuller"

[n gé]me á-diri-ta **nam-^{lú}ázlag**-šè, "[n] workwomen at additional wages for fulling," 714:1–2

---

9 On the reading ^{ğeš}ásal see F. Carroué 1986, 53 n. 102, with references.

10 Steinkeller 1995, 52.

2. PN ^{lú}ázlag, "PN, the fuller" > *Personal Name Index*

bu-lu-za | *la-qì-ip*
ḫal-lí-a | *puzur$_4$-a-gu$_5$-um*

– B –

ba, *qiāšu, zâzu*, "to allot; to divide into shares; to give, present" > *Verb Index*

^{dug}**ba**, "(a vessel)"[11]

12 ^{dug}**b[a-x]** ⌜mu⌝ diğir-re-e-ne-šè gaz-dè, "12 [x]-vessels to be broken for the gods," 1013:6–7

^{ğeš}**ba**, *suppīnu*, "(a cutting tool)"

20 ma-na gu-^{ğeš}**ba** *zi-ba-tum* mu sa-par$_4$-šè, "20 minas of (?) cord for a net," 1162:'55-'56

ba-al, *herû*, "to dig, bail out (a cistern); to unload (a boat)" > *Verb Index*

^{gi}**ba-an-du$_8$-du$_8$**, "(a basket)"[12]

^{gi}**ba-an-du$_8$-du$_8$** ésir šub-ba, "a basket coated with bitumen," 1299:7, 1376:13

ba-an-gi$_4$, "taper, bevel, slant, incline"[13]

n nindan gíd n kùš dağal n kùš (**ba-an-**)**gi$_4$**-bi n kùš sukud saḫar-bi n sar (n gín n še) (. . .) n sar im-du$_8$-a, "n nindan long, n kùš wide, n kùš tapered from n kùš high, its dirt is n sar (n gín (and) n še); (the total volume) of the adobe wall is n sar," 366:'1-'3, 366:'7-'8, '13, 366:'9-'10, '13, 366:'11-'13, 366:'17–19

^{ğeš}**ba-an-la**, "(a wooden object)," 1349:3

ba-ba, "(a kind of porridge)"[14]

1. **ba-ba-munu$_4$**, "malt porridge," 511:61, 523:10, 972:60, 972:84, 975:61, 975:85, 1046:3
2. **ba-ba-še**, "barley porridge," 494:15, 509:6, 511:55, 972:13, 972:78, 975:14, 975:79, 999:7, 1025:29, 1025:48, 1025:104
3. **zì-ba-ba**, "(a kind of porridge made of flour)"

   zì-ba-ba-sig$_5$, "fine flour porridge," 511:49, 972:55, 972:72, 975:58, 975:73, 1033:7, 1134:4, 1394:12

---

11 For dug-ba as a variant dug-bán, "Gefäss (mit einem Volumen) von 1 Seah," see Sallaberger 1996, 98.

12 Civil 1994, 1.21 and commentary p. 74. He interprets this as the "basket used to carry the seed for the plow funnel and also to measure the seed beforehand."

13 Heimpel 2004.

14 Brunke 2008, 154–159 (§3.2).

ba-rí-ga, *parsiktu*, "a unit of capacity; a measuring container"

^{gi}gur **ba-rí-ga**, "(a gur-measuring basket)" > **^{gi}gur**

ba-tab *tuḫ-ḫu-um*, "(a specification of textiles)"

^{túg}bar-si túg **ba-tab *tuḫ-ḫu-um***, "band of a ba-tab *tuḫ-ḫu-um* textile" > **^{túg}bar-si**

^{túg}gú-è **ba-tab *tuḫ-ḫu-um***, "ba-tab *tuḫ-ḫu-um* cape" > **^{túg}gú-è**

^{túg}sagšu **ba-tab *tuḫ-ḫu-um***, "ba-tab *tuḫ-ḫu-um* cap" > **^{túg}sagšu**

siki túg **ba-tab *tuḫ-ḫu-um***, "wool (for) a ba-tab *tuḫ-ḫu-um* textile" > **siki**

^{túg}šà-ga-dù **ba-tab *tuḫ-ḫu-um***, "ba-tab *tuḫ-ḫu-um* belt" > **^{túg}šà-ga-dù**

^{túg}šà-gi$_4$-dab$_6$ **ba-tab *tuḫ-ḫu-um***, "ba-tab *tuḫ-ḫu-um* šà-gi$_4$-dab$_6$ textile" > **^{túg}šà-gi$_4$-dab$_6$**

túg **ba-tab *tuḫ-ḫu-um***, "ba-tab *tuḫ-ḫu-um* textile," 818:3, 1394:1

túg **ba-tab *tuḫ-ḫu-um*** 3-kam-ús, "3rd-quality ba-tab *tuḫ-ḫu-um* textile," 570:1, 578:6, 579:6, 618:3, 643:1, 662:1, 753:5, 757:1, 758:2, 806:2, 810:1, 814:5, 835:'2, 1162:'12

túg **ba-tab *tuḫ-ḫu-um*** 3-kam-ús ^{d}inana, "3rd-quality ba-tab *tuḫ-ḫu-um* textile of Inana," 1028:31

túg **ba-tab *tuḫ-ḫu-um*** 4-kam-ús, "4th-quality ba-tab *tuḫ-ḫu-um* textile," 578:8, 579:8, 701:7, 746:1, 758:9, 786:6

túg **ba-tab *tuḫ-ḫu-um*** [4]-kam-ús [lú]-KAŠ$_4$, "[4th]-quality ba-tab *tuḫ-ḫu-um* textile (for) the runner," 579:10

túg **ba-tab *tuḫ-ḫu-um*** [n]-kam-ús, "[nth]-quality ba-tab *tuḫ-ḫu-um* textile," 694:1, 709:2

túg **ba-tab *tuḫ-ḫu-um***-[gen], "[ordinary] ba-tab *tuḫ-ḫu-um* textile," 764:3

1 túg **ba-tab *tuḫ-ḫu-u*[*m* ?]** ki-lá-bi 1 ma-na [n gín], "1 ba-tab *tuḫ-ḫu-um* textile, its weight is 1 mina (and) [n gín]," 747:3–4

túg [**ba-tab *t*]*uḫ-ḫu-um*** ⌜lugal⌝-ra, "[ba-tab] *tuḫ-ḫu-um* textile for the king," 609:6

túg **ba-tab *tuḫ-ḫu-um***-PI-ús, "ba-tab *tuḫ-ḫu-um*-PI textile," 578:2

túg **ba-tab *tuḫ*-[*ḫu-um*]**-PI-ús-tur *simat*-[^{d}*ištaran*], "small ba-tab *tuḫ-ḫu-um*-PI textile of *Simat-Ištaran*," 610:1

túg **ba-tab *tuḫ-ḫu-um***-PI *simat*-^{d}*ištaran*, "ba-tab *tuḫ-ḫu-um*-PI textile of *Simat-Ištaran*," 608:1

túg **ba-tab *tuḫ-ḫu-um*-PI-UD-DINGIR[?], 1254:'37

túg **ba-tab *tuḫ-ḫu-um*** *simat*-^{d}*ištaran*, "ba-tab *tuḫ-ḫu-um* textile of *Simat-Ištaran*," 618:1, 801:1, 823:1

túg **ba-tab *tuḫ-ḫu-um*** tab-ba-gen ^{geš}gu-za *šu-kab-tá*, "ordinary double ba-tab *tuḫ-ḫu-um* textile (for) the chair of *Šu-Kabta*," 737:3–4

[túg **ba**]**-tab *tuḫ-ḫ*[*u-um***-tur 4-kam-ús], "[4th-quality small] ba-tab *tuḫ-ḫu-um* [textile]," 578:10

túg **ba-tab *tuḫ-ḫu-um***-tur-gen pi-lu-da, "small ordinary ba-tab *tuḫ-ḫu-um* textile (for) ritual (use)," 787:3

túg **ba-tab *tuḫ-ḫu-u*[*m*** . . .], 403:9, 579:2

túg **ba-tab *tuḫ-ḫu-um*** [?], 654:2

^{gi}*ba-ti-um*, "(a reed container)"

1 **^{gi}*ba-ti-um*** búr 3-sìla gi-bi x x IB? búr x x ma-x x x [x . . . á-bi u$_4$]-3-[kam], "1 reed container with a volume(?) of 3 liters. (Manufacture required:) reeds, [. . .] (and) 3 [days of labor], 374:'8-'12

babbar, *peṣû*, "(to be) white"

kuš-udu-**babbar**, "white sheep skin" > **kuš-udu**

^{túg}sagšu-**babbar**, "white cap" > $^{\textbf{túg}}$**sagšu**

^{kuš}súḫub-**babbar**, "white shoes" > $^{\textbf{kuš}}$**súḫub**

udu-**babbar**, "white sheep" > **udu**

bàd, *dūru*, "(enclosure) wall"

da **bàd**, "the side of the (enclosure) wall"

iz-zi **bàd**, "the iz-zi wall of the (enclosure) wall"

sag̃ **bàd**, "the head of the (enclosure) wall"

ù-ru-a **bàd**, "the urua wall"

uš **bàd**, "the foundation of the (enclosure) wall"

1. **bàd**, "the (enclosure) wall"

al-tar **bàd**, "construction of the (enclosure) wall" > **al-tar**

bàd egir é-a, "the (enclosure) wall behind the house" > **egir**, *Household Index*

bàd im sumur aka, "to plaster the (enclosure) wall" > **aka**

bàd-šè mu-DU, "delivery of bricks for the (enclosure) wall" > **mu-DU**

gi-sal **bàd** gul "to trim thin reeds at the (enclosure) wall" > **gul**

gi-sal **bàd** tà(g), "to stucco thin reeds on the (enclosure) wall" > **tà(g)**

kurum$_7$ aka éren al-tar **bàd** gub-ba, "inspection (of the work) of workers employed (for) construction of the (enclosure) wall" > **al-tar**

kurum$_7$ aka éren šu dím **bàd** gub-ba, "inspection (of the work) of workers employed to build the (enclosure) wall" > **šu dím**

šeg$_{12}$ **bàd** tab, "to lay bricks at the (enclosure) wall" > **tab**

sízkur **bàd**, "(ceremonial) offering (for) the (enclosure) wall" > **sízkur**

u$_4$ *tak-ri-ib-tum* **bàd**, "on the occasion of (the performance of) a *takribtum* at(?) the (enclosure) wall" > ***takribtum***

1.1 Construction Work of the (Enclosure) Wall: Broken Context

3 géme im ga$_6$-g̃á-[dè gub-ba] **bàd** x-[. . .], 47:39–40

2 g̃uruš i[m-. . .] g̃á-g̃á **b[àd** . . .] 1-kam? éren? dù-dè [gub-ba], 49:34

1 g̃uruš šidim ká im š[eg$_{12}$] ⌜ku$_4$⌝-ra **bàd** x-[. . .] ká sè-g[é-dè gub-ba], "1 builder [employed] to place [. . .] at the 'service entrance' of the gate," 200:'11-'12

1.2 Offerings(?) for the (Enclosure) Wall

0.0.1. [. . .] 3 [. . .] **bàd**-[šè], 1035:'1-'3

1.3 Thin Reeds for the (Enclosure) Wall

4800 sa gi-izi gu-[níg̃in] 13-sa-ta gi-sa[l **bà]d**-šè ba-g̃ar, "4800 bundles of fuel reeds, bales of 13 bundles each, thin reeds placed for the (enclosure) wall," 1259:1–3

3600+3000+40[+n sa] gi-[izi] gu-níg̃in 20-sa-[ta] gi-sal **bàd**-šè, "9640[+n bundles] of [fuel] reeds, bales of 20 bundles each, thin reeds for the (enclosure) wall," 1288:1–3

660 sa gi-[izi] gu-níĝin [n sa-ta] gi-sal-[x] **bàd**-šè, "660 bundles of [fuel] reeds, bales of [n bundle(s) each], thin reeds for the (enclosure) wall," 1316:1–3

2. **da bàd**, "the side of the (enclosure) wall"

da bàd gub-ba, "employed at the side of the (enclosure) wall" > **gub**

da bàd saḫar sè(g_{10}), "to tamp dirt at the side of the (enclosure) wall" > **sè(g_{10})**

šeg$_{12}$ **da bàd** ĝar, "to place bricks at the side of the (enclosure) wall" > **ĝar**

3. **iz-zi bàd**, "the iz-zi wall of the (enclosure) wall" > **iz-zi**

4. **saĝ bàd**, "the head of the (enclosure) wall"

saĝ bàd im sumur aka, "to plaster the head of the (enclosure) wall" > **aka**

5. **ù-ru-a bàd**, "the urua wall" > **ù-ru-a**

6. **uš bàd**, "the foundation of the (enclosure) wall"

saḫar **uš bàd** zi(g), "to move dirt at the foundation of the (enclosure) wall" > **zi(g)**

sízkur **uš bàd**, "(ceremonial) offering (for) the foundation of the (enclosure) wall" > **sízkur**

uš bàd aka, "to make the foundation of the (enclosure) wall" > **aka**

uš bàd tà(g), "to apply stucco to the foundation of the (enclosure) wall" > **tà(g)**

báḫar, *pahāru*, "potter"

ĝuruš **báḫar**, "potter" > *Craftsmen Index*

bala, "to rotate, turn over, cross" > *Verb Index*

n sìla še-**bala**-bi šà-gal mušen-na, "n liter(s) of barley of the bala, fodder of birds" > **šà-gal**

^{dug}úgur **bala**, "bala vessel" > **^{dug}úgur**

balag, *balangu*, "a large drum"

2 sìla dabin 1 sìla A.[TIR **ba]**lag**-x-[x?], 506:14–15

bán, *sūtu*, "unit of capacity"[15]

n zíz gur **ba-na** zì-KAL n sìla-ta ì-ĝál, "n bushel(s) of emmer wheat, in each ban (=10 liters) of it there are n liter(s) of KAL-flour" > **ĝál**

^{ĝeš}banšur, *paššūru*, "table"

[. . .] ì-ĝeš [. . .] $^{[ĝe]š}$gu-za ù **^{ĝeš}banšur**, "[. . .] sesame oil [. . .] chair and table," 562:'77-'78

[1] gi é-KU-**^{ĝeš}banšur** gi-bi ½ sa ésir-é-a-bi ⅓ sìla á-bi u$_4$-⅓-kam, "1 (reed object for? a table). (Manufacture required:) ½ bundle of reeds, ⅓ liter of house bitumen (and) ⅓ of a day of labor," 1381:58–61

---

15 For the interpretation of ba-na as bán-a (locative), see Brunke 2008, 25 (§2.1.5) n. 35.

báppir, *báppiru*, "beer bread, an ingredient in beer-making"

báppir du_8, "to bake beer bread" > **du_8**

báppir dirig $sila_{11}$(g̃), "to knead additional beer bread" > **$sila_{11}$(g̃)**

báppir $sila_{11}$(g̃), "to knead beer bread" > **$sila_{11}$(g̃)**

báppir-gen, "ordinary beer bread," 511:36, 511:59, 972:31, 972:47, 972:82, 975:33, 975:50, 975:83, 1036:'19, 1036:'34, 1036:'68, 1206:2, 1210:1, 1242:1, 1247:2, 1254:'23

báppir-sig_5, "fine beer bread," 511:58, 972:46, 972:81, 975:32, 975:49, 975:82, 1020:1, 1025:1, 1025:107, 1036:'18, 1036:'24, 1036:'67, 1131:1, 1230:1, 1254:'22

1. **Barley Equivalents**

23⅓ ma-na **báppir**-sig_5 še-bi 0.0.3.5 sìla, "23⅓ minas of fine beer bread, its barley (equivalent) is 35 liters," 1527:6–7

2. **Beer Bread for Additional Beer**

1 gú **báppir** kaš dirig-šè, "1 talent of beer bread for additional beer," 1244:1–2

bar, *warkatu*, "outside, (other) side"

dùb bar-ra, "outer knee" > **dùb**

bar, "fleece"

1. **bar-udu**, "sheep fleece"

19 ma-na siki-gen ⅓ ma-na siki-g̃e$_6$ **bar-udu** 32-kam "19 minas of ordinary wool (and) ⅓ mina of black wool of 32 sheep fleeces," 634:1–3

$^{\text{g̃eš}}$**bar**, *mayāru*, "(a type of plow)"

⋆⋆$^{\text{g̃eš}}$**bar**-bi éš-g̃ar, 635:8

bar-da, *mušelû*, "crossbar"

bar-da $^{\text{g̃eš}}$ig-g̃e$_6$ ba-a-kéše, "to bind the crossbar of a black door" > **kéše**

^{túg}**bar-dul$_5$**, *ṣubātu*, "(a textile)"

^{túg}**bar-dul$_5$**-gen, "ordinary bar-dul$_5$ textile," 654:7, 662:6, 663:5, 669:8, 673:6, 676:3, 691:2, 694:4, 738:14, 748:10, 758:13, 760:6, 765:5, 778:8, 786:12, 793:7, 796:7, 799:3, 800:4, 801:5, 802:2, 814:10, 821:9

^{túg}**bar-dul$_5$**-ús, "2nd-quality bar-dul$_5$ textile," 569:11

^{túg}**bar-dul$_5$**-⌜ús⌝ *šu-kab-ta*, "2nd-quality bar-dul$_5$ textile of *Šu-Kabta*," 588:3

^{túg}**bar-dul$_5$** 3-kam-ús, "3rd-quality bar-dul$_5$ textile," 658:2, 673:3, 698:6, 748:4, 753:6, 800:1, 1162:'11

^{túg}**bar-dul$_5$** 4-kam-ús, "4th-quality bar-dul$_5$ textile," 578:9, 579:9, 649:5, 654:5, 742:4, 753:10, 778:5, 786:5, 810:2, 829:'4

^{túg}**bar-dul$_5$** 4-kam-ús al-bi-ra, "shredded? 4th-quality bar-dul$_5$ textile," 698:26

⋆⋆^{túg}**bar-dul$_5$** abzu? *a-ši-um*, "abzu? *a-ši-um* bar-dul$_5$ textile," 571:1

^{túg}**bar-dul$_5$** ba-tab *tuḫ-ḫu-um* 3-kam-ús, "3rd-quality ba-tab *tuḫ-ḫu-um* bar-dul$_5$ textile," 569:13

^{túg}**bar-dul$_5$** *šu-kab-ta*, "bar-dul$_5$ textile of *Šu-Kabta*," 608:2, 654:1

★★^{túg}**bar-dul$_5$** *šu-kab-tá a-ši-um*, "*a-ši-um* bar-dul$_5$ textile of *Šu-Kabta*," 762:1

^{túg}**bar-dul$_5$**-AB *šu-kab-tá*, "bar-dul$_5$-AB textile of *Šu-Kabta*," 591:5, 677:1, 698:2, 794:1

^{túg}**bar-dul$_5$**-gal 3-kam-ús, "large 3rd-quality bar-dul$_5$ textile," 646:3, 796:2

^{túg}**bar-dul$_5$**-gal 4-kam-ús, "large 4th-quality bar-dul$_5$ textile," 771:4

★★^{túg}**bar<-dul$_5$**>-níĝ-lám-x-[. . .], 829:'6

^{túg}**bar-dul$_5$**-túg-⸢sig$_5$?-tur⸣, "small fine? bar-dul$_5$ textile," 727:1

^{túg}**bar-dul$_5$**-tur, "small bar-dul$_5$ textile,"676:4

^{túg}**bar-dul$_5$**-tur-gen, "ordinary small bar-dul$_5$ textile," 674:7, 680:2, 722:1, 734:4, 786:13, 793:3, 800:5, 801:6

^{túg}**bar-dul$_5$**-tur 3-kam-ús, "small 3rd-quality bar-dul$_5$ textile," 651:4, 743:2

^{túg}**bar-dul$_5$**-tur 4-kam-ús, "small 4th-quality bar-dul$_5$ textile," 743:6, 803:3, 804:1

[n ^{túg}**bar-dul$_5$**]-tur 4-kam-ús [ki-lá]-bi 14½ ma-na, "[n] small 4th-quality bar-dul$_5$ textile(s), their [weight] is 14½ minas," 738:12–13

^{túg}**bar-dul$_5$**-ús-sa [. . .], 746:8

^{túg}**bar-dul$_5$**-[. . .], 591:9, 669:1, 765:2

^{túg}**bar-dul$_5$**-x-[. . .], 654:8

^{túg}**bar-dul$_5$**-[x] 3-kam-ús, 713:1

^{túg}**bar-d[ul$_5$**-. . .] ki-lá-bi 18 [. . .], 724:1–2

^{túg}**bar-si**, "woven band, ribbon"

3 ^{túg}**bar-si** 3 ma-n[a-ta], "3 bands (weighing) 3 minas [each]," 701:10

^{túg}**bar-si**-gen, "ordinary band," 692:6, 739:6

^{túg}**bar-si**-ús, "2nd-quality band," 636:1, 708:1, 709:1, 718:1, 726:1, 742:1, 786:1, 1162:'19

^{túg}**bar-si**-ús-nin, "2nd-quality lady's band," 814:4

^{túg}**bar-si** 3-kam-ús, "3rd-quality band," 636:4, 646:5, 647:2, 674:4, 701:3, 744:1, 745:1, 758:8, 760:3, 771:3, 775:2, 778:2

1 ^{túg}**bar-si** [3-kam-ús] ki-lá-bi 4-gín, "1 [3rd-quality] band, its weight is 4 shekels," 747:1–2

^{túg}**bar-si** 4-kam-ús, "4th-quality band," 618:11, 636:6, 764:5

^{túg}**bar-si** ba-tab *tuḫ-ḫu-um*, "ba-tab *tuḫ-ḫu-um* band," 674:5

^{túg}**bar-si** ba-tab *tuḫ-ḫu-um* 3-kam-ús, "3rd-quality ba-tab *tuḫ-ḫu-um* band," 617:3, 696:1, 778:3, 827:6, 835:'6

^{túg}**bar-si** ba-tab *tuḫ-ḫu-um* 4-kam-ús, "4th-quality ba-tab *tuḫ-ḫu-um* band," 835:'10

^{túg}**bar-si**-gal 3-kam-ús, "large 3rd-quality band," 786:2

^{túg}**bar-si**-gal ba-tab *tuḫ-ḫu-um* 3-kam-ús, "large 3rd-quality ba-tab *tuḫ-ḫu-um* band," 690:4, 811:6, 834:15

^{túg}**bar-si**-gal ba-tab *tuḫ-ḫu-um* 4-kam-ús, "large 4th-quality ba-tab *tuḫ-ḫu-um* band," 569:14

^{túg}**bar-si** gú-è é-ba-an, "pair of ties (for) a cape," 649:3, 748:9

^{túg}**bar-si** gú-è 3-kam-ús é-ba-an, "3rd-quality ties (for) a cape," 802:1

^{túg}**bar-si** gú-è-tur-lugal, "small royal ties (for) a cape," 821:2

^{túg}**bar-si** gùn-a 3-kam-ús, "3rd-quality multicolored band," 577:2

^{túg}**bar-si** gùn-a 4-kam-ús, "4th-quality multicolored band," 564:2, 565:2, 568:2, 577:4, 786:11

^{túg}**bar-si** níĝ-lá-gen, "ordinary níĝ-lá band," 569:15, 586:3, 587:3, 663:6, 834:16, 835:'14

^{túg}**bar-si** níĝ-lá-gen sumun, "old ordinary níĝ-lá band," 1272:9

^{túg}**bar-si** níĝ-lá 3-kam-ús, "3rd-quality níĝ-lá band," 580:1

^{túg}**bar-si** níĝ-lá 4-kam-ús, "4th-quality níĝ-lá band," 580:2

^{túg}**bar-si** níĝ-lá ba-tab *tuḫ-ḫu-um* 3-kam-ús, "3rd-quality níĝ-lá ba-tab *tuḫ-ḫu-um* band," 572:4

1 **bar-si** siki-ud$_5$ šà-tuku$_5$ é-ba-an ki-lá-bi 2 ma-na, "1 pair of bands (for) a mattress, their weight is 2 minas," 740:3–4

^{túg}**bar-si** túg ba-tab *tuḫ-[ḫu]-um* 3-[kam]-ús, "band of a 3rd-quality ba-tab *tuḫ-ḫu-um* textile," 572:3

^{túg}**bar-si** [túg] ba-tab *tuḫ-[ḫu]-um* 4-k[am-ús], "band of a 4th-quality ba-tab *tuḫ-ḫu-um* [textile]," 565:3

^{túg}**bar-si** túg-gíd-[da], "band of a long textile," 793:11

^{túg}**bar-si**-ĝe$_6$, "black band," 651:7

^{túg}**bar-si**-nin, "lady's band," 646:2, 821:3

^{túg}**bar-si** [. . .], 663:1, 765:3

^{túg}gú-è ba-tab *tuḫ-ḫu-um* **bar-si** ĝar-ra 3-kam-ús, "3rd-quality ba-tab *tuḫ-ḫu-um* cape fashioned with bands," 586:2, 587:2

^{túg}gú-è-níĝ-lám **bar-si** ĝar-ra 3-kam-ús, "3rd-quality níĝ-lám cape fashioned with bands," 579:16

^{túg}gú-è-níĝ-lám **bar-si** ĝar-ra 4-kam-ús, "4th-quality níĝ-lám cape fashioned with bands," 1162:'18

^{túg}gú-è *tá-ki-ru-um* **bar-s[i** ĝar-r]a-tur lugal, "small royal *takkirum* cape fashioned with bands," 824:1

barag, "to press, to mix" > *Verb Index*

barag, *bašamu*, "sack; a part of an animal's body," 848:1, 1272:10

^{kuš}a-ĝá-lá **barag**-bi maš-dà, "leather sack, its barag of gazelle skin" > ^{kuš}**a-ĝá-lá**

^{kuš}a-ĝá-lá **barag**-bi udu, "leather sack, its barag of sheep skin" > ^{kuš}**a-ĝá-lá**

barag-siki-ud$_5$, "goat-hair sack" > **siki**

^{ĝeš}***be-rum***, "(a wooden object)"

★★4 túg-*bu-ti-um*(?) ^{ĝeš}***be-rum*** siki ^{ĝeš}garig aka gen ki-lá-bi ⅔ ma-na, 807:1–3

bí-ni-tum, *binītu*, "a crossbeam"[16]

bí-ni-tum gíd, "to haul crossbeams" > **gíd**

bí-ni-tum im sumur aka, "to plaster crossbeams" > **im sumur aka**

---

16 For a different interpretation cf. Heimpel 2008, §4.11.

bíl, *qalû*, "to burn" > *Verb Index*

bir$_7$, *šarāṭu*, "to shred" > **al-bi-ra**

^{gi}bisağ, *pisannu*, "basket, container"

bisağ im sar-ra im ga$_6$(ğ), "to carry earth in the clay tablet coffer" > **ga$_6$(ğ)**

1. **Types of Baskets**

1.1 **^{ğeš}bisağ**, "a wooden basket or container"

1 **bisağ**?(ğeš?)-[. . .], 1337:7

1 **^{ğeš}bisağ**-tur gíd-da na$_4$, "small, long basket (for) stone," 1372:36, 1372:93

1.2 **bisağ^{zabar}**, "a bronze container"

1 **bisağ^{zabar}** dub-x zabar ğar-⌜ra⌝, "1 bronze container of tablets(?), covered in bronze," 1337:6

1.3 **bisağ-dub-ba**, "tablet basket"

4.0.0. dabin gur ⌜**bisağ**⌝**-dub-ba**-ka ğál-la, "there are 4 bushels of semolina in the tablet basket," 1233:12–13

bisağ-dub-ba gaba-ri kurum$_7$ aka éren al-tar-ra gub-ba, "a tablet basket of copies of inspection (of the work) of workers employed for construction," 1314:1–4

1.4 **^{gi}bisağ-gíd-da**, "long basket," 1311:1

4 **^{gi}bisağ-gíd-da**-tur sa-ḫa gíd-2-kùš dağal-1-kùš, "4 small, long, canvas-lined baskets, 2 kùš in length, 1 kùš in width," 1006:1

n **^{gi}bisağ-gíd-da**-tur sa-ḫa, "n small, long, canvas-lined basket(s)," 1011:4, 1011:9, 1347:1

1.5 **^{gi}bisağ-gíd-da túg-ga**, "long basket (for) textiles," 834:19

2 **^{gi}bisağ-gíd-da** [**túg**]**-ga** sa-ḫa, "2 long canvas-lined baskets (for) textiles," 602:2

1 **^{gi}bisağ-gíd-da túg-ga**-tur ésir šub-ba ka-bi kuš-ğar-ra, "1 long, small basket coated with bitumen (for) textiles, its opening covered with leather," 798:1–3

1.6 **^{gi}bisağ-im-sar-ra**, "clay tablet coffer"

1 **^{gi}bisağ-im-sar-ra** [sa-ḫ]a ⅔ kùš íb-sá im-sar ğá-ğá-dè u$_4$ é-[e] im sumur ba-aka, "1 canvas-lined clay tablet coffer—it is ⅔ kùš square—(in which) to deposit clay tablets when the house was plastered," 1318:1–3

1 **^{gi}bisağ-im-sar-ra** sa-ḫa ⅔ kùš íb-sá im-sar ğá-ğá-dè, "1 canvas-lined clay tablet coffer—it is ⅔ kùš square—(in which) to deposit clay tablets," 1331:1–2, 1365:1–3

1.7 **^{gi}bisağ ninda-gur$_4$-ra**, "basket (for) thick bread"

1 **^{gi}bisağ ninda-gur$_4$-ra** ésir šub-ba, "1 basket coated with bitumen (for) thick bread," 1376:44

1 **^{gi}bisağ ninda-gur$_4$-ra** [peš]-múrgu-bi 1 [pa] ^{ğeš}nimbar-bi 3, "1 basket (for) thick bread. (Manufacture required:) 1 date palm spine (and) 3 date palm fronds," 1381:25–27

1.8 **^{gi}bisağ túg-aš**, "single textile basket," 749:3, 751:3, 913:3, 1352:1, 1376:15

120 **^{gi}bisağ**-gíd-da **túg-**[**aš**], "120 long single textile baskets," 1292:8

1 **^{gi}bisağ túg-aš** pa ^{ğeš}nimbar-bi 3, "1 single-textile basket. (Manufacture required:) 3 date palm fronds," 1381:28–29

1.9 Reading Uncertain

⋆⋆1 ^{gi}**bisağ**? é-ĞAR kuš ğar-ra, "1 (?) basket, covered with leather," 1332:2

⋆⋆1 ^{gi}**bisağ**-BÚR-tab-ba ğeš-tab-ba, 1336:1

1.10 Broken Context

^{gi}**bisağ**-[. . .], 1292:'18, 1292:'21

[BOVINES]

gu$_4$, "bull"

[BREADS AND CAKES]

níğ-ì-dé-a, "(a dessert, pastry)"
níğ-*lá-lá-rum*, "(a dessert, pastry)"
ninda-dabin, "semolina bread"
ninda-*e-bi-a-tum*, "thick bread"
ninda-gal, "large (loaf of) bread"
ninda-gúg, "(a cake)"
ninda-gur$_4$-ra, "thick bread"
ninda-ğeš-AŠ, "(a bread)"
ninda-ne-mur, "bread (baked in) ash"
ninda-sal-la, "thin bread"
ninda-šu-ra, "half(-loaf) bread"
ninda-tuḫ, "bran bread"
ninda-*u$_4$-tuḫ-ḫu-um*, "(a bread)"
ninda-zì-gu, "gu-flour bread"

bù(r), *nasāḫu*, "to cut, trim; to pull out" > *Verb Index*

^{gi}**bunin-bunin**, *kuninu, pattû*, "trough, bowl, bucket," 592:3

bùr, *būru*, "a unit of area; a unit of volume"

n kùš **bùr** saḫar-bi n, "n kùš in area, its dirt (volume) is n bùr" > **saḫar**

a-šà 1 (**bùr**) 2 (iku) GÁNA, "a field of 1 bur (and) 2 iku of acreage," 1051:3

1 (**bùr**) GÁNA zàr tab-ba nu-de$_5$-de$_5$-ga, "the sheaves stacked on 1 bur of acreage are not to be collected," 1398:1–3

1 ^{gi}*ba-ti-um* **búr**[17] 3-sìla gi-bi x x IB? **búr** x x ma-x x x [x . . . á-bi u$_4$] 3-[kam], "1 reed container with a volume? of 3 liters. (Manufacture required:) reeds, [. . .] (and) 3 [days of labor], 374:'8-'12

---

[17] The writing búr is a phonetic variant of bùr.

buru$_{14}$, *ebūru*, "harvest"

ezem-gur-**buru**$_4$, "bushel harvest festival" > **ezem**
egir **buru**$_{14}$ gi$_4$, "to be paid back after the harvest" > **gi**$_4$

[CANALS] > **i**$_7$**(íd)**

[CAPRIDS]

gukkal, "fat-tailed sheep"
maš-dà, "gazelle"
máš, "goat"
u$_8$, "ewe"
ud$_5$, "goat"
udu, "sheep"

[CEREALS AND GRAINS]

ar-za-na, "barley-grits, groats"
dabin, "semolina, barley grits"
eša, "(a fine flour)"
img̃ag̃a$_3$, "emmer"
níg̃-àr-ra, "groats"
še, "barley"
tuḫ, "bran"
zì, "flour"
zíz, "emmer wheat"

– D –

da, *idu*, "side"

da bàd, "the side of the (enclosure) wall" > **bàd**
da-iz-zi, "the side of the iz-zi wall" > **iz-zi**
da-ki-sá-a, "the side of the foundation terrace" > **ki-sá-a**
iz-zi-**da**, "side-wall" > **iz-zi**

$^{g̃eš}$**da**, "(a tree)"

1 ḪAR $^{g̃eš}$**da** 1, "1 da tree seedling of 1 (unit)," 1256:38

^{kuš}**da-lá**, "(a leather object)," 968:4

da-na, *bêru*, "a unit of length, double-hour (distance), double-mile"

1 má-80-gur [x? d]a-na** gur a 1 sìla-ta še-bi 2.0.4. gur, 561:'35-'37

1 ⸢má⸣-60-gur [da-na**] gur a 1 sìla-ta [še-bi n.n.n.] gur, 561:'38-'40

(. . .) [gú] i_7-⸢*ma*⸣-*an-iš-ti-šu*-ta gar-ša-an-na[ki]-⸢šè⸣ má diri-ga **da-na**-bi 9-àm, "{barley in boats} floated from the [bank] of the *Maništišu* canal to Garšana, (a distance of) 9 double-miles," 561:'41-'44

gú i_7-me-kal-kal-ta 1 **da-na** 1200 nindan ús bàd-[d]šul-gi-šè, "1 da-na (and) 1200 nindan, the length from the bank of the Mekalkal canal to Bad-Šulgi," 1382:1–3

šu+níĝin 3 ⸢**da**⸣**-n**[**a** 240+]120 nindan ús gú i_7-me-kal-kal *simat-é-a* a-da-ga-ta ká-[d]*šu*-[d]*suen*-šè, "In total: 3 da-na (and) 360 nindan, the length from the bank of the Mekalkal canal of *Simat-Ea* (and its) irrigation ditch to the *Šu-Suen* gate," 1382:14–16

dab$_5$, *ṣabātu*, "to take in charge" > *Verb Index*

dabin, *tappinu*, "semolina, barley grits," 383:2, 383:6, 383:9, 385:2, 385:8, 396:13, 399:14, 399:23, 426:1, 435:1, 436:1, 437:2, 439:1, 440:1, 440:5, 441:1, 446:2, 464:1, 465:2, 479:2, 479:10, 488:8, 493:3, 493:13, 494:3, 494:11, 506:1, 506:6, 506:10, 506:12, 506:14, 511:47, 512:2, 514:2, 520:3, 523:4, 524:2, 533:2, 537:2, 539:2, 552:2, 879:1, 950:1, 972:3, 972:52, 972:70, 975:6, 975:55, 975:71, 981:6, 987:1, 988:1, 989:1, 990:1, 991:1, 992:1, 993:1, 994:1, 995:1, 999:2, 1001:4, 1007:2, 1007:6, 1008:4, 1016:1, 1016:10, 1016:15, 1016:18, 1017:3, 1027:5, 1027:9, 1028:28, 1030:3, 1030:6, 1030:13, 1030:20, 1030:27, 1030:33, 1033:5, 1034:'4, 1034:'8, 1035:'4, 1072:2, 1080:1, 1082:1, 1088:1, 1096:1, 1097:1, 1100:4, 1106:1, 1108:1, 1111:1, 1114:1, 1117:2, 1118:1, 1121:1, 1122:1, 1124:1, 1132:1, 1134:2, 1136:1, 1137:1, 1141:1, 1144:2, 1151:1, 1157:1, 1164:4, 1166:1, 1167:3, 1167:12, 1182:2, 1186:1, 1196:2, 1203:1, 1226:1, 1249:1, 1251:10, 1254:'19, 1297:11, 1379:'14, 1527:29, 1527:31

dabin al-ús-sa, "processed semolina," 1086:2, 1100:3, 1182:1

dabin dub-dub-ne, "semolina for the grain heap" > **dub-dub**

dabin ninda túg ù ì ḫi-a má gíd, "to tow a boat (with) various (amounts of) semolina, bread, textiles and oil" > **gíd**

dabin zì-dub-dub-šè, "semolina for the small flour heap" > **zì-dub-dub**

[giš]ma-an-sim **dabin**, "semolina sieve" > [giš]**ma-an-sim**

4.0.0. **dabin** gur ⸢bisaĝ⸣-dub-ba-ka ĝál-la, "there are 4 bushels of semolina in the tablet basket," 1233:12–13

1. Semolina Distributed as Rations, Wages, or Provisions

n (sìla) **dabin**-ta, "n (liters) of semolina each," 381:5, 386:13, 387:4, 396:1, 396:5, 397:1, 397:5

dabin-bi n (sìla), "their semolina is n (liters)," 381:18, 386:26, 387:17, 396:16, 397:16

dabin šà-gal, "semolina (as) fodder/provisions" > **šà-gal**

(. . .) 1.2.2. gur mu **dabin**-šè šu ba-ti, "(10 individuals) received 1 bushel (and) 140 liters (of barley) in place of semolina," 560:11–13

0.1.0. **dabin** šà-⸢gal⸣ nam-ra-ak, "60 liters of semolina, provisions of the booty," 1085:1–2

[0.n.n.] **dabin** [n] sìla še-bi, "[n] liter(s) of semolina, their barley (equivalent) is [n] liter(s) of barley," 1254:'19-'20

2. Semolina in Manufacture

2.1 For Bread

n **dabin** ninda-šè, "n liter(s) of semolina for bread" > **ninda**

n **dabin** ninda ne-mur-šè, "n liter(s) of semolina for bread (baked in) ash" > **ninda**

n **dabin** ninda-sal-la-gen, "n liter(s) of semolina for ordinary thin bread" > **ninda**

ninda-**dabin**, "semolina bread" > **ninda**

ninda-sal-la-**dabin**, "semolina (for) thin bread" > **ninda**

ninda **dabin** ḫi, "to mix bread from semolina" > **ḫi**

n sìla zì **dabin** ḫi, "to mix n liter(s) of flour (together with) semolina" > **ḫi**

n sìla zì-šà-gen **dabin** ḫi, "to mix n liter(s) of šà-flour (together with) semolina" > **ḫi**

[0.3].3. ninda-šu-ra **dabin** ù š[à-g]en ½ sìla du_8, "210 liters of half(-loaf) bread of semolina and ordinary šà-flour to bake (in) ½ liter (loaves)," 548:4

2.2 For Processing Skins

dabin kuš a-g̃ar gu_7-a(-šè), "semolina (for) de-hairing skins" > **a-g̃ar gu_7**

dabin mu kuš-šè, "semolina for (processing) skins," 952:1–2, 961:1–2

dabin mu kuš-udu-niga-šè, "semolina for (processing) skins of fattened sheep," 954:1–2

dabin kuš-udu-niga, "semolina (for processing) skins of fattened sheep," 957:1–2

2.3 Wages for (Milling) Semolina

si-ì-tum á **dabin**, "the remainder of wages (for processing) semolina," 453:2–3

še á **dabin**-šè, "barley, wages for (milling) semolina," 475:1–2

2.4 Mixed with Fine Flour and Dates

n sìla **dabin** n sìla eša n sìla zú-lum eša ḫi, "to mix n liter(s) of semolina, n liter(s) of fine flour (and) n liter(s) of dates with fine flour" > **ḫi**

3. Broken Context

[. . .] **dabin**, 1279:2

dag̃, *nagāšu*, "to wander, travel" > *Verb Index*

dag̃al, *rapāšu*, "(to be) wide; width, breadth"

ab-ba **dag̃al** tà(g), "to widen (the opening of) the roof vent" > **tà(g)**

dag̃al n kùš, "n kùš in width," 374:'4, 374:'15, 1381:1, 1381:7, 1381:30, 1381:35, 1381:40, 1381:54, 1381:62 (in reference to the width of **^{giš}gida$_x$**, **^{giš}ig**, **^{giš}kid**)

^{gi}dur-**dag̃al**, "wide ropes" > **^{gi}dur**

n nindan **dag̃al** saḫar-bi n, "n nindan in width, its dirt (volume) is n (units)" > **saḫar**

n nindan gíd n kùš **dag̃al** n kùš (ba-an-)gi_4-bi n kùš sukud saḫar-bi n sar (n gín n še) (. . .) n sar im-du_8-a, "n nindan long, n kùš wide, n kùš tapered from n kùš high, its dirt is n sar (n gín (and) n še); (the total volume) of the adobe wall is n sar," 366:'1-'3, 366:'7-'8, '13, 366:'9-'10, '13, 366:'11-'13, 366:'17–19 n nindan gíd n kùš **dağal** n kùš sukud saḫar-bi n sar (n gín n še) (. . .) n sar im-du$_8$-a, "n nindan long, n kùš wide, n kùš high, its dirt is n sar (n gín (and) n še); (the total volume) of the adobe wall is n sar," 366:'5-'6, '13, 366:'15-'16, '19

[. . . kùš] **dağal** 3 [. . . n sar] im-du$_8$-a [. . .], 366:'22-'23

dal, "part of a container (shelves or other compartments)"

120 ^{ğeš}zé-na 10 ^{ğeš}dal-ásal 2 kùš-ta 5 ^{ğeš}ú-bíl-lá 10 ^{ğeš}ù-suḫ$_5$ mi-rí-za mu **dal** é-túg-ga-šè, "120 date palm frond midribs, 10 poplar beams of 2 kùš in length each, 5 (units) of charcoal wood (and) 10 pine boards, for the shelves(?) of a textile container," 779:1–5

^{dug}**dal**, *tallu*, "a vessel for oil, perfume, or wine"[18] > **dal**

^{dug}**dal** n, "an oil vessel of n liter(s)," 1266:1, 1266:2

^{ğeš}**dal**, *gištallu*, "crossbar, beam, dividing line"

10 ^{ğeš}**dal**-ásal 2 kùš-ta (. . .) mu dal é-túg-ga-šè, "10 poplar beams, 2 kùš in length each (and) {other materials}, for the shelves(?) of a textile container," 779:2, 5

^{ğeš}**dal** ká, "beam of gate wood," 1380:2

dal-ba-na, *birītu*, "property held in common; space between"

1. **e-sír dal-ba-na**, "alley-way"

a-za-bu-um a im še-ğá **e-sír dal-ba-na** bàd ù é-*šu-eš$_4$-tár* dù, "to construct a cistern for rain-water (in) the alley-way, a wall and the house of *Šu-Eštar*" > **dù**

dam, *aššatu*, *mutu*, "wife, spouse"

1. **PN dam PN**, "PN, wife of PN" > *Personal Name Index*

ama-kal-la **dam** *a-al-lí*, "Ama-kala, wife of *Alli*"

é-dam-*zé-ra-ra*, "house of the wife of *Zerara*" > *Household Index*

ga-su-su **dam** *a-ḫu-a*, "*Gasusu*, wife of *Aḫu'a*"

šu-bu-ul-tum **dam** *a-da-làl*, "*Šubultum*, wife of *Adallal*"

dam-gàr, *tamkaru*, "merchant"

1. **PN dam-gàr**, "PN, the merchant" > *Personal Name Index*

ilum-ra-pi$_5$ ur-^{d}*suena*

dar, *pênu*, *pêṣu*, *salātu*, *šatāqu*, "to break up, crush, grind; to split" > **al-dar-ra**

dé, orthographic writing for de$_6$(GUB), "to bring" > **de$_6$**

[18] Sallaberger 1996, 99.

dé, *šapāku*; *šaqû*, "to pour" > *Verb Index*
kaš-**dé-a**, "banquet" > **kaš**

de$_5$(g), *laqātu*, "to collect, gather up, glean" > *Verb Index*

de$_6$, *babālu*, "to bring, carry" > *Verb Index*

de$_9$(TI), orthographic writing for de$_6$(GUB), "to bring" > **de$_6$**

[DEITIES]

^{d}*adad* (PN only)
^{d}*al-la-tum*
^{d}alim-[. . .]
$^{(d)}$àš-gi$_5$ (GN only)
^{d}*ba-ú*[19] (PN only)
^{d}*da-at-sir-tum*
^{d}*da-gan* (PN only)
^{d}da-mu
^{d}dumu-zi (PN only)
^{d}en-líl
^{d}*eš$_4$-tár* (PN only)
^{d}gu-la
^{d}gu$_4$-an-na (GN only)
^{d}ḫa-ìa (PN only)
^{d}inana
^{d}iškur (PN only)
^{d}*ištaran*
^{d}*kab-ta*[20]
^{d}*ma-lik* (PN only)
^{d}*ma-mi-tum*
^{d}na-na
^{d}nergal$_x^{\text{eri11-gal}}$[21]
^{d}nin-a-zu (PN only)
^{d}nin-ḫur-sag̃
^{d}nin-kar-ak (PN only)
^{d}nin-líl (PN only)
^{d}nin-unug
^{d}nin-^{d}si$_4$-an-na
^{d}nin-šubur (PN only)
^{d}nisaba (PN only)
^{d}nu-muš-da (PN only)
^{d}*suen* (PN only)
^{d}*šamaš* (PN only)
^{d}šára
^{d}šu-bu-la
^{d}*šu*-^{d}*suen*
^{d}šul-gi (PN only)
^{d}*tá-ad-muṣ-tum*
^{d}utu (PN only)

19 The proper reading of this divine name has long been debated. For the most recent discussion, see G. Marchesi 2002. For the sake of convenience, the reading ^{d}ba-ú will be used here.

20 For discussion of the indeterminate *Kabta*, see W. Lambert 1976–80, 284. At Garšana the personal name *Ummi-Kabta* ("My mother is Kabta"), shows that, at least here, *Kabta* was considered a female deity. Cf. also P. Steinkeller 1985, 196 and 2004, 183 n. 31.

21 For this reading see Steinkeller 2004.

dì-um, "wattle and daub"

dì-um aka, "to make wattle and daub" > **aka**

dì-um ga_6(g̃), "to carry wattle and daub" > **ga_6(g̃)**

dì-um g̃ar, "to place wattle and daub" > **g̃ar**

605 sa gi-izi ***dì-um***-šè, "605 bundles of fuel reeds for wattle and daub," 1286:11, 1289:11

1. **im *dì-um***, "an adobe mix"

   im *dì-um* ga_6(g̃), "to carry the adobe mix" > **ga_6(g̃)**

   im *dì-um* lu, "to mix adobe" > **lu**

2. **Broken Context**

   [n g̃uruš šidim n] g̃uruš šu [dím . . .] ***dì-um*** [. . .], 147:37–38

di_4-di_4-la, *ṣeḫru*?, "young child(ren)"

⅓ sìla ì-⌜šáḫ⌝ **di_4-di_4-la** àga-ús *simat-^{d}ištaran* ba-ab-$šeš_4$ (. . .) u_4 é-e im sumur ba-aka, "⅓ liter of lard (used by) *Simat-Ištaran* (when) she anointed the small child(ren) of the gendarme (. . .) when the house was plastered," 472:8–9, 14

$dida_x$(Ú.SA), *billatu*, "sweet wort, an ingredient for beer making; beer for transport"[22]

0.1.4. **$dida_x$**-gen, "100 liters of ordinary dida beer," 548:10

1. **dug $dida_x$**, *ḫittu*, "jug of dida beer"

   dug **$dida_x$**-gen, "n jug(s) of ordinary dida beer," 377:1, 506:7, 548:10, 548:11, 548:12, 1009:2, 1009:5, 1009:10, 1009:13, 1009:19, 1028:3, 1034:'3, 1117:3, 1251:9, 1379:'13

dug **$dida_x$**-gen zì-dub-dub-šè, "jug(s) of ordinary dida beer for the small flour heap" > **zì-dub-dub**

n dug **$dida_x$**-gen 0.0.3-ta, "n jug(s) of 30 liters of ordinary dida beer each," 548:11, 629:1, 1007:1

1 dug **$dida_x$**-gen 0.0.3. še-bi 0.1.0., "1 jug of 30 liters of ordinary dida beer, its barley (equivalent) is 60 liters," 1098:1–2

n dug **$dida_x$**-gen a-níg̃in-šè, "n jug(s) of ordinary dida beer for the a-níg̃in ceremony," 437:1, 1028:15–17, 1028:40–41

1 dug **$dida_x$**-sig_5 a-níg̃in-šè, "1 jug of fine dida beer for the a-níg̃in ceremony," 1028:15, 17

didli, *mādūtu*, "several, various"

a-gàr-**didli**, "various meadows" > **a-gàr**

é-**didli**, "various houses" > *Household Index*

iri^{ki}-**didli**, "various cities" > **iri**

sízkur-**didli**, "various (ceremonial) offerings" > **sízkur**

zi(g) **didli**, "additional (dirt) removal" > **zi(g)**

---

[22] Brunke 2008, 37–40 (Bemerkung 2.28).

zì-dub-dub-**didli**, "various small flour heaps" > **zì-dub-dub**

diğir, *ilu*, "god" > *Deities Index*

$^{\tilde{g}e\check{s}}$**dim**, *maḫrašu*; *makūtu*; *timmu*, "post, pillar, pole"

$^{\tilde{g}e\check{s}}$**dim**-šinig, "tamarisk post," 1334:2

[n] ^{gi}**dim**-gal-bi ésir šub-ba, "[n] large reed post(s) coated with bitumen," 1376:12

★★1 ^{gi}**dim** ab-ba ba-ḫa, 1376:42

dím, *epēšu*, "to make, fashion" > *Verb Index*

diri(g), *atru*, "(to be) surplus, additional"

á-**dirig**, "additional wages" > **á**

báppir **dirig** sila$_{11}$(g̃), "to knead additional beer bread" > **sila$_{11}$(g̃)**

dirig g̃ál-la, "there is additional" > **g̃ál**

dirig sá-du$_{11}$, "surplus of the regular offerings" > **sá-du$_{11}$**

dirig še-ba-ne-ne mu zì nu-g̃ál-la-šè ba-na-ḫa-la, "additional barley rations were divided because there was no flour" > **ḫal**

iti **dirig**, "month 13" > **iti**

kaš **dirig**, "additional beer" > **kaš**

ninda **dirig**, "additional bread" > **ninda**

pad-**dirig** "(meaning uncertain)" > **pad**

siki-gen **dirig** sa$_{10}$ siki-a-šè, "supplementary ordinary wool for the purchase of (more) wool" > **sa$_{10}$**

1. **Additional Barley (for) Bread**

šu+níg̃in 15.0.3.4 sìla še ninda gur zi-ga-[àm] **dirig** 3.1.5.[9 sìla gur] **diri-[ga**-àm], "In total: 15 bushels (and) 34 liters of barley (for) bread was expended. [There are] an additional 3 bushels (and) 109 liters," 1527:41–45

2. **Broken Context**

★★[. . .] x [. . .] **dirig**? 6 [. . .] 60 udu lá-ìa 10 **dirig** lá-ìa **dirig** KA×Ú-a (. . .) níg̃-kas$_7$-aka ^{d}*adad-tillati* šabra, "{animals delivered and expended}, {tabulation of the remainder}. (This is) the balanced account of *Adad-tillati*, the majordomo," 984:'68-'76

diri(g), *neqelpû*, "to float, glide (along/down)" > *Verb Index*

[DIVINE NAMES > DEITIES]

du-ú-um, *du'u*, "(an unidentified structure)"

du-ú-um aka, "to make a *du-ú-um*" > **aka**

dú(TU), *marāṣu*, "to be sick" > *Verb Index*

^{ĝeš}***dú-ul-bu-um***, "a plane tree," 1375:31

HAR ^{ĝeš}***dú-ul-bu-um*** n-ta, "n plane tree seedling(s), n (units) each," 1256:29–30, 1375:31

dù, *banû*, *epēšu*,"to construct" > *Verb Index*

dù-a-tar, "a type of orchard workman"[23]

ĝuruš **dù-a-tar** > *Craftsman Index*

du$_6$, *tīlu*, "(ruin) mound"

(a-šà) **du$_6$**-ba-an-du$_8$-du$_8$ > *Field Index*

du$_6$-saḫar-ra^{ki} > *Toponym Index*

é-**du$_6$**-gur$_4$-*i-din-*^{d}*adad*, "round-hill-house of *Iddin-Adad*" > *Household Index*

du$_6$-lugal-pa-è^{ki} > *Toponym Index*

du$_8$, *epû*, "to bake (bread), to mold (bricks)" > *Verb Index*

du$_8$-ši-a, *dušû*, "turquoise green"[24]

^{kuš}e-sír **du$_8$-ši-a**, "turquoise sandals" > **^{kuš}e-sír**

^{túg}íb-lá **du$_8$-ši-a**, "turquoise belt" > **túg-íb-lá**

^{kuš}súḫub **du$_8$-ši-a**, "turquoise shoes" > **^{kuš}súḫub**

du$_{10}$(g$_3$), *ṭābu*, "(to be) good; (to be) sweet; goodness, good (thing)"

ì-**du$_{10}$**-nun-na, "good-quality ghee" > **ì**

^{kuš}du$_{10}$-gan, *tu(k)kannu*, "leather bag," 906:1

^{kuš}du$_{10}$-gan-⌈šağan⌉, "leather flask," 906:5

^{kuš}du$_{10}$-gan-ti-bal, *šutablakkutu*(?), "leather bag with a marking?," 917:4, 932:3

^{kuš}du$_{10}$-gan-ti-bal-babbar, "white leather bag with a marking?," 838:2, 849:1, 864:5, 871:1, 892:3, 897:1, 900:1, 965:4, 1517:2

^{kuš}du$_{10}$-gan UD?.X.LÚ, 968:6

du$_{10}$-ús, *narmaku*, "bath (within a house)"

du$_{10}$-ús é-didli, "bath of additional houses" > **é-didli**

du$_{10}$-ús ésir du$_8$, "to seal a bath with bitumen" > **du$_8$**

---

23 Yamamoto 1981, 105–6.

24 Following van de Mieroop 1987, 31, 145.

du$_{11}$(g$_{4}$), *qabû*, "to speak" > *Verb Index*

dub, *ṭuppu*, "tablet"

bisağ^{zabar} **dub**, "bronze container of tablets" > **bisağ^{zabar}**

bisağ-**dub-ba**, "tablet basket" > **^{gi}bisağ**

dub du$_{8}$, "to bake a tablet" > **du$_{8}$**

dub tur, "to subtract (from) a tablet" > **tur**

1. **dub PN**, "tablet of PN" > *Personal Name Index*

i-din-^{d}adad
^{d}*ma-lik-ba-ni*
šar-ru-um-ì-lí

2. **Broken Context**

gaba-ri **dub** [. . .] um-ma [. . .], 1052:2

dub, *šapāku*, "to heap up, pile, pour" > *Verb Index*

zì-**dub-dub**, "a small heap of flour" > **zì**

dub-sar, *ṭupšarru*, "scribe"

1. **PN dub-sar**, "PN, the scribe" > *Personal Name Index*

a-ḫu-ma
a-ḫu-wa-qar
a-ḫu-[*x*]
a-kal-la
a-wi-lum-ma
^{d}*adad-tillati*
ba-ba-ni
é-a-bu
é-a-dan
é-a-šar
^{d}en-líl-*ba-za-du*
en-um-ì-lí
èr-ra-ba-ni
i-ṣur-^{d}suen
ì-lí-an-dùl
ib-ni-^{d}adad
ilum-ba-ni
la-qì-ip
nu-úr-^{d}adad
puzur$_{4}$-^{d}en-líl
puzur$_{4}$-^{d}nin-kar-ak
su-mi-it-ìl
šar-ru-um-ba-ni
^{d}šára-kam
še-lí-a-núm
šu-^{d}adad
šu-^{d}dumu-zi
šu-èr-ra
šu-eš$_{4}$-tár
šu-ku-bu-um
tu-ra-am-ì-lí
ù-ṣí-na-wi-ir
ur-é-an-na

2. **Provisions for Scribes**

2.1 Barley

še-ba **dub-sar-e-ne**, "barley rations of scribes," 394:7, 408:2

2.2 Barley and Sheep Carcasses

0.1.3. še 3 ádda-udu-ta *puzur$_{4}$*-^{d}nin-kar-ak 1 *la-qì-ip* 1 *é-a-dan* **dub-sar-me-éš** (. . .) [šà-gal šidim] ù **dub-sar-e-ne**, "90 liters of barley (and) 3 sheep carcasses each (for) *Puzur-Ninkarak*, *Laqip* (and) *Ea-dan*, the scribes, (and for) {other workers}, [food (for) builders] and scribes," 399:16–20, 24

2.3 Barley, Lard and Sheep Carcasses

0.1.3. še-ta [n s]ìla ì-ĝeš-ta [n] ádda-udu-ta [*pù*]-*zur*$_8$-^{d}nin-kar-ak [*é*]-*a-dan* **du[b-s]ar-me-éš**, "13 liters of barley each, [n] liter(s) sesame oil each (and) [n] sheep carcass(es) each (for) *Puzur*-Ninkarak (and) *Ea-dan*, the scribes," 406:1–6

3. Workmen (employed for) Scribal Work: Provisions

3 ĝuruš **dub-sar** 2 sìla kaš-ninda ½ sìla tu$_7$ 1 ĝuruš **dub-sar** 1 sìla kaš-ninda ⅓ sìla tu$_7$ (. . .) kaš-ninda ḫa-la-a? al-⌜tar⌝ gub-ba, "2 liters of beer (and) bread (and) ½ liter of soup for 3 workmen (employed for) scribal (work and) 1 liter of beer (and) bread (and) ⅓ liter of soup for 1 workman (employed for) scribal (work and) {provisions for other workers}, beer (and) bread divided (for workers) employed (for) construction," 379:12–13, 20

3 ĝuruš **dub-sar** 2 sìla ninda-dabin 2 sìla zú-lum-ta (. . .) ḫa-la-a ĝuruš árad-é-a-e-[ne], "2 liters of semolina bread (and) 2 liters of dates each (for) 3 workmen (employed for) scribal (work, and for) {other workers, provisions} divided for the household servants," 402:9, 17

3 ĝuruš **dub-sar** 2 sìla kaš-ninda ½ sìla tu$_7$-ta, "3 workmen (employed for) scribal (work:) 2 liters of beer (and) bread (and) ½ liter of soup each," 556:'6

2 ĝuruš **dub-sar** 1 sìla kaš-ninda ⅓ sìla tu$_7$-ta, "2 workmen (employed for) scribal (work:) 1 liter of beer (and) bread (and) ⅓ liter of soup each," 556:'7

dúb, "to extract" > **al-dúb-ba**

dùb, "knee"

u$_4$ **dùb** bar-ra-ni in-na-gig-ga, "when his 'outer knee' was hurting him" > **gig**

dug, *karpatu*, "clay jug,"[25] 1068:4

1 **dug** 0.0.3 kéše-ra, "1 bound 30 liter jug," 595:6

n **dug** 0.0.3.-ta, "n jug(s) of 30 liters each," 1069:3, 1072:7, 1074:7, 1075:5, 1134:9, 1203:3, 1300:1, 1304:1, 1340:6

1. Types of Vessels

^{dug}ba, "(a vessel)"

^{dug}dal, "a vessel for oil, perfume or wine"

dug, "clay jug"

dug-a-kúm, "hot-water bottle"

dug dida$_x$, "jug of dida beer" > **dida$_x$**

dug kaš, "jug of beer" > **kaš**

^{dug}dúr-bùr, "fermenting vat"

^{dug}epig, "drinking vessel, sprinkling vessel, watering can for animals"

^{dug}gur$_4$-gur$_4$-ĝeštin, "a vase for wine"

^{dug}ĝeš-ŠÀ/UD?, "(a vessel)"

^{dug}*ku-kur-rú*, "(a vessel)"

---

25 Sallaberger 1996, 97.

^{dug}laḫtan, "a beer vat"
^{dug}ma-an-ḫara$_4$, "a large container (for beer)"
^{dug}níĝ n-sìla-ta, "a jug of n liter(s)"
^{dug}sìla-bàn-da, "(a vessel)"
^{dug}sìla-bur-zi, "1-liter (offering) bowl"
^{dug}sìla-gal, "large liter-jug
^{dug}ù-lu-lu, "pipe, conduit"
^{dug}úgur, "(a vessel)"
^{dug}útul, "tureen"
^{dug}útul-gal, "large tureen"

2. Broken Context

n **dug** [. . .], 602:1, 1036:'39, 1376:73, 1376:74, 1376:75
^{dug}ḪI?-x-[. . .], 1268:1

dug-a-kúm, "hot-water bottle,"[26] 1334:7

duḫ, *paṭāru*, "to loosen, release, free" > *Verb Index*

dumu, *māru*, "son"

1. PN dumu PN, "PN, son of PN" > *Personal Name Index*

a-da-làl **dumu** *si-um*, "*Adallal*, son of *Si'um*"
a-da-làl **dumu** *še-um*, "*Adallal*, son of *Še'um*"
a-da-làl **dumu** *šu*-ma-ma, "*Adallal*, son of *Šu*-Mama"
á-ni-á **dumu** *ùr*?-[x], "*Ani'a*, son of *Ur*-[x]"
^{d}nergal$_x^{eri_{11}\text{-gal}}$ **dumu** *da-da*-AN, "Nergal, (the personal deity of) the son of *Dada*-AN"
^{d}nergal$_x^{eri_{11}\text{-gal}}$ **dumu** e$_{(2)}$-é-zi, "Nergal, (the personal deity of) the son of Ezi"
ḫu-lu-lu **dumu** *da-da-a*, "*Hululu*, son of *Dada'a*"
šu-eš$_4$-tár **dumu** *da-da-a*, "*Šu-Eštar*, son of *Dada'a*"

dumu-munus, *mārtu*, "daughter"

1 **dumu-munus** (. . .) ^{d}*adad-tillati* ì-dab$_5$, "*Adad-tillati* took in charge 1 daughter," 1515:2, 4–5

1. PN dumu-munus PN, "PN, daughter of PN" > *Personal Name Index*

eš$_4$-tár-um-mi **dumu-munus** *šu-kab-ta*, "*Eštar-ummi*, daughter of *Šu-Kabta*"
um-mi-kab-tá **dumu-munus** é-a, "*Ummi-Kabta*, daughter of the household"

^{gi}**dur**, *markasu*, *ṭurru*, "binding, knot, bond, tie; rope"

1. Types of Rope

---

26 Sallaberger 1996, 97.

1.1 ^{gi}**dur-dağal**, "wide rope"

^{gi}**dur-dağal** a-rá-3-tab-ba gíd 5 nindan-ta, "30-meter 3-ply wide rope," 1008:1, 1273:3, 1291:1, 1305:2, 1308:3, 1376:45, 1379:'5, 1380:7

1.2 ^{gi}**dur-gazi**, "gazi rope"

^{gi}**dur-gazi** a-rá-2-tab-ba gíd 1½ nindan-ta, "9-meter 2-ply gazi rope," 1008:2, 1286:9, 1287:2, 1289:9, 1291:3, 1297:1, 1328:3, 1378:'1, 1379:'6, 1380:8

^{gi}**dur-gazi** a-rá 2 tab-ba gíd 1½ nindan-ta ğeš ùr kéše gíd, "9-meter 2-ply gazi rope to tighten bound roof beams" > **gíd**

^{gi}**dur-gazi** a-rá-3-tab-ba gíd 1½ nindan-ta, "9 meter 3-ply gazi rope," 1291:2, 1293:4

2. **Used to Manufacture Other Reed Products**

n ^{gi}**dur**-bi ½ sa, "n bundle(s) of rope," 1381:3, 1381:42 (in reference to the amount of bitumen required to manufacture ^{gi}**ig-dur**)

dúr, *pūqu*, *šuburru*, "back, behind"

dúr SIG_4.ANŠE-šè ğar, "to place for (use as) the bottom of a brick stack" > **ğar**
dúr ^{ğeš}ig $šeš_4$, "to anoint the back of a door" > **$šeš_4$**

^{dug}**dúr-bùr**, *namzītu*, "fermenting vat"[27]

4 ^{dug}**dúr-bùr** 0.1.0.-ta, "4 fermenting vats of 60 liters each," 1376:77

$duru_5$, *labāku*, *raṭbu*, "(to be) soft, (to be) wet, irrigated, fresh, damp"

^{ğeš}ḫašḫur-**$duru_5$**, "fresh apples" > ^{ğeš}**ḫašḫur**
tuḫ-**$duru_5$**, "fresh chaff" > **tuḫ**

^{ğeš}**dusu**, *tupšikku*, "brick-carrying frame; earth basket," 1299:14, 1340:4

– E –

e-bi-a-tum < *ebbiatu*, "thick"

ninda-***e-bi-a-tum***, "thick bread" > **ninda**

e-lu-núm, "(a festival)"

e-lu-núm-$^{d}nergal_x$, "*Elunum* festival of Nergal" > *Deities Index*
udu $^{d}nergal_x$ u_4 ***e-lu-núm-ma***, "a sheep (for) Nergal during the *Elunum* festival" > *Deities Index*

e-pe-eš, *epēšu*, "to do, make" > *Verb Index*

---

27 Sallaberger 1996, 72–73, 99.

e-rí-na, “root-tanned”[28]

★★kuš **é-ri-na** ka-la > **ka-la**

kuš-máš **e-rí-na**, “root-tanned goat skin” > **kuš-máš**

kuš-udu **e-rí-na**, “root-tanned sheep skin” > **kuš-udu**

kuš-udu **e-rí-na** ka-tab, “root-tanned sheep skin cover” > **ka-tab**

^{kuš}šà-ga-dù **e-rí-na**, “root-tanned leather belt” > ^{kuš}**šà-ga-dù**

e-ri-um, “frond, leaf of a date palm,” 511:42, 1036:'45, 1036:'75

^{kuš}**e-sír**, *šēnu*, “sandal, shoe”

^{kuš}**e-sír** du$_8$-ši-a, “turquoise sandals,” 782:3

^{kuš}**e-sír** é-ba-an, “pair of sandals,” 855:21

^{kuš}**e-sír**-gen é-ba-an, “pair of ordinary sandals,” 839:1, 853:2, 858:1, 897:2, 912:2, 931:1, 955:3

^{kuš}**e-sír**-níta túg-du$_8$-a du$_8$-ši-a é-ba-an, “pair of man’s meshwork turquoise sandals,” 925:3

^{kuš}**e-sír**-tur-gen, “pair of ordinary small sandals,” 968:14

^{kuš}**e-sír**-ús, “2nd-quality sandals,” 1376:59

^{kuš}**e-sír**-ús é-ba-an, “pair of 2nd-quality sandals,” 912:1, 955:2

^{kuš}**e-sír** [. . .], “[. . .] sandals,” 892:4, 968:13

^{kuš}**e-sír** [. . .] é-ba-an, “pair of [. . .] sandals,” 782:6

^{kuš}súḫub-**e-sír**, “sandals” > ^{kuš}**súḫub**

1. **Sandals of *Šu-Kabta***

^{kuš}**e-sír** du$_8$-ši-a *šu-kab-tá* é-ba-an, “pair of turquoise sandals of *Šu-Kabta*,” 1376:57

^{kuš}**e-sír** du$_8$-ši-[a] túg-du$_8$-a-su$_4$-a *šu-kab-*[*ta* é]-ba-an, “pair of turquoise sandals lined with red meshwork of *Šu-Kabta*,” 782:3

^{kuš}**e-sír** *šu-kab-tá* é-ba-an, “pair of sandals of *Šu-Kabta*,” 1376:58

^{kuš}**e-sír** túg-[du$_8$-a] *šu-kab-tá* é-ba-an, “pair of meshwork sandals of *Šu-Kabta*,” 782:5

e-sír, *esēru*, “square (of town), confined space”

1. **e-sír dal-ba-na**, “alley-way”

a-za-bu-um a im še-g̃á **e-sír dal-ba-na** dù, “to construct a cistern for rain-water (in) the alley-way” > **dù**

é, *bītu*, “house, household, building, temple” > *Household Index*

é-agrig, “house of the steward”

é-báḫar, “potter’s house”

é-didli, “various houses”

é-en-^{d}inana-gal, “house of the senior priest of Inana”

[28] Stol 1980–83, 535.

é-gal, "palace"
é-gašam(-e-ne), "craftsmen's house"
é-*gi-na-tum*, "barracks"
é-gul, "demolished house"
é-^{ĝeš}gu-za, "chair house"
é-ki-ba-ĝar-ra, "replacement house"
(**é**-)ki-mur-ra, "textile depository"
é-kíkken, "mill"
é-^{ĝeš}kiri$_6$, "garden house"
é-kìšib, "warehouse"
é-kù, "bright temple"
é-lùnga, "brewery"
é-lùnga ù **é**-kíkken, "brewery and mill"
é-lùnga **é**-muḫaldim ù **é**-kíkken, "brewery-kitchen-mill complex" > *Triple Complex*
é-muḫaldim, "kitchen"
é-munus, "house of the women"
é-mušen-na, "bird house"
é-^{d}nin-si$_4$-an-na, "Nin-Siana temple"
é-šáḫ, "piggery"
é-^{d}šára, "Šara temple"
é-šu-i-e-ne, "house of the barbers"
é-šu-sum-ma, "storehouse"
é-tab-tab, "double house"
é-til-la, "finished house"
é-udu-niga, "sheep-fattening pen"
é-ùr ku$_6$ al-ús-sa, "fish-sauce roof house"
é-uš-bar, "textile mill"
é-uš-bar ù **é**-gašam-e-ne, "textile mill and craftsmen's house"
é-PN, "house of PN"

é-*a-a-lú-a*
é-*a-bí-a-ti*
é-*a-gu-a*
é-*a-lí-a-bi*
é-*ba-ḫa-a*
é-*bí-za-a*
é-*da-da*
é-dam-*zé-ra-ra*
é-*du-gu-a*
é-du$_6$-gur$_4$-*i-din-*^{d}*adad*, "round-hill-house of *Iddin-Adad*"
é-géme-tur
é-*ḫa-bi-ṣa-nu-um*
é-*ḫa-bu-ra-tum*
é-*ḫu-lu-lu*
é-*i-ti-rum*
é-*ì-lí-bi-šu*
é-*pí-ša-aḫ-ilum*
é-*pu-ta-nu-um*
é-*puzur$_4$-ra-bi*
é-*simat-*^{d}*ištaran*
é-*šu-bu-la-num*
é-*šu-eš$_4$-tár*
é-*šu-eš$_4$-tár* ù *za-ki-ti*
é-*šu-i-ti-rum*
é-*šu-ku-bu-um*
é-*šu-ma-mi-tum*
é-*u-bar-ri-a*
é-*u-bar-rum*
é-*zu-zu-tum*

é-ba-an, *tāpalu*, "pair"

^{kuš}á-si g̃ar-ra **é-ba-an**, "pair of leather covered hinges" > **^{kuš}á-si**
^{túg}bar-si gú-è **é-ba-an**, "pair of ties (for) a cape" > **^{túg}bar-si**
^{kuš}e-sír **é-ba-an**, "pair of sandals" > **^{kuš}e-sír**
éš-túg-gíd **é-ba-an**, "pair of cords, used to extend a textile (on a loom)" > **éš**
$^{g̃eš}$garig **é-ba-an**, "pair of combs" > **$^{g̃eš}$garig**
^{túg}g̃eštu **é-ba-an**, "pair of g̃eštu textiles" > **^{túg}g̃eštu**
^{kuš}súḫub **é-ba-an**, "pair of shoes" > **^{kuš}súḫub**
★★túg-tùn túg-lugal **é-ba-an**, "container of a pair of royal textiles" > **tùn**
★★$^{g̃eš}$zúm nu-úr-ma **é-ba-an** > **$^{g̃eš}$zúm**

$^{g̃eš}$é-da, "board, plank; joist (side-ḫouse timber)"[29]

$^{g̃eš}$é-da ásal, "poplar joist," 1273:1, 1286:2, 1286:6, 1289:2, 1289:6, 1293:2, 1297:4, 1303:2, 1380:1
$^{g̃eš}$é-da ⌜asal$_x$⌝ (A.[TU.NIR]), "poplar joist," 1379:'1
$^{g̃eš}$é-da šinig, "tamarisk joist," 1286:4, 1289:4, 1368:3, 1379:'2

é-duru$_5$, *kapru*, "village" > *Toponym Index*

é-duru$_5$-kab-bi^{ki}
é-duru$_5$-*simat-^{d}ištaran*
é-duru$_5$-ul-luḫ-uri$_5^{ki}$

é-g̃ar, "(meaning uncertain)"

★★1 ^{gi}bisag̃? **é-g̃ar** kuš g̃ar-ra, "1 (?) basket, covered with leather,"1332:2
★★12 sar 18 gín ⌜apin⌝? šà **é-g̃ar**, 1397:'3-'4

é-šu-sum-ma, "storehouse" > *Household Index*

é-túg-ga, "textile container"

dal **é-túg-ga**, "the shelves(?) of a textile container" > **dal**

é-u$_4$-7, "half-moon (day)"[30]

1 udu-niga **é-u$_4$-7** iti u$_4$-[7]-ba-zal (. . .) sá-du$_{11}$-ku$_5$-rá ^{d}nin-^{d}si$_4$-an-na, "1 fattened sheep at the end of the [7th] day of the month, i.e. the half-moon day, (and) {other offerings}, deducted regular offerings of Nin-Siana," 985:1–2, 5–6

---

[29] See F. Carroué 1986, 53 n. 102 with references.
[30] Sallaberger 1993, 39f.; Sigrist 1992, 148–154.

é-u$_4$-10, " 3/4? moon (day)"[31]

1 [ud]u-niga **é-[u$_4$]-10** iti u$_4$-10-⌜ba⌝-zal sá-du$_{11}$-ku$_5$-rá ^{d}nin-^{d}si$_4$-an-na, "1 fattened sheep at the end of the 10th day of the month, i.e. the 3/4? moon day, deducted regular offerings of Nin-Siana," 985:3–6

é-u$_4$-15, "full moon (day)"

1 *mu-du-lum* udu-niga **é-u$_4$-15** sá-du$_{11}$ *simat-^{d}ištaran* é-gal-ta, "1 salted fattened sheep on the full moon day, regular offerings of *Simat-Ištaran* from the palace," 375:3–6

60 ^{dug}sìla-bur-zi níĝ-dab$_5$ saĝ u$_4$-sakar ù **é-u$_4$-15** (. . .) sá-du$_{11}$-ki-a-naĝ-*šu-kab-tá*, "60 1-liter offering bowls, requisitions on the new moon day and the full moon day (and) {other comestibles}, regular offerings of the funerary libation place of *Šu-Kabta*," 972:65–66, 107

60 ^{dug}sìla-bur-zi tu$_7$-šè níĝ-dab$_5$ saĝ u$_4$-sakar ù **é-u$_4$-15** (. . .) sá-du$_{11}$-ki-a-naĝ-*šu-kab-tá*, "60 1-liter offering bowls for soup, requisitions on the new moon day and the full moon day (and) {other comestibles}, regular offerings of the funerary libation place of *Šu-Kabta*," 975:66–67, 108

[1] šáḫ-zé-d[a K]A-⌜dé⌝-[x] 1 {erasure} **é-u$_4$-15** (. . .) sá-du$_{11}$-ki-a-naĝ-*šu-kab-tá*, "[1] piglet (?) on the full moon day, (and) {other comestibles}, regular offerings of the funerary libation place of *Šu-Kabta*," 981:1–4, 33

è, *waṣû*, *erēbu*, "to bring out, to enter" > *Verb Index*

ég, *iku*, "dike, levee"

ég-tab aka, "to make a double dike" > **aka**

ki-**ég**, "place of the dike" > **ki-ég**

má saḫar **ég** a-ab-ba sè(g$_{10}$), "to tamp dirt (delivered by) boat at the sea dike" > **sè(g$_{10}$)**

egir, *arkatu*, "back, rear; after"

egir buru$_{14}$ gi$_4$, "to be paid back after the harvest" > **gi$_4$**

u$_4$ bàd **egir** é-a dù-dè, "when the (enclosure) wall behind the house was being constructed" > **dù**

^{ĝeš}**eme-sig**, "boat plank"[32]

^{ĝeš}**eme-sig** al-dúb-ba, "extracted boat plank," 1303:3

^{ĝeš}**eme-sig** má-30-ta, "boat plank from a 30-bushel boat," 1380:3

en, *ēnu*, *ēntu*, "priest, priestess"

é-ki-ba-ĝar-ra **en**-^{d}inana-gal, "the replacement house of the senior priest of Inana" > *Household, Deities Index*

---

[31] é-u$_4$-10 is otherwise unattested but may be an indication of the celebration of the third-quarter moon.

[32] Literally "low-tongues," designating part of a wooden boat.

en-šè šu bar, "to release for the priest" > **šu ... bar**

g̃uruš šidim lú-**en**-^{d}inana-unu^{ki}-ga, "the builder of the priest of Inana of Uruk" > *Deities Index*

en-nu-g̃á, *maṣṣartum*, "watch, guard"

en-nu aka, "to perform guard duty, to guard" > **aka**

ensi(EN.ME.LI), *šā'ilu/šā'iltu*, "dream interpreter"

še **ensi**-šè, "barley for the dream interpreter," 484:10, 484:17

énsi, *iššaku*, "governor"

g̃uruš šidim lú-**énsi**-marad^{ki}, "the builder, the man of the governor of Marad" > *Toponym Index*

^{lú}kíg̃-gi$_{4}$-a-**énsi**-nibru^{ki}, "the messenger of the governor of Nippur" > *Toponym Index*

^{dug}**epig**(SIG), *mašqû*, "drinking vessel; sprinkling vessel, watering can for animals,"[33] 449:4, 595:7

[EQUIDS]

anše, "donkey"

^{anše}kúnga, "equid, probably a donkey-onager cross"

ér, *takribtu*, "(performance of) an Emesal lament"[34]

ér iri ni$_{10}$-ni$_{10}$, "(performance of) a *takribtum* (involving) circling around the city" > **níg̃in**

éren, *ṣabu*, "people; (soldier-)workers (used for corvee labor)"

ba-úš mu **éren**-na-šè, "(animals) slaughtered for the workers" > **úš**

éren íb-gu$_{7}$, "the workers ate" > **gu$_{7}$**

kurum$_{7}$ aka **éren** al-tar bàd gub-ba, "inspection (of the work) of workers employed (for) construction of the (enclosure) wall" > **al-tar**

kurum$_{7}$ aka **éren** al-tar-ra gub-ba, "inspection (of the work) of workers employed for construction" > **al-tar**

kurum$_{7}$ aka **éren** šu dím bàd gub-ba, "inspection (of the work) of workers employed to build the (enclosure) wall" > **šu ... dím**

še-ba **éren**-na sum, "to give barley rations to the workers" > **sum**

2 g̃uruš i[m-. . .] g̃á-g̃á b[àd . . .] 1-kam? **éren**? dù-dè [gub-ba], "2 workmen to place [. . .] earth, [. . .] workers? [employed] to build," 49:34

[33] Sallaberger 1996, 51, 100.

[34] Gabbay, *forthcoming*.

^{ĝeš}**éren**, *ṣimittu*, "yoke"

1 ^{ĝeš}**éren** 1 gú še-du$_{10}$, "1 yoke of 1 talent of šedu (wood?)," 1372:30, 1372:87

1 ^{ĝeš}**éren** 30 ma-na še-du$_{10}$, "1 yoke of 30 minas of šedu (wood?)," 1372:31, 1372:88

1 ^{ĝeš}**éren** 1 gú ésir-ásal, "1 yoke of 1 talent of bitumen (coated) poplar," 1372:32, 1372:89

1 ^{ĝeš}**éren**-DU$_8$ ḫašḫur, "1 (?) yoke of apple wood," 1372:33, 1372:90

^{ĝeš}ḫašḫur **éren** n-kùš-ta, 1327:1, 1327:2, 1327:3, 1327:4

★★^{ĝeš}ḫašḫur **éren** n-kùš-ta šà **éren** ^{ĝeš}ig-šè, 1327:1–5

^{na4}**esi**, *ušû*, "diorite, dolerite"

(. . .) ^{na4}**esi**-kam, "{stones of various weight} of diorite," 1372:25, 1372:82

ésir, *kupru*, "bitumen, asphalt"

du$_{10}$-ús **ésir** du$_8$, "to seal a bath with bitumen" > **du$_8$**

^{ĝeš}éren 1 gú **ésir**-ásal, "yoke of 1 talent of bitumen (coated) poplar" > ^{ĝeš}**éren**

ésir sim, "to filter bitumen" > **sim**

ésir šeĝ$_6$, "to boil bitumen" > **šeĝ$_6$**

ésir šub, "to coat with bitumen" > **šub**

ésir zuḫ, "to steal bitumen" > **zuḫ**

gum-**ésir**, "pestle (for crushing) bitumen,"[35] 592:1

kíĝ **ésir**-ra,"bitumen work" > **kíĝ**

peš-**ésir**, "bitumen(-sealed) palmleaflet (mat)" > **peš**

★★1 ^{ĝeš}ĜEŠ/ĜEŠ 1 gú **ésir**-⌜ásal⌝, 1372:29, 1372:86

1. **ésir-é-a**, "house bitumen," 534:6, 1008:7, 1249:7, 1257:1, 1260:2, 1299:2, 1302:2, 1325:12, 1329:1, 1329:6, 1338:1, 1343:1, 1353:1, 1355:1, 1357:1, 1358:1, 1363:1, 1373:1, 1374:1

   ésir-é-a-bi n sìla, "its house bitumen is n liter(s)," 1381:23, 1381:32, 1381:38, 1381:46, 1381:52, 1381:56, 1381:60 (in reference to the amount of bitumen required to manufacture é-KU-^{ĝeš}banšur, ^{gi}gida$_x$, ^{gi}kid)

   ésir-é-a peš-šè, "house bitumen for palmleaflet (mats)" > **peš**

   ésir-é-a ù im-bábbar ^{ĝeš}ig bí-ib-sù-ub, "the door was coated with house bitumen and gypsum" > **sù(b)**

2. **ésir-ḫád**, "dry bitumen," 1260:1, 1299:1, 1302:1, 1325:11, 1359:1

   ésir-ḫád lá, "to transport dry bitumen" > **lá**

3. **Other**

0.1.0. še 2 ma-na siki-gen 2 sìla ì-ĝeš luḫ 60.0.0. gur-kam mu **ésir** šeg$_{12}$-al-ur$_x$-ra-šè, "60 liters of barley, 2 minas of ordinary wool (and) 2 liters of sesame oil – cleaning(?) of 60 bushels – for the bitumen of the bricks," 1296:1–5

[35] Waetzoldt and Sigrist 1993, 272.

éš, *eblu*, "string, cord, rope"

éš g̃eš ùr kéše, "to bind ropes to roof beams" > **kéše**

1. Types of Rope

1 **éš** ^{gi}kid-aš-rin siki-ud$_5$, 1334:4

[n] **éš**-maḫ [*ḫa*]-*bu-u*[*m* k]i-lá-bi ½ ⸢gú⸣ 15⅓ ma-⸢na⸣, "[n] large *ḫabum* fabric rope(s)—their weight is ½ talent and 15⅓ minas," 831:1–2

20 **éš**-túg-gíd é-ba-an, "20 pairs of cords, used to extend textiles (on a loom)" 1376:53

[n+]2 **éš**-túg-gíd-siki-ud$_5$, "[n+]2 goat-hair cords, used to extend textiles (on a loom)," 628:1

14 **éš**-ú, "14 grass ropes," 1376:54

2 **éš-ú-nin$_9$, "2 ú-nin$_9$-plant ropes," 1376:55

n **éš-ú-nin$_9$-siki-ud$_5$, 628:3

[n+]1 **éš-ú-siki-ud$_5$, 628:2

2. A Missing Rope

1 má 60.0.0. gur ba-gul ésir-bi zuḫ-a ba-g̃ar g̃eš **éš**-bi <<BI>> nu-g̃ál, "1 60-bushel boat was dismantled, its stolen bitumen was replaced (but) its wood (and) ropes are (still) missing," 1369:1–4

3. Ropes for Towing Boats

1 **éš** má g[íd . . .], "1 boat towing rope [. . .]," 1306:2

4 **éš** má gíd-ús, "4 2nd-quality boat towing ropes," 1376:56

4. As a Distance Measurement

ús-bi n nindan n **éš**, "the distance (carried) is n nindan (and) n éš" > **ús**

5. Broken Context

x-**éš**-x-[. . .], 1328:'6

éš-g̃ar, "(meaning uncertain)"

10 $^{\text{g̃eš}}$taskarin-bi **éš-g̃ar, 635:7

10 $^{\text{g̃eš}}$bar-bi **éš-g̃ar, 635:8

èš, *bītu*, *eššu*, "shrine"

1. èš-ta-gur-ra, "(offerings) returned from the shrine"

èš-ta-gur-ra ^{d}*adad-tillati* šu ba-an-ti, "*Adad-tillati* received offerings returned from the shrine," 980:8–10, 997:12–14, 1002:13–15, 1022:15–16, 1023:15–16, 1024:17–19, 1026:13–14

^{kuš}**èš**, "tent, pavilion"

1 ^{kuš}**èš**-ú-ḫáb kuš-12, "1 madder-tanned leather tent of 12 skins," 1334:1

eša, *saskû*, "(a fine flour)," 383:9, 385:8, 435:2, 436:1, 437:2, 439:2, 440:2, 440:6, 441:2, 457:1, 487:5, 488:9, 506:6, 506:10, 506:12, 506:14, 511:62, 970:4, 972:61, 972:85, 975:62, 975:86, 987:2, 988:2, 989:2, 990:2, 991:2, 992:2, 993:2, 994:2, 995:2, 999:6, 1001:5, 1007:3, 1007:7,

1008:4, 1016:2, 1016:10, 1016:13, 1016:15, 1016:19, 1017:4, 1027:4, 1027:10, 1028:28, 1030:3, 1030:7, 1030:14, 1030:21, 1030:27, 1030:33, 1034:'5, 1034:'9, 1035:'5, 1036:'14, 1036:'66, 1046:2, 1077:2, 1100:5, 1164:5, 1166:2, 1182:5, 1193:1, 1249:2, 1251:11, 1254:'21, 1297:11, 1379:'15, 1517:9, 1517:17

eša dub, "to heap up fine flour" > **dub**

eša šub, "to pour fine flour" > **šub**

eša zì-dub-dub-šè, "fine flour for the small flour heap" > **zì-dub-dub**

zú-lum **eša** hi, "to mix dates (with) fine flour" > **ḫi**

n sìla dabin n sìla **eša** n sìla zú-lum **eša** ḫi, "to mix n liter(s) of semolina, n liter(s) of fine flour (and) n liter(s) of dates (with) fine flour" > **ḫi**

20 ^{gi}gur sal-la zì **eša** ésir šub-ba, "20 thin baskets coated with bitumen (containing) flour (and) fine flour," 1299:10

ezem, *issinu*, "festival"

1. **ezem-*a-bu-um-ma***, "*Abum* Festival"

1.1 Assorted Grains

(. . .) níĝ-dab$_5$ **ezem**-*a-bu-um-ma*-šè u$_4$-10-lá-1-kam, "{assorted grains}, requisitions for the *Abum* festival on the 9th day," 999:12–13

0.1.1.7$^5/_6$ sìla še 9 sìla tuḫ-duru$_5$-sig$_5$ 0.0.4.2 sìla tuḫ-duru$_5$-gen lá-ìa kaš zi-ga **ezem**-*a-bu-um*, "77$^5/_6$ liters of barley, 9 liters of fine fresh bran (and) 42 liters of ordinary fresh bran, the remainder from the beer expended (for) the *Abum* festival," 1047:1–5

1.2 A Braider to Beat His Breast

1 ĝuruš túg-du$_8$ u$_4$-12-šè gaba sàĝ-dè [gu]b-ba u$_4$ **ezem**-*a-bu-um-ma*, "1 braider employed for 12 days to beat (his) breast during the *Abum* festival," 278:1–4

1.3 Requisitions

(. . .) 28 [. . .] níĝ-dab$_5$ **ezem**-*a-bu-um-ma* (. . .) níĝ-kas$_7$-aka ^{d}*adad-tillati* šabra, "(In total:) 28 [. . .], requisitions of the *Abum* festival, (and) {other allotments}, the balanced account of *Adad-tillati*, the majordomo," 984:'41-'42, '75-'76

1.4 Surplus Regular Offerings

(. . .) dirig sá-du$_{11}$-u$_4$-[n-šè] *ra-ba-tum* ù ^{d}*šu*-^{d}E[N.ZU-*e*]-*te-íl-pi*$_4$-^{d}en-lí[l sugal$_7$] ⌜u$_4$⌝ **ezem**-*a-bu-um*, "{assorted commodities}, surplus of the regular offerings on the [nth] day of *Rabatum* and *Šu-Suen-etelpi*-Enlil, [the sugal], during the *Abum* festival," 509:'12-'14

2. **ezem-*e-lu-núm***, "*Elunum* Festival"

[. . .] ^{d}nin-unu?-g[a? n] sìla ninda [n] kuš-u[du-nig]a ki-a-naĝ *šu-kab-*⌜*ta*⌝ èš-ta-gur-ra ^{d}*adad-tillati* šu ba-ti u$_4$ **ezem-*e-lu-núm***-^{d}nergal$_x^{eri_{11}\text{-gal}}$, "*Adad-tillati* received [. . .] (of?) Nin-unug (and) [n] liter(s) of bread (and) [n] skin(s) of fattened sheep of the funerary libation place of *Šu-Kabta*, offerings returned from the shrine during the *Elunum* festival of Nergal," 980:1–11

3. **ezem-gur-buru$_{14}$**, "the bushel harvest festival"

1 udu abzu-šè 1 máš ká kù-^{d}inana-zabala$_4^{ki}$ u$_4$ **ezem-gur-buru$_{14}$**, "1 sheep for the abzu (and) 1 goat (for) the gate of bright Inana of Zabala, during the bushel harvest festival," 996:1–4

4. ezem níĝ-ab-e, "níĝ-ab-e Festival"

1 udu-[ni]ga iti-u_4-11-ba-zal 0.0.2. zì-KAL 5 sìla dabin 5 sìla eša [d]šára **ezem-níĝ-ab-e**, "1 fattened sheep at the end of the 11th day of the month, 20 liters of KAL-flour, 5 liters of semolina (and) 5 liters of fine flour (for) Šara (during) the níĝ-ab-e festival," 1001:1–7

5. ezem-pa-è, "the emergence festival"

1 udu-niga u_4-12-kam 0.0.1 zì-KAL 3 sìla dabin 2 sìla eša ⅔ sìla zú-lum [d]šára u_4 **ezem-pa-è**, "1 fattened sheep on the 12th day, 10 liters of KAL-flour, 3 liters of semolina, 2 liters of fine flour (and) ⅔ liter of dates (for) Šara during the emergence festival," 1030:1–5

6. Festival Unspecified

10 {erasure} gín kuš-gu_4-[úh]áb 5 gín sa-udu 2½ gín eša x x **ezem**-da-šè ba-a-ĝar, "10 shekels of madder-tanned ox hide, 5 shekels sheep sinew (and) 2½ shekels of fine flour, placed for (?) of the festival," 1517:7–10

[FIELDS] > **a-šà**

[FOWL]

ir_7[mušen], "pigeon"
kur-gi[mušen], "goose"
mušen-tur, "young bird"
sim[mušen], "swallow"
tu-gur_4[mušen], "dove"
tum_{12}[mušen], "wild dove"
uz-tur, "duckling"

– G –

ga, *šizbu*, "milk; suckling"

máš-**ga**, "suckling goat" > **máš**
$sila_4$-**ga**, "suckling lamb" > **$sila_4$**

ga-ga-ra, *kumurrû*, "capital; total"

(. . .) [x i]m **ga-ga-ra-a** zi-[ga? mu e]n-[d]inana-unu[ki]-[ga] máš-e ì-pàd, "{activities in each month} of *Ibbi-Suen* Year 2, the total [having been?] expended," 1029:'9-'10

(. . .) iti u_5-bí-gu_7 (. . .) iti ki-siki-[d]nin-[a-zu] úgu-a ĝá-ĝá **ga-ga-ra-a** ki [d]*adad-tillati*-ta ⌜ba⌝-zi "*Adad-tillati* disbursed {finished textiles, supplies for processing fish, chaff for burning, cord for a net, and reed bundles}, in months 4 and 5, the total placed in the account," 1162:'50, '64-'70

(. . .) [úg]u-a ĝá-[ĝá **ga]-ga-ra-a** [ki [d]]*adad-tillati*-[ta ba-zi], "*Adad-tillati* [disbursed] {animals, assorted comestibles and finished textiles}, the total placed in the account," 1254:'47-'51

ga-ḫar, "round cheese," 1036:'10, 1036:'73

n sìla **ga-ḫar** (. . .) níĝ-ì-dé-a-šè, "n liter(s) of round cheese (and) {other ingredients} for pastry" > **níĝ-ì-dé-a**

ga-na-na, (meaning uncertain)

5 gín ì-šáḫ-ta 15 gín níĝ-àr-ra-sig$_5$ 1⅓ ma-na tuḫ-ĝeš-ì-[ḫád-ta] 10 gín ádda-u[du-ta] 10 gín mun-ta 3 gín luḫ-lá-⌜ta⌝ **ga-na-⌜na⌝** 1 *lu-l*[*u*?] 1 *ni-a-ma* 1 *ni-a-ma* [min?] 1 *simat-*^{d}*ištaran* nu-x 1 *simat-*^{d}*ištaran* zi-[x] 1 *simat-*^{d}*ištaran* [x]-ti 1 *lu-l*[*u*?] min munus-me-éš {indent}10, "5 shekels of lard each, 15 shekels of fine groats, 1⅓ minas of [dried] sesame chaff [each], 10 shekels of sheep carcasses [each], 10 shekels of salt each, 3 shekels of luḫ-lá each (?), (provisions for) *Lulu*, *Ni'ama*, *Ni'ama* [the 2nd], *Simat-Ištaran* [x], *Simat-Ištaran* [x] (and) *Lulu*, the 2nd, 10(?) women," 562:'40-'55

ga$_6$(ĝ)(ÍL), *nasû*, "to bring; to lift, carry; to haul" > *Verb Index*

gag, *sikkatu*, *ūṣu*, "peg, nail"

60 ^{ĝeš}**gag**-ásal 1 kùš-⌜ta⌝, "60 poplar pegs, 1 kùš each," 1380:4

120 **gag** ma-nu 2 kùš-[ta], "120 manu wood pegs, 2 kùš each," 1380:5

gaba . . . ri, "to confront, meet" > *Verb Index*

gaba-ri-a, "meeting" > **gaba-ri-a**

gaba . . . sàg, "to beat one's breasts (in mourning)" > *Verb Index*

gaba-ri, *miḫru*, "copy," *passim*

bisaĝ-dub-ba **gaba-ri**, "a tablet basket of copies" > **bisaĝ-dub-ba**

****gaba-ri** dub [. . .] um-ma [. . .], 1052:2

2 **gaba-ri**, "2nd copy," 1104:10

nu-ĝál **gaba-ri**, "there is no copy" > **ĝál**

****gaba-ri** dub [. . .] um-ma [. . .], 1052:2

gaba-ri-a, "meeting"[36]

1. At the Place of the Stele

1 sila$_4$ kuš-bi ba-zi 0.0.1. zì-KAL ninda-gur$_4$-ra-šè 1 dug dida$_x$-gen a-níĝin-šè **gaba-ri-a** ki na-rú-a (. . .) šà zabala$_4^{ki}$ u$_4$-2-kam, "1 lamb, its skin was disbursed, 10 liters of KAL-flour for thick bread (and) 1 jug of ordinary dida beer for the a-níĝin ceremony at the meeting at the place of the stele (and) {other "offerings"} in Zabala on the 2nd day," 1028:38–41, 45

36 Sallaberger 1993.

2. At the Gates

6 sìla dabin 1 sìla eša **gaba-ri-a** ká-bar-ra ù ká im šeg$_{12}$ ku$_4$-ra, "6 liters of semolina (and) 1 liter of fine flour (for) a meeting at the outer gate and the 'service entrance,'" 1035:'4-'6

3. Location Unspecified

0.0.1. kaš-sig$_5$ 0.0.1. kaš-gen 0.4.0. kaš-ninda 5 sìla-ta kaš ba-an-dé *ri-im-ilum* sugal$_7$ **gaba-ri-a** unug^{ki}-ta du-ni, "10 liters of fine beer, 10 liters of ordinary beer (and) 240 liters of beer (and) bread, 5 liters each; he poured the beer when *Rim-ilum*, the sugal, came from Uruk (for) a meeting," 517:1–6

gaba-tab, "breastwork fence"

gaba-tab é-ùr-ra ku$_6$ al-ús-sa, "the breastwork fence of the fish-sauce roof house" > *Household Index*

gaba-tab gi-sig dù, "to construct the breastwork fence of the reed hut" > **dù**

gada, *kitū*, "flax, linen"

1 **gada**-gen, "1 ordinary linen," 659:1, 664:1, 674:10, 688:1, 707:1, 731:5, 742:11, 793:12

2 **gada**-gen-sumun, "2 old ordinary linens," 825:3

4 **gada**-gen ki-lá-bi 7⅓ ma-na, "4 ordinary linens, their weight is 7⅓ minas," 575:1–2

[n+]4 **gada**-g[en] *a-gi$_4$-um*, "[n+]4 ordinary *a-gi$_4$-um* linens," 573:1

1 **gada** 3-kam-ús, "3rd-quality linen," 825:2

3 gín šudum-**gada** é-munus-šè, "3 shekels of linen warp-thread for the house of the women," 541:1–2

gal, *rabû*, "(to be) big, great; large"

en-**gal**, "senior priest" > **en**

★★gi-ĝír-ab-ba tab-ba **gal** > **gi-ĝír-ab-ba**

^{ĝeš}ig mi-rí-za-**gal**, "large door plank" > **^{ĝeš}ig mi-rí-za**

ka-**gal**, "large opening" > **ka(g)**

^{gi}ma-sá-ab-**gal**, "large ma-sab basket" > **^{gi}ma-sab**

^{ĝeš}nimbar-**gal**, "large date palm" > **^{ĝeš}nimbar**

ninda-**gal**-gen, "ordinary large (loaf) of bread" > **ninda**

^{dug}sìla-**gal**, "large liter-jug" > **^{dug}sìla-gal**

★★46 ^{gi}ma-sab **gal**-ir dù-a, 1299:15

gal, "large cup"[37]

1. gal-kù-babbar, "large silver cup"

1 **gal-kù-babbar** ½ ma-na 5½ gín, "1 large silver cup (weighing) ½ mina (and) 5½ shekels," 1339:1

---

37 Sallaberger 1996, 100.

1 **gal ka-balag-a-bar?? kù-babbar 19 gín, "1 large silver ka-balag-a-bar?? cup (weighing) 19 shekels," 1339:2

2. **gal-zabar**, "large bronze cup"

2 **gal-zabar** ⅔ ma-na 9-gín-ta, "2 large bronze cups (weighing) ⅔ minas (and) 9 shekels each," 1337:2

1 **gal-zabar** ⅔ ma-na 8½ gín, "1 large bronze cup (weighing) ⅔ minas (and) 8½ shekels," 1337:3

gala(UŠ.KU), *kalû*, "lamentation singer"

1. **Provisions for the Lamentation Singers**

0.0.3. ninda-šu-ra-gen ½ sìla du$_8$ **gala** ù kur-ĝá-ra-a-ne, "30 liters of ordinary half(-loaf) bread baked (in) ½-liter (loaves) for the lamentation singers and the cultic performers," 541:14–15

1.1 **Delivery of the Brewery, Kitchen and Mill Complex**

0.0.1.2 sìla ninda 0.0.1. kaš-gen ½ sìla níĝ-àr-ra-sig$_5$ 1 ku$_6$ al-dar-ra ^{dug}útul-šè **gala-e-ne** *táq-ri-ib-tum* é-⌜lùnga⌝ é-muḫaldim ù é-kíkken, "12 liters of bread, 10 liters of ordinary beer, ½ liter of fine groats (and) 1 split (dried) fish for the tureen of the lamentation singers (for their performance of) a *takribtum*; (delivery from) the brewery-kitchen-mill complex," 437:7–13

1.2 **For Circling the City**

5 sìla kaš 5 sìla ninda **gala-e-ne** a-rá-1-kam (. . .) ér iri ni$_{10}$-ni$_{10}$, "5 liters of beer (and) 5 liters of bread (for) the lamentation singers for the 1st time, (and) {4 other times}, (performance of) a *takribtum* (involving) circling around the city," 1030:10–12, 17–19, 30–32, 36–39

0.0.3. ninda 0.0.3. kaš **gala** ù kur-ĝar-e-ne [a]-rá-3-kam (. . .) ér iri ni$_{10}$-ni$_{10}$, "30 liters of bread (and) 30 liters of beer (for) the lamentation singers and cultic performers for the 3rd time, (and for) {lamentation singers 4 other times}, (performance of) a *takribtum* (involving) circling around the city," 1030:20–26, 39

1.3 **On the Occasion of Offerings for the Wall**

0.0.2. dabin ninda-sal-la-⌜gen⌝ 1 sìla níĝ-àr-ra-sig$_5$ tu$_7$-šè **gala** ù ama-gal-e-ne íb-gu$_7$ u$_4$ *tak-ri-ib-tum* bàd, "the lamentation singers and the female mourners ate ordinary thin bread (made from) 20 liters of semolina (and) soup (made from) 1 liter of fine groats on the occasion of (their performance) of a *takribtum* at? the (enclosure) wall," 1035:'7-'11

^{ĝeš}**galam**, *simmiltu*, "staircase, ladder; step"

1 ^{ĝeš}kuĝ$_5$ **ga-lam**-8, "1 ladder of 8 steps," 808:1

^{ú}**gámun**, *kamûnu*, "cumin," 1178:3

^{ú}**gámun** mu ku$_6$ al-ús-sa-šè, "cumin for fish-sauce" > **ku$_6$**

gán(a), *eqlu*, "field"

5.4.0. še gur á al aka ù gu$_4$-ḫuĝ-ĝá a-šà 1 (bùr) 2 (iku) **gána**, "5 bushels and 240 liters of barley, wages (for) hoeing and the hired oxen, (and) a field of 1 bur (and) 2 iku of acreage," 1051:1–3 še-**gána**-bi 36.1.0. še gur 11.1.0. zíz gur, "their barley of the field: 36 bushels (and) 60 liters of barley (and) 11 bushels (and) 60 liters of emmer wheat," 1233:8–10

1 (bùr) **gána** zàr tab-ba nu-de_5-de_5-ga, "the sheaves stacked on 1 bur of acreage are not to be collected," 1398:1–3

garaš, *karašu*, "leek"[38]

numun **ga**, "leek? seed" > **numun**

kàr-šum, "leek" > **kàr-šum**

[GARDENS] > **ĝeškiri₆**

ĝešgarig(ZUM.SI), *mušṭu*, "comb"

siki **ĝešgarig** aka, "combed wool" > **siki**

29½ **ĝešgarig** šà-kal é-ba-an, "29½ pairs of wooden comb cores," 598:1

★★4 túg-*bu-ti-um*(?) ĝeš*be-rum* siki **ĝešgarig** aka gen ki-lá-bi ⅔ ma-na, 807:1–3

8 **ĝešgari[g**-x]-x é-ba-an, "8 pairs of (?) combs," 1376:49

[GARMENTS] > [TEXTILES]

gašam, *ummiānu*, "craftsman, specialist"

é-**gašam**, "craftsmen's house" > *Household Index*

[GATES] > **ká**

gaz, *dâku*, *šagāšu*, "to kill, slaughter; beat; thresh (grain)" > *Verb Index*

gazi, *kasû*, "(a condiment, mustard seed or licorice),"[39] 511:70, 972:20, 972:92, 975:21, 975:94, 1092:4, 1105:1, 1130:2, 1162:'39, 1162:'45, 1190:3, 1204:1

gidur-**gazi** a-rá-n-tab-ba gíd 1½ nindan-ta, "9-meter n-ply gazi rope" > **gidur**

n sìla **gazi** al-$naĝ_4$-ĝá, "n liter(s) of crushed gazi," 981:21, 1028:6, 1028:23

n sìla **gazi** mu ku_6 al-ús-sa-šè, "n liter(s) of gazi for fish-sauce" > **ku₆**

gigur **gazi**?, "basket (for the transport of) gazi?" 1340:7

géme, *amtu*, "female worker," *passim*

géme á-⅔, "workwomen at ⅔ wages," *passim*

---

[38] Leeks (garaš) are only sparsely attested in the Ur III corpus, where the term is written ga-raš(KASKAL) or $garaš_4$(ga:raš). Several texts (e.g. Syracuse 285:1) mention "leek seeds" (numun $garaš_4^{sar}$). The appearance of numun ga here may be a reference to leeks, perhaps an abbreviation for ga-raš. However, Stol (personal communication) has suggested that at Garšana the term for "leek" is *kàr-šum* and not garaš.

[39] Brunke 2008, 165, n.185 with references.

géme-árad *simat-^{d}ištaran*, "female and male servants of *Simat-Ištaran*" > *Personal Name Index*

géme ḫuĝ-ĝá, "hired workwoman," *passim*

géme saĝ-dub, "full-time workwoman," *passim*

1. **Craftswomen** > *Craftswomen Index*

   géme é-kíkken, "workwoman of the mill" > *Household Index*

   géme gu, "female spinner"

   géme ĝeš-ì-sur-sur, "female sesame presser"

   géme kíkken, "female miller"

   géme kisal-luḫ, "female courtyard sweeper"

   géme uš-bar, "female weaver"

2. **Rations for Workwomen**

   n **géme** ḫuĝ-ĝá n sìla kaš-ninda n sìla tu_7-ta, "n hired workwomen: n liter(s) of beer (and) bread (and) n liter(s) of soup each," 379:8, 556:'4

   ì-ba ù níĝ-dab_5 **géme**-árad, "oil rations and requisitions of female and male servants" > **ì-ba, níĝ-dab_5**

   ninda-ba **géme**-árad, "bread rations of female and male servants" > **ninda**

   siki-ba **géme**-árad, "wool rations of female and male servants" > **siki**

   še-ba **géme**-árad, "barley rations of female and male servants" > **še**

   túg-ba **géme**-árad, "textile rations of female and male servants" > **túg**

3. **Workwomen Days**

   [5]6⅔ 4⅓ gín **géme** u_4-1-šè, "[5]6⅔ 4⅓ gín workwomen days," 342:79

   [šu+níĝin n+]46 [sar] ⅚ gín **géme** u_4-1-šè, "[In total: n+]46 [sar] ⅚ gín workwomen days," 351:137

   207½ 2 gín igi-6-ĝál **géme** u_4-1-šè, "207½ 2⅙ gín workwomen days," 593:4

4. **géme-bi**, "its workwomen"

   á géme n-$šeg_{12}$-ta **géme-bi** n u_4-n-šè, "the workwomen wages (are) for each n bricks (carried); its workwomen (equal) n workerdays" > **á**

   šu+níĝin 60+20+7 sar 6 gín igi-6-ĝál á 1⅓ [u_4]-1-šè á 100-ta **géme-bi** 347½ 7 gín igi-4-ĝál, "In total: 87 sar (and) 6⅙ gín (bricks), wages for 1⅓ workerdays, wages for 100 (bricks) each, its workwomen (equal) 347½ 7¼ gín," 346:69–72

gen, "medium, ordinary quality"

dug $dida_x$-**gen**, "jug of ordinary dida beer" > **$dida_x$**

^{kuš}e-sír-**gen**, "ordinary sandals" > **^{kuš}e-sír**

gada-**gen**, "ordinary linen" > **gada**

gu-**gen**, "ordinary cord" > **gu**

ì-**gen**, "ordinary oil" > **ì**

kaš-**gen**, "ordinary beer" > **kaš**

mun-**gen**, "ordinary salt" > **mun**

ninda-**gen**, "ordinary bread" > **ninda**

siki-**gen**, "ordinary wool" > **siki**

^{kuš}súḫub-**gen**, "ordinary shoes" > **^{kuš}súḫub**
túg-**gen**, "ordinary textile" > **túg**
tuḫ-**gen**, "ordinary bran" > **tuḫ**
zì-**gen**, "ordinary flour" > **zì**

gen$_{6}$, *kânu*, "to confirm, verify" > *Verb Index*

[GEOGRAPHICAL NAMES] > *Toponym Index*

gi, *qanû*, "reed"

gi-bi n sa, "its reeds are n bundle(s)," 374:'5, 374:'16, 1381:2, 1381:8, 1381:20, 1381:31, 1381:36, 1381:41, 1381:50, 1381:55, 1381:60, 1381:63 (in reference to the amount of reeds required to manufacture é-KU-^{ĝeš}banšur, ^{gi}gida$_{x}$, ^{gi}ig, ^{gi}kid)
gi-bi x x IB?, 374:'9 (in reference to the amount of reeds required to manufacture ^{gi}*ba-ti-um*)
gi bù(r), "to cut reeds" > **bù(r)**
gi de$_{6}$, "to bring reeds" > **de$_{6}$**
gi ga$_{6}$(ĝ), "to carry reeds" > **ga$_{6}$(ĝ)**
gi-guru$_{5}$, "reedwork panel" > **guru$_{5}$**
gi ka-tab gúrdub, "n reed cover(s) of reed baskets," 815:9, 1292:4
gi ma-lá-a gíd, "to tow a freight boat of reeds" > **gíd**
gi šeg$_{12}$-al-ur$_{x}$-ra šeĝ$_{6}$, "reeds (used) to bake bricks" > **šeĝ$_{6}$**
sa **gi**, "bundle of reeds," 1356:1
gi tùm-dè ĝen, "to go in order to bring reeds" > **ĝen**

1. **Reed Products**

^{gi}ba-an-du$_{8}$-du$_{8}$, "(a basket)"
^{gi}*ba-ti-um*, "(a reed container)"
^{gi}bisaĝ, "basket"
^{gi}bisaĝ túg-aš, "single textile basket"
^{gi}bisaĝ-gíd-da-tur sa-ḫa, "small, long, canvas-lined basket"
^{gi}bunin-bunin, "trough, bowl, bucket"
^{gi}dim, "reed pole" > **^{ĝeš}dim**
^{gi}dur, "rope"
gi é-KU-^{ĝeš}banšur, "(reed object for? a table)"
gi-guru$_{5}$, "reedwork panel"
gi-izi-lá, "torch"
gi-ka-du, "a type of reed shelter"
gi-nindan, "measuring rod"
gi-sig, "reed hut"
^{gi}gida$_{x}$, "(a reed object)"
^{gi}gilim, "rope of twined reeds"
^{gi}gur, "a reed basket; a measuring container"

^{gi}gur-dub, "a reed basket"
^{gi}gur-sal-la, "a reed basket (especially for dates, bread)"
^{gi}gúrdub, "a reed basket (for fish, wool)"
^{gi}ḫal, "(a basket)"
^{gi}ig, "reed door"
^{gi}kid, "reed mat"
^{gi}ku-ni-na, "drinking straw"
^{gi}ma-an-sim, "sieve"
^{gi}ma-sá-ab, "(a basket)"
^{gi}níĝ-si-ga, "panel"
^{gi}zar-zar(-zar), "(a basket)"

2. Type of Reeds

2.1 **gi-izi**, "fuel reeds"[40]

sa **gi-izi**, "bundles of fuel reeds," 409:4, 416:4, 436:11, 473:1, 473:3, 479:12, 483:12, 483:23, 506:8, 509:'11, 511:81, 516:1, 523:14, 972:11, 972:57, 972:104, 975:60, 975:105, 1013:15, 1013:20, 1014:'8, 1014:'13, 1025:12, 1025:35, 1025:52, 1025:70, 1025:87, 1025:112, 1028:9, 1028:33, 1033:12, 1036:'76, 1162:'61, 1273:2, 1282:1, 1286:8, 1289:8, 1294:1, 1294:3, 1294:5, 1297:8, 1297:14, 1297:17, 1299:24, 1308:2, 1309:2. 1309:5, 1309:8, 1321:1, 1322:1, 1328:1, 1332:1, 1378:'2, 1379:'10, 1380:6, 1396:43, 1527:35

605 sa **gi-izi** *dì-um*-šè, "605 bundles of fuel reeds for wattle and daub," 1286:11, 1289:11

n sa **gi-izi gi-izi**-lá-šè, "n bundle(s) of fuel reeds for torches" > **gi-izi-lá**

n sa **gi-izi** gi-guru$_5$-šè, "n bundle(s) of fuel reeds for reedwork panels" > **guru$_5$**

n sa **gi-izi** gi-ka-du-šè, "n bundle(s) of fuel reeds for a reed shelter" > **gi-ka-du**

sa **gi-izi** gi-sal-šè gul, "to cut bundle(s) of fuel reeds for thin reeds" > **gul**

n sa **gi-izi** gir$_4$, "n bundle(s) of fuel reeds (for) the oven" > **gir$_4$**

n sa **gi-izi** gu-níĝin n-sa-ta, "n bundle(s) of fuel reeds, bales of n bundle(s) each," 1259:1–2, 1261:1–2, 1262:1–2, 1264:1–2, 1276:1–2, 1277:1–2, 1278:1–2, 1288:1–2, 1316:1–2, 1323:1–2, 1325:1–2, 1325:4–5

n sa **gi-izi** ĝar, "to place n bundle(s) of fuel reeds" > **ĝar**

n sa **gi-izi** ku$_6$ šeĝ$_6$, "n bundle(s) of fuel reeds to cook fish" > **šeĝ$_6$**

n sa **gi-izi** ^{ĝeš}lam gub, "n bundle(s) of fuel reeds to prop up (young) trees" > **gub**

n sa **gi-izi** níĝ-sù-a ^{urudu}šen-šè, "n bundle(s) of fuel reeds for the níĝ-sù-a cauldron" > **^{urudu}šen**

n sa **gi-izi** ninda du$_8$, "n bundle(s) of fuel reeds to bake bread" > **du$_8$**

n sa **gi-izi** sa$_{10}$ še n n sa gi-ta, "n bundle(s) of fuel reeds, the price of which is n liter(s) of barley for each n bundle(s) of reeds" > **sa$_{10}$**

n sa **gi-izi** tu$_7$ šeĝ$_6$, "n bundle(s) of fuel reeds to cook soup" > **šeĝ$_6$**

---

40 Sallaberger 1989, 315. For gi-izi, "mixed or unsorted reeds," see H. Waetzoldt 1992, 134f.

2.2 **gi-šid**, "dry reed (fully matured on the stem)"

n sa **gi-šid**, "n bundle(s) of dry reeds," 1348:1, 1357:2, 1358:2, 1360:1, 1363:2, 1364:1, 1366:1, 1373:2, 1374:2

600 sa **gi-šid** gu-níĝin 20-sa-ta, "600 bundles of dry reeds, bales of 20 bundles each," 1278:3–4

[. . .] **gi-šid** 3255 sa sa_{10} gi-zi 0.0.1. še gi 13 sa-ta, "[. . .] 3255 bundles of dry reeds, the price of fresh reeds is 10 liters of barley for reeds of 13 bundles each," 1320:4–5

2.3 **gi-zi**, "fresh reed (used primarily for fodder)"

sa **gi-zi**, "bundle of fresh reeds," 1081:2, 1081:12, 1109:3, 1109:15, 1179:3, 1179:19, 1199:3, 1199:15, 1208:3, 1208:17, 1386:2

n sa **gi-zi** gu-níĝin n-sa-ta, "n bundle(s) of fresh reeds, bales of n bundle(s) each," 1276:3–4, 1277:3–4, 1335:1–2

1470 sa **gi-zi** gu-níĝin 10-sa-ta gu-níĝin-bi 147-àm, "1470 bundles of fresh reeds, bales of 10 bundles each, its bales are 147," 1361:1–3

n sa **gi-zi** šà-gal udu-niga, "n bundle(s) of fresh reeds, fodder of fattened sheep" > **šà-gal**

gi-zi! (GI_4)-bi 524 sa šà-gal udu-niga, "its fresh reeds are 524 bundles, fodder of fattened sheep," 1189:5–6

[. . .] gi-šid 3255 sa sa_{10} **gi-zi** 0.0.1. še gi 13 sa-ta, "[. . .] 3255 bundles of dry reeds, the price of fresh reeds is 10 liters of barley for reeds of 13 bundles each," 1320:4–5

2.4 **Broken Context**

sa **gi**-[x], 1313:1

1 **g**[**i**-x x . . .], 1376:35

3. **gi é-KU-**^{ĝeš}**banšur**, "(reed object for? a table)"

[1] **gi é-KU-**^{ĝeš}**banšur** gi-bi ½ sa ésir-é-a-bi ⅓ sìla á-bi u_4-⅓-kam, "[1] (reed object for? a table). (Manufacture required:) ½ bundle of reeds, ⅓ liter of house bitumen (and) ⅓ of a day of labor," 1381:58–61

4. **gi-izi-lá**, *dipāru*, *gizillû*, "torch"

n ⸢sa⸣ gi-izi **gi-izi-lá**-šè, "n reed bundle(s) for torches," 972:43–44, 1299:24

5. **gi-ka-du**, "(a type of reed shelter)"

45 sa gi-izi **gi-ka-du**-šè, "45 bundles of fuel reeds for a reed shelter," 1324:1–2

6. **gi-nindan**, "measuring rod"

1 **gi-nindan** šu-luḫ ésir šub-ba, "1 ritual cleansing measuring rod coated with bitumen," 1376:14

7. **gi-sal**, *gisallu*, "thin reeds (formed into mats and layered in the construction of walls between layers of bricks or packed earth)"

gi-sal ga_6(ĝ), "to carry thin reeds (to the construction site)" > **ga_6(ĝ)**

gi-sal gi-ir aka, "(meaning uncertain)" > **aka**

gi-sal gul, "to trim thin reeds" > **gul**

gi-sal ĝar, "to place thin reeds (on top of layers of mortar)" > **ĝar**

gi-sal im sumur aka, "to plaster thin reeds (in situ)" > **aka**

gi-sal tà(g), "to stucco thin reeds (in situ)" > **tà(g)**

sa gi **gi-sal**-šè gul, "to cut bundles of reeds for thin reeds" > **gul**

7.1 **gi-sal bàd-šè**, "thin reeds for the wall"

3600+3000+40[+n sa] gi-[izi] gu-níĝin 20-sa-[ta] **gi-sal bàd-šè**, "9640[+n bundle(s)] of [fuel] reeds, bales of 20 bundles each, thin reeds for the (enclosure) wall," 1288:1–3

660 sa gi-[izi] gu-níĝin [n sa-ta] **gi-sal**-[x] **bàd-šè**, "660 bundles of fuel reeds of [n bundles each], [x] thin reeds for the (enclosure) wall," 1316:1–3

7.2 **Broken Context**

n ĝuruš n géme **gi-sal** [. . .], 102:33, 142:31

1 ĝuruš šidim [n ĝuruš] **gi-sal** [. . .], 192:'12-'13

8. **gi-sig**, "reed hut"

gi-sig dù, "to construct a reed hut" > **dù**

gi-sig im sumur aka, "to plaster a reed hut" > **aka**

[n] ĝuruš 2 géme[1 ĝuruš **gi?-si**]**g**? ĝá-nun-na, "[n] workmen (and) 2 workwomen at the reed hut? of the storehouse," 50:8–9

gi-ĝír-ab-ba, "(meaning uncertain)"

[n+]240 **gi-ĝír-ab-ba tab-ba gal zikum šub, 1292:5

[n] **gi-ĝír-ab-ba tab-ba ús ésir šub, 1292:6

[n] **gi-ĝír-ab-b[**a** ésir šub], 1292:7

gi-ir, "(meaning uncertain)"

gi-ir aka, "to make a gi-ir" > **aka**

gi-sal, *gisallu*, "thin reeds (formed into mats and layered in the construction of walls between layers of bricks or packed earth)" > **gi**

gi$_4$, *apālu*, "to send back, return" > *Verb Index*

gibil, *edēšu*, "(to be) new"

é-gal **gibil**, "the new palace" > *Household Index*

é-**gibil** ùr ku$_6$ al-ús-sa, "new roof of the fish-sauce roof house"[41] > *Household Index*

tuḫ-duru$_5$-sig$_5$ **gibil**, "fine fresh new bran" > **tuḫ**

zíz **gibil**, "new emmer wheat" > **zíz**

[41] For the syntax of this passage see Heimpel 2008, §3.17.

gíd, *arāku*, "(to be) long; to tighten; to survey, measure out a field; to quarry (clay); to tow/pull a boat upstream" > *Verb Index*

1. **As an Adjective**

bisağ-**gíd-da**, "long basket" > **bisağ**

túg-íb-lá-su$_4$-a-**gíd**, "long red/brown belt" > **túg-íb-lá**

2. **Length**

^{gi}dur-dağal a-rá-3-tab-ba **gíd** 5 nindan, "30-meter 3-ply wide rope" > **^{gi}dur**

^{gi}dur-gazi a-rá-2-tab-ba **gíd** 1½ nindan-ta, "9-meter 2-ply gazi rope" > **^{gi}dur**

^{gi}dur-gazi a-rá-3-tab-ba **gíd** 1½ nindan-ta, "9-meter 3-ply gazi rope" > **^{gi}dur**

gíd n kùš, "n kùš in length," 1381:1, 1381:7, 1381:30, 1381:35, 1381:40, 1381:54, 1381:62 (in reference to ^{gi}gida$_x$, ^{gi}ig-dur, ^{gi}kid)

gíd n nindan, "n nindan in length," 1381:49 (in reference to ^{gi}gida$_x$)

n kùš **gíd** saḫar-bi n, "n kùš in length, its dirt (volume) is n (units)" > **saḫar**

n nindan **gíd** n kùš dağal n kùš (ba-an-)gi$_4$-bi n kùš sukud saḫar-bi n sar (n gín n še) (. . .) n sar im-du$_8$-a, "n nindan long, n kùš wide, n kùš tapered from n kùš high, its dirt is n sar (n gín (and) n še); (the total volume) of the adobe wall is n sar," 366:'1-'3, 366:'7-'8, '13, 366:'9-'10, '13, 366:'11-'13, 366:'17–19

n nindan **gíd** n kùš dağal n kùš sukud saḫar-bi n sar (n gín n še) (. . .) n sar im-du$_8$-a, "n nindan long, n kùš wide, n kùš high, its dirt is n sar (n gín (and) n še); (the total volume) of the adobe wall is n sar," 366:'5-'6, '13, 366:'15-'16, '19

^{gi}gida$_x$(KWU-844),[42] "(a reed object)"

1 **^{gi}gida$_x$** ésir šub-ba gíd 1 nindan gi-bi 4 sa ésir-é-a-bi 2 sìla á-bi u$_4$-1⅓-[kam], "1 (reed object) coated with bitumen, 1 nindan in length. (Manufacture required:) 4 bundles of reeds, 2 liters of house bitumen (and) 1⅓ days of labor," 1381:49–53

60 **^{gi}gida$_x$** ésir š[ub-ba] gíd 4 kùš dağal ⅔ kùš gi-bi 2 sa ésir-é-a-bi ⅔ sìla á-bi u$_4$-⅔-kam, "60 (reed objects) coated with bitumen, 4 kuš long (and) ⅔ kuš wide. (Manufacture required:) 2 bundles of reeds, ⅔ liter of house bitumen (and) ⅔ of a day of labor," 1381:54–57

gig, *marāṣu*, "to be sick" > *Verb Index*

^{gi}gilim, *kilimbu*, "rope of twined reeds"

****^{gi}gilim** kisal-lá, 1282:2

gín, *šiqlu*, "a unit of weight, shekel; a unit of area; a unite of volume," *passim*

GÍN-bal, "(an unidentified garden structure)"[43]

1. **GÍN-bal GN**

GÍN-bal a-šà gar-ša-an-na^{ki}, "the GÍN-bal of the Garšana field" > *Field Index*

---

[42] For the reading gida$_x$ = KWU-844 see Lafont 1992, 43f. For ^{gi}gida$_x$ see also *RA* 16, 19 rev. col. vi. l.2.

GÍN-bal *a-za-bu-um* šà é-a, "the GÍN-bal of the cistern in the house" > *Household Index*

GÍN-bal gar-ša-an-na^{ki}, "the GÍN-bal of Garšana" > *Toponym Index*

GÍN-bal ^{ĝeš}kiri$_6$, "the GÍN-bal of the garden" > *Garden Index*

GÍN-bal ^{ĝeš}kiri$_6$ ĝá-nun-na, "the GÍN-bal of the garden of the storehouse" > *Garden Index*

GÍN-bal ^{ĝeš}kiri$_6$ gar-ša-an-na^{ki}, "the GÍN-bal of the Garšana garden" > *Garden Index*

2. Construction Projects

GÍN-bal dù, "to construct a GÍN-bal" > **dù**

ḫu-ur-da **GÍN-bal** aka, "to make reed screens (for) the GÍN-bal" > **aka**

saḫar zi-ga **GÍN-bal**, "dirt moved at the GÍN-bal" > **zi(g)**

gir-ga, "(an agricultural product)," 1066:2, 1092:1, 1102:3, 1190:7, 1215:5, 1237:5, 1376:52

gir-ra, "Girra, i.e. fire"

gir-ra ba-ab-gu$_7$, "fire consumed" > **gu$_7$**

sízkur **gir-ra**, "(ceremonial) offerings of the fire" > **sízkur**

gír-siki-gul-la^{zabar}, "bronze wool-sheering knife," 1272:11

gir$_4$(U.AD), *kīru*, "kiln; oven"

gir$_4$ šeg$_{12}$-al-ur$_x$-ra dù, "to construct a kiln for baking bricks" > **dù**

sízkur **gir$_4$**, "(ceremonial) offerings of the oven" > **sízkur**

šeg$_{12}$-al-ur$_x$-ra **gir$_4$**-ta i$_7$-šè ga$_6$(ĝ), "to carry bricks from the kiln to the canal" > **ga$_6$(ĝ)**

šeg$_{12}$-al-ur$_x$-ra úgu **gir$_4$**-ta ĝar, "to set bricks down from the top of the kiln" > **ĝar**

1. Reeds for the Oven

2 sa gi-izi 2 gu-níĝin A.ZI/ZI(.ÉŠ) **gir$_4$**-1-kam, "2 bundles of fuel reeds, 2 bales of rushes, (for) the 1st oven," 436:11–13

240 sa gi-izi 420 gu-níĝin ^{ĝeš}kišig **gir$_4$**-2-kam, "240 bundles of fuel reeds (and) 420 bales of shok (for) the 2nd oven," 1297:14–16

gu, *qû*, "cord, net; unretted flax stalks"

géme **gu**, "female spinner" > *Craftswomen Index*

siki-**gu** kéše, "wool cord binding," 665:2

★★20 ma-na **gu**-^{ĝeš}ba *zi-ba-tum* mu sa-par$_4$-šè, "20 minas of (?) cord for a net," 1162:'55-'56

---

43 Cf. Sallaberger 1996, 10. The meaning here is obscure, but perhaps is to be understood as a garden arbor. For the difference between the signs GÍN (*REC* 448) and TÙN (*REC* 447), see Selz 1997 and Braun-Holzinger 1989, 3. According to Hh 11 375, ^{urudu}gín has to be equated with *pāšu* "adze"; Aa VIII/1 130 provides the equivalence gi-in = TÙN = *pāšu*. Since Ur III differentiates between GÍN and TÙN, and there also is a different entry for ^{urudu}tùn = *quddu* in Ḫh 11 376, the reading for this object must be ^{urudu}gín. Conversely, the word ^{urudu}tùn is rare in Ur III texts; it is mentioned as a part of a gal-container in *BCT* 2 143:ii.4; tùn^{zabar} is attested in *SAT* 3 1331, which might also be read as gín^{zabar}. Finally, ^{urudu}TÙN-sal (*BRM* 3 144, *Ontario* 1 179, *SAT* 2 1143), has a possible variant in ^{urudu}GÍN-sal (*HUCA* 29 88 15, UET 3 20).

1 ma-na **gu**-gen a-rá-11-ta ì-tab-ba(!), "1 mina of ordinary cord of 11 strands each," 836:7–8

gu-níĝin, "bale"[44]

2 **gu-níĝin** A.ZI/ZI(.ÉŠ), "2 bales of rushes," 436:12

gu-níĝin ĝeškišig, "bale of shok" > **ĝeškišig**

n sa gi-izi **gu-níĝin** n-sa-ta, "n bundle(s) of fuel reeds, bales of n bundle(s) each" > **gi-izi**

n sa gi-zi **gu-níĝin** n-sa-ta, "n bundle(s) of fresh reeds, bales of n bundle(s) each" > **gi-zi**

260 **gu-níĝin** ùZI/ZI.ŠÈ, "260 bales of rushes," 1308:4

u_4-1-àm má ĝar-ra u_4-⅔-àm má diri-ga **gu-níĝin**-bi 647½, "the one-day boat was placed (i.e. loaded with shok), the ⅔ day boat 'floated,' (in total: they transported) 647½ bales," 236:10–12[45]

ĝešgu-za, *kussû*, "chair, stool, throne"

é-**ĝešgu-za** (*šu-kab-tá*), "chair house (of *Šu-Kabta*)" > *Household Index*

ĝešgu-za kéše-da-šè, "(supplies) for binding a chair" > **kéše**

ì-ĝeš barag aka ì-ba **ĝešgu-za**, "pressed sesame oil, the oil allotment of the chair" > **ì-ĝeš**

1. **Types of Chairs**

ĝešgu-za-munus, "woman's chair" > see sec. 4 below

ĝešgu-za-níta, "man's chair" > see sec. 3 below

ĝešgu-za *šu-kab-ta*, "a chair (for) *Šu-Kabta*" > *Personal Name Index*

ĝešgu-za-zà-bi-ús, "armchair"[46] > see sec. 2 below

2. **(Leather) Chair Mats**

1 kuš-[udu?]-babbar gikid **ĝešgu-za**, "1 white [sheep?] skin (for) a chair mat," 855:9–10

1½ [kuš-udu] e-rí-na gikid **ĝešgu-za**-šè, "1½ root-tanned [sheep skins] for a chair mat," 855:13–14

1½ kuš-udu e-rí-na gikid **ĝešgu-za**-zà?-bi-ús-a, "1½ root-tanned sheep skins (for) the mat of an armchair," 912:6–7

★★2 gikid **ĝešgu-za**-zà-bi-ús tùn?-ba kuš ĝar-ra, "2 mats of an armchair, (?), covered with leather," 1376:8–9

1 gikid **ĝešgu-za**-zà-bi-ús gíd 5 kùš ⌜dağal⌝ 4 kùš gi-b[i . . .], "1 mat of an armchair, 5 kùš in length, 4 kùš in width [. . .]," 1381:7–9

[1] gikid **ĝešgu-za** ⌜gíd⌝-10-kùš dağal-1½-kùš ⌜gi⌝-bi 4 sa [x]-x siki ud_5 [x] 10 gín [ésir-é]-a-bi [n sìl]a [á-b]i u_4-[n-kam], "[1] chair mat, 10 kùš in length, 1½ kùš in width. (Manufacture required:) 4 bundles of reeds, 10 shekels goat hair [x?], [n] liter(s) of house bitumen (and) [n] day(s) of labor," 1381:35–39

---

44 On this reading and translation, rather than the more common gu-kilib, "bundle," see Heimpel 2003, 3.

45 Translation courtesy of Heimpel, personal communication. See má ĝar-ra, "to place a boat (as terminus technicus for loading bales of shok)" in the *Verb Index*.

46 Röllig and Waetzoldt 1993–97, 328.

1 ^{gi}kid-KU $^{\check{g}e\check{s}}$**gu-za** gíd-2-kùš dağal-1-kùš gi-bi 1 sa á-bi u_4-⅓-kam, "1 KU mat (for) a chair, 2 kùš in length, 1 kùš in width. (Manufacture required:) 1 bundle of reeds (and) ⅓ day of labor," 1381:62–64

1+n kuš-udu e-rí-na ^{gi}kid? $^{\check{g}e\check{s}}$**gu-za**-šè ba-a-ğar, "1+n root-tanned sheep skin(s) were (used to) cover a mat for a chair," 1517:11–12

3. Chair Coverings

1 ^{túg}*ḫa-um* $^{\check{g}e\check{s}}$**g[u-za]** uri_5^{ki} 3-k[am-ús], "1 3rd-quality *ḫa'um* fabric of the throne of Ur," 631:3

1 ^{túg}*ḫa-bu-um* 3-kam-ús $^{\check{g}e\check{s}}$**gu-za** uri_5^{ki}-ma, "1 3rd-quality *ḫabum* fabric of the throne of Ur," 821:5

4. ğír-gul Wool Meshworks

5 túg-du_8-a siki-ğír-gul $^{\check{g}e\check{s}}$**gu-za**-munus šà!-kal ki-lá-bi 3⅔ ma-na, "5 meshworks of ğír-gul wool (for) a wooden woman's chair, their weight is 3⅔ minas," 761:1–2

5. Other Textiles and Leather Products for Chairs

1 túg ba-tab *tuḫ-ḫu-um* tab-ba-gen $^{\check{g}e\check{s}}$**gu-za** *šu-kab-tá*, "1 ordinary double ba-tab *tuḫ-ḫu-um* textile of the chair of *Šu-Kabta*," 737:3–4

★★5½ ĞAR kuš-pa_5 udu-niga-ú-túl $^{\check{g}e\check{s}}$**gu-za** ŠEŠ.[AB^{ki}-ma], 968:8–9

2 kuš-udu-pu-uš x 1 $^{ku\check{s}}du_{10}$-gan-ti-bal-babbar 1 kuš-máš-gal-niga1 kuš-máš-niga 5 gín sa-udu $^{\check{g}e\check{s}}$**gu-za**-níta $^{\check{g}e\check{s}}$ku!(TÚG)-ku!(TÚG) ba-a-ğar, "2 (?) sheep skins, 1 white leather bag with a marking(?), 1 fattened billy-goat skin, 1 fattened-goat skin (and) 5 shekels of sheep sinew were (used to) cover the man's chair (and?) the loom piece," 1517:1–6

6. A Table and Chair: Broken Context

[. . .] ì-ğeš [. . .] $^{[\check{g}e]\check{s}}$**gu-za** ù $^{\check{g}e\check{s}}$banšur, "[. . .] sesame oil [. . .] chair and table," 562:'77-'78

gú, "pulse, bean"

★★ 4 **gú**-ús-sa sullim, 1143:1

1. gú-gal, *ḫallūru*, "(broad) bean"[47]

gú-gal al-àr-ra, "milled beans," 479:5, 483:4, 483:21, 493:7, 493:16, 494:13, 511:56, 972:14, 972:79, 975:15, 975:80, 981:16, 999:10, 1025:6, 1025:30, 1025:65, 1025:83, 1025:105, 1074:5, 1075:3, 1167:14

gú-gal al-àr-ra šu-gíd,[48] "milled šu-gíd beans," 529:8

gú-gal al-ús-sa, "processed beans," 494:7

★★1 sìla **gú-gal gú-gal** SA+A-bi 1⅓ sìla, 836:13–14

2. gú-tur, *kakkû*, "pea,"[49] 1192:2

gú-tur al-ús-sa, "processed peas," 409:3, 416:3, 479:7, 483:6, 483:22, 493:8, 493:17, 523:9, 972:15, 972:80, 975:16, 975:81, 981:17, 999:11, 1025:7, 1025:31, 1025:66, 1025:84, 1025:106, 1075:4, 1193:2, 1396:57

---

47 Brunke 2008, 91 (§3.1.1).

48 For the unusual notation šu-gíd modifying beans see Brunke 2008, 177 (§3.3.5.6, Bemerkung 3.50).

49 Brunke 2008, 91 (§3.1.1).

gú-tur al-ús, "processed peas," 1074:6

gú-tur al-al(sic!)-sa, "processed peas," 1167:7

1 sìla **gú-tur gú-tur SA+A-bi 1 sìla 15 gín, 836:15–16

gú, "side, bank"

gú kíĝ aka, "to do work on the side" > **aka**

gú $\mathbf{i_7}$, "bank of a canal" > *Canal Index*

gú $\mathbf{i_7}$-*a-ga-mu-um*

gú $\mathbf{i_7}$-^{d}amar-^{d}*suena*

^{túg}**gú-è**, "cape"[50]

^{túg}bar-si **gú-è**, "ties (for) a cape" > ^{túg}**bar-si**

^{túg}**gú-è** 3-kam-ús, "3rd-quality cape," 618:6

^{túg}**gú-è** ba-tab *tuḫ-ḫu-um* 3-kam-ús, "3rd-quality ba-tab *tuḫ-ḫu-um* cape," 748:7, 834:7

$^{\text{⌜túg⌝}}$**gú-è** ba-tab *t*[*uḫ-ḫu-um*] ì-n[e-. . .], 609:5

^{túg}**gú-è** ba-tab *tuḫ-ḫu-um* bar-si ĝar-ra 3-kam-ús, "3rd-quality ba-tab *tuḫ-ḫu-um* cape fashioned with bands," 586:2, 587:2

^{túg}**gú-è**-bar-dul_5-gen, "ordinary cape of bar-dul_5 (material)," 698:24, 567:1

^{túg}**gú-è**-bar-dul_5-tur-gen, "small ordinary bar-dul_5 cape," 698:25

^{túg}**gú-è**-$ĝe_6$ 4<-kam>-ús, "4th-quality black cape," 796:9

^{túg}**gú-è**-guz-za-gen, "ordinary tufted cape," 649:9, 803:4, 804:3

^{túg}**gú-è**-guz-za 3-kam-ús, "3rd-quality tufted cape," 631:2 647:3, 758:5

^{túg}**gú-è**-guz-za 4-kam-ús, "4th-quality tufted cape," 617:7, 647:4, 649:7, 731:1, 742:6, 743:7, 773:4, 786:8

^{túg}**gú-è**-níĝ-lám 3-kam-ús, "3rd-quality cape of níĝ-lám (material)," 618:5, 748:6, 793:3

^{túg}**gú-è**-níĝ-lám 4-kam-ús, "4th-quality níĝ-lám cape," 793:6, 829:'5

^{túg}**gú-è**-níĝ-lám bar-si ĝar-ra 3-kam-ús, "3rd-quality níĝ-lám cape fashioned with bands," 579:16

^{túg}**gú-è**-níĝ-lám bar:si ĝar-ra 4-kam-ús, "4th-quality níĝ-lám cape fashioned with bands," 1162:'18

^{túg}**gú-è**-níĝ-lám-tur 3-kam-ús, "small 3rd-quality níĝ-lám cape," 649:2

^{túg}**gú-è**-níĝ-lám-tur 4-kam-ús, "small 4th-quality níĝ-lám cape," 639:2

^{túg}**gú-è**-[níĝ-lám]-tur-lugal, "small royal [níĝ-lám] cape," 821:1

^{túg}**gú-è** *tá-ki-ru-um* bar-s[i ĝar-r]a-tur lugal, "small royal *takkirum* cape fashioned with bands," 824:1

gú-gal, *ḫallūru*, "broad bean" > **gú**

---

[50] *Apud* Waetzoldt "Schulterumhang?"

^{túg}**gú-lá**, "(a textile)"

^{túg}**gú-lá**-PI 3-kam-ús ^{d}*kab-tá*, "3rd-quality gú-lá-PI textile of *Kabta*," 738:7, 811:4

^{túg}**gú-lá**-PI-tur 3-kam-ús ^{d}*kab-ta*, "small 3rd-quality gú-lá-PI textile of *Kabta*," 690:3

gú(n), *biltu*, "load; yield; rent, tax, tribute; a unit of weight," *passim*

^{ĝeš}**gú-ne(-saĝ-ĝá)**, "a cupboard or chest for drinking utensils," 1376:46[51]

0.0.1. kaš-sig$_5$ u$_4$-28-kam 0.0.1. kaš-sig$_5$ u$_4$-29-kam **gú-ne-saĝ-ĝá**-šè, "10 liters of fine beer on the 28th day (and) 10 liters of fine beer on the 29th day for the cupboard," 541:20–24

10 gú ^{ĝeš}[A.T]U.GAB.LIŠ šu aka **gú-ne**-šè, "10 talents of processed poplar wood for a cupboard," 975:46–47

gú-tur, *kakkû*, "pea" > **gú**

gu$_4$(d), *alpu*, "bull, ox; cattle"

gu$_4$-gaz bàd-šè, "slaughered ox for the (enclosure) wall," 992:3

gu$_4$-ḫuĝ-ĝá, "hired ox" > **ḫuĝ**

gu$_4$-niga, "fattened ox," 1125:1

gu$_4$-niga tùm, "to bring a fattened ox" > **tùm**

gu$_4$-ú, "range-fed ox," 1214:1

i$_7$-**gu$_4$**, "ox canal" > *Canal Index*

kuš-**gu$_4$**, "ox-hide"

kuš-kun-**gu$_4$**, "ox-tail" > **kuš**

mur-**gu$_4$**, "ox fodder" > **mur**

si **gu$_4$**, "ox horn" > **si**

^{urudu}šim-da **gu$_4$**-udu, "sheep and cattle brand" > ^{urudu}**šim-da**

^{ĝeš}šudul-**gu$_4$**, "ox yoke" > ^{ĝeš}**šudul**

★★[n] ^{ĝeš}ig mi-r[í-za x?] **gu$_4$** du$_{11}$-g[a x] **gu$_4$**-ta 24, "[n] door plank(s) decorated? with (?) from an ox," 1307:1–2

★★še-gán-bi 36.1.0. še gur 11.1.0. zíz gur lá-ìa su-ga še **gu$_4$** e-na-am-DU ur-^{d}dumu-zi ù *i-din-èr-ra*, "their barley of the field: 36 bushels (and) 60 liters of barley (and) 11 bushels (and) 60 liters of emmer wheat; the remainder was replaced, Ur-Dumuzi and *Iddin-erra* (?) barley and oxen," 1233:8–11

gu$_4$-e-ús-sa, "(fed) following the oxen"[52]

máš-gal-niga **gu$_4$-e-ús-sa**, "fattened billy-goat(s) '(fed) following the oxen'," 984:'58, 1254:5

---

51 For this term, cf. Heimpel 1994, 83.

52 This is a designation of low-quality sheep fed with barley after the cattle had grazed (Steinkeller 1995, 57).

udu-niga **gu$_4$-e-ús-sa**, "fattened sheep '(fed) following the oxen'," 506:3, 970:1, 970:7, 984:'38, 984:'54, 1025:23, 1025:93, 1254:4, 1394:5

1 udu-niga **gu$_4$-e-ús-sa** kuš-[bi] ba-zi, "1 fattened sheep '(fed) following the oxen', its skin was disbursed," 1027:2

^{urudu}**gu$_4$-zi-bi-ir**, *merdētu*, "step-ladder"

1 ^{urudu}**gu$_4$-zi-bi-ir** ½ ma-na 1 gín, "1 step-ladder (weighing) ½ mina and 1 shekel," 1269:1

gu$_7$, *akālu*, "to eat" > *Verb Index*

a-g̃ar **gu$_7$-a**, "de-haired (skin)" > **a-g̃ar gu$_7$-a**

NE-**gu$_7$**, "wastage" > **NE-gu$_7$**

gub, *izuzzu*, "to stand; (to be) assigned (to a task), (to be) employed at" > *Verb Index*

gudu$_4$, *pašīšu*, "a priest"

1. **PN gudu$_4$**, "PN, the gudu$_4$-priest" > *Personal Name Index*
   al-la
   li-bur

gúg, *kukku*; *niqû*, "(an offering; cake)"

ninda-**gúg**, "(a cake)" > **ninda**

gukkal, *gukkallu*, "fat-tailed sheep," 1154:1, 1521:2, 1522:2

kir$_{11}$-**gukkal**, "fat-tailed female lamb" > **kir$_{11}$**

sila$_4$-**gukkal**, "fat-tailed lamb" > **sila$_4$**

u$_8$-**gukkal**, "fat-tailed ewe" > **u$_8$**

gul, *abātu*, "to raze, demolish (a building); to cut" > *Verb Index*

é-**gul**, "demolished house" > *Household Index*

gum, "to crush"

gum-ésir, "pestle (for crushing) bitumen" > **ésir**

gùn, *barmu*, "(to be) speckled, multicolored"

^{túg}bar-si **gùn-a**, "multicolored band" > ^{túg}**bar-si**

lulim-**gùn**, "speckled stag" > **lulim**

túg-**gùn-a**, "multicolored textile" > **túg**

gur, *saḫāru*; *târu*, "to reject (legal evidence), to turn away; to turn, return; to argue" > *Verb Index*

èš-ta-**gur-ra**, "(offerings) returned from the shrine" > **èš** ku-úr **gu-ru-dè**, "to be returned in the future," 1090:3

gur, *kurru*, "a unit of capacity, bushel," *passim*

ezem-**gur**-buru$_{14}$, "bushel harvest festival" > **ezem**

^{gi}**gur**, *gigurru*; *pānu*, "a reed basket; a measuring container"

^{gi}**gur** gazi, "basket (for the transport of) gazi" > **gazi**

^{gi}**gur** in-u-da, "basket (for the transport of) straw" > **in-u-da**

1. ^{gi}**gur a bala**, "reed basket for pouring water," 1255:3

^{gi}**gur a bala** ésir šub-ba, "reed basket coated with bitumen for pouring water," 1271:1, 1299:6, 1349:2

2. ^{gi}**gur ba-rí-ga**, "gur-measuring basket"

^{gi}**gur ba-rí-ga** ka-ba si g̃ar-ra, "gur-measuring basket whose opening is covered (in) horn," 1372:34, 1372:92

^{gi}**gur ba-rí-ga** ka-ba urudu g̃ar-ra, "gur-measuring basket whose opening is covered (in) cooper," 1372:35, 1372:91

3. ^{gi}**gur sal-la**, *sellu*, "thin reed basket"

20 ^{gi}**gur sal-la** zì eša ésir šub-ba, "20 thin baskets coated with bitumen (containing) flour (and) fine flour," 1299:10

n ^{gi}**gur-sal-la** n-sìla-ta, "n thin basket(s) of n liter(s) each," 1367:1, 1367:2

4. ^{gi}**gur še**, "reed basket of barley," 1087:1, 1299:22

^{gi}gur še** á-ág̃-[g̃á] ésir šub-ba, 1376:40

^{gi}**gur še** ésir šub-ba, "reed basket coated with bitumen (containing) barley," 1274:1–4, 1301:1

5. **Baskets of Various Types, Coated with Bitumen**

2 ^{gi}**gur** ki gub-ba ésir šub-ba, "2 baskets—set in place—coated with bitumen," 1272:8

1 ^{gi}**gur**-^{dug}útul ésir šub-ba, "1 basket shaped like a tureen coated with bitumen," 1370:1

6. **Broken Context**

[x] ^{gi}**gur**-bi-kam, 374:'19

[0.n.n.] zú-lum ^{gi}**gur**-ra, "[n] liter(s) of dates in a basket," 1231:1

⌜^{gi}⌝**gur** [. . .], 1292:16

163 ^{gi}**gur** [x]-1-ta, 1376:23

^{gi}**gur-dub**, "(a basket)," 595:5

27 ^{gi}**gur-dub** 0.1.0-ta, "27 gur-dub baskets of 60 liters each," 1134:8

30 ^{gi}**g[ur?-dub?** . . .], 1292:'19

[n] ^{gi}**gur-dub** [. . .], 1292:'20

gur$_4$, *ebû*; *rabû*; *kabru*, "(to be) thick; (to be) big, to feel big"

ninda-**gur**$_4$-ra, "thick bread" > **ninda**

^{dug}**gur$_4$-gur$_4$-g̃eštin**, "a vase for wine,"[53] 1263:1

gur$_7$, *karū*, "granary"

še kar-ta **gur$_7$**-šè ga$_6$(g̃), "to carry barley from the quay to the granary" > **ga$_6$(g̃)**
ki-sá-a **gur$_7$** tà(g), "to apply stucco to the foundation terrace of the granary" > **tà(g)**

gur$_{10}$, *eṣēdu*, "to reap, sickle" > *Verb Index*

^{gi}**gúrdub**(G̃Á×GI$_4$), *gurduppu*, "a reed basket (for fish, wool)"

n gi ka-tab **gúrdub**, "n reed cover(s) of reed baskets," 815:9, 1292:4
[n+]480 ^{gi}**gúrdub** ka-tab sè-ga, "[n+]480 reed baskets fitted with covers," 1292:3
10 ^{gi}**gúrdub** siki, "10 reed baskets of wool," 1376:22
n ^{gi}**gúrdub** siki ka-tab sè-ga, "n reed basket(s) of wool fitted with a cover," 502:1, 1279:1, 1285:2, 1376:20
4 ^{gi}**gúrdub**-siki ba-tab *tuḫ-ḫu-um*, "4 reed baskets of ba-tab *tuḫ-ḫu-um* wool," 625:14
2 ^{gi}**gúrdub** ⌜siki⌝-gi, "2 reed baskets of wool of an eme-GI sheep," 616:2

guru$_5$(URU×GU=KWU-771), "to separate, divide; to cut, pull, trim (weeds)" > *Verb Index*

1. **gi-guru$_5$**, "reedwork panel"
   7 gi-**guru$_5$** a-rá-3-tab-ba, "7 triple reedwork panels," 1328:4
   gi-**guru$_5$** aka, "to make a reedwork panel" > **aka**

guz, "(to be) tufted"

túg-**gu-za**, "tufted textile" > **túg**

– G̃ –

g̃á, *bītu*, "house"

g̃á-nun(-na), "storehouse" > *Household Index*
g̃á-udu, "sheep-shearing shed" > *Household Index*

g̃á-nun(-na), *ganūnu*, "storehouse" > *Household Index*

g̃á-rí-na, *garinnu*, "pit or basin in which mortar or plaster was mixed" > **a-g̃á-ri-na**

---

[53] Sallaberger 1996, 49.

g̃á šub-ba, *isqu*, "lot, share; brickyard"

1. Count of Bricks in the Lot

37⅔ sar 4 gín igi-4-g̃ál šeg$_{12}$ u$_4$-1-kam 37 sar 1 gín šeg$_{12}$ u$_4$-2-kam ⸢NE⸣-gu$_7$-bi nu-ub-ta-zi šeg$_{12}$ šid-da **g̃á šub-ba** g̃á-g̃ál, "37⅔ (volume) sar (and) 4¼ gín of bricks for 1 day, 37 (volume) sar (and) 1 shekel of bricks for 2 days, the damaged bricks were not deducted; the count of bricks took place in the brickyard," 357:1–7

270 sar 13 gín šeg$_{12}$ ús-⸢sa⸣ i$_7$-*a*-⸢*ga*⸣-*mu-um* 60 sar 13 gín šeg$_{12}$ ⸢é⸣-^{d}[x]-SAḪAR [NE?]-gu$_7$-bi ù PA [NE-gu$_7$]-bi nu-zi [šid-d]a šà **g̃á šub-ba**, "270 (volume) sar (and) 13 gín of bricks along the *Agamum* canal, 60 (volume) sar (and) 13 shekels of bricks of the [DN] temple, damaged bricks and damaged (?) not deducted; the count (of bricks) in the brickyard," 358:1–7

188 sar 10 gín šeg$_{12}$ NE-gu$_7$-bi nu-zi šid-da šà **g̃á šub-ba** (. . .) ús-sa i$_7$-*a-ga-mu-um*, "188 sar (and) 10 gín of bricks along the *Agamum* canal, damaged bricks not deducted; the count (of bricks) in the brickyard," 359:1–3, 5

g̃á-udu, "sheep-shearing shed" > *Household Index*

g̃ál, *bašû*; *šakānu*, "to be (there, at hand, available); to exist; to put, place, lay down; to have" > *Verb Index*

g̃ar, *šakānu*, "to put, place, lay down; to deposit" > *Verb Index*

g̃e$_6$, *mūšu*, "(to be) black, dark"

^{túg}gú-è-**g̃e$_6$**, "black textile" > **^{túg}gú-è**

$^{g̃eš}$ig-**g̃e$_6$**, "black door" > **$^{g̃eš}$ig**

kaš-**g̃e$_6$**, "dark beer" > **kaš**

kuš-gu$_4$-**g̃e$_6$**, "black ox hide" > **kuš**

siki-**g̃e$_6$**, "black wool" > **siki**

^{túg}sagšu-**g̃e$_6$**-sig$_5$, "fine black cap" > **^{túg}sagšu**

šáḫ-**g̃e$_6$**, "black pig" > **šaḫ**

túg-**g̃e$_6$**, "black textile" > **túg**

tuḫ-duru$_5$-sig$_5$-**g̃e$_6$**, "fine fresh dark bran" > **tuḫ**

^{túg}uš-bar-**g̃e$_6$**, "black uš-bar textile" > **^{túg}uš-bar**

g̃en, *alāku*, "to go, to come" > *Verb Index*

g̃eš, *iṣu*, "wood"

g̃eš gul, "to cut wood" > **gul**

ki-**g̃eš** gub-ba, "the place of planted trees" > **ki-g̃eš**

1. Wood Products

^{ğeš}apin, "(seed) plow"
^{ğeš}ba, "(a cutting tool)"
^{ğeš}ba-an-la, "(a wooden object)"
^{ğeš}banšur, "table"
^{ğeš}bar, "(a type of plow)"
^{ğeš}*be-rum*, "(a wooden object)"
^{ğeš}bisağ, "a wooden basket or container"
^{ğeš}dal, "cross-bar, beam"
^{ğeš}dim, "post, pillar, pole"
^{ğeš}dusu, "brick-carrying frame; earth basket"
^{ğeš}é-da, "joist"
^{ğeš}eme-sig, "plank"
^{ğeš}éren, "yoke"
^{ğeš}éš, "rope"
^{ğeš}gag, "arrowhead; peg, nail"
^{ğeš}galam, "ladder"
^{ğeš}gú-ne-sağ-ğá, "cupboard"
^{ğeš}garig, "comb"
ğeš-gan, "pestle (or door-bolt?)"
ğeš-ğar, "(a wooden object)"
ğeš-íb(-ra), "(type of plank)"
ğeš-íl, "(a wooden object)"
ğeš-ká, "gate timber"
ğeš-níğ, "(a wooden container)"
ğeš-rín, "scales"
^{ğeš}ḫal, "(a basket)"
^{ğeš}*ḫu-pu-um*, "wheel rim"
^{ğeš}ig, "door"
^{ğeš}ig mi-rí-za, "door plank"
^{ğeš}kuğ$_5$, "stair(case), ladder, threshold"
^{ğeš}*la-ri-um*, "branch?"
^{ğeš}mud, "bridle, strap"
^{ğeš}nu-kúš, "door pivot"
^{ğeš}sağ-du, "a wooden beam (part of a loom)"
^{ğeš}suḫuš-ig, "sole/foundation of a door"
^{ğeš}šeg$_{12}$, "(a wooden object)"
^{ğeš}šudul, "yoke"
^{ğeš}túg-túg, "a designation of looms"
^{ğeš}ú-bíl-lá, "charcoal"
^{ğeš}ù, "planking"
^{ğeš}ù-šar, "point/crescent (of a door)"
^{ğeš}ù-šub, "brick mold"
^{ğeš}*zi-ri-qum*, "shaduf"

2. Types of Wood / Trees

^{ğeš}ásal, "poplar"
^{ğeš}da, "(a tree)"
^{ğeš}*dú-ul-bu-um*, "a plane tree"
^{ğeš}EGER, "(a tree)"
^{ğeš}ği$_6$-par$_4$, "(a fruit tree; fruit)"
^{ğeš}ḫal-bi, "(a tree)"
^{ğeš}ḫašḫur, "apple, apricot (tree)"
^{ğeš}HAŠḪUR.KUR, "quince, quince tree"
^{ğeš}ildáğ, "a type of poplar"
^{ğeš}*kà-na-at-ḫu-um*, "(a tree or aromatic product from a tree)"
^{ğeš}kab, "willow"
^{ğeš}kíğ, "(a tree)"
^{ğeš}kíğ-sig-ḫi-a, "(a tree)"
^{ğeš}kišig, "shok"
^{ğeš}lam, "sapling; a nut-bearing tree"
^{ğeš}ma-nu, "(a tree, perhaps willow)"
^{ğeš}maš, "(a tree)"
^{ğeš}nimbar, "date palm"
^{ğeš}nu-nir, "(a tree)"
^{ğeš}nu-úr-ma, "pomegranate"
^{ğeš}pa-kab, "(a tree)"
^{ğeš}pèš, "fig, fig tree"
^{ğeš}*sé-er-dum*, "olive tree"
^{ğeš}šà-kal, "(a wood used for furniture)"
^{ğeš}še-du$_{10}$, "(a tree)"
^{ğeš}šennur, "plum"
^{ğeš}šim, "(a resinous tree)"
^{ğeš}šinig, "tamarisk"
^{ğeš}taskarin, "boxwood"
^{ğeš}tir, "forest, wood"
^{ğeš}ù-suḫ$_5$, "pine tree"
^{ğeš}ÚR×A.NA, "mulberry"
^{ğeš}zúm, "(a tree)"

3. **Wood (Type Unspecified)**

(. . .) še gur$_{10}$-gur$_{10}$-dè zàr-tab-ba-dè ù **ĝeš** ra-ra-dè a-šà *ṣé-ru-um* gub-ba, "{craftsmen} employed at the *Ṣerum* field to harvest, to stack grain, and to split wood," 262:19–22

1 má 60.0.0. gur ba-gul ésir-bi zuḫ-a ba-ĝar **ĝeš** éš-bi <<BI>> nu-ĝál, "1 60-bushel boat was dismantled, its stolen bitumen was replaced (but) its wood (and) ropes are (still) missing," 1369:1–4

ĝeš é-⌜^{ĝeš}kiri$_6$⌝-a gub-ba šu-sum-ma ^{ĝeš}kiri$_6$ igi-érim-iri^{ki}, "wood stored in the garden house, the inventory of the Igi-erim-iri garden," 1375:45–46

4. **Broken Context**

[. . .]-x ^{ĝeš}gi-[x?], 505:869

⌜sa$_{10}$⌝-bi **ĝeš** 1 [x], 536:25

[n] **ĝeš** [. . .], 925:8

^{ĝeš}[. . .], 1368:1, 1368:2

1 **ĝeš**-gi [. . .], 1376:48

ĝeš . . . ra(ḫ$_2$), *rapāsu*, "to beat; to thresh (grain-with a flail)" > *Verb Index*

ĝeš-gan, *bukānu*, "pestle," 1280:4

ĝeš-ĝar, "(a wooden object)"

n **ĝeš-ĝar n sìla um-mi, 1272:5, 1272:6, 1272:7

ĝeš-ì, *šamaššammū*, "sesame," 1192:1

1. **géme ĝeš-ì-sur-sur**, "female sesame presser" > *Craftswomen Index*
2. **ĝeš-ì barag aka**, "pressed sesame," 972:59, 972:99
3. **tuḫ-ĝeš-ì-ḫád**, "dried sesame chaff," 403:4, 438:8, 442:4, 445:4, 510:4, 511:'103, 521:4, 528:10, 535:4, 549:4, 981:26, 1196:4

   n ma-na **tuḫ-ĝeš-ì-ḫád**-ta, "n mina(s) of dried sesame chaff each," 536:4, 536:9, 536:16, 562:'7, 562:'42, 562:'62

   tuḫ-ĝeš-ì-ḫád-bi n ma-na, "(in total) its dried sesame chaff is n mina(s)," 536:20, 562:'18, 562:'58, 562:'72, 562:'83
4. **tuḫ-ĝeš-ì-sig$_5$**, "fine sesame chaff," 1194:4

ĝeš-íb(**-ra**), "(type of plank)," 592:2

4 **ĝeš-íb-ra** má-[20?-g]ur, "4 íb-ra planks of a [20?]-bushel boat," 1359:2

ĝeš-íl, "(a wooden object)," 1275:4, 1292:1, 1376:47

ĝeš-ká, "gate timber," 1287:1, 1293:3

g̃eš-níg̃, "a wooden container"

1 **g̃eš-níg̃** n sìla, "1 n-liter wooden container," 1372:37, 1372:38, 1372:39, 1372:40, 1372:41, 1372:42, 1372:43, 1372:44, 1372:45, 1372:94, 1372:95, 1372:96, 1372:97, 1372:98, 1372:99, 1372:100, 1372:101

g̃eš-rín, *gišrinnu*, "scales"

1⅔ [kuš-g]u_4 10 gín še-gín 10 gín sa-udu **g̃eš-rín-⌜na⌝**? gú 2 ù 30 ma-na 7 gín, "1⅔ ox [skins], 10 shekels of glue (and) 10 shekels of sheep sinew for a scale of 2 talents and 30 minas," 855:1–4

^{dug}g̃eš-ŠÀ/UD?, "(a vessel)"

[9 ^{dug}]**g̃eš-ŠÀ/UD?** gub-ba, "[9] g̃eš-ŠÀ/UD-vessels on-hand," 1072:5

g̃eš-tab-ba, "(meaning uncertain)"

★★1 ^{gi}bisag̃-BÚR-tab-ba **g̃eš-tab-ba**, 1336:1

g̃eštin, *karānu*, "vine, wine"

^{dug}gur$_4$-gur$_4$-**g̃eštin**, "a vase for wine," 1263:1

^{túg}g̃eštu, "(a textile)"

^{túg}**g̃eštu**$_x$(PI!.TÚG!)-gen! é-ba-an, "pair of ordinary g̃eštu textiles,"511:'122

^{túg}**g̃eštu** 3-kam-ús é-ba-an, "pair of 3rd-quality g̃eštu textiles," 673:8, 778:4, 786:4, 799:1, 803:2

^{túg}**g̃eštu** 3-kam-ús é-ba-an [ki-l]á-bi 4 ma-na 5 gín, "pair of 3rd-quality g̃eštu textiles, their weight is 4 mina and 5 gin," 738:8–9

^{túg}**g̃eštu**-lugal é(!)-[ba-an], "pair of royal g̃eštu textiles," 663:2

^{túg}**g̃eštu**$_x$(PI.TÚG) *simat-^{d}ištaran* é-ba-an, "pair of g̃eštu textiles of *Simat-Ištaran*," 720:2

^{túg}**g̃eštu**-túg 3-kam-ús é(!)-ba-[an], "pair of 3rd-quality g̃eštu-túg textiles," 814:8

^{túg}**g̃eštu**-[. . .] 811:7

$^{g̃eš}$g̃i$_6$-par$_4$, *libāru*, "(a fruit tree; fruit)"[54]

n ḫar $^{g̃eš}$**g̃i$_6$-par$_4$** n(-ta), "n g̃i$_6$-par$_4$ tree seedling(s), n (units) each,"1256:16, 1256:17, 1256:18

7 ḫar lam $^{g̃eš}$**g̃i$_6$-par$_4$**, "7 seedling containers of g̃i$_6$-par$_4$ (seedlings)," 1375:22

g̃iri, "via, by means of, under the authority of someone"

1. g̃iri PN, "under the authority of PN" > *Personal Name Index*

54 Brunke 2008, 207, n. 246 with references.

a-gu-a
a-ḫu-DU$_{10}$
a-ḫu-wa-qar
a-ḫu-[x]
a-wi-lum-ma
^{d}*adad-tillati*
ba-ba-ni
ba-zi
be-lí-ì-lí
é-a-šar
en-nam-^{d}*ma-lik*
en-um-ì-lí
gù-zi-dé-a
g̃ìri-^{d}ba-ú-ì-dab$_{5}$
g̃ìri-né-ì-dab$_{5}$
i-gi-zu-tum
i-ku-nu-um
i-ṣur-^{d}*suen*
ì-lí-aš-ra-ni
ì-lí-ku
ì-lí-[. . .]
ib-ni-^{d}*adad*
ìl-su-ba-ni
im-[. . .]
la-ma-súm
li-bur
lú-kal-la
lugal-ḫa-ma-ti
^{d}*ma-lik-ba-ni*
nin-zi-šà-g̃ál
nu-úr-^{d}*adad*
nu-úr-ì-lí
^{d}*puzur*$_{4}$*-a-gu*$_{5}$*-um*
puzur$_{4}$-^{d}nin-kar-ak
simat-^{d}*ištaran*
sù-kà-lí
^{d}*suen-a-bu-šu*
ṣa-al-lum
šar-ru-zu-DU$_{10}$
^{d}šára-ì-ša$_{6}$
šu-^{d}*adad*
šu-^{d}en-líl
šu-kab-ta
šu-^{d}nisaba
^{d}*šu-*^{d}*suen-e-te-íl-pi*$_{4}$-^{d}en-líl
u-bar-tum
ù-ṣí-na-wi-ir
ur-é-an-na
za-ak-ì-lí

g̃uruš, *eṭlu*, *wardu*, "male worker," *passim*

á g̃uruš-a n gín-ta **g̃uruš**-bi n (gín) u$_{4}$-1-šè, "the workmen wages are n gín each; its workmen (equal) n workerdays" > **á**

g̃uruš á-⅔, "workman at ⅔ wages" > *passim*

g̃uruš dub-sar, "workman (employed for) scribal (work)" > **dub-sar**

g̃uruš ḫi-a, "various workmen" > **ḫi-a**

g̃uruš ḫug̃-g̃á, "hired workman" > *passim*

g̃uruš ^{lú}kíg̃-gi$_{4}$-a-lugal, "royal messenger" > $^{\mathbf{lú}}$**kíg̃-gi$_{4}$-a-lugal**

g̃uruš sag̃-dub, "full-time workman" > **sag̃-dub**

g̃uruš sag̃-tag, "full-time workman" > **sag̃-tag**

g̃uruš ugula, "overseer" > **ugula**

g̃uruš ugula lú-ḫug̃-g̃á, "overseer of hired workers" > **ugula**

1. **Craftsmen** > *Craftsmen Index*

g̃uruš ad-kub$_{4}$, "reed craftsman"

g̃uruš ašgab, "leather worker"

g̃uruš ^{lú}ázlag, "fuller"

g̃uruš báḫar, "potter"

g̃uruš dù-a-tar, "(a type of orchard workman)"

g̃uruš é-kíkken, "workmen of the mill" > *Household Index*

g̃uruš ì-du$_{8}$, "doorkeeper"

g̃uruš lú-kíkken, "miller"

g̃uruš má-gíd, "boat tower"

g̃uruš má-laḫ$_{4}$, "sailor"

g̃uruš nagar, "carpenter"
g̃uruš níg̃-ga, "(class of worker)"
g̃uruš si_x-a, "(class of worker)"
g̃uruš simug, "smith"
g̃uruš šà-gu_4, "ox-driver"
g̃uruš túg-du_8, "braider"
g̃uruš um-mi-a, "craftsman"
g̃uruš un-ga_6, "porter"

2. **g̃uruš šidim**, "builder" > *passim*
g̃uruš šidim um-mi-a, "master builder" > *passim*

2.1 **g̃uruš šidim GN**, "builder from GN" > *Toponym Index*
g̃uruš šidim lú-*dì-ma-at-kál-bu-um*^{ki}, "builder from *Dimat-kalbum*"
g̃uruš šidim lú-é-^{d}*šu*-^{d}*suen*^{ki}, "builder from *Bit-Šu-Suen*"
g̃uruš šidim lú-énsi-marad^{ki}, "builder of the governor of Marad"
g̃uruš šidim lú-ì-si-in^{ki}, "builder from Isin"
g̃uruš šidim lú-*i-zi-in-èr-ra*^{ki}, "builder from *Izin-Erra*"
g̃uruš šidim lú-níg̃-^{d}ba-ú, "builder from Nig̃-Ba'u"
g̃uruš šidim lú-*tu-lí-um*^{ki}, "builder from *Tulium*"
g̃uruš šidim lú-ur-^{d}šul-pa-è, "builder from Ur-Šul-pa'e"

3. **Provisions for Workmen and Builders**
n **g̃uruš šidim** n sìla kaš n sìla ninda n sìla tu_7-ta, "n builder(s): n liter(s) of beer, n liter(s) of bread (and) n liter(s) of soup each," 379:1

n **g̃uruš** n sìla kaš n sìla ninda n sìla tu_7-ta, "n workmen: n liter(s) of beer, n liter(s) of bread (and) n liter(s) of soup each," 379:2, 379:4

n **g̃uruš** ḫug̃-g̃á n sìla kaš-ninda n sìla tu_7-ta, "n hired workmen: n liter(s) of beer (and) bread (and) n liter(s) of soup each," 379:7, 556:'3

n **g̃uruš** n sìla kaš-ninda n sìla tu_7-ta, "n workmen, n liter(s) of beer (and) bread (and) liters of soup each," 556:'1

– Ḫ –

^{túg}***ḫa-bu-um***, ^{túg}***ḫa-um*** >*ḫa'um, ḫapum, ḫawu*, "(a fabric, textile)"

1. **Fabrics**
n ^{túg}***ḫa(-bu)-um*** 3-kam-ús, "n 3rd-quality *ḫa(-bu)-um* fabric(s)," 725:4, 771:5, 796:3
1 ^{túg}***ḫa-bu-um*** 4-kam-ús, "1 4th-quality *ḫabum* fabric," 607:1
[. . . ^{túg}***ḫa***]-***bu-um***-šè, "[(wool)] for a *ḫabum* fabric," 755:9

1.1 **For Ropes**
[n] éš-maḫ [***ḫa***]-***bu-u***[***m*** k]i-lá-bi ½ ⌜gú⌝ 15⅓ ma-⌜na⌝, "[n] large *ḫabum* fabric rope(s)—their weight is ½ talent and 15⅓ minas," 831:1–2

1.2 For the Throne of Ur

1 ^{túg}***ḫa-um*** ^{ĝeš}g[u-za] uri$_5$^{ki} 3-k[am-ús], "1 3rd-quality *ḫa'um* fabric of the throne of Ur," 631:3

1 ^{túg}***ḫa-bu-um*** 3-kam-ús ^{ĝeš}gu-za uri$_5$^{ki}-ma, "1 3rd-quality *ḫabum* fabric of the throne of Ur," 821:5

2. Textiles

[1 ^{túg}***ḫa***]***-bu-um*** $^{\text{[d]}}$da-mu, "[1] *ḫabum* textile of Damu," 594:2–3

1 ^{túg}***ḫa-um*** *a-gi$_4$-um simat-^{d}ištaran*, "1 *a-gi$_4$-um ḫa'um* textile of *Simat-Ištaran*," 581:1

[n] ^{túg}[níĝ-lá]m-ús [n-ka]m [n] túg-guz-za-ús-1-kam t[úg?-ba]r?-r[a-n]i? ***ḫa-um*** *na-wi-ir-ilum*, "{assorted textiles}, *ḫa'um* textiles of *Nawir-ilum*," 650:2–5

ḫa-šu-um, "(a spice plant)," 548:14

^{urudu}**ḫa-zi-in**, *ḫaṣṣinu*, "axe," 1258:1

3 ^{urudu}**ḫa-zi-in** 2 ma-na-ta, "3 copper axes of 2 minas each," 1283:1–2

ḫád, *abālu*; *šābulu*, "(to be) dried (out), dry; to dry"

ésir-**ḫád**, "dried bitumen" > **ésir**

tuḫ-ĝeš-ì-**ḫád**, "dried sesame chaff" > **ĝeš-ì**

ḫal, *zâzu*, "to divide" > *Verb Index*

^{gi}**ḫal**, "(a basket)"

^{gi}**ḫal**-^{ĝeš}ḫašḫur, "a basket of apple wood," 1162:'41

3 ^{gi}**ḫal** ĝar-r[a? . . .], 1376:32

2 ^{gi}**ḫal** x-[. . .], 1376:33

1 ^{gi}**ḫal** im-x-[. . .], 1376:34

^{ĝeš}**ḫal-bi**, "(a tree)"

n ḫar ^{ĝeš}**ḫal-bi** n-ta, "n ḫal-bi tree seedling(s), n (units) each," 1256:33, 1375:34

ḫar, "seedling"

1. Types of Seedlings

ḫar ^{ĝeš}ásal, "poplar seedling"

ḫar ^{ĝeš}da, "da tree seedling"

ḫar ^{ĝeš}*dú-ul-bu-um*, "plane tree seedling"

ḫar ^{ĝeš}ĝi$_6$-par$_4$, "fruit tree seedling"

ḫar ^{ĝeš}ḫal-bi, "ḫal-bi tree seedling"

ḫar ^{ĝeš}ḫašḫur, "apple tree seedling"

ḫar ^{ĝeš}ḪAŠḪUR.KUR, "quince tree seedling"

ḫar ^{ĝeš}*kà-na-at-ḫu-um*, "*kanatḫum* tree seedling"

ḫar ^{ğeš}kab, "kab tree seedling"
ḫar ^{ğeš}kíĝ-sig-ḫi-a, "kíĝ-sig-ḫi-a tree seedling"
ḫar ^{ğeš}pa-kab, "pa-kab tree seedling"
ḫar ^{ğeš}pèš, "fig tree seedling"
ḫar ^{ğeš}*sé-er-dum*, "olive tree seedling"
ḫar sum-sikil, "onion sprout?"
ḫar ^{ğeš}*ša-pá-ar-gi-lum*, "quince tree seedling"
ḫar ^{ğeš}šennur, "plum tree seedling"
ḫar ^{ğeš}šinig, "tamarisk seedling"
ḫar ^{ğeš}taskarin, "boxwood seedling"
ḫar ^{ğeš}ÚR×A.NA, "mulberry seedling"

2. **ḫar lam**, "seedling container" > **lam**

3. **Broken Context**

[n] **ḫar**-tur [. . .] x x, "[n] small seedling(s) of [x]," 1362:19
n **ḫar** [^{ğeš} . . .], "n seedling(s) of [. . .],"1362:'40, 1362:'41

^{ğeš}**ḫašḫur**, *ḫašḫûru*, "apple (tree),"[55] 1362:'66

★★^{ğeš}éren-DU$_8$ **ḫašḫur** > ^{ğeš}**éren**
^{gi}ḫal-^{ğeš}**ḫašḫur**, "basket of apple wood," 1162:'41
^{ğeš}**ḫašḫur**-duru$_5$, "fresh apples," 415:1, 1190:2, 1173:1
[n ha]r ^{ğeš}**ḫašḫur**, "[n] apple tree seedling(s)," 1362:15
n ḫar ^{ğeš}**ḫašḫur** n(-ta), "n apple tree seedling(s), n (units each)," 1256:7–13, 1375:10–16
[n ḫar] ^{ğeš}**ḫašḫur**-tur, "[n] small apple tree [seedling(s)]," 1362:17
475 ḫar ^{ğeš}**ḫašḫur**-[x], "475 [x] apple tree seedlings," 1362:'65
★★^{ğeš}**ḫašḫur** éren n-kùš-ta, 1327:1, 1327:2, 1327:3, 1327:4
★★^{ğeš}**ḫašḫur** éren n-kùš-ta šà éren ^{ğeš}ig-šè, 1327:1–5

ḫi, *balālu*, "to mix" > *Verb Index*

ḫi-a, "various, collective plural"

dabin ninda túg ù ì **ḫi-a** má gid, "to tow a boat (with) various (amounts of) semolina, bread, textiles and oil" > **gíd**
ĝuruš **ḫi-a**, "various workmen" > **ĝuruš**
sar **ḫi-a**, "various vegetables" > **sar**
^{ğeš}šim **ḫi-a**, "various resinous woods" > ^{ğeš}**šim**
^{kuš}*maš-lí-um* ^{kuš}a-ĝá-lá **ḫi-a**, "various leather buckets (and) leather sacks" > ^{kuš}**a-ĝá-lá**, ^{kuš}***maš-lí-um***

[55] Brunke 2008 207, n. 246 with references.

sila$_4$-máš **ḫi-a**, "various lambs (and) goats" > **máš**, **sila$_4$**
šà-gal udu šáḫ mušen péš **ḫi-a**, "fodder of various sheep, pigs, birds (and) mice" > **šà-gal**
še-zíz **ḫi-a**, "various barley (and) emmer wheat" > **še**, **zíz**
^{ĝeš}ù-suḫ$_5$ **ḫi-a**, "various pine trees" > **^{ĝeš}ù-suḫ$_5$**
udu-máš **ḫi-a**, "various sheep (and) goats" > **udu**, **máš**

[HOUSES] > **é**

^{ĝeš}*ḫu-pu-um*, *hūpu*, "wheel rim"

1½ kuš-udu é-rí-na **^{ĝeš}*ḫu-pu-um*** 14-kam, "1½ waterproof sheep skins (for) 14 wheel rims," 855:15–16

ḫu-ri-um, *ḫurium*, *ḫuriānu*, "(a spice)," 1092:6, 1190:4

ḫu-ur-da, *ḫurdu*, "(reed) mat/screen (for a door)"

ḫu-ur-da GÍN-bal šà é-a aka, "to make reed screens for the GÍN-bal in the house" > **aka**

ḫuĝ, *agāru*, "to hire, rent" > *Verb Index*

ḫur-saĝ, *ḫursānu*, "mountain, foothills; steppe"

ì-**ḫur-saĝ-ĝá**, "mountain oil" > **ì**

1. **Broken Context**

[. . . **ḫu**]**r?-saĝ-ĝá**, 1251:7

– I –

ì, *šamnu*, "oil"

ì de$_6$, "to bring oil" > **de$_6$**
ì gu$_7$, "to consume oil" > **gu$_7$**
ì má gíd, "to tow a boat (with) oil" > **gíd**
ì sá-du$_{11}$-diĝir-re-e-ne, "oil, regular offerings of the gods" > **sá-du$_{11}$**

1. **ì-ba**, *piššatu*, "oil allotment, rations"

ì-ĝeš barag aka **ì-ba** ^{ĝeš}gu-za, "pressed sesame oil, the oil allotment of the chair" > **ì-ĝeš**

1.1 **For Boat Towers**

[n.n.n.n (sìla n gín)] ì-šáḫ [**ì-ba**] má gíd-e-ne, "[n liter(s)] of lard, [oil rations] of the boat towers," 419:1–2

1.2 **For Builders**

ì-ba šidim-e-[ne], "oil rations of the builders," 482:13

1.3 Requisitions for Household Servants

ì-ba ù níĝ-dab$_5$ géme-árad, "oil rations and requisitions of female and male household servants," 403:10, 510:9, 511:'108, 521:9, 535:8, 549:8

1.4 Unspecified Recipients

(. . .) še-ba **ì-b**[**a** ù níĝ-dab$_5$], "{assorted commodities} (for) barley (and) oil rations [and requisitions]," 446:9

2. Types of Oil

ì-gen, "ordinary oil"
ì-ĝeš, "sesame oil"
ì-ĝeš barag aka, "pressed sesame oil"
ì-ḫur-saĝ-ĝá, "mountain oil"
ì-nun, "ghee, clarified butter"
ì-šáḫ, "lard"
ì-udu, "mutton fat"

2.1 ì-gen, "ordinary oil," 1008:13, 1194:1

2.2 ì-ĝeš, *šamnu*, "sesame oil," 403:1, 444:1, 444:4, 445:1, 446:3, 466:1, 482:1, 510:1, 511:'100, 521:1, 528:8, 535:1, 549:1, 562:'77, 595:1, 695:2, 712:1, 774:1, 809:1, 970:14, 1008:10, 1011:3, 1011:8, 1011:13, 1036:'9, 1036:'72, 1042:4, 1044:4, 1062:1, 1062:2, 1181:1, 1246:1, 1296:3

n sìla **ì-ĝeš**-ta, "n liter(s) of sesame oil each," 406:2, 562:'6

[**ì**]-**ĝeš**-bi ½ sìla, "their sesame oil is ½ liter," 562:'16

ì-ĝeš-ĝeš-a-rá-me, "1 liter of a-rá sesame oil," 1004:2

(. . .) n sìla **ì-ĝeš** níĝ-ì-dé-a-šè, "n liter(s) sesame oil (and) {other ingredients} for pastry" > **níĝ-ì-dé-a**

2.2.1 ì-ĝeš barag aka, "pressed sesame oil," 511:40, 511:76, 972:8, 972:63, 972:100, 975:9, 975:64, 975:100, 981:1, 981:11

n sìla **ì-ĝeš barag aka** (. . .) níĝ-ì-dé-a-šè, "n liter(s) of pressed sesame oil (and) {other ingredients} for pastry" > **níĝ-ì-dé-a**

ì-ĝeš barag aka ì-ba ^{ĝeš}gu-za (. . .) sá-du$_{11}$-ki-a-naĝ-*šu-kab-tá*, "pressed sesame oil, the oil allotment of the chair (and) {other commodities}, regular offerings of the funerary libation place of *Šu-Kabta*," 972:41–42, 107, 975:42–43, 108, 981:30–33

2.2.2 Barley Equivalents

2 sìla **ì-ĝeš** še 0.0.4.-ta, "2 liters of sesame oil, the equivalent of 40 liters of barley each," 457:3

2.2.3 For (Processing) Textiles

n sìla **ì-ĝeš** mu túg-ga-šè, "n liter(s) of sesame oil for (processing) textiles," 699:2, 5, 705:1, 5, 770:1–2

2.3 ì-ḫur-saĝ-ĝá, "mountain oil," 157:20, 1260:3, 1299:4

ì-ḫur-saĝ-ĝá íl, "to bring mountain oil" > **íl**

2.4 ì-nun, "ghee, clarified butter"

10 gín **ì-du$_{10}$-nun-na**, "10 shekels good-quality ghee," 1004:3

1 sìla **ì-nun**-g̃eš-a-rá-me, "1 liter a-rá ghee," 1004:1

2.5 ì-šáḫ, *naḫu*, "lard," 403:2, 419:1, 438:3, 442:13, 445:2, 472:8, 482:2, 510:2, 511:'101, 521:2, 535:2, 549:2, 557:13, 595:2, 822:1, 891:1, 898:1, 943:1, 946:1, 947:1, 972:36, 972:101, 1005:3, 1194:2, 1196:3, 1299:3, 1520:1

n sìla **ì-šáḫ**-ta, "n liter(s) of lard each," 557:2, 562:'40, 562:'81

ì-šáḫ-bi n sìla, "its lard is n liter(s)," 562:'17, 562:'56, 562:'70

ì-šáḫ di_4-di_4-la àga-ús $šeš_4$, "to anoint the children of the gendarme with lard" > **$šeš_4$**

2.5.1 Barley Equivalents

15 gín sa_{10}+didli 10 še **ì-šáḫ**, "10 shekels of lard, worth 10 barley corns," 828:4

2.5.2 For (Processing) Skins

2 sìla **ì-šáḫ** mu kuš-šè, "2 liters of lard for (processing) skins," 878:1–2, 899:1–2

2.5.3 For (Processing) Textiles

0.0.1 sìla **ì-šáḫ** mu túg-ga-šè, "10 liters of lard for (processing) textiles," 712:2–3

2.6 ì-udu, "mutton fat," 511:77, 876:1, 975:38, 975:101, 1319:1, 1325:14

ì-udu dúr $^{g̃eš}$ig $šeš_4$, "mutton fat (with which) to anoint the back of a door " > **$šeš_4$**

ì-du$_8$, *atû*, "doorkeeper"

g̃uruš **ì-du$_8$**, "doorkeeper" > *Craftsmen Index*

1. **PN ì-du$_8$**, "PN, the doorkeeper" > *Personal Name Index*

nu-úr-zu

šu-^{d}ma-mi-tum

ì-dub, *našpaku*, "granary, grain bin"

ì-dub šà *dì-im-bu-na*-aš-gi_5, "the granary in *Dimbun*-Ašgi" > *Toponym Index*

ì-dub a-šà mí-mí, "the granary of the Mimi field" > *Field Index*

21.4.3 še gur **ì-dub** še-ba iti-3-kam, "21 bushels (and) 270 liters of barley of the granary, barley rations (for) 3 months," 542:1–3

80.0.0. še gur **ì-dub** 1-kam 60.0.0. še gur **ì-dub** 2-kam 19.3.3. še gur **ì-dub** 3-kam 21.4.3. še gur **ì-dub** [4-kam] 10.0.0. zíz gur **ì-dub** 5-[kam] 4.1.4. kib_x gur **ì-dub** 6-kam {indent}181.3.0. še gur {indent}10.0.0. zíz gur {indent}4.1.4. kib_x gur, "80 bushels of barley of the granary for the 1st time, 60 bushels of barley of the granary for the 2nd time, 19 bushels (and) 210 liters of barley of the granary for the 3rd time, 21 bushels (and) 270 liters of barley of the granary [for the 4th time], 10 bushels of emmer wheat of the granary for the 5th time (and) 4 bushels (and) 100 liters of wheat of the granary for the 6th time; (in total:) 181 bushels (and) 180 liters of barley, 10 bushels of emmer wheat (and) 4 bushels (and) 100 liters of wheat," 1233:1–7

10.0.0. zíz gur **ì-dub**, "10 bushels of emmer wheat of the granary," 1234:1–2

ì-ḫur-saĝ-ĝá, "mountain oil" > **ì**

ì-ĝeš, *šamnu*, "sesame oil" > **ì**

ì-nun, "ghee, clarified butter" > **ì**

ì-šaḫ, *naḫu*, "lard" > **ì**

i_7(íd), *nāru*, "canal" > *Canal Index*

i_7-*a-ga-mu-um*, "*Agamum* Canal"
i_7-a-gàr-ús-sa, "Agar-usa Canal"
i_7-^{d}amar-^{d}*suena*, "Amar-*Suena* Canal"
i_7-è, "the 'Outgoing' Canal"
i_7-gu_4, "Ox Canal"
i_7-*ì-diš$_x$-tum*, "*Idištum* Canal"
i_7-ir-ni-na, "Irnina Canal"
i_7-kar_4-na, "Karna Canal"
i_7-*ma-an-iš-tu-šu*, "*Maništišu* Canal"
i_7-ma-ma-*šar-ra-at*, "Mama-*šarrat* Canal"
i_7-me-kal-kal, "Mekalkal Canal"
i_7-mi-me-er, "Mimer Canal"
i_7-nar-e-ne, "Singers' Canal"
i_7-^{d}nin-ḫur-saĝ-ĝá, "Ninḫursag Canal"
i_7-sur, "Sur Canal"
i_7-*šu-suen*-ḫe-ĝál, "*Šu-Suen* Canal of Abundance"

ib-šu, "(meaning uncertain)"

★★0.2.0. ninda šuku **ib-šu**-bi u_4-4-kam, "20 liters of bread of the food allocation, its (?) on the 4th day," 1031:11

^{túg}íb-lá, "belt"

1 **^{túg}íb-lá** siki-a-[gíd] siki ^{ĝeš}garig aka gen ki-lá-bi 16 gín, "ordinary combed wool for a belt of a-gíd wool, its weight is 16 shekels," 756:7–9

1. **^{túg}íb-lá-kaskal**, "traveling belt"

   [1] **^{túg}íb-[lá]-kaskal** ⌜siki⌝-bi ⅓ ma-⌜na⌝ 1 gín, "[1] traveling belt, its wool is ⅓ mina and 1 shekel," 702:1–2

2. **^{túg}íb-lá-su_4-a**, "red/brown belt"

   [n] **^{túg}íb-lá-su_4-a** siki ^{ĝeš}ZUM.[SI aka 4-kam-ús], "[4th-quality combed wool] (for) [n] red/brown belt(s)," 833:3–4

⅔ kuš-máš-g[al-ni]ga 4 ^{túg}**íb-lá-su$_4$-a**-gíd 4 kùš 2 šu-dù 1-šè ba-a-ĝar "⅔ of a fattened billy-goat skin were (used for) covering 4 long red/brown belts of 4 kùš and 2 šu-dù in length," 939:1–2

2 ^{túg}**íb-lá-su$_4$-a** KWU-809-ba du$_8$-ši-a ĝar-ra, "2 red/brown belts covered with turquoise (?)," 782:7

^{gi}ig, "reed door"

[n] ^{gi}**ig**-x [n+]3 kùš daĝal 1⅔ kùš [x gi]-bi 3 sa ⌜peš⌝-múrgu-bi x? 1 á-bi u$_4$-1-kam, "[n] reed [x] door(s), [n+]3 kùš in width, 1⅔ kùš in [x]. (Manufacture required:) 3 bundles of reeds, [n] date palm spines (and) 1 day of labor," 374:'3-'7

[n+]1 ^{gi}**ig**-dur sa-ḫa gíd 3⅔-kùš daĝal 1½ kùš gi-bi 5 sa ^{gi}dur-bi ½ sa ^{gi}níĝ-si-ga-bi 1½ sa peš-múrgu-bi 3 á-bi u$_4$-2½ kam, "[n+]1 reed doors with canvas ropes, 3⅔ kùš in length, 1½ kùš in width. (Manufacture required:) 5 bundles of reeds, ½ a bundle of rope, 1½ bundles of panels, 3 date palm spines (and) 2½ days of labor," 1381:1–6

^{ĝeš}ig, *daltu*, "door"

bar-da ^{ĝeš}**ig** kéše, "to bind the cross-bar of a door" > **kéše**

dúr ^{ĝeš}**ig** šeš$_4$, "to anoint the back of a door" > **šeš$_4$**

$^{⌜ĝeš⌝}$**ig** NI-m[i-. . .], 925:7

^{ĝeš}**ig** bù(r), "to pull out a door" > **bù(r)**

^{ĝeš}**ig** sù(b), "to coat a door" > **sù(b)**

1. Commodities for the Door

[n] gín še-gín mu x-šè [. . . n ma]-na šu-sar m[angaga? $^{ĝeš?}$]**ig** ^{ĝeš}kuĝ$_5$-šè u$_4$ é-e im sumur ba-aka, "[n] gín of glue for x, [. . .] (and) [n mina(s)] of cord (made from) date palm fibers for the door (and) ladder[56] when the house was plastered," 472:10–14

★★4 ^{ĝeš}ḫašḫur éren 6-kùš-[ta] 7 ^{ĝeš}ḫašḫur éren 5-kùš-[ta] 11 ^{ĝeš}ḫašḫur éren 4-kùš-ta 11 ^{ĝeš}ḫašḫur éren 3-kùš-ta šà éren ^{ĝeš}**ig**-šè, 1327:1–5

2. Door Parts

^{ĝeš}apin-**ig**-ù-suḫ$_5$, "frame of pine wood," 1333:1

^{ĝeš}ù-šar-**ig**-ù-suḫ$_5$, "door point/crescent of pine wood," 1333:2

^{ĝeš}suḫuš-**ig**-ù-suḫ$_5$, "door foundation of pine wood," 1333:3

2.1 ^{ĝeš}ig mi-rí-za, "door plank"

^{ĝeš}**ig mi-rí-za** sù(b), "to coat the door plank" > **sù(b)**

4 kuš-gu$_4$ šu-gíd ^{ĝeš}**ig mi-rí-za**-šè, "4 šu-gíd ox skins for door planks," 912:9–10

★★[n ^{ĝeš}]**ig mi-r[í-za** x?] gu$_4$ du$_{11}$-⌜ga⌝ [x] gu$_4$-ta 24, "[n] door plank(s) (decorated?) with (?) from an ox," 1307:1–2

1 ^{ĝeš}**ig mi-rí-za**-gal ésir šub-ba, "1 large door plank coated with bitumen," 1307:3

---

56 Heimpel 2008, §4.7, "ladder door."

igi, *šību*, "witness" > *Personal Name Index*

a-a-mu
a-da-làl
a-na-aḫ-ì-lí
a-wi-lí
^{d}*adad-tillati*
ba-zi
be-lí-ì-lí
bu-lu-za
dub-si-ga
èr-ra-ba-ni
g̃ìri-né-ì-dab$_{5}$
i-ri-bu-um
i-sú-a-ri-iq
ì-lí-bi-la-ni
ìl-su-ba-ni
la-ma-gir$_{11}$
la-qì-ip
làl-la
li-bur
li-bur-be-lí
lú-^{d}nin-šubur
^{d}*ma-lik-ba-ni*
ma-šum
nu-úr-zu
puzur$_{4}$*-a-gu*$_{5}$*-um*
puzur$_{4}$*-é-a*
puzur$_{4}$*-*^{d}*nin-kar-ak*
si-mu
si-na-ti
^{d}šára-kam
šu-^{d}dumu-zi
šu-eš$_{4}$*-tár*
šu-ku-bu-um
šu-ma-mi-tum
šu-^{d}nin-girim$_{x}$
ur-^{d}en-líl-lá
ur-^{d}šul-pa-è
ur-zikum-ma
a?-⸢al⸣-la-[x?]. 1056:6
a[b?-. . .], 609:22
NE-[. . .], 609:21
[. . .]-na-x, 1059:6

igi . . . g̃ál, "(fractional notation)," *passim*

igi . . . sag̃, "to sort" > *Verb Index*

íl, *našû*, "to raise, carry" > *Verb Index*

im, *ṭīdu*, "earth"[57]

bisag̃ **im** sar-ra, "clay tablet coffer" > **bisag̃**
im-bábbar, "gypsum" > **im-bábbar**
im *dì-um*, "an adobe mix" > ***dì-um***
im-du$_{8}$-a "adobe wall" > **im-du$_{8}$-a**
im ga$_{6}$(g̃), "to carry earth" > **ga$_{6}$(g̃)**
im gíd, "to haul earth" > **gíd**
im g̃ar, "to place earth" > **g̃ar**
im íl, "to lift earth" > **íl**
im-kù-sig$_{17}$, "reddish clay; ointment; rouge (cosmetic)" > **im-kù-sig$_{17}$**
im ku$_{4}$, "to bring in earth" > **ku$_{4}$**
im lu, "to mix earth" > **lu**
im sumur, "plaster" > **sumur**
im šeg$_{12}$, "brick earth" > **šeg$_{12}$**
im šu dím-ma sum, "to hand earth for building" > **sum**

---

57 Earth (im) designates the mixture of dirt (saḫar), temper (in-u) and water (a) from which mortar and plaster were made (Heimpel, personal communication).

im zi(l), "to strip earth" > **zi(l)**

1. **im-sar**, "clay tablet"

im-sar g̃ar, "to deposit clay tablets" > **g̃ar**

2. **Broken Context**

1 g̃uruš **im** [. . .], 53:53

im-bábbar, *gaṣṣu*, "gypsum," 595:4, 695:1, 768:2, 783:4, 785:1, 791:2, 1329:2, 1343:3

n ma-na **im-bábbar** lu-luḫ-dè, "n mina(s) of gypsum for cleaning" > **luḫ**

1. **For Coating the Door**

1⅓ g̃uruš ad-kub$_4$ u$_4$-1-[šè] ésir-é-a ù **im-bábbar** $^{\text{g̃eš}}$ig bí-ib-sù-ub, "1⅓ reed craftsmen [for] 1 day coated the door with house bitumen and gypsum," 1329:5–7

2. **For (Processing) Textiles**

n gú **im-bábbar** mu túg-ga-šè, "n talent(s) of gypsum for textiles," 642:1–2, 689:1–2, 699:4–5, 705:3, 5

im-du$_8$-a, *pitqu*; *pitiqtu*, "adobe (earth) wall; mud wall"

im-du$_8$-a $^{\text{g̃eš}}$kiri$_6$ gar-ša-an-na^{ki}, "the adobe wall of the Garšana garden" > *Garden Index*

im-du$_8$-a $^{\text{g̃eš}}$kiri$_6$ *šu-eš$_4$-tár*, "the adobe wall of the garden of *Šu-Eštar*" > *Garden Index*

im-du$_8$-a $^{\text{g̃eš}}$kiri$_6$ zabala$_4^{\text{ki}}$, "the adobe wall of the Zabala garden" > *Garden Index*

n sar **im-du$_8$-a**, "n sar (of dirt for) the adobe wall," 1362:5, 1362:'28

1. **Delivery of Dirt for the Adobe Wall**

[20+2+]3 sar 10+[5 gín] 5 še **im-d[u$_8$-a]** á g̃uruš 3⅔ gín 15 še-ta g̃uruš-bi 404 [u$_4$-1-šè] še 6-sìla-ta ba-[ḫug̃] **im-du$_8$-a** $^{\text{g̃eš}}$[kiri$_6$] zabala$_4^{\text{[ki]}}$ mu-[DU], "[25] sar 1[5] gín (and) 5 še (of dirt for) the adobe wall. Workmen wages of 3⅔ gín (and) 15 še each, its workmen (equal) 404 workerdays, hired (for) 6 liters of barley each. Delivery for the adobe wall of the Zabala garden," 356:1–6

2. **Volumes of Dirt for the Wall**

n nindan gíd n kùš dag̃al n kùš (ba-an-)gi$_4$-bi n kùš sukud saḫar-bi n sar (n gín n še) (. . .) n sar **im-du$_8$-a**, "n nindan long, n kùš wide, n kùš tapered from n kùš high, its dirt is n sar (n gín (and) n še); (the total volume) of the adobe wall is n sar," 366:'1-'3, 366:'7-'8, '13, 366:'9-'10, '13, 366:'11-'13, 366:'17–19

n nindan gíd n kùš dag̃al n kùš sukud saḫar-bi n sar (n gín n še) (. . .) n sar **im-du$_8$-a**, "n nindan long, n kùš wide, n kùš high, its dirt is n sar (n gín (and) n še); (the total volume) of the adobe wall is n sar," 366:'5-'6, '13, 366:'15-'16, '19

[. . . kùš] dag̃al 3 [. . . n sar] **im-du$_8$-a** [. . .], 366:'22-'23

im-kù-sig$_{17}$, *šaršerrum*, *illur pani*, "reddish clay; ointment; rouge (cosmetic)," 891:2

img̃ag̃a$_3$(ZÍZ.AN), *kunāšu*, *dišiptuḫḫu*, "emmer," 1110:3

n zíz gur ba-na **img̃ag̃a$_3$** n sìla-ta ì-g̃ál, "n bushel(s) of emmer wheat, in each ban (=10 liters) of it there are n liter(s) of emmer" > **g̃ál**

in-u, *tibnu*, "straw"

in-u de_6, "to bring straw" > **de_6**

in-u en-nu aka, "to guard straw" > **aka**

in-u en-nu aka g̃en, "to go (in order) to guard straw" > **aka**, **g̃en**

in-u ga_6(g̃), "to carry straw" > **ga_6(g̃)**

in-u g̃en, "to go (for) straw" > **g̃en**

in-u íl, "to lift straw" > **íl**

in-u lá, "to transport straw" > **lá**

in-u tùm, "to bring straw" > **tùm**

1. [gi]**gur in-u-da**, "basket (for the transport of) straw," 1292:2, 1299:13, 1340:5, 1376:19
2. **Broken Context**

6 g̃uruš **in-[u** (x x)] ka i_7-ir-ni-na-š[è x x], "6 workmen [having transported/carried] straw to the mouth of the Irnina canal," 40:32–33

20-lá-1 [. . .] **in-u** i[m-. . .], 53:49–50

6 g̃uruš **in-u** [i_7]-kar-na_4-ta in-[. . .], "6 workmen [. . .] straw from the Karna [canal]," 81:9

[. . .] DU [x] **in-u** [. . .], 191:34

ir-dù-a, "(meaning uncertain)"

★★2 [gi]kid ésir BE-a **ir-dù-a** tab-⌜ba⌝ ésir šub-ba, 1376:43

★★[. . .] **ir-dù-[a** 1]-ta, 1376:31

ir_7(KASKAL)**[mušen]**, *uršānu*, "pigeon," 470:2, 522:1, 522:3, 526:2, 526:4, 526:7, 1055:1, 1092:3, 1126:1, 1394:8

ir_7[mušen]-niga, "fattened pigeon," 1053:3, 1060:1, 1253:'4

★★2 **ir_7[mušen]** sag̃-x-du, 1220:1–2

iri, *ālu*, "city"

[d]inana-šà-**iri[ki]**, "Inana of the city" > *Deities Index*

iri níg̃in, "to circle around the city" > **níg̃in**

iri-šè g̃en, "to go to the city" > **g̃en**

iri[ki] sá, "to arrive at the city" > **sá**

lú-ḫug̃-g̃á **iri[ki]**-didli-ke_4-ne íb-gu_7, "the hired workers of various cities ate" > **gu_7**

u_4 *e-lu-núm*-[d]ner[gal_x[eri11-gal]] šà **iri[ki]**, "during the *Elunum* festival of Nergal in the city" > *Deities Index*

2 (iku) gána 20 sar **iri[ki]** sumun, "2 iku (and) 20 sar (of land) in the old city," 1362:'53

iti(d), *arḫu*, "month," *passim*

iti u_4-n-ba-zal, "at the end of the nth day of the month" > **zal**

šu-a-gi-na u_4 **iti-da**, "offering of the month" > **šu-a-gi-na**

1. In Month 1

(. . .) [sá-d]u$_{11}$ **iti-1-kam** (. . .) sá-du$_{11}$-ki-a-nağ-*šu-kab-tá*, "{assorted comestibles}, regular offerings in the 1st month, (and) {other comestibles}, regular offerings of the funerary libation place of *Šu-Kabta*, 972:45, 107

2. From Month 3

0.4.0. ninda **iti šeš-da-gu$_7$**-⸢ta⸣, "40 liters of bread from month 3," 1031:6

3. In Month 4

0.1.3. ninda šuku *šu*-^{d}nin-súmun **iti 4-kam**, "63 liters of bread are the food allocation of *Šu*-Ninsumun in the 4th month," 1031:16

4. In Months 4 and 5

(. . .) **iti u$_5$-bí-gu$_7$** (. . .) **iti ki-siki-^{d}nin-[a-zu]** úgu-a ğá-ğá ga-ga-ra-a ki ^{d}*adad-tillati*-ta ⸢ba⸣-zi "*Adad-tillati* disbursed {finished textiles, supplies for fish-sauce, chaff for burning, cord for a net, and reed bundles}, in months 4 and 5, the total placed in the account," 1162:'50, '64-'70

iti u$_5$-bí-[gu$_7$] ù **iti ki-siki-^{d}n[in-a-zu** x?] še-zíz-ḫi-a 720 g[ur (. . .)] *dì-im-bu-na*-á[š-gi$_5$-ta] é-duru$_5$-kab-bí-šè lá-[a], "(in) month 4 and month 5 720 bushels of various barley (and) emmer wheat were transported from *Dimbun*-Ašgi to the Kabbi village," 1029:'1-'5

5. In Month 6

0.2.0. dabin *a-da-làl* **iti 6-kam** šu ba-ti, "in the 6th month *Adallal* received 120 (liters) of semolina," 1527:31–34

(. . .) **[iti]-6-kam** 23⅓ ma-na báppir-sig$_5$ še-bi 0.0.3.5 sìla sá-du$_{11}$ ku$_5$-rá **iti-6-kam** [šu+nígin 10+]1.3.3.5 sìla še ninda gur [sag-níğ]-gur$_{11}$-ra-kam [šà-b]i-ta, "{regular offerings of deities} of the 6th month, 23⅓ minas of fine beer bread, their barley (equivalent) is 35 liters, deducted regular offerings of the 6th month—in total: 11 bushels (and) 215 liters of barley (for) bread—are the available assets. From among it: {barley rations and requisitions of various individuals}," 1527:6–13

6. From Month 7 to 12

1.1.3. ninda gur **iti á-ki-ti**-ta **iti ezem-^{d}me-ki-ğál**-šè iti 6-kam, "1 bushel (and) 90 liters of bread from month 7 to month 12 – (in total:) 6 months," 1031:7–10

7. In Month 8

[. . . x? **iti ez]em-^{d}šul-g[i x? . . . im] sumur aka [gar]-ša-an-na$^{[ki]}$ ù ğír-[su]^{ki}-⸢šè⸣ D[U-x?], 1029:'11-'14

8. In Month 9

****iti ezem-^{d}[*šu*]-^{d}EN.[ZU** x?] kaš-dé-a diğir-re-e-[ne] sa gi$_4$-gi$_4$ a[ka?], "preparations made? for the banquet of the gods (in) month 9," 1029:'15-'17

9. In Month 10

iti ezem-maḫ še túm-dè é-duru$_5$-ul-luḫ-uri$_5$^{ki}-[ma-šè ğen-na], "(workers) [having gone to] the Ulluḫ-Urim village to bring barley (in) month 10," 1029:'18-'19

10. In Months 11 and 12

1 ğuruš ⸢ašgab⸣ u$_4$-14-[šè] **iti ezem-an-⸢na⸣** 1 ğuruš ⸢ašgab⸣ ⸢u$_4$⸣-[n-šèn ğuruš] ašgab **i[ti ezem]-m[e-ki-ğ]ál** ⸢saḫar⸣ zi-⸢ga⸣ i$_7$-ma-ma-*šar-ra-at*, "1 leather worker for 14 days in month 11 (and) 1 leather worker for [n] day(s) (and) [n] leather worker(s) in month 12 having moved dirt at the Mama-*šarrat* canal," 281:1–8

11. In Month 12

0.2.0. ninda šuku ib-šu-bi u_4-4-kam 1.0.2. ninda gur sá-du_{11} ù ninda dirig ba-ab-daḫ-a **iti ezem-me-ki-g̃ál**, "20 liters of bread of the food allocation, its (?) on the 4th day; 1 bushel (and) 20 liters of bread, regular offerings and additional bread that were added in the 12th month," 1031:11–12

12. After Month 12

iti ezem-me-ki-g̃ál ba-zal, "month 12 having passed" > **zal**

13. In Month 13

5[0 ud]u-máš ḫi-a gub-ba [é-š]u-sum-ma g̃ìri *a-ḫu*-[x] dub-sar **iti dirig ezem-me-ki-g̃ál** ba-zal mu ^{d}*i-bí-*^{d}*suen* lugal, "(In total:) 50 various sheep (and) goats present in the storehouse under the authority of *Aḫu*-[x], the scribe, at the end of the 13th month of *Ibbi-Suen* Year 1," 984:5–9

[. . .] x-x [. . . é]-^{d}šára-G̃EŠ.KÚŠ[U^{ki} . . . o.n.n.]6⅔ sìla [ninda] **iti dirig ezem-**^{d}**me-ki-g̃ál**-šè mu ^{d}*i-bí-*^{d}*suen* ⌜lugal⌝, "[. . .] Šara [temple] of G̃EŠ.KÚŠU, [n+]6⅔ liters of [bread] for month 13, *Ibbi-Suen* Year 1" 1031:1–5

1 udu-níta mu kù-^{d}⌜šára ⌜ba⌝-šè **iti dirig** sum-mu-dam, "1 ram for the purification of Šara, to be provided in month 13," 1078:1–4

14. Uncertain Context

****iti** ezem-^{d}nin-a-z[u x? x] še-ba **iti** 4-k[am x? še?]-ninda bí-in-n[a-x?], 1029:'6-'8

iz-zi, *igāru*, "a (brick) wall (of a building)"

iz-zi bàd tà(g), "to touch up the iz-zi wall of the (enclosure) wall" > **tà(g)**

iz-zi dù, "to construct the iz-zi wall" > **dù**

iz-zi gul, "to demolish the iz-zi wall" > **gul**

iz-zi im sumur aka, "to plaster the iz-zi wall" > **aka**

iz-zi ù-ru, "to level the iz-zi wall" > **ù-ru**

úgu **iz-zi-da** a g̃ar, "to waterproof the top of the iz-zi wall" > **a . . . g̃ar**

1. iz-zi gub-ba, "employed at the iz-zi wall"

1 g̃uruš šidim **iz-zi** bàd **gub-ba**, "1 builder employed at the iz-zi wall of the (enclosure) wall," 29:'16

1 g̃uruš šidim um-mi-a 4 g̃uruš šidim é-*u-bar-ri-a* gub-ba 1 g̃uruš šidim **iz-zi** šà é-a **gub-ba**, "1 master builder (and) 4 builders employed at the house of *Ubarria*, 1 builder employed at the iz-zi wall in the house," 91:6–9

5 [g̃uruš šidim] **iz-zi** š[à é-a **gub-ba**], "5 [builders employed at] the iz-zi wall in [the house]," 185:12–13

2. da-iz-zi, "the side of the iz-zi wall"

da-iz-zi g̃ar, "to place at the side of the iz-zi wall" > **g̃ar**

3. iz-zi-da, "side iz-zi wall"

[n géme da]-**iz-zi-da**-šè an-za-qar-$^{g̃eš}$$kiri_6$-$zabala_4$$^{⌜ki⌝}$ [gub-ba], "[n workwomen] for [the side] of the side iz-zi wall, (workers) employed at the tower of the Zabala garden," 201:'5-'6

– K –

ka(g), *pû*, "mouth; opening (of a river, canal; of a box/basket)"

ka gi-sal im sumur aka, "(meaning uncertain)"

ka-ga-na gen$_6$, "to confirm" > **gen$_6$**

1. Opening of Baskets

1 ^{gi}bisağ-gíd-da túg-ga-tur ésir šub-ba **ka**-bi kuš-ğar-ra, "1 long, small basket coated with bitumen (for) textiles, its opening covered with leather," 798:1–3

^{gi}gur ba-rí-ga **ka**-ba si ğar-ra, "reed basket whose opening is covered (in) horn," 1372:34, 1372:92

^{gi}gur ba-rí-ga **ka**-ba urudu ğar-ra, "reed basket whose opening is covered (in) cooper," 1372:35, 1372:91

2. ka i$_7$ "Opening of the Canal" > *Canal Index*

ka i$_7$-è, "opening of the 'Outgoing' Canal"

ka i$_7$-nar-e-ne, "opening of the Singers' Canal"

ka i$_7$-^{d}nin-ḫur-sağ-ğá, "opening of the Ninḫursağ Canal"

ka i$_7$-da ka-gal, "large opening of the canal" > **i$_7$**

ka i$_7$ de$_6$, "to come (to) the opening of the canal" > **de$_6$**

ka i$_7$ in-u lá, "to transport straw to the opening of the canal" > **lá**

ka i$_7$-šè má gíd, "to tow a boat to the opening of the canal" > **gíd**

in-u **ka i$_7$** en-nu aka tuš, "to sit at the opening of the canal to guard straw" > **aka**, **tuš**

3. Broken or Uncertain Context

★★1 gal **ka**-balag-a-bar?? kù-babbar 19 gín, "1 large silver ka-balag-a-bar?? cup (weighing) 19 shekels," 1339:2

★★2 ^{ğeš}maš DI-[. . .] **ka**-ba UD.K[A.BAR. . .], 1342:4–5

ka-al-la-ka, **ka-la$_{(2)}$-ka**, "dirt quarry (the excavation site from which dirt was quarried)"

in-u **ka-lá**-šè ga$_6$(ğ), "to carry straw to the dirt quarry" > **ga$_6$(ğ)**

ka-la$_{(2)}$-ka gub-ba, "employed at the dirt quarry" > **gub**

saḫar zi-ga **ka-la-ka** gub-ba, "employed to remove dirt at the dirt quarry" > **zi(g)**

saḫar zi-ga **ka-la-ka** si(g), "to pile up excavated dirt at the dirt quarry" > **si(g)**

1. At the Quarry (Task Unspecified)

5 ğuruš im lu-a 3 ğuruš **ka-al-la-ka** 2 ğuruš bisağ im sar-ra im ga$_6$-ğá, "5 workmen having mixed earth, 3 workmen at the dirt quarry (and) 2 workmen having carried earth in the clay tablet coffer," 103:28–30

ka-la, "(meaning uncertain)"

★★kuš é-ri-na **ka-la**, "root-tanned ka-la leather," 855:17

^{kuš}**ka-tab**, *katammu*; *katappû*, "lid, cover; bridle," 1072:7, 1074:8

^{gi}gúrdub (siki) **ka-tab** sè(g), "a gúrdub basket (of wool) fitted with a cover" > **sè(g)**

1. **Reed Covers**

gi **ka-tab** gúrdub, "n reed cover(s) of reed baskets," 815:9

2. **Sheep Skin Covers**

kuš-udu **ka-tab**, "sheep skin cover," 900:2, 912:8, 1068:6, 1075:6, 1272:3

kuš-udu e-rí-na **ka-tab**, "root-tanned sheep skin cover," 969:'1

kuš-udu **ka-tab** e-rí-na, "root-tanned sheep skin cover," 1525:3

2.1 **Sheep Skins for Leather Covers**

3 kuš-udu 3 kuš-sila$_{4}$ **ka-tab**-šè, "3 sheep skins (and) 3 lamb skins for covers," 906:2–4

1 kuš-[udu] ú-ḫáb 4 kuš-udu e-rí-na ⸢**ka**⸣**-tab**-šè, "1 madder tanned [sheep] skin (and) 4 root-tanned sheep skins for covers," 917:1–3

ká, *bābu*, "gate"

^{ĝeš}dal **ká**, "beam of gate wood" > ^{ĝeš}**dal**

ĝeš-**ká** kéše, "to bind the wood of a gate" > **kéše**

ĝeš **ká**-šè gul, "to cut wood for a gate" > **gul**

ká-é-gal-ka, "palace gate" > *Household Index*

ká im sumur aka, "to plaster a gate" > **aka**

ká sè(g$_{10}$), "set in place at the gate" > **sè(g$_{10}$)**

Gates

ká-bar-ra, "outer gate"

ká-bil-lí-a, "*Billia'a* gate"

ká-dedal-lí-a, "gate of the emerging date palm heart"

ká é-gašam, "gate of the craftsmen's house"

ká é-lùnga é-muḫaldim ù é kíkken, "gate of the brewery-kitchen-mill complex"

ká-ḫu-lu-lu, "*Ḫululu* gate"

ká-*ilum-qá-qá-da-nu-um*, "gate of the big-headed god"

ká kù-^{d}Inana-zabala$_{4}^{\text{ki}}$, "gate of bright Inana of Zabala"

ká-suḫur, "tree-top gate"

ká-^{d}*šu*-^{d}*suen*, "*Šu-Suen* gate"

1. **ká-bar-ra**, "outer gate"

6 sìla dabin 1 sìla eša gaba-ri-a **ká-bar-ra** ù ká im šeg$_{12}$ ku$_{4}$-ra, "6 liters of semolina (and) 1 liter of fine flour (for) a meeting at the outer gate and the 'service entrance,'" 1035:'4-'6

2. **ká-bil-lí-a**

é-*gi-na-tum* **ká-bil-lí-a**, "*Billi'a* gate barracks" > *Household Index*

3. **ká-dedal-lí-a**, "gate of the emerging date palm heart"

é-*gi-na-tum* **ká-dedal-i-a**, "Dedali'a gate barracks" > *Household Index*

4. **ká é-lùnga é-muḫaldim ù é kíkken**, "gate of the brewery, kitchen and mill complex" > *Household Index*

5. **ká é-gašam**, "gate of the craftsmen's house" > *Household Index*

6. **ká-*ḫu-lu-lu***, "*Ḫululu* gate"

10 g̃eš-ká 3 [gi]dur-gazi a-rá-2-tab-ba gíd-1½ [ni]ndan-ta **ká-*ḫu-lu-lu*** im $šeg_{12}$ ku_4-ra-šè ba-a-[g̃ar], "10 gate timbers (and) 3 double-standed gazi ropes, 1½ nindan long each were placed at the *Ḫululu* gate for the 'service entrance'," 1287:1–4

7. **ká-*ilum-qá-qá-da-nu-um***, "gate of the big-headed god"

7.1 **As the Colophon of Brick Texts**

ká-*ilum-qá-qá-da-nu-um*, 309:82, 312:42, 316:80, 318:'57, 321:'41, 323:132, 326.1:'10, 367:'129, 322:'89

ká-*ìl-lum-qá-qá-da-ni-um*, 313:30, 362:'28

ká-*ilum-qá-qá-da-nu-um*-ta, 317:38, 335:47, 345:'22, 369:'27

8. **ká im $šeg_{12}$ ku_4-ra**, "the 'service entrance' of the gate"[58]

ká-*ḫu-lu-lu* im **$šeg_{12}$ ku_4-ra**-šè, "at the *Hululu* gate for the 'service entrance'" > **ká-*ḫu-lu-lu***

gaba-ri-a ká-bar-ra ù **ká im $šeg_{12}$ ku_4-ra**, "{provisions} (for) a meeting at the outer gate and the 'service entrance'" > **ká-bar-ra**

1 g̃uruš šidim **ká im ⌜$šeg_{12}$⌝ ⌜ku_4⌝-ra** bàd x-[. . .] ká sè-g[é-dè gub-ba], "1 builder [employed] to place [. . .] at the 'service entrance' of the gate," 200:'11-'12

9. **ká kù-[d]Inana-$Zabala_4$[ki]**, "gate of bright Inana of Zabala"

1 udu abzu-šè 1 máš **ká kù-[d]inana-$zabala_4$[ki]** u_4 ezem-gur-$buru_{14}$, "1 sheep for the abzu, (and) 1 goat (for) the gate of bright Inana of Zabala, during the bushel harvest festival," 996:1–4

10. **ká suḫur**, "tree-top gate"

8 [gi]dur-gazi a-rá 2 tab-ba gíd 1½ nindan-ta g̃eš ùr kéše gíd-da 3 [g̃eš]ù-$suḫ_5$ 3-kam-ús 15 [g̃eš]é-da ásal **ká-suḫur** é-lùnga-šè ba-a-g̃ar, "8 9-meter 2-ply gazi ropes, to tighten bound roof beams, 3 3rd-quality pine boards (and) 15 poplar side house planks that were placed for the tree-top gate of the brewery," 1297:1–5

11. **ká-[d]*šu*-[d]*suen***, "*Šu-Suen* Gate"

šu+nígin 3 ⌜da⌝-n[a 240+]120 nindan ús gú i_7-me-kal-kal *simat-é-a* a-da-ga-ta **ká-[d]*šu*-[d]*suen***-šè, "In total: 3 da-na (and) 360 nindan, the length from the bank of the Mekalkal canal of *Simat-Ea* (and its) irrigation ditch to the *Šu-Suen* gate," 1382:14–16

kà-ma-am-tum, *kamamtum/kammantu*, "(a vegetable)," 442:15, 445:7, 511:'106, 557:17, 1194:7

6 gín ***kà-ma-am-tum***-ta, "6 shekels of (vegetable) each," 557:6

---

[58] Literally "the gate where earth and bricks enter."

^{ğeš}***kà-na-at-ḫu-um***, "(a tree or aromatic product from a tree)"

n ḫar ^{ğeš}***kà-na-at-ḫu-um*** n-ta, "n *kanatuḫum* tree seedling(s), n (units) each," 1375:35, 1375:36, 1375:37

^{ğeš}**kab**, "willow"[59]

1 ḫar ^{ğeš}**kab** 1, "1 willow seedling, 1 (unit)," 1375:43

káb . . . du$_{11}$(g), "to check, to measure or count commodities for accounting or taxation" > *Verb Index*

kala(g), *dannu*, *kubbû*, "(to be) strong, powerful, mighty; to reinforce, repair" > *Verb Index*

kala-kala aka, "to reinforce" > **aka**

kar, *kâru*, "harbor, quay"

kar dù, "to construct a quay" > **dù**

kar-ki-mu-ra, "quay of the textile depository" > *Household Index*

kar-ta ga$_6$(g̃), "to carry (barley, shok, straw, the commodity tax) from the quay" > **ga$_6$(g̃)**

kàr-šum, "leek,"[60] 511:74, 972:28, 972:97, 975:30, 975:98

kaskal, *ḫarrānu*, "way, road; journey, caravan"

u$_4$ **kaskal**-šè i-re-sa-a, "when they went on a journey" > **ri**

1. **Specifying the Length of a Trip**

1.1 From Du-saḫar to Enzu-babbar (12-Day Trip)

1 g̃uruš túg-du$_8$ u$_4$-12-šè du$_6$-saḫar-ra^{ki}-ta en-zu-bábbar^{ki}-šè [. . .] íb-ga$_6$ [ús-b]i 1500 éš **kaskal** š[u+níg̃in]-na-bi, "1 braider for 12 days carried [. . .] from Du-saḫara to Enzu-babbar. Its distance: 1500 ropes is the entire trip," 263:1–6

1.2 From *Bit-Šu-Suen* to Nippur (10-Day Trip)

3 g̃uruš ^{lú}ázlag siki é-^{d}*šu*-^{d}*suen*^{ki}-ka-ta nibru^{ki}-šè de$_6$-a **kaskal** šu+níg̃in-na-bi u$_4$-10!-kam u$_4$-2 kaš-dé-[a] á-⌜ki⌝-ti šu-numun, "3 fullers having brought wool from *Bit-Šu-Suen* to Nippur, a trip of 10 days in total, on day 2 of the banquet of the Akiti festival of month 4," 240:1–6

1.3 From Nippur to Garšana (4-Day Trip)

1 g̃uruš ^{lú}ázlag nibru^{ki}-ta gar-ša-an-na^{ki}-šè túg de$_6$-a **kaskal** šu+níg̃in-na-bi u$_4$-4-àm, "1 fuller having brought textiles from Nippur to Garšana, a trip of 4 days in total," 224:1–6

---

59 Heimpel, *forthcoming*.

60 M. Stol, personal communication.

1.4 From Nippur to *Šu-Suen-ṭabu* (11 Day Trip)

1 g̃uruš ^{lú}ázlag nibru^{ki}-ta ^{d}*šu*-^{d}*suen*-DU$_{10}$^{ki}-šè ^{urudu}šim-da gu$_{4}$-udu de$_{6}$-a **kaskal** šu+níg̃in-na-bi, "1 fuller having brought a sheep and cattle brand from Nippur to *Šu-Suen-ṭabu*, a trip of 11 days in total," 219:1–6

2. Meals along the Journey

4 sìla níg̃-àr-ra-⌜sig$_{5}$⌝ á-u$_{4}$-te-na u$_{4}$-3-kam šà **kaskal**-na àga-ús [*ri-im*]-*ilum* íb-gu$_{7}$ u$_{4}$ má-*simat*-^{d}*ištaran* gar-ša-an-na^{ki}-ta *puzur*$_{4}$-*iš*-^{d}*da-gan*[^{ki}-šè] in-gíd-sa-a, "the gendarme, *Rim-ilum*, ate 4 liters of fine groats in the evening on the 3rd day of the journey when they towed the boat of *Simat-Ištaran* from Garšana to *Puzriš-Dagan*," 551:9–15

3. Broken Context

[. . .] x u$_{4}$ **kaskal**-na, 955:5

kaš, *šikaru*, "beer," 379:1, 379:2, 379:4, 395:1, 507:13, 1030:10, 1030:17, 1030:24, 1030:30, 1030:36

kaš dé, "to pour beer" > **dé**

kaš nag̃, "to drink beer" > **nag̃**

la-ìa **kaš** zi-ga ezem-*a-bu-um*, "the deficit of the beer expended (for) the *Abum* festival," 1047:4–5

1. dug kaš, "jug of beer"

[n **dug**] **kaš** 0.0.3.–ta, "[n] 30 liter [jug(s)] of beer," 1312:1

2. kaš dirig, "additional beer"

5.0.0. munu$_{4}$-si-è gur **kaš dirig**-šè, "5 bushels of sprouted malt for additional beer," 1227:1–2

1 gú báppir **kaš** dirig-šè, "1 talent of beer malt for additional beer," 1244:1–2

3. kaš-gen, "ordinary beer," 377:3, 379:17, 393:1, 398:1, 400:1, 401:1, 418:1, 425:1, 428:1, 430:2, 435:4, 436:7, 437:8, 437:14, 439:4, 440:3, 440:10, 441:4, 471:2, 478:1, 505:2, 505:5, 507:2, 507:5, 507:7, 507:12, 508:2, 508:5, 517:2, 528:7, 548:9, 550:'3, 550:'5, 550:'8, 550:'13, 550:'20, 550:'22, 1009:1, 1009:4, 1009:7, 1009:9, 1009:12, 1025:3, 1025:16, 1025:40, 1025:57, 1025:75, 1025:109, 1028:18

n (sìla) **kaš-gen**-ta, "n (liters) of ordinary beer each," 378:9, 380:1, 384:1, 389:1, 536:3, 536:8, 536:15

kaš-gen-bi n (sìla), "(in total:) its ordinary beer is n liter(s)," 378:15, 380:7, 384:6, 389:7, 536:19

0.0.1. **kaš-gen** níg̃ ki-zàḫ-šè, "10 liters of ordinary beer, provisions for the cultic place," 986:1–2

0.0.3.1⅔ sìla [. . .] **kaš-gen** [. . .], 1036:'36-'37

4. kaš-g̃e$_{6}$, "dark beer," 1046:5

5. kaš-níg̃-àr-ra-gen, "ordinary groat beer," 1103:2

6. kaš ninda, "beer (and) bread,"[61] 379:6, 379:7, 379:8, 379:9, 379:10, 379:11, 379:12, 379:13, 379:14, 379:15, 1324:4

[61] Brunke 2008, 191 (§3.3.8.1).

o.n.n. **kaš-ninda** n sìla-ta, “n units(s) of beer (and) bread, n liter(s) each,” 517:3

n sìla **kaš-ninda**-ta, “n liter(s) of beer (and) bread each,” 556:'1, 556:'3, 556:'4, 556:'5, 556:'6, 556:'7, 556:'8, 556:'9, 556:'10, 556:'11

0.0.5. **ninda-kaš** á-u$_4$-[te-na], “50 liters of bread (and) beer in the evening,” 551:1

7. kaš-sig$_5$, “fine-quality beer,” 505:1, 505:4, 507:1, 507:4, 508:1, 508:4, 517:1, 541:20, 541:22, 661:1, 1025:2, 1334:6

0.0.3. **kaš-sig$_5$** 0.0.1.-ta, “30 liters of fine beer, 10 liters each,” 1025:15

šu+níĝin 0.0.3. **kaš-sig$_5$** 1½-ta, “In total: 30 liters of fine beer, 1½ liters each,” 1025:108

2 **kaš-sig$_5$** ^{dug}níĝ 5-sìla-ta, “2 5-liter pots of fine beer,” 1180:2

8. še kaš, “barley (for) beer,” 442:9, 449:3

n sìla **še kaš**-ta, “n liter(s) of barley (for) beer each,” 442:3

9. Beer Production: for the Funerary Libations of *Šu-Kabta*

1 gú 20 ma-na šim-sig$_5$ 1 gú 40 ma-na šim-gen 1.2.2.2½ sìla munu$_4$-si-è gur 0.4.0 níĝ-àr-ra-sig$_5$ 1.0.0. níĝ-àr-ra-gen gur **kaš**-sig$_5$ 2-ta 1.0.0. gur-kam ù **kaš**-gen 2.0.0. gur-kam (. . .) sá-du$_{11}$-ki-a-naĝ-*šu-kab-tá*, “1 talent (and) 20 minas of fine beer malt, 1 talent (and) 40 minas of ordinary beer malt, 1 bushel (and) 142½ liters of sprouted malt, 240 liters of fine groats (and) 1 bushel of ordinary groats (for) fine beer—2 (units) each of 1 bushel—and ordinary beer—2 bushels, (and) {other comestibles}, regular offerings for the funerary libation place of *Šu-Kabta*,” 972:30–35, 106, 975:32–37, 108

5 ma-na šim-sig$_5$ 8 ma-[na š]im-gen 0.0.2.4 sìla munu$_4$-si-è 0.0.1.5 sìla níĝ-àr-ra-sig$_5$ 0.0.2.4 sìla níĝ-àr-ra-gen **kaš**-sig$_5$ 2-ta 0.0.2.-kam ù **kaš**-gen 0.0.4.-kam (. . .) sá-du$_{11}$-ki-a-naĝ-*šu-kab-tá*, “5 minas of fine beer malt, 8 minas of ordinary beer malt, 24 liters of sprouted malt, 15 liters of fine gorats (and) 24 liters of ordinary groats (for) fine beer—2 (units) each of 20 liters – and ordinary beer – 40 liters, (and) {other comestibles}, regular offerings for the funerary libation place of *Šu-Kabta*,” 972:46–51, 106, 975:49–54, 108

½ sìla zà-ḫi-li ½ sìla *sí-mi-*⸢*tum*⸣ 1 gú 23⅓ ma-na t[uḫ-ĝeš-ì-ḫád] 4[+n/n sìl]a munu$_4$-si-UD.[DU] 0.3.3. níĝ-àr-ra-sig$_5$ **kaš**-sig$_5$ 2-ta 1.0.0. gur-kam (. . .) sá-du$_{11}$-ki-a-naĝ-*šu-kab-tá*, “½ liter of zà-ḫi-li seeds, ½ liter of *sí-mi-tum*, 1 talent (and) 23⅓ minas of dried sesame chaff, 4[+n/n] liter(s) of sprouted malt (and) 210 liters of fine groats (for) fine beer – 2 (units) each of 1 gur, (and) {other comestibles}, regular offerings for the funerary libation place of *Šu-Kabta*,” 981:24–29, 33

10. Broken or Uncertain Context

30 **kaš**-UD+*gunu*-gi, 1180:1

[n] ^{dug}níĝ 2-sìla-ta **kaš**-[x?]-šè, “[n] pot(s) of 2 liters each were disbursed for [x?] beer,” 1330:1–3

kaš-dé-a, *qerītu*, “banquet”[62]

1. kaš-dé-a á-ki-ti šu-numun, “banquet of the Akiti festival of month 4”

3 ĝuruš ^{lú}ázlag siki é-^{d}*šu*-^{d}*suen*^{ki}-ka-ta nibru^{ki}-šè de$_6$-a kaskal šu+níĝin-na-bi u$_4$-10!-kam u$_4$-2 **kaš-dé-[a] á-⸢ki⸣-ti šu-numun**, “3 fullers having brought wool from *Bit-Šu-Suen* to

62 Brunke 2008, 211–213 (§4.1.1).

Nippur, a trip of 10 days in total, on day 2 of the banquet of the Akiti festival of month 4," 240:1–6

2. kaš-dé-a diĝir-re-e-ne, "banquet of the gods"

šu+níĝin 680 ^{dug}sìla-bur-zi **kaš-dé-a diĝir-re-e-ne**, "In total: 680 1-liter offering bowls of soup (for) the banquets of the gods," 1025:113–115

iti ezem-^{d}[*šu*]-^{d}EN.[ZU x?] **kaš-dé-a diĝir-re-e-[ne] sa gi$_4$-gi$_4$ a[ka?], "preparations made? for the banquet of the gods (in) month 9," 1029:'15-'17

[. . .] **kaš-d[é-a . . .]** (. . .) sá-du$_{11}$-**diĝir-re-e-ne**, "[. . . (for)] the banquet, (and) {other comestibles}, regular offerings of the gods," 1036:'21, '78

3. kaš-dé-a ^{d}inana, "banquet of Inana"

380 ^{dug}sìla-bur-⌈zi⌉ tu$_7$ ba-aka **kaš-dé-a ^{d}inana**-zabala$_4^{ki}$, "380 1-liter offering bowls of soup were served at the banquet of Inana of Zabala," 1025:37–39

60 ^{dug}sìla-bur-zi tu$_7$ ba-aka **kaš-dé-a ^{d}inana**-iri^{ki}, "60 1-liter offering bowls of soup were served at the banquet of Inana of the City," 1025:72–74

4. kaš-dé-a lugal, "royal banquet"

2 ĝuruš ^{lú}ázlag u$_4$-1-šè zi-ga **kaš-dé-a lugal** šà á-<ki->ti gub-ba, "2 fullers employed for 1 day, expended (for) the royal banquet of the Akiti festival," 221:1–2

5. kaš-dé-a ^{d}nergal, "banquet of Nergal"

120 ^{dug}sìla-bu[r-zi] tu$_7$ ba-⌈aka⌉ **kaš-dé-a ^{d}nergal$_x^{[eri11-gal]}$** dumu *da-d*[*a*-AN], "120 1-liter offering bowls of soup were served at the banquet of Nergal (the personal deity of) the son of *Dada*-AN," 1025:54–56

120 ^{dug}sìla-bur-zi tu$_7$ ba-aka **kaš-dé-a ^{d}nergal$_x^{eri11-[gal]}$** dumu é-é-⌈zi⌉, "120 1-liter bur-zi bowls of soup were served at the banquet of Nergal (the personal deity of) the son of E-ezi," 1025:89–91

6. kaš-dé-a ^{d}nin-^{d}si$_4$-an-na *a-ḫu-a*, "banquet of Nin-Siana, (the personal deity of) *Aḫu'a*"

[0.0.1. báppir-sig$_5$ 0.n.n] kaš-⌈sig$_5$⌉ 0.0.3. kaš-gen 0.0.2. níĝ-àr-ra-⌈sig$_5$⌉ 0.0.2.5 sìla ar-za-na 5 sìla gú-gal al-àr-ra 5 sìla gú-tur al-ús-sa 3 udu ba-úš [n+]1 ádda-udu [0.n.]1. mun-gen $^{⌈dug⌉}$útul-gal-šè 30 sa gi-izi [tu$_7$] ba-ra-šeĝ$_6$ **⌈kaš⌉-dé-a ^{d}nin-^{d}si$_4$-an-na** *a-ḫu-a*, "[10 liters of fine beer bread, n] liter(s) of fine beer, 30 liters of ordinary beer, 20 liters of fine groats, 25 liters of barley-grits, 5 liters of milled beans, 5 liters of processed peas, 3 slaughtered sheep, [n+]1 sheep carcasses (and) [n+]10 liters of ordinary salt for the large tureen (and) 30 bundles of fuel reeds were (used) to cook [soup] (for) the banquet of Nin-Siana, (the personal deity of) *Aḫu'a*," 1025:1–14

^{lú}**kaš$_4$**, *lāsimu*, "runner"

1. PN ^{lú}kaš$_4$, "PN, the runner" > *Personal Name Index*

ìl-su-ba-ni

za-ak-ì-lí

2. Provisions for the Runner

(. . .) ba-ra-šeĝ$_6$ maš-en-gag ^{lú}**kaš$_4$** ká-é-gal-ka gub-ba ⌈*simat*⌉-^{d}*ištaran* íb-gu$_7$ u$_4$ má-*simat*-^{d}*ištaran* é-^{d}šára-ta gar-ša-an-na^{ki}-šè mu-un-gíd-ša-a, "the *muškenu* (and?) the runner, stationed by *Simat-Ištaran* at the gate of the palace, ate {soup} when they towed the boat of *Simat-Ištaran* from the Šara temple to Garšana," 529:13–18

3 túg ba-tab *tuḫ-ḫu-um* 4-kam-ús ^{lú}**kaš$_4$**, "3 4th-quality ba-tab *tuḫ-ḫu-um* textiles (for) the runner," 578:11[63], 579:10

kéše, *rakāsu*, "to bind" > *Verb Index*

ki, *ašru*; *erṣetu*; *mātu*; *qaqqaru*; *šaplû*, "place; ground, earth, land"

2 ^{gi}gur **ki** gub-ba ésir šub-ba, "2 reed baskets—set in place—coated with bitumen," 1272:8

ki-ba sè(g$_{10}$), "to set it in its place" > **sè(g$_{10}$)**

ki-ég, "place of the dike" > **ki-ég**

ki-g̃eš, "dike land" > **ki-g̃eš**

ki ^{lú}lùnga, "place of the brewer" > ^{lú}**lùnga**

ki na-rú-a, "place of the stele" > **na-rú-a**

****ki**-siki, "meaning uncertain" > **siki**

ki-a-nag̃, "funerary libation place"[64]

ki-a-nag̃ PN, "funerary libation place of PN" > *Personal Name Index*

a-la-tum | *na-wi-ir-ilum*
árad-^{d}nana | *šu-kab-tá*
da-da

ki-ég, "place of the dike"

12½ sar **ki-ég**, "12½ sar (of land at) the place of the dike," 1362:'55

ki-g̃eš, "dike land"

3 iku **ki-g̃eš** gub-ba, "3 iku of cultivated dike land," 1362:'52

5 iku 32 sar **ki-g̃eš** gub-ba, "5 iku (and) 32 sar of cultivated dike land," 1362:1, 1362:'25

ki-lá, *šuqultu*, "weight"

1. Bread

0.2.5.5 sìla ninda-gal-gen 1-sìla du$_8$ **ki-lá**-bi 2 gú 50 ma-na, "175 liters of ordinary large bread baked (in) 1 liter (loaves), their weight is 2 talents and 50 minas," 528:1–2

1.1.0. ninda-dabin ù zì-šà-gen gur **ki-lá**-bi 4 gú 30 ma-na, "1 bushel (and) 60 liters of semolina and ordinary šà-flour bread, their weight is 4 talents (and) 30 minas," 528:3–4

2.0.1.5 sìla ninda-zì-kum ù zì-šà-gen gur **ki-lá**-bi 6 gú 40 ma-na, "2 bushels (and) 15 liters of kum and ordinary šà-flour bread, their weight is 6 talents (and) 40 mana," 528:5–6

---

63 Restoration based on no. 579:10.

64 Brunke 2008, 213–215 (§4.1.2).

2. Linen

gada **ki-lá** tà-ga, "weighed linen having been woven" > **tà(g)**

4 gada-gen **ki-lá**-bi 7⅓ ma-na, "4 ordinary linens, their weight is 7⅓ minas," 575:1–2

3. Textiles

túg **ki-lá** tà-ga, "weighed textiles having been woven" > **tag**

5 ^{túg}níĝ-lám 3-kam-ús **ki-lá**-bi 9⅓ ma-na [n gín] "5 3rd-quality níĝ-lám textiles, their weight is 9⅓ minas [(and) n shekel(s)]," 582:1–2

★★1 túg-^{d}*al-la-tum*-gùn-a ù zi-in-bi **ki-lá**-bi 9 ma-[na] 12 gín *a-ku$_8$-a-nu-ri*, "1 colored textile of *Allatum* and its zi-in weighing 9 minas (and) 12 shekels (for) *Akua-nuri*," 584:1–3

[2? túg-guz-za-g]en 2 ^{túg}saĝ-uš-bar 2 ^{túg}uš-bar 4 ma-na-ta 2 ^{túg}uš-bar 1½ ma-na-ta **ki-lá**-bi 36⅔ ma-na ⸢túg⸣ **ki-lá** tà-ga, "[2?] ordinary [tufted textiles], 2 saĝ-uš-bar textiles, 2 uš-bar textiles—4 minas each—(and) 2 uš-bar textiles—1½ minas each—their weight is 36⅔ minas, weighed textiles having been woven," 730:1–6

1 bar-si siki-ud$_5$ šà-tuku$_5$ é-ba-an ki-lá-bi 2 ma-na, "1 pair of goat-hair bands (for) a mattress, their weight is 2 minas," 740:3–4

1 ^{túg}bar-si 3-k[am-ús] 5 ^{túg}sagšu ba-tab *tuḫ-ḫu-⸢um⸣* **ki-lá**-bi ⅓ ma-na 4 gín, "1 3rd-quality band (and) 5 ba-tab *tuḫ-ḫum* caps, their weight is ⅓ of a mina (and) 4 shekels," 744:1–3

1 ^{túg}níĝ-lám 4-kam-ús 4 túg-guz-za 4-kam-ús **ki-lá**-bi 26⅓ ma-na, "1 4th-quality níĝ-lám textile (and) 4 4th-quality tufted textiles, their weight is 26⅓ minas," 744:4–6

7 túg-guz-za-gen 7 ^{túg}uš-bar 4 ma-na-ta 2 ^{túg}šà-ga-dù **ki-lá**-bi 58! ma!-[na], "7 ordinary tufted textiles, 7 uš-bar textiles – 4 mina each – (and) 2 belts, their weight is 58 mina," 744:7–10

1 túg-mug **ki-lá** siki-gen šudum-bi 1-ma-na **ki-lá** mug-bi n ma-na, "1 textile of poor-quality wool, its weight is 1 mina of warp-thread of ordinary wool (and) n mina(s) of wool combings," 744:11–3, 747:13–15

1 túg-gùn-a *ilum-ma-⸢zi⸣* **ki-lá**-bi 11½ ma-na, "1 multi-colored textile (for) *Ilum-mazi*, its weight is 11½ minas," 747:16–17

4. Tools

4 ^{urudu}ku-gi-im **ki-lá**-bi 12 gín, "4 copper objects, their weight is 12 shekels," 1255:4

1 ^{urudu}šum **ki-lá**-bi ½ ma-na, "1 saw, its weight is 1½ minas," 1310:3–4

5. Wool

siki **ki-lá** -bi n ma-na, "wool, its weight is n mina(s)" > **siki**

siki ^{ĝeš}garig aka **ki-lá**-bi n ma-na, "combed wool, its weight is n mina(s)" > **siki**

6. Other Weighed Objects

barag-siki-ud$_5$ **ki-lá**-bi n ma-na, "goat-hair sacks, their weight is n mina(s)" > **siki**

éš-siki-ud$_5$ **ki-lá**-bi n ma-na, "goat-hair ropes, their weight is n mina(s)" > **siki**

n ma-na **ki-lá** mun, "salt weighing n mina(s)" > **mun**

n ma-na **ki-lá** šeg$_{12}$ naga, "brick of potash weighing n mina(s)" > **naga**

[n] éš-maḫ [*ha*]-*bu-u*[*m* **k**]**i-lá**-bi ½ ⸢gú⸣ 15⅓ ma-⸢na⸣, "[n] large *ḫabum* fabric rope(s)—their weight is ½ talent and 15⅓ minas," 831:1–2

[n ^{ĝeš}]ú-bíl-lá **ki-lá**-bi 10 ma-⸢na⸣, "[n (units)] of charcoal, their weight is 10 minas," 1162:'59-'60

7. Broken or Uncertain Context

^{túg}bar-d[ul$_5$-. . .] **ki-lá**-bi 18 [. . .], 724:1–2

n [. . .] **ki-lá**-bi [. . .], 740:5–6, 740:7–8

4 túg-*bu-ti-um*(?) ^{ĝeš}*be-rum* siki ^{ĝeš}garig aka gen **ki-lá-bi ⅔ ma-na, 807:1–3

1 apin!(GÍN) UD.K[A.B]AR **ki-lá**-bi 1 ma-[na] 3 gín, "1 bronze plow, its weight is 1 mina (and) 3 shekels," 1310:1–2

ki-mu-ra, "textile depository" > *Household Index*

KI.NE, "fireplace"

KI.NE sè(g$_{10}$), "to place (dirt) around the fireplace" > **sè(g$_{10}$)**

ki-ri-ip, *kirippu*, "a (oil) jar"

ki-ri-ip *ar-gi$_5$-núm*, "(oil) jar of *arginnum*," 511:65, 972:17, 972:87, 975:18, 975:89

ki-sá-a, "foundation terrace"[65]

1. Work on the Foundation Terrace

a bal **ki-sá-a**-šè, "to pour water for (construction of) the foundation terrace" > **a ... bal**

ki-sá-a saḫar zi(g), "to move dirt at the foundation terrace" > **zi(g)**

šeg$_{12}$ ga$_6$(ĝ) **ki-sá-a**-šè, "to carry bricks for the foundation terrace" > **ga$_6$(ĝ)**

2. da-ki-sá-a, "the side of the foundation terrace"

da-ki-sá-a é-uš-bar, "the side of the foundation terrace of the textile mill" > *Household Index*

šeg$_{12}$ **da-ki-sá-a** ĝar, "to place bricks at the side of the foundation terrace" > **ĝar**

3. ki-sá-a é, "the foundation terrace of the house" > *Household Index*

é-lùnga é-muḫaldim ù é-kíkken

é-lùnga ù é-kíkken

é-*pu-ta-nu-um*

é-uš-bar

é-uš-bar ù é-gašam-e-ne

65 Cf. Akk. *kisû*, "retaining wall."

ki-zàḫ, "(a cultic place)"[66]

0.0.1. kaš-gen níĝ **ki-zàḫ**-šè sízkur ⌜bàd⌝-šè, "10 liters of ordinary beer, provisions for the cultic place, (ceremonial) offerings for the (enclosure) wall," 986:1–3[67]

kib$_x$(GIG), *kibtu*, "wheat," 532:6, 1065:3, 1081:5, 1081:11, 1109:6, 1109:12, 1197:2, 1232:2, 1232:5, 1232:8, 1233:7, 1233:22, 1235:2

4.1.4. **kib**$_x$ gur ì-dub 6-kam, "4 bushels (and) 64 liters of wheat of the granary for the 6th time," 1233:6

1 sìla **kib**$_x$ **kib**$_x$-bi 1 sìla 15 gín, "1 liter of wheat, its wheat is 1 liter (and) 15 shekels," 836:17–18

kíb$_x$ šà-gal mušen-na, "wheat, fodder of birds" > **šà-gal**

^{gi}kid, *kītu*, "reed mat"

★★1 éš **^{gi}kid**-aš-rin siki-ud$_5$, 1334:4

^{gi}kid-aš-rin ésir šub-ba, "an ašrin reed mat coated with bitumen," 1334:3

★★**^{gi}kid** ésir BE-a ir-dù-a tab-⌜ba⌝ ésir šub-ba, 1376:43

^{gi}kid ésir šub-ba, "reed mat coated with bitumen," 1376:41

^{gi}kid ^{ĝeš}gu-za, "chair mat" > **^{ĝeš}gu-za**

31 **^{gi}kid**-ka-ḫa-ra gir-ra ba-ab-gu$_7$, "31 ka-ḫa-ra mats were consumed by fire," 1299:25–26

^{gi}kíd-kíd ésir šub-ba, "reed mat coated with bitumen," 1376:21

★★**^{gi}kid**-KU-ka KWU-737-ga, 1299:12

^{gi}kid má ⌜gíd⌝, "a mat for towing boats," 1376:11

^{gi}kid-maḫ, "large reed mat," 1328:2

^{gi}kid-maḫ-sun, "(a type of reed mat)," 1119:2

^{gi}kid sum?-x kur-⌜ra⌝, "(a type of reed mat)," 1376:10

^{gi}kid titab, "reed mat for malted barley" > **titab**

^{gi}kid-uzu, "(a type of reed mat)," 834:20, 1284:1, 1299:11

^{gi}kid-[. . .], "a [. . .] reed mat," 1249:5

kíĝ, *šipru*, "work; to work" > *Verb Index*

kíĝ aka, "to do work" > **aka**

1. **kíĝ ésir-ra**, "bitumen work"

11 ĝuruš **kíĝ ésir**!-**ra** ki-⌜mu⌝-ra dù-a, "11 workmen (for) bitumen work, having constructed the textile depository," 158:37

---

[66] Sallaberger 1993, 43–44.

[67] Reading and interpretation of níĝ ki-zàḫ-šè suggested by H. Brunke (personal communication) with reference to Sallaberger 1993, 190, "Gabe für den Fluchtort," and Westenholz 1997, 62, "the provisions for the place of disappearance."

2. kíĝ-til, "completed work"

6 ĝuruš du_{10}-ús ⸢e_2⸣?-[did]li? **kíĝ-til** ba-al, "6 workmen having completed the work of digging the baths of additional? houses?," 158:40

(. . .) **kíĝ-til-la** mu-DU é-kišib-ba-šè, "{leather products}, delivery of completed work for the warehouse," 932:7–9

kíĝ, *še'û*, "to look for, seek" > *Verb Index*

^{ĝeš}kíĝ, "(a tree)"

pa ^{ĝeš}**kíĝ** ku_5, "to prune kíĝ trees" > **ku_5**

★★[. . . ^{ĝeš}]**kíĝ**-tur, "[. . .] small kíĝ tree," 1362:19

^{lú}kíĝ-gi_4-a, *šipru*, "messenger"

^{lú}**kíĝ-gi_4-a** énsi-nibru^{ki}, "the messenger of the governor of Nippur" > *Toponym Index*

^{lú}**kíĝ-gi_4-a** *šu-kab-ta*, "the messenger of *Šu-Kabta*" > *Personal Name Index*

1. PN ^{lú}kíĝ-gi_4-a-lugal, "PN, the royal messenger" > *Personal Name Index*

na-sìm
ṣa-al-lum
šu-eš₄-tár

1.1 Provisions

0.0.2. še ^{lú}**kíĝ-gi_4-a-lugal** ⸢u_4⸣-3-kam, "20 liters of barley (for) the royal messenger on the 3rd day," 488:1–3

1.2 Uncertain Context

★★[o.n.n. š]e ensi-šè [PN] ^{lú}**kíĝ-gi_4-a-lugal** [x].GA.URU ⸢níĝ⸣-šu-$taka_4$-lugal [mu]-un-de_9-a, "[n liter(s)] of barley for the dream interpreter, [PN], the royal messenger, who brought (?), the royal consignment," 484:10–13

^{ĝeš}kíĝ-sig-ḫi-a, "(a tree)"

ḫar ^{ĝeš}**kíĝ-sig-ḫi-a**, "kíĝ-sig-ḫi-a tree seedling," 1256:31, 1375:32

kíkken(ḪAR.ḪAR), *sāmidu*, "mill(er)"

é-**kíkken**, "mill" > *Household Index*

géme **kíkken**, "female miller" > *Craftswomen Index*

ĝuruš lú-**kíkken**, "miller" > *Craftsmen Index*

ugula **kíkken** ĝar, "to place (in the account) of the overseer of the mill" > **ĝar**

1. **PN géme é-kíkken**, "PN, the workwoman of the mill" > *Personal Name Index*

   a-na-a
   lu_5-zi-lá
   za-a-za

2. **PN géme kíkken**, "PN, the female miller" > *Personal Name Index*

   bu-za-du-a
   na-na
   dšára-sá-$\tilde{g}u_{10}$

kilib, *napḫaru*, "total, sum"

kilib-ba 316 [. . .] **kilib**-ba [n . . .] **kilib**-ba 37 [. . .] **kilib**-ba 360 ud_5 **kilib**-ba 306 udu-máš-ḫi-a [sag̃]-níg̃-ga-ra (. . .) níg̃-kas_7-aka d*adad-tillati* šabra, "In total: 316 [. . .], [n . . .], 37 [. . .], 360 goats (and) 306 various sheep (and) goats are the available assets (and) {other commodities}, the balanced account of *Adad-tillati*, the majordomo," 984:'30-'35, '75-'76

na4**kinkin**, "a millstone"

na4**kinkin** á-da-bar šu sè-ga, "'hand-held' black basalt millstone," 1372:4, 1372:61

na4**kinkin**-GI-bí šu sè-ga, "'hand-held' GI-bí millstone," 1341:1, 1372:3, 1372:60

na4**kinkin**-GI-bí zà-ḫi-li, "(a millstone)," 1372:5, 1372:62

na4**kinkin**-zi-bí g̃eš-dù šu sè-ga, "'hand-held' zi-bí g̃eš-dù millstone," 1372:2, 1372:59

na4**kinkin**-zi-bí šu sè-ga, "'hand-held' zi-bí millstone," 601:1, 615:1–4, 1372:1, 1372:58

kir_{11}, *buqamtu*, "female lamb"

kir_{11}-gukkal, "fat-tailed female lamb," 1154:4

g̃eš**$kiri_6$**, *kirû*, "(fruit) plantation, orchard" > *Garden Index*

kisal, *kiṣallu*, "courtyard"

kisal-lá dinana-$zabala_4$ki, "the courtyard of Inana of Zabala" > *Deities Index*

★★gigilim **kisal-lá**, 1282:2

kisal-luḫ, *kisaluḫḫu*, "courtyard sweeper"

géme **kisal-luḫ**, "female courtyard sweeper" > *Craftswomen Index*

kislaḫ, *maškanu*; *nidûtu*; *terīqtu*; *turbalû*, "threshing floor; uncultivated, uninhabited, cleared land; empty house lot"

kislaḫ saḫar zi(g), "to move dirt (to/from) the lot" > **zi(g)**

1. **Plots of Land**

   1 eše 3½ ¼ (iku) gána **kislaḫ**, 1362:3, 1362:'26

   36 sar **kislaḫ**, 1362:'54

2. Land Prices

[n+]⅓ ma-na 9 gín siki-gen sa_{10} **kis[la]ḫ** 1 sar 9? gín-kam, "[n+]⅓ minas and 9 shekels of ordinary wool, the price of 1 sar and 9? gín of uncultivated land," 681:1–2

kìšib, *kunukku*, "seal, sealed tablet"

1. **kìšib PN**, "seal(ed tablet) of PN" > *Personal Name Index*

a-ḫu-wa-qar
amar-^{d}da-mu
^{d}ba-ú-*da*
ilum-ra-pi$_{5}$
lú-kìri-zal
puzur$_{4}$-^{d}en-líl
šu-^{d}en-líl
šu-eš$_{4}$*-tar*
tu-ra-a

é-**kìšib**-ba, "warehouse" > *Household Index*
kìšib de_6, "to bring a sealed tablet" > **de_6**
kìšib ra, "to roll a seal" > **ra**
kìšib šu . . . te(g̃), "to take a seal(ed tablet)" > **šu . . . te(g̃)**
kìšib zi(r), "to cancel a sealed tablet" > **zi(r)**

$^{g̃eš}$**kišig**(Ú.ÁD), *ašāgu*, "shok (*prosopis stephaniana*, Arabic shok < šauk), a thorny shrub"

$^{g̃eš}$**kišig** dúr SIG_4.ANŠE-šè g̃ar, "to place shok at the back of the brick pile" > **g̃ar**
$^{g̃eš}$**kišig** ga_6(g̃), "to carry shok" > **ga_6(g̃)**
$^{g̃eš}$**kišig** iri-ki-gíd-da-šè g̃en, "to go to Irikigida for shok" > **g̃en**
$^{g̃eš}$**kišig** ku_5, "to cut shok" > **ku_5**
$^{g̃eš}$**kišig** tùm, "to bring shok" > **tùm**

1. **Bales of Shok**

10 gu-níg̃in $^{g̃eš}$**kišig** á g̃uruš-a 4 gu-níg̃in-ta, "(In total:)10 bales of shok. The workmen wages were for 4 bales each," 235:1–2

420 gu-níg̃in $^{g̃eš}$**kišig** gir_4-2-kam, "420 bales of shok (for) the 2nd oven," 1297:15–16

ku-bu > **gub**, "to prop up" > *Verb Index*

ku-bu-gu, "(meaning uncertain)"

11 g̃uruš sag̃-[tag] 2 g̃uruš á-⅔-ta 2 g̃uruš á-½-ta u_4-2-šè iz-zi sumun **ku-bu-gu gul-dè gub-ba, "11 full-time workmen, 2 workmen at ⅔ wages (and) 2 workmen at ½ wages employed for 2 days to demolish the old ku-bu-gu iz-zi wall," 244:1–5

^{urudu}**ku-gi-im**, "(a copper object)"

4 ^{urudu}**ku-gi-im** ki-lá-bi 12 gín, "4 copper objects, their weight is 12 shekels," 1255:4

^{ĝeš}**ku-ku**, *mukānu*, "(part of the loom)"[68]

2 kuš-udu-pu-uš x 1 ^{kuš}du$_{10}$-gan-ti-bal-babbar 1 kuš-máš-gal-niga1 kuš-máš-niga 5 gín sa-udu ^{ĝeš}gu-za-níta ^{ĝeš}**ku!**(TÚG)-**ku!**(TÚG) ba-a-ĝar, "2 (?) sheep skins, 1 white leather bag with a marking?, 1 skin of a fattened billy-goat, 1 skin of a fattened goat, (and) 5 shekels of sheep sinew were (used to) cover the man's chair (and?) the loom piece," 1517:1–6

^{dug}***ku-kur-rú***, SB/NA *kurkurru*, "(a vessel),"[69] 1267:1

^{gi}**ku-ni-na**, *kunin(n)u*, "drinking straw," 1345:1

^{gi}**ku-ni-na** [. . .] ⅓ sìla-[ta], 1292:'22

130 ^{gi}**ku-ni-na** ⅔ sìla-ta, "130 drinking straws, ⅔ of a liter each," 1299:8

^{gi}**ku-ni-n**[**a** . . .], 1312:3

kù, *ellu*, "metal, silver; (to be) bright, shiny; (to be) pure"

ká **kù**-^{d}inana-zabala$_{4}^{\text{ki}}$, "the gate of bright Inana of Zabala" > **ká**

kù-bi n gín n še, "(in total:) n shekel(s) and n barley corn of silver," 540:5

kù-^{d}šára, "bright Šara" > *Deities Index*

kù-babbar, *kaspu*, "silver," 1224:1

gal **kù-babbar**, "large silver cup" > **gal**

sa$_{10}$ **kù-babbar**, "price (in) silver" > **sa$_{10}$**

^{zabar}saĝ-kul **kù-babbar**, "silver bolt" > ^{zabar}**saĝ-kul**

n gín n še **kù-babbar**, "n shekel(s) (and) n barley corn(s) of silver," 540:8

n gín n še **kù-babbar**-ta, "n shekel(s) (and) n barley corn(s) of silver each," 540:2, 540:4

ku$_{4}$(r), *erēbu*, "to enter" > *Verb Index*

ku$_{5}$(d^{r}), *parāsu*, "to cut, break off, deduct" > *Verb Index*

ku$_{6}$, *nūnu*, "fish"

ku$_{6}$ du$_{6}$-lugal-pa-è^{ki}-ta de$_{6}$, "to bring fish from Du-lugalpa'e" > **de$_{6}$**

ku$_{6}$ šeĝ$_{6}$, "to cook fish" > **šeĝ$_{6}$**

šu-**ku$_{6}$**, "fisherman" > **šu-ku$_{6}$**

1. **ku$_{6}$ al-dar$_{(2)}$-ra**,[70] "split (dried) fish," 427:1, 437:10, 446:5, 472:1, 489:1, 511:66, 972:18, 972:88, 975:19, 975:90, 1070:3, 1198:1

---

[68] Waetzoldt 1972, 135.

[69] Reading based on a late Akkadian equivalent. For dug-kur-ku-dù see P. Steinkeller and J.N. Postgate, 1992, 53–4, and Sallaberger 1996, 102.

[70] Brunke 2008, 164 (§3.3.14).

2. ku$_6$ al-ús-sa, "fish-sauce,"[71] 14:21

é-ùr **ku$_6$ al-ús-sa**, "fish-sauce roof house" > *Household Index*

[n.n.n.] gazi ⌜mu⌝ **ku$_6$ al-ús-sa**-šè, "[n] liter(s) of gazi for fish-sauce," 1105:1–2

n Ú.KUR n gazi n gú ki-lá šeg$_{12}$-mun-sig$_5$ mu **ku$_6$ al-ús-sa**-šè, "n liter(s) of Ú.KUR, n liter(s) of gazi (and) a brick of fine salt weighing n talent(s) for fish-sauce," 1162:'37-'40, 1162:'44-'47

0.0.3. gín [. . .] 0.1.0. [. . .] 2 sìla ^{ú}gámun [. . .] 6 gú ki-lá mun-sig$_5$ mu **ku$_6$ al-ús-sa**-šè, "30 shekels [. . .], 60 [. . .] 2 liters of cumin [. . .] (and) fine salt weighing 6 talents for fish-sauce," 1178:1–5

3. ku$_6$-sim, "flying (swallow) fish," 511:64, 972:16, 972:87, 975:17, 975:88

ku$_6$-sim sa$_{10}$-sa$_{10}$-dè gú-ab-ba^{ki}-šè, "{workers having gone} to purchase flying fish in Gu'abba" > **sa$_{10}$**

^{ĝeš}**kuĝ$_5$**(TUR.ÉŠ), *askuppu*, *simmiltu*, "stair(case), ladder, threshold"

^{ĝeš}**kuĝ$_5$** dù, "to install a ladder" > **dù**

[n] gín še-gín mu x-šè [. . . n ma]-na šu-sar m[angaga? $^{ĝeš?}$]ig ^{ĝeš}**kuĝ$_5$**-šè ⌜u$_4$⌝ é-e im sumur ba-aka, "[n] gín of glue for x, [. . .] (and) [n mina(s)] of cord (made from) date palm fibers for the door (and) ladder when the house was plastered," 472:10–14

1 ^{ĝeš}**kuĝ$_5$** ga-lam-8, "1 ladder with 8 steps," 808:1

kun, *zibbatu*, "tail"

kuš-**kun**-gu$_4$, "ox-tail" > **kuš**

kun-zi, *miḫru*, "weir"

kun-zi-da a-pi$_4$-sal$_4$-la^{ki}, "weir of Apisal" > *Toponym Index*

kun-zi-da i$_7$-a-gàr-ús-sa, "weir of the Agar-usa Canal" > *Canal Index*

kun-zi-id-šè ga$_6$(ĝ), "to carry (reeds) to the weir" > **ga$_6$(ĝ)**

^{anše}**kúnga**, *parû*, "equid, probably a donkey-onager cross"

šà-gal ^{anše}**kúnga**, "fodder of equids" > **šà-gal**

kur, *erṣetu*, *mātu*, *šadû*, "land, country; mountain(s); east"

★★^{gi}kid sum?-x **kur**-⌜ra⌝, 1376:10

kur-ĝá-ra, *kurgarrû*, "cultic performer"

1. Provisions for the Lamentation Singers and Cultic Performers

---

71 Brunke 2008, 194–197 (§3.4).

0.0.3. ninda-šu-ra-gen ½ sìla du$_8$ gala ù **kur-ĝá-ra-a-ne**, "30 liters of ordinary half(-loaf) bread baked (in) ½ liter (loaves) for the lamentation singers and the cultic performers," 541:14–15

0.0.3. ninda 0.0.3. kaš gala ù **kur-ĝar-e-ne** [a]-rá-3-kam (. . .) ér iri ni$_{10}$-ni$_{10}$, "30 liters of bread (and) 30 liters of beer (for) the lamentation singers and cultic performers for the 3rd time, (and for) {lamentation singers 4 other times}, (performance of a) *takribtum* (involving) circling around the city," 1030:24–26, 39

kur-gi^{mušen}, *kurkû*, "goose," 1127:1

kur-gi^{mušen}-niga, "fattened goose," 1053:2

kúr, "in the future"[72]

ku-úr gur, "to return" > **gur**

kurum$_7$,[73] *pāqadu, piqittu*, "inspection"

kurum$_7$ aka, "inspection" > **aka**

kurum$_7$ aka al-tar, "inspection of construction" > **al-tar**

kurum$_7$ aka šidim-e-ne, "inspection (of the work) of builders," 1:19, 3:19, 4:24

kurušda, *mārû*, "animal fattener"

1. **PN kurušda**, "PN, the animal fattener" > *Personal Name Index*

ì-lí-bi-la-ni	*si-mu*
li-bur-ni-rum	*šar-ru-um-ba-ni*

kuš, *mašku*, "skin; leather"[74]

kuš má gíd, "to tow a boat with leather" > **gíd**

1. **Leather Products**

^{kuš}a-ĝá-lá, "leather sack" > ^{kuš}**a-ĝá-lá**

^{kuš}á-si, "hinge" > ^{kuš}**á-si**

^{kuš}da-lá, "(a leather object)" > ^{kuš}**da-lá**

^{kuš}du$_{10}$-gan, "leather bag" > ^{kuš}**du$_{10}$-gan**

^{kuš}e-sír, "sandals" > ^{kuš}**e-sír**

^{kuš}èš, "tent, pavilion" > ^{kuš}**èš**

kuš-ka-^{ĝeš}mud, "socket mouth leather (i.e. a piece of leather that lines or covers the open part of a socket)," 968:7

---

[72] Selz 1993, 186.

[73] See Steinkeller 1982a, 14–15, whose conclusions will have to be modified in light of the new evidence from this archive where the distinct writing IGI.ÉREN for gúrum / kurum$_7$ is attested earlier than the reign of *Ibbi-Suen*.

[74] V.E. Crawford 1948, Stol 1980–83, van de Mieroop 1987, and R. K. Englund 2003.

kuš-sila$_4$ ka-tab, "lamb skin cover" > **ka-tab**

kuš-udu ka-tab, "sheep skin cover" > **ka-tab**

^{kuš}*maš-lí-um*, "leather bucket" > ^{kuš}***maš-lí-um***

^{kuš}*na-aḫ-ba-tum*, "leather case (for precious objects)" > ^{kuš}***na-aḫ-ba-tum***

^{kuš}súḫub, "shoes" > ^{kuš}**súḫub**

^{kuš}šà-ga-dù, "leather belt" > ^{kuš}**šà-ga-dù**

^{kuš}ummu$_x$, "waterskin" > ^{kuš}**ummu$_x$**

1.1 **Basket Covers**

1 ^{gi}bisağ-gíd-da túg-ga-tur ésir šub-ba ka-bi **kuš** ğar-ra, "1 long, small basket coated with bitumen (for) textiles, its opening covered with leather," 798:1–3

1.2 **Meaning Uncertain**

5½ ĞAR **kuš-pa$_5$ udu-niga ú-ḫáb, 968:8

2. **Treatments**

kuš a-ğar gu$_7$-a, "dehaired skin" > **a-ğar gu$_7$-a**

kuš é-ri-na, "root-tanned skin" > **e-rí-na**

kuš ú-ḫád, "madder-tanned leather" > **ú-ḫád**

2.1 **mu kuš-šè**, "for (processing) skins"

dabin **kuš** a-ğar gu$_7$-a(-šè), "semolina (for) de-hairing skins" > **a-ğar gu$_7$-a, dabin**

dabin mu **kuš**-šè, "semolina for (processing) skins" > **dabin**

ì-šáḫ mu **kuš**-šè, "lard for (processing) skins" > **ì-šáḫ**

3. **Skins**

3.1 **kuš-anše**, "donkey skin," 927:3

kuš-amar-**anše**, "donkey-foal skin," 927:4

3.2 **kuš-gu$_4$**, "ox hide," 247:1, 855:1, 855:5, 855:18, 857:1, 880:1, 881:1, 910:1, 915:1

kuš-amar-**gu$_4$**, "calf skin," 910:2, 911:1, 927:2

kuš-gu$_4$ ^{ğeš}gu-za, "ox hide for a chair" > ^{ğeš}**gu-za**

kuš-gu$_4$-ğe$_6$, "black ox hide," 925:6

kuš-gu$_4$ x-x-KA×X, "(?) ox hide," 864:6

kuš-gu$_4$ šu-gíd, "šu-gíd ox hide," 912:9

kuš-gu$_4$ ú-ḫáb, "madder-tanned ox hide" > **ú-ḫáb**

kuš-kun-**gu$_4$**, "ox-tail," 846:1, 857:2, 880:3, 881:3

3.3 **kuš-máš**, "goat skin," 844:3, 847:4, 857:7, 888:3, 903:2, 908:2, 915:3, 916:2, 923:5, 935:2, 948:3

kuš-máš e-rí-na, "root-tanned goat skin," 855:6

kuš-máš-niga, "fattened-goat skin," 851:2, 922:3, 944:2, 1517:4

kuš-máš sá-du$_{11}$, "goat skin (for) regular offerings" > **sá-du$_{11}$**

kuš-m[**áš** . . .], 1022:4

3.4 **kuš-máš-gal**, "billy-goat skin," 844:3, 847:3, 853:3, 857:6, 877:2, 887:3, 902:2, 922:2, 934:2, 936:1, 1524:2

kuš-máš-gal-niga, "skin of a fattened billy-goat," 841:1, 842:1, 852:2, 861:2, 870:2, 875:2, 885:2, 890:2, 909:1, 914:1, 918:1, 939:1, 1022:11, 1517:3

kuš-máš-gal-niga sá-du_{11}, "skin of a fattened billy-goat (for) regular offerings" > **sá-du_{11}**

3.5 **kuš-$sila_4$**, "lamb skin," 840:2, 843:1, 844:2, 847:2, 857:5, 887:2, 888:2, 903:1, 926:2, 941:1, 948:2, 951:2, 959:2

kuš-$sila_4$ a-g̃ar gu_7, "de-haired lamb skin" > **a-g̃ar gu_7**

kuš-$sila_4$ ka-tab-šè, "lamb skin for a leather cover" > **ka-tab**

kuš-$sila_4$-niga, "skin of a fattened lamb," 861:1, 922:4, 949:2

1 **$sila_4$ kuš**-bi ba-zi, "the skin of 1 lamb was disbursed," 1028:38

3.6 **kuš-šáḫ**, "pig skin," 901:1

kuš-šáḫ-babbar, "white pig skin," 1517:14

kuš-šáḫ-niga, "skin of a fattened pig," 953:1

kuš-šáḫ-zé-da-ga, "skin of a milk-fed piglet," 968:3

3.7 **kuš-ud_5**,"female goat skin," 921:1

3.8 **kuš-udu**, "sheep skin," 459:2, 840:1, 844:1, 857:4, 859:1, 862:1, 867:2, 867:5, 869:2, 872:1, 877:1, 882:1, 885:3, 886:1, 887:1, 888:1, 893:1, 905:1, 906:2, 908:1, 911:2, 915:2, 916:1, 919:1, 920:1, 926:1, 927:1, 928:1, 929:1, 951:1, 960:1, 1517:13, 1524:1

kuš-udu a-g̃ar gu_7-a "dehaired sheep skin" > **a-g̃ar gu_7-a**

kuš-udu ba-úš, "skin of dead sheep," 844:4, 852:3, 894:1–2, 922:9, 956:1

kuš-udu-babbar, "white sheep skin," 838:1, 855:9, 864:1, 884:1–2, 923:3, 933:1, 942:1, 1517:16

kuš udu e-rí-na, "root-tanned sheep skin," 855:13, 855:15, 864:3, 892:2, 912:6, 917:2, 923:1, 945:1, 1517:11

kuš-udu ka-tab, "sheep-skin cover" > **ka-tab**

****kuš-udu**-pu-uš x, 1517:1

kuš-udu *qí-il-pu-um*, "bark tanned sheep-skin," 892:1

kuš-udu sá-du_{11}, "sheep skin (for) regular offerings" > **sá-du_{11}**

****kuš-udu**-si_4-gu_4, 955:1

kuš-udu-ú, "skin of a range-fed sheep," 847:1, 1285:3

kuš-udu ú-ḫáb, "madder-tanned sheep skin" > **ú-ḫáb**

kuš-udu uš, "skin of a dead sheep," 843:2

kuš-udu zi-ga, "expended sheep skin" > **zi(g)**

3.8.1 **kuš-udu-niga**, "skin of a fattened sheep," 845:1, 851:1, 852:1, 856:1, 863:1, 865:1, 866:1, 869:1, 870:1, 875:1, 885:1, 889:1, 890:1, 902:1, 904:1, 907:1, 922:1, 922:6, 922:8, 934:1, 935:1, 937:1, 944:1, 948:1, 949:1, 959:1, 968:2, 974:3, 980:5, 1022:4, 1022:13, 1023:4, 1023:11, 1023:13, 1024:3, 1024:12, 1024:15, 1026:2, 1026:9, 1026:11, 1516:1

kuš-udu-niga a-g̃ar gu_7, "dehaired sheep skin from a fattened sheep" > **a-g̃ar** $\mathbf{gu_7}$

kuš-udu-niga ba-úš, "skin of a dead fattened sheep," 850:1, 854:1

kuš-udu-niga-bábbar, "white skin of a fattened sheep," 912:3

kuš-udu-niga *ma-ad-li-um* g̃ar 2-šè ba-a-g̃ar, "1 fattened sheep skin placed to cover 2 buckets," 968:17

kuš-udu-niga sá-du_{11}, "skin of a fattened sheep (for) regular offerings" > **sá-**$\mathbf{du_{11}}$

1 **udu-niga** gu_4-e-ús-sa **kuš**-[bi] ba-zi, "1 fattened sheep '(fed) following the oxen', its skin was disbursed," 1027:2

1 **udu-niga kuš**-bi ba-zi, "1 fattened sheep, its skin was disbursed" > **zi(g)**

3.9 Broken Context

kuš-[x], 887:4, 960:2, 1376:64

**1 ^{kuš}[x]-x-apin? *ak-lu-um*, 925:'14

[**kuš**-am]ar?-[x], 927:5

kuš-[. . .], 964:'2, 967:1

kuš-[x]-ka-[. . .], 965:3

[n **kuš**-. . .] 974:1, 974:2

^{kuš}EDIN-[. . .], 1376:63

$^{⸢kuš⸣}$[. . .], 1376:65

2 **ku**[š-. . .]-šè, 1521:3

10 ^{kuš}maš-NI-x-x-gal-še, 1525:1

kùš, *ammatu*, "forearm, cubit; a unit of length"

n $^{g̃eš}$gag n **kùš**-ta, "n peg(s), n kùš each" > $^{g̃eš}$**gag**

⅔ kuš-máš-g[al-ni]ga 4 túg-íb-lá-si_4-a-gíd 4 **kùš** 2 šu-dù 1-šè ba-a-g̃ar "⅔ of a fattened billy-goat skin were (used for) covering 4 long red/brown belts of 4 kùš and 2 šu-dù in length," 939:1–2

n **kùš** bùr, "n kùš in area" > **bùr**

n **kùš** dag̃al, "n kùš in width" > **dag̃al**

n **kùš** gíd, "n kùš in length" > **gíd**

n **kùš** sukud, "n kùš in height" > **sukud**

– L –

^{ğeš}*la-ri-um*, *larû*, "branch?"

★★**^{ğeš}*la-ri-um***-^{ğeš}apin, 1255:2

lá, "to transport" > *Verb Index*

lá, *šaqālu*, "to weigh out, to pay" > *Verb Index*

lá-ìa, *ribbatu*, "remainder; arrears; surplus"

lá-ìa de_9, "to bring the remainder" > **de_6**

lá-ìa (. . .) **lá-ìa**-àm PN in-da-ğál, "remaining {commodities}; the remainder are with PN" > **ğál**

lá-ìa su(g), "to repay the remainder" > **su(g)**

[. . .] x [. . .] dirig? 6 [. . .] 60 udu **lá-ìa** 10 dirig **lá-ìa** dirig KAxÚ-a (. . .) níğ-kas_7-aka ^{d}*adad-tillati* šabra, "{animals delivered and expended, tabulation of the remainder}. (This is) the balanced account of *Adad-tillati*, the majordomo," 984:'68-'76

lá-ìa kaš zi-ga ezem-*a-bu-um*, "the remainder of the beer expended (for) the *Abum* festival," 1047:4–5

lah_4/lah_5, *babālu*, plural stem of de_6 "to bring" > *Verb Index*

^{dug}lahtan, *lahtanu*, "a beer vat"[75]

16 **^{dug}lahtan** kéše-rá, "16 bound beer vats," 1334:5

lam, "(a container)"

1. **har lam**, "seedling container"

har lam ^{ğeš}ù-suh_5 ke_4-dè, "{workers gone} to prepare a seedling container of pine trees" > **aka**

4 **har lam** ^{ğeš}ù-suh_5-tur-tur 3-ta ù har-bi, "4 seedling containers of very young pine trees, 3 each, and their seedlings," 1255:6

7 **har lam** $^{ğeš}ği_6$-par_4, "7 seedling containers of $ği_6$-par_4 (seedlings)," 1375:22

^{ğeš}lam, *lammu*, "sapling, a nut-bearing tree"

n sa gi-izi **^{ğeš}lam** gub, "n bundle(s) of fuel reeds to prop up (young) trees" > **gub**

[LEATHER PRODUCTS]

^{kuš}a-ğá-lá, "leather sack"

---

75 Sallaberger 1996, 58, 74, 103.

^{kuš}á-si, "hinge"
^{kuš}da-lá, "(a leather object)"
^{kuš}du$_{10}$-gan, "leather bag"
^{kuš}e-sír, "sandals"
^{kuš}èš, "tent, pavilion"
kuš-ka-^{ĝeš}mud, "socket mouth leather"
^{kuš}ka-tab, "lid, cover"
^{kuš}*maš-lí-um*, "leather bucket"
^{kuš}*na-aḫ-ba-tum*, "leather carrying case (for precious objects)"
^{kuš}súḫub, "shoes"
^{kuš}šà-ga-dù, "leather belt"
^{kuš}ummu$_x$, "waterskin"

li-iq-tum, *liqtu*, "leftovers?"[76]

2 ma-na *al-lu-ḫa-ru-um* ***li-iq-tum***, "2 minas of *alluḫaru* leftovers?," 668:1

lu, *balālu*; *dalāḫu*; *katāmu*, "to disturb, stir up; to cover completely; to mix" > **lu**

lú, *awīlu*, "man"

^{lú}ázlag, "fuller" > **^{lú}ázlag**
^{lú}kaš$_4$, "runner" > **^{lú}kaš$_4$**
^{lú}kíĝ-gi$_4$-a, "messenger" > **^{lú}kíĝ-gi$_4$-a**
lú é-ne-ne, "men of the household" > *Household Index*
lú gaba sàg-dè, "the man who beats (his) breast" > **gaba … sàg**
lú-ḫuĝ-ĝá iri^{ki}-didli-ke$_4$-ne, "hired workers of various cities" > **iri**
lú-ḫuĝ-ĝá, "hired worker" > **lú-ḫuĝ-ĝá**
lú-kíkken, "miller" > *Craftsmen Index*
lú-ùr-ra, "fish-sauce manufacturer" > **lú-ùr-ra**
lú-^{ĝeš}tir, "forester" > **lú-^{ĝeš}tir**
^{lú}lùnga, "brewer" > **^{lú}lùnga**

1. **The Man of *Adad-tillati***

ĝìri gù-zi-dé-a **lú**-na, "Under the authority of Guzidea, his man" > *Personal Name Index*

2. **lú-GN**, "man from GN" > *Toponym Index*

lú-*dì-ma-at-kál-bu-um*^{ki}
lú-du$_6$-lugal-pa-è^{ki}
a-ḫu-wa-qar **lú**-du$_6$-lugal-pa-è-a^{ki} > *Personal Name Index*
zàḫ *ku-du-du-ú* **lú**-du$_6$-lugal-pa-è^{ki} > *Personal Name Index*

[76] Steinkeller, 1980, 79–100, esp. p. 96 n. 33.

lú-é-^{d}*šu*-^{d}*suen*^{ki}
lú-énsi-marad^{ki}
lú-*i-zi-in-èr-ra*^{ki}
lú-ì-si-in^{ki}
lú-kabšu^{ki}
lú-karkar^{ki}
lú-níĝ-^{d}ba-ú
lú-*tu-lí-um*^{ki}
lú-ur-^{d}šul-pa-è
lú-zabala$_{4}$^{ki}

lú-ḫuĝ-ĝá, "hired worker," *passim*

lú-ḫuĝ-ĝá-me-éš, "hired workers," *passim*

ugula **lú-ḫuĝ-ĝá**, "overseer of hired workers" > **ugula**

1. Provisions

á **lú-ḫuĝ-ĝá**(**-e-ne**), "wages of hired workers" > **á**

šidim ù **lú-ḫuĝ-ĝá-e-ne** ḫal, "to divide {assorted comestibles} for builders and hired workers" > **ḫal**

0.1.5.9⅔ sìla ninda-zì-šà-gen dabin íb-ta-ḫi 0.0.1. níĝ-àr-ra-sig$_{5}$ ^{urudu}šen-šè 50 sa gi-[izi ninda ba-ra-d]u$_{8}$ ù tu$_{7}$ ba-[ra]-šeĝ$_{6}$ mu **lú-**⌜**ḫuĝ**⌝**-ĝá-e-ne**-šè u$_{4}$ igi *šu-kab-tá* ninda in-gu$_{7}$-ša-a, "119⅔ liters of bread mixed from ordinary šà-flour and semolina, 10 liters of fine groats for the (soup) cauldron, (and) 50 bundles of [fuel] reeds with which [bread] was baked and soup was cooked for the hired men when they ate before *Šu-Kabta*," 479:10–16

[ninda ba-ra-du$_{8}$ ù tu$_{7}$ ba-ra-šeĝ$_{6}$ mu] **lú-ḫuĝ-ĝ**[**á-e-ne**-šè] (. . .) mu šidim ù lú-ḫuĝ-ĝ[á-šè], "{assorted comestibles} with which [bread was baked and soup was cooked for] the hired workers; {totals of comestibles}, [for] the builders and hired workers," 483:13–14, 24

2. Broken Context

[... ú] **lú-ḫuĝ-ĝ**[**á-e-ne**], 483:13–14

lú-^{ĝeš}**tir**, "forester"

0.0.2. še 5 sila 5 ninda **lú-**^{ĝeš}**tir**, "20 liters of barley (and) 5 liters of bread (for) the forester," 436:4–6

5 sìla ninda 0.0.2. zú-lum 10 ma-na tuḫ-ĝeš-ì-ḫád **lú-**^{ĝeš}**tir**, "5 liters of bread, 20 liters of dates (and) 10 minas of dried sesame chaff (for) the forester," 438:7–9

lú-ùr-ra, "fish-sauce manufacturer"[77]

1. **PN lú-ùr-ra**, "PN, the fish-sauce manufacturer" > *Personal Name Index*
   a-da-làl
   i-din-^{d}šamaš

lugal, *šarru*, "king, master; royal"

àga-ús **lugal**, "royal gendarme" > **àga-ús**
kaš-dé-a **lugal**, "royal banquet" > **kaš-dé-a**
^{ĝeš}kiri$_{6}$-**lugal**, "the master's garden" > ^{ĝeš}**kiri$_{6}$**
^{lú}kíĝ-gi$_{4}$-a-**lugal**, "royal messenger" > ^{lú}**kíĝ-gi$_{4}$-a**
má-**lugal** laḫ$_{4}$, "to bring the royal boat" > **laḫ$_{4}$**
mu **lugal**-bi pàd, "to swear by the name of the king" > **pàd**
níĝ-šu-taka$_{4}$-**lugal**, "royal consignment" > **níĝ-šu-taka$_{4}$**

1. **alam-lugal**, "royal statue"
   1 máš **alam-lugal**, "1 goat (for) the royal statue," 1012:3
   sá-du$_{11}$ **alam-lugal**, "regular offerings of the royal statue" > **sá-du$_{11}$**
   sá-du$_{11}$ **alam-lugal** èš-ta-gur-ra, "regular offerings of the royal statue, returned from the shrine" > **sá-du$_{11}$**
2. **The Death of the King**
   85 géme-⸢saĝ⸣-dub 16-géme á-⅓-⸢ta⸣ u$_{4}$-1-šè géme uš-bar-me-éš gaba sàg-dè gub-ba u$_{4}$ **lugal**-e ba-úš-[a], "85 full-time female weavers (and) female weavers at ⅔ wages employed for 1 day to beat (their) breasts when the king died," 257:1–6
3. **Wool for Textiles of Royal Quality**
   siki bar-dul$_{5}$-**lugal**, "wool (for) a royal bar-dul$_{5}$ (textile)," 585:4
   siki ^{túg}níĝ-lám-**lugal**, "wool (for) a royal níĝ-lám (textile)," 585:2, 625:5, 667:2
   siki šudum-ma-túg-**lugal**, "wool (for) warp-thread (for) a royal textile," 620:3
   siki šudum-túg-**lugal**, "wool (for) warp-thread (for) a royal textile," 667:4
   siki túg-*á-gu$_{4}$-ḫu-um*-**lugal**, "wool (for) a royal belt," 620:1
   siki túg-guz-za-**lugal**, "wool (for) a royal tufted textile," 625:1
   siki túg-⸢šudum⸣-ma-túg-**lugal**, "wool (for) warp-thread (for) a royal textile," 633:3
   siki t[úg-x]-**lugal**, "wool (for) a royal [x] textile," 625:2
   siki [^{túg}. . .] túg-⸢**lugal**⸣, "wool (for) a royal [. . .] textile," 826:1
   siki-za-rí-in túg-**lugal**-gen, "coarse wool (for) textiles of royal to ordinary quality," 836:1

---

[77] Lit. "person of the roof," indicating that this person was associated with the é ùr ku$_{6}$ al-ús-sá, "fish-sauce roof house," and so involved in the production of fish-sauce (Heimpel 2008, §3.17). In the Iri-saĝrig texts Lugal-amarku, lú-ùr-ra, frequently is sent to obtain mun-gazi, presumably to be used to make sauce. See Owen 2009.

4. Textiles of Royal Quality

túg-**lugal**-gen *simat-*[d]*ištaran šu-kab-tá*, "ordinary textile of royal quality of *Simat-Ištaran* (and) *Šu-Kabta*" > *Personal Name Index*

1 [túg]*á-gu*$_4$*-ḫu-um*-PI-**lugal**, "royal PI-belt," 578:1, 579:1, 591:1

[túg]bar-si gú-è-tur-**lugal**, "small royal ties (for) a cape," 821:2

[túg]gú-è-[níĝ-lám]-tur-**lugal**, "small royal [níĝ-lám] cape," 821:1

[túg]gú-è *tá-ki-ru-um* bar-s[i-ĝar-r]a-tur **lugal**, "small royal *takkirum* cape fashioned with bands," 824:1

[túg]ĝeštu-**lugal** é(!)-[ba-an], "pair of royal ĝeštu textiles," 663:2

[túg]níĝ-lám-AB.PI-**lugal**, "royal níĝ-lám-AB.PI textile," 569:1

[túg]níĝ-lám tab-ba AB.PI-za-**lugal**, "royal double níĝ-lám AB.PI-za textile," 591:2

túg [ba-tab *t*]*uḫ-ḫu-um* ⸢lugal⸣-ra, "[ba-tab] *tuḫ-ḫu-um* textile for the king," 609:6

túg-tùn túg-lugal** é-ba-an, "container of a pair of royal textiles," 748:2

t[úg . . .]-PI-**lugal**, 748:1

luḫ, *mesû*, "to wash, clean" > *Verb Index*

luḫ-lá, "(meaning uncertain)"

n sìla **luḫ-lá** (. . .) ì-ba ù níĝ-dab$_5$ géme-árad, "n liter(s) of luḫ-lá (and) {other commodities}, oil rations and requisitions of female and male servants," 403:7, 10, 510:7, 9, 521:7, 9, 535:7–8, 549:7–8,

n sìla **luḫ-lá**-ta, "n liter(s) luḫ-lá each," 562:'10, 562:'32, 562:'45, 562:'65

luḫ-lá-bi n sìla, "its luḫ-lá is n liter(s)," 562:'75

lulim, *aggalu*; *lulīmu*, "stag"

lulim?-gùn?-[x], "speckled stag?," 983:9, 983:22

[lú]**lùnga**(ŠIM), *sâlu*, "brewer"

é-**lùnga**, "brewery" > *Household Index*

1. PN [lú]**lùnga**, "PN, the brewer" > *Personal Name Index*

a-da-làl

dan-ḫi-li

èr-ra-ba-ni

2. Employed Brewer(s)

[n ĝuru]š [lú]**lùnga** gub-ba, "[n] employed brewer(s)," 206:21

3. Employed at the Place of the Brewers

10-lá-1 ĝuruš ugula *šu-*[d]dumu-zi 4 ĝuruš ugula *simat-é-a* ki [lú]**lùnga**(!) gub-ba kurum$_7$ aka, "inspection (of the work) of 9 workmen, supervised by *Šu*-Dumuzi, (and) 4 workmen, supervised by *Simat-Ea*, employed at the place of the brewer," 169:1–7

4. Inspection

[. . . ki] *šu-*^{d}⸢*adad*-ta⸣ zì $^{⸢\text{lú}⸣}$**lùnga** [x?] kurum$_{7}$ [aka], "inspection of [. . .], flour (for?) the brewer from *Šu-Adad*," 1145:1–5

– M –

ma-ad-li-um, *madlā'u*, "bucket"

1 kuš-udu-niga ***ma-ad-li-um*** ĝar 2-šè ba-a-ĝar, "1 fattened sheep skin placed to cover 2 buckets," 968:17

^{dug}**ma-an-ḫara**$_{4}$(KWU-893), *namḫarû*, "a large (wheeled?) container (for beer),"[78] 1334:10, 1376:78

5 kuš-udu e-rí-na **ma-an-ḫara**$_{4}$-3-šè ba-a-ĝar, "5 root-tanned sheep skins were (used) for covering 3 manḫara containers," 923:1–2

^{gi}**ma-an-sim**, *maḫḫaltum, nappītu*, "a sieve"

^{gi}**ma-an-sim** dabin, "semolina sieve," 1270:1, 1280:2, 1299:17

$^{<\text{gi}>}$**ma-an-sim** BÚR dabin ésir šub-ba, "semolina BÚR sieve coated with bitumen," 1376:17

^{gi}**ma-an-sim** níĝ-àr-ra, "groats sieve," 1280:3, 1299:18

^{gi}**ma-an-sim** níĝ-àr-ra ésir šub-ba, "groats sieve coated with bitumen," 1376:18

$^{<\text{gi}>}$**⸢ma⸣-an-sim** BÚR zì-gu-sig$_{5}$ ésir šub-ba, "fine gu-flour BÚR sieve coated with bitumen," 1376:16

^{gi}**ma-sim** dabin, "semolina sieve," 592:4

ma-aZ-ḫa-ru-um, "(a vessel? a sieve?)"

26.2.1.5 sìla ésir-ḫád gur 0.2.2.5 ⸢sìla⸣ ésir-é-a 0.0.0.8½ sìla ì-šáḫ 0.0.2. ì-ḫur-saĝ-ĝá *šit-tum* é-lùnga é-kíkken ù ***ma-aZ-ḫa-ru-um*** é-muḫaldim-šè ba-a-ĝar, "26 bushels (and) 135 liters of dried bitumen, 145 liters of house bitumen, 8½ liters of lard (and) 20 liters of mountain fat, the balance (of the settled account), were placed for the brewery, the mill and the *maZḫarum* of the kitchen," 1299:1–5

ma-na, *manû*, "a unit of weight, mina," *passim*

^{ĝeš}**ma-nu**, *ēru*, "(a tree, perhaps willow)"

n gú ^{ĝeš}**ma-nu** šu aka, "n talent(s) of processed manu wood" > **šu … aka**

120 gag **ma-nu** 2 kùš-[ta], "120 pegs of manu wood, 2 kùš [each]," 1380:4

---

[78] Sallaberger 1996, 57, 104.

^{gi}ma-sab, **ma-sá-ab**, *masabbu*, "(a basket)," 1265:4, 1311:2, 1312:2, 1376:39

[120?+]5 **^{gi}m[a-sá]-ab** ½-[sìla-ta], "[120?+]5 ma-sab baskets of ½ liter [each]," 1371:1

11 **^{gi}ma!**(KU)**-sá-ab** 5-⸢sìla-ta⸣, "11 ma-sab baskets of 5 liters each," 1371:3

n **^{gi}ma-sab** n sìla-ta, "n ma-sab baskets of n liter(s) each," 1299:19, 1299:20, 1299:21, 1345:2

10? **^{gi}ma-sá-⸢ab⸣** ésir šub-[ba], "10? ma-sab baskets coated with bitumen," 1376:38

46 **^{gi}ma-sab gal-ir dù-a, 1299:15

[n **^{gi}m]a-sá-ab**-gal [. . .], "[n] large ma-sab basket(s) [. . .]," 1292:9

^{gi}ma-sá-ab ninda, "ma-sab basket of bread," 1135:2, 1299:16

[**^{gi}m]a-sá-ab**[. . .], "[. . .] ma-sab basket," 1292:10, 1292:11, 1292:12, 1292:13, 1292:14, 1292:15

ma šub-ba, "brickyard"[79]

ma šub-ba gub-ba, "employed at the brickyard" > **gub**

[n g̃u]ruš šidim **ma šub-ba** šeg$_{12}$-al-ur$_x$-ra, "[n builder(s)] (to mold) bricks at the brickyard," 88:5

má, *eleppu*, "ship, boat"

^{gi}kid **má** ⸢gíd⸣, "a mat for towing boats," 1376:11

má dirig, "to float a boat (downstream)" > **dirig**

má en-nu aka, "to guard a boat" > **aka**

má gaba . . . ri, "to meet a boat" > **gaba . . . ri**

má gíd, "to tow a boat" > **gíd**

má-gín, "boat builder" > **má-gín**

má gul, "to dismantle a boat" > **gul**

má g̃ar, "to place a boat (as terminus technicus for loading bales of shok)" > **g̃ar**

má-laḫ$_5$, "sailor" > **má-laḫ**

má saḫar sè(g$_{10}$), "to tamp dirt (delivered by) boat" > **sè(g$_{10}$)**

má si(g), "to load a boat" > **si(g)**

má sù, "to sink a boat" > **sù**

$^{g̃eš}$ù-**má**, "boat planks" > **$^{g̃eš}$ù**

1. Boats of Deities and Individuals

3 g̃uruš **má** ^{d}*šu*-^{d}E[N.ZU . . .] é-^{d}nin?-si$_4$-in-[na . . . t]a^{ki}-ta gar-ša-[an-na^{ki}-šè] D[U-x], 206:24–25

má *na-wi-ir-ilum*, "boat of *Nawir-ilum*" > *Personal Name Index*

má nin-zi-šà-g̃ál, "boat of Nin-zišag̃al" > *Personal Name Index*

má *simat-*^{d}*ištaran*, "boat of *Simat-Ištaran*" > *Personal Name Index*

2. má gíd-e-ne, "boat towers" > **gíd**

[79] ma šub-ba is likely an alternative spelling of g̃á šub-ba, designating the work area where bricks were molded.

[n.n.n.n (sìla n gín)] ì-šáḫ [ì-ba] **má gíd-e-ne**, "[n liter(s)] of lard, [oil rations] of boat towers," 419:1–2

2.1 ugula má-gíd, "overseer of boat towers" > *Personal Name Index*

be-lí-ì-lí

lugal-ḫa-ma-ti

3. Types of Boats

3.1 má a-a-ba, "sea(-going) boat"

sízkur **má a-a-ba**, "(ceremonial) offerings of the sea(-going) boat" > **sízkur**

3.2 má ḫuĝ-ĝá, "hired boat" > **ḫuĝ**

á **má ḫuĝ-ĝá** ù má-laḫ$_5$-bi, "wages of the hired boat and its sailors" > **ḫuĝ**

3.3 má-lá, *malallû*, "freight boat"

má-lá gíd, "to tow a freight boat" > **gíd**

má-lá tùm, "to bring a freight boat" > **tùm**

3.4 má-lugal, "royal boat"

má-lugal laḫ$_4$, "to bring a royal boat" > **laḫ$_4$**

3.5 má-n-gur, "n-bushel boat," **1359:2, 1359:3, 1369:1**

1 **má-n-gur da-na gur a 1 sìla-ta še-bi n gur, 561:'35-'37, 561:'38-'40

má-n-gur gíd, "to tow a n-bushel boat" > **gíd**

má-n-gur n sìla, "boat of n bushel(s) (and) n liter(s)," 553:8, 553:9, 553:10, 553:27, 553:28, 561:'9, 561:'18, 561:'27

má-n-gur n sìla-ta, "boats of n bushel(s) (and) n liter(s) each," 561:'8, 561:'17, 561:'26

^{ğeš}ù-suḫ$_5$ mi-rí-za **má-n-gur**, "pine board of a n-bushel boat" > **^{ğeš}ù-suḫ$_5$**

3.5.1 Wood of Boats

[n] ^{ğeš}[. . .] 4 [^{ğeš}. . . n] ^{ğeš}é-da-[šinig?] 20 ^{ğeš}ù **má-**[. . .] 2 ^{ğeš}šeg$_{12}$ **má-**[. . .] **má-40-gur** 1-kam [?], "{assorted wood} of 1 40-bushel boat," 1368:1–6

^{ğeš}eme-sig **má-30**-ta, "boat plank from a 30(-bushel) boat," 1380:3

má-gín, "boat builder"[80]

1. Provisions for the Boat Builder of the Sugal-maḫ

0.2.0. **má-gín** sugal$_7$-maḫ (. . .) [šu+níĝin n+]7.0.0. gur še-ba *ba-zi-tum* šu+níĝin 47.1.[n.] še-ba é, "120 liters of (barley) (for) the boat builder of the sugal-maḫ (and) {barley for other individuals}; [in total: n+]7 bushels of the barley rations of *Bazitum*. In total: 47 bushels (and) 60[+n] liter(s) of barley rations of the household," 555:10, 24–25

[80] Sigrist 1984, 78.

má-laḫ$_5$(DU.DU), *malaḫḫu*, "sailor"

lú-^{d}*suena* **má-laḫ$_5$**, "Lu-*Suena*, the sailor" > *Personal Name Index*

n sìla še-bi sa$_{10}$ **má-laḫ$_5$**, "n liter(s) of (barley) is the (hiring) price of the sailor(s)" > **sa$_{10}$**

má-laḫ$_5$ ésir si-mi-dè gub-ba, "sailors employed to filter bitumen" > **sim**

šà-gal **má-laḫ$_5$**, "provisions of sailors" > **šà-gal**

1. **g̃uruš má-laḫ$_5$**

á má ḫug̃-g̃á ù **má-laḫ$_5$**-bi, "wages of the hired boat and its sailors" > **ḫug̃**

[1] **g̃uruš má-DU.[DU]**, "[1] sailor," 71:25

2 **g̃uruš má-laḫ$_5$**, "2 sailors," 61:9, 158:38, 161:'23, 175:31, 160:'17

g̃uruš má-laḫ$_5$ *ì-lí-aš-ra-ni* ì-dab$_5$, "sailor taken in charge by *Ili-ašranni*" > *Personal Name Index*

g̃uruš má-laḫ$_5$ ugula *za-la-a*, "sailor supervised by *Zala'a*" > *Personal Name Index*

1.1 **Work Assignments for Sailors**

[3 **g̃uruš] **má-laḫ$_5$** 1 g̃uruš 3 géme *ra-ṭum-a* KU-[x] g[ub-ba], "[3] sailors, 1 workman (and) 3 workwomen employed to (?) a drain(-pipe)," 59:46–49

1 **g̃uruš má-laḫ$_5$ g̃[en-na] ésir-g̃[e$_6$? . . .], 60:41–42

[n **g̃uruš**] **má-laḫ$_5$** 1 g̃uruš [im] ga$_6$-g̃á-dè, "[n] sailor(s) (and) 1 workman to carry [earth]," 66:'11

maḫ, *kabtu*; *mādu*; *rabû*; *ṣīru*, "(to be) great"

éš-**maḫ**, "large rope" > **éš**

^{gi}kid-**maḫ**, "large mat" > ^{gi}**kid**

mangaga(KA×SA), *mangagu*, "date palm fibers"

[n ma]-na šu-sar **m[angaga**? $^{geš?}$]ig ^{geš}kug̃$_5$-šè ⌜u$_4$⌝ é-e im sumur ba-aka, "[n mina(s)] of cord (made from) date palm fibers for the door (and) ladder when the house was plastered," 472:12–14

^{geš}**maš**, *giṣṣu*, "(a tree)"

2? ^{geš}**maš**-sá-d[a?. . .], 1342:1

2 ^{geš}**maš**-sá-[. . .] ka-ba UD.K[A.BAR. . .], 1342:4–5

2 ^{geš}**maš**-sá-da šinig, 1376:50

maš-dà, *ṣabītu*, "gazelle"

^{kuš}a-g̃á-lá barag-bi **maš-dà**, "leather sack, its barag of gazelle skin" > ^{kuš}**a-g̃á-lá**

mu-du-lum **maš-dà**, "salted gazelle" > ***mu-du-lum***

maš-en-gag, *muškēnu*, "dependant"

1. **Provisions for the *Muškenu*, Stationed at the Palace**

(. . .) **maš-en-gag** ^{lú}kaš$_4$ ká-é-gal-ka gub-ba ⌜*simat*⌝-^{d}*ištaran* íb-gu$_7$ u$_4$ má-*simat*-^{d}*ištaran* é-^{d}šára-ta gar-ša-an-na^{ki}-šè mu-un-gíd-ša-a, "the *muškenu* (and?) the runner, stationed by *Simat-Ištaran* at the gate of the palace, ate {soup} when they towed the boat of *Simat-Ištaran* from the Šara temple to Garšana," 529:13–18

0.0.2.6 sìla <ninda->šu-ra-gen ½ sìla du$_8$ **maš-en-gag** ká-é-gal-ka gub-ba íb-gu$_7$, "the *muškenu*, employed at the gate of the palace, ate 26 liters of ordinary half(-loaf) <bread> baked (in) ½ liter (loaves)," 541:17–19

^{kuš}***maš-lí-um***, *mašlû*, "leather bucket," 930:1

^{kuš}***maš-lí-um*** ^{kuš}a-g̃á-lá ḫi-a, "various leather buckets (and) leather sacks," 963:1

^{kuš}***maš-lí-um***-udu-niga, "leather bucket (made) of fattened sheep skin," 912:4, 932:1, 968:15

máš, *urīṣu*, "(male) goat," 448:3, 497:2, 984:'20, 984:'25, 984:'52, 984:'66, 1003:7, 1003:9, 1019:1, 1025:25, 1025:95, 1165:3, 1171:5, 1216:1, 1217:3, 1518:2, 1519:3

máš-ga, "suckling goat," 421:1

sila$_4$-**máš** ḫi-a, "various lambs (and) goats," 1041:3

udu-**máš** ḫi-a, "various sheep (and) goats," 984:5, 984:12, 984:'21, 984:'26, 984:'34

1. **Alloted for Various Purposes**

máš alam-lugal, "goat (for) the royal statue" > **lugal**

máš ká-kù ^{d}inana-zabala$_4^{ki}$, "goat (for) the gate of bright Inana of Zabala" > **ká**

máš sá-du$_{11}$ ^{d}nin-ḫur-sag̃-g̃á, "goat, regular offerings of Ninḫursag̃a" > **sá-du$_{11}$**

máš sá-du$_{11}$ ^{d}nin-^{d}si$_4$-an-na, "goat, regular offerings of Nin-Siana" > **sá-du$_{11}$**

máš-gal, *mašgallu*, "billy-goat," 448:2, 984:11, 984:17, 984:'19, 984:'24, 984:'57, 984:'65, 1019:4, 1154:5, 1175:2, 1519:3

kuš-**máš-gal**-niga, "skin of a fattened billy-goat" > **kuš**

máš-gal-niga, "fattened billy-goat," 973:3, 983:5, 983:20, 984:3

n **máš-gal**-niga 4-kam-ús, "n 4th-quality fattened billy-goat(s)," 984:39, 984:'56

n **máš-gal**-niga gu$_4$-e-ús-sa, "n fattened billy-goat(s) '(fed) following the oxen'," 984:'58, 1254:5

[n] **máš-gal** [UD.K]A.BAR-dab$_5$, "[n] billy-goat(s) (for) the zabar-dab$_5$ official," 469:1–2

maškim, *rābiṣu*, "an administrative position – secretary, bailiff, deputy"

1. **PN maškim**, "PN, the deputy" > *Personal Name Index*

a-bu-DU$_{10}$
a-ḫu-a
a-ḫu-ni
a-na-a
^{d}*adad-tillati*
be-lí-ì-lí
é-a-šar
èr-ra-ba-ni
g̃ìri-^{d}ba-ú-ì-dab$_5$
i-ṣur-^{d}*suen*
ì-lí-ku
išdum-ki-in
li-bur-ni-rum
^{d}*ma-lik-ba-ni*
^{d}*ma-lik-tillat-sú*
nin-lu-lu
nu-úr-^{d}*adad*
še-da

še-lí-a-núm	*šu-*^{d}nisaba	*ta-ḫu-lam*
šu-èr-ra	*šu-*^{d}*suen-ba-ni*	ur-é-an-na
šu-^{d}nin-in-si	^{d}šul-gi-*wa-qar*	ur-^{d}nin-^{d}si$_{4}$-an-na

me, "to be" > *Verb Index*

^{tumu}**mer**, *ištānu*, "north"

da bàd sè(g$_{10}$) á ^{tumu}**mer**, "to tamp (dirt) at the north side of the (enclosure) wall" > **sè(g$_{10}$)**

[METALS]

BRONZE OBJECTS

bisag̃^{zabar}, "bronze container"

gal-zabar, "large bronze cup"

gír-siki-gul-la^{zabar}, "bronze, wool sheering knife"

^{zabar}sag̃-kul, "bronze bolt"

sà-ḫum^{zabar}, "(a bronze drinking or cooking vessel)"

šen-da-lá^{zabar}, "(a bronze vessel)"

COPPER OBJECTS

^{urudu}gu$_{4}$-zi-bi-ir, "copper ladder"

^{urudu}ḫa-zi-in, "copper axe"

^{urudu}ku-gi-im, "(a copper object)"

^{urudu}šen, "copper (soup) cauldron"

^{urudu}šim-da, "a copper (cattle) branding iron"

^{urudu}šum, "saw"

SILVER OBJECTS

gal kù-babbar, "large silver cup"

^{zabar}sag̃-kul kù-babbar, "silver bolt"

mi-rí-za, *parīsu*, "plank, board; boat pole"

$^{g̃eš}$ig **mi-rí-za**, "door plank" > **$^{g̃eš}$ig**

$^{g̃eš}$ù-suḫ$_{5}$ **mi-rí-za**, "pine board" > **$^{g̃eš}$ù-suḫ$_{5}$**

mu, *šattu*, "year," *passim*

zà-**mu**-bi, "the beginning of the year" > **zà-mu**

1. Age

n $^{g̃eš}$ ù-suḫ$_{5}$ **mu**-n, "n n-year-old pine tree(s)" > **$^{g̃eš}$ ù-suḫ$_{5}$**

n ḫar $^{g̃eš}$ù-suḫ$_{5}$ **mu**-n, "n n-year-old pine seedling(s)" > **$^{g̃eš}$ù-suḫ$_{5}$**

2. In Reference to Specific Years

2.1 From *Šu-Suen* 6 to *Šu-Suen* 7

tu-ra-am-ì-lí ù-na-a-du$_{11}$ níĝ-kas$_7$ ^{d}*adad-tillati* šabra **mu na-rú-a-maḫ**-ta **mu *si-mu-ru-um*^{ki} ba-ḫulu**-šè ḫé-en-ĝá-ĝá ú-lá-bi, "Say to *Turam-ili* that 'the account of *Adad-tillati*, the majordomo, for the years *Šu-Suen* 6 to *Šu-Suen* 7, should be brought forth quickly," 1040:1–7

2.2 *Ibbi-Suen* 1

[. . .]x-x [. . . é]-^{d}šára-ĜEŠ.KUŠ[Ú^{ki} . . . o.n.n.]6⅔ sìla [ninda] iti dirig ezem-^{d}me-ki-ĝál-šè **mu ^{d}*i-bí-*^{d}*suen* ⌜lugal⌝**, "[. . .] Šara [temple], [n+]6⅔ liters of [bread] for month 13, *Ibbi-Suen* Year 1" 1031:1–5

5[0 ud]u-máš ḫi-a gub-ba [é-š]u-sum-ma ĝìri *a-ḫu*-[x] dub-sar iti dirig ezem-me-ki-ĝál ba-zal **mu ^{d}i-bí-^{d}suen lugal** (. . .) níĝ-kas$_7$-aka^{d}*adad-tillati* šabra, "(In total:) 50 various sheep (and) goats present in the storehouse under the authority of *Aḫu*-[x], the scribe, at the end of the 13th month of *Ibbi-Suen* Year 1 (and) {other commodities}, the balanced account of *Adad-tillati*, the majordomo," 984:5–9, '75-'76

2.3 *Ibbi-Suen* 2

(. . .) šu-sum-ma ĝìri *ib-ni-*^{d}*adad* d[ub-sar] iti ezem-me-ki-ĝál ba-zal **mu en-^{d}inana-unu^{ki}-ga máš-e ì-pàd** 0.0.1.2½ sìla ^{na4}ŠEM? še-ta sa$_{10}$-a saĝ-níĝ-gur$_{11}$-ra-kam (. . .) ⌜diri⌝ ĝál-la níĝ-kas$_7$-aka ^{d}*adad-tillati* šabra, "{millstones, diorite stones, woods, yokes, and wooden containers}, the consignment under the authority of *Ibni-Adad*, the scribe, at the end of the 12 month of *Ibbi-Suen* Year 2; (and) 12½ liters ^{na4}ŠEM, the price from barley; (these) are the available assets. There are additional {millstones, diorite stones, woods, yokes, and wooden containers}; the account of *Adad-tillati*, the majordomo," 1372:46–53, 103–106

(. . .) [x i]m *ga-ga-ra-a* zi-[ga? **mu e]n-^{d}inana-unu^{ki}-[ga] máš-e ì-pàd**, "{activities in each month} of *Ibbi-Suen* Year 2, the total [having been?] expended," 1029:'9-'10

3. Yearly Accounting

(. . .) á de$_6$-a ad-kub$_4$ taḫ-ḫe-dam **mu-2-kam**, "{assorted mats, baskets and other finished reed products}; 'incoming' labor of the reed craftsman, to be added (to) the 2 year (account)," 1381:66–69

mu, *šumu*, "name"

mu lugal . . . pàd, *nīš šarrim tamû*, "to swear by the name of the king" > **pàd**

mu-DU, *šurubtu*, "delivery"

1. mu-DU PN, "delivery of PN" > Personal Name Index

a-na-aḫ-ì-lí
ak-ba-zum
árad-é-a > **árad**
ba-zi
ḫal-lí-a
i-din-é-a
ìl-su-dan
li-la-a
lú-kìri-zal
puzur$_4$-a-gu$_5$-um
simat-é-a
simat-^{d}nana
ša-at-bi-zi-il
šál-maḫ
šu-^{d}dumu-zi
šu-kab-tá
za-la-a
zi-ti-a

2. **á mu-DU**, "delivery of (completed) work"

á **mu-DU** ki PN-ta, "delivery of (completed) work from PN" > *Personal Name Index*

a-na-aḫ-ì-lí

puzur$_4$-a-gu$_5$-um

3. **ì-DU PN**, "delivery of PN" > *Personal Name Index*

a-da-làl dumu *šu*-ma-ma

a-da-làl dumu *si-um*

[x-x?]-ti-en

4. **túg-sa-gi$_4$-a mu-DU**, "delivery of finished textiles"

túg-sa-gi$_4$-a mu-DU ki *puzur$_4$-a-gu$_5$-um*-ta *šu*-^{d}*adad* šu ba(-an)-ti, "*Šu-Adad* received a delivery of finished textiles from *Puzur-agum*," 568:4–9, 577:5–9

5. **Other**

5.1 **Delivery of Bricks**

mu-DU ki-sá-a [é-uš-bar] ù é-NUN.[ME.TAG-e]-ne [PN ugula] lú-ḫuĝ-ĝá "delivery (of bricks) for the foundation terrace of the [textile mill] and craftsmen's house by [PN, overseer] of hired workers," 321:'33-'35

[ki]-sá-a é-uš-bar-šè **mu-DU** árad-é-a ugula, "delivery (of bricks) for the foundation terrace of the textile mill by the overseer of the household servants," 322:'83-'84

5.2 **Delivery of (Earth)**

mu-[DU . . .], 349:'17

5.3 **Leather**

(. . .) kíĝ-til-la **mu-DU** é-kišib-ba-šè, "{leather products}, delivery of completed work for the warehouse," 932:7–9

5.4 **Linen**

4 gada-gen ki-lá-bi 7 ma-na ki-lá tag-a **mu-DU** kišib lú-kìri-zal, "4 ordinary linens, their weight is 7 minas. Delivery of weighed (linen) having been woven, seal of Lu-kirizal," 575:1–5

5.5 **Onions**

15 sum-sikil!-mar-ḫa-ši^{ki} **mu-DU** $^{[d]}$*adad-tillati* šabra šu ba-an-ti "*Adad-tillati*, the major-domo, received a delivery of 15 Marhaši onions," 1113:1–4

5.6 **Textiles**

5 ^{túg}níĝ-lám 3-kam-ús ki-lá-bi 9⅓ ma-na [n gín] túg ki-lá tag-a ki *šu-ì-lí-su*-ta **mu-DU**, "5 3rd-quality níĝ-lám textiles, their weight is 9⅓ minas [(and) n shekel(s)], delivery of weighed textiles having been woven from *Šu-ilissu*," 582:1–5

6. **Broken or Uncertain Context**

[. . .]x-*še-en* [x] dú-ra-a [. . .] 6 sìla gíd-[. . .] 0.0.2. [á]-bi ḫ[uĝ-ĝ]á ^{lú}ázlag-me-éš ⌜mu-DU**⌝ NE-KU, 477:1–7

mu-du-lum, *muddulu*,"pickled, salted (meat, grain)"

1 ***mu-du-lum*** udu-niga, "1 salted, fattened sheep," 375:1, 375:3

5 sìla zì-kum ***mu-du-lum***, "5 liters of salted kum-flour," 1090:1–2

[. . .] ***mu-du-lum***, 1188:1–2

mu-gu, "(meaning uncertain)"

n ğuruš šidim n ğuruš n géme [x] ***mu-gu* dù-a, "n builder(s), n workmen (and) n workwomen having constructed (?)," 146:'32-'33, 147:34–35

^{ğeš}**mud**, *uppu*, "bridle, strap"

kuš-ka-^{ğeš}**mud**, "socket mouth leather" > **kuš**

mug, *mukku*, "wool combings, (textile made of) poor-quality wool"

6 ma-na ⅔ gín **mug**, "6 minas (and) ⅔ shekel of wool combings," 593:2

1. Wool Combings from Textile Manufacture

1 ma-na siki-za-rí-in túg-lugal-gen *simat-^{d}ištaran šu-kab-tá* **mug**-bi ⅓ ma-na 4 gín-ta NE-gu$_7$-bi 6 gín-ta, "1 mina of coarsely cleaned wool material (for) textiles of royal to ordinary quality of *Simat-Ištaran* (and) *Šu-Kabta*; its wool combings are ⅓ of a mina (and) 4 shekels each, its wastage is 6 shekels each," 836:1–3

1 ma-na siki-za-rí-in 3-kam-ús 4-kam-ús **mug**-bi ⅓ mana 1 gín-ta NE-gu$_7$-bi 8 gín-ta, "1 mina of 3rd and 4th-quality coarsely cleaned wool material; its wool combings are ⅓ mina (and) 1 shekel each, its wastage is 8 shekels each," 836:4–6

2. túg-mug, "textile of poor-quality wool," 569:19, 654:9, 658:8, 662:10, 669:10, 680:5, 691:5, 694:8, 701:12, 708:9, 725:6, 742:10, 745:8, 748:14, 753:15, 758:16, 764:11, 771:7, 786:15, 796:12, 799:5, 814:12, 827:8, 835:'15

1 **túg-mug** ki-lá siki-gen šudum-bi 1-ma-na ki-lá mug-bi 4$\frac{5}{6}$ ma-na, "1 textile of poor-quality wool, its weight is 1 mina of ordinary wool warp-thread (and) 4$\frac{5}{6}$ minas of wool combings," 744:11–3

1 **túg-[mug** ki-lá] siki-gen šudum-[bi 1 ma-na] ki-lá mug-bi 4⅔ [ma-na], "1 textile [of poor-quality wool, its weight is 1 mina] of ordinary wool warp-thread (and) 4⅔ [minas] of wool combings," 747:13–15

2 **túg-mug**-tur, "2 small textiles of poor-quality wool," 827:9

muḫaldim, *nuḫatimmu*, "cook"

é-**muḫaldim**, "kitchen" > *Household Index*

1. PN muḫaldim, "PN, the cook" > *Personal Name Index*

a-da-làl *da-a-a* *ì-lí-bi-la-ni*

mul-ṭum, *mulṭum/mušṭu*, "a comb"

1 kuš-máš ***mul-ṭum***-šè ba-a-ğar, "1 goat skin (used for) covering a comb," 923:5–6

mun, *ṭabtu*, "salt," 403:6, 442:14, 445:6, 510:6, 511:'105, 521:6, 535:6, 549:6, 557:16, 1194:6, 1325:9

n sìla **mun**-ta, "n liter(s) of salt each," 557:5, 562:'9, 562:'31, 562:'44, 562:'64

mun-bi n sìla, "its salt is n liter(s)," 562:'74

mun-gen, "ordinary salt," 529:9, 1025:10, 1025:33, 1025:50, 1025:68, 1025:111

mun-gen ^{urudu}šen-šè, "ordinary salt for the cauldron" > $^{\mathbf{urudu}}$**šen**

n sìla **mun**-sig$_5$ al-nağ$_4$-ğá, "n liter(s) of fine crushed salt," 511:67, 529:19, 529:89, 975:20, 975:91, 981:20, 1028:5, 1028:22

n ma-na ki-lá šeg$_{12}$-**mun**-sig$_5$, "brick of fine (quality) salt weighing n mina(s)," 1130:4, 1162:'39, 1162:'46

6 gú ki-lá **mun**-sig$_5$, "fine salt weighing 6 talents," 1178:4

(šeg$_{12}$-)**mun**-sig$_5$ mu ku$_6$ al-ús-sa-šè, "(brick of) fine salt for fish-sauce" > **ku**$_6$

saḫar **mun**, "salty dirt" > **saḫar**

mun-gazi, "(a class of agricultural products)"

níğ-kas$_7$-aka **mun-gazi** nu-^{ğeš}kiri$_6$ a-pí-sal$_4^{ki}$-ke$_4$-ne, "the balanced account of mun-gazi agricultural products of the gardeners of Apisal," 540:11–12

munu$_4$, *buqlu*, "malt"

ba-ba-**munu**$_4$, "malt porridge" > **ba-ba**

munu$_4$ nağa$_4$, "to crush malt" > **nağa**$_4$

1. **Barley for Malt**

n še gur mu **munu**$_4$-šè, "n bushel(s) of barley for malt," 1123:1–2, 1133:1–2

2. **munu**$_4$**-si-è**, "sprouted malt," 511:37, 511:60, 972:32, 972:48, 972:83, 975:34, 975:51, 975:84, 981:27, 1036:'35, 1036:'54, 1036:'69, 1250:1, 1254:'24

2.1 **Sprouted Malt for Beer**

5.0.0. **munu**$_4$**-si-è** gur kaš-dirig-šè, "5 bushels of sprouted malt for additional beer," 1227:1–2

munu$_4$**-mú**, *bāqilu*, "maltster"

šu-la-núm **munu**$_4$**-mú**, "*Šulanum*, the maltster" > *Personal Name Index*

munus, *sinništu*, "woman"

dumu-**munus**, "daughter" > **dumu-munus**

é-**munus**, "house of the women" > *Household Index*

1. **PN munus**, "PN, the woman" > *Personal Name Index*

lu-lu

ni-a-ma

2. **Female, as a Commodity Designation**

^{ğeš}gu-za-**munus**, "woman's chair" > $^{\mathbf{ğeš}}$**gu-za**

^{kuš}súḫub-**munus**-babbar é-ba-an, "pair of woman's white shoes" > $^{\mathbf{kuš}}$**súḫub**

^{kuš}súḫub-e-sír-**munus**-babbar é-ba-an, "pair of woman's white sandals" > $^{\mathbf{kuš}}$**súḫub**

mur, *imrû*, "fodder"

27.1.4. še gur **mur**-gu_4-šè, "27 bushels (and) 100 liters of barley for ox fodder," 1236:1–2

mušen, *iṣṣūru*, "bird, fowl, poultry"

mušen-dù, "bird warden" > **mušen-dù**

mušen-tur, "young bird," 1183:1, 1183:3

sipa-**mušen**-na, "bird warden" > **sipa**

šà-gal **mušen**-na, "bird fodder" > **šà-gal**

šà-gal udu šáḫ **mušen** péš ḫi-a, "fodder of various sheep, pigs, birds (and) mice" > **šà-gal**

še **mušen**-[na . . .], "barley (for) birds [. . .]," 1253:'2

{erasure}^{mušen}, 1059:1

1. **Types of Birds**

$ir_7^{mušen}$, "pigeon"

kur-$gi^{mušen}$, "goose"

$sim^{mušen}$, "swallow"

tu-$gur_4^{mušen}$, "dove"

$tum_{12}^{mušen}$, "wild dove"

mušen-dù, "bird warden"

šu-^{d}šamaš **mušen-dù**, "*Šu-Šamaš*, the bird warden" > *Personal Name Index*

– N –

^{kuš}***na-aḫ-ba-tum***, *naḫbātu*, "leather case (for precious objects)," 1376:60

7 gín kuš-gu_4 ⅓ kuš-máš e-rí-na 1 gín sa-udu $^{kuš⌈}$***na⌉-aḫ-ba-⌈tum⌉***, "7 shekels of ox skin, ⅓ of a root-tanned goat skin (and) 1 shekel of sheep sinew (for) a leather case," 855:5–8

na-gada, *naqidu*, "herdsman" > *Personal Name Index*

ur-^{d}šul-pa-è **na-gada**, "Ur-Šulpa'e, the herdsman" > *Personal Name Index*

na-kab-tum, *naqabtu*, "administrative structure responsible for collection, storage and redistribution"[81]

[81] Brunke, *forthcoming*.

1. **níĝ-*na-kab-tum*-šè**, "for the *nakabtum*"

1.1 **Assorted Grains for the *Nakabtum***

0.4.4. zì-kum-sig$_5$ 1.1.2. zì gur 0.0.3. dabin al-ús-sa 13.4.0. dabin gur 0.0.2. eša **níĝ-*na-kab-tu*[*m*-šè]**, "280 liters of fine kum-flour, 1 bushel and 80 liters of flour, 30 liters of processed semolina, 13 bushels (and) 240 liters of semolina (and) 20 liters of fine flour, for the *nakabtum*," 1100:1–6

1.2 **Semolina for the *Nakabtum***

n dabin gur **níĝ-*na-kab-tum*-šè**, "n bushel(s) of semolina for the *nakabtum*," 1080:1–2, 1084:1–2, 1099:1–2, 1107:1–2, 1115:1–2, 1136:1–2

na-rú-a, *narû*, "stele"

gaba-ri-a ki **na-rú-a**, "meeting at the place of the stele" > **gaba-ri-a**

na$_4$, *abnu*, "stone; stone weight"

1 **na$_4$** n gú, "1 stone of n talent(s)," 1372:6, 1372:63

1 **na$_4$** n ma-na, "1 stone of n mina(s)," 1372:7, 1372:8, 1372:9, 1372:10, 1372:11, 1372:12, 1372:13, 1372:14, 1372:15, 1372:16, 1372:64, 1372:65, 1372:66, 1372:67, 1372:68, 1372:69, 1372:70, 1372:71, 1372:72, 1372:73

1 **na$_4$** n gín, "1 stone of n shekel(s)," 1372:17, 1372:18, 1372:19, 1372:20, 1372:21, 1372:22, 1372:23, 1372:24, 1372:74, 1372:75, 1372:76, 1372:77, 1372:78, 1372:79, 1372:80, 1372:81

1. **Types of Stones**

^{na4}EDEN, "(a stone)"

^{na4}esi-kam, "diorite"

^{na4}kinkin á-da-bar šu sè-ga, "'hand-held' black basalt millstone"

^{na4}kinkin-GI-bí šu sè-ga, "'hand-held' GI-bí millstone"

^{na4}kinkin-GI-bí zà-ḫi-li, "(a millstone)"

^{na4}kinkin-zi-bí ĝeš-dù šu sè-ga, "'hand-held' zi-bí ĝeš-dù millstone"

^{na4}kinkin-zi-bí šu sè-ga, "'hand-held' zi-bí millstone"

^{na4}ŠEM, "(a stone)"

^{na4}zú, "flint"

nagar, *nagārum*, "carpenter"

làl-la **nagar**, "Lala, the carpenter" > *Personal Name Index*

ĝuruš **nagar**, "carpenter" > *Craftsmen Index*

naĝ, *šatû*, "to drink" > *Verb Index*

naĝ(a)$_4$(KUM), "to crush/grind (in a mortar with a pestle)" > *Verb Index*

nag̃a, *uḫūlu*, "potash, soap," 630:1, 791:1, 1013:3

1. **Potash for the House of the Barbers**

   2 sìla x-x **nag̃a**? é-šu-i-e-ne-šè, "2 liters of x-x potash? for the house of the barbers," 492:1–2

2. **nag̃a-si-è**, *uḫūlu*, "sprouted nag̃a," 595:4, 621:1, 733:2, 768:1, 774:3, 783:3, 809:2

   n sìla **nag̃a-si-è** mu túg-ga-šè, "n liter(s) of sprouted nag̃a for (processing) textiles," 699:3, 5, 705:2, 5

   n ma-na **nag̃a-si-è** lu-luḫ-dè, "n mina(s) of sprouted nag̃a for cleaning" > **luḫ**

3. **šeg$_{12}$ nag̃a**, "brick of potash"

   [x]-ru [. . . ma-n]a ki-lá šeg$_{12}$ **[na]g̃a, 505:11

   1 gú ki-lá šeg$_{12}$ **nag̃a**, "a brick of potash weighing 1 talent," 774:2

   1⅔ ma-na ki-lá šeg$_{12}$ **nag̃a**, "a brick of potash weighing 1⅔ minas," 788:3

nag̃ar, "(a plant)"

1 gú [x] **nag̃ar mu-x, 733:1

nam-10, *uš̌urtu*, *wākil uš̌urtu*, "overseer of a group of ten"

ugula **nam-10**, "overseer of a group of 10" > **ugula**

1. **nam-10 PN**, "overseer: PN" > *Brick Hauler Index*

a-a-lí
a-ḫu-ni
a-lí-a-bi
^{d}*adad-nu-ri*
al-du-ru-um
bu-ga-núm
eš$_4$-tár-im-ti
ilum-ba-ni
im-ti-dam
ku-ku-zam
la-al-ku-da
la-ma-za-tum
na-ab-ri-tum
ša-at-bi-zi-il
ša-at-ì-lí
ši-nu-ri
šu-eš$_4$-tár
šu-gur-tum
ta-tù-ru-um
ud-du-ur(-um)
un-du-ru-um
wu-nu-ri
zi-ti-ma

nam-60, "overseer of a group of sixty"

1. **PN nam-60**, "PN, the overseer of a group of 60" > *Personal Name Index*

*a-bu-*DU$_{10}$
nu-úr-^{d}*adad*

nam-^{lú}ázlag, "the craft of the fuller" > **^{lú}ázlag**

nam-dú-ra, *marṣūtu*, "being sick" > **dú**

nam-ra-ak, "booty"

0.1.0. dabin šà-g[al] **nam-ra-ak**, "60 liters of semolina, provisions of the booty," 1085:1–2

nam-ša-ra-ab-du, "administration"

30 ĝuruš u$_4$-1-šè **nam-ša-ra-ab<-du>** a-šà-pa$_4$-lugal- ĝu$_{10}$-ka gub-ba, "30 workmen for 1 day employed for the administration of the Palugalĝu field," 276:1–3

30 ĝuruš túg-du$_8$ u$_4$-1-[šè] **nam-ša-ra-ab-du** a-šà-pa$_4$-lugal-ĝu$_{10}$-ka gub-ba, "30 braiders [for] 1 day employed for the administration of the Palugalĝu field," 306:1–2

nar, *nāru*, "singer"

i$_7$-**nar**-e-ne, "singers' canal" > *Canal Index*

ur-^{d}nin-^{d}si$_4$-an-na **nar**, "Ur-Nin-Siana, the singer" > *Personal Name Index*

NE-gu$_7$, "wastage"

NE-gu$_7$-bi zi "to deduct damaged (bricks)" > **zi(g)**

NE-gu$_7$-bi nu-zi "damaged (bricks) not deducted" > **zi(g)**

1. Wastage from Textile Manufacture

1 ma-na siki-za-rí-in túg-lugal-gen *simat-^{d}ištaran šu-kab-tá* mug-bi ⅓ ma-na 4 gín-ta **NE-gu$_7$**-bi 6 gín-ta, "1 mina of coarsely cleaned wool material (for) textiles of royal to ordinary quality of *Simat-Ištaran* (and) *Šu-Kabta*; its wool combings are ⅓ of a mina (and) 4 shekels each, its wastage is 6 shekels each," 836:1–3

1 ma-na siki-za-rí-in 3-kam-ús 4-kam-ús mug-bi ⅓ mana 1 gín-ta **NE-gu$_7$**-bi 8 gín-ta, "1 mina of 3rd and 4th-quality coarsely cleaned wool material; its wool combings are ⅓ mina (and) 1 shekel each, its wastage is 8 shekels each," 836:4–6

1 ma-na siki-za-rí-in-gen **NE-gu$_7$**-bi 6⅔ gín, "1 mina of ordinary coarsely cleaned wool material; its wastage is 6⅔ shekels," 836:9–10

1 ma-na ĝír-⌜gul⌝ **NE-gu$_7$**-bi 15 gín, "1 mina ĝír-gul (wool); its wastage is 15 shekels," 836:11–12

2. Translation Uncertain

[. . .] 1 gíd-[. . .] 12 sar 18 gín ⌜apin⌝? šà é-ĝar 16½ sar 5 gín [*pe*]-*ṣe-ti* **NE-gu$_7$-bi, 1397:'1-'8

ne-mur, *idrānu*, *tumru*, "alkali, potash; coal; ashes; charcoal"

0.0.1. dabin ninda **ne-mur**-šè, "10 liters of semolina for bread (baked in) ash," 437:5

niga, *marû*, "(to be) fattened"

^{munus}áš-gàr **niga**, "fattened female kid" > **^{munus}áš-gàr**

ir$_7^{mušen}$-**niga**, "fattened pigeon" > **ir$_7^{mušen}$**

kur-gi^{mušen}-**niga**, "fattened goose" > **kur-gi^{mušen}**

máš-gal-**niga**, "fattened billy-goat" > **máš-gal**

máš-**niga**, "fattened goat" > **maš**

sila$_4$-**niga**, "fattened lamb" > **sila$_4$**

šáh-**niga**, "fattened pig" > **šáh**

tu-gur$_4^{mušen}$-**niga**, "fattened dove" > **tu-gur$_4^{mušen}$**

u_8-**niga**, "fattened ewe" > $\mathbf{u_8}$
udu-**niga**, "fattened sheep" > **udu**
uz-tur **niga**, "fattened duckling" > **uz-tur**

níĝ, *bušu*; *mimma*, "thing, possession; something"
dug**níĝ** n-sìla-ta, "jug of n liter(s)"
níĝ al-zi-ra, "used goods" > **al-zi-ra**
níĝ-àr-ra, "groat"
níĝ-dab_5, "requisition"
níĝ-GA, "(meaning uncertain)"
níĝ-gú-na, "commodity tax"
níĝ-gu_7, "food"
níĝ-gur_{11}, "property"
níĝ-ì-dé-a, "(a dessert, pastry)"
níĝ-kas_7, "account"
níĝ ki-zàḫ-šè, "provisions for the cultic place" > **ki-zàḫ**
níĝ-lá, "(a qualification of textiles)"
níĝ-*lá-lá-rum*, "(a dessert, pastry)"
túg**níĝ**-lam, "(a textile)"
níĝ-*na-kab-tum*-šè, "material for the *nakabtum*" > ***na-kab-tum***
túg**níĝ**-saĝ-lá-mí, "cap"
níĝ-si-ga, "panel"
níĝ-sù-a, "(a metal object)"
níĝ-šu-$taka_4$, "gift; shipment, consignment"
níĝ-U.NU-a, "thread"
níĝ-ú-ba, "corner piece"
níĝ-zuḫ-a, "stolen good" > **zuḫ**

dug**níĝ n-sìla**, "jug of n liter(s)"[82]
2 kaš-sig_5 dug**níĝ** 5-sìla-ta, "2 5-liter jugs of fine beer," 1180:2
n dug**níĝ** 2-sìla-ta, "n jug(s) of 2 liters each," 1013:12, 1014:'5, 1180:3, 1330:1
n dug**níĝ** 5-sìla-ta, "n jug(s) of 5 liters each," 1013:11, 1014:'4
★★7 dug**níĝ** 5-sìla-ta l[ú?-S]U?.A-šè, 1317:1–2

níĝ-àr-ra, *mundu*, "groats," 416:1, 562:'82, 1073:1, 1100:7, 1103:1, 1280:3
á **níĝ-àr-ra**-ra, "wages for (milling) groats" > **á**
gišma-an-sim **níĝ-àr-ra**, "groats sieve" > **gišma-an-sim**

[82] Sallaberger 1996, 105.

níĝ-àr-ra àra, "to grind groats" > **àra**

1. **níĝ-àr-ra-gen**, "ordinary groats," 511:39, 511:53, 972:34, 972:50, 972:76, 975:36, 975:53, 975:77, 1036:'71

2. **níĝ-àr-ra-sig$_5$**, "fine groats," 381:13, 383:4, 385:4, 391:1, 403:3, 409:1, 437:9, 442:16, 445:3, 479:6, 483:5, 483:11, 483:20, 493:5, 494:5, 494:14, 510:3, 511:38 511:52, 511:'102, 521:3, 523:7, 529:7, 535:3, 549:3, 550:'12, 551:2, 551:5, 551:8, 557:14, 562:'41, 562:'57, 972:11, 972:35, 972:49, 972:75, 975:12, 975:35, 975:52, 975:76, 981:14, 981:28, 999:8, 1016:5, 1025:4, 1025:27, 1025:46, 1025:63, 1025:81, 1025:102, 1027:7, 1028:4, 1028:21, 1036:7, 1036:'70, 1046:1, 1134:7, 1167:5, 1167:15, 1194:3

   níĝ-àr-ra-sig$_5$-bi n (sìla), "their fine groats are n (liters)," 381:20, 386:28, 387:19, 396:18, 396:18, 397:18, 562:'71

   níĝ-àr-ra-sig$_5$ ^{dug}útul, "fine groats (for) the tureen," 383:7, 386:22, 387:13, 396:14, 397:14

   0.0.1. **níĝ-àr-ra-sig$_5$** ^{uruduх}šen-šè, "10 liters of fine groats for the (soup) cauldron," 479:11, 490:3

   n sìla **níĝ-àr-ra-sig$_5$**-ta, "n liter(s) of fine groats each," 557:3

   níĝ-àr-ra-sig$_5$ tu$_7$-šè, "fine groats for soup," 1035:'8

3. **še níĝ-àr-ra**, "barley groats," 381:14

   še níĝ-àr-ra ^{dug}útul, "barley groats (for) the tureen," 386:23, 387:14

   še níĝ-àr-ra-sig$_5$ ^{dug}útul, "fine barley groats (for) the tureen," 399:13

4. **Broken Context**

   níĝ-àr-ra-x, 1036:'53

níĝ-dab$_5$, "requisitions"

níĝ-dab$_5$ ezem-*a-bu-um-ma*-šè, "requisitions for the *Abum* festival" > **ezem**

níĝ-dab$_5$ saĝ u$_4$-sakar ù é-u$_4$-15, "requisitions on the new moon day and the full moon day" > **é-u$_4$-15**, **saĝ u$_4$-sakar**

níĝ-dab$_5$ zà-mu-bi sum, "to give requisitions at the beginning of the year" > **sum**

(. . .) še-ba ì-b[a ù **níĝ-dab$_5$**], "{assorted commodities} (for) barley (and) oil rations [and requisitions]," 446:9

1. **Requisitions of the Boat Towers**

   (. . .) **níĝ-dab$_5$** ĝuruš má gíd-e-ne u$_4$ al-tar-ra gub-ba šà gar-ša-an-na^{ki}, "{assorted comestibles}, requisitions of the boat towers when they were employed for construction in Garšana," 442:19–20

2. **Requisitions of the Gendarmes**

   12 ^{kuš}[e-sí]r-gen é-ba-an **níĝ-dab$_5$** àga-ús-e-ne, "12 pairs of regular sandals, requisitions of the gendarmes," 858:1–2

3. **Requisitions of Individuals**

   níĝ-dab$_5$ *um-mi-kab-tá*, "requisitions of *Ummi-Kabta*" > *Personal Name Index*

   níĝ-dab$_5$ ur-^{d}nin-^{d}si$_4$-an-na, "requisitions of Ur-Nin-Siana" > *Personal Name Index*

4. **Requisitions, Regular Offerings of *Šu-Kabta***

   0.0.5. sìla dabin 4 sìla zì-KAL 4 sìla [zì]-kum-sig$_5$ 2 sìla zì-ba-ba-sig$_5$ **níĝ-dab$_5$** (. . .) sá-du$_{11}$-ki-a-naĝ-*šu-kab-tá*, "50 liters of semolina, 4 liters of KAL-flour, 4 liters of fine kum-[flour]

(and) 2 liters of fine flour porridge, requisitions, (and) {other comestibles}, regular offerings for the funerary libation place of *Šu-Kabta*," 972:52–56, 106, 975:55–59, 108

5. **Requisitions of Servants**

ì-ba ù **níĝ-dab$_5$** géme-árad, "oil rations and requisitions of female and male servants," 403:10, 445:10, 510:9, 511:'108, 521:9, 535:8, 549:8, 1194:8

níĝ-GA, "(meaning uncertain)"

ĝuruš **níĝ-GA**, "(a class of worker)," 21:'30

níĝ-gú-na, *biltu*, "commodity tax (of processed items and processed foods)"

níĝ-gú-na de$_6$, "to bring the commodity tax" > **de$_6$**

níĝ-gú-na ga$_6$(ĝ), "to carry the commodity tax" > **ga$_6$(ĝ)**

níĝ-gú-na ĝar, "to deposit the commodity tax" > **ĝar**

níĝ-gú-na má gíd, "to tow a boat (with) the commodity tax" > **gíd**

níĝ-gu$_7$, "food"

[10+]10 ku$_6$ al-dar-ra **níĝ-gu$_7$** šidim-e-ne, "20 split (dried) fish, food of builders," 427:1–2

níĝ-gur$_{11}$, *makkuru*, "property"

níĝ-gur$_{11}$ *na-wi-ir-ilum-ma*, "property of *Nawir-ilum*" > *Personal Name Index*

níĝ-ì-dé-a, *mirsu*, "(a dessert, pastry)"[83]

1. **Recipes for níĝ-ì-dé-a**

n sìla zì-gú-nida n sìla ì-ĝeš barag aka n sìla zú-lum **níĝ-ì-dé-a**-šè, "n liter(s) of hulled grain, n liter(s) of pressed sesame oil (and) n liter(s) of dates, (ingredients) for a dessert," 972:7–10, 975:7–11, 981:10–13

0.0.3. zì-KAL 5 sìla ì-ĝeš 5 sìla ga-ḫar [n.n.n.] zú-lum **[níĝ-ì-d]é-a**-šè, "30 (liters) KAL-flour, 5 liters sesame oil, 5 liters of round cheese (and) [n] (liters) of dates, (ingredients) for a dessert," 1036:'8-'12

níĝ-kas$_7$, *nikkassu*, "account"

1. **níĝ-kas$_7$-aka** "balanced account"

níĝ-kas$_7$-aka mun-gazi, "the balanced account of mun-gazi agricultural products" > **mun-gazi**

2. **níĝ-kas$_7$-aka PN**, "balanced account of PN" > *Personal Name Index*

da-a-a	*li-la-á*
ì-lí-bi-la-ni	*šu*-^{d}dumu-zi

[83] Brunke 2008, 198–206 (§3.5.1).

2.1 The Account of *Adad-tillati*

tu-ra-am-ì-lí ù-na-a-du$_{11}$ **níĝ-kas$_7$** ^{d}*adad-tillati* šabra mu na-rú-a-maḫ-ta mu *si-mu-ru-um*^{ki} ba-ḫulu-šè ḫé-en-ĝá-ĝá ú-lá-bi, "Say to *Turam-ili* that 'the account of *Adad-tillati*, the majordomo, for the years *Šu-Suen* 6 to *Šu-Suen* 7, should be brought forth quickly," 1040:1–7

(. . .) šu-sum-ma ĝìri *ib-ni-*^{d}*adad* d[ub-sar] iti ezem-me-ki-ĝál ba-zal mu en-^{d}inana-unu^{ki}-ga máš-e ì-pàd 0.0.1.2½ sìla ^{na4}ŠEM? še-ta sa$_{10}$-a saĝ-níĝ-gur$_{11}$-ra-kam šà-bi-ta 0.0.1.2½ sìla ^{na4}EDEN ugula EDEN šu ba-ti (. . .) ⸢diri⸣ ĝál-la **níĝ-kas$_7$-aka** ^{d}*adad-tillati* šabra, "{millstones, diorite stones, woods, yokes, and wooden containers}, the consignment under the authority of *Ibni-Adad*, the scribe, at the end of the 12 month of *Ibbi-Suen* Year 2; (and) 12½ liters ^{na4}ŠEM, the price from barley; (these) are the available assets. From among it: the supervisor of EDEN received 12½ liters of ^{na4}EDEN. There are additional {millstones, diorite stones, woods, yokes, and wooden containers}; the balanced account of *Adad-tillati*, the majordomo," 1372:46–57, 103–106

(. . .) [n] sar gíd-da [**níĝ**]-**kas$_7$-da** $^{[d]}$*adad-tillati* šabra [ì]-dab$_5$,"{parcels of land in Zabala and Garšana; in it: date palm, pine boards of boats, seedlings, and planks, the delivery of 3 craftsmen, the delivery of [PN], the craftsman, in Garšana}; (in total:) [n] sar (of land) surveyed. *Adad-tillati*, the majordomo, took in charge the account," 1362:'73-'76

(. . .) gub-ba [é-š]u-sum-ma ĝìri *a-ḫu-*[x] dub-sar iti dirig ezem-me-ki-ĝál ba-zal mu ^{d}i-bí-^{d}suen lugal (. . .) [saĝ]-níĝ-ga-ra [šà]-bi-ta (. . .) níĝ-dab$_5$ ezem-*a-bu-um-ma* (. . .) sá-du$_{11}$-^{d}na-na-*a-ḫu-a* (. . .) sá-du$_{11}$-^{d}[. . .] (. . .) [. . .] x [. . .] dirig? 6 [. . .] 60 udu lá-ìa 10 dirig lá-ìa dirig KA×Ú-a (. . .) **níĝ-kas$_7$-aka** ^{d}*adad-tillati* šabra, "{animals} present in the storehouse under the authority of *Aḫu-*[x], the scribe, at the end of the 13th month of *Ibbi-Suen* year 1 (and) {animal deliveries from other indiviudals}, these are the available assets. From among it {animals}, requisitions of the *Abum* festival, regular offerings of Nana, (the personal deity of) *Aḫu'a*, (and) regular offerings of [. . .]; {tabulation of the remainder}. (This is) the balanced account of *Adad-tillati*, the majordomo," 984:6–9, '35-'36, '42, '45, '48, '68-'76

2.2 Expended from the Balanced Account

[n.n.n.n sìl]a ḫašḫur-duru$_5$ gur ⸢*ilum*⸣*-ra-pi$_5$* dam-gàr šu ba-ti **níĝ-kas$_7$-aka**-ta ^{d}ba-ú-da ba-⸢na⸣-zi kišib *ilum-ra-pi$_5$* u$_4$-um-de$_6$ kišib ^{d}ba-ú-da zi-re-dam, "*Ilum-rapi*, the merchant, received [n] bushel(s) (and) [n] liter(s) of fresh apples which Ba'uda expended from the account for him. When the sealed tablet of *Ilum-rapi* is brought, Ba'uda's sealed tablet will be canceled," 1173:1–10

níĝ-lá, "(a qualification of textiles)"

^{túg}bar-si **níĝ-lá**, "níĝ-lá band" > **^{túg}bar-si**

níĝ-*lá-lá-rum*, "(a dessert, pastry)"[84]

1. Recipes for níĝ-*lá-lá-rum*

6 sìla ĝeš-ì ba[rag aka] 4 sìla [ba-ba-munu$_4$] 4 sìla [eša] 4 sìla z[ú-lum] ⅓ sìla ì-ĝeš b[arag ak]a **níĝ-*lá-lá-rum*-šè** (. . .) sá-du$_{11}$-ki-a-naĝ-*šu-kab-tá*, "6 liters of pressed sesame, 4 liters

[84] Brunke 2008, 209–210(§3.5.3). Perhaps from *lallāru*, "white honey."

of [malt porridge], 4 liters of [fine flour], 4 liters of [dates] (and) ⅓ liter of pressed sesame oil; (ingredients) for a dessert (and) {other comestibles}, regular offerings of the funerary libation place of *Šu-Kabta*," 972:59–64, 106

4 sìla ba-ba-⸢munu$_4$⸣ 4 sìla eša 4 sìla zú-lum ⅓ sìla ì-g̃eš barag aka **níg̃-*lá-lá-rum*-**šè (. . .) ⸢sá⸣-du$_{11}$-ki-a-nag̃-*šu-kab-tá*, "4 liters of malt porridge, 4 liters of fine flour, 4 liters of dates (and) ⅓ liter of pressed sesame oil; (ingredients) for a dessert (and) {other comestibles}, regular offerings of the funerary libation place of *Šu-Kabta*," 975:61–65, 108

^{túg}**níg̃-lam**, *lamḫuššu*, "(a textile)"

★★^{túg}bar<-dul$_5$>-**níg̃-lám**-x-[. . .], 829:'6

^{túg}gú-è-**níg̃-lám**, "níg̃-lám cape" > ^{túg}**gú-è**

^{túg}**níg̃-lám**-gen, "ordinary níg̃-lám textile," 588:1

^{túg}**níg̃-lám**-ús, "2nd-quality níg̃-lám textile," 569:10, 651:1, 698:15

^{túg}**níg̃-lám**-ús-ni, "2nd-quality níg̃-lám textile," 711:2

^{túg}**níg̃-lám** 3-kam-ús, "3rd-quality níg̃-lám textile," 569:5, 570:2, 578:7, 579:7, 582:1, 590:1, 608:4, 618:2, 649:1, 651:2, 662:2, 663:3, 669:3, 673:2, 674:1, 686:1, 691:1, 693:1, 698:6, 708:2, 737:1, 738:3, 739:1, 746:2, 748:3, 758:3, 760:1, 764:4, 766:2, 773:2, 790:1, 793:2, 794:2, 806:1, 811:2, 821:4, 823:3, 827:4, 829:'3, 835:'3, 1394:2

^{túg}**níg̃-lám** 3-kam-ús *a-gi$_4$-um*, "3rd-quality *a-gi$_4$-um* níg̃-lám textile,"737:2

★★^{túg}**níg̃-lám** 3-kam-ús nu?-gu$_4$?-x[. . .ta]k?-[. . .], 609:1–2

1½ ma-na šudum U.NU.A ^{túg}**níg̃-⸢lám⸣** 3-kam-ús, "½ mina of warp-thread (for) a 3rd-quality níg̃-lám textile," 596:3

^{túg}**níg̃-lám** 4-kam-ús, "4th-quality níg̃-lám textile," 569:6, 570:3, 579:11, 609:3, 626:1, 636:5, 639:1, 658:4, 662:4, 693:3, 698:7, 698:17, 700:3, 701:6, 708:4, 709:3, 743:4, 744:4, 745:3, 746:3, 753:3, 753:8, 758:10, 760:4, 764:6, 765:4, 778:6, 786:7, 790:2, 796:5, 806:5, 821:7, 835:'7, 1162:'17

^{túg}**níg̃-lám** 4-kam-ús-ni, "4th-quality níg̃-lám textile," 749:2, 751:2, 754:1

^{túg}**níg̃-lám** 4-kam-ús ^{d}da-mu, "4th-quality níg̃-lám textile of Damu," 17:6

^{túg}**níg̃-lám** 4-kam-ús ^{d}šu-bu-la, "4th-quality níg̃-lám textile of Šubula," 834:10

^{túg}**n[íg̃-lám** 4-kam-ú]s ^{d}x-[. . .]-šè, "[4th-quality] níg̃-lám textile for [. . .]," 609:7

^{túg}**níg̃-[lám** n-kam-ús], "[n^{th}-quality] níg̃-lám textile," 834:5

^{túg}**[níg̃-lá]m**-ús [n-ka]m, "[n^{th}-quality] níg̃-lám textile," 650:2

15 gín šudum U.NU.A ^{túg}**níg̃-lám** 4-kam-ús, "15 shekels of warp-thread (for) a 4th-quality níg̃-lám textile," 596:4

^{túg}**níg̃-lám**-AB *simat-^{d}ištaran*, "níg̃-lam-AB textile of *Simat-Ištaran*," 720:1, 811:1, 814:1

^{túg}**níg̃-lám**-AB *šu-kab-tá*, "níg̃-lam-AB textile of *Šu-Kabta*," 569:4, 578:5, 579:5, 676:1, 736:1, 823:2, 827:2, 1254:'38

^{túg}**níg̃-lám**-AB-ús, "2nd-quality níg̃-lam-AB textile," 814:2

^{túg}**níg̃-lám**-AB.[PI-g]en, "ordinary níg̃-lam-AB.PI textile," 569:3

^{túg}**níg̃-lám**-AB.PI-lugal, "royal níg̃-lam-AB.PI textile," 569:1

^{túg}**níg̃-lám**-AB.PI-ús, "2nd-quality níg̃-lam-AB.PI textile," 569:2, 673:1, 1254:'36

^{túg}**níg̃-lám** ba-tab *tuḫ-ḫu-um* 3-kam-ús, "3rd-quality ba-tab *tuḫ-ḫu-um* níg̃-lam textile," 579:18

^{túg}**níĝ-lám**-PI-ús, "2nd-quality níĝ-lam-PI textile," 578:3, 579:3, 591:3
^{túg}**níĝ-lám**-PI-ús-ni, "2nd-quality níĝ-lam-PI textile," 711:1, 749:1, 751:1
^{túg}**níĝ-lám** *simat-*^{d}*ištaran*, "níĝ-lám textile of *Simat-Ištaran*," 753:1
^{túg}**níĝ-lám** *šu-kab-tá*, "níĝ-lám textile of *Šu-Kabta*," 591:6, 698:3, 789:1
^{túg}**níĝ-lám** tab-ba AB.PI-za-lugal, "double royal níĝ-lam-AB.PI-za textile," 591:2
★★^{túg}**níĝ-lám** tab-ba ús x-ḪI?, 819:1
^{túg}**níĝ-lam**-tur-gen pi-lu-da, "small ordinary níĝ-lam textile (for) ritual (use)," 787:4
^{túg}**níĝ-lam**-tur 3-kam-ús, "small 3rd-quality níĝ-lám textile," 658:3
^{túg}**níĝ-lam**-tur 4-kam-ús, "small 4th-quality níĝ-lám textile," 674:6, 685:1, 687:1, 692:5, 738:11, 773:3, 796:6
^{túg}**níĝ-lam**-tur 4-kam-ús ^{d}šu-bu-⸢la⸣, "small 4th-quality níĝ-lám textile of Šubula," 608:6
^{túg}**níĝ-lam**-tur *simat-*^{d}*ištaran*, "small níĝ-lám textile of *Simat-Ištaran*," 591:4
^{túg}**níĝ-lam** [?] *šu-kab-*⸢*ta*⸣, "[?] níĝ-lam textile of *Šu-Kabta*," 781:1
^{túg}**níĝ-lam** x-[. . .], 572:1
^{túg}**níĝ-lam** [. . .], 747:5
^{túg}**níĝ-[lám**. . .], 759:2
^{túg}**níĝ-⸢lám⸣**-[. . .]-ni-[. . .], 759:3
^{túg}sagšu-**níĝ-lám** 3-kam-ús, "3rd-quality níĝ-lám cap" > ^{túg}**sagšu**
^{túg}šà-gi$_4$-dab$_6$ **níĝ-lám**, "níĝ-lám šà-gi$_4$-dab$_6$ textile" > ^{túg}**šà-gi$_4$-dab$_6$**
★★túg-šà-^{kuš}súḫub-**níĝ-lám** > ^{kuš}**súḫub**
[túg . . . **níĝ-lá**]**m** 3-kam-[ús], 773:1

^{túg}níĝ-saĝ-lá-mí, "cap," 825:1

^{túg}**níĝ-saĝ-lá-mí** 3-kam-ús, "3rd-quality cap," 569:12, 701:4

níĝ-si-ga, "panel"

níĝ-si-ga ZI/ZI aka, "to make a panel of rushes" > **aka**
^{gi}**níĝ-si-ga**-bi n sa, "n bundle(s) of panels," 1381:4, 1381:43 (in reference to the amount of panels required to manufacture ^{gi}ig-dur)

níĝ-sù-a, "(a metal object)"

12 sa gi-izi **níĝ-sù-a** ^{urudu}šen-šè, "12 bundles of fuel reeds for the níĝ-sù-a (soup) cauldron," 1297:17–18

níĝ-šu-taka$_4$, *šūbultu*, "gift; shipment, consignment"

★★[o.n.n. š]e ensi-šè [PN] ^{lú}kíĝ-gi$_4$-a-lugal [x].GA.URU ⸢**níĝ**⸣**-šu-taka$_4$**-lugal [mu]-un-de$_9$-a, "[n liter(s)] of barley for the dream interpreter, [PN], the royal messenger, who brought (?), the royal consignment," 484:10–13

níĝ-U.NU-a, "thread," 755:8

níĝ-U.NU-a siki-ud$_5$, "goat-hair thread," 716:2, 1343:2

níĝ-u$_{2/3}$-ba, "corner piece"

níĝ-ú-ba A.ZI/ZI.ÉŠ sur, "to twist rushes (for use as) corner pieces" > **sur**

níĝ-ù-ba sur, "to twist corner pieces" > **sur**

níĝin, *esēru*, *lawû*, "to enclose, confine; to encircle" > *Verb Index*

sa-**níĝin** ^{ĝeš}àsal, "bundle of poplar wood" > $^{\mathbf{ĝeš}}$**asal**

^{ĝeš}**nimbar**, *gišimmaru*, "date palm," 1362:8, 1362:'31, 1362:'59

^{ĝeš}**nimbar**-gal, "large date palm," 1256:1, 1375:1

20 ĝuruš ^{ĝeš}nimbar** sumun te-[x? gub]-ba, 36:20

13 ĝuruš ^{ĝeš}**nimbar** zi-zi-dè [gub-ba], "13 workmen [employed] to strip date palm wood," 35:36

pa ^{ĝeš}**nimbar**-bi n, "n date palm frond(s)," 1381:22, 1381:27, 1381:29, (in reference to the amount of date palm fronds required to manufacture ^{gi}bisaĝ túg-aš, ^{gi}bisaĝ ninda-gur$_4$-ra)

nin, *bēltu*, "lady"

^{túg}bar-si **nin**, "lady's band" > $^{\mathbf{túg}}$**bar-si**

nin$_9$, *aḫātu*, "sister"

a-ga-ti **nin$_9$** *šu-kab-tá*, "*Agati*, sister of *Šu-Kabta*" > *Personal Name Index*

ninda, *akalu*, "bread," 379:18, 383:1, 385:1, 385:6, 386:21, 402:2, 402:5, 402:13, 430:1, 436:5, 437:7, 438:7, 440:9, 465:2, 476:1, 480:1, 494:25, 512:3, 514:3, 520:3, 524:3, 537:3, 539:3, 552:3, 997:8, 1022:11, 1022:13, 1023:11, 1024:3, 1030:10, 1030:17, 1030:24, 1030:30, 1030:36, 1031:3, 1031:6, 1031:7, 1031:20, 1062:4, 1209:1, 1243:1, 1527:1, 1527:17, 1527:19, 1527:21, 1527:23, 1527:25, 1527:27

ninda-bi n (sìla), "their bread is n (liters)," 386:25, 387:16, 381:17

n (sìla) **ninda**-ta, "n (liters) of bread each," 381:1, 386:1

dabin **ninda** túg ù ì ḫi-a má gíd, "to tow a boat (with) various (amounts of) semolina, bread, textiles and oil" > **gíd**

ninda du$_8$, "to bake bread" > **du$_8$**

1. **kaš-ninda**, "beer (and) bread"[85] > **kaš**

2. **še-ninda**, "barley (for) bread,"[86] 997:1, 997:5, 1022:1, 1022:6, 1022:8, 1023:1, 1023:6, 1023:8, 1023:10, 1023:13, 1024:5, 1024:9, 1024:11, 1024:14, 1026:1, 1026:4, 1026:5, 1026:7, 1527:10, 1527:41

še-**ninda**-gen, "barley (for) ordinary bread" 1024:1

še-**ninda** sá-du$_{11}$, "barley (for) bread of regular offerings" > **sá-du$_{11}$**

---

85 Brunke 2008, 191 (§3.3.8.1).

86 Brunke 2008, 161 (Bemerkung 3.37).

3. "Bread Baskets"

20-lá-1 ^{gi}ma-sá-ab **ninda**, "19 ma-sá-ab baskets of bread," 1135:2

4. Bread Rations and Allotments

5.0.1. [še gur] **ninda**-ba géme-⌜árad⌝ é-[a], "5 bushels of barley, bread rations of the female (and) male servants of the house," 468:1–2

[1 *w*]*a-qar-dan* 1 *á-pil-lí-a* **ninda**-ta nu-tuku, "*Waqar-dan* (and) *Apilli'a*, they each did not get bread," 559:30–32

0.2.0. **ninda** šuku ib-šu-bi u_4-4-kam 1.0.2. **ninda** gur sá-du_{11} ù **ninda** dirig ba-ab-daḫ-a iti ezem-me-ki-g̃ál, "20 liters of bread of the food allocation, its (?) on the 4th day; 1 bushel (and) 20 liters of bread, regular offerings and additional bread that was added in the 12th month," 1031:11–12

šu+níg̃in 3.0.1.5½ sìla **ninda** gur šà-bi-ta 0.1.3. **ninda** šuku *šu*-^{d}nin-súmun iti 4-kam 2.4.3.6 sìla **ninda** gur [é]-kišib-ba-šè ba-an-ku_4, "In total: 3 bushels (and) 15½ liters of bread; from among it 63 liters of bread are the food allocation of *Šu*-Ninsumun in the 4th month (and) 2 bushels (and) 276 liters of bread entered the storeroom," 1031:14–18

5. Types of Bread

ninda-dabin, "semolina bread"

ninda-*e-bi-a-tum*, "thick bread"

ninda-gal, "large (loaf of) bread"

ninda-gúg, "cake"

ninda-gur_4, "thick bread"

ninda-g̃eš-AŠ, "(a bread)"

ninda-ne-mur, "bread (baked in) ash"

ninda-sal-la, "thin bread"

ninda-šu-ra, "half(-loaf) of bread"

ninda-tuḫ, "bran bread"

ninda-u_4-*tuḫ-ḫu-um*, "(a bread)"

ninda-zì-gu, "gu-flour bread"

5.1 ninda-dabin, "semolina bread,"[87] 402:1, 402:4, 402:8, 402:11, 402:12, 483:2, 501:2, 550:'7, 550:'11, 550:'20, 1025:20, 1025:44, 1025:61, 1025:79, 1025:100

ninda-dabin-bi n (sìla), "their semolina bread is n liter(s)," 402:14

ninda-sal-la-**dabin**, "thin semolina bread," 485:2, 548:6, 899:2

5.1.1 Bread of Semolina and šà-flour[88]

ninda-dabin ù zì-šà-gen ½ sìla du_8-bi 0.0.2.8 ⌜sìla⌝, "their bread of semolina and ordinary šà-flour is 28 liters baked (in) ½-liter loaves," 402:15

ninda-dabin ù zì-šà-gen(-ta), "bread from semolina and ordinary šà-flour," 442:2, 442:8

---

[87] Brunke 2008, 119 (§3.1.4.5).

[88] Brunke 2008, 119–120 (§3.1.4.6).

0.4.0. **ninda-dabin** ù zì-šà-gen íb-ta-ḫi, "240 liters of bread were mixed from semolina and ordinary šà-flour," 490:1

1.1.0. **ninda-dabin** ù zì-šà-gen gur ki-lá-bi 4 gú 30 ma-na, "1 bushel (and) 60 liters of semolina and ordinary šà-flour bread, their weight is 4 talents (and) 30 minas," 528:3–4

5.2 ninda-*e-bi-a-tum*, "thick bread," 1209:2

5.3 ninda-gal, "large (loaf of) bread"[89]

ninda-gal-gen, "ordinary large (loaf of) bread," 479:4, 483:3, 483:19, 493:9, 1033:8, 1184:2

n sìla **ninda-gal**-gen 1 sìla du_8, "n liter(s) of ordinary large bread baked (in) 1-liter (loaves)" > **du_8**

n sìla **ninda-gal**-gen 1 sìla du_8 ki-lá-bi n gú n ma-na, "n liter(s) of ordinary large bread baked (in) 1-liter (loaves), their weight is n talents and n mina(s)" > **du_8**

5.3.1 Flour for Large (Loaves)

ninda-gal zì-gen, "large (loaf of) bread of ordinary flour," 1248:1

ninda-gal zì-kum, "large (loaf of) bread of kum-flour," 1248:2

n **ninda-gal** zì-kum ù šà-gen n sìla du_8, "n liter(s) of large bread of kum and ordinary šà-flour baked (in) 1 liter (loaves)" > du_8

5.4 ninda-gúg, *kukku*, "cake"[90]

ninda-gúg-zì-KAL, "cake of KAL-flour," 495:2:1

ninda-gúg ù **ninda**-gur_4-ra zì-KAL, "cake and thick bread of KAL-flour," 548:7

5.5 ninda-gur_4, "thick bread"[91]

^{gi}bisağ **ninda-gur_4-ra**, "basket (for) thick bread" > **^{gi}bisağ**

ninda-gúg ù **ninda-gur_4-ra** zì-KAL, "cake and thick bread of KAL-flour," 548:7

5.5.1 Flour for Thick Bread

0.1.3.2 sìla **ninda-gur_4-ra** zì-KAL, "92 liters of thick bread of KAL-flour," 490:2

ninda-gúg ù **ninda-gur_4-ra** zì-KAL, "cake and thick bread of KAL-flour," 548:7

0.0.2. zì-KAL 0.0.1. zì-gu-ús **ninda-gur_4-ra**-šè, "20 liters of KAL-flour (and) 10 liters of 2nd-quality gu-flour for thick bread," 1015:1–3, 1018:1–3

0.0.3.5⅓ sìla **ninda-gur_4-ra** zì-KAL, "35⅓ liters of KAL-flour (for) thick bread," 1033:9

5.6 ninda-ğeš-AŠ, "(a bread)"

n sìla **ninda**-gal-**ğeš-AŠ** 1 sìla du_8, "n liter(s) of large ğeš-AŠ bread baked (in) 1 liter (loaves)" > **du_8**

---

89 Brunke 2008, 124 (§3.1.4.10).

90 Brunke 2008, 127 (§3.1.4.15).

91 Brunke 2008, 132–133 (§3.1.4.19).

5.7 ninda ne-mur, "bread (baked in) ash"[92]

0.0.1. dabin **ninda ne-mur**-šè, "10 liters of semolina for bread (baked in) ash," 437:5

5.8 ninda-sal-la, "thin bread"[93]

dabin-**ninda-sal-la**, "semolina (for) thin bread," 483:17

ninda-sal-la-dabin, "thin semolina bread" > **ninda-dabin**

ninda-sal-la-zì-gu, "thin gu-flour bread" > **ninda-zì-gu**

0.0.5. zì-gu-⌈ús⌉ 0.0.5. dabin **ninda-sal-la**-šè, "50 liters of 2nd-quality gu-flour (and) 50 liters of semolina for thin bread," 479:1–3

0.0.2. dabin **ninda-sal-la**-⌈gen⌉, "20 liters of semolina for ordinary thin bread," 1035:'7

5.9 ninda-šu-ra, "half(-loaf) bread,"[94] 463:1, 507:9

n **ninda-šu-ra** ½ sìla du_8, "n liter(s) of half(-loaf) bread, baked (in) ½-liter (loaves)" > **du_8**

ninda-šu-ra-gen, "ordinary half(-loaf) bread," 449:8, 495:2, 529:1, 529:5, 1025:19, 1025:45, 1025:62, 1025:98, 1135:1

ninda-šu-ra-gen ^{kuš}a-g̃á-lá kéše, "ordinary half(-loaf) bread in bound leather sacks" > **kéše-rá**

n **ninda-šu-ra**-gen ½ sìla du_8, "n liter(s) of ordinary half(-loaf) bread baked (in) ½-liter (loaves)" > **du_8**

ninda-šu-ra-sig_5, "fine half(-loaf) bread," 449:7, 509:5, 509:'10

5.9.1 Flour for Half(-Loaf) Bread

n **ninda-šu-ra** dabin ù šà-gen ½ sìla du_8, "n liter(s) of half(-loaf) bread of dabin and ordinary šà-flour baked (in) ½-liter (loaves)" > **du_8**

n **ninda-šu-ra** zì-kum ù šà ½ sìla du_8, "n liter(s) of half(-loaf) bread of kum and šà-flour baked (in) ½-liter (loaves)" > **du_8**

5.10 ninda-tuḫ, "bran bread,"[95] 548:8, 1025:22, 1025:80, 1025:101

5.11 ninda-*u*$_4$*-tuḫ-ḫu-um*, "(a bread),"[96] 449:6

5.11.1 Flour for *utuḫḫum* Bread

0.1.0 zì-kum-sig_5 0.1.0. eša **ninda-*u*$_4$*-tuḫ-ḫu-um***-šè, "60 liters of fine kum-flour (and) 10 liters of fine flour for *utuḫḫum*-bread," 1077:1–3

5.12 ninda-zì-gu, "gu-flour bread,"[97] 999:1

ninda-zì-gu-ús, "2nd-quality gu-flour bread," 483:1, 1025:19, 1025:43, 1025:60, 1025:78, 1025:99

ninda-sal-la-**zì-gu**, "thin gu-flour bread," 485:1

---

92 Brunke 2008, 138 (§3.1.4.34).

93 Brunke 2008, 139 (§3.1.4.37).

94 Brunke 2008, 142 (§3.1.4.4.6).

95 Reading ninda-tuḫ instead of ninda-du_8 (Brunke 2008, 121, §3.1.4.8).

96 Brunke 2008, 144–146 (§3.1.4.51).

97 Brunke 2008, 148–149 (§3.1.4.59).

5.13 Breads of Various Flours[98]

0.1.5.9⅔ sìla **ninda**-zì-šà-gen dabin íb-ta-ḫi, "119⅔ liters of bread were mixed from ordinary šà-flour (and) semolina," 479:10, 483:9–10

2.0.1.5 sìla **ninda**-zì-kum ù zì-šà-gen gur ki-lá-bi 6 gú 40 ma-na, "2 bushels (and) 15 liters of kum and ordinary šà-flour bread, their weight is 6 talents (and) 40 minas," 528:5–6

n sìla **ninda** zì-milla ù zì-šà-gen-ta, "n liter(s) of bread of milla-flour and ordinary šà-flour each," 536:7, 536:14

ninda zì-milla ù zì-šà-gen-bi n-sìla, "(In total:) their bread of milla-flour and ordinary šà-flour is n liter(s)," 536:18

0.3.3. zì-gu-sig$_5$ 1.0.0. zì-gu-ús gur 0.3.3. dabin 0.0.4.5 sìla zì-KAL 0.1.0.0 sìla zì-kum-sig$_5$ **ninda**-šè, "210 liters of of fine gu-flour, 1 bushel of 2nd-quality gu-flour, 210 liters of semolina, 45 liters of KAL-flour, (and) 60 liters of fine kum-flour for bread," 972:1–6, 975:1–6

0.3.0. zì-gu-sig$_5$ 0.4.2 dabin 0.0.5.4 sìla zì-KAL 0.1.0. zì-kum **ninda**-šè, "180 liters of fine gu-flour, 260 liters of semolina, 54 liters of KAL-flour (and) 60 liters of kum-flour for bread," 981:5–9

0.2.0. zì-KAL 0.2.3. zì-gu-ús **ninda**-šè, "120 liters of KAL-flour (and) 150 liters 2nd-quality gu-flour for bread," 1036:'5-'7

0.4.0. **ninda**-zì-šà-gen zì-milla íb-ta-ḫi ½ sìla du$_8$, "240 liters of bread baked (in) ½-liter (loaves) were mixed from ordinary šà-flour (and) milla-flour," 1079:2

6. Broken Context

0.0.1. **ninda** [. . .] ki? [. . .], 507:8

0.0.3. **ninda** [. . .], 509:'9

[. . .] x-NE **ninda** x [. . .], 550:'15

0.1.0. zì-[x] 0.0.2. [. . .] **ninda** [. . .], 1036:'27-'29

0.0.1. **ninda** [. . .], 1036:'52

0.0.1.2 sìla [. . .] **ninda**, 1379:'17

nindan, *nindanu*, "a unit of length," *passim*

gi-**nindan**, "measuring rod" > **gi**

n **nindan** dağal, "n nindan in width"

n **nindan** gíd, "n nindan in length"

n **nindan** ús, "n nindan (is) the length"

ús-bi n **nindan**, "the distance (carried) is n nindan"

[98] Brunke 2008, 147–153 (§§3.1.4.54 – 3.1.4.71).

níta, *zikaru*, "male"

1. PN níta, "PN, the man" > *Personal Name Index*

ad-da-ni	*bi-za-tum*	*ì-lí-[. . .]*
be-lí-a-sú	*i-din-^{d}šamaš*	*in-ga-la*

2. Male, as a Commodity Designation

^{ĝeš}gu-za-**níta**, "man's chair" > **^{ĝeš}gu-za**

^{kuš}e-sír-**níta**, "man's sandals" > **^{kuš}e-sír**

^{kuš}súḫub-**níta**, "man's shoes" > **^{kuš}súḫub**

nu-bànda, *laputtû*, "overseer, captain"

1. PN nu-bànda, "PN, the overseer" > *Personal Name Index*

a-bu-DU$_{10}$	*lu-ša-lim*

nu-bànda-gu$_{4}$, "ox-herder"

1. PN nu-bànda-gu$_{4}$, "PN, the ox-herder" > *Personal Name Index*

a-bí-a-ti	*mu-na-núm*	*šu-^{d}adad*
AN.TAG.KAL	*puzur$_{4}$-a-bi*	*ti-ga-an*
i-me-èr-ra	*puzur$_{4}$*-^{d}en-líl	ur-^{d}dumu-zi
ilum-ba-ni	*puzur$_{4}$-šu-ba*	*za-bu-la*
^{d}*ma-lik-tillati*	*su-ga-ni-a*	

nu-^{ĝeš}kiri$_{6}$, *nukaribbu*, "gardener"

nu-^{ĝeš}kiri$_{6}$ a-pí-sal$_{4}$^{ki}, "gardener of Apisal" > *Toponym Index*

1. PN nu-^{ĝeš}kiri$_{6}$, "PN, the gardener" > *Personal Name Index*

a-da-làl	*ak-ba-zum*	ĜAR-šà-*ti*
a-ḫu-wa-qar	^{d}ba-ú-da	*li-bur-be-lí*

2. Orders for Gardeners

^{d}*adad-tillati* ù-na-a-du$_{11}$ káb-du$_{11}$-ga ĝìri *é-a-šar* ^{ĝeš}zé-na ù peš-[múrgu] **nu-^{ĝeš}kiri$_{6}$-ke$_{4}$-ne** na-ba-ab-sum-mu-⌜dè⌝ šà dub-za ḫa-ba-tur-re, "Say to *Adad-tillati* that 'the gardeners should not give date palm frond midrib(s) and date palm spine(s), commodities (that were) measured for accounting under the authority of *Ea-šar*. Let it be subtracted in your tablet,'" 1037:1–9

^{ĝeš}nu-kúš, "door pivot," 1307:4

^{ĝeš}nu-nir, "(a tree)," 635:6

****^{ĝeš}nu-nir** 1 ĜAR, 1290:3

^{ĝeš}nu-úr-ma, *nurmû*, "pomegranate, pomegranate tree"

^{ĝeš}nu-úr-ma-sig$_{5}$, "fine pomegranate," 1298:1

^{ĝeš}nu-úr-ma-ús, "lesser-quality pomegranate," 1298:2

★★½ ^{ğeš}zúm **nu-úr-ma** é-ba-an, 593:3

numun, *zēru*, "seed"

33.4.1. še gur **numun**-šè, "33 bushels (and) 250 liters of barley for seed," 543:1–2

numun ga, "leek? seed," 1129:1

– O –

[OCCUPATIONS] > [PROFESSIONS]

[OIL PRODUCTS] > **ì**

– P –

pa, *agappu, aru*, "branch, frond"

pa ku_5, "to cut branches, prune" > **ku_5**

pa ^{ğeš}nimbar, "date palm frond" > **^{ğeš}nimbar**

^{ğeš}pa-kab, "(a tree)"

ḫar **^{ğeš}pa-kab**, "pa-kab seedling," 1256:32, 1375:33

pad, "(meaning uncertain)"

★★[o.n.n.] še [n sì]la ì-ğeš [ğuruš?] SI ^{ğeš}sìg-ga **pad**-dirig [?] ğír-su^{ki} a-a-ba-[šè? . . .] níğ-^{d}b[a-ú-šè?], 970:13–16

pàd, *atû*; *nabû*, "to find, discover; to name, nominate" > *Verb Index*

peš, "date palm heart, palmleaflet (mat)"

5 sìla ésir-é-a **peš**-šè mu GÍN-bal $^{ğeš}kiri_6$-[šè], "5 liters of house bitumen for palmleaflet (mats) [for] the GÍN-bal of the garden," 1008:7–8

16.0.0. **peš** gur IB?-ğar, "16 bushels (of) date palm hearts (?) ," 1248:3

peš-ésir dù, "to plait bitumen(-sealed) palmleaflet (mats)" > **dù**

peš-ésir é dù, "to construct a house with bitumen(-sealed) palmleaflet (mats)" > **dù**

peš ésir ù-ru, "to soak palmleaflet (mats) with bitumen" > **ù-ru**

šu-SAR-**peš**, "palmleaf cord" > **šu-SAR**

1. **peš-múrgu**, "date palm spine," 1037:6, 1190:8, 1215:4, 1237:4, 1306:1, 1350:3

peš-múrgu-bi n, "n date palm spines," 374:'6, 1381:5, 1381:21, 1381:26, 1381:33, 1381:44 (in reference to the amount of date palm spines required to manufacture ^{gi}bisağ ninda-gur_4-ra, ^{gi}ig, ^{gi}kid titab)

péš, *ḫumṣīru*, "a type of large, edible (field) mouse"

šà-gal udu šáḫ mušen **péš** ḫi-a, "fodder of various sheep, pigs, birds (and) mice" > **šà-gal**

1. **péš-g̃eš-gi**, *ušummu*, "a type of large, edible (field) mouse," 472:3, 472:5, 526:10, 979:1, 979:5, 1059:3, 1104:2, 1127:3, 1170:1, 1172:4, 1254:'30

   péš-g̃eš-gi-niga, "fattened mouse,"1053:5

2. **péš-igi-gùn**, "striped-eyed mouse," 541:7, 1059:4, 1127:15, 1138:2, 1152:1, 1172:5, 1254:'31

   péš-igi-gùn-niga, "fattened, striped-eyed mouse," 1053:6, 1060:4

$^{g̃eš}$**pèš**, *tittu*, "fig, fig tree"

ḫar $^{g̃eš}$**pèš** n(-ta), "fig tree seedling(s), n (units) each," 1256:3, 1256:4, 1256:5, 1256:6, 1375:3, 1375:4, 1375:5, 1375:6, 1375:7, 1375:8

peš$_5$, *napāšu*, "(to be) plucked"

lá-ìa 3⅔ [ma-n]a 6⅔ gín siki g̃ír-gul **peš**$_5$**-a**, "the remainder of 3⅔ minas and 6⅔ shekels of plucked g̃ír-gul wool," 593:1

pi-lu-da, *parṣu*; *pilludû*, "ritual, rites"

1 túg ba-tab *tuḫ-ḫu-um*-tur-gen **pi-lu-da**, "1 small ordinary ba-tab *tuḫ-ḫu-um* textile (for) ritual (use)," 787:3

1 ^{túg}níg̃-lam-tur-gen **pi-lu-da**, "1 small ordinary níg̃-lam textile (for) ritual (use)," 787:4

1 túg-guz-za-tur-gen **pi-lu-da**, "1 small ordinary tufted textile (for) ritual (use)," 787:5

pù-sú-LUM, "(a food product?)," 511:79, 972:103, 975:103, 1272:4

5 sìla ì-šáḫ ½ ma-na ***pù-sú-LUM pù-sú-LUM***-šè, "5 liters lard (and) ½ mina *pusuLUM* for *pusulum*," 972:36–38

5 sìla ì-udu ½ ma-n[a ***pù***]***-sú-LUM pù-***⸢***sú***⸣***-LUM***-šè, "5 liters mutton fat (and) ½ mina *pusuLUM* for *pusuLUM*," 975:38–40

[PLANTS] > [AGRICULTURAL PRODUCTS]

[PROFESSIONS and FUNCTIONS]

ad-kub$_4$, "craftsman making reed objects"
àga-ús, "gendarme"
agrig, "steward (of a private household)"
ašgab, "leatherworker"
^{lú}ázlag, "fuller"
dù-a-tar, "type of orchard workman"
dub-sar, "scribe"
géme, "workwoman"
gudu$_4$, "priest"
g̃ìri, "facilitator"
g̃uruš, "workman"
ì-du$_8$, "doorkeeper"
^{lú}kaš$_4$, "runner"
^{lú}kíg̃-gi$_4$-a, "messenger"
^{lú}kíg̃-gi$_4$-a-lugal, "royal messenger"
lú-$^{g̃eš}$tir, "forester"
lú-ùr-ra, "fish-sauce manufacturer"
^{lú}lùnga, "brewer"
má-laḫ$_5$, "sailor"
maškim, "deputy"

muḫaldim, "cook"
na-gada, "herdsman"
nagar, "carpenter"
nam-10, "overseer of 10"
nam-60, "overseer of 60"
nar, "singer"
nu-bànda, "overseer"
nu-bànda-gu$_4$, "oxherder"
nu-^{ĝeš}kiri$_6$, "gardener"
ra$_{(2)}$-gaba, "courier, rider, mounted messenger"
sagi, "cupbearer"
santana, "date orchard administrator"
sipa-mušen, "bird warden"
šà-gu$_4$, "ox-driver"
šabra, "majordomo"
šu-i, "barber"
šu-ku$_6$, "fisherman"
túg-du$_8$, "braider"
ugula, "overseer"

– Q –

qí-il-pu-um, *qilpu*, "skin, peel; bark for tanning?"

kuš-udu ***qí-il-pu-um***, "bark tanned sheep-skin" > **kuš-udu**

– R –

ra, *kanāku*, "to roll (seal)" > *Verb Index*

ra-ṭum, *rāṭu*, "drain(-pipe)"

ra-ṭum dù, "to construct a drain(-pipe)" > **dù**

★★[3 ĝuruš] má-laḫ$_5$ 1 ĝuruš 3 géme ***ra-ṭum****-a* KU-[x] g[ub-ba], "[3] sailors, 1 workman (and) 3 workwomen employed to (?) a drain(-pipe)," 59:46–49

ra$_{(2)}$-gaba, *rākibu*, "courier, rider, mounted messenger"

1. **PN ra$_{(2)}$-gaba**, "PN, the courier" > *Personal Name Index*

ĝìri-né-ì-dab$_5$
^{d}*ma-lik-ba-ni*
nu-úr-ma-ti-šu
pa?-da-^{d}šul-gi

[REEDS] > **gi**

[REED PRODUCTS]

^{gi}ba-an-du$_8$-du$_8$, "(a basket)"
^{gi}*ba-ti-um*, "(a reed container)"
^{gi}bisaĝ, "basket"
^{gi}bisaĝ túg-aš, "single textile basket"
^{gi}bisaĝ-gíd-da-tur sa-ḫa, "small, long, canvas-lined baskets"
^{gi}bunin-bunin, "trough, bowl, bucket"
^{gi}dim, "reed pole" > **^{ĝeš}dim**

^{gi}dur, "rope"
gi é-KU-^{ĝeš}banšur, "reed object (for?) a table"
^{gi}gida$_{x}$, "(a reed object)"
^{gi}gilim, "rope of twined reeds"
^{gi}gur, "a reed basket, a measuring container"
^{gi}gur-dub, "a reed basket"
^{gi}gur-sal-la, "a reed basket (especially for dates, bread)"
^{gi}gúrdub, "a reed basket (for fish, wool)"
gi-guru$_{5}$, "reedwork panel"
^{gi}ḫal, "(a basket)"
^{gi}ig, "reed door"
gi-izi-lá, "torch"
gi-ka-du, "a type of reed shelter"
^{gi}kid, "reed mat"
^{gi}ku-ni-na, "drinking straw"
^{gi}ma-an-sim, "sieve"
^{gi}ma-sá-ab, "(a basket)"
^{gi}níĝ-si-ga, "panel"
gi-nindan, "measuring rod"
gi-sig, "reed hut"
^{gi}zar-zar(-zar), "(a basket)"

[RELATIVE CLAUSES]

1. During Construction

1.1 Disbursal of Building Supplies

u$_{4}$ é-e im sumur ba-aka, "when the house was plastered" > **aka**

u$_{4}$ ĝeš ùr i-im-de$_{6}$-a, "when the roof beams were brought" > **de$_{6}$**

1.2 Disbursal of Rations, Wages, and Commodities

u$_{4}$ al-tar bàd gub-ba, "when they were employed for construction of the (enclosure) wall" > **al-tar**

u$_{4}$ al-tar é-lùnga é-muḫaldim ù é-kíkken gub-ba, "when they were employed for construction of the brewery-kitchen-mill complex" > *Household Index*

u$_{4}$ al-tar-ra gub-ba, "when they were employed for construction > **al-tar**

u$_{4}$ bàd ba-dù-a, "when the (enclosure) wall was constructed" > **dù**

u$_{4}$ bàd (egir) é-a dù-dè, "when the (enclosure) wall (behind) the house was being constructed" > **dù**

u$_{4}$ bàd in-dù-sa-a, "when they constructed the (enclosure) wall" > **dù**

u$_{4}$ é-e im sumur ba-aka, "when the house was plastered" > **aka**

u$_{4}$ ĝeš ùr ba-kéše-rá, "when the roof beams were bound" > **kéše**

u$_{4}$ ká é-lùnga é-muḫaldim ù é kíkken kéše-rá, "when the gate of the brewery-kitchen-mill complex was bound" > **kéše**, *Household Index*

2. During Special Occasions and under Unusual Circumstances

2.1 Disbursal of Assorted Comestibles

u_4 dú-ra i-me-a, "when he was sick" > **me**

u_4 dú-ra i-me é-gal-šè, "when they were sick at the palace" > **me**

u_4 dùb bar-ra-ni in-na-gig-ga, "when his 'outer knee' was hurting him" > **gig**

u_4 igi *šu-kab-tá* ninda in-gu_7-ša-a, "when they ate bread before *Šu-Kabta*" > **gu_7**

u_4 iri-ni-šè ì-g̃en-na-a, "when he went to his city" > **g̃en**

u_4 kaskal-šè i-re-sa-a, "when they went on a journey" > **ri**

u_4 lú é-ne-ne ba-an-ši-sa_{10}-a íb-gu_7, "when the men who bought their houses ate (bread)" > **sa_{10}, gu_7**

u_4 má *ra-ba-tum* $nibru^{ki}$-ta gar-ša-an-na^{ki}-šè in-gíd-sa-a, "when they towed the boat of *Rabatum* from Nippur to Garšana" > **gíd**

u_4 má *simat-^{d}ištaran* é-^{d}šára-ta gar-ša-an-na^{ki}-šè mu-un-gíd-ša-a, "when they towed the boat of *Simat-Ištaran* from the Šara temple to Garšana" > **gíd**

u_4 má *simat-^{d}ištaran* gar-ša-an-na^{ki}-ta *$puzur_4$-iš-^{d}da-gan^{ki}*-šè in-gíd-sa-a, "when they towed the boat of *Simat-Ištaran* from Garšana to *Puzriš-Dagan*" > **gíd**

u_4 má *simat-^{d}ištaran $puzur_4$-iš-^{d}da-gan^{ki}*-ta gar-ša-an-na^{ki}-šè mu-un-gíd-ša-a, "when they towed the boat of *Simat-Ištaran* from *Puzriš-Dagan* to Garšana" > **gíd**

u_4 *šu-kab-ta* G̃EŠ.$KÚŠU^{ki}$-šè du-ni u_4 *šu-kab-ta* G̃EŠ.$KÚŠU^{ki}$-ta du-ni, "when *Šu-Kabta* went to G̃EŠ.KÚŠU and when *Šu-Kabta* came form G̃EŠ.KÚŠU" > **g̃en**

2.2 Employment of Workers

u_4 dabin *i-zi-in-èr-ra^{ki}*-ta g̃ar-ša-an-na^{ki}-šè de_6-a, "when semolina was brought from *Izin-Erra* to Garšana" > **de_6**

u_4 *e-lu-núm*-$^{d}nergal_x^{eri11\text{-}gal}$ šà iri^{ki}, "during the *Elunum* the festival of Nergal in the city" > *Deities Index*

2.2.1 Errands to be Run

u_4 *šu-kab-tá* é-dam-*zé-ra-ra* šu sum-mu-dè ì-g̃en-na-a, "when *Šu-Kabta* came to the house of the wife of *Zerara* in order to take inventory" > **g̃en**

2.2.2 Workers Employed to Mourn

u_4 dig̃ir-re gaba *na-wi-ir-ilum* ba-a-g̃ar-ra, "when the god made the breast of *Nawir-ilum* subside (i.e. when he died)" > **g̃ar**

u_4 lugal-e ba-úš-a, "when the king died" > **úš**

u_4 PN ba-úš-a, "when PN died" > **úš**

Nawir-ilum

Šu-Kabta

3. Broken Context

**u_4 *ša-lim-a-ḫu-um* [. . .] nu-un-na-an-[. . .] in-na-RU-[. . .], 1052:5–7

ri, *alāku*, "to go, walk along" > *Verb Index*

– S –

sa, *kiššu*, "bundle (of reeds)"

sa gi-izi, "bundle of fuel reeds" > **gi-izi**

sa gi-šid, "bundle of dry reeds" > **gi-šid**

sa gi-zi, "bundle of fresh reeds" > **gi-zi**

n **sa** gi-zi gu-níĝin n-**sa**-ta, "n bundle(s) of fresh reeds, bales of n bundle(s) each" > **gi-zi**

sa-níĝin ^{ĝeš}ásal, "bundle of poplar wood" > **^{ĝeš}ásal**

sa ^{ú}sullim, "bundle of fenugreek" > **^{ú}sullim**

[. . .]-da-tur [. . .]-x nu-ub-kíĝ [n+]½ kùš daĝal 1 kùš [x]-bi 3 **sa [šeg$_{12}$]-bi 60 [ús-bi] u$_{4}$-2½-kam [x] ^{gi}gur-bi-kam, 374:'14-'18

sa, *matnu*, "sinew, tendon"

sa-udu, "sheep sinew," 459:3, 840:3, 855:3, 855:7, 855:18, 898:4, 926:3, 943:4, 958:2, 1517:5, 1517:8

14 gín **sa-udu** udu ba-úš-ta, "14 shekels of sheep sinew from dead sheep," 1091:1–2

sa . . . gi$_{4}$, *šutērušû*, "to prepare" > *Verb Index*

sa-gi$_{4}$-a, *eršû*, "prepared or finished (textiles)" > **túg-sa-gi$_{4}$-a**

sa-ḫa, "canvas, cloth"[99]

^{gi}bisaĝ-gíd-da **sa-ḫa**, "long canvas-lined basket" > **^{gi}bisaĝ**

^{gi}bisaĝ-im-sar-ra **sa-ḫa**, "canvas-lined clay tablet coffer" > **^{gi}bisaĝ**

^{gi}ig-dur **sa-ḫa**, "reed door (with) canvas ropes" > **^{gi}ig**

sa-par$_{4}$, *sapāru*, "a net"

20 ma-na gu-^{ĝeš}ba *zi-ba-tum* mu **sa-par$_{4}$-šè, "20 minas of (?) cord for a net," 1162:'55-'56

sá, *kašādu*, "to equal; to reach, arrive" > *Verb Index*

sá-du$_{11}$, *sattukku*, "regular offering; provision"

1. Regular Offerings for Deities

1.1 For Enlil

1 [udu] **sá-du$_{11}$**-^{d}en-[líl?], "1 [sheep], regular offerings of Enlil," 1003:3–4

---

[99] For sa-ḫa, "canvas, cloth," compare *CAD* A/1 96 s.v. *šaḫḫû* (Heimpel, personal communication).

1.2 For Inana of Zabala

1 udu **sá-du$_{11}$**-^{d}inana-zabala$_{4}^{ki}$, "1 sheep, regular offerings of Inana of Zabala," 1000:1–2, 1010:1–2, 1012:1, 1021:1–2

3 sìla níĝ-àr-ra-sig$_{5}$ [n sìla] zì [n sìla] dabin [n sìla] eša [. . .]-rú?-maḫ [**sá-du$_{11}$**-^{d}ina]na-zabala$_{4}^{ki}$, "3 liters of fine groats, [n liter(s)] of flour, [n liter(s)] of semolina (and) [n liter(s)] of fine flour, [... regular offerings] of Inana of Zabala," 1027:7–12

1.3 For Multiple Deities

(. . .) [**sá**]-**du$_{11}$**-diĝir-re-e-ne, "{assorted comestibles}, regular offerings of deities," 511:44, 1036:'78

1 udu abzu-šè 1 máš ká kù-^{d}inana-zabala$_{4}^{ki}$ u$_{4}$ ezem-gur-buru$_{14}$ ĝìri nin-zi-šà-ĝál 1 u$_{8}$ **sá-du$_{11}$**-^{d}inana-zabala$_{4}^{ki}$ 1 udu **sá-du$_{11}$**-^{d}šára sá-du$_{11}$-diĝir-re-ne, "regular offerings of the gods: 1 sheep for the abzu, 1 goat for the gate of bright Inana of Zabala during the bushel harvest festival under the authority of Nin-zišaĝal (and) 1 ewe, regular offerings of Inana of Zabala (and) 1 sheep, regular offerings of Šara," 996:1–9

1.4 For Nana

12 udu **sá-du$_{11}$**-^{d}na-na *a-ḫu-a*, "(In total:) 12 sheep, regular offerings of Nana, (the personal deity of) *Aḫu'a*," 984:'44-'45

1.5 For Nin-Siana

1 gú [n ma-na] báppir-sig$_{5}$ **sá-du$_{11}$**-^{d}nin-^{d}si$_{4}$-an-na, "1 talent (and) [n mina(s)] of fine beer bread, regular offerings of Nin-Siana," 1020:1–2

[6.2.0. ninda gur **sá-du$_{11}$** ^{d}nin-^{d}si$_{4}$-an-na], "[6 bushels (and) 120 liters of bread, regular offerings of Nin-Siana]," 1527:1–2

1.5.1 For Nin-Siana, (the personal deity of) *Aḫu'a*

[n] udu ⌜**sá**⌝-**du$_{11}$**-^{d}nin-$^{[d]}$si$_{4}$-an-na *a-ḫu-a*, "[n] sheep, regular offerings of Nin-Siana, (the personal deity of) *Aḫu'a*," 982:1–2

1.5.2 For the Sanctuary of Nin-Siana

[2.2.0. **sá-du$_{11}$** zà-gu-lá ^{d}nin-^{d}si$_{4}$-an-na], "[2 bushels (and) 120 liters, regular offerings of the sanctuary of Nin-Siana]," 1527:3

1.5.3 Deducted Offerings

1 udu-niga é-u$_{4}$-7 iti u$_{4}$-[7]-ba-zal 1 ⌜udu⌝-niga é-[u$_{4}$]-10 iti u$_{4}$-10-⌜ba⌝-zal **sá-du$_{11}$**-ku$_{5}$-rá ^{d}nin-^{d}si$_{4}$-an-na, "1 fattened sheep at the end of the [7th] day of the month, i.e. the half-moon day, 1 fattened sheep at the end of the 10th day of the month, i.e. the 3/4? moon day, deducted regular offerings of Nin-Siana," 985:1–8

1.6 For the Royal Statue

[2.4.0. **sá-du$_{11}$** a]lam-lugal, "[2 bushels (and) 240 liters, regular offerings] of the royal statue," 1527:4

1.7 For Šara of ĜEŠ.KÚŠU

1 udu **sá-du$_{11}$**-^{d}šára-ĜEŠ.KÚŠU^{ki}, "1 sheep, regular offerings of Šara of ĜEŠ.KÚŠU," 1000:3–4, 1010:3–4, 1012:2, 1021:3–4

1.8 Divine Name Broken

12 udu **sá-du$_{11}$**-^{d}[. . .], "(In total:) 12 sheep, regular offerings of [. . .]," 984:'47-'48

1 udu **sá-[du$_{11}$**-^{d}. . .], "1 sheep, regular offering of [. . .]," 1003:1–2, 1003:5–6

0.1.[n . . .] x x [. . .] 30 [ma-na báppir-sig$_5$] SAḪAR? munu$_4$-[si-è] **sá-du$_{11}$**-[^{d}. . .] (. . .) **sá-du$_{11}$**-diğir-re-e-ne, " 60[+n liters . . .], 30 [minas of fine beer bread], (?), sprouted malt, regular offerings of [. . .], (and) {other offerings}, regular offerings of the gods," 1036:'22-'26, '78

12 ma-n[a báppir-gen] 0.0.2. munu$_4$-[si-è] 0.0.3.1⅔ sìla [. . .] kaš-gen [. . .] 1 sìla [. . .] 30 dug [. . .] **sá-du$_{11}$**-^{d}n[in-. . .] (. . .) **sá-du$_{11}$**-diğir-re-e-ne, "12 minas [of ordinary beer bread], 20 liters [of sprouted] malt, 31⅔ liters [. . .], [. . .] ordinary beer, 1 liter [. . .], (and) 30 pots [. . .], regular offerings of Nin-[. . .], (and) {other offerings}, regular offerings of the gods," 1036:'34-'40, '78

[. . .] **sá-[du$_{11}$**-^{d}. . .] (. . .) **sá-du$_{11}$**-diğir-re-e-ne, "[. . .], regular offerings of [. . .], (and) {other offerings}, regular offerings of the gods," 1036:'42, '78

3⅓ [sìla . . .] 0.0.1. ninda [. . .] 0.0.1. níğ-[àr-ra-x] 0.0.1. munu$_4$-[si-è] **sá-du$_{11}$**-^{d}[. . .] šà MÙŠ.ZA.[UNUG^{ki} . . .] (. . .) **sá-du$_{11}$**-diğir-re-e-ne, "3⅓ [liters . . .], 10 liters [. . .] bread, 10 liters [x] groats, (and) 10 liters [sprouted] malt, regular offerings of [. . .] in Zabala [. . .], (and) {other offerings}, regular offerings of the gods," 1036:'51-'56, '78

2. Regular Offerings for Funerary Libation Places

2.1 Of *Nawir-ilum*

12 udu **sá-du$_{11}$**-ki-a-nağ-*na-wi-ir-ilum*, "12 sheep, regular offerings of the funerary libation place of *Nawir-ilum*," 982:3–4

2.2 Of *Šu-Kabta*

2.2.1 Animals

1 šáḫ-zé-da iti u$_4$-1-ba-zal 1 máš-gal-niga iti u$_4$-10-ba-zal 1 šáḫ-zé-da iti u$_4$-15-ba-zal 1 udu-aslum$_x$-niga-babbar iti u$_4$-20-ba-zal 1 udu-niga-babbar iti u$_4$-28-ba-zal **sá-du$_{11}$**-ki-a-nağ-*šu*-[*kab*]-*tá*, "1 piglet at the end of the 1st day of the month, 1 fattened billy-goat at the end of the 10th day of the month, 1 piglet at the end of the 15th day of the month, 1 fattened white long fleeced sheep at the end of the 20th day of the month (and) 1 fattened white sheep at the end of the 28th day of the month, regular offerings of the funerary libation place of *Šu-Kabta*," 973:1–8

1 šáḫ-zé-[da] u$_4$-1-[kam] 1 udu-niga u$_4$-10-kam 1 tum$_{12}$mušen u$_4$-15-kam 1 udu-niga u$_4$-20-kam 1 udu-niga 1 tum$_{12}$^{mušen} u$_4$-28-kam **sá-du$_{11}$**-ki-a-nağ-*šu-kab-tá*, "1 piglet on the 1st day, 1 fattened sheep on the 10th day, 1 wild dove on the 15th day, 1 fattened sheep on the 20th day (and) 1 fattened sheep (and) 1 wild dove on the 28th day, regular offerings of the funerary libation place of *Šu-Kabta*," 976:1–9

[1] udu-niga u$_4$-10-kam 1 šáḫ-zé-da 1 tu-gur$_4$mušen u$_4$-15-kam 1 udu-niga u$_4$-20-[kam] 1 udu-[niga 1] šáḫ-zé-[da 1] tu-gur$_4$$^{m[ušen]}$ [u$_4$-n-kam] **sá-du$_{11}$**-ki-[a-nağ-*šu-kab-tá*], "[1] fattened sheep on the 10th day, 1 piglet (and) 1 dove on the 15th day, 1 fattened sheep on the 20th day (and) 1 [fattened] sheep, [1] piglet (and) [1] dove [on the nth day], regular offerings of the [funerary libation] place of [*Šu-Kabta*]," 978:1–11

1 péš-ĝeš-gi u$_4$-1-kam 1 udu-niga u$_4$-10-kam 1 péš-ĝeš-gi u$_4$-15-[kam] 1 ^{munus}áš-[gàr u]4-20-[kam] 1 udu-[niga] 1 [. . .] u$_4$-[n-kam] **sá-du$_{11}$**-ki-[a-nağ]-⸢*šu*⸣-[*kab-tá*], "1 mouse on the 1st day, 1 fattened sheep on the 10th day, 1 mouse on the 15th day, 1 female goat on the 20th day, 1 [fattened] sheep (and) 1 [. . .] [on the nth] day, regular offerings of the [funerary libation] place of *Šu-Kabta*," 979:1–14

2.2.2 Assorted Comestibles

(. . .) [**sá-d**]**u**$_{11}$ iti-1-kam (. . .) **sá-du**$_{11}$-ki-a-nağ-*šu-kab-tá*, "{assorted comestibles} regular offerings of the 1st month (and) {other comestibles}, regular offerings of the funerary libation place of *Šu-Kabta*," 972:45, 107, 975:48, 108

(. . .) **sá-du**$_{11}$-ki-a-nağ-*šu-kab-tá*, "{assorted comestibles} regular offerings of the funerary libation of place of *Šu-Kabta*," 981:33

2.2.3 Skins

[n kuš- . . .] 3 kuš-udu-niga **sá-du**$_{11}$-ki-a-nağ-*šu-kab-ta*-ta(sic!?), "[n . . . skin(s)] (and) 3 skins of fattened-sheep, regular offerings of the (funerary) libation place of *Šu-Kabta*," 974:1–4

3. Regular Offerings, Donatee Unspecified

3.1 Animals

16 udu 1 sila$_4$ 7 máš-gal 6 máš **sá-du**$_{11}$-šè ki ^{d}*adad*-⌜SIG$_5$⌝-ta ^{d}*adad-tillati* ì-dab$_5$, "*Adad-tillati* took in charge 16 sheep, 1 lamb, 7 billy-goats, (and) 2 goats for regular offerings from *Adad-ṭabu*," 448:1–7

24 udu-niga 1-sìla-[ta] **sá-du**$_{11}$-šè, "24 fattened sheep, 1 liter of (fodder) [each] for regular offerings," 525:1–2

šu+níğin 60 ^{munus}áš-gàr-niga **sá-du**$_{11}$ (. . .) níğ-kas$_7$-aka ^{d}*adad-tillati* šabra, "In total: 60 female kids, regular offerings, (and) {other animals}, the balanced account of *Adad-tillati*, the majordomo," 984:'59, '75–'76

3.2 Assorted Commodities

(. . .) **sá-du**$_{11}$-šè *ì-lí-aš-ra-ni* šu ba-ti ki ^{d}*adad-tillati*-ta ba-zi, "*Ili-ašranni* received {assorted comestibles and other commodities} for regular offerings from *Adad-tillati*," 523:16–18

(. . .) **sá-du**$_{11}$-[šè] *ba-la-a* šu ba-⌜ti⌝ ki ^{d}*adad-tillati*-ta ⌜ba⌝-zi, "*Bala'a* received {assorted comestibles and other commodities} [for] regular offerings from *Adad-tillati*," 1033:15–18

3.3 Bread, from the Account of *Da'a*, the Cook

0.2.0. ninda šuku ib-šu-bi u$_4$-4-kam 1.0.2. ninda gur **sá-du**$_{11}$ ù ninda dirig ba-ab-daḫ-a iti ezem-me-ki-ğál (. . .) níğ-kas$_7$-aka *da-a-a* muḫaldim, "20 liters of bread of the food allocation, its (?) on the 4th day; 1 bushel (and) 20 liters of bread, regular offerings and additional bread that was added in the 12th month (and) {other allotments}; the balanced account of *Da'a*, the cook," 1031:11–12, 26

3.4 Wood

3 gú ^{ğeš}ma-nu šu aka **sá-du**$_{11}$-šè *ì-lí-aš-ra-ni* šu ba-ti ki ^{d}*adad*-[*tillati*-ta], "*Ili-ašranni* received 3 talents of processed manu wood for regular offerings from *Adad-tillati*," 1351:1–5

4. Regular Offerings Returned from the Shrine

4.1 Of Inana of Zabala

4.1.1 Bread and Skins

9 sìl[a . . .] 8 sìla ninda 1 kuš-máš-gal-niga **sá-du**$_{11}$-^{d}inana-zabala$_4^{ki}$ (. . .) èš-ta-gur-⌜ra⌝, "9 liters [. . .], 8 liters of bread, (and) 1 skin of a fattened billy-goat, regular offerings of Inana of Zabala, (and) {offerings of other deities}, offerings returned from the shrine," 1022:10–12, 15

6 sìla ninda 1 kuš-udu-niga **sá-du$_{11}$**-^{d}inana-zabala$_{4}^{[ki]}$ (. . .) èš-ta-gur-ra, "6 liters of bread (and) 1 skin of a fattened sheep, regular offerings of Inana of Zabala, (and) {offerings of other deities}, offerings returned from the shrine," 1023:11–12, 15

5? sìla š[e-ninda]1 kuš-u[du-niga] **sá-du$_{11}$**-^{d}inana-MÙŠ.ZA.[UNUG]^{ki} (. . .) èš-ta-gur-⸢ra⸣, "5? liters of barley [(for) bread] (and) 1 skin of a [fattened] sheep, regular offerings of Inana of Zabala, (and) {offerings of other deities}, offerings returned from the shrine," 1024:11–13, 17

4.1.2 Grains

(. . .) 0.0.1.7⅔ sìla tuḫ-[duru$_{5}$] **sá-du$_{11}$**-^{d}inana-zabala$_{4}^{ki}$ èš-ta-gur-ra, "{offerings of other deities} (and) 17⅔ liters of [fresh] bran, regular offerings of Inana of Zabala, offerings returned from the shrine," 997:10–12, 1002:11–13

4.1.3 Skins

2 kuš-udu-niga **sá-du$_{11}$**-^{d}inana-zabala$_{4}^{ki}$ (. . .) èš-ta-gur-ra, "2 sheep skins, regular offerings of Inana of Zabala, (and) {offerings of other deities}, offerings returned from the shrine," 1026:9–10, 13

4.2 Of Ninḫursaĝa

9 sìla še-ninda **sá-du$_{11}$**-^{d}nin-ḫ[ur-s]aĝ-ĝá (. . .) èš-ta-gur-ra, "9 liters of barley (for) bread, regular offerings of Ninḫursaĝa (and) {offerings of other deities}, offerings returned from the shrine," 997 :8–9, 12, 1023:10, 15, 1024:9–10, 17, 1026:7–8, 13

4.3 Of Nin-Siana

4.3.1 Grains

0.4.3. še-ninda [?] 0.3.2. tuḫ-duru$_{5}$-sig$_{5}$ [. . .] 0.3.2. tuḫ-duru$_{5}$-sig$_{5}$ [. . .] **sá-du$_{11}$**-^{d}nin-^{d}[si$_{4}$-an-na] èš-ta-gur-ra, "270 liters of [?] barley (for) bread, 200 liters of [. . .] fine fresh bran (and) 200 liters of [. . .] fine fresh bran, regular offerings of Nin-Siana, (and) {offerings of other deities}, offerings returned from the shrine," 997:1–4, 12

[0.n].3. ⸢še⸣ 0.3?.2. tuḫ-duru$_{5}$-⸢sig$_{5}$⸣ 0.3.2. tuḫ-duru$_{5}$-⸢sig$_{5}$⸣-ĝe$_{6}$ **sá-du$_{11}$**-^{d}nin-^{d}[si$_{4}$]-an-na (. . .) èš-ta-gur-ra, "[n+]30 liters of barley, 200 liters of fine fresh bran (and) 200 liters of fine fresh dark bran, regular offerings of Nin-Siana, (and) {offerings of other deities}, offerings returned from the shrine," 1002:1–4, 13

0.2.0. še-ninda 0.1.0. tuḫ-duru$_{5}$-gen **sá-du$_{11}$**-zà-gú-lá-^{d}nin-^{d}si$_{4}$-an-na (. . .) èš-ta-gur-⸢ra⸣, "120 liters of barley (for) bread (and) 60 liters of ordinary fresh bran, regular offerings of the sanctuary of Nin-Siana, (and) {offerings of other deities}, offerings returned from the shrine," 1024:5–6, 17

0.2.0. še-ninda **sá-du$_{11}$**-zà-gú-lá-^{d}nin-^{d}s[i$_{4}$-a]n-⸢na⸣ (. . .) èš-ta-gur-ra, "120 liters of barley (for) bread, regular offerings of the sanctuary of Nin-Siana, (and) {offerings of other deities}, offerings returned from the shrine," 1026:4, 13

4.3.2 Grains and Skins

1.0.2. še-ninda gur 0.3.2. tuḫ-duru$_{5}$-si[g$_{5}$] 0.4.2. tuḫ-duru$_{5}$-si[g$_{5}$-ĝe$_{6}$] 1 kuš-udu-niga 1 kuš-m[áš . . .] **sá-du$_{11}$**-^{d}nin-[^{d}si$_{4}$-an-na] (. . .) èš-ta-gur-⸢ra⸣, "1 bushel (and) 20 liters of barley (for) bread, 200 liters of fine fresh bran, 260 liters of fine fresh [dark] bran, 1 skin of a fattened sheep (and) 1 skin of a [. . .] goat, regular offerings of Nin-Siana, (and) {offerings of other deities}, offerings returned from the shrine," 1022:1–5, 15

1.0.2. še-ninda gur 0.2.3. tuḫ-duru$_5$-sig$_5$ 0.3.2. tuḫ-duru$_5$-sig$_5$-g̃e$_6$ 2 kuš-udu-niga **sá-du$_{11}$**-^{d}nin-^{d}si$_4$-an-na (. . .) èš-ta-gur-ra, "1 bushel (and) 20 liters of barley (for) bread, 150 liters of fine fresh bran, 200 liters of fine fresh dark bran (and) 2 skins of fattened sheep, regular offerings of Nin-Siana, (and) {offerings of other deities}, offerings returned from the shrine," 1023:1–5, 15, 1024:1–4, 17

1.0.2. še-ninda gur 1 kuš-udu-niga **sá-du$_{11}$**-^{d}nin-^{d}si$_4$-an-na (. . .) èš-ta-gur-ra, "1 bushel (and) 120 liters of barley (for) bread (and) 1 skin of a fattened sheep, regular offerings of Nin-Siana, (and) {offerings of other deities}, offerings returned from the shrine," 1026:1–3, 13

4.3.3 Of Nin-Siana's Sanctuary

0.2.0. še-[ninda . . .] 0.1.0. tuḫ-duru$_5$-gen **sá-du$_{11}$**-zà-gú-lá-^{d}nin-^{d}si$_4$-an-na šà é-a (. . .) èš-ta-gur-ra, "120 liters of barley [(for) bread...] (and) 60 liters of ordinary fresh bran, regular offerings of the sanctuary of Nin-Siana in the house, (and) {offerings of other deities}, offerings returned from the shrine," 997:5–7, 12

0.2.0. še [ninda . . .] **sá-du$_{11}$**-z[à-g]ú-lá-^{d}[nin-si$_4$]-an-na š[à é-a] (. . .) èš-ta-gur-⸢ra⸣, "20 liters of barley [(for) bread], regular offerings of the sanctuary of Nin-Siana in [the house], (and) {offerings of other deities}, offerings returned from the shrine," 1022:6–7, 15

0.2.0. še-ninda 0.1.0. tuḫ-duru$_5$-gen **sá-du$_{11}$**-zà-gú-lá-^{d}nin-^{d}si$_4$-an-na (. . .) èš-ta-gur-ra, "120 liters of barley (for) bread (and) 60 liters of ordinary fresh bran, regular offerings of the sanctuary of Nin-Siana, (and) {offerings of other deities}, offerings returned from the shrine," 1023:6–7, 15

4.4 Of the Royal Statue

1 sìla še-[ninda . . .] **sá-du$_{11}$**-ala[m-lugal] (. . .) èš-ta-gur-⸢ra⸣, "1 liter of barley [(for) bread . . .], regular offerings of the royal statue, (and) {offerings of other deities}, offerings returned from the shrine," 1022:8–9, 15

n še-ninda n tuḫ-duru$_5$-gen **sá-du$_{11}$**-alam-lugal (. . .) èš-ta-gur-ra, "n liter(s) of barley (for) bread (and) n liter(s) of ordinary fresh bran, regular offerings of the royal statue, (and) {offerings of other deities}, offerings returned from the shrine," 1023:8–9, 15, 1024: 7-8,17

0.1.3. še-ninda **sá-du$_{11}$**-alam-lugal (. . .) èš-ta-gur-ra, "90 liters of barley (for) bread, regular offerings of the royal statue, (and) {offerings of other deities}, offerings returned from the shrine," 1026:5–6, 13

4.5 Of Šara of G̃EŠ.KÚŠU

(. . .) 5 sìla še-ninda 1 kuš-udu-niga **sá-du$_{11}$**-^{d}šára-G̃EŠ.KUŠÚ èš-ta-gur-ra, "5 liters of barley (for) bread (and) 1 skin of a fattened sheep, (and) {offerings of other deities}, regular offerings of Šara of G̃EŠ.KÚŠU, offerings returned from the shrine," 1022:13–15, 1023:13–15, 1024:14–17

(. . .) 1 kuš-udu-niga **sá-du$_{11}$**-^{d}šára-G̃EŠ.KÚŠU^{ki} èš-ta-gur-ra, "{offerings of other deities} (and) 1 skin of a fattened sheep, regular offerings of Šara of G̃EŠ.KÚŠU, offerings returned from the shrine," 1026:10–13

4.6 Divine Name Broken

0.2.0. š[e. . .] 0.1.0. tuḫ-[duru$_5$-. . .] **sá-d[u$_{11}$** . . .] 0.0.1. [. . .] 0.0.1.5 sìla [. . .] **sá-du$_{11}$** ^{d}nin-[. . .] (. . .) èš-ta-gur-ra, , "120 liters [. . .] barley (and) 60 liters [. . . fresh] bran, regular offerings of [. . .], (and) 10 liters [. . .] (and) 15 liters [. . .], regular offerings of

Nin-[. . .], (and) {offerings of other deities}, offerings returned from the shrine," 1002:5–10, 13

5. Redistribution of Commodities of Regular Offerings

5.1 Animals

5.1.1 From the Regular Offerings of *Šu-Kabta*, Recipient Unspecified

šu+níĝin 1 udu-⌜niga⌝ šu+níĝin 1 udu-ú šu+níĝin 1 máš-gal-niga šu+níĝin 2 [. . .] šu+níĝin 3 lulim?-dar?-[x] šu+níĝin 1 šáḫ-zé-da **sá-du$_{11}$**-ta?-*šu-kab-tá*, "In total: 1 fattened sheep, 1 range-fed sheep, 1 fattened billy-goat, 2 [. . .], 3 speckled stags (and) 1 piglet from? the regular offerings of *Šu-Kabta*," 983:18–24

5.2 Assorted Commodities

5.2.1 For the House of the Steward

(. . .) dirig **sá-du$_{11}$**-é-agrig-šè, "{assorted comestibles on the nth and nth days}, surplus of the regular offerings for the house of the steward," 493:19, 494:17

0.0.2. [. . .] 0.1.0. ninda dabin dirig **sá-du$_{11}$**-é-agrig-[šè], "20 liters [. . .] (and) 60 liters of semolina bread, surplus of the regular offerings [for] the house of the steward," 501:1–9

5.2.2 For *Rabatum* and *Šu-Suen-etelpi*-Enlil

(. . .) dirig **sá-du$_{11}$**-u$_4$-[n-šè] *ra-ba-tum* ù ^{d}*šu*-^{d}E[N.ZU]-[*e*]-*te-íl-pi$_4$*-^{d}en-lí[l sugal u]4 ezem-*a-bu-um*, "{assorted commodities}, surplus of the regular offerings on the [nth] day of *Rabatum* and *Šu-Suen-etelpi*-Enlil, [the sugal], during the *Abum* festival," 509:'12–'14

5.2.3 For Various Individuals

(. . .) [iti]-6-kam 23⅓ ma-na báppir-sig$_5$ še-bi 0.0.3.5 sìla **sá-du$_{11}$** ku$_5$-rá iti-6-kam [šu+níĝin 10+]1.3.3.5 sìla še ninda gur [sag-níĝ]-gur$_{11}$-ra-kam [šà-b]i-ta, "{regular offerings of deities} of the 6th month, 23⅓ minas of fine beer bread, their barley (equivalent) is 35 liters, deducted regular offerings of the 6th month—in total: 11 bushels (and) 215 liters of barley (for) bread—are the available assets. From among it: {barley rations and requisitions for various individuals}," 1527:6–13

5.3 Skins

5.3.1 Receipt of *Adad-tillati*

2 kuš-udu-niga 2 kuš-udu kuš-udu **sá-du$_{11}$** ^{d}*adad-tillati* šu ba-an-ti, "*Adad-tillati* received 2 skins of fattened sheep (and) 2 sheep skins, sheep skins of regular offerings," 869:1–5

1 kuš-udu-niga 1 kuš-máš-gal-niga 2 kuš-udu kuš-udu **sá-du$_{11}$** ^{d}*adad-tillati* šu ba-a[n-t]i, "*Adad-tillati* received 1 skin of a fattened sheep, 1 skin of a fattened billy-goat (and) 2 sheep skins, caprid skins of regular offerings," 885:1–6

5.3.2 Receipt of *Anaḫ-ili*, Disbursal of *Adad-tillati*

1 kuš-udu-niga 1 kuš-máš-niga kuš-udu **sá-du$_{11}$** ki ^{d}*adad-tillati*-ta *a-na-aḫ-ì-lí* šu ba-an-ti, "*Anaḫ-ili* received 1 skin of a fattened sheep (and) 1 skin of a fattened billy-goat, caprid skins of regular offerings, from *Adad-tillati*," 851:1–6

1 kuš-sila$_4$-niga 1 kuš-máš-gal-niga kuš-udu **sá-du$_{11}$** ki ^{d}*adad-tillati*-ta *a-na-aḫ-ì*-[*lí*] šu ba-an-ti, "*Anaḫ-ili* received 1 skin of a fattened lamb skin (and) 1 skin of a fattened billy-goat, caprid skins of regular offerings, from *Adad-tillati*," 861:1–6

1 kuš-[x] 1 kuš-⌜udu⌝ 2 kuš-[x] kuš-udu zi-[ga] 2 kuš-udu kuš-udu **sá-du$_{11}$** ki ^{d}*adad-tillati*-ta *a-na-aḫ-ì-lí* šu ba-an-ti, "*Anaḫ-ili* received an expenditure of caprid skins (consisting) of 1 [x] skin, 1 sheep skin, (and) 2 [x] skins (and) 2 sheep skins, sheep skins of regular offerings, from *Adad-tillati*," 867:1–9

1 kuš-udu 1 kuš-máš-gal kuš-udu **sá-du$_{11}$** ki ^{d}*adad-tillati*-ta *a-*[*na-aḫ*]*-ì-lí* šu ba-an-ti, "*Anaḫ-ili* received 1 sheep skin (and) 1 billy-goat skin, caprid skins of regular offerings, from *Adad-tillati*," 877:1–6

51 kuš-udu-niga 10 kuš-máš-gal 1 kuš-máš-niga 1 kuš-sila$_4$-niga [kuš]-udu zi-ga [n kuš]-udu-niga [kuš]-udu **sá-du$_{11}$** 2 kuš-udu-niga kuš-udu ba-úš ki ^{d}*adad-tillati*-ta *a-na-aḫ-ì-lí* šu ba-ti, "*Anaḫ-ili* received 51 skins of fattened sheep, 10 billy-goat skins, 1 skin of a fattened goat, (and) 1 skin of a fattened lamb, expended caprid skins, [n] [skin(s)] of fattened sheep, caprid skins of regular offerings, (and) 2 skins of fattened sheep, skin of dead sheep, from *Adad-tillati*," 922:1–11

2 kuš-udu-niga kuš-udu **sá-du$_{11}$** ki ^{d}*adad-tillati*-ta *a-na-aḫ-ì-lí* šu ba-an-ti, "*Anaḫ-ili* received 2 skins of fattened sheep, sheep skins of regular offerings, from *Adad-tillati*," 1516:1–5

5.3.2.1 The Offerings of Inana of Zabala and Šara of ĞEŠ.KÚŠU

1 kuš-udu **sá-du$_{11}$**-^{d}inana-zabala$_4$^{ki} 1 kuš-máš sá-du$_{11}$-^{d}šára-ĞEŠ.KÚŠU^{ki} ki ^{d}*adad-tillati*-ta *a-na-aḫ-ì-lí* šu ba-ti, "*Anaḫ-ili* received 1 sheep skin, regular offerings of Inana of Zabala, (and) 1 goat skin, regular offerings of Šara of ĞEŠ.KÚŠU, from *Adad-tillati*," 860:1–7

5.3.2.2 The Offerings of Nin-Siana

1 kuš-máš-gal-niga **sá-du$_{11}$**-^{d}nin-^{d}si$_4$-an-na ki ^{d}*adad-tillati*-ta [*a-na*]*-aḫ-ì-lí* [šu ba]-ti, "*Anaḫ-ili* received 1 skin of a fattened billy-goat, regular offerings of Nin-Siana, from *Adad-tillati*," 842:1–5

2 kuš-udu-niga **sá-du$_{11}$**-^{d}nin-^{d}si$_4$-an-na ki ^{d}*adad-tillati*-ta *a-na-aḫ-ì-lí*, "*Anaḫ-ili* received 2 skins of fattened sheep, regular offerings of Nin-Siana, from *Adad-tillati*," 874:1–4

5.4 Commodity Broken

5.4.1 For *Libur*, the Gudu-priest: the Offerings of Nin-Siana

[lá-ì]a 2.1.1.5 sìla [x lá]-ìa šà **sá-du$_{11}$**-^{d}nin-[^{d}si$_4$]-an-na-ta lá-ìa-àm *li-bur* gudu$_4$ in-[da]-ĝál, "the remainder of 2 bushels (and) 75 liters of [x], the remainder of the regular offerings from Nin-Siana are with *Libur*, the gudu-priest," 998:1–5

6. Regular Provisions

6.1 Animals: Provisions of *Simat-Ištaran*

1 *mu-du-lum* udu-niga saĝ u$_4$-sakar 1 *mu-du-lum* udu-niga é-u$_4$-15 **sá-du$_{11}$** *simat-*^{d}*ištaran* é-gal-ta *lú-ša-lim* šu ba-an-ti, "*Lušallim* received 1 salted fattened sheep on the new moon day (and) 1 salted fattened sheep on the full moon day, regular provisions of *Simat-Ištaran*, from the palace," 375:1–8

6.2 Assorted Commodities: Provisions of *Ummi-Kabta*

3⅓ sìla níĝ-àr-ra 3⅓ sìla ar-za-na [3?] ⅓ sìla gú-tur al-ús-sa 60 sa gi-izi ⌜**sá**⌝**-du$_{11}$**-*um-mi-kab-ta* dumu-[munus] é-a, "3⅓ liters of groats, 3⅓ liters of barley-grits, [3?] ⅓ liters of processed peas (and) 60 bundles of fuel reeds, regular provisions of *Ummi-Kabta*, daughter of the house," 416:1–5

6.3 Beer

6.3.1 Provisions for Construction Workers

7 sìla kaš-gen dirig **sá-du$_{11}$** šidim ù ugula lú-ḫuĝ-ĝá-e-ne íb-naĝ, "the builders and overseer of hired workers drank 7 liters of ordinary beer, surplus of the regular provisions," 400:1–3

0.0.1.6 sìla kaš-gen **sá-du$_{11}$** šidim-e-ne u$_4$ bàd ba-dù-a, "16 liters of ordinary beer, regular provisions of the builders, when the (enclosure) wall was constructed," 478:1–6

6.3.2 Provisions for Individuals

0.0.1. kaš-sig$_5$ 0.0.4. kaš-gen **sá-du$_{11}$**-*ra-ba-tum*, "10 liters of fine beer (and) 40 liters of regular beer, regular provisions of *Rabatum*," 505:1–3, 507:1–3, 508:1–3

5 sìla kaš-sig$_5$ 0.0.1. kaš-[gen **sá**]-**du$_{11}$**-^{d}*šu*-^{d}[*suen*]-*e-te-íl-pi$_4$*-^{d}en-líl, "5 liters of fine beer (and) 10 liters of regular beer, regular provisions of *Šu-Suen-etelpi*-Enlil," 505:4–6, 507:4–6, 508:4–6

6.4 Reeds: for *Tadin-Eštar*

300 sa gi-izi **sá-du$_{11}$**-*tá-din-eš$_4$-tár*, "300 bundles of fuel reeds, regular provisions of *Tadin-Eštar*," 516:1–3

6.5 Commodity Broken: for *Tadin-Eštar*

1 [. . .] **sá-du$_{11}$** *tá*-⸢*din*⸣-*eš$_4$-tár*, "1 [. . .], regular provisions of *Tadin-Eštar*," 513:1–3

sà-ḫum^{zabar}, *šāḫu*, "(a bronze drinking or cooking vessel)"

1 ***sà-ḫum***^{zabar} 5/6 ma-na, "1 *sa-ḫum* vessel of 5/6 mina," 1337:5

2 ***sà-ḫum***^{zabar} 5/6 ma-na 4-gín-ta, "2 *sa-ḫum* vessels of 5/6 mina (and) 4 shekels each," 1337:4

sa$_{10}$, *šâmu*, "to buy/purchase" > *Verb Index*

1. Prices: Barley Equivalents

15 gín **sa$_{10}$**+didli 10 še ì-šáḫ, "10 barley corn of lard (worth) 15 shekels," 828:4

[n+]⅓ ma-na 9 gín siki-gen **sa$_{10}$** ⸢kislaḫ⸣ 1 sar 9? gín-kam, "[n+]⅓ minas and 9 shekels of ordinary wool, the price of 1 sar and 9? gín of uncultivated land," 681:1–2

[n.n.n.] še gur **sa$_{10}$** saḫar 48-kam *tá-din-eš$_4$-tár* 0.4.0. še **sa$_{10}$** saḫar 12-kam *ša-at-èr-ra* ninda du$_8$-dè-⸢šè⸣, "[n] bushel(s) (and) [n liter(s)] of barley, the price of 48 units of dirt for *Tadin-Eštar* (and) 240 liters of barley, the price of 12 units of dirt for *Šat-Erra* to bake bread," 1169:1–6

[n.n.n] še [. . . n.n.n.] siki-gen [n.n.]3?. ⸢gur?⸣ [. . .] gi-šid 3255 sa **sa$_{10}$** gi-zi 0.0.1. še gi 13 sa-ta, "[n] liter(s) of [. . .] barley, [n] liter(s) of ordinary wool, [. . .] (and) 3255 bundles of dry reeds, the price of fresh reeds is 10 liters of barley for reeds of 13 bundles each," 1320:1–5

(. . .) šu-sum-ma ĝìri *ib-ni*-^{d}*adad* d[ub-sar] iti ezem-me-ki-ĝál ba-zal mu en-^{d}inana-unu^{ki}-ga máš-e ì-pàd 0.0.1.2½ sìla ^{na4}ŠEM? še-ta **sa$_{10}$-a** saĝ-níĝ-gur$_{11}$-ra-kam, "{millstones, diorite stones, woods, yokes (and) wooden containers}, the consignment under the authority of *Ibni-Adad*, the scribe, at the end of the 12th month of *Ibbi-Suen* Year 2; (and) 12½ liters ^{na4}ŠEM, the price from barley; (these) are the available assets," 1372:46–53

★★0.2.1.3⅓ sìla [. . . -g]en **sa$_{10}$** ki-siki ½ [. . .]-kam ù é-^{d}[. . .], "133⅓ liters of ordinary [. . .], the (?) price of ½ [. . .] and the [DN] temple," 1391:1–2

540 sa gi-izi **sa$_{10}$** še 0.0.1. 20 sa gi-ta še-bi 0.4.3., "540 bundles of fuel reeds, the price of which is 10 liters of barley for each 20 bundles of reeds, their barley is 270 (liters)," 1527: 35–37

2. Prices: Silver Equivalents

★★0.3.2.4 sìla [x] **sa$_{10}$** kù-babbar 1⅓ šar kam?, "204 liters [x], the price (in) silver is 1⅓ (?)," 1139:1–2

3. Prices: Hire of Sailors

[. . .] 0.1.0.8 s[ìla š]e-bi **sa$_{10}$** má-laḫ$_{5}$-e-ne 6.1.1.4 sìla še gur še ù-dag-ga[^{ki}-ta gar]-ša-an-na[^{ki}-šè] de$_{6}$-[a], "[. . . (and)] 68 liters of barley is the (hiring) price of the sailors. (In total:) 6 bushels (and) 74 liters of barley having been brought [from] Udaga [to] Garšana," 553:54–59

[. . .] á g̃uruš-[a . . .] 0.0.1.6 sìla še-bi **sa$_{10}$** má-laḫ$_{5}$-e-ne u$_{4}$-1-[šè] é-duru$_{5}$-kab-⌜bí⌝-ta é-duru$_{5}$-*simat*-^{d}*ištarān*-šè má diri-ga, "[. . .] wages of workmen [. . .], 16 liters of barley is the (hiring) price of the sailors [for] 1 day having floated boats from the Kabbi village to the village of *Simat-Ištaran*," 561:'1-'5

0.2.3. á má-ḫug̃-g̃á 0.2.0. á g̃uruš ḫug̃-g̃á 0.0.1.6 šà-gal má-laḫ$_{5}$ 0.0.1.6 <še->bi **sa$_{10}$** má-laḫ$_{5}$ u$_{4}$-1-šè gú i$_{7}$-^{d}nin-ḫur-sag̃-g̃á-ta [gar-ša-an-na^{ki}-šè má] gíd-da, "150 liters (of barley), wages of the hired boat (and) 120 liters, wages of hired workmen; 16 liters, food (for) sailors, 16 liters of <barley> is the (hiring) price of the sailors [for] 1 day having towed [boats] from the bank of the Ninḫursag̃a canal [to Garšana]," 561:'19-'23

0.2.3. á má-ḫug̃-g̃á 0.2.0. á g̃uruš ḫug̃-g̃á 0.0.1.6 sìla šà-gal má-laḫ$_{5}$ 0.0.1.6 sìla < še->b[i **s]a$_{10}$** má-⌜laḫ$_{5}$⌝ u$_{4}$-1-šè é-duru$_{5}$-ka[b-bí-ta] gú i$_{7}$-[*ma-an-iš-ti-šu*-šè] má gí[d-da], "140 liters (of barley), wages of the hired boat (and) 120 liters, wages of hired workmen; 16 liters, food (for) sailors, 16 liters <of barley> is the (hiring) price of the sailors for 1 day having towed boats [from] the Kabbi village [to] the bank of the [*Maništišu*] canal," 561:'28-'32

4. Broken or Uncertain Context

★★⌜**sa$_{10}$**⌝-bi g̃eš 1 [x x]-na-[x], 536:22–26

sagi, *šāqû*, "cupbearer"

1. PN sagi, "PN, the cupbearer" > *Personal Name Index*

i-sú-a-ri-iq	^{d}nin-^{d}si$_{4}$-an-na	še-da
išdum-ki-in	SIPAD-*si-in*	*šu*-^{d}nin-girim$_{x}$
nam-ḫa-ni		

^{túg}**sagšu**, *kubšu*, "cap"

^{túg}**sagšu** ba-tab *tuḫ-ḫu-um*, "ba-tab *tuḫ-ḫu-um* cap," 744:2, 773:9

^{túg}**sagšu** ba-tab *tuḫ-ḫu-um* 3-kam-ús, "3rd-quality ba-tab *tuḫ-ḫu-um* cap," 511:'121 578:17, 645:2, 647:5, 692:2, 700:2, 708:3, 742:3, 745:2, 746:7, 793:5, 801:2, 803:1, 806:4, 835:'4, 1254:'41

^{túg}**sagšu** ba-tab *tuḫ-ḫu-um* 4-kam-ús, "4th-quality ba-tab *tuḫ-ḫu-um* cap," 708:6, 709:5, 799:2

^{túg}**sagšu** ba-tab *tuḫ-ḫu-um* [n-kam-ús], "[nth-quality] ba-tab *tuḫ-ḫu-um* cap," 701:5

1 ^{túg}**sagšu** ba-tab *tuḫ-ḫu-*⌜*um*⌝ ki-lá-bi 10⁵⁄₆ ma-[na], "1 ba-tab *tuḫ-ḫu-um* cap, its weight is 10⁵⁄₆ mina," 747:7

^{túg}**sagšu**-ĝe$_6$-sig$_5$, "fine black cap," 782:1, 783:12

^{túg}**sagšu**-níĝ-lám 3-kam-ús, "3rd-quality níĝ-lám cap," 646:4, 669:5, 674:3, 1254:'42

^{túg}**sagšu** *tá-ki-ru-um simat-*^{d}*ištaran*, "*takkirum* cap of *Simat-Ištaran*," 563:2, 569:16, 579:17, 591:8, 617:2, 636:2, 669:2, 753:2, 764:2, 789:2, 793:1, 796:1, 814:3, 1162:'14

^{túg}**sagšu**-u[š-bar], "uš-bar cap," 834:12

^{túg}**sagšu** [. . .], "[. . .] cap," 773:8

1. Wool for Caps

5 ^{túg}**sagšu**-babbar siki-⌜ĝír⌝-gul ki-lá-bi ⅔ ma-na, "ĝír-gul wool (for) 5 white caps, their weight is ⅔ mina," 679:1–2

n ^{túg}**sagšu** siki ^{ĝeš}garig aka 4-kam-ús ki-lá-bi n ma-na, "4th-quality combed wool (for) n cap(s), their weight is n mina(s)," 702:3–4, 741:1–3, 755:1–2, 756:4–6

saĝ, *qaqqadu*; *rēšu*, "head; servant"

saĝ bàd, "head of the (enclosure) wall" > **bàd**

1 géme-^{d}en-ki géme uš-bar **saĝ**-ba *ga-su-su* dam *a-ḫu-a*, "Geme-Enki, the female weaver, the servant of *Gasusu*, the wife of *Aḫu'a*," 270:1–2

[n+]1 udu-**saĝ** *šu-kab-tá*, "[n+]1 lead sheep of *Šu-Kabta*," 484:8

⋆⋆2 ir$_7$^{mušen} **saĝ**-x-du, 1220:1–2

saĝ u$_4$-sakar, *uskāru*; *warḫu*, "crescent moon; new moon day; moon"

1 *mu-du-lum* udu-niga **saĝ u$_4$-sakar** (. . .) sá-du$_{11}$ *simat-*^{d}*ištaran* é-gal-ta, "1 salted fattened sheep on the new moon day (and) {other comestibles} regular offerings of *Simat-Ištaran* from the palace," 375:1–2, 5–6

60 ^{dug}sìla-bur-zi níĝ-dab$_5$ **saĝ u$_4$-sakar** ù é-u$_4$-15 (. . .) sá-du$_{11}$-ki-a-nag-*šu-kab-tá*, "60 1-liter offering bowls, requisitions on the new moon day and the full moon day, (and) {other comestibles}, regular offerings of the funerary libation place of *Šu-Kabta*," 972:65–66, 107

60 ^{dug}sìla-bur-zi tu$_7$-šè níĝ-dab$_5$ **saĝ u$_4$-sakar** ù é-u$_4$-15 (. . .) sá-du$_{11}$-ki-a-nag-*šu-kab-tá*, "60 1-liter offering bowls for soup, requisitions on the new moon day and the full moon day, (and) {other comestibles}, regular offerings of the funerary libation place of *Šu-Kabta*," 975:66–67, 108

[. . .] sá-[du$_{11}$-^{d}. . .] **saĝ u$_4$**-[**sakar**], "[. . .], regular offerings of [. . .] on the new moon day," 1036:'42-'43

^{ĝeš}**saĝ-du**, "a wooden beam (part of a loom)"

⋆⋆2 ^{ĝeš}**saĝ-du** šà-ga-dù 3-kùš-ta, 1290:4

n ^{ĝeš}**saĝ-du** túg-ga gíd n-kùš-ta, "n saĝ-du beam(s) n kuš each used to extend textiles (as part of a loom)," 635:1, 635:2, 635:3, 635:4, 635:5

saĝ-dub, "full-time worker > *Craftswomen Index*

géme **saĝ-dub** géme gu-me-éš, "full-time female spinners"

géme **sağ-dub** géme uš-bar-me-éš, "full-time weavers"

ğuruš **sağ-dub**, "full-time workman" > *passim*

1. **Orders Involving Full-time Workmen**

^{d}*a*[*dad-till*]*ati* ù-n[a-a]-du$_{11}$ 3 ğuruš ḫi-a **sağ-dub** ğír-su^{ki}-šè ù níğ-dab$_5$ zà-mu-bi *i-mi-iq*-^{d}šul-gi [ḫé]-na-ab-sum-mu, "Say to *Adad-tillati* that '*Imiq*-Šulgi should give 3 various full-time workmen in Ĝirsu and the requisitions at the beginning of its year,'" 1038:1–7

^{zabar}**sağ-kul**, "bolt"

1 ^{zabar}**sağ-kul** kù-babbar ⅓ ma-na 9½ gín, "1 silver bolt (weighing) ⅓ mina (and) 9½ shekels," 1337:1

sağ-níğ-gur$_{11}$-ra, "available assets"

1. **From the Account of *Adad-tillati***

kilib-ba 316 [. . .] kilib-ba [n . . .] kilib-ba 37 [. . .] kilib-ba 360 ud$_5$ kilib-ba 306 udu-máš-ḫi-a [**sağ**]**-níğ-gur$_{11}$-ra** (. . .) níğ-kas$_7$-aka ^{d}*adad-tillati* šabra, "In total: 316 [. . .], [n . . .], 37 [. . .], 360 goats (and) 306 various sheep (and) goats are the available assets, (and) {other comestibles}, the balanced account of *Adad-tillati*, the majordomo," 984:'30-'35, '75-'76

(. . .) šu-sum-ma ğìri *ib-ni-*^{d}*adad* d[ub-sar] iti ezem-me-ki-ğál ba-zal mu en-^{d}inana-unu^{ki}-ga máš-e ì-pàd 0.0.1.2½ sìla ^{na_4}ŠEM? še-ta sa$_{10}$-a **sağ-níğ-gur$_{11}$-ra-kam** (. . .) níğ-kas$_7$-aka ^{d}*adad-tillati* šabra, "{millstones, diorite stones, woods, yokes, and wooden containers}, the consignment under the authority of *Ibni-Adad*, the scribe, at the end of the 12 month of *Ibbi-Suen* Year 2; (and) 12½ liters ^{na_4}ŠEM, the price from barley; (these) are the available assets (and) {other comestibles}, the balanced account of *Adad-tillati*, the majordomo," 1372:46–53, 105–106

2. **From Other Accounts**

[21 ma]-na siki-gen siki 1 [ma-n]a še 0.0.3.-ta še-bi [2.0].3. gur 0.0.4. še šu+níğin 2.1.1. še gur **sağ-níğ-gur$_{11}$-ra-kam** (. . .) níğ-kas$_7$-aka *šu*-^{d}dumu-zi ugula lú-ḫuğ-ğá, "[21] minas of ordinary wool, 1 mina of wool (is the equivalent of) 30 liters of barley; (therefore) their barley is [2] bushels (and) 30 liters (plus an additional) 40 liters of barley (is) in total: 2 bushels (and) 70 liters of barley. These are the available assets, {assignment of workers}, the balanced account of *Šu*-Dumuzi, overseer of hired workers," 336:1–6, 55–56

sá-du$_{11}$ ku$_5$-rá iti-6-kam [šu+níğin 10+]1.3.3.5 sìla še ninda gur [**sag-níğ**]**-gur$_{11}$-ra-kam** [šà-b]i-ta (. ..) [níğ-kas$_7$]-aka [*ì-lí*]*-bi-la-ni* muḫaldim, "{regular offerings of deities} deducted regular offerings of the 6th month—in total: 11 bushels (and) 215 liters of barley (for) bread—are the available assets. From among it: {barley rations and requisitions for various individuals}. The balanced account of *Ili-bilani*, the cook," 1527:8–13, 47–48

sağ-tag, "full-time (worker)"

ğuruš **sağ-tag** ^{lú}ázlag-me-éš, "full-time fullers" > *Craftsmen Index*

ğuruš **sağ-tag** ğuruš á-½-ta nam-60 *nu-úr-*^{d}*adad*, "full-time workmen (and) workmen at ½ wages (supervised by) *Nur-Adad*, the overseer of 60" > *Personal Name Index*

^{túg}**sağ-uš-bar**, "(a textile)," 658:6, 660:1, 662:7, 692:7, 693:6, 730:2, 731:2, 732:2, 734:2, 738:15, 766:5, 773:6, 778:9, 795:2, 796:8, 804:2, 806:7

3 ^{túg}**sağ-uš-bar** [n ma-na-ta], "3 sağ-uš-bar textiles, [(weighing) n mina(s) each]," 701:8

★★⌈siki⌉-bala-dè in-na-[kéše t]úg-gen-kam ì-in-⌈DU⌉? 1 ^{túg}**sağ-uš-bar** sa-gi$_4$-[àm], "{assorted textiles}, the wool was bound up to be baled, the ordinary textiles were delivered, they are finished sağ-uš-bar textiles," 609:7–9 (envelope)

saḫar, *eperu*, "dirt (used or removed in construction)"

saḫar è, "to extract dirt" > **è**

saḫar sè(g$_{10}$), "to tamp, trample dirt" > **sè(g$_{10}$)**

saḫar si(g), "to pile up dirt" > **si(g)**

saḫar tùm, "to bring dirt" > **tùm**

saḫar zi(g), "to (re)move dirt" > **zi(g)**

saḫar zi-ga im lu, "to mix excavated dirt (with) clay" > **lu**

1. Volumes of Dirt

½ nindan 2 kùš íb-sá 1½ kùš bùr **saḫar**-bi ⅔ sar, "½ nindan (and) 2 kùš in length, it is 1½ kùš square, its dirt (volume) is ⅔ sar," 329:6–7, 331:1–2, 331:8–9, 331:14–15, 331:16–17, 331:22–23, 333:9–10, 333:13–14

{indent} 2⅔ sar 7⅔ gín 20 še **saḫar**, "(in total:) 2⅔ sar, 7⅔ gín (and) 20 še of dirt," 329:8

7½ gín **saḫar** [. . .] ½ nindan 2 kùš gíd ½ nindan ⌈dağa]l⌉ ½ [kùš bùr] **saḫar**-bi 10 gín, "7½ gín of dirt [. . .], ½ nindan (and) 2 kùš in length (and) ½ nindan in width (and) ½ [kùš in area], its dirt (volume) is 10 gín," 331:3–5

n nindan gíd n nindan dağal n kùš bùr **saḫar**-bi n sar n gín, "n nindan in length, n nindan in width, n kùš in area, its dirt (volume) is n sar (and) n gín," 331:6–7, 331:10–11, 331:12–13, 331:18–19, 331:25–16, 333:1–2, 333:3–4, 333:5–6, 333:7–8, 333:11–12, 349:1–2, 349:3–4

n nindan gíd n kùš dağal n kùš (ba-an-)gi$_4$-bi n kùš sukud **saḫar**-bi n sar (n gín n še) (. . .) n sar im-du$_8$-a, "n nindan long, n kùš wide, n kùš tapered from n kùš high, its dirt is n sar (n gín (and) n še); (the total volume) of the adobe wall is n sar," 366:'1-'3, 366:'7-'8, '13, 366:'9-'10, '13, 366:'11-'13, 366:'17–19

n nindan gíd n kùš dağal n kùš sukud **saḫar**-bi n sar (n gín n še) (. . .) n sar im-du$_8$-a, "n nindan long, n kùš wide, n kùš high, its dirt is n sar (n gín (and) n še); (the total volume) of the adobe wall is n sar," 366:'5-'6, '13, 366:'15-'16, '19

1.1 Broken Context

[n] nindan gíd [. . . **saḫar**-bi] 2 sar [n gín . . .], 329:1–3

[. . .] kùš gíd [. . .] 2 [. . .] **saḫar**-bi ⅓ [sar], 329:4–5

[. . . **saḫa**]**r**-bi ½ [sar], 331:20–21

[n+]1⅔ kùš gíd ½ [kùš dağal] 2 kùš 10 [. . . **saḫ**]**ar**-bi ½ sar 7 [. . .], 332:'3-'4

[n nind]an gíd 4 kùš dağal n? [. . . **saḫar**]-bi ⅓ s[ar . . .], 332:'5-'6

2. Wages for (Removing or Delivering) Earth

{indent} 1 sar 10 gín **saḫar** ús-bi 30 nindan á g̃uruš-a 6 gín-ta ½ nindan gíd [. . .], "(In total:) 1 sar (and) 10 gín of dirt, its base is 30 nindan (long), workmen wages at 6 gín each (for) ½ nindan in length [. . .]," 349:5–8

[á-g̃]uruš-a 3⅓ ⸢gín⸣ 15 še-ta **saḫar**-bi 128⅓ <sar> u_4-1-šè [šu+]níg̃in 139 g̃uruš u_4-1-šè, "workmen [wages] at 3⅓ gín (and) 15 še each, its dirt is 128⅓ (units) for 1 day; in total: 139 worker days," 349:'12-'14

še á lú-ḫug̃-g̃á mu saḫar-šè, "barley, wages of hired workers for (moving?) dirt," 545:1–3

3. Broken or Uncertain Context

2 g̃uruš **saḫar** [. . .]-uš ù-ru-a b[àd], 46:'27

****SAḪAR**? $munu_4$-[si-è], 1036:'25

sal, *raqāqu*, "(to be) thin"

ninda **sal-la**, "thin bread" > **ninda**

^{gi}gur **sal-la**, "thin basket" > **^{gi}gur**

santana(GAL+NI), *šandanakku*, "date orchard administrator"

1. **PN santana**, "PN, the date orchard administrator" > *Personal Name Index*

^{d}*ma-lik-ba-ni* ur-me

sar, *mūšaru*, "a determinative for vegetables and plants"

5 gú ⸢**sar**⸣ ḫi-a, "5 talents of various vegetables," 1041:4

sar, *šaṭāru*, "to write"

bisag̃ im **sar-ra**, "clay tablet coffer" > **bisag̃**

[SCRIBES] > **dub-sar**

$^{g̃eš}$***sé-er-dum***, "olive tree"

ḫar $^{g̃eš}$***sé-er-dum*** n(-ta), "olive tree seedling(s) n (units) each," 1256:22, 1256:23, 1256:24, 1256:25, 1256:26, 1256:27, 1256:28, 1375:27, 1375:28, 1375:29, 1375:30

sè(g_{10}), *šakānu*, "to apply, place, set" > *Verb Index*

si, *qarnu*, "horn"

^{gi}gur ba-rí-ga ka-ba **si** g̃ar-ra, "a measuring container whose opening is covered (in) horn," 1372:34, 1372:92

si gu_4, "ox horn," 857:3, 880:2, 881:2, 927:6

si(g), "to fill, load up; to pile up (e.g., earth for a levee or temple foundation)" > *Verb Index*

si-ì-tum, *šittu*, "balance (of a settled account); left-over surplus; remainder"

šit-ì-tum[100] g̃ar, "to place the balance (of a settled account)" > **g̃ar**

1. **Barley, the Remainder of Wages**

1.1 **For Carrying Bricks**

1.2.5 še gur **si-ì-tum** á šeg$_{12}$ [ga$_6$-g̃á] á 5 sìla-⌜ta⌝, "1 bushel (and) 170 liters of barley, the remainder of wages (of workers) [having carried] bricks, wages of 5 liters each," 499:1–4

1.2 **(For Processing) Semolina**

0.3.4.5 še **si-ì-tum** á dabin, "225 liters of barley, the remainder of wages (for processing) semolina," 453:1–3

1.3 **For Construction Work and Carrying Bricks**

šu+níg̃in+ba 2.0.3.7½ sìla še gur zi-ga-àm 0.0.3.2½ sìla še ⌜**si**⌝**-ì-tum** níg̃-kas$_7$-aka *šu*-^{d}dumu-zi ugula lú-ḫug̃-g̃á, "In total: 2 bushels and 37½ liters of barley were expended. 32½ liters of barley were the remainder, the balanced account of *Šu*-Dumuzi, overseer of hired workers," 336:50–56

n (sìla) še **si-ì-tum** á šeg$_{12}$ ga$_6$-g̃á ù al-tar-ra, "n (liters) of barley, the remainder of wages of (workers) having carried bricks and (employed) for construction," 452:1–4, 498:1–4

2. **Other Remaining Commodities**

šu+níg̃in 7.4.0. š[e gur] šà-bi-⌜ta⌝ 124⅔ sar [šeg$_{12}$] NE-gu$_7$-bi í[b-ta-zi] á g̃uruš-a ⅓ sa[r-ta] g̃uruš-bi 360+14 [u$_4$-1-šè] še 5 sìla-ta [ba-ḫug̃ še-bi] 6.1.1. [gur š]eg12-bi 124⅔ [sar 1].2.5. še gur [**si**]**-ì-tum** "In total: 7 bushels (and) 240 liters of barley. From among it 124⅔ sar [bricks] were deducted as its wastage. Workman wages at ⅓ sar [each], its workmen (equal) 374 workerdays, [hired (for)] 5 liters of barley each. Their barley is 6 bushels (and) 70 liters. Their bricks are 124⅔. 1 bushel and 170 liters is the remainder," 496:5–16

3⅓ gín 3 še kù-babbar 1.0.0. zíz gur 3.0.0. tuḫ-hád-gen gur **si-ì-tum** [ur-^{d}]*suena* dam-[gàr] i[n-d]a-g̃ál, "the remainder of 3⅓ shekels (and) 3 barley corn of silver, 1 bushel of emmer (and) 3 bushels of ordinary dried bran are with Ur-*Suena*, the merchant," 1224:1–6

sí-mi-tum, ^{ú}**sumun-dar** = *šimittum* <**šumuttu*, "(a kind of plant),"[101] 511:75, 972:29, 972:98, 975:31, 975:99, 981:25

si$_{12}$(SIG$_7$), *baqāmu*; *barāšu*, *naṭāpu*, *nasāḫu*, "to cut, remove; to erase" > *Verb Index*

sig, *enšu*, *qatnu*, "(to be) weak, low, thin, narrow"

$^{g̃eš}$eme-**sig**, "plank" > $^{g̃eš}$**eme-sig**

$^{g̃eš}$ù-suḫ$_5$-**sig**, "narrow pine plank" > $^{g̃eš}$**ù-suḫ$_5$**

---

[100] Var: *šit-tum.*

[101] Civil 1961, 94 N407:9, numun *sí-me-tum.*

^{ğeš}**sìg-ga**, "(a tree?)," 970:15

SIG$_4$.ANŠE >*amara, *amāru*, "a type of brick stack"

al-tar **SIG$_4$.ANŠE**, "construction of the brick stack" > **al-tar**

SIG$_4$.ANŠE dù, "to construct a brick stack" > **dù**

SIG$_4$.ANŠE ĝar, "to place a brick stack" > **ĝar**

SIG$_4$.ANŠE im ga$_6$(ĝ), "to carry earth to a brick stack" > **ga$_6$(ĝ)**

SIG$_4$.ANŠE im sumur aka, "to plaster a brick stack" > **aka**

SIG$_4$.ANŠE kurum$_7$ aka al-tar, "inspection (of the work of workmen employed at) the brick stack (for) construction" > **al-tar**

SIG$_4$.ANŠE (šà) zabala$_4^{ki}$, "the brick stack of Zabala" > *Toponym Index*

im lu-a **SIG$_4$.ANŠE**(-šè), "having mixed earth (for) a brick stack" > **lu**

[n ĝuruš] 1 géme **KA.ANŠE** [im sumur] ke$_4$-dè gub-ba, "[n workmen] (and) 1 workwoman employed to plaster the brick stack," 66:10[102]

1. Building Supplies for the Brick Stack

[600?+12]0+27 g[u-níĝin] ^{ğeš}kišig dúr **SIG$_4$.ANŠE**-šè ba-a-ĝar, "[74]7 bales of shok placed for (use as) the bottom of a brick stack," 1295:1–2

sig$_5$, "(to be) fine, high quality"

báppir-**sig$_5$**, "fine beer bread" > **báppir**

dug dida$_x$-**sig$_5$**, "jug of fine dida beer" > **dida$_x$**

kaš-**sig$_5$**, "fine beer" > **kaš**

mun-**sig$_5$**, "fine salt" > **mun**

níĝ-àr-ra-**sig$_5$**, "fine groats" > **níĝ-àr-ra**

ninda-šu-ra-**sig$_5$**, "fine half(-loaf) bread" > **ninda**

^{ğeš}nu-úr-ma-**sig$_5$**, "fine pomegranate plank" > ^{ğeš}**nu-úr-ma**

^{túg}sagšu-ĝe$_6$-**sig$_5$**, "fine black cap" > ^{túg}**sagšu**

^{kuš}súḫub e-sír túg-du$_8$-a-babbar-**sig$_5$** é-ba-an, "pair of fine white, meshwork-lined shoes" > ^{kuš}**súḫub**

šim-**sig$_5$**, "fine aromatic" > **šim**

tuḫ-duru$_5$-**sig$_5$**, "fine fresh bran" > **tuḫ**

zì-**sig$_5$**, "fine flour" > **zì**

[. . .] x-**sig$_5$**, 1254:'25

siki, *šipātu*, "wool, hair"

siki-a-gíd, "(a specification of wool)"

---

102 KA-anše is likely a mistake for SIG$_4$.ANŠE.

siki ba-tab *tuḫ-ḫu-um*, "(a specification of wool)"

siki bar-dul$_5$, "(a specification of wool)"

siki é-^{d}*šu*-^{d}*suen*^{ki}-ta, "wool from *Bit-Šu-Suen*" > *Toponym Index*

siki-gen, "ordinary wool"

siki-gi, "wool of an eme-GI sheep"

siki-g̃e$_6$, "black wool"

siki $^{g̃eš}$garig aka, "combed wool"

siki-g̃ír-gul, "(a specification of wool)"

siki níg̃-lám, "(a specification of wool)"

siki šudum, "wool (for) warp-thread"

siki túg-du$_8$-a, "wool meshwork"

siki-ud$_5$, "goat hair"

siki-ús, "2nd-quality wool"

siki-za-rí-in, "coarsely cleaned wool material"

1. **Hair**

1.1 **siki-ud$_5$**, "goat hair," 704:2, 716:1, 772:1, 783:9

[x]-x **siki-ud$_5$** [x] 10 gín, "10 shekels [x] goat hair," 1381:37, (in reference to the amount of [x] required to manufacture ^{gi}kid $^{g̃eš}$gu-za > ^{gi}**kid**)

1.1.1 **Goat-Hair Mattresses**

1 šà-tuku$_5$ **siki-ud$_5$** ki-lá-bi 5 ma-na 10 gín, "1 goat-hair mattress, its weight is 5 minas and 10 shekels," 706:1–2

1 bar-si **siki-ud$_5$** šà-tuku$_5$ é-ba-an ki-lá-bi 2 ma-na, "1 pair of bands (for) a goat-hair mattress, their weight is 2 minas," 740:3–4

1.1.2 **Goat-Hair Ropes**

éš-túg-gíd-**siki-ud$_5$**, "goat-hair cord, used to extend a textile (on a loom)," 628:1

éš-ú-siki-ud$_5$**, 628:2

éš-ú-nin$_9$-siki-ud$_5$**, 628:3

éš-**siki-ud$_5$**, "goat-hair ropes," 717:3

5 éš-**siki-ud$_5$** ki-lá-bi 15⅔ ma-na, "5 goat-hair ropes, their weight is 15⅔ minas," 740:1–2

eše ^{gi}kid-aš-rin **siki-ud$_5$, 1334:4

1.1.3 **Goat-Hair Sacks**

6 barag-**siki-ud$_5$** ki-lá-bi 18 ma-na, "6 goat-hair sacks, their weight is 18 minas," 717:1–2

1.1.4 **Goat-Hair Thread**

níg̃-U.NU-a **siki-ud$_5$**, "goat-hair thread," 716:2, 1343:2

2. **Wool**

2 gú **siki**, "2 talents of wool," 616:1

siki de$_6$, "to bring wool" > **de$_6$**

siki g̃en, "to go (for) wool" > **g̃en**

siki igi sag̃, "to sort wool" > **igi . . . sag̃**

siki íl, "to carry wool" > **íl**

u$_4$ **siki**-ba-ka šu bar, "to release {workers} on the day of the wool rations" > **šu . . . bar**

siki tùm, "to bring wool" > **tùm**

2.1 Baskets of Wool

2 ^{gi}gúrdub ⸢**siki**⸣-gi, "2 reed baskets of wool of an eme-GI sheep," 616:2

4 ^{gi}gúrdub **siki** ba-tab *tuḫ-ḫu-um*, "4 reed baskets of ba-tab *tuḫ-ḫu-um* wool," 625:14

^{gi}gúrdub **siki** ka-tab sè(g$_{10}$), "to fit a reed basket of wool with a cover" > **sè(g$_{10}$)**

2.2 Deliveries, Equivalents and Purchases

★★(. . .) **siki** bala-[dè i]n-na-⸢keše⸣ ^{túg}uš-ba[r sa-gi$_4$-àm], "{assorted textiles}, the wool was bound up to be baled, they are finished uš-bar textiles," 609:8 (tablet)

★★(. . .) ⸢**siki**⸣-bala-dè in-na-[kéše t]úg-gen-kam ì-in-⸢DU⸣? 1 ^{túg}sag̃-uš-bar sa-gi$_4$-[àm], "{assorted textiles}, the wool was bound up to be baled, he delivered the ordinary textile, they are finished sag̃-uš-bar textiles," 609:7–9 (envelope)

★★(. . .) kišib íb-ra é-kišib-ba-ta dub-bi in-du$_8$ **siki** bala-dè in-kéše é-gal-šè, "{assorted textiles} He rolled the seal, baked its tablet in the storeroom, (and) bound up the wool to be baled," 609:11–13

$^{[d]}$*adad-tillati ù-na-a*-du$_{11}$ 5.0.0. še gur 0.0.1.2 sìla ì-g̃eš [n] ma-na **siki** [níg̃]-dab$_5$ *zà-mu-⸢ka⸣-ni a-ḫa-ni-šu* ḫé-na-ab-sum-mu, "Say to *Adad-tillati* that '5 bushels of barley, 12 liters of sesame oil (and) [n] mina(s) of wool, the requisitions at the beginning of the year, should be given to *Ahanišu*,'" 1042:1–8

2.2.1 Barley Equivalents

[21 ma]-na siki-gen **siki** 1 [ma-n]a še 0.0.3.-ta, "[21] minas of ordinary wool, 1 mina of wool (is the equivalent of) 30 liters of barley," 336:1

5 ma-na **siki** še 0.0.3.-ta, "5 minas of wool is (the equivalent of) 30 liters of barley each," 431:2

10 ma-na **siki** [1 ma-na še 0.0.3.-ta], "10 minas of wool, [1 mina (is the equivalent of) 30 liters each]," 496:2

2.2.2 Wool to Purchase More Wool

5 ma-na siki-gen dirig sa$_{10}$ **siki**-a-šè *pu-ta-nu-um*, "5 minas of supplementary ordinary wool for the purchase of (more) wool (for) *Putanum*," 1005:7–9

2.3 Wool Rations and Wages

2.3.1 For Baking Bricks

0.4.3. eša 12 ma-na **siki** še-0.0.3!.-[ta] 2 sìla ì-g̃eš še-0.0.4.-ta šeg$_{12}$ du$_8$-dè á 5-sìla-ta, "270 liters of fine flour, 12 minas of wool, the equivalent of 30 liters of barley each, (and) 2 liters of sesame oil, the equivalent of 40 liters of barley each, wages of 5 liters each (for workers) to mold bricks," 457:1–5

2.3.2 For Carrying Bricks

15 ma-na **siki** šeg$_{12}$ ga$_6$-g̃á-[dè], "15 minas of wool [to] carry bricks," 638:2–3

2.3.3 For Servants

1½ ma-na siki-gen **siki-ba** árad *šu-eš$_4$-tár*, "1½ minas of ordinary wool, wool rations of the servant of *Šu-Eštar*," 627:1–2

8 gú 1½ ma-na siki-gen ⸢**siki**⸣**-ba** géme-árad, "8 talents (and) 1½ minas of ordinary wool, wool rations of female (and) male servants," 721:1–2

2.4 Wool and Textile Rations: for the Servants of *Simat-Ištaran*

(. . .) {indent} 131 túg-⸢ḫi⸣-a [n] ma-na ⸢siki-gen⸣ túg-⸢ba⸣ **siki-**⸢**ba**⸣ géme-á[rad *simat-*^{d}K]A.⸢DI⸣, "{assorted textiles}, (in total:) 131 textiles (and) [n] mina(s) of ordinary wool, the textile and wool rations of the female and male servants of *Simat-Ištaran*," 734:1–9

8 gú 33 m[a-na] siki-gen (. . .) túg-ba **siki-ba** géme-árad *simat-*^{d}K[A.DI], "8 talents and 33 minas of ordinary wool, (and) {assorted textiles}, the textile and wool rations of the female and male servants of *Simat-Ištaran*," 795:1–6

8 gú 27½ m[a-n]a siki-⸢gen⸣ (. . .) tú[g-ba] **siki-ba** géme-árad *simat-*$^{\text{[d]}}$*ištaran*, "8 talents (and) 27 minas of ordinary wool (and) {assorted textiles}, the textile and wool rations of the female and male servants of *Simat-Ištaran*," 818:1–8

3. Types of Wool

3.1 siki-a-gíd, "(a specification of wool)"

1 túg-íb-lá **siki-a-[gíd]** siki ^{ĝeš}garig aka gen ki-lá-bi 16 gín, "ordinary combed wool for a belt of a-gíd wool, its weight is 16 shekels," 756:7–9

3.2. siki ba-tab *tuḫ-ḫu-um*, "(a specification of wool)"

4 ^{gi}gúrdub **siki ba-tab *tuḫ-ḫu-um***, "4 reed baskets of ba-tab *tuḫ-ḫu-um* wool," 625:14

3.3 siki bar-dul$_5$, "(a specification of wool)"

siki bar-dul$_5$-lugal, "royal(-quality) bar-dul$_5$ wool," 585:4

3.4 siki-gen, "ordinary wool," 438:2, 623:3, 627:1, 634:2, 641:1, 670:1, 672:1, 681:1, 721:1, 728:1, 734:7, 752:1, 763:2, 784:2, 795:1, 815:6:7, 817:1, 818:1, 1005:2, 1005:7, 1011:2, 1011:7, 1011:12, 1052:4, 1285:1, 1296:2, 1320:2

****siki-gen** šudum-bi, "warp-thread of ordinary wool" > see 4.2.1 below

3.5 siki-gi, "wool of an eme-GI sheep"[103]

2 ^{gi}gúrdub ⸢**siki**⸣**-gi**, "2 reed baskets of wool of an eme-GI sheep," 616:2

3.6 siki-gu, "wool cord" > see 5.7 below.

3.7 siki ^{ĝeš}garig aka, "combed wool" > see also 4.2.2 below

siki ^{ĝeš}garig aka 4-kam-ús, "4th-quality combed wool," 671:2, 710:1

siki ^{ĝeš}garig aka gen, "ordinary combed wool," 710:2

3.8 siki-ĝe$_6$, "black wool," 634:1, 728:2

3.9 siki-ĝír-gul, "(a specification of wool),"[104] 605:1, 632:1, 640:1, 657:1, 703:1, 704:1, 777:1, 784:3, 805:1 > see also 4.2.3 below

túg-du$_8$-a **siki-ĝír-gul** ki-lá-bi ⅓ ma-na 3 gín, "1 meshwork of ĝír-gul wool, its weight is ⅓ mina (and) 3 shekels," 776:1

---

103 Stępień 1996, 17; Waetzoldt 1972.

104 Waetzoldt 1972, 54–55. Waetzoldt (personal communication) further qualifies this term as "es handelt sich um minderwertige Wolle, die mit einem Messer von der Hautverendeter und geschlachteter Tiere abgeschabt wird. Die Woll-qualität ist schlechter als gen und mug."

1 ma-na **g̃ír-⌜gul⌝** NE-gu$_7$-bi 15 gín, "1 mina of g̃ír-gul (wool); its wastage is 15 shekels," 836:11–12

3.9.1 For Mattresses

12 gín **siki-g̃ír-gul** šà-tuku$_5$ kala-kala-ke$_4$-dè, "12 shekels of g̃ír-gul wool to reinforce a mattress," 783:1–2

3.10 **siki níg̃-lám**, "(a specification of wool)"

siki níg̃-⌜lám⌝ 4-kam-ús, "4th-quality níg̃-lam wool," 750:1

3.11 **siki šudum**, "wool (for) warp-thread" > see also 4.2.1 below

siki šudum 3-kam-ús, "3rd-quality wool (for) warp-thread," 625:11

siki šudum-ma 4-kam-ús, "4th-quality wool (for) warp-thread," 815:4

siki šudum-⌜má⌝-túg 3-kam-ús, "3rd-quality wool (for) warp-thread (for) textiles," 719:4

siki šudum-má-túg-lugal, "wool (for) warp-thread (for) royal textiles,"620:30

siki šudum-túg, "wool (for) warp-thread (for) textiles," 667:5

siki šudum-túg 3-[kam-ús], "3rd-[quality] wool (for) warp-thread (for) textiles," 667:12

siki šudum-túg-lugal, "wool (for) warp-thread (for) royal textiles," 667:4

siki túg-⌜**šudum**⌝-má-túg-lugal 3-kam-ús, "3rd-[quality] wool (for) warp-thread (for) royal textiles," 633:3

3.12 **siki túg-du$_8$-a**, "wool meshwork"

siki túg-du$_8$-a 4-kam-ús, "4th-quality wool meshwork," 623:1

3.13 **siki-ús**, "2nd-quality wool," 603:1, 613:1, 614:1, 675:1

3.14 **siki-za-rí-in**, *zarinnu*, "coarsely cleaned wool material"

siki-za-rí-in-gen, "ordinary coarsely cleaned wool material," 671:1

1 ma-na **siki-za-rí-in** túg-lugal-gen *simat-^{d}ištaran šu-kab-tá* mug-bi ⅓ ma-na 4 gín-ta NE-gu$_7$-bi 6 gín-ta, "1 mina of coarsely cleaned wool material (for) textiles of royal to ordinary quality of *Simat-Ištaran* (and) *Šu-Kabta*; its wool combings are ⅓ of a mina (and) 4 shekels each, its wastage is 6 shekels each," 836:1–3

1 ma-na **siki-za-rí-in** 3-kam-ús 4-kam-ús mug-bi ⅓ mana 1 gín-ta NE-gu$_7$-bi 8 gín-ta, "1 mina of 3rd and 4th-quality coarsely cleaned wool material; its wool combings are ⅓ mina (and) 1 shekel each, its wastage is 8 shekels each," 836:4–6

1 ma-na **siki-za-rí-in**-gen NE-gu$_7$-bi 6⅔ gín, "1 mina of ordinary coarsely cleaned wool material; its wastage is 6⅔ shekels," 836:9–10

3.15 Broken Context

[**siki** . . .] 3-kam-ús, "3rd-quality [. . . wool]," 666:1

siki [. . .] 4-k[am-ús], "4th-quality [. . . wool]," 671:3

4. Wool Designated for Textiles

4.1 In General

(. . .) **siki**-túg-àm, "{assorted} wools are (for) textiles," 585:13

1 gú 24 ma-na **siki** túg-g̃e$_6$, "1 talent (and) 24 minas of wool (for) a black textile," 648:2

siki túg 3-kam-ús, "wool (for) a 3rd-quality textile," 719:3

4.2 Specific Types of Wool Designated for Textiles

4.2.1 siki-gen, "ordinary wool"

n gín **siki-gen** mu-túg-ga-šè, "n shekel(s) of ordinary wool for textiles," 699:1, 5, 705:4–5

1 túg-mug ki-lá **siki-gen** šudum-bi 1 ma-na ki-lá mug-bi n ma-na, "1 textile of poor-quality wool, its weight is 1 mina of warp-thread of ordinary wool (and) n mina(s) of wool combings," 744:1–3, 747:13–15

1 túg 1⅓ <ma->na **siki-gen**, "1 textile of ⅓ mina of ordinary wool," 817:1

4.2.2 siki ^{ğeš}garig aka, "combed wool"

4.2.2.1 For Belts

1 túg-íb-lá siki-a-[gíd] **siki ^{ğeš}garig aka** gen ki-lá-bi 16 gín, "ordinary combed wool for a belt of a-gíd wool, its weight is 16 shekels," 756:7–9

[n] túg-íb-lá-su$_4$-a **siki ^{ğeš}ZUM.[SI aka** 4-kam-ús], "[4th-quality combed wool] (for) [n] red/brown belt(s)," 833:3–4

4.2.2.2 For Textiles

2⅔ ma-na **siki ^{ğeš}garig aka** túg 3-kam-ús, "2⅔ mina combed wool (for) a 3rd-quality textile," 596:1

[. . .]x-ka-ğe$_6$-sig$_5$ [. . .**siki**] **^{ğeš}garig aka** 4-kam-ús, "4th-quality combed wool (for) a fine black [textile]," 833:1–2

4.2.2.3 For Shoes

1 $^{\text{<kuš>}}$súḫub-túg-du$_8$-a-⸢babbar⸣? **siki ^{ğeš}garig aka** 3-kam-ús ki-lá-bi ½ ma-na 2 gín, "3rd-quality combed wool (for) 1 (pair) of white meshwork shoes, its weight is ½ mina and 2 shekels," 756:1–3

4.2.2.4 For Caps

[1] ^{túg}sagšu **siki ^{ğeš}garig aka** 4-kam-ús ⸢siki⸣-bi ⅓ ma-na, "4th-quality combed wool (for) [1] cap, its weight is ⅓ mina," 702:3–4

2 ^{túg}sagšu **siki ^{ğeš}garig aka** 4-kam-ús ki-lá-bi 13 gín, "4th-quality combed wool (for) 2 caps, its weight is 13 shekels," 741:1–3, 756:4–6

4 ^{túg}sagšu [. . .] **siki ^{ğeš}garig a[ka** . . .], "combed wool (for) 4 [. . .] caps, [its weight is n mina(s)]," 755:1–2

4.2.2.5 Meshworks of Combed Wool

1 túg-d[u$_8$-a . . .] **siki ^{ğeš}gari[g aka]** 4-kam-ús ki-lá-bi ½ ma-na, "1 [. . .] meshwork of 4th-quality combed wool, its weight is ½ mina," 583:1–3

1 túg-du$_8$-a-babbar é-ba-an <**siki**> **^{ğeš}garig aka** gen ki-l[á-bi n] ma-na [n gín], "1 pair of white meshworks of ordinary combed <wool>, their weight is [n] mina(s) [and n shekel(s)]," 583:4–7

1 túg-du$_8$-a-babbar túg-tur **siki ^{ğeš}garig aka** 3-kam-ús ki-lá-bi 7 gín, "1 white meshwork (for) a small textile of 3rd-quality combed wool, its weight is 7 shekels," 583:7–9

1 túg-du$_8$-a ⸢siki**⸣ ^{ğeš}NÍĞIN-**garig aka** 4-kam-ús ki-lá-bi ½ ma-na, "1 meshwork of 4th-quality (?) combed wool, its weight is ½ mina," 767:3–4

6 túg-du$_8$-a **siki ^{geš}garig aka** 1 túg-du$_8$-a siki-g̃ír-gul [ki-lá-bi n ma]-na 5 gín [igi]-12-g̃ál, "6 meshworks of combed wool (and) 1 meshwork of g̃ír-gul wool, [their weight is n] mina(s) and 5 $^{1}/_{12}$ shekels," 883:1–4

4.2.3 siki-g̃ír-gul, "(a specification of wool)"

4.2.3.1 For White Turbans

5 ^{túg}sagšu-babbar **siki-⸢g̃ír⸣-gul** ki-lá-bi ⅔ ma-na, "g̃ír-gul wool (for) 5 white caps, its weight is ⅔ mina," 679:1–2

4.2.3.2 Meshworks of g̃ír-gul Wool

5 túg-du$_8$-a **siki-g̃ír-gul** ^{geš}gu-za-munus šà!-kal ki-lá-bi 3⅔ ma-na, "5 meshworks of g̃ír-gul wool (for) a wooden woman's chair, their weight is 3⅔ minas," 761:1–2

6 túg-du$_8$-a siki ^{geš}garig aka 1 túg-du$_8$-a **siki-g̃ír-gul** [ki-lá-bi n ma]-na 5 gín [igi]-12-g̃ál, "6 meshworks of combed wool (and) 1 meshwork of g̃ír-gul wool, [their weight is n] mina(s) and 5 $^{1}/_{12}$ shekels," 883:1–4

2 túg-du$_8$-a [**siki**]-**g̃ír-gul**, "2 meshworks of g̃ír-gul wool," 924:3

4.2.3.2.1 For Chairs

5 túg-du$_8$-a **siki-g̃ír-gul** ^{geš}gu-za MÍ.U$_4$.KAL ki-lá-bi 3⅔ ma-na, "5 meshworks of g̃ír-gul wool (for) MÍ.U$_4$.KAL chairs, their weight is 3⅔ minas," 761:1–2

4.2.3.3 Textiles of g̃ír-gul Wool

^{túg}uš-bar **siki-g̃ír-gul**, "uš-bar textile of g̃ír-gul wool," 694:9, 708:7, 588:4

^{túg}uš-bar-tur **siki-g̃ír-gul**, "small uš-bar textile of g̃ír-gul wool," 674:9

4.2.3.4 Plucked g̃ír-gul Wool

lá-ìa 3⅔ [ma-n]a 6⅔ gín **siki-g̃ír-gul** peš$_5$-a, "the remainder of 3⅔ minas and 6⅔ shekels of plucked g̃ír-gul wool," 593:1

5. Wool Designated for Specific Textiles

5.1 ^{túg}*á-gu$_4$-hu-um*

siki ^{túg}*á-gu$_4$-hu-um*-⸢PI⸣, "wool (for) a *á-gu$_4$-hu-um*-PI textile," 667:1

siki ^{túg}*á-gu$_4$-hu-um*-lugal, "wool (for) a royal *á-gu$_4$-hu-um* textile," 620:1

5.2 ^{túg}aktum

siki ^{túg}aktum 3-kam-ús, "wool (for) a 3rd-quality aktum textile," 667:11

siki ^{túg}aktum 4-kam-ús, "wool (for) a 4th-quality aktum textile," 585:12, 667:16

5.3 ^{túg}bar-dul$_5$

siki ^{túg}bar-dul$_5$ *šu-kab-ta*, "wool (for) a bar-dul$_5$ textile of *Šu-Kabta*," 585:5

5.4 ^{túg}níg̃-lám

siki ^{túg}níg̃-lám, "wool (for) a níg̃-lám textile," 667:3

siki ^{túg}níg̃-lám-lugal, "wool (for) a royal níg̃-lám textile," 585:2, 625:5, 667:2

siki ^{túg}níg̃-lám *simat-^{d}ištaran*, "wool (for) a níg̃-lám textile of *Simat-Ištaran*," 815:1

siki ^{túg}níg̃-lám *šu-kab-tá*, "wool (for) a níg̃-lám textile of *Šu-Kabta*," 585:6, 619:2, 620:4, 625:6, 667:6

siki ^{túg}níĝ-lám-gen, "wool (for) an ordinary níĝ-lám textile," 813:1

siki ^{túg}níĝ-lám-ús, "wool (for) a 2nd-quality níĝ-lám textile," 585:3, 620:2, 625:3, 633:1

siki ^{túg}níĝ-lám 3-kam-ús, "wool (for) a 3rd-quality níĝ-lám textile," 585:9, 620:5, 624:1, 625:9, 667:9, 815:2, 826:3

siki ^{túg}níĝ-lám 4-kam-ús, "wool (for) a 4th-quality níĝ-lám textile," 585:11, 625:13, 667:14

5.5 túg ba-tab *tuḫ-ḫu-um*

siki túg ba-tab *tuḫ-ḫu-um*, "wool (for) a ba-tab *tuḫ-ḫu-um* textile," 585:10

siki túg ba-tab *tuḫ-ḫu-um* 3-kam-ús, "wool (for) a 3rd-quality ba-tab *tuḫ-ḫu-um* textile," 585:8, 619:3, 667:8, 719:1

siki túg ba-tab *tuḫ-ḫu-um* 4-kam-ús, "wool (for) a 4th-quality ba-tab *tuḫ-ḫu-um* textile," 625:12, 666:2, 667:13, 719:2

siki túg ba-tab *tuḫ-ḫu-um* [n]-kam-ús, "wool (for) a [n^{th}]-quality ba-tab *tuḫ-ḫu-um* textile," 625:8

siki túg ba-tab *tuḫ-ḫu-um* *simat-^{d}ištaran*, "wool (for) a ba-tab *tuḫ-ḫu-um* textile of *Simat-Ištaran*," 826:2

5.6 túg-gen

siki túg-gen, "wool (for) an ordinary textile," 815:6

5.7 túg-guz-za

siki túg-gu[z-za], "wool (for) a tufted textile," 769:3

siki túg-guz-za-gen, "wool (for) an ordinary tufted textile," 623:2, 667:17, 763:1, 784:1, 826:7

siki túg-guz-za-ús, "wool (for) a 2nd-quality tufted textile," 619:1, 620:6, 625:4, 633:2

siki túg-guz-za 3-kam-ús, "wool (for) a 3rd-quality tufted textile," 625:10, 648:1, 667:10, 815:3, 826:4

siki túg-guz-za 4-kam-ús, "wool (for) a 4th-quality tufted textile," 620:7, 666:5, 667:15, 719:5, 815:5, 826:6

siki túg-guz-za-lugal, "wool (for) a royal tufted textile," 625:1

siki túg-guz-za *šu-kab-ta*, "wool (for) a tufted textile of *Šu-Kabta*," 585:7, 625:7, 667:7

****siki túg-guz-za** siki túg-ĝír-su^{ki} 5 g[i-x]-x-ka-du-ga, 585:14–16

20 ma-na **siki túg-guz-za**-gen mu siki-gu kéše-šè, "20 minas of wool (for manufacturing) ordinary tufted cloth (to be used) for wool cord bindings," 665:1–2

5.8 túg-ĝír-su^{ki}, "textile of Ĝirsu"

siki túg-guz-za **siki túg-ĝír-su^{ki} 5 g[i-x]-x-ka-du-ga, 585:14–16

5.9 túg-íb-lá-kaskal, "traveling belt"

[1] **túg-íb-[lá]-kaskal** ⸢siki⸣-bi ⅓ ma-⸢na⸣ 1 gín, "[1] traveling belt, its wool is ⅓ mina (and) 1 shekel," 702:1–2

5.10 túg-ša-aktum

****siki** túg?-ša??-**aktum** [. .], 671:4

5.11 ^{túg}**uš-bar**

[**siki** ^{tú}]^{g}**uš-bar**, "[wool] (for) an uš-bar textile," 596:7

4 ^{túg}**uš-bar siki**-[bi] 5 ma-na-[ta? ki]-lá-bi 17 m[a-na], "4 uš-bar textiles, [their] wool is 5 minas [each?], their weight is 17(sic!) minas," 747:11–12

5.12 Context Uncertain

★★⅔ ma-na 5 gín **siki** šu-gan-túg 3-kam-ús, 596:2

5.13 Broken Context

siki t[úg-x]-lugal, "wool (for) a royal [x] textile," 625:2

siki túg-x-g̃e$_{6}$, "wool (for) a black [x] textile," 596:8

[**siki**]-túg-x-[x?], "wool for a x-[x?] textile," 585:1

siki túg-[. . .], "wool for a [. . .] textile," 666:4

siki [^{túg} . .] túg-⌜lugal⌝, "wool for a [. . .] royal textile," 826:1

★★[x-*t*]*um*?? ANŠE+BAR+MUL [$^{g̃eš}$g̃a]rig̃ aka gen [**siki**-bi] ⅔ ma-[na] 4 gín, "⅔ mina (and) 4 shekels of ordinary combed wool for (?)," 702:5–7

6. Context Uncertain

★★0.2.1.3⅓ sìla [. . . -g]en sa$_{10}$ ki-**siki** ½ [. . .]-kam ù é-^{d}[. . .], "133⅓ of liter of ordinary [. . .], the price of ½ [. . .] and the temple of [. . .]," 1391:1–6

sila, *sūqu*, "street"

★★3.0.0. še gur-⌜ta⌝? i$_{7}$-gu$_{4}$ **sila**-a g̃ál-la, 1233:17–18

sìla, *mīšertu*; *qû*, "a unit of capacity (liter); a vessel," *passim*

1. ^{dug}**sìla-bàn-da**,[105] "(a vessel)," 1334:8

2. ^{dug}**sìla-bur-zi**, *pursû*, "1-liter (offering) bowl,"[106] 511:82, 523:15, 972:105, 975:106, 1013:17, 1014:10, 1025:37, 1025:54, 1025:72, 1025:89, 1025:113, 1025:113, 1033:14, 1334:12

2.1 ^{dug}**sìla-bur-zi tu$_{7}$-(šè), "1-liter (offering) bowl for soup"**[107]

n ^{dug}**sìla-bur-zi tu$_{7}$** ba-aka kaš-dé-a, "n 1-liter offering bowl(s) of soup were made (for) the banquet" > **kaš-dé-a, aka**

n ^{dug}**sìla-bur-zi tu$_{7}$** si(g), "to fill soup into n 1-liter offering bowl(s)" > **si(g)**

60 ^{dug}**sìla-bur-zi** (**tu$_{7}$-šè**) níg̃-dab$_{5}$ sag̃ u$_{4}$-sakar ù é-u$_{4}$-15 (. . .) sá-du$_{11}$-ki-a-nag-*šu-kab-tá*, "60 1-liter offering bowls (for soup), requisitions on the new moon day and the full moon day (and) {other comestibles}, regular offerings of the funerary libation place of *Šu-Kabta*," 972:65–66, 107, 975:66–67, 108

60 ^{dug}**sìla**-bur-zi tu$_{7}$-šè šà kisal-lá ^{d}inana-zabala$_{4}^{ki}$, "60 1-liter offering bowls for soup in the courtyard of Inana of Zabala," 1028:35–37

---

105 Sallaberger 1996, 106.

106 Sallaberger 1996, 98f.

107 Brunke 2008, 167 (§3.3.3).

^{dug}**sìla-gal**, "large liter-jug,"[108] 1033:13, 1281:1, 1334:11

sila$_4$, *puḫādu*, "lamb," 448:1, 984:'62, 1003:11, 1160:1, 1165:3, 1171:3
kuš-**sila$_4$**, "lamb skin" > **kuš**
kuš-**sila$_4$** a-g̃ar gu$_7$, "de-haired lamb skin" > **a-g̃ar gu$_7$**
sila$_4$ ba-úš, "dead lamb" > **úš**
sila$_4$-ga, "suckling lamb," 984:'63, 1083:2
sila$_4$-gukkal, "fat-tailed lamb," 1154:3
1 **sila$_4$** kuš-bi ba-zi, "the skin of 1 lamb was disbursed," 1028:38
sila$_4$-máš ḫi-a, "various lambs (and) goats," 1041:3
sila$_4$ sá-du$_{11}$-^{d}inana-zabala$_4^{ki}$, "lamb, regular offerings of Inana of Zabala" > **sá-du$_{11}$**

sila$_{11}$(g̃)(ŠID), *lâšu*, "to knead (dough/clay)" > *Verb Index*

sim, *napû*, "to sieve, filter" > *Verb Index*

sim-da, "brand, branding mark"
sim-da *da-da-a* sipa-mušen-na, "branding mark of *Dada'a*, the bird warden" > *Personal Name Index*

simug, *nappāḫu*, "smith, metalworker"
g̃uruš **simug** > *Craftsmen Index*

sipa(d)-mušen-na, "bird warden"
1. **PN sipa(d)-mušen-na**, "PN, the bird warden" > *Personal Name Index*
a-ta-li-ku
da-da-a
šu-^{d}na-zi

sízkur, *nīqu*, "(ceremonial) offering, sacrifice; libation"
Commodities Offered

dida$_x$-gen, "ordinary dida beer"	ninda, "bread"
dabin, "semolina"	zì-gu-ús, "2nd-quality gu-flour"
eša, "fine flour"	zì-KAL, "KAL-flour"
kaš-gen, "ordinary beer"	zú-lum, "dates

[108] Sallaberger 1996, 106.

1. During Construction of the Brewery-Kitchen-Mill Complex: Beer, Semolina, and Fine Flour

1 sìla [dabin] ½ sìla eša **sízkur** é-lù[ng]a é-[muḫaldim ú] é-kíkken (. . .) u_4 al-tar é-lùnga é-muḫaldim é-kíkken, "1 liter of [semolina] (and) ½ liter of fine flour, (ceremonial) offerings of the brewery-kitchen-mill complex, (and) {other disbursals}, construc-tion of the brewery-kitchen-mill-complex," 440:5–7, 12

1 dug $dida_x$-gen 0.0.3?-[ta] 1 sìla dabin [1 sìl]a eša [**síz**]**kur**-šè u_4 ká é-lùnga é-muḫaldim ù é kíkken kéše-⌜rá⌝, "1 jug of ordinary dida beer, 30? liters [each], 1 liter of semolina, (and) [1] liter of fine flour, for (ceremonial) offerings when the gate of the brewery-kitchen-mill complex was bound," 1007:1–5

2. For the Fire and the Oven: Semolina and Fine Flour

[2 sìla] dabin 1 sìla eša 0.0.1. kaš-gen **sízkur** gir-ra (. . .) u_4 al-tar é-lùnga é-muḫaldim é-kíkken, "[2 liters] of semolina, 1 liter of fine flour (and) 10 liters of ordinary beer, (ceremonial) offerings of the fire, (and) {other disbursals} during the construction of the brewery-kitchen-mill complex," 440:1–4, 12

1 [sì]la dabin 1 sìla eša **sízkur** gir_4?, "1 liter of semolina (and) 1 liter of fine flour, (ceremonial) offerings of the oven?," 1007:6–8

3. For the Gods: Assorted Grains

0.0.5. zì-KAL 0.0.2. zì-gu-ús 0.0.4.3 sìla dabin 0.0.2.4 sìla eša 7⅓ sìla zú-lum eša ḫi-dè **sízkur** diğir-re-[e?]-ne [. . .], "50 liters of KAL-flour, 20 liters of 2nd-quality gu-flour, 43 liters of semolina, 24 liters of fine flour (and) 7⅓ liters of dates to mix (with) fine flour, (ceremonial) offerings of the [. . .] gods," 1017:1–6

4. For the Sea(-going) Boat: Fine Flour, Beer, Semolina, and Dates

[n] sìla ⌜eša⌝ a-rá-1-[kam] 1 dug $dida_x$-g[en] 2 sìla dabin 1 sìla eša ½ sìla zú-lum a-rá-2-kam 3 sìla dabin 2 sìla eša 1 sìla zú-lum zì-dub-dub-didli-šè **sízkur** má a-a-ba, "[n] liter(s) of fine flour for the 1st time, 1 jug of ordinary dida beer, 2 liters of semolina, 1 liter of fine flour (and) ½ liter of dates for the 2nd time (and) 3 liters of semolina, 2 liters of fine flour (and) 1 liter of dates for various small heaps of flour, (ceremonial) offerings of the sea(-going) boat," 1034:'1-'12

5. For the (Enclosure) Wall

5.1 Ordinary Beer

0.0.1. kaš-gen níğ ki-zàḫ-šè **sízkur** ⌜bàd⌝-šè, "10 liters of ordinary beer, provisions for the cultic place, (ceremonial) offerings for the (enclosure) wall," 986:1–3

5.2 Semolina and Fine Flour

1 sìla dabin ½ sìla eša **sízkur** bàd-šè, "1 liter of semolina (and) ½ liter of fine flour, (ceremonial) offerings for the (enclosure) wall," 987:1–3, 988:1–3, 989:1–3, 990:1–3, 993:1–3, 995:1–3

[0.n.n.] dabin [0.n.n.] eša ⌜**SIZKUR**⌝.**SIZKUR** bàd-šè, "[n] liter(s) of semolina (and) [n] liter(s) of fine flour, (ceremonial) offerings for the (enclosure) wall," 992:1–3

5.3 For the Foundation of the Enclosure Wall: Beer

1 dug $dida_x$-gen **sízkur** uš bàd, "1 jug of ordinary dida beer, (ceremonial) offerings for the foundation of the (enclosure) wall," 377:1–2

6. For the (Enclosure) Wall and Textile Mill: Semolina and Fine Flour

1 sìla dabin ½ sìla eša **sízkur** bàd ù é-uš-bar, "1 liter of semolina (and) ½ liter of fine flour, (ceremonial) offerings for the (enclosure) wall and the textile mill," 991:1–3, 994:1–3

7. Various (Ceremonial) Offerings: Dates Mixed with Fine Flour

0.0.1. zú-lum eša ba-ḫi ⌜**sízkur**⌝-didli-šè, "10 liters of dates were mixed (with) fine flour for various (ceremonial) offerings," 1013:9–10, 1014:'2-'3

8. Context Unspecified, Eaten by the Builders

0.0.1. dabin ninda ne-mur-šè **sízkur**-šè šidim-e-ne íb-gu$_7$, "the builders ate 10 liters of semolina bread (baked in) ash for offerings," 437:5–6

9. Recipient Unspecified: Semolina and Fine Flour

1 sìla dabin ½ sìla eša **sízkur**-šè, "1 liter of semolina (and) ½ liter of fine flour for (ceremonial) offerings," 435:1–3, 439:1–3, 441:1–3

[STONES]

^{na_4}EDEN,"(a stone)"

^{na_4}esi-kam,"diorite"

^{na_4}kinkin á-da-bar šu sè-ga, "'hand-held' black basalt millstone"

^{na_4}kinkin-GI-bí šu sè-ga, "'hand-held' GI-bí millstone"

★★^{na_4}kinkin-GI-bí zà-ḫi-li, "(a millstone)"

^{na_4}kinkin-zi-bí g̃eš-dù šu sè-ga, "'hand-held' ZI-bí g̃eš-dù millstone"

^{na_4}kinkin-zi-bí šu sè-ga, "'hand-held' ZI-bí millstone"

^{na_4}zú, "flint"

^{na_4}ŠEM, "(a stone)"

su(g$_6$), *apālu*, *riābu*, "to repay a loan; to replace" > *Verb Index*

sù, *ṭebû*, "to submerge, sink" > *Verb Index*

sù(b), "to rub, to coat" > *Verb Index*

su$_4$, *pelû*; *sāmu*, "(to be) red, brown"

^{kuš}e-sír túg-du$_8$-a-**su$_4$-a**, "red/brown meshwork sandals" > **^{kuš}e-sír**

^{kuš}súḫub túg-du$_8$-a-**su$_4$-a**, "red/brown meshwork shoes" > **^{kuš}súḫub**

túg-íb-lá-**su$_4$-a**, "red/brown belt" > **túg-íb-lá**

sugal$_7$, *sugallu*, "secretary, civil servant"

1. PN sugal$_7$, "PN, the sugal" > *Personal Name Index*

ri-im-ilum

^{d}*šu*-^{d}*suen-e-te-el-pi$_5$*-^{d}en-líl

sugal$_7$-maḫ, *sugalmaḫu*, "an official, chief minister"

má-gín **sugal$_7$-maḫ**, "the boat builder of the sugal-maḫ" > **má-gín**

1. **Provisions**

0.0.3. ninda-*u$_4$-tuḫ-ḫu-um* 0.0.3. ninda-šu-ra-sig$_5$ 0.2.0. ninda-šu-ra-gen árad-géme **sugal$_7$-maḫ** g̃ír-su^{ki}-šè du-ni, "30 liters of *utuḫḫum* bread, 30 liters of fine half(-loaf) bread (and) 120 liters of ordinary half(-loaf) bread when the male and female servants of the sugal-maḫ came to G̃irsu," 449:6–10

1 udu-niga 2.0.0. ninda-gal-gen gur 0.1.0. zì-gu-ús **sugal$_7$-maḫ**, "1 fattened sheep, 2 bushels of large ordinary bread (and) 60 liters of 2nd-quality gu-flour (for) the sugal-maḫ," 1184:1–5

^{kuš}**súḫub**, *šuḫuppatu*, "boots, shoes"

^{kuš}**súḫub**-gen é-ba-an, "pair of ordinary shoes," 855:11, 855:22, 913:1, 925:1

^{kuš}**súḫub** e-sír-munus-babbar é-ba-an, "pair of woman's white sandals," 932:4

^{kuš}**súḫub** e-sír túg-du$_8$-a-babbar-sig$_5$ é-ba-an, "pair of fine white meshwork-lined sandals," 853:1

^{kuš}**súḫub**-níta du$_8$-ši-a é-ba-an, "pair of man's turquoise shoes," 925:4

^{kuš}**súḫub**-munus-babbar é-ba-an, "pair of woman's white shoes," 932:5

^{kuš}**súḫub**-munus-e-sír é-ba-an, "pair of woman's white sandals," 932:6

^{kuš}**súḫub**-túg-du$_8$-a-su$_4$-a *šu-kab-tá* é-ba-an, "pair of red/brown meshwork shoes of *Šu-Kabta*," 782:2

^{kuš}**súḫub**-tur-gen é-ba-an, "pair of small/children's ordinary shoes," 913:2, 925:2

1. **túg-šà-^{kuš}súḫub**

★★**túg-šà-^{kuš}súḫub** 3-kam-ús, 680:1

★★**túg-šà-^{kuš}súḫub**-níg̃-lám 3-kam-ús, 649:4, 725:5, 771:6

★★**túg-šà-^{kuš}súḫub**-[níg̃?-lám?] é-b[a-an], 572:2

2. **Wool for Shoes**

1 $^{\text{<kuš>}}$**súḫub**-túg-du$_8$-a-[babb]ar? siki $^{\text{g̃eš}}$garig aka 3-kam-ús ki-lá-bi ½ ma-na 2 gín, "3rd-quality combed wool (for) 1 (pair) of white meshwork shoes, its weight is ½ mina and 2 shekels," 756:1–3

suḫur, *qimmatu*, "tuft, plume; crown (of a tree)"

★★a-g̃á-ri-in SUḪUR im g̃ar-ra, 192:'17, 194:58–59

ká-**suḫur**, "tree-top gate" > **ká**

$^{\text{g̃eš}}$**suḫuš-ig**, *ḫapḫappu*, "foundation of a door"

3 $^{\text{g̃eš}}$**suḫuš-ig**-ù-suḫ$_5$, "3 door foundations of pine wood," 1333:3

sukud, *mēlû*, "height"

n nindan gíd n kùš dag̃al n kùš (ba-an-)gi$_4$-bi n kùš **sukud** saḫar-bi n sar (n gín n še) (. . .) n sar im-du$_8$-a, "n nindan long, n kùš wide, n kùš tapered from n kùš high, its dirt is n sar (n gín (and) n še); (the total volume) of the adobe wall is n sar," 366:'1-'3, '13, 366:'7-'8, '13, 366:'9-'10, '13, 366:'11-'13, 366:'17–19

n nindan gíd n kùš dağal n kùš **sukud** saḫar-bi n sar (n gín n še) (. . .) n sar im-du$_8$-a, "n nindan long, n kùš wide, n kùš high, its dirt is n sar (n gín (and) n še); (the total volume) of the adobe wall is n sar," 366:'5-'6, '13, 366:'15-'16, '19

ᵘsullim(U.EN), *šambalitu*, "fenugreek"

★★4 gú-ús-sa **sullim**, 1143:1

lá-ìa 40 ma-na 10⅔ gín **ᵘsullim**-a, "40 minas (and) 10 1⅔ shekels of fenugreek remaning," 1350:1

40 ma-na 10⅔ gín **ᵘU.[EN]**, "40 minas (and) 10⅔ shekels of fenugreek," 1092:9

n sa **ᵘsullim**, "n bundle(s) of fenugreek," 511:68, 972:23, 972:91, 975:24, 975:92, 981:22

sum, *nadānu*, "to give" > *Verb Index*

sum-sikil, *šamaškilu*, "a type of onion," 511:71, 972:25, 972:94, 975:27, 975:95

sum-sikil-mar-ḫa-ši, "Marhaši onion," 1113:1

ḫar **sum-sikil** mar-ḫa-ši, "Marhaši onion sprout?," 1168:1

sumun, *labāru*, "(to be) old"

ᵏᵘˢ̌a-g̃á-lá-**sumun**, "old leather sack" > **ᵏᵘˢ̌a-g̃á-lá**

ᵗᵘ́ᵍbar-si **sumun**, "old band" > **ᵗᵘ́ᵍbar-si**

gada **sumun**, "old linen" > **gada**

g̃á-nun-na **sumun**, "old storehouse" > *Household Index*

é-lùnga **sumun**, "old brewery" > *Household Index*

é-kišib-ba **sumun**, "old storeroom" > *Household Index*

é-*zu-zu-tum* **sumun**, "old house of *Zuzutum*" > *Household Index*

iri^{ki} **sumun**, "old city" > **iri^{ki}**

iz-zi **sumun**, "old iz-zi wall" > **iz-zi**

$^{g̃eš}$nimbar **sumun**, "old date palm" > **$^{g̃eš}$nimbar**

šeg$_{12}$ **sumun**, "old brick" > **šeg$_{12}$**

túg **sumun**, "old textile" > **túg**

ᵗᵘ́ᵍuš-bar **sumun**, "old uš-bar textile" > **ᵗᵘ́ᵍuš-bar**

zíz **sumun**, "old emmer wheat" > **zíz**

sumur, *ṣulūlu*, "protection"

1. **im sumur**, "plaster"

im sumur aka, "to plaster (with mud or clay)" > **aka**

im sumur tà(g), "to apply plaster" > **tà(g)**

sumur iz-zi ù-ru, "to level the plastered wall" > **ù-ru**
1 ĝuruš šidim 2 ĝuruš 1 géme **i[m sumur**...], 112:'18-'19

sur, "to twist, twine (rope)" > *Verb Index*

sur, *ṣaḫātu*, "to press, squeeze" > *Verb Index*
géme ĝeš-ì-**sur-sur**, "female oil presser" > *Craftswomen Index*

[SYLLABICALLY WRITTEN SUMERIAN]
^{dug}alalu > ^{dug}ù-lu-lu
alur(a) > al-ur_{x}(BÁḪAR)-ra
^{ĝeš}galam > ga-lam
gub > ku-bu
gur > gu-ru-dè
ḫal > ba-na-ḫa-la
íl > ì-li-de_{9}(TI)/dè
kúr > ku-úr
$še\tilde{g}_{6}$ > šé-$\tilde{g}e_{6}$-dè
šu . . . te(ĝ) > šu ḫa-ba-ab-ti-ĝá
šu . . . te(ĝ) > šu te-$\tilde{g}e_{6}$-dè
ùr > ù-ru-dè

– Š –

^{ĝeš}***ša-pá-ar-gi-lum***, *šapargillu / supurgi(l)lu*, "quince, quince tree wood"
2 ḫar ^{ĝeš}***ša-pá-ar-gi-lum*** 1-ta, "2 quice tree seedlings, 1 (unit) each," 1375:9

ša-ra-ab-du, *šarrabtû*, "(an official)"
nu-úr-ì-lí **ša-ra-ab-du**, "*Nur-ili*, the šarabdu official" > *Personal Name Index*
nam-**ša-ra-ab-du**, "administration" > **nam-ša-ra-ab-du**

šà, *libbu*, "in, inside of," *passim*
šà-bi-ta, "from among it," *passim*

^{túg}**šà-ga-dù**, *šakattû*, "a textile; waist-binding (cloth),"[109] 744:9
^{kuš}**šà-ga-dù**, "leather belt," 912:5, 1376:61

---

[109] Steinkeller 1982b, 362.

kuš**šà-ga-dù** e-rí-na, "root-tanned leather belt," 968:5

túg**šà-ga-dù**-gen, "ordinary belt," 639:5, 680:3, 683:1, 693:7, 694:7, 742:9, 745:7, 748:13, 753:14, 800:7, 801:7, 818:6

túg**šà-ga-dù**-ús, "2nd-quality belt," 793:10

túg**šà-[ga-dù** ba-tab *tuḫ-ḫu-um*], "[ba-tab *tuḫ-ḫu-um*] belt," 765:1

túg**šà-ga-dù** ba-tab *tuḫ-ḫu-um*-gen, "ordinary ba-tab *tuḫ-ḫu-um* belt," 764:1

túg**šà-ga-dù** ba-tab *tuḫ-ḫu-um*-ús, "2nd-quality ba-tab *tuḫ-ḫu-um* belt," 746:5, 758:1

túg**šà-ga-dù** ba-tab *tuḫ-ḫu-um* 3-kam-ús, "3rd-quality ba-tab *tuḫ-ḫu-um* belt," 569:8, 579:14, 618:4, 669:4, 692:1, 738:4, 742:2, 746:6, 753:7, 758:6, 760:3, 771:2, 778:1, 786:3, 806:3, 811:5, 814:7, 821:6, 1162:'16

túg**šà-ga-dù** ba-tab *tuḫ-ḫu-um* 4-kam-ús, "4th-quality ba-tab *tuḫ-ḫu-um* belt," 579:15, 649:8, 692:3, 708:5, 709:4, 747:6, 834:9, 835:'9

túg**šà-ga-dù** ba-tab *tuḫ-ḫu-um* [n-kam-ú]s, "[nth]-quality ba-tab *tuḫ-ḫu-um* belt," 511:'120, 743:1, 743:3

túg**šà-ga-dù**-níĝ-lám 3-kam-ús, "3rd-quality níĝ-lám belt," 569:9, 637:1, 662:3, 673:4, 674:2, 693:2, 701:2, 738:5, 739:3, 758:7, 793:4, 834:8, 1162:'15

túg**šà-ga-dù**-níĝ-lám 4-kam-ús, "4th-quality níĝ-lám belt," 739:5

túg**šà-ga-dù**-níĝ-lám [n-kam-ú]s, "[nth]-quality níĝ-lám belt," 569:7

túg**šà-ga-dù**-níĝ-lám *šu-kab-tá*, "níĝ-lám belt of *Šu-Kabta*," 579:13, 590:3, 591:7, 608:3, 636:3, 647:1, 658:1, 676:2, 690:1, 698:4, 698:14, 736:2, 827:3, 829:'2

[n túg**š]à-ga-dù**-níĝ-lám *šu-kab-tá* [ki-lá-b]i ⅓ mana [2 gín], "[n] níĝ-lám belt(s) of *Šu-Kabta*, their weight is ⅓ mina (and) 2 shekels," 738:1–2

túg**šà-ga-dù** [. . .], "[. . .] belt," 591:'10, 829:'7

1 túg**šà-ga-dù** [. . .] *šu-kab-*[*tá*], "1 [. . .] belt of *Šu-Kabta*," 759:4

šà-gal, *ukullû*, "food, fodder; provisions"

šà-gal anšekúnga, "equid fodder"

šà-gal má-laḫ5, "food (for) sailors"

šà-gal mušen-na, "bird fodder"

šà-gal nam-ra-ak, "provisions of the booty"

šà-gal šáḫ, "pig fodder"

šà-gal šidim-e-ne, "food (for) builders"

šà-gal udu-niga, "fattened sheep fodder"

šà-gal udu šáḫ mušen péš ḫi-a, "fodder of various sheep, pigs, birds (and) mice"

1. **šà-gal** anše**kúnga**, "equid fodder"

0.0.1. še šà-gal anše**kúnga**, "10 liters of barley, fodder of equids," 534:1–2

2. **šà-gal má-laḫ5**, "food (for) sailors"

0.2.3. še á má-ḫuĝ-ĝá 0.2.0. á ĝuruš ḫuĝ-ĝá 0.0.1.6 sìla **šà-gal má-la[ḫ5** . . .] ⸢u4⸣-1-[šè] é-duru5-*simat*-d[*ištaran*-ta] ka i7-d[nin-ḫur-saĝ-ĝá-šè] má gíd-da, "150 liters of barley, wages of the hired boat (and) 120 liters, wages of hired workmen; 16 liters, food (for) sailors [. . .]

(workers) [for] 1 day having towed boats [from] *Simat-Ištaran*'s village [to] the opening of the [Ninḫursaĝa] canal," 561:'10–'14

0.2.3. á má-ḫuĝ-ĝá 0.2.0. á ĝuruš ḫuĝ-ĝá 0.0.1.6 **šà-gal má-laḫ$_5$** 0.0.1.6 <še->bi sa$_{10}$ má-laḫ$_5$ u$_4$-1-šè gú i$_7$-^{d}nin-ḫur-sag-ĝá-ta [gar-ša-an-na^{ki}-šè má] gíd-da, "150 liters (of barley), wages of the hired boat (and) 120 liters, wages of hired workmen, 16 liters, food (for) sailors, 16 liters <of barley> is the (hiring) price of the sailors [for] 1 day having towed [boats] from the bank of the Ninḫursaĝa canal [to Garšana]," 561:'19-'23

0.2.3. á má-ḫuĝ-ĝá 0.2.0. á ĝuruš ḫuĝ-ĝá 0.0.1.6 sìla **šà-gal má-laḫ$_5$** 0.0.1.6 sìla < še->b[i s]a$_{10}$ má-⌜laḫ$_5$⌝ u$_4$-1-šè é-duru$_5$-ka[b-bí-ta] gú i$_7$-[*ma-an-iš-ti-šu*-šè] má gí[d-da], "140 liters (of barley), wages of the hired boat (and) 120 liters, wages of hired workmen, 16 liters, food for sailors, 16 liters is the (hiring) price of the sailors for 1 day having towed boats [from] the Kabbi village [to] the bank of the [*Maništišu*] canal," 561:'28-'32

3. **šà-gal mušen-na**, "bird fodder"

3.1 Assorted Grains

n sìla še gur n sìla n gín kib$_x$ **šà-gal mušen-na**, "n bushel(s) (and) n liter(s) of barley, (and) n liter(s), (and) n shekel(s) of wheat, fodder of birds," 1081:4–6, 1109:5–7

3.2 Barley and Groats

n sìla še n sìla ar-za-na n sìla še-bala-bi **šà-gal mušen-na**, "n liter(s) of barley, n liter(s) of barley-grits, (and) n liter(s) (and) n shekel(s) of barley of the bala, fodder of birds," 1179:1–14, 1199:8–11, 1208:10–13

3.3 Semolina

0.0.2. dabin **šà-gal mušen-na**, "20 liters of semolina, fodder of birds," 1161:1–2

4. **šà-gal nam-ra-ak**, "provisions of the booty"

0.1.0. dabin **šà-g[al] nam-ra-ak**, "60 liters of semolina, provisions of the booty," 1085:1–2

5. **šà-gal šáḫ**, "pig fodder"

5.1 Assorted Grains for Range-fed Pigs

0.3.3. še 0.1.1. zì-milla 0.3.3. tuḫ-duru$_5$-gen **šà-gal šáḫ**-ú, "210 liters of barley, 70 liters of low-quality flour (and) 210 liters of ordinary fresh chaff, fodder of range-fed pigs," 1179:7–10

0.3.3 še 0.1.3. tuḫ-duru$_5$-gen **šà-gal šáḫ**-ú, "210 liters of barley (and) 90 liters of ordinary fresh bran, fodder of range-fed pigs," 1199:5–7

0.3.4.5. sìla še 0.1.3. tuḫ-duru$_5$-gen **šà-gal šáḫ**-ú, "225 liters of barley (and) 90 liters of ordinary fresh bran, fodder of range-fed pigs," 1208:7–9

5.2 Barley for Fattened Pigs

0.4.3. še **šà-gal šáḫ**-niga, "270 liters of barley, fodder of fattened pigs," 1179:5–6

[2] šáḫ-munus-ama-gan-da-bi de$_6$-a 2 sìla-ta {indent} 2 ⌜še⌝-bi 0.2.0. **[šà-ga]l šáḫ-niga, "[2] female breeding pigs having been brought at 2 liters each; (total:) 2 (pigs). Their barley equivalent for the fodder of the fattened pigs is 180 liters," 1189:7–10

1.1.0. še gur **šà-gal šáḫ**-niga, "1 bushel and 60 liters of barley, fodder of fattened pigs," 1208:5–6

5.3 Fresh Bran for Female Breeding Pigs

[n **š]áḫ**-munus-ama-gan ½ sìla še-[ta n]+1 sìla tuḫ-duru$_5$-ta [. . . **š]à-gal** ½ ⸢sìla⸣-[ta], "[n] female breeding pig(s): ½ liter of barley [each] (and) [n]+1 liter of fresh chaff each; [. . .] fodder of ½ liter [each]," 1189:11–12

5.4 Fresh Dates for Range-fed Pigs

0.n.0. u$_4$-ḫi-in **šà-gal šáḫ**-ú, "n liter(s) of fresh dates, fodder of range-fed pigs," 1081:7–8, 1109:8–9

5.5 Broken Context

[. . .] x [. . . **šà-ga**]**l šáḫ**-[ú], "[. . .], fodder of [range-fed] pigs," 1189:'14-'15

6. **šà-gal šidim-e-ne**, "food (for) builders"

6.1 Animals

10 ádda-udu 1 uz-tur 3 péš-g̃eš-gi ba-úš iti u$_4$-8-ba-zal **šà-gal šidim-e-ne** (. . .) ⸢u$_4$⸣ é-e im sumur ba-aka, "10 sheep carcasses, 1 dead duckling (and) 3 dead mice, at the end of the 8th day of the month, food (for) builders (and) {other allotments} when the house was plastered," 472:3–7, 14

6.2 Assorted Grains

ninda-bi [5-sìla] dabin-bi 0.0.1. še-bi 0.0.1.1 sìla níg̃-àr-ra-sig$_5$-bi ⅓ sìla **šà-gal šidim-e-ne**, "(In total:) their bread is [5 liters], their semolina is 10 liters, their barley is 11 liters, their fine groats are 1⅓ liters, food (for) builders," 381:17–21

5 sìla ninda 0.0.1. dabin 0.0.1.1 sìla še⅓ sìla níg̃-àr-ra-sig$_5$ **šà-gal šidim-e-ne** (. . .) u$_4$ bàd é-a dù-dè, "5 liters of bread, 10 liters of semolina, 11 liters of barley, ⅓ liter of fine groats, food (for) builders, (and) {other allotments}, when they were constructiong the (enclosure) wall of the house," 383:1–5, 11

[0.0.5.5] sìla ninda [0.0.1.] dabin [0.0.1.1] sìla še 1 sìla 10 gín níg̃-àr-ra-sig$_5$ **šà-gal šidim-e-ne** (. . .) bà[d egi]r é-a dù-dè, "[55] liters of bread, [10] liters of semolina, [11] liters of barley (and) 1 liter and 10 shekels of fine groats, food (for) builders, (and) {other allotments}, (provisions for workers) to construct the (enclosure) wall behind the house," 385:1–5, 9

ninda-bi n-sìla dabin-bi n še-bi n sìla níg̃-àr-ra-sig$_5$-bi n sìla **šà-gal šidim-e-ne** ⸢u$_4$⸣ bàd egir é-a dù-dè, "(In total:) their bread is n liters(s), their semolina is n liter(s), their barley is n liter(s), their fine groats are n liter(s), food (for) builders when they were constructing the (enclosure) wall behind the house," 386:25–30, 387:16–21

dabin-bi 0.0.1.5 sìla še-bi 0.0.1. níg̃-àr-ra-sig$_5$-bi 1-sìla **šà-gal šidim-e-ne** u$_4$ bàd in-dù-sa-a, "(In total:) their semolina is 15 liters, their barley is 10 liters (and) their fine groats are 1 liter, food (for) builders when they constructed the (enclosure) wall," 396:16–20, 397:16–20

6.3 Birds

2 uz-tur 1 ir$_7^{\text{mušen}}$ ba-úš **šà-gal šidim-e-ne**, "2 dead ducklings (and) 1 dead pigeon, food (for) builders," 470:1–4

6.4 Fish

30 ku$_6$ al-dar-ra **šà-gal šidim-e-ne**, "30 split (dried) fish, food (for) builders," 489:1–2

6.5 Salt

[n sìl]a mun [**šà-ga**]**l šidim-e-ne**, "[n] liter(s) of salt, food (for) builders," 1325:9–10

7. **šà-gal šidim ù dub-sar-e-ne**, "food (for) builders and scribes"

[šu-nígin 2.2].4. še gur [šu-nígin 1.3.3.] dabin gur [šu-nígin 36] ádda-udu [**šà-gal šidim**] **ù dub-sar-e-ne**, "[In total: 2 bushel(s) (and) 120+]40 liters of barley, [1 bushel(s) (and) 210 liter(s)] of semolina (and) [36] sheep carcassses, [food (for) builders] and scribes," 399:22–25

8. **šà-gal udu-niga**, "fattened sheep fodder"

8.1 Barley and Reeds

9.2.1. [še gur] 1680 sa gi-zi **šà-gal udu-niga**, "9 bushels (and) 130 liters [of barley] (and) 1680 bundles of fresh reeds, fodder of fattened sheep," 1081:1–3

še-bi 3.2.3. gur gi-zi(!)-bi 524 sa **šà-gal udu-niga**, "(In total:) their barley is 3 bushels (and) 150 liters, their fresh reeds are 524 bundles, fodder of fattened sheep," 1189:1–6

8.2 Barley, Bran, and Reeds

n sìla še gur n tuḫ-duru$_5$-gen n sa gi-zi **šà-gal udu-niga**, "n bushel(s) (and) n liter(s) of barley, n liter(s) of ordinary fresh bran, (and) n bundle(s) of fresh reeds, fodder of fattened sheep," 1109:1–4, 1179:1–4, 1199:1–4, 1208:1–4

9. **šà-gal udu šáḫ mušen péš ḫi-a**, "fodder of various sheep, pigs, birds (and) mice"

9.1 Barley, Bran, and Reeds

šu+nígin n sìla gur šu+nígin n tuḫ-duru$_5$-gen gur šu+nígin n sa gi-zi **šà-gal udu šáḫ mušen péš** ḫi-a, "In total: n bushel(s) (and) n liter(s) of barley, n bushel(s) (and) n liter(s) of ordinary fresh bran, (and) n bundle(s) of fresh reeds, fodder of various sheep, pigs, birds (and) mice," 1199:13–16, 1208:15–18

9.2 Barley, Flour, Bran, and Reeds

šu+nígin 10.1.2.9 sìla še gur šu+nígin 0.1.1. zì-milla šu+nígin 1.2.3. tuḫ-duru$_5$-gen gur š[u+nig̃]in$_2$ 1230 sa gi-zi [**šà-gal u**]**du šáḫ mušen péš** ḫi-a, "In total: 10 bushels (and) 89 liters of barley, 70 liters of milla-flour, 1 bushel (and) 150 liters of ordinary fresh bran (and) 1230 bundles of fresh reeds, [fodder] of various sheep, pigs, birds (and) mice," 1179:16–20

9.3 Barley, Wheat, Reeds, and Dates

šu+nígin [10.4].2.3½ sìla še gur šu+nígin 0.0.1.5⅔ sìla 5 gín kib$_x$ šu+nígin 1680 sa ⌜gi⌝-zi šu+nígin 0.0.4. u$_4$-ḫi-[in] **šà-gal udu šáḫ mušen [péš]** ḫi-a, "In total: 10 bushels (and) 263½ liters of barley, 15⅔ liters (and) 5 shekels of wheat, 1680 bundles of fresh reeds (and) 40 liters of fresh dates, fodder of various sheep, pigs, birds (and) [mice]," 1081:10–14

šu+nígin 14.0.5. 1½ sìla še gur šu+nígin 0.1.1.4 sìla 15 gín kib$_x$ šu+nígin 0.3.0. tuḫ-duru$_5$-[gen] šu+nígin 0.3.0. u$_4$-ḫi-in šu+nígin 2130 [sa gi-z]i **šà-gal udu šáḫ mušen pé[š** ḫi-a], "In total: 14 bushels (and) 51½ liters of barley, 74 liters and 15 shekels of wheat, 180 liters of [ordinary] fresh bran, 30 liters of fresh dates, and 2130 [bundles] of fresh [reeds], fodder of various sheep, pigs, birds (and) mice," 1109:11–16

^{túg}**šà-gi$_4$-dab$_6$**, "(a textile)"

^{túg}**šà-gi$_4$-dab$_6$** ba-tab *tuḫ-ḫu-um* 3-kam-ús, "3rd-quality ba-tab *tuḫ-ḫu-um* šà-gi$_4$-dab$_6$ textile," 775:1

^{túg}**šà-gi$_4$-dab$_6$** ba-tab *tuḫ-ḫu-um* 4-kam-ús, "4th-quality ba-tab *tuḫ-ḫu-um* šà-gi$_4$-dab$_6$ textile," 786:9

^{túg}**šà-gi**(!)**-dab$_6$** níĝ-lám 3-kam-ús, "3rd-quality níĝ-lám šà-gi-dab$_6$ textile," 835:'5

^{túg}**šà-gi$_4$-dab$_6$** níĝ-lám 3-kam-ús, "3rd-quality níĝ-lám šà-gi$_4$-dab$_6$ textile," 594:4, 697:1

^{túg}**šà-gi$_4$-dab$_6$** níĝ-lám-AB 3-kam-ús, "3rd-quality níĝ-lám-AB šà-gi$_4$-dab$_6$ textile," 590:2

šà-gu$_4$, *kullizu*, "ox-driver"

ĝuruš **šà-gu$_4$**, "ox-driver," *passim*

še **šà-gu$_4$-me-éš** ḫal, "to divide barley for ox-drivers" > **ḫal**

1. **šà-gu$_4$-me-éš ugula PN šabra**, "ox-drivers supervised by PN, the majordomo" > *Personal Name Index*

ba-ba-ni

nu-úr-^{d}adad

2. **Orders for the Ox-Driver**

ur-^{d}dumu-zi ù *a-ḫu-wa-qar* ù-na-a-⌜du$_{11}$⌝ 0.0.2. ku-[x] *šu*-^{d}nisaba ḫé-na-ab-sum-mu 1 ĝuruš **šà-gu$_4$** iri^{ki}-ta iri^{ki}-šè ḫé-eb-sá-e nam-mi-gur-re, "Say to Ur-Dumuzi and *Aḫu-waqar* that '20 liters of [x] should be given to *Šu*-Nisaba. 1 ox-driver from the city should arrive at the city. They should not argue!'" 1045:1–11

šà-kal, *šakkullu*, "(a wood used for furniture)"

29½ ^{ĝeš}garig **šà-kal** é-ba-an, "29½ pairs of wooden combs," 598:1

^{ĝeš}gu-za-munus **šà!-kal**, "wooden woman's chair," 761:1

šà-maḫ, *šammāhu*, "large intestine?"

[1 ^{kuš}EDIN].A.LÁ **šà-⌜maḫ⌝**, "[1] waterskin (made) of a large intestine?," 925:'12

šà-tuku$_5$, *še'ītu*, "mattress"

1. **Cleaning Supplies to Wash a Mattress**

5½ naga-si-è 2 ma-na im-bábbar **šà-tuku$_5$** lu-luḫ-dè, "5⅓ (liters) of sprouted naĝa (and) 2 minas of gypsum in order to wash a mattress," 783:3–5

2. **Wool to Reinforce a Mattress**

12 gín siki-ĝír-gul **šà-tuku$_5$** kala-kala-gé-dè, "12 shekels of ĝír-gul wool to reinforce a mattress," 783:1–2

3. **šà-tuku$_5$ siki-ud$_5$**, "goat-hair mattress"

1 **šà-tuku$_5$** siki-ud$_5$ ki-lá-bi 5 ma-na 10 gín, "1 goat-hair mattress, its weight is 5 minas and 10 shekels," 706:1–2

1 bar-si siki-ud$_5$ **šà-tuku$_5$** é-ba-an ki-lá-bi 2 ma-na, "1 pair of goat-hair bands (or) a mattress, their weight is 2 minas," 740:3–4

šabra(PA.AL), *šabrû*, "majordomo; chief administrator of a temple or other household"

še **šabra** sum, "to give barley to the majordomo" > **sum**

ugula PN **šabra**, "supervised by PN, the majordomo" > **ugula**

1. **PN šabra**, "PN, the majordomo" > *Personal Name Index*

^{d}adad-tillati	*èr-ra-ba-ni*	*nu-úr-^{d}adad*
ba-ba-ni	ḫa-ma-ti	*šu-^{d}adad*
ba-la-a	*ilum-ba-ni*	*za-ak-ì-lí*
é-a-šar	lú-dingir-ra	
ì-lí-aš-ra-ni	*na-sìm*	

šag̃an, *šikkatu*, "a flask"

^{kuš}du$_{10}$-gan-⌜**šag̃an**⌝, "a leather flask," 906:5

šáḫ, *šaḫû*, "pig"[110]

é-**šáḫ**, "piggery" > *Household Index*

ì-**šáḫ**, "lard" > **ì**

kuš-**šáḫ**, "pig skin" > **kuš**

šà-gal **šáḫ**, "pig fodder" > **šà-gal**

šà-gal **šáḫ**-niga, "fodder of fattened pigs"

šà-gal **šáḫ**-ú, "fodder of range-fed pigs"

šà-gal udu **šáḫ** mušen péš ḫi-a, "fodder of various sheep, pigs, birds (and) mice" > **šà-gal**

****šáḫ**-g̃e$_{6}$ TAG$_{4}$.ALAM, 421:2

šáḫ-munus-ama-gan, "female breeding pig," 1189:7, 1189:11, 1211:1

šáḫ-niga, "fattened pig," 1189:10

šáḫ-níta, "male pig," 1211:2

šáḫ-ú, "range-fed pig," 1189:15

šáḫ-zé-da, "piglet," 511:86, 541:6, 541:9

1. **šáḫ-zé-da**, "piglet"

1.1 **For the Kitchen**

1 **šáḫ-zé-da** é-muḫaldim-⌜šè⌝, "1 piglet for the kitchen," 507:15

[1] **šáḫ-zé-da** é-muḫaldim mu *simat-^{d}ištaran*<-šè>, "[1] piglet (for) the kitchen for *Simat-Ištaran*," 529:22–23

1.2 **For the Funerary Libation Place of Dada**

1 **šáḫ-zé-da**-ga ki-a-nag-*da-da*-šè, "1 suckling piglet for the funerary libation place of *Dada*," 970:10–11

1.3 **Offerings of the Funerary Libation Place of *Šu-Kabta***

šáḫ-zé-da sá-du$_{11}$-ki-a-nag̃-*šu-kab-tá*, "piglet, regular offerings of the funerary libation place of *Šu-Kabta*" > **sá-du$_{11}$**

110 For pigs at Garšana see Owen 2006.

[1] **šáḫ-zé-d[a** K]A-⌜dé⌝-[x] 1 {erasure} é-u$_4$-15 (. . .) sá-du$_{11}$-ki-a-nag-*šu-kab-tá*, "[1] piglet (?) on the full moon day, (and) {other comestibles}, regular offerings of the funerary libation place of *Šu-Kabta*," 981:1–4, 33

^{ĝeš}**šar**(NE)-**ša$_4$**(DU)-**bìd**(KU),[111] *šaršabiṭṭu*, "(a tree)"

n ḫar ^{ĝeš}**šar-ša$_4$-bìd**, "n šar-ša$_4$-bìd seedling(s)," 1256:21, 1362:18, 1362:'37, 1362:'38, 1362:'39

n ḫar ^{ĝeš}**šar-ša$_4$-bìd** n-ta, "n šar-ša$_4$-bìd seedling(s), n (units) each," 1256:19, 1256:20, 1375:24, 1375:25, 1375:26

še, *še'u*, "barley"

še ba-al, "to unload barley" > **ba-al**

še de$_6$, "to bring barley" > **de$_6$**

še è,"to bring out barley" > **è**

še en-nu aka, "to guard barley" > **aka**

še ga$_6$(ĝ), "to carry barley" > **ga$_6$(ĝ)**

še-gán-bi, "their barley of the field" > **gán**

še ĝen, "to go (for) barley" > **ĝen**

še gur$_{10}$, "to reap barley" > **gur$_{10}$**

še ì-dub, "barley of the granary" > **ì-dub**

še nu-ĝál, "there was not barley" > **ĝál**

še su(g), "to repay a loan of barley" > **su(g)**

še sum, "to give barley" > **sum**

še-zíz-ḫi-a lá, "to transport various barley (and) emmer wheat" > **lá**

še zuḫ, "to steal barley" > **zuḫ**

1. Barley as Animal Fodder

še mur-gud-šè, "barley for ox fodder" > **mur-gud**

še mušen, "barley (for) birds" > **mušen**

še šà-gal, "barley (as) fodder" > **šà-gal**

n sìla **še**-bala-bi šà-gal mušen-na, "n liter(s) of barley of the bala, fodder of birds" > **šà-gal**

2. Barley Equivalents

še-bi n (sìla), "their barley is n (liters)," 381:19, 386:26, 387:18, 396:17, 397:17, 1527:7

n dug dida n še-bi n, "n jug(s) of dida beer, their barley (equivalent) is n liter(s)" > **dida**

n dabin n sìla **še**-bi, "n liter(s) of semolina, their barley (equivalent) is n liter(s) of barley," 1254:'19-'20

5 ma-na siki **še** 0.0.3.-ta, "5 minas of wool, the equivalent of 30 liters of barley each," 431:2

[111] For this reading, see Bauer 1992.

540 sa gi-izi sa$_{10}$ **še** 0.0.1. 20 sa gi-ta še-bi 0.4.3., "540 bundles of fuel reeds, the purchase price of which is 10 liters of barley for each 20 bundles of reeds, their barley is 270 (liters)," 1527: 35–37

★★0.0.1.2½ sìla ^{na_4}ŠEM? **še**-ta sa$_{10}$-a, "12½ liters (?), the price from barley," 1372:50–51

3. Barley for Food Production

še mu munu$_4$-šè, "barley for malt" > **munu$_4$**

še mu ninda du$_8$, "barley to bake bread" > **du$_8$**

4. še(-ba), "barley rations"

dirig **še-ba**-ne-ne mu zì nu-g̃ál-la-šè ḫal, "to divide additional barley rations because there was no flour" > **ḫal**

še-ba árad *šu-eš$_4$-tár*, "barley rations for the servant(s) of *Šu-Eštar*" > *Personal Name Index*

še-ba é, "barley rations of the household" > **é**

še-ba géme-árad *simat-^{d}ištaran*, "barley rations of the female and male servants of *Simat-Ištaran*" > *Personal Name Index*

še-ba éren-na, "barley rations of the workers" > **éren**

še-ba g̃en-na mu še-ba-ne-ne-šè, "(workers) having gone for barley for barley rations" > **g̃en**

še-ba éren-na sum, "to give barley rations to the workers" > **sum**

še mu dabin-šè, "barley in place of semolina" > **dabin**

n (sìla) **še**-ta, "n (liters) of barley each," 381:6, 386:14, 387:5, 396:6, 397:6, 557:1

še-ba dub-sar-e-ne, "barley rations of scribes," 394:7, 408:2

še-ba géme-árad, "barley rations of female and male household servants," 465:4, 511:'99, 512:4, 514:4, 520:4, 524:4, 527:2

(. . .) **še-ba** ì-b[a ù níg̃-dab$_5$], "{assorted commodities} (for) barley (and) oil rations [and requisitions]," 446:9

21.4.3 še gur ì-dub **še-ba** iti-3-kam, "21 bushels (and) 270 liters of barley of the granary (for) barley rations (for) 3 months," 542:1–3

4.1 še-ba PN, "barley rations (for) PN" > *Personal Name Index*

ad-da-kal-la	*ba-zi-tum*	*in-ga-la*
aḫ-dam-ì-lí	*ḫa-la-ša*	lú-^{d}*suena*
		SIG$_7$-a ḪA?.[A?]

5. Barley Wages

še á, "barley as wages" > **á**

5.1 For Specific Work Assignments

še á al aka ù gu$_4$-ḫug̃-g̃á, "barley, wages of hoers and rented oxen" > **aka**

še á dabin-šè, "barley, wages for (milling) semolina," 475:1–2

še al aka, "barley (for workers) to hoe" > **aka**

še apin-lá, "barley of the cultivator" > **apin-lá**

še šeg$_{12}$ ga$_6$(g̃), "barley (for workers) to carry bricks" > **ga$_6$(g̃)**

5.2 Hiring Rates

á n-ta **še**-bi n u$_4$-1-šè, "{workwomen} wages for each n (bricks carried), their barley (rations are) for n workerday(s)" > **á**

še n sìla-ta ba-ḫuĝ, "hired (for) n liter(s) of barley each" > **ḫuĝ**

še n-sìla-ta ba-ḫuĝ še-bi n sìla n gín, "{workwomen / workmen} hired (for) n liter(s) of barley each, their barley is n liter(s) (and) n shekel(s)" > **ḫuĝ**

še-bi n sìla ba-ḫuĝ, "hired (for barley), their barley is n liter(s)" > **ḫuĝ**

še 3-sìla-[ta] še-bi 0.3.0.-ta, "{workwomen} (hired for) 3 liters of barley [each], their barley is 30 liters each," 338:18–19

5.3 Remainder of Barley Wages

n (sìla) **še** *si-ì-tum* á, "n (liters) of barley, the remainder of wages" > ***si-ì-tum***

6. Other

ba-ba-**še**, "barley porridge" > **ba-ba**

^{gi}gur **še**, "measuring container of barley" > **^{gi}gur**

^{gi}gur **še** ésir šub-ba, "measuring container coated with bitumen (containing) barley" > **šub**

^{gi}gur **še á-áĝ-ĝá ésir šub-ba > **^{gi}gur**

še níĝ-àr-ra, "barley groats" > **níĝ-àr-ra**

še-ninda, "barley (for) bread" > **ninda**

še numun-šè, "barley for seed" > **numun**

7. Broken Context

[. . .] še-bi, 1036:'65

še-du$_{10}$, "(a tree)"

1 ^{ĝeš}éren n ma-na **še-du$_{10}$**, "1 yoke of n mina(s) of šedu (wood?)" > **^{ĝeš}éren**

še-gín, *šimtu*, "wax, glue," 855:2, 855:19, 1520:2

[n] gín **še-gín** mu x-šè (. . .) ⸢u$_4$⸣ é-e im sumur ba-aka, "[n] shekels of glue for x, (and) {other allotments} when the house was plastered," 472:10, 14

še-lú, *kisibirru*, "coriander," 511:69, 972:21, 972:93, 975:22, 975:93, 981:19, 1130:3

še-lú al-ús-sa, "processed coriander," 523:11

šeg$_{12}$(SIG$_4$), *libittu*, "mud brick"

ká im **šeg$_{12}$** ku$_4$-ra, "the 'service entrance' of the gate" > **ká**

šeg$_{12}$-al-ur$_x$-ra, "(baked) brick" > **al-ur$_x$-ra**

šeg$_{12}$ du$_8$, "to mold bricks" > **du$_8$**

šeg$_{12}$ en-nu aka, "to guard bricks" > **aka**

šeg$_{12}$ ga$_6$(ĝ), "to carry bricks" > **ga$_6$(ĝ)**

šeg$_{12}$ gub-ba, "employed (to mold) bricks" > **gub**

šeg$_{12}$ ĝar, "to place bricks" > **ĝar**

šeg$_{12}$ ma šub-ba gub-ba, "employed at the brick yard" > **gub**

šeg$_{12}$ mun, "brick of salt" > **mun**

šeg$_{12}$ naĝa, "brick of potash" > **naĝa**

šeg$_{12}$ NE-gu$_7$-bi zi(g), "to deduct damaged bricks" > **zi(g)**

šeg$_{12}$ šu dím-ma sum, "to hand (up) bricks for building" > **sum**

šeg$_{12}$ tab, "to lay bricks" > **tab**

^{ĝeš}ù-šub **šeg$_{12}$**, "brick mold (for) bricks" > **^{ĝeš}ù-šub**

1. **In Brick Worker Texts**

á géme n-**šeg$_{12}$**-ta géme-bi n u$_4$-n-šè, "workwomen wages for each n brick(s) (carried), its workwomen (equal) n workerday(s)" > **á**

n sar **šeg$_{12}$** NE-gu$_7$-bi íb-ta-zi, "n sar of damaged bricks deducted" > **zi**

šu+níĝin n sar n gín **šeg$_{12}$** ús-bi n nindan, "In total: n sar (and) n gín of bricks, its base is n nindan (long)" > **ús-bi**

šu+níĝin n sar **šeg$_{12}$** sumun ús-bi n nindan, "In total: n sar of old bricks, its base is n nindan (long)" > **ús-bi**

2. **Receipts**

20 ma-na ki-lá **šeg$_{12}$** [ki ^{d}]*adad-tillati*-ta *a-na-aḫ-ì-lí* šu ba-ti, "*Anaḫ-ili* received 20 minas of brick from *Adad-tillati*," 891:3–6

3. **Broken Context**

1 ĝuruš **šeg$_{12}$**-[. . .], 160:'16

1 ĝuruš **šeg$_{12}$**-[. . .], 213:'13

^{ĝeš}**šeg$_{12}$**, "(a wooden object)"

★★2 ^{ĝeš}**šeg$_{12}$** má-[. . .], 1368:5

šeĝ$_6$(NE), *bašālu*, "to cook" > *Verb Index*

^{urudu}**šen**, *ruqqu*, "(soup) cauldron"

2 ádda-udu ^{urudu}**šen**-šè, "2 sheep carcasses for the (soup) cauldron," 382:1–2, 388:1–2

0.0.1. níĝ-àr-ra-sig$_5$ ^{urudu}**šen**-šè, "10 liters of fine groats for the (soup) cauldron," 479:11, 483:11, 490:3

0.0.2.6 sìla ninda-šu-ra-gen 2 ádda-udu 5 sìla níĝ-àr-ra-sig$_5$ 0.0.1. gú-gal al-àr-ra šu-gíd 1 sìla mun-gen ^{urudu}**šen**-šè 8 sa gi-izi tu$_7$ ba-ra-šeg$_6$, "26 liters of ordinary half(-loaf) bread, 2 sheep carcasses, 5 liters of fine groats, 10 liters of milled šu-gíd beans (and) 1 liter of ordinary salt for the (soup) cauldron (and) 8 bundles of fuel reeds with which soup was cooked," 529:5–12

0.0.3. níĝ-àr-ra-⌜sig$_5$⌝ 5 sìla ar-za-na 2 sìla ba-ba-še 3 ádda-udu 5 sìla mun-gen ^{urudu}**šen**-šè 60 sa gi-izi tu$_7$ ba-ra-šeĝ$_6$, "30 liters of fine groats, 5 liters of barley-grits, 2 liters of barley porridge, 3 sheep carcasses (and) 5 liters of ordinary salt for the (soup) cauldron (and) 60 bundles of fuel reeds with which soup was cooked," 1025:46–53

1 udu-niga 0.0.1. zì-KAL ninda-[gur$_4$-ra]-šè 1 dug dida-g[en] 5 sìla níĝ-àr-ra-⌜sig$_5$⌝ ⅓ sìla mun-sig$_5$ al-naĝ$_4$-ĝá 10 gín gazi al-naĝ$_4$-ĝá ^{urudu}**šen**-šè 7 sa+níĝin ^{ĝeš}ásal 5 sa gi-izi ninda ba-ra-du$_8$ uzu ù tu$_7$ ba-ra-šeĝ$_6$, "1 fattened sheep, 10 liters of KAL-flour for [thick] bread, 1 jug of ordinary dida beer, 5 liters of fine groats, 13 liter of fine crushed salt (and) 10 shekels of crushed gazi for the (soup) cauldron (and) 7 bundles of poplar (and) 5 bundles of fuel reeds with which bread was baked and meat and soup were cooked," 1028:1–10

12 sa gi-izi níĝ-sù-a ^{urudu}**šen**-šè, "12 bundles of fuel reeds for the níĝ-sù-a (soup) cauldron," 1297:17–18

šen-da-lá^{zabar}, *šandalu*, "a bronze vessel"

n **šen-da-lá**^{zabar} n ma-na n gín, "n bronze vessel(s) (weighing) n mina(s) (and) n shekel(s)," 977:1, 977:2, 1346:1, 1346:2

n **šen-da-lá-gur$_8$-da^{zabar} n gín, 977:3, 977:4, 977:5

^{ĝeš}**šennur** (GÁN/GÁN), *šallūru*, "plum, plum tree wood"

ḫar ^{ĝeš}**šennur**, "plum tree seedling," 1256:15, 1375:21

šeš, *aḫu*, "brother"

a-ba **šeš**-ĝu$_{10}$-gin$_7$, "who is like my brother?" 1526:7

šeš$_4$(ERIN), *pašāšu*, "to anoint (with oil)" > *Verb Index*

šid(šita$_5$), *minûtu*, "number, count; to count" > *Verb Index*

šidim, *itinnu*, "builder, architect"

á-áĝ **šidim-e-ne** ĝír-su^{ki}-šè de$_6$, "to bring a message concerning builders to Ĝirsu" > **de$_6$**
ĝuruš **šidim**, "builder," *passim*
ĝuruš **šidim** dú-ra, "sick builder" > **dú**
ĝuruš **šidim** zàḫ, "runaway builder" > **zàḫ**
kurum$_7$ aka **šidim-e-ne**, "inspection (of the work) of builders," 85:14, 87:17
šidim la-ḫa-dè ĝen, "to go in order to bring builders" > **ĝen**, **laḫ$_4$**/**laḫ$_5$**

1. **PN šidim**, "PN, the builder" > *Personal Name Index*

a-a-mu	*šal-maḫ*	ur-mes
ma-šum	*tu-ku-lí*	ur-^{d}nanše

2. **šidim lú-GN**, "builder from GN" > *Toponym Index*

dí-ma-at-kál-bu-um	ì-si-in^{ki}	*tu-lí-um*^{ki}
é-^{d}*šu*-^{d}*suen*	níĝ-^{d}ba-ú	ur-^{d}šul-pa-è
i-zi-in-èr-ra^{ki}		

3. **Rations, Wages, and Allotments**

níĝ-gu$_7$ **šidim-e-ne**, "food of builders" > **níĝ-gu$_7$**
sá-du$_{11}$ **šidim**(-e-ne), "regular offerings of the builders" > **sá-du$_{11}$**
šà-gal **šidim-e-ne**, "food (for) builders" > **šà-gal**
šidim-e-ne-šè in-gu$_7$-ša-a, "{comestibles} that the builders ate" > **gu$_7$**
šidim-e-ne íb-nag, "the builders drank" > **nag**
šidim ù lú-ḫuĝ-ĝá-e-ne ḫal, "to divide {comestibles} for builders and hired workers" > **ḫal**

^{dug}útul-gal 2-šè mu **šidim-e-ne**-šè, "{assorted comestibles} for 2 large tureens for the builders" > **^{dug}útul-gal**

(. . .) mu **šidim** ù lú-ḫuĝ-ĝ[á-šè], "{assorted comestibles} [for] builders and hired workers," 483:24

(. . .) lú-é-ki-ba-ĝar-ra **šidim** ugula lú-ḫuĝ-[ĝá . . .]-ka é-ka gub-ba [. . .]-e-ne, "{assorted breads} for the man of the replacement house, the builder, the overseer of the hired workers, employed in the [. . .] of the house," 485:5

šim, *rīqu*, "aromatic substance"

n sìla **šim**-sig$_5$ al-naĝ$_4$-ĝá, "n liter(s) of crushed fine aromatic," 511:63, 972:22, 972:86, 975:23, 975:87, 981:18, 1182:8

šim-sig$_5$ al-ús-sa, "processed fine aromatic," 523:12

^{ĝeš}šim, *kanakku*, "(a resinous tree)"

má **^{ĝeš}šim** ḫi-a, "boat of various resinous woods," 253:4

^{urudu}šim-da, "a (cattle) branding iron"

^{urudu}šim-da gu$_4$-udu de$_6$, "to bring a sheep (and) cattle brand" > **de$_6$**

^{ĝeš}šinig, *bīnu*, "tamarisk," 635:9

^{ĝeš}dim-**šinig**,"tamarisk pillar" > **^{ĝeš}dim**

^{ĝeš}é-da-**šinig**, "tamarisk joist" > **^{ĝeš}é-da**

★★^{ĝeš}maš-sá-da **šinig** > **^{ĝeš}maš**

ĝeš ùr **šinig**, "tamarisk roof beam" > **ĝeš ùr**

1. Tamarisk Seedlings

140 ḫar **^{ĝeš}⌜šinig⌝**-tur, "140 seedlings of small tamarisk trees," 1362:'21

170 ḫar **^{ĝeš}šinig** [. . .], "170 seedlings of [. . .] tamarisk trees," 1362:'47

2. Tamarisk Wood

★★1 ^{ĝeš}ĜEŠ/ĜEŠ 30 ma-na **šinig**, 1372:28 1372:85

90 **^{ĝeš}šinig** ma?-[. . .], 1362:'45

34 **^{ĝeš}šinig** za-[. . .], 1362:'44

104 **^{ĝeš}šinig** KA-[. . .], 1362:'46

šíta-ùr, "door knob"

1 ĝuruš [. . .] šà **šíta-ùr** [. . .], "1 workman [. . .] (work done) for door knobs," 58:32–33

šu, *qātu*, "hand"

^{na4}kinkin **šu** sè-ga, "'hand-held' millstone > **^{na4}kinkin**

šu . . . aka, "to manufacture" > **aka**

šu+níĝin, *napḫaru*, "total, sum," *passim*

šu . . . bala, *šupêlu*, "to change" > *Verb Index*

šu . . . bar, "to release, set free" > *Verb Index*

šu . . . dím, "to build" > *Verb Index*

šu . . . ra(ḫ$_2$), *maḫāṣu*, "to beat" > *Verb Index*

šu . . . sum, "to inventory" > *Verb Index*

šu . . . tag, *lapātu*, "to touch, take hold of" > *Verb Index*

šu . . . ti, *leqû*, *maḫāru*, "to accept, take, receive" > *Verb Index*

šu-a-gi-na, *šuginû*, "a type of offering"

24 udu-niga 1-sìla-[ta] sá-du$_{11}$-šè 26 udu-niga 1-sìla-ta [x] -šè é-⸢udu⸣-niga **šu-a-⸢gi⸣-na** u$_4$ iti-da ⸢gíd⸣-gíd-⸢dam⸣, "24 fattened sheep, 1 liter (of fodder) [each] for regular offerings (and) 26 fattened sheep, 1 liter (of fodder) each for [x]; (sheep), of the sheep-fattening pen, to be transferred (for) the offering of the month," 525:1–7

šu-dù-a, *šīzu*, "a unit of length"

⅔ kuš-máš-g[al-ni]ga 4 túg-íb-lá-su$_4$-a-gíd 4 kùš 2 **šu-dù** 1-šè ba-a-ĝar "⅔ of a fattened billy-goat skin were (used for) covering 4 long red/brown belts of 4 kùš and 2 šu-dù in length," 939:1–2

šu-gíd, "designation of animals, unfit for work(?)"[112]

4 kuš-gu$_4$ **šu-gíd** ^{ĝeš}ig mi-rí-za-šè, "4 šu-gíd ox skins for a door plank," 912:9–10

0.0.1. gú-gal al-àr-ra **šu-gíd** (. . .) ^{urudu}šen-šè, "10 liters of milled šu-gíd beans (and) {other comestibles} for the (soup) cauldron," 529: 8, 10

šu?-ĝar, "(meaning uncertain)"

1 sìla dabin 1 sìla A.[TIR] **šu?-ĝar sa-[. . .], "1 liter of semolina (and) 1 liter of fine flour (?) [. . .]," 506:12–13

šu-i, *gallābu*, "barber"

1. **PN šu-i**, "PN, the barber" > *Personal Name Index*

*a-bu-*DU$_{10}$	*en-nam-*^{d}*ma-lik*	*šu-*^{d}nin-in-si
be-lí-ì-lí	^{d}*ma-lik-illat-sú*	*šu-*^{d}*suen-ba-ni*

[112] Brunke 2008, 177 (§3.3.5.6, Bemerkung 3.50) with references.

šu-ku$_{6}$, *bā'eru*, "fisherman"

1. **PN šu-ku$_{6}$**, "PN, the fisherman" > *Personal Name Index*

šu-ba-ra-ni *šu-eš$_{4}$-tár*

šu-luḫ, "ritual cleansing"

1 gi-nindan **šu-luḫ** ésir šub-ba, "1 ritual cleansing measuring rod coated with bitumen," 1376:14

šu-numun, "(month 4)"

á-ki-ti **šu-numun**, "Akiti festival of month 4" > **á-ki-ti**

šu-sar, *pitiltu*, "string, cord, wire"

[n] gú 6½ ma-na 5 gín **šu-sar** peš, "[n] talent(s), 6½ minas (and) 5 shekels of palmleaf cord," 1343:5

[n ma]-na **šu-sar** m[angaga? $^{ğeš?}$]ig ^{ğeš}kuğ$_{5}$-šè ⸢u$_{4}$⸣ é-e im sumur ba-aka, "[n mina(s)] of cord (made from) date palm fibers for the door (and) ladder when the house was plastered," 472:12–14

šu-sum-ma, *puquddû*, "inventory; a type of consignment"

é-**šu-sum-ma**, "storehouse" > *Household Index*

šu-sum-ma ^{ğeš}kiri$_{6}$ igi-érim-iri^{ki}, "inventory of the Igi-erim-iri garden" > *Garden Index*

20 ^{kuš}a-ğá-lá-udu 9 ^{kuš}a-ğá-lá-máš 7 kuš-⸢udu⸣ ka-tab 5 gú *pù-su-lum* (. . .)2 ^{gi}gur ki gub-ba ésir šub-ba 19 ^{túg}bar-si níğ-lá-gen sumun 15 barag 1 ğír-siki-gul-la-zabar **šu-sum-ma** ^{d}*adad-tillati* šabra šu ba-ti, "*Adad-tillati*, the majordomo, received the inventory: 20 sheep-skin sacks, 9 goat-skin sacks, 7 sheep-skin covers, 5 talents of *pusulum*, {assorted wooden boards}, 2 reed baskets set in place for pouring bitumen, 19 old ordinary níğ-lá bands, 15 sacks (and) 1 bronze sheering knife," 1272:1–14

(. . .) **šu-sum-ma** ğìri *ib-ni-*^{d}*adad* d[ub-sar] iti ezem-me-ki-ğál ba-zal mu en-^{d}inana-unu^{ki}-ga máš-e ì-pàd 0.0.1.2½ sìla ^{na_4}ŠEM? še-ta sa$_{10}$-a sağ-níğ-gur$_{11}$-ra-kam, "{millstones, diorite stones, woods, yokes, and wooden containers}, the consignment under the authority of *Ibni-Adad*, the scribe, the 12 month of *Ibbi-Suen* Year 2 having passed; (and) 12½ liters ^{na_4}ŠEM, the price from barley; (these) are the available assets," 1372:46–53

šu tag . . . dug$_{4}$, *za'ānu*, "to decorate" > *Verb Index*

šu-ur$_{4}$, *kisittu*, "branch, wing?"

uz-tur **šu-ur$_{4}$**-ra, "duckling wing?," 529:20

šub, *nadû*, "to pour (water, bitumen, etc.); to lay down (bricks)" > *Verb Index*

^{ĝeš}šudul, *nīru*, "yoke"

1. **^{ĝeš}šudul-gu$_4$**, "ox yoke"

3 kuš-udu-babbar **^{ĝeš}šudul-gu$_4$**-šè ba-a-ĝar, "3 white sheep skins were (used) for covering an ox yoke," 864:1–2, 923:3–4

šudum(ŠID) (**U.NU.A**), *šutû*, "warp-thread"

siki **šudum**, "wool (for) warp-thread" > **siki**

šudum-gada, "linen warp-thread" > **gada**

1½ ma-na **šudum U.NU.A** ^{túg}níĝ-⌜lám⌝ 3-kam-ús, "½ mina of warp-thread (for) a 3rd-quality níĝ-lám textile," 596:3

15 gín **šudum U.NU.A** ^{túg}níĝ-lám 4-kam-ús, "15 shekels of warp-thread (for) a 4th-quality níĝ-lám textile," 596:4

13 gín **šudum U.NU.A** túg-guz-[za] 4-kam-ús, "13 shekels of warp-thread (for) a 4th-quality tufted textile," 596:5

[n]+5/6 ma-na 7 gín **šudum** [**U.NU.A**] túg-guz-za-gen, "[n]+5/6 minas (and) 7 shekels of warp-thread (for) an ordinary tufted textile," 596:6

šuku, *kurummatu*, "food allocation, ration"

šuku *šu*-^{d}nin-súmun, "the food allocation of *Šu*-Ninsumun" > *Personal Name Index*

★★0.2.0. ninda **šuku** ib-šu-bi u$_4$-4-kam, "120 liters of bread of the food allocation, its (?) on the 4th day," 1031:11

^{urudu}šum, *šaššāru*, "saw"

1 **^{urudu}šum** ki-lá-bi ½ ma-na, "1 saw, its weight is ½ mina," 1310:3–4

šùš, "equerry"

puzur$_4$-a-bi **šùš**, "*Puzur-abi*, the equerry" > *Personal Name Index*

– T –

tá-ki-ru-um, *takkīru*, "(a textile)"

^{túg}gú-è ***tá-ki-ru-um*** bar-s[i g̃ar-r]a-tur lugal, "small royal *takkirum* cape fashioned with bands," 824:1

^{túg}sagšu ***tá-ki-ru-um*** *simat-^{d}ištaran*, "*takkirum* cap of *Simat-Ištaran*" > **^{túg}sagšu**

^{túg}*tá-ki-ru-um* 3-kam-ús ^{d}nin-^{d}si$_{4}$-an-na, "3rd-quality *takkirum* textile of Nin-Siana," 739:2, 684:1

^{túg}*tá-ki-ru-um*-tur ^{d}nin-^{d}si$_{4}$-an-na, "small *takkirum* textile of Nin-Siana," 766:1

^{túg}*tá-ki-ru-um*-tur ^{d}nin-^{d}si$_{4}$-an-na 3-kam-ús, "small 3rd-quality *takkirum* textile of Nin-Siana," 608:5, 796:4

tab, *eṣēpu*, "to twine (rope, thread), to line up (bricks in rows), to stack (sheaves of grain); to double; to repeat" > *Verb Index*

tà(g), *rakāsu*, *sêru*, "to bind; to touch up; to apply stucco" > *Verb Index*

tag, "to beat; to weave" > *Verb Index*

TAG$_{4}$.ALAM, "(meaning uncertain)"

1. **šáḫ-g̃e$_{6}$ TAG$_{4}$.ALAM**

3 udu 1 máš-ga **šáḫ-g̃e$_{6}$ TAG$_{4}$.ALAM 2 udu-ú *um-mi-kab-tá* dumu-munus é-a, "3 sheep, 1 suckling goat, (1?) TAG$_{4}$.ALAM black pig (and) 2 range-fed sheep (for) *Ummi-Kabta*, daughter of the house," 421:1–4

taḫ, *aṣābu*, "to add, increase" > *Verb Index*

tak-ri-ib-tum, *taqribtu*, "(performance of) an Emesal lament"[113]

1. **Provisions for the Performance of a *Takribtum***

0.0.1.2 sìla ninda 0.0.1. kaš-gen ½ sìla níg̃-àr-ra-sig$_{5}$ 1 ku$_{6}$ al-dar-ra ^{dug}útul-šè gala-e-ne ***tak-ri-ib-tum*** é-⸢lùnga⸣ é-muḫaldim ù é-kíkken, "12 liters of bread, 10 liters of ordinary beer, ½ liter of fine groats (and) 1 split (dried) fish for the tureen of the lamentation singers (for their performance of) a *takribtum*; (delivery from) the brewery-kitchen-mill complex," 437:7–13

8 sìla dabin 4 sìla eša 1 sìla zú-lum eša ḫi-dè ***tak-ri-ib-tum*** iri^{ki} ne-ne-de$_{4}$, "8 liters of semolina, 4 liters of fine flour (and) 1 liter of dates to mix (with) fine flour, (for the performance of) a *takribtum* (involving) circling around the city," 1016:18–21

0.0.2. dabin ninda-sal-la-⸢gen⸣ 1 sìla níg̃-àr-ra-sig$_{5}$ tu$_{7}$-šè gala ù ama-gal-e-ne íb-gu$_{7}$ u$_{4}$ ***tak-ri-ib-tum*** bàd, "the lamentation singers and the female mourners ate ordinary thin

[113] Gabbay, *forthcoming*.

bread (made from) 20 liters of semolina (and made from) 1 liter of fine groats for soup on the occasion of (their performance of) a *takribtum* at? the (enclosure) wall," 1035:'7-'11

ták-si/ši-ru-um, *takšīru*, "repair (of architecture)"

1. **du_{10}-ús é-didli *ták-si-ru-um-šè***, "for repair of the bathroom of various houses" > *Household Index*

2. ***ták-si-ru-um* šà é-a**, "repair in the house"

   1 g̃uruš šidim um-mi-a 7 g̃uruš šidim 10-lá-1 g̃uruš šu dím gub-⌜ba⌝ ***ták-si-ru-um* šà é-a**, "1 master builder, 7 builders (and) 9 workmen employed to build (for) repair in the house," 45:13–16

3. ***ták-si-ru-um* šà é-gal**, "repair in the palace" > *Household Index*

4. ***ták-ši-ru-um* é-*gi-na-tum***, "repair of the barracks" > *Household Index*

5. **Unspecified Location**

   1 g̃uruš šidim [um-mi-a] 1 g̃uruš šidim ***ták-*[*si-ru-um*]**, "1 master builder (and) 1 builder (for) repair," 160:'5-'6

6. **Contents Lost**

   [1] g̃uruš [šidim. . .] ***ták-ši-ru-um*** [. . .] gub-[ba], "[1 builder . . .] employed (for) repair [. . .]," 50:2

   1 g̃uruš šidim 1 g̃uruš 2 géme ***ták-ši-ru-um*** šà x x (x), "1 builder, 1 workman (and) 2 workwomen (for) repair in [. . .]," 53:34–36

   1 g̃uruš šidim 1 [g̃uruš. . .] ***ták-ši-ru-um*** [. . .], "1 builder, 1 [workman . . .] (for) repair [. . .]," 54:22

   2 g̃uruš šidim 2 g̃uruš šu dím 6 géme im ga_6-[g̃á-dè] gub-[ba] 1 g̃uruš im ì-l[i-de_9 gub-ba] ***ták-ši-ru-*[*um*** . . .] ù [. . .], "2 builders (and) 2 workmen having built, 6 workwomen employed [to] carry earth, 1 workman [employed to] lift earth, (for) repair [. . .] and [. . .]," 58:40–44

$^{g̃eš}$**taskarin**, *taskarinnu*, "box tree, boxwood"

n ḫar $^{g̃eš}$**taskarin** n-ta, "n boxwood seedling(s), n (units) each," 1375:23

★★$^{g̃eš}$**taskarin**-bi éš-g̃ar, 635:7

te($g̃_3$), *ṭeḫû*, "to be near, to approach" > *Verb Index*

[TEMPLES] > *Household Index*

é-kù, "bright temple"

é-^{d}nin-si_4-an-na, "Nin-Siana temple"

é-^{d}šára, "Šara temple"

[TEXTILES] > **túg**[114]

til, *gamāru*; *labāru*; *qatû*, "(to be) complete(d); (to be) old, long-lasting; to end" > *Verb Index*

^{ĝeš}**tir**, *luḫummû*, "mud; forest, wood"

[1 eše 2¼] (iku) gána 10 sar ^{ĝeš}**tir**, "[1 eše 2¼] gána (and) 10 sar of wood," 1362:2

titab, *titāpū*, "(an ingredient in beer-making); malted barley"

1. ^{gi}**kid titab**, "reed mat for malted barley"

^{gi}**kid titab** ésir šub-ba, "reed mat coated with bitumen for malted barley," 1376:7

1 ^{gi}**kid titab** ⌜gíd⌝ 7 kùš dağal 4 kùš gi-bi 2[+n sa] ésir-é-a-bi 5 sìla peš-múrgu-bi 1⅔ á-bi u_4-1⅓-kam, "1 reed mat for malted barley, 7 kùš in length, 4 kùš in width. (Manufacture required:) 2[+n bundles] of reeds, 5 liters of house bitumen, 1⅔ date palm spines (and) 1⅓ days of labor," 1381:30–34

[TOOLS]

^{ĝeš}al, "hoe"

^{ĝeš}dusu, "brick-carrying frame"

gír-siki-gul-la^{zabar}, "a bronze, wool sheering knife"

^{urudu}gu_4-zi-bi-ir, "ladder"

^{urudu}ḫa-zi-in, "axe"

^{urudu}šim-da, "a (cattle) branding iron"

^{urudu}šum, "saw"

[TOPONYMS] > *Toponym Index*

adab^{ki}
a-pi_4-sal_4-la^{ki}
bàd-ga-zi^{ki}
bàd-^{d}šul-gi
ba-la-nu^{ki}
dì-ma-at-kál-bu-um^{ki}
du_6-ba-an-du_8-du_8 > *Field Index*
du_6-lugal-pa-è^{ki}
du_6-saḫar-ra^{ki}
é-da-na^{ki}
é-$duru_5$-^{d}ba-ú
é-$duru_5$-kab-bi$_{(2)}$
é-$duru_5$-*simat*-^{d}*ištaran*
é-$duru_5$-ul-luḫ-uri_5^{ki}
é-kab-ba^{ki}
é-lugal-eden-na
é-^{d}*šu*-^{d}*suen*^{ki}
é-ù-ri-a^{ki}
Elam^{ki}
en-zu-bábbar^{ki}
gar-ša-an-na^{ki}
gú-ab-ba^{ki}
gú-saḫar^{ḫar}.DU^{ki}
^{d}gu_4-an-na
ĜEŠ.KÚŠU^{ki}
ĝír-su^{ki}
ì-si-in^{ki}
i-zi-in-èr-ra^{ki}
igi-érim-iri^{ki}
iri^{ki}-gíd-da
iri-sağ-rig_7^{ki}
ka-saḫar-ra^{ki}

[114] For a more detailed discussion of the textile terminology at Garšana, see the forthcoming commentary by H. Waetzoldt.

kab-šu^{ki}
kàr-da-ḫi
karkar^{ki}
marad^{ki}
mar-ḫa-ši^{ki}
maš-kán^{ki}
maš-kán-šar-ru-um^{ki}
nağ-su^{ki}
nibru^{ki}
níğ-^{d}ba-ú
puzur$_4$*-iš-*^{d}*da-gan*^{ki}
^{d}*šu-*^{d}*suen*-am-ma-ra^{ki}
^{d}*šu-*^{d}*suen-ṭabu*^{ki}
tár-ra-um^{ki}
tum-ma-al^{ki}
tu-lí-um^{ki}
ù-dag-ga^{ki}
unug^{ki}
ur-^{d}šul-pa-è
uri$_5$^{ki}
*ù-ṣa-ar-*é-ú-ra^{ki}
zabala$_4$^{ki}

tu-gur$_4$^{mušen}, *sukannīnu*, “dove,” 511:87, 526:5, 526:9, 978:4, 978:9, 1058:2, 1138:1, 1172:3, 1254:'29, 1394:9

tu-gur$_4$^{mušen}-niga, “fattened dove,” 1053:4, 1060:3, 1253:'5
tu-gur$_4$^{mušen} ba-úš, “dead dove” > **úš**

tu$_7$, *ummaru*, “soup, broth,”[115] 379:12, 379:13, 379:15, 379:19

níğ-àr-ra-sig$_5$ **tu$_7$**-šè, “fine groats for soup,” 391:1–2, 1035:'8
tu$_7$ aka, “to serve soup” > **aka**
tu$_7$ si(g), “to fill (a bowl with) soup” > **si(g)**
tu$_7$ šeğ$_6$, “to cook soup” > **šeğ$_6$**
n (sìla) **tu$_7$**-ta, “n liter(s) of soup each,” 379:1, 379:2, 379:4, 379:6, 379:7, 379:8, 379:9, 379:10, 379:11, 379:14, 556:'1, 556:'3, 556:'4, 556:'5, 556:'6, 556:'7, 556:'8, 556:'9, 556:'10, 556:'11

túg, *ṣubātu*, “cloth, textile”

^{túg}*á-gu*$_4$*-ḫu-um*, “belt, sash”
^{túg}aktum, “(a textile)”
^{túg}bar-dul$_5$, “(a textile)”
^{túg}bar-si, “woven band, ribbon”
éš-**túg**-gíd, “cord, used to extend a textile (on a loom)” > **éš**
^{túg}gú-è, “cape”
^{túg}gú-lá, “(a textile)”
^{túg}ğeštu, “(a textile)”
^{túg}*ḫa-bu-um* > ^{túg}***ḫa-um***
^{túg}íb-lá, “belt”
^{túg}*ḫa-um*, “(a fabric, textile)”
^{túg}KU.KA.GA?, “(a textile)”
^{túg}níğ-lám, “(a textile)”

---

115 Brunke 2008, 160–193 (§3.3).

^{túg}níĝ-saĝ-lá-mí, "cap"
^{túg}sagšu, "cap"
^{túg}saĝ-uš-bar, "(a textile)"
^{túg}šà-ga-dù, "belt"
^{túg}šà-gi$_4$-dab$_6$, "(a textile)"
^{túg}*tá-ki-ru-um*, "(a textile)"
túg ba-tab *tuḫ-ḫu-um*, "(a specification of textiles)" > **ba-tab**
túg-*bu-ti-um*, "(a specification of textiles)"
túg-du$_8$-a, "meshwork" > **túg-du$_8$-a**
túg-gen, "ordinary textile"
túg-gùn-a, "multi-colored textile"
túg-guz-za, "tufted textile"
túg-ĝe$_6$, "black textile"
túg-ĝir-su^{ki}, "Ĝirsu textile" > **siki**
túg-*ḫa-la*, "(a specification of textiles)"
túg-*ḫu-la-um*, "(a specification of textiles)"
túg-lugal, "royal textile" > **lugal**
túg-ma-dur$_7$-ra, "mourning textile" > **túg-ma-dur$_7$-ra**
túg-mug, "textile of poor-quality wool" > **mug**
túg-sa-gi$_4$-a, "finished textiles"
túg-sumun, "old textile"
****túg**-šà-^{kuš}súḫub > **^{kuš}súḫub**
túg-tùn, "textile container?" > **tùn**
túg-tur, "small textile" > **siki**
^{túg}uš-bar, "(a textile)"
^{túg}zi-lí-ḫi, "(a textile)"

1. Textiles, Type Unspecified

1.1 Baskets

^{gi}bisaĝ **túg**-aš, "single textile basket" > **^{gi}bisaĝ**

2 ^{gi}bisaĝ-gíd-da [**túg**]-ga sa-ḫa, "2 long canvas-lined baskets (for) textiles," 602:2

1 ^{gi}bisaĝ-gíd-da **túg**-ga-tur ésir šub-ba ka-bi kuš-ĝar-ra, "1 long, small basket coated with bitumen (for) textiles, its opening covered with leather," 798:1–3

1.2 Textiles Brought to Garšana from Nippur

1 ĝuruš ^{lú}ašlaĝ nibru^{ki}-ta gar-ša-an-na^{ki}-šè **túg** de$_6$-a kaskal šu+níĝin-na-bi u$_4$-4-àm, "1 fuller having brought textiles from Nippur to Garšana, a trip of 4 days in total," 224:1–6

1.3 Textiles Brought to Nippur

3 ĝuruš **túg** nibru^{ki}-šè de$_6$-a, "3 workmen having brought textiles to Nippur," 148:'20

1.4 **túg-ba**, "textile rations"

780 ^{túg}uš-bar 12 ^{túg}uš-bar-dul$_5$-⸢gen⸣? **túg-ba** géme-árad šà nibru^{ki}, "780 uš-bar textiles (and) 12 ordinary? uš-bar-dul$_5$ textiles, textile rations of male (and) female servants in Nippur," 589:1–4

1.5 **túg-ba siki-ba**, "textile and wool rations"

1.5.1 **For the Servants of *Simat-Ištaran***

(. . .) {indent}131 túg-⸢ḫi⸣-a [n] ma-na ⸢siki-gen⸣ **túg-⸢ba⸣ siki-⸢ba⸣** géme-á[rad *simat*-^{d}K]A.⸢DI⸣, "{assorted textiles}, 131 textiles (and) [n] mina(s) of ordinary wool, the textile and wool rations of the female and male servants of *Simat-Ištaran*," 734:6–9

(. . .) **túg-ba siki-ba** géme-árad *simat*-$^{\text{[d]}}$*ištaran*, "{wool and assorted textiles}, the textile and wool rations of the female and male servants of *Simat-Ištaran*," 795:5–6, 818:7–8

1.6 **Wool for Textile Production**

siki **túg** / **túg** siki ki-lá-bi n mina(s), "wool (designated for) a textile, its weight is n mina(s)" > **siki**

n gín siki-gen mu-**túg**-ga-šè, "n shekel(s) of ordinary wool for textiles," 699:1, 5, 705:4–5

1 **túg** 1⅓ <ma->na siki-gen, "1 textile of ⅓ mina of ordinary wool," 817:1

2. **Types of Textiles and Other Woolen Materials**

2.1 **túg-*bu-ti-um***, "(a specification of textiles)"

4 **túg-*bu-ti-um***(?) ^{ĝeš}*be-rum* siki ^{ĝeš}garig aka gen ki-lá-bi ⅔ ma-na, 807:1–3

2.2 **túg-gen**, "ordinary textile," 818:2, 1187:1

★★⸢siki⸣-bala-dè in-na-[kéše **t**]**úg-gen**-kam ì-in-⸢DU⸣? 1 ^{túg}saĝ-uš-bar sa-gi$_4$-[àm], "{assorted textiles}, the wool was bound up to be baled, he delivered the ordinary textiles, they are finished ^{túg}saĝ-uš-bar textiles," 609:7–9 (envelope)

2.3 **túg-gùn**, "multi-colored textile"

túg-gùn-a 3-kam-ús, "3rd-quality multi-colored textile," 568:1, 577:1

túg-gùn-a 4-kam-ús, "4th-quality multi-colored textile," 564:1, 565:1, 577:3, 786:10

★★1 **túg**-^{d}*al-la-tum*-**gùn-a** ù zi-in-bi ki-lá-bi 9 ma-[na] 12 gín *a-ku$_8$-a-nu-ri*, "1 colored textile of *Allatum* and its zi-in weighing 9 minas (and) 12 shekels (for) *Akua-nuri*," 584:1–3

1 **túg-gùn-a** *ilum-ma-⸢zi⸣* ki-lá-bi 11½ ma-na, "1 multi-colored textile (for) *Ilum-mazi*, its weight is 11½ minas," 747:16–17

2.4 **túg-guz-za**, "tufted textile," 645:1

túg-guz-za-gen, "ordinary tufted textile," 511:'123, 606:1, 644:1, 645:3, 646:1, 651:6, 654:6, 673:7, 674:8, 676:5, 685:3, 686:2, 687:2, 690:5, 693:5, 694:3, 698:10, 698:22, 725:1, 730:1, 732:1, 734:1, 742:7, 744:7, 745:5, 746:9, 748:11, 753:11, 758:12, 760:5, 764:7, 765:6, 766:4, 773:5, 780:1, 800:3, 801:4, 810:3, 834:11

[n]+5/6 ma-na 7 gín šudum [U.NU.A] **túg-guz-za**-gen, "[n]+5/6 minas (and) 7 shekels of warp-thread (for) an ordinary tufted textile," 596:6

túg-guz-za-ús, "2nd-quality tufted textile," 578:4, 579:4, 698:16

túg-guz-za-ús [*šu-kab-tá*], "2nd-quality tufted textile of [*Šu-Kabta*]," 698:1

túg-guz-za 3-kam-ús, "3rd-quality tufted textile," 571:2, 631:1, 651:3, 663:4, 698:20, 700:1, 701:1, 753:4, 758:4, 771:1, 814:6, 827:5, 1162:'13

túg-guz-za 4-kam-ús, "4th-quality tufted textile," 609:4, 626:3, 631:6, 649:6, 651:5, 654:3, 658:5, 662:5, 669:6, 692:4, 693:4, 694:2, 697:2, 698:9, 738:10, 742:5, 743:5, 744:5, 745:4, 748:8, 753:9, 758:11, 778:7, 806:6, 814:9, 821:8, 834:6, 835:'8

túg-guz-za 4-kam-ús ^{d}*tá-ad-muṣ-tum*, "4th-quality tufted textile of *Tadmuṣtum*," 617:5

túg-guz-za 4-ka[m-ú]s diĝir-re-e-ne, "4th-quality tufted textiles of the gods,"739:4

túg-guz-za 4-kam-ús ^{d}*ma-mi-tum*, "4th-quality tufted textile of *Mamitum*," 608:7, 617:4

túg-guz-za 4-kam-ús *šu-kab-tá*, "4th-quality tufted textile of *Šu-Kabta*," 698:21

túg-guz-za 4-kam-ús-tur tà-[ga], "small 4th-quality tufted textile having been woven," 618:10

13 gín šudum U.NU.A **túg-guz-[za]** 4-kam-ús, "13 shekels of warp-thread (for) a 4th-quality tufted textile," 596:5

túg-guz-za *šu-kab-tá*, "tufted textile of *Šu-Kabta*," 586:1, 587:1, 588:2, 723:1

túg-guz-za-AB-gen, "ordinary AB tufted textile," 801:3

túg-guz-za tab-ba-gen, "ordinary double tufted textile," 608:8, 617:8, 793:9, 800:2, 802:3, 835:'11

túg-guz-za-tur-gen pi-lu-da, "small ordinary tufted textile (for) ritual (use)," 787:5

túg-guz-za-tur 4-kam-ús, "small 4th-quality tufted textile," 654:4, 669:7, 685:2

túg-guz-za-tur 4-kam-ús ^{d}*ištaran*, "small 4th-quality tufted textile of *Ištaran*," 576:1–2

túg-guz-za-tur [n-kam]-ús, "small [nth]-quality tufted textile," 766:3

túg-guz-za-ús-n-kam, "nth-quality tufted textile," 650:3

túg-guz-[za . . .], "[. . .] tufted textile," 597:1

20 ma-na siki **túg-guz-za**-gen mu siki-gu kéše-šè, "20 minas of wool (for manufacturing) ordinary tufted textile (to be used) for wool cord bindings," 665:1–2

2.5 túg-ĝe$_6$, "black textile"

1 gú 24 ma-na siki **túg-ĝe$_6$**, "1 talent (and) 24 minas of wool (for) a black textile," 648:2

túg-ĝe$_6$ ^{d}nin-ḫur-saĝ-ĝá, "black textile of Ninḫursaĝ," 787:1–2

2.6 túg-*ḫa-la*, "(a specification of textiles)"

****túg-*ḫa-la*** ù-x-x-tur 3-kam-ús ^{d}*kab-ta*, 690:2

****túg-*ḫa-la-um*** ⌜u$_3$⌝? zi-lí-ḫi 3-kam-ús, 811:3

2.7 túg-*ḫu-la-um*, "(a specification of textiles)"

****túg-*ḫu-la-um*** ù zi-lí-ḫi 3-kam-ús ^{d}*kab-tá*, 738:6

2.8 túg-sumun, "old textile"

túg-sumun-tur 3-kam-ús, "3rd-quality small old textile," 746:4

2.9 Broken Context

túg-[. . .], 511:'119, 631:5, 631:6, 645:4, 811:12, 811:15, 829:'1, 829:'7, 829:'8, 1162:'31

[n ^{túg} . . .], 594:1, 617:1, 618:8, 618:9, 811:13, 811:14, 827:1, 834:1, 834:2, 834:3, 834:4

[n ^{túg} . . .]-x 3-kam-ús, 618:7

[n . . .**tú**]**g**?-ga-x, 655:1

^{túg}[. . .], 663:8, 832:1, 811:8, 811:9, 811:10, 811:11

[^{túg} . . .]-PI-[. . .], 682:3

túg-x, 690:7

[^{túg}x]-an 3-kam-ús, 698:11

t[**úg** . . .]-PI-lugal, 748:1

túg x-x-x ba-tab [*tuḫ-ḫu-um*] 3-kam-[ús], 773:7

[n **túg** . . .] 3-kam-[ús], 773:10

[n **túg**?-]x-níĝ–1-gen, 1254:'43

[. . .**t**]**úg**?-x, 1383:4

túg-[. . . n-kam]-ús, 1394:3

3. Processing Textiles

3.1 Assorted Commodites for Processing

1 ma-na 15 gín siki-ĝen 3⅓ sìla 5 gín ì-ĝeš 0.0.3.½ sìla naĝa-si-è 23 ma-na im-bábbar mu **túg-ga**-šè, "1 mina (and) 15 shekels of ordinary wool, 3⅓ liters (and) 5 shekels of sesame oil, 3½ liters of sprouted naĝa (and) 23 minas of gypsum for (processing) textiles," 699:1–5

1 sìla 11 gín ì-ĝeš 0.0.5.2 sìla 15 gín naĝa-si-è 9 ma-na im-bábbar 7½ gín siki-gen mu **túg-ga**-šè, "1 liter (and) 11 shekels of sesame oil, 52 liters (and) 15 shekels of sprouted naĝa, 9 minas of gypsum (and) 7½ shekels of ordinary wool for textiles," 705:1–5

3.2 Fats

ì-ĝeš mu **túg-ga**-šè, "sesame oil for (processing) textiles" > **ì-ĝeš**

0.0.1. ì-ĝeš 0.0.1. ì-šáḫ mu **túg-ga**-šè, "10 liters of sesame oil (and) 10 liters of lard for (processing) textiles," 712:1–3

3.3 Gypsum

n gú im-bábbar mu **túg-ga**-šè, "n talent(s) of gypsum for (processing) textiles" > **im-bábbar**

4. Translation Uncertain

★★[n] ^{túg}[níĝ-lá]m-ús [n-ka]m [n] **túg**-guz-za-ús-1-kam **t**[**úg**?-ba]r?-r[a-n]i? *ḫa-um na-wi-ir-ilum*, "{assorted textiles}, *ḫa'um* textiles of *Nawir-ilum*," 650:2–5

túg-du$_8$, "braider, ropemaker"

ĝuruš **túg-du$_8$**, "braider" > *Craftsmen Index*

ḫa-lí **túg-du$_8$**, "*Hali*, the braider" > *Personal Name Index*

túg-du$_8$-a, "network, mesh"[116]

^{kuš}e-sír **túg-du$_8$-a**, "meshwork sandals" > **^{kuš}e-sír**

^{kuš}súḫub-**túg-du$_8$-a**, "meshwork shoes" > **^{kuš}súḫub**

túg-du$_8$-a siki gír-gul, "meshwork of g̃ír-gul wool" > **siki**

túg-du$_8$-a siki $^{g̃eš}$garig aka, "meshwork of combed wool" > **siki**

túg-ma-dur$_7$-ra, *ṣubat arišti*, "mourning textile"[117]

7 ^{túg}uš-bar *a-gi$_4$-um* **túg-ma-dur$_7$-ra** (. . .) á mu-DU, "7 *a-gi$_4$-um* uš-bar mourning textiles, {authorizing official}, delivery of (completed) work. *Šelianum*, the scribe, was the deputy," 566:1–2, 4

[n+]4 gada-g[en] *a-gi$_4$-um* **túg-ma-dur$_7$-ra** á mu-DU, "[n]+4 ordinary *a-gi$_4$-um* mourning linens, delivery of (completed) work," 573:1–3

4 ^{túg}bar-si níg̃-lá 3-kam-ús 4 ^{túg}bar-si níg̃-lá 4-kam-ús túg **túg-ma-dur$_7$-ra**-àm á mu-DU, "4 ordinary níg̃-lá bands (and) 4 4th-quality níg̃-lá bands, mourning textiles, delivery of (completed) work," 580:1–4

1 ^{túg}*ḫa-um a-gi$_4$-um simat-^{d}ištaran* túg **túg-ma-dur$_7$-ra**-àm á mu-DU-⸢ra⸣?, "1 *a-gi$_4$-um ḫa'um* textile of *Simat-Ištaran*, a mourning textile, delivery of (completed) work," 581:1–3

(. . .) túg-sumun-àm 53 **túg-ma-dur$_7$-ra**, "{assorted textiles, many belonging to *Šu-Kabta*, in the month of his death}, old textiles, 53 mourning textiles," 698:28–30

túg-sa-gi$_4$-a, "finished textiles"

1. Delivery of *Adat-tillati*

1.1 Receipt of *Amrini*

(. . .) {indent} 21 **túg-sa-gi$_4$-àm** ⸢*am*⸣*-ri-ni* šu ba-ti ki ^{d}*adad-tillati*-ta ba-zi, "*Amrini* received 21 {assorted} finished textiles from *Adad-tillati*," 746:10–15

1.2 Receipt of *Nuruš-eli*

[**túg-s**]**a-gi$_4$-àm** [*nu*]*-ru-uš-e-lí* ⸢šu⸣ ba-ti ki ^{d}*adad-tillati*-ta ba-zi, "*Nuruš-eli* received {assorted} finished [textiles] from *Adad-tillati*," 773:12–16, 790:3–6

1.3 Receipt of *Puzur-agum*

103 ⸢**túg**⸣**-sa-gi$_4$-àm** 2 ^{gi}bisag̃-gíd-da túg-ga 2 ^{gi}kid-uzu ki ^{d}*adad-tillati*-ta *puzur$_4$-a-gu$_5$-*[*um*] šu [ba-ti], "From *Adad-tillati*, *Puzur-agum* received 103 finished textiles, 2 long textile baskets (and) 2 reed uzu-mats," 834:17–23

1.4 Receipt of *Šu-Adad*

(. . .) **túg-sa-gi$_4$-àm** *šu-^{d}adad* šu ba-ti (. . .) iti u$_5$-bí-gu$_7$ (. . .) úgu-a g̃á-g̃á ga-ga-ra-a ki ^{d}*adad-tillati*-ta ⸢ba⸣-zi, "From *Adad-tillati* in month 4, *Šu-Adad* received {assorted

[116] Waetzoldt (personal communication), rather than the previous interpretation as felt, now understands túg-du$_8$-a as "Flechtwerk, Geflecht," and the profession túg-du$_8$ as "Seiler und Flechter."

[117] This term is not attested in the Ur III corpus. However, túg-mu-dur$_7$-ra is attested in OB literary texts (Waetzoldt 1972, XXI).

textiles}, finished textiles, (and) {other deliveries to other people}, the total placed in the account," 1162:'34-'36, '50, '66-'70

(. . .) **[túg]-sa-gi$_4$-a** [*šu*]-^{d}*adad* [šu] ba-an-ti ⌜úgu⌝-a g̃á-[g̃á ga]-ga-ra-a [ki ^{d}]*adad-tillati*-[ta ba-zi], "[From] *Adad-tillati, Šu-Adad* received {assorted textiles}, finished textiles, the total placed in the account," 1254:'44-'51

2. Delivery of ***Puzur-agum***

2.1 Receipt of ***Šu-Adad***

túg-sa-gi$_4$-àm ki *puzur$_4$-a-gu$_5$-um*-ta *šu*-^{d}*adad* šu ba-(an-)ti, "*Šu-Adad* received {assorted} finished textiles from *Puzur-agum*," 567:2–5, 570:4–8, 578:19–22, 579:20–24, 586:4–7, 587:4–7, 590:4–7

túg-sa-gi$_4$-a mu-DU *šu*-^{d}*adad* šu ba-an-ti ki *puzur$_4$-a-gu$_5$-um*-ta ba-zi, "*Šu-Adad* received a delivery of {assorted} finished textiles from *Puzur-agum*," 568:4–9

túg-sa-gi$_4$-a mu-DU ki *puzur$_4$-a-gu$_5$-um*-ta *šu*-^{d}*adad* šu ba-ti, "*Šu-Adad* received a delivery of {assorted} finished textiles from *Puzur-agum*," 577:5–9

túg-sa-gi$_4$-[àm] ki *puzur$_4$-a-gu$_5$-um*-[ta] *šu*-^{d}*adad* šu ba-an-ti šà tum-ma-al^{ki}, "*Šu-Adad* received {assorted} finished textiles from *Puzur-agum* in Tumal," 591:'12-'15

2.2 The Textiles of ***Šu-Eštar***

túg-sa-gi$_4$-a ⌜mu⌝-DU *puzur$_4$-a-gu$_5$-um* ^{lú}ázlag túg-*šu-eš$_4$-tár*, "{assorted} finished textiles, the delivery of *Puzur-agum*, the fuller, (are) the textiles of *Šu-Eštar*," 823:4–7

3. Bound Up to be Baled

★★(. . .) ⌜siki⌝-bala-dè in-na-[kéše t]úg-gen-kam ì-in-⌜DU⌝? 1 ^{túg}sag̃-uš-bar **sa-gi$_4$-[àm]**, "{assorted textiles}, the wool was bound up to be baled, he delivered the ordinary textiles, they are finished sag̃-uš-bar textiles," 609:7–9 (envelope)

★★(. . .) siki bala-[dè i]n-na-k[éše] ^{túg}uš-ba[r **sa-gi$_4$-àm**], "{assorted textiles}, the wool was bound up to be baled, they are finished uš-bar textiles," 609:8 (tablet)

túg-tùn, "a cloth container?" > **tùn**

tuḫ, *tuḫḫū*, "bran; husks, residue, chaff," 1128:1

ninda-**tuḫ**, "bran bread" > **ninda**

1. **tuḫ-bi**, "its bran"

★★[. . .] NE-x[. . . n] dida$_x$-g[en . . . x]-ki-ri?-šè šà é-duru$_5$-^{d}b[a?-ú? (x)] **tuḫ-bi** ba-zi, "[. . . n (liters?) . . .] ordinary dida beer for [x] in the B[a'u?] village, its bran was disbursed," 1009:18–21

2. **tuḫ-duru$_5$**, "fresh bran," 997:10, 1002:11

tuḫ-[**duru$_5$**...], 1002:6

n sìla **tuḫ-duru$_5$**-ta, "n liter(s) of fresh bran each," 1189:11

tuḫ-duru$_5$ šà-gal, "fresh bran (as) fodder" > **šà-gal**

3. **tuḫ-duru$_5$-gen**, "ordinary fresh bran," 997:6, 1023:6, 1023:6, 1024:5, 1024:7, 1047:3, 1109:2, 1109:13, 1179:2, 1179:9, 1179:18, 1199:2, 1199:6, 1199:14, 1208:2, 1208:8, 1208:15

tuḫ-duru$_5$-gen bíl-šè, "ordinary fresh bran for burning" > **bíl**

tuḫ-duru$_5$-gen sá-du$_{11}$, "ordinary fresh bran, regular offerings" > **sá-du$_{11}$**

tuḫ-duru$_5$-gen šà-gal šáḫ-ú, "ordinary fresh bran, fodder of range-fed pigs" > **šà-gal**

tuḫ-duru$_5$-gen šà-gal udu-niga, "ordinary fresh bran, fodder of fattened sheep" > **šà-gal**

4. **tuḫ-duru$_5$-sig$_5$**, "fine fresh bran," 442:12, 445:9, 1002:2, 1022:2, 1023:2, 1024:2, 1047:2, 1150:1, 1162:50, 1162:'51, 1218:1

tuḫ-duru$_5$-sig$_5$ bíl-šè, "fine fresh chaff for burning" > **bíl**

tuḫ-duru$_5$-sig$_5$ gibil, "fine fresh new bran," 436:9

tuḫ-duru$_5$-sig$_5$ sá-du$_{11}$, "fine fresh bran, regular offerings" > **sá-du$_{11}$**

tuḫ-duru$_5$-sig$_5$-ĝe$_6$, "fine fresh dark bran," 403:8, 510:8, 511:'107, 521:8, 1002:3, 1022:3, 1023:3, 1024:3, 1046:6

3 sìla **tuḫ-duru$_5$-sig$_5$**-ta, "3 liters of fine fresh dark bran each," 442:6

tuḫ-duru$_5$-sig$_5$ [. . .], 997:2, 997:3, 1022:2, 1022:3

5. **tuḫ-ĝeš-ì**, "sesame chaff" > ĝeš-ì

6. **tuḫ-hád-gen**, "ordinary dried bran," 1116:1, 1224:3

7. **zì-tuḫ**, "bran flour," 1074:3

tuḫ-ḫu-um, *tuḫḫu*, "bran, husks, residue, waste products"

túg ba-tab *tuḫ-ḫu-um*, "(a specification of textiles)" > **ba-tab**

tuku, *rašû*, "to acquire, get" > *Verb Index*

túl, *būrtu*; *ḫirītu*; *kalakku*, "well; ditch; trench"

túl dù, "to construct a well" > **dù**

á-ĝã-ĝá še **túl**-tur é-^{d}*šu*-^{d}*suen*^{ki}-šè de$_6$<-a>, "having gone to *Bit-Šu-Suen* (to receive) instruction (about) barley (and?) the small well," 175:28

túm, **tùm**, *babālu*, sg. imperfect stem of de$_6$, "to bring" > *Verb Index*

tum$_{12}$(TU)^{mušen}, *summatu*, "wild dove," 526:8, 976:4, 976:7, 1058:1, 1059:2, 1172:2, 976:4

tum$_{12}$^{mušen}-niga, "fattened wild dove," 1060:2

tum$_{12}$^{mušen} ba-úš, "dead wild dove" > **úš**

tùn, *tākaltu*, "bag; a container"

★★2 ^{gi}kid ^{ĝeš}gu-za-zà-bi-ús **tùn**?-ba kuš ĝar-ra, "2 mats of an armchair, (?), covered with leather," 1376:8–9

★★1 túg-**tùn** túg-lugal é-ba-an, "1 container of a pair of royal textiles," 748:2

tùn-lá, "a device/container used for pouring dirt"[118]

sabar zi-ga in-lá **tùn-lá** ^{ĝeš}kiri$_6$-zabala$_4$^{ki} kurum$_7$ [aka], "Inspection (of the work of workers). They transported dirt removed via a tùn-lá device at the Zabala garden," 178:6–8

saḫar zi-ga **tùn-lá** da bàd sè-ga, "dirt removed via a tùn-lá device, tamped at the side of the (enclosure) wall" > **sè(g$_{10}$)**

tur, *ṣehēru*, "(to be) small, young; to reduce" > *Verb Index*

^{gi}bisaĝ-**tur** , "small basket" > **^{gi}bisaĝ**

^{kuš}e-sír-**tur**, "small sandals" > **^{kuš}e-sír**

gú-**tur**, "peas" > **gú-tur**

gu$_4$-**tur**, "small ox" > **gu$_4$**

ḫar-**tur**, "small seedling" > **ḫar**

^{ĝeš}kíĝ-**tur**, "small/young kíĝ tree" > **^{ĝeš}kíĝ**

mušen-**tur**, "small bird" > **mušen**

^{kuš}súḫub-**tur**, "small shoes" > **^{kuš}súḫub**

túg-**tur**, "small textile" > **túg**

túl-**tur**, "small well" > **túl**

^{ĝeš}ù-suḫ$_5$-**tur**, "small/young pine tree" > **^{ĝeš}ù-suḫ$_5$**

uz-**tur**, "duckling" > **uz-tur**

★★[. . .]-da-**tur** [. . .] x x x nu-ub-kíĝ, 374:'14

tuš, *wašābu*, "to sit; to dwell; to be idle" > *Verb Index*

– U –

u-še-er-ḫa-lum, "(meaning uncertain)"

★★[n] ^{ĝeš}ú-bíl-lá [*u-še-er*]-*ḫa-lum*-šè, "[n] (units) of charcoal for *ušerḫalum*," 1379:'8-'9

ú, *šammu*, "grass"

éš-**ú**, "grass ropes" > **éš**

1. **As a Determinative**

^{ú}gámun, "cumin" > **^{ú}gámun**

^{ú}sullim, "fenugreek" > **^{ú}sullim**

^{ú}ZI/ZI, "rushes" > **A.ZI/ZI**

2. **Range-fed Animals**

gu$_4$-**ú**, "range-fed ox" > **gu$_4$**

šáḫ-**ú**, "range-fed pig" > **šáḫ**

udu-**ú**, "range-fed sheep" > **udu**

[118] Heimpel 2008, §5.18.3.

^{ĝeš}**ú-bíl-lá**, *upillû*, "charcoal, charcoal wood," 1305:1, 1308:1

[n ^{ĝeš}]**ú-bíl-lá** ki-lá-bi 10 ma-⌜na⌝, "[n (units)] of charcoal, its weight is 10 minas," 1162:'59-'60

^{ĝeš}**ú-bíl-lá** (. . .) mu dal é-túg-ga-šè, "charcoal wood (and) {other materials} for the shelves? of a textile container," 779:3, 5

★★60 ^{ĝeš}**ù-bil-lá** *ZA*-ḫa-*LUM*-šè, "60 (units) of charcoal for *ZA-ḫa-LUM*," 1297:6–7

★★[n] ^{ĝeš}**ú-bíl-lá** [*u-še-er*]-*ḫa-lum*-šè, "[n] (units) of charcoal for *ušerḫalum*," 1379:'8-'9

ú-ḫáb, *ḫûratu*, "madder (dye)," 828:3, 898:5, 943:5, 947:2

^{kuš}èš **ú-ḫáb**, "madder-tanned tent" > ^{kuš}**èš**

kuš-gu$_4$ **ú-ḫáb**, "madder-tanned ox hide," 839:2, 923:7, 925:5, 1517:7, 1517:19

kuš-udu **ú-ḫáb**, "madder-tanned sheep skin," 917:1

★★5½ ĜAR kuš-pa$_5$ udu-niga **ú-ḫáb**, 968:8

ú-la-bi (<ul$_4$-lá-bi), "quickly"

1. Orders to Quickly Provide the Account

tu-ra-am-ì-lí ù-na-a-du$_{11}$ níĝ-kas$_7$ ^{d}*adad-tillati* šabra mu na-rú-a-maḫ-ta mu *si-mu-ru-um*^{ki} ba-ḫulu-šè ḫé-en-ĝá-ĝá **ú-lá-bi**, "Say to *Turam-ili* that 'the account of *Adad-tillati*, the majordomo, for the years *Šu-Suen* 6 to *Šu-Suen* 7, should be brought forth quickly,'" 1040:1–7

ú-nin$_9$, "(a plant)"

éš-**ú-nin$_9$**, "ú-nin$_9$-plant rope" > **éš**

^{ĝeš}**ù**, "planking"

20 ^{ĝeš}**ù** má-[. . .], "20 [. . .] boat planks," 1368:4

ù-dug$_4$, *kakku*, "stick; a weapon"

^{ĝeš}ù-suḫ$_5$-sig **ù-du$_{11}$-ga**, "narrow pine stick" > ^{ĝeš}**ù-suḫ$_5$**

^{dug}**ù-lu-lu**, *alallû*, "pipe, conduit"

63 ^{dug}**ù-lu-lu** 2-kùš-ta *a-za-bu-um* šà é-a-šè ba-a-ĝar, "63 pipes of 2 cubits each were placed for the cistern in the house," 1325:7–8

ù-ru (< ùr), *sapānu*, "to level; to saturate/soak (with bitumen); to manufacture (bricks)" > *Verb Index*

ù-ru-a, "section of a wall, perhaps a feature protecting the approach to the gate"

ù-ru-a bàd aka, "to make the urua wall" > **aka**

1. Work for the urua wall

25 géme [im ga$_6$-ĝá]-dè [gub-ba] **ù-ru-a** bàd-šè, "25 workwomen [employed] to [carry earth] for the urua wall,"43:'24-'25, 44:24–25

2 ĝuruš šidim 2 ĝuruš šu dím gub-ba 4 géme im ga_6-ĝá-dè gub-ba 1 ĝuruš im i-⌜le⌝?-dè gub-[ba] **ù-ru-a** bàd-[šè], "2 builders (and) 2 workmen employed to build, 4 workwomen employed to carry earth (and) 1 workman employed to lift earth [for] the urua wall," 46:'22-'26

ù-suḫ$_5$, *ašūḫu*, "pine tree"

1. Types of Pine Trees

★★1 ^{ĝeš}ĜEŠ/ĜEŠ 1 gú-na **ú-suḫ**$_5$, 1372:27, 1372:84

1800 $^{\mathbf{ĝeš}}$**ù-⌜suḫ**$_5$⌝-tur-tur, "1800 very small/young pine trees," 1056:1

$^{\mathbf{ĝeš}}$**ù-suḫ**$_5$-sig ḫi-a, "various narrow pine boards," 1256:2, 1375:2

3 $^{\mathbf{ĝeš}}$**ù-suḫ**$_5$ 3-kam-ús, "3 3rd-quality pine trees," 1297:3

$^{\mathbf{ĝeš}}$**ù-suḫ**$_5$-sig ú-du_{11}-ga, "narrow pine stick," 1362:13, 1362:'36, 1362:'62

[n ^{ĝe}]^{š}**ù-suḫ**$_5$ [. . .] mu-4(aš), "[n] 4-year-old [. . .] pine tree(s)," 1362:14

2. Pine Seedlings

[n] ĝuruš u_4-[n-šè] ḫar lam $^{\mathbf{ĝeš}}$**ù-suḫ**$_5$ ke_4-[dè] $^{d}gu_4$-an-na-⌜ta⌝ gar-ša-an-na^{ki}-šè d[e_6-a], "[n] workmen [for n] day(s) having brought a seedling container of pine trees from Guanna to Garšana," 272:10–15

n ḫar $^{\mathbf{ĝeš}}$**ù-suḫ**$_5$ mu-n, "n n-year-old pine seedlings," 1362:'63, 1362:'64

4 ḫar lam $^{\mathbf{ĝeš}}$**ù-suḫ**$_5$-tur-tur 3-ta ù ḫar-bi, "4 seedling containers of very young pine trees, 3 each, and their seedlings," 1255:6

3. Pine Planks

$^{\mathbf{ĝeš}}$**ù-suḫ**$_5$ mi-rí-za mu dal é-túg-ga-šè, "pine planks for the shelves(?) of a textile container," 779:4–5

n $^{\mathbf{ĝeš}}$**ù-suḫ**$_5$ mi-rí-za má-n-gur, "n pine plank(s) of a n-bushel boat," 1362:9, 1362:10, 1362:11, 1362:12, 1362:'32, 1362:'33, 1362:'34, 1362:'35, 1362:'60, 1362:'61

4. Pine Door Parts

^{ĝeš}apin-ig-**ù-suḫ**$_5$, "door frame of pine wood," 1333:1

^{ĝeš}ù-šar-ig-**ù-suḫ**$_5$, "door point/crescent of pine wood," 1333:2

^{ĝeš}suḫuš-ig-**ù-suḫ**$_5$, "door foundation of pine wood," 1333:3

$^{\mathbf{ĝeš}}$**ù-šar**, "point/crescent (of a door)"

$^{\mathbf{ĝeš}}$**ù-šar**-ig-ù-suḫ$_5$, "door point/crescent of pine wood," 1333:2

$^{\mathbf{ĝeš}}$**ù-šub**, "brick mold"

$^{\mathbf{ĝeš}}$**ù-šub** $šeg_{12}$, "brick mold," 1340:2

$^{\mathbf{ĝeš}}$**ù-šub** $šeg_{12}$-al-ur_x-ra, "brick mold (for baked) brick," 1340:1

u$_4$, "day, occasion; during the time of day of," *passim*; see also [Relative Clauses]

1. During Construction

ba-na-ḫa-la **u**$_4$ al-tar é-lùnga é-muḫaldim ù é-kíkken, "{comestibles} were divided during construction of the brewery-kitchen-mill complex" > **ḫal** ba-na-ḫa-la **u_4** al-tar SIG$_4$.ANŠE, "{comestibles} were divided (for) {workers} during construction of the brick stack" > **ḫal**

íb-gu$_7$ **u_4** al-tar é-lùnga é-muḫaldim é-kíkken, "{workers} ate during construction of the brewery-kitchen-mill complex" > **gu$_7$**

íb-nağ **u_4** al-tar é-lùnga é-muḫaldim ù é-kíkken, "{workers} drank during construction of the brewery-kitchen-mill-complex" > **nağ**

sízkur **u_4** al-tar é-lùnga é-muḫaldim é-kíkken, "regular offerings during construction of the brewery-kitchen-mill complex" > **sízkur**

2. During a Festival > ezem

u_4 ezem-*a-bu-um-ma*, "during the *Abum* festival"

u_4 ezem-*e-lu-núm*-^{d}nergal$_x^{eri_{11}\text{-}gal}$, "during the *Elunum* Festival of Nergal" > *Deities Index*

u_4 ezem-gur-buru$_{14}$, "during the bushel harvest festival"

u_4 ezem-pa-è, "during the emergence festival"

3. On the Occasion of a Performance of a *Takribtum*

íb-gu$_7$ **u_4** *tak-ri-ib-tum* bàd, "(they) ate on the occasion of (the performance of) a *takribtum* at? the (enclosure) wall" > **gu$_7$**, ***tak-ri-ib-tum***

4. Workers Released for a Day

u_4 du$_8$-ḫa a im še-ğá-a, "{workers} released for a day (because of) rain" > **duḫ**

u_4 siki ba-a-ka šu bar-ra, "{workers} released on the day of the wool rations" > **šu . . . bar**

u_4-ḫi-in, *uḫinnu*, "fresh dates," 1081:7, 1081:13, 1102:2, 1109:8, 1109:14, 1215:2, 1237:2

u_4-ḫi-in šà-gal šáḫ-ú, "fresh dates, fodder of range-fed pigs" > **šà-gal**

u_4-sakar, *uskāru*; *warḫu*, "crescent moon; moon"

sağ **u_4-sakar**, "new moon day" > **sağ u_4-sakar**

u_4-tuḫ-ḫu-um, "(meaning uncertain)"[119]

ninda-***u_4-tuḫ-ḫu-um***, "(a bread)" > **ninda**

u_8, *immertum*, *laḫru*, "ewe," 984:'64, 1019:2, 1083:1, 1165:2, 1171:1, 1217:2, 1254:'16

u_8-gukkal, "fat-tailed ewe," 1154:2

u_8-niga, "fattened ewe," 511:25, 984:2

ud$_5$, *enzu*, "female goat," 984:'33, 1019:3, 1019:9, 1025:24, 1025:94, 1154:6, 1171:4, 1519:1

siki-ud$_5$, "goat hair," 704:2, 772:1

éš-túg-gíd-**siki-ud$_5$**, "goat-hair cord, used to extend a textile (on a loom)," 628:1

★★éš-ú-**siki-ud$_5$**, 628:2

---

119 Brunke 2008, 144–146 (§3.1.4.51).

éš-ú-nin$_9$-**siki-ud$_5$**, 628:3

udu, *immeru*, "sheep," *passim*

^{kuš}a-g̃á-lá-barag-bi **udu**, "leather sack, its barag of sheep skin" > **^{kuš}a-g̃á-lá**

bar-**udu**, "sheep fleece" > **bar**

kuš-**udu**, "sheep skin" > **kuš**

sa-**udu**, "sheep sinew" > **sa**

šà šà-gal **udu** šáḫ mušen péš ḫi-a, "fodder of various sheep, pigs, birds (and) mice" > **šà-gal**

^{urudu}šim-da gu$_4$-**udu**, "sheep and cattle brand" > **^{urudu}šim-da**

udu abzu-šè, "sheep for the abzu" > **abzu**

udu-aslum$_x$-niga-babbar, "fattened white long-fleeced sheep," 973:6

udu ba-úš, "dead sheep" > **úš**

udu de$_6$, "to bring a sheep" > **de$_6$**

udu-máš ḫi-a, "various sheep (and) goats," 984:5, 984:12, 984:'21, 984:'26, 984:'34

udu ^{d}nergal$_x$, "sheep (for) Nergal" > *Deities Index*

udu sá-du$_{11}$, "sheep (for) regular offerings" > **sá-du$_{11}$**

1. **udu-niga**, "fattened sheep," 420:1, 449:1, 511:21, 511:23, 511:83, 519:1, 976:3, 976:5, 976:6, 978:1, 978:6, 978:7, 979:3, 979:9, 983:1, 983:18, 984:1, 984:'37, 984:'55, 985:1, 985:3, 1001:1, 1028:1, 1028:12, 1030:1, 1067:1, 1159:1, 1184:1, 1189:6, 1207:1, 1245:1, 1394:4

é-**udu-niga**, "sheep-fattening pen" > *Household Index*

5½ G̃AR kuš-pa$_5$ **udu-niga ú-háb, 968:8

kuš-**udu-niga**, "skin of a fattened sheep" > **kuš**

mu-du-lum **udu-niga**, "salted fattened sheep" > ***mu-du-lum***

šà-gal **udu-niga**, "fodder of fattened sheep" > **šà-gal**

26 **udu-niga** 1-sìla-ta, "26 fattened sheep, 1 liter (of fodder) each," 525:3

24 **udu-niga** 1-sìla-[ta] sá-du$_{11}$-šè, "24 fattened sheep, 1 liter (of fodder) [each] for regular offerings," 525:1–2

udu-niga ba-úš, "dead fattened sheep," 896:1–2

udu-niga-babbar, "white fattened sheep," 973:7

udu-niga é-**udu-niga**-šè, "fattened sheep for the sheep-fattening pen" > *Household Index*

udu-niga gu$_4$-e-ús-sa, "fattened sheep '(fed) following the oxen'," 506:3, 970:1, 970:7, 984:'38, 984:'54, 1025:23, 1025:93, 1254:4, 1394:5

1 **udu-niga** gu$_4$-e-ús-sa kuš-[bi] ba-zi, "1 fattened sheep '(fed) following the oxen', [its] skin was disbursed," 1027:2

n **udu-niga** iti u$_4$-n-ba-zal, "n fattened sheep at the end of the nth day of the month" > **zal**

udu-niga kuš-bi zi, "to disburse the skin of a fattened sheep" > **zi(g)**

udu-ú-niga, "fattened range-fed sheep," 411:3

2. **udu-níta**, "ram," 1078:1

3. **udu-sag̃**, "lead sheep"

[n+]1 **udu-sag̃** *šu-kab-tá*, "[n+]1 lead sheep of *Šu-Kabta*," 484:8

4. **udu-ú**, "range-fed sheep," 411:1, 421:3, 422:1, 971:1, 983:3, 983:19,, 1028:13 1067:2, 1521:1, 1522:1

kuš-**udu-ú**, "skin of a range-fed sheep" > **kuš**

udu-ú-niga, "fattened range-fed sheep," 411:3

5. **Broken Context**

1? **udu**?-x-x-x, 469:3

2? **udu** *šu*-ka-[. . .], 1342:2

[n] **udu**-[. . .], 1394:6

udug, "caretaker"

1. **The Caretaker of the House of *Dada***

0.1.0. še 4 ma-na siki-gen ½ sìla ì-šáḫ 5 sìla zì-kum 5 sìla zú-lum **udug** é-*da-da* dumu *na-sìm*, "60 liters of barley, 4 minas of ordinary wool, ½ liter of lard, 5 liters of kum-flour (and) 5 liters of dates for the caretaker of the house of *Dada*, son of *Nasim*," 438:1–6

2. **The Caretaker of the Replacement House**

0.1.0. še 4 ma-na siki-gen 1 sìla ì-šáḫ 5 sìla zì-kum 5 sìla zú-lum **udug** é-ki-ba-g̃ar-ra *u-bar-ri-a*, "60 liters of barley, 4 minas of ordinary wool, 1 liter of lard, 5 liters of kum-flour (and) 5 liters of dates (for) the caretaker of the replacement house of *Ubarria*," 1005:1–6

4 ^{gi}bisag̃-gíd-da-tur sa-ḫa gíd-2-kùš dag̃al-1-kùš **udug** é-ki-ba-g̃ar-ra-a *al-lu-a*-šè ba-a-g̃ar, "4 small, long, canvas-lined baskets, 2 kùš in length, 1 kùš in width, were placed for the caretaker of the replacement house of *Alua*," 1006:1–2

0.1.0. še 1 sìla ì-g̃eš ⌜**udug**⌝ é-ki-ba-g̃ar-ra [*a-lí*]-*a-bi*, "60 liters of barley (and) 1 liter of sesame oil (for) the caretaker of the replacement house of *Aliabi*," 1008:9–12

3. **Provisions for Caretakers**

(. . .) *ba-da*?-[erasure]-*a* (. . .) *šu-eš$_4$-tár* dumu *da-da-a* (. . .) ur-me s[an]tana mu **udug** kislaḫ saḫar zi-zi-dè-šè, "{barley, ordinary wool, oil and baskets} (for) *Bada'a*, *Šu-Eštar*, son of *Dada'a* (and) Ur-me, the date orchard administrator, (provisions) for caretakers moving dirt (to/from) the lot," 1011:5, 10, 14–15

úgu, *eli; muḫḫu; qaqqadu*, "first section of a balanced account, capital; on, over, above; against; more than; top"

šeg$_{12}$-al-ur$_x$-ra **úgu** gir$_4$-ta g̃ar, "to set bricks down from the top of the kiln" > **g̃ar**

úgu-a g̃ar, "to place (something) in the account" > **g̃ar**

úgu iz-zi-da a g̃ar, "to waterproof the top of the iz-zi wall" > **a . . . g̃ar**

úgu . . . dé, *ḫalāqu*, "to disappear, to be lost" > *Verb Index*

ugula, *waklu*, "overseer, foreman"

1 g̃uruš **ugula**, "1 overseer," *passim*

2 g̃uruš **ugula** 1½ sìla kaš-ninda [⅓ sìla tu$_7$]-ta, "2 overseers: 1½ liters beer (and) bread (and) [⅓ liter of soup] each," 379:6

1. **PN ugula árad-é-a**, "overseer of household servants" > *Personal Name Index*
   be-lí-ì-lí
   i-ri-ib
2. **ugula àga-ús-e-ne**, "overseer of gendarmes" > **àga-ús**
   Rim-ilum **ugula àga-ús-e-ne**, "*Rim-ilum*, overseer of gendarmes" > *Personal Name Index*
3. **ugula-é**, "overseer of the house"
   ur-^{d}dumu-zi nu-bànda-gu$_{4}$ ù **ugula-é**, "Ur-Dumuzi, ox-herder and overseer of the house" > *Personal Name Index*
4. **ugula-ĝéš-da**, "overseer of 60"
   a-gu-a **ugula-ĝéš-da**, "*Agua*, overseer of 60" > *Personal Name Index*
5. **ugula-gu$_{4}$**, "overseer of oxen"
   ì-lí-a-núm **ugula-gu$_{4}$**, "*Ili-anum*, overseer of oxen" > *Personal Name Index*
6. **ugula kíkken**, "mill overseer"
   ugula kíkken ĝar, "to place (something in the account) of the overseer of the mill" > **ĝar**
7. **ugula lú-ḫuĝ-ĝá**, "overseer of hired workers" > *Personal Name Index*
   ^{d}*adad-tillati* ĝuruš šidim **ugula**, 202:1–2, 203:1–2, 205:1, 206:1, 207:1, 209:1

aḫ-dam-ì-lí
ba-ba-ti-a
ba-zi
ḫal-lí-a
ib-ni-ilum
i-din-é-a
ilum-ba-ni
ilum-dan
la-qì-ip
la-te-ni-iš
li-la-a$_{(2)}$
simat-^{d}*nana*
simat-é-a
ša-lim-a-ḫu-um
šal$_{(2)}$*-maḫ*
šat-erra
šu-^{d}dumu-zi
šu-^{d}nisaba
za-la-a

7.1 Provisions

ugula lú-ḫuĝ-ĝá-e-ne íb-gu$_{7}$, "the overseer of hired workers ate" > **gu$_{7}$**

ugula lú-ḫuĝ-ĝá-e-ne íb-nag, "the overseer of the hired workers drank" > **nag**

n ĝuruš **ugula** lú-ḫuĝ-ĝá n sìla kaš-ninda n sìla tu$_{7}$-ta, "n overseer(s) of hired workmen: n liter(s) of beer (and) bread (and) n liter(s) of soup each," 379:9, 556:'5

7.2 Other

(. . .) lú-é-ki-ba-ĝar-ra šidim **ugula** lú-ḫuĝ-[ĝá . . .]-ka é-ka gub-ba [. . .]-e-ne, "{assorted breads} for the man of the replacement house, the builder, the overseer of the hired workers, employed in the [. . .] of the house," 485:5

8. **ugula lú-karkar^{ki}-me**, "overseer of men from Karkar" > *Personal Name Index*

á-ni-dam
ir$_{11}$*-dam*
šu-la-núm

9. **ugula má-gíd**, "overseer of boat towers"
   be-lí-ì-lí **ugula má-gíd**, "*Beli-ili*, overseer of boat towers" > *Personal Name Index*
10. **ugula-nam-10**, "overseer of 10"
   šu+níĝin 27.1.1.3 sìla še gur ki **ugula-nam-10-ka** ⌜ĝál⌝-la, "{barley for individuals}; in total: there are 27 bushels (and) 73 liters of barley at the place of the overseer of 10," 504:20–22

11. **ugula nu-bànda-gu$_4$**, "overseer of ox-herders" > *Personal Name Index*

a-bí-a-ti
AN. ŠUM.TAG.KAL
ilum-ba-ni
i-me-èr-ra
^{d}*ma-lik-tillati*
mu-na-núm
puzur$_4$-a-bi
puzur$_4$-^{d}en-líl
su-ga-ni-a
šu-^{d}*adad*
ti-ga-an
ur-^{d}dumu-zi
za-bu-la

12. **ugula PN šabra**, "supervised by PN, the majordomo" > *Personal Name Index*

ugula *ba-ba-ni* **šabra**, "{ox-herders} supervised by *Babani*, the majordomo"

His work gang: *Abiati*, *Imerra*, Lu-Ea, Lu-Inana, *Munanum*, *Puzur-abi*, *Puzur*-Enlil, *Zabula*

ugula *nu-úr*-^{d}*adad* **šabra**, "{ox-herders} supervised by *Nur-Adad*, the majordomo"

His work gang: *Ilum-bani*, *Malik-tillati*, *Sugania*, *Tigan*, Ur-Dumuzi

13. **PN ugula uš-bar**, "overseer of weavers" > *Personal Name Index*

aš-tá-qar
ku-un-si-ma-at

^{dug}**úgur**(SIG$_7$), "(a vessel)"

8 ^{dug}**úgur** bala, "8 bala vessels," 1376:76

um-ma, "(meaning uncertain)"

★★gaba-ri dub [. . .] **um-ma** [. . .], 1052:2

um-mi, "(meaning uncertain)"

★★n g̃eš-g̃ar n sìla **um-mi**, 1272:5, 1272:6, 1272:7

um-mi-a, *ummānu*, "expert, master craftsman" > *Personal Name Index*

a-da-làl
ak-ba-zum
G̃AR-šà-*ti*
ma-šum
si-um
šu-ma-ma
[x-x?]-ti-en

g̃uruš šidim **um-mi-a**, "master builder," *passim*

g̃uruš **um-mi-a**, "craftsman" > *Craftsmen Index*

^{kuš}**ummu$_x$**(A.U.EDIN.LÁ), "waterskin," 932:2

^{kuš}**ùmmu**(EDIN.A.LÁ), "waterskin," 938:1, 940:1, 968:16

^{kuš}**ummu$_x$** é-$^{<g̃eš>}$gu-za-šè, "waterskin for the house of the chair," 925:'15

^{kuš}**ummu$_x$** ^{d}inana-unug^{ki}, "waterskin (for) Inana of Uruk," 925:'13

^{kuš}**ummu$_x$** šà-mah̬, "waterskin (made) of a large intestine?," 925:'12

ÚR×A.NA(KWU-739) > ***murana**, *murrānu*, "mulberry"

n ḫar ^{ĝeš}**ÚR×A.NA** n-ta, "n mulberry seedling(s), n (units) each," 1256:14, 1375:17, 1375:18, 1375:19, 1375:20

ùr, *sapānu*, "to level, to pave (with paving bricks)" > **ú-ru**

ùr, *ūru*, "roof"

ùr a ĝar, "to waterproof a roof" > **a . . . ĝar**

ùr dù, "to construct a roof" > **dù**

ùr é-udu-niga, "the roof of the sheep-fattening pen" > *Household Index*

ùr im sumur aka, "to plaster a roof" > **aka**

ùr tùm, "to bring roof (beams)" > **tùm**

ùr zi(l), "to strip a roof" > **zi(l)**

1. **ĝeš ùr**, *gušūru*, "roof beam, rafter"

éš ĝeš **ùr** kéše, "to bind ropes to roof beams" > **kéše**

ĝeš **ùr** gíd, "to haul roof beams" > **gíd**

ĝeš **ùr** kéše, "to bind roof beams" > **kéše**

ĝeš **ùr** kéše gíd, "to tighten bound roof beams" > **gíd**

1.1 **Types of Beams**

ĝeš **ùr** ásal, "poplar roof beam," 1286:1, 1289:1, 1303: 1, 1309:1, 1309:4, 1309:7

ĝeš **ùr** šinig, "tamarisk roof beam," 1286:3, 1289:3, 1293:1

1.2 **Broken Context**

[. . .] **ùr** ésir šub-ba [gi]-bi ½ sa? [peš]-múrgu-[bi] ½ [pa] ^{ĝeš}nimbar-bi 4 ésir-é-a-bi 0.0.1 [. . .] á-bi u_4-½-kam, "[n object(s)] coated with bitumen. (Manufacture required:) ½ bundles of [reeds], ½ date palm spine, 4 date palm fronds, 10 [+n? liters] of house bitumen (and) ½ a day of labor," 1381:19–24

urudu, *erû*, "copper"

1 ^{gi}gur ba-rí-ga ka-ba **urudu** ĝar-ra, "a measuring container whose opening is covered (in) copper," 1372:35, 1372:92

[n] gú UD.KA.B[AR x?] **urudu** ĝar-⌜ra⌝, "[n] talent(s) of bronze [(and?) x] covered (with) copper," 1377:1

1. **Copper Objects**

^{urudu}gu$_4$-zi-bi-ir, "ladder"

^{urudu}ḫa-zi-in, "axe"

^{urudu}ku-gi-im, "(a copper object)"

^{urudu}šen, "(soup) cauldron"

^{urudu}šim-da, "(cattle-)branding iron"

^{urudu}šum, "saw"

4. udu-ú, "range-fed sheep," 411:1, 421:3, 422:1, 971:1, 983:3, 983:19,, 1028:13 1067:2, 1521:1, 1522:1

kuš-**udu-ú**, "skin of a range-fed sheep" > **kuš**

udu-ú-niga, "fattened range-fed sheep," 411:3

5. Broken Context

1? **udu**?-x-x-x, 469:3

2? **udu** *šu*-ka-[. . .], 1342:2

[n] **udu**-[. . .], 1394:6

udug, "caretaker"

1. The Caretaker of the House of *Dada*

0.1.0. še 4 ma-na siki-gen ½ sìla ì-šáh̬ 5 sìla zì-kum 5 sìla zú-lum **udug** é-*da-da* dumu *na-sìm*, "60 liters of barley, 4 minas of ordinary wool, ½ liter of lard, 5 liters of kum-flour (and) 5 liters of dates for the caretaker of the house of *Dada*, son of *Nasim*," 438:1–6

2. The Caretaker of the Replacement House

0.1.0. še 4 ma-na siki-gen 1 sìla ì-šáh̬ 5 sìla zì-kum 5 sìla zú-lum **udug** é-ki-ba-g̃ar-ra *u-bar-ri-a*, "60 liters of barley, 4 minas of ordinary wool, 1 liter of lard, 5 liters of kum-flour (and) 5 liters of dates (for) the caretaker of the replacement house of *Ubarria*," 1005:1–6

4 ^{gi}bisag̃-gíd-da-tur sa-h̬a gíd-2-kùš dag̃al-1-kùš **udug** é-ki-ba-g̃ar-ra-a *al-lu-a*-šè ba-a-g̃ar, "4 small, long, canvas-lined baskets, 2 kùš in length, 1 kùš in width, were placed for the caretaker of the replacement house of *Alua*," 1006:1–2

0.1.0. še 1 sìla ì-g̃eš ⸢**udug**⸣ é-ki-ba-g̃ar-ra [*a-lí*]-*a-bi*, "60 liters of barley (and) 1 liter of sesame oil (for) the caretaker of the replacement house of *Aliabi*," 1008:9–12

3. Provisions for Caretakers

(. . .) *ba-da*?-[erasure]-*a* (. . .) *šu-eš*$_4$*-tár* dumu *da-da-a* (. . .) ur-me s[an]tana mu **udug** kislah̬ sah̬ar zi-zi-dè-šè, "{barley, ordinary wool, oil and baskets} (for) *Bada'a*, *Šu-Eštar*, son of *Dada'a* (and) Ur-me, the date orchard administrator, (provisions) for caretakers moving dirt (to/from) the lot," 1011:5, 10, 14–15

úgu, *eli; muh̬h̬u; qaqqadu*, "first section of a balanced account, capital; on, over, above; against; more than; top"

šeg$_{12}$-al-ur$_x$-ra **úgu** gir$_4$-ta g̃ar, "to set bricks down from the top of the kiln" > **g̃ar**

úgu-a g̃ar, "to place (something) in the account" > **g̃ar**

úgu iz-zi-da a g̃ar, "to waterproof the top of the iz-zi wall" > **a . . . g̃ar**

úgu . . . dé, *h̬alāqu*, "to disappear, to be lost" > *Verb Index*

ugula, *waklu*, "overseer, foreman"

1 g̃uruš **ugula**, "1 overseer," *passim*

2 g̃uruš **ugula** 1½ sìla kaš-ninda [⅓ sìla tu$_7$]-ta, "2 overseers: 1½ liters beer (and) bread (and) [⅓ liter of soup] each," 379:6

1. **PN ugula árad-é-a**, "overseer of household servants" > *Personal Name Index*
   be-lí-ì-lí
   i-ri-ib

2. **ugula àga-ús-e-ne**, "overseer of gendarmes" > **àga-ús**
   Rim-ilum **ugula àga-ús-e-ne**, "*Rim-ilum*, overseer of gendarmes" > *Personal Name Index*

3. **ugula-é**, "overseer of the house"
   ur-^{d}dumu-zi nu-bànda-gu$_4$ ù **ugula-é**, "Ur-Dumuzi, ox-herder and overseer of the house" > *Personal Name Index*

4. **ugula-g̃éš-da**, "overseer of 60"
   a-gu-a **ugula-g̃éš-da**, "*Agua*, overseer of 60" > *Personal Name Index*

5. **ugula-gu$_4$**, "overseer of oxen"
   ì-lí-a-núm **ugula-gu$_4$**, "*Ili-anum*, overseer of oxen" > *Personal Name Index*

6. **ugula kíkken**, "mill overseer"
   ugula kíkken g̃ar, "to place (something in the account) of the overseer of the mill" > **g̃ar**

7. **ugula lú-ḫug̃-g̃á**, "overseer of hired workers" > *Personal Name Index*
   ^{d}*adad-tillati* g̃uruš šidim **ugula**, 202:1–2, 203:1–2, 205:1, 206:1, 207:1, 209:1

aḫ-dam-ì-lí	*ilum-dan*	*šal*$_{(2)}$*-maḫ*
ba-ba-ti-a	*la-qì-ip*	*šat-erra*
ba-zi	*la-te-ni-iš*	*šu-*^{d}dumu-zi
ḫal-lí-a	*li-la-a*$_{(2)}$	*šu-*^{d}nisaba
ib-ni-ilum	*simat-*^{d}*nana*	*za-la-a*
i-din-é-a	*simat-é-a*	
ilum-ba-ni	*ša-lim-a-ḫu-um*	

7.1 Provisions

ugula lú-ḫug̃-g̃á-e-ne íb-gu$_7$, "the overseer of hired workers ate" > **gu$_7$**

ugula lú-ḫug̃-g̃á-e-ne íb-nag, "the overseer of the hired workers drank" > **nag**

n g̃uruš **ugula** lú-ḫug̃-g̃á n sìla kaš-ninda n sìla tu$_7$-ta, "n overseer(s) of hired workmen: n liter(s) of beer (and) bread (and) n liter(s) of soup each," 379:9, 556:'5

7.2 Other

(. . .) lú-é-ki-ba-g̃ar-ra šidim **ugula** lú-ḫug̃-[g̃á . . .]-ka é-ka gub-ba [. . .]-e-ne, "{assorted breads} for the man of the replacement house, the builder, the overseer of the hired workers, employed in the [. . .] of the house," 485:5

8. **ugula lú-karkar^{ki}-me**, "overseer of men from Karkar" > *Personal Name Index*

á-ni-dam	*ir*$_{11}$*-dam*	*šu-la-núm*

9. **ugula má-gíd**, "overseer of boat towers"
   be-lí-ì-lí **ugula má-gíd**, "*Beli-ili*, overseer of boat towers" > *Personal Name Index*

10. **ugula-nam-10**, "overseer of 10"
    šu+nígin 27.1.1.3 sìla še gur ki **ugula-nam-10-ka** ⌜g̃ál⌝-la, "{barley for individuals}; in total: there are 27 bushels (and) 73 liters of barley at the place of the overseer of 10," 504:20–22

ús, *redû*, "to process (emmer)" > *Verb Index*

ús, "(to be) of a lesser quality"

gi-g̃ír-ab-ba tab-ba **ús > **gi-g̃ír-ab-ba**
ninda zì-gu-**ús**, "2nd-quality gu-flour bread" > **ninda**
g̃ešnu-úr-ma-**ús**, "2nd-quality pomegranate" > **g̃ešnu-úr-ma**
túg-**ús**, "2nd-quality textile" > **túg**
zì-**ús**, "2nd-quality flour" > **zì**

ús, *diāšu*; *redû*; *šadādu*, "to drag; to stretch; to accompany, follow; flank, (long) side" > *Verb Index*

ús-sa i_7-*a-ga-mu-um*, "following the *Agamum* canal" > *Canal Index*
ús-bi, "carrying (distance of bricks or earth)" > *Verb Index*

uš, *uššu*, "foundation"

1. **uš bàd**, "the foundation of the (enclosure) wall"
   gi-sal **uš** bàd gul, "to trim thin reeds (for) the foundation of the (enclosure) wall" > **gul**
   sízkur **uš** bàd, "offering (for) the foundation of the (enclosure) wall" > **sízkur**
   uš bàd tà(g), "to touch-up the foundation of the (enclosure) wall" > **tà(g)**
   uš bàd zi(g), "to move (dirt at) the foundation of the (enclosure) wall > **zi(g)**
2. **uš é-*ba-ḫa-a***, "the foundation of the house of *Baḫa'a*"
   uš é-*ba-ḫa-a* dù, "to construct the foundation of the house of *Baḫa'a*" > *Household Index*
3. **uš é-uš-bar-ra**, "the foundation of the textile mill" > *Household Index*
   gi-sal **uš** ki-sá-a é-uš-bar-šè g̃ar, "to place thin reeds for the foundation of the foundation terrace of the textile mill" > **g̃ar**
4. **uš ki-sá-a**, "the foundation of the foundation terrace"
   uš ki-sá-a saḫar zi(g), "to move dirt at the foundation of the foundation terrace" > **zi(g)**

uš-bar, *išparu*, "weaver"

géme **uš-bar**, "female weaver" > *Craftswomen Index*

1. **PN ugula uš-bar**, "PN, overseer of weavers" > *Personal Name Index*
   aš-tá-qar *ku-un-si-ma-at*

túguš-bar, "(a textile)," 568:3, 569:17, 572:5, 579:12, 589:1, 597:2, 608:9, 617:9, 618:12, 637:3, 639:3, 646:6, 647:6, 649:10, 658:7, 669:9, 680:4, 685:4, 686:3, 690:6, 691:3, 692:8, 693:8, 694:5, 698:27, 725:2, 731:3, 732:3, 734:3, 739:7, 745:6, 753:12, 758:14, 760:7, 764:9, 765:7, 778:10, 786:14, 795:3, 796:10, 804:4, 806:8, 810:4, 814:11, 818:4, 821:10, 827:7, 834:13, 1162:'32

túgsag̃-**uš-bar**, "(a textile)" > **túgsag̃-uš-bar**
siki **túguš-bar**, "wool (for) an uš-bar textile" > **siki**
n **túguš-bar** n ma-na-ta, "n uš-bar textile(s), (weighing) n mina(s) each," 662:8, 701:1, 701:9, 730:3, 730:4, 742:8, 744:8

n ^{túg}**uš-bar** n ma-na-ta ki-lá-bi n ma-na, "n uš-bar textile(s), (weighing) n mina(s) each, their weight is n mina(s) (in total)," 738:16–17, 747:9–10

^{túg}**uš-bar** *a-gi$_4$-um*, "*a-gi$_4$-um* uš-bar textile," 566:1

^{túg}**uš-bar**-dul$_5$-gen, "ordinary uš-bar-dul$_5$ textile," 589:2, 764:8

^{túg}**uš-bar**-g̃e$_6$, "black uš-bar textile," 569:18, 662:9, 663:7, 725:3, 753:13, 758:15, 760:8, 764:10, 796:13, 804:5

^{túg}**uš-bar**-g̃e$_6$ sumun, "old black uš-bar textile," 678:2

4 ^{túg}**uš-bar** siki-[bi] 5 ma-na-[ta? ki]-lá-bi 17(sic!) m[a-na], "4 uš-bar textiles, [their] wool is 5 minas [each?]; their weight is 17(sic!) minas," 747:11–12

^{túg}**uš-bar**-siki-g̃ír-gul, "uš-bar textile of g̃ír-gul wool," 588:4, 694:9, 708:7

^{túg}**uš-bar** sumun, "old uš-bar textile," 678:1

^{túg}**uš-bar**-tur, "small uš-bar textile," 636:7, 637:4, 639:4, 691:4, 694:6, 731:4, 732:4, 734:5, 748:12, 766:6, 795:4, 796:11, 799:4, 800:6, 818:5, 834:14, 835:'13

^{túg}**uš-bar**-tur siki-g̃ír-gul, "small uš-bar textile of g̃ír-gul wool," 674:9

^{túg}**uš-bar**-1(sic!?), "1? uš-bar textile," 835:'12

★★(. . .) siki bala-[dè i]n-na-⸢keše⸣ ^{túg}**uš-ba**[**r** sa-gi$_4$-àm], "{assorted textiles}, the wool was bound up to be baled, they are finished uš-bar textiles," 609:8 (tablet)

úš(TIL), *mâtu*, "to die" > *Verb Index*

^{dug}**útul**(KWU-452/489), *diqāru*, "tureen"[120]

1 ^{dug}**útul** n-sìla, "1 n-liter tureen," 1265:1, 1265:2, 1334:9, 1344:1, 1344:2

n ^{dug}**útul** n sìla-ta, "n tureen(s) of n-liter(s) each," 1376:79, 1376:80

1 ^{gi}gur-^{dug}**útul** ésir šub-ba, "1 container shaped like a tureen coated with bitumen," 1370:1

1. Assorted Commodities for the Tureen

1.1 Regular Offerings of *Šu-Kabta*

(. . .) ^{dug}**útul**-šè (. . .) sá-du$_{11}$-ki-a-nag-*šu-kab-tá*, "{grains, fish, salt, spices, aromatics and reed bundles} for the tureen (and) {other comestibles}, regular offerings of the funerary libation place of *Šu-Kabta*," 972:24, 107, 975:25, 108

0.0.1. [níg̃-àr-ra-sig$_5$] 0.0.1. [ar]-za-⸢na⸣ [0.0.1 g]ú-⸢gal⸣ al-à[r-r]a 0.0.1. gú-tur al-ú[s-s]a 5 sìla šim-sig$_5$ al-nag̃$_4$-g̃á 6 sìla še-lú {x-x-x erased} 5 sìla mun-sig$_5$ al-nag̃$_4$-g̃á 0.0.1. ⅓ sìla gazi al-nag̃$_4$-g̃á 30 sa ^{ú}sullim ^{dug}**útul**-šè (. . .) sá-du$_{11}$-ki-a-nag-*šu-kab-tá*, "10 (liters) [of fine groats], 10 liters of barley-grits, [10 liters] of milled beans, 10 liters of processed peas, 5 liters of crushed fine aromatic, 6 liters of coriander, 5 liters of crushed fine salt, 10⅓ liters of crushed gazi (and) 30 bundles of fenugreek for the tureen, (and) {other comestibles}, regular offerings of the funerary libation place of *Šu-Kabta*," 981:14–23, 33

120 Sallaberger 1996, 108; Brunke 2008, 165 (§3.3.2).

1.2 Requisitions of the Boat Towers

(. . .) ^{dug}**útul**-šè níĝ-dab$_5$ ĝuruš má gíd-e-ne u$_4$ al-tar-ra gub-ba šà gar-ša-an-na^{ki}, "{grains, dates, lard, salt and sheep carcasses} for the tureen, requisitions of the boat towers when they were employed for construction in Garšana," 442:18–19

1.3 The Tureen of the Lamentation Singers

0.0.1.2 sìla ninda 0.0.1. kaš-gen ½ sìla níĝ-àr-ra-sig$_5$ 1 ku$_6$ al-dar-ra ^{dug}**útul**-šè gala-e-ne *táq-ri-ib-tum* é-⸢lùmgi⸣ é-muḫaldim ù é-kíkken, "12 liters of bread, 10 liters of ordinary beer, ½ liter of fine groats (and) 1 split (dried) fish for the tureen of the lamentation singers (for their performance of) a *takribtum*; (delivery from) the brewery-kitchen-mill complex," 437:7–13

2. Flour for the Tureen

0.0.1.5 sìla zì-gu-sig$_5$ 0.0.4. zì-gu-ús 0.1.5.5 sìla dabin 0.0.2 zì-KAL 3 sìla níĝ-àr-ra-sig$_5$ 2 sìla ar-za-na 2½ sìla gú-tur al-al(sic!)-sa ^{dug}**útul**-šè u$_4$-2-kam, "15 liters of fine gu-flour, 40 liters 2nd-quality gu-flour, 115 liters of semolina, 20 liters of KAL-flour 3 liters of fine groats, 2 liters of barley-grits, (and) 2½ liters of processed peas for the tureen on the 2nd day," 1167:1–9

0.0.1.5 sìla zì-gu-sig$_5$ 0.0.4. sìla zì-g[u-ús] 0.1.5.5 sìla ZÌ.⸢ŠE⸣ 0.0.2?. zì-⸢KAL⸣ 5 sìla gú-gal al-à[r-ra] 2 sìla níĝ-àr-⸢ra⸣-sig$_5$ 2½ sìla ar-za-na ^{dug}**útul**-šè u$_4$-3-kam, "65 liters of fine gu-flour, 40 liters of 2nd-quality gu-flour, 115 liters of semolina, 20? liters of KAL-flour, 5 liters of milled beans, 2 liters of fine groats (and) 2½ liters of barley-grits for the tureen on the 3rd day," 1167:10–17

3. Groats for the Tureen

níĝ-àr-ra-sig$_5$ ^{dug}**útul**, "fine groats (for) the tureen," 383:7, 386:22, 387:13, 396:14, 397:14

še níĝ-àr-ra ^{dug}**útul**, "barley groats (for) the tureen," 386:23, 387:14

še níĝ-àr-ra-sig$_5$ ^{dug}**útul**, "fine barley groats (for) the tureen," 399:13

^{dug}**útul-gal**, "large tureen"[121]

1. For the Builders

0.1.1.6 sìla ninda-gal-gen 0.0.1. gú-gal al-àr-ra 4 sìla níĝ-àr-ra-sig$_5$ 3 sìla gú-tur al-ús-sa ^{dug}**útul-gal** 2-šè mu šidim-e-ne-šè, "76 liters of ordinary large bread, 10 liters of milled beans, 4 liters of fine groats (and) 3 liters of processed peas for 2 large tureens for the builders," 479:4–9

0.0.5. ninda zì-g[u-ús] 0.0.5. ninda-dabin 0.1.1.6 sìla ninda-gal-[gen] 0.0.1. gú-⸢gal⸣ al-àr-ra 4 sìla níĝ-àr-ra-⸢sig$_5$⸣ 3 sìla gú-tur ⸢al⸣-ús-sa ^{dug}**útul-gal** 2-šè mu šidim-e-ne-šè, "50 liters of [2nd-quality] gu-flour bread, 50 liters of semolina bread, 76 liters of [ordinary] large bread, 10 liters of milled beans, 3 liters of fine groats (and) 3 liters of processed peas for 2 large tureens for the builders," 483:1–8

---

[121] Brunke 2008, 165 (§3.3.2).

2. To Cook Soup

2.1 For the Banquet of Inana

0.2.1. níĝ-àr-ra-sig$_5$ 0.0.1.5 sìla ar-za-na 5 sìla ba-ba-še 5 sìla gú-gal al-àr-ra [5 sìla] gú-tur al-ús-sa [n] ádda-udu [n sìla mun-gen ^{dug}**útul-gal**]-šè [n sa gi]-izi [tu$_7$] ba-⸢ra⸣-šeĝ$_6$ 380 ^{dug}sìla-bur-⸢zi⸣ tu$_7$ ba-aka kaš-dé-a ^{d}inana-zabala$_4^{ki}$, "130 liters of fine groats, 15 liters of barley-grits, 5 liters of barley porridge, 5 liters of milled beans, [5 liters] of processed peas, [n] sheep carcass(es), [n liter(s) of ordinary salt] for [the large tureen] (and) [n bundle(s)] of fuel [reeds] with which [soup] was cooked; 380 1-liter offering bowls of soup were served at the banquet of Inana of Zabala," 1025:27–39

5 sìla níĝ-àr-ra-⸢sig$_5$⸣ 5 sìla ar-za-⸢na⸣ 5 sìla gú-gal al-àr-ra 5 sìla gú-tur al-⸢ús⸣-sa 2 ádda-[udu] 5 sìla mun-[gen] ^{dug}**útul-gal**-šè 20 sa gi-izi tu$_7$ ba-ra-šeĝ$_6$ 60 ^{dug}sìla-bur-zi tu$_7$ ba-aka kaš-dé-a ^{d}inana-iri^{ki}, "5 liters of fine groats, 5 liters of barley-grits, 5 liters of milled beans, 5 liters of processed peas, 2 [sheep] carcasses (and) 5 liters of [ordinary] salt for the large tureen (and) 20 bundles of fuel reeds with which soup was cooked; 60 1-liter offering bowls of soup were served at the banquet of Inana of the city," 1025:63–74

2.2 For the Banquet of Nin-Siana

[0.0.1. bappir?-sig$_5$ 0.n.n] kaš-⸢sig$_5$⸣ 0.0.3. kaš-gen 0.0.2. níĝ-àr-ra-⸢sig$_5$⸣ 0.0.2.5 sìla ar-za-na 5 sìla gú-gal al-àr-ra 5 sìla gú-tur al-ús-sa 3 udu ba-úš [n+]1 ádda-udu [0.n.]1. mun-gen ⸢^{dug}⸣**útul-gal**-šè 30 sa gi-izi [tu$_7$] ba-ra-šeĝ$_6$ [ka]š-dé-a ^{d}nin-^{d}si$_4$-an-na-a-ḫu-a, "[10 liters of fine beer bread?, n] liter(s) of fine beer, 30 liters of ordinary beer, 20 liters of fine groats, 25 liters of barley-grits, 4 liters of milled beans, 5 liters of processed peas, 3 slaughtered sheep, [n+]1 sheep carcasses (and) [n+]10 liters of ordinary salt for the large tureen (and) 30 bundles of fuel reeds with which [soup] was cooked (for) the banquet of Nin-Siana, (the personal deity of) *Aḫu'a*," 1025:1–14

2.3 For the Banquet of Nergal

5 sìla níĝ-àr-ra-sig$_5$ 5 sìla ar-za-na 5 sìla gú-gal al-àr-ra 2 sìla gú-tur al-ú[s-sa] 2 ádda-⸢udu⸣ ^{dug}**útul-gal**-[šè] 50 sa gi-izi tu$_7$ ba-ra-šeĝ$_6$ 120 ^{dug}sìla-bur-zi tu$_7$ ba-aka kaš-dé-a ^{d}nergal$_x^{eri11-[gal]}$ dumu é-é-⸢zi⸣, "5 liters of fine groats, 5 liters of barley-grits, 5 liters of milled beans, 2 liters of processed peas (and) 2 sheep carcasses [for] the large tureen (and) 50 bundles of fuel reeds with which soup was cooked; 120 1-liter offering bowls of soup were served at the banquet of Nergal, (the personal deity of) the son of E-ezi," 1025:81–91

uz-tur, "duckling," 470:1, 472:4, 511:85, 1104:1, 1127:2, 1172:1, 1176:1, 1176:3, 1176:5, 1176:7, 1254:'27, 1254:'28, 1394:7

uz-tur niga, "fattened duckling," 1053:1, 1112:1

uz-tur šu-ur$_4$-ra, "duckling wings(?)," 529:20

[VERBS] (see below s. v. COMPOUND VERBS, REDUPLICATED VERBS)

aka, "to do, to make"

àra, "to mill, grind"

ba, "to allot; to divide into shares; to give, present"

ba-al, "to dig, bail out (a cistern); to unload (a boat)"

babbar, "(to be) white" (adjective only)

bala, "to rotate, turn over, cross"
barag, "to press, to mix"
bíl, "to burn"
bir_7, "to shred" > **al-bi-ra**
bù(r), "to cut, trim; to pull out"
dab_5, "to take in charge"
dağ, "to wander, travel"
dağal, "(to be) wide" (adjective only)
dar, "to break up, crush, grind; to split" > **al-dar-ra**
dé, orthographic writing for de_6, "to bring" > **de_6**
dé, "to pour"
de_5(g), "to collect, gather up, glean"
de_6, "to bring, carry"
de_9, orthographic writing for de_6, "to bring" > **de_6**
dím, "to create, make, manufacture"
diri(g), "(to be) surplus, additional" (adjective only)
diri(g), "to float, glide (along/down)"
dú, "to be sick"
dù, "to construct"
du_8, "to bake (bread); to (mold bricks)"
du_{10}(g_3) "(to be) good; (to be) sweet" (adjective only)
du_{11}(g_4), "to speak"
dub, "to heap up, pile, pour"
dúb, "to extract" > **al-dúb-ba**
duḫ, "to loosen, release, free"
$duru_5$, "(to be) soft, wet, irrigated, fresh, damp" (adjective only)
e-pe-eš, "to do, make"
è, "to bring out; to enter"
ga_6(ğ), "to bring; to lift, carry, haul"
gal, "(to be) big, great, large" (adjective only)
gaz, "to kill, slaughter; beat; thresh (grain)"
gen_6, "to confirm, verify"
gi_4, "to send back, return"
gibil, "(to be) new" (adjective only)
gíd, "(to be) long; to tighten; to survey, measure out a field; to quarry (clay); to tow/pull a boat upstream"
gig, "to be sick"
gu_7, "to eat"
gub, "to stand; (to be) assigned (to a task), (to be) employed at"
gukkal, "(to be) fat-tailed" (adjective only)

gul, "to raze, demolish (a building); to cut"
gum, "to crush" > **ésir**
gùn, "(to be) speckled, multi-colored" (adjective only)
gur, "to reject (legal evidence), to turn away; to turn, return; to argue"
gur$_4$, "(to be) thick; (to be) big, feel big" (adjective only)
gur$_{10}$, "to reap, sickle"
guru$_5$, "to separate, divide; to cut, pull, trim (weeds)"
guz, "(to be) tufted" (adjective only)
g̃ál, "to be (there, at hand, available); to exist; to put, place, lay down; to have"
g̃ar, "to put, place, lay down; to deposit"
g̃e$_6$, "(to be) black" (adjective only)
g̃en, "to go, to come"
ḫa-la < ḫal, "to divide"
ḫád, "(to be) dried (out), dry; to dry" (adjective only)
ḫi, "to mix"
ḫug̃, "to hire, rent"
íl, "to raise, carry"
kala(g), "(to be) strong, powerful, mighty; to reinforce; repair"
kéše, "to bind"
kíg̃, "to work" > **aka**
kíg̃, "to look for, seek"
ku$_4$(r), "to enter"
ku$_5$(d^r), "to cut, break off, deduct"
lá, "to transport"
lá, "to weigh out, to pay"
laḫ$_4$/laḫ$_5$, plural stem of de$_6$ "to bring"
lu, "to disturb, stir up; to cover completely; to mix"
maḫ, "(to be) great" (adjctive only)
me, "to be"
nag, "to drink"
nag̃(a)$_4$, "to crush, grind (in a mortar with a pestle)"
niga, "(to be) fattened" (adjective only)
níg̃in, "to enclose, confine; to encircle"
pàd, "to find, discover; to name, nominate"
peš$_5$, "(to be) plucked" (adjective only)
ra, "to roll (seal)"
ri, "to go, walk along"
sá, "to equal; to reach, arrive"
sa$_{10}$, "to buy, purchase"
sal, "(to be) thin" (adjective only)

sar, "to write" > **bisag̃**
sè(g$_{10}$), "to apply, place, set"
si(g), "to fill, load up; to pile up (e.g., earth for a levee or temple foundation)"
si$_{12}$(SIG$_7$), "to cut, remove; to erase"
sig, "(to be) weak, low, trim, narrow" (adjective only)
sig$_5$, "(to be) fine, high quality" (adjective only)
sila$_{11}$(g̃), "to knead (dough/clay)"
sim, "to sieve, filter"
su(g$_6$), "to repay a loan; to replace"
sù, "to submerge, sink"
sù(b), "to rub, coat"
su$_4$, "(to be) red, brown" (adjective only)
sum, "to give"
sumun, "(to be) old" (adjective only)
sur, "to twist, twine (rope)"
sur, "to press, squeeze"
šeg̃$_6$, "to cook"
šeš$_4$, "to anoint (with oil)"
šid, "to count"
šub, "to pour (water, bitumen, etc.); to lay down (bricks)"
tab, "to twine (rope, thread), to line up (bricks in rows), to stack (sheaves of grain); to double; to repeat"
tà(g), "to bind, to touch up; to apply stucco"
tag, "to beat; to weave"
taḫ, "to add, increase"
te(g̃$_3$),"to be near, to approach"
til, "(to be) complete(d); (to be) old, long-lasting; to end"
tuku, "to acquire, get"
túm, tùm, sg. imperfect stem of de$_6$, "to bring"
tur, "(to be) little, small, young; to reduce"
ú, "(to be) range (fed)" (adjective only)
ù-ru (< ùr), "to level; to saturate/soak (with bitumen); to manufacture (bricks)"
ús, "(to be) second quality" (adjective only)
ús, "to process"
ús, "to drag; to stretch; to accompany, follow; flank, (long) side"
úš, "to die"
záḫ/zàḫ, "to disappear, (to be) lost"
zi(g), "to expend"
zi(l), "to strip"
zi(r), "to break, destroy; to erase/cancel (seal, tablet)"
zuḫ, "to steal"

[COMPOUND VERBS]

a . . . bal, "to pour water; to irrigate"
a . . . g̃ar, "to waterproof"
gaba . . . ri, "to confront, meet"
gaba . . . sàg, "to beat one's breasts (in mourning)"
g̃eš . . . ra(h_2), "to beat; to thresh (grain with a flail)"
igi . . . sag̃, "to sort"
káb . . . du_{11}(g_4), "to measure or count commodities for accounting or taxation"
sa . . . gi_4, "to prepare"
šu . . . bala, "to change"
šu . . . bar, "to release, set free"
šu . . . dím, "to build"
šu . . . sum, "to inventory"
šu . . . tag, "to touch, take hold of"
šu . . . ti, "to accept, take, receive"
šu tag . . . dug_4, "to decorate"
úgu . . . dé, "to disappear, to be lost"

[REDUPLICATED VERBS]

de_5(g)-de_5(g), "to glean" > **de_5(g)**
g̃eš . . . ra($ḫ_2$)-ra($ḫ_2$), "to beat; to thresh (grain with a flail)" > **g̃eš . . . ra($ḫ_2$)**
gi_4-gi_4, "to return" > **gi_4**
g̃á-g̃á, "to place, deposit" > **g̃ar**
kala-kala aka, "to reinforce" > **aka**
ne-ne (ni_{10}-ni_{10}), "to enclose, confine; to encircle" > **níg̃in**
su(g_6)-su(g_6), "to replace" > **su(g_6)**
sur-sur, "to press" > **sur**
tà(g)-tà(g), "to bind, to touch up; to apply stucco" > **tà(g)**
te($g̃_3$)-te($g̃_3$), "to accept, receive" > **te($g̃_3$)**

[VESSELS]

dugba, "a vessel (with a capacity of) 1 seah"
dugdal, "a vessel for oil, perfume or wine"
dug, "clay jug"
dug-a-kúm, "hot-water bottle"
dug $dida_x$, "jug of dida beer"
dug kaš, "a jug of beer"
dugdúr-bùr, "fermenting vat"
dugepig, "drinking vessel; sprinkling vessel, watering can for animals"

gal, "large cup"
^{dug}gur$_4$-gur$_4$-ĝeštin, "a vase for wine"
^{dug}ĝeš-ŠÀ/UD? "(a vessel)"
^{dug}*ku-kur-rú*, "(a vessel)"
^{dug}laḫtan, "a beer vat"
^{dug}ma-an-ḫara$_4$, "a large container (for beer)"
^{dug}níĝ n-sìla-ta, "a jug of n liter(s)"
sà-ḫum^{zabar}, "(bronze drinking or cooking vessel)"
^{dug}sìla-bàn-da, "(a vessel)"
^{dug}sìla-bur-zi, "1-liter (offering) bowl"
^{dug}sìla-gal, "large liter-jug"
^{urudu}šen, "(soup) cauldron"
šen-da-lá^{zabar}, "(bronze vessel)"
^{dug}ù-lu-lu, "pipe, conduit"
^{dug}úgur, "a kind of pot"
^{dug}útul, "tureen"
^{dug}útul-gal, "large tureen"

[WOOD PRODUCTS]

^{ĝeš}apin, "(seed) plow"
^{ĝeš}ba, "(a cutting tool)"
^{ĝeš}ba-an-la, "(a wooden object)"
^{ĝeš}banšur, "table"
^{ĝeš}bar, "(a type of plow)"
^{ĝeš}*be-rum*"(a wooden object)"
^{ĝeš}bisaĝ, "wooden basket or container"
^{ĝeš}dal, "cross-bar, beam"
^{ĝeš}dim, "post, pillar, pole"
^{ĝeš}dusu, "brick-carrying frame; earth basket"
^{ĝeš}é-da, "joist"
^{ĝeš}eme-sig, "plank"
^{ĝeš}éren, "yoke"
^{ĝeš}éš, "rope"
^{ĝeš}gag, "arrowhead; peg, nail"
^{ĝeš}galam, "ladder"
^{ĝeš}garig, "comb"
ĝeš-gan, "pestle (or door-bolt?)"
ĝeš-ĝar, "(a wooden object)"
ĝeš-íb-ra, "(type of plank)"
ĝeš-íl, "(a wooden object)"
ĝeš-ká, "gate timber"
ĝeš-níĝ, "(a wooden container)"
ĝeš-rín, "scales"
^{ĝeš}gú-ne-saĝ-ĝá, "cupboard"
^{ĝeš}ḫal, "(a basket)"
^{ĝeš}*hu-pu-um*, "wheel rim"
^{ĝeš}ig, "door"
^{ĝeš}ig mi-rí-za, "door plank"
^{ĝeš}kuĝ$_5$, "stair(case), ladder, threshold"
^{ĝeš}*la-ri-um*, "branch?"
^{ĝeš}mud, "bridle, strap"
^{ĝeš}nu-kúš, "door pivot"
^{ĝeš}saĝ-du, "a wooden beam (part of a loom)"
^{ĝeš}suḫuš-ig, "sole/foundation of a door"
^{ĝeš}šeg$_{12}$, "(a wooden object)"
^{ĝeš}šudul, "yoke"
^{ĝeš}túg-túg, "a designation of looms"
^{ĝeš}ú-bíl-lá, "charcoal"

^{ĝeš}ù, "planking"
^{ĝeš}ù-šar, "point/crescent (of a door)"
^{ĝeš}ù-šub, "brick mold"
^{ĝeš}*zi-ri-qum*, "shaduf"

[TYPES OF WOOD / TREES]

^{ĝeš}ásal, "poplar"
^{ĝeš}da, "(a tree)"
^{ĝeš}*dú-ul-bu-um*, "a plane tree"
^{ĝeš}EGER, "(a tree)"
^{ĝeš}ĝi$_6$-par$_4$, "(a fruit tree; fruit)"
^{ĝeš}ḫal-bi, "(a tree)"
^{ĝeš}ḫašhur, "apple, apricot (tree)"
^{ĝeš}ḪAŠḪUR.KUR, "quince, quince tree"
^{ĝeš}ildáĝ, "a type of poplar"
^{ĝeš}*kà-na-at-ḫu-um*, "(a tree or aromatic product from a tree)"
^{ĝeš}kab, "willow"
^{ĝeš}kíĝ, "(a tree)"
^{ĝeš}kíĝ-sig-ḫi-a, "(a tree)"
^{ĝeš}kišig, "shok"
^{ĝeš}lam, "sapling; a nut-bearing tree"
^{ĝeš}ma-nu, "(a tree, perhaps willow)"
^{ĝeš}maš, "(a tree)"
^{ĝeš}nimbar, "date palm"
^{ĝeš}nu-nir, "(a tree)"
^{ĝeš}nu-úr-ma, "pomegranate"
^{ĝeš}pa-kab, "(a tree)"
^{ĝeš}pèš, "fig, fig tree"
^{ĝeš}*sé-er-dum*, "olive tree"
šà-kal, "(a wood used for furniture)"
^{ĝeš}še-du$_{10}$, "(a tree)"
^{ĝeš}šennur, "plum"
^{ĝeš}šim, "(a resinous tree)"
^{ĝeš}šinig, "tamarisk"
^{ĝeš}taskarin, "boxwood"
^{ĝeš}tir, "forest, woods"
^{ĝeš}ù-suḫ$_5$, "pine tree"
^{ĝeš}ÚR×A.NA, "mulberry"
^{ĝeš}zúm, "(a tree)"

[WOOL] > **siki**

– Z –

za-ḫa-din, *nušû*; *šuḫatinnu*, "a plant, a leek?," 511:72, 972:26, 972:95, 975:28 975:96

za-rí-in, *zarinnu*, "coarsely cleaned material"

siki-**za-rí-in**, "coarsely cleaned wool material" > **siki**

zà-gú-lá, *sāgu*, "sanctuary, cella"

1. **Regular Offerings of the Sanctuary of Nin-Siana**

[2.2.0. sá-du$_{11}$-**zà-gu-lá** ^{d}nin-^{d}si$_4$-an-na], "[2 bushels (and) 120 liters, regular offerings of the sanctuary of Nin-Siana]," 1527:3

1.1 **Offerings Returned from the Shrine**

0.2.0. še-ninda 0.1.0. tuḫ-duru$_5$-gen sá-du$_{11}$-**zà-gú-lá**-^{d}nin-^{d}si$_4$-an-na (. . .) èš-ta-gur-ra, "120 liters of barley (for) bread (and) 60 liters of ordinary fresh bran, regular offerings of the sanctuary of Nin-Siana (and) {offerings of other deities}, offerings returned from the shrine," 997:5–7, 12, 1023:6–7, 15, 1024:5–6, 17

0.2.0. še [ninda . . .] sá-du$_{11}$-**z[à-g]ú-lá**-^{d}[nin-si$_4$]-an-na š[à é-a] (. . .) èš-ta-gur-ra, "120 liters of barley [(and) bread . . .], regular offerings of the sanctuary of Nin-Siana in [the house] (and) {offerings of other deities}, offerings returned from the shrine," 1022:6–7, 15

0.2.0. še-ninda sá-du$_{11}$-**zà-gú-lá**-^{d}nin-^{d}s[i$_4$-a]n-⌜na⌝ (. . .) èš-ta-gur-ra, "120 liters of barley (for) bread, regular offerings of the sanctuary of Nin-Siana (and) {offerings of other deities}, offerings returned from the shrine," 1026:4, 13

zà-ḫi-li, *saḫliu / saḫlû*, "edible seed used for flavoring," 511:73, 972:27, 972:96, 975:29, 975:97, 981:24, 1092:8, 1190:5

★★^{na4}kinkin-GI-bí **zà-ḫi-li**, "(a millstone)" > **^{na4}kinkin**

zà-mu, "the beginning of the year"

níĝ-dab$_5$ **zà-mu-bi** sum, "to give requisitions at the beginning of the year > **sum**

zabar, *siparru*, "bronze"

zabar ĝar-ra, "covered in bronze" > **ĝar**

[n] gú **UD.KA.B[AR** x?] urudu ĝar-⌜ra⌝, "[n] talent(s) of bronze [(and?) x] covered (with) copper," 1377:1

1 apin!(GÍN) **UD.K[A.B]AR** ki-lá-bi 1 ma-[na] 3 gín, "1 bronze plow(?), its weight is 1 mina (and) 3 shekels," 1310:1–2

★★2 ^{ĝeš}maš DI-[. . .] ka-ba **UD.K[A.BAR. . .]**, 1342:4–5

1. **Bronze Objects**

bisaĝ$^{\textbf{zabar}}$, "container of bronze"

gal-**zabar**, "large bronze cup"

gír-siki-gul-la$^{\textbf{zabar}}$, "bronze, wool sheering knife"

$^{\textbf{zabar}}$saĝ-kul, "bolt"

sà-ḫum$^{\textbf{zabar}}$, "(bronze drinking or cooking vessel)"

šen-da-lá$^{\textbf{zabar}}$, "(bronze vessel)"

zabar-dab$_5$, *zabardabbû*, "an official"

[n] máš-gal **[UD.K]A.BAR-dab$_5$**, "[n] billy-goat(s) (for) the zabar-dab$_5$ official," 469:1–2

záḫ/zàḫ, *ḫalāqu*, "to disappear, (to be) lost" > *Verb Index*

zàḫ, *nābutu*, "runaway"

1. **Runaway Builders**

1 ĝuruš šidim **zàḫ** lú-*dì-ma-at-kál-bu-um*^{ki}, "1 runaway builder from *Dimat-kalbum*," 13:3

2 ĝuruš šidim **zàḫ** lú-*i-zi-in-èr-ra*^{ki}-me-éš, "2 runaway builders from *Izin-Erra*," 13:4

2 ĝuruš šidim **zàḫ** lú-*tu-lí-um*^{ki}-me-éš, "2 runaway builders from *Tulium*," 13:1–2

2. Runaway Builders and Workmen

5 g̃uruš šidim **zàḫ** 1 g̃uruš **zàḫ**, "5 runaway builders and 1 runaway workman," 13:'22

3. Runaway Individuals > *Personal Name Index*

a-bu-DU_{10}	*ir-du-du*	*šu-*^{d}*i-šum*
a-da-làl	*ki-du-du-ú*	*šu-qá-qá*
a-ḫu-wa-qar	*ku-ru-ub-*^{d}*Adad*	*u-bar-um*
AN.ŠUM.TAG.KAL	lugal-ḫa-ma-ti	zàḫ [PN], "the runaway [PN]," 52:63
i-la-ak-nu-id	*puzur*$_{4}$*-šu-ba*	
ilam-šu-mur		

4. Runaway Workmen

1 g̃uruš **zàḫ**, "1 runaway workman," 10:23, 114:49

3 g̃uruš {erasure} **zàḫ**, "3 runaway workmen," 14:34

n g̃uruš **zàḫ** ugula PN, "n runaway workmen, supervised by PN" > *Personal Name Index*

i-ri-ib *ilum-dan*

5. Sick and Runaway Workmen

5.1 From Specific Work Gangs

n g̃uruš dú-ra n g̃uruš **zàḫ** ugula *ilum-dan*, "n sick workmen (and) n runaway workmen, supervised by *Ilum-dan*" > *Personal Name Index*

n g̃uruš šidim dú-ra n g̃uruš **zàḫ** ugula *i-ri-ib*, "n sick builder(s) (and) n runaway workmen, supervised by *Irib*" > *Personal Name Index*

zal, *qatû*, "to come to an end" > *Verb Index*

^{gi}**zar-zar(-zar)**, "(a basket)"

^{gi}**zar-zar(-zar)** ésir šub-ba, "a zar-zar-basket coated with bitumen," 1280:1, 1299:9

zàr, *zarru*, "sheaf (of barley); stack of sheaves"

zàr tab, "to stack sheaves (of grain for drying)" > **tab**

$^{g̃eš}$**zé-na**, *zinû*, "date palm frond midrib," 1037:5, 1092:2, 1190:6, 1215:3, 1237:3, 1265:3, 1350:2, 1376:51

120 $^{g̃eš}$**zé-na** (. . .) mu dal é-túg-ga-šè, "120 date palm frond midribs (and) {other materials} for the shelves(?) of a textile container," 779:1, 5

zi-ba-tum, "rear part (of certain implements)"

20 ma-na gu-$^{g̃eš}$ba ***zi-ba-tum*** mu sa-par$_{4}$-šè, "20 minas of (?)-cord for a net," 1162:'55-'56

zi(g), *nasāḫu*, "to expend" > *Verb Index*

zi(l), "to strip" > *Verb Index*

zi(r), *pasāsu*, "to break, destroy; to erase, cancel (seal, tablet)" > *Verb Index*

zi-in, "(a specification of textiles)"

★★1 túg-^{d}*al-la-tum*-gùn-a ù **zi-in**-bi ki-lá-bi 9 ma-[na] 12 gín *a-ku$_8$-a-nu-ri*, "1 colored textile of *Allatum* and its zi-in weighing 9 minas (and) 12 shekels (for) *Akua-nuri*," 584:1–3

^{túg}**zi-lí-ḫi**, "(a textile)"

★★túg-*ḫu-la-um* ù **zi-lí-ḫi** 3-kam-ús ^{d}*kab-tá*, 738:6

★★túg-*ḫa-la-um* ⌜ù⌝? **zi-lí-ḫi** 3-kam-ús, 811:3

^{túg}**zi-li-ḫi** túg-^{d}*al-la*-tum, "zi-lí-ḫi textile of *Allatum*," 715:1

^{túg}**zi-lí-ḫi**-tur 3-kam-ús, "small 3rd-quality zi-lí-ḫi textile," 673:5

^{ĝeš}***zi-ri-qum***, "an irrigation device, shaduf," 1255:1, 1271:2

^{ĝeš}***zi-ri-qum***-ásal, "poplar shaduf," 1349:1

zì, "flour," 484:4, 1013:3, 1027:8, 1072:3, 1100:1, 1140:1, 1144:1, 1325:13

dirig še-ba-ne-ne mu **zì** nu-ĝál-la-šè ḫal, "to divide additional barley rations because there was no flour" > **ḫal**

zì àra, "to grind flour" > **àra**

zì dabin ḫi, "to mix flour and semolina" > **ḫi**

zì de$_6$, "to bring flour" > **de$_6$**

zì-dub-dub, "a small heap of flour" > **zì-dub-dub**

zì ĝar, "to place flour" > **ĝar**

zì tùm, "to bring flour" > **tùm**

1. Flour Rations

21.1.0. dabin gur **zì**-ba má gíd-e-ne, "21 bushels (and) 60 liters of semolina, flour rations for boat towers," 426:1–2

2 Types of Flour

2.1 zì-ba-ba, "a kind of porridge made of flour"[122] > **ba-ba**

2.2 zì-gu, "gu-flour,"[123] 1069:2

2.2.1 zì-gu-gen, "ordinary gu-flour," 1074:2, 1153:1, 1254:'18

2.2.2 zì-gu-sig$_5$, "fine gu-flour," 493:1, 493:11, 494:1, 494:9, 511:45, 523:2, 526:5, 972:1, 972:68, 975:1, 975:69, 1033:3, 1069:1, 1074:1, 1075:1, 1134:1, 1167:1, 1167:10, 1394:10

0.3.0. **zì-gu-sig$_5$** 0.4.2 dabin 0.0.5.4 sìla zì-KAL 0.1.0. zì-kum ninda-šè, "180 liters of fine gu-flour, 260 liters of semolina, 54 liters of KAL-flour (and) 60 liters of kum-flour for bread," 981:5–9

---

122 Brunke 2008, 157–158 (§3.2.2).

123 Brunke 2008, 115–117 (§3.1.3.2.2.2), 148–150 (§§3.14.59–3.1.4.63).

^{giš}ma-an-sim **zì-gu-sig$_5$**, "fine gu-flour sieve" > **^{giš}ma-an-sim**

2.2.3 zì-gu-ús, "2nd-quality gu-flour," 479:1, 483:16, 493:2, 493:12, 494 :2, 494:10, 511:27, 511:46, 523:3, 816:1, 972:2, 972:69, 975:2, 975:70, 1017:2, 1033:4, 1072:1, 1086:1, 1128:4, 1167:2, 1167:11, 1184:3

ninda **zì-gu-ús**, "2nd-quality gu-flour bread," 483:1

0.0.2. zì-KAL 0.0.1. **zì-gu-ús** ninda-gur$_4$-ra-šè, "20 liters of KAL-flour (and) 10 liters of 2nd-quality gu-flour for thick bread," 1015:1–3, 1018:1–3

0.2.0. zì-KAL 0.2.3. **zì-gu-ús** ninda-šè, "120 liters of KAL-flour (and) 150 liters 2nd-quality gu-flour for bread," 1036:'5-'7

2.2.4 0.1.0. **zì-gu-[x?]**, "60 liters of [x?] gu-flour," 1221:1

2.3 zì-gú-nida, "hulled grain," 511:50, 523:6, 972:7, 972:73, 975:8, 975:74, 1033:10, 1134:6

6 sìla **zì-gú-nida** 1 sìla ì-g̃eš barag aka 2 sìla zú-lum níg̃-ì-dé-a-šè, "6 liters of hulled grain, 1 liter of pressed sesame oil (and) 2 liters of dates; (ingredients for) a dessert," 981:10–13

2.4 zì-KAL,[124] *ḫišlētu*, "KAL-flour (cracked barley mixed with wheat flour(?))," 493:4, 493:14, 494:12, 506:5, 511:48, 523:5, 970:2, 972:4, 972:39, 972:53, 972:71, 975:4, 975:41, 975:56, 975:72, 999:3, 1001:3, 1017:1, 1016:9, 1027:3, 1030:2, 1033:6, 1128:2, 1134:3, 1167:4, 1167:13, 1182:3, 1203:2, 1209:1, 1226:2, 1254:'17, 1395:1

0.0.1 zíz gur ba-na **zì-KAL**-ta, "10 liters of emmer wheat in each ban (=10 liters) (there is) KAL-flour," 467:2

ninda-gúg ù ninda-gur$_4$-ra **zì-KAL**, "cake and thick bread of KAL-flour," 548:7

0.3.0. zì-gu-sig$_5$ 0.4.2 dabin 0.0.5.4 sìla **zì-KAL** 0.1.0. zì-kum ninda-šè, "180 liters of fine gu-flour, 260 liters of semolina, 54 liters of KAL-flour (and) 60 liters of kum-flour for bread," 981:5–9

0.0.2. **zì-KAL** 0.0.1. zì-gu-ús ninda-gur$_4$-ra-šè, "20 liters of KAL-flour (and) 10 liters of 2nd-quality gu-flour for thick bread," 1015:1–3, 1018:1–3

0.0.1. **zì-KAL** ninda-gur$_4$-ra-šè, "10 liters of KAL-flour for thick bread," 1028:2, 1028:14, 1028:39

0.0.4. **zì-KAL** ninda-gur$_4$-ra-šè, "40 liters of KAL-flour for thick bread," 1028:14

0.0.3.5⅓ sìla ninda-gur$_4$-ra **zì-KAL**, "35⅓ liters of KAL-flour (for) thick bread," 1033:9

0.2.0. **zì-KAL** 0.2.3. zì-gu-ús ninda-šè, "120 liters of KAL-flour (and) 150 liters 2nd-quality gu-flour for bread," 1036:'5-'7

0.0.3. **zì-KAL** 5 sìla ì-g̃eš 5 sìla ga-ḫar [n.n.n.] zú-lum [níg̃-ì-d]é-a-šè, "30 liters of KAL-flour, 5 liters sesame oil, 5 liters of round cheese (and) [n] liter(s) of dates for pastry," 1036:'8-'12

n zíz gur ba-na **zì-KAL** n sìla-ta ì-g̃ál, "n bushel(s) of emmer wheat, in each ban (=10 liters) of it there are n liter(s) of KAL-flour" > **zíz**

---

[124] Brunke 2008, 115–117 (§3.1.3.2.2.2).

2.5 zì-kum, "kum-flour,"[125] 438:4, 1005:4, 1074:4, 1128:3, 1182:4

zì-kum-sig$_5$, "fine kum-flour," 511:51, 972:5, 972:54, 972:74, 975:5, 975:57, 975:75, 999:5, 1033:11, 1072:4, 1075:2, 1077:1, 1100:1, 1134:5, 1394:13

[0].4.2. ninda-šu-ra **zì-kum** [ù šà] ½ sìla du$_8$, "260 liters of half(-loaf) bread of kum [and šà]-flour baked (in) ½ liter (loaves)," 548:2

[0.n.n] ninda-gal **zì-kum** ù šà-[gen] 1 sìla d[u$_8$], "[n] liter(s) of large bread of kum and [ordinary] šà-flour baked (in) 1-liter (loaves)," 548:3

0.3.0. zì-gu-sig$_5$ 0.4.2 dabin 0.0.5.4 sìla zì-KAL 0.1.0. **zì-kum** ninda-šè, "180 liters of fine gu-flour, 260 liters of semolina, 54 liters of KAL-flour (and) 60 liters of kum-flour for bread," 981:5–9

5 sìla **zì-kum** *mu-du-lum*, "5 liters of salted kum-flour,"1090:1–2

★★[n+]240 gi-ĝír-ab-ba tab-ba gal **zikum**[126] šub, 1292:5

2.6 zì-milla, *kukkušu*, "milla-flour (a low-quality flour),"[127] 1079:4, 1179:8, 1179:17, 1182:7

[2] sìla **zì-milla** ù zì-šà-gen-ta, "[2] liter(s) of milla-flour and ordinary šà-flour each," 536:2

0.4.0. ninda-zì-šà-gen **zì-milla** íb-ta-ḫi ½ sìla du$_8$, "240 liters of bread baked (in) ½-liter (loaves) were mixed from ordinary šà-flour (and) milla-flour," 1079:2

n sìla ninda **zì-milla** ù zì-šà-gen-ta, "n liter(s) of bread of milla-flour and ordinary šà-flour each" > **ninda**

ninda **zì-milla** ù zì-šà-gen-bi n-sìla, "(In total:) their bread of milla-flour and ordinary šà-flour is n liter(s)" > **ninda**

2.7 zì-šà, "šà-flour"[128]

zì-šà-gen, "ordinary šà-flour," 383:6, 1079:3, 1182:6

n sìla ninda zì-milla ù **zì-šà**-gen-ta, "n liter(s) of bread of milla-flour and ordinary šà-flour each" > **ninda**

ninda zì-milla ù **zì-šà**-gen-bi n-sìla, "(In total:) their bread of milla-flour and ordinary šà-flour is n liter(s)" > **ninda**

n sìla **zì-šà**-gen dabin íb-ta-ḫi, "n liter(s) of ordinary šà-flour mixed with semolina" > **ḫi**

[0].4.2. ninda-šu-ra **zì**-kum [ù **šà**] ½ sìla du$_8$, "260 liters of half(-loaf) bread of kum [and šà]-flour baked (in) ½-liter (loaves)," 548:2

[0.n.n] ninda-gal **zì**-kum ù **šà**-[gen] 1 sìla d[u$_8$], "[n] liter(s) of large bread of kum and [ordinary] šà-flour baked (in) 1-liter (loaves)," 548:3

[0.3].3. ninda-šu-ra dabin ù **š[à**-g]en ½ sìla du$_8$, "210 liters of half(-loaf) bread of semolina and ordinary šà(-flour) baked (in) ½-liter (loaves)," 548:4

[2] sìla zì-milla ù **zì-šà**-gen-ta, "[2] liter(s) of milla-flour and ordinary šà-flour each," 536:2

---

[125] Brunke 2008, 114–115 (Bemerkung 3.11); 151–152 (§§3.1.4.66–3.1.4.68).

[126] zikum(LAGAB.ḪAL), *isqūqu*, "a flour"?

[127] Brunke 2008, 114–115 (Bemerkung 3.11), 152–153 (§§3.1.4.69–3.1.4.70).

[128] Brunke 2008, 141 (§3.1.4.43), 153 (§§3.1.4.71–3.1.4.73).

0.4.0. ninda **zì-šà**-gen zì-milla íb-ta-ḫi ½ sìla du$_8$, "240 liters of bread baked (in) ½-liter (loaves) were mixed from ordinary šà-flour (and) milla-flour," 1079:2

ninda-dabin ù **zì-šà**-gen, "bread of semolina and ordinary šà-flour" > **ninda**

ninda **zì-šà**-gen, "bread of ordinary šà-flour" > **ninda**

ninda-zì-kum ù **zì-šà**-gen, "bread of kum-flour and ordinary šà-flour" > **ninda**

2.8 zì-tuḫ, "bran flour," 1074:3

2.9 zì-ús, "2nd-quality flour," 494:4

2.10 Broken Context

zì-[x], 970:3, 1036:'27

zì-[x]-sig$_5$, 999:4

zì-[. . .], 1036:'30, 1036:'46, 1036:'58

[. . .] **zì**-[x], 1036:'64

3. Other

[. . .] [ki] *šu*-[dr]*adad*˺-˹ta˺ **zì** [lú]lùnga [x?] kurum$_7$ [aka], "inspection of [. . .], flour (for?) the brewer from *Šu-Adad*," 1145:1–5

20 [gi]gur sal-la **zì** eša ésir šub-ba, "20 thin baskets coated with bitumen (containing) flour (and) fine flour," 1299:10

zì-dub-dub, *zidubdubbû*, "a small heap of flour"

Commodities for the Small Flour Heap

dabin, "semolina"

dug dida$_x$-gen, "jug of ordinary dida beer"

eša, "fine flour"

zì-KAL, "KAL-flour"

zú-lum, "dates"

1. The Small Flour Heap, Location Unspecified

5 sìla dabin 3 sìla eša 1 sìla zú-lum **zì-dub-dub**-šè, "5 liters of semolina, 3 liters of fine flour (and) 1 liter of dates for the small flour heap," 437:1–3

0.0.2. zì-KAL 2 sìla eša 4 sìla dabin **zì-dub-dub**-šè, "20 liters of KAL-flour, 2 liters of fine flour (and) 4 liters of semolina for the small flour heap," 1027:3–6

[n] dug dida$_x$-gen [n] dabin [n] eša ˹**zì**˺**-dub-dub**-šè, "[n] jug(s) of ordinary dida beer, [n] unit(s) of dabin (and) [n] unit(s) of fine flour, for the small flour heap," 1379:'13-'16

1.1 Offerings of the Gods

[n.n.n. ZI.]ŠE [n.n.n.] eša 0.0.1. zú-lum eša ḫi-dè **zì-dub-dub**-šè (. . .) sá-du$_{11}$-diĝir-re-e-ne, "[n liter(s)] of semolina, [n liter(s)] of fine flour (and) 10 liters of dates to mix (with) fine flour for the small flour heap, (and) {other comestibles}, regular offerings of the gods," 1036:'13-'17, '78

0.1.0. zì-[. . .] 0.0.3. [. . .] 0.0.1. zú-lum **zì-dub-du**[**b**-šè] (. . .) sá-du$_{11}$-diĝir-re-e-ne, "60 liters [x]-flour, 30 liters [x] (and) 10 liters of dates [for] the small flour heap, (and) {other comestibles}, regular offerings of the gods," 1036:'30-'33, '78

[. . .] **zì-dub-du[b**-šè] (. . .) sá-du$_{11}$-diğir-re-e-ne, "[. . . for] the small flour heap, (and) {other comestibles}, regular offerings of the gods," 1036:'46-'50, '78, 1036:'57-'62, '78

1.2 Offerings of Lamentation Singers and Cultic Performers

0.0.1. dabin 5 sìla eša 1 sìla zú-lum eša ba-ḫi **⌜zì⌝-dub-dub**-šè 5 sìla kaš 5 sìla ninda gala-e-ne a-rá-5-kam ér iri ni$_{10}$-ni$_{10}$, "10 liters of semolina, 5 liters of fine flour (and) 1 liter of dates mixed (with) fine flour for the small flour heap (and) 5 liters of beer (and) 5 liters of bread (for) the lamentation singers and cultic performers for the 5th time, {and 4 other times}, (performance of) a *takribtum* (involving) circling around the city," 1030:16, 23, 29, 33–39

1.3 When the (Enclosure) Wall was Constructed

[1] sìla dabin ½ sìla eša **zì-dub-dub**-šè u$_4$ bàd é-a dù-dè, "[1] liter of semolina (and) ½ liter of fine flour for the small heap of flour, when the (enclosure) wall of the house was being constructed," 383:9–11

1.4 When Roof Beams were Bound

1 dug dida$_x$-gen 1 sìla dabin 0.0.1 eša **zì-dub-dub**-šè u$_4$ ĝeš ùr ba-kéše-rá é-lùnga é-muḫaldim ù é-kíkken, "1 jug of ordinary dida beer, 1 liter of semolina (and) 10 liters of fine flour for the small flour heap when the roof beams of the brewery-kitchen-mill complex were bound," 1251:9–14

1.5 The Small Flour Heap in Zabala

[n] sìla dabin 7 sìla eša [n] ⅓ sìla zú-lum eša ba-ḫi **zì-dub-dub**-šè (. . .) šà zabala$_4^{ki}$ u$_4$-2-kam, "[. . .], [n] liter(s) of semolina, 7 liters of fine flour (and) [n+]⅓ liters of dates were mixed (with) fine flour for the small flour heap (and) {other offerings} in Zabala on the 2nd day," 1028:28–30, 45

2. The Small Flour Heap of Various Installations

zì-dub-dub-šè é-lùnga é-muḫaldim ù é-kíkken, "for the small flour heap of brewery-kitchen-mill complex" > *Household Index*

3. zì-dub-dub-didli, "various small flour heaps"

[. . . n.n.n. A.TI]R zú-lu[m ba-ḫi **zì-dub]-dub-didli**-[šè], "[... n liter(s)] fine flour [mixed (with)] dates [for] various small [flour] heaps," 484:1–3

3.1 (Ceremonial) Offerings of the Sea(-going) Boat

[n] sìla ⌜eša⌝ a-rá-1-[kam] 1 dug dida$_x$-⌜gen⌝ 2 sìla dabin 1 sìla eša ½ sìla zú-lum a-rá-2-kam 3 sìla dabin 2 sìla eša 1 sìla zú-lum **zì-dub-dub-didli**-šè sízkur má a-a-ba, "[n] liter(s) of fine flour for the 1st time, 1 pot of ordinary dida beer, 2 liters of semolina, 1 liter of fine flour (and) ½ liter of dates for the 2nd time (and) 3 liters of semolina, 2 liters of fine flour (and) 1 liter of dates for various small flour heaps, (ceremonial) offerings of the sea(-going) boat," 1034:'1-'12

3.2 When *Šu-Kabta* Travelled

0.0.4.4 sìla dabin 0.0.2.8 sìla eša 0.0.1. zú-lum eša {erasure} ba-ḫi **zì-dub-dub**-didli-šè u$_4$ *šu-kab-ta* ĜEŠ.KÚŠU^{ki}-šè du-ni {erasure} u$_4$ *šu-kab-ta* ĜEŠ.KÚŠU^{ki}-ta du-ni, "44 liters of semolina, 28 liters of fine flour and 10 liters of dates were mixed (with) fine flour for various small flour heaps when *Šu-Kabta* went to ĜEŠ.KÚŠU (and) when *Šu-Kabta* came from ĜEŠ.KÚŠU," 488:8–23

ZI/ZI(KWU-127) and variants **A.ZI/ZI(.ÉŠ)**, "a kind of grass or rush (used for making ropes)" > **A.ZI/ZI(.ÉŠ)**

zíz, *kiššātu*; *kunšu*, "emmer wheat," 412:1, 433:2, 509:4, 532:2, 532:4, 1039:4, 1065:2, 1197:1, 1224:2, 1228:2, 1232:1, 1232:4, 1232:8, 1233:7, 1233:10, 1233:15, 1233:21, 1234:1, 1235:1

zíz gibil, "new emmer wheat,"[129] 461:1

zíz sumun, "old emmer wheat," 461:3

10.0.0. **zíz** gur ì-dub 5-[kam], "10 bushels of emmer wheat of the granary for the 5th time," 1233:5

še-**zíz** ḫi-a lá, "to transport various barley (and) emmer wheat" > **lá**

zíz ús, "to process emmer wheat" > **ús**

zíz ús-sa nağ(a_4), "to grind processed emmer wheat" > **nağ(a)**$_4$

n **zíz** gur ba-na zì-KAL n sìla-ta ì-ğál, "n bushel(s) of emmer wheat, in each ban (=10 liters) of it there are n liter(s) of KAL-flour" > **ğál**

n **zíz** gur ba-na imğağa$_3$ n sìla-ta ì-ğál, "n bushel(s) of emmer wheat, in each ban (=10 liters) of it there are n liter(s) of emmer" > **ğál**

0.0.1 **zíz** gur ba-na zì-KAL-ta, "10 liters of emmer wheat in each ban (=10 liters) (there is) KAL-flour," 467:2

9.4.0. **zíz** gur [**zíz** b]a-[na] zì-KAL 5 [sìla-t]a, "9 bushels (and) 240 liters of emmer wheat, in each ban (=10 liters) [of emmer wheat] (there are) 5 [liters] of KAL-flour," 532:4–5

13.2.5. [**zíz** gur] **zíz** ba-na 5-sìla-[ta ì-ğál], "13 bushels (and) 170 liters of [emmer wheat], in [each] ban (=10 liters) [there are] 5 liters," 1110:1–2

zíz [. . .], 1147:1

^{na_4}**zú**, "flint"

0.1.3. ^{na_4}**zú**, "90 (units) of flint," 1372:26, 1372:83

zú-lum, *suluppû*, "date," 402:1, 402:4, 402:7, 402:12, 424:1, 429:1, 437:3, 438:5, 438:7, 442:11, 471:3, 511:41, 511:78, 515:1, 528:9, 972:9, 972:62, 972:102, 975:10, 975:63, 975:102, 1005:5, 1016:20, 1017:5, 1030:4, 1030:8, 1030:15, 1030:22, 1030:28, 1030:34, 1034:'6, 1034:'10, 1036:'11, 1036:'15, 1036:'32, 1036:'74, 1066:1, 1071:1, 1102:1, 1190:1, 1205:1, 1215:1, 1237:1, 1240:1

zú-lum-bi n (sìla), "its dates are n (liters)," 402:16, 536:21

zú-lum eša ḫi, "to mix dates (and) fine flour" > **ḫi**

(. . .) n sìla **zú-lum** níğ-ì-dé-a-šè, "{other ingredients} (and) n liter(s) dates for pastry" > **níğ-ì-dé-a**

n (sìla) **zú-lum**-ta, "n (liters) of dates each," 402:2, 402:5, 402:9, 402:11, 402:13, 442:5, 536:5, 536:10, 536:17

0.0.1. **zú-lum** eša ba-ḫi ⸢sízkur⸣-didli-šè, "10 liters of dates were mixed (with) fine flour for various (ceremonial) offerings," 1013:9–10, 1014:'2-'3

[0.n.n.] **zú-lum** ^{gi}gur-ra, "[n] liter(s) of dates in a basket," 1231:1

---

[129] Brunke 2008, 25, n. 35.

zú-si, "plucking, plucking time"

30 ^{gi}gúrdub siki ka-tab sè-ga **zú-si** g̃ír-su^{ki}-šè, "30 baskets fitted with a cover (were sent) to G̃irsu (to pack) plucked (wool)," 502:1–2

zuḫ, *šarāqu*, "to steal" > *Verb Index*

$^{g̃eš}$**zúm**, "(a tree)"

★★½ $^{g̃eš}$**zúm** nu-úr-ma é-ba-an, 593:3

— Uncertain Readings —

1. AS.AS

★★**AS.AS** NE-ku-nu šu aka, 1371:4

2. **BÚR**[130]

34⅔ ma-na **BÚR**, 1343:4

3. ^{na4}**EDEN**, "a stone"

0.0.1.2½ sìla ^{na4}**EDEN**, 1372:55

4. **e-na-am-DU**

★★še-gán-bi 36.1.0. še gur 11.1.0. zíz gur lá-ìa su-ga še gu_4 **e-na-am-DU** ur-^{d}dumu-zi ù *i-din-èr-ra*, "their barley of the field: 36 bushels (and) 60 liters of barley (and) 11 bushels (and) 60 liters of emmer wheat; the remainder was replaced. Ur-Dumuzi and *Iddin-Erra* (?) barley and oxen," 1233:8–11

5. **É**

[n] géme [$šeg_{12}$ d]a-bàd g̃á-g̃á [n] g̃uruš [. . .] é-kíkken ù é-lùnga [. . .] **É**, "[n] workwomen having placed [bricks] at the side of the (enclosure) wall (and) [n] workmen [. . .] the mill and brewery [. . .],98:'12-'15

6. $^{g̃eš}$**EGER**, "(a tree)," 35:36

7. **G̃AR**

★★5½ **G̃AR** kuš-pa_5 udu-niga-ú-ḫáb, 968:8

★★g̃eš-nu-nir 1 **G̃AR**, 1290:3

8. $^{g̃eš}$**G̃EŠ/G̃EŠ**

★★1 $^{g̃eš}$**G̃EŠ/G̃EŠ** 1 gú ésir-⌜ásal⌝, 1372:29, 1372:86

★★1 $^{g̃eš}$**G̃EŠ/G̃EŠ** 1 gú-na ú-$suḫ_5$, 1372:27, 1372:84

★★1 $^{g̃eš}$**G̃EŠ/G̃EŠ** 30 ma-na šinig, 1372:28, 1372:85

9. $^{g̃eš}$**ḪAŠḪUR.KUR**, "quince, quince tree"

[n ḫar] $^{g̃eš}$**ḪAŠḪUR.KUR**, "[n] quince tree [seedling(s)], 1362:16

---

130 A variant for barag, "sack, container" (*PSD* B 191)?

10. ÌR, "servant?"

^{kuš}e-sír-**ÌR**, "servant? sandals" > ^{kuš}**e-sír**

^{kuš}súḫub-**ÌR**, "servant? shoes" > ^{kuš}**súḫub**

11. KA

★★ 2 uz-tur-niga 1 kur-gi^{mušen}-niga 6 ir$_{7}^{\text{mušen}}$-niga 10 tu-gur$_{4}^{\text{mušen}}$-niga 5 péš-g̃eš-gi-niga 30-lá-1 péš-igi-gùn-niga *da-da-a* sipa-mušen-na in-**KA**-[x] ù ba-an-d[u$_{11}$-ga] ka-ga-[na ba-gen], "*Dada*, the bird warden, confirmed that he [. . .] and [. . .] 2 fattened ducklings, 1 fattened goose, 6 fattened pigeons, 10 fattened doves, 5 fattened mice (and) 29 fattened, striped-eyed mice," 1053:1–9

12. KA×Ú

★★[. . .] x [. . .] dirig? 6 [. . .] 60 udu lá-ìa 10 dirig lá-ìa dirig **KA×Ú**-a, 984:'68-'73

13. KU

[3 g̃uruš] má-laḫ$_{5}$ 1 g̃uruš 3 géme *ra-ṭum-a* **KU**-[x] g[ub-ba], "[3] sailors, 1 workman (and) 3 workwomen employed to (?) a drain(-pipe)," 59:46–49

14. ^{túg}**KU.KA.GA?**, "(a textile)"

^{túg}**KU.KA.GA**? PI-gùn-a 4-kam-ús, "4th-quality multicolored **KU.KA.GA**? PI textile," 563:1

15. NE-KU

★★[. . .]x-*še-en* [x] dú-ra-a [. . .] 6 sìla gíd-[. . .] 0.0.2. á-bi ḫ[ug̃-g̃]á lú-ašlág̃-me-éš ⸢mu-DU⸣ **NE-KU**, 477:1–7

★★AS.AS **NE-KU**-nu šu aka, 1371:4

16. $^{\text{g̃eš}}$**NÍGIN-garig**, "(a type of comb?)"

★★1 túg-du$_{8}$-a ⸢siki⸣ $^{\text{g̃eš}}$**NÍGIN-garig** aka 4-kam-ús ki-lá-bi ½ ma-na, "1 meshwork of 4th-quality (?) combed wool, its weight is ½ mina," 767:3–4

17. $^{\text{na}_4}$**ŠEM**, "(a stone)"

0.0.1.2½ sìla $^{\text{na}_4}$**ŠEM**(?) [or BI-X], 1372:50

18. Ú.KUR, 1092:5, 1117:4, 1162:'37, 1162:'44

Ú.KUR mu ku$_{6}$ al-ús-sa-šè, "Ú.KUR for fish-sauce" > **ku$_{6}$**

19. *ZA-ḫa-LUM*

★★60 $^{\text{g̃eš}}$ù-bil-lá ***ZA-ḫa-LUM***-šè, "60 (units) of charcoal for *ZA-ḫa-LUM*," 1297:6–7

20. [x].GA.URU

[PN] ^{lú}kíg̃-gi$_{4}$-a-lugal **[x].GA.URU** ⸢níg̃⸣-šu-taka$_{4}$-lugal [mu]-un-de$_{9}$-a, "[PN], the royal messenger, brought (?), the royal consignment," 484:11–13

Analytical Index of Verbs

a . . . bal, *dalû*, "to pour water; to irrigate"
a . . . g̃ar, "to waterproof"
ak(a), *epēšu*, "to do, to make"
àra, *samādu*, "to mill, grind"
ba, *qiāšu, zâzu*, "to allot; to divide into shares; to give, present"
ba-al, *ḫerû*, "to dig, bail out (a cistern); to unload (a boat)"
babbar, *peṣû*, "(to be) white" > *Glossary* (adjective only)
bala, "to rotate, turn over, cross"
barag, "to press, to mix"
bíl, *qalû*, "to burn"
bir$_7$, *šarāṭu*, "to shred" > **al-bi-ra**
bù(r), *nasāḫu*, "to cut, trim; to pull out"
dab$_5$, *ṣabātu*, "to take in charge"
dag̃, *nagāšu*, "to wander, travel"
dag̃al, *rapašu*, "(to be) wide; width, breadth" > *Glossary* (adjective only)
dar, *pênu, pêṣu, salātu, šatāqu*, "to break up, crush, grind: to split" > **al-dar-ra**
dé, orthographic writing for de$_6$, "to bring" > **de$_6$**
dé, *šapāku*; *šaqû*, "to pour"
de$_5$(g), *laqātu*, "to collect, gather up, glean"
de$_6$, *babālu* "to bring, carry"
de$_9$, orthographic writing for de$_6$, "to bring" > **de$_6$**
dím, *banû*, "to create, make, manufacture" > **šu dím**
diri(g), *atru*, "(to be) surplus, additional" > *Glossary* (adjective only)
diri(g), *neqelpû*, "to float, glide (along/down)"
dú, *marāṣu*, "to be sick"
dù, *banû, epēšu*, "to construct"
du$_8$, *epû*, "to bake (bread); to mold (bricks)"
du$_{10}$(g$_3$), *ṭābu*, "(to be) good; (to be) sweet; goodness, good (thing)" > *Glossary* (adjective only)
du$_{11}$(g$_4$), *qabû*, "to speak"
dub, *šapāku*, "to heap up, pile, pour"
dúb, *napāṣu*, "to extract" > **al-dúb-ba**
duḫ, *paṭāru*, "to loosen, release, free"

duru$_5$, *labāku, raṭbu*, "(to be) soft, wet, irrigated, fresh, damp" > *Glossary* (adjective only)
e-pe-eš, *epēšu*, "to do, make"
è, *waṣû, erēbu*, "to bring out; to enter"
ga$_6$**(g̃)**, *babālum; nasû*, "to bring; to lift, carry, haul"
gaba . . . ri, "to confront, meet"
gaba . . . sàg, "to beat one's breasts (in mourning)"
gal, *rabû*, "(to be) big, great; large" > *Glossary* (adjective only)
gaz, *dâku, šagāšu*, ”to kill, slaughter; beat; thresh (grain)"
gen, "(to be) medium, ordinary quality" > *Glossary* (adjective only)
gen$_6$, *kânu*, "to confirm, verify"
gi$_4$, *apālu*, "to send back, return"
gibil, *edēšu*, "(to be) new" > *Glossary* (adjective only)
gíd, *arāku*, "(to be) long; to tighten; to survey, measure out a field; to quarry (clay); to tow/pull a boat upstream"
gig, *marāṣu*, "to be sick"
gu$_7$, *akālu*, "to eat"
gub, *izuzzu*, "to stand; (to be) assigned (to a task), (to be) employed at"
gukkal, "(to be) fat-tailed" > *Glossary* (adjective only)
gul, *abātu*, "to raze, demolish (a building); to cut"
gum, "to crush" > **ésir**
gùn, *barmu*, "(to be) speckled, multicolored" > *Glossary* (adjective only)
gur, *sahāru; târu*, "to reject (legal evidence), to turn away; to turn, return; to argue"
gur$_4$, *ebû; rabû; kabru*, "(to be) thick; (to be) big, to feel big" > *Glossary* (adjective only)
gur$_{10}$, *esēdu*, "to reap, sickle"
guru$_5$, "to separate, divide; to cut, pull, trim (weeds)"
guz, "(to be) tufted" > *Glossary* (adjective only)
g̃ál, *bašû; šakānu*, "to be (there, at hand, available); to exist; to put, place, lay down; to have"
g̃ar, *šakānu*, "to put, place, lay down; to deposit"
g̃e$_6$, *mūšu*, "(to be) black, dark" > *Glossary* (adjective only)
g̃en, *alāku*, "to go, to come"
g̃eš . . . ra(ḫ$_2$**)**, *rapāsu*, "to beat; to thresh (grain with a flail)"
ḫa-la < ḫal, *zâzu*, "to divide"
ḫád, *abālu; šābulu*, "(to be) dried (out), dry; to dry" > *Glossary* (adjective only)
hi, *balālu*, "to mix"
ḫug̃, *agāru*, "to hire, rent"
igi . . . sag̃, "to sort"
íl, *našû*, "to raise, carry"
káb . . . du$_{11}$**(g**$_4$**)**, "to check, to measure or count commodities for accounting or taxation"
kala(g), *dannu, kubbû*, "(to be) strong, powerful, mighty; to reinforce, repair" > **aka**
kéše, *rakāsu*, "to bind"
kíg̃, "to work" > **aka**
kíg̃, "to look for, seek"

ku$_4$(r), *erēbu*, "to enter"
ku$_5$(d^r), *parāsu*, "to cut, break off, deduct"
lá, "to transport"
lá, *šaqālu*, "to weigh out, to pay"
laḫ$_4$/laḫ$_5$, *babālu*, plural stem of de$_6$ "to bring"
lu, *balālu*; *dalāḫu*; *katāmu*, "to disturb, stir up; to cover completely; to mix"
luḫ, *mesû*, "to clean, to wash"
maḫ, *kabtu*, *mādu*, *rabû*, *ṣīru*, "(to be) great" > *Glossary* (adjective only)
me, "to be"
nağ, *šatû*, "to drink"
nağ(a)$_4$, "to crush, grind (in a mortar with a pestle)"
niga, "(to be) fattened" > *Glossary* (adjective only)
níğin, *esēru*, *lawû*, "to enclose, confine; to encircle"
pàd, *atû*; *nabû*, "to find, discover; to name, nominate"
peš$_5$, *napāšu*, "to pluck" > *Glossary* (adjective only)
ra, "to roll (seal)"
ri, *alāku*, "to go, walk along"
sa . . . gi$_4$, *šutērušû*, "to prepare"
sá, *kašādu*, "to equal; to reach, arrive"
sa$_{10}$, *šâmu*, "to buy, purchase"
sal, *raqāqu*, "(to be) thin" > *Glossary* (adjective only)
sar, *šaṭāru*, "to write" > **bisağ**
sè(g$_{10}$), *šakānu*, "to apply, place, set"
si(g), "to fill, load up; to pile up (e.g., earth for a levee or temple foundation)"
si$_{12}$, *baqāmu*; *barāšu*, *naṭāpu*, *nasāḫu*, "to cut, remove; to erase"
sig, *enšu*, *qatnu*, "(to be) weak, low, thin, narrow" > *Glossary* (adjective only)
sig$_5$, "(to be) fine, high quality" > *Glossary* (adjective only)
sila$_{11}$(ğ), *lâšu*, "to knead (dough/clay)"
sim, *napû*, "to sieve, filter"
su(g$_6$), *apālu*; *riābu*, "to repay a loan; to replace"
sù, *ṭebû*, "to submerge, sink"
sù(b), "to rub, coat"
su$_4$, *pelû*; *sāmu*, "(to be) red, brown" > *Glossary* (adjective only)
sum, *nadānu*, "to give"
sumun, *labāru*, "(to be) old" > *Glossary* (adjective only)
sur, "to twist, twine (rope)"
sur, *ṣaḫātu*, "to press, squeeze"
šeğ$_6$, *bašālu*, "to cook"
šeš$_4$, *pašāšu*, "to anoint (with oil)"
šid, "to count"
šu . . . bala, *šupêlu*, "to change"
šu . . . bar, "to release, set free"

šu . . . dím, "to build"
šu . . . sum, "to inventory"
šu . . . tag, *lapātu*, "to touch, take hold of"
šu . . . ti, *leqû*, *maḫāru*, "to accept, take, receive"
šu tag . . . dug$_4$, *za'ānu*, "to decorate"
šub, *nadû*, "to pour (water, bitumen, etc.); to lay down (bricks)"
tà(g), *rakāsu*, *sêru*, "to bind, to touch up; to apply stucco"
tab, *eṣēpu*, "to twine (rope, thread), to line up (bricks in rows), to stack sheaves of grain; to double; to repeat"
tag, "to beat; to weave"
taḫ, *aṣābu*, "to add, increase"
te(g̃$_3$), *ṭeḫû*, "to be near, to approach"
til, *gamāru*; *labāru*; *qatû*, "(to be) complete(d); (to be) old, long-lasting; to end"
tuku, *rašû*, "to acquire, get"
túm, **tùm**, *babālu*, sg. imperfect stem of de$_6$, "to bring"
tur, *ṣeḫēru*, "(to be) small, young; to reduce"
tuš, *wašābu*, "to sit; to dwell; to be idle"
ú, "(to be) range fed" > *Glossary* (adjective only)
ù-ru (< ùr), *sapānu*, "to level; to saturate/soak (with bitumen); to manufacture (bricks)"
úgu . . . dé, *ḫalāqu*, "to disappear, to be lost"
ús, "(to be) second quality" > *Glossary* (adjective only)
ús, *redûm*, "to process"
ús, *diāšu*; *redû*; *šadādu*, "to drag; to stretch; to accompany, follow; flank, (long) side"
úš, *mâtu*, "to die"
záḫ/zàḫ, *ḫalāqu*, "to disappear, (to be) lost"
zi(g), *nasāḫu*, "to expend"
zi(l), "to strip"
zi(r), *pasāsu*, "to break, destroy; to erase/cancel (seal, tablet)"
zuḫ, *šarāqu*, "to steal"

– A –

a. . . **bal**, *dalû*, "to pour water, to irrigate"

1. Water-Pourers

2 ĝuruš **a bal-a-dè** gub-ba, "2 workmen employed to pour water," 39:38

2 géme **a bala-dè** gub-ba, "2 workwomen employed to pour water," 72:21

1.1 Construction

1.1.1 Of the Brick Stack

1.1.1.1 Drawing Water to Mix with Earth

[1 ĝ]uruš níĝ-GA **a bal-a** im lu-a SIG$_4$.ANŠE-šè gub<-ba>, "[1] employed níĝ-GA workman having poured water for mixing (with) earth for the brick stack," 21:'30

1.1.1.2 To Plaster the Brick Stack

[4] géme im [ga$_6$]-ĝá 1 ĝuruš im lu-a 1 ĝuruš **a bal-[a]** 1 ĝuruš in-u ga$_6$-[ĝá] im lu-a SIG$_4$.⸢ANŠE⸣ im sumur aka, "[4] workwomen having carried earth, 1 workman having mixed earth, 1 workman having poured water (and) 1 workman having carried straw (and) having mixed (it with) earth to plaster the brick stack," 209:27–32

1.1.2 Of the Foundation Terrace

10 ĝuruš im lu-a 2 ĝuruš 2 géme *a-za-bu-um* a im še-ĝá ba-al-dè 1 ĝuruš **a bal-a** ki-sá-a-šè, "10 workmen having mixed earth, 2 workmen (and) 2 workwomen to bail out rain-water from a cistern (and) 1 workman having poured water for the foundation terrace," 104:36–38, 105:34–36

1.1.3 Of the House of *Ili-bišu*

*See *Household Index* for the complete context of the following passages.

1 ĝuruš **a bal-a(-e-dè)** al-tar é-*ì-lí-bi-šu*, "1 workman having poured/to pour water (for) construction of the house of *Ili-bišu*," 202:28–29, 203:28–29

2 ĝuruš **a bal-a** (. . .) é-*ì-lí-bi-šu*, "2 workmen having poured water (. . .), (for) the house of *Ili-bišu*," 204:'7, '9

1.1.4 Of the Tower of the Zabala Garden

*See *Garden Index* for the complete context of the following passages.

[n] ĝuruš **a bal-a-e-dè** úgu iz-zi-da a ĝá-ĝá an-za-qar-^{ĝeš}kiri$_6$-zabala$_4$^{ki}, "[n] workmen to pour water having waterproofed the top of the iz-zi wall at the tower of the Zabala garden," 200:'7-'9

[n] ĝuruš **a bal-a-e-dè** (. . .) an-za-qar-^{ĝeš}kiri$_6$-zabala$_4$$^{⸢ki⸣}$ [gub-ba], "[n] workmen to pour water (. . .), (workers) [employed] at the tower of the Zabala garden," 201:'2, '6

3 ĝuruš **a bal-a(-e-dè)** im sumur aka an-za-qar-^{ĝeš}kiri$_6$-za[bala$_4$^{ki}], "3 workmen having poured/to pour water, (workers) having plastered the tower of the Zabala garden," 202:18, 20–21, 203:19–21

1.1.5 Construction Site Broken or Unspecified

2 ĝuruš **a bal-[a** . . .], "2 workmen having poured water [. . .]," 46:'29

5 ĝuruš *šu-kab-tá* 5 ĝuruš *a-a-ni* [n ĝuruš ugula] *ba-zi* [n ĝu]ruš ugula *simat-é-a* [**a**] **bal-a**, "5 workmen of *Šu-Kabta*, 5 workmen of *A'ani*, [n workmen supervised by] *Bazi* (and) [n] workmen supervised by *Simat-Ea* having poured [water]," 181:1–5

[. . .n ĝuruš] **a bal-[a-e-dè** gub-ba], "[. . . n workmen employed to] pour water," 198:'20

1.1.5.1 Pouring Water to Mix with Earth

2 ĝuruš im [a-ĝá]-ri-na lu-dè gub-ba [n ĝuruš **a ba**]**l-a** ⌜gub⌝-ba, "2 workmen employed to mix earth in the *agarinnum* (and) [n] employed [workmen] having poured [water]," 43:'33-'34

7 ĝuruš im lu-a 1 ĝuruš **a bal-a**, "7 workmen having mixed earth (and) 1 workman having poured water," 101:26–27

2 ĝuruš im lu-a [n] ĝuruš **a bal-a** im lu-a-šè, "2 workmen having mixed earth (and) [n] workmen having poured water for mixing (with) earth," 106:39–40

3 ĝuruš **a bal-[a]** im lu-[a-šè], "3 workmen having poured water [for] mixing (with) earth," 194:45

1.2 Garden Irrigation

1.2.1 The Ba'uda Garden

n ĝuruš **a bal-a** ^{geš}kiri$_6$ ^{d}ba-ú-da, "n workmen having irrigated the garden of Ba'uda," 14:32, 16:27, 17:27, 28:26, 29:30, 32:38, 33:42, 35:40, 36:40

1.2.2 The Garšana Garden

1⅔ guruš ašgab u$_4$-2-šè **a bal-e-dè** gub-ba ^{geš}kiri$_6$ šà gar-ša-an-na^{ki}, "1⅔ leather workers employed for 2 days to irrigate the garden in Garšana," 1523:1–4

1.2.3 The Garšana and Zabala Gardens

0.4.0. še á lú-ḫug-ĝá **a bal-e-dè** gub-ba ^{geš}kiri$_6$ šà ĝar-š[a-an-na]^{ki} ú ^{geš}kiri$_6$ šà zabala$_4$^{ki}, "240 liters of barley, wages of hired workers employed to irrigate the gardens in Garšana and Zabala," 390:1–3

1.2.4 The Zabala Garden

n ĝuruš **a bal-a** ^{geš}kiri$_6$ zabala$_4$^{ki}, "n workmen having irrigated the Zabala garden," 13:'20, 14:33, 16:28, 17:28

[n ĝuruš **a**] **bal-a** ^{geš}kiri$_6$ [zabala$_4$]^{ki}-šè, "[n workmen] having poured [water] for the [Zabala] garden," 31:39

2. Baskets for Pouring Water

^{gi}gur **a bal**, "reed basket for pouring water," 1255:3

^{gi}gur **a bal** ésir šub-ba, "reed basket coated with bitumen for pouring water," 1271:1, 1299:6, 1349:2

a . . . ĝar, "to waterproof"

úgu iz-zi-da a ĝar, "to waterproof the top of the iz-zi wall"

ùr a ĝar, "to waterproof the roof"

1. **úgu iz-zi-da a ĝar**, "to waterproof the top of the iz-zi wall"

   1 ĝuruš šidim ⸢um⸣-m[i-a] 1 ĝuruš šidim ⸢10⸣ ĝuruš im šu dím-ma sum-mu-dè 11 ĝuruš im ga$_6$-ĝá 3 ĝuruš im lu-a [n] ĝuruš a bal-a-e-dè **úgu iz-zi-da a ĝá-ĝá** an-za-qar-^{ĝeš}kiri$_6$-zabala$_4$^{ki}, "1 master builder, 1 builder, 10 workmen to hand earth for building, 11 workmen having carried earth, 3 workmen having mixed earth (and) [n] workmen to pour water, (workers) having waterproofed the top of the iz-zi wall at the tower of the Zabala garden," 200:'2-'9

2. **ùr a ĝar**, "to waterproof the roof"

2.1 The Roof of the Brewery-Kitchen-Mill Complex

*See *Household Index* for complete context of the following passages.

1 ĝuruš šidim um-mi-a 4 ĝuruš šidim 4 ĝuruš 60 géme **ùr a ĝá-ĝá** (. . .) é-lùnga é-muḫaldim ù é-kíkken, "1 master builder, 4 builders, 4 workmen (and) 60 workwomen having waterproofed the roof (. . .), (construction of) the brewery-kitchen-mill complex," 150:26–28, 36

[n] ĝuruš šidim 10 ⸢géme⸣ **ùr a ĝá-ĝá** (. . .) é-lùnga é-muḫaldim ù é-kíkken, "[n] builder(s) (and) 10 workwomen having waterproofed the roof (. . .), (construction of) the brewery-kitchen-mill complex," 151:30–31, 33

2 ĝuruš šidim 2 ĝuruš 50 géme **ùr a ĝá-ĝá** (. . .) é-lùnga é-muḫaldim ù [é-kíkken], "2 builders, 2 workmen (and) 50 workwomen having waterproofed the roof (. . .), (construction of) the brewery-kitchen-mill complex," 152:'7-'8, '19, 153:'20-'21, '32

2.2 The Roof of the Fish-sauce Roof House

1 ĝuruš šidim 1 ĝuruš šu dím 10-lá-1 géme im ga$_6$-ĝá gub-ba é-gibi[l **ù**]**r** ku$_6$ al-ús-sa **a [ĝá]-ĝá-dè** gub-ba, "1 builder, 1 workman having built (and) 9 employed workwomen having carried earth, (workers) employed to waterproof the new (roof) of the fish-sauce roof house," 49:39–42

2.3 The Roof of the Palace

2 ĝuruš šidim **ùr** é-gal **a ĝá-ĝá**, "2 builders having waterproofed the roof of the palace," 110:30, 111:29, 112:'10, 113:'7, 114:41–42, 117:23, 121:33

[n ĝu]ruš šidim 2 ĝuruš 10 géme **ùr** é-[gal **a**] **ĝ[á-ĝá]**, "[n] builder(s), 2 workmen (and) 10 workwomen [having waterproofed] the roof [of the palace]," 146:'41

2.4 The Roof of the New Palace

[. . . n ĝur]uš [. . . n+]4 ĝuruš šidim [n] ĝuruš im ì-li-de$_9$ gub-ba [n] ĝuruš 25 géme im ga$_6$ [**ùr** é-gal gib]il **a ĝá-ĝá**, "[. . . n] workmen [. . .], [n+]4 builders (and) [n] workmen employed to lift earth (and) [n] workmen (and) 25 workwomen having carried earth, (workers) having waterproofed [the roof of the] new [palace]," 74:'1-'6

[1 ĝuruš šidi]m um-[mi]-a [1 ĝuru]š šidim 1 ĝuruš šu d[ím gub-ba] 23 ĝuruš 20-lá-1 géme im sumur ga$_6$-ĝá-⸢dè⸣ [gub-ba] 7 ĝuruš im sumur lu-dè gub-ba **ùr** é-gal gibil **a ĝá-ĝ[á-d]è** gub-⸢ba⸣, "[1] master builder, [1] builder (and) 1 workman [employed] to build, 23 workmen (and) 19 workwomen [employed] to carry plaster (and) 7 workmen employed to mix plaster, (workers) employed to waterproof the roof of the new palace," 75:15–21

2.5 The Roof of the Storeroom

1 g̃uruš šidim 18 géme im ga_6-[g̃á] **ùr** é-kišib-ba **a g̃á-g̃á**, "1 builder (and) 18 workwomen having carried earth, (workers) having waterproofed the roof of the storeroom," 122:'26-'27

2.6 The Roof of the Textile Mill

1 g̃uruš šidim **ùr** é-uš-bar **a g̃á-g̃á**, "1 builder having waterproofed the roof of the textile mill," 109:24–25, 110:31

2.7 The Roof of the Textile Mill and Craftsmen's House

*See *Household Index* for the complete context of the following passage.

7 g̃uruš šidim im ì-li-de_9 gub-ba **ùr a g̃á-g̃á-[dè]** g[ub-ba] (. . .) é-uš-bar ù é-gašam-šè, "7 builders employed to lift earth, (workers) employed [to] waterproof the roof (. . .), (work) for the textile mill and craftmen's house," 59:36–38, 43

[. . . n g̃uruš i]m ì-li-de_9 [gub-ba n g̃uruš] im sumur tà-tà-dè gub-ba **[úr] a g̃á-g̃á-dè** [é-uš]-bar ù é-gašam-e-[ne], "[n workmen employed] to lift earth (and) [n workmen] employed to apply plaster, (workers) having waterproofed [the roof] of the textile mill (and) craftmen's house," 65:'15-'19

3. Other: the Barracks

[1] g̃uruš šidim 1 g̃uruš 4 [géme *ták-si-ru-um*] é-*gi-na-tum* $^{g̃eš}$kiri$_6$ [gar-š]a-an-na^{ki} **a g̃á-[g̃á]**, "[1] builder, 1 workman (and) 4 [workwomen (for) repair], (workers) having waterproofed the Garšana garden barracks," 65:'10-'11

ak(a) / ke_4, *epēšu*, "to do, make"

al aka, "to hoe"
bàd aka, "to make the (enclosure) wall"
barag aka, "to press"
***du-ú-um* aka**, "to make a *du-ú-um*"
ég-tab aka, "to make a double dike"
en-nu aka, "to perform guard duty, to guard"
gi-$guru_5$ aka, "to make a reedwork panel"
gi-ir aka, "(meaning uncertain)"
ḫar lam aka, "to make a seedling container(?)"
ḫu-ur-da aka, "to make a reed screen"
im sumur aka, "to plaster"
kala-kala aka, "to reinforce"
kíg̃ aka, "to do work"
$kurum_7$ aka, "to make an inspection"
níg̃ si-ga A.ZI/ZI.ÉŠ aka, "to make a panel of rushes"
ninda aka, "to make bread"
sa gi_4 aka, "to make preparations"
siki $^{g̃eš}$garig aka, "to comb wool"
šu aka, "to manufacture"
tu_7 aka, "to serve soup"

1\. **al aka**, "to hoe"

1.1 **Wages for Workers Assigned to Hoe**

4.4.0. še gur **al aka** ^{ĝeš}kiri$_6$, "4 bushels (and) 240 liters of barley (for workers) having hoed the garden," 500:1–2

5.4.0. še gur á **al aka** ù gu$_4$-ḫuĝ-ĝá, "5 bushels and 240 liters of barley, wages of hoers and rented oxen," 1051:1–2

2\. **bàd aka**, "to make the (enclosure) wall"

ù-ru-a **bàd aka**, "to make the urua wall"

uš **bàd aka**, "to make the foundation of the (enclosure) wall"

2.1. **ù-ru-a bàd aka**, "to make the urua wall"

2 ĝuruš [. . . n ĝuruš im ì-lí]-dè gub-ba 6 géme im ga$_6$-ĝá-dè gub-⌈ba⌉ **ù-[ru]-a bàd ke$_4$-dè**, "2 workmen [. . ., n workmen] employed to [lift earth] (and) 6 workwomen employed to carry earth, (workers) to make the urua wall," 39:31–34

2 ĝuruš [šidim] 6 ĝuruš šu [dím] gub-[ba] 5 géme im ga$_6$-[ĝá]-dè gub-[ba] **ú-ru-á**(!) **bàd** [**ke$_4$-dè**], "2 [builders] (and) 6 workmen employed to build (and) 5 workwomen employed to carry earth, (workers) [to make] the urua wall," 40:26–29

1 ĝuruš šidim 1 ĝuruš šu dím gub-ba 5 géme im ga$_6$-ĝá-dè gub-ba 2 ĝuruš im ì-li-de$_9$ gub-ba **ù-ru-a bàd ke$_4$-dè**, "1 builder (and) 1 workman employed to build, 5 workwomen employed to carry earth (and) 2 workmen employed to lift earth, (workers) to make the urua wall," 47:27–31

2.2 **uš bàd aka**, "to make the foundation of the (enclosure) wall"

1 ĝuruš šidim uš **bàd** [**ke$_4$**]**-dè** g[ub-ba], "1 builder employed to [make] the foundation of the (enclosure) wall," 93:'25

3\. **barag aka**, "to press"

ì-ĝeš **barag aka**, "pressed sesame oil" > **ì-ĝeš**

4\. ***du-ú-um* aka**, "to make a *du-ú-um*"

*See *Household Index* for the complete context of the following passages.

4.1 **Construction of the Brewery-Kitchen-Mill Complex**

n géme ***du-ú-um* aka** (. . .) al-tar ki-sá-a é-lùnga é-muḫaldim ù é-kíkken, "n workwomen having made a *du-ú-um* (. . .), (for) construction of the foundation terrace of the brewery-kitchen-mill complex," 125:23, 26, 126:23, 28

n géme ***du-ú-um* aka** (. . .) al-tar é-lùnga é-muḫaldim ù é-kíkken, "n workwomen having made a *du-ú-um* (. . .), (for) construction of the brewery-kitchen-mill complex," 128:21–23, 28, 129:24, 29, 131:'18, '23, 132:25, 30, 133:25, 29, 135:26, 30, 138:26, 31, 143:28, 34

1 géme ***du-ú-um* aka** (. . .) al-tar gub-ba (. . .) é-lùnga é-muḫaldim ù [é]-kíkken, "1 workwoman having made a *du-ú-um* (. . .), (workers) employed for construction (. . .), of the brewery-kitchen-mill complex," 140:33, 36, 39

4.2 **Construction of the Foundation Terrace of the Brewery and Mill**

1 géme ***du-ú-um* aka** (. . .) [ki-sá-a é]-báppir ù é-kíkken, "1 workwoman having made a *du-ú-um* (. . .), (work for) [the foundation terrace of] the brewery and mill," 123:27, 30

n géme ***du-ú-um*** **aka** (. . .) al-tar ki-sá-a é-lùnga ù é-kíkken, "n workwomen having made a *du-ú-um* (. . .), (for) construction of the foundation terrace of the brewery and mill," 113:'11, '15, 115:'18, '21, 121:28, 31

4.3 Construction of the Textile Mill

2 g̃uruš *du-ú-um* **ke$_4$-dè** gub-ba (. . .) é-uš-[bar . . .], "2 workmen employed to make a *du-ú-um* (. . .), [(work for)] the textile mill," 33:23, 30

n géme ***du-ú-um*** **ke$_4$-dè** gub-ba (. . .) é-uš-bar-šè, "n workwomen employed to make a *du-ú-um* (. . .), (work) for the textile mill," 37:22, 26, 38:23, 27

[n g̃ur]uš ***du-ú-um*** **ke$_4$-⸢dè⸣** gub-ba (. . .) al-t[ar] é-[uš-bar-ra], "[n] workmen employed to make a *du-ú-um* (. . .), (for) construction of the [textile] mill," 52:31, 35

[n géme] ***du-ú-*[*um* aka]** (. . .) al-ta[r u]š é-bar-ra, "[n workwomen having made] a *du-ú-um* (. . .), (for) construction of the textile mill," 53:23, 29

4.3.1 Construction of the Foundation Terrace of the Textile Mill

1 g̃uruš ***du-ú-um*** **ke$_4$-dè** gub-ba (. . .) ki-sá-a é-uš-bar (. . .), "1 workman employed to make a *du-ú-um*, (. . . work for) the foundation terrace of the textile mill," 35:23, 28

6 g̃uruš ***du-ú-um*** **⸢ke$_4$⸣-dè** gub-ba (. . .) ki-sá-a é-uš-bar-šè, "6 workmen employed to make a *du-ú-um* (. . .), (work) for the foundation terrace of the textile mill," 43:'28, '32

3 g̃ur[uš šidim] 15 g̃uru[š šu dím] 6 g̃uru[š ***du-ú-um*** **ke$_4$-dè**] gu[b-ba] 2 [g̃uruš im gíd-dè gub-ba], "3 [builders], 15 workmen [having built], 6 workmen employed [to make a *du-ú-um*], 2 workmen [employed to haul earth], (work for) the foundation terrace of the textile mill,[1]" 44:26–29

4.4 Construction of Various Houses

1 géme ***du-ú-um*** **[aka]** (. . .) é-*ba-ḫa-a* dù-[a], "1 workwoman [having made] a *du-ú-um* (. . .), (workers) having constructed the house of *Baḫa'a*," 114:33, 36

2 géme ***du-ú-⸢um⸣*** **aka** (. . .) al-tar é-*pu-ta-nu-um*, "2 workwomen having made a *du-ú-um* (. . .), (for) construction of the house of *Putanum*," 121:23, 26

4.5 Construction of the (Enclosure) Wall

1 géme ***du-ú-um*** **ke$_4$-dè** al-tar bàd gub-ba, "1 workwoman to make a *du-ú-um*, (workers) employed (for) construction of the (enclosure) wall," 102:22–23, 103:19–20

4.5.1 Construction of the urua wall

2 géme ***du-ú-um*** **aka** (. . .) ù-ru-a bàd aka, "2 workwomen having made a *du-ú-um* (. . .), (workers) having made the urua wall," 104:24, 26, 105:23, 25

4.6 Construction Site Unspecified

n g̃uruš ***du-ú-um*** **ke$_4$-dè** gub-ba, "n workmen employed to make a *du-ú-um*," 14:25, 16:24, 20:25, 31:22, 32:22

n géme ***du-ú-um*** **ke$_4$-dè** gub-ba, "n workwomen employed to make a *du-ú-um*," 26:'13, 37:22

---

1 Restoration of worksite based on duplicate text, no. 43:'26–:'32.

4.7 Construction Site Broken

2 g̃uruš ***du-ú-um*** **ke$_4$-dè** gub-ba, "2 workmen employed to make a *du-ú-um*," 51:'15

1 géme ***du-ú-um*** [**ke$_4$-dè** gub-ba], "1 workwoman [employed to make] a *du-ú-um*," 93:'20

1 g̃uruš šidim um-m[i-a] 2 g̃uruš šidim 6 g̃uruš šu dím-ma 2 géme ***du-<ú->um*** **aka** 2 géme [im gíd n] géme im ga$_6$-[g̃á-dè] 1 g̃uruš šidim [2 g̃uruš šu dím n] géme im ga$_6$-g̃[á-dè a]l-tar [. . .], "1 master builder, 2 builders, 6 workmen having built, 2 workwomen having made a *du-ú-um*, 2 workwomen [having hauled earth, n] workwomen [to] carry earth, 1 builder (and) [2 workmen having built], (and) [n] workwomen [to] carry earth, (workers for) construction [of . . .]," 106:22–28

5. ég-tab aka, "to make a double dike"

5.1. A Double Dike in the Palace

3 g̃uruš šidim 3 g̃uruš 3 géme **ég-tab** šà é-gal-la **ke$_4$-dè** gub-ba, "3 builders, 3 workmen (and) 3 workwomen employed to make a double dike in the palace," 21:'25-'26

1 g̃uruš šidim 3 g̃uruš **ég-tab** šà é-gal-la **ke$_4$-dè** gub-ba, "1 builder (and) 3 workmen employed to make a double dike in the palace," 28:'14

[n g̃uruš] šidim **ég-tab** šà é-gal-la **ke$_4$-dè** gub-ba, "[n] builder(s) employed to make a double dike in the palace," 29:'22

6. en-nu aka, "to perform guard duty, to guard"

in-u en-nu aka, "to guard straw"
má en-nu aka, "to guard a boat"
še en-nu aka, "to guard barley"
šeg$_{12}$ en-nu aka, "to guard bricks"

6.1. in-u en-nu aka, "to guard straw"

1 g̃uruš **in-u** [ka] i$_7$-è-šè **e[n-n]u aka** tuš-a, "1 workman having sat at [the opening] of the 'Outgoing' canal having guarded straw," 194:56–57

1 g̃uruš **in-u** ka i$_7$-[ta] gub-ba **en-n[u ke$_4$-dè]** g̃en-[na], "1 employed workman having gone to guard straw [at] the opening of the canal," 196:'27-'28

1 g̃uruš **in-u** ka i$_7$-ta UD.[DU]-šè **en-nu-g̃á ak-a** [gub-ba], "1 [employed] workman having guarded straw between the opening of the canal (and) the "entrance," 198:'30

6.2. má en-nu aka, "to guard a boat"

1 g̃uruš **má en-nu ke$_4$-dè** tuš-a, "1 workman having sat in order to guard a boat," 26:'20

6.3. še en-nu aka, "to guard barley"

1 *a-lí-aḫ* 1 *ta-tù-ri* **še** šà g̃ír-su[ki] **en-nu ke$_4$-dè** gub-ba, "*Ali-aḫ* (and) *Tatturi* employed to guard barley in G̃irsu," 51:'19-'21, 52:56–58, 53:58–60

[1 *a*]-*lí-a*[*ḫ* 1 *ta-tù*]-⸢*ri*⸣ **še** šà [g̃ír]-su[ki] **en-nu k[e$_4$-dè]** tuš-[a], "*Ali-aḫ* (and) *Tatturi* having sat [in order to] guard grain in G̃irsu," 56:'29-'31

6.4. šeg$_{12}$ en-nu aka, "to guard bricks"

n g̃uruš **šeg$_{12}$ en-nu aka**, "n workmen having guarded bricks," 98:'25, 102:4, 102:31, 103:4, 103:36, 104:4, 104:43, 105:4, 105:41, 106:4, 106:42, 107:7, 108:4, 108:37 109:4, 109:34, 110:6, 110:35, 111:6, 111:42, 114:6, 114:47, 115:'25, 116:6, 117:6, 117:34, 118:6, 118:27, 119:6, 119:24, 120:6, 120:'36, 121:6, 121:36, 123:7, 123:43, 125:6,

125:38, 126:6, 126:34, 127:6, 128:6, 128:36, 129:6, 129:40, 130:6, 130:'20, 132:6, 132:38, 133:6, 133:37, 134:6, 134:18, 135:6, 135:37, 136:6, 136:43, 137:6, 138:6, 139:6, 140:6, 140:45, 141:6, 141:40, 142:6, 142:36, 143:6, 145:6, 145:43, 146:'1, 146:'44, 147:6, 147:49, 149:6, 150:6, 150:42, 151:6, 151:41, 154:6, 154:44, 156:38, 157:23, 158:42, 159:36, 161:'22, 162:32

[n] g̃uruš šeg$_{12}$ **en-nu ke$_4$-dè**, "[n] workmen to guard bricks," 97:'21

6.4.1 Workmen Employed to Guard Bricks

n g̃uruš **šeg$_{12}$ en-nu ke$_4$-dè** gub-ba, "n workmen employed to guard bricks," 14:31, 16:26, 20:30, 26:'15, 29:'33, 35:41, 37:29, 38:34, 39:41, 40:34–35, 43:'39, 45:20, 46:'36, 47:50, 48:55, 49:54, 52:50, 57:'24, 93:'28, 94:30, 99:30, 101:31

6.4.2 Workmen Sitting in order to Guard Bricks

n g̃uruš **šeg$_{12}$ en-nu ke$_4$-dè** tuš-a, "n workmen having sat in order to guard bricks," 28:'24, 31:34, 32:34, 33:37, 36:35, 50:'14, 58:60, 59:50, 65:'24

6.5. Broken Context

[. . .]-x-a x DU? ka [. . .] **en-nu-g̃á aka [tuš]-a, 197:34

7. gi-guru$_5$ aka, "to make a reedwork panel"

7.1. For the Brewery-Kitchen-Mill Complex

*See *Household Index* for the complete context of the following passages.

12 ⸢g̃uruš⸣ **gi-guru$_5$ aka** [. . . é-lùnga é-muḫaldim] ù é-kíkken, "12 workmen having made reedwork panels, [. . . (work for) the brewery-kitchen]-mill complex," 144:'20-'21

12 g̃uruš 12 géme **gi-guru$_5$ ⸢aka⸣** al-tar é-lùnga é-muḫaldim ù é-⸢kíkken⸣, "12 workmen (and) 12 workwomen having made reedwork panels, (for) construction of the brewery-kitchen-mill complex," 145:35–36

10 géme **gi-guru$_5$ aka** ⸢al⸣-tar é-lùnga é-muḫaldim ù [é-kíkken], "10 workwomen having made reedwork panels, (for) construction of the brewery-kitchen-mill complex," 146:'34-'35

10 géme **g[i-guru$_5$ aka]** (. . .) [é]-⸢lùnga⸣ é-muḫaldim ù é-[kíkken], "10 workwomen [having made] reedwork [panels] (. . .), (work for) the brewery-kitchen-mill complex," 147:36, 40

7.2. Construction Site Unspecified

5 g̃uruš [n] géme **gi-guru$_5$ aka**, "5 workmen (and) [n] workwomen having made reedwork panels," 136: 40

8. gi-ir aka, "(meaning uncertain)"

8.1. Construction the Brewery-Kitchen-Mill Complex

*See *Household Index* for the complete context of the following passage.

2 g̃uruš 2 géme gi-sal **gi-ir ke$_4$-dè (. . .) al-tar é-lùnga é-muḫaldim ù é-kíkken, "2 workmen (and) 2 workwomen to (?) thin reeds (. . .), (for) construction of the brewery-kitchen-mill complex," 136:32, 34

8.2. Thin Reeds of the (Enclosure) Wall

1 g̃uruš g[i-sa]l bàd **gi-ir ke$_4$-dè gub-ba, "1 workman employed to (?) thin reeds of the (enclosure) wall," 28:'19, 40:30

★★[n ĝuruš] gi-sal **gi-ir** bàd **ke$_4$-dè** gub-ba, "[n workmen] employed to (?) thin reeds of the (enclosure) wall," 31:27

★★2 ĝuruš 2 géme gi-sal **gi-ir** bàd **ke$_4$-dè** gub-ba, "2 workmen (and) 2 workwomen employed to (?) thin reeds of the (enclosure) wall," 32:27, 35:34

8.3. Construction Site Unspecified

★★[n] ĝuruš g[i-sal **g]i-ir ⌜ke$_4$⌝-dè** gub-ba, "[n] workmen employed to (?) [thin] reeds," 39:35–36

9. **ḫar lam aka**, "to make a seedling container?"

★★[n] ĝuruš u$_4$-[n-šè] **ḫar lam** ^{geš}ù-suḫ$_5$ **ke$_4$-[dè]** ^{d}gu$_4$-an-na-⌜ta⌝ gar-ša-an-na^{ki}-šè ⌜de$_6$⌝-[a], "[n] workmen [for n] day(s) having brought a seedling container of pine trees from Guanna to Garšana," 272:10–15

10. **ḫu-ur-da aka**, "to make a reed screen"

10.1. For the GÍN-bal in the House

1 ĝuruš šidim 2 ĝuruš **ḫu-ur-da** GÍN-bal šà é-a **ke$_4$-dè**, "1 builder (and) 2 workmen to make a reed screen for the GÍN-bal in the house," 58:57–59

11. **im sumur aka**, "to plaster (with mud or clay)"

bàd im sumur aka, "to plaster the (enclosure) wall"

bí-ni-tum **im sumur aka**, "to plaster cross-beams"

é-e im sumur aka, "to plaster the house"

gi-sal im sumur aka, "to plaster thin reeds (in situ)"

gi-sig im sumur aka, "to plaster the reed hut"

iz-zi im sumur aka, "to plaster the iz-zi wall"

ká im sumur aka, "to plaster the gate"

SIG$_4$.ANŠE im sumur aka, "to plaster the brick stack"

ùr im sumur aka, "to plaster the roof"

11.1 bàd im sumur aka, "to plaster the (enclosure) wall"

1 ĝuruš šidim um-mi-a tà-tà-dè gub-⌜ba⌝ 5 ĝuruš šidim 4 ĝuruš 8 géme im ga$_6$-ĝá-dè gub-ba 3 ĝuruš im lu-dè gub-ba **bàd** {erasure} **im sumur ke$_4$-d[è** gub]-ba, "1 master builder employed to apply stucco, 5 builders, 4 workmen (and) 8 workwomen employed to carry earth (and) 3 workmen employed to mix earth, (workers) employed to plaster the (enclosure) wall," 36:26–30

1 ĝuruš šidim um-mi-a 4 ĝuruš šidim 6 ĝuruš šu dím-ma gub-ba 4 ĝuruš im sumur tà-tà-dè gub-ba [n] géme im ga$_6$-ĝá-dè gub-ba **bàd [im sumur] ke$_4$-[dè]**, "1 master builder, 4 builders (and) 6 workmen employed to build, 4 workmen employed to apply plaster (and) [n] workwomen employed to carry earth, (workers) [to] plaster the (enclosure) wall," 40:20–25

[. . .] 6 ĝuruš šu dím-ma ⌜gub⌝-ba [n ĝuruš] im sumur [tà-tà]-dè gub-ba 1 ĝuruš ⌜im⌝ ì-⌜li⌝-de$_9$ [gub-ba] 10-lá-1 géme i[m ga$_6$]-ĝá-dè gub-ba **bàd im sumur ke$_4$-dè**, "[. . .] 6 workmen employed to build, [n workmen] employed to [apply] plaster, 1 workman [employed] to lift earth (and) 9 workwomen employed to carry earth, (workers) to plaster the (enclosure) wall," 41:'18-'22

11.1.1 The Head of the (Enclosure) Wall

n g̃uruš šidim sag̃ **bàd im sumur ke$_4$-dè** gub-ba, "n builder(s) employed to plaster the head of the (enclosure) wall," 27:'13, 28:'11, 29:'17

n g̃uruš šidim n g̃uruš n géme sag̃ **bàd im sumur ke$_4$-dè** gub-ba, "n builder(s), n workmen (and) n workwomen employed to plaster the head of the (enclosure) wall," 31:28, 32:28, 35:30

*See *Household Index* for the complete context of the following passage.

1 g̃uruš 11 g[éme s]ag̃ **bàd i[m sumur ke$_4$]-d[è** g]ub-ba (. . .) é-uš-[bar . . .], "1 workman (and) 11 workwomen employed to plaster the head of the (enclosure) wall (. . .), [(workers employed for)] the textile mill," 33:28–30

11.1.2 The urua wall

1 g̃uruš šidim 1 g̃uruš šu dím gub-ba 4 géme im ga$_6$-g̃á-dè gub-ba 2 g̃uruš im ì-li-de$_9$ <<dè>> gub-ba ù-ru-a **bàd im sumur ke$_4$-dè**, "1 builder (and) 1 workman employed to build, 4 workwomen employed to carry earth (and) 2 workmen employed to lift earth, (workers) to plaster the urua wall," 47:32–36

11.2. ***bí-ni-tum* im sumur aka**, "to plaster cross-beams"

11.2.1 Crossbeams for the Brewery-Kitchen-Mill Complex

*See *Household Index* for the complete context of the following passage.

n g̃uruš šidim n g̃uruš n géme ***bí-ni-tum* im sumur aka** (. . .) é-lùnga é-muḫaldim ù é-kíkken, "n builder(s), n workmen (and) n workwomen having plastered crossbeams (. . .), (work for) the brewery-kitchen-mill complex," 147:30–31, 40, 151:24–25, 33, 154:30–31, 36

11.2.2 Crossbeams for the Textile Mill and Craftsmen's House

[n g̃uruš šidim] 8 g̃uruš šu dím-[ma? n] géme im ga$_6$<-g̃á>-dè g[ub-bá] g̃uruš im ì-li-de$_9$ [gub-ba ***b*]*í-ni-tum* im sumur ke$_4$-dè** é-uš-bar ù é-gašam-[e-ne(-šè)], "[n builder(s)] (and) 8 workmen having built, [n] workwomen employed to carry earth (and) 2 workmen [employed] to lift earth, (workers) to plaster crossbeams [(for)] the textile mill and craftsmen's house," 71:21–24

11.3. **é-e im sumur aka**, "to plaster the house"

11.3.1 Supplies Expended when the House Was Plastered

1 ^{gi}bisag̃-im-sar-ra [sa-ḫ]a ⅔ kùš íb-sá im-sar g̃á-g̃á-dè u$_4$ **é-[e] im sumur ba-aka**, "1 canvas-lined clay tablet coffer—it is ⅔ kùš square—(in which) to deposit clay tablets when the house was plastered," 1318:1–3

11.3.2 Rations Expended when the House was Plastered

11.3.2.1 Assorted Commodities for the Household Servants

0.1.0.8 sìla ninda-g[al-gen] 1 sìla [du$_8$] 0.0.5.4 sìla kaš-gen 0.0.5.4 sìla zú-lum ⸢g̃uruš⸣ árad-é-a ù lú-ḫug̃-g̃á-e-ne ba-na-ḫa-la u$_4$ **é<-e> im sumur <ba->aka**, "68 liters of [ordinary] large bread [baked] (in) 1 liter (loaves), 54 liters of ordinary beer (and) 54 liters of dates were divided for the household servants and hired workers when the house was plastered," 471:1–5

11.3.2.2 Barley for the Ox-Drivers

0.3.0. še šà-gu$_4$-me-éš (. . .) u$_4$ **é-e i[m sumur ba-aka]**, "180 liters of barley for the ox-drivers, {authorizing officials}, when the house was plastered," 481:1, 6

11.3.2.3 Bread

11.3.2.3.1 Bread for *Abu-ṭabu*, the Overseer

0.0.2.6 sìla ninda ^{kuš}a-ĝá-lá kéše-rá ĝuruš nam–60 *a-*⸢*bu*⸣-DU$_{10}$ u$_4$ é-^{d}*šu-*^{d}*suen*^{ki}-šè i-⸢re⸣-ša-a u$_4$ **é-e im sumur ba-aka**, "26 liters of bread in bound leather sacks (for) *Abu-ṭabu*, the overseer of 60 workmen, when (his workers) went to *Bit-Šu-Suen* when the house was plastered," 480:1–3

11.3.2.3.2 Bread for the Man Bringing Fish

3 sìla ninda lú ku$_6$ du$_6$-lugal-pa-è^{ki}-ta de$_6$-a u$_4$ **é-e im sumur ba-aka**, "3 liters of bread (for) the man who brought fish from Du-lugalpa'e when the house was plastered," 476:1–4

11.3.2.4 Groats for the Men from *Bit-Šu-Suen*

[n sìl]a níĝ-àr-r[a-sig$_5$ t]u$_7$-šè lú-é-^{d}*šu*-^{d}E[N.ZU]^{ki}-ke$_4$-ne ba-na-ḫa-la u$_4$ **[é]-e [im sumur ba-aka]**, "[n] liter(s) of [fine] barley groats for soup were divided among the men from *Bit-Šu-Suen*, when the house was plastered," 391:1–5

11.3.2.5 Oil for the Builders

[n.n].1.[n].6½ [sìla ì-ĝeš gur] 4? sìla 5 gín [ì-šaḫ] ì-ba šidim-e-[ne] u$_4$ **é-e im sumur ba-aka**, "[n bushel(s) (and) n liter(s) of sesame oil] (and) 4? liters (and) 5 shekels [of lard], oil rations (for) builders when the house was plastered," 482:1–4

11.3.2.6 Recipient Unspecified

11.3.2.6.1 Bread and Soup

24 sa gi-[izi] ninda ba-ra-⸢du$_8$⸣ 10 sa gi-[izi] tu$_7$ [ba]-ra-⸢šeĝ$_6$⸣ u$_4$ **é-e im sumur ⸢ba⸣-aka**, "24 bundles of [fuel] reeds, with which bread was baked, (and) 10 bundles of [fuel] reeds, with which soup was cooked, when the house was plastered," 473:1–5

11.3.2.6.2 Mutton Fat

½ sìla ì-udu dúr ^{ĝeš}ig-[x] ba-ab-šeš$_4$ u$_4$ **é-e im sumur ba-aka**, "½ liter of mutton fat (with which) the back of the [x] door was oiled when the house was plastered," 1319:1–4

11.3.3 Building Supplies and Rations

(. . .) ba-úš iti-u$_4$-8-ba-zal šà-gal šidim-e-ne ⅓ sìla ì-⸢šáḫ⸣ di$_4$-di$_4$-la àga-ús *simat-*^{d}*ištaran* ba-ab-šeš$_4$ [n] gín še-gín mu x-šè [. . . n ma]-na šu-sar m[angaga? $^{ĝeš?}$]ig ^{ĝeš}kuĝ$_5$-šè ⸢u$_4$⸣ **é-e im sumur ba-aka**, "{assorted animals} were slaughtered at the end of the 8th day of the month, food (for) builders, ⅓ liter of lard (used by) *Simat-Ištaran* (when) she anointed the small child(ren) of the gendarme, [n] shekel(s) of glue for (?) [. . .] (and) [n mina(s)] of cord (made from) date palm fibers for the door (and) ladder when the house was plastered," 472:6–14

11.4. gi-sal im sumur aka, "to plaster thin reeds (in situ)"

[4] g̃uruš šidim 4 g̃uruš [4] géme gi-sal šà **é-a im sumur ke$_4$-dè** gub-ba, "[4] builders, 4 workmen and [4] workwomen employed to plaster thin reeds in the house," 14:18–19

11.4.1 ka gi-sal im sumur aka, "(meaning uncertain)"

n g̃uruš šidim n g̃uruš šu dím-ma gub-ba **ka gi-sal-la im sumur aka (gub-ba), "n builder(s) (and) n workmen employed to build, (employed workers) having (?)," 5:16–17, 6:16–18

11.5. gi-sig im sumur aka, "to plaster the reed hut"

2 g̃uruš šidim **gi-sig ki-mu-ra im sumur ke$_4$-dè** gub-ba, "2 builders employed to plaster the reed hut of the textile depository," 85:9–10

11.6. iz-zi im sumur aka, "to plaster the iz-zi wall"

[. . .] 2 g̃uruš im [ì-li]-de$_9$ gub-⸢ba⸣ **iz-zi im sumur ke$_4$-dè**, "[. . .] (and) 2 workmen employed to [lift] earth, (workers) to plaster the iz-zi wall," 51:'10-'11

1 g̃uruš šidim um-mi-a 4 g̃uruš ⸢šidim⸣ 4 g̃uruš šu dím-[ma] 3 g̃uruš im sumur ì-⸢li-de$_9$⸣ gub-ba 10 g̃u[ruš n géme?] im ga$_6$-g̃á-dè gu[b-ba] **iz-⸢zi⸣ im sumur ke$_4$-dè**, "1 master builder, 4 builders (and) 4 workmen having built, 3 workmen employed to lift plaster (and) 10 workmen [(and) n workwomen?] employed to carry earth, (workers) to plaster the iz-zi wall," 52:20–26

[. . .] 8 géme im ga$_6$-⸢g̃á⸣-dè gub-[ba] 2 g̃uruš im ì-li-de$_9$ [gub-b]a **iz-zi im [sumur k]e$_4$-⸢dè⸣**, "[. . .] (and) 8 workwomen employed to carry earth (and) 2 workmen employed to lift earth, (workers) to plaster the iz-zi wall," 56:'20-'22

11.6.1 Of the Brewery-Kitchen-Mill Complex

*See *Household Index* for the complete context of the following passage.

n géme im ga$_6$-g̃á **iz-zi im sumur aka** (. . .) al-tar é-lùnga é-muḫaldim ù é-kíkken, "n workwomen having carried earth having plastered the iz-zi wall (. . .), (for) construction of the brewery-kitchen-mill complex," 136:30–31, 34, 142:23–24, 29

11.6.2 Of the Craftsmen's House

*See *Household Index* for the complete context of the following passages.

2 g̃uruš im ì-li-dè gub-ba **iz-zi im sumur ke$_4$-dè** é-gašam-e-ne-šè, "2 workmen employed to lift earth to plaster the iz-zi wall for the craftsmen's house," 53:32–33

3 géme im ga$_6$-g̃á-dè gub-ba **iz-zi im sumur ke$_4$-dè** (. . .) é-uš-bar ù é-gašam-e-ne-šè, "3 workwomen employed to carry earth to plaster the iz-zi wall (. . .), (work) for the textile mill and craftsmen's house," 58:36–37, 39

11.6.3 Of the Storehouse

[n g̃uruš] im ⸢ga$_6$⸣-g̃á šu dím gub-ba [n g̃uruš šid]im 7 g̃uruš 7 géme [**iz-zi**?] **im sumur ke$_4$-dè** gub-ba [n g̃uruš] im lu-a SIG$_4$.ANŠE gub-ba [n g̃uruš] šidim iz-zi g̃á-nun-na dù-dè gub-ba, "[n workmen] employed to carry earth (for) building, [n] builder(s), 7 workmen (and) 7 workwomen employed to plaster [the iz-zi wall?], [n workmen] employed to mix earth at the brick stack (and) [n] builder(s) employed to construct the iz-zi wall of the storehouse," 29:'23-'27

11.6.4 For General Construction

*See **al-tar** for the complete context of the following passage.

n géme im ga_6-g̃á **iz-zi im sumur aka** (. . .) al-tar gub-ba, "n workwomen having carried earth—(workers) having plastered the iz-zi wall—(. . .), (workers) employed for construction," 140:27–28, 36, 144:'9-'10, '15

11.7. **ká im sumur aka**, "to plaster the gate"

*See *Household Index* for the complete context of the following passages.

11.7.1 Of the Brewery-Kitchen-Mill Complex

1 g̃uruš šidim 3 géme **ká ⸢im⸣ sumur aka** (. . .) [. . . é-lùnga é-muḫaldim] ù é-kíkken, "1 builder (and) 3 workwomen having plastered the gate (. . .), [. . . (work for) the brewery-kitchen]-mill complex," 144:'16-'17, '21

2 g̃uruš šidim 3 g̃uruš 3 géme **ká im sumur aka** é-lùnga é-muḫaldim ù é-kíkken, "2 builders, 3 workmen (and) 3 workwomen having plastered the gate, (work for) the brewery-kitchen-mill complex," 155:29–31

11.8. **SIG_4.ANŠE im sumur aka**, "to plaster the brick stack"

11.8.1 For Construction of the Brewery and Mill

1 g̃uruš šidim u[m-mi-a] 1 g̃uruš šidim **SIG_4.ANŠE [im sumur aka]** 2 g̃[uruš šidim] 16 g̃[uruš n géme . . .] im su[mur aka n g̃uruš n] géme im [ga_6-g̃á al-tar ki]-sá-a é-[lùnga ù é-kíkken], "1 master builder, 1 builder [having plastered] the brick stack, 2 [builders], 16 [workmen (and) n workwomen] having plastered [. . .] (and) [n workmen (and) n] workwomen [having carried] earth, (for) [construction of] the foundation terrace of [the brewery and mill]," 112:'4-'9

11.8.2 For Construction of the Palace

[n g̃uruš] 1 géme **SIG_4.ANŠE [im sumur] ke_4-dè** gub-ba [n g̃uruš] má-$laḫ_5$ 1 g̃uruš [im] ga_6-g̃á-dè [n g̃uruš x] x šà? é?-gal ke_4-dè, "[n workmen] (and) 1 workwoman employed to plaster the brick stack, [n] sailor(s) (and) 1 workman having carried [earth] (and) [n workmen] having made [x] in? the palace," 66:'10-'12

11.8.3 For Construction of Various Houses

11.8.3.1 The House of *Alua*

[2] g̃uruš šidim 10 g̃uruš 20 géme **SIG_4.ANŠE im sumur aka** 1 g̃uruš šidim 2 g̃uruš 10 géme *é-a-lu-a*, "[2] builders, 10 workmen (and) 20 workwomen having plastered the brick stack (and) 1 builder, 2 workmen (and) 10 workwomen at the house of *Alua*," 110:26–29

11.8.3.2 The House of *Baḫa'a*

3 g̃uruš šidim 15 g̃uruš 30 [géme] **SIG_4.ANŠE im sum[ur aka]** 3 g̃uruš šidim 16 g̃uruš šu dím 34 géme im ga_6-g̃á al<-tar> *é-ba-ḫa-a*, "3 builders, 15 workmen (and) 30 [workwomen] having plastered the brick stack, 3 builders (and) 16 workmen having built (and) 34 workwomen having carried earth, (for) construction of the house of *Baḫa'a*," 117:24–28

11.8.3.3 The House of *Ili-bišu*

7 ⸢g̃uruš⸣ **SIG_4.ANŠE i[m su]mur aka** 1 g̃uruš šidim 2 g̃uruš šu dím 6 g̃uruš im ga_6-g̃á 2 g̃uruš im lu-a 2 g̃uruš a bal-a 1 g̃uruš in-u ga_6-g̃á im lu-a *é-ì-lí-bi-šu*, "7 workmen having plastered the brick stack, 1 builder (and) 2 workmen having built, 6 workmen having carried earth, 2 workmen having mixed

earth, 2 workmen having poured water (and) 1 workman having carried straw (for) mixing (with) earth, (work for) the house of *Ili-bišu*," 204:'1-'9

11.8.3.4 The House of *Ubarria*

[n] g̃uruš šidim 10 g̃uruš 13 [géme] **SIG_4.ANŠE im sumur ⸢aka⸣** 1 g̃uruš šidim SIG_4.ANŠE šà zaba[la_4^{ki}] 26 g̃uruš im lu-a 1 g̃uruš šidim 2 g̃uruš šu ⸢dím⸣ 5 géme im ga_6-g̃á é-*u-bar-⸢ri⸣-a* dù-a, "[n] builder(s), 10 workmen (and) 13 [workwomen] having plastered the brick stack, 1 builder at the brick stack in Zabala, 26 workmen having mixed earth, 1 builder, 2 workmen having built (and) 5 workwomen having carried earth, (workers) having constructed the house of *Ubarria*," 111:30–36

11.8.4 Construction Project Unspecified

11.8.4.1 Plastering the Brick Stack

1 g̃uruš šidim **SIG_4.ANŠE im sumur ke_4-dè** gub-ba, "1 builder employed to plaster the brick stack," 35:37

n g̃uruš šidim n g̃uruš n géme **SIG_4.ANŠE im sumur aka**, "n builder(s), n workmen (and) n workwomen having plastered the brick stack," 109:30–31, 113:'3-'4, 114:37–40

n g̃uruš šidim um-mi-a n g̃uruš šidim n g̃uruš n géme **SIG_4.ANŠE im sumur aka**, "n master builder(s), n builder(s), n workmen (and) n workwomen having plastered the brick stack," 118:20–24, 120:21–23

n g̃uruš šidim n g̃uruš **SIG_4.ANŠE im sumur aka**, "n builder(s) (and) n workmen having plastered the brick stack," 207:18–21, 209:24–26

2 g̃uruš [u_4-1-šè] **SIG_4.ANŠE im [sumur ke_4-dè]** gub-[ba], "2 workmen employed [for 1 day to] plaster the brick stack," 336:33–34

11.8.4.2 Mixing Earth to Plaster the Brick Stack

n g̃uruš šidim n g̃uruš n géme **SIG_4.ANŠE im sumur ke_4-dè** gub-ba n g̃uruš im lu-a SIG_4.ANŠE-šè, "n builder(s), n workmen (and) n workwomen employed to plaster the brick stack (and) n workmen having mixed earth, (work) for the brick stack," 28:'16-'18, 31:31–32, 32:31–32

[10] géme im ga_6-g̃á 3 g̃uruš im lu-a **SIG_4.ANŠE im sumur aka**, "[10] workwomen having carried earth (and) 3 workmen having mixed earth, (workers) having plastered the brick stack," 199:12–14

[4] géme im [ga_6]-g̃á 1 g̃uruš im lu-a 1 g̃uruš a bal-[a] 1 g̃uruš in-u ga_6-[g̃á] im lu-a **SIG_4.⸢ANŠE⸣ im sumur aka**, "[4] workwomen having carried earth, 1 workman having mixed earth, 1 workman having poured water (and) 1 workman having carried straw (and) having mixed (it with) earth, (workers) having plastered the brick stack," 209:27–32

11.9. ùr im sumur aka, "to plaster the roof"

2 g̃uruš šidim **ùr** é-*u-bar-ri-a* **im sumur ke_4-dè** gub-ba, "2 builders employed to plaster the roof of the house of *Ubarria*," 92:19

11.10. Plastering, Multiple Objects for Specific Construction Projects

11. 10.1 For the Brewery-Kitchen-Mill Complex

*See *Household Index* for the complete context of the following passages.

11.10.1.1 Plastering Crossbeams and the Gate

1 ĝuruš šidim 1 ĝuruš 7 géme ká **im sumur aka** 5 ĝuruš šidim 7 ĝuruš 20 géme *bí-ni-tum* **im sumur ⸢aka⸣** (. . .) é-lùnga é-muḫaldim ù é-kíkken, "1 builder, 1 workman (and) 7 workwomen having plastered the gate, 5 builders, 7 workmen (and) 20 workwomen having plastered crossbeams (. . .), (work for) the brewery-kitchen-mill complex," 152:'13-'16, '19, 153:'26-'29, '32

11.10.1.2 Plastering Crossbeams and the iz-zi Wall

3 ĝuruš šidim 12 ĝuruš 12 [géme] *bí-ni-⸢tum⸣* **i[m sumur aka]** (. . .) 2 ĝuruš šidim 3 ĝur[uš n géme?] iz-zi im **sum[ur a]ka** (. . .) ⸢al⸣-tar é-lùnga é-muḫaldim ù [é-kíkken], "3 builders, 12 workmen (and) 12 [workwomen having plastered] crossbeams, (. . .), 2 builders, 3 workmen [(and) n workwomen?] having plastered the iz-zi wall (. . .), (for) construction of the brewery-kitchen-mill complex," 146:'24-'25, '27-'28, '35

n ĝuruš šidim n ĝuruš n géme *bí-ni-tum* **im sumur aka** n ĝuruš šidim n ĝuruš n géme iz-zi im sumur **aka** (. . .) é-lùnga é-muḫaldim ù é-kíkken, "n builder(s), n workmen (and) n workwomen having plastered crossbeams, n builder(s), n workmen (and) n workwomen having plastered the iz-zi wall (. . .), (work for) the brewery-kitchen-mill complex," 147:30–33, 40, 150:31–34, 36

11.11. Plastering for Specific Construction Projects, Object Unspecified

11.11.1 The Brewery-Kitchen-Mill Complex

[n ĝuru]š **im sumur [ke$_4$-dè]** (. . .) [é-lùn]ga é-kíkken [ù é-muḫaldim], "[n] workmen [to] plaster (. . .), (work for) the brewery-kitchen-mill complex," 106:30, 32

11.11.2 The Sheep-Fattening Pen

1 ĝuruš [šidim n] ĝur[uš. . .] 1 ĝuruš **im sumur [aka]** 1 ĝuruš šidim gi-sig é-udu-niga [dù-a], "1 builder, [n] workmen [having. . .], 1 workman having plastered (and) 1 builder [having constructed] the reed hut of the sheep-fattening pen," 206:12–171

11.11.3 The Tower at the Zabala Garden

2 ĝuruš šidim [im] šu dím-ma sum-mu-dè 2 ĝuruš im ga$_6$-ĝá 2 ĝuruš im lu-a 3 ĝuruš a bal-a-e-dè 8 ĝuruš saḫar šà é-a sè-ĝé-dè **im sumur aka** an-za-qar-^{ĝeš}kiri$_6$-zabala$_4^{ki}$, "2 builders to hand [earth] for building, 2 workmen having carried earth, 2 workmen having mixed earth, 3 workmen to pour water (and) 8 workmen to tamp dirt in the house, (workers) having plastered the tower of the Zabala garden," 202:14–21

1 ĝuruš šidim um-mi-a 3 ĝuruš šidim 3 ĝuruš im šu dím-ma [sum]-mu-dè 7 ĝuruš im ga$_6$-ĝá 3 ĝuruš im lu-a 3 ĝuruš a bal-a **im sumur aka** an-za-qar-^{ĝeš}kiri$_6$-za[bala$_4^{ki}$], "1 master builder, 3 builders (and) 3 workmen to hand earth for building, 7 workmen having carried earth, 3 workmen having mixed earth (and) 3 workmen having poured water, (workers) having plastered the tower of the Zabala garden," 203:14–21

*See *Toponymn Index* for the complete context of the following passage.

[n g̃uruš i]m **sumur aka** (. . .) an-za-qar-^{geš}kiri$_6$-zabala$_4$$^{⌜ki⌝}$ [gub-ba], "[n workmen] having plastered (. . .), (workers) [employed] at the tower of the Zabala garden," 201:'3, '6

11.11.4 Various Houses

11.11.4.1 The House of *Putanum*

*See *Household Index* for the complete context of the following passage.

1 g̃uruš šidim 2 [g̃uruš] 1 géme **im [sumur aka]** (. . .) é-*pu*-[*ta-nu-um* dù-a], "1 builder, 2 [workmen] (and) 1 workwoman having plastered (. . .), (workers) [having constructed] the house of *Putanum*," 112:'14-'15, '17

11.11.4.2 The House of *Ubarria*

2 g̃uruš šidim 1 g̃uruš x-[. . .] 5 géme **im [sumur aka]** é-*u-bar-ri*-[*a* dù-a], "2 builders, 1 workman [having. . .] (and) 5 workwomen [having plastered], (workers) [having constructed] the house of *Ubarria*," 112:'11-'13

11.11.5 Plastering, Construction Site Broken or Unspecified

2 g̃uruš šidim **im su[mur ke$_4$]-dè** gub-[ba], "2 builders employed to plaster," 6:21

n g̃uruš **im sumur ke$_4$-dè** gub-ba, "n workmen employed to plaster," 15:31, 46:'28, 48:44, 59:44–45, 62:'11

[n g̃uruš] **im sumur ⌜aka⌝**, "[n workmen] having plastered," 205:23

11.12. Broken Context

15 g̃uruš 33 géme ⌜SIG$_4$⌝.ANŠE g̃á-g̃á [3 g̃uruš] **im sumur aka** [. . .]-zu?, "15 workmen (and) 33 workwomen having placed the brick stack (and) [3 workmen] having plastered (?)," 199:9–11

[. . . x? iti ez]em-^{d}šul-g[i x? . . . **im] sumur aka [gar]-ša-an-na$^{[ki]}$ ù g̃ír-[su]^{ki}-⌜šè⌝ D[U-x?], 1029:'11-'14

12. **kíg̃ aka**, "to do work"

gú-ba **kíg̃ bí-na**, "he did work on its side," 1048:5

13. **kurum$_7$ aka**, "to make an inspection," *passim*

kurum$_7$ aka al-tar, "inspection of construction" > al-tar

14. **níg̃ si-ga A.ZI/ZI.ÉŠ aka**, "to make a panel of rushes"

4 g̃uruš **níg̃ si-ga A.ZI/ZI.ÉŠ aka**, "4 workmen having made a panel of rushes," 47:49

4 g̃uruš **níg̃ si-ga A.ZI/ZI.ÉŠ aka** gub-ba, "4 workmen employed to make a panel of rushes," 48:54

15. **ninda aka**, "to make bread"

60 ninda-gúg-zì-KAL 3 sìla **ni[nda-š]**u-ra-gen lú-*i-zi-in-èr-ra*^{ki} **ke$_4$-dè** u$_4$ dabin *i-zi-in-*[*èr-ra*]^{ki}-ta gar-ša-an-na^{ki}-šè de$_6$-a, "the man of *Izin-Erra* (was assigned) to make 60 cakes of KAL-flour (and) 3 liters of ordinary half (loaf) bread, when semolina was brought from *Izin-Erra* to Garšana," 495:1–5

16. **sa gi$_4$ aka**, "to make preparations"

16.1 Preparations for a Banquet

iti ezem-^{d}[*šu*]-^{d}EN.[ZU x?] kaš-dé-a dig̃ir-re-e-[ne] **sa gi$_4$-gi$_4$ a[ka?], "preparations made? for the banquet of the gods (in) month 9," 1029:'15-'17

17. siki ^{ĝeš}garig aka, "to comb wool"

siki ^{ĝeš}garig aka, "combed wool" > **siki**

18. šu aka, "to manufacture; to process"

^{ĝeš}ásal šu aka, "processed poplar wood"

^{ĝeš}ma-nu šu aka, "processed manu wood"

18.1. ^{ĝeš}ásal šu aka, "processed poplar wood"

10 gú ^{ĝeš}**[A.T]U.GAB.LIŠ šu aka** gú-ne-šè, "10 talents of processed poplar wood for a cupboard," 975:46–7

šu+níĝin 10 gú **^{ĝeš}ásal šu aka**, "In total: 10 talents of processed poplar wood," 975:104

18.2. ^{ĝeš}ma-nu šu aka, "processed manu wood"

n gú **^{ĝeš}ma-nu šu aka**, "n talent(s) of processed manu wood," 511:80, 523:13, 1223:3, 1351:1

18.3. Object Uncertain

★★[120?+]5 ^{gi}m[a-sá]-ab ½-[sìla-ta] 120 ^{gi}ku-[ni-na] 5-sìla-ta 11 ^{gi}ma!(KU)-sá-ab 5-s[ìla-t]a AŠ.AŠ NE-ku-nu **šu aka**, "[120?+]5 ma-sab baskets of ½ liter [each], 120 drinking straws of 5 liters each (and) 11 ma-sab baskets of 5 liters each, to process (?)," 1371:1–7

19. tu$_7$ aka, "to serve soup"

19.1. Offering Bowls of Soup

19.1.1 For the Banquet of Inana

380 ^{dug}sìla-bur-⌜zi⌝ **tu$_7$ ba-aka** kaš-dé-a ^{d}inana-zabala$_4^{ki}$, "380 1-liter offering bowls of soup were served at the banquet of Inana of Zabala," 1025:37–39

60 ^{dug}sìla-bur-zi **tu$_7$ ba-aka** kaš-dé-a ^{d}inana-iri^{ki}, "60 1-liter offering bowls of soup were served at the banquet of Inana of the city," 1025:72–74

19.1.2 For the Banquet of Nergal

120 ^{dug}sìla-bu[r-zi] **tu$_7$ ba-a⌜ka⌝** kaš-dé-a ^{d}nergal$_x^{[eri11-gal]}$ dumu *da-d*[*a*-AN], "120 1-liter offering bowls of soup were served at the banquet of Nergal, (the personal deity of) the son of *Dada*-AN," 1025:54–56

120 ^{dug}sìla-bur-zi **tu$_7$ ba-aka** kaš-dé-a ^{d}nergal$_x^{eri11-[gal]}$ dumu é-é-⌜zi⌝, "120 1-liter offering bowls of soup were served at the banquet of Nergal, (the personal deity of) the son of E-ezi," 1025:89–91

20. [. . .] aka, "to make [x]"

[. . .] **ke$_4$-dè** [gub-ba], 17:23

1 ĝuruš [. . .] **ke$_4$-[dè]** gub-ba, 17:26

[. . .] **ke$_4$-dè** [gub-ba], 46:'18

2 ĝuruš šidim 2 ĝuruš šu dím [n ĝuruš] i[m-. . .] **ke$_4$-dè** [gub-ba. . .], 57:'17-'19

[. . .] **ke$_4$-d[è** . . .], 101:20–21

20.1. For the Craftsmen's House

[n] ĝuruš šidim [n] ĝuruš šu dím-ma gub-ba [n ĝuruš] im ga$_6$<-ĝá>-dè gub-ba [n ĝuruš im] ⌜ì⌝-li-de$_9$ gub-ba [. . .] **ke$_4$-dè** [. . . é]-gašam, "[n] builder(s) (and) [n] workmen employed to build, [n workmen] employed to carry earth, [n] workmen employed to lift [earth] (and) [. . .] to make [. . .] [(for)] the craftsmen's [house]," 66:'4-'9

20.2. In the Palace

[n g̃uruš x] x šà? é?-gal **ke$_4$-dè**, "[n workmen] to make [x] in? the palace," 66:'12

20.3. Translation Uncertain

[n s]ìla g̃eš-ì [x]-ga$_6$? a[ka** x?], "[n] liter(s) of (?) sesame," 1181:1–2

àra, *samādu*, "to mill, grind"

géme **àr-ra**, "female grinder" > *Craftswomen Index*

gú-gal **al-àr-ra**, "milled beans" > **gú-gal**

níg̃-**àr-ra**, "groats" > **níg̃-àr-ra**

níg̃-àr-ra àra, "to grind groats"

zì-da àra, "to mill flour"

1. **níg̃-àr-ra àra**, "to grind groats"

7 géme u$_4$-1-šè še 3-sìla-ta ba-ḫug̃ ⌜**níg̃**⌝**-àr-ra àr-ra-**⌜**dè**⌝ ⌜gub⌝-ba [ugula] *li-la-á*, "7 workwomen, [supervised] by *Lila'a*, hired for 1 day for 3 liters of barley each, employed to grind groats," 423:4

2 géme u$_4$-1-šè še 3-sìla ⌜ús⌝-sa-šè ⌜**níg̃**⌝**-àr-ra àr-ra-dè** ús-sa, "2 workwomen for 1 day, 3 liters of barley for processing, (the women) having processed (the barley) in order to grind groats," 434:1–2

2. **zì-da àra**, "to mill flour"

1 géme **zì-da àra-**⌜**dè**⌝ gub-ba zàḫ *ku-du-du-ú* lú-du$_6$-lugal-pa-è^{ki}(-me-éš), "1 workwoman employed to mill flour (and) *Kududu*, the runaway, workers of Du-lugal-pa'e," 45:34–36, 46:'51-'53, 47:69–71, 48:75–77

– B –

ba, *qiāšu, zâzu*, "to allot; to divide into shares; to give, present"

1. **Allotments**

[6]9 ádda-udu 69 kuš-udu 2 ma-na 18 gín sa ⌜udu⌝ *a-ḫu-a* **mu-na-**⌜**ba**⌝?, "6[9] sheep carcasses, 69 sheep skins, (and) 2 minas (and) 18 shekels of sheep sinews alloted for *Aḫu'a*," 459:1–4

2. **Rations**

ì-**ba**, "oil rations" > **ì**

ninda-**ba**, "bread rations" > **ninda**

siki-**ba**, "wool rations" > **siki**

še-**ba**, "barley rations" > **še**

ba-al, *ḫerû*, "to dig, bail out (a cistern); to unload (a boat)"

***a-za-bu-um* ba-al**, "to bail out a cistern"

še ba-al, "to unload barley"

1. **Digging Assignments**

1.1 **The Baths**

6 ĝuruš du_{10}-ús é[?-did]li? kíĝ-til **ba-al**, "6 workmen having completed the work of digging the baths of additional? houses?," 158:40

1.2 **The Mimer Canal**

13 ĝuruš saĝ-tag 3 ĝuruš á-⅔-ta [lú]ázlag-me-éš u_4-2-šè i_7-mi-me-er gub-ba **ba-al-la** (. . .) šà nibru[ki], "13 full-time fullers and 3 fullers at ⅔ wages employed for 2 days having dug the Mimer canal. {Expenditure} in Nippur," 227:1–5, 7

2. ***a-za-bu-um* ba-al**, "to bail out a cistern"

*See *Household Index* for the complete context of the following passage.

[n ĝur]uš šidim 3 ĝuruš 6 géme [***a-za-b***]***u-um*** šà é-a **ba-a[l-dè]** (. . .) é-lùnga é-muḫaldim ù é-kíkken, "[n] builder(s), 3 workmen (and) 6 workwomen [to] bail out the cistern in the house (and) (. . .), (work for) the brewery-kitchen-mill complex," 155:25–26, 31

3. **še ba-al**, "to unload barley"

1 ĝuruš túg-du_8 u_4-[1-šè] gú-saḫar[ḫar].DU[ki]-ta a[n-za-qar]-*da-da*-šè má gíd-da ù [**še ba-al**], "1 braider [for 1] day having towed a boat from Gu-saḫar.DU to the fortified tower of *Dada* and [having unloaded barley]," 298:11–12

2 ĝuruš ašgab u_4-1-šè gú-saḫar[ḫar].DU[ki]-ta an-za-qar-*da-da*-šè má gíd-da ù **še ba-al**, "2 leather workers for 1 day having towed a boat from Gu-saḫar.DU to the fortified tower of *Dada* and having unloaded barley," 299:11–12

4. **Broken Context**

[n] ĝuruš [. . .] é?-a im-[. . .] ⌜x⌝ **ba-al-dè, 106:36

bala, "to rotate, turn over, cross"

[dug]úgur **bala, "bala vessel" > **[dug]úgur**

še-**bala**-bi šà-gal mušen-na, "barley of the bala, fodder of birds" > **šà-gal**

1. **siki bala**, "to bale wool"

(. . .) ⌜siki**⌝ **bala-dè** in-na-[kéše t]úg-gen-kam ì-in-⌜DU⌝? 1 [túg]saĝ-uš-bar sa-gi_4-[àm], "{assorted textiles}, the wool was bound up to be baled, he delivered the ordinary textiles, they are finished uš-bar textiles," 609:7–9 (envelope)

(. . .) **siki bala-[dè i]n-na-⌜kéše⌝ [túg]uš-ba[r sa-gi_4-àm], "{assorted textiles}, the wool was bound up to be baled, they are finished uš-bar textiles," 609:8 (tablet)

(. . .) kìšib íb-ra é-kìšib-ba-ta dub-bi in-du_8 **siki bala-dè in-kéše é-gal-šè mu-DU, "{assorted textiles}. He rolled the seal, baked its tablet in the warehouse, (and) bound up the wool to be baled (for) delivery for the palace," 609:11–14

barag, "to press, to mix" > *Verb Index*

ì-ĝeš **barag** aka, "pressed sesame oil" > **ì-ĝeš**

bíl, *qalû*, "to burn"

1. **Chaff for Burning**

tuḫ-$duru_5$-gen **bíl**-šè, "ordinary fresh chaff for burning," 1219:1–2 tuḫ-duru$_5$-sig$_5$ **bíl**-šè, "fine fresh chaff for burning," 511:'127-'128, 1150:1–2, 1162:'51-'52, 1218:1–2

bù(r), *nasāḫu*, "to cut, trim; to pull out"

gi bù(r), "to pull out reeds"

^{ĝeš}**ig bù(r)**, "to pull out a door"

1. **gi bù(r)**, "to pull out reeds (from a small plot)"

4 ĝuruš **gi bù-ra-dè** gub-ba, "4 workman employed to pull out reeds," 26:'19

2. ^{ĝeš}**ig bù(r)**, "to pull out a door"

3 ĝuruš šidim 1 ĝuruš 3 [géme] ^{ĝeš}**ig** šà é-a [**bu-ra**], "3 builders, 1 workman (and) 3 [workwomen having pulled out] a door in the house," 15:21–22

1 ĝuruš ašgab u$_4$-3-šè ^{ĝeš}**ig** šà é-a **bu-ra**, "1 leather worker for 3 days having pulled out a door in the house," 239:1–2

– D –

dab$_5$, *ṣabātu*, "to take in charge"

PN **ì-dab$_5$**, "taken in charge by PN" > *Personal Name Index*

a-da-làl
a-na-aḫ-ì-lí
^{d}*adad-tillati*
ak-ba-zum
aš-tá-qar
ba-la-a
ì-lí-an-dùl
ì-lí-aš-ra-ni
ì-lí-bi-la-ni
ilum-mu-tá-bíl
^{d}*ma-lik-ba-ni*
puzur$_4$-a-gu$_5$-um
si-mu
^{d}šára-kam

1. **Barley Not to Be Taken**

iti u$_4$-29-ba-zal še nu-ĝál bí-in-gi$_4$ u$_4$-1-àm mu-[un-ĝál] še šabra in-na-an-sum šu te-ĝe$_6$-dè **nu-un-dab$_5$**?, "At the end of the 29th day of the month there was no barley. (Someone) returned it. On the 1st day, it was there. (Then) the barley was given to the majordomo. In order for him to receive it, it will not (first) be taken (by someone else)," 1057:1–7

daĝ, *nagāšu*, "to wander, travel"

1. **Errands: Bringing the Man from the King**

1 ĝuruš ^{lú}ázlag u$_4$-25-šè *na-sìm* ^{lú}kíĝ-gi$_4$<-a>-lugal-ta lú te-te-dè **in-da-ĝe$_6$-en**, "1 fuller for 25 days. *Nasim*, the royal messenger, went to bring the man (i.e. the fuller) from the king," 222:1–5

dé, *šapāku*; *šaqû*, "to pour"

kaš-**dé-a**, "(beer) banquet" > **kaš-dé-a**

1. **kaš dé**, "to pour beer"

0.1.0. še-kaš 3 ^{dug}epig **kaš ba-an-dé** (. . .) árad-géme sugal$_7$-maḫ g̃ír-su^{ki}-šè du-ni, "60 liters of barley (for) beer (and) 3 drinking vessels, he poured the beer (and) {disbursed other comestibles} when the male and female servants of the sugal-maḫ came to G̃irsu," 449:2–5, 9–10

0.0.1. kaš-sig$_5$ 0.0.1. kaš-gen 0.4.0. kaš-ninda 5 sìla-ta **kaš ba-an-dé** *ri-im-ilum* sugal gaba-ri-a unug^{ki}-ta du-ni, "10 liters of fine beer, 10 liters of ordinary beer (and) 240 liters of beer (and) bread, 5 liters each; he poured the beer when *Rim-ilum*, the sugal, came from Uruk (for) a meeting," 517:1–6

de$_5$(g), *laqātu*, "to collect, gather up, glean"

1 (bùr) GÁNA zàr tab-ba **nu-de$_5$-de$_5$-ga**, "the sheaves stacked on 1 bur of acreage are not to be collected," 1398:1–3

de$_6$, *babālu*, "to bring, to carry"

1. **á-ág̃(-g̃á) de$_6$-a**, "having brought a message"

1.1 Messages Brought to *Aḫu-waqar*

1 *šu-^{d}belum* **á-ág̃** ki *a-ḫu-wa-qar* lú-du$_6$-lugal-pa-è^{ki} **de$_6$-a**, "*Šu-Belum* having brought a message to the place of *Aḫu-waqar*, the man from Du-lugal-pa'e," 45:28–29, 46:'44, 47:56, 48:62–63

1.2 Messages Brought to *Šu-Eštar*

1.2.1 E'igara and *Ḫilua*

1 *ḫi-lu-a* 1 é-ì-gára **á-ág̃** ki *šu-e*[*š$_4$-tár*-šè] **d**[**e$_6$-a**], "*Ḫilua* (and) E'igara having brought a message [to] the place of *Šu-Eštar*," 37:31–33

[1] é-ì-gára 1 *ḫi-lu-a* 1 **á-ág̃** ki *šu-eš$_4$-tár*-[šè] **de$_6$-a**, "E'igara (and) *Ḫilua* having brought a message [to] the place of *Šu-Eštar*," 38:37–39

1.2.2 *Ḫilua*

1 *ḫi-lu-a* **á-ág̃** *šu-eš$_4$-tár* ù-dag-ga^{ki}-šè **de$_6$-a**, "*Ḫilua* having brought a message to *Šu-Eštar* in Udaga," 43:'47, 45:24–25, 46:'42-'43, 47:55, 48:60–61

1 *ḫi-lu-a* **á-ág̃** [ki *š*]*u-eš$_4$-tár*-šè **de$_6$-a**, "*Ḫilua* having brought a message to [the place] of *Šu-Eštar*," 52:52–53, 53:55

1.3 Messages Brought to *Šu-Kabta*

1.3.1 A Builder

1 g̃uruš šidim **á-ág̃(-g̃á)** ki *šu-kab-ta*$_{(2)}$-šè **de$_6$-a**, "1 builder having brought a message to the place of *Šu-Kabta*," 2:19, 3:15, 4:20

1.3.2 E'igara

1 é-ì-gára **á-ág̃(-g̃á)** nibru^{ki}-šè ki *šu-kab-ta*-šè **de$_6$-a**, "E'igara having brought a mesage to the place of *Šu-Kabta* in Nippur," 31:40, 32:39, 33:43, 34:'17, 35:46

1 é-ì-gára **á-ág̃(-g̃á)** ki *šu-kab-tá*-šè **de$_6$-a**, "E'igara having brought a message to the place of *Šu-Kabta*," 36:41, 47:53–54, 48:58–59, 49:57, 50:'16-'17, 59:52, 60:48–49, 102:5, 103:5, 107:9, 108:6, 108:40, 109:6

1.3.3 E'igara and Companions

1 *i-ṭib-ší-na-at* 1 é-ì-gára **á-áĝ** ki *šu-kab-tá*-šè **de$_6$-a**, "*Iṭibšinat* and E'igara having brought a message to the place of *Šu-Kabta*," 43:'43-'44, 44:41–43, 46:'39-'41

1 *i-ṭib-ší-na-at* 1 é-ì-gára **á-áĝ** [ki] *šu-kab-tá*-ta ⌜**de$_6$**⌝**-a**, "*Iṭibšinat* (and) E'igara having brought a message from [the place] of *Šu-Kabta*," 45:22–23

1 é-ì-gára 1 *šu-^{d}belum* **á-áĝ(-ĝá)** ki *šu-kab-ta*-šè **de$_6$-a**, "E'igara (and) *Šu-Belum* having brought a message to the place of *Šu-Kabta*," 71:32–34, 110:7–8, 111:7–9

1 é-ì-gára 1 *šu*-^{d}nin-kar-ak **á-áĝ** ki *šu-kab-ta*-šè **de$_6$-a**, "E'igara (and) *Šu*-Ninkarak having brought a message to the place of *Šu-Kabta*," 106:6–8, 106:45–47

1 *be-lí-ì-lí* 1 é-ì-gára **á-áĝ-ĝá** ki *šu-kab-ta*-šè **de$_6$-a**, "*Beli-ili* and E'igara having brought a message to the place of *Šu-Kabta*," 123:8–10

1.3.4 *Šu-Belum*

1 *šu-^{d}belum* **á-áĝ-ĝá** ki *šu-kab-ta*-šè **de$_6$-a**, "*Šu-Belum* having brought a message to the place of *Šu-Kabta*," 39:45, 114:7–8

[1 *š*]*u-^{d}belum* [á-áĝ** ki] *šu-kab-t*[*a*-š]è šu?-x-[x?]-x ĜEŠ.KÚŠU[^{ki}-šè?] **de$_6$-[a]**, "*Šu-Belum* having brought [a message] to [the place of] *Šu-Kabta* (?) [in?] ĜEŠ.KÚŠU," 56:'36-'38

1.3.5 *Šu*-Ninkarak

1 *šu*-^{d}nin-kar-ak **á-áĝ** ki *šu-kab-ta*-šè **de$_6$-a**, "*Šu*-Ninkarak having brought a mesage to the place of *Šu-Kabta*," 104:7, 104:47, 105:7, 105:45

1.3.6 *Tatturi*

1 *ta-tù-ri* **á-áĝ** ki *šu-kab-ta*-šè nibru^{ki}-šè **de$_6$-a**, "*Tatturi* having brought a message to the place of *Šu-Kabta* in Nippur," 24:'25

1.3.7 Workmen

n ĝuruš **á-áĝ** ki *šu-kab-ta*-šè **de$_6$-a**, "n workmen having brought a message to the place of *Šu-Kabta*," 21:'28, 153:'36

1.3.8 Personal Name Lost

[1 PN] **á-áĝ** ki *šu-kab-ta*-šè **de$_6$-a**, "[PN] having brought a message to the place of *Šu-Kabta*," 162:30

1.4 Message Recipient Unspecified

1.4.1 Messages Brought to *Bit-Šu-Suen*

[n] ĝuruš **á-áĝ-ĝá** še túl-tur é-^{d}*šu*-^{d}*suen*^{ki}-šè **de$_6$<-a>**, "[n] workmen having brought a message to *Bit-Šu-Suen* concerning barley (and?) the small well," 175:28

1.4.2 Messages Brought to Ĝirsu

1 ĝuruš šidim **á-áĝ** ĝír-su^{ki}-šè **de$_6$-a**, "1 builder having brought a message to Ĝirsu," 20:34, 148:'22, 150:44

1 *ḫi-lu-a* **á-áĝ** ĝír-su^{ki}-šè **de$_6$-a**, "*Ḫilua* having brought a message to Ĝirsu," 24:'26, 25:'13, 27:'18, 26:'22, 28:'29, 29:'34

1.4.2.1 Messages Concerning Builders

1 lug[al-ḫ]a-ma-ti **á-á[g̃** ši]dim-e-ne g̃ír-su$^{[ki]}$-šè **de$_6$-a**, "Lugal-ḫamati having brought a message concerning builders to G̃irsu," 52:67–79

1 g̃uruš šidim lú-níg̃-^{d}ba-ú **á-ág̃** šidim-e-ne g̃ír-su^{ki}-šè **de$_6$-a**, "1 builder from Nig̃-Ba'u having brought a message concerning builders to G̃irsu," 52:71–73

1.4.3 Messages Brought to Nippur

n g̃uruš **á-ág̃(-g̃á)** nibru^{ki}-šè **de$_6$-a**, "n workmen having brought a message to Nippur," 150:41, 152:'23, 154:43, 160:'14, 161:'20

1.4.4 Messages Brought to Udaga

1 *ḫi-lu-a* **á-ág̃-[g̃á]** ù-dag-ga$^{<ki>}$-šè **de$_6$-a**, "*Ḫilua* having brought a message to Udaga," 44:46

1 *šu-eš$_4$-[tár]* **á-ág̃-g̃á** ù-[dag-ga]^{ki}-[šè **de$_6$-a**], "*Šu-Eštar* [having brought] a message [to] U[daga]," 54:31–32

1 *šu*-^{d}nin-kar-ak **á-ág̃-g̃á** ù-dag-ga^{ki}-šè **de$_6$-a**, "*Šu*-Ninkarak having brought a message to Udaga," 105:6, 105:45, 107:10, 107:'17, 108:7, 108:41, 109:7

1 g̃uruš **á-ág̃(-g̃á)** ù-dag-ga^{ki}-šè **de$_6$-a**, "1 workman having brought a message to Udaga," 148:'21, 150:43, 156:34, 157:21, 159:32

1.4.5 Location of Delivery Broken or Unspecified

1 *šu-eš$_4$-tár* [x-x-x]^{ki}-šè [x]-šè? **de$_6$-a**, "*Šu-Eštar* having brought (a message) to [GN] for? [x],"53:57

1 [PN] 1 *ḫi-lu-[a]* 1 *šu*-^{d}⌜*belum*⌝ **á-ág̃-g̃á** ki [. . .–šè **de$_6$-a**], "[PN], *Ḫilua* (and) *Šu-belum* [having brought] a message [to] the place of [. . .]," 54:'27-'30

n g̃uruš **á-ág̃(-g̃á) de$_6$-a**, "n workmen having brought a message," 102:32, 103:38, 109:36, 110:36, 111:43, 114:44, 123:44, 155:36, 174:29

2. To Bring: Commodities Away from Garšana

2.1 The Commodity Tax

2 g̃uruš ⌜u$_4$⌝-[1-š]è níg̃-gú-na é-d[a-na^{ki}-šè **d]e$_6$-a**, "2 workmen for [1] day having brought the commodity tax [to] Edana," 246:3–4

1 g̃uruš túg-du$_8$ u$_4$-6-šè še en-zu-bábbar$^{<ki>}$-ta 1 g̃uruš túg-du$_8$ u$_4$-6-šè níg̃-gú-na tum-ma-al^{ki}-šè **de$_6$-a** 1 g̃uruš túg-du$_8$ u$_4$-11-šè níg̃-gú-na é-da-na^{ki}-šè **de$_6$-a** 1 g̃uruš túg-du$_8$ u$_4$-6-šè níg̃-gú-na nag̃-su^{ki}-ta **de$_6$-a**, "1 braider for 6 days (having brought) barley from Enzu-babbar, 1 braider for 6 days having brought the commodity tax to Tumal, 1 braider for 11 days having brought the commodity tax to Edana (and) 1 braider for 6 days having brought the commodity tax from Nag̃su," 267:1–11

2.2 Oil to Nippur

0.0.1.1 sìla ì-g̃eš ⌜lá⌝-ìa šà ì-g̃eš 2.0.0. gur-kam gar-ša-an-na^{ki}-ta nibru^{ki}-šè **in-de$_9$-ša-a**, "11 liters of sesame oil, the remainder of 2 bushels that they brought from Garšana to Nippur," 1062:1–4

2.3 Tablets

2.3.1 The Tablet of *Iddin-Adad* Brought to Nippur

1 *ḫi-lu-a* dub *i-din-*^{d}*adad* nibru^{ki}-šè **de$_6$-a**, "*Ḫilua* having brought the tablet of *Iddin-Adad* to Nippur," 33:44, 34:'18, 35:47, 36:42, 39:44, 40:42

2.3.2 The Tablet of *Malik-bani* to Edana

1 *be-lí-ì-lí* 1 *šu-*^{d}nin-kar-ak dub ^{d}*ma-lik-ba-ni* é-[da]-na^{ki}-šè **de$_6$-a**, "*Beli-ili* and *Šu*-Ninkarak having brought the tablet of *Malik-bani* to Edana," 51:'22-'24, 52:59–62, 53:61–63, 56:'32-'35

2.4 Textiles to Nippur

3 g̃uruš túg nibru^{ki}-šè **de$_6$-a**, "3 workmen having brought textiles to Nippur," 148:'20

2.5 Commodity Uncertain

5 g̃uruš sag̃-t[ag 1+]1 g̃uruš á-⅔ 1 g̃uruš á-½ 1 g̃uruš á-⅓ u$_4$-2-šè gar-ša-an-na^{ki}-ta tum-ma-al^{ki}-šè x x a 140-àm **de$_6$-a**, "5 full-time workmen, 2 workmen at ⅔ wages, 1 workman at ½ wages (and) 1 workman at ⅓ wages for 2 days having brought 140 (?) from Garšana to Tumal," 266:1–7

5 g̃uruš sag̃-tag 2 g̃uruš á-[⅔ 1] g̃uruš [á]-½ [1 g̃uruš á-⅓ u$_4$]-5-šè tum-ma-al$^{[ki]}$ **de$_6$-a**, "5 full-time workmen, 2 workmen at [⅔] wages, [1] workman at ½ [wages] (and) [1 workman at ⅓ wages] for 5 [days] having brought (items) (to/from?) Tumal," 266:8–12

3. To Bring: Commodities to Garšana

3.1 Barley

3.1.1 From *Bit-Šu-Suen*

0.4.4.5 sìla [še?] 0.0.3. zíz 0.0.1. kib$_x$ *dan-ḫi-li* ⌜^{lú}lùnga⌝ in-⌜da⌝-g̃ál še é-^{d}*šu-*^{d}*suen*^{ki}-ta **de$_6$-a**, "285 liters of [barley?], 30 liters of emmer wheat (and) 10 liters of wheat are with *Danḫili*, the brewer, who brought barley from *Bit-Šu-Suen*," 1065:1–6

3.1.2 From Du-saḫara

2 g̃uruš ad-kub$_4$ 1½ g̃uruš báḫar u$_4$-5-šè [še] du$_6$-saḫar-ra^{ki}-ta gar-ša-an-na^{ki}-šè **de$_6$-a**, "2 reed craftsmen (and) 1½ potters for 5 days having brought [barley] from Du-saḫara to Garšana," 233:4–8

3.1.3 From the Kabbi Village

2 g̃uruš ad-kub$_4$ u$_4$-20-šè še é-duru$_5$-kab-bí-ta gar-ša-an-na^{ki}-šè **de$_6$-a**, "2 reed craftsmen for 20 days having brought barley from the Kabbi village to Garšana," 300:1–4

4 géme kíkken u$_4$-20-šè še é-duru$_5$-kab-bi^{ki}-ta gar-ša-an-na^{ki}-šè **de$_6$-a**, "4 female millers for 20 days having brought barley from the Kabbi village to Garšana," 301:1–3

[n g̃uruš] túg-d[u$_8$ u$_4$]-20-[šè še é]-duru$_5$-kab-bi[^{ki}-ta g̃ar]-ša-an-na^{ki}-[šè] **de$_6$-a**, "[n] braider(s) [for] 20 [days] having brought [barley from] the Kabbi village [to] Garšana," 302:1–3

3 géme uš-bar u$_4$-20-šè še é-duru$_5$-ka[b-bí]-ta gar-š[a-an]-n[a^{k}]^{i}-šè [**de$_6$**]-**a**, "3 female weavers for 20 days having [brought] barley from the Kabbi village to Garšana," 303:1–4

3 géme uš-bar 3 géme kíkken 1 g̃uruš lú-kíkken 1 g̃uruš túg-du$_8$ 2 g̃uruš ašgab 2 g̃uruš ad-kub$_4$ u$_4$-20-šè še é-duru$_5$-kab-bi-ta gar-ša-an-na^{ki}-šè **mu-un-de$_9$-sa-a**, "3 female weavers, 3 female millers, 1 miller, 1 braider, 2 leather workers (and) 2 reed craftsmen for 20 days who brought barley from the Kabbi village to Garšana," 304:1–10

[n g̃uru]š ašgab [u$_4$]-20-šè [še é]-duru$_5$-kab-bi-ta^{ki} [gar-ša]-an-na^{ki}<-šè> **de$_6$-a**, "[n] leather worker(s) for 20 [days] having brought [barley] from the Kabbi village to Garšana," 305:1–4

3.1.4 From Ekabba and Karkar

9 g̃uruš sag̃-tag 1 g̃uruš á-⅔ 1 g̃uruš á-⅓ ^{lú}ázlag-me-éš u$_4$-1-šè še é-kab-ba^{ki} ⸢karkar⸣^{ki}-ta ⸢g̃ar-ša-an-na⸣⸢^{ki}⸣-šè **de$_6$-a**, "9 full-time fullers, 1 fuller at ⅔ wages, (and) 1 fuller at ⅓ wages for 1 day having brought barley from Ekabba (and) Karkar <to> Garšana," 237:1–8

3.1.5 From the Fortified Tower of *Dada*

10 géme kíkken u$_4$-1-šè a-rá-1-kam 10 géme kíkken u$_4$-1-šè a-rá-2-kam 10 géme kíkken u$_4$-1-šè a-rá-3-kam še an-za-qar-*da-da*-ta gar-ša-an-na^{ki}-šè **de$_6$-a**, "10 female millers for 1 day for the 1st time, 10 female millers for 1 day for the 2nd time (and) 10 female millers for 1 day for the 3rd time having brought barley from the fortified tower of *Dada* to Garšana," 296:1–9

2 g̃uruš [ašgab] u$_4$-[1-šè] a-rá-1-[kam] 2 g̃uruš ašgab [u$_4$-1-šè] a-rá-2-kam 2 g̃uruš ašgab u$_4$-1-šè a-rá-3-kam 2 g̃uruš ašgab u$_4$-1-šè a-rá-4-kam 2 g̃uruš ašgab u$_4$-1-šè a-rá-5-kam še an-za-qar-*da-da*-[ta] gar-ša-an-na^{ki}-šè **de$_6$-a**, "2 [leather] workers [for 1] day having brought barley [from] the fortified tower of *Dada* to Garšana (on) {5 different occasions}," 297:1–14

3.1.6 From *Šu-Suen*-ammara

8 g̃uruš sag̃-tag 2 g̃uruš á-⅔-ta 4 g̃uruš á-½ ta ^{lú}ázlag-me-éš [u$_4$]-1-šè ⸢še⸣ ^{d}*šu*-^{d}*suen*-am-ma-ar^{ki}-ta **de$_6$-a** íb-[ga$_6$], "8 full-time fullers, 2 fullers at ⅔ wages, (and) 4 fullers at ½ wages for 1 [day carried] barley brought from *Šu-Suen*-ammara," 248:1–6

3 géme g̃eš-ì-sur-sur u$_4$-1-šè še ^{d}*šu*-^{d}*suen*-am-ma-ar^{ki}-ta **de$_6$-a** íb-ga$_6$, "3 female oil pressers for 1 day carried barley brought from *Šu-Suen*-ammara," 249:1–3

3.1.7 From *Šu-Suen*-ammara and Bad-gazi

1 g̃uruš ašgab 1 g̃uruš ad-kub$_4$ 1 géme kíkken u$_4$-[2]7-šè še, ^{d}*šu*-^{d}*suen*-<am->ma-ra$^{[ki]}$ ù bàd-ga-zi^{ki}-⸢ta⸣ gar-ša-an-na^{ki}-šè **de$_6$-a**, "1 leather worker, 1 reed craftsman (and) 1 female miller for [2]7 days having brought barley from *Šu-Suen*-ammara and Bad-gazi to Garšana," 259:1–7

3.1.8 From *Darra'um*

0.4.0. še á má ḫug̃-g̃á [40-gur-kam] ù má-la[ḫ$_5$-bi] á 0.1.2.-ta u$_4$-3-šè še *dar-ra-um*^{ki}-⸢ta⸣ gar-ša-an-na^{ki}-[šè] **de$_6$-[a]**, "240 liters of barley as wages (for) the hired [40 bushel] boat and [its] sailors, wages of 80 liters each for 3 days (for sailors) having brought barley from *Darra'um* [to] Garšana," 462:1–6

3.1.9 From Udaga

[n] g̃uruš tú[g-d]u$_8$ u$_4$-9-šè še ù-dag-ga^{ki}-ta gar-ša-an-na^{ki}-šè **de$_6$-a** ù kar-[ta] g̃á-nun-šè íb-⸢ga$_6$⸣, "[n] braider(s) for 9 days having brought barley from Udaga to Garšana and carried it [from] the quay to the storehouse," 261:1–6

3 g̃uruš ašgab 2 g̃uruš ad-kub$_4$ 2 g̃uruš ^{lú}ázlag 15⅓ géme uš-bar 6 géme kíkken 2 géme g̃eš-ì-sur-sur u$_4$-10-šè še ù-dag-ga^{ki}-ta gar-ša-an-na^{ki}-šè **de$_6$-a**, "3 leather workers, 2 reed craftsmen, 2 fullers, 15⅓ female weavers, 6 female millers (and) 2 female oil pressers for 10 days having brought barley from Udaga to Garšana," 287:1–9

2 g̃uruš [ad-kub$_4$ u$_4$]-10-šè ⸢še⸣ ù-dag-ga^{ki}-t[a gar-ša]-an-na^{ki}-šè **de$_6$-a**, "2 [reed craftsmen] for 10 [days] having brought barley from Udaga to Garšana," 288:1–4

6 géme kíkken u$_4$-10-šè še ù-dag-ga^{ki}-ta gar-ša-an-na^{ki}-šè **de$_6$-a** 6 géme kíkken u$_4$-[n-šè] še [GN-ta GN-šè **de$_6$-a**], "6 female millers for 10 days having brought barely from Udaga to Garšana (and) 6 female millers for [n] day(s), [having brought] barley [from GN to GN]," 289:1–8

16⅓ géme uš-bar u$_4$-10-šè še ù-dag-ga^{ki}-ta gar-ša-an-na^{ki}-šè **de$_6$-a**, "16⅓ female weavers for 10 days having brought barley from Udaga to Garšana," 290:1–4

[1.1.4.] še gur [á má-ḫug̃]-g̃á má 50-gur-ta 2-kam ù má-laḫ$_5$-bi [0].1.2.5 sìla-ta [á] 0.0.2.5 sìla-ta á má-ḫug̃-g̃á má 40-gur-ta 2-kam ù má-laḫ$_5$-bi á 0.0.2.-ta [u$_4$]-8-šè ⸢še⸣ ù-dag-ga^{ki}-ta [gar-ša]-an-na^{ki}-šè **de$_6$-a**, "[1] bushel (and) 100 liters of barley, [wages] (for) each of 2 hired 50-bushel boats and their sailors, 85 liters each; [wages] of 25 liters each, wages (for) each of 2 hired 40-bushel boats and their sailors, 20 liters each; (wages for sailors) for 8 [days] having brought barley from Udaga to Garšana," 414:1–11

[. . .] 0.1.0.8 s[ìla š]e-bi sa$_{10}$ má-laḫ$_5$-e-ne 6.1.1.4 sìla še gur še ù-dag-ga[^{ki}-ta gar]-ša-an-na[^{ki}-šè] **de$_6$-[a]**, "[. . . (and)] 68 liters of barley is the (hiring) price of the sailors. (In total:) 6 bushels (and) 74 liters of barley having been brought [from] Udaga [to] Garšana," 553:54–59

3.1.10 From Ur-Šulpa'e

14 g̃uruš še ki ur-^{d}šul-pa-UD.⸢DU⸣-ta **de$_6$-a** kar-ta gur$_7$-šè íb-[ga$_6$], "14 workmen, having brought barley from Ur-Šulpa'e, [carried] it from the quay to the granary," 192:'18-'19

3.1.11 Origin Broken

1⅔ g̃uruš ašg[ab] u$_4$-4-⸢šè⸣ še [GN]^{ki}-ta gar-[ša-an-na^{ki}]-šè **de$_6$-a**, "1⅔ leather workers for 4 days having brought barley from [GN] to Garšana," 229:1–4

3.2 Fish from Du-lugalpa'e

3 sìla ninda lú ku$_6$ du$_6$-lugal-pa-è^{ki}-ta **de$_6$-a** u$_4$ é-e im sumur ba-aka, "3 liters of bread (for) the man who brought fish from Du-lugalpa'e when the house was plastered," 476:1–4

3.3 Oil, Origin Unspecified

2 g̃uruš ad-kub$_4$ u$_4$-1-šè ì **de$_6$-a** a-rá-1-kam, "2 reed craftsmen for 1 day having brought oil for the 1st time," 285:4–6, 286:4–6

2 g̃uruš túg-du$_8$ u$_4$-1-šè ì **de$_6$-a** a-rá-1-kam, "2 braiders for 1 day having brought oil for the 1st time," 306: 6–8

3.4 Reeds

3.4.1 From the Šara Temple

1⅔ ĝuruš ašgab 1 ĝuruš túg-du$_8$ 1 ĝuruš simug u$_4$-1-šè ⸢gi⸣ ù gi-zi é-^{d}šára-ta gar-ša-an-na^{ki}-šè [**de$_6$**]**-a**, "1 leather worker, 1 braider (and) 1 smith for 1 day having [brought] reeds and fresh reeds from the Šara temple to Garšana," 232:1–7

3.4.2 From Udaga

1 ĝuruš ašgab 1 ĝuruš ad-kub$_4$ 1½ ĝuruš báḫar 1 ĝuruš simug 1 ĝuruš túg-du$_8$ u$_4$-10-še gi-izi ù-dag^{ki}-ga-ta gar-ša-an-na^{ki}-šè [**de$_6$**]**-a**, "1 leather worker, 1 reed craftsman, 1½ potters, 1 smith (and) 1 braider for 10 days having [brought] fuel reeds from Udaga to Garšana," 230:1–9

3 ĝuruš saĝ-tag 1 ĝuruš á-⅔ ^{lú}ázlag-me-éš u$_4$-10-šè gi-izi ù-dag^{ki}-ga-ta [gar-š]a-an-na^{ki}-šè **de$_6$-a**, "3 full-time fullers (and) 1 fuller at ⅔ wages for 10 days having brought fuel reeds from Udaga to Garšana," 231:1–6

3.4.3 Reeds and a Container of Seedlings

1 ĝuruš u$_4$-1-šè gi-zi ĜEŠ.KÚŠU^{ki}-[ta] **de$_6$-[a** n] ĝuruš u$_4$-[n-šè] ḫar lam ^{ĝeš}ù-suḫ$_5$ ke$_4$-[dè] ^{d}gu$_4$-an-na-⸢ta⸣ gar-ša-an-na^{ki}-šè ⸢**de$_6$**⸣**-[a]**, "1 worker for 1 day having brought fresh reeds [from] ĜEŠ.KÚŠU, (and) [n] workmen for [n] day(s) having brought a seedling container of pine trees from Guanna to Garšana," 272:8–15

3.4.4 Reeds and Straw

[n ĝuruš] gi-zi [é-^{d}]šára-ta [gar-ša-an]-na^{ki}-šè **de$_6$-a** [in-u] é-ù-ri-a^{ki}-ta [ka i$_7$ UD].DU-šè **de$_6$-a**, "[n workmen] having brought fresh reeds from the Šara [temple] to Garšana (and) having brought [straw] from E-uri'a to [the opening] of the 'Out-going' canal," 193:29–32

3.5 Semolina from *Izin-Erra*

60 ninda-gúg-zì-KAL 3 sìla ni[nda-š]u-ra-gen lú-*i-zi-in-èr-ra*^{ki} ke$_4$-dè u$_4$ dabin *i-zi-in-*[*èr-ra*]^{ki}-ta gar-ša-an-na^{ki}-šè **de$_6$-a**, "The man of *Izin-Erra* (was assigned) to make 60 cakes of KAL-flour (and) 3 liters of ordinary half (loaf) bread, when semolina was brought from *Izin-Erra* to Garšana," 495:1–5

3.6 Straw

3.6.1 From the Agili Field

40 ĝuruš u$_4$-1-šè še 6 sìla-ta ba-ḫuĝ a-šà a-gi-li-⸢ta⸣ gar-⸢ša⸣-an-na^{ki}-šè in-u **de$_6$-a**, "40 workmen were hired for 1 day for 6 liters of barley each having brought straw (from) the Agili field to Garšana," 443:1–5

3.6.2 From *Šu-Suen*-ammara

6 ĝuruš in-u [^{d}*šu*]-^{d}*suen*-am-ma-ar-ra^{ki}-ta **de$_6$-a** kar-ta ĝá-nun-šè íb-ga$_6$, "6 workmen, having brought straw from *Šu-Suen*-ammara, carried it from the quay to the storehouse," 198:'28

3.6.3 Origin Broken or Unspecified

15 ĝuruš in-u **de$_6$-a** ĝen-na, "15 workmen having come back (with) straw," 150:40

[. . .]-*um*-ta [. . . š]è in-u ⸢**de$_6$**⸣**-a**, "[. . .] having brought straw from [. . .] to [. . .]," 197:33

3.7 Textiles from Nippur

1 ĝuruš ^{lú}ázlag nibru^{ki}-ta gar-ša-an-na^{ki}-šè túg **de$_6$-a** kaskal šu+níĝin-na-bi u$_4$-4-àm, "1 fuller having brought textiles from Nippur to Garšana, a trip of 4 days in total," 224 :1–6

3.8 Wool from *Bit-Šu-Suen*

4 ĝuruš saĝ-tag 1 ĝuruš á-⅔ ^{lú}ázlag-me-éš u$_4$-2-šè siki é-^{d}*šu*-^{d}*suen*^{ki}-ta **de$_6$-a,** "4 full-time workmen (and) 1 workman at ⅔ wages, fullers for 2 days having brought wool from *Bit-Šu-Suen*," 241:1–4

8 ĝuruš ^{lú}ázlag u$_4$-1-šè siki é-^{d}*šu*-^{d}*suen*- ta gar-ša-an-n[a^{ki}]-šè **mu-un-de$_9$-sa-a,** "8 fullers for 1 day who brought wool from *Bit-Šu-Suen* to Garšana," 243:1–4

8 géme u$_4$-1-šè [siki] igi saĝ-ĝá šà é-^{d}*šu*-^{d}*suen*^{ki}-ka **de$_6$-a,** "8 workwomen for 1 day having brought [wool] sorted in *Bit-Šu-Suen*," 279:1–3

2 ĝuruš ad-kub$_4$ u$_4$-1-šè a-rá-2-kam 2 ĝuruš ad-kub$_4$ u$_4$-1-šè a-rá-3-kam siki **de$_6$-a** é-^{d}*šu*-^{d}*suen*^{ki}-ta gar-ša-an-na^{ki}-šè (ĝen-a), "2 reed craftsmen for 1 day for the 2nd time, 2 reed craftsmen for 1 day for the 3rd time having brought wool, (reed craftsmen having gone) from *Bit-Šu-Suen* to Garšana," 285:7–13, 286:7–13

2 ĝuruš túg-du$_8$ u$_4$-1-šè ⌜siki⌝ **de$_6$-a** a-rá-2-kam é-^{d}*šu*-^{d}*suen*^{ki}-ta gar-ša-an-na^{ki}-šè ĝen-a, "2 braiders for 1 day having brought wool for the 2nd time, (braiders) having gone from *Bit-Šu-Suen* to Garšana," 306:9–13

4. To Bring: Commodities Transferred between Various Places outside Garšana

4.1 Barley

4.1.1 From *Dimbun*-Ašgi to the Kabbi Village

3 ĝuruš ašgab 2 ĝuruš ad-kub$_4$ 1 ĝuruš túg-du$_8$ 5 géme uš-bar 6 géme ḪAR.[ḪAR] 2 géme ĝeš-ì-[sur-sur] u$_4$-1-[šè] še *dì-im-bu-na*-^{d}àš-gi$_5$-ta é-duru$_5$-kab-bi-šè(!) <**de$_6$-**>**a,** "3 leather workers, 2 reed craftsmen, 1 braider, 5 female weavers, 6 female millers (and) 2 female oil pressers [for] 1 day having brought barley from *Dimbun*-Ašgi to the Kabbi village," 287:10–18

5 géme uš-bar u$_4$-1-šè še *dì-im-bu-na*-^{d}àš-gi$_5$-ta [é]-duru$_5$-kab-bí$^{<ki>}$-šè **de$_6$-a,** "5 female weavers for 1 day having brought barley from *Dimbun*-Ašgi to the Kabbi village," 290:5–8

4.1.2 To Udaga

[1 ĝuruš u$_4$-n]-šè še ù-dag-ga^{ki}-šè **de$_6$-a,** "[1 workman] for [n day(s)] having brought barley to Udaga," 162:31

4.2 Earth Brought to Zabala for the Houses of the Gardeners

[*ak-b*]*a-zum* nu-^{ĝeš}kiri$_6$-⌜ke$_4$⌝ má-lugal-na saḫar tùm-dè zabala$_4$^{ki}-šè in-la-aḫ saḫar **mu-un-de$_9$** ^{ĝeš}kiri$_6$-lugal-na-šè nu-un-ni-ku$_4$ é-ni-šè ba-an-dé ka-ga-na ba-ge-en, "*Akbazum*, the gardener, confirmed that they took a boat of his master to Zabala in order to bring dirt, that he brought the dirt, that it did not enter the garden of his master but was brought for his (own) house," 1049:1–10

^{d}ba-ú-da [nu]-^{ĝeš}kiri$_6$-ke$_4$ má-lugal-na saḫar tùm-dè zabala$_4$^{ki}-šè in-la-aḫ saḫar **mu-un-de$_9$** ^{ĝeš}kiri$_6$-lugal-na nu-un-ni-ku$_4$ é-ni-šè ba-an-dé ka-ga-na ba-ge-en, "Ba'uda, the gardener, confirmed that they took a boat of his master to Zabala in order to bring dirt, that he brought the dirt, that it did not enter the garden of his master but was brought for his (own) house," 1050:1–10

4.3 Reeds

4.3.1 Reeds from Da-*siḫum* and the Commoditiy Tax to Zabala

5 géme u$_4$-1-[šè] gi da-*si-ḫu-um*-ta **de$_6$-a** 4 géme u$_4$-1-šè níĝ-gú-na zabala$_4$$^{[ki]}$-šè **d[e$_6$-a]**, "5 workwomen [for] 1 day having brought reeds from Da-*siḫum* (and) 4 workwomen for 1 day having brought the commodity tax to Zabala," 258:1–6

4.3.2 Reeds to Zabala

2 ĝuruš u$_4$-1-[šè] gi zabala$_4$$^{[ki]}$-[šè] **de$_6$-[a]**, "2 workmen [for] 1 day having brought reeds [to] Zabala," 246:8–9

4.4 A Sheep and Cattle Brand from Nippur to *Šu-Suen-ṭabu*

1 ĝuruš ^{lú}ázlag nibru^{ki}-ta ^{d}*šu*-^{d}*suen*-DU$_{10}$^{ki}-šè, ^{urudu}šim-da gu$_4$-udu **de$_6$-a** kaskal šu+níĝin-na-bi u$_4$-11-kam u$_4$ *šu-kab-tá* é-dam-*zé-ra-ra* šu sum-mu-dè ì-ĝen-na-a "1 fuller having brought a sheep and cattle brand from Nippur to *Šu-Suen-ṭabu*, a trip of 11 days in total, when *Šu-Kabta* went to the house of the wife of *Zerara* in order to take inventory," 219:1–10

4.5 Wool: from *Bit-Šu-Suen* to Nippur

1 ĝuruš ^{lú}ázlag saĝ-tag u$_4$-2-šè u$_4$-2-šè 2 ĝuruš saĝ-tag 2 ĝuruš á-½-ta u$_4$-2-šè siki é-^{d}*šu*-^{d}*suen*^{ki}-ta nibru^{ki}-šè <<DU>> **de$_6$-a**, "1 full-time fuller for 2 days (and) 2 full-time workmen (and) 2 half-time workmen having brought wool from *Bit-Šu-Suen* to Nippur," 226:1–8

3 ĝuruš ^{lú}ázlag siki é-^{d}*šu*-^{d}*suen*^{ki}-ka-ta nibru^{ki}-šè **de$_6$-a** kaskal šu+níĝin-na-bi u$_4$-10!-kam u$_4$-2 kaš-dé-[a] á-⸢ki⸣-ti šu-numun, "3 fullers having brought wool from *Bit-Šu-Suen* to Nippur, a trip of 10 days in total, on day 2 of the banquet of the Akiti festival of month 4," 240:1–6

5. To Bring: Destination and Origin of Transfer Unspecified

5.1 Pigs

★★[2] šáḫ-munus-ama-gan-da-bi **de$_6$-a** 2 sìla-ta {indent} 2 ⸢še⸣-bi 0.2.0. [šà-ga]l šáḫ-niga, "[2] female breeding pigs having been brought at 2 liters each; (total:) 2 (pigs). Their barley equivalent for the fodder of the fattened pigs is 180 liters," 1189:7–10

5.2 Roof Beams

(. . .) u$_4$ ĝeš ùr **i-im-de$_6$-a**, "{delivery of date palm spines and a rope} when the roof beams were brought," 1306:6

5.3 The Royal Consignment

★★[PN] ^{lú}kíĝ-gi$_4$-a-lugal [x].GA.URU ⸢níĝ⸣-šu-taka$_4$-lugal **[mu]-un-de$_9$-a**, "[PN], the royal messenger, who brought (?), the royal consignment," 484:11–13

5.4 A Sealed Tablet[2]

[n.n.n.n sìl]a ḫašḫur-duru$_5$ gur ⸢*ilum*⸣-*ra-pi$_5$* dam-gàr šu ba-ti níĝ-kas$_7$-aka-ta ^{d}ba-ú-da ba-⸢na⸣-zi kìšib *ilum-ra-pi$_5$* **u$_4$-um-de$_6$** kìšib ^{d}ba-ú-da zi-re-dam, "*Ilum-rapi*, the merchant, received [n] bushel(s) (and) [n] liter(s) of fresh apples which Ba'uda expended

2 Reading u$_4$-um-de$_6$ according to a suggestion by H. Waetzoldt (personal communication). Note similar spellings at Umma, MVN 16, 1037 and 1530.

from the account for him. When the sealed tablet of *Ilum-rapi* is brought, Ba'uda's sealed tablet will be canceled," 1173:1–10

1470 sa gi-zi gu-níĝin 10-sa-ta gu-níĝin-bi 147-àm ᵈ*adad-tillati* šu ba-ti ki *puzur*$_4$-ᵈen-líl-ta ba-zi ĝìri *a-ḫu-wa-qar* dub-sar kìšib *a-ḫu-wa-qar-ra*! **u$_4$-um-de$_6$** kìšib *puzur*$_4$-ᵈen-líl zi-re-dam, "Under the authority of *Aḫu-waqar*, the scribe, *Adad-tillati* received from *Puzur*-Enlil 1470 bundles of fresh reeds, bales of 10 bunches each, its bales are 147. When the sealed tablet of *Aḫu-waqar* is brought, *Puzur*-Enlil's sealed tablet will be canceled," 1361:1–12

5.5 Textiles

(. . .) ⌜túg⌝-gen-kam **ì-in-⌜DU⌝**? 1 ᵗᵘ́ᵍsaĝ-uš-bar sa-gi$_4$-[àm], "{assorted textiles}. He delivered the ordinary textiles, they are finished uš-bar textiles," 609:8–9 (envelope)

6. Other: 'Incoming' Labor

(. . .) á **de$_6$-a** ad-kub$_4$ taḫ-ḫe-dam mu–2-kam, "{assorted mats, baskets, and other finished reed products}; 'incoming' labor of the reed craftsmen, to be added (to) the 2-year (account)," 1381:66–69

diri(g), *neqelpû*, "to float, glide (along/down)"

⌜ka⌝ i$_7$ è-ta [gar-ša-an]-naᵏⁱ-šè má di[ri-ga], "{boats} having floated from the opening of the 'Outgoing' canal to Garšana," 195:'21–'22

76 ĝuruš 4 má-10-gur-ta gar-ša-an-naᵏⁱ-ta karkarᵏⁱ-šè gíd-da u$_4$-1-àm má ĝar-ra u$_4$-⅔-àm má **diri-ga** gu-níĝin-bi 647½, "76 workmen towed 4 10-bushel boats from Garšana to Karkar, the one-day boat was placed (i.e. loaded with shok), the ⅔ day boat "floated," (in total: they transported) 647½ bales," 236:7–12

[. . .] á-ĝuruš-[a . . .] 0.0.1.6 sìla še-bi sa$_{10}$ má-laḫ$_5$-e-ne u$_4$-1-[šè] é-duru$_5$-kab-⌜bí⌝-ta é-duru$_5$-*simat*-ᵈ*ištaran*-šè má **diri-ga**, "[. . .] wages of workmen [. . .], 16 liters of barley is the (hiring) price of the sailors [for] 1 day having floated boats from the Kabbi village to the *Simat-Ištaran* village," 561:'1-'5

(. . .) [gú] i$_7$-⌜*ma*⌝-*an-iš-ti-šu*-ta gar-ša-an-naᵏⁱ-⌜šè⌝ má **diri-ga** da-na-bi 9-àm, "{barley in boats} having floated from the [bank] of the *Maništišu* canal to Garšana, (a distance of) 9 double-miles," 561:'41-'44

dú(TU), *marāṣu*, "to be sick"

1. Rations for Sick Workers

½ sìla ì-[ĝeš] *tu-ku-lí* šidim u$_4$ **dú-ra** i-[me-a], "½ liter of sesame oil (for) *Tukulli*, the builder, when he was sick," 444:1–2

[n] gín ì-ĝeš-ta ᵈšára-sá-ĝu$_{10}$ 1 *bu-za-du-a* géme kíkken-me-éš u$_4$ **dú-ra** i-me é-gal?-šè, "[n] shekel(s) of sesame oil each (for) Šara-saĝu (and) *Buzadua*, female millers, when they were sick at the palace," 466:3–7

2. Sick Builders

1 ĝuruš šidim **dú-ra**, "1 sick builder," 5:25, 6:24, 31:43, 35:49, 102:35, 189:31, 202:30

2 ĝuruš šidim **dú-ra**, "2 sick builders," 36:38, 85:11, 215:'4

1 *en-ni-ma* šidim **dú-ra**, "*Enima*, the sick builder" > *Personal Name Index*

1 *šu*-ma-ma šidim **dú-ra**, "*Šu*-Mama, the sick builder" > *Personal Name Index*

n ĝuruš šidim **dú-ra** n ĝuruš zàḫ ugula *i-ri-ib*, "n sick builder(s) (and) n runaway workmen supervised by *Irib*" > *Personal Name Index*

3. Sick Workmen

n ĝuruš **dú-ra**, "n sick workmen," 10:22, 13:'21, 15:36, 92:16, 93:'31, 94:33, 95:28, 96:'8, 97:'23, 98:'26, 99:28, 100:'32, 101:34, 103:40, 109:37, 110:38, 111:46, 114:48, 115:'26, 117:35, 118:28, 119:25, 120:'37, 121:37, 123:47, 125:39, 126:35, 128:37, 129:41, 130:'21, 132:39, 133:38, 134:19, 135:38, 136:44, 140:46, 141:41, 142:37, 143:44, 145:45, 146:'46, 147:50, 148:'23, 150:46, 156:36, 157:24, 158:44, 159:34 160:'19, 161:'25, 162:33, 173:32, 174:31, 186:'10, 194:60, 205:34, 206:28, 207:29, 209:35

1 [ĝuruš] **dú-ra-a**, "1 sick [workman]," 36:49

3.1 From the Gang of *Abiati*

1 ĝuruš **dú-ra** *a-bí-a-ti* nu-bànda-gu$_4$, "1 sick workman (from the gang of) *Abiati*, the ox-herder" > *Personal Name Index*

3.2 From the Gang of *Beli-ili*

1 ĝuruš **dú-ra** ugula *be-lí-ì-lí*, "1 sick workman, supervised by *Beli-ili*" > *Personal Name Index*

1 ar-ri-az **dú-ra** ugula *be-lí-ì-lí*, "*Arriaz*, the sick (workman), supervised by *Beli-ili*" > *Personal Name Index*

1 *en-nim-ma* šidim 1 *šál-maḫ* šidim **dú-ra-me-éš** 1 *e-pe-eš* **na-am-dú-ra** ugula *be-lí-ì-lí*, "*Enima* (and) *Šal-maḫ*, sick builders, (and) 1 (workman) satisfying the allowance of sick leave, supervised by *Beli-ili*," 24:'28-'31

3.3 From the Gang of *Ilum-dan*

1 ĝuruš **dú-ra** 2 ĝuruš zàḫ ugula *ilum-dan*, "1 sick workman (and) 2 runaways, supervised by *Ilum-dan*" > *Personal Name Index*

3.4 From the Gang of *Irib*

1 PN **dú-ra** ugula *i-ri-ib*, "PN, the sick (workman), supervised by *Irib*" > *Personal Name Index*

ar-ri-az	šeš-kal-la	*ta-tù-ri*
be-lí-a-sú	*šu-eš$_4$-tar*	

1 *be-[lí]-a-sú* 1 *e-pe-eš* ^{na}nam!?<-dú?-ra?> ugula *i-[ri]-ib* 1 géme lú-du$_6$-lugal-pa-è$^{\langle ki\rangle}$ **⸢dú⸣-ra-m[e-é]š**, "*Beli-asu*, satisfying the allowance of sick leave, supervised by *Irib* (and) 1 workwoman, a worker from Du-lugal-pa'e, sick workers," 36:44–47

3.5 From the Gang of *Malik-tillati*

1 ĝuruš **dú-ra** ^{d}*ma-li[k-til]lati* nu-bànda-gu$_4$ ugula *nu-úr-^{d}adad* šabra, "1 sick workman (from the gang of) *Malik-tillati*, the ox-herder, supervised by *Nur-Adad*, the majordomo," 195:'28-'29, 196:'31-'32, 197:40–41

1 ĝuruš **dú-ra** *šu-*^{d}dumu-zi nu-bànda-g[u$_4$ 1 ĝuruš] **dú-ra** 1 *ú-bar-⸢um⸣* 1 *bí-za-⸢tum⸣* 1 *šu-^{d}⸢adad⸣* 1 AN.TAG.⸢KAL⸣ ^{d}*ma-lik-tillati* [nu-bànda]-gu$_4$ ugula *nu-úr-^{d}adad* šabra, "1 sick workman (from the gang of) *Šu*-Dumuzi, the ox-herder, [1] sick [workman], *Ubarum*, *Bizatum*, *Šu-Adad*, (and) AN.TAG.KAL (workers from the gang of) *Malik-tillati*, the ox-herder, supervised by *Nur-Adad*, the majordomo," 198:'31-'38

3.6 From the Gang of Ur-Dumuzi

[n] ĝuruš **dú-ra-éš** [ur-^{d}]dumu-zi nu-bànda-gu$_4$ ù ugula-é, "[n] sick workmen (from the gang of) Ur-Dumuzi, the ox-herder and overseer of the house," 194:68–69

4. **Sick Workwomen**

4.1 **From Du-lugal-pa'e**

1 géme **dú-ra** lú-du$_6$-lugal-pa-è^{ki}, "1 sick workwoman from Du-lugal-pa'e" > *Toponym Index*

5. **Broken Context**

[1 x]-ga?-x ⌜**dú**⌝**-ra**, 52:65

[x] **dú-ra-a**, 477:2

6. **na-am-dú-ra**, *marṣūtu*, "being sick"

e-pe-eš **na-am-dú-ra**, "(worker) satisfying the allowance of sick leave" > ***e-pe-eš***

dù, *banû, epēšu*, "to construct, to build; to make"

a-za-bu-um **dù**, "to construct a cistern"

al-tar dù, "to do construction work"

bàd dù, "to construct the (enclosure) wall"

é dù, "to construct a house (or installation)"

gaba-tab dù, "to construct a breastwork fence"

gi-sig dù, "to construct a reed hut"

GÍN-bal dù, "to construct a GÍN-bal"

gir$_4$ dù, "to construct an oven"

im dù, "to construct (with) earth"

im-du$_8$-a dù, "to construct an adobe wall"

iz-zi dù, "to construct an iz-zi wall"

kar dù, "to construct a quay"

^{ĝeš}kuĝ$_5$ dù, "to install a ladder"

peš-ésir dù, "to plait bitumen(-sealed) palmleaflet (mats)"

ra-ṭum **dù**, "to construct a drain"

SIG$_4$.ANŠE dù, "to construct a brick stack"

túl dù, "to construct a well"

1. ***a-za-bu-um*** **dù**, "to construct a cistern"

1.1. **For Rain-water**

[n ĝuruš šidim] ***a-za-bu-um*** a im [še-ĝá] e-sír dal-ba-na ⌜bàd⌝ ù é-*šu-eš$_4$-tár* **dù**-[**a**], "[n builder(s)] having constructed a cistern for rain-water (in) the alley-way, a wall and the house of *Šu-Eštar*," 53:45–46

n ĝuruš u$_4$-n-šè ***a-za-bu-um*** a im še-ĝá e-sír dal-ba-na bàd ù é-*šu-eš$_4$-tár* **dù-a**, "n workmen for n day(s) having constructed a cistern for rain-water (in) the alley-way, a wall and the house of *Šu-Eštar*," 58:47–50, 336:36–37

[2] ĝuruš šidim ***a-za-bu-um*** a im še-ĝá **dù-a**, "[2] builders having constructed a cistern for rain-water," 121:32

2. al-tar dù, "to do construction work"

2.1. Construction of the Brewery-Kitchen-Mill Complex

*See *Household Index* for the complete context of the following passage.

n g̃uruš šidim n g̃uruš n géme **al-tar dù-a** (. . .) é-lùnga é-muḫaldim ù é-kíkken, "n builder(s), n workmen (and) n workwomen having done construction work (. . .), (for) the brewery-kitchen-mill complex," 151:28–29, 33, 152:'17-'19, 153:'30-'32, 154:32–33, 36

3. bàd dù, "to construct the (enclosure) wall"

3.1. Provisions when the (Enclosure) Wall was Constructed

3.1.1 For Builders

šà-gal šidim-e-ne ⸢u_4⸣ **bàd** egir é-a **dù-dè**, "food (for) builders when they were constructing the (enclosure) wall behind the house," 386:29–30, 387:20–21

dabin-bi 0.0.1.5 sìla še-bi 0.0.1. sìla 0.0.1. níg̃-àr-ra-sig_5-bi 1-sìla šà-gal šidim-e-ne u_4 **bàd in-dù-sa-a**, "(In total:) their semolina is 15 liters, their barley is 10 liters, (and) their fine groats are 1 liter, food (for) builders when they constructed the (enclosure) wall," 396:16–20, 397:16–20

0.0.1.6 sìla kaš-gen sá-du_{11} šidim-e-ne u_4 **bàd ba-dù-a**, "16 liters of ordinary beer, provisions of builders when the (enclosure) wall was constructed," 478:1–6

3.1.2 For Builders, Overseers and Other Workers

(. . .) šà-gal šidim-e-ne (. . .) árad-é-[a lú-ḫug̃]-g̃á ù ugula lú-[ḫug̃-g̃á-e-n]e íb-gu_7 [1] sìla dabin ½ sìla eša zì-dub-dub-šè u_4 **bàd** é-a **dù-dè**, "{assorted grains}, food (for) builders, {assorted grains}—the servants, hired workers and overseer of the hired workers ate (the grains)—1 liter of semolina (and) ½ liter of fine flour for the small flour heap, (rations for workers) when they were constructing the (enclosure) wall of the house," 383:5, 8–11

(. . .) šà-gal šidim-e-ne 5 sìla ninda ugula lú-ḫug̃-g̃á-e-ne íb-gu_7 3 sìla [lú]kíg̃-gi_4-a *šu-kab-ta* 1 sìla dabin ½ sìla eša dub-dub-dè **bà[d** egi]r é-a **dù-dè**, "{assorted grains}, food (for) builders, 5 liters of bread—the overseer of hired workers ate (the bread)—3 liters (of bread for) the messenger of *Šu-Kabta* (and) 1 liter of semolina (and) ½ liter of fine flour for heaping, (rations for the workers) to construct the (enclosure) wall behind the house," 385:5–9

4. é dù, "to construct a house (or installation)" > *Household Index*

é-*a-bu-ṭabu*
é-*a-gu-a*
é-*a-lí-a-bi*
é-*a-lu-a*
é-*ba-ḫa-a*
é-báḫar
é-*bu-ta-nu-um*
é-géme-tur
é-*ḫa-bu-ra-tum*
é-*ḫa-bi-ṣa-nu-um*
é-*ḫu-lu-lu*
é-*i-ti-rum*
é-ki-ba-g̃ar-ra
é-kìšib-ba
é-ki-mu-ra
é-mušen-na
é-*pu-ta-nu-um*
é-šáḫ
é-*šu-bu-la-núm*
é-*šu-i-ti-rum*
é-*šu-ma-mi-tum*
é-*u-bar-ri-a*
é-udu-niga
é-ùr ku_6 al-ús-sa
é-*zu-zu-tum*

4.1. Household Designation Lost

n g̃uruš šidim n g̃uruš n géme **é**-[PN **dù-a**], "n builder(s), n workmen, (and) n workwomen [having constructed] the house of [PN]," 158:24, 158:26–27

1 g̃uruš šidim gi-sal šà é-a gul-la [1] g̃uruš šidim šeg$_{12}$ ma šub-[ba] gub-ba [n+]5 g̃uruš ⌜saḫar⌝ šà é-a è-d[è n] g̃uruš [**é**-PN] **dù-a**, "1 builder having trimmed thin reeds in the house, [1] builder employed at the brick yard, [n+]5 workmen to extract dirt (from) inside the house (and) [n] workmen having constructed [the house of PN]," 191:26–33

5. **gaba-tab dù**, "to construct a breastwork fence"

5.1. Of the Fish-sauce Roof House

1 g̃uruš šidim 1 g̃uruš 3 géme **gaba-tab** é-ùr-ra ku$_6$ a[l-ús-sa] **dù-dè** gu[b-ba], "1 builder, 1 workman (and) 3 workwomen employed to construct the breastwork fence of the fish-sauce roof house," 15:23–24

5.2. Of the Reed Hut

2 ⌜g̃uruš⌝ 3 ⌜géme⌝ **gaba-tab** gi-sig **dù**-⌜**dè**⌝ gu[b-b]a, "2 workmen (and) 3 workwomen employed to construct the breastwork fence of the reed hut," 47:42–44

[. . .] **gaba-tab** g[i-sig **dù-dè**] gu[b-b]a, "[. . .] employed [to construct] the breastwork fence of the reed hut," 48:47–48

6. **gi-sig dù**, "to construct a reed hut"

6.1. Of the Sheep-Fattening Pen

1 g̃uruš [šidim n] g̃ur[uš. . .] 1 g̃uruš im sumur [aka] 1 g̃uruš šidim **gi-sig** é-udu-niga [**dù-a**], "1 builder, [n] workmen [. . .], 1 workman having plastered (and) 1 builder [having constructed] the reed hut of the sheep-fattening pen," 206:12–17

1 g̃uruš [ši]dim 5 g̃uruš **gi-sig** é-udu-niga **dù-a**, "1 builder (and) 5 workmen having constructed the reed hut of the sheep-fattening pen," 207:26–28

6.2. Of the Storehouse

1 g̃uruš šidim **gi-sig** g̃á-nun-na **dù-dè** gub-ba, "1 builder employed to construct a reed hut at the storehouse," 6:23

2 g̃uruš [šidim] **gi-sig** g̃[á-nun-na] **dù**-[**a**], "2 [builders] having constructed a reed hut at the storehouse, 60:27–28

6.3. Construction Site Unspecified

7 g̃uruš **gi-sig dù**-[**a**], "7 workmen having constructed a reed hut," 72:22

7. **GÍN-bal dù**, "to construct a GÍN-bal"

7.1. The GÍN-bal of the Garden

n g̃uruš šidim n g̃uruš n géme **GÍN-bal** ^{geš}kiri$_6$ **dù-a**, "n builder(s), n workmen (and) n workwomen having constructed the GÍN-bal of the garden," 151:36–37, 154:39–40, 159:27–28

13 g̃uruš 10 géme **GÍN-bal** ^{geš}kiri$_6$ **dù-a**, "13 workmen and 10 workwomen having constructed the GÍN-bal of the garden," 155:32

20 g̃uruš **GÍN-bal** ^{geš}kiri$_6$ **dù-a**, "20 workmen having constructed the GÍN-bal of the garden," 158:41

7.2. The GÍN-bal of the Garšana Garden

1 ĝuruš šidim [n] ĝuruš **GÍN-bal** šà ^{ĝeš}kiri$_6$ gar-ša-a[n-n]a^{ki} **dù-a**, "1 builder (and) [n] workmen having constructed the GÍN-bal of the Garšana garden," 129:33–34

n ĝuruš šidim n ĝuruš n géme **GÍN-bal** ^{ĝeš}kiri$_6$ gar-ša-an-na^{ki} **dù-a**, "n builder(s), n workmen (and) n workwomen having constructed the GÍN-bal of the Garšana garden," 131:'24-'25, 133:32–33, 135:31–32, 136:35–36, 146:'36-'37, 147:41–42

1 ĝuruš šidim 6 ĝuruš **[GÍN]-bal** ^{ĝeš}kiri$_6$ gar-ša-an-na^{ki} **dù-a**, "1 builder (and) 6 workmen having constructed the [GÍN]-bal of the Garšana garden," 132:33–34

7.2.1. Construction Supplies

7.2.1.1. Baskets

(. . .) [GÍN]-bal ^{ĝeš}ki[ri$_6$ gar-ša-an-na^{ki} **dù-a**], "{assorted baskets} [(used by workers) having constructed the GÍN-bal of the Garšana] garden," 1292:'25

7.2.1.1. Bitumen

21.0.0. ésir-ḫád ⸢gur⸣ 2.1.3. ésir-é-a gur **GÍN-bal** ^{ĝeš}kiri$_6$ gar-[ša-an-na^{ki} **dù-a**], "21 bushels of dry bitumen (and) 2 bushels (and) 90 liters of house bitumen, [(used by workers) having constructed] the GÍN-bal of the Garšana garden," 1302:1–3

8. gir$_4$ dù, "to construct an oven"

1 ĝuruš šidim 2 ĝuruš 4 géme **gir$_4$** šeg$_{12}$-al-ur$_x$-ra **dù-dè** gub-ba, "1 builder, 2 workmen (and) 4 workwomen employed to construct an oven for baking bricks," 94:27–28

[n ĝuruš] šidim 3 ĝuruš **gir$_4$** šeg$_{12}$-al-ur$_x$<-ra> **dù-dè**, "[n] builder(s) (and) 3 workmen to construct an oven for baking bricks," 97:'19

9. im dù, "to construct (with) earth"

6 ĝuruš **im** a-ĝá-ri-na **dù-dè** gub-ba, "6 workmen employed to construct (with) earth (mixed) in the *agarinnum*," 9:27

10. im-du$_8$-a dù, "to construct an adobe wall"

1 ĝuruš šidim um-mi-a 1 ĝuruš šidim **im-du$_8$-a** ^{ĝeš}kiri$_6$ zabala$_4$^{ki} **dù-a**, "1 master builder (and) 1 builder having constructed the adobe wall at the Zabala garden," 146:'20-'21

11. iz-zi dù, "to construct an iz-zi wall"

11.1. The Wall of the House of *Ḫabiṣanum*

5 [ĝuruš] **iz-zi** é-*ḫa-bi-ṣa-nu-um* **dù-a**, "5 [workmen] having constructed the iz-zi wall of the house of *Ḫabiṣanum*," 158:30–31

11.2. The Wall of the Storehouse

[n ĝuruš] im ⸢ga$_6$⸣-ĝá šu dím gub-ba [n ĝuruš šid]im 7 ĝuruš 7 géme [. . .] im sumur ke$_4$-dè gub-ba [n ĝuruš] im lu-a SIG$_4$.ANŠE gub-ba [n ĝuruš] šidim **iz-zi** ĝá-nun-na **dù-dè** gub-ba, "[n] employed [workmen] having carried earth (for) building, [n] builder(s), 7 workmen (and) 7 workwomen employed to plaster [. . .], [n employed workmen] having mixed earth at the brick stack (and) [n] builder(s) employed to construct the iz-zi wall of the storehouse," 29:'23-'27

12. kar dù, "to construct a quay"

12.1. The Quay of the Laundry

6 g̃uruš im lu-a 10 g̃uruš **kar**-ki-mu-ra **dù-a**, "6 workmen having mixed earth (and) 10 workmen having constructed the quay of the laundry," 163:31–32

[n] g̃uruš **kar**-ki-mu-ra **dù-a**, "[n] workmen having constructed the quay of the laundry," 173:33, 174:32

13. $^{\text{g̃eš}}$**kug̃**$_5$ **dù**, "to install a ladder"

*See *Household Index* for the complete context of the following passage.

[n] g̃uruš šidim 2 g̃uruš 10 géme **kug̃**$_5$ **dù-a** (. . .) ⸢al⸣-tar é-lùnga é-muḫaldim ù [é-kíkken], "[n] builder(s), 2 workmen (and) 10 workwomen having installed a ladder (. . .), (for) construction of the brewery-kitchen-mill complex," 146:'31, '35

14. peš-ésir dù, "to plait bitumen(-sealed) palmleaflet (mats)"

1 g̃uruš šidim **peš-ésir dù-a**, "1 builder having plaited bitumen(-sealed) palmleaflet (mats)," 123:34

1 [g̃uruš n gém]e **peš-ésir** é **dù-a**, "1 [workman (and) n] workwomen having constructed a house with bitumen(-sealed) palmleaflet (mats)," 125:34

15. ***ra-ṭum*** **dù**, "to construct a drain"

15.1. For the Brewery-Kitchen-Mill Complex

*See *Household Index* for the complete context of the following passage.

1 g̃uruš šidim um-mi-a 4 g̃uruš šidim 4 g̃uruš 60 géme ùr a g̃á-g̃á 1 g̃uruš šidim 3 g̃uruš 3 géme ***ra-ṭum***-bi **dù-a** (. . .) é-lùnga é-muḫaldim ù é-kíkken, "1 master builder, 4 builders (and) 60 workwomen having waterproofed the roof, 1 builder, 3 workmen (and) 3 workwomen having constructed its drains (. . .), (work for) the brewery-kitchen-mill complex," 150:26–30, 36

15.2. Construction Site Unspecified

2 g̃uruš 2 géme ***ra-ṭum***-bi **dù-a**, "2 workmen (and) 2 workwomen having constructed its drains," 156:33

16. SIG$_4$.ANŠE dù, "to construct a brick stack"

1 g̃uruš šidim 16 ⸢g̃uruš⸣ **SIG$_4$.ANŠE dù-dè** g[ub-ba], "1 builder (and) 16 workmen employed to construct the brick stack," 20:27–28

17. túl dù, "to construct a well"

[n] g̃uruš šidim [n g̃uru]š šu dím gub-ba 5 géme im ga$_6$-g̃á-dè gub-ba **túl** šà é-a **dù-a**, "[n] builder(s), [n] workmen employed to build (and) 5 workwomen employed to carry earth to construct the well in the house," 210:'25-'28

18. Broken or Uncertain Context

2 g̃uruš i[m-. . .] g̃á-g̃á b[àd . . .] 1-kam? éren? **dù-dè [gub-ba], "2 workmen to place [. . .] earth, [. . .] workers? [employed] to build," 49:34

n g̃uruš šidim n g̃uruš n géme [x] *mu-gu* **dù-a, "n builder(s), n workmen (and) n workwomen having constructed (?)," 146:'32-'33, 147:34–35

46 ^{gi}ma-sab gal-ir **dù-a, 1299:15

[. . . níg̃]-ša i$_7$ **dù-a, 1383:1–2

du$_{8}$, *epû*, "to bake (bread, bricks), to spread out mud (to make bricks), to caulk"

báppir du$_{8}$, "to bake beer bread"
dub du$_{8}$, "to bake a tablet"
é du$_{8}$, "to caulk a house"
ésir du$_{8}$, "to seal with bitumen"
ninda du$_{8}$, "to bake bread"
šeg$_{12}$ du$_{8}$, "to mold bricks"

1. **báppir du$_{8}$**, "to bake beer bread"

3 g̃uruš **báppir du$_{8}$-dè** gub-[ba], "3 workmen employed to bake beer bread," 190:29

2. **dub du$_{8}$**, "to bake a tablet"

kìšib íb-ra é-kìšib-ba-ta **dub**-bi **in-du$_{8}$**, "He rolled the seal (and) baked its tablet in the storeroom," 609:11–13

3. **é du$_{8}$**, "to caulk a house"

šar-ru-um-ì-lí ù-na-a-du$_{11}$ [x]-g̃ál-la [x?] é-za ì-g̃ál **é**-ki-ba-g̃ar-ra **du$_{8}$-dè** ^{d}*adad-tillati* ḫé-na-ab-sum-mu a-ba šeš-g̃u$_{10}$-gin$_{7}$, "Say to *Šarrum-ili* that '(?) that is in your house should be given to *Adad-tillati* in order to caulk the replacement house. Who is like my brother?'" 1526:1–7

4. **ésir du$_{8}$**, "to seal with bitumen"

[n.n.n.] ésir-ḫád gur [0.n.n.n] sìla ésir-é-a [0.0.]1 zì 1 sìla 10 gín ì-udu du$_{10}$-ús **ésir du$_{8}$-dè**, "[n] bushel(s) (and) [n liter(s)] of dry bitumen, [n] liter(s) of house bitumen, 10 liters of flour (and) 1 liter and 10 shekels of mutton fat to seal the bath with bitumen," 1325:11–15

5. **ninda du$_{8}$**, "to bake bread"

5.1 Barley for Baking Bread

1?.2.3. še gur mu **ninda du$_{8}$-dè**, "1? bushel (and) 150 liters of barley to bake bread," 1163:1–2

[n.n.n.] še gur sa$_{10}$ saḫar 48-kam *tá-din-eš$_{4}$-tár* 0.4.0. še sa$_{10}$ saḫar 12-kam *ša-at-èr-ra* **ninda du$_{8}$-dè-**⌜šè⌝, "[n] bushel(s) (and) [n liter(s)] of barley, the price of 48 units of dirt for *Tadin-Eštar* (and) 240 liters of barley, the price of 12 units of dirt for *Šat-erra* to bake bread," 1169:1–6

5.2 Reeds for Baking Bread

12 sa gi-izi **ninda ba-ra-du$_{8}$**, "12 bundles of fuel reeds with which bread was baked," 972:57–58, 975:60

70 sa gi-izi **ninda du$_{8}$-dè**, "70 bundles of fuel reeds (to be used) to bake bread," 1322:1–2

5.2.1 Baking Bread and Cooking Soup

24 sa gi-[izi] **ninda ba-ra-**⌜**du$_{8}$**⌝ 10 sa gi-[izi] tu$_{7}$ [ba]-ra-⌜šeg̃$_{6}$⌝ u$_{4}$ é-e im sumur ⌜ba⌝-aka, "24 bundles of [fuel] reeds, with which bread was baked, (and) 10 bundles of [fuel] reeds, with which soup was cooked when the house was plastered," 473:1–5

0.1.5.9⅔ sìla ninda-zì-šà-gen dabin íb-ta-ḫi 0.0.1. níg̃-àr-ra-sig$_{5}$ ^{urudu}šen-šè 50 sa gi-[izi **ninda ba-ra-d**]**u$_{8}$** ù tu$_{7}$ ba-[ra]-šeg̃$_{6}$ mu lú-⌜ḫug̃⌝-g̃á-e-ne-šè, "119⅔ liters of bread mixed from ordinary šà-flour and semolina, 10 liters of fine groats for the (soup) cauldron, (and) 50 bundles of [fuel] reeds with which [bread] was baked and soup was cooked for the hired workers," 479:10–13, 483:9–14

[n+]119 sa gi-izi [**ninda ba]-ra-du$_8$** ù tu$_7$ ba-ra-šeĝ$_6$, "[n+]119 bundles of fuel reeds with which [bread] was baked and soup was cooked," 1013:15–16, 1014:'8-'9

5.2.2 Baking Bread and Cooking Meat and Soup

7 sa+níĝin ^{ĝeš}ásal 5 sa gi-izi **ninda ba-ra-du$_8$** uzu ù tu$_7$ ba-ra-šeĝ$_6$ é-kù-ga, "7 bundles of poplar wood (and) 5 bundles of fuel reeds with which bread was baked (and) meat and soup were cooked in the bright temple," 1028:9–11

10 sa-níĝin ^{ĝeš}⸢ásal⸣ 30 sa gi-izi **ninda ba-ra-du$_8$** uzu ù tu$_7$ ba-ra-šeĝ$_6$ 60 ^{dug}sìla-bur-zi tu$_7$-šè šà kisal-lá ^{d}inana-zabala$_4^{ki}$, "10 bundles of poplar wood (and) 30 bundles of fuel reeds with which bread was baked (and) meat and soup were cooked; 60 1-liter offering bowls for soup in the courtyard of Inana of Zabala," 1028:32–37

5.3 Bread Baked in Loaves

5.3.1 In Half-Liter Loaves

5.3.1.1 Half(-Loaf) Bread

n sìla **ninda**-šu-ra-gen ½ sìla **du$_8$**, "n liter(s) of ordinary half(-loaf) bread baked (in) ½-liter (loaves)," 541:14, 541:17, 548:1, 1028:20

[0].4.2. **ninda**-šu-ra zì-kum [ù šà] ½ sìla **du$_8$**, "260 liters of half(-loaf) bread of kum [and šà-]flour baked (in) ½-liter (loaves)," 548:2

[0.3].3. **ninda**-šu-ra dabin ù š[à-g]en ½ sìla **du$_8$**, "210 liters of half(-loaf) bread of dabin and ordinary šà-flour baked (in) ½-liter (loaves)," 548:4

0.1.2. **ninda**-šu-ra ½ sìla **du$_8$**, "80 liters of half(-loaf) bread baked (in) ½-liter (loaves)," 1079:1

5.3.1.2 Mixed Flour Bread

ninda-dabin ù zì-šà-gen ½ sìla **du$_8$**-bi 0.0.2.8 ⸢sìla⸣, "their bread of dabin and ordinary šà-flour is 28 liters baked (in) ½-liter loaves," 402:15

0.4.0. **ninda**-zì-šà-gen zì-milla íb-ta-ḫi ½ sìla **du$_8$**, "240 liters of bread baked (in) ½-liter (loaves) were mixed from ordinary šà-flour (and) milla-flour," 1079:2

5.3.2 In Liter Loaves: Large Breads

5.3.2.1 ĝeš-AŠ Breads

n sìla **ninda**-gal-ĝeš-AŠ 1 sìla **du$_8$**, "n liter(s) of large ĝeš-AŠ bread baked (in) 1 liter (loaves)," 485:3, 1025:17, 1025:41, 1025:58, 1025:76, 1028:19

[šu+níĝin 0.n].4.7 sìla **ninda**-gal-ĝeš-AŠ 1 sìla **du$_8$**, "[In total: n+]47 liters of large ĝeš-AŠ bread baked (in) 1 liter (loaves)," 1025:96

5.3.2.2 Ordinary Large Breads

n sìla **ninda**-gal-gen 1 sìla **du$_8$**, "n liter(s) of ordinary large bread baked (in) 1 liter (loaves)," 471:1, 485:4, 491:1, 1025:18, 1025:42, 1025:59

0.2.5.5 sìla **ninda**-gal-gen 1-sìla **du$_8$** ki-lá-bi 2 gú 50 ma-na, "175 liters of ordinary large bread baked (in) 1 liter (loaves), their weight is 2 talents and 50 minas," 528:1–2 [šu+níĝin] 2.0.4.4 sìla **ninda**-gal-gen 1 sìla **du$_8$** gur, "[In total:] 2 bushels (and) 44 liters of ordinary large bread baked (in) 1 liter (loaves)," 1025:97

5.3.2.3 Large Breads of Various Flours

[0.n.n] **ninda**-gal zì-kum ù šà-[gen] 1 sìla ⸢**du$_8$**⸣, "[n] liter(s) of large bread of kum and [ordinary] šà-flour baked (in) 1 liter (loaves)," 548:3

5.4 Workers Assigned to Bake Bread

1 *lu-kà-dum* **ninda du$_8$-dè** gub-ba, "*Lukadum* employed to bake bread," 24:'27, 25:'4, 26:'23, 27:'19, 28:'30, 29:'35, 31:41, 32:40, 33:45, 34:'19, 35:48, 36:43, 39:47, 40:45, 41:'27, 52:66, 53:64, 57:'28-'29, 58:66, 59:54–55, 60:51, 62:'12-'13, 71:36, 73:'17

1 ĝuruš **ninda du$_8$-dè**, "1 workman to bake bread," 103:37, 104:5, 104:44, 105:5, 105:42

1 ĝuruš **ninda du$_8$-dè** gub-ba, "1 workman employed to bake bread," 93:'29, 98:'24, 99:26, 101:30

6. šeg$_{12}$ du$_8$, "to mold bricks"

6.1 Workers to Mold Bricks

1 ĝuruš šidim **šeg$_{12}$**-al-ur$_x$-ra **du$_8$-dè** gub-ba, "1 builder employed to mold bricks," 86:16–17, 87:11–12

[n ĝuruš] šidim 17 ĝuruš [**šeg$_{12}$**-al-ur$_x$-ra] **du$_8$**-⸢**dè**⸣, "[n] builder(s) (and) 17 workmen to mold [bricks]," 98:'21-'22

[n] ĝur[uš **še**]**g$_{12}$**-al-ur$_x$-ra [**du$_8$**]**-dè** g[ub-ba], "[n] workmen employed to [mold] bricks," 100:'19-'20

6.2 Wages for Molding Bricks

6.2.1 Assorted Commodities

0.4.3. eša 12 ma-na siki še-0.0.3!.-[ta] 2 sìla ì-ĝeš še-0.0.4.-ta **šeg$_{12}$ du$_8$-dè** á 5-sìla-ta, "270 liters of fine flour, 12 minas of wool, the equivalent of 30 liters of barley [each], (and) 2 liters of sesame oil, the equivalent of 40 liters of barley each, (to pay) wages of 5 liters each (for workers) to mold bricks," 457:1–5

6.2.2 Barley

á sar 1-a še 0.0.1.[n sìla] še-bi 125.2.3. gur **šeg$_{12}$ du$_8$-[a]** lú-ḫuĝ-ĝá-e-⸢ne⸣, "Wages of 10[+n liters] of barley. Their barley is 125 bushels (and) 150 liters, (barley for) hired workers having molded bricks," 350:'23-'26

0.2.3 še 5 ma-na siki še 0.0.3.-ta **šeg$_{12}$ du$_8$-dè**, "170 liters of barley (and) 5 minas of wool, the equivalent of 30 liters of barley each, (for workers) to mold bricks," 431:1–3

[n+]5.0.0. še gur á 5-sìla-ta [**šeg$_{12}$ d**]**u$_8$-a**-šè, "[n+]5 bushels of barley, wages of 5 liters each for (workers) having molded [bricks]," 447:1–3

n še gur **šeg$_{12}$ du$_8$-dè** á 5-sìla-ta, "n bushel(s) of barley, wages of 5 liters each (for workers) to mold bricks," 451:1–3, 456:1–3, 458:1–3; 530:1–3; 531:1–3

[n.n.n.] še gur ⸢**šeg$_{12}$**⸣ **du$_8$-dè** á 5-sìla-ta ba-ḫuĝ, "[n] bushel(s) of barley were (used to) hire (workers) to mold bricks at wages of 5 liters each," 454:1–3

du$_{11}$(g$_4$), *qabû*, "to speak, talk, say; to order"

ù-na-a-du$_{11}$, "Say (to PN)" > *Personal Name Index*

^{d}*adad-tillati*, 1037:1–2, 1038:1–2, 1042:1–2, 1044:1–2

a-ḫu-wa-qar	*šar-ru-um-ì-lí*
i-la-ak-nu-id	*tu-ra-am-ì-lí*
ì-lí-aš-ra-ni	ur-^{d}dumu-zi

1. **Additional Barley Rations, Ordered by *Šu-Kabta***

0.3.0. še šà-gu$_4$-me-éš dirig še-ba-ne-ne mu zì nu-g̃ál-la-šè ba-na-ḫa-la *šu-kab-tá* **bí-in-dug$_4$**, "180 liters of barley for the ox-drivers. *Šu-Kabta* had ordered that additional barley rations were to be divided for them because there was no flour," 481:1–4

2. **Translation Uncertain**

★★ 2 uz-tur-niga 1 kur-gi^{mušen}-niga 6 ir$_7$^{mušen}-niga 10 tu-gur$_4$^{mušen}-niga 5 péš-g̃eš-gi-niga 30-lá-1 péš-igi-gùn-niga *da-da-a* sipa-mušen-na in-KA-[x] ù **ba-an-d[u$_{11}$-ga]** ka-ga-[na ba-gen$_7$], "*Dada*, the bird warden, confirmed that he (?) and (?) 2 fattened ducklings, 1 fattened goose, 6 fattened pigeons, 10 fattened doves, 5 fattened mice (and) 29 fattened, striped-eyed mice," 1053:1–9

dub, *šapāku*, "to heap up, pile, pour"

zì-**dub-dub**, "small flour heap" > **zì-dub-dub**

1. **Flour for Heaping**

1 sìla dabin ½ sìla eša **dub-dub-dè**, "1 liter semolina (and) ½ liter fine flour for heaping," 385:8

duḫ, *paṭāru*, "to loosen, release, free"

1. **Release of Workers**

1.1 **Because of Rain**

1 [guru]š šidim u$_4$ **du$_8$-ḫa** a im še-g̃á-a, "1 builder released for the day (because of) rain," 180:15

1.2 **During the Festival of Nergal**

6 g̃uruš šidim u$_4$ *e-lu-núm*-^{d}nergal$_x$$^{[eri_{11}\text{-}g]al}$ **du$_8$**-[**dè**], "6 builders [to be] released during the *Elunum* festival of Nergal," 90:6–7

1.3 **Under the Authority of *Nawir-ilum***

[n g̃u]ruš **du$_8$-ḫa-me-éš** ⸢g̃iri⸣ *na-wi-ir-ilum*, "[n] workmen released under the authority of *Nawir-ilum*," 65:'22-'23

1.4 **Reason for Release Unspecified**

6 g̃uruš šidim **du$_8$**-[**ḫa**], "6 released builders," 145:44

– E –

e-pe-eš, *epēšu*, "to do, make"

1 ***e-pe-eš*** na-am-dú-ra, "1 (workman) satisfying the allowance of sick leave," 24:'31, 104:8, 104:48, 105:8, 106:9, 106:48, 107:11, 107:'18, 108:8, 108:42, 109:8, 110:9, 111:10, 114:9, 116:7, 117:7, 120:7, 121:7, 123:11, 125:7, 126:7, 127:7, 128:7, 129:7, 130:7, 131:'1, 132:7, 133:7, 134:7, 135:7, 136:7, 137:7, 138:7, 139:7, 140:7, 141:7, 142:7, 143:7, 145:7, 146:2, 147:7, 149:7, 150:7

1 ***e-pe-eš*** ^{na}nam!?<-dú?-ra?>, "1 (workman) satisfying the allowance of sick leave," 36:44

1 ***e-pe-eš*** nam-dú-ra, "1 (workman) satisfying the allowance of sick leave," 118:7, 119:7

è, *waṣû, erēbu*, "to bring out; to enter"

saḫar è, "to extract dirt"

še è, "to bring out barley"

1. **saḫar è**, "to extract dirt"

1.1 Construction of the Potter's House

3 [g̃uruš šidim] sumur iz-zi šà [é-a ù-ru-dè] 14 [g̃uruš] **saḫar** šà é-a **è-[dè]** 1 g̃uruš šidim 3 ⸢g̃uruš⸣ é-báḫar dù-a, "3 [builders to level] the plastered iz-zi wall in [the house], 14 [workmen to] extract dirt (from) inside the house (and) 1 builder (and) 3 workmen having constructed the potter's house," 190:22–27

1.2 Construction of Individual Households

1 g̃uruš šidim gi-sal šà é-a gul-la [1] g̃uruš šidim šeg$_{12}$ ma šub-[ba] gub-ba [n+]5 g̃uruš ⸢**saḫar**⸣ šà é-a **è-d[è** n] g̃uruš [é-PN] dù-a, "1 builder having trimmed thin reeds in the house, [1] builder employed at the brickyard, [n+]5 workmen to extract dirt (from) inside the house (and) [n] workmen having constructed [the house of PN]," 191:26–31

1.3 Household Unspecified

n g̃uruš **saḫar** šà é-a **è-dè**, "n workmen to extract dirt (from) inside the house," 192:'16, 193:26–27, 1376:6

2. **še è**, "to bring out barley"

1 *ta-tù-ri* ù *a-lí-aḫ* **še è-dè** g̃ír-su^{ki}-šè g̃en-na, "*Tatturi* and *Aliaḫ* having gone to G̃irsu to bring out barley," 31:37, 32:37, 33:40, 35:44, 36:39

1 *a-lí-aḫ* **še è(-dè)** g̃ír-su^{ki}-šè g̃en-na, "*Aliaḫ* having gone to G̃irsu to bring out barley," 37:34–35, 38:40–41, 43:'45-'46, 44:44–45, 45:26–27, 47:57, 48:64–65

– G –

ga_6(g̃)(ÍL), *babālum*; *nasû*, "to bring; to lift, carry, haul"[3]

gi ga_6(g̃), "to carry reeds"
gi-sal ga_6(g̃), "to carry thin reeds"
im *dì-um* ga_6(g̃), "to carry the adobe mix"
im ga_6(g̃), "to carry earth"
im sumur ga_6(g̃), "to carry plaster"
in-u ga_6(g̃), "to carry straw"
$^{g̃eš}$kišig ga_6(g̃), "to carry shok"
níg̃-gú-na ga_6(g̃), "to carry the commodity tax"
še ga_6(g̃), "to carry barley"
$šeg_{12}$-al-ur_x-ra ga_6(g̃), "to carry bricks"
ùr ga_6(g̃), "to carry roof beams"

*See *Household Index* for the complete context of the following passages.

1. **gi ga_6(g̃)**, "to carry reeds"

1.1 **Carried from the Sheep-Shearing Shed to the Weir**

30 géme uš-bar u_4-1-šè **gi** g̃á-udu-ta kun-zi-id(Á)-šè **íb-ga_6**, "30 female weavers for 1 day carried reeds from the sheep-shearing shed to the weir," 273:7–9

1.2 **Construction of the (Enclosure) Wall**

[1 g̃uruš šidim 6 g̃uruš šu dím-ma gub-ba 6 géme **g]i ⌜ga_6⌝-g̃á-⌜dè⌝** 5 g̃uruš šidim 6 g̃uruš gi-sal uš bàd gul-dè g[ub-ba], "[1 builder, 6 workmen employed to build, 6 workwomen] to carry reeds (and) 5 builders (and) 6 workmen employed to trim thin reeds at the foundation of the (enclosure) wall," 9:17–21

2. **gi-sal ga_6(g̃)**, "to carry thin reeds"

2.1 **Construction of the Brewery-Kitchen-Mill Complex**

n g̃uruš **gi-sal ga_6-g̃á** al-tar é-lùnga é-muḫaldim ù é-kíkken, "n workmen having carried thin reeds (for) construction of the brewery-kitchen-mill complex," 128:27–28, 129:28–29, 131:'21, '23

4 g̃uruš **gi-sal** [bàd **ga_6-g̃á-dè**] (. . .) al-tar é-lùnga é-mu[ḫaldim ù é-kík]ken, "4 workmen [to carry] thin reeds [for the (enclosure) wall] (. . .), (for) construction of the brewery-kitchen-mill complex," 138:29, 31

---

3 On the use and meaning of ga_6-g̃á (=ÍL-g̃á), *babālum*, "to lift up (a thing above one's head) > to bring, to carry," see M. Yoshikawa 1993, 300–302. The pronunciation, ga_6(g̃), not $g̃a_6$(g̃), was demonstrated by Heimpel 1986, 565. The "standard" Sumerian form, íl-la, occurs in the G̃EŠ.KÚŠU text, M. Molina, 1452:7 (ŠS 8/-/-). Its scribe, Gududu, is well known at G̃EŠ.KÚŠU. Line 5 records flour for the household of *Šu-Kabta* that was brought/carried (íl-la) from G̃EŠ.KÚŠU to Garšana. According to Yoshikawa, ga_6(g̃)-g̃á is the G̃EŠ.KÚŠU dialect form of "standard" Sumerian íl-la. However, in this G̃EŠ.KÚŠU text we have a clear example of the use of íl-la, while at nearby Garšana, ga_6-g̃á is found regularly to the exclusion of the form íl-la.

2.2 Construction of the House

1 g̃uruš šidim 8 g̃uruš gi-sal ⌜bàd⌝ gul-dè gub-ba 3 géme **gi-sal** $\mathbf{ga_6}$**-g̃á-d[è** gub-ba] 3 g̃uruš šidim 1 g̃uruš 3 [géme] $^{g̃eš}$ig šà é-a [bu-ra], "1 builder (and) 8 workmen employed to trim thin reeds at the (enclosure) wall, 3 workwomen [employed] to carry thin reeds (and) 3 builders, 1 workman (and) 3 [workwomen having pulled out] a door in the house," 15:19–22

3. **g̃eš ùr** $\mathbf{ga_6}$**(g̃)**, "to carry roof beams"

1 g̃uruš u_4-2-šè **g̃eš ùr** $\mathbf{ga_6}$**-g̃á**, "1 workman for 2 days having carried roof beams," 272:3–4

4. **im *dì-um*** $\mathbf{ga_6}$**(g̃)**, "to carry the adobe mix"

4.1 Construction of the House

1 g̃uruš šidim 6 g̃uruš **im [*dì*]-*um*** **g[**$\mathbf{a_6}$**-g̃]á** [é]-*ì-lí-b[i-š]u* dù-a, "1 builder (and) 6 workmen having carried the adobe mix, (workers) having constructed the house of *Ili-bišu*," 209:16–18

4.2 Construction of the Tower

[4] g̃uruš **im *dì-um*** $\mathbf{ga_6}$**-g̃á** (. . .) an-za-qar-$^{g̃eš}$kiri$_6$ zabala$_4$$^{⌜ki⌝}$ [gub-ba], "[4] workmen having carried the adobe mix (. . .), (workers) [employed] at the tower of the Zabala garden," 201:'4, '6

5. **im** $\mathbf{ga_6}$**(g̃)**, "to carry earth"

5.1 Construction of the Brewery-Kitchen-Mill Complex

n géme **im** $\mathbf{ga_6}$**-g̃á** (. . .) al-tar é-lùnga é-muḫaldim ù é-kíkken, "n workwomen having carried earth (. . .), (for) construction of the brewery-kitchen-mill complex," 128:25, 28, 129:26, 28–29, 131:'20, '23, 132:28, 30, 133:27, 29, 135:28, 30, 138:28, 31, 143:30, 34

11 g̃uruš 11 géme **im** $\mathbf{ga_6}$**-g̃á** é-lùnga é-muḫaldim ù [é]-kíkken, "11 workmen (and) 11 workwomen having carried earth, (work for) the brewery-kitchen-mill complex," 140:38–39

5.1.1 Carrying Earth to Bind Roof Beams

20 [g̃uruš 16] géme **im** $\mathbf{ga_6}$**-g̃[á** g̃eš ùr] kéše-rá (. . .) al-[tar] é-lùnga é-muḫaldim [ù] é-kíkken, "20 [workmen (and) 16] workwomen having carried earth—(workers) having bound [roof beams]—(. . .), (for) construction of the brewery-kitchen-mill complex," 141:30–31, 33

5.1.2 Carrying Earth for its Foundation Terrace

n géme **im** $\mathbf{ga_6}$**-g̃á** (. . .) al-tar ki-sá-a é-lùnga é-muḫaldim ù é-kíkken, "n workwomen having carried earth (. . .), (for) construction of the foundation terrace of the brewery-kitchen-mill complex," 125:25–26, 126:25, 28

5.1.3 Carrying Earth to Plaster the iz-zi Wall

n géme **im** $\mathbf{ga_6}$**-g̃á** iz-zi im sumur aka (. . .) al-tar é-lùnga é-muḫaldim ù é-kíkken, "n workwomen having carried earth to plaster the iz-zi wall (. . .), (for) construction of the brewery-kitchen-mill complex," 136:20–31, 34, 142:23–24, 29

5.2 Construction of the Brewery and Mill

[n] g̃uruš [n] géme **im** $\mathbf{ga_6}$**-g̃á** [al-tar é-lùn]ga ù é-kíkken(!), "[n] workmen (and) [n] workwomen having carried earth (for) [construction of the] brewery and mill," 122:'15-'16

5.2.3 Carrying Earth for its Foundation Terrace

n géme **im ga$_6$-g̃á** al-tar ki-sá-a é-lùnga ù é-kíkken, "n workwomen having carried earth (for) construction of the foundation terrace of the brewery and mill," 111:25–26, 113:'14-'15, 114:26–27, 115:'20-'21, 121:30–31, 123:29–30

[n g̃uruš n] géme **im** [**ga$_6$-g̃á** al-tar ki]-sá-a é-[lùnga ù é-kíkken], "[n workmen (and) n] workwomen [having carried] earth (for) [construction of] the foundation terrace of [the brewery and mill]," 112:'8-'9

5.3 Construction of the Craftsmen's House

10-lá-1 géme **im ga$_6$-g̃á-dè** gub-ba (. . .) é-gašam-e-ne-šè, "9 workwomen employed to carry earth (. . .), (work) for the craftsmen's house," 53:31, 33

[n g̃uruš] **im ga$_6$-dè** gub-ba [. . . é]-gašam, "[n workmen] employed to carry earth (. . .), [(work for)] the craftsmen's [house]," 66:'6,'9

5.4 Construction of the House

5 géme **im ga$_6$-g̃á-dè** gub-ba túl šà é-a dù-a, "5 workwomen employed to carry earth, (workers) having constructed the well in the house," 210:'27-'28

5.5 Construction of the Palace

[n g̃uruš] má-laḫ$_5$ 1 g̃uruš [**im**] **ga$_6$-g̃á-dè** [n g̃uruš x] x šà? é?-gal ke$_4$-dè, "[n] sailor(s) (and) 1 workman to carry [earth] (and) [n workmen] to make [x] in? the palace," 66:'11-'12

[n] g̃uruš 25 géme **im ga$_6$** [ùr é-gal gib]il a g̃á-g̃á, "[n] workmen (and) 25 workwomen having carried earth, (workers) having waterproofed [the roof of the] new [palace]," 74:'5-'6

5.6 Construction of the Storehouse

[n g̃uruš] **im** ⌈**ga$_6$**⌉**-g̃á** šu dím gub-ba (. . .) [n g̃uruš] šidim iz-zi g̃á-nun-na dù-dè gub-ba, "[n workmen] employed to build, having carried earth (. . .), (and) [n] builder(s) employed to construct the iz-zi wall of the storehouse," 29:'23, '27

5.7 Construction of the Textile Mill

30 géme **im ga$_6$-g̃á-dè** [gub-ba] (. . .) [. . .] é-uš-[bar . . .], "30 workwomen [employed] to carry earth (. . .), [(work for)] the textile mill," 33:26, 30

n géme **im ga$_6$-g̃á-dè** gub-ba (. . .) é-uš-bar-šè, "n workwomen employed to carry earth (. . .), (work) for the textile mill," 37:23, 26, 38:24, 27

n géme **im ga$_6$-g̃á-dè** gub-ba al-tar é-uš-bar-ra, "n workwomen employed to carry earth, (for) construction of the textile mill," 52:34–35, 53:26, 29

5.7.1 Carrying Earth for its Foundation

[4?] géme **im** gíd **ga$_6$**<**-g̃á**>**-dè** gub-ba (. . .) 30 géme **im ga$_6$-g̃**[**á-dè**] gub-ba (. . .) ⌈uš⌉ é-uš-bar-ra, "[4?] workwomen having hauled earth, employed to carry it, (. . .), 30 workwomen employed [to] carry earth (. . .), (work) for the foundation of the textile mill," 47:22, 24, 26

5.7.2 Carrying Earth for its Foundation Terrace

1 [g̃uruš] **im ga$_6$-g̃á-dè** gub-ba (. . .) [17] g̃uruš 40 géme šeg$_{12}$ da-ki-sá-a é-uš-bar g̃á-g̃á-dè gub-[ba], "1 [workman] employed to carry earth (. . .), (and) [17] workmen (and) 40 workwomen employed to place bricks at the side of the foundation terrace of the textile mill," 35:26, 28

18 géme **im ga$_6$-g̃á-dè** g[ub-b]a (. . .) ki-sá-a é-uš-bar-šè, "18 workwomen employed to carry earth (. . .), (work) for the foundation terrace of the textile mill," 43:'30, '32

5.8 Construction of the Textile Mill and Craftsmen's House

3 géme **im ga$_6$-g̃á-dè** gub-ba iz-zi im sumur ke$_4$-dè (. . .) é-uš-bar ù é-gašam-e-ne-šè, "3 workwomen employed to carry earth to plaster the iz-zi wall (. . .), (work) for the textile mill and craftsmen's house," 58:36–37, 39

30 ⸢géme⸣ 10 ⸢g̃uruš⸣ **im ga$_6$-g̃á-dè** gu[b-b]a (. . .) é-uš-bar ù é-gašam-šè, "30 workwomen (and) 10 workmen employed to carry earth (. . .), (work) for the textile mill and craftmen's house," 59:33–35, 43

4 géme **im ga$_6$-g̃á-dè** gub-[ba] ab-ba dag̃al t[à-tà-dè gub-ba] é-uš-bar ù é-[NUN].ME.TAG-[e-ne-šè], "4 workwomen employed to carry earth, [(workers) employed] to widen (the opening of) the roof vent, [(work) for] the textile mill and craftsmen's house," 60:36–40

[n] géme **im ga$_6$<-g̃á>-dè** g[ub-bá] (. . .) é-uš-bar ù é-gašam-[e-ne(-šè)], "[n] workwomen employed to carry earth (. . .), [(work for)] the textile mill and the craftsmen's house," 71:22, 24

5.9 Construction of Various Houses and Installations

5.9.1 The Brick Stack

[n] g̃uruš 21 géme [SIG$_4$].ANŠE g̃á-g̃á [1]8 géme **im ⸢ga$_6$⸣-g̃á** ⸢gú⸣-i$_7$-[*a*]-*ga-mu-um-ta* é-*gi-na-tum* ká-bil-[lí]-a-šè, "[n] workmen (and) 21 workwomen having placed the brick stack (and) 18 workwomen having carried earth from the bank of the *Agamum* canal to the barracks of the Billi'a gate," 208:13–19

5.9.2 The Fish-sauce Roof House

10-lá-1 géme **im ga$_6$-g̃á** gub-ba é-gibi[l ù]r ku$_6$ al-ús-sa a [g̃á]-g̃á-dè gub-ba, "9 employed workwomen having carried earth, (workers) employed to waterproof the new roof of the fish-sauce roof house," 49:41–42

5.9.3 Individual Houses

6 géme **im g[a$_6$-g̃á-dè** gub-ba] (. . .) é-*pí-ša-aḫ-ilum* gub-[ba], "6 workwomen [employed to] carry earth (. . .), (workers) employed at the house of *Pišaḫ-ilum*," 84:15, 17

6 géme **im ga$_6$-g̃á-dè** gub-ba (. . .) é-*u*-⸢*bar*⸣-*ri-a* gub-[ba], "6 workwomen employed to carry earth (. . .), (workers) employed at the house of *Ubarria*," 94:18, 20

5 géme **im ga$_6$-g̃á** é-*u-bar*-⸢*ri*⸣-*a* dù-a, "5 workwomen having carried earth, (workers) having constructed the house of *Ubarria*," 111:35–36

10 géme **im ga$_6$-g̃á** é-*a-al-lu*-[*a*] dù-a, "10 workwomen having carried earth, (workers) having constructed the house of *A'allua*," 111:38–39

n géme **im ga$_6$-g̃á** é-*pu-tá-nu-um* dù-a, "n workwomen having carried earth, (workers) having constructed the house of *Putanum*," 112:'16–'17, 120:'28–'29, 156:21–22

17 géme **im [ga$_6$-g̃á]** é-*ba-ḫa-a* dù-[a], "17 workwomen [having carried] earth, (workers) having constructed the house of *Baḫa'a*," 114:35–36

34 géme **im ga$_6$-ĝá** al<-tar> é-*ba-ḫa-a*, "34 workwomen having carried earth, (for) construction of the house of *Baḫa'a*," 117:27–28

6 géme **im ga$_6$-ĝá** al-tar é-*pu-ta-nu-um*, "6 workwomen having carried earth, (for) construction of the house of *Putanum*," 121:25–26

3 ⌈géme⌉ **im ga$_6$-ĝá** é-*pu-ta-nu-um*, "3 workwomen having carried earth, (work for) the house of *Putanum*," 122:'19-'20

10 géme **im ga$_6$-ĝá** é-*zu-zu-tum* dù-a, "10 workwomen having carried earth, (workers) having constructed the house of *Zuzutum*," 123:32–33, 156:24–25

3 ĝuruš **im ga$_6$-ĝá** (. . .) al-tar é-*ì-lí-bi-šu*, "3 workmen having carried earth (. . .), (for) construction of the house of *Ili-bišu*," 202:26, 29, 203:26, 29

6 ĝuruš **im ga$_6$-ĝá** (. . .) é-*ì-lí-bi-šu*, "6 workmen having carried earth (. . .), (work for) the house of *Ili-bišu*," 204:'5, '9

5.9.4 Replacement Houses

5 ĝuruš 2 géme **im ga$_6$-dè** gub-ba é-ki-ba-ĝar-ra en-^{d}inana-gal, "5 workmen (and) 2 workwomen employed to carry earth, (work for) the replacement house of the senior priest of Inana," 78:12–13, 79:11–12

[11 gém]e **im ga$_6$-[ĝá]-dè** gub-ba [é-ki-b]a-ĝar-ra ⌈*bí*⌉-*za-a* gub-ba, "[11] workwomen employed to carry earth, (workers) employed at the replacement house of *Biza'a*," 86:13–15

5.9.5 The Sheep-Fattening Pen

1 ĝuruš šidim 5 géme **im ga$_6$<-ĝá>-dè** gub-ba (. . .) ùr é-udu-niga-šè, "1 builder (and) 5 workwomen employed to carry earth (. . .), (work) for the roof for the sheep-fattening pen," 53:37–38, 40

5.9.6 The Tower of the Zabala Garden

11 ĝuruš **im ga$_6$-ĝá** (. . .) úgu iz-zi-da a **ĝá-ĝá** an-za-qar-^{ĝeš}kiri$_6$ zabala$_4^{ki}$, "11 workmen having carried earth (. . .), (workers) to waterproof the top of the iz-zi wall at the tower of the Zabala garden," 200:'5, '8-'9

n ĝuruš **im ga$_6$-ĝá** (. . .) im sumur aka an-za-qar-^{ĝeš}kiri$_6$ zabala$_4^{ki}$, "n workmen having carried earth (. . .), (workers) having plastered the tower of the Zabala garden," 202:16, 20–21, 203:17, 20–21

5.10 Construction of the (Enclosure) Wall

1 ĝuruš šidim 2 ĝuruš šu dím gub-[ba] 3 géme **im g[a$_6$-ĝá-dè** gub-ba] bàd x-[. . .], "1 builder (and) 2 workmen employed to build (and) 3 workwomen [employed to] carry earth [(for) construction? of] the (enclosure) wall," 47:37–40

*See **al-tar** for the complete context of the following passages.

10 géme **im ga$_6$-ĝá-d[è** a]l-tar bàd gub-ba, "10 workwomen to carry earth, (workers) employed for construction of the (enclosure) wall," 99:15–16

20 géme **im ga$_6$-ĝá** (. . .) al-tar bàd gub-ba, "20 workwomen having carried earth (. . .), (workers) employed (for) construction of the (enclosure) wall," 102:19, 23, 103:17, 20

5.10.1 Carrying Earth to the *Agarinnum*

3 gé[me **im** *a-ga-ri*]-*nu-um* **ga$_6$-ĝá-dè** gub-[ba] al-tar uš bàd tà-tà-dè gub-ba, "3 workwomen employed to carry [earth to the *agarinnum*], (workers) employed

(for) construction to apply stucco to the foundation of the (enclosure) wall," 7:'25-'27

2 g̃uruš šidim 3 g̃uruš ḫug̃-g̃á šu dím-ma gub-ba 3 géme ḫug̃-g̃á **im** *a-ga-ri-nu-um* **ga$_6$-g̃á-dè** gub-ba [. . .g]ub-ba [n g̃uruš **im**] *a-ga-ri-n*[*u-um* **ga$_6$-g̃**]**á-dè** gub-[ba a-rá]-2-kam u[š bàd] tà-tà-dè gub-ba, "2 builders (and) 3 hired workmen employed to build, 3 hired workwomen employed to carry earth to the *agarinnum*, [. . .] (and) [n workmen] employed to carry [earth] to the *agarinnum* for the 2nd time, (workers) employed to apply stucco to the foundation [of the (enclosure) wall]," 8:23–32

5.10.2 Carrying Earth to Make and Plaster the urua wall

2 g̃uruš [. . . n g̃uruš im ì-lí]-dè gub-ba 6 géme **im ga$_6$-g̃á-dè** gub-⸢ba⸣ ù-[ru]-a bàd ke$_4$-dè, "2 workmen [. . ., n workmen] employed to [lift earth] (and) 6 workwomen employed to carry earth, (workers) to make the urua wall," 39:31–34

2 g̃uruš [šidim] 6 g̃uruš šu [dím-ma] gub-[ba] 5 géme **im ga$_6$-[g̃á]-dè** gub-[ba] ú-ru-á(!) bàd [ke$_4$-dè], "2 [builders] (and) 6 workmen employed to build (and) 5 workwomen employed to carry earth, (workers) [to make] the urua wall," 40:26–29

25 géme **im ga$_6$-g̃á-dè** gub-ba ù-ru-a bàd-šè, "25 workwomen employed to carry earth, (work) for the urua wall,"43:'24-'25, 44:24–25

2 g̃uruš šidim 2 g̃uruš šu dím gub-ba 4 géme **im ga$_6$-g̃á-dè** gub-ba 1 g̃uruš im i-⸢li⸣?-dè gub-[ba] ú-ru a bàd-[šè], "2 builders (and) 2 workmen employed to build, 4 workwomen employed to carry earth (and) 1 workman employed to lift earth, (work) [for] the urua wall," 46:'22-'26

1 g̃uruš šidim 1 g̃uruš šu dím gub-ba 5 géme **im ga$_6$-g̃á-dè** gub-ba 2 g̃uruš im ì-li-de$_9$ gub-ba ù-ru-a bàd ke$_4$-dè, "1 builder (and) 1 workman employed to build, 5 workwomen employed to carry earth (and) 2 workmen employed to lift earth, (workers) to make the urua wall," 47:27–31

1 g̃uruš šidim 1 g̃uruš šu dím gub-ba 4 géme **im ga$_6$-g̃á-dè** gub-ba 2 g̃uruš im ì-li-de$_9$ <<dè>> gub-ba ù-ru-a bàd im sumur ke$_4$-dè, "1 builder (and) 1 workman employed to build, 4 workwomen employed to carry earth (and) 2 workmen employed to lift earth, (workers) to plaster the urua wall," 47:32–36

1 g̃uruš šidim um-mi-a 2 g̃uruš šidim 2 g̃uruš šu dím 2 géme im gíd-me 2 géme *du-ú-um* aka 10 géme **im ga$_6$-g̃á** ù-ru-a bàd aka, "1 master builder, 2 builders (and) 2 workmen having built, 2 workwomen having hauled earth, 2 workwomen having made a *du-ú-um* (and) 10 workwomen having carried earth, (workers) having made the urua wall," 104:20–26, 105:24–25

5.10.3 Carrying Earth to Plaster the (Enclosure) Wall

1 g̃uruš šidim um-mi-a tà-tà-dè gub-⸢ba⸣ 5 g̃uruš šidim 4 g̃uruš 8 géme **im ga$_6$-g̃á-dè** gub-ba 3 g̃uruš im lu-dè gub-ba bàd {erasure} im sumur ke$_4$-d[è gub]-ba, "1 master builder employed to apply stucco, 5 builders, 4 workmen (and) 8 workwomen employed to carry earth (and) 3 workmen employed to mix, (workers) employed to plaster the (enclosure) wall," 36:26–30

1 g̃uruš šidim um-mi-a 4 g̃uruš šidim 6 g̃uruš šu dím-ma gub-ba 4 g̃uruš im sumur tà-tà-dè gub-ba [n] géme **im ga$_6$-g̃á-dè** gub-ba bàd [im sumur] ke$_4$-[dè], "1

master builder, 4 builders (and) 6 workmen employed to build, 4 workmen employed to apply plaster (and) [n] workwomen employed to carry earth, (workers) [to] plaster the (enclosure) wall," 40:20–25

6 ĝuruš šu dím-ma ⌈gub⌉-ba [n ĝuruš] im sumur [tà-tà]-dè gub-ba 1 ĝuruš ⌈im⌉ ì-⌈li⌉-de_9 [gub-ba] 10-lá-1 géme **i[m ga_6]-ĝá-dè** gub-ba bàd im sumur ke_4-dè, "6 workmen employed to build, [n workmen] employed to [apply] plaster, 1 workman [employed] to lift earth (and) 9 workwomen employed to carry earth, (workers) to plaster the (enclosure) wall," 41:'18-'22

5.10.4 Carrying Earth to Plaster the iz-zi Wall

1 ĝuruš šidim um-mi-a 4 ĝuruš ⌈gub-ba⌉ 4 ĝuruš šu dím-[ma] 3 ĝuruš im sumur ì-⌈li⌉-[d]e_9 gub-ba 10 ĝu[ruš n géme?] **im ga_6-ĝá-dè** gu[b-ba] iz-⌈zi⌉ im sumur ke_4-dè, "1 master builder, 4 employed workmen (and) 4 workmen having built, 3 workmen employed to lift plaster (and) 10 workmen [(and) n workwomen?] employed to carry earth, (workers) to plaster the iz-zi wall," 52:20–26

8 géme **im ga_6-⌈ĝá⌉-dè** gub-[ba] 2 ĝuruš im ì-li-de_9 [gub-b]a iz-zi im [sumur k]e_4-⌈dè⌉, "8 workwomen employed to carry earth (and) 2 workmen employed to lift earth, (workers) to plaster the iz-zi wall," 56:'20-'22

5.11 Construction of the Warehouse

3 ĝuruš 14 géme **im ga_6-ĝá-dè** gub-ba (. . .) é-kišib-ba ugula kíkken, "3 workmen (and) 14 workwomen employed to carry earth (. . .), (work for) the warehouse (under the authority of?) the overseer of the mill," 36:23, 25

10 géme **im ga_6-ĝá-dè** gub-ba é-⌈kìšib⌉-ba ĝá-nun-na sumun ĝeš ùr kéše-rá, "10 workwomen employed to carry earth, (workers) having bound roof beams for the warehouse of the old storehouse," 49:37–38

1 ĝuruš šidim 18 géme **im ga_6-[ĝá]** ùr é-kìšib-ba a ĝá-ĝá, "1 builder (and) 18 workwomen having carried earth, (workers) having waterproofed the roof of the warehouse," 122:'26-'27

5.12 Construction Site Broken or Unspecified

3 ĝuruš x-[. . .] **im g[a_6?-. . .]**, 6:19–20

n géme **im ga_6-ĝá-dè** gub-ba, "n workwomen employed to carry earth," 14:23, 15:29, 17:21, 20:24, 31:25, 32:25, 48:31, 49:20, 53:41, 72:19, 80:'10, 93:'17, 95:16

[n ĝuruš] má-$la\underset{\smile}{h}_5$ 1 ĝuruš **[im] ga_6-ĝá-dè**, "[n] sailor(s) (and) 1 workman to carry [earth]," 66:'11

[n géme] **im [ga_6]-ĝá**, "[n workwomen] having [carried] earth," 115:'16

5.12.1 Carrying Earth to the *Agarinnum*

3 ĝuruš a-ĝá-ri-in **ga_6-ĝá-dè** gub-ba, "3 workmen employed to carry (earth) to the *agarinnum*," 189:29

5.12.2 Carrying Earth for Binding Roof Beams

1 ĝuruš šidim um-mi-a 3 ĝuruš šidim 6 ĝuruš šu dím gub-[ba] 6 géme **im g[a_6-ĝá** gub-ba] 1 ĝuruš im [. . .] ĝeš ùr ké[še-rá], "1 master builder, 3 builders (and) 6 workmen employed to build, 6 workwomen [employed] to carry earth (and) 1 workman [. . .], (workers) having bound roof beams," 54:11–16

2 g̃uruš šidim 4 g̃uruš šu dím-[ma] 4 géme **im ga$_6$-[g̃á]-dè** gu[b-ba] 1 g̃uruš im ì-[li]-de$_9$ gu[b-ba] éš g̃eš ùr kéše-[rá], "2 builders (and) 4 workmen having built, 4 workwomen employed to carry earth (and) 1 workman employed to lift earth, (workers) having bound ropes to roof beams," 57:'12-'16

5.12.3 Carrying Earth for Building

n g̃uruš 10 géme **im ga$_6$-g̃á** šu dím-ma gub-ba, "n workmen (and) 10 workwomen employed to carry earth (for) building," 29:'18, 29:'28

5.12.4 Carrying Earth in the Clay-Tablet Coffer

2 g̃uruš bisag̃ im sar-ra **im ga$_6$-g̃á**, "2 workmen having carried earth in the clay tablet coffer," 103:30

5.12.5 Carrying Earth to Plaster the Brick Stack

[10] géme **im ga$_6$-g̃á** 3 g̃uruš im lu-a SIG$_4$.ANŠE im sumur aka, "[10] workwomen having carried earth (and) 3 workmen having mixed earth, (workers) having plastered the brick stack," 199:12–14

[4] géme **im [ga$_6$]-g̃á** 1 g̃uruš im lu-a 1 g̃uruš a bal-[a] 1 g̃uruš in-u ga$_6$-[g̃á] im lu-a SIG$_4$.⌜ANŠE⌝ im sumur aka, "[4] workwomen having carried earth, 1 workman having mixed earth, 1 workman having poured water (and) 1 workman having carried straw (and) having mixed (it with) earth, (workers) having plastered the brick stack," 209:27–32

5.12.6 Carrying Earth For Repair

2 g̃uruš šidim 2 g̃uruš šu dím 6 géme **im ga$_6$-[g̃á-dè]** gub-[ba] 1 g̃uruš im ì-l[i-de$_9$ gub-ba] *ták-ši-ru-[um . . .]* ù [. . .], "2 builders (and) 2 workmen having built, 6 workwomen employed [to] carry earth, 1 workman [employed to] lift earth, (for) repair (work) [. . .]," 58:40–44

5.12.7 Employed for Construction

*See **al-tar** for the complete context of the following passages.

8 géme **im ga$_6$-g̃á-dè** (. . .) al-tar gub-ba, "8 workwomen to carry earth (. . .), (workers) employed for construction," 58:24, 26

[n] géme **im ga$_6$-[g̃á-dè]** (. . .) [n] géme **im ga$_6$-g̃[á-dè]** ⌜al⌝-tar [. . .], "[n] workwomen [to] carry earth (. . .) (and) [n] workwomen [to] carry earth, (for) construction [. . .]," 106:25, 27–28

11 géme **im ga$_6$-g̃á** g̃eš ùr kéše-rá (. . .) al-tar gub-ba, "11 workwomen having carried earth to bind roof beams (. . .), (workers) employed for construction," 140:27–28, 36

24 géme **im ga$_6$-g̃á** iz-zi im sumur aka (. . .) al-[tar] gub-ba, "24 workwomen having carried earth—(workers) having plastered the iz-zi wall—(. . .), (workers) employed for construction," 144:'9-'10, '15

6. im sumur ga$_6$(g̃), "to carry plaster"

6.1 Construction of the House

2 g̃uruš **im sumur** šà é-a-šè **ga$_6$-g̃á**, "2 workmen having carried plaster for the interior of the house," 5:22

6.2 Construction of the New Palace

23 ĝuruš 20-lá-1 géme **im sumur** $\mathbf{ga_6}$**-ĝá-**⸢**dè**⸣ [gub-ba] (. . .) ùr é-gal gibil a ĝá-ĝ[á-d]è gub-⸢ba⸣, "23 workmen (and) 19 workwomen [employed] to carry plaster (. . .), (workers) employed to waterproof the roof of the new palace," 75:19, 21

7. in-u $\mathbf{ga_6}$(ĝ), "to carry straw"

7.1 Carried from the Canal

[10]-lá-1 ĝuruš ⸢**in**⸣**-u** i[$_7$-k]ar-na$_4$-t[a **g**]$\mathbf{a_6}$**-ĝá-dè** gub-ba, "9 workmen employed to carry straw from the Karna canal," 83:14–16

3 ĝuruš [**in**]**-u** gú i$_7$-^{d}amar-^{d}E[N.ZU]-ta im lu-a-šè **íb-**$\mathbf{ga_6}$, "3 workmen carried straw from the bank of the Amar-*Suen* canal for mixing (with) earth," 194:49–51

3 ĝuruš **in-**[**u**] i$_7$-^{d}šu-^{d}*suen*-⸢ḫé⸣-ĝál-ta im lu-a-šè **íb-**$\mathbf{ga_6}$, "3 workmen carried straw from the *Šu-Suen* Canal of Abundance for mixing (with) earth,'" 198:'24-'25

7.2 Carried from the Storehouse to the Dirt Quarry

n ĝuruš **in-u** ĝá-nun-ta ka-lá(-ka)-šè **íb-**$\mathbf{ga_6}$, "n workmen carried straw from the storehouse to the dirt quarry," 185:'15-'16, 196:'24

7.3 Carried to the Storehouse

7.3.1 From the Bank of the Canal

20? ĝuruš gú i$_7$-da-ta ĝá-nun-sè **in-u** $\mathbf{ga_6}$**-ĝá**, "20? workmen having carried straw from the bank of the canal to the storehouse," 16:25

7.3.2 From the Quay

n ĝuruš **in-u** kar-ta ĝá-nun-šè **íb-**$\mathbf{ga_6}$, "n workmen carried straw from the quay to the storehouse," 28:'23, 39:39, 43:'35-'37, 187:22–24

n ĝuruš **in-u** kar-ta ĝá-nun-šè $\mathbf{ga_6}$**-ĝá**, "n workmen having carried straw from the quay to the storehouse," 35:39, 188:'18-'20

6 ĝuruš **in-u** [^{d}*šu*]-^{d}*suen*-am-ma-ar-ra^{ki}-ta de$_6$-a kar-ta ĝá-nun-šè **íb-**$\mathbf{ga_6}$, "6 workmen, having brought straw from *Šu-Suen*-ammara, carried it from the quay to the storehouse," 198:'28

7.4 Construction of Individual Households

[n ĝuruš] **in-u** $\mathbf{ga_6}$**-**[**ĝá-dè**] (. . .) é-*a*-[*lu*]-*a*, "[n workmen to] carry straw (. . .), (work for) the house of *Alua*," 101:23, 25

[n g]éme **in-**[**u**] $\mathbf{ga_6}$**-ĝá-dè** (. . .) é-⸢*pi*$_5$-*ša-aḫ*⸣-*ilum*, "[n] workwomen to carry straw (. . .), (work for) the house of *Pišaḫ-ilum*," 108:31, 33

1 ĝuruš **in-u** $\mathbf{ga_6}$**-ĝá** im lu-a é-*ì-lí-bi-šu*, "1 workman having carried straw (and) having mixed (it with) earth, (work for) the house of *Ili-bišu*," 204:'8-'9

7.5 Construction of the Enclosure Wall

9 ĝuruš šidim 14 ĝuruš 18 géme šeg$_{12}$ šu dím-ma sum-mu-dè gub-ba 2 ĝuruš 2 géme im a-ĝá-ri-na ì-li-de$_9$ gub-ba 20 géme im ga$_6$-ĝá-dè gub-ba 3 ĝuruš 3 géme im lu-dè gub-ba 1 ĝuruš **in-u** $\mathbf{ga_6}$**-ĝá** im lu-a 7 géme šeg$_{12}$ ⸢da⸣-b[àd ĝá-ĝá-dè gub-ba], "9 builders, 14 workmen (and) 18 workwomen employed to hand (up) bricks for building, 2 workmen (and) 2 workwomen employed to lift earth into the *agarinnum*, 20 workwomen employed to carry earth, 3 workmen (and) 3 workwomen employed to mix earth, 1

workman having carried straw (and) having mixed (it with) earth (and) 7 workwomen [employed to place] bricks at the side of the (enclosure) wall," 16:17–23

7.6 To Plaster the Brick Pile

[4] géme im [ga$_6$]-g̃á 1 g̃uruš im lu-a 1 g̃uruš a bal-[a] 1 g̃uruš **in-u ga$_6$-[g̃á]** im lu-a SIG$_4$.⸢ANŠE⸣ im sumur aka, "[4] workwomen having carried earth, 1 workman having mixed earth, 1 workman having poured water (and) 1 workman having carried straw (and) having mixed (it with) earth, (workers) having plastered the brick pile," 209:27–32

8. ^{ğeš}**kišig ga$_6$(g̃)**, "to carry shok"

8.1 From the Quay to the Storehouse

n g̃uruš ^{ğeš}**kišig** kar-ta g̃á-nun-šè **ga$_6$-g̃á**, "n workmen having carried shok from the quay to the storehouse," 147:46, 155:34

30-lá-1 g̃uruš [4 gém]e ^{ğeš}**kišig** kar-ta g̃á-nun-šè **ga$_6$-g̃á**, "29 workmen and [4] workwomen having carried shok from the quay to the storehouse," 154:42

4 g̃uruš u$_4$-1-šè kar-ta g̃á-nun-šè **ga$_6$-⸢g̃á⸣**,"4 workmen for 1 day having carried (shok) from the quay to the storehouse," 235:11–12

9. **níg̃-gú-na ga$_6$(g̃)**, "to carry the commodity tax"

17 g̃uruš níg̃-gú-na kar-ta é-kišib-ba-šè **ga$_6$-g̃á**, "17 workmen having carried the commodity tax from the quay to the storeroom," 129:5, 129:39, 130:5, 130:'19, 131:'30, 132:5, 132:37

10. **še ga$_6$(g̃)**, "to carry barley"

10.1 From Du-saḫara to Enzu-babbar

1 g̃uruš túg-du$_8$ u$_4$-12-šè du$_6$-saḫar-ra^{ki}-ta en-zu-bábbar^{ki}-šè **[še] íb-ga$_6$**, "1 braider for 12 days carried [barley] from Du-saḫara to Enzu-babbar," 263:1–5

10.2 From Ekabba and Karkar to Garšana

3 g̃uruš u$_4$-1-šè **še** é-kab-[ba^{ki}] karkar^{ki}-[ta] gar-ša-an-na^{ki}-[šè] **íb-ga$_6$**, "3 workmen for 1 day carried barley [from] Ekabba (and) Karkar [to] Garšana," 884:6–10

10.3 From the Quay to the Granary

14 g̃uruš **še** ki ur-^{d}šul-pa-UD.⸢DU⸣-ta de$_6$-a kar-ta gur$_7$-šè **íb-[ga$_6$]**, "14 workmen, having brought barley from Ur-Šulpa'e, [carried] it from the quay to the granary," 192:'18-'19

1⅔ g̃uruš ašgab u$_4$-3-šè kar-ta gur$_7$-šè **še íb-ga$_6$**, "1⅔ leather workers for 3 days carried barley from the quay to the granary," 229:5–7

10.4 From the Quay to the Storehouse

12 g̃uruš **še** kar?-ta g̃á-nun-šè **ga$_6$-g̃á**, "12 workmen having carried barley from the quay? to the storehouse," 104:42, 105:40

[n] g̃uruš tú[g-d]u$_8$ u$_4$-9-šè **še** ù-dag-ga^{ki}-ta gar-ša-an-na^{ki}-šè de$_6$-a ù kar-[ta] g̃á-nun-šè **íb-⸢ga$_6$⸣**, "[n] braider(s) for 9 days having brought barley from Udaga to Garšana and carried it [from] the quay to the storehouse," 261:1–6

10.5 From *Šu-Suen*-ammara

8 g̃uruš sag̃-tag 2 g̃uruš á-⅔-ta 4 g̃uruš á-½ ta ^{lú}ázlag-me-éš [u$_4$]-1-šè **⸢še⸣** ^{d}*šu*-^{d}*suen*-amma-ar^{ki}-ta de$_6$-a **íb-[ga$_6$]**, "8 full-time fullers, 2 fullers at ⅔ wages, (and) 4 fullers at ½ wages for 1 [day carried] barley brought from *Šu-Suen*-ammara," 248:1–6

3 géme g̃eš-ì-sur-sur u_4-1-šè **še** ^{d}*šu*-^{d}*suen*-am-ma-ar^{ki}-ta de_6-a **íb-ga_6**, "3 female oil pressers for 1 day carried barley brought from *Šu-Suen*-ammara," 249:1–3

10.6 From the Tower to the Weir

(. . .) [u_4]-3-šè [**še** x] x x x an-za-qar-ta kun-zi-da i_7-a-gàr-ús-sa a-šà lú-maḫ-šè **íb-ga_6** ù má-a si-ga, "{workers and boats} for 3 day; (the boats) carried [barley . . .] from the fortified tower to the weir of the Agar-usa Canal of the Lu-maḫ field and (the workers) having loaded the boat(s)," 553:11–15

11. **$šeg_{12}$ ga_6(g̃)**, "to carry bricks"

11.1 Carried from the Kiln to the Canal

20 géme **$šeg_{12}$**-al-ur_x-ra gir_4-ta i_7-šè **ga_6-g̃á**, "20 workwomen having carried bricks from the kiln to the canal," 113:'16, 145:37

[n g̃]uruš **$šeg_{12}$**-al-ur_x-⌜ra⌝ gir_4-ta i_7-šè **ga_6-[g̃á]**, "[n] workmen having carried bricks from the kiln to the canal," 143:35

[n] g̃uruš 17 géme **$šeg_{12}$**-al-ur_x-r[a gir_4-ta] i_7-šè **ga_6-[g̃á]**, "[n] workmen (and) 17 workwomen having carried bricks [from the kiln] to the canal," 146:'38

11.2 Construction of the Brewery-Kitchen-Mill Complex

[n] géme **$šeg_{12}$ ga_6-[g̃á-dè]** (. . .) [é-lùn]ga é-kíkken [ù é-muḫaldim], "[n] workwomen [to] carry bricks (. . .), (work for) the brewery-kitchen-mill complex," 106:31, 32

11.3 Construction of the House of *Šu-Eštar* and *Zakiti*

30 géme **$šeg_{12}$ ga_6-g̃á** [n] g̃uruš 6 géme iz-zi é-*šu-eš*$_4$-*tár* ù *za-ki-ti* gul-la, "30 workwomen having carried bricks (and) [n] workmen (and) 6 workwomen having demolished the iz-zi wall of the house of *Šu-Eštar* and *Zakiti*," 104:27–29, 105:26–28

11.4 Wages for Carrying Bricks

11.4.1 Sample with Full Context

šu+níg̃in 3⅔ ⌜sar⌝-ta ús-bi 90 nindan á-géme–1-[a] 120-$šeg_{12}$-ta géme-bi 22 u_4-1-še še 3-sìla-ta ba-ḫug̃ še-bi 0.1.0.6 sìla á **$šeg_{12}$ ga_6-g̃á** ki-sá-a é-uš-bar-šè mu-DU *za-la-a* ugula lú-ḫ[ug̃-g̃á] g̃iri ^{d}*adad-tillati* [ù] *puzur*$_4$-^{d}nin-kar-ak du[b-sar], "In total: 3⅔ sar (of bricks) each, its base is 90 nindan (long), workwomen wages for each 120 bricks, its workwomen (equal) 22 workerdays, hired for 3 liters of barley each. Their barley is 66 liters, wages of (workers) having carried bricks. *Zala'a*, overseer of hired workers having delivered (bricks) for the foundation terrace of the textile mill under the authority of *Adad-tillati* [and] *Puzur*-Ninkarak, the scribe," 311:14–24

11.4.2 References

á **$šeg_{12}$ ga_6-g̃á**, "wages of (workers) having carried bricks," 310:'16, 311:20, 312:34, 316:71, 317:29, 318:'49, 320:10, 321:'32, 322:'82, 323:123, 324:93, 325:17, 327:81, 328:13, 330:26, 334:64, 335:40, 336:21, 336:27, 337:29, 338:20, 339:12, 340:32, 341:11, 342:82, 343:10, 344:'24, 347:'16, 352:39, 353:16, 362:'19, 368:'59, 373:'11, 452:3, 498:3, 499:3, 503:5

11.4.3 The Remainder of Wages

n še *si-ì-tum* á **šeg$_{12}$ ga$_6$-g̃á** ù al-tar-ra PN ugula lú-ḫug̃-g̃á in-da-g̃ál, "n liter(s) of barley, the remainder of wages of (workers) having carried bricks and (employed) for construction are with PN, overseer of hired workers" > *Personal Name Index*

li-la-a *simat-é-a* *ša-at-èr-ra*

1.2.5. še gur *si-ì-tum* á **šeg$_{12}$ [ga$_6$-g̃á]** á 5 sìla-⸢ta⸣ *li-l*[*a-tum*] ⸢in⸣-d[a-g̃ál], "1 bushel (and) 170 liters of barley, the remainder of wages of (workers) [having carried] bricks—wages of 5 liters each—are with *Lilatum*," 499:1–6

2.2.3. še-gur 15 ma-na siki **šeg$_{12}$ ga$_6$-g̃á-[dè]** ki ^{d}*adad-tillati*-ta [*puzur$_4$-a-gu$_5$*]-*um* šu ba-ti, "*Puzur-agum* received 2 bushels (and) 150 liters of barley (and) 15 minas of wool from *Adad-tillati* [to] carry bricks," 638:1–6

12. Other Objects, Broken Context

12.1 Grass

[x-r]a?-ra-am ú **ga$_6$-[g̃á . . .], 1062:7–8

12.2 Sesame

[n s]ìla g̃eš-ì [x]-ga$_6$**? a[ka x?], "n liter(s) (?) sesame," 1181:1–2

13. Commodity Broken

[. . .] **ga$_6$-g̃á**, 15:33

[n g̃uruš . . .] **ga$_6$-⸢g̃á⸣**, 26:'12, 193:33

[n géme] **ga$_6$-g̃á-[dè** gub-ba], 65:'13

[. . .] 10 g̃uruš **ga$_6$-g̃á**, 109:29

1 [g̃uruš. . .] **ga$_6$-g̃á**, 138:39

14. un-ga$_6$, "carrier" > *Personal Name Index*

da-da-a *ì-lí-aš-ra-ni*
el-pa-dan *tu-ra-am-ì-lí*

g̃uruš **un-ga$_6$**, "carrier" > *Craftsmen Index*

gaba . . . ri, "to confront, to meet"

gaba-ri-a, "meeting" > **gaba-ri-a**

12 g̃uruš má **gaba ri-a** igi *šu-kab-tá*-šè g̃en-⸢na⸣, "12 workmen having gone before *Šu-Kabta*, having met the boat," 163:37

gaba . . . sàg, "to beat one's breasts (in mourning)"

1. During the *Abum* Festival

1 g̃uruš túg-du$_8$ u$_4$-12-šè **gaba sàg-dè** ⸢gub⸣-ba u$_4$ ezem-*a-bu-um-ma*, "1 braider employed for 12 days to beat (his) breast during the *Abum* festival," 278:1–4

2. When the King Died

85 géme-⸢sag̃⸣-dub 16 géme á-⅓-⸢ta⸣ u$_4$-1-šè géme uš-bar-me-éš **gaba sàg-dè** gub-ba u$_4$ lugal-e ba-úš-[a], "85 full-time female weavers (and) 16 female weavers at ⅓ wages employed for 1 day to beat (their) breasts when the king died," 257:1–6

3. When *Nawir-ilum* Died

11 g̃uruš sa[g̃-tag] 2 g̃uruš á-⅔-ta 4 g̃uruš á-½-ta 1 g̃uruš á-⅓<-ta> ^{lú}ázlag-me-éš u_4-1-šè **gaba sàg-gé-dè** [gub-ba] u_4 *na-wi-ir-*[*ilum* ba-úš-a], "11 full-time fullers, 2 fullers at ⅔ wages, 4 fullers at ½ wages (and) 1 fuller at ⅓ wages [employed] for 1 day to beat (their) breasts when *Nawir-ilum* [died]," 250:1–8

(. . .) ⸢u_4⸣-1-šè **gaba sàg-dè** gub-ba u_4 dig̃ir-re gaba *na-wi-ir-ilum* ba-a-g̃ar-ra, "{craftsmen} employed for 1 day to beat (their) breasts when the god made the breast of *Nawir-ilum* subside (i.e. when he died)," 251:8–10

4. When *Šu-Kabta* Died

97 géme sag-dub 15 géme á-⅓-ta géme uš-bar-me-éš [n] géme gu [u_4]-9½-šè [**gaba**] **sàg-dè** gub-[ba u_4 *šu*]-*kab-tá* ba-ú[š-a], "97 full-time female weavers (and) 15 female weavers at ⅓ wages (and) [n] female spinners employed for 9½ days to beat (their) [breasts when] *Šu-Kabta* died," 252:1–7

5. When Šulgi-*rama* Died

3 g̃uruš u_4-1-šè **gaba sàg-dè** gub-ba u_4 ^{d}šul-gi-*r*[*a-ma* ba-uš-a], "3 workmen employed for 1 day to beat (their) breasts when Šulgi-*rama* [died]," 246:5–7

6. Occasion Unspecified

0.1.0. kaš-gen 0.0.2.1½ ⸢sìla kaš⸣ lú **gaba sàg-dè** íb-nag̃, "The men who beat (their) breasts drank 60 liters of ordinary beer (and) 21½ liters of beer," 507:12–13

3 g̃uruš u_4-9½-šè **gaba sàg-dè** gub-ba, "3 workmen employed for 9½ days to beat (their) breasts," 968:18–19

gaz, *dâku*, *šagāšu*, "to break; beat; thresh (grain)"

1. Damaged(?) Commodities

(. . .) [. . .]-**gaz**-a-ḫi? [x]-**gaz-gaz** [. . .]-zi-ra é-tab-tab-ba [?] x-šè ba-an-ku_4, "{baskets and other reed products, ropes, palm products, leather products, pots and other containers}; [. . .] broken(? vessels?) entered the double house for [x]," 1376:87–90

2. Pots to be Broken[4]

12 ^{dug}b[a-x] ⸢mu⸣ dig̃ir-re-e-ne-šè **gaz-dè**, "12 [x]-vessels to be broken for the gods," 1013:6–7

gen_6, *kânu*, "to confirm, verify"

PN ka-ga-na **ba-ge-en**, "confirmed by PN" > *Personal Name Index*

a-na-aḫ-ì-lí	*da-da-a*	^{d}*ma-lik-ba-ni*
a-ta-li-ku	*ḫal-lí-a*	*na-na*
ak-ba-zum	*ì-lí-an-dùl*	
^{d}ba-ú-da	*li-bur-i-du-ni*	

[4] For this interpretation note ^{dug}sìla gaz, "zerbrechendes Litergefäss" (Sallaberger 1996,106).

gi$_4$, *apālu*, "to send back, return"

egir buru$_{14}$ **gi$_4$-gi$_4$-dè** su-su-dam, "after the harvest he shall pay (it) back" > **su-su**

1. To be Returned after the Harvest

1.1 Dida Beer, from *Adad-tillati*

1 dida-gen 0.0.3. še-bi 0.1.0. ki ^{d}*adad-tillati*-[ta] *a-da-làl* [muḫaldim] šu ba-⸢ti⸣ egir bu[ru$_{14}$ **gi$_4$-gi$_4$-dè**], "From *Adad-tillati, Adallal*, the cook, received 1 (container) of 30 liters of ordinary dida beer—its barley (equivalent) is 60 liters—[to be paid back] after the harvest," 1098:1–6

11 dug dida$_x$-g̃en 0.0.3.-ta še-bi 2.1.0. gur ki ^{d}*adad-tillati*-ta *aš-tá-qar* šu ba-an-ti egir buru$_{14}$ **g[i$_4$-gi$_4$-dè]**, "From *Adad-tillati, Aštaqqar* received 11 jugs of 30 liters of ordinary dida beer each—their barley (equivalent) is 2 bushels and 60 liters—[to be] paid back after the harvest," 629:1–6

1.2 Sheep Skins, from *Awilumma*

[n] kuš-udu ki *á-wi-lu*[*m-ma*-ta] ^{d}*adad-tillati* ⸢šu⸣ ba-ti [egir bu]ru$_{14}$ **gi$_4$-gi$_4$-[dè]**, "From *Awilumma, Adad-tillati* received [n] sheep skin(s) [to be] paid back after the harvest," 893:1–5

2. Returned Barley

iti u$_4$-29-ba-zal še nu-g̃ál **bí-in-gi$_4$** u$_4$-1-àm mu-[un-g̃ál] še šabra in-na-an-sum šu te-g̃e$_6$-dè nu-un-dab$_5$?, "At the end of the 29th day of the month there was no barley. (Someone) returned it. On the 1st day, it was there. (Then) the barley was given to the majordomo. In order for him to receive it, it will not (first) be taken (by someone else)," 1057:1–7

gíd, *arāku*, "(to be) long; to tighten; to survey, measure out a field; to quarry (clay); to tow/pull a boat upstream"

bí-ni-tum **gíd**, "to tighten crossbeams"

g̃eš ùr gíd, "to tighten roof beams"

im gíd, "to haul earth"

má gíd, "to tow/pull a boat upstream"

sar gíd, "to survey land"

túg gíd, "to extend a textile (on a loom)"

1. *bí-ni-tum* gíd, "to tighten crossbeams"

1.1 For Construction of the Brewery-Kitchen-Mill Complex

*See *Household Index* for the complete context of the following passages.

20 g̃uruš [***bí-n***]***i-tum*** **gíd-dè** (. . .) [. . . é-lùnga é-muḫaldim] ù é-kíkken, "20 workmen to tighten crossbeams (. . .), [. . . (work for) the brewery-kitchen]-mill complex," 144:'18, '21

10 g̃uruš ***bí-ni-tum*** **gíd-[da]** (. . .) al-tar é-lùnga é-muḫaldim ù é-kík[ken], "10 workmen having tightened crossbeams (. . .), (for) construction of the brewery-kitchen-mill complex," 145:34, 36

2. g̃eš ùr gíd, "to tighten roof beams"

*See *Household Index* for the complete context of the following passages.

2.1 Construction of the Brewery-Kitchen-Mill Complex

13 [g̃uruš **g̃eš**] **ùr** kéše **gíd-da** (. . .) [. . . é-lùnga é-muḫaldim] ù é-kíkken, "13 [workmen] having tightened bound roof [beams] (. . .), [. . . (work for) the brewery-kitchen]-mill complex," 144:'19, '21

2 g̃uruš 7 géme **g̃eš** [**ùr** kéše **gíd-dè**] (. . .) ⸢al⸣-tar é-lùnga é-muḫaldim ù [é-kíkken], "2 workmen (and) 7 workwomen [to tighten bound roof] beams (. . .), (for) construction of the brewery-kitchen-mill complex," 146:'26-'35

2.2 Construction of the Textile Depository

1 g̃uruš šidim um-mi-a 2 g̃uruš šidim 22 g̃uruš 6 géme **g̃eš ùr** kéše **gíd-da** gub-ba (. . .) $kurum_7$ aka al-tar ki-mu-ra gub-ba, "1 master builder, 2 builders, 22 workmen (and) 6 workwomen employed to tighten bound roof beams (. . .) inspection (of the work) of (workers) employed (for) construction of the textile depository," 76:10–14, 19

2.3 Ropes to Tighten Roof Beams

8 [gi]dur-gazi a-rá tab-ba gíd 1½ nindan-ta **g̃eš ùr** kéše **gíd-da** (. . .) ká-suḫur é-lùnga-šè ba-a-g̃ar, "8 9-meter 2-ply gazi ropes having tightened bound roof beams (and) {other planks} were placed for the tree-top gate of the brewery," 1297:1–2, 5

3. im gíd, "to haul earth"

3.1 For Construction (al-tar)

*See **al-tar** for the complete context of the following passages.

1 g̃uruš **im gíd-dè** (. . .) al-tar gub-ba, "1 workman to haul earth (. . .), (workers) employed for construction," 58:23, 26

n géme **im gíd** (. . .) al-tar gub-ba, "n workwomen having hauled earth (. . .), (workers) employed for construction," 106:24, 28, 140:34, 36

3.2 Construction of the Foundation Terrace of the Brewery and Mill

*See *Household Index* for the complete context of the following passage.

n géme **im gíd** (. . .) al-tar ki-sá-a é-lùnga ù é-kíkken, "n workwomen having hauled earth (. . .), (for) construction of the foundation terrace of the brewery and mill," 113:'12, '15, 115:'19, '21, 121:29, 31, 123:28, 30

3.3 Construction of the Brewery-Kitchen-Mill Complex

*See *Household Index* for the complete context of the following passages.

n géme **im gíd** (. . .) ⸢al⸣-tar ki-sá-a é-lùnga é-muḫaldim ù é-kíkken, "n workwomen having hauled earth (. . .), (for) construction of the foundation terrace of the brewery-kitchen-mill complex," 125:24, 26, 126:24, 28, 132:26, 30

n géme **im gíd** (. . .) al-tar é-lùnga é-muḫaldim ù é-kíkken, "n workwomen having hauled earth (. . .), (for) construction of the brewery-kitchen-mill complex," 128:24, 28, 129:25, 29, 131:'19, '23, 133:26, 29, 135:27, 30, 138:27, 31, 143:29, 34

3.4 Construction of the Textile Mill

*See *Household Index* for the complete context of the following passages.

4 g̃uruš **im gíd-dè** gub-ba (. . .) é-uš-[bar . . .], "4 workmen employed to haul earth (. . .), [(work for)] the textile mill," 33:24, 30

6 géme **im** [**gíd-dè** gub-ba] (. . .) é-uš-bar-⸢šè⸣, "6 workwomen [employed to haul] earth (. . .), (work) for the textile mill," 38:22, 27

1 ĝuruš **im ⌜gíd-dè⌝** gub-ba (. . .) al-t[ar] é-[uš-bar-ra], "1 workman employed to haul earth, (. . .) (for) construction of the textile mill," 52:32, 35

3.4.1 Its Foundation

[4?] géme **im gíd** ga_6-dè gub-ba (. . .) ⌜uš⌝ é-uš-bar-ra, "[4?] workwomen having hauled earth, employed to carry it (. . .), (work) for the foundation of the textile mill," 47:22, 26

3.4.2 Its Foundation Terrace

1 ĝuruš **im gíd-dè** gub-ba (. . .) 40 géme $šeg_{12}$ da-ki-sá-a é-uš-bar ĝá-ĝá-dè gub-[ba], "1 workman employed to haul earth (. . .), (and) 40 workwomen employed to place bricks at the side of the foundation terrace of the textile mill," 35:24, 28

2 ĝuruš **im gíd-dè** gub-ba (. . .) ki-sá-a é-uš-bar-šè, "2 workmen employed to haul earth (. . .), (work) for the foundation terrace of the textile mill," 43:'29, '32, 44:29[5]

3.5 Construction of Various Houses

*See *Household Index* for the complete context of the following passages.

3.5.1 The House of *Baḫa'a*

2 géme **im gíd** (. . .) é-*ba-ḫa-a* dù-[a], "2 workwomen having hauled earth (. . .), (workers) having constructed the house of *Baḫa'a*," 114:34, 36

3.5.2 The House of *Putanum*

2 géme **im gíd** (. . .) é-*pu-tá-nu-um* dù-a, "2 workwomen having hauled earth (. . .), (workers) having constructed the house of *Putanum*," 120:'27, '29

2 géme **im gíd** (. . .) al-tar é-*pu-ta-nu-um*, "2 workwomen having hauled earth (. . .), (for) construction of the house of *Putanum*," 121:24, 26

[n géme] **im gíd** (. . .) é-*pu-ta-nu-um*, "[n workwomen] having hauled earth (. . .), (for) the house of *Putanum*," 122:'18, '20

3.6 Construction of the (Enclosure) Wall

*See **al-tar** for the complete context of the following passage.

2 géme **im gíd-dè** (. . .) al-tar bàd gub-ba, "2 workwomen to haul earth (. . .), (workers) employed (for) construction of the (enclosure) wall," 102:21, 23, 103:18, 20

3.7 Construction of the urua wall

1 ĝuruš šidim um-mi-a 2 ĝuruš šidim 2 ĝuruš šu dím 2 géme **im gíd(-me)** 2 géme *du-ú-um* aka 10 géme im ga_6-ĝá ù-ru-a ⌜bàd⌝ aka, "1 master builder, 2 builders (and) 2 workmen having built, 2 workwomen having hauled earth, 2 workwomen having made a *du-ú-um* (and) 10 workwomen having carried earth, (workers) having made the urua wall," 104:20–26, 105:21–25

3.8 Construction of the Warehouse

*See *Household Index* for the complete context of the following passage.

---

5 Restored from duplicate, no. 43:'26-'32.

1 ĝuruš **im gíd-dè** gub-ba (. . .) é-kišib-ba ugula kíkken, "1 workman employed to haul earth (. . .), (for) the warehouse (under the authority of?) the overseer of the mill," 36:22, 25

3.9 Construction Site Broken or Unspecified

2 ĝuruš **im gíd-d[è** gub-ba], "2 workmen [employed] to haul earth," 32:22

1 géme **im gíd-d[è** gub-ba], "1 workwoman [employed] to haul earth," 93:'19

57 ĝuruš **im ⸢gíd⸣**, "57 workmen having hauled earth," 152:'22, 153:'35

1 ĝuruš šidim um-m[i-a] 2 ĝuruš šidim 6 ĝuruš šu dím-ma 2 géme *du-<ú->um* aka 2 géme [**im gíd** n] géme im ga$_6$-[ĝá-dè] 1 ĝuruš šidim [2 ĝuruš šu dím n] géme im ga$_6$-ĝ[á-dè a]l-tar [. . .], "1 master builder, 2 builders, 6 workmen having built, 2 workwomen having made a *du-ú-um*, 2 workwomen [having hauled earth, n] workwomen [to] carry earth, 1 builder (and) [2 workmen having built], (and) [n] workwomen [to] carry earth, (for) construction [. . .]," 106:22–28

4. **má gíd**, "to tow a boat (upstream)"

^{gi}kid **má ⸢gíd⸣**, "a mat for towing boats" > **^{gi}kid**

éš **má gíd**, "boat towing rope" > **éš**

4.1 From Garšana

4.1.1 To Karkar

9 ĝuruš gar-ša-an-na^{ki}-ta karkar^{ki}-šè **má gíd-⸢da⸣**, "9 workmen having towed a boat from Garšana to Karkar," 209:33–34

4 ĝuruš u$_4$-1-šè gar-ša-an-na^{ki}-ta karkar^{ki}-šè **má gíd-da**, "4 workmen for 1 day having towed a boat from Garšana to Karkar," 235:5–6

76 ĝuruš 4 **má**-10-gur-ta gar-ša-an-na^{ki}-ta karkar^{ki}-šè **gíd-da**, "76 workmen having towed 4 10-bushel boats from Garšana to Karkar," 236:6–9

4.1.2 To Nippur

2 ĝuruš ašgab 1 ĝuruš ad-kub$_4$ u$_4$-4-[šè] **má** ^{ĝeš}šim ḫi-a gar-ša-an-na^{ki}-ta nibru^{ki}-šè **in-gíd-sa-a**, "2 leather workers (and) 1 reed craftsman [for] 4 days who towed a boat (with) various resinous woods from Garšana to Nippur," 253:1–7

1 ĝuruš u$_4$-7-šè **má gíd má**-40-gur-ta 2-àm gar-ša-an-na^{ki}-ta nibru^{ki}-šè **in-gíd-sa-a**(sic!), "1 workman for 7 days who towed 2 40-bushel boats from Garšana to Nippur," 255:1–5

3.4.5. ninda šu-r[a gur lú]-é-^{d}šu-^{d}EN.[ZU^{ki} l]ú-*dì-ma-a*[*t-kál-bu*]*-um*$^{⸢ki⸣}$ lú-^{d}*šu*-^{d}EN.Z[U-am-ma]-ar-[ra^{ki} **má**-n-gur gar-ša-an-na^{ki}-ta] nibru^{ki}-[šè] **in-gíd-s[a-a]**, "3 bushels (and) 290 liters of half (loaf) bread (for) the [men] from *Bit-Šu-Suen*, the men from *Dimat-kalbum* (and) the men from *Šu-Suen*-ammara who towed [a n-bushel boat from Garšana to] Nippur," 463:1–8

3 ĝuruš u$_4$-11-šè dabin ninda túg ù ì ḫi-a gar-ša-an-na^{ki}-ta nibru^{ki}-šè **má gíd-da**, "3 workmen for 11 days having towed a boat (with) various (amounts of) semolina, bread, textiles (and) oil from Garšana to Nippur," 931:2–6

4.1.3 To *Puzriš-Dagan*

(. . .) àga-ús [*ri-im*]*-ilum* íb-gu$_7$ u$_4$ **má** *simat-*^{d}*ištaran* gar-ša-an-na^{ki}-ta *puzur*$_4$*-iš-*^{d}*da-gan*[^{ki}-šè] **in-gíd-sa-a**, "the gendarme *Rim-ilum* ate {assorted comestibles} when they towed the boat of *Simat-Ištaran* from Garšana to *Puzriš-Dagan*," 551:12–15

4.1.4 Other

1 [g̃uruš . . .] **má**-20-gur-bi 2-à[m gar-š]a-an-na^{ki}-ta [. . . ka] i_7-è-šè **gíd-⌜da**, "1 [workman . . .] having towed 2 20-bushel boats from Garšana [. . . to the opening] of the 'Outgoing' canal," 195:'17-'20

2 [g̃uruš gar-ša]-an-na^{ki}-ta ka A.[ENGUR]-šè **má gíd-da**, "2 [workmen] having towed a boat from Garšana to the opening of the canal," 198:'26-'27

9 g̃uruš gar-ša-an-na^{ki}-ta adab^{ki}-šè **má gíd-da** é-du_6-gur_4-*i-din-^{d}adad*-šè, "9 workmen having towed a boat from Garšana to Adab, to the round-hill-house of *Iddin-Adad*," 207:23–25

[. . . x] g̃uruš á-[n-ta] ^{lú}ázlag-me-[éš] u_4-1-[šè] **má**-nin-zi-šà-g̃ál gar-ša-an-na^{ki}-ta G̃EŠ.KÚŠU^{ki}-šè **in-gíd-ša-a**, "[. . .] (and) [n] fuller(s) [at n] wages [for] 1 day who towed the boat of Nin-zišag̃al from Garšana to G̃EŠ.KÚŠU," 238:1–7

7 g̃uruš ašgab u_4-1-šè é-da-na^{ki}-šè **má gíd-da**, "7 leather workers for 1 day having towed a boat to Edana," 884:3–4

4.2 To Garšana

4.2.1 From Nippur

0.0.4. ⅔ sìla [. . . àga]-ús é-gal-la gub-ba [íb]-gu_7 u_4 **⌜má⌝** *ra-ba-tum* nibru^{ki}-ta gar-ša-an-na^{ki}-šè **i[n-g]íd-sa-a**, "The gendarme employed at the palace ate 4⅔ liters [. . .] when they towed the boat of *Rabatum* from Nippur to Garšana," 506:22–26

4.2.2 From *Puzriš-Dagan*

0.0.1. kaš-gen ugula àga-ús-e-ne á-u_4-te-na u_4-2-kam àga-ús *ri-im-ilum* íb-nag̃ (. . .) u_4 **má** *simat-^{d}ištaran puzur$_4$-iš-^{d}da-gan*^{ki}-ta gar-ša-an-na^{ki}-šè **mu-un-gíd-š[a-a]**, "10 liters of ordinary beer, in the evening on the 2nd day—the supervisor of the gendarmes, the gendarme, *Rim-ilum* drank (the beer)—{authorizing official}, when they towed the boat of *Simat-Ištaran* from *Puzriš-Dagan* to Garšana," 550:'23-'25, '27-'29

4.2.3 From Udaga

6 g̃uruš gub-ba še ù-da[g-ga]^{ki}-ta gar-ša-a[n-na]^{ki}-šè **má gíd-da**, "6 employed workmen having towed a boat (with) barley from Udaga to Garšana," 185:16–19

6 g̃uruš gi **má**-⌜lá⌝-a ù-dag-⌜ga^{ki}⌝-ta gar-ša-an-na^{ki}-⌜šè⌝ **gíd-[da]**, "6 workmen having towed reeds in a freight boat from Udaga to Garšana," 189:25–28

4.2.4 Other

6 g̃uruš še *ù-ṣa-ar*-é-ú-ra-ta gar-ša-an-na^{ki}-šè **má gíd-da**, "6 workmen having towed a boat with barley from *Uṣar*-E'ura to Garšana," 6:25

[6?] g̃uruš má níg̃-gú-na [GN-ta] gar-ša-an-na$^{\langle ki\rangle}$-šè **má gíd-⌜da⌝**, "[6?] workmen having towed a boat with the commodity tax [from GN] to Garšana," 206:26–27

1 g̃uruš u_4-11-šè má ú-sa unug^{ki}-ta gar-ša-an-na$^{\langle ki\rangle}$-šè **má gíd-da**, "1 workman for 11 days having towed a "processed" boat from Uruk to Garšana," 272:5–7

(. . .) maš-en-gag ^{lú}$kaš_4$ ká-é-gal-ka gub-ba ⌜*simat*⌝-*^{d}ištaran* íb-gu_7 u_4 **má**-*simat-^{d}ištaran* é-^{d}šára-ta gar-ša-an-na^{ki}-šè **mu-un-gíd-ša-a**, "The *muškenu* (and?) the runner, stationed by *Simat-Ištaran* at the gate of the palace, ate {soup} when they towed the boat of *Simat-Ištaran* from the Šara temple to Garšana," 529:13–18

(. . .) u$_4$-[n-šè] še má-a [si-ga] kun-zi-⌜da⌝ a-pi$_4$-sal$_4$-la^{ki}-[ta] gar-ša-an-na^{ki}-[šè] **má** še **[g]íd-da**, "{workmen and boats} [for n] day(s), (the workers) having towed boats [loaded] with barley [from] the weir of Apisal [to] Garšana," 553:45–52

0.2.3. á má-ḫuĝ-ĝá 0.2.0. á ĝuruš ḫuĝ-ĝá 0.0.1.6 šà-gal má-laḫ$_5$ 0.0.1.6 <še->bi sa$_{10}$ má-laḫ$_5$ u$_4$-1-šè gú i$_7$-^{d}nin-ḫur-saĝ-ĝá-ta [gar-ša-an-na^{ki}-šè **má**] **gíd-da**, "150 liters (of barley), wages of the hired boat (and) 120 liters, wages of hired workmen; 16 liters, food (for) sailors, 16 liters <of barley> is the (hiring) price of the sailors [for] 1 day having towed [boats] from the bank of the Ninḫursaĝa canal [to Garšana]," 561:'19-'23

4.3 Between Locations outside Garšana

4.3.1 From *Bit-Šu-Suen* to Gu-saḫar.DU

1 ĝuruš túg-du$_8$ u$_4$-[1-šè] é-^{d}šu-^{d}suen$^{⌜ki⌝}$-[ta] gú-saḫar^{har}.DU^{ki}-šè **m[á gíd-da]**, "1 braider [for 1] day [having towed] a boat [from] *Bit-Šu-Suen* to Gu-saḫar.DU," 298:6–8

3 ĝuruš ašgab u$_4$-1-šè é-^{d}šu-[^{d}EN].ZU^{ki}-ta gú-saḫar^{har}.DU^{ki}-šè **má gíd-da**, "3 leather workers for 1 day having towed a boat from *Bit-Šu-Suen* to Gu-saḫar.DU," 299:6–8

4.3.2 From Gu-saḫar.DU to the Tower of *Dada*

1 ĝuruš túg-du$_8$ u$_4$-[1-šè] gú-saḫar^{har}.DU^{ki}-ta a[n-za-qar]-*da-da*-šè **má gíd-da** ù [še ba-al], "1 braider for 1 day having towed a boat from Gu-saḫar.DU to the fortified tower of *Dada* and [having unloaded barley]," 298:11–12

2 ĝuruš ašgab u$_4$-1-šè gú-saḫar^{har}.DU^{ki}-ta an-za-qar-*da-da*-šè **má gíd-da** ù še ba-al, "2 leather workers for 1 day having towed a boat from Gu-saḫar.DU to the fortified tower of *Dada* and having unloaded barley," 299:11–12

4.3.3 Between Other Locations

3 ĝuruš ^{lú}ázlag u$_4$-2½-šè nibru^{ki}-ta é-^{d}šu-^{d}suen-šè **má** *na-wi-ir-ilum* **íb-gíd**, "3 fullers for 2½ days towed the boat of *Nawir-ilum* from Nippur to *Bit-Šu-Suen*," 220:1–6

[n] ĝuruš ^{lú}[ázlag n] ĝuruš ašgab [n] ĝuruš ad-kub$_4$ [n] ĝ[uruš tú]g-du$_8$ [. . .]-x-šè [x]-zi-[x]-x maš-kán^{ki}-⌜šè⌝ **má gíd-⌜da⌝, "[n fuller(s)], [n] leather worker(s), [n] reed craftsmen (and) [n] braider(s) having towed a boat [. . .] to *Maškan*," 260:11–17

(. . .) [u$_4$]-3-šè [še x] x x x an-za-qar-ta kun-zi-da i$_7$-a-kàr-ús-sa a-šà-lú-maḫ-šè íb-ga$_6$ ù má-a si-ga ⌜ús⌝-bi 36 nindan ⌜kun⌝-zi-da an-za-qar-ta [GN-šè] **má** še **gíd-[da** . . .] ús-bi 290 [nindan], "{workers and boats} for 3 [days], (the boats) carried [barley . . .] from the fortified tower to the weir of the Agar-usa Canal of the Lu-maḫ field and (the workers) loaded the boat(s). Its distance is 36 nindan from the weir of the fortified tower [to GN], boats of barley having been towed a distance of 290 [nindan]," 553:11–20

(. . .) u$_4$-2-[šè] a-pi$_4$-sal$_4$-[la^{ki}-ta] ù-dag-[ga^{ki}-šè] **má** sù **[gíd-da]** še má-[a si-ga] ù-dag-[ga^{ki}-ta] kun-zi-[da] a-pi$_4$-[sal$_4$-la^{ki}-šè] má-[a si-ga], "{workmen and boats} for 2 days, (the workers) [having towed] the sunken boats [from] Apisal [to] Udaga, [having loaded] the boats with barley (and then having towed) [the loaded] boats from Udaga [(back) to] the weir of Apisal," 553:29–38

[. . . u]$_4$-1-[šè] é-duru$_5$-*simat*-^{d}[*ištaran*-ta] ka i$_7$-^{d}[nin-ḫur-sag̃-g̃á-šè] **má gíd-da**, "[(wages of sailors) for] 1 day having towed [boats] from the *Simat-Ištaran* village [to the] mouth of the [Ninḫursag̃] canal," 561:'11-'14

0.2.3. á má-ḫug̃-g̃á 0.2.0. á g̃uruš ḫug̃-g̃á 0.0.1.6 sìla šà-gal má-laḫ$_5$ 0.0.1.6 sìla <še->b[i s]a$_{10}$ má-⸢laḫ$_5$⸣ u$_4$-1-šè é-duru$_5$-ka[b-bí-ta] gú i$_7$-[*ma-an-iš-ti-šu*-šè] **má gí[d-da]**, "150 liters (of barley), wages of the hired boat (and) 120 liters, wages of hired workmen; 16 liters, food (for) sailors, 16 liters <of barley> is the (hiring) price of the sailors for 1 day having towed boats [from] the Kabbi village [to] the bank of the [*Maništišu*] canal," 561:'28-'32

4.3.4 Location Unspecified

[n] g̃uruš ka i$_7$-da ka-gal kuš **má gíd**, "[n] workmen having towed a boat (with?) leather through the large opening of the canal," 175:27

1 g̃uruš túg-du$_8$ u$_4$-6-šè **má gíd-da**, "1 braider having towed a boat for 6 days," 783:6–7

4.4 Boat Towers

g̃uruš **má-gíd**, "boat tower" > *Craftsmen Index*

g̃uruš ugula **má-gíd**, "overseer of boat towers" > *Craftsmen Index*

ḫi-li **má-gíd**, "*Ḫili*, the boat tower" > *Personal Name Index*

4.4.1 Rations and Requisitions for Boat Towers

[n.n.n.n (sìla n gín)] ì-šáḫ [níg̃-dab$_5$] **má-gíd-e-ne**, "[n (liters and n shekels)] of lard, [requisitions] of the boat towers," 419:1–2

21.1.0. dabin gur zì-ba **má-gíd-e-ne**, "21 bushels (and) 60 liters of semolina, flour rations of the boat towers," 426:1–2

5. sar gíd, "to survey land"

(. . ..) [n] **sar gíd-da**,"{parcels of land in Zabala and Garšana}; (in total:) [n] sar (of land) surveyed," 1362:'73

6. túg gíd, "to extend a textile (on a loom)"

éš-**túg-gíd**, "cord, used to extend a textile (on a loom)" > **éš**

$^{g̃eš}$sag̃-du **túg-ga gíd**, "sag̃-du beam, used to extend a textile (on a loom)" > **$^{g̃eš}$sag̃-du**

7. To Transfer

24 udu-niga 1-sìla-[ta] sá-du$_{11}$-šè 26 udu-niga 1-sìla-ta [x]-šè é-⸢udu⸣-niga šu-a-⸢gi⸣-na u$_4$ iti-da **⸢gíd⸣-gíd-⸢dam⸣**, "24 fattened sheep, 1 liter (fodder) [each] for regular offerings (and) 26 fattened sheep, 1 liter (fodder) each for [x]; (sheep), of the sheep-fattening pen, to be transferred (for) the offering of the month," 525:1–7

8. Broken Context

6 g̃uruš **me(!)-gíd** al-[. . .]-la, 147:47

[. . .] 6 sìla **gíd**-[. . .], 477:3

gig, *marāṣu*, "to be sick, injured"

1. Oil Allotments for an Injured Knee

½ sìla ì-g̃eš *ḫi-li* má gíd u$_4$ dùb bar-ra-ni **in-na-gig-ga**, "½ liter of sesame oil (for) *Ḫili*, the boat tower, when his 'outer knee' was hurting him," 444:4–5

10 gín ì-g̃eš *da-da-a* un-ga$_6$ u$_4$ dùb bar-ra-ni **in-na-gig-ga**, "10 shekels of sesame oil (for) *Dada'a*, the porter, when his 'outer knee' was hurting him," 466:1–2

gu$_7$, *akālu*, "to eat"

níg̃-gu$_7$, "food" > **níg̃-gu$_7$**

1. Eaten by the Builders

1.1 Assorted Commodities

[x]-2-bi [n] sìla ì-gen [šidim-e-n]e **íb-gu$_7$**, "The builders ate (?) (and) [n] liter(s) of ordinary oil," 1008:12–14

1.2 Bread

5 sìla ninda ugula lú-ḫug̃-g̃á-e-ne **íb-gu$_7$** (. . .) bà[d egi]r é-a dù-dè, "The overseer of hired workers ate 5 liters of bread, (and) {other allotments}, (provisions for workers) to construct the (enclosure) wall behind the house," 385:6, 9

0.0.1. dabin ninda ne-mur-šè sízkur-šè šidim-e-ne **íb-gu$_7$**, "10 liters of semolina for bread (baked in) ash for offerings; the builders ate (the bread)," 437:5–6

1.3 Bread and Beer

5 sìla ninda 0.0.2. kaš-gen šidim-e-ne **íb-gu$_7$** ù íb-nag̃ [u$_4$] al-tar é-lùnga é-muḫaldim ù é-kíkken gub-ba, "The builders ate and drank 5 liters of bread (and) 20 liters of ordinary beer [when] they were employed (for) construction of the brewery-kitchen-mill complex," 430:1–4

5 sìla ninda [0.n.n.] kaš-gen ⸢šidim⸣-e-ne **íb-gu$_7$** u$_4$ al-tar é-lùnga é-muḫaldim é-kíkken, "The builders consumed 5 liters of bread (and) [n] liter(s) of ordinary beer during construction of the brewery-kitchen-mill-complex," 440:9–12

2. Eaten by Other Workers

2.1 Eaten by the Builders and Hired Workers

(. . .) mu šidim-e-ne-šè (. . .) [ninda ba-ra-d]u$_8$ ù tu$_7$ ba-[ra]-šeg̃$_6$ mu lú-⸢ḫug̃⸣-g̃á-e-ne-šè u$_4$ igi šu-kab-tá ninda **in-gu$_7$-ša-a**, "{assorted comesibles} for the builders (and) {flour, groats and reeds} with which bread was baked and soup was cooked for the hired workers when they ate bread before *Šu-Kabta*," 479:9, 13–16

2.2 Eaten by the Gendarmes

0.0.4. ⅔ sìla [. . . àga]-ús é-gal-la gub-ba [**íb**]-**gu$_7$** ⸢u$_4$ má⸣ *ra-ba-tum* nibru[ki]-ta gar-ša-an-na[ki]-šè i[n-g]íd-sa-a, "The gendarme employed at the palace ate 4⅔ liters [. . .] when they towed the boat of *Rabatum* from Nippur to Garšana," 506:22–26

0.0.5. ninda-kaš á-u$_4$-[te-na] 2 sìla níg̃-àr-[ra-sig$_5$] šà zabala$_4$[[ki]] u$_4$-1-[kam] 4 sìla níg̃-àr-ra-[sig$_5$] u$_4$-2-[kam] á-gú-zi-⸢ga⸣ 4 sìla níg̃-àr-ra-⸢sig$_5$⸣ á-u$_4$-te-na u$_4$-3-kam šà kaskal[ki] àga-ús [*ri-im*]-*ilum* **íb-gu$_7$**, "The gendarme *Rim-ilum* consumed 50 liters of bread (and) beer [in] the evening (and) 2 liters of fine barley groats in Zabala on the 1st day, 4 liters of [fine] groats at dawn on the 2nd day (and) 4 liters of fine groats in the evening on the 3rd day in Kaskal," 551:1–12

2.3 Eaten by the Hired Workers

0.4.0. ninda-dabin ù zì-šà-gen íb-ta-ḫi 0.1.3.2 sìla ninda-gur$_4$-ra zì-KAL 0.0.1. níg̃-àr-ra-sig$_5$ [urudu]šen-šè lú-ḫug̃-g̃á iri[ki]-didli-ke$_4$-ne **íb-gu$_7$**, "The hired workers of various cities ate 240 liters of bread of mixed semolina and ordinary šà-flour, 92 liters of thick bread of KAL-flour (and) 10 liters of fine groats for the (soup) cauldron," 490:1–4

2.4 Eaten by the Home-owners

0.0.1.2? sìla ninda-gal-gen 1 sìla du$_8$ [u$_4$ l]ú é-ne-ne ba-an-ši-sa$_{10}$-a **íb-gu$_7$**, "The men who bought their houses ate 12? liters of ordinary large bread baked (in) 1 liter (loaves)," 491:1–3

2.5 Eaten by the Lamentation Singers and the Mourners

0.0.2. dabin ninda-sal-la-ge[n] 1 sìla níĝ-àr-ra-sig$_5$ tu$_7$-šè gala ù ama-gal-e-ne **íb-gu$_7$** u$_4$ *tak-ri-ib-tum* bàd, "The lamentation singers and female mourners ate ordinary thin bread (made from) 20 liters of semolina (and) soup (made from) 1 liter of fine groats on the occasion of (their performance) of a *takribtum* at? the (enclosure) wall," 1035:'7-'11

2.6 Eaten by *Libur-iduni*

1 ir$_7$^{mušen} *li-bur-i-du-ni* **in-gu$_7$-a** ka-ga-na ba-a-ge-en, "*Libur-iduni* confirmed that he ate 1 pigeon," 1055:1–4

2.7 Eaten by those Stationed at the Palace Gate

0.0.2.6 sìla ninda-šu-ra-gen 2 ádda-udu 5 sìla níĝ-àr-ra-sig$_5$ 0.0.1. gú-gal al-àr-ra šu-gíd 1 sìla mun-gen ^{urudu}šen-šè 8 sa gi-izi tu$_7$ ba-ra-šeg$_6$ maš-en-gag ^{lú}kaš$_4$ ká-é-gal-ka gub-ba [*si*]*mat*-^{d}*ištaran* **íb-gu$_7$**, "The *muškenu* (and?) the runner, stationed by *Simat-Ištaran* at the gate of the palace, ate 26 liters of ordinary half (loaf) bread (and) soup cooked with 2 sheep carcasses, 5 liters of fine groats, 10 liters of šu-gíd milled beans, 1 liter of ordinary salt for the cauldron (and) 8 bundles of fuel reeds," 529:5–14

0.0.2.6 sìla <ninda->šu-ra-gen ½ sìla du$_8$ maš-en-gag ká-é-gal-ka gub-ba **íb-gu$_7$**, "The *muškenu*, employed at the gate of the palace, ate 26 liters of ordinary half (loaf) <bread> baked (in) ½ liter (loaves)," 541:17–18

2.8 Eaten by the Servants and Hired Workers

(. . .) árad-é-[a lú-ḫuĝ]-ĝá ù ugula lú-[ḫuĝ-ĝá-e-n]e **íb-gu$_7$** (. . .) u$_4$ bàd é-a dù-dè, "The servants, hired workers and overseer of the hired workers ate {assorted grains, and provisions for other workers}, when they were constructing the (enclosure) wall of the house," 383:8, 11

[n] sìla 10 gín [kaš?] árad-é-a ù lú-ḫuĝ-ĝá-e-ne **ib-gu$_7$** u$_4$ al-tar bàd gub-ba, "The household servants and hired workers consumed [n] liter(s) (and) 10 shekels of [beer?] when they were employed (for) construction of the (enclosure) wall," 392:1–7

2.9 Eaten by the Workers

2 ádda-udu ^{urudu}šen-šè éren al-tar bàd gub-ba **íb-gu$_7$**, "The workers, employed for construction of the (enclosure) wall, ate 2 sheep carcasses for the (soup) cauldron," 382:1–4, 388:1–4

3. Consumed by Fire

(. . .) [níĝ] al-zi-ra [. . . gir-r]a **ba-ab-⸢gu$_7$⸣**, "{assorted baskets and containers}, fire consumed the used goods," 1292:'23-'24

(. . .) níĝ al-⸢zi⸣-ra 70 ⸢sa⸣ gi-izi gi-izi-lá-šè 31 ^{gi}kid-ka-ḫa-ra gir-ra **ba-ab-gu$_7$**, "{assorted baskets}—used goods—70 bundles of reeds for torches (and) 31 reed mats—fire consumed (the used goods)," 1299:25–26

gub, *izuzzu*, "to stand; (to be) assigned (to a task), (to be) employed at"

gub, "to be present, on-hand"
gub-ba, "employed," *passim*
****á-áĝ-dè gub-ba**, "instructions to follow"
da bad gub-ba, "employed at the side of the (enclosure) wall"
ka-la$_{(2)}$-ka gub-ba, "employed at the dirt quarry"
ki-ĝeš **gub-ba**, "cultivated dike land" > **ki-ĝeš**
ku-bu, "to prop up"
ma šub-ba gub-ba, "employed at the brickyard"
šeg$_{12}$-al-ur$_x$-ra gub-ba, "employed (to mold) bricks"

1. **gub**, "to be present, on-hand"

 5[0 ud]u-máš-ḫi-a **gub-ba** [é-š]u-sum-ma, "(In total:) 50 various sheep (and) goats present in the storehouse," 984:5–6

 [9 ^{dug}]ĝeš-ŠÀ/UD? **gub-ba**, "[9] ĝeš-ŠÀ/UD-vessels on-hand," 1072:5

 (ĝeš) é-^{ĝeš}kiri$_6$-a **gub-ba**, "(wood) stored in the garden house," 1256:39, 1375:45

2. **á-áĝ-dè gub-ba**, "instructions to follow"

 1 ĝuruš túg-du$_8$ [u$_4$-1-šè] še 120 gur **á-á[ĝ-d]è gub-b[a ù má si-ga], "1 braider [for 1 day], instructions about the 120 gur of barley followed [and the boat was loaded]," 298:4–5

 3 ĝuruš ašgab u$_4$-1-šè še 120 gur **á-áĝ-dè gub-ba ù má si-ga, "3 leather workers for 1 day, instructions about the 120 gur of barley followed and the boat was loaded," 299:4–5

3. **da bad gub-ba**, "employed at the side of the (enclosure) wall"

 3 ĝuruš **da bàd DU-a**, "3 workmen employed at the side of the (enclosure) wall," 163:34

4. **ka-la$_{(2)}$-ka gub-ba**, "employed at the dirt quarry"

 1 ĝuruš ḫuĝ-ĝá 1 géme ḫuĝ-ĝá im *a-ga-ri-nu-um* **ka-la$_{(2)}$-ka gub-ba**, "1 hired workman (and) 1 hired workwoman employed at the dirt quarry (to dig) earth for the *agarinnum*," 7:'30, 8:37

 1 ĝuruš šidim **ka-lá-ka gub-ba**, "1 builder employed at the dirt quarry," 9:23, 8:36, 196:'21

 1 ĝuruš šidim [um-mi-a] 1 [ĝuruš šidim **k]a-lá-ka [gub-ba]**, "1 [master] builder and 1 [builder employed] at the dirt quarry," 195:'12-'14

5. **ku-bu**, "to prop up"[6]

 60 sa gi-izi ^{ĝeš}lam **ku-bu-dè**, "60 bundles of fuel reeds to prop-up (young) trees," 1309:10–11

6. **ma šub-ba gub-ba**, "employed at the brickyard"

 1 ĝuruš šidim **ma šub-ba** šeg$_{12}$ **gub-ba**, "1 builder employed at the brickyard," 1:14–15, 3:11–12, 4:16–17

 1 ĝuruš šidim **ma šub-ba gub-ba**, "1 builder employed at the brickyard," 2:15–16, 5:18, 7:'32, 9:26

---

6 Heimpel, personal communication.

[n g̃uruš] šidim šeg$_{12}$ **ma šub-ba gub-ba**, "[n] builder(s) employed at the brickyard," 8:39, 25:10, 187:20–21, 193:28

1 g̃uruš **ma šub-ba gub-ba**, "1 workman employed at the brickyard," 14:30

1 g̃uruš šidim šeg$_{12}$ **ma šub-ba gub-ba**, "1 builder employed at the brickyard," 86:18–19, 87:13–14, 185:14–15, 188:'17, 189:23–24, 190:28, 196:'20, 197:38

6.1 For Construction of the Textile Depository

1 g̃uruš šidim šeg$_{12}$ ma **šub-ba gub-⸢ba⸣** 1 g̃uruš šidim é-ki-mu-ra d[ù-a], "1 builder employed at the brickyard (and) 1 builder having constructed the textile depository," 194:35–38

1 g̃uruš ⸢šidim⸣ šeg$_{12}$ **ma šub-ba gub-ba** 3 g̃uruš ⸢ùr⸣ é-ki-mu-ra dù-a, "1 builder employed at the brickyard (and) 3 workmen having constructed the roof of the textile depository," 198:'17-'18

6.2 For Construction of Various Houses

*See *Household Index* for the complete context of the following passages.

[n g̃u]ruš šidim **ma šub-ba** šeg$_{12}$ **gub-ba** [n g̃u]ruš šidim é-ki-ba-g̃ar-ra [dù]-dè gub-ba, "[n] builder(s) employed at the brickyard (and) [n] builder(s) employed to [construct] the replacement house," 88:6–7

1 g̃uruš **ma šub-ba** še[g$_{12}$ **gub-ba**] 4 g̃uruš šidim [. . .] é-ki-ba-g̃ar-ra *u-bar-ri-a* tà-tà<-dè> gub-ba, "1 workman [employed] at the brickyard (and) 4 builders [. . .], (workers) employed <to> apply stucco to the replacement house of *Ubarria*," 89:7–8

[1] g̃uruš šidim šeg$_{12}$ **ma šub-[ba] gub-ba** (. . .) [é-PN] dù-a, "[1] builder employed at the brickyard (. . .), (workers) having constructed [the house of PN]," 191:28–29, 33

7. **šeg$_{12}$ gub-ba**, "employed (to mold) bricks"

*See *Household Index* for the complete context of the following passage.

1 g̃uruš šidim [**šeg$_{12}$**-a]l-ur$_x$-ra **gub-ba** (. . .) é-ki-ba-g̃ar-ra *u-bar-ri-a* tà-tà<-dè> gub-ba, "1 builder employed (to mold) bricks, (. . .) (workers) employed <to> apply stucco to the replacement house of *Ubarria*," 89:6, 8

gul, *abātu*, "to raze, demolish (a building); to cut"

é gul, "to demolish a house"

gi-sal gul, "to trim thin reeds"

g̃eš gul, "to cut wood"

iz-zi gul, "to demolish an iz-zi wall"

má gul, "to dismantle a boat"

1. **é gul**, "to demolish a house"

é-gul, "demolished house" > *Household Index*

7 g̃uruš 6 géme **é**-*u-bar-ri-a* **gul-[dè** gub-ba], "7 workmen (and) 6 workwomen [employed to] demolish the house of *Ubarria*," 93:'26

3 g̃uruš šidim 6 g̃uruš 13 géme **é**-*zu-zu-⸢tum* sumun⸣ <<til>> **gul-dè**, "3 builders, 6 workmen (and) 13 workwomen to demolish the old house of *Zuzutum*," 161:'13-'14

6 ĝuruš ašgab 8 ĝuruš lúázlag 24 géme uš-bar u_4-1-šè al-tar **é**-*a-bí-a-ti* **gul-dè** gub-ba, "6 leather workers, 8 fullers (and) 24 female weavers employed for 1 day of construction to demolish the house of *Abiati*," 273:1–6

2. **gi-sal gul**, "to trim thin reeds"

*See *Household Index* for the complete context of the following passages.

2.1 Construction of the Brewery-Kitchen-Mill Complex

5 ĝuruš **gi-[sal] gul-la** ⸢al⸣-tar ki-sá-[a é-lùnga] é-muḫaldim [ù é]-kíkken, "5 workmen having trimmed [thin] reeds, (for) construction of the foundation terrace of [the brewery]-kitchen-mill complex," 126:27–28

n ĝuruš n géme **gi-sal(-la) gul-la** (. . .) al-tar é-lùnga é-muḫaldim ù é-kíkken, "n workmen (and) n workwomen having trimmed thin reeds (. . .), (for) construction of the brewery-kitchen-mill complex," 129:27, 29, 131:'21, '23, 132:29–30, 133:28–29, 135:29–30

[n] géme **gi-sal gul-[dè** al-tar é-ba]ppir é-muḫaldim [ù é-kíkken], "[n] workwomen [to] trim thin reeds, [(for) construction of] the brewery-kitchen-[mill] complex," 143:33–34

2.2 Construction of the House

5 ĝuruš šidim **gi-sal** šà é-a ⸢**gul**⸣**-dè** gub-ba, "5 builders employed to trim thin reeds in the house," 7:'35

[n ĝuruš] **gi-sal** šà é-a **[gul]-dè** [gub-ba], "[n workmen employed] to trim thin reeds in the house," 8:40

1 ĝuruš šidim **gi-sal** šà é-a **gul-la**, "1 builder having trimmed thin reeds in the house," 191:26

2.3 Construction of the Textile Mill

n ĝuruš n géme **gi-sal** é-uš-bar **gul-dè** gub-ba, "n workmen and n workwomen employed to trim thin reeds at the textile mill," 47:45–46, 48:50–51

2.4 Construction of Various Houses

n ĝuruš šidim **gi-sal** é-til-la **gul-dè** (gub-ba), "n builder(s) (employed) to trim thin reeds at the finished house," 1:10–11, 2:13–14, 3:9–10, 4:14–15

10 ĝuruš im a-ĝá-ri-[na] lu-dè [gub-ba] 3 ⸢ĝuruš⸣ 3 ⸢géme⸣ **gi-sal-[la]** é-*al*<-*lu*>-*a* **g[ul-dè** gub-ba], "10 workmen [employed] to mix earth in the *agarinnum* (and) 3 workmen (and) 3 workwomen [employed to] trim thin reeds, (work for) the house of *Alua*," 38:28–32

300 sa gi-izi **gi-sal**-šè **ba-gul** (. . .) é-ki-ba-ĝar-ra é-*u-bar-ri-a*-šè ba-a-ĝar, "300 bundles of fuel reeds were cut for thin reeds (and) {other reed and wood products} were placed for the replacement house of the house of *Ubarria*," 1286:8, 12, 1289:8, 12

2.5 Construction of the (Enclosure) Wall

1 ĝuruš šidim 8 ĝuruš **gi-sal** ⸢bàd⸣ **gul-dè** gub-ba, "1 builder (and) 8 workmen employed to trim thin reeds at the (enclosure) wall," 15:19

n ĝuruš **gi-sal** bàd **gul-dè** gub-ba, "n workmen employed to trim thin reeds at the (enclosure) wall," 24:23, 26:'17

2 ĝuruš 2 géme **gi-sal** bàd **gul-la**, "2 workmen and 2 workwomen having trimmed thin reeds at the (enclosure) wall," 103:32

3 g̃uruš u_4-1-šè **gi-sal** bàd **gu[l-d]è** gub-ba, "3 workmen for 1 day employed to trim thin reeds at the (enclosure) wall," 336:8–9

2.5.1 Carrying, Trimming, and Depositing Reeds at the (Enclosure) Wall

[1 g̃uruš šidim 6 g̃uruš šu dím-ma gub-ba 6 géme g]i ⸢ga_6⸣-g̃á-⸢dè⸣ 5 g̃uruš šidim 6 g̃uruš **gi-sal** uš bàd **gul-dè** g[ub-ba], "[1 builder, 6 workmen employed to build, 6 workwomen] to carry reeds, (and) 5 builders (and) 6 workmen employed to trim thin reeds at the foundation of the (enclosure) wall," 9:17–21

1 g̃uruš šidim 4 g̃uruš gi-sal bàd g̃á-g̃á-dè gub-ba [n g̃uru]š **gi-sal** bàd **gul-dè** gub-ba [n g̃uru]š **gi-sal** bàd **gul-dè** gub-ba, "1 builder (and) 4 workmen employed to place thin reeds at the (enclosure) wall (and) [n] workmen employed to trim thin reeds at the (enclosure) wall," 29:'19-'20

2.6 Construction Site Broken or Unspecified

4 [g̃uruš] 4 [géme] **gi-sal-la**? é-[. . . **gul-dè** gub-ba], "4 [workmen] (and) 4 [workwomen employed to trim] thin reeds at the house [of. . .]," 49:46–48

1 g̃uruš 2 géme **gi-sal gul-dè** gub-ba, "1 workman (and) 2 workwomen employed to trim thin reeds," 94:26

[n] g̃uruš 1 géme **gi-sal gul-dè**, "[n] workmen (and) 1 workwoman to trim thin reeds," 97:'18

3. g̃eš gul, "to cut wood"

24 [g̃eš]é-da-ásal **g̃eš** ká-šè **ba-gul** (. . .) é-ki-ba-g̃ar-ra é-*u-bar-ri-a*-šè ba-a-g̃ar, "24 poplar joists were cut for gate timber (and) {other reed and wood products} were placed for the replacement house of the house of *Ubarria*," 1286:6–7, 12, 1289:6–7, 12

4. iz-zi gul, "to demolish an iz-zi wall"

11 g̃uruš sag̃-[tag] 2 g̃uruš á-⅔-ta 2 g̃uruš á-½-ta u_4-2-šè **iz-zi** sumun ku-bu-gu **gul-dè** gub-ba, "11 full-time workmen, 2 at ⅔ wages (and) 2 at ½ wages employed for 2 days to demolish the old ku-bu-gu iz-zi wall," 244:1–5

4.1 Of Various Houses

3 g̃uruš **iz-zi** é-⸢*zu*⸣-*zu*-⸢*tum*⸣ **gul-dè** g[ub-ba], "3 workmen employed to demolish the iz-zi wall of the house of *Zuzutum*," 58:53–54

10-lá-1 g̃uruš **iz-zi** é-*du-gu*-[*a*?] **gul-dè** gub-ba, "9 workmen employed to demolish the iz-zi wall of the house of *Dugua*," 58:55–56

5 g̃uruš 10 géme **iz-zi** šà é-a **gul-la** 1 g̃uruš 8 géme é-*a-al-lu-a*, "5 workmen (and) 10 workwomen having demolished the iz-zi wall in the house (and) 1 workman (and) 8 workwomen at the house of *Alua*," 103:24–27

30 géme $šeg_{12}$ ga_6-g̃á [n] g̃uruš 6 géme **iz-zi** é-*šu-eš₄-tár* ù *za-ki-ti* **gul-la**, "30 workwomen having carried bricks (and) [n] workmen (and) 6 workwomen having demolished the iz-zi wall of the house of *Šu-Eštar* and *Zakiti*," 104:27–29, 105:26–28

2 ⸢g̃uruš⸣ é-*bí-za-a* **iz-zi gul-la**, "2 workmen having demolished the iz-zi wall of the house of *Biza'a*," 108:34–35

3 g̃uruš 10 géme **iz-zi** é-*pí-ša-aḫ-ilum* **gul-la**, "3 workmen (and) 10 workwomen having demolished the iz-zi wall of the house of *Pišaḫ-ilum*," 113:'5-'6

5 guruš **iz-zi** é-*a-lu*-[*a* **gul-la**], "5 workmen [having demolished] the iz-zi wall of the house of *Alua*," 120:'32

3 ĝuruš **iz-˹zi˺** é-*zu-zu-tum* **gul-la**, "3 workmen having demolished the iz-zi wall of the house of *Zuzutum*," 122:'21

[n] ĝuru[š **iz**]**-zi** é-*al-lu-a* **gul-la**, "[n] workmen having demolished the iz-zi wall of the house of *Alua*," 129:32

4.2 Construction Site Unspecified

6 guruš **iz-zi gul-la**, "6 workmen having demolished an iz-zi wall," 163:33

5. má gul, "to dismantle a boat"

1 ĝuruš túg-du$_{8}$ u$_{4}$-3-˹šè˺ **má gul-dè** gub<-ba>, "1 braider for 3 days employed to dismantle a boat," 272:1–2

8.1.0. ésir-ḫád [gur] 4 ĝeš-íb-ra má-[20?-g]ur 28 ^{ĝeš}ù-má má-20-gur **má gul-la**-ta, "8 bushels (and) 60 liters of dry bitumen, 4 íb-ra planks of a [20?]-bushel boat (and) 28 boat planks of a 20-bushel boat, (wood) from dismantled boats," 1359:1–4

1 **má**-60-gur **ba-gul** ésir-bi zuḫ-a ba-ĝar ĝeš éš-bi <<BI>> nu-ĝál, "1 60-bushel boat was dismantled, its stolen bitumen was replaced (but) its wood (and) ropes are (still) missing," 1369:1–4

gur, *saḫāru, târu*, "to reject (legal evidence), to turn away; to turn, return; to argue"

èš-ta-**gur-ra**, "(offerings) returned from the shrine" > **èš**

ku-úr gur, "to return in the future"

1. Instructions in Letter Orders not to Argue

ì-lí-aš-ra-ni ù-na-a-du$_{11}$ 30.0.0. še gur 30.0.0. zíz gur ^{d}*Adad-tillati* ḫé-na-ab-sum-mu kìšib-ba-a-ni [šu] ḫa-ba-ab-ti-ĝe$_{26}$ **[nam-m]i-gur-re**, "Say to *Ili-ašranni* that '30 bushels of barley (and) 30 bushels of emmer wheat should be given to *Adad-tillati*. He should take his seal(ed tablet). He should not argue!'" 1039:1–9

ur-^{d}dumu-zi ù *a-ḫu-wa-qar* ù-na-a-˹du$_{11}$˺ 0.0.2. ku-[x] *šu*-^{d}nisaba ḫé-na-ab-sum-mu 1 ĝuruš šà-gu$_{4}$ iri^{ki}-ta iri^{ki}-šè ḫé-eb-sá-e **nam-mi-gur-re**, "Say to Ur-Dumuzi and *Aḫu-waqar* that '20 liters of (?) should be given to *Šu*-Nisaba. 1 ox-driver from the city should arrive at the city. They should not argue!'" 1045:1–11

2. ku-úr gur, "to return in the future"

2 sìla zì-KAL TÚG-NI [ku-ú]r **gu-ru-dè**, "2 liters of KAL-flour (?) to be returned in the future," 972:39–40, 975:41–42

5 sìla zì-kum *mu-du-lum* ku-úr **gu-ru-dè**, "5 liters of salted kum-flour to be returned in the future," 1090:1–3

gur$_{10}$, *eṣēdu*, "to reap, sickle"

1. Craftsmen Assigned to Reap Barley

(. . .) še **gur$_{10}$-gur$_{10}$-dè** zàr tab-ba-dè ù ĝeš ra-ra-dè a-šà *ṣe-ru-um* gub-ba, "{craftsmen} employed at the *Ṣerum* field to reap barley, stack (its) sheaves (for drying) and reap (them)," 262:19–22

1 ĝuruš ašgab u$_{4}$-1-šè še **gur$_{10}$-gur$_{10}$-dè** a-šà *dì-im-bu*-na-àš-gi$_{5}$ gub-ba, "1 leather worker employed for 1 day to reap barley at the field of *Dimbun*-Ašgi," 282:1–3

1 ĝuruš ad-kub$_4$ u$_4$-4-šè *dì-im-bu-na*-àš-gi$_5$-ta a-šà *ṣe-r*[*u-u*]*m*-šè še **gur$_{10}$-gur$_{10}$-[dè]** gub-ba, "1 reed craftsman (having gone) from *Dimbun*-Ašgi to the *Ṣerum* field, employed for 4 days [to] reap barley," 284:5–10

guru$_5$(URU×GU=KWU–771), "to separate, divide; to cut, pull, trim (weeds)"

gi-guru$_5$ aka, "to make reedwork panels" > **aka**

1. **gi-guru$_5$**, "to trim reeds"

300 sa gi-izi 40 sa A.ZI/ZI **gi-guru$_5$**-šè, "300 bundles of fuel reeds (and) 40 bundles of rushes for trimming," 1297:8–10

[n+]4 sa gi-izi [n+]20 sa A.ZI/ZI(.ÉŠ) **[gi]-guru$_5$**-šè, "[n+]4 bundles of fuel reeds (and) [n+]20 bundles of rushes for trimming," 1379:'10-'12

– G̃ –

ĝál, *bašû*; *šakānu*, "to be (there, at hand, available); to exist; to put, place, lay down; to have"

1. **Commodities in Individual Accounts**

PN **in-da-ĝál**, "{commodities} are with PN" > *Personal Name Index*

a-ḫu-DU$_{10}$	*ì-lí-an-dùl*	*simat-é-a*
a-da-làl	*ì-lí-bi-la-ni*	*šál-maḫ*
da-a-a	*ku-un-si-ma-at*	*ša-at-èr-ra*
dan-ḫi-li	*li-bur*	*šu-la-núm*
ĜAR-*šà-ti*	*li-la-a*	*zi-ti-a*
ḫa-lí	lugal-ezem	ur-^{d}*suen*

1.1 **The Account of *Adad-tillati***

(. . .) šu-sum-ma ĝiri *ib-ni-^{d}adad* d[ub-sar] iti ezem-me-ki-ĝál ba-zal mu en-^{d}inana-unu^{ki}-ga máš-e ì-pàd (. . .) ⌜diri⌝ **ĝál-la** níĝ-kas$_7$-aka ^{d}*adad-tillati* šabra, "{millstones, diorite stones, woods, yokes, and wooden containers}, the consignment under the authority of *Ibni-Adad*, the scribe, the 12th month of *Ibbi-Suen* Year 2 having passed; There are additional {millstones, diorite stones, woods, yokes, and wooden containers}; the account of *Adad-tillati*, the majordomo," 1372:46–49, 103–106

1.2 **The Account of the Overseer**

šu+níĝin 27.1.1.3 sìla še gur ki ugula-nam–10-ka ⌜**ĝál**⌝**-la**, "{barley for individuals}; in total: there are 27 bushels (and) 73 liters of barley at the place of the overseer of 10," 504:20–22

2. **Flour Production**[7]

13.2.5. [zíz gur] zíz ba-na 5-sìla-[ta **ì-ĝál**], "13 bushels (and) 170 liters of [emmer wheat], in [each] ban (=10 liters) [there are] 5 liters," 1110:1–2

---

7 Brunke 2008, 25 (§2.1.5) n. 35.

2.1 Emmer

14.2.0. zíz gibil gur zíz ba-na imĝaĝa$_{3}$ 5 sìla 7-gín-ta **ì-ĝál**, "14 bushels (and) 120 liters of new emmer wheat, in each ban (=10 liters) of the emmer wheat there are 5 liters (and) 7 shekels of emmer," 461:1–2

5.3.0 zíz sumun gur zíz ba-na imĝaĝa$_{3}$ 4-sìla-ta **ì-ĝál**, "5 bushels (and) 180 liters of old emmer wheat, in each ban (=10 liters) of emmer wheat there are 4 liters of emmer," 461:3–4

20.0.0. zíz gur zíz ba-na imĝaĝa$_{3}$ 3⅓ sìla-ta **ì-ĝál**, "20 bushels of emmer wheat, in each ban (=10 liters) of the emmer wheat there are 3⅓ liters of emmer," 532:2–3

2.2 KAL-flour

4.0.0. zíz gur zíz ba-na zì-KAL 4½ sìla 5 gín-ta **ì-ĝál**, "4 bushels of emmer wheat, in each ban (=10 liters) of the emmer wheat there are 4½ liters and 5 shekels of KAL-flour," 412:1–2

10.0.0. zíz gur ba-na zì-KAL 5 sìla-ta **ì-ĝál**, "10 bushels of emmer wheat, in each ban (=10 liters) of it there are 5 liters of KAL-flour," 433:2

3. Count of Bricks

37⅔ sar 4 gín igi-4-ĝál šeg$_{12}$ u$_{4}$-1-kam 37 sar 1 gín šeg$_{12}$ u$_{4}$-2-kam ⸢NE⸣-gu$_{7}$-bi nu-ub-ta-zi šeg$_{12}$ šid-da ĝá šub-ba **ĝá-ĝál**, "37⅔ sar (and) 4¼ gín of bricks for 1 day, 37 sar (and) 1 shekel of bricks for 2 days, the damaged bricks were not deducted; the count of bricks took place in the brickyard," 357:1–7

4. Used for Negation

4.1 Missing Items

1 má-60-gur ba-gul ésir-bi zuḫ-a ba-ĝar ĝeš eše-bi <<BI>> **nu-ĝál**, "1 60-bushel boat was dismantled, its stolen bitumen was replaced (but) its wood (and) ropes are (still) missing," 1369:1–4

4.2 Lost and Found

iti u$_{4}$-29-ba-zal še **nu-ĝál** bí-in-gi$_{4}$ u$_{4}$-1-àm **mu-[un-ĝál]** še šabra in-na-an-sum šu te-ĝe$_{6}$-dè nu-un-dab$_{5}$?, "At the end of the 29th day of the month there was no barley. (Someone) returned it. On the 1st day, it was there. (Then) the barley was given to the majordomo. In order for him to receive it, it will not (first) be taken (by someone else)," 1057:1–7

4.3 When a Copy was not Made

gaba-ri **nu-ĝál**, "there is no copy," 1024:23, 1195:8, 1214:8

nu-ĝál gaba-ri, "there is no copy," 880:10, 1135:9, 1315:9, 1515:8

4.4 When there was no Flour

0.3.0. še šà-gu$_{4}$-me-éš dirig še-ba-ne-ne mu zì **nu-ĝál-la**-šè ba-na-ḫa-la *šu-kab-tá* bí-in-dug$_{4}$, "180 liters of barley for the ox-drivers. *Šu-Kabta* had ordered that additional barley rations were to be divided for them because there was no flour," 481:1–4

5. Other

1 tum$_{12}^{mušen}$ 2 tu-gur$_{4}^{mušen}$ ba-úš mušen-bi ki záḫ **ì-ĝál**, "1 wild dove and 2 doves, slaughtered birds that had escaped (previsiously)," 1058:1–4

4.0.0. dabin gur ⸢bisag̃⸣-dub-ba-ka **g̃ál-la**, "there are 4 bushels of semolina in the tablet basket," 1233:12–13

šar-ru-um-ì-lí ù-na-a-du$_{11}$ [x]-**g̃ál-la** [x] é-za **ì-g̃ál** é-ki-ba-g̃ar-ra du$_8$-dè ^{d}*adad-tillati* ḫé-na-ab-sum-mu a-ba šeš-g̃u$_{10}$-gin$_7$, "Say to *Šarrum-ili* that '(?) that is in your house should be given to *Adad-tillati* in order to caulk the replacement house. Who is like my brother?'" 1526:1–7

6. Uncertain Translation

★★3.0.0. še gur-⸢ta⸣? i$_7$-gu$_4$ sila-a **g̃ál-la,** 1233:17–18

g̃ar, *šakānu*, "to put, place, lay down; to deposit"

***dì-um* g̃ar**, "to place wattle and daub"

gi-sal g̃ar, "to place thin reeds (on top of layers of mortar)"

im g̃ar, "to place earth"

má g̃ar, "to place a boat (as terminus technicus for loading bales of shok)"

níg̃-kas$_7$ / *šit-tum* / úgu g̃ar, "to place in the account"

SIG$_4$.ANŠE g̃ar, "to place the brick stack"

šeg$_{12}$ g̃ar, "to place bricks"

1. ***dì-um* g̃ar**, "to place wattle and daub"

1.1 Construction of the Brewery-Kitchen-Mill Complex

★See *Household Index* for the complete context of the following passage.

1 g̃uruš šidim 11 g̃uruš [5] géme ***dì-um* g̃á-g̃á** é-lùnga é-muḫaldim ù é-kíkken, "1 builder, 11 workmen (and) [5] workwomen having placed wattle and daub, (work for) the brewery-kitchen-mill complex," 154:34–36

1.2 Construction of the House of *Dugu'a*

1 g̃uruš šidim 1 g̃uruš šu dím 3 géme ***dì-um* [g̃á]-g̃á-dè** [gub-ba] é-*du-gu-a*[? . . .] é-g̃ar-r[a x?], "1 builder (and) 1 workman having built (and) 3 workwomen [employed] to place wattle and daub, (work for) the house of *Dugu'a* [. . .]," 210:'29-'32

1.3 Construction Site Broken

1 g̃uruš ⸢šidim⸣ 7 g̃uruš ***dì-um* [g̃a]r-ra**, "1 builder (and) 7 workmen having placed wattle and daub," 82:11

2. **gi-sal g̃ar**, "to place thin reeds (on top of layers of mortar)"

2.1 At the (Enclosure) Wall

2 g̃uruš **gi-sal** [bàd **g̃á-g̃á-dè** gub-ba], "2 workmen [employed to place] thin reeds [at the (enclosure) wall]," 20:26

n g̃uruš šidim n g̃uruš **gi-sal** bàd **g̃á-g̃á-dè** gub-ba, "n builder(s) and n workmen employed to place thin reeds at the (enclosure) wall," 28:'13, 29:'19

1 g̃uruš šidim 1 g̃uruš 5 géme **gi-sal** bàd **g̃á-g̃á**, "1 builder, 1 workman (and) 5 workwomen having placed thin reeds at the (enclosure) wall," 103:21–22

3. **im g̃ar**, "to place earth"

3.1 suḫur im g̃ar, "(meaning uncertain)"

★★n g̃uruš a-g̃á-ri-in **suḫur im g̃ar-ra**, 192:'17, 194:58–59

4. má ĝar, "to place a boat (as terminus technicus for loading bales of shok)"

4 ĝuruš u$_4$-1-šè gar-ša-an-na^{ki}-ta karkar^{ki}-šè má gíd-da 4 ĝuruš u$_4$-1-šè **m[á ĝa]r-ra**, "4 workmen for 1 day having towed a boat from Garšana to Karkar (and then) 4 workmen for 1 day having placed the boat (i.e. loaded it with shok)," 235:5–7

76 ĝuruš 4 má-10-gur-ta gar-ša-an-na^{ki}-ta karkar^{ki}-šè gíd-da u$_4$-1-àm **má ĝar-ra** u$_4$-⅔-àm má diri-ga gu-níĝin-bi 647½, "76 workmen having towed 4 10-bushel boats from Garšana to Karkar, the one-day boat was placed (i.e. loaded with shok), the ⅔ day boat "floated," (in total: they transported) 647½ bales," 236:7–12

4.1 Broken Context

6 ĝuruš **má ĝar-r[a . . .]** ĜEŠ.⸢KÚŠU⸣^{ki}-[. . .], 193:36–37

5. níĝ-kas$_7$ / *šit-tum* / úgu ĝar, "to place in the account"

úgu lú-^{d}ḫa-ìa **ba-a-ĝar**, "placed in the account of Lu-Ḫa'ia" > *Personal Name Index*

5.1 The Account of *Adad-tillati*

tu-ra-am-ì-lí ù-na-a-du$_{11}$ **níĝ-kas$_7$** ^{d}*adad-tillati* šabra mu na-rú-a-maḫ-ta mu *si-mu-ru-um*^{ki} ba-ḫulu-šè **ḫé-en-ĝá-ĝá** ú-lá-bi, "Say to *Turam-ili* that 'the account of *Adad-tillati*, the majordomo, for the years *Šu-Suen* 6 to *Šu-Suen* 7, should be brought forth quickly,'" 1040:1–7

5.2 The Account of the Brewery-Kitchen-Mill Complex

26.2.1.5 sìla ésir-ḫád gur 0.2.2.5 ⸢sìla⸣ ésir-é-a 0.0.0.8½ sìla ì-šáḫ 0.0.2. ì-ḫur-saĝ-ĝá ***šit-tum*** é-lùnga é-kíkken ù *ma-aZ-ḫa-ru-um* é-muḫaldim-šè **ba-a-ĝar**, "26 bushels (and) 135 liters of dried bitumen, 145 liters of house bitumen, 8½ liters of lard (and) 20 liters of mountain oil, the balance (of the settled account), were placed for the brewery, the mill and the *maZḫarum* of the kitchen," 1299:1–5

5.3 The Account of the Overseer of the Mill

7.4.0. ésir-ḫád gur 0.0.4.6 sìla ésir-é-a 0.0.0.7 sìla ì-ḫur-saĝ-ĝá ***⸢šit⸣-tum*** é-lùnga ***⸢šit⸣-tum*** é-kìšib-ba ugula kíkken [?] du$_{10}$-ús é-didli *ták-si-[ru-um]*-šè **ba-a-ĝar**, "7 bushels (and) 240 liters of dried bitumen, 46 liters of house bitumen (and) 7 liters of mountain oil, the balance (of the settled account) of the brewery (and) of the warehouse, were placed (in the account of) the overseer of the mill for repair of the bathroom of various houses," 1260:1–4

5.4 Assorted Commodities Placed in the Account

(. . .) iti u$_5$-bí-gu$_7$ (. . .) iti ki-siki-^{d}nin-[a-zu] **úgu-a ĝá-ĝá** ga-ga-ra-a, "{finished textiles, supplies for processing fish, chaff for burning, cord for a net, and reed bundles}, in months 4 and 5, the total placed in the account," 1162:'50, '64-'68

(. . .) **⸢úgu⸣-a ĝá-[ĝá** ga]-ga-ra-a, "{animals, assorted comestibles and finished textiles}, the total placed in the account," 1254:'47-'49

0.3.0. **KA:A**[8] **ĝá-ĝá**, "30 liters placed in the account," 1372:57

---

8 Perhaps a mistake for úgu(A.KA), "account."

5.5 Not Placed

0.1.2. zú-lum é-munus-šè *šar-ru-sú-ṭa-ba-at* šu ba-ti **úgu-a nu-um-g̃ar** ki ^{d}*adad-tillati*-ta ba-zi, "*Šarrussu-ṭabat* received 80 liters of dates for the house of the women from *Adad-tillati*. It was not placed on the account," 515:1–7

6. SIG$_4$.ANŠE g̃ar, "to place the brick stack"

n g̃uruš šidim n g̃uruš n géme **SIG$_4$.ANŠE g̃á-g̃á-dè** gub-ba, "n builder(s), n workmen (and) n workwomen employed to place the brick stack," 24:20–22, 28:'21-'22, 99:23–24, 102:27–29

[. . .] **SIG$_4$.ANŠE g̃á-g̃á-dè** g[ub-ba], "[. . .] employed to place the brick stack," 26:'14

n g̃uruš n géme **SIG$_4$.ANŠE g̃á-g̃á**, "n workmen (and) n workwomen having placed the brick stack," 101:28–29, 199:9–11

n g̃uruš šidim n g̃uruš n géme **SIG$_4$.ANŠE g̃á-g̃á(-me-éš)**, "n builder(s), n workmen (and) n workwomen having placed the brick stack," 103:32–34, 104:40–41, 105:38–39, 106:37–38

6.1 Erected at the Billi'a Gate Barracks

[n] g̃uruš 21 géme [**SIG$_4$**].**ANŠE g̃á-g̃á** [1]8 géme im ⸢ga$_6$⸣-g̃á ⸢gú⸣-i$_7$-[*a*]-*ga-mu-um*-ta é-*gi-na-tum* ká-bil-[lí]-a-šè, "[n] workmen (and) 21 workwomen having placed the brick stack (and) 18 workwomen having carried earth from the bank of the *Agamum* canal to the Billi'a gate barracks," 208:13–19

6.2 Erected in Zabala

[1 g̃uruš šidim u]m-mi-a [1 g̃uruš š]idim **SIG$_4$.ANŠE** šà zabala$_4^{ki}$ **g̃ar-ra**, "[1] master [builder] (and) [1] builder having placed the brick stack in Zabala," 113:'1-'2

6.3 Erected for Work on *Pišaḫ-ilum*'s House

1 g̃uruš šidim 11 g̃uruš 2 ⸢géme **SIG$_4$**⸣.**ANŠE g̃á-g̃á** [n+]5 g̃uruš i[m lu]-a [n g]éme in-[u] ga$_6$-g̃á-dè 2 g̃uruš 1 géme é-⸢*pi$_5$-ša-aḫ*⸣-*ilum*, "1 builder, 11 workmen (and) 2 workwomen having placed the brick stack, [n+]5 workmen having mixed earth, [n] workwomen to carry straw (and) 2 workmen (and) 1 workwoman at the house of *Pišaḫ-ilum*," 108:28–33

7. šeg$_{12}$ g̃ar, "to place bricks"

*See *Household Index* for the complete context of the following passages.

7.1 Construction of the Brewery-Kitchen-Mill Complex: The Side of the iz-zi Wall

10 géme **šeg$_{12}$** da iz-zi **g̃á-g̃á** (. . .) é-lùnga é-muḫaldim ù [é]-kíkken, "10 workwomen having placed bricks at the side of the iz-zi wall (. . .), (work for) the brewery-kitchen-mill complex," 140:37–39

[8] géme **šeg$_{12}$** da iz-zi **g̃á-g̃á** ⸢al⸣-tar é-lùnga é-muḫaldim ù é-kíkken, "[8] workwomen having placed bricks at the side of the iz-zi wall, (for) construction of the brewery-kitchen-mill complex," 141:32–33, 142:28–29

7.2 Construction of the Brewery and Mill

[n] géme [**šeg$_{12}$** d]a bàd **g̃á-g̃á** [n] g̃uruš [. . .] é-kíkken ù é-lùnga [. . .] é, "[n] workwomen having placed [bricks] at the side of the (enclosure) wall (and) [n] workmen [. . .], (work for) the mill and brewery [. . .]," 98:'12-'15

30 géme **šeg$_{12}$** da ki-sá-a ⸢**g̃á**⸣-**g̃á** (. . .) al-tar ki-sá-a é-lùnga ù é-kíkken, "30 workwomen having placed bricks at the side of the foundation terrace (. . .), (for) construction of the foundation terrace of the brewery and mill," 113:'13, '15

7.3 Construction of the GÍN-bal

203 **šeg$_{12}$**-al-ur$_{x}$-ra GÍN-bal ^{ĝeš}kiri$_{6}$-ĝá-nun-na-šè **ba-a-ĝar**, "203 bricks were placed for GÍN-bal of the garden of the storehouse," 1326:1–2

7.4 Construction of the Textile Mill

[17] ĝuruš 40 géme **šeg$_{12}$** da-ki-sá-a é-uš-bar **ĝá-ĝá-dè** gub-[ba], "[17] workmen (and) 40 workwomen employed to place bricks at the side of the foundation terrace of the textile mill," 35:28

7.5 Construction of the Textile Mill and Craftsmen's House

10 géme **šeg$_{12}$** šà é-a **ĝá-ĝá-dè** gub-ba é-uš-bar ù é-gašam-e-ne-šè, "10 workwomen employed to place bricks in the house, (work) for the textile mill and craftsmen's house," 58:38–39

7.6 Construction of Various Walls

7.6.1 At the Side of the (Enclosure) Wall

10 géme **šeg$_{12}$** da bàd **ĝá-ĝá-[dè]** gub-[ba], "10 workwomen employed to place bricks at the side of the (enclosure) wall," 15:30

9 ĝuruš šidim 14 ĝuruš 18 géme šeg$_{12}$ šu dím-ma sum-mu-dè gub-ba 2 ĝuruš 2 géme im a-ĝá-ri-na ì-li-de$_{9}$ gub-ba 20 géme im ga$_{6}$-ĝá-dè gub-ba 3 ĝuruš 3 géme im lu-dè gub-ba 1 ĝuruš in-u ga$_{6}$-ĝá im lu-a 7 géme **šeg$_{12}$** ⌜da⌝ b[àd **ĝá-ĝá-dè** gub-ba], "9 builders, 14 workmen (and) 18 workwomen employed to hand (up) bricks for building, 2 workmen (and) 2 workwomen employed to lift earth into the *agarinnum*, 20 workwomen employed to carry earth, 3 workmen (and) 3 work-women employed to mix earth, 1 workman having carried straw (and) having mixed (it with) earth (and) 7 workwomen [employed to place] bricks at the side of the (enclosure) wall," 16:17–23

8 ĝuruš **šeg$_{12}$** da ⌜bàd⌝ **ĝá-ĝ[á-dè]**, "8 workmen [to] place bricks at the side of the (enclosure) wall," 20:29

1 ĝuruš šidim um-mi-[a] 2 ĝuruš šidim 10-lá-1 ĝuruš šu dím-ma 20 géme im ga$_{6}$-ĝá 10 géme **šeg$_{12}$** da bàd **ĝá-ĝá-dè** 2 géme im gíd-dè 1 géme *du-ú-um* ke$_{4}$-dè al-tar bàd gub-ba, "1 master builder, 2 builders (and) 9 workmen having built, 20 workwomen having carried earth, 10 workwomen to place bricks at the side of the (enclosure) wall, 2 workwomen to haul earth (and) 1 workwoman to make a *du-ú-um*, (workers) employed for construction of the (enclosure) wall," 102:16–23

1 ĝuruš šidim 1 ĝuruš 5 géme gi-sal bàd ĝá-ĝá [2]0 géme **šeg$_{12}$** da bàd **ĝá-ĝá**, "1 builder, 1 workman (and) 5 workwomen having placed thin reeds at the (enclosure) wall (and) 20 workwomen having placed bricks at the side of the (enclosure) wall," 103:21–23

7.6.2 At the Side of the iz-zi Wall

17 géme da-iz-zi-da **šeg$_{12}$** **ĝá-ĝá-dè** gub-ba, "17 workwomen employed to place bricks at the side of the side iz-zi wall,"14:27

7.7 Bricks Taken Down from the Kiln

n ĝuruš **šeg$_{12}$**-al-ur$_{x}$-ra úgu gir$_{4}$-ta **ĝá-ĝá**, "n workmen having set bricks down from the top of the kiln," 145:38, 146:'40, 148:'17, 155:35

8. Deposit of Building Supplies

8.1 (. . .) **é-šè ba-a-g̃ar**, "{building supplies} were placed for the house" > *Household Index*

8.1.1 Gardens

^{ĝeš}kiri$_6$ gar-ša-an-na^{ki}, "at the Garšana garden" > *Garden Index*

8.1.2 Houses

é-a-šè, "for the house"

é-*gi-na-tum*-šè, "for the barracks"

é-*gi-na-tum* ká-dedal-lí-a-šè, "for the barracks of the Dedali'a gate"

é-ki-ba-g̃ar-ra-šè, "for the replacement house"

é-ki-mu-ra-šè, "for the textile depository"

é-lùnga é-muḫaldim ù é-kíkken-šè, "for the brewery-kitchen-mill complex"

é-uš-bar-šè, "for the textile mill"

é-uš-bar ù é-gašam-e-ne-šè, "for the textile mill and craftsmen's house"

ká-suḫur é-lùnga-šè, "for the tree-top gate of the brewery"

8.1.3 Other

bàd-šè, "for the (enclosure) wall" > **bàd**

ká-*ḫu-lu-lu* im šeg$_{12}$ ku$_4$-ra-šè, "at the *Ḫululu* gate for the 'service entrance'" > **ká**

SIG$_4$.ANŠE-šè, "for the brick stack" > **SIG$_4$.ANŠE**

8.2. Buidling Supplies Placed

^{gi}bisag̃-gíd-da, "long basket"
^{gi}dur, "rope"
^{ĝeš}é-da-ásal, "poplar joist"
ésir, "bitumen"
g̃eš, "wood, plank"
g̃eš ùr, "roof beam"
gi-guru$_5$, "reedwork panel"
gi-sal, "thin reeds"
ì-ḫur-sag̃-g̃á, "mountain oil"
ì-šáḫ, "lard"
^{gi}kid, "reed mat"
^{ĝeš}kišig, "shok"
sa gi-izi, "bundle of fuel reeds"
ú, "grass"
^{ĝeš}ú-bíl-lá, "charcoal"
^{dug}ù-lu-lu, "pipe"
ZI/ZI.ÉŠ, "rushes"

9. Assorted Commodities

9.1 Leather Products

10 {erasure} gín kuš-gu$_4$ ú-ḫáb 5 gín sa-udu 2½ gín eša x x ezem-da-šè **ba-a-g̃ar**, "10 shekels of madder-tanned ox-hide, 5 shekels sheep sinew (and) 2½ shekels of fine flour, were placed for (?) of the festival," 1517:7–10

2 kuš-udu 2 kuš-šáḫ-babbar *bí-du-lu-um*-šè **ba-a-g̃ar**, "2 sheep skins (and) 2 white pig skins were placed for *Bidulum*," 1517:13–15

½ kuš-udu-babbar ½ gín eša *hu-im*-šè **ba-a-g̃ar**, "½ of a white sheep skin (and) ½ shekel of fine flour were placed for *Ḫu'im*," 1517:16–18

5 gín [kuš]-gu$_4$-^{ú}ḫáb *ib-du-um*-šè **ba-a-g̃ar**, "5 shekels of madder-tanned ox-[hide] were placed for *Ibdum*," 1517:19–20

9.2 Tablets: Deposited in Baskets

1 ^{giš}bisaĝ-im-sar-ra [sa-ḫ]a ⅔ kùš íb-sá im-sar **ĝá-ĝá-dè** u$_4$ é-[e] im sumur ba-aka, "1 canvas-lined clay tablet coffer—it is ⅔ kùš square—(in which) to deposit clay tablets when the house was plastered," 1318:1–3

1 ^{giš}bisaĝ-im-sar-ra sa-ḫa ⅔ kùš íb-sá im-sar **ĝá-ĝá-dè**, "1 canvas-lined clay tablet coffer—it is ⅔ kùš square—(in which) to deposit clay tablets," 1331:1–2, 1365:1–3

10. Errands to Make Deposits

10.1 Depositing the Commodity Tax

17 ĝuruš níĝ-gú-na **ĝá-ĝá** é-da-na^{ki}-šè ĝen-na, "17 workmen having gone to Edana (and) deposited the commodity tax," 125:5, 125:37, 126:5, 126:32, 127:5, 128:5, 128:35

10.2 Depositing Flour

2 ĝuruš *ṣa-al-*[*lum* ^{lú}kíĝ-gi$_4$-a]-⌜lugal⌝ zì **ĝá-ĝá-dè** karkar^{ki}-šè in-tùm-uš, "2 workmen of *Ṣallum*, the royal [messenger], brought flour to Karkar in order to deposit it," 28:'27

11. Coverings

11.1 Of Metal

1 bisaĝ^{zabar} dub-x zabar **ĝar-⌜ra⌝**, "1 bronze covered container of x tablets," 1337:6

1 ^{giš}gur ba-rí-ga ka-ba urudu **ĝar-ra**, "1 bushel-measuring container whose opening is covered (in) copper," 1372:35, 1372:92

11.2 Of Horn

1 ^{giš}gur ba-rí-ga ka-ba si **ĝar-ra**, "1 bushel-measuring container whose opening is covered (in) horn," 1372:34, 1372:92

11.3 Of Leather

11.3.1 Basket and Container Covers

1 ^{giš}bisaĝ-gíd-da túg-ga-tur ésir šub-ba ka-bi kuš **ĝar-ra**, "1 long, small textile basket (for) pouring bitumen, its opening covered with leather," 798:1–3

5 kuš-udu e-rí-na ma-an-ḫara$_4$–3-šè **ba-a-ĝar**, "5 root-tanned sheep skins were (used for) covering 3 manḫara containers," 923:1–2

1 kuš-udu-niga *ma-ad-li-um* **ĝar** 2-šè **ba-a-ĝar**, "1 fattened-sheep skin was (used for) covering 2 covered buckets," 968:17

1 ^{giš}bisaĝ? é-ĜAR kuš **ĝar-ra, "1 (?) basket, covered with leather," 1332:2

11.3.2 Belt Coverings

2 ^{túg}íb-lá-su$_4$-a KWU–809-ba du$_8$-ši-a **ĝar-ra**, "2 red/brown belts covered with turquoise (?)," 782:7

⅔ kuš-máš-g[al-ni]ga 4 ^{túg}íb-lá-si$_4$-a-gíd 4 kùš 2 šu-dù 1-šè **ba-a-ĝar** "⅔ of a fattened-billy-goat skin were (used for) covering 4 long red/brown belts of 4 kùš and 2 šu-dù in length," 939:1–2

11.3.3 Comb Coverings

1 kuš-máš *mul-tum*-šè **ba-a-ĝar**, "1 kid skin was (used for) covering a comb," 923:5–6

11.3.4 Hinge Coverings

^{kuš}á-si **ĝar-ra** é-ba-an, "pair of leather covered hinges," 853:4

11.3.5 Leather-Covered Chair Mats

★★2 ^{gi}kid ^{ĝeš}gu-za-zà-bi-ús tùn?-ba kuš **ĝar-ra**, "2 mats of an armchair, (?), covered with leather," 1376:8–9

2 kuš-udu-pu-uš x 1 ^{kuš}du$_{10}$-gan-ti-bal-babbar 1 kuš-máš-gal-niga 1 kuš-máš-niga 5 gín sa-udu ^{ĝeš}gu-za-níta ^{ĝeš}ku!(TÚG)-ku!(TÚG) **ba-a-ĝar**, "2 (?) sheep skins, 1 white leather bag with a marking?, 1 skin of a fattened billy-goat, 1 skin of a fattened goat, (and) 5 shekels of sheep sinew were (used for) covering the man's chair (and?) the loom piece," 1517:1–6

1+n kuš-udu e-rí-na ^{gi}kid? ^{ĝeš}gu-za-šè **ba-a-ĝar**, "1[+n?] root-tanned sheep skin(s) were (used for) covering a mat? for a chair," 1517:11–12

11.3.6 Ox Yoke Coverings

3 kuš-udu-babbar ^{ĝeš}šudul-gu$_4$-šè **ba-a-ĝar**, "3 white sheep skins were (used for) covering an ox yoke," 864:1–2, 923:3–4

11.4 Other

★★^{ĝeš}taskarin-bi éš-**ĝar**, 635:7

★★^{ĝeš}bar-bi éš-**ĝar**, 635:8

★★3 ^{gi}ḫal **ĝar-r**[**a**? . . .], 1376:32

12. Other

12.1 As a Euphemism for "To Die"

(. . .) ⌜u$_4$⌝-1-šè gaba sàg-dè gub-ba u$_4$ diĝir-re gaba *na-wi-ir-ilum* **ba-a-ĝar-ra**, "{craftsmen} employed for 1 day to beat (their) breasts when the god made the breast of *Nawir-ilum* subside (i.e. when he died)," 251:8–10

12.2 Fashioned With

^{túg}gú-è-níĝ-lám bar-si **ĝar-ra** 3-kam-ús, "3rd-quality níĝ-lám cape fashioned with bands," 579:16

^{túg}gú-è ba-tab *tuḫ-ḫu-um* bar-si **ĝar-ra** 3-kam-ús, "3rd-quality ba-tab *tuḫ-ḫu-um* cape fashioned with bands," 586:2, 587:2

^{túg}gú-è *tá-ki-ru-um* bar-s[i **ĝar-r**]**a** tur lugal, "small royal *takkirum* cape fashioned with bands," 824:1

1 ^{túg}gú-è-níĝ-lám bar:si **ĝar-ra** 4-kam-ús, "4th-quality níĝ-lám cape fashioned with bands," 1162:'18

12.3 Replacements: Stolen Bitumen

1 má-60-gur ba-gul ésir-bi zuḫ-a **ba-ĝar** ĝeš eše-bi <<BI>> nu-ĝál, "1 60-bushel boat was dismantled, its stolen bitumen was replaced (but) its wood (and) ropes are (still) missing," 1369:1–4

13. Broken or Uncertain Context

[n ĝuruš šidim] 30-lá-1 ĝuruš [n] géme [. . .] **ĝá-ĝá**, 98:'19-'20

1 ĝuruš **ĝá**-[. . .], 213:'14

★★16.0.0. peš gur IB?-**ĝar**, "16 bushels (?) date palm hearts," 1248:3

g̃en, *alāku*, "to go, to come"

1. Errands

1.1 Errands for Builders

1.1.1 Gone to G̃irsu

2 g̃uruš šidim šidim la-ḫa-dè g̃ír-su^{ki}-šè **g̃en-na**, "2 builders having gone to G̃irsu in order to bring builders," 40:50–51, 41:'31-'32

1.1.2 Gone to Edana

1 g̃uruš šidim é-da-na^{ki}-šè **g̃en-na**, "1 builder having gone to Edana," 190:30, 195:'26, 196:'29, 197:39

1.2 Errands for Craftsmen

1.2.1 Gone for Barley

80 géme sag̃-dub 17 géme á ⅔-ta géme uš-bar-me-éš 12 géme kíkken 3 g̃uruš lú-kíkken 4 géme g̃eš-ì-sur-sur 10 10 gín? g̃uruš ^{lú}ázlag 1 g̃uruš túg-du$_8$ 3 g̃uruš ašgab 2 g̃uruš ad-kub$_4$ 1 g̃uruš báḫar u$_4$-2-šè še é-duru$_5$-ul-luḫ-ŠEŠ.AB^{ki}-ma-šè **g̃en-⸢na⸣** mu še-ba-ne-ne-šè, "80 full-time female weavers, 17 female weavers at ⅔ wages, 12 female millers, 3 male millers, 4 female sesame pressers, 10 1/6 fullers, 1 braider, 3 leather workers, 2 reed craftsmen (and) 1 potter for 2 days having gone to the Ulluḫ-Urim village for barley for barley rations," 291:1–14, 292:1–14

1 g̃uruš báḫar u$_4$-2-šè še é-duru$_5$-ul-luḫ-ŠEŠ.AB^{ki}-ma-šè **g̃en-na** mu še-ba-ne-ne-šè, "1 potter for 2 days having gone to the Ulluḫ-Urim village for barley for barley rations," 293:1–4

2 g̃uruš ad-kub$_4$ u$_4$-2-šè še é-duru$_5$-ul-luḫ-ŠEŠ.AB^{ki}-ma-šè **g̃en-na** mu še-ba-ne-ne-šè, "2 reed craftsmen for 2 days having gone to the Ulluḫ-Urim village for barley for barley rations," 294:1–4

1.2.2 Gone to Bring a Sheep

1 g̃uruš ad-kub$_4$ udu la-ḫe-dè iri-sag̃-⸢rig$_7$⸣^{ki}-šè **⸢g̃en-na⸣**, "1 reed craftsman having gone to Iri-sag̃rig in order to bring a sheep," 260:1–2

1.2.3 Gone to Plow and Irrigate

[n] g̃uruš ^{lú}ázlag á-½ ⸢u$_4$⸣-8-šè (. . .) še apin-lá-a ⸢káb⸣ dì-de$_4$ **ì-im-g̃en-na-a**, "[n] fuller(s) at ½ wages for 8 days, {authorizing official}, went to check on the grain of the leased fields," 271:1–2, 5–7

1.2.4 Traveling, Task Unspecified

1 g̃uruš [túg-du$_8$ u$_4$-1-šè] gar-ša-an-na^{ki}-ta é-^{d}*šu*-^{d}*suen*[^{ki}-a] **g̃en-[na]**, "1 [braider for 1 day] having gone from Garšana [into] *Bit-Šu-Suen*," 298:1–3

3 g̃uruš ašgab u$_4$-1-šè gar-ša-an-na^{ki}-ta é-^{d}*šu*-^{d}*suen*^{ki}-a **g̃en-a**, "3 leather workers for 1 day having gone from Garšana into *Bit-Šu-Suen*," 299:1–3

1.3 Errands for Individuals

1.3.1 Gone to Bring Various Commodities: E'igara

1 é-ì-gára siki tùm-dè é-^{d}*šu*-^{d}*suen*^{ki}-[ta] **g̃en-a**, "E'igara having gone to bring wool [from] *Bit-Šu-Suen*," 39:46

1 é-ì-gára é-^{d}*šu*-^{d}*suen*^{ki}-ta siki tùm-dè **g̃en-na**, "E'igara having gone to bring wool from *Bit-Šu-Suen*," 40:40–41

1 é-ì-gára g̃eš ùr tùm-dè **g̃en-na**, "E'igara having gone to bring roof beams," 51:'18, 52:54–55, 53:56, 54:33–34

1.3.2 Gone to G̃irsu to Bring Out Barley

1 *a-lí-aḫ* še è(-dè) g̃ír-su^{ki}-šè **g̃en-na**, "*Ali-aḫ* having gone to G̃irsu to bring out barley," 37:34–35, 38:40–41, 43:'45-'46, 44:44–45, 45:26–27, 47:57, 48:64–65

1 *ta-tù-ri* ù *a-lí-aḫ* še è-dè g̃ír-su^{ki}-šè **g̃en-na**, "*Tatturi* and *Ali-aḫ* having gone to G̃irsu to bring out barley," 31:37, 32:37, 33:40, 35:44, 36:39

1.3.3 Gone to the Place of *Šu-Kabta*

1 *ma-šum* šidim ki *šu-kab-ta*-šè **g̃en-na**, "*Mašum*, the builder, having gone to the place of *Šu-Kabta*," 59:58–59, 60:54–55, 61:15, 62:'16

1 *šu-^{d}belum* á-ág̃ ki *šu-kab-ta*-šè **g̃en-na**, "*Šu-Belum* having gone to the place of *Šu-Kabta* (to bring) a message," 40:38–39

1.3.4 Gone to Gu'abba to Purchase Flying Fish

1 šeš-kal-la 1 *lu-kà-dum* ku$_{6}$-sim sa$_{10}$-sa$_{10}$-dè gú-ab-ba^{ki}-šè **g̃en-na**, "Šeš-kala (and) *Lukadum* having gone to Gu'abba to purchase flying fish," 37:35–37, 47:58–61, 48:66–69, 49:60–62

1 *ša-lim-be-lí* ku$_{6}$-sim sa$_{10}$(-sa$_{10}$)-dè gú-ab-ba^{ki}-šè **g̃en-na**, "*Šalim-Beli* having gone to Gu'abba to purchase flying fish," 37:41–44, 38:48–50, 47:64–65, 48:71–73, 49:65–67

1 šeš-kal-la 1 *lu-kà-dum* ku$_{6}$-sim sa$_{10}$-sa$_{10}$-dè gú-ab-ba^{ki}-šè **g̃en-a**, "Šeš-kala (and) *Lukadum* having gone to Gu'abba to purchase flying fish," 38:42–44

1 *lu-kà-dum* [1] šeš-kal-la [ku$_{6}$-sim] sa$_{10}$-sa$_{10}$-dè [gú-ab-ba]^{ki}-šè **g̃en-na**, "*Lukadum* (and) Šeš-kala having gone to [Gu'abba] to purchase [flying fish]," 46:'45-'47

1.4 For Workmen

1.4.1 Gone to Bring Shok

n g̃uruš ^{geš}kišig iri-ki-gíd-da-šè **g̃en-na**, "n workmen having gone to Irikigida for shok," 128:34, 129:36, 131:'29, 132:36, 133:35, 134:16, 143:41

12[+n?] g̃uruš ^{geš}kišig iri-ki-gíd-da **g̃en-na**, "12[+n?] workmen having gone (to) Irikigida for shok," 130:'16

n g̃uruš ^{geš}kišig iri-ki-gíd-da-šè lá-e-dè **g̃en-na**, "n workmen having gone to Irikigida to transport shok," 133:36, 134:17, 135:36

n g̃uruš ^{geš}kišig iri-ki-gíd-da tùm-dè **g̃en-na**, "n workmen having gone to Irikigida to bring shok," 145:41, 146:'43

10-lá-1 g̃uruš ^{geš}kišig tù[m-d]è **g̃en-⸢na⸣**, "9 workmen having gone to bring shok," 151:40

1.4.2 Gone to Bring Reeds

1.4.2.1 From Ka-saḫara

15 g̃uruš ka-saḫar-ra^{ki}-šè gi tùm-dè **g̃en-na**, "15 workmen having gone to Ka-saḫara to bring reeds," 136:41, 138:39–40,[9] 140:43, 141:38, 143:40

9 No. 138:40 has ka-saḫar-ra^{ki}-TA, but this is almost certainly a mistake for -šè.

1.4.2.2 From Udaga

6 g̃uruš má-lá-a gi ù-da[g-ga^{ki}-ta] tùm-dè **g̃e[n-na]**, "6 workmen having gone to bring a freight boat of reeds [from] Udaga," 205:26–27

1.4.2.3 From Various Fields

6 [g̃uruš . . .] a-šà pa$_4$-lu[gal-g̃]u$_{10}$-k[a-ta] gi tùm-⸢dè⸣ **g̃en-[na]**, "6 [workmen . . .] having gone to bring reeds [from] the Palugalg̃u field," 57:'22-'23

[n] g̃uruš gi-zi tùm(-dè) a-šà *ši-ḫu-um*-šè **g̃en-na(-me)**, "[n] workmen having gone to the *Šihum* field to bring fresh reeds," 74:'8, 75:26–27

30 g̃uruš gi-zi a-šà pa$_5$-lugal-g̃u$_{10}$ tùm-dè **g̃en-na**, "30 workmen having gone to bring fresh reeds of the Palugalg̃u field," 148:'19

1.4.3 Gone to Bring Straw

n g̃uruš in-u kàr-da-ḫi-šè **g̃en-na(-me-éš)**, "n workmen having gone to Kardaḫi (for) straw," 26:'18, 29:'29, 31:33, 32:33, 36:34

15 g̃uruš in-u de$_6$-a **g̃en-na**, "15 workmen having come back (with) straw," 150:40

37 g̃uruš in-u tùm-dè ^{d}*šu*-^{d}*suen*-am-ma-ar-ra^{ki}-šè **g̃en-na**, "37 workmen having gone to *Šu-Suen*-ammara to bring straw," 196:'25-'26, 197:36–37

1.4.4 Gone to Bring Wool

6 g̃uruš siki é-^{d}*šu*-^{d}*suen*^{ki}-ka-šè **g̃en-[na]**, "6 workmen having gone for *Bit-Šu-Suen* wool," 122:'30, 123:6, 123:42

[2] g̃uruš ad-kub$_4$ u$_4$-[1-šè a]-⸢rá⸣-2-kam [2 g̃ur]uš ad-kub$_4$ u$_4$-1-šè [a]-rá-3-kam siki de$_6$-a é-^{d}*šu*-^{d}*suen*^{ki}-ta gar-ša-an-na^{ki}-šè **g̃en-[a]**, "[2] reed craftsmen [for 1] day for the 2nd time (and) 2 reed craftsmen for 1 day for the 3rd time having brought wool, (reed craftsmen having gone) from *Bit-Šu-Suen* to Garšana," 286:7–13

2 g̃uruš túg-du$_8$ u$_4$-1-šè ⸢siki⸣ de$_6$-a a-rá-2-kam é-^{d}*šu*-^{d}*suen*^{ki}-ta gar-ša-an-na^{ki}-šè **g̃en-a**, "2 braiders for 1 day having brought wool for the 2nd time, (braiders) having gone from *Bit-Šu-Suen* to Garšana," 306:9–13

1.4.5 Gone to Collect Wages

1 g̃uruš á-ne nag̃-su$^{⸢ki⸣}$-šè **g̃en-a**, "1 workman having gone to Nag̃su for his wages," 96:'9

2 g̃uruš še á-ne nag-su^{ki}-šè **g̃en**, "2 workmen having gone to Nagsu for their barley wages," 189:30

1.4.6 Gone to Deposit the Commodity Tax

17 g̃uruš níg̃-gú-na g̃á-g̃á é-da-na^{ki}-šè **g̃en-na**, "17 workmen having gone to Edana (and) deposited the commodity tax," 125:5, 125:37, 126:5, 126:32, 127:5, 128:5, 128:35

1.4.7 Gone to Guard Straw

1 g̃uruš in-u ka i$_7$-[ta] gub-ba en-n[u ke$_4$-dè] **g̃en-[na]**, "1 employed workman having gone to guard straw [at] the opening of the canal," 196:'27-'28

1.4.8 Gone to Meet the Boat

12 g̃uruš má gaba ri-a igi *šu-kab-tá*-šè **g̃en-⸢na⸣**, "12 workmen having gone before *Šu-Kabta*, having met the boat," 163:37

1.4.9 Traveling, Task Unspecified

[n] g̃uruš [GN]^{ki}-ta [gar-ša]-an-⸢na⸣^{ki}-[šè **g̃en-na**], "[n] workmen [having gone] from [GN to] Garšana," 184:17–19

7 g̃uruš é-ù-ri-a[^{ki}-ta] ka i_7-è **g̃[en-na]**, "7 workmen having gone [from] E-uri'a (to) the opening of the 'Outgoing' canal," 192:'21

[n g̃uruš . . .] *ba?-la-nu*^{ki}-ta [. . . iri-sag̃]-$rig_7$$^{[ki]}$-šè **g̃en-na**, "[n workmen . . .] having gone from *Balanu* [. . .] to Iri-sag̃rig," 193:34–35

2 g̃uruš s[ag̃-tag] 1 g̃uruš á-[⅔] u_4-1½-[šè] gar-ša-an-[na^{ki}-ta] nibru^{ki}-šè **g̃[en-na]** 2 g̃uruš [sag̃-tag] 1 [g̃uruš á-⅔] u_4-[n-šè] nibru^{ki}-[ta GN-šè **g̃en-na**] 2 g̃uruš sag̃-[tag] 1 g̃uruš á-⅔ u_4-1-šè gar-ša-an-na^{ki}-šè? [?], "2 full-time workmen (and) 1 workman at [⅔] wages [for] 1½ days having gone [from] Garšana to Nippur, 2 [full-time] workmen (and) 1 [workman at ⅔ wages for n] day(s) [having gone from] Nippur [to GN] (and) 2 full-time workmen (and) 1 workman at ⅔ wages for 1 day (having gone?) to? Garšana," 223:1–14

[n] g̃uruš sag̃-tag [n] g̃uruš á-⅔ [n] g̃uruš á-½ [n] g̃uruš á-⅓ [tum-ma]-al^{ki}-ta [gar-š]a-an-na^{ki}-šè **g̃en-na** u_4-2-šè, "[n] full-time workmen, [n] workmen at ⅔ wages, [n] workmen at ½ wages (and) [n] workmen at ⅓ wages for 2 days having gone from Tumal to Garšana for 2 days," 266:13–17

[n+]1 g̃uruš u_4-1-šè [gar]-ša-an-na^{ki}-ta ù-dag-ga^{ki}-šè **g̃en-na**, "[n+]1 workmen for 1 day having gone from Garšana to Udaga," 553:3–5

22½ g̃uruš u_4-[1-šè] gar-ša-an-na^{ki}-[ta] ù-dag-ga^{ki}-[šè **g̃en-na**], "22½ workmen [for 1] day [having gone from] Garšana [to] Udaga," 553:23–25

1.5 Errand Runner Unspecified or Broken

[. . .] in-u tùm-d[è **g̃en-na**], "[. . . having gone] to bring straw," 52:48–49

iti ezem-maḫ še tùm-dè é-$duru_5$-ul-luḫ-uri_5^{ki}-[ma-šè **g̃en-na**], "(workers) [having gone to] the Ulluḫ-Urim village to bring barley (in) month 10," 1029:'18-'19

2. The Travels of *Šu-Kabta*

2.1 To and from G̃EŠ.KÚŠU

0.0.4.4 sìla dabin 0.0.2.8 sìla eša 0.0.1. zú-lum eša {erasure} ba-ḫi zì-dub-dub-didli-šè u_4 *šu-kab-ta* G̃EŠ.KÚŠU^{ki}-šè **du-ni**[10] {erasure} u_4 *šu-kab-ta* G̃EŠ.KÚŠU^{ki}-ta **du-ni**, "44 liters of semolina, 28 liters of fine flour (and) 10 liters of dates were mixed (with) fine flour for various small flour heaps when *Šu-Kabta* went to G̃EŠ.KÚŠU (and) when *Šu-Kabta* came from G̃EŠ.KÚŠU," 488:8–23

2.2 To the House of *Zerara*'s Wife

1 g̃uruš ^{lú}ázlag nibru^{ki}-ta ^{d}*šu*-^{d}*suen*-DU_{10}^{ki}-šè ^{urudu}šim-da gu_4-udu de_6-a kaskal šu+níg̃in-na-bi u_4-11-kam u_4 *šu-kab-tá* é-dam-*zé-ra-ra* šu sum-mu-dè **ì-g̃en-na-a**, "1 fuller having brought a sheep and cattle brand from Nippur to *Šu-Suen-ṭabu*, a trip of 11 days in total,

---

10 For the writing du-ni for g̃en-né see Hilgert 2003, 52 with reference to Attinger 1993, §205.

when *Šu-Kabta* went to the house of the wife of *Zerara* in order to take inventory," 219:1–10

3. The Travels of Various Individuals

3.1 *Beli-arik*

2 udu *be-lí-a-ri-ik* u$_4$ iri-ni-šè **ì-g̃en-na-a**, "2 sheep (for) *Beli-arik* when he went to his city," 410:1–3

3.2 *Nasim*, the Royal Messenger

na-sìm ^{lú}kíg̃-gi$_4$<-a>-lugal-ta lú te-te-dè **in-da-g̃e$_{26}$-en**, "*Nasim*, the royal messenger, went to bring the man from the king," 222:3–5

3.3 *Rim-Ilum*

(. . .) kaš ba-an-dé *ri-im-ilum* sugal$_7$ gaba-ri-a unug^{ki}-ta **du-ni**, "{assorted beer}, he poured the beer when *Rim-ilum*, the sugal, came from Uruk (for) a meeting," 517:4–6

3.4 The Servants of the Sugal-maḫ

2 udu-˹niga˺ iti u$_4$-27-ba-zal 0.1.0. še-kaš 3 ^{dug}epig kaš ba-an-dé 0.0.3. ninda-*u$_4$-tuḫ-ḫu-um* 0.0.3. ninda-šu-ra-sig$_5$ 0.2.0. ninda-šu-ra-gen árad-géme sugal$_7$-maḫ g̃ír-su^{ki}-šè **du-ni**, "2 fattened sheep at the end of the 27th day of the month, 60 liters of barley (for) beer (and) 3 drinking vessels (into which) he poured beer, 30 liters of *utuhhum* bread, 30 liters of fine half(-loaf) bread (and) 20 liters of ordinary half(-loaf) bread when the male and female servants of the sugal-maḫ came to G̃irsu," 449:1–10

4. Broken Context

★★[. . . x? iti ez]em-^{d}šul-g[i x? . . . im] sumur aka [gar]-ša-an-na$^{[ki]}$ ù g̃ír-[su]^{ki}-˹šè˺ D[U-x?], 1029:'11-'14

g̃eš . . . ra(ḫ$_2$), *rapāsu*, "to beat; to thresh (grain with a flail)"

1. Craftsmen Assigned to Flail Barley

(. . .) še gur$_{10}$-gur$_{10}$-dè zàr tab-ba-dè ù **g̃eš ra-ra-dè** a-šà *ṣe-ru-um* gub-ba, "{craftsmen} employed at the *Ṣerum* field to reap barley, stack (its) sheaves (for drying) and flail (them)," 262:19–22

– Ḫ –

ḫal, *zâzu*, "to divide"

1. Division of Assorted Commodities as Rations during Construction Work

šu+níg̃in 0.1.0.3 sìla 10 gín kaš-gen šu+níg̃in 0.0.5.3⅔ sìla ninda šu+níg̃in 0.0.3.8 sìla tu$_7$ kaš-ninda **ḫa-la-a**? al-˹tar˺ gub-ba, "In total: 63 liters (and) 10 shekels of ordinary beer, 53⅔ liters of bread (and) 38 liters of soup, beer (and) bread divided (for workers) employed (for) construction," 379:17–20

1.1 Construction of the Brick Stack

[n.n.n.n sìla] zú-lum ˹gur˺ šidim ù lú-ḫug̃-g̃á-e-ne **ba-na-ḫa-la** u$_4$ al-tar SIG$_4$.˹ANŠE˺, "[n] bushel(s) (and) [n liter(s)] of dates were divided for the builders and hired workers during construction of the brick stack," 424:1–3

1.2 Construction of the Brewery-Kitchen-Mill Complex

1.2.2.5 sìla zú-lum <gur> šidim ù lú-ḫuĝ-ĝá-e-ne **ba-na-ḫa-la** u$_4$ al-tar é-lùnga é-muḫaldim ù é-kíkken, "1 bushel (and) 145 liters of dates were divided for the builders and hired workers during construction of the brewery-kitchen-mill complex," 429:1–4

1.3 When the House was Plastered

[n sìl]a níĝ-àr-r[a-sig$_5$ t]u$_7$-šè lú-é-^{d}*šu*-^{d}E[N.ZU]^{ki}-ke$_4$-ne **ba-na-ḫa-la** u$_4$ [é]-e [im sumur ba-aka], "[n] liter(s) of [fine] barley groats for soup were divided among the men from *Bit-Šu-Suen* when [the house] was plastered," 391:1–5

0.1.0.8 sìla ninda-g[al-gen] 1 sìla [du$_8$] 0.0.5.4 sìla kaš-gen 0.0.5.4 sìla zú-lum ˹ĝuruš˺ árad-é-a ù lú-ḫuĝ-ĝá-e-ne **ba-na-ḫa-la** u$_4$ é<-e> im sumur <ba->aka, "68 liters of [ordinary] large bread [baked] (in) 1 liter (loaves), 54 liters of ordinary beer (and) 54 liters of dates were divided for the household servants and hired workers when the house was plastered," 471:1–5

0.3.0. še šà-gu$_4$-me-éš dirig še-ba-ne-ne mu zì nu-ĝál-la-šè **ba-na-ḫa-la** *šu-kab-tá* bí-in-dug$_4$, "180 liters of barley for the ox-drivers. *Šu-Kabta* had ordered that additional barley rations were to be divided for them because there was no flour," 481:1–4

2. Division of Provisions: Occasion Unspecified

2.1 For Craftswomen

ninda zì-milla ù zì-šà-gen-bi 4 [sìla] kaš-gen-bi [0.n.n(.n sìla)] tuḫ-ĝeš-ì-ḫád-bi [n ma-na] zú-lum-bi 1.3.5.[(n sìla) gur] **ba-na-ḫa-[la]**, "(In total:) their bread of milla and ordinary šà-flour is 4 [liters], their ordinary beer is [n liter(s)], their dried sesame chaff is [n mina(s)] (and) their dates are 1 bushel (and) 130[+n liters]; (provisions) were divided for the {female weavers, millers and sesame pressers}," 536:18–22

2.2 For Hired Workers

0.0.4. tuḫ-duru$_5$-sig$_5$ gibil lú-ḫuĝ-ĝá-e-ne **ba-na-ḫa-[la]**, "40 liters of fine fresh new bran were divided for the hired workers," 436:9–10

2.3 For Household Servants

šu+níĝin 6 ĝ[uruš 2 sìla ninda-dabin] 2 sìla [zú-lum-ta šu+níĝin 9] ĝuruš 1 sìla ninda-˹dabin˺ 2 ˹sìla˺ zú-lum šu+níĝin 28 ĝuruš 1 sìla [ninda] 2 sìla zú-lum-ta ninda-dabin-bi 0.0.1.8 sìla ninda-dabin ù zì-šà-gen ½ sìla du$_8$-bi 0.0.2.8 ˹sìla˺ zú-lum-bi 0.1.2.4 ˹sìla˺ **ḫa-la-a** ĝuruš árad-é-a-e-[ne], "In total: 6 workmen, [2 liters of semolina bread] (and) 2 liters [of dates, each; in total: 9] workmen, 1 liter of semolina bread (and) 2 liters of dates; in total: 28 workmen, 1 liter of [bread] (and) 2 liters of dates each; (in total:) their semolina bread is 18 liters, their bread of semolina and ordinary šà-flour is 28 liters baked (in) ½-liter loaves, (and) their dates are 84 liters; divided (provisions) of household servants," 402:11–17

(. . .) 0.3.2. kaš-gen 0.0.2.7½ sìla ì-ĝeš 1.2.0. zú-lum gur 7.0.0. gú tuḫ-ĝeš-ì-ḫád 112 [ádda udu géme]-árad-é-[a **ba-na-ḫ]a-la**, "{assorted breads}, 32 liters of ordinary beer, 27½ liters of sesame oil, 1 bushel (and) 120 liters of dates, 7 talents of dried sesame chaff (and) 112 [sheep carcasses] were divided for the [female] and male household servants," 528:7–12

(. . .) géme-árad-é-a **ba-na-ḫa-la**, "{assorted breads, ordinary beer, jugs of dida beer, sheep carcasses (and) spice plants} were divided for the female and male household servants," 548:15–16

3. Portioned out to Individuals

0.0.1.1 sìla zú-lum eša b[a-ḫ]i ½ x géme-tur **ba-na-ḫa-la**, "11 liters of dates were mixed (with) fine flour, ½ x. They were portioned out to Geme-tur," 506:16–19

ḫi, *balālu*, "to mix"

1. To Mix Dates and Fine Flour

n eša zú-lum **ba-ḫi**, "n liter(s) of fine flour were mixed (with) dates," 484:2

n zú-lum eša **ba-ḫi**, "n liter(s) of dates were mixed (with) fine flour," 506:16–17, 1013:9, 1014:2, 1028:29, 1030:22, 1030:28, 1030:34

n zú-lum eša **ḫi-dè**, "n liter(s) of dates to mix (with) fine flour," 1016:20, 1017:5, 1030:8, 1030:15

2. To Mix Dates, Fine Flour, and Semolina

0.0.4.4 sìla dabin 0.0.2.8 sìla eša 0.0.1. zú-lum eša {erasure} **ba-ḫi** zì-dub-dub-didli-šè, "44 liters of semolina, 28 liters of fine flour and 10 liters of dates were mixed (with) fine flour for various small flour heaps," 488:8–11

[n] sìla dabin 7 sìla eša [n+]⅓ sìla zú-lum eša **ba-ḫi** zì-dub-dub-šè, "[n] liter(s) of semolina, 7 liters of fine flour (and) [n+]⅓ liters of dates were mixed (with) fine flour for the small flour heap," 1028:28–30

[0.n.n. ZÌ.]ŠE [0.n.n.] eša 0.0.1. zú-lum eša **ḫi-dè** zì-dub-dub-šè, "[n liter(s)] of semolina, [n liter(s)] of fine flour (and) 10 liters of dates to mix (with) fine flour for the small flour heap," 1036:'13-'17

0.0.3. ZÌ.[ŠE] 0.0.2. eša zú-lum eša **ḫi-dè**, "30 liters of semolina (and) 20 liters of fine flour in order to mix dates (and) fine flour," 1166:1–4

3. To Mix Flour for Bread

3.1 Ordinary Flour

0.4.0. ninda-zì-šà-gen zì-milla **íb-ta-ḫi** ½ sìla du_8, "240 liters of bread baked (in) ½ liter (loaves) were mixed from ordinary šà-flour (and) milla-flour," 1079:2

3.2 Semolina

0.1.5.9⅔ sìla ninda-zì-šà-gen dabin **íb-ta-ḫi**, "119⅔ liters of bread were mixed from ordinary šà-flour (and) semolina," 479:10

0.1.5.9⅔ sìl[a zì]-š[à-gen] dabin **íb-ta-[ḫi]**, "119⅔ liters of [ordinary] šà-[flour] were mixed with semolina," 483:9–10

[šu+níĝin 0.1.5].9⅔ ⌜sìla⌝ zì-[šà-gen] dabin **ì-ḫi**, "[In total: 11]9⅔ liters of [ordinary šà]-flour were mixed (with) semolina," 483:18

0.4.0. ninda-dabin ù zì-šà-gen **íb-ta-ḫi**, "240 liters of bread were mixed from semolina and ordinary šà-flour," 490:1

ḫuĝ, *agāru*, "to hire, rent"

1. Hired Animals

5.4.0. še gur á al aka ù gu_4 **ḫuĝ-ĝá**, "5 bushels and 240 liters of barley, wages (for) hoeing and the hired oxen," 1051:1–2

2. Hired Workers

géme **ḫuĝ-ĝá**, "hired workwoman" > *passim*

ĝuruš **ḫuĝ-ĝá**, "hired workman" > *passim*

lú-**ḫuĝ-ĝá**(-e-ne), "hired worker(s)" > *passim*

ugula lú-**ḫuĝ-ĝá**, "overseer of hired workers" > **ugula**

3. Provisions for Hired Workers

n ĝuruš ḫuĝ-ĝá n sìla kaš-ninda n sìla tu$_7$-ta, "n hired workmen: n liter(s) of beer (and) bread (and) n liter(s) of soup each," 379:7, 556:'3

n géme ḫuĝ-ĝá n sìla kaš-ninda n sìla tu$_7$-ta, "n hired workwomen: n liter(s) of beer (and) bread (and) n liter(s) of soup each," 379:8, 556:'4

4. Wages for Hired Workers

á ^{lú}ázlag **ḫuĝ-ĝá**, "wages of hired fullers" > *Craftsmen Index*

á ĝuruš **ḫuĝ-ĝá**, "wages of hired workmen" > **á**

4.1 Barley Wages

4.1.1 To Break up Earth

9 ĝuruš u$_4$-1-šè še 6 sìla-ta **ba-ḫuĝ** im si-le ˹gub˺-ba, "9 workmen hired for 1 day for 6 liters of barley each, employed to break up earth," 474:1–3

4.1.2 To Bring Straw

40 ĝuruš u$_4$-1-šè še 6 sìla-ta **ba-ḫuĝ** a-šà a-gi-li-˹ta˺? gar-˹ša˺-an-na^{ki}-šè in-u de$_6$-a, "40 workmen were hired for 1 day for 6 liters of barley each having brought straw [from?] the Agili field to Garšana," 443:1–5

4.1.3 To Carry Bricks

4.1.3.1 Sample Texts with Full Context

[šu+níĝin] 16 sar 2½ gín šeg$_{12}$ ús-bi 72 nindan á-géme 150-šeg$_{12}$-ta géme-bi 77 u$_4$-1-šè še 3-sìla-ta **ba-ḫuĝ** še-bi 0.3.5.1 sìla [4 gín] mu-DU bàd-šè *simat-é-a* ugula lú-**ḫuĝ-ĝá** ĝìri ^{d}*adad-tillati* šabra ù *puzur*$_4$-^{d}nin-kar-ak dub-sar, "In total: 16 sar (and) 2½ gin of bricks, its base is 72 nindan (long), workwomen wages for each 150 bricks, its workwomen (equal) 77 workerdays, hired for 3 liters of barley each. Their barley is 231 liters (and) 4 shekels. Delivery (of bricks) for the (enclosure) wall by *Simat-Ea*, overseer of hired workers, under the authority of *Adad-tillati*, the majordomo, and *Puzur*-Ninkarak, the scribe," 308:41–51

šu+níĝin 9½ sar 4 gín igi-6-ĝál ús-bi 30 nindan á-ĝuruš-a 6 gín-ta ĝuruš-bi 95⅔ 1⅔ gín u$_4$-1-šè še 6 sìla-ta **ba-ḫuĝ** še-bi 1.4.3.4 sìla 10 gín gur saḫar zi-ga tùn-[lá] da bàd sè-ga á ^{tumu}mer mu-DU *ba-zi* ugula lú-**ḫuĝ-ĝá** ĝìri ^{d}*adad-tillati* šabra ù *puzur*$_4$-^{d}nin-kar-ak dub-sar, "In total: 9½ sar (and) 4⅙ gín, its base is 30 nindan (long), workmen wages at 6 gín each, its workmen (equal) 95⅔ (and) 1⅔ gín workerdays, hired for 6 liters of barley each. Their barley is 1 bushel, 274 liters (and) 10 shekels. Dirt removed via a tùn-lá device, tamped at the north side of the (enclosure) wall. Delivery (of dirt) by *Bazi*, overseer of hired workers, under the authority of *Adad-tillati*, the majordomo, and *Puzur*-Ninkarak, the scribe," 331:28–38

4.1.3.2 References

še n-sìla-ta **ba-ḫuĝ̃** še-bi n sìla (n gín), "{workwomen / workmen} hired for n liter(s) of barley each. Their barley is n liter(s) (and n shekel(s))," 308:45–46, 309:72–73, 311:18–19, 312:32–33, 313:21–22, 316:27–28, 316:69–70, 318:'47-'48, 321:'30-'31, 322:'81, 323:121–122, 324:91–92, 325:15–16, 327:79–80, 328:11–12, 329:11–12, 330:24–25, 331:32–33, 333:19–20, 334:62–63, 335:38–39, 337:27–28, 339:10–11, 340:30–31, 341:10–11, 342:80–81, 343:8–9, 344:'22-'23, 345:'13-'14, 347:'14-'15, 349:'15-'16, 352:37–38, 353:14–15, 361:'11-'12, 362:'17-'18, 367:'127-'128, 368:'57-'58, 369:'25-'26, 373:'9-'10

še-bi n sìla **ba-ḫuĝ̃**, "{workwomen} hired (for barley). Their barley is n liter(s)," 310:'16

še n sìla-ta **ba-ḫuĝ̃**, "{workmen} hired for barley (rations) of n liter(s) each," 355:5, 356:4, 496:12

4.1.4 To Grind and Process Grains

4.1.4.1 Beer Bread

2 géme u$_4$-1-šè še 3-sìla-ta **ba-ḫuĝ̃** bappir-ra àr-ra-dè ús-sa, "2 workwomen were hired for 1 day for 3 liters of barley each to grind and process beer bread," 434:1–2

4.1.4.2 Groats

7 géme u$_4$-1-šè še 3-sìla-ta **ba-ḫuĝ̃** ⸢níĝ⸣-àr-ra àr-ra-⸢dè⸣ ⸢gub⸣-ba, "7 workwomen were hired for 1 day for 3 liters of barley each, (workwomen) employed to grind groats," 423:1–3

90-lá-1 géme še 3 sìla-ta **ba-[ḫuĝ̃]** á níĝ-àr-ra-ra, "89 workwomen were [hired] for 3 liters of barley each as wages for (milling) groats," 432:1–3

4.1.5 To Mold Bricks

[n.n.n.] še gur ⸢šeg⸣$_{12}$ du$_8$-dè á 5-sìla-ta **ba-ḫuĝ̃**, "[n] bushel(s) of barley were (used to) hire (workers) to mold bricks at wages of 5 liters each," 454:1–3

4.1.6 To Pile Earth

[. . .] á [ĝuruš]-a 10 gín-ta ĝuruš-bi 4 u$_4$-1-šè še 6-sìla-ta **ba-ḫuĝ̃** saḫar zi-ga kar-ki-mu-ra si-ga "[. . . workmen] wages of 10 shekels each, its workmen (equal) 4 workerdays, (workers) hired for 6 liters of barley each, having piled up excavated dirt at the quay of the textile depository," 354:1–5

4.1.7 For Sailors of Hired Boats

0.2.3. ⸢še⸣ á má **ḫuĝ̃-ĝá** 4[0]-gur-kam ù má-laḫ$_5$-bi á 0.0.3.-ta, "150 liters of barley, wages of the hired 40-bushel boat and its sailors, wages of 30 liters each," 233:1–3

2.2.0. še gur á má **ḫuĝ̃-ĝá** má-90-gur-kam á 0.0.4-ta ù má-laḫ$_5$-bi u$_4$-18-šè in-u é-ù-ri-a<ki>-ta gú i$_7$-da lá-a, "2 bushels (and) 120 liters of barley, wages of the hired 90-bushel boat and its sailors, wages of 40 liters each for 18 days (for sailors) having transported straw from E-uri'a to the bank of the canal," 413:1–7

[1.1.4.] še gur [á má-**ḫuĝ̃**]-**ĝá** má 50-gur-ta 2-kam ù má-laḫ$_5$-bi [0].1.2.5 sìla-ta [á] 0.0.2.5 sìla-ta á má-**ḫuĝ̃-ĝá** má 40-gur-ta 2-kam ù má-laḫ$_5$-bi á 0.0.2.-ta [u$_4$]-8-šè

˹še˺ ù-dag-ga^{ki}-ta [gar-ša]-an-na^{ki}-šè de$_6$-a, "[1] bushel (and) [100 liters] of barley, [wages] (for) each of 2 hired 50-bushel boats and their sailors, 85 liters each; [wages] of 25 liters each, wages (for) each of 2 hired 40-bushel boats and their sailors, 20 liters each; (wages for sailors) for 8 days having brought barley from Udaga to Garšana," 414:1–11

0.4.0. še á má **ḫug̃-g̃á** [40-gur-kam] ù má-la[ḫ$_5$-bi] á 0.1.2.-ta u$_4$-3-šè še *dar-ra-um*^{ki}-˹ta˺ gar-ša-an-na^{ki}-[šè] de$_6$-[a], "40 liters of barley, wages of the hired [40 bushel] boat and [its] sailors, wages of 80 liters each for 3 days (for sailors) having brought barley from *Darra'um* [to] Garšana," 462:1–6

0.2.3. še á má-**ḫug̃-g̃á** 0.2.0. á g̃uruš **ḫug̃-g̃á** 0.0.1.6 sìla šà-gal má-la[h$_5$. . .], "150 liters of barley, wages of hired boats (and) 120 liters, wages of hired workmen; 16 liters, food (for) sailors [. . .]," 561:'10

0.2.3. á má-**ḫug̃-g̃á** 0.2.0. á g̃uruš **ḫug̃-g̃á** 0.0.1.6 šà-gal má-laḫ$_5$ 0.0.1.6 <še->bi sa$_{10}$ má-laḫ$_5$ u$_4$-1-šè gú i$_7$-^{d}nin-ḫur-sag̃-g̃á-ta [gar-ša-an-na^{ki}-šè má] gíd-da, "150 liters (of barley), wages of the hired boat (and) 120 liters, wages of hired workmen; 16 liters, food (for) sailors, 16 liters <of barley> is the (hiring) price of the sailors [for] 1 day having towed [boats] from the bank of the Ninhursag̃a canal [to Garšana]," 561:'19-'23

0.2.3. á má-**ḫug̃-g̃á** 0.2.0. á g̃uruš **ḫug̃-g̃á** 0.0.1.6 sìla šà-gal má-laḫ$_5$ 0.0.1.6 sìla < še->b[i s]a$_{10}$ má-˹laḫ$_5$˺ u$_4$-1-šè é-duru$_5$-ka[b-bí-ta] gú i$_7$-[*ma-an-iš-ti-šu*-šè] má gí[d-da], "140 liters (of barley), wages of the hired boat (and) 120 liters, wages of hired workmen; 16 liters, food (for) sailors, 16 liters is the (hiring) price of the sailors for 1 day having towed boats [from] the Kabbi village [to] the bank of the [*Maništišu*] canal," 561:'28-'32

4.1.8 For Workmen: Work Unspecified

šu+níg̃in 62 g̃uruš u$_4$-1-˹šè˺ še 6-sìla-ta **ba-ḫug̃** še-bi 1.1.1.2 sìla gur, "In total: 62 workmen for 1 day, hired for 6 liters of barley each. Their barley is 1 bushel and 72 liters," 336:43–45

šu+níg̃in 99½ [géme] u$_4$-1-[šè] še 3-sìla-[ta **ba-ḫug̃**] še-bi 0.4.2.5½ sìla, "In total: 99½ [workwomen for] 1 day [were hired] for 3 liters of barley [each]. Their barley is 265½ liters," 336:46–48

4.2 Broken or Uncertain Context

[. . .]x-*še-en* [x] dú-ra-a [. . .] 6 sìla gíd-[. . .] 0.0.2. [á]-bi **ḫ[ug̃-g̃]á ^{lú}ázlag-me-éš ˹mu-DU˺ NE-KU, 477:1–7

– I –

igi . . . sag̃, "to sort"

siki igi sag̃, "to sort wool"

1. Wool Sorted in *Bit-Šu-Suen*

4 géme uš-bar u_4-1-šè **siki igi sag̃-g̃á** šà é-^{d}*šu*-^{d}*suen*^{ki}, "4 female weavers for 1 day having sorted wool in *Bit-Šu-Suen*," 264:1–3

8 géme u_4-1-šè **[siki] igi sag̃-g̃á** šà é-^{d}*šu*-^{d}*suen*^{ki}-ka de_6-a, "8 workwomen for 1 day having brought [wool] sorted in *Bit-Šu-Suen*," 279:1–3

íl, *našû*, "to raise, carry"[11]

ì-ḫur-sag̃-g̃á íl, "to bring mountain oil"

im íl, "to lift earth"

im a-g̃á-ri-na íl, "to lift earth into the *agarinnum*"

im sumur íl, "to lift plaster"

in-u íl, "to lift straw"

siki íl, "to bring wool"

1. **ì-ḫur-sag̃-g̃á íl**, "to bring mountain oil"

[1] g̃uruš **ì-ḫur-sag̃-g̃[á. . .] ì-li-[de_9]** gub-[ba], "[1] workman employed to bring [. . .] mountain oil," 157:16–20

2. **im ìl**, "to lift earth"

*See *Household Index* for the complete context of the following passages.

2.1 Construction of the Craftsmen's House

[n g̃uruš **im] ì-li-de_9** gub-ba (. . .) [. . . é]-gašam, "[n workmen] employed to lift [earth] (. . .), [(work for)] the craftsmen's house," 66:'4-'9

2.2 Construction of the Roof

2 g̃uruš šidim 4 g̃uruš šu dím-[ma] 4 géme im ga_6-[g̃á]-dè gu[b-ba] 1 g̃uruš **im ì-[li]-de_9** gu[b-ba] éš g̃eš ùr kéše-[rá], "2 builders (and) 4 workmen having built, 4 workwomen employed to carry earth (and) 1 workman employed to lift earth, (workers) having bound ropes to roof beams," 57:'12-'16

[. . . n g̃ur]uš [. . . n+]4 g̃uruš šidim [n] g̃uruš **im ì-li-de_9** gub-ba (. . .) [ùr é-gal gib]il a g̃á-g̃á, "[. . . n] workmen [. . .], [n+]4 builders (and) [n] workmen employed to lift earth (. . .), (workers) having waterproofed [the roof of the] new [palace]," 74:'1-'4, '6

2.3 Construction of the Textile Mill

4 g̃uruš **im ì-li-de_9** gub-ba é-uš-bar-šè, "4 workmen employed to lift earth, (work) for the textile mill," 37:25–26, 38:26–27

n g̃uruš **im ì-li-de_9** gub-ba (. . .) al-tar é-uš-bar-ra, "n workmen employed to lift earth (. . .), (for) construction of the textile mill," 52:33, 35, 53:27, 29

---

11 Written syllabically, ì-li, at Garšana to differentiate the verb from ÍL, which is written /gag̃/.

2.3.1 The Foundation of the Textile Mill

6 ĝuruš im **ì-li-[de$_9$]** gub-ba ⸢uš⸣ é-uš-bar-ra, "6 workmen employed [to] lift earth, (work) for the foundation of the textile mill," 47:25–26

2.3.2 The Foundation Terrace of the Textile Mill

n ĝuruš **im ì-li-de$_9$** gub-ba ki-sá-a é-uš-bar-šè, "n workmen employed to lift earth, (work) for the foundation terrace of the textile mill," 43:'31-'32, 46:'20-'21

2.4 Construction of the Textile Mill and Craftsmen's House

2.4.1 To Plaster Crossbeams

[n ĝuruš šidim] 8 ĝuruš šu dím-[ma? n] géme im ga$_6$<-ĝá>-dè g[ub-bá 2] ĝuruš **im ì-li-de$_9$** [gub-ba *b*]*í-ni-tum* im sumur ke$_4$-dè é-uš-bar ù é-gašam-[e-ne(-šè)], "[n builder(s)], 8 workmen having built, [n] workwomen employed to carry earth, [2] workmen [employed] to lift earth, (workers) to plaster crossbeams [(for)] the textile mill and craftsmen's house," 71:21–24

2.4.2 To Waterproof its Roof

4 ĝuruš ⸢šidim⸣ 3 ĝu[ruš . . .] gub-ba 30 ⸢géme⸣ 10 ⸢ĝuruš⸣ im ga$_6$-ĝá-dè gu[b-b]a 7 ĝuruš šidim **im ì-li-de$_9$** gub-ba ùr a ĝá-ĝá-[dè] g[ub-ba] (. . .) é-uš-bar ù é-gašam-šè, "4 builders, 3 workmen employed [to . . .], 30 workwomen (and) 10 workmen employed to carry earth, 7 builders employed to lift earth—(workers) employed to waterproof the roof—(. . .) (work) for the textile mill and craftmen's house," 59:31–35, 43

[n ĝuruš **i]m ì-li-de$_9$** [gub-ba n ĝuruš] im sumur tà-tà-dè gub-ba [ùr] a ĝá-ĝá-dè [é-uš]-bar ù é-gašam-e-[ne], "[n workmen employed] to lift earth, [n workmen] employed to apply plaster, (workers) to waterproof [the roof] of the textile mill (and) craftmen's house," 65:'15-'19

2.5 Construction of Various Houses and Installations

2.5.1 The House of *Ubarria*

1 ĝuruš **im ì-li-d[e$_9$** gub-ba] é-*u*-⸢*bar*⸣-*ri-a* gub-[ba], "1 workman [employed] to lift earth, (workers) employed at the house of *Ubarria*," 94:19–20

2.5.2 The Roof of the Sheep-Fattening Pen

1 ĝuruš **im ì-li-dè** gub-ba ùr é-udu-niga-šè, "1 workman employed to lift earth, (work) for the roof for the sheep-fattening pen," 53:39–40

2.6 Construction of the (Enclosure) Wall

6 ĝuruš šu dím-ma ⸢gub⸣-ba [n ĝuruš] im sumur [tà-t]à-dè gub-ba 1 ĝuruš **⸢im⸣ ì-⸢li⸣-de$_9$** [gub-ba] 10-lá-1 géme i[m ga$_6$]-ĝá-dè gub-ba bàd im sumur ke$_4$-dè, "6 workmen employed to build, [n workmen] employed to apply stucco, 1 workman [employed] to lift earth (and) 9 workwomen employed to carry earth, (workers) to plaster the (enclosure) wall," 41:'18-'22

2.7 Construction of the iz-zi Wall

2 ĝuruš **im [ì-li]-de$_9$** gub-⸢ba⸣ iz-zi im sumur ke$_4$-dè, "2 workmen employed to lift earth, (workers) to plaster the iz-zi wall," 51:'10-'11

8 géme im ga$_6$-⸢ĝá⸣-dè gub-[ba] 2 ĝuruš **im ì-li-de$_9$** [gub-b]a iz-zi im [sumur k]e$_4$-⸢dè⸣, "8 workwomen employed to carry earth (and) 2 workmen employed to lift earth, (workers) to plaster the iz-zi wall," 56:'20-'22

2.8 Construction of the urua wall

[n ĝuruš **im ì-lí]-dè** gub-ba 6 géme im ga_6-ĝá-dè gub-⌜ba⌝ ù-[ru]-a bàd ke_4-dè, "[n workmen] employed to [lift] earth (and) 6 workwomen employed to carry earth, (workers) to make the urua wall," 39:32–34

2 ĝuruš šidim 2 ĝuruš šu dím gub-ba 4 géme im ga_6-ĝá-dè gub-ba 1 ĝuruš **im i-⌜li⌝-dè** gub-[ba] ù-ru-a bàd-[šè], "2 builders (and) 2 workmen employed to build, 4 workwomen employed to carry earth (and) 1 workman employed to lift earth, (work) [for] the urua wall," 46:'22-'26

1 ĝuruš šidim 1 ĝuruš šu dím gub-ba 5 géme im ga_6-ĝá-dè gub-ba 2 ĝuruš **im ì-li-de_9** gub-ba ù-ru-a bàd ke_4-dè, "1 builder (and) 1 workman employed to build, 5 workwomen employed to carry earth (and) 2 workmen employed to lift earth, (workers) to make the urua wall," 47:27–31

2.9 For Repair

2 ĝuruš šidim 2 ĝuruš šu dím 6 géme im ga_6-[ĝá-dè] gub-[ba]1 ĝuruš **im ì-l[i-de_9** gub-ba] *ták-ši-ru-[um . . .]* ù [. . .], "2 builders (and) 2 workmen having built, 6 workwomen employed [to] carry earth, 1 workman [employed] to lift earth, repair (work for) [. . .] and [. . .]," 58:40–44

2.10 Construction Site Lost or Unspecified

2 ĝuruš šidim 6 ĝuruš šu dím-ma gub-ba 1 ĝuruš im a-ĝá-ri-⌜na⌝ lu-dè gub-ba 1 ĝuruš **im ì-li-de_9**, "2 builders (and) 6 workmen employed to build, 1 workman employed to mix earth at the *agarinnum* (and) 1 workman having lifted earth," 41:'23-'26

1 ĝuruš **im ì-li-de_9** al-tar gub-ba, "1 workman having lifted earth, (workers) employed for construction," 58:25–26

n ĝuruš **im ì-li-de_9** gub-ba, "n workmen employed to lift earth," 72:18, 95:17

3. **im a-ĝá-ri-na íl**, "to lift earth into the *agarinnum*"

3.1 Construction of the Textile Mill

*See *Household Index* for the complete context of the following passages.

6 ĝuruš **im a-ĝá-ri-na ì-li-de_9** gub-ba (. . .) é-uš-[bar . . .], "6 workmen employed to lift earth into the *agarinnum* (. . .), [(work for)] the textile mill," 33:25, 30

1 [ĝuruš] **im a-ĝá-ri-na ì-li-de_9** gub-ba (. . .) 40 géme $šeg_{12}$ da-ki-sá-a é-uš-bar ĝá-ĝá-dè gub-[ba], "1 [workman] employed to lift earth into the *agarinnum* (. . .), (and) 40 workwomen employed to place bricks at the side of the foundation terrace of the textile mill," 35:25, 28

3.2 Construction of the (Enclosure) Wall

9 ĝuruš šidim 14 ĝuruš 18 géme $šeg_{12}$ šu dím-ma sum-mu-dè gub-ba 2 ĝuruš 2 géme **im a-ĝá-ri-na ì-li-de_9** gub-ba 20 géme im ga_6-ĝá-dè gub-ba 3 ĝuruš 3 géme im lu-dè gub-ba 1 ĝuruš in-u ga_6-ĝá im lu-a 7 géme $šeg_{12}$ ⌜da⌝ b[àd ĝá-ĝá-dè gub-ba], "9 builders, 14 workmen (and) 18 workwomen employed to hand (up) bricks for building, 2 workmen (and) 2 workwomen employed to lift earth into the *agarinnum*, 20 workwomen employed to carry earth, 3 workmen (and) 3 workwomen employed to mix earth, 1 workman having carried straw (and) having mixed (it with) earth (and) 7 workwomen [employed to place] bricks at the side of the (enclosure) wall," 16:17–23

3.3 Construction Site Unspecified

2 g̃uruš 2 géme **im a-g̃á-ri-na ì-li-de$_9$** gub-ba, "2 workmen (and) 2 workwomen employed to lift earth into the *agarinnum*," 16:19, 17:20

n g̃uruš **im a-g̃á-ri-na ì-li-de$_9$** gub-ba, "n workmen employed to lift earth into the *agarinnum*," 20:23, 21:23, 26:'11, 31:24, 32:24

4. im sumur íl, "to lift plaster"

4.1 Construction of the iz-zi Wall

1 g̃uruš šidim um-mi-a 4 g̃uruš ⸢šidim⸣ 4 g̃uruš šu dím-[ma] 3 g̃uruš **im sumur ì-⸢li-de$_9$⸣** gub-ba 10 g̃u[ruš n géme?] im ga$_6$-g̃á-dè gu[b-ba] iz-⸢zi⸣ im sumur ke$_4$-dè, "1 master builder, 4 builders (and) 4 workmen having built, 3 workmen employed to lift plaster (and) 10 workmen [(and) n workwomen?] employed to carry earth, (workers) to plaster the iz-zi wall," 52:20–26

5. in-u íl, "to lift straw"

[n guru]š **in-u ì-l[i-de$_9$** gub-ba], "[n] workmen [employed to] lift straw," 195:'24

6. siki íl, "to bring wool"

★★1⅔ g̃uruš ašgab u$_4$-6-šè **siki** é-^{d}*šu*-^{d}*suen*^{ki}-ka-ta **mu-un-li-sa-a**, "1⅔ leather workers for 6 days who brought wool from *Bit-Šu-Suen*," 228:1–4

– K –

káb . . . du$_{11}$(g$_4$), "to check; to measure or count commodities for accounting or taxation"

1. To Check

[n] g̃uruš ^{lú}ázlag á-½ ⸢u$_4$⸣-8-šè (. . .) še apin-lá-a **⸢káb⸣ dì-de$_4$** ì-im-g̃en-na-a, "[n] fuller(s) at ½ wages for 8 days, {authorizing official}, went to check on the grain of the leased fields," 271:1–2, 5–7

2. To Measure For Taxation

2.1 Assorted Grains

2 sìla níg̃-àr-ra-sig$_5$ 4 sìla eša 4 sìla ba-ba-munu$_4$ šà-bi-ta 0.0.1.2½ sìla kaš-g̃e$_6$ 2-ta 0.0.1.5 s[ìla x] tuḫ-duru$_5$-sig$_5$-g̃e$_6$ **káb du$_{11}$-ga**, "2 liters of fine groats, 4 liters of fine flour, (and) 4 liters of malt porridge. From among it: 12½ liters of dark beer, 2 liters each (and) 15 liters of dark fine fresh bran, commodities measured for accounting," 1046:1–7

2.2 Commodities of the Garden

n.n.n.n sìla zú-lum gur n.n.n. u$_4$-ḫi-in gur n gín ${}^{g̃eš}$zé-na n peš-múrgu n gín peš-ga n á-an-zú-lum **káb du$_{11}$-ga** ${}^{g̃eš}$kiri$_6$, "n bushel(s) (and) n liter(s) of dates, n bushel(s) and n liter(s) of fresh dates, n shekel(s) of date palm frond midribs, n date palm spine(s), n shekel(s) of date palm hearts (and) n date cluster(s), commodities of the garden measured for accounting," 1215:1–7, 1237:1–7

2.2.1 Of *Eštar-ummi*'s Garden

4.3.0. zú-lum gur 0.0.5. u$_4$-ḫi-in [n+]3 gín peš-ga 5? sìla á-an-zú-lum **[káb d]u$_{11}$-ga** ${}^{g̃eš}$kiri$_6$ *eš$_4$-tár-<um->mi* dumu-munus *šu-kab-tá*, "4 bushels (and) 180 liters of dates, 50 liters of fresh dates, [n+]3 shekels of date palm hearts (and) 5? liters of date clusters, commodities of the garden of *Eštar-ummi*, the daughter of *Šu-Kabta*, measured for accounting," 1102:1–6

2.2.2 Instructions Regarding the Garden Commodities

^{d}*adad-tillati* ù-na-a-du$_{11}$ **káb du$_{11}$-ga** g̃ìri *é-a-šar* ^{geš}zé-na ù peš-[múrgu] nu-$^{g̃eš}$kiri$_6$-ke$_4$-ne na-ba-ab-sum-mu-⸢dè⸣ šà dub-za ḫa-ba-tur-re, "Say to *Adad-tillati* that 'the gardeners should not give date palm frond midribs and date palm spines, commodities (that were) measured for accounting under the authority of *Ea-šar*. Let it be subtracted in your tablet,'" 1037:1–9

kala(g), *dannu*, *kubbû*, "(to be) strong, powerful, mighty; to reinforce, repair"

1. A Mattress

12 gín siki-g̃ír-gul šà-tuku$_5$ **kala-kala-gé-dè**, "12 shekels of shaved wool in order to reinforce a mattress," 783:1–2

2. Textiles

1 ^{túg}níg̃-lám-gen 1 túg-guz-za *šu-⸢kab⸣-ta* 1 ^{túg}bar-dul$_5$-⸢ús⸣ *šu-kab-ta* 3 ^{túg}uš-bar ⸢siki⸣-g̃ír-⸢gul⸣ **kala-kala-gé-dè**, "{receipt of} 1 ordinary níg̃-lam textile, 1 tufted textile of *Šu-Kabta*, 1 2nd-quality bar-dul$_5$ textile of *Šu-Kabta*, (and) 3 uš-bar textiles of g̃ír-gul wool, in order to repair (them)," 588:1–5

kéše, *rakāsu*, "to bind"

bar-da ^{geš}ig-g̃e$_6$ kéše, "to bind the crossbar of a door"

éš g̃eš ùr kéše, "to bind ropes to roof beams"

g̃eš kéše, "to bind wooden planks"

g̃eš ùr kéše, "to bind roof beams"

ká kéše, "to bind a gate"

1. bar-da $^{g̃eš}$ig kéše, "to bind the crossbar of a door"

4 kuš-gu$_4$ kuš a-g̃ar nu-gu$_7$-a **bar-da ^{geš}ig-g̃e$_6$** 1-àm **ba-a-kéše** 3 g̃uruš ašgab u$_4$-2-⸢šè⸣ **bar-da ^{geš}ig-⸢g̃e$_6$⸣ kéše-⸢rá⸣**, "4 ox-hides, skins whose hair has not been removed, were (used) to bind the cross bar of 1 black door and 3 leather workers for two days having bound the crossbar of the black door," 247:1–5

2. éš g̃eš ùr kéše, "to bind ropes to roof beams"

2 g̃uruš šidim 4 g̃uruš šu dím-[ma] 4 géme im ga$_6$-[g̃á]-dè gu[b-ba] 1 g̃uruš im ì-[li]-de$_9$ gu[b-ba] **éš g̃eš ùr kéše-[rá]**, "2 builders (and) 4 workmen having built, 4 workwomen employed to carry earth (and) 1 workman employed to lift earth, (workers) having bound ropes to roof beams," 57:'12-'16

3. g̃eš kéše, "to bind wooden planks"

84 $^{g̃eš}$é-da ⸢asal$_x$⸣ 38 $^{g̃eš}$é-da ⸢šinig⸣ {indent} 430 **⸢g̃eš⸣ kéše-⸢rá⸣**, "84 poplar joists (and) 38 tamarisk joists; (in total:) 430 bound planks," 1379:'1-'4

4. g̃eš ùr kéše, "to bind roof beams"

4.1 Construction of the Brewery

1 g̃uruš šidim 2 g̃uruš 10 géme é-lù[nga **g̃eš]** **ùr kéše-rá**, "1 builder, 2 workmen (and) 10 workwomen having bound roof beams, (work for) the brewery," 205:'22-'23

4.2 Construction of the Brewery-Kitchen-Mill Complex

*See *Household Index* for the complete context of the following passages.

n g̃uruš **g̃eš ùr kéše-rá** (. . .) al-tar é-lùnga é-muḫaldim ù é-kíkken, "n workmen having bound roof beams (. . .), (for) construction of the brewery-kitchen-mill complex," 138:30–31, 145:33, 36

[n g̃uruš] 15 [géme **g̃eš ùr]** **kéše-⌜rá⌝** (. . .) [al-tar é-lù]nga é-muḫaldim [ù é-kíkken], "[n workmen] (and) 15 [workwomen] having bound [roof beams] (. . .), [(for) construction of] the brewery-kitchen-mill complex," 143:31–32, 34

4.2.1 Carrying Earth in order to Bind Roof Beams

[n] géme im ga_6-g̃á **g̃eš ùr kéše-rá** (. . .) al-tar é-lùnga é-muḫaldim ù é-kíkken, "[n] workwomen having carried earth—(workers) having bound roof beams—(. . .), (for) construction of the brewery-kitchen-mill complex," 136:27–28, 34

2 g̃uruš šidim 20 g̃uruš 16 géme im ga_6-g̃á **g̃eš ùr kéše-rá** (. . .) al-tar é-lùnga é-muḫaldim ù é-kíkken, "2 builders, 20 workmen (and) 16 workwomen having carried earth—(workers) having bound roof beams—(. . .), (for) construction of the brewery-kitchen-mill complex," 141:29–31, 33, 142:25–27, 29

4.2.2 Tightening Bound Roof Beams

13 [g̃uruš **g̃eš]** **ùr kéše** gíd-da (. . .) [. . . é-lùnga é-muḫaldim] ù é-kíkken, "13 [workmen] having tightened bound roof [beams] (. . .), [. . . (work for) the brewery-kitchen]-mill complex," 144:'19, '21

4.2.3 For the Grain Heap when the Roof Beams were Bound

1 dug $dida_x$-gen 1 sìla dabin ½ sìla eša zì-dub-dub-šè u_4 **g̃eš ùr ba-kéše-rá** é-lùnga é-muḫaldim ù é-kíkken, "1 jug of ordinary dida beer, 1 liter of semolina (and) ½ liter of fine flour for the small flour heap when the roof beams of the brewery-kitchen-mill complex were bound," 1251:9–14

4.3 Construction of Replacement Houses: Woods for Roof Beams

27 g̃eš ùr ásal 57 $^{g̃eš}$é-da-ásal 13 g̃eš ùr šinig 31 $^{g̃eš}$é-da-šinig **g̃eš ùr kéše-rá** (. . .) é-ki-ba-g̃ar-ra é-*u-bar-ri-a*-šè ba-a-g̃ar, "27 poplar roof beams, 57 poplar joists, 13 tamarisk roof beams (and) 31 tamarisk joists, roof beams having been bound, (and) {other reed and wood products} were placed for the replacement house of the house of *Ubarria*," 1286:1–5, 12, 1289:1–5, 12

4.4 Construction of the Warehouse

2 g̃uruš [šidim] 6 g̃uruš šu dím gub-ba 10 géme im ga_6-g̃á gub-ba é-⌜kišib⌝-ba g̃á-nun-na sumun **g̃eš ùr kéše-rá**, "2 [builders], 6 workmen employed to build (and) 10 workwomen employed to carry earth, (workers) having bound roof beams (for) the warehouse of the old storehouse," 49:35–38

2 [. . .] é-kišib-ba [. . . **g̃eš]** **ùr kéše-⌜rá⌝**, "2 [(workers) . . .], (workers) having bound roof [beams] (for) the warehouse," 49:51–52

4.5 Construction, Site Unspecified

*See **al-tar** for the complete context of the following passages.

11 géme im ga$_6$-g̃á **g̃eš ùr kéše-rá** (. . .) al-tar gub-ba, "11 workwomen having carried earth—(workers) having bound roof beams—(. . .), (workers) employed for construction," 140:30–31, 36

2 g̃uruš šidim 10 g̃uruš 10 ⸢géme⸣ **g̃eš ùr kéše-rá** (. . .) al-[tar] gub-ba, "2 builders, 10 workmen (and) 10 workwomen having bound roof beams (. . .), (workers) employed for construction," 144:'11-'12, '15

4.5.1 Tightening Bound Roof Beams

1 g̃uruš šidim um-mi-a 2 g̃uruš šidim 22 g̃uruš 6 géme **g̃eš ùr kéše** gíd-da gub-ba, "1 master builder, 2 builders, 22 workmen (and) 6 workwomen employed to tighten bound roof beams," 76:10–14

4.5.2 Ropes for Binding Roof Beams

50 ^{gi}dur-dag̃al a-rá-3-[tab-ba] gíd 5 nindan-ta 590 ^{gi}dur-gazi a-rá-2-tab-ba gíd 1½ nindan-ta **g̃eš ùr kéše-dè**, "50 30-meter 3-ply wide ropes (and) 590 9-meter 2-ply gazi ropes to bind roof beams," 1008:1–3

4.5.3 Ropes for Tightening Bound Roof Beams

8 ^{gi}dur-gazi a-rá 2-tab-ba gíd 1½ nindan-ta **g̃eš ùr kéše** gíd-da (. . .) ká-suḫur é-lùnga-šè ba-a-g̃ar, "8 9-meter 2-ply gazi ropes having tightened bound roof beams (and) {other planks} were placed for the tree-top gate of the brewery," 1297:1–2, 5

4.5.4 Wood and Ropes for Binding Roof Beams

84 $^{g̃eš}$é-da ⸢asal$_x$⸣ 38 $^{g̃eš}$é-da ⸢šinig⸣ {indent} 430 ⸢g̃eš⸣ kéše-⸢rá⸣ 55 ^{gi}dur-dag̃al a-rá-3-tab-ba gíd 5-nindan-ta 1530 ^{gi}dur-gazi a-rá-2-tab-ba gíd 1½ nindan-ta **g̃eš ùr kéše-da**(sic!), "84 poplar joists (and) 38 tamarisk joists; (in total:) 430 bound planks; (and) 55 30-meter 3-ply wide ropes, (and) 1530 9-meter 2-ply gazi ropes in order to bind roof beams," 1379:'1-'7

4.6 Construction Site Lost

1 g̃uruš im [. . .] **g̃eš ùr ké[še-rá]**, "1 workman [. . .] earth, (workers) having bound roof beams," 54:15–16

[. . .] **g̃eš ùr kéše-⸢rá⸣**, "[. . .] having bound roof beams," 57:'11

5. ká kéše, "to bind a gate"

5.1 The Gate of the Brewery-Kitchen-Mill Complex

5.1.1 Offerings when the Gate was Bound

1 dug dida$_x$-gen 0.0.3?-[ta] 1 sìla dabin [1 sìl]a eša ⸢sízkur⸣-šè u$_4$ **ká** é-lùnga é-muḫaldim ù é kíkken **kéše-⸢rá⸣**, "1 jug of ordinary dida beer, 30? liters [each], 1 liter of semolina, (and) [1] liter of fine flour for (ceremonial) offerings when the gate of the brewery-kitchen-mill complex was bound," 1007:1–5

5.1.2 Binding the Wood of the Gate

[n] g̃eš ùr šinig 31 $^{g̃eš}$é-da-ásal 56 g̃eš-ká 260 ^{gi}dur-gazi a-rá-3-tab-ba gíd 1½ nindan-⸢ta⸣ g̃eš **ká kéše-dè** é-lùnga é-muḫaldim ù é-kíkken, "[n] tamarisk roof beam(s), 31 poplar joists, 56 gate timbers (and) 260 9 meter 3-ply gazi ropes in order to bind the gate timbers of the brewery-kitchen-mill complex," 1293:1–6

5.2 Binding Gate Timbers

1 g̃uruš [šidim] 1 g̃uruš 2 géme g̃eš **ká kéše-[rá** . . .], "1 [builder], 1 workman, (and) 2 workwomen having bound gate timbers [. . .]," 52:36–39

6. Other

6.1 (Barley) Bound in Leather Sacks

n g̃uruš u_4-n-šè ^{kuš}a-g̃á-lá **kéše-rá**, "n workmen for n day(s) having bound (barley) in leather sacks," 553:1–2, 553:21–22

6.2 Bread in Bound Leather Sacks

0.0.2.6 sìla ninda ^{kuš}a-g̃á-lá **kéše-rá** g̃uruš nam-60 *a*-⌜*bu*⌝-DU$_{10}$ u_4 é-^{d}*šu*-^{d}*suen*^{ki}-šè i-⌜re⌝-ša-a u_4 é-e im sumur ba-aka, "36 liters of bread in bound leather sacks (for) *Abu-ṭabu*, the overseer of 60 workmen, when (his workers) went to *Bit-Šu-Suen* when the house was plastered," 480:1–3

[0.n.n sìla] ninda-šu-ra-gen ^{kuš}a-g̃á-lá **kéše-rá** g̃uruš 7-kam u_4 kaskal-šè i-re-sa-a, "[n liter(s)] of ordinary half (loaf) bread in bound leather sacks (for) 7 workmen when they went on a journey," 529:1–3

6.3 Jugs

1 dug 0.0.3. **kéše-rá**, "1 bound 30 liter jug," 595:6

16 ^{dug}laḫtan **kéše-rá**, "16 bound beer vats," 1334:5

6.4 Supplies for Binding a Chair

1 kuš e-rí-na ka-la 10 gín kuš-gu_4 5 gín sa-udu 5 gín še-gín ${}^{g̃eš}$gu-za **kéše-da**-šè, "1 root-tanned ka-la skin, 10 shekels of ox-hide, 5 shekels of sheep sinew (and) 5 shekels of glue for binding a chair," 855:17–20

[10?+]5 gín k[uš-g]u_4 ú-ḫáb ${}^{g̃eš}$gu-za **kéš[e-da**-š]è ⌜*šu*⌝?-*kab*?-⌜*ta*⌝?, "[10?+]5 shekels of madder-tanned ox-hides for binding a chair of *Šu-Kabta*," 923:7–8

6.5 Wool

★★(. . .) ⌜siki⌝-bala-dè **in-na-[kéše** t]úg-gen-kam ì-in-⌜DU⌝? 1 ^{túg}sag̃-uš-bar sa-gi_4-[àm], "{assorted textiles}, the wool was bound up to be baled, he delivered the ordinary textiles, they are finished uš-bar textiles," 609:7–9 (envelope)

★★(. . .) siki bala-[dè **i]n-na-k[éšè]** ^{túg}uš-ba[r sa-gi_4-àm], "{assorted textiles}, the wool was bound up to be baled, [they are finished] uš-bar textiles," 609:8 (tablet)

★★(. . .) kìšib íb-ra é-kìšib-ba-ta dub-bi in-du_8 siki bala-dè **in-kéše** é-gal-šè mu-DU, "{assorted textiles}, he rolled the seal, baked its tablet in the warehouse, (and) bound up the wool to be baled (for) delivery for the palace," 609:11–14

20 ma-na siki túg-guz-za-gen mu siki-gu **kéše**-šè, "20 minas of wool (for manufacturing) ordinary tufted textiles (to be used) for wool cord bindings," 665:1–2

kíg̃, *še'û*, "to look for, seek"

★★[. . .]-da-tur x x x **nu-ub-kíg̃**, 374:'14

ku_4(r), *erēbu*, "to enter"

ká im šeg$_{12}$ **ku_4-ra**, "the 'service entrance' of the gate" > **ká**

1. **Assorted (Damaged?) Commodities for the House**

★★ (. . .) [. . .]-gaz-a-ḫi? [x]-gaz-gaz [. . .]-zi-ra é-tab-tab-ba [?] x-šè **ba-an-ku$_4$**, "{baskets and other reed products, ropes, palm products, leather products, pots, and other containers}; [. . .] broken(? vessels?) entered the double house for (?)," 1376:87–90

2. **Bread for the Warehouse**

2.4.3.6 sìla ninda gur [é]-kišib-ba-šè **ba-an-ku$_4$**, "2 bushels (and) 276 liters of bread entered the warehouse," 1031:17–18

3. **Earth that did not Enter the Garden**

[*ak-b*]*a-zum* nu-^{ğeš}kiri$_6$-⌜ke$_4$⌝ má-lugal-na saḫar tùm-dè zabala$_4$^{ki}-šè in-la-aḫ saḫar mu-un-de$_9$ ^{ğeš}kiri$_6$-lugal-na-šè **nu-un-ni-ku$_4$** é-ni-šè ba-an-dé ka-ga-na ba-ge-en, "*Akbazum*, the gardener, confirmed that they took a boat of his master to Zabala in order to bring dirt, that he brought the dirt, that it did not enter the garden of his master but was brought for his (own) house," 1049:1–10

^{d}ba-ú-da [nu]-^{ğeš}kiri$_6$-ke$_4$ má-lugal-na saḫar tùm-dè zabala$_4$^{ki}-šè in-la-aḫ saḫar mu-un-de$_9$ ^{ğeš}kiri$_6$-lugal-na **nu-un-ni-ku$_4$** é-ni-šè ba-an-dé ka-ga-na ba-ge-en, "Ba'uda, the gardener, confirmed that they took a boat of his master to Zabala in order to bring dirt, that he brought the dirt, that it did not enter the garden of his master but was brought for his (own) house," 1050:1–10

ku$_5$(d^r), *parāsu*, "to cut, break off, deduct"

^{ğeš}kišig ku$_5$, "to cut shok"

pa ku$_5$, "to cut branches, prune"

sá-du$_{11}$ ku$_5$, "to deduct offerings"

1. **$^{ğeš/ú}$kišig ku$_5$**, "to cut shok"

n ğuruš **^{ğeš}kišig ku$_5$-ru-dè** gub-ba, "n workmen employed to cut shok," 93:'27, 94:31, 95:26, 99:29, 100:'30, 101:32, 102:30

12 ğuruš **^{ğeš}kišig ku$_5$-ru-dè**, "12 workmen to cut shok," 103:35

n ğuruš **$^{ğeš/ú}$kišig ku$_5$-rá**, "n workmen having cut shok," 106:41, 108:36, 109:33, 115:'24, 118:26, 123:41, 125:36, 126:31

10 gu-níğin ^{ğeš}kišig á-ğuruš-a 4 gu-níğin-ta á-bi 2½ u$_4$-1-šè a-šà karkar^{ki}-šè **^{ğeš}kišig ku$_5$-rá**, "(In total:) 10 bales of shok. The workmen wages were for 4 bales each. Their wages were for 2½ days (for workers) having cut shok at the field of Karkar," 235:1–4

2. **pa ku$_5$**, "to cut branches, prune"

2 **pa** ^{ğeš}kíğ ^{ğeš}kiri$_6$-*simat-*^{d}*ištaran* gar-ša-an-na^{ki} *šu-eš$_4$-tár* ^{lú}kíğ-gi$_4$-[a-lugal] **in-ku$_5$**, "*Šu-Eštar*, the [royal] messenger, pruned 2 kíğ trees in the garden of *Simat-Ištaran* at Garšana," 1354:1–6

3. **sá-du$_{11}$ ku$_5$**, "to deduct offerings"

1 udu-niga é-u$_4$-7 iti u$_4$-[7]-ba-zal 1 ⌜udu⌝-niga é-[u$_4$]-10 iti u$_4$-10-⌜ba⌝-zal **sá-du$_{11}$-ku$_5$-rá** ^{d}nin-^{d}si$_4$-an-na, "1 fattened sheep at the end of the [7th] day of the month, i.e. the half-moon day, 1 fattened sheep at the end of the 10th day of the month, i.e. the 3/4? moon day, deducted regular offerings of Nin-Siana," 985:1–6

(. . .) [iti]-6-kam 23⅓ ma-na báppir-sig$_5$ še-bi 0.0.3.5 sìla **sá-du$_{11}$ ku$_5$-rá** iti-6-kam, "{regular offerings of deities} of the 6th month, 23⅓ minas of fine beer bread, their barley (equivalent) is 35 liters, deducted regular offerings of the 6th month," 1527:6–8

– L –

lá, "to transport"

1. Transport of Bitumen

2 g̃uruš ésir-ḫád **lá-e-dè**, "2 workmen having transported dry bitumen," 129:38, 130:'18

2. Transport of Dirt

saḫar zi-ga **in-lá** tùn-lá ^{geš}kiri$_6$ zabala$_4^{ki}$ kurum$_7$ [aka], "Inspection (of the work of workers). They transported dirt removed via a tùn-lá device at the Zabala garden," 178:6–8

3. Transport of Grain

iti u$_5$-bí-[gu$_7$] ù iti ki-siki-^{d}n[in-a-zu x?] še-zíz ḫi-a 720 g[ur (. . .)] *dì-im-bu-na*-á[š-gi$_5$-ta] é-duru$_5$-kab-bí-šè **lá-[a]**, "(in) month 4 and month 5 720 bushels of various barley (and) emmer wheat having been transported [from] *Dimbun*-Ašgi to the Kabbi village," 1029:'1-'5

4. Transport of Shok from Irikigida

17 g̃uruš ^{geš}kišig iri-ki-gíd-da-šè **lá-e-dè** g̃en-na, "17 workmen having gone to Irikigida in order to transport shok," 133:36, 134:17, 135:36

5. Transporting Straw

6 g̃uruš [GN-ta] gar-ša-a[n-na]^{ki}-[šè] in-u **l[á-a]**, "6 workmen having transported straw [from GN to] Garšana," 194:46–48

2 g̃uruš gar-ša-an-na^{ki}-ta ka i$_7$-è-šè in-u **lá-a**, "2 workmen having transported straw from Garšana to the opening of the 'Outgoing' canal," 194:52–55

[n g̃uruš . . .]-bi? bala um-[. . .] gar-š[a-an-na]^{ki}-šè in-u **lá-[a]**, "[n workmen . . .] having transported straw [from GN?] to Garšana," 198:'22-'23

2 g̃uruš ad-kub$_4$ u$_4$-1-šè in-u a-gàr-didli-ta gar-ša-an-na^{ki}-šè **lá-a**, "2 reed craftsmen for 1 day having transported straw from various meadows to Garšana," 285:1–3, 286:1–3

10 g̃uruš túg-du$_8$ u$_4$-1-šè in-u a-gàr-didli-ta gar-ša-an-na^{ki}-šè **lá-a**, "10 braiders for 1 day having transported straw from various meadows to Garšana," 306:3–5

2.2.0. še gur á má ḫug̃-g̃á má-90-gur-kam á 0.0.4-ta ù má-laḫ$_5$-bi u$_4$-18-šè in-u é-ù-ri-a<ki>-ta gú i$_7$-da **lá-a**, "2 bushels (and) 120 liters of barley, wages of the hired 90-bushel boat and its sailors, wages of 40 liters each for 18 days (for sailors) having transported straw from E-uri'a to the bank of the canal," 413:1–7

6. Context Uncertain

★★4 g̃uruš ⸢šidim⸣ 5 g̃uruš ⸢dub⸣?-lá? šà é-[a] **lá-[a]** x, 194:39–41

lá, *šaqālu*, "to weigh out, to pay"

1. Commodities Weighed by *Ḫali*, the Braider

1.1 Goat Hair

1 šà-tuku$_5$-siki-ud$_5$ ki-lá-bi 5 ma-na 10 gín *ḫa-lí* túg-du$_8$ **ì-lá**, "*Ḫali*, the braider, weighed out 1 goat hair mattress, its weight is 5 minas (and) 10 shekels," 706:1–3

6 barag-siki-ud$_5$ ki-lá-bi 18 ma-na 1$\frac{5}{6}$ma-na éš-siki-ud$_5$ *ḫa-lí* **in-lá**, "*Ḫali* weighed out 6 sacks of goat hair—their weight is 18 minas—(and) 1$\frac{5}{6}$ minas of goat hair ropes," 717:1–4

5 éš-siki-ud$_5$ ki-lá-bi 15⅔ ma-na 1 bar-si siki-ud$_5$ šà-tuku$_5$ é-ba-an ki-lá-bi 2 ma-na 1 [. . .] ki-lá-b[i . . .] 10 [. . .] ki-lá-bi [. . .] *ḫa-lí* **ì-[lá]**, "*Ḫali* [weighed out] 5 goat hair ropes, —their weight is 15⅔ minas—1 pair of goat-hair bands (for) a mattress—their weight is 2 minas—1 [. . .]—their weight is [. . .]—(and) 10 [. . .]—their weight is [. . .]," 740:1–9

1.2 Combed Wool

1.2.1 For Assorted Commodities

[1] túg-íb-[lá]-kaskal ⌜siki⌝-bi ⅓ ma-⌜na⌝ 1 gín [1] ^{túg}sagšu siki ^{ĝeš}garig aka 4-kam-ús ⌜siki⌝-bi ⅓ ma-na [x-*t*]*um*?? ANŠE+BAR+MUL [^{ĝeš}ga]rig aka gen [siki-bi] ⅔ ma-[na] 4 gín [*ḫa-l*]*í* túg-du$_8$ **ì-lá**, "*Ḫali*, the braider, weighed out ⅓ mina (and) 1 shekel wool (for) [1] traveling belt, 4th-quality combed wool (weighing) ⅓ mina (for) [1] cap (and) ⅔ mina (and) 4 shekels of ordinary combed wool for (?)," 702:1–8

1 $^{\text{<kuš>}}$súhub-túg-du$_8$-a-⌜babbar⌝? siki ^{ĝeš}garig aka 3-kam-ús ki-lá-bi ½ ma-na 2 gín 2 túg-sagšu-ĝe$_6$ siki ^{ĝeš}garig aka 4-kam-ús ki-lá-bi 13 gín 1 ^{túg}íb-lá siki-a-[gíd] siki ^{ĝeš}garig aka ĝen ki-lá-bi 16 gín *ḫa-lí* túg-du$_8$ **ì-lá**, "*Ḫali*, the braider, weighed out 3rd quality combed wool—its weight is ½ mina (and) 2 shekels—(for) 1 (pair) of white? meshwork shoes, 4th-quality combed wool—its weight is 13 shekels—(for) 2 black caps (and) ordinary combed wool—its weight is 16 shekels—(for) 1 belt of a-gíd wool," 756:1–11

1.2.2 For Caps

2 ^{túg}sagšu siki ^{ĝeš}garig aka 4-kam-ús ki-lá-bi 13 gín *ḫa-l*[*í* túg-d]u$_8$ **ì-[lá]**, "*Ḫali*, the braider, [weighed out] 4th-quality combed wool—its weight is 13 shekels—(for) 2 caps," 741:1–5

4 ^{túg}sagšu siki ^{ĝeš}garig a[ka . . .] ⅔ [. . .níĝ]-U.NU-a [. . . túg-*ḫa*]-*bu-um*-šè [. . . *ḫa-lí* túg-d]u$_8$ **[ì]-lá**, "[*Ḫali*], the braider, weighed out combed wool (for) 4 caps, ⅔ [. . .] (for) thread, [. . .] for *ḫa-bu-um* [textiles, (and) . . .]," 755:1–11

1.2.3 Broken Context

[. . .] 1 túg-du$_8$-a ⌜siki⌝ ^{ĝeš}NÍĜIN-garig aka 4-kam-ús ki-lá-bi ½ ma-na *ḫa-lí* **ì-lá**, "*Ḫali* weighed out [. . .] (and) 1 meshwork of 4th-quality combed wool weighing ½ mina," 767:1–5

1.3 gír-gul Wool

5 ^{túg}sagšu-babbar siki-⌜ĝír⌝-gul ki-lá-bi ⅔ ma-na *ḫa-lí* túg-du$_8$ **ì-lá** "*Ḫali*, the braider, weighed out gír-gul wool—its weight is ⅔ mina—(for) 5 white caps," 679:1–3

1.4 **Wool Meshworks**

5 túg-du$_8$-a siki-g̃ír-gul $^{g̃eš}$gu-za-munus šà!-kal ki-lá-bi 3⅔ ma-na *ḫa-lí* túg-du$_8$ **[ì]-lá**, "*Ḫali*, the braider, weighed out 5 meshworks of gír-gul wool—their weight is 3⅔ minas—(for) a wooden woman's chair," 761:1–4

1 túg-du$_8$-a siki-g̃ír-gul ki-lá-bi ⅓ ma-na 3 gín *ḫa-lí* **ì-lá**, "*Ḫali* weighed out 1 meshwork of gír-gul wool—its weight is ⅓ mina (and) 3 shekels," 776:1–4

2. **Commodities Weighed by *Ili-uṣranni***

★★[n] éš-maḫ [*ḫa*]-*bu-u*[*m* k]i-lá-bi ½ ⸢gú⸣ 15⅓ ma-⸢na⸣ **ì-lá**-1-a-ni ki *ì-lí*-[*uṣ-ra-ni*-t]a [PN šu ba(-an)-ti], "[PN received n] large *habum*-fabric ropes—their weight is ½ talent (and) 15⅓ minas—from *Ili*-[*uṣranni*], which he had weighed out," 831:1–6

laḫ$_4$/laḫ$_5$, *babālu*, plural stem of de$_6$ "to bring"

1. **Builders, Brought from G̃irsu**

2 g̃uruš šidim šidim **la-ḫa-dè** g̃ír-su^{ki}-šè g̃en-na, "2 builders having gone to G̃irsu to bring builders," 40:50–51, 41:'31-'32

2. **Earth, Brought to Zabala for the Houses of the Gardeners**

[*ak-b*]*a-zum* nu-$^{g̃eš}$kiri$_6$-⸢ke$_4$⸣ má-lugal-na saḫar tùm-dè zabala$_4^{ki}$-šè **in-la-aḫ** saḫar mu-un-de$_9$ $^{g̃eš}$kiri$_6$-lugal-na-šè nu-un-ni-ku$_4$ é-ni-šè ba-an-dé ka-ga-na ba-ge-en, "*Akbazum*, the gardener, confirmed that they took a boat of his master to Zabala in order to bring dirt, that he brought the dirt, that it did not enter the garden of his master but was brought for his (own) house," 1049:1–10

^{d}ba-ú-da [nu]-$^{g̃eš}$kiri$_6$-ke$_4$ má-lugal-na saḫar tùm-dè zabala$_4^{ki}$-šè **in-la-aḫ** saḫar mu-un-de$_9$ $^{g̃eš}$kiri$_6$-lugal-na nu-un-ni-ku$_4$ é-ni-šè ba-an-dé ka-ga-na ba-ge-en, "Ba'uda, the gardener, confirmed that they took a boat of his master to Zabala in order to bring dirt, that he brought the dirt, that it did not enter the garden of his master but was brought for his (own) house," 1050:1–10

3. **A Sheep, Brought from Iri-sag̃rig**

1 g̃uruš ad-kub$_4$ udu **la-ḫe-dè** iri-sag̃-⸢rig$_7$⸣^{ki}-šè ⸢g̃en-na⸣, "1 reed craftsman having gone to Iri-sag̃rig in order to bring a sheep," 260:1–2

lu, *balālu*; *dalāḫu*; *katāmu*, "to disturb, stir up; to cover completely; to mix"

im lu, "to mix earth"

im a-g̃á-ri-na lu, "to mix earth in the *agarinnum*"

im *dì-um* lu, "to mix adobe"

im sumur lu, "to mix plaster"

1. **im lu**, "to mix earth"

★See *Household Index* for the complete context of the following passages.

1.1 **Construction of the Brewery and Mill**

1 g̃uruš šidim um-mi-a 2 g̃uruš šidim 7 g̃uruš 40 géme ki-sá-a **im lu-a** é-lùnga ù é-kíkken, "1 master builder, 2 builders, 7 workmen (and) 40 workwomen having mixed earth at the foundation terrace of the brewery and mill," 109:21–23

1.2 Construction of the Mill

[n g̃uruš] **im lu-a** gub-⸢ba⸣ [. . . é]-[ḪAR].ḪAR-šè [. . .] gub-[ba], "[n workmen] employed to mix earth [. . .], (workers) employed for the mill," 99:21–22

1.3 Construction of the Foundation Terrace

10 g̃uruš **im lu-a** 2 g̃uruš 2 géme *a-za-bu-um* a im še-g̃á ba-al-dè 1 g̃uruš a bal-a ki-sá-a-šè, "10 workmen having mixed earth, 2 workmen (and) 2 workwomen to bail out rain-water from a cistern (and) 1 workman having poured water, (work) for the foundation terrace," 104:36–38, 105:34–36

1.4 Construction of the Warehouse

1 g̃uruš **im lu-dè** gub-ba é-kišib-ba ugula kíkken, "1 workman employed to mix earth (for) the warehouse (under the authority of?) the overseer of the mill," 32:24–25

1.5 Construction of the Textile Mill

6 g̃uruš **im lu-dè** gub-[ba] (. . .) [. . .] é-uš-[bar . . .], "6 workmen employed to mix earth (. . .), [(work for)] the textile mill," 33:27, 30

[1 g̃uruš] **im lu-dè** gub-ba [17] g̃uruš 40 géme šeg$_{12}$ da-ki-sá-a é-uš-bar g̃á-g̃á-dè gub-[ba], "[1 workman] employed to mix earth (and) [17] workmen (and) 40 workwomen employed to place bricks at the side of the foundation terrace of the textile mill," 35:27–28

1.6 Construction of Various Houses and Installations

1.6.1 The House of *Alua*

6 g̃uruš **im lu-a** (. . .) é-*a-lu-a* gub-ba, "6 workmen having mixed earth (. . .), (workers) employed at the house of *Alua*, 102:24, 26

1.6.2 The House of *Ili-bišu*

2 g̃uruš **im lu-a** (. . .) al-tar é-*ì-lí-bi-šu*, "2 workmen having mixed earth (. . .), (for) construction of the house of *Ili-bišu*," 203:27, 29

2 g̃uruš **im lu-a** (. . .) 1 g̃uruš in-u ga$_6$-g̃á **im lu-a** é-*ì-lí-bi-šu*, "2 workmen having mixed earth (. . .), (and) 1 workman having carried straw (and) having mixed (it with) earth, (work for) the house of *Ili-bišu*," 204:'6, '8-'9

1.6.3 The House of *Pišaḫ-ilum*

3 g̃uruš **im lu-a** g[ub-ba] é-*pí-ša-aḫ-ilum* gub-[ba], "3 workmen employed to mix earth, (workers) employed at the house of *Pišaḫ-ilum*," 84:16–17

[n+]5 g̃uruš **i[m lu]-a** (. . .) é-⸢*pi$_5$-ša-aḫ*⸣-*ilum*, "[n+]5 workmen having mixed earth (. . .), (work for) the house of *Pišaḫ-ilum*," 108:30, 33

1.6.4 The House of *Putanum*

13 g̃uruš **im lu-a** (. . .) é-*pu-ta-nu-um*, "13 workmen having mixed earth (. . .), (work for) the house of *Putanum*," 123:37, 38

1.6.5 The House of *Šukubum*

1 g̃uruš 4 géme **im lu-a** gub-ba [é]-*šu-ku-bu-um* gub-ba, "1 employed workman (and) 4 employed workwomen having mixed earth, (workers) employed at the the [house] of *Šukubum*," 84:21–22

1.6.6 The House of *Ubarria*

2 ĝuruš **im ⌜lu⌝-dè** gub-ba (. . .) é-*u*-⌜*bar*⌝-*ri*-*a* gub-[ba], "2 workmen employed to mix earth (. . .), (workers) employed at the house of *Ubarria*," 94:17, 20

26 ĝuruš **im lu-a** (. . .) é-*u*-*bar*-⌜*ri*⌝-*a* dù-a, "26 workmen having mixed earth (. . .), (workers) having constructed the house of *Ubarria*," 111:33, 36

1.6.7 The Piggery

[n] ĝuruš **im lu-a** (. . .) é-⌜šáḫ⌝ dù-a, "[n] workmen having mixed earth (. . .), (workers) having constructed the piggery," 125:27, 29

1.6.8 The Quay of the Textile Depository

6 ĝuruš **im lu-a** 10 ĝuruš kar-ki-mu-ra dù-a, "6 workmen having mixed earth (and) 10 workmen having constructed the quay of the textile depository," 163:31–32

1.6.9 The Replacement House of *Biza'a*

1 ĝuruš **im lu-a** gub-ba (. . .) [é-ki-b]a-ĝar-ra ⌜*bí*⌝-*za*-*a* gub-ba, "1 workman employed to mix earth (. . .), (workers) employed at the replacement house of *Biza'a*," 86:12, 14–15

1.7 Construction of the Tower of Zabala

*See *Garden Index* for the complete context of the following passages.

3 ĝuruš **im lu-a** (. . .) úgu iz-zi-da a ĝá-ĝá an-za-qar-^{ĝeš}kiri$_6$-zabala$_4^{ki}$, "3 workmen having mixed earth (. .), (workers) having waterproofed the top of the iz-zi wall at the tower of the Zabala garden," 200:'6, '8-'9

[n] ĝuruš **im lu-a** (. . .) an-za-qar-^{ĝeš}kiri$_6$-zabala$_4^{⌜ki⌝}$ [gub-ba], "[n] workmen having mixed earth (. . .), (workers) [employed] at the tower of the Zabala garden," 201:'1, '6

n ĝuruš **im lu-a** (. . .) im sumur aka an-za-qar-^{ĝeš}kiri$_6$-zabala$_4^{ki}$, "n workmen having mixed earth (. . .), (workers) having plastered the tower of the Zabala garden," 202:17, 20–21, 203:18, 20–21

1.8 Construction of the (Enclosure) Wall

9 ĝuruš šidim 14 ĝuruš 18 géme šeg$_{12}$ šu dím-ma sum-mu-dè gub-ba 2 ĝuruš 2 géme im a-ĝá-ri-na ì-li-de$_9$ gub-ba 20 géme im ga$_6$-ĝá-dè gub-ba 3 ĝuruš 3 géme **im lu-dè** gub-ba 1 ĝuruš in-u ga$_6$-ĝá **im lu-a** 7 géme šeg$_{12}$ ⌜da⌝ b[àd ĝá-ĝá-dè gub-ba], "9 builders, 14 workmen (and) 8 workwomen employed to hand (up) bricks for building, 2 workmen (and) 2 workwomen employed to lift earth into the *agarinnum*, 20 workwomen employed to carry earth, 3 workmen (and) 3 workwomen employed to mix earth, 1 workman having carried straw (and) having mixed (it with) earth (and) 7 workwomen [employed to place] bricks at the side of the (enclosure) wall," 16:17–23

1 ĝuruš šidim um-mi-a tà-tà-dè gub-⌜ba⌝ 5 ĝuruš šidim 4 ĝuruš 8 géme im ga$_6$-ĝá-dè gub-ba 3 ĝuruš **im lu-dè** gub-ba bàd {erasure} im sumur ke$_4$-d[è gub]-ba, "1 master builder employed to apply stucco, 5 builders, 4 workmen (and) 8 workwomen employed to carry earth (and) 3 workmen employed to mix earth, (workers) employed to plaster the (enclosure) wall," 36:26–30

1.9 Construction Site Lost or Unspecified

n ĝuruš **im lu-a**, "n workmen having mixed earth," 14:28, 101:26–29, 103:28, 110:32, 115:'22, 117:31, 129:35, 130:'15, 132:35, 133:34, 135:35, 136:38, 138:37, 140:41, 145:40,

146:'42, 148:'16, 150:37, 151:38, 154:41, 155:33, 156:32, 158:36, 159:3, 160:'13, 161:'19, 162:28, 174:26, 175:26

n g̃uruš **im lu-dè** gub-ba, "n workmen employed to mix earth," 5:23, 28:'20, 29:'21, 31:26, 32:26, 35:32, 35:35, 36:32, 39:23, 72:16, 72:20, 80:'9, 93:'18, 95:15, 131:'26, 198:'19, 198:'21

23 g̃uruš **im lu**, "23 workmen having mixed earth," 114:43

1.9.1 Mixing Earth and Water

2 g̃uruš **im lu-a** {erasure} g̃uruš a bal-a **im lu-a**-šè, "2 workmen having mixed earth (and) [n] workmen having poured water for mixing (with) earth," 106:39–40

3 g̃uruš a bal-[a] **im lu-**[**a**-šè], "3 workmen having poured water [for] mixing (with) earth," 194:45

1.9.2 Mixing Earth and Excavated Dirt

[n g̃uruš **im**] **lu-dè** gub-ba [n g̃uruš n] géme saḫar zi-ga **im lu**-šè, "[n workmen] employed to mix [earth] (and) [n workmen (and) n] workwomen for mixing excavated dirt (with) earth," 17:24–25

8 g̃uruš saḫar zi-ga **im lu-**[**dè** gub-ba], "8 workmen [employed to] mix excavated dirt (with) earth," 26:'16

1.9.3 Mixing Earth and Straw

3 g̃uruš [in]-u gú i_7-^{d}amar-^{d}E[N.ZU]-ta **im lu-a**-šè íb-ga_6, "3 workmen carried straw from the bank of the Amar-*Suena* canal for mixing (with) earth," 194:49–51

3 g̃uruš in-[u] i_7-^{d}*šu*-^{d}*suen*-⸢ḫé⸣-g̃ál-ta **im lu-a**-šè íb-ga_6, "3 workmen carried straw from the *Šu-Suen* Canal of Abundance for mixing (with) earth," 198:'24-'25

2. im a-g̃á-ri-na lu, "to mix earth in the *agarinnum*"

2.1 Construction of the House of *Alua*

10 g̃uruš **im a-g̃á-ri-[na] lu-dè** [gub-ba] 3 ⸢g̃uruš⸣ 3 ⸢géme⸣ gi-sal-[la] é-*al*<-*lu*>-*a* g[ul-dè gub-ba], "10 workmen [employed] to mix earth in the *agarinnum* (and) 3 workmen (and) 3 workwomen [employed to] trim thin reeds, (work for) the house of *Alua*," 38:28–32

2.2 Construction of the Textile Mill

*See *Household Index* for the complete context of the following passages.

n g̃uruš **im a-g̃á-ri-na lu-dè** gub-ba (. . .) é-uš-bar-šè, "n workmen employed to mix earth in the *agarinnum* (. . .), (work) for the textile mill," 37:24, 26, 38:25, 27

[n] g̃uruš **im a-g̃á-ri-⸢na⸣ lu-dè** gub-ba (. . .) ki-sá-a é-uš-bar-šè, "[n] workmen employed to mix earth in the *agarinnum* (. . .), (work) for the foundation terrace of the textile mill," 46:'19, '21

2.3 Construction Site Lost or Unspecified

n g̃uruš **im** (**a-**)**g̃á-rí-na lu-dè** gub-ba, "n workmen employed to mix earth in the *agarinnum*," 10:'21, 14:24, 15:28, 39:37, 41:'25, 43:'33, 45:17, 48:45, 99:25

2 g̃uruš 3 géme **im a-g̃á-ri-na lu-dè**, "2 workmen (and) 3 workwomen to mix earth in the *agarinnum*," 104:39, 105:37

3. (im) ***dì-um*** **lu**, "to mix adobe"

3.1 **Construction of Various Houses**

3.1.1 **The House of *Baḫa'a***

2 g̃uruš 4 géme ***dì-um*** **lu-dè** gub-ba é-*ba-ḫa-a* gub-ba, "2 workmen (and) 4 workwomen employed to mix adobe, (workers) employed at the house of *Baḫa'a*," 84:18–20

3.1.2 **The House of *Ili-bišu***

1 g̃uruš šidim 6 g̃uruš **im** ***dì-um*** **lu-a** é-*ì-lí-bi-šu*, "1 builder (and) 6 workmen having mixed adobe, (work for) the house of *Ili-bišu*," 207:15–17

3.2 **Construction Site Unspecified**

2 g̃uruš 4 géme ***dì-um*** **lu-dè** gub-ba, "2 workmen (and) 4 workwomen employed to mix adobe," 84:17–18

4. **im lu SIG$_4$.ANŠE(-šè)**, "to mix earth for the brick stack"

n g̃uruš **im lu-a SIG$_4$.ANŠE**-šè, "n workmen having mixed earth for the brick stack," 28:'18, 31:32, 32:32

[n g̃uruš] **im lu-a SIG$_4$.ANŠE** gub-ba, "[n] employed [workmen] having mixed earth at the brick stack," 29:26

4.1 **Mixing Earth and Water for the Brick Stack**

[1 g̃]uruš níg̃-GA a bal-a **im lu-a SIG$_4$.ANŠE**-šè gub<-ba>, "[1] employed níg̃-GA workman having poured water (for) mixing (with) earth for the brick stack," 21:'3

4.2 **Mixing Earth to Plaster the Brick Stack**

[10] géme im ga$_6$-g̃á 3 g̃uruš **im lu-a SIG$_4$.ANŠE** im sumur aka, "[10] workwomen having carried earth (and) 3 workmen having mixed earth, (workers) having plastered the brick stack," 199:12–14

[4] géme im [ga$_6$]-g̃á 1 g̃uruš im lu-a 1 g̃uruš a bal-[a] 1 g̃uruš in-u ga$_6$-[g̃á] **im lu-a SIG$_4$.⸢ANŠE⸣** im sumur aka, "[4] workwomen having carried earth, 1 workman having mixed earth, 1 workman having poured water (and) 1 workman having carried straw (for) mixing (with) earth, (workers) having plastered the brick stack," 209:27–32

5. **im sumur lu-dè**, "to mix plaster"

5.1 **Construction of the Palace**

[1 g̃uruš šidi]m um-[mi]-a [1 g̃uru]š šidim 1 g̃uruš šu d[ím gub-ba] 23 g̃uruš 20-lá-1 géme im sumur ga$_6$-g̃á-⸢dè⸣ [gub-ba] 7 g̃uruš **im sumur lu-dè** gub-ba ùr é-gal gibil a g̃á-g̃[á-d]è gub-⸢ba⸣, "[1] master builder, [1] builder (and) 1 workman [employed] to build, 23 workmen (and) 19 workwomen [employed] to carry plaster (and) 7 workmen employed to mix plaster, (workers) employed to waterproof the roof of the new palace," 75:15–21

5.2 **Construction Site Unspecified**

10 g̃uruš **im sumur lu-⸢dè⸣** gub-ba, "10 workmen employed to mix plaster," 53:48

luḫ, *mesû*, "to clean, to wash"

1. Cleaning Supplies for a Mattress

5½ naĝa-si-è 2 ma-na im-bábbar šà-tuku$_5$ **lu-luḫ-dè**, "5½ (liters of) sprouted naĝa (and) 2 minas of gypsum in order to clean a mattress," 783:3–5

2. Context Uncertain

0.1.0. še 2 ma-na siki-gen 2 sìla ì-ĝeš **luḫ 60.0.0. gur-kam mu ésir šeg$_{12}$-al-ur$_x$-ra-šè, "60 liters of barley, 2 minas of ordinary wool (and) 2 liters of sesame oil—cleaning? of 60 bushels—for the bitumen of the bricks," 1296:1–5

– M –

me, "to be"

dú-ra me, "to be sick"

1. Oil for Sick Builders and Millers

½ sìla ì-[ĝeš] *tu-ku-lí* šidim u$_4$ **dú-ra i-[me-a]**, "½ liter of sesame oil (for) *Tukulli*, the builder, when he was sick," 444:1–2

[n] gín ì-ĝeš-ta ^{d}šára-sá-ĝu$_{10}$ 1 *bu-za-du-a* géme kíkken-me-éš u$_4$ **dú-ra i-me** é-gal-šè, "[n] shekel(s) of sesame oil each (for) Šara-saĝu (and) *Buzadua*, female millers, when they were sick at the palace," 466:3–7

– N –

naĝ, "to drink"

kaš-gen naĝ, "to drink ordinary beer"

1. Drunk by the Builders

n sìla **kaš-gen** šidim-e-ne **íb-naĝ**, "The builders drank n liter(s) of ordinary beer," 398:1–3, 401:1–3, 418:1–3, 425:1–3, 436:7–8

1.1 During Construction of the Brewery-Kitchen-Mill Complex

0.0.1.5 sìla **kaš-gen** šidim-e-ne **íb-naĝ** u$_4$ al-tar ki-sá-a é-lùnga ù é-[kíkken], "The builders drank 15 liters of ordinary beer during construction of the foundation terrace of the brewery and [mill]," 428:1–4

5 sìla ninda 0.0.2. **kaš-gen** šidim-e-ne íb-gu$_7$ ù **íb-naĝ** [u$_4$] al-tar é-lùnga é-muḫaldim ù é-kíkken gub-ba, "The builders ate and drank 5 liters of bread (and) 20 liters of ordinary beer [when] they were employed (for) construction of the brewery-kitchen-mill complex," 430:1–4

0.0.n. **kaš-gen** šidim-e-ne **íb-naĝ** u$_4$ al-tar é-lùnga é-muḫaldim ù é-kíkken, "The builders drank n liter(s) of ordinary beer during construction of the brewery-kitchen-mill complex," 435:4–6, 439:4–6, 441:4–6

1.2 Drunk by Specific Builders

2 sìla **kaš-gen**-ta *en-ni-ma* 1 *be-lí-a-sú* lú-ì-si-in[ki] 1 sìla *ma-šum* árad-é-a **kaš-gen**-bi 5-sìla šidim-e-ne **íb-nağ**, "2 liters of ordinary beer each (for) *Enima* (and) *Beli-asu*, men from Isin (and) 1 liter (for) *Mašum*, the household servant. (In total:) their ordinary beer is 5 liters. The builders drank (the beer)," 378:9–16, 380:1–11, 389:1–11

2 sìla **kaš-gen**-ta *en-ni-ma* 1 *be-lí-a-sú* 1 sìla *ma-šum* árad-é-a {indent} 3 [**kaš-gen**-b]i 5-sìla [šidim-e-ne] **íb-nağ**, "2 liters of ordinary beer each (for) *Enima* (and) *Beli-asu* (and) 1 liter (for) *Mašum*, the household servant, (sub-total): 3 disbursals. (In total:) their [ordinary beer] is 5 liters. [The builders] drank (the beer)," 384:1–7

3. Drunk by the Builders and the Overseer of Hired Workers

7 sìla **kaš-gen** dirig sá-du$_{11}$ šidim ù ugula lú-ḫug̃-g̃á-e-ne **íb-nağ**, "The builders and overseer of hired workers drank 7 liters of ordinary beer, surplus of the regular offerings," 400:1–3

4. Drunk by the Overseer of Hired Workers

n sìla **kaš-gen** ugula lú-ḫug̃-g̃á-e-ne **íb-nağ**, "The overseer of hired workers drank n liter(s) of ordinary beer," 377:3–5, 393:1–2, 437:14–15

5. Drunk by Individuals

4.1 The Gendarme, *Rim-ilum*

0.0.1. **kaš-gen** ugula àga-ús-e-ne á-u$_4$-te-na u$_4$-2-kam àga-ús *ri-im-ilum* **íb-nağ** (. . .) u$_4$ má *simat-*[d]*ištaran puzur*$_4$*-iš-*[d]*da-gan*[ki]-ta gar-ša-an-na[ki]-šè mu-un-gíd-š[a-a], "The overseer of the gendarmes—the gendarme, *Rim-ilum*—drank 10 liters of ordinary beer in the evening of the 2nd day when they towed the boat of *Simat-Ištaran* from *Puzriš-Dagan* to Garšana, {authorizing official}," 550: '22-'25, '27-'29

4.2 The Men who Beat their Breasts

0.1.0. **kaš-gen** 0.0.2.1½ ⌜sìla kaš⌝ lú gaba sàg-dè **íb-nağ**, "The men who beat (their) breasts drank 60 liters of ordinary beer (and) 21½ liters of beer," 507:12–14

nağ(a)$_4$(KUM), "to crush/grind (in a mortar with a pestle)"

gazi **al-nağ$_4$-g̃á**, "crushed gazi" > **gazi**

mun **al-nağ$_4$-g̃á**, "crushed salt" > **mun**

munu$_4$ nağa$_4$, "to crush malt"

šim **al-nağ$_4$-g̃á**, "crushed aromatic" > **šim**

zíz nağa$_4$, "to grind emmer wheat"

1. munu$_4$ nağa$_4$, "to crush malt"

1.1 Female Weavers Assigned to Crush Malt

n géme uš-bar u$_4$-1-šè **munu$_4$ nağ$_4$-g̃á-dè** gub-ba, "n female weaver(s) for 1 day employed to crush malt," 245:1–2, 277:1–2

1.2 Household Servants, Supervised by *Beli-ili*

6 [géme] ugula *be-lí-ì-[lí]* árad-é-a-me-éš (. . .) **munu$_4$ al-nağ$_4$-g̃á-dè** ⌜gub⌝-ba, "6 [workwomen], household servants supervised by *Beli-ili*, *(and) {other workers} employed to crush malt," 217:'1-'3, '7-'8

1.3 Household Servants and Hired Workers

n ĝuruš n géme ugula *ba-zi* **munu$_4$ (al-)nağ$_4$-ĝá-dè** gub-ba, "n workmen (and) n workwomen, supervised by *Bazi*, employed to crush malt" > *Personal Name Index*

n ĝuruš n géme ugula *simat-é-a* **munu$_4$ nağ$_4$-ĝá-dè**, "n workmen (and) n workwomen, supervised by *Simat-Ea*, to crush malt" > *Personal Name Index*

2 ĝuruš **munu$_4$ nağa$_4$-dè** [gub-ba], "2 workmen [employed] to crush malt," 92:14

6 ĝuruš **munu$_4$ nağ$_4$-ĝá-[dè]**, "6 workmen [to] crush malt," 205:24

1.3.1 Inspection of the Work of Malt Crushers

3 ĝuruš ugula *za-l[a-a]* 3 ĝuruš ugula *šu-*^{d}[dumu-zi] lú-ḫuĝ-ĝá-me-[éš] 6 ĝuruš ugula *b[e!-lí-ì-lí]* árad-é-a-me-[éš] **munu$_4$ nağ$_4$-ĝá-dè** ⌜kurum$_7$ aka⌝, "Inspection (of the work) of 3 hired workmen, supervised by *Zala'a*, 3 hired workmen, supervised by *Šu*-[Dumuzi], (and) 6 household servants, supervised by *Beli-ili*, to crush malt," 170:1–8

3 ĝuruš ugula *šu-*^{d}dumu-zi 3 géme ugula *z[a-la]-a* lú-ḫuĝ-ĝá-[me-éš] 3 ĝuruš ugula *be-lí-ì-[lí]* [árad-é-a-me-éš] **munu$_4$ nağ$_4$-ĝá-⌜dè⌝** kurum$_7$ aka, "Inspection (of the work) of 3 hired workmen, supervised by *Šu*-Dumuzi, 3 hired workwomen supervised by *Zala'a*, (and) 3 [household servants], supervised by *Beli-ili*, to crush malt," 171:1–7

[n ĝuruš] ugula *be-lí-ì-[lí]* árad-é-a-me-éš 3 ĝuruš ugula *šu-*^{d}dumu-zi 2 géme ugula *ba-zi* lú-ḫuĝ-ĝá-me-[éš] **munu$_4$ nağ$_4$-ĝá** kurum$_7$ aka, "Inspection (of the work) of [n] household servant(s) supervised by *Beli-ili*, 3 hired workmen, supervised by *Šu*-Dumuzi, (and) 2 hired workwomen, supervised by *Bazi*, having crushed malt," 172:1–8

šu+níĝin 12 ĝuruš šu+níĝin 6 géme **munu$_4$ al-nağ$_4$-ĝá-dè** ⌜gub⌝-ba I[GI].Ĝ[AR] a[ka l]ú?-[. . .], "Inspection (of the work) of a total of 12 workmen (and) 6 workwomen employed to crush malt, men? [. . .]," 217:'5-'10

2. **zíz nağa$_4$**, "to grind emmer wheat"

n ĝuruš **zíz** ús-sa **nağa$_4$-dè** gub-ba, "n workmen employed to grind processed emmer wheat," 92:15, 110:33

3. Object Broken

1 s[ìla? . . .**al-n]ağ$_4$-ĝá**, 1394:15

0.0.1. [. . . **al-nağ$_4$-ĝ]á**, 1394:16, 1394:17

níĝin, *esēru*, *lawû*, "to enclose, confine, to encircle"[12]

1. **iri níĝin**, "to circle the city"

8 sìla dabin 4 sìla eša 1 sìla zú-lum eša ḫi-dè *tak-ri-ib-tum* **iri^{ki} ne-ne-de$_4$**, "8 liters of semolina, 4 liters of fine flour (and) 1 liter of dates to mix (with) fine flour, (for the performance of) a *takribtum* (involving) circling around the city," 1016:18–21

12 For ne-ne / ni$_{10}$(NÍGIN)-ni$_{10}$(NÍGIN) = *saḫārum*, "to circle, circumambulate," see *CAD* S s.v. 37. On the circling of cities and temples, see Heimpel 1998, 13–16.

(. . .) gala-e-ne a-rá-5-kam ér **iri ni$_{10}$-ni$_{10}$**, "{assorted comestibles} of the lamentation singers (for the performance of) a *takribtum* (involving) circling around the city for the 5th time (and on) {4 prior occasions}," 1030:37–39

– P –

pàd, *atû*; *nabû*, "to find, discover; to name, nominate"

mu lugal-bi pàd, "to swear by the name of the king"

(. . .) [d]*adad-tilla*[*ti* P]A.⌜AL⌝ **[mu] lugal-bi in-**IGI.[RU] zi-ga [*simat*]-dKA.[DI] ki d*adad-*[*tillati*]-ta ba-[zi], "*Adad-tillati* disbursed {craftsmen for various tasks in different cities}. (It was) the expenditure of *Simat-Ištaran*. *Adad-tillati*, the majordomo, swore by the name of the king," 260:34–37

– R –

ra, "to roll (seal)"

kìšib íb-ra, "the seal was rolled"

1. **The Seal of *Ḫallia***

kìšib íb-ra é-kìšib-ba-ta dub-bi in-du$_8$ siki bala-dè in-kéše é-gal-šè mu-DU *ḫal-lí-a* lúázlag ka-ga-na ba-gi-in, "He rolled the seal, baked its tablet in the warehouse, (and) bound up the wool to be baled (for) delivery for the palace," 609:11–16

2. **The Seal of *Tura'a***

1 túg-guz-za-gen ki *aš-tá-qar*-ta *puzur$_4$-a-gum*! šu ba-an-ti **kìšib** *tu-ra-a* **íb-ra**, "*Puzur-agum* received 1 ordinary tufted textile from *Aštaqqar*. *Tura'a* rolled (his) seal," 644:1–5

3. **kìšib nu-ub-ra**, "the seal was not rolled," 1268:8

ri, *alāku*, "to go, walk along"

1. **Provisisions for Going on a Journey**

0.0.2.6 sìla ninda kušа-g̃á-lá kéše-rá g̃uruš nam–60 *a-*⌜*bu*⌝-DU$_{10}$ u$_4$ é-d*šu*-d*suen*ki-šè **i-**⌜**re**⌝**-ša-a** u$_4$ é-e im sumur ba-aka, "26 liters of bread in bound leather sacks (for) *Abu-ṭabu*, the overseer of 60 workmen, when his workers went to *Bit-Šu-Suen* when the house was plastered," 480:1–3

[n.n.n sìla] ninda-šu-ra-gen kuša-g̃á-lá kéše-rá g̃uruš 7-kam u$_4$ kaskal-šè **i-re-sa-a**, "[n liter(s)] of ordinary half (loaf) bread in bound leather sacks (for) 7 workmen when they went on a journey," 529:1–3

– S –

sá, *kašādu*, "to equal; to reach, arrive"

1. **Area and Volume Measurements**

½ nindan 2 kùš **íb-sá** 1½ [kùš bùr] saḫar-bi ⅔ [sar], "½ nindan (and) 2 kùš in length, it is 1½ kùš square, its dirt (volume) is ⅔ [sar]" > **saḫar**

1 ^{giš}bisag̃-im-sar-ra sa-ḫa ⅔ kùš **íb-sá** im-sar g̃á-g̃á-dè, "1 canvas-lined clay tablet coffer—it is ⅔ kùš square—(in which) to deposit clay tablets," 1318:1–2, 1331:1–2, 1365:1–3

2. **To Arrive**

ur-^{d}dumu-zi ù *a-ḫu-wa-qar* ù-na-a-⌜du$_{11}$⌝ 0.0.2. ku-[x] *šu*-^{d}nisaba ḫé-na-ab-sum-mu 1 g̃uruš šà-gu$_{4}$ iri^{ki}-ta iri^{ki}-šè **ḫé-eb-sá-e** nam-mi-gur-re, "Say to Ur-Dumuzi and *Aḫu-waqar* that '20 liters of (?) should be given to *Šu*-Nisaba. 1 ox-driver from the city should arrive at the city. They should not argue!'" 1045:1–11

sa$_{10}$, *šâmu*, "to buy, purchase"

é sa$_{10}$, "to purchase a house"

ku$_{6}$-sim sa$_{10}$, "to purchase flying fish"

siki sa$_{10}$, "to purchase wool

1. **é sa$_{10}$**, "to purchase a house"

0.0.1.2 sìla [. . .] 5 sìla ninda-sal-la-dabin lú é-ne-ne <**é**->⌜ki⌝-ba-gar-ra **sa$_{10}$-a**, "12 liters of [. . .], 5 liters of thin semolina bread, (for) men having bought their houses as replacements," 487:1–4

0.0.1.2? sìla ninda-gal-gen 1 sìla du$_{8}$ [u$_{4}$ l]ú **é**-ne-ne **ba-an-ši-sa$_{10}$-a** íb-gu$_{7}$, "The men who bought their houses ate 12? liters of ordinary large bread baked (in) 1 liter (loaves)," 491:1–3

2. **ku$_{6}$-sim sa$_{10}$**, "to purchase flying fish"

PN **ku$_{6}$-sim sa$_{10}$-sa$_{10}$-dè** gú-ab-ba^{ki}-šè g̃en-na, "PN having gone to Gu'abba to purchase flying fish" > *Personal Name Index*

lu-kà-dum *ša-lim-be-lí* šeš-kal-la

3. **siki sa$_{10}$**, "to purchase wool"

3.1 **Wool, to Purchase Additional Wool**

5 ma-na **siki**-gen dirig **sa$_{10}$** siki-a-šè *pu-ta-nu-um*, "5 minas of supplementary ordinary wool for the purchase of (more) wool (for) *Putanum*," 1005:7–9

sa . . . gi$_{4}$, *šutērušû*, "to prepare"

sa gi$_{4}$. . .aka, "to make preparations" > **aka**

túg-**sa-gi$_{4}$-a**, "finished textiles" > **túg-sa-gi$_{4}$-a**

sar, *šatāru*, "to write"

bisag̃ im **sar-ra**, "clay tablet coffer" > **bisag̃**

sè(g_{10}), *šakānu; sapānu,* "to apply, place, set; to tamp"

[gi]gúrdub ka-tab sè(g_{10}), "to fit a basket (with) a cover"

ká sè(g_{10}), "to set in place at the gate"

ki-ba sè(g_{10}), "to tamp the floor"

[na4]kinkin šu **sè**(g_{10}), "'hand-held' millstone" > **[na4]kinkin**

saḫar sè(g_{10}), "to tamp dirt"

siki túg sè(g_{10}), "to fit wool (for) a textile"

1. **[gi]gúrdub ka-tab sè**(g_{10}), "to fit a basket (with) a cover"

n **[gi]gúrdub** siki **ka-tab sè-ga**, "n reed basket(s) of wool fitted with a cover," 502:1, 600:1, 603:2, 613:2, 614:2, 620:8, 623:4, 624:2, 633:6, 641:2, 648:3, 665:3, 666:6, 670:2, 672:2, 675:2, 667:18, 719:6–10, 750:2, 763:3, 784:4, 815:8, 826:8, 1279:1, 1285:2

[n+]480 **[gi]gúrdub ka-tab sè-ga**, "[n+]480 reed baskets fitted with a cover," 1292:3

2. **ki-ba sè**(g_{10}), "to tamp the floor"

2.1 For Construction of the Brewery-Kitchen-Mill Complex

*See *Household Index* for the complete context of the following passage.

n g̃uruš n géme **ki-ba sè-ga** é-lùnga é-muḫaldim ù é-kíkken, "n workmen (and) n workwomen having tamped the floor, (work for) the brewery-kitchen-mill complex," 150:35–36, 151:32–33

3. **ká sè**(g_{10}), "to set in place at the gate"

1 g̃uruš šidim ká im ⌜šeg$_{12}$ ku$_4$⌝-ra bàd x-[. . .] **ká sè-g[é-dè** gub-ba], "1 builder [employed] to place [. . .] at the 'service entrance' of the gate," 200:'11-'12

4. **saḫar sè**(g_{10}), "to tamp dirt"

4.1 Around the Fireplace

1 g̃u[ruš šidim n g̃uruš] 18 [géme] KI.NE [**saḫar**?] **sè-gé-d[è** gub-ba] é-uš-bar [ù é]-gaša[m-e-ne-šè], "1 builder, [n workmen], and 18 [workwomen employed] to tamp [dirt?] around the fireplace [for] the textile mill [and] craftsmen's house," 54:'18-'20

4.2 At the Foundation Terrace of the Brewery and Mill

1 g̃uruš šidim 10 g̃uruš 10 géme ki-sá-a é-lùnga ù é-kíkken **saḫar sè-ga**, "1 builder, 10 workmen (and) 10 workwomen having tamped dirt at the foundation terrace of the brewery and mill," 104:34–35, 105:32–33

4 g̃uruš 30 géme ki-sá-a é-lùnga ù é-kíkken **saḫar sè-ga**, "4 workmen (and) 30 workwomen having tamped dirt at the foundation terrace of the brewery and mill," 117:29–30

4.3 At the Sea Dike

2 g̃uruš má-laḫ$_5$ u$_4$-30-šè má **saḫar** ég a-ab-ba **se-gé-dè** gub-ba, "2 sailors employed for 30 days to tamp dirt (delivered by) boat at the sea dike," 274:1–3, 275:1–3

4.4 At the Side of the Wall

4.4.1 Delivery of Earth: Sample Text with Full Context

šu+níg̃in 9½ sar 4 gín igi-6-g̃ál ús-bi 30 nindan á-g̃uruš-a 6 gín-ta g̃uruš-bi 95⅔ 1⅔ gín u$_4$-1-šè še 6 sìla-ta ba-ḫug̃ še-bi 1.4.3.4 sìla 10 gín gur **saḫar** zi-ga tùn-[lá] da bàd **sè-ga** á [tumu]mer mu-DU *ba-zi* ugula lú-ḫug̃-g̃á g̃iri [d]*adad-tillati* šabra ù *puzur*$_4$-^{d}nin-kar-ak dub-sar "In total: 9½ sar (and) 4¹⁄₆ gín, its base is 30 nindan (long), workmen wages at 6 gín each, its workmen (equal) 95⅔ (and) 1⅔ gín workerdays, hired (for) 6 liters barley each. Their barley is 1 bushel, 274 liters (and) 10 shekels. Dirt removed via a tùn-lá device, tamped at the north side of the (enclosure) wall. Delivery (of dirt) by *Bazi*, overseer of hired workers, under the authority of *Adad-tillati*, the majordomo, and *Puzur*-Ninkarak, the scribe," 331:28–38

4.4.2 Related References

saḫar zi-ga tùn-lá da bàd [**sè-ga** m]u-DU *ba-zi* ugula l[ú-ḫug̃-g̃á], "Dirt removed via a tùn-lá device [tamped] at the side of the (enclosure) wall. Delivery (of dirt) by *Bazi*, overseer of [hired] workers," 329:13–15

saḫar zi-ga tùn-[lá] da bàd **sè-ga** á ^{tumu}mer mu-DU *ba-zi* ugula lú-ḫug̃-g̃á, "Dirt removed via a tùn-lá device, tamped at the north side of the (enclosure) wall. Wages for clay. Delivery (of dirt) by *Bazi*, overseer of hired workers," 333:21–24

4.4.3 Worker Assignments

2 ⌈g̃uruš⌉ da bàd **saḫar sè-g[é-dè]** gub-[ba], "2 workmen employed [to] tamp dirt at the side of the (enclosure) wall," 58:51–52

4.5 To Plaster the Garden Tower of Zabala

2 g̃uruš šidim [im] šu dím-ma sum-mu-dè 2 g̃uruš im ga$_6$-g̃á 2 g̃uruš im lu-a 3 g̃uruš a bal-a-e-dè 8 g̃uruš **saḫar** šà é-a **sè-gé-dè** im sumur aka an-za-qar-^{geš}kiri$_6$-zabala$_4$^{ki}, "2 builders to hand [earth] for building, 2 workmen having carried earth, 2 workmen having mixed earth, 3 workmen to pour water, 8 workmen to tamp dirt in the house, (workers) having plastered the tower of the Zabala garden," 202:14–21

5. Object Broken

*See *Household Index* for the complete context of the following passage.

[n g̃u]ruš šidim 31 g̃uruš šu dím [x] **sè-gé-dè** (. . .) ⌈al⌉-tar é-lùnga é-muḫaldim ù [é-kíkken], "[n] builder(s) (and) 31 workmen, having built, (worked) to place [x], (. . .), (for) construction of the brewery-kitchen-mill complex," 146:'29, '35

6. Translation Uncertain

1 g̃uruš x x x x-⌈dè⌉ **sè-g[é-dè gub-ba], 92:11

si(g), "to fill, load up; to pile up (e.g., earth for a levee or temple foundation)"

má(-a) si(g), "to load a boat"

saḫar si(g), "to pile up dirt"

tu$_7$ si(g), "to fill (a bowl with) soup"

1. **má(-a) si(g)**, "to load a boat"

1 g̃uruš túg-du$_8$ [u$_4$-1-šè] še 120 gur á-á[g̃-d]è gub-b[a ù **má si-ga], "1 braider [for 1 day], instructions about the 120 gur of barley followed [and the boat was loaded]," 298:4–5

3 g̃uruš ašgab u$_4$-1-šè še 120 gur á-ág̃-dè gub-ba ù **má si-ga, "3 leather workers for 1 day, instructions about the 120 gur of barley followed and the boat was loaded," 299:4–5

(. . .) [u$_4$]-3-šè [še x] x x x an-za-qar-ta kun-zi-da i$_7$-a-gàr-ús-sa a-šà lú-maḫ-šè íb-ga$_6$ ù **má-a si-ga**, "{workers and boats} for 3 day; (the boats) carried [barley . . .] from the fortified tower to the weir of the Agar-usa Canal of the Lu-maḫ field and (the workers) having loaded the boat(s)," 553:11–15

(. . .) u_4-2-[šè] a-pi_4-sal_4-[la^{ki}-ta] ù-dag-[ga^{ki}-šè] má sù [gíd-da] še **má-[a si-ga]** ù-dag-[ga^{ki}-ta] kun-zi-[da] a-pi_4-[sal_4-la^{ki}-šè] **má-[a si-ga]**, "{workmen and boats} for 2 days, (the workers) [having towed] the sunken boats [from] Apisal [to] Udaga, [having loaded] the boats with barley (and then having towed) [the loaded] boats from Udaga [(back) to] the weir of Apisal," 553:29–38

(. . .) u_4-[n-šè] še **má-a [si-ga]** kun-zi-⌜da⌝ a-pi_4-sal_4-la^{ki}-[ta] gar-ša-an-na^{ki}-[šè] má še ⌜gíd⌝-da, "{workmen and boats} [for n] day(s), (the workers) having towed boats [loaded] with barley [from] the weir of Apisal [to] Garšana," 553:45–52

2. **saḫar si(g)**, "to pile up dirt"[13]

2.1 At the Dirt Quarry

2 g̃u[ruš ḫug̃]-g̃á **saḫar** zi-ga ka-$la_{(2)}$-ka **si-ga**, "2 hired workman having piled up excavated dirt at the dirt quarry," 7:'30, 8:35

13 g̃uruš **saḫar** zi-ga ka-lá-ka **si-ga**, "13 workmen having piled up excavated dirt at the dirt quarry," 196:'22-'23

2.2 At the Quay

[. . .] á [g̃uruš]-a 10 gín-ta g̃uruš-bi 4 u_4-1-šè še 6-sìla-ta ba-ḫug̃ **saḫar** zi-ga kar-ki-mu-ra **si-ga**, "[. . . workmen] wages of 10 shekels each, its workmen (equal) 4 workerdays, (workers) hired for 6 liters of barley each, having piled up excavated dirt at the quay of the textile depository," 354:1–5

3. **tu_7 si(g)**, "to fill (a bowl with) soup"[14]

n sa gi-izi ninda ba-ra-du_8 ù tu_7 ba-ra-$šeg̃_6$ n ^{dug}sìla-bur-zi tu_7 **ba-a-si**, "n bundle(s) of fuel reeds with which bread was baked and soup was cooked; n 1-liter offering bowls into which the soup was filled," 1013:15–18, 1014:'8-'11

si_{12}(SIG_7), *baqāmu*; *barāšu*, *naṭāpu*, *nasāḫu*, "to cut, remove; to erase"

g̃uruš **si_{12}-a**, "a class of worker" > *Craftsmen Index*

$sila_{11}$(g̃)(ŠID), *lâšu*, "to knead (dough/clay)"

báppir dirig $sila_{11}$, "to knead additional beer bread"

n g̃uruš **báppir dirig $sila_{11}$-g̃á-dè** gub-ba, "n workmen employed to knead additional beer bread," 197:35, 198:'29

sim, *napû*, "to sieve, filter"

ésir sim, "to filter bitumen"

[1 g̃uruš m]á-$laḫ_5$ [n g̃uru]š **ésir si-mi-dè** gub-ba, "[1] sailor (and) [n] workmen employed to filter bitumen," 65:'20-'21

[13] Civil 1994, 111.

[14] Brunke 2008, 167 (Bemerkung 3.42).

sù, *ṭebû*, "to submerge, sink"

má sù, "to sink a boat"

(. . .) u$_4$-2-[šè] a-pi$_4$-sal$_4$-[la^{ki}-ta] ù-dag-[ga^{ki}-šè] **má sù** [gíd-da] še má-[a si-ga] ù-dag-[ga^{ki}-ta] kun-zi-[da] a-pi$_4$-[sal$_4$-la^{ki}-šè] má-[a si-ga], "{workmen and boats} for 2 days, (the workers) [having towed] the sunken boats [from] Apisal [to] Udaga, [having loaded] the boats with barley (and then having towed) [the loaded] boats from Udaga [(back) to] the weir of Apisal," 553:29–38

sù(b), "to rub, coat"

^{geš}ig sù, "to coat a door"

0.0.1.6 sìla ésir-é-a 7½ ma-na im-bábbar **^{geš}ig** mi-rí-za **ba-ab-sù-ub** 1⅓ g̃uruš ad-kub$_4$ u$_4$-1-[šè] ésir-é-a ù im-bábbar **^{geš}ig bí-ib-sù-ub**, "16 liters of house bitumen, 7½ minas of gypsum (with which) the door plank was coated. 1⅓ reed craftsmen [for] 1 day coated the door with house bitumen and gypsum," 1329:1–7

su(g$_6$), *apālu*; *riābu*, "to repay a loan; to replace"

1. To Replace Lost Birds and Mice

5 tu-gur$_4$^{mušen} 31 péš-igi-gùn úgu dé-a *da-da-a* sipa-mušen-⸢na⸣ **íb-su-su**, "*Dada'a*, the bird warden will replace 5 lost doves (and) 31 lost striped-eyed mice," 1138:1–4

23 péš-i[gi-gùn] úgu dé-a *da-da-a* sipa-mušen-na **íb-su-su**, "*Dada'a,* the bird warden, will replace 23 lost striped-eyed mice," 1152:1–3

2. To Replace the Remainder

še-gán-bi 36.1.0. še gur 11.1.0. zíz gur lá-ìa **su-ga še gu$_4$ e-na-am-DU ur-^{d}dumu-zi ù *i-din-èr-ra*, "their barley of the field: 36 bushels (and) 60 liters of barley (and) 11 bushels (and) 60 liters of emmer wheat; the remainder having been replaced. Ur-Dumuzi and *Iddin-erra* (?) barley and oxen," 1233:8–11

sum, *nadānu*, "to give"

im šu dím-ma sum, "to hand earth for building"

šeg$_{12}$ šu dím-ma sum, "to hand (up) bricks for building"

1. To Give

1.1 Assorted Commodities

1.1.1 Barley to the Majordomo

iti u$_4$-29-ba-zal še nu-g̃ál bí-in-gi$_4$ u$_4$-1-àm mu-[un-g̃ál] še šabra **in-na-an-sum** šu te-g̃e$_6$-dè nu-un-dab$_5$?, "At the end of the 29th day of the month there was no barley. (Someone) returned it. On the 1st day, it was there. (Then) the barley was given to the majordomo. In order for him to receive it, it will not (first) be taken (by someone else)," 1057:1–7

1.1.2 Barley Groats to the Workers

0.0.2.5 sìla níg̃-àr-ra-s[ig$_5$ **su]m-mu-da-éš** ⸢mu⸣ éren-na-šè, "25 liters of fine barley groats to be given to the workers," 1016:5–7

1.1.3 A Ram to Šara

1 udu-níta mu kù-^{d}⸢šára⸣-šè iti dirig **sum-mu-dam**, "1 ram for bright Šara, to be provided in month 13," 1078:1–4

1.2 In Letter Orders

1.2.1 Animals

a-ḫu-wa-qar ù-na-a-⸢du$_{11}$⸣ 1 sila$_4$-máš [ḫi-a] 5 gú ⸢sar⸣ ḫi-a *a-na-*[*a*?] **ḫé-na-ab-sum-mu**, "Say to *Aḫu-waqar* that '[various] lambs (and) goats (and) 5 talents of various vegetables(?) should be given to *Ana'a*,'" 1041:1–6

1.2.2 Barley and Other Comestibles

ì-lí-aš-ra-ni ù-na-a-du$_{11}$ 30.0.0. še gur 30.0.0. zíz gur ^{d}*adad-tillati* **ḫé-na-ab-sum-mu** kišib-ba-a-ni [šu] ḫa-ba-ab-ti-ğe$_{26}$ [nam-m]i-gur-re, "Say to *Ili-ašranni* that '30 bushels of barley (and) 30 bushels of emmer wheat should be given to *Adad-tillati*. He should take his seal(ed tablet). He should not argue!'" 1039:1–9

$^{[d]}$*adad-tillati* ù-na-a-du$_{11}$ 5.0.0. še gur 0.0.1.2 ì-ğeš [n] ma-na siki [níğ]-dab$_5$ *zà-mu-*⸢*ka*⸣*-ni a-ḫa-ni-šu* **ḫé-na-ab-sum-mu**, "Say to *Adad-tillati* that '5 bushels of barley, 12 liters of sesame oil (and) [n] mina(s) of wool, the requisitions at the beginning of the year, should be given to *Aḫanišu*,'" 1042:1–8

i-la-ak-nu-id ù-na-a-du$_{11}$ 5.1.4. še gur še-ba éren-na *šu-*^{d}nin-in-[si **ḫé-na**]**-ab-**[**sum-m**]**u**, "Say to *Ilak-nu''id* that '5 bushels (and) 100 liters of barley, barley rations of the workers, should be given to *Šu*-Nininsi,'" 1043:1–6

^{d}*adad-tillati* ù-na-a-du$_{11}$ 10.0.0. še gur 0.0.1. ì-ğeš ma-ma-*ri-be* **ḫé-na-ab-sum-mu**, "Say to *Adad-tillati* that '10 bushels of barley (and) 10 liters of sesame oil should be given to Mama-*ribe*,'" 1044:1–6

1.2.3 Building Supplies

šar-ru-um-ì-lí ù-na-a-du$_{11}$ [x]-ğál-la [x?] é-za ì-ğál é-ki-ba-ğar-ra du$_8$-dè ^{d}*adad-tillati* **ḫé-na-ab-sum-mu** a-ba šeš-ğu$_{10}$-gin$_7$, "Say to *Šarrum-ili* that '(?) that is in your house should be given to *Adad-tillati* in order to caulk the replacement house. Who is like my brother?'" 1526:1–7

1.2.4 Garden Products: An Order not to Give

^{d}*adad-tillati* ù-na-a-du$_{11}$ káb du$_{11}$-ga ğìri *é-a-šar* ^{ğeš}zé-na ù peš-[múrgu] nu-^{ğeš}kiri$_6$-ke$_4$-ne **na-ba-ab-sum-mu-**⸢**dè**⸣ šà dub-za ḫa-ba-tur-re, "Say to *Adad-tillati* that 'the gardeners should not give date palm frond midrib(s) and date palm spine(s), commodities (that were) measured for accounting under the authority of *Ea-šar*. Let it be subtracted in your tablet,'" 1037:1–9

1.2.5 Workmen and Other Requisitions at the Beginning of the Year

^{d}*a*[*dad-till*]*ati* ù-n[a-a]-du$_{11}$ 3 ğuruš ḫi-a sağ-dub ğír-su^{ki}-šè ù níğ-dab$_5$ zà-mu-bi *i-mi-iq-*^{d}šul-gi [**ḫé**]**-na-ab-sum-mu**, "Say to *Adad-tillati* that '3 various full-time workmen in Ğirsu and the requisitions at the beginning of its year should be given to *Imiq*-Šulgi,'" 1038:1–7

1.2.6 Commodity Broken

ur-^{d}dumu-zi ù *a-ḫu-wa-qar* ù-na-a-⸢du$_{11}$⸣ 0.0.2. ku-[x] *šu-*^{d}nisaba **ḫé-na-ab-sum-mu** 1 ğuruš šà-gu$_4$ iri^{ki}-ta iri^{ki}-šè ḫé-eb-sá-e nam-mi-gur-re, "Say to Ur-Dumuzi and *Aḫu-waqar* that '20 liters of (?) should be given to *Šu*-Nisaba. 1 ox-driver from the city should arrive at the city. They should not argue!'" 1045:1–11

2. im šu dím-ma sum, "to hand earth for building"

2.1 Construction of the Garden Tower of Zabala

*See *Garden Index* for the complete context of the following passages.

1 ğuruš šidim ⸢um⸣-m[i-a] 1 ğuruš šidim [1]0 ğuruš **im šu dím-ma sum-mu-dè** (. . .) úgu iz-zi-da a ğá-ğá an-za-qar-^{ğeš}kiri$_6$-zabala$_4^{ki}$, "1 master builder, 1 builder, (and) [1]0 workmen to hand earth for building (. . .), (workers) having waterproofed the top of the iz-zi wall at the tower of the Zabala garden," 200:'2-'4, '9

2 ğuruš šidim **[im] šu dím-ma sum-mu-dè** (. . .) im sumur aka an-za-qar-^{ğeš}kiri$_6$-zabala$_4^{ki}$, "2 builders to hand [earth] for building (. . .), (workers) having plastered the tower of the Zabala garden," 202:14–15, 20–21

1 ğuruš šidim um-mi-a 3 ğuruš šidim 3 ğuruš **im šu dím-ma [sum]-mu-dè** (. . .) im sumur aka an-za-qar-^{ğeš}kiri$_6$-za[bala$_4^{ki}$], "1 master builder, 3 builders (and) 3 workmen to hand earth for building (. . .), (workers) having plastered the tower of the Zabala garden," 203:14–16, 20–21

3. šeg$_{12}$ šu dím-ma sum, "to hand (up) bricks for building"

*See *Household Index* for the complete context of the following passages.

3.1 Construction of the Brewery-Kitchen-Mill Complex

10 ⸢ğuruš⸣ 1 géme **šeg$_{12}$ šu dím sum-mu-dè** al-tar é-lùnga é-muḫaldim ù é-kíkken, "10 workmen (and) 1 workwoman to hand (up) bricks for building, (for) construction of the brewery-kitchen-mill complex," 136:33–34

3.2 Construction of the Textile Depository

8 ğuruš sağ-tag 2 ğuruš á-⅔-ta lú-ašlağ-me-éš u$_4$-[1-šè] **šeg$_{12}$ šu dím sum-mu-dè** gub-ba al-tar é-[ki-m]u-ra, "8 full-time fullers (and) 2 fullers at ⅔ wages employed [for 1] day to hand (up) bricks for building, (for) construction of the textile depository," 242:1–5

3.3 Construction of the Textile Mill

20 ğuruš **šeg$_{12}$ šu dím-ma sum-mu-dè** gub-ba (. . .) [. . .] é-uš-[bar . . .], "20 workmen employed to hand (up) bricks for building (. . .), [(work for)] the textile mill," 33:22, 30

1 ğuruš **šeg$_{12}$ šu dím-ma sum-mu-dè** gub-ba (. . .) 40 géme šeg$_{12}$ da-ki-sá-a é-uš-bar ğá-ğá-dè gub-[ba], "1 workman employed to hand (up) bricks for building (. . .), (and) 40 workwomen employed to place bricks at the side of the foundation terrace of the textile mill," 35:22, 28

1 ğuruš šidim 8 ğuruš 4 géme **šeg$_{12}$ šu dím-[ma sum-mu-dè** gub-ba] (. . .) ki-sá-a é-uš-bar-šè, "1 builder, 8 workmen, (and) 4 workwomen [employed to hand (up)] bricks for building (. . .), (work) for the foundation terrace of the textile mill," 46:'15–'17, '21

3.4 Construction of Various Houses

1 ğuruš šidim u[m-mi-a] 1 ğuruš <šidim> 5 ğuruš **[šeg$_{12}$ šu dím-ma] sum-m[u-dè** gub-ba] (. . .) é-*pu-ta-nu-um* dù-[a], "1 master builder, 1 <builder> (and) 5 workmen [employed to] hand (up) [bricks for building] (. . .), (workers) having constructed the house of *Putanum*," 156:19–20, 22

3 ĝuruš šidim 5 ĝuruš 3 géme **šeg$_{12}$ šu dím-ma sum-mu-dè** (. . .) é-*zu-zu-tum* dù-[a], "3 builders, 5 workmen (and) 3 workwomen to hand (up) bricks for building (. . .), (workers) having constructed the house of *Zuzutum*," 156:23, 25

3.5 Construction of the (Enclosure) Wall

9 ĝuruš šidim 14 ĝuruš 18 géme **šeg$_{12}$ šu dím-ma sum-mu-dè** gub-ba 2 ĝuruš 2 géme im a-ĝá-ri-na ì-li-de$_9$ gub-ba 20 géme im ga$_6$-ĝá-dè gub-ba 3 ĝuruš 3 géme im lu-dè gub-ba 1 ĝuruš in-u ga$_6$-ĝá im lu-a 7 géme šeg$_{12}$ ⌜da⌝ b[àd ĝá-ĝá-dè gub-ba], "9 builders, 14 workmen (and) 18 workwomen employed to hand (up) bricks for building, 2 workmen (and) 2 workwomen employed to lift earth into the *agarinnum*, 20 workwomen employed to carry earth, 3 workmen (and) 3 workwomen employed to mix earth, 1 workman having carried straw (and) having mixed (it with) earth (and) 7 workwomen [employed to place] bricks at the side of the (enclosure) wall," 16:17–23

*See **al-tar** for the complete context of the following passage.

4 ĝuruš šidim 10-lá-1 ĝuruš 10 géme **šeg$_{12}$ šu dím-ma su[m-mu-dè]** (. . .) ⌜al⌝-tar bàd gub-ba, "4 builders, 9 workmen (and) 10 workwomen [to] hand (up) bricks for building (. . .), (workers) employed (for) construction of the (enclosure) wall," 99:13–14, 16

3.6 For the Warehouse

2 ĝuruš šidim 7 ĝuruš **šeg$_{12}$ šu dím-ma sum-mu-dè** gub-ba (. . .) é-kìšib-ba ugula kíkken, "2 builders (and) 7 workmen employed to hand (up) bricks for building (. . .), (work for) the warehouse (under the authority of?) the overseer of the mill," 36:21, 25

3.7 Construction Site Broken or Unspecified

5 ĝuruš šidim 9 ĝuruš **šeg$_{12}$ šu dím-ma sum-mu-dè** gub-ba, "5 builders (and) 9 workmen employed to hand (up) bricks for building," 14:22

[n] ĝuruš 3 géme **šeg$_{12}$ [šu dí]m-ma ⌜sum⌝-mu-[dè** gub-ba], "[n] workmen (and) 3 workwomen [employed] to hand (up) bricks for building," 17:19

n ĝuruš **šeg$_{12}$ šu dím(-ma) sum-mu-dè** gub-ba, "n workmen employed to hand (up) bricks for building," 20:22, 25:'10, 26:'10, 31:21, 32:21, 72:17

sur, "to twist, twine (rope)"

níĝ-ú-ba A.ZI/ZI.ÉŠ sur, "to twist rushes (for use as) corner pieces"

níĝ-ù-ba sur, "to twist corner pieces"

1. níĝ-ú-ba A.ZI/ZI.ÉŠ sur, "to twist rushes (for use as) corner pieces"

n ĝuruš **níĝ-ú-ba A.ZI/ZI.ÉŠ sur-dè** gub-ba, "n workmen employed to twist rushes (for use as) corner pieces," 36:33, 37:27, 39:40, 40:31, 43:'38, 45:19, 49:53

n ĝuruš n géme **níĝ-ú-ba A.ZI/ZI(.ÉŠ) sur-dè** (gub-ba), "n workmen (and) n workwomen (employed) to twist rushes (for use as) corner pieces," 136:39, 141:34, 142:30

2. níĝ-ù-ba sur, "to twist corner pieces"

[n ĝuruš **n]íĝ-ù-ba su[r-r]a**, "[n workmen] having twisted corner pieces," 98:'23

sur, *ṣaḫātu*, "to press, squeeze"

géme ĝeš-ì-**sur-sur**, "female sesame presser" > *Craftswomen Index*

– Š –

šeg̃$_6$, *bašālu*, “to cook”

ésir šeg̃$_6$, “to boil bitumen”

ku$_6$ šeg̃$_6$, “to cook fish”

šeg$_{12}$-al-ur$_x$-ra šeg̃$_6$, “to bake bricks”

tu$_7$ šeg̃$_6$, “to cook soup”

1. **ésir šeg̃$_6$**, “to boil bitumen”

[n g̃uru]š **ésir šé-g̃e$_6$-dè** gub-ba, “[n] workmen employed to boil bitumen,” 65:'21

2. **ku$_6$ šeg̃$_6$**, “to cook fish”

2.1 Fuel Reeds for Cooking Fish

80 sa gi-izi **ku$_6$ šé-g̃e$_6$-dè**, “80 bundles of fuel reeds to cook fish,” 1013:20–21, 1014:'13-'14, 1321:1–2

3. **šeg$_{12}$-al-ur$_x$-ra šeg̃$_6$**, “to bake bricks”

10 g̃uruš **šeg$_{12}$-al-ur$_x$-ra šé-g̃e$_6$-dè**, “10 workmen to bake bricks,” 110:34

120 sa gi-[x] 240 gu-níg̃in $^{g̃eš}$[ásal?] **šeg$_{12}$-al-ur$_x$-ra šé-g̃e$_6$-dè**, “120 bundles of [x] reeds (and) 240 bales of [poplar?] wood in order to bake bricks,” 1313:1–3

4. **tu$_7$ šeg̃$_6$**, “to cook soup”[15]

4.1 Ingredients with which to Cook Soup

4.1.1 For Banquets

4.1.1.1 Of Inana

0.2.1. níg̃-àr-ra-sig$_5$ 0.0.1.5 sìla ar-za-na 5 sìla ba-ba-še 5 sìla gú-gal al-àr-ra [5 sìla] gú-tur al-ús-sa [n] ádda-udu [n sìla mun-gen ^{dug}útul-gal]-šè [n sa gi]-izi [**tu$_7$**] **ba-⸢ra⸣-šeg̃$_6$** 380 ^{dug}sìla-bur-⸢zi⸣ tu$_7$ ba-aka kaš-dé-a ^{d}inana-zabala$_4^{ki}$, “130 liters of fine groats, 15 liters of barley-grits, 5 liters of barley porrige, 5 liters of milled beans, [5 liters] of processed peas, [n] sheep carcass(es), [n liter(s) of ordinary salt] for [the large tureen] (and) [n bundle(s)] of fuel [reeds] with which soup was cooked; 380 1-liter offering bowls of soup were served at the banquet of Inana of Zabala,” 1025:27–39

5 sìla níg̃-àr-ra-⸢sig$_5$⸣ 5 sìla ar-za-⸢na⸣ 5 sìla gú-gal al-àr-ra 5 sìla gú-tur al-⸢ús⸣-sa 2 ádda-[udu] 5 sìla mun-[gen] ^{dug}útul-gal-šè 20 sa gi-izi **tu$_7$ ba-ra-šeg̃$_6$** 60 ^{dug}sìla-bur-zi tu$_7$ ba-aka kaš-dé-a ^{d}inana-iri^{ki}, “5 liters of fine groats, 5 liters of barley-grits, 5 liters of milled beans, 5 liters of processed peas, 2 [sheep] carcasses (and) 5 liters of [ordinary] salt for the large tureen (and) 20 bundles of fuel reeds with which soup was cooked; 60 1-liter offering bowls of soup were served at the banquet of Inana of the city,” 1025:63–74

4.1.1.2 Of Nergal

0.0.3. níg̃-àr-ra-⸢sig$_5$⸣ 5 sìla ar-za-na 2 sìla ba-ba-še 3 ádda-udu 5 sìla mun-gen ^{urudu}šen-šè 60 sa gi-izi **tu$_7$ ba-ra-šeg̃$_6$** 120 ^{dug}sìla-bu[r-zi] tu$_7$ ba-⸢aka⸣ kaš-

[15] Brunke 2008, 160–193 (§3.3).

dé-a ^{d}nergal$_{x}^{[eri11-gal]}$ dumu *da-d*[*a*-AN], "30 liters of fine groats, 5 liters of barley-grits, 2 liters of barley porridge, 3 sheep carcasses (and) 5 liters of ordinary salt for the cauldron (and) 60 bundles of fuel reeds with which soup was cooked; 120 1-liter offering bowls of soup were served at the banquet of Nergal, (the personal deity of) the son of *Dada*-AN," 1025:46–56

5 sìla níĝ-àr-ra-sig$_5$ 5 sìla ar-za-na 5 sìla gú-gal al-àr-ra 2 sìla gú-tur al-ú[s-sa] 2 ádda-⸢udu⸣ ^{dug}útul-gal-[šè] 50 sa gi-izi **tu$_7$ ba-ra-šeĝ$_6$** 120 ^{dug}sìla-bur-zi tu$_7$ ba-aka kaš-dé-a ^{d}nergal$_{x}^{eri11-[gal]}$ dumu é-é-⸢zi⸣, "5 liters of fine groats, 5 liters of barley grits, 5 liters of milled beans, 2 liters of processed peas (and) 2 sheep carcasses [for] the large tureen (and) 50 bundles of fuel reeds with which soup was cooked; 120 1-liter offering bowls of soup were served at the banquet of Nergal, (the personal deity of) the son of E-ezi," 1025:81–91

4.1.1.3 Of Nin-Siana

[0.0.1. bappir?-sig$_5$ 0.n.n] kaš-⸢sig$_5$⸣ 0.0.3. kaš-gen 0.0.2. níĝ-àr-ra-⸢sig$_5$⸣ 0.0.2.5 sìla ar-za-na 5 sìla gú-gal al-àr-ra 5 sìla gú-tur al-ús-sa 3 udu ba-úš [n+]1 ádda-udu [0.n.]1. mun-gen ⸢^{dug}⸣útul-gal-šè 30 sa gi-izi [**tu$_7$**] **ba-ra-šeĝ$_6$** ⸢kaš⸣-dé-a ^{d}nin-^{d}si$_4$-an-na-a-ḫu-a, "[10 liters of fine beer bread?, n] liter(s) of fine beer, 30 liters of ordinary beer, 20 liters of fine groats, 25 liters of barley-grits, 4 liters of milled beans, 5 liters of processed peas, 3 slaughtered sheep, [n+]1 sheep carcasses (and) [n+]10 liters of ordinary salt for the large tureen (and) 30 bundles of fuel reeds, with which [soup] was cooked (for) the banquet of Nin-Siana, (the personal deity of) *Aḫu'a*," 1025:1–14

4.1.2 For the *Muškenu* and the Runner

0.0.2.6 sìla ninda-šu-ra-gen 2 ádda-udu 5 sìla níĝ-àr-ra-sig$_5$ 0.0.1. gú-gal al-àr-ra šu-gíd 1 sìla mun-gen ^{urudu}šen-šè 8 sa gi-izi **tu$_7$ ba-ra-šeĝ$_6$** maš-en-gag ^{lú}kaš$_4$ ká-é-gal-ka gub-ba ⸢*simat*⸣-^{d}*ištaran* íb-gu$_7$, "the *muškenu* (and?) the runner, stationed by *Simat-Ištaran* at the gate of the palace, ate 26 liters of ordinary half (loaf) bread, (and) soup cooked with 2 sheep carcasses, 5 liters of fine groats, 10 liters of milled šu-gíd beans, 1 liter of ordinary salt for the (soup) cauldron (and) 8 bundles of fuel reeds," 509:5–14

4.2 Fuel Reeds with which to Bake Bread and Cook Soup

4.2.1 Served in Liter Bowls, Occassion Unspecified

n sa gi-izi ninda ba-ra-du$_8$ ù **tu$_7$ ba-ra-šeĝ$_6$** n ^{dug}sìla-bur-zi tu$_7$ ba-a-si, "n bundle(s) of fuel reeds with which bread was baked and soup was cooked; n 1-liter offering bowl(s) into which the soup was filled," 1013:15–18, 1014:'8-'11

4.2.2 For the Hired Workers

0.1.5.9⅔ sìla ninda-zì-šà-gen dabin íb-ta-ḫi 0.0.1. níĝ-àr-ra-sig$_5$ ^{urudu}šen-šè 50 sa gi-[izi ninda ba-ra-d]u$_8$ ù **tu$_7$ ba-[ra]-šeĝ$_6$** mu lú-⸢ḫuĝ⸣-ĝá-e-ne-šè, "119⅔ liters of bread mixed from ordinary šà-flour and semolina, 10 liters of fine groats for the cauldron, (and) 50 bundles of [fuel] reeds with which the [bread] was baked and soup was cooked for the hired workers," 479:10–13, 483:9–14

4.2.3 When the House was Plastered

24 sa gi-[izi] ninda ba-ra-⸢du$_8$⸣ 10 sa gi-[izi] **tu$_7$ [ba]-ra-⸢šeĝ$_6$⸣** u$_4$ é-e im sumur ⸢ba⸣-aka, "24 bundles of [fuel] reeds, with which bread was baked, (and) 10

bundles of [fuel] reeds, with which soup was cooked, when the house was plastered," 473:1–5

4.3 Reeds and Wood with which to Bake Bread and Cook Meat and Soup

4.3.1 In the Bright Temple

7 sa+níĝin ^{ĝeš}ásal 5 sa gi-izi ninda ba-ra-du$_{8}$ uzu ù **tu$_{7}$ ba-ra-šeĝ$_{6}$** é-kù-ga, "7 bundles of poplar wood (and) 5 bundles of fuel reeds with which bread was baked (and) meat and soup were cooked in the bright temple," 1028:9–11

4.3.2 In the Courtyard of Inana of Zabala

10 sa-níĝin ^{ĝeš}⸢ásal⸣ 30 sa gi-izi ninda ba-ra-du$_{8}$ uzu ù **tu$_{7}$ ba-ra-šeĝ$_{6}$** 60 ^{dug}sìla-bur-zi tu$_{7}$-šè šà kisal-lá ^{d}inana-zabala$_{4}$^{ki}, "10 bundles of poplar wood (and) 30 bundles of fuel reeds with which bread was baked (and) meat and soup were cooked; 60 1 liter offering bowls for soup in the courtyard of Inana of Zabala," 1028:32–37

šeš$_{4}$(ERIN), *pašāšu*, "to anoint (with oil)"

1. To Anoint the Child(ren)

⅓ sìla ì-⸢šáḫ⸣ di$_{4}$-di$_{4}$-la àga-ús *simat-^{d}ištaran* **ba-ab-šeš$_{4}$** (. . .)⸢u$_{4}$⸣ é-e im sumur ba-aka, "⅓ liter of lard (used by) *Simat-Ištaran* (when) she anointed the small child(ren) of the gendarme (and) {other commodities} when the house was plastered," 472:8–9, 14

2. To Oil the Door

½ sìla ì-udu dúr ^{ĝeš}ig-[x] **ba-ab-šeš$_{4}$** u$_{4}$ é-e im sumur ba-aka, "½ liter of mutton fat (with which) the back of the [x] door was oiled when the house was plastered," 1319:1–4

šid, "to count"

1. Bricks

1.1 Counted in the Brickyard

37⅔ sar 4 gín igi-4-ĝál šeg$_{12}$ u$_{4}$-1-kam 37 sar 1 gín šeg$_{12}$ u$_{4}$-2-kam ⸢NE⸣-gu$_{7}$-bi nu-ub-ta-zi šeg$_{12}$ **šid-da** ĝá šub-ba ĝá-ĝál, "37⅔ sar (and) 4¼ gín of bricks for 1 day, 37 sar (and) 1 shekel of bricks for 2 days, the damaged bricks were not deducted; the count of bricks took place in the brickyard," 357:1–7

270 sar 13 gín šeg$_{12}$ ús-⸢sa⸣ i$_{7}$-*a*-⸢*ga*⸣-*mu-um* 60 sar 13 gín šeg$_{12}$ é-^{d}[x]-SAḪAR [NE?]-gu$_{7}$-bi ù PA [NE-gu$_{7}$]-bi nu-zi [**šid-d**]**a** šà ĝá šub-ba, "270 sar (and) 13 gín of bricks along the *Agamum* canal, 60 sar (and) 13 gín of bricks of the temple of [DN], damaged bricks and damaged (?) not deducted; the count (of bricks) in the brickyard," 358:1–7

188 sar 10 gín šeg$_{12}$ NE-gu$_{7}$-bi nu-zi **šid-da** šà ĝá šub-ba (. . .) ús-sa i$_{7}$-*a-ga-mu-um*, "188 sar (and) 10 gín of bricks along the *Agamum* canal, damaged bricks not deducted; the count (of bricks) in the brickyard," 359:1–3, 5

1.2 Counted under *Bazi*

73⅓ sar šeg$_{12}$ NE-gu$_{7}$-bi íb-ta-zi mu-DU *i-din-é-a* ugula lú-ḫuĝ-ĝá ĝìri *ba-zi* **šid-da**, "73⅓ sar of bricks, damaged bricks deducted. Delivery of *Iddin-Ea*, overseer of hired workers. The count (of bricks) was under the authority of *Bazi*," 315:1–8

2. Fodder

(. . .) é-a **šid-da**, "{assorted grains, fodder for sheep and pigs,} counted in the house," 1189:17

šu . . . bala, *šupêlu*, "to change"

[. . .] še mušen-[na . . .] **šu bala-dè [. . .] 6 ir_7^{mušen}-niga 30 $tu\text{-}gur_4$^{mušen}-niga *da-da-a* sipa-mušen-na é-[a . . .] *šu*-^{d}na-zi sipa-mušen-na é-[a . . .], 1253:'1-'7

šu . . . bar, "to release, set free"

1. Craftmen Released on the Day of the Wool Rations

2 géme sag̃-dub-ba 1 géme á-⅔ géme gu-me-éš u_4-1-šè u_4 siki-ba-ka [**šu bar**]-**ra**, "2 full-time female spinners (and) 1 female spinner at ⅔ wages [released] for 1 day on the day of the wool rations," 234:1–5

3 g̃uruš ašgab u_4-1-šè u_4 siki-ba-a-ka **šu bar-ra**, "3 leather workers released for 1 day on the day of the wool rations," 246:1–2

1 g̃uruš [túg-du_8] u_4-1-šè u_4 siki-ba-a-ka **šu bar-ra**, "1 [braider] released for 1 day on the day of the wool rations," 265:1–3

(. . .) [u_4-1-šè $u]_4$ siki-ba-ka **šu bar-**⌜**ra**⌝, "{craftsmen} released [for 1 day] on the day of the wool rations," 280:17–23

2. Craftsmen Released for the Priest

(. . .) u_4-15-šè ⌜ki⌝ en-šè **šu bar-ra**, "{craftsmen} released for 15 days for the priest," 225:6–7

šu . . . dím, "to build"

im $\mathbf{ga_6}$**-g̃á šu dím**, "to carry earth (for) building"

im **šu dím-ma** sum, "to hand earth for building" > **sum**

$šeg_{12}$ **šu dím-ma** sum, "to hand (up) bricks for building" > **sum**

$\mathbf{šeg_{12}}$ **šu dím**, "to build with bricks"

1. im ga_6-g̃á šu dím, "to carry earth (for) building"

1.1 Construction of the Storehouse Wall

*See *Household Index* for the complete context of the following passage.

[n g̃uruš] **im** ⌜$\mathbf{ga_6}$⌝**-g̃á šu dím** gub-ba (. . .) [n g̃uruš] šidim iz-zi g̃á-nun-na dù-dè gub-ba, "[n workmen] employed to build, having carried earth (. . .), (and) [n] builder(s) employed to construct the iz-zi wall of the storehouse," 29:'23, '27

1.2 Work Site Unspecified

1 g̃uruš 10 géme ⌜**im**⌝ $\mathbf{ga_6}$**-g̃á šu dím-ma** gub-ba, "1 workman (and) 10 workwomen employed to build, having carried earth," 29:'18, 29:'28

2. $šeg_{12}$ šu dím, "to build with bricks"

*See *Household Index* for the complete context of the following passage.

[n g̃uruš] $\mathbf{šeg_{12}}$ **šu dím-ma** [al-tar é-lù]nga é-muḫaldim [ù é-kíkken], "[n workmen] having built with bricks, (. . .) [(for) construction of] the brewery-kitchen-mill complex," 143:27, 34

3. To Build, Object Unspecified

n g̃uruš **šu dím**(**-ma**) gub-ba, "n workmen employed to build," *passim*

n g̃uruš šu dím gub-⌜ba⌝ *ták-si-ru-um*, "n workmen employed to build (for) repair" > ***ták-si-ru-um***

2 ĝuruš šidim 3 ĝuruš ḫuĝ-ĝá **šu dím-ma** gub-ba, "2 hired builders and 3 hired workmen employed to build," 8:23–24

4 ĝuruš šidim 5 ĝuruš [n géme] **šu dím-ma** gub-ba, "4 builders, 5 workmen (and) [n workwomen] employed to build," 15:25–26

šu . . . sum, "to inventory"

é-**šu-sum-ma**, "storehouse" > *Household Index*

šu-sum-ma, "inventory; a type of consignment" > **šu-sum-ma**

1 ĝuruš ^{lú}ázlag nibru^{ki}-ta ^{d}*šu*-^{d}*suen*-DU$_{10}$^{ki}-šè ^{uruduš}šim-da gu$_{4}$-udu de$_{6}$-a kaskal šu+níĝin-na-bi u$_{4}$-11-kam u$_{4}$ *šu-kab-tá* é-dam-*zé-ra-ra* **šu sum-mu-dè** ì-ĝen-na-a, "1 fuller having brought a sheep and cattle brand from Nippur to *Šu-Suen-ṭabu*, a trip of 11 days in total, when *Šu-Kabta* went to the house of the wife of *Zerara* in order to take inventory," 219:1–10

šu . . . tag, *lapātu*; *za'ānu*, "to touch, take hold of"

1. Uncertain Context

[x?] **šu tag-a ki *na-bu-tum*-šè, 529:21

šu . . . ti, *leqû, maḫāru*, "to accept, take, receive"

PN **šu ba(-an)-ti**, "PN received" > *Personal Name Index*

a-a-kal-la
a-al-lu-ú
a-da-làl
a-ḫu-DU$_{10}$
a-ḫu-wa-qar
a-lim-kal-la
a-na-aḫ-ì-lí
a-wi-lum-ma
^{d}*adad*-SIG$_{5}$
^{d}*adad-tillati* > *passim*
ak-ba-zum
am-ri-ni
ama-kal-la
aš-tá-qar
da-a-a
ĜAR-*šà-ti*
ḫi-lu-lu
i-din-a-bu-um
i-din-^{d}*šamaš*
i-sú-a-ri-iq
ì-lí-aš-ra-ni
ì-lí-si-na-at
ilum-ba-ni
ilum-mu-tá-bìl
ilum-ra-pi$_{5}$
ip-qú-ša
ki-ùr-en-mur
làl-la
lu-ba
lú-ša-lim
^{d}*ma-lik-ba-ni*
ma-nu-um-ki-^{d}šul-gi
nu-ru-uš-e-lí
puzur$_{4}$*-a-gu*$_{5}$*-um*
simat-é-a
ša-at-kab-tá
šar-ru-sú-ṭa-ba-at
^{d}šára-kam
šu-^{d}*adad*
šu-ba-ra-ni
šu-la-núm
šu-^{d}nin-girim$_{x}$
šu-^{d}nin-in-si
šu-^{d}nisaba
^{d}*šu*-^{d}*suen*-ḫa-ma-ti
^{d}šul-gi-*wa-qar*
ud-du-ur
ur-^{d}dumu-zi
zi-ti-a

ugula **šu ba-ti**, "the overseer received" > **ugula**

1. Barley to be Received by the Majordomo

iti u$_{4}$-29-ba-zal še nu-ĝál bí-in-gi$_{4}$ u$_{4}$-1-àm mu-[un-ĝál] še šabra in-na-an-sum **šu te-ĝe$_{6}$-dè** nu-un-dab$_{5}$?, "At the end of the 29th day of the month there was no barley. (Someone) returned it. On the 1st day, it was there. (Then) the barley was given to the majordomo. In order for him to receive it, it will not (first) be taken (by someone else)," 1057:1–7

2. Instructions to Take a Seal(ed Tablet)

ì-lí-aš-ra-ni ù-na-a-du$_{11}$ 30.0.0. še gur 30.0.0. zíz gur ^{d}*adad-tillati* ḫé-na-ab-sum-mu kìšib-ba-a-ni [**šu**] **ḫa-ba-ab-ti-ĝe$_{26}$** [nam-m]i-gur-re, "Say to *Ili-ašranni* that '30 bushels of barley (and) 30 bushels of emmer wheat should be given to *Adad-tillati*. He should take his seal(ed tablet). He should not argue!'" 1039:1–9

šu tag . . . dug$_4$, *za'ānu*, "to decorate"

1. To Decorate

★★[n ^{ĝeš}]ig mi-⌜ri⌝-[za x?] gu$_4$ **du$_{11}$-⌜ga⌝** [x] gu$_4$-ta 24, "[n] door plank(s) decorated? with (?) from an ox," 1307:1–2[16]

šub, *nadû*, "to pour (water, bitumen, etc.); to lay down (bricks)"

ésir šub-ba, "coated with bitumen"

Commodities Made with Bitumen

^{gi}ba-an-du$_8$-du$_8$, "(a basket)"

^{gi}bisaĝ, "basket"

^{gi}dim-gal-bi, "large reed pole"

^{gi}gur, "reed basket"

gi-ĝír-ab-ba tab-ba, "(meaning uncertain)"

gi-nindan šu-luḫ, "measuring rod for ritual cleansing"

^{ĝeš}ig mi-rí-za-gal, "large door plank"

^{gi}kid, "reed mat"

^{gi}ma-sá-ab, "(a basket)"

^{gi}ma-an-sim, "sieve"

^{gi}zar-zar, "(a basket)"

1 Baskets Coated with Bitumen

^{gi}bisaĝ-gíd-da túg-ga-tur **ésir šub-ba** ka-bi kuš ĝar-ra, "long basket coated with bitumen (for) small textiles, its opening covered with leather," 798:1–3

^{gi}gur a bala **ésir šub-ba**, "reed basket coated with bitumen for pouring water," 1271:1, 1299:6

^{gi}gur ki gub-ba **ésir šub-ba**, "reed basket—set in place—coated with bitumen," 1272:8

^{gi}gur še **ésir šub-ba**, "reed basket coated with bitumen (containing) barley," 1274:1, 1301:1

^{gi}zar-zar(-zar) **ésir šub-ba**, "basket coated with bitumen," 1280:1, 1299:9

^{gi}ba-an-du$_8$-du$_8$ **ésir šub-ba**, "basket coated with bitumen," 1299:7

^{gi}gur sal-la zì eša **ésir šub-ba**, "thin basket coated with bitumen (containing) flour (and) fine flour," 1299:10

^{gi}gur-^{dug}útul **ésir šub-ba**, "reed basket shaped like a tureen coated with bitumen," 1370:1

★★2 ^{gi}gur še á-áĝ-[ĝá] **ésir šub-ba**, 1376:40

^{gi}ma-sá-⌜ab⌝ **ésir šub-[ba]**, "basket coated with bitumen," 1376:38

^{gi}bisaĝ ninda-gur$_4$-ra **ésir šub-ba**, "basket coated with bitumen for thick bread," 1376:44

---

16 Understood as an abbreviation for of šu-tag. . .dug$_4$.

2. Reed Mats Coated with Bitumen

^{gi}kid-aš-rin **ésir šub-ba**, "aš-rin reed mat coated with bitumen," 1334:3

^{gi}kid titab **ésir šub-ba**, "reed mat coated with bitumen for malted barley," 1376:7

^{gi}kíd-kíd **ésir šub-ba**, "reed mat coated with bitumen," 1376:21

^{gi}kid **ésir šub-ba**, "reed mat coated with bitumen," 1376:41

^{gi}kid ésir BE-a ir-dù-a tab-⸢ba⸣ **ésir šub-ba, 1376:43

3. Sieves Coated with Bitumen

$^{<gi>}$⸢ma⸣-an-sim BÚR zì-gu-sig$_{5}$ **ésir šub-ba**, "fine gu-flour BÚR sieve coated with bitumen," 1376:16

$^{<gi>}$ma-an-sim BÚR dabin **ésir šub-ba**, "semolina BÚR sieve coated with bitumen," 1376:17

^{gi}ma-an-sim níĝ-àr-ra **šub-ba**, "groats sieve coated (with bitumen)," 1376:18

4. Other Reed Items Coated with Bitumen

[n] gi-ĝír-ab-b[a **ésir šub], 1292:7

[n+]240 gi-ĝír-ab-ba tab-ba gal zikum **šub, 1292:7

[n] gi-ĝír-ab-ba tab-ba ús **ésir šub, 1292:6

^{ĝeš}ig mi-rí-za-gal **ésir šub-ba**, "large door plank coated with bitumen," 1307:3

^{gi}dim-gal-bi **ésir šub-ba**, "large reed pole coated with bitumen," 1376:12

gi-nindan šu-luh **ésir šub-ba**, "ritual cleansing measuring rod coated with bitumen," 1376:14

5. Bitumen Needed to Manufacture Coated Objects

[. . .] ùr **ésir šub-ba** (. . .) ésir-é-a-bi 0.0.1 [. . .], "[n object(s)] coated with bitumen. (Manufacture required:) {assorted commodities} 10 [+n? liters] of house bitumen (and) {labor}," 1381:19, 23

1 ^{gi}gida$_{x}$ **ésir šub-ba** gíd 1 nindan (. . .) ésir-é-a-bi 2 sìla, "1 (reed object) coated with bitumen, 1 nindan in length. (Manufacture required:) {reeds}, 2 liters of house bitumen (and) {labor}," 1381:49, 52

60 ^{gi}gida$_{x}$ **ésir š[ub-ba]** gíd 4 kùš daĝal ⅔ kùš (. . .) ésir-é-a-bi, "60 (reed objects) coated with bitumen, 4 kuš long (and) ⅔ kuš wide. (Manufacture required:) {reeds}, ⅔ liter of house bitumen (and) {labor}," 1381:54, 56

– T –

tà(g), *rakāsu*, *sêru*, "to bind, to touch up; to apply stucco"

ab-ba daĝal tà(g), "to widen (the opening of) the roof vent"

gi-sal tà(g), "to stucco thin reeds (in situ)"

im sumur tà(g), "to apply plaster"

1. To Apply Stucco

1.1 The Replacement House

4 ĝuruš šidim [. . .] é-ki-ba-ĝar-ra *u-bar-ri-a* **tà-tà<-dè>** gub-ba, "4 builders [. . .] employed to apply stucco to the replacement house of *Ubarria*," 89:8

1.2 The Foundation Terrace of the Granary

1.2.1 Of the Granary

1 g̃uruš šidim ki-sá-a gur$_7$ **tà-tà-dè**, "1 builder to apply stucco to the foundation terrace of the granary," 191:24–25

1.2.2 Of the Textile Mill

1 g̃uruš šidim um-mi-a ki-sá-a é-uš-bar **tà-ga** gub-ba, "1 employed master builder having applied stucco to the foundation terrace of the textile mill," 35:20

1.3 The (Enclosure) Wall

1 g̃uruš šidim um-mi-a **tà-tà-dè** gub-⸢ba⸣ 5 g̃uruš šidim 4 g̃uruš 8 géme im ga$_6$-g̃á-dè gub-ba 3 g̃uruš im lu-dè gub-ba bàd im sumur ke$_4$-d[è gub]-ba, "1 master builder employed to apply stucco, 5 builders, 4 workmen (and) 8 workwomen employed to carry earth (and) 3 workmen employed to mix earth, (workers) employed to plaster the (enclosure) wall," 36:26–30

1.3.1 The Foundation of the (Enclosure) Wall

2 g̃uruš šidim uš bàd **tà-tà-dè** gub-ba, "2 builders employed to apply stucco to the foundation of the (enclosure) wall," 6:22, 7:'31, 8:38

3 gé[me im *a-ga-ri*]-*nu-um* ga$_6$-g̃á-dè gub-[ba] al-tar uš bàd **tà-tà-dè** gub-ba, "3 workwomen employed to carry [earth] to the *agarinnum*, (workers) employed (for) construction to apply stucco to the foundation of the (enclosure) wall," 7:'25-'27

2 g̃uruš šidim 3 g̃uruš ḫug̃-g̃á šu dím-ma gub-ba 3 géme ḫug̃-g̃á im *a-ga-ri-nu-um* ga$_6$-g̃á-dè gub-ba [. . .g]ub-ba [n g̃uruš im] *a-ga-ri-n*[*u-um* ga$_6$-g̃]á-dè gub-[ba a-rá]-2-kam u[š bàd] **tà-tà-dè** gub-ba, "2 builders (and) 3 hired workmen employed to build, 3 hired workwomen employed to carry earth to the *agarinnum*, [. . .] employed [to . . .] (and) [n workmen] employed to carry [earth] to the *agarinnum* for the 2nd time, (workers) employed to apply stucco to the foundation [of the (enclosure) wall]," 8:23–32

1 g̃uruš šidim um-⸢mi⸣-a 3 g̃uruš [gub-ba] uš bàd **tà-t[à-dè]** ⸢gub⸣-ba, "1 master builder (and) 3 [employed] workmen, (workers) employed [to] apply stucco to the foundation of the (enclosure) wall," 92:8–10

1.3.2 The Gate of the (Enclosure) Wall

1 g̃uruš šidim 3 g̃uruš 5 géme ká bàd **tà-tà-dè**, "1 builder, 3 workmen (and) 5 workwomen to apply stucco to the gate of the (enclosure) wall," 104:32–33, 105:30–31

1.3.3 The iz-zi Wall

1 g̃uruš šidim iz-zi **tà-tà-dè** gub-ba, "1 builder employed to apply stucco to the iz-zi wall," 14:26

n g̃uruš šidim iz-zi bàd **tà-tà-dè** gub-ba, "n builder(s) employed to apply stucco to the iz-zi wall of the (enclosure) wall," 15:27, 16:16, 17:17, 20:19, 21:19, 25:'7, 26:'7, 27:'12, 28:'10, 31:19, 32:19

*See *Household Index* for the complete context of the following passage.

1 g̃uruš šidim iz-zi bàd **tà-tà-dè** gub-ba (. . .) [. . .] é-uš-[bar . . .], "1 builder employed to apply stucco to the iz-zi wall of the (enclosure) wall (. . .), [(work for)] the textile mill," 33:20, 30

2. **ab-ba dag̃al tà(g)**, "to widen (the opening of) the roof vent"

2.1 Construction of the Textile Mill and Craftsmen's House

[n] g̃uru[š šidim] 2 [g̃uruš] 3 ⸢géme⸣ **ab-ba dag̃al t[à-tà-dè]** gub-ba é-uš-bar ù é-gašam-šè, "[n builder(s)], 2 [workmen] (and) 3 workwomen employed [to] widen (the opening of) the roof vent, (work) for the textile mill and craftsmen's house," 59:39–40

2 g̃uruš ⸢šidim⸣ 2 g̃uruš šu dím-m[a gub-ba] 4 géme im ⸢ga$_6$⸣-g̃á-dè gub-[ba] **ab-ba dag̃al t[à-tà-dè** gub-ba] é-uš-bar ù é-[NUN].ME.TAG-[e-ne-šè], "2 builders, 2 workmen [employed] to build, 4 workwomen employed to carry earth, (workers) [employed to] widen (the opening of) the roof vent, (work) [for] the textile mill and craftsmen's house," 60:36–40

2 g̃uru[š] 3 [géme] **ab-ba dag̃[al tà-tà]-dè** [gub-ba] é-uš-bar [ù] é-gašam-[šè] "2 workmen (and) 3 [workwomen employed] to [widen] (the opening of) the roof vent, (work) [for] the textile mill [and] craftsmen's house," 62:'21-'24

3. **gi-sal tà(g)**, "to stucco thin reeds"

2 g̃uruš **gi-sal** bàd **tà-tà-[dè** gub]-ba, "2 workmen employed [to] stucco thin reeds on the (enclosure) wall," 36:31

4. **im sumur tà-tà-dè**, "to apply plaster"

4.1 To Plaster the (Enclosure) Wall

1 g̃uruš šidim um-mi-a 4 g̃uruš šidim 6 g̃uruš šu dím-ma gub-ba 4 g̃uruš **im sumur tà-tà-dè** gub-ba [n] géme im ga$_6$-g̃á-dè gub-ba bàd [im sumur] ke$_4$-[dè], "1 master builder, 4 builders (and) 6 workmen employed to build, 4 workmen employed to apply plaster (and) [n] workwomen employed to carry earth, (workers) [to] plaster the (enclosure) wall," 40:20–25

6 g̃uruš šu dím-ma ⸢gub⸣-ba [n g̃uruš] **im sumur [tà-t]à-dè** gub-ba 1 g̃uruš ⸢im⸣ ì-⸢li⸣-de$_9$ [gub-ba] 10-lá-1 géme i[m ga$_6$]-g̃á-dè gub-ba bàd im sumur ke$_4$-dè, "6 workmen employed to build, [n workmen] employed to apply plaster, 1 workman [employed] to lift earth (and) 9 workwomen employed to carry earth, (workers) to plaster the (enclosure) wall," 41:'18-'22

4.2 To Waterproof the Roof of the Textile Mill and Craftsmen's House

[n g̃uruš i]m ì-li-de$_9$ [gub-ba n g̃uruš] **im sumur tà-tà-dè** gub-ba [ùr] a g̃á-g̃á-dè [é-uš]-bar ù é-gašam-e-[ne], "[n workmen employed] to lift earth, [n workmen] employed to apply plaster, (workers) to waterproof [the roof] of the textile mill (and) craftmen's house," 65:'15-'19

4.3 Construction Site Broken or Unspecified

1 g̃uruš **im sumur tà-tà-dè** gub-ba, "1 workman employed to apply plaster," 49:21

1 g̃uruš ⸢šidim⸣ **im sumur tà-[tà]-⸢dè⸣** gu[b-ba], "1 builder employed to apply plaster," 194:42–43

tab, *eṣēpu*, "to twine (rope, thread), to line up (bricks in rows), to stack sheaves of grain; to double; to repeat"

1. **To Twine Rope**

1.1 2-Ply Ropes

^{gi}dur-gazi a-rá-2-**tab-ba** gíd 1½ nindan-ta, "9-meter 2-ply gazi rope" > **^{gi}dur**

^{gi}dur-gazi a-rá-3-**tab-ba** gíd 1½ nindan-ta, "9-meter 3-ply gazi rope" > **^{gi}dur**

1.2 3-Ply Ropes and Reed Panels

^{gi}dur dağal a-rá-3-**tab-ba** gíd 5 nindan-ta, "30 meter 3-ply wide rope" > **^{gi}dur**

1.3 Cord

1 ma-na gu-gen a-rá-11-ta **ì-tab-ba**(!), "1 mina of ordinary cord of 11 strands each," 836:7–8

1.4 Triple Reedwork Panels

gi-guru$_5$ a-rá-3-**tab-ba**, "triple reedwork panel" > **guru$_5$**

2. **To line up (bricks in rows)**

2.1 Construction of the Textile Mill and its Foundation Terrace

*See *Household Index* for the complete context of the following passages.

3 ğuruš šidim 10 ğuruš 28 géme [ki]-sá-a é-uš-bar šeg$_{12}$ **tab-bé-dè** gub-ba, "3 builders, 10 workmen (and) 28 workwomen employed to line up bricks at the foundation terrace of the textile mill," 32:29–30

5 ğuruš š[idim šeg$_{12}$ bà]d **tab-bé-dè** gub-ba (. . .) [. . .] é-uš-[bar . . .], "5 builders employed to line-up [bricks] at the (enclosure) wall (. . .), [(work for)] the textile mill," 33:21, 30

1 ğuruš šidim ki-sá-a é-uš-bar šeg$_{12}$ **tab-bé-dè** gub-ba, "1 builder employed to line up bricks at the foundation terrace of the textile mill," 35:21

2.2 Construction of the (Enclosure) Wall

n ğuruš šidim šeg$_{12}$ bàd **tab-bé-dè** gub-ba, "n builder(s) employed to line up bricks at the (enclosure) wall," 21:20, 31:20, 32:20

3. **To Stack Sheaves of Grain**

(. . .) še gur$_{10}$-gur$_{10}$-dè zàr **tab-ba-dè** ù ğeš ra(ḫ$_2$)-ra(ḫ$_2$)-dè a-šà *ṣe-ru-um* gub-ba, "{craftsmen} employed at the *Ṣerum* field to reap barley, stack (its) sheaves (for drying) and flail (them)," 262:19–22

1 (bùr) gána zàr **tab-ba** nu-de$_5$-de$_5$-ga, "the sheaves stacked on 1 bur of acreage are not to be collected," 1398:1–3

4. **To Double**

é-**tab-tab**, "double house" > *Household Index*

ég-**tab**, "double dike" > **ég**

^{túg}níğ-lam **tab-ba**, "double níğ-lam textile" > **^{túg}níğ-lam**

túg-guz-za **tab-ba**, "double tufted textile" > **túg-guz-za**

túg ba-tab *taḫ-ḫu-um* **tab-ba**, "double ba-tab *taḫ-ḫu-um* textile" > **ba-tab *taḫ-ḫu-um***

5. Translation Uncertain

[n+]240 gi-g̃ír-ab-ba **tab-ba gal zikum šub, 1292:5

8 [n] gi-g̃ír-ab-ba **tab-ba ús ésir šub, 1292:6

1 [gi]bisag̃-BÚR-tab-ba** g̃eš-**tab-ba**, 1336:1

2 [gi]kid ésir BE-a ir-dù-a **tab-⸢ba⸣ ésir šub-ba, 1376:43

tag, "to beat; to weave"

1. Woven Linen

4 gada-gen ki-lá-bi 7⅓ ma-na ki-lá **tag-a** mu-DU, "4 ordinary linens, their weight is 7⅓ minas. Delivery of weighed (linen) having been woven," 575:1–4

2. Woven Textiles

túg ki-lá **tà(g-ga)**, "weighed textiles having been woven," 582:3, 594:5, 597:3, 608:10, 617:11, 618:13, 685:5, 686:4, 687:3, 690:8, 708:11, 724:3, 730:6, 738:18, 744:14, 747:18, 765:8, 778:11, 803:5, 804:6, 821:11, 832:2, 835:'17

[n túg-guz]-za 4-kam-ús-tur **tà-[ga]**, "[n] 4th-quality small tufted textile(s) having been woven," 618:10

taḫ, *aṣābu*, "to add, increase"

1. Additional Bread

1.0.2. ninda gur sá-du$_{11}$ ù ninda dirig **ba-ab-taḫ-a** iti ezem-me-ki-g̃ál, "1 bushel (and) 20 liters of bread, regular offerings and additional bread that were added in the 12th month," 1031:11–12

2. Labor Added to the Account

(. . .) á de$_6$-a ad-kub$_4$ **taḫ-ḫe-dam** mu–2-kam, "{assorted mats, baskets, and other finished reed products}; 'incoming' labor of the reed craftsmen, to be added (to) the 2 year (account)," 1381:66–69

te(g̃$_3$), *ṭeḫû*, "to be near, to approach"

na-sìm [lú]kíg̃-gi$_4$<-a>-lugal-ta lú **te-te-dè** in-da-g̃e$_{26}$-en, "*Nasim*, the royal messenger, went to bring the man from the king," 222:3–5

til, *gamāru*; *labāru*; *qatû*, "(to be) complete(d); (to be) old, long-lasting; to end"

kíg̃-**til**, "completed work" > **kíg̃**

tuku, *rašû*, "to acquire, get"

1. Individuals who did not Get Bread

[1 *w*]*a-qar-dan* 1 *á-pil-lí-a* ninda-ta **nu-tuku**, "*Waqar-dan* (and) *Apilli'a*, they each did not get bread," 559:30–32

2. Broken Context

4.0.0. zíz gur zíz-ba-na zì-KAL 4½ sìla 5 gín-ta ì-g̃ál 7.4.0. kib$_x$ gur ⸢sag̃⸣? g̃ál-la **nu-ub-tuku á géme kíkken-šè, "4 bushels of emmer, in each ban (=10 liters) of the emmer there are 4½ liters and 5 shekels of KAL-flour (and) 7 bushels (and) 240 liters of wheat, which did not have (?), for labor of the female millers," 412:1–4

túm, **tùm**, *babālu*, sg. imperfect stem of de_6, "to bring"

1. Errands

1.1 Bringing Barley

2 g̃uruš ^{lú}kíg̃-gi_4-a *šu-kab-ta* še karkar^{ki}-ta nibru^{ki}-šè **ba-an-tùm**, "2 messengers of *Šu-Kabta* brought barley from Karkar to Nippur," 20:33, 21:'27[17]

iti ezem-maḫ še **tùm-dè** é-$duru_5$-ul-luḫ-uri_5ki-[ma-šè g̃en-na], "(workers) [having gone to] the Ulluḫ-Urim village to bring barley (in) month 10," 1029:'18-'19

1.2 Bringing Shok

10-lá-1 g̃uruš$^{g̃eš}$kišig **tù[m-d]è** g̃en-⸢na⸣, "9 workmen having gone to bring shok," 151:40

1.3 Bringing Flour

[2 g̃uruš] *ṣa-a-l[um* ^{lú}kíg̃-gi_4-a-lugal zì] karkar^{ki}-šè **i[n-tùm-uš]**, "[2 workmen] of *Ṣallum*, [the royal messenger], brought [flour] to Karkar," 27:'16

2 g̃uruš *ṣa-al-[lum* ^{lú}kíg̃-gi_4-a-lu]gal zì g̃á-g̃á-dè karkar^{ki}-šè **in-tùm-uš**, "2 workmen of *Ṣallum*, the royal messenger, brought flour to Karkar in order to deposit it," 28:'27

1.4 Bringing Oxen to Nippur

1 g̃uruš gu_4-niga g̃ar-ša-an-na^{ki}-ta nibru^{ki}-šè **ba-an-tùm**, "1 workman brought a fattened ox from Garšana to Nippur," 17:29, 20:32

1.5 Bringing Reeds

1.5.1 From Ka-saḫara

15 g̃uruš ka-saḫar-ra^{ki}-šè gi **tùm-dè** g̃en-na, "15 workmen having gone to Ka-saḫara to bring reeds," 136:41, 138:39–40,[18] 140:43, 141:38, 143:40

1.5.2 From Udaga

6 g̃uruš má-lá-a gi ù-da[g-ga^{ki}-ta] **tùm-dè** g̃e[n-na], "6 workmen having gone to bring a freight boat of reeds [from] Udaga," 205:26–27

1.5.3 Bringing Fresh Reeds from the Fields

6 [g̃uruš . . .] a-šà pa_4-lu[gal-g̃]u_{10}-k[a-ta] gi **tùm-⸢dè⸣** g̃en-[na], "6 [workmen. . .] having gone to bring reeds [from] the Palugalg̃u field," 57:'22-'23

[n] g̃uruš gi-zi **tùm(-dè)** a-šà *ši-ḫu-um*-šè g̃en-na(-me), "[n] workmen having gone to the *Šiḫum* field to bring fresh reeds," 74:'8, 75:26–27

30 g̃uruš gi-zi a-šà pa_5-lugal-$g̃u_{10}$ **tùm-dè** g̃en-na, "30 workmen having gone to bring fresh reeds of the Palugalg̃u field," 148:'19

---

17 Literally, "messengers of *Šu-Kabta* were escorted from Karkar (to bring) barley to Nippur." As Sallaberger 2004 demonstrated, the *ḫamṭu* form of $túm_{3/4}$ was used to bring objects that can move themselves. As such, the messengers here must be the objects of the verb. However, at Garšana commodities such as grain or reeds are being moved as well indicating a wider use for the verb.

18 No. 138:40 has ka-saḫar-ra^{ki}-TA, but this is almost certainly a mistake for -šè.

1.6 Bringing Straw

37 ĝuruš in-u **tùm-dè** ^{d}*šu*-^{d}*suen*-am-ma-ar-ra^{ki}-šè ĝen-na, "37 workmen having gone to *Šu-Suen*-ammara to bring straw," 196:'25-'26, 197:36–37

[. . .] in-u **tùm-d**[**è** ĝen-na], "[. . .having gone] to bring straw," 52:48–49

1.7 Errands for E'igara

1.7.1 Bringing Roof Beams

1 é-ì-gára ĝeš ùr **tùm-dè** ĝen-na, "E'igara having gone to bring roof beams," 51:'18, 52:54–55, 53:56, 54:33–34

1.7.2 Bringing Wool

1 é-ì-gára siki **tùm-dè** é-^{d}*šu*-^{d}*suen*^{ki}-[ta] ĝen-a, "E'igara having gone to bring wool [from] *Bit-Šu-Suen*," 39:46

1 é-ì-gára é-^{d}*šu*-^{d}*suen*^{ki}-ta siki **tùm-dè** ĝen-na, "E'igara having gone to bring wool from *Bit-Šu-Suen*," 40:40–41

1.8 Commodity Broken

[. . .]-da nibru^{ki}-šè ⌜**ba**⌝-**tùm**, "[. . .] brought [. . .] to Nippur," 24:'24

2. In Legal Texts

2.1 To Bring a Tablet

1 (bùr) gána zàr-tab-ba nu-de$_5$-de$_5$-ga dub *šar-ru-um-ì-lí ì-lí-an-dùl* **tùm-dam**, "The (grain) stacked on 1 bur of acreage is not to be collected. *Ili-andul* brought *Šarrum-ili's* tablet," 1398:1–6

2.2 Earth, Brought to Zabala for the Houses of the Gardeners

[*ak-b*]*a-zum* nu-^{ĝeš}kiri$_6$-⌜ke$_4$⌝ má-lugal-na saḫar **tùm-dè** zabala$_4$^{ki}-šè in-la-aḫ saḫar mu-un-de$_9$ ^{ĝeš}kiri$_6$-lugal-na-šè nu-un-ni-ku$_4$ é-ni-šè ba-an-dé ka-ga-na ba-ge-en, "*Akbazum*, the gardener, confirmed that they took a boat of his master to Zabala in order to bring dirt, that he brought the dirt, that it did not enter the royal garden but was brought for his (own) house," 1049:1–10

^{d}ba-ú-da [nu]-^{ĝeš}kiri$_6$-ke$_4$ má-lugal-na saḫar **tùm-dè** zabala$_4$^{ki}-šè in-la-aḫ saḫar mu-un-de$_9$ ^{ĝeš}kiri$_6$-lugal-na nu-un-ni-ku$_4$ é-ni-šè ba-an-dé ka-ga-na ba-ge-en, "Ba'uda, the gardener, confirmed that they took a boat of his master to Zabala in order to bring dirt, that he brought the dirt, that it did not enter the royal garden but was brought for his (own) house," 1050:1–10

tur, *ṣeḫēru*, "(to be) small, young; to reduce"

1. Commodities Subtracted from the Account of the Gardeners

^{d}*adad-tillati* ù-na-a-du$_{11}$ káb du$_{11}$-ga ĝìri *é-a-šar* ^{ĝeš}zé-na ù peš-[múrgu] nu-^{ĝeš}kiri$_6$-ke$_4$-ne na-ba-ab-sum-mu-⌜dè⌝ šà dub-za **ḫa-ba-tur-re**, "Say to *Adad-tillati* that 'the gardeners should not give date palm frond midrib(s) and date palm spine(s), commodities (that were) measured for accounting under the authority of *Ea-šar*. Let it be subtracted in your tablet,'" 1037:1–9

tuš, *wašābu*, "to sit; to dwell; to be idle"

1. **Sitting to Guard**

1.1 Boats

1 g̃uruš má en-nu ke_4-dè **tuš-a**, "1 workman having sat to guard a boat," 26:'20

1.2 Bricks

n g̃uruš $šeg_{12}$ en-nu ke_4-dè **tuš-a**, "n workmen having sat in order to guard bricks," 28:'24, 31:34, 32:34, 33:37, 58:60, 59:50, 65:'24

1.3 Grain

[1 *a*]-*lí-a*[*ḫ* 1 *ta-tù*]-⸢*ri*⸣ še šà [g̃ír]-su[ki] en-nu k[e_4-dè] **tuš-[a]**, "*Ali-aḫ* (and) *Tatturi* having sat [in order to] guard grain in G̃irsu," 56:'29-'31

1.4 Straw

1 g̃uruš in-u [ka] i_7-è-šè e[n-n]u aka **tuš-a**, "1 workman having sat at [the opening of] the 'Outgoing' canal having guarded straw," 194:56–57

1.5 Broken Contents

[. . .]-x-a x DU? ka [. . .] en-nu-g̃á aka [**tuš**]-**a**, 197:34

2. **Sitting (Idle)**

2.1 At the *agarinnum*

1 g̃uruš šidim 2 g̃uruš šu dím-ma 3 g̃uruš im ga_6-g̃á 2 g̃uruš im a-ga-ri-in-na **tuš-a** 1 g̃uruš a bal-a al-tar é-*ì-lí*<-*bi*?>-*šu*, "1 builder (and) 2 workmen having built, 3 workmen having carried earth, 2 workmen having sat (idle) at the *agarinnum* (and) 1 workman having poured water (for) construction of the house of *Ili-bišu*," 202:24–29

2.2 At the Gate of the Craftsmen's House

n g̃uruš ká é-gašam **tuš-a,** "n workmen having sat (idle) at the gate of the craftsmen's house," 71:31, 74:'10, 75:30

2.3 At the Storehouse

1 g̃uruš g̃á-nun-na **tuš-a**, "1 workman having sat (idle) at the storehouse," 27:'17, 28:'28, 29:'32, 31:35, 32:35, 33:38, 35:42, 36:36, 37:30, 38:35, 39:42, 40:36, 43:'40, 44:39, 45:21, 46:37, 47:51, 48:56, 49:55, 50:'15, 52:51, 57:'25-'26, 58:61, 59:51, 60:47, 65:'25, 74:'11, 75:29

2.4 Because of Rain in Gu-saḫar.DU

1 g̃uruš túg-d[u_8 u_4-1-šè] šà [gú-saḫar[ha]]⸢r⸣.DU[ki] **tuš**-[a šà] a im še-g̃á, "1 braider for 1 day having sat (idle) in Gu-saḫar.DU because of rain," 298:9–10

3 g̃uruš ašgab u_4-2-šè šà gú-saḫar[har].DU[ki] **tuš-a** šà a im še-g̃á, "3 leather workers for 2 days having sat (idle) in Gu-saḫar.DU because of rain," 299:9–10

– U –

ù-ru (< **ùr**), *sapānu*, "to level; to saturate/soak (with bitumen); to manufacture (bricks)"

peš ésir ù-ru, "to soak palmleaflet (mats) with bitumen"

$šeg_{12}$-al-ur_x-ra ù-ru, 'to manufacture bricks"

1. To Level

1.1 The iz-zi Wall in the House

6 g̃uruš šidim iz-zi šà é-a **ù-[ru-dè]**, "6 builders [to] level the iz-zi wall in the house," 184:15–16

n g̃uruš šidim n g̃uruš (sumur) iz-zi šà é-a **ù-ru-dè** gub-ba, "n builder(s) (and) n workmen employed to level the (plastered) iz-zi wall in the house," 183:12–14, 189:20–22

n g̃uruš šidim n g̃uruš sumur iz-zi šà é-a **ù-ru-dè**, "n builder(s) (and) n workmen to level the plastered iz-zi wall in the house," 187:17–19, 188:'14-'16, 193:23–25

1.2 The Wall in the Potter's House

*See *Household Index* for the complete context of the following passage.

3 [g̃uruš šidim] sumur iz-zi šà [é-a **ù-ru-dè**] (. . .) é-báḫar dù-a, "3 [builders having leveled] the plastered iz-zi wall in [the house] (. . .), (workers) having constructed the potter's house," 190:22–23, 27

2. **peš ésir ù-ru**, "to soak palmleaflet (mats) with bitumen"

n g̃uruš **peš ésir ù-ru-dè**, "n workmen having soaked palmleaflet (mats) with bitumen," 136:42, 140:44, 141:39, 142:35, 145:42, 146:'45, 147:48, 150:45

3. **$šeg_{12}$ al-ur_x-ra ú-ru**, "to manufacture bricks"

n g̃uruš **$šeg_{12}$-al-ur_x-ra ù-ru**, "n workmen having manufactured bricks," 111:41, 114:46, 117:33, 121:35

úgu . . . dé, *halāqu*, "to disappear, to be lost"

1. Lost Birds and Mice

5 tu-$gur_4^{mušen}$ 31 péš-igi-gùn **úgu dé-a** *da-da-a* sipa-mušen-⌜na⌝ íb-su-su, "*Dada'a*, the bird warden, will replace 5 lost doves (and) 31 lost striped-eyed mice," 1138:1–4

23 péš-i[gi-gùn] **úgu dé-a** *da-da-a* sipa-mušen-na íb-su-su, "*Dada'a*, the bird warden, will replace 23 lost striped-eyed mice," 1152:1–3

3 uz-tur 7 $tum_{12}^{mušen}$ 4 tu-$gur_4^{mušen}$ 15 péš-g̃eš-gi 23 péš-igi-gùn **úgu d[é-a]** *da-da-a* sipa-mušen-na, "3 ducklings, 7 wild doves, 4 doves, 15 mice (and) 23 striped-eyed mice—lost (animals) of *Dada'a*, the bird warden," 1172:1–7

ús, *redûm*, "to process"

dabin **al-ús-sa**, "processed semolina" > **dabin**

é-ùr ku_6 **al-ús-sa**, "fish-sauce roof house" > *Household Index*

gú-gal **al-ús-sa**, "processed beans" > **gú-gal**

gú-tur **al-ús-sa**, "processed peas" > **gú-tur**

ku$_6$ **al-ús-sa**, "fish-sauce" > **ku$_6$**

má ús, "to process a boat"

še ús, "to process barley"

še-lú **al-ús-sa**, "crushed coriander" > **še-lú**

šim-sig$_5$ **al-ús-sa**, "crushed fine aromatics" > **šim**

zíz ús, "to process emmer wheat"

1. **má ús**, "to process a boat"

   1 g̃uruš u$_4$-11-šè **má ú-sa** unug^{ki}-ta gar-ša-an-na$^{<ki>}$-šè má gíd-da, "1 workmen for 11 days having towed a processed boat from Uruk to Garšana," 272:5–7

2. **še ús**, "to process barley"

   2 géme u$_4$-1-šè **še** 3-sìla **⸢ús⸣-sa**-šè ⸢níg̃⸣-àr-ra àr-ra-dè ús-sa, "2 workwomen for 1 day, 3 liters of barley for processing, (the women) having processed (the barley) in order to grind groats," 434:1–2

3. **zíz ús**, "to process emmer wheat"

   n g̃uruš **zíz ús-sa** nag̃a$_4$-dè gub-ba, "n workmen employed to grind processed emmer wheat," 92:15, 110:33

   n g̃uruš **zíz ús-sa**, "n workmen having processed emmer wheat," 111:40, 114:45, 115:'23, 118:25, 121:34, 123:40

ús, *diāšu*; *redû*; *šadādu*, "to drag; to stretch; to accompany, follow; flank, (long) side"

ús-bi, "carrying (distance of bricks or earth)"

ús-sa i$_7$-*a-ga-mu-um*, "along the *Agamum* canal" > *Canal Index*

1. **Carrying Distance of Bricks**

1.1 **Simple with Full Context**

šu+níg̃in n sar n gín šeg$_{12}$ **ús-bi** n nindan, "In total: n sar (and) n gín of bricks, the distance (carried) is n nindan"

[šu+níg̃in] 16 sar 2½ gín šeg$_{12}$ **ús-bi** 72 nindan á-géme 150-šeg$_{12}$-ta géme-bi 77 u$_4$-1-šè še 3-sìla-ta ba-ḫug̃ še-bi 0.3.5.1 sìla [4 gín] mu-DU bàd-šè *simat-é-a* ugula lú-ḫug̃-g̃á g̃iri ^{d}*adad-tillati* šabra ù *puzur$_4$*-^{d}nin-kar-ak dub-sar, "In total: 16 sar (and) 2½ gín of bricks, the distance (carried) is 72 nindan, workwomen wages for each 150 bricks, its workwomen (equal) 77 workerdays, hired (for) 3 liters of barley each. Their barley is 231 liters (and) 4 shekels. Delivery (of bricks) by *Simat-Ea*, overseer of hired workers, for the (enclosure) wall under the authority of *Adad-tillati*, the majordomo, and *Puzur-*Ninkarak, the scribe," 308:41–51

1.1.1 **Related References**

šu+níg̃in n sar (n gín) šeg$_{12}$ **ús-bi** n nindan, "In total: n sar (and n gín) of bricks, the distance (carried) is n nindan," 310:'11-'12, 312:28–29, 313:17–18, 316:65–66, 321:'26-'27, 322:'77-'78, 323:117–118, 324:87–88, 325:11–12, 327:75–76, 330:20–21, 334:58–59, 336:36–37, 337:23–24, 338:15–16, 339:6–7, 340:26–27, 341:6–7, 342:70–71, 342:74–75, 343:4–5, 344:'18-'19, 346:120–121, 347:'10-'11, 351:132–133, 352:32–33, 361:'7-'8, 364:'27-'28, 367:114–115, 368:'53-'54, 369:'21-'22, 373:'5-'6

1.1.2 Variants

šu+níĝin n sar-ta **ús-bi** n nindan, "In total: n sar (of bricks) each, the distance (carried) is n nindan," 311:14–15, 353:10–11

šu+níĝin n sar (n gín) **ús-bi** n nindan, "In total: n sar (and n gín of bricks), the distance (carried) is n nindan ," 328:7–8

šu+níĝin n sar šeg$_{12}$ sumun **ús-bi** n nindan, "In total: n sar of old bricks, the distance (carried) is n nindan," 335:34–35

n sar šeg$_{12}$ **ús-bi** n nindan, "n sar of bricks, the distance (carried) is n nindan," 336:17–18, 336:23–24

2. Carrying Distance of Dirt

2.1 Sample Text with Full Context

šu+níĝin n sar (n gín) **ús-bi** n nindan, "In total: n sar (and n gín), the distance carried is n nindan"

šu+níĝin 9½ sar 4 gín igi-6-ĝál **ús-bi** 30 nindan á-ĝuruš-a 6 gín-ta ĝuruš-bi 95⅔ 1⅔ gín u$_4$-1-šè še 6 sìla-ta ba-ḫuĝ še-bi 1.4.3.4 sìla 10 gín gur saḫar zi-ga tùn-[lá] da bàd sè-ga á ^{tumu}mer mu-DU *ba-zi* ugula lú-ḫuĝ-ĝá ĝìri ^{d}*adad-tillati* šabra ù *puzur*$_4$-^{d}nin-kar-ak dub-sar, "In total: 9½ sar (and) 4⅙ gín, the distance carried is 30 nindan, workmen wages at 6 gín each, its workmen (equal) 95⅔ (and) 1⅔ gín workerdays, hired (for) 6 liters of barley each. Their barley is 1 bushel, 274 liters (and) 10 shekels. Dirt removed via a tùn-lá device, tamped at the north side of the (enclosure) wall. Delivery (of dirt) by *Bazi*, overseer of hired workers, under the authority of *Adad-tillati*, the majordomo, and *Puzur*-Ninkarak, the scribe," 331:28–38

2.1.1 Related References and Variants

1 sar **ús-bi** 30 nindan, "1 sar (of dirt), the distance carried is 30 nindan," 333:15–16

n sar (n gín n še) saḫar **ús-bi** n nindan, "n sar (and n gín and n še) of dirt, the distance carried is n nindan," 355:1–2, 363:'24-'26

3. Distance Measurements

gú i$_7$-me-kal-kal-ta 1 da-na 1200 nindan **ús** bàd-^{d}šul-gi-šè, "1 da-na (and) 1200 nindan, the length from the bank of the Mekalkal canal to Bad-Šulgi," 1382:1–3

bàd-^{d}šul-gi-ta 1200 nindan **ús** é-lugal-eden-na-šè, "1200 nindan, the length from Bad-Šulgi to the E-lugal-edena," 1382:4–6

é-lugal-eden-na-ta 1200 nindan **ús** gú i$_7$-*ì-diš$_x$-tum*-šè, "1200 nindan, the length from E-lugal-edena to the bank of the *Idištum* canal," 1382:7–9

i$_7$-*ì-diš$_x$-tum*-ta 360 [nindan **ú**]**s** ká-^{d}*šu*-^{d}*suen*-šè, "360 nindan, the length from the *Idištum* canal measured to the *Šu-Suen* gate," 1382:12–10

šu+níĝin 3 ⌜da⌝-n[a 240+]120 nindan **ús** gú i$_7$-me-kal-kal *simat-é-a* a-da-ga-ta ká-^{d}*šu*-^{d}*suen*-šè, "In total: 3 da-na (and) 360 nindan, the length from the bank of the Mekalkal canal of *Simat-Ea* (and its) irrigation ditch to the *Šu-Suen* gate," 1382:14–16

4. The Length of a Journey

1 ĝuruš túg-du$_8$ u$_4$-12-šè du$_6$-saḫar-ra^{ki}-ta en-zu-bábbar^{ki}-šè [. . .] íb-ga$_6$ [**ús-b**]**i** 1500 éš kaskal š[u+níĝin]-na-bi, "1 braider for 12 days carried [. . .] from Du-saḫara to Enzu-babbar. Its distance: 1500 ropes is the entire trip," 263:1–6

(. . .) [u$_4$]-3-šè [še x] x x x an-za-qar-ta kun-zi-da i$_7$-a-kàr-ús-sa a-šà-lú-maḫ-šè íb-ga$_6$ ù má-a si-ga ⸢**ús**⸣**-bi** 36 nindan [ku]n-zi-da an-za-qar-ta [GN-šè] má še gíd-[da . . .] **ús-bi** 290 [nindan], "{workers and boats} for 3 [days], (the boats) carried [barley . . .] from the fortified tower to the weir of the Agar-usa Canal of the Lu-maḫ field and (the workers) having loaded the boats. Its distance is 36 nindan from the weir of the fortified tower [to GN], boats of barley having been towed a distance of 290 [nindan]," 553: 11–20

úš(TIL), *mâtu*, "to die, to slaughter"

1. Dead Individuals

u$_4$ lugal-e **ba-úš-a**, "when the king died" > **lugal**

u$_4$ PN **ba-úš-a**, "when PN died" > *Personal Name Index*

šu-kab-tá ^{d}šul-gi-*ra-ma* *na-wi-ir-ilum*

2. Slaughtered Animals

2.1 For the House of the Steward

2 ir$_7^{mušen}$ u$_4$-20-kam 2 ir$_7^{mušen}$ u$_4$-10-kam **[ba]-úš** é-⸢agrig⸣-šè, "2 pigeons on the 20th day (and) 2 pigeons on the 10th day were slaughtered for the house of the steward," 522:1–5

1 [x^{mušen}] 1 ir$_7^{mušen}$ u$_4$-20-kam 2 ir$_7^{mušen}$ 5 tu-gur$_4^{mušen}$ u$_4$-25-kam 1 ir$_7^{mušen}$ 1 tum$_{12}^{mušen}$ 5 tu-gur$_4^{mušen}$ [2 péš]-g̃eš-⸢gi⸣ u$_4$-28-kam **ba-úš** é-agrig-šè, "1 [bird] (and) 1 pigeon on the 20th day, 2 pigeons (and) 5 doves on the 25th day (and) 1 pigeon, 1 wild dove, 5 doves (and) 2 mice on the 28th day were slaughtered for the house of the steward," 526:1–12

2.2 For the Warehouse

★★4 ⸢máš⸣ 4 u$_8$ [n] ud$_5$ [n] máš-gal **ba-úš** bi+šu-ab-ta? ^{d}inana-zabala$_4^{ki}$ u$_4$-1-šè é-šu-^{d}E[N.Z]U 32 udu 1 ud$_5$ **b[a-úš]** é-kišib-ba-šè, "4 goats, 4 ewes, [n] female goat(s), [n] billy-goat(s) were slaughtered (?) (for) Inana of Zabala for one day (in) *Bit-Šu-Suen*, (and) 32 sheep (and) 1 female goat were slaughtered for the warehouse," 1019:1–10

1 uz-tur 1 péš-g̃eš-gi iti u$_4$-28-ba-zal **ba-úš** é-kišib-ba-šè, "1 duckling (and) 1 mouse were slaughtered at the end of the 28th day of the month for the warehouse," 1104:1–4

1 uz-tur iti u$_4$-22-ba-zal **ba-úš** é-kišib-ba-šè, "1 fattened duckling was slaughtered at the end of the 22nd day of the month for the warehouse," 1112:1–3

1 uz-t[ur] iti u$_4$-11-ba-zal 1 uz-tur iti u$_4$-13?-ba-zal 1 uz-tur iti u$_4$-20-ba-zal 1 uz-tur [iti u$_4$-2]8-ba-zal **[ba-úš** é]-kišib-ba-[šè], "1 duckling at the end of the 11th day of the month, 1 duckling at the end of the 13th? day of the month, 1 duckling at the end of the 20th day of the month (and) 1 duckling at the end of the 28th day of [the month] were [slaughtered for] the warehouse," 1176:1–9

1 ⸢mušen⸣-tur u$_4$-24-kam 1 ⸢mušen⸣-tur u$_4$-30-kam **ba-úš** é-kišib-ba-šè, "1 young bird on the 24th day and 1 young bird on the 30th day were slaughtered for the warehouse," 1183:1–5

1 uz-tur u$_4$-14-kam 5 uz-tur u$_4$-27-kam 4 tu-gur$_4^{mušen}$ 2 péš-g̃eš-gi 2 péš-igi-gùn u$_4$-30-kam **ba-úš** é-kišib-ba-šè, "1 duckling on the 14th day, 5 ducklings on the 27th day, 4 doves, 2 mice (and) 2 striped-eyed mice on the 30th day were slaughtered for the warehouse," 1254:'27-'33

2.3 Provisions for Builders

2 uz-tur 1 ir$_7^{\text{mušen}}$ **ba-úš** šà-gal šidim-e-ne, "2 ducklings (and) 1 pigeon were slaughtered, food (for) builders," 470:1–4

10 ádda-udu 1 uz-tur 3 péš-g̃eš-gi **ba-úš** iti u$_4$-8-ba-zal šà-gal šidim-e-ne (. . .) ⸢u$_4$⸣ é-e im sumur ba-aka, "10 sheep carcasses, 1 duckling (and) 3 mice were slaughtered at the end of the 8th day of the month, food (for) builders (and) {other commodities} when the house was plastered," 472:3–7, 14

2.4 For the Workers

1 udu-niga-gu$_4$-e-ús-sa 1 ud$_5$ 1 máš **ba-úš** mu éren-na-šè, "1 fattened sheep '(fed) following the oxen', 1 female goat (and) 1 (male) goat were slaughtered for the workers," 1025:23–26

2.5 Purpose / Destination Unspecified

2.5.1 Birds

1 tum$_{12}^{\text{mušen}}$ 2 tu-gur$_4^{\text{mušen}}$ **ba-úš** mušen-bi ki záḫ ì-g̃ál, "1 wild dove and 2 doves, slaughtered birds that had escaped (previously)," 1058:1–4

2.5.2 Sheep

n udu **ba-úš**, "n dead sheep," 1025:8, 1142:1–2

2.5.3 Sheep and Lambs

1 udu 1 sila$_4$ **ba-úš**, "1 dead sheep (and) 1 dead lamb," 1095:1–3

2.5.4 Sinews of Dead Animals

14 gín sa-udu udu **ba-úš**-ta, "14 shekels of sheep sinew from each dead sheep," 1091:1–2

2.5.5 Skins of Dead Animals

kuš-sila$_4$ kuš-udu <ba->úš, "lamb skin, skin of a dead caprid," 843:1–2

kuš-udu **ba-úš**, "skin of a dead caprids," 844:4, 852:3, 894:1, 956:1

kuš-udu-niga **ba-úš**, "skin of a dead fattened sheep," 850:1, 854:1

– Z –

záḫ, *ḫalāqu*, "to disappear, (to be) lost"

g̃uruš **zàḫ**, "runaway workman" > **zàḫ** (in glossary)

1. Lost Birds

1 tum$_{12}^{\text{mušen}}$ 2 tu-gur$_4^{\text{mušen}}$ ba-úš mušen-bi ki **záḫ** ì-g̃ál, "1 wild dove and 2 doves, slaughtered birds that had escaped (previously)," 1058:1–4

zal, *qatû*, "to come to an end"

iti ba-zal, "the end of the month"

iti u$_4$-n-ba-zal, "the end of the nth day of the month"

1. iti ba-zal, "the end of the month"

1.1 Assets Available at the End of the Month

5[0 ud]u-máš ḫi-a gub-ba [é-š]u-sum-ma g̃ìri *a-ḫu*-[x] dub-sar **iti** dirig ezem-me-ki-g̃ál **ba-zal** mu ^{d}i-bí-^{d}suen lugal, "(In total): 50 various sheep (and) goats present in the storehouse under the authority of *Aḫu*-[x], the scribe, at the end of the 13th month of *Ibbi-Suen* year 1," 984:5–9

(. . .) šu-sum-ma g̃ìri *ib-ni-^{d}adad* d[ub-sar] **iti** ezem-me-ki-g̃ál **ba-zal** mu en-^{d}inana-unu^{ki}-ga máš-e ì-pàd, "{millstones, diorite stones, woods, yokes, and wooden containers}, the consignment under the authority of *Ibni-Adad*, the scribe, at the end of the 12th month of *Ibbi-Suen* Year 2," 1372:46–49

2. iti u$_4$-n-ba-zal, "the end of the nth day of the month"

2.1 Disbursal of Animals at the End of the Day

2.1.1 For the Builders

1 udu-[niga] **iti u$_4$-10-ba-zal** [lú-níg̃-^{d}]ba-ú šidim, "1 [fattened] sheep at the end of the 10th day of the month (for) the builder from Nig̃-Ba'u," 420:1–3

10 ádda-udu 1 uz-tur 3 péš-g̃eš-gi ba-úš **iti u$_4$-8-ba-zal** šà-gal šidim-e-ne (. . .) ⌜u$_4$⌝ é-e im sumur ba-aka, "10 sheep carcasses, 1 duckling (and) 3 mice were slaughtered at the end of the 8th day of the month, food (for) builders (and) {other commodities} when the house was plastered," 472:3–7, 14

2.1.2 For Deities

[n] udu-niga gu$_4$-e-ús-[sa] **iti u$_4$-17-ba-[zal]** (. . .) šà kisal-lá-^{d}inana-za[bala$_4$^{ki}], "[n] fattened sheep '(fed) following the oxen' at the end of the 17th day of the month (and) {other commodities} in the courtyard of the temple of Inana of Zabala," 506:3–4, 9

1 udu-niga gu$_4$-e-ús-[sa] ^{d}nin-^{d}si$_4$-an-na šà [é]-⌜gal⌝ **iti u$_4$-6-ba-zal**, "1 fattened sheep '(fed) following the oxen' (for) Nin-Siana in the palace at the end of the 6th day of the month," 970:7–9

1 udu-niga é-u$_4$-7 **iti u$_4$-[7]-ba-zal** 1 ⌜udu⌝-niga é-[u$_4$]-10 **iti u$_4$-10-⌜ba⌝-zal** sá-du$_{11}$-ku$_5$-rá ^{d}nin-^{d}si$_4$-an-na, "1 fattened sheep at the end of the [7th] day of the month, i.e. the half-moon day, 1 fattened sheep at the end of the 10th day of the month, i.e. the 3/4 moon day, deducted regular offerings of Nin-Siana," 985:1–6

1 udu-⌜niga⌝ **iti u$_4$-11-ba-zal** 0.0.2. zì-KAL 5 sìla dabin 5 sìla eša ^{d}šára ezem-níg̃-ab-e, "1 fattened sheep at the end of the 11th day of the month, 20 liters of KAL-flour, 5 liters of semolina (and) 5 liters of fine flour (for) Šara (during) the níg̃-ab-e festival," 1001:1–7

2.1.3 For Regular Offerings of *Šu-Kabta*

1 šáḫ-zé-da **iti u$_4$-1-ba-zal** 1 máš-gal-niga **iti u$_4$-10-ba-zal** 1 šáḫ-zé-da iti **u$_4$-15-ba-zal** 1 udu-aslum$_x$-niga-babbar **iti u$_4$-20-ba-zal** 1 udu-niga-babbar **iti u$_4$-28-ba-zal** sá-du$_{11}$-ki-a-nag-*šu*-[*kab*]-*tá*, "1 piglet at the end of the 1st day of the month, 1 fattened billy-goat at the end of the 10th day of the month, 1 piglet at the end of the 15th day of the month, 1 fattened white long-fleeced sheep at the end of the 20th day of the month (and) 1 fattened white sheep at the end of the 28th day of the month, regular offerings of the funerary libation place of *Šu-Kabta*," 973:1–8

[1 udu-niga **iti u$_4$-n]-ba-[zal** 1 udu-ú **iti u$_4$-n]-ba-[zal]** 1 [máš-gal-niga] **iti u$_4$-[n-ba-zal . . .] iti u$_4$-[n-ba-zal]** 1 lulim?-[gùn(DAR)?-x] **iti u$_4$-[n-ba-zal]** 1 šá[ḫ-zé-da] iti u_4-[n-ba-**zal**] 1[. . .] iti u_4-[n-ba-**zal** n . . . iti u_4-ba-**zal**] (. . .) sá-du_{11}-ta?-*šu-kab-tá*, "[1 fattened sheep at the end of the nth day of the month 1 range fed sheep at the end of the nth day of the month], 1 [fattened billy-goat at the end of the nth] day of the month, [. . . at the end of the nth] day of the month, 1 [speckled?] stag [at the end of the nth] day of the month, 1 pig[let at the end of the nth] day of the month, 1 [. . . at the end of the nth] day of the month [(and) n . . . at the end of the nth day of the month]; {totals of animals}, regular offerings of *Šu-Kabta*," 983:1–16, 24

2.1.4 For the Warehouse: Birds

1 uz-tur 1 péš-g̃eš-gi **iti u_4-28-ba-zal** ba-úš é-kìšib-ba-šè, "1 duckling (and) 1 mouse were slaughtered for the warehouse at the end of the 28th day of the month," 1104:1–4

1 uz-tur **iti u_4-22-ba-zal** ba-úš é-kìšib-ba-šè, "1 fattened duckling was slaughtered at the end of the 22nd day of the month for the warehouse," 1112:1–3

1 uz-⸢tur⸣ **iti u_4-11-ba-zal** 1 uz-tur **iti u_4-13?-ba-zal** 1 uz-tur **iti u_4-20-ba-zal** 1 uz-tur [**iti u_4-2**]**8-ba-zal** [ba-úš é]-kìšib-ba-[šè], "1 duckling at the end of the 11th day of the month, 1 duckling at the end of the 13th? day of the month, 1 duckling at the end of the 20th day of the month (and) 1 duckling at the end of the 28th day of [the month were slaughtered for] the warehouse," 1176:1–9

2.1.5 Purpose Unspecified

2.1.5.1 Assorted Caprids

1 gukkal 3 u_8-gukkal 4 $sila_4$-gukkal 2 kir_{11}-gukkal 2 máš-gal 3 ud_5 **iti u_4-15-ba-zal**, "1 fat-tailed sheep, 3 fat-tailed ewes, 4 fat-tailed lambs, 2 fat-tailed female lambs, 2 billy-goats (and) 3 goats at the end of the 15th day of the month," 1154:1–7

2.1.5.2 Birds and Mice

2 $ir_7^{mušen}$ **iti u_4-7-ba-zal**, "2 pigeons at the end of the 7th day of the month," 1126:1–2

2 ⸢kur⸣-$gi^{mušen}$ 3 uz-tur 6 péš-g̃eš-gi *e-sí-tum* 15 péš-igi-gùn ⸢*lú*⸣*-ša-lim* **iti u_4-13-ba-zal**, "2 geese, 3 ducklings (and) 6 mice (from) *Esitum* (and) 15 striped-eyed mice (from) *Lušallim*, at the end of the 13th day of the month," 1127:1–7

4? péš-g̃eš-gi **iti u_4-22-ba-zal**, "4? mice at the end of the 22nd day of the month," 1170:1–2

2.1.5.3 Oxen

2 gu_4-niga **iti u_4-5-ba-zal**, "2 fattened oxen at the end of the 5th day of the month," 1125:1–2

2.1.5.4 Sheep

2 udu-⸢niga⸣ **iti u_4-27-ba-zal**, "2 fattened sheep at the end of the 27th day of the month," 449:1–2

[1]4 udu-niga [n?+]4 udu-ú **iti u_4-12-ba-zal**, "[1]4 fattened sheep (and) [n?+]4 range fed sheep at the end of the 12th day of the month," 1067:1–3

1 udu-niga **iti** $\mathbf{u_4}$**-5-ba-zal**, "1 fattened sheep at the end of the 5th day of the month," 1159:1–2

2.2 Disbursal of Grains at the End of the Day

[n] dabin [. . .] **[iti]** $\mathbf{u_4}$**-[n-ba-z]al** (. . .) šà kisal-lá-^{d}inana-za[bala$_4^{ki}$], "[n (units)] semolina at the end of the [nth day of the month] (and) {other commodities} in the courtyard of the temple of Inana of Zabala," 506:1–2, 9

iti $\mathbf{u_4}$**-29-ba-zal** še nu-g̃ál bí-in-gi$_4$ u$_4$-1-àm mu-[un-g̃ál] še šabra in-na-an-sum šu te-g̃e$_6$-dè nu-un-dab$_5$?, "At the end of the 29th day of the month there was no barley. (Someone) returned it. On the 1st day, it was there. (Then) the barley was given to the majordomo. In order for him to receive it, it will not (first) be taken (by someone else)," 1057:1–7

3. Broken Context

[. . .] é-gul **⸢iti⸣** $\mathbf{u_4}$**-18 ba-zal** (. . .) sá-du$_{11}$-dig̃ir-re-e-ne, "[. . .] the demolished house at the end of the 18th day of the month, {assorted comestibles}, regular offerings of the gods," 1036:'1-'4, '78

zi, *baqāmu*; *barāšu*; *naṭāpu*; *nasāḫu*, "to cut, remove, erase"

NE-gu$_7$-bi zi, "to deduct damaged (bricks)"

NE-gu$_7$-bi nu-zi, "damaged bricks not deducted"

1. NE-gu$_7$-bi zi, "to deduct damaged (bricks)"

73⅓ sar šeg$_{12}$ **NE-gu$_7$-bi íb-ta-zi**, "73⅓ sar of bricks, the damaged bricks were deducted," 315:1–2

šu+nígin 7.4.0. š[e gur] šà-bi-⸢ta⸣ 124⅔ sar [šeg$_{12}$] **NE-gu$_7$-bi í[b-ta-zi]**, "In total: 7 bushels (and) 240 liters of barley. From among it 124⅔ sar of damaged [bricks] were deducted," 496:5–9

2. NE-gu$_7$-bi nu-zi, "damaged bricks not deducted"

113 sar 16 gín šeg$_{12}$ **NE-gu$_7$-bi nu-zi** [. . .]-IR?–2-kam [x]-da, "113 sar (and) 16 shekels of bricks, damaged bricks not deducted [. . .]," 360:1–4

2.1 Count of Bricks in the Brickyard

37⅔ sar 4-gín igi-4-g̃ál šeg$_{12}$ u$_4$-1-kam 37 sar 1 gín šeg$_{12}$ u$_4$-2-kam **⸢NE⸣-gu$_7$-bi nu-ub-ta-zi** šeg$_{12}$ šid-da g̃á šub-ba g̃á-g̃ál, "37⅔ sar (and) 4¼ gín of bricks for 1 day, 37 sar (and) 1 gín of bricks for 2 days, the damaged bricks were not deducted; the count of bricks took place in the brickyard," 357:1–7

270 sar 13 gín šeg$_{12}$ ús-⸢sa⸣ i$_7$-*a*-⸢*ga*⸣-*mu-um* 60 sar 13 gín šeg$_{12}$ é-^{d}[x]-SAḪAR [NE?]-gu$_7$-bi ù PA **[NE-gu$_7$]-bi nu-zi** [šid-d]a šà g̃á šub-ba, "270 sar (and) 13 gín of bricks along the *Agamum* canal, 60 sar (and) 13 gín of bricks of the temple of [DN], damaged bricks and damaged (?) not deducted; the count (of bricks) in the brickyard," 358:1–7

188 sar 10 gín šeg$_{12}$ **NE-gu$_7$-bi nu-zi** šid-da šà g̃á šub-ba (. . .) ús-sa i$_7$-*a-ga-mu-um*, "188 sar (and) 10 gín of bricks along the *Agamum* canal, damaged bricks not deducted; the count (of bricks) in the brickyard," 359:1–3, 5

zi(g), *nasāḫu*, "to expend, disburse"

ki PN-ta ba-zi, "disbursed by PN"

PN zi-ga, "expenditure of PN"

saḫar zi(g), "to (re)move dirt"

zi-ga-àm, "expended," *passim* (in worker inspection texts)

1. **ki PN-ta ba-zi,** "disbursed by PN" > *Personal Name Index*

a-a-kal-la
a-da-làl
a-ḫu-wa-qar
a-lim-ma
a-ma-a
a-na-aḫ-ì-lí
a$_{(2)}$*-wi-lum-ma*
^{d}*adad*-SIG$_5$
^{d}*adad-tillati*
aš-tá-qar
ba-la-a
é-a-šar
èr-ra-ba-ni
ḫa-lí
i-dì-èr-ra
i-din-^{d}*adad*
i-din-^{d}*suen*
i-ṣur-^{d}*suen*
ì-lí-a-núm
ì-lí-an-dùl
ì-lí-aš-ra-ni
ì-lí-bi-la-ni
ì-lí-uz-ra-ni
išdum-ki-in
^{d}iškur-SIG5
ki-ùr-re-en
la-ša?-[x]
lú-^{d}nana
ma-lik-ba-ni
pu-šu-ki-in
puzur$_4$*-a-gu*$_5$*-um*
puzur$_4$-^{d}en-líl
si-mu
šar-ru-um-ba-ni
šu-^{d}*adad*
šu-èr-ra
šu-ì-lí
šu-ì-lí-su
šu-^{d}*šamaš*
^{d}šul-gi-*wa-qar*
ud-du-ur
ur-mes
ur-ni$_9$-g̃ar
za-bu-la
za-la-a

1.1 Disbursals, Name of Responsible Party Unspecified

1.1.1 Beer

[n] ^{dug}níg̃ 2-sìla-ta kaš-[x?]-šè *ta-ḫu-lam* maškim **ba-zi**, "[n] pot(s) of 2 liters each were disbursed for [x?] beer. *Tahulam* was the deputy official," 1330:1–5

1.1.2 Bran

[. . .] NE-x[. . . n] dida$_x$-g[en . . . x]-ki-ri?-šè šà é-duru$_5$-^{d}b[a?-ú? (x)] tuḫ-bi **ba-zi, "[. . . n (liters?) . . .] ordinary dida beer for (?) in the B[a'u?] village, its bran was disbursed," 1009:18–21

1.1.3 Skins

1 udu-niga kuš-bi **ba-zi**, "the skin of 1 fattened sheep was disbursed," 1027:1

1 udu-niga gu$_4$-e-ús-sa kuš-[bi] **ba-zi**, "1 fattened sheep '(fed) following the oxen', its skin was disbursed," 1027:2

1 sila$_4$ kuš-bi **ba-zi**, "the skin of 1 lamb was disbursed," 1028:38

1.1.4 Workmen

1 g̃uruš šidim 15 g̃uruš u$_4$ *e-lu-núm-*^{d}n[è-eri$_{11}$-gal] šà iri^{ki} **ba-zi**, "1 builder (and) 15 workmen disbursed during the *Elunum* festival of Nergal in the city," 19:14–16

2. PN **zi-ga**, "expenditure of PN" > *Personal Name Index*

simat-^{d}*ištaran*
šu-kab-ta
⸢*šu*⸣?*-x-ki?-ra?-ta?-ni?*
tá-ki-il-ì-lí-ís-sú

2.1 Expenditures of Assorted Commodities

[. . . **zi**]**-ga** é-$^{g̃eš}$gu-za *šu-kab-tá*-me-šè, "{assorted commodities} expended for the house of the chair of *Šu-Kabta*," 562:'76

2.1.1 Barley

šu+níg̃in+ba 2.0.3.7½ sìla še gur **zi-ga-àm** 0.0.3.2½ sìla še ⸢*si*⸣*-ì-tum* níg̃-kas$_7$-aka *šu-*^{d}dumu-zi ugula lú-ḫug̃-g̃á, "In total: 2 bushels and 37½ liters of barley was expended. 32½ liters of barley is the remainder, the balanced account of *Šu-Dumuzi*, overseer of hired workers," 336:50–56

2.1.2 Beer

0.0.1. kaš-gen ugula àg[a-ús-e-ne] á-[u$_4$]-te-⸢na⸣ **zi-[ga]**, "10 liters of ordinary beer (for) the overseer of the gendarmes, expended in the evening," 550:'5-'6

0.1.1.7$\frac{5}{6}$ sìla še 9 sìla tuḫ-duru$_5$-sig$_5$ 0.0.4.2 sìla tuḫ-a-ĝen lá-ìa kaš **zi-ga** ezem-*a-bu-um šu-la-núm* munu$_4$-mú in-da-ĝál, "77$\frac{5}{6}$ liters of barley, 9 liters of fine fresh bran (and) 42 liters of ordinary fresh bran, the deficit from the beer expended (for) the *Abum* festival, is with *Šulanum*, the maltster," 1047:1–7

2.1.3 Bread from *Da'a*'s Balanced Account

[šu+níĝin n.]1.0.6 sìla ninda gur **[zi-ga]-àm** [šu+níĝin] 9½ sìla **[zi-ga]-àm** níĝ-kas$_7$-aka *da-a-a* muḫaldim, "[In total: n] bushel(s) (and) 66 liters of bread were expended; [in total] 9½ liters were expended; the balanced account of *Da'a* the cook," 1031:20–26

2.1.4 Craftsmen for the Banquet

2 ĝuruš ^{lú}ašláĝ u$_4$-1-šè **zi-ga** kaš-dé-a lugal šà á-<ki->ti gub-ba, "2 fullers employed for 1 day, expended (for) the royal banquet of the Akiti festival," 221:1–2

2.1.5 Fresh Apples

[n.n.n.n sìl]a ḫašḫur-duru$_5$ gur ⸢*ilum*⸣*-ra-pi$_5$* dam-gàr šu ba-ti níĝ-kas$_7$-aka-ta ^{d}ba-ú-da **ba-⸢na⸣-zi**, "*Ilum-rapi*, the merchant, received [n] bushel(s) (and) [n] liter(s) of fresh apples. Ba'uda expended (them) from the account for him," 1173:1–6

2.1.6 Skins

kuš-udu **zi-ga**, "expended caprid skins," 863:2, 867:4, 922:5, 948:4

2.2 Broken Context

[x i]m *ga-ga-ra-a* **zi-[ga?]** [mu e]n-^{d}inana-unu^{ki}-[ga] máš-e ì-pàd, "{activities in each month} of *Ibbi-Suen* Year 2, the total [. . . having been?] expended," 1029:'9-'10

3. saḫar zi(g), "to (re)move dirt"

saḫar zi-ga im lu, "to mix excavated dirt (with) earth" > **lu**

saḫar zi-ga ka-la-ka si(g), "to pile up excavated dirt at the dirt quarry" > **si(g)**

saḫar zi-ga tùn-[lá] da bàd sè(g$_{10}$), "to tamp dirt removed via a tùn-lá device having been tamped at the side of the (enclosure) wall" > **sè(g$_{10}$)**

3.1 Inspection of (Re)moved Earth

kurum$_7$ aka **saḫar zi-ga** ^{ĝeš}kiri$_6$-gar-ša-an-na^{ki}, "Inspection of dirt moved at the Garšana garden," 176:16–17, 179:17–18

saḫar zi-ga in-lá tùn-lá ^{ĝeš}kiri$_6$-zabala$_4^{\text{ki}}$ kurum$_7$ [aka], "Inspection (of the work of workers). They transported dirt removed via a tùn-lá device at the Zabala garden," 178:6–8

saḫar zi-g[a kurum$_7$ aka], "[Inspection of] moved dirt," 181:6–8

3.2 Workers Assigned to (Re)move Earth

3.2.1 At the Barracks of the Dedali'a Gate

n g̃uruš **saḫar zi-ga** é-*gi-na-tum* ká-dedal-i-a, "n workmen having moved dirt at the barracks of the Dedali'a gate," 206:22–23, 207:22

[. . . **saḫar z**]**i-ga** é-[*gi-na-tum*] ká-dedal-i-a, "[(workers)] having moved [dirt] at the [barracks] of the Dedali'a gate," 209:19–21

3.2.2 At the Brewery-Kitchen-Mill Complex

⋆ See *Household Index* for the complete context of the following passage.

[n g̃uruš n] géme **saḫar z**[**i-zi-dè** é-lùn]ga é-kíkken [ù é-muḫaldim], "[n workmen (and) n] workwomen [to] move dirt at the brewery-kitchen-mill complex," 106:32

3.2.3 At a Canal

3.2.3.1 At the Mama-*šarrat* Canal

1 g̃uruš ⸢ašgab⸣ u_4-14-[šè] iti ezem-an-⸢na⸣ 1 g̃uruš ⸢ašgab u_4⸣-[n-šè n g̃uruš] ašgab i[ti ezem]-m[e-ki-g̃]ál ⸢**saḫar**⸣ **zi**-⸢**ga**⸣ i_7-ma-ma-*šar-ra-at*, "1 leather worker [for] 14 days in month 11 (and) 1 leather worker for [n] day(s) (and) [n] leather worker(s) in month 12 having moved dirt at the Mama-*šarrat* canal," 281:1–8

1 g̃uruš túg-[du_8] u_4-13-šè **saḫar zi-ga** i_7-ma-ma-*šar-ra-at*, "1 braider for 13 days having moved dirt at the Mama-*šarrat* canal," 283:1–3

[1] g̃uruš ad-kub_4 [u_4]-13-šè **saḫar zi-ga** i_7-ma-ma-*šar-ra-at*, "[1] reed craftsman for 13 [days] having moved dirt at the Mama-*šarrat* canal," 284:1–3

3.2.3.2 At the Sur Canal

1 g̃uruš túg-du_8 [u_4]-21-šè **saḫar zi-ga** i_7-sur du_6-ba-an-du_8-du_8 a-⸢šà⸣-sum-túl-túl, "1 braider for 21 [days] having moved dirt at the Sur canal of Dubandudu (and?/in?) the Sum-tultul field," 268:1–5

3.2.4 At the Dirt Quarry

n g̃uruš ugula *ilum-dan* **saḫar zi-ga** ka-la-ka gub-ba, "n workmen, supervised by *Ilum-dan*, having moved dirt (while) employed at the dirt quarry," 7:'36, 8:41

3.2.5 At the Foundation of the (Enclosure) Wall

[2] g̃uruš šidim 2 g̃uruš [**saḫar**] uš bàd **zi-zi-dè** ⸢gub⸣-ba, "[2] builders and 2 workmen employed to move [dirt] at the foundation of the (enclosure) wall," 5:19–21

3 g̃uruš 2 géme **saḫar** uš bàd [**zi**]-**zi-dè** gu[b-ba], "3 workmen (and) 2 workwomen employed to move dirt at the foundation of the (enclosure) wall," 9:22

3.2.6 At the Foundation Terrace of the Brewery and Mill

1 g̃uruš šidim 10 g̃[uruš n géme] **saḫar zi-ga** ki-sá-a é-bapp[ir ù é-kíkken], "1 builder, 10 workmen [(and) n workwomen] having moved dirt at the foundation terrace of the brewery [and mill]," 108:26–27

saḫar zi-ga [ki-s]á-a é-l[ùnga ù é-kíkken] mu-⸢DU⸣ *li-la-a* ugula lú-ḫug̃-g̃á, "delivery of moved dirt (for) the foundation terrace of the house of the brewery [and mill] (by) *Lila'a*, overseer of hired workers," 355:6–8

3.2.7 At the Foundation Terrace of the Textile Mill

2 ĝuruš šidim 14 ĝuruš uš ki-sá-a é-uš-bar **saḫar zi-zi-dè** gub-ba, "2 builders (and) 14 workmen employed to move dirt at the foundation of the foundation terrace of the textile mill," 28:'15

1 ĝuruš 4 géme **saḫar zi-zi-dè** ki-[sá-a] é-uš-bar gub-ba, "1 workman (and) 4 workwomen employed to move dirt at the foundation terrace of the textile mill," 35:29

3.2.8 At the GÍN-bal

[3] ĝuruš **saḫar** GÍN?-[bal?] **zi-zi-d[è** gub-ba], "[3] workmen [employed] to move dirt at GÍN-bal?," 92:12

12 ĝuruš **saḫar zi-ga** GÍN-bal a-šà ^{ğeš}kiri$_6$ ĝar-ša-an-na^{ki}, "12 workmen having moved dirt at the GÍN-bal of the field of the Garšana garden," 123:39

14 [ĝuruš **saḫar**] **zi-ga** GÍN-bal [^{ğeš}ki]ri$_6$ ĝar-ša-an-na^{ki}, "14 [workmen] having moved [dirt] at the GÍN-bal of the Garšana garden," 125:35

[n ĝuruš **saḫar**] **zi-ga** GÍN-ba[l a]-šà ĝar-ša-an-n[a^{ki}], "[n workmen] having moved [dirt] at the GÍN-bal of the field of Garšana" 126:30

1 ĝuruš šidim 14 [ĝuruš 3 géme] **saḫar zi-ga** GÍN-bal ^{ğeš}kiri$_6$ ĝar-ša-an-na^{ki}-a,"1 builder, 14 [workmen (and) 3 workwomen] having moved dirt at the GÍN-bal of the Garšana garden," 128:31–32

3.2.9 At the Kiln

[n] ĝuruš **saḫar** mun **zi-⸢zi⸣-dè**, "[n] workmen to remove salty dirt," 146:'39

3.2.10 At the Lot

(. . .) *ba-da?*-{erasure}-*a* (. . .) *šu-eš*$_4$*-tár* dumu *da-da-a* (. . .) ur-me ⸢santana⸣ mu udug kislaḫ **saḫar zi-zi-dè**-šè, "{barley, ordinary wool, oil and baskets} (for) *Bada'a*, *Šu-Eštar*, son of *Dada'a*, (and) Ur-me, the date orchard administrator, (provisions) for caretakers moving dirt (to/from) the lot," 1011:5, 10, 14–15

3.2.11 At Various Houses

1 ĝuruš šidim **saḫar** <é->*šu-eš*$_4$*-tár* **zi-zi-dè** gub-[ba], "1 builder employed to move dirt at <the house of> *Šu-Eštar*," 92:20

13 ĝuruš im lu-a 3 ĝuruš 3 géme **saḫar zi-ga** é-*pu-ta-nu-um*, "13 workmen having mixed earth (and) 3 workmen (and) 3 workwomen having moved dirt at the house of *Putanum*," 123:37–38

4 ĝuru[š **sa]ḫar zi-ga** é-*zu-zu-tum*, "4 workmen having moved dirt at the house of *Zuzutum*," 125:30

[n ĝuruš **saḫ]ar zi-ga** é-*pu-ta-nu-um*, "[n workmen] having moved dirt at the house of *Putanum*," 125:31

3.2.12 Construction Site Broken or Unspecified

1 ĝuruš **saḫar** x [. . .] **zi-zi-d[è** gub-ba], "1 workman [employed] to move [. . .] dirt," 92:13

[n ĝuruš . . . **saḫar zi-z]i-dè** g[ub-ba], "[n workmen . . .] employed to move [dirt]," 100:'29

[n ĝuruš **saḫa]r zi-ga** gub-ba, "[n] employed [workmen] having moved dirt," 1386:3

3.2.13 Rations for Moving Dirt

2.0.0 še gur **saḫar zi-ga**-šè, "2 bushels of barley for having moved dirt," 1201:1–2

4. Object Unspecified

[n] ĝuruš **zi-ga** gub-ba, "[n] employed workmen having moved (dirt?)," 74:'9

[n] ĝuruš **zi-ga** didli gub-ba, "[n] employed workmen having moved additional (dirt?)," 75:28

zi(l), "to strip"

ĝeš zi(l), "to strip wood"

im zi(l), "to strip earth"

ùr zi(l), "to strip a roof"

1. ĝeš zi(l), "to strip wood"

13 ĝuruš ^{ĝeš}nimbar **zi-zi-dè** [gub-ba], "13 workmen [employed] to strip date palm wood," 35:36

2. im zi(l), "to strip earth"

9 ĝuruš u_4-1-šè še 6 sìla-ta ba-ḫuĝ **im si-le** ⸢gub⸣-ba, "9 workmen hired for 1 day (for) 6 liters of barley each, employed to strip earth," 474:1–3[19]

3. ùr zi(l), "to strip a roof"

5 ĝuruš **ùr** é-kìšib-ba ĝá-n[un-na] sumun **zi-le-dè** gu[b-ba], "5 workmen employed to strip the roof of the warehouse of the old storehouse," 47:47–48

n ĝuruš **ùr** é-kìšib-ba sumun **zi-le-**de_9 gub-ba, "n workmen employed to srip the roof of the old warehouse," 48:52–53, 140:40

n ĝuruš **ùr** é-kìšib-ba sumun **zi-lé-dè**, "n workmen to strip the roof of the old warehouse," 136:37, 138:34, 141:37

zi(r), *pasāsu*, "to break, destroy; to erase, cancel (seal, tablet)"

kìšib zi(r), "to cancel a tablet"

niĝ **al-zi-ra**, "used goods" > **al-zi-ra**

1. kìšib zi(r), "to cancel a tablet"

[n.n.n.n sìl]a ḫašḫur-$duru_5$ gur ⸢*ilum*⸣-*ra-*pi_5 dam-gàr šu ba-ti níĝ-kas_7-aka-ta ^{d}ba-ú-da ba-⸢na⸣-zi kìšib *ilum-ra-*pi_5 u_4-um-de_6 **kìšib** ^{d}ba-ú-da **zi-re-dam**, "*Ilum-rapi*, the merchant, received [n] bushel(s) (and) [n] liter(s) of fresh apples. Ba'uda expended (them) from the account for him. When the sealed tablet of *Ilum-rapi* is brought, Ba'uda's sealed tablet will be canceled," 1173:1–10

1470 sa gi-zi gu-níĝin 10-sa-ta gu-níĝin-bi 147-àm ^{d}*adad-tillati* šu ba-ti ki *puzur*$_4$-^{d}en-líl-ta ba-zi ĝìri *a-ḫu-wa-qar* dub-sar kìšib *a-ḫu-wa-qar-ra*! u_4-um-de_6 **kìšib** *puzur*$_4$-^{d}en-líl **zi-re-dam**, "Under the authority of *Aḫu-waqar*, the scribe, *Adad-tillati* received from *Puzur-*

---

19 si-le is probably a variant spelling of zi-le.

Enlil 1470 bundles of fresh reeds, bales of 10 bunches each, its bales are 147. When the sealed tablet of *Aḫu-waqar* is brought, *Puzur*-Enlil's sealed tablet will be canceled," 1361:1–12

zuḫ, *šaraqu*, "to steal"

1. **níĝ-zuḫ-a**, "stolen goods"

1.1 **Stolen Goods of *Dada'a*, the Bird Warden: Birds and Mice**

4 $tum_{12}^{mušen}$ 1 péš-ĝeš-gi 1 péš-igi-gùn **[níĝ-z]uḫ-a** *[da-d]a-a* sipa-⌜mušen⌝-na, "4 wild doves, 1 mouse (and) 1 striped-eyed mouse; stolen goods of *Dada'a*, the bird warden," 1059:2–5

[n] ⌜ir_7⌝^{mušen}-niga [n] $tum_{12}^{mušen}$-niga 47 $tu\text{-}gur_4^{mušen}$-niga 21 péš-igi-gùn-niga **níĝ-zuḫ-a** *da-da-a* sipa-mušen-na, "[n] fattened pigeon(s), [n] fattened wild dove(s), 47 fattened doves (and) 21 fattened striped-eyed mice; stolen goods of *Dada'a*, the bird warden," 1060:1–6

2. **Thefts**

2.1 **Confimed by *Anaḫ-ili*, the Leather Worker**

2.1.1 **Barley**

0.2.0. še **zuḫ-a** *a-na-aḫ-ì-[lí]* ašgab šà ka i_7-nar-e-⌜ne⌝ ka-ga-na ba-ge-en, "*Anaḫ-ili*, the leather worker, confirmed at the opening of the Singers' canal that (there were) 120 liters of stolen barley," 1063:1–4

2.1.2 **Skins**

1 kuš-udu-niga a-ĝar gu_7 *nu-úr-*^{d}*adad* ašgab **ba-an-zuḫ** *a-na-aḫ-ì-lí* ašgab in-ge-en, "*Nur-Adad*, the leather worker, stole 1 de-haired skin of a fattened sheep. *Anaḫ-ili*, the leather worker, confirmed it," 1061:1–4

2.2 **Confirmed by *Ili-andul***

0. 3.1. [. . .] é-kìšib-ba é-udu-[. . .] *ì-lí-an-dùl* [. . .] **ba-an-z[uḫ(-a)]** ka-ga-na ba-a-[ge-en], "[. . .] in the storehouse, the sheep pen [. . .] *Ili-andul* [. . .] he stole it. He confirmed it," 1064:1–5

2.3 **Stolen Bitumen**

1 má 60.0.0. gur ba-gul ésir-bi **zuḫ-a** ba-ĝar ĝeš ešé-bi <<BI>> nu-ĝál, "1 60-bushel boat was dismantled, its stolen bitumen was replaced (but) its wood (and) ropes are (still) missing," 1369:1–4

Analytical Index of Personal Names

a-a-kal-la
a-a-mu
a-a-ni
a-al-lí
a-al-lu-a (household only)
a-al-lu-ú
a-bí-a-ti
a-bu-DU$_{10}$
a-bu-um-ilum
a-da-làl
a-ga-ti
a-gu-a
a-ḫa-ni-šu
a-ḫu-a
a-ḫu-ba-qar
a-ḫu-DU$_{10}$
a-ḫu-ma
a-ḫu-ni
a-ḫu-wa-qar
a-ku$_{8}$-a-nu-ri
a-la-tum
a-lí-a-bi
a-lí-aḫ
a-lim-ma
a-ma-a
a-na-a
a-na-aḫ-ì-lí
a-ta-li-ku
a-wi-lí
a-wi-lum[1]
á-g̃eš-u
á-ni-á
á-pil-la-núm
á-pil-lí-a
ad-da-ka-la
ad-da-ni

1 Var: *á-wi-lum-ma*.

^{d}*adad*-SIG$_{5}$
^{d}*adad-tillati*,[2] *passim*
aḫ-dam-ì-lí
ak-ba-zum
al-la
al-la-ša-ru-um
am-ri-ni
ama-kal-la
amar-^{d}da-mu
AN.ŠUM.TAG.KAL[3]
an-ta-lú
ar-ri-az
árad-g̃u$_{10}$
árad-^{d}nana
aš-tá-qar

ba-aḫ-zi-gi
ba-ba-ni[4]
ba-ba-ti-a
ba-da-a
ba-ḫa-a (household only)
ba-la-a
^{d}ba-ú-da
ba-zi[5]
be-lí-a-ri-ik
be-lí-a-sú
be-lí-ì-lí

2 On the reading KASKAL+ KUR = *tillatī*, see Stol 1991, 192.

3 Var: AN.TAG.KAL.

4 This name should perhaps be read as *ba-ba-lí* as in CUNES 55-01-048:19 (AS 8/vi/30). See Owen 2009 for the complete text.

5 Var: *ba-zi-tum*.

bi-dạ-sa$_{6}$-sa$_{6}$
bí-du-lu-um
bí-za-a (household only)
bí-za-tum
bu-lu-za
bu-za-du-a

da-a-a
da-da
da-da-a
da-da-AN
dan-ḫi-li
du-du-gu
du-gu-a (household only)
dub-si-ga

e-é-zi[6]
e-ri-ib-bu-um
e-ṣí-dum
é-a-bu
é-a-dan
é-a-ra-bí
é-a-šar
é-ì-gára
el-pa-dan
^{d}en-líl-*ba-za-du*
en-nam-^{d}ma-lik
en-nim-ma
en-um-ì-lí
ér-kal-la
èr-ra-ba-ni
eš$_{4}$-tár-im-dì
eš$_{4}$-tár-um-mi

ga-su-su
géme-^{d}en-ki
géme-tur

6 Var: é-é-zi.

gù-zi-dé-a
G̃AR-*šà-ti*
g̃ìri-^{d}ba-ú-ì-dab$_5$
g̃ìri-né-ì-dab$_5$
ḫa-bi-ṣa-nu-um (household only)
ḫa-bu-ra-tum (household only)
ḫa-la-ša
ḫa-lí
ḫal-lí-a
ḫi-li
ḫi-lu-a
ḫu-im
ḫu-lu-lu

i-ba-a-a
i-dì-èr-ra
i-din-a-bu-um
i-din-^{d}*adad*
i-din-é-a
i-din-èr-ra
i-din-^{d}*šamaš*
i-gi-zu-tum
i-ku-núm
i-la-ak-nu-id
i-me-èr-ra
i-mi-iq-^{d}šul-gi
i-ri-ib[7]
i-sú-a-ri-iq
i-ṣur-^{d}*suen*
i-ti-rum (household only)
i-ṭib-ší-na-at
ì-lí-a-núm
ì-lí-an-dul
ì-lí-aš-ra-ni
ì-lí-bi-la-ni
ì-lí-bi-šu (household only)
ì-lí-ra-bí
ì-lí-si-na-at
ì-lí-uṣ-ra-ni
ì-sum-a-bi
ib-du-um
ib-ni-^{d}*adad*
ib-ni-ilum
ìl-su-ba-ni
ìl-su-dan

ilam-šu-qir$_x$
ilum-ba-ni
ilum-dan
ilum-ma-zi
ilum-mu-tá-bíl
ilum-ra-pi$_5$
in-ga-la
ip-qú-ša
ir-du-du
ir$_{11}$*-dam*
išdum-ki-in

kà-al-ma-ti
ki-ùr-en-mur[8]
ku-du-du-ú
ku-ru-ub-^{d}*adad*
ku-un-si-ma-at

la-la-a
la-lum
la-ma-gir$_{11}$
la-ma-sà-tum
la-ma-súm
la-qì-ip[9]
la-te-ni-si
làl-la
li-bur
li-bur-be-lí
li-bur-i-du-ni
li-bur-ni-rum
li-la-a
lu-ba
lu-kà-dum[10]
lu-lu
lú-^{d}ḫa-ìa
lú-^{d}inana
lú-kal-la
lú-kìri-zal
lú-me-lám
lú-^{d}nana
lú-^{d}nin-šubur
lú-^{d}*suena*
lú-ša-lim
lu$_5$*-zi-lá*
lugal-ezem

lugal-ḫa-ma-ti
lugal-ú-šim-e

ma-aš-rum
ma-áš-tum
ma-at-ì-lí
ma-la-ti
^{d}*ma-lik-ba-ni*
^{d}*ma-lik-tillati*
^{d}*ma-lik-tillat-sú*
ma-ma-*ri-be*
ma-nu-um-ki-^{d}šul-gi
ma-šum
mu-na-núm

na-bu-tum
na-na
na-sìm
na-wi-ir-ilum
nar-^{d}inana
ni-a-ma
nin-lu-lu
nin-zi-šà-g̃ál
nu-ru-uš-e-lí
nu-úr-^{d}*adad*
nu-úr-ì-lí
nu-úr-ma-ti-šu
nu-úr-zu

pa-da-^{d}šul-gi
pe-ṣe-ti
pi$_5$*-ša-aḫ-ilum*[11] (household only)
pu-šu-ki-in
pu-ta-nu-um
puzur$_4$*-a-bi*
puzur$_4$*-a-gu*$_5$*-um*
puzur$_4$*-é-a*
puzur$_4$-^{d}en-líl
puzur$_4$*-èr-ra*
puzur$_4$-^{d}nin-kar-ak
puzur$_4$*-ra-bi* (household only)
puzur$_4$*-šu-ba*

ra-ba-tum
ra-qa-šu-bu-um

---

7 Var: *i-ri-bu-um*.

8 Var: *kì-ùr-re-en*.

9 Var: *la-qì-pu-um*.

10 Var: *lu-kà-du-um*.

11 Var: *pí-ša-aḫ-ilum*.

ri-im-ilum
ru-ba-ti-a

sa$_{10}$-é-ama-tu
si-mu
si-na-ti
si-um[12]
simat-é-a
simat-^{d}*ištaran*
simat-^{d}nana
simat-^{d}nin-šubur
su-kà-lí-a[13]
^{d}*suen-a-bu-šu*

ṣa-al-lum
ṣú-mi-id-ilum

ša-at-bi-zi-il
ša-at-èr-ra
ša-at-ì-lí
ša-at-kab-tá
ša-bar-zi-na-at
ša-lim-a-ḫu-um
ša-lim-be-lí
šà-gu$_{4}$
šál-maḫ[14]
^{d}*šamaš-a-bi*
^{d}*šamaš-di-in*
šar-ru-sú-ṭa-ba-at
šar-ru-um-ba-ni
šar-ru-um-ì-li
^{d}šára-ì-ša$_{6}$
^{d}šára-kam
^{d}šára-sá-g̃u$_{10}$
še-da
še-lí-a-núm
šeš-kal-la
šu-a-ku
šu-^{d}*adad*
šu-ba-ra-ni
šu-^{d}*belum*
šu-bu-la-núm (household only)
šu-bu-ul-tum
šu-^{d}dumu-zi
šu-^{d}en-líl
šu-èr-ra
šu-eš$_{4}$-tár
šu-^{d}*i-šum*
šu-i-ti-rum (household only)
šu-ì-lí-su[15]
šu-kà-kà
šu-kab-ta[16]
šu-ku-bu-um
šu-la-núm
šu-ma-ma
šu-^{d}*ma-mi-tum*
šu-^{d}na-zi
šu-^{d}nin-girim$_{x}$
šu-^{d}nin-in-si
šu-^{d}nin-kar-ak
šu-^{d}nin-súmun
šu-^{d}nin-šubur
šu-^{d}nisaba
šu-^{d}*suen-ba-ni*
^{d}*šu-*^{d}*suen-dan*
^{d}*šu-*^{d}*suen-e-te-íl-pi$_{4}$-*^{d}en-líl
^{d}*šu-*^{d}*suen-*ḫa-ma-ti
^{d}*šu-*^{d}*suen-na-ra-am-*^{d}en-líl
šu-^{d}*šamaš*
^{d}šul-gi-*ra-ma*
^{d}šul-gi-*wa-qar*

ta-ḫu-lam
ta-tù-ri
tá-di-na
tá-din-eš$_{4}$-tár
tá-ḫi-iš-a-tal
tá-ki-il-ì-lí-ís-sú
ti-ga-an
tu-ku-lí
tu-ra-a
tu-ra-am-ì-lí

u-bar-ri-a (household only)
u-bar-tum
u-bar-um[17]
ù-ṣí-na-wi-ir
ud-du-ur
um-mi-kab-ta
ur-^{d}asar-lu-ḫi
ur-^{d}dumu-zi
ur-é-an-na
ur-^{d}en-líl-lá
ur-gi-a-zu
ur-me
ur-mes
ur-^{d}nanše
ur-ni$_{9}$-g̃ar
ur-^{d}nin-^{d}si$_{4}$-an-na
ur-^{d}*suena*
ur-ša-lu-ḫi
ur-^{d}šul-pa-è
ur-te-me-na
ur-zikum-ma
^{d}utu-sá-bí

wa-qar-dan

za-a-za
za-ak-ì-lí
za-bu-la
za-ki-ti (household only)
za-ki-tum
za-la-a
za-la-tum
zé-ra-ra (household only)
zi-ti-a
zu-zu-tum (household only)

---

12 Var: *še-um*.
13 Var: *sù-kà-lí*.
14 Var: *šal-maḫ*.
15 Var: *šu-ì-lí*.
16 Var: *šu-kab-tá*.
17 Var: *ú-bar-um*.

– A –

a-a-kal-la

1. Deliveries: Broken Context

34 [. . .] 1 *ra-ab-*[*su* . . .] ki **a-a-kal-la**-ta $^{[d]}$*adad-tillati* [šu ba-ti], "*Adad-tillati* received [. . .] from A'akala," 1390:1–4

2. Receipts: Charcoal and Reeds

[n ^{geš}]ú-bíl-lá ki-lá-bi 10 ma-⸢na⸣ 10 sa gi-⸢izi⸣ **a-a-kal-⸢la⸣** šu ba-⸢ti⸣ iti ki-siki-^{d}nin-[a-zu] úgu a g̃á-g̃á ga-ga-ra-a ki ^{d}*adad-tillati*-ta ⸢ba⸣-zi, "In month 5, A'akala received [n (units)] of charcoal, their weight is 10 minas, (and) 10 bundles of fuel reeds from *Adad-tillati*; the total placed in the account," 1162:'59–'70

a-a-mu

A'amu, the Builder

1. As a witness

igi ***a-a-mu*** šidim, "witnessed by *A'amu*, the builder," 1063:6, 1064:7

a-a-ni

1. Inspection (of the Work) of his Workmen

n g̃uruš ***a-*[*a-ni*]** (. . .) kurum$_7$ aka saḫar zi-ga ^{geš}kiri$_6$ gar-ša-an-na^{ki}, "Inspection (of the work) of n workmen of *A'ani*, (and) {other workers} having moved dirt at the Garšana garden," 176:5–6, 16–17, 179:2, 17–18

5 g̃uruš ***a-a-ni*** (. . .) a bal-a (. . .) [kurum$_7$ aka], "[Inspection] (of the work) of 5 workmen of *A'ani*, (and) {other workers} having poured water," 181:2, 5, 8

a-al-lí

A'alli, the husband of Ama-kala

1. Receipts: Sprouted Malt

0.2.0. munu$_4$-si-è ama-kal-la dam ***a-al-lí*** šu ba-ti, "Ama-kala, the wife of *A'alli*, received 120 liters of sprouted malt," 1250:1–4

a-al-lu-ú

1. Receipts: Pine Trees

1800 ^{geš}ù-su[ḫ$_5$]-tur-tur ki *a-da-làl-*[ta] ***a-al-lu-ú*** šu ba-an-ti, "*A'allu* received 1800 small pine trees from *Adallal*," 1056:1–4

a-bí-a-ti

é-***a-bí-a-ti***, "the house of *Abiati*" > *Household Index*

1. *Abiati*, the Ox-Herder, Supervised by *Babani*, the Majordomo

1.1 Ox-Drivers from his Gang

2 g̃uruš šà-gu$_4$ ***a-bí-a-ti*** nu-bànda-gu$_4$ ugula *ba-ba-ni* PA.[AL] árad-é-a-me-[éš], "2 ox-drivers (from the gang of) *Abiati*, the ox-herder, household servants supervised by *Babani*, the majordomo," 183:4–7

n g̃uruš ugula, ***a-bí-a-ti*** nu-bànda-gu$_4$ (. . .) (šà-gu$_4$-me-éš ugula) *ba-ba-ni* šabra, "n workmen, supervised by *Abiati*, the ox-herder, (and) {other gangs}, (ox-drivers supervised by) *Babani*, the majordomo," 184:1–2, 5–6, 185:1, 4–5, 186:1, 4–5, 187:1, 4, 189:1, 5, 190:1, 7, 191:1–2, 10, 194:1, 7, 15

n g̃uruš ***a-bí-a-ti*** nu-bànda-gu$_4$ (. . .) šà-gu$_4$-me-éš (. . .) ugula *ba-ba-ni* šabra, "n workmen (from the gang of) *Abiati*, the ox-herder, (and) {other gangs}, ox-drivers (and) {hired workers} supervised by *Babani*, the majordomo," 193:1, 7, 9, 197:1, 8, 11

1.2 Overseer of *Adallal*, the Runaway

zàḫ *a-da-làl* ***a-bí-a-ti*** nu-bànda-gu$_4$ (. . .) ugula *ba-ba-ni* šabra, "*Adallal*, the runaway, (from the gang of) *Abiati*, the ox-herder, (and) {other runaways}, supervised by *Babani*, the majordomo," 192:'22,'26, 195:'30, '34, 196:'33, '37, 197:42, 46

1.3 Overseer of a Sick Worker

1 g̃uruš dú-ra ***a-bí-a-ti*** nu-bànda-gu$_4$ (. . .) ugula *ba-ba-ni* šabra, "1 sick workman (from the gang of) *Abiati*, the ox-herder (and) {other runaways}, supervised by *Babani*, the majordomo," 194:60–61, 198:'39, '44

2. *Abiati*, Overseer of Hired Workmen

[n g̃uruš] šidim gub<-ba> [ugula ***a-bí-a-t***]***i*** (. . .) lú-ḫug̃-g̃á-me-éš kurum$_7$ aka, "Inspection (of the work) of [n] employed builder(s), [supervised by *Abiati*], (and) {other gangs}, (all) hired workmen," 182:1–2, 5–7

a-bu-DU$_{10}$

é-***a-bu***-DU$_{10}$, "the house of *Abu-ṭabu*" > *Household Index*

1. *Abu-ṭabu*, the Barber

1.1 As a Deputy

[o.n.n.] še [n+]1 udu-sag̃ *šu-kab-tá* [***a-b***]***u***-DU$_{10}$ šu-i maškim, "[n] liter(s) of barley (and) [n+]1 lead-sheep of *Šu-Kabta*. *Abu-ṭabu*, the barber, was the deputy," 484:7–9

1.2 As a Witness

igi ***a-bu***-DU$_{10}$ šu-i, "witnessed by *Abu-ṭabu*, the barber," 1061:10

2. *Abu-ṭabu*, the Overseer

2.1 Builders Supervised by *Abu-ṭabu*

3 ⸢g̃uruš⸣ šidim l[ú-é-^{d}*š*]*u*-^{d}EN.ZU-me-éš ugula ***a-bu***-DU$_{10}$, "3 builders from *Bit-Šu-Suen* supervised by *Abu-ṭabu*," 187:11–12[18]

3 g̃uruš šidim lú-é-^{d}*š*[*u*-^{d}EN.ZU]^{ki}-me-éš ***a-bu***-DU$_{10}$ nu-⸢bànda⸣, "3 builders from *Bit-Šu-Suen* (from the gang of) *Abu-ṭabu*, the overseer" 188:'7–'8, 189:13–15

3 g̃uruš šidim nu-bànda ***a-bu***-DU$_{10}$, "3 builders (from the gang of) the overseer, *Abu-ṭabu*," 190:16–17, 193:18

---

18 For unknown reasons this text uses ugula instead of nu-bànda. Nevertheless *Abu-ṭabu*'s activities are the same as in nos. 188, 189, and 190 below.

2.2 Provisions

0.0.2.6 sìla ninda ^{kuš}a-g̃á-lá kéše-rá g̃uruš nam–60 ***a-⸢bu⸣*-DU**$_{10}$ u$_4$ é-^{d}*šu*-^{d}EN.ZU^{ki}-šè i-⸢re⸣-ša-a u$_4$ é-e im sumur ba-aka, "26 liters of bread in bound leather sacks (for) *Abu-ṭabu*, the overseer of 60 workmen, when (his workers) went to *Bit-Šu-Suen* when the house was plastered," 480:1–3[19]

[erased number] kaš-gen 0.0.1. ninda [. . .] ki? [. . .] 0.0.1. ninda-šu-ra-g̃en ***a-bu*-DU**$_{10}$ nu-bànda, "ordinary beer, 10 liters of [. . .] bread (and) 10 liters of ordinary half (loaf) bread (for) *Abu-ṭabu*, the overseer," 507:7–10

3. *Abu-ṭabu*, the Runaway from the Gang of *Puzur-abi*

zàḫ ***a-bu*-DU**$_{10}$ *puzur$_4$-a-bi* nu-bànda-gu$_4$, "*Abu-ṭabu*, the runaway (from the gang of) *Puzur-abi*, the ox-herder," 194:62–63, 198:'40

4. *Abu-ṭabu*, Title Unspecified

4.1 As a Deputy

0.0.1. še nin-lu-lu ***a-bu*-DU**$_{10}$ maškim ba-[zi], "10 liters of barley were disbursed (for) Ninlulu. *Abu-ṭabu* was the deputy," 486:1–4

a-bu-um-ilum

1. *Abum-ilum*, Man from Kabšu

1.1 Provisions: Barley

12.0.0. gur ***a-bu-um-ilum*** lú-kab-šu^{ki} (. . .) [šu+níg̃in n+]7.0.0. gur še-ba *ba-zi-tum* šu+níg̃in 47.1.[n.] še-ba é, "8 bushels of (barley) (for) *Abum-ilum*, the man from Kabšu, (and barley for) {other individuals}; [in total: n+]7 bushels of the barley rations of *Bazitum*; in total: 47 bushels (and) 60[+n] liters of barley rations of the household," 555:13, 24–25

2. *Abum-ilum*, Title Unspecified

2.1 Provisions: Barley

8.0.0. gur iti-4-kam ***a-bu-um-ilum*** (. . .) [šu+níg̃in n+]7.0.0. gur še-ba *ba-zi-tum* šu+níg̃in 47.1.[n.] še-ba é, "8 bushels of (barley) in the 4th month (for) *Abum-ilum* (and barley for) {other individuals}; [in total: n+]7 bushels of the barley rations of *Bazitum*; in total: 47 bushels (and) 60[+n] liters of barley rations of the household," 555:11–12, 24–25

a-da-làl

1. *Adallal*, the Brewer

1.1 Receipts

1.1.1 Semolina

0.0.3. dabin ki ^{d}*adad-tillati*-ta ***a-da-làl*** ^{lú}lùnga šu ba-ti, "*Adallal*, the brewer, received 30 liters of semolina from *Adad-tillati*," 1157:1–4

---

19 This text appears to use nam-60 in place of nu-bànda.

1.1.2 Workers to Crush Malt

[n] g̃uruš 2? géme ugula *simat-é-a* $munu_4$ $nag̃_4$-g̃á-dè ***a-da-làl*** [lú]lùnga ì-dab_5 $kurum_7$ aka, "Inspection (of the work) of [n] workmen (and) 2? workwomen, supervised by *Simat-Ea*. *Adallal*, the brewer, took (the workers) in charge to crush malt," 167:1–6

2. *Adallal*, the Craftsman, and Son of *Šu*-Mama

2.1 Deliveries: Wood

(. . .) ì-DU ***a-da-làl*** dumu *šu*-ma-ma um-mi-a (. . .) [n] sar gíd-da [níg̃]-šid-da [[d]]*adad-tillati* šabra [ì]-dab_5 [zi-ga *sí*]*mat*-[d]*ištaran* [g̃ìri *a-h*]*u-ma* dub-sar, "{parcels of land; in it: date palm, pine boards of boats, and seedlings}, the delivery of *Adallal*, the son of *Šu*-Mama, the craftsman, (and) {2 other deliveries of similar commodities}. (In total:) [n] sar (of land) having been surveyed. *Adad-tillati*, the majordomo, took in charge the account. (It was) [the expenditure] of *Simat-Ištaran* [under the authority of] *Aḫuma*, the scribe," 1362:'23–'24, '73–'78

2.2 Receipts: Assorted Commodities

9.1.1.5 sìla zú-lum gur 1.0.1. u_4-ḫi-in gur 10⅚ 6 gín [g̃eš]zé-na 656 peš-múrgu 3½ 3 gín peš-ga 1065 á-an-zú-lum káb du_{11}-ga [g̃eš]⌜$kiri_6$⌝ ki [d]*adad-tillati*-ta ***a-da-làl*** um-mi-a dumu *šu*-ma-ma šu ba-ti g̃ìri *ù-ṣí-na-wi-ir* dub-sar, "Under the authority of *Uṣi-nawir*, the scribe, *Adallal*, the craftsman, the son of *Šu*-Mama, received from *Adad-tillati* 9 bushels (and) 75 liters of dates, 1 bushel and 10 liters of fresh dates, 10⅚ (minas and) 6 shekels of date palm frond midribs, 656 date palm spines, 3½ (minas and) 3 shekels of date palm hearts (and) 1065 date clusters; commodities of the garden measured for accounting," 1215:1–11

2.3 Orchard Products in his Possession

(. . .) lá-ìa-àm ***a-da-làl*** dumu *šu*-ma-ma in-da-g̃ál, "The remainder of {assorted commodities} are with *Adallal*, the son of *Šu*-Mama," 1092:10–12

3. *Adallal*, the Cook (as specified on text or seal)

3.1 Receipts

3.1.1 Assorted Grains

3.1.1.1 From *Adad-tillati*

0.4.4. zì-kum-sig_5 1.1.2. zì gur 0.0.3. dabin al-ús-sa 13.4.0. dabin gur 0.0.2. eša níg̃-*na-kab-tu*[*m*-šè] 0.1.0. níg̃-àr-[ra] ki [d]*adad-tillati*-ta ***a-da-làl*** šu ba-an-ti, "*Adallal* received 280 liters of fine kum-flour, 1 bushel and 80 liters of flour, 30 liters of processed semolina, 13 bushels (and) 240 liters of semolina (and) 20 liters of fine flour [for] the *nakabtum* (and) 60 liters of groats from *Adad-tillati*," 1100:1–10

1.2.0. dabin gur 2.0.0. zì-KAL gur ki [d]*adad*-[*tillati*-ta] ***a-⌜da-làl⌝*** šu [ba-ti], "*Adallal* received 1 bushel and 120 liters of semolina (and) 2 bushels of KAL-flour from *Adad-tillati*," 1226:1–5

3.1.0. še gur 2.2.3. zíz gur ki [d]*adad-tillati*-ta ***a-da-làl*** šu ⌜ba⌝-ti, "*Adallal* received 3 bushels (and) 60 liters of barley (and) 2 bushels and 150 liters of emmer wheat from *Adad-tillati*," 1228:1–5

3.1.1.2 From *Ili-andul*

0.3.0. dabin al-ús-sa 5.0.5. dabin gur 0.3.0.8 sìla zì-KAL 0.3.4.1 sìla zì-kum 0.2.0.4 sìla eša 3.3.0 zì-šà-gen gur 5?.3.4. zì-milla gur 4 sìla [šim-sig$_5$] al-nag̃-g̃á ki *ì-lí-an-dùl*-ta ***a-da-làl*** muḫaldim šu ba-ti, "*Adallal,* the cook, received from *Ili-andul* 180 liters of processed semolina, 5 bushels (and) 50 liters of semolina, 188 liters of KAL-flour, 221 liters of kum-flour, 124 liters of fine flour, 3 bushels (and) 180 liters of ordinary šà-flour, 5? bushels (and) 220 liters of milla-flour, (and) 4 liters of crushed [fine aromatic]," 1182:9–11

3.1.1.3 From *Malik-bani*

0.2.0. zì-gu-ús 0.2.0. dabin al-ús-sa ki ^{d}*ma-lik-ba-ni*-ta ***a-da-làl*** šu ba-an-ti, "*Adallal* received 120 liters of 2nd-quality gu-flour (and) 120 liters of processed semolina from *Malik-bani*," 1086:1–5

[0].1.1. tuḫ [0.n].2. zì-KAL [0].3.2. zì-kum [0].0.1. zì-gu-ús [ki] ^{d}*ma-lik-ba-ni*-ta [***a-d***]***a-làl*** ⌜šu⌝ ba-an-ti, "*Adallal* received 70 liters of bran, [n+]20 liters of KAL-flour, 200 liters of kum-flour, (and) 10 liters of 2nd-quality gu-flour from *Malik-bani*," 1128:1–7

3.1.1.4 From an Unspecified Source

0.1.2. ninda-šu-ra ½ sìla tuḫ 0.4.0. ninda-zì-šà-gen zì-milla íb-ta-ḫi ½ sìla du$_8$ 1.0.0. zì-šà-gen gur 0.1.0. zì-milla é-[muḫaldim-šè?] ***a-da-làl*** muḫaldim šu ba-an-ti, "*Adallal,* the cook, received 80 liters of half (loaf) bread, baked (in) ½ liter (loaves), 240 liters of bread mixed from ordinary šà-flour and milla-flour, baked (in) ½ liter (loaves), 1 bushel of ordinary šà-flour (and) 60 liters liters of milla-flour [for the kitchen?]," 1079:1–7

3.1.2 Barley from *Adad-tillati*

n še ki ^{d}*adad-tillati*-ta ***a-da-làl*** šu ba-ti, "*Adallal* received n liter(s) of barley from *Adad-tillati*," 1229:1–4, 1241:1–4

3.1.3 Beer and Beer Bread from *Adad-tillati*

1 dug dida$_x$-gen 0.0.3. še-bi 0.1.0. ki ^{d}*adad-tillati*-[ta] ***a-da-làl*** [muḫaldim] šu ba-⌜ti⌝ egir bu[ru$_{14}$ gi$_4$-gi$_4$-dè], "From *Adad-tillati*, *Adallal*, [the cook], received 1 jug of 30 liters of ordinary dida beer—its barley (equivalent) is 60 liters—[to be paid back] after the harvest," 1098:1–6

1 gú báppi[r-gen] ki ^{d}*adad-tillati*-ta ***a-da-làl*** šu ba-ti, "*Adallal* received 1 talent of [ordinary] beer bread from *Adad-tillati*," 1242:1–4

3.1.4 Chaff from *Adad-tillati*

1.0.4. tuḫ-duru$_5$-sig$_5$ bil-šè ki ^{d}*adad-tillati*-ta ***a-da-làl*** šu ba-an-ti, "*Adallal* received 1 bushel and 40 liters of fine fresh chaff for burning from *Adad-tillati*," 1150:1–5

3.1.5 Containers from *Adad-tillati*

5 ^{dug}gur$_4$-gur$_4$-g̃eštin ki ^{d}*adad-tillati*-ta ***a-da-làl*** muḫaldim šu ba-an-ti, "*Adallal*, the cook, received 5 wine vessels from *Adad-tillati*," 1263:1–4

1 ^{dug}útul-0.0.2. 1 ^{dug}útul-0.0.1. 1 $^{g̃eš}$zé-na 2 ^{gi}ma-sab ugula *ḫal-lí-a* ki ^{d}*adad-tillati*-ta ***a-da-làl*** muḫaldim šu ba-an-ti, "*Adallal*, the cook, received from *Adad-tillati* 1 20-liter tureen, 1 10-liter tureen, 1 date palm frond midrib (and) 2 ma-sab baskets of the overseer, *Ḫallia*," 1265:1–7

300 ^{gi}gur še ésir šub-[ba] ki ^{d}*adad-tillati*-⸢ta⸣ ***a-da-làl*** muḫaldim šu ba-an-ti, "*Adallal*, the cook, received 300 reed baskets coated with bitumen (containing) barley from *Adad-tillati*," 1274:1–4

[1] ^{gi}zar-zar-zar ésir šub-ba 1 ^{gi}ma-an-sim dabin 1 ^{gi}ma-an-sim níĝ-àr-ra 1 ĝeš-gan ki ^{d}*adad-tillati*-ta ***a-da-làl*** muḫaldim šu ba-an-ti, "*Adallal*, the cook, received [1] zar-zar basket coated with bitumen, 1 semolina sieve, 1 groats sieve (and) 1 pestle from *Adad-tillati*," 1280:1–7

20 ^{dug}sìla-gal 3 sìla-ta ki ^{d}*adad-tillati*-ta ***a-da-làl*** muḫaldim šu ba-an-ti, "*Adallal*, the cook, received 20 large liter-jugs of 3 liters each from *Adad-tillati*," 1281:1–4

3.1.6 Dates and Containers from *Adad-tillati*

[o.n.n.] zú-lum ^{gi}gur-ra ki ^{d}*adad-tillati*-ta ***a-da-làl*** šu ba-ti, "*Adallal* received [n] liter(s) of dates in a measuring container from *Adad-tillati*," 1231:1–4

0.0.3. zú-lum 2 ^{kuš}a-ĝá-lá ki ^{d}*adad-tillati*-⸢ta⸣ ***a-da-làl*** šu ba-ti, "*Adallal* received 30 liters of dates (and) 2 leather sacks from *Adad-tillati*," 1240:1–5

3.1.7 Flour from *Malik-bani*

0.1.0 zì-kum-sig$_5$ 0.1.0. eša ninda-*u$_4$-tuḫ-ḫ*[*u-um*-šè] ki ^{d}*ma-lik-ba-ni*-ta ***a-da-làl*** mu[ḫaldim] šu ba-an-ti, "*Adallal*, the cook, received 60 liters of fine kum-flour (and) 60 liters of fine flour [for] *utuḫḫum*-bread from *Malik-bani*," 1077:1–6

3.1.8 Gazi

3.1.8.1 From *Adad-tillati*

[n.n.n.] gazi ⸢mu⸣ ku$_6$ al-ús-sa-šè ***a-da-làl*** muḫaldim [šu b]a-an-ti [ki ^{d}*adad-til*]*lati*-ta [ba]-zi, "*Adallal*, the cook, received [n] liter(s) of gazi for fish-sauce from *Adad-tillati*," 1105:1–6

3.1.8.2 From *Erra-bani*

1.2.[n. g]azi gur ki *èr-ra-ba-ni*-ta ***a-da-làl*** muḫaldim šu ba-ti, "*Adallal*, the cook, received 1 bushel and 120[+n] liters of gazi from *Erra-bani*," 1204:1–4

3.1.9 Labor for Female Millers from *Adad-tillati*

10.0.0. še gur 20.0.0. zíz gur zíz ba-na imĝaĝa$_3$ 3⅓ sìla-ta ì-ĝál 9.4.0. zíz gur [zíz b]a-[na] zì-KAL 5 [sìla-t]a 1.4.4. kib$_x$ gur á géme kíkken-šè ki ^{d}*adad-tillati*-ta *a-da-lal* šu ba-ti, "*Adallal* received from *Adad-tillati* 10 bushels of barley, 20 bushels of emmer wheat, in each ban (=10 liters) of the emmer wheat there are 3⅓ liters of emmer, 9 bushels (and) 240 liters of emmer wheat, in each ban (=10 liters) of emmer wheat (there are) 5 liters of KAL-flour (and) 1 bushel (and) 280 liters of wheat for labor of female millers," 532:1–10

3.1.10 Reeds from *Adad-tillati*

70 sa gi-izi ninda du$_8$-dè ki ^{d}*adad-tillati*-ta ***a-da-làl*** šu ba-ti, "*Adallal* received 70 bundles of fuel reeds to bake bread from *Adad-tillati*," 1322:1–5

3.1.11 Requisitions for the *Abum* Festival from *Malik-bani*

(. . .) níĝ-dab$_5$ ezem-*a-bu-um-ma*-šè u$_4$-10-lá-1-kam ki ^{d}*ma-lik-ba-ni*-ta ***a-da-làl*** šu ba-an-ti, "*Adallal* received {assorted grains}, requisitions for the *Abum* festival on the 9th day from *Malik-bani*," 999:12–15

3.1.12 Semolina

3.1.12.1 From *Adad-tillati*

n.n.n dabin gur ki ^{d}*adad-tillati*-ta ***a-da-làl*** (muḫaldim) šu ba-an-ti, "*Adallal*, (the cook), received n bushel(s) (and) n liter(s) of semolina from *Adad-tillati*," 1096:1–4, 1106:1–5, 1111:1–4

13.1.5. dabin gur še *dar-ra-um*^{ki} ki ^{d}*adad-tillati*-ta ***a-da-làl*** muḫaldim [šu] ba-an-ti, "*Adallal*, the cook, received 13 bushels (and) 110 liters of semolina, grain of *Darra'um*, from *Adad-tillati*," 1097:1–5

3.1.12.2 From *Malik-bani*

n dabin gur níĝ-*na-kab-tum*-šè ki ^{d}*ma-lik-ba-ni*-ta ***a-da-làl*** muḫaldim šu ba-an-ti, "*Adallal*, the cook, received n bushel(s) of semolina for the *nakabtum* from *Malik-bani*," 1080:1–5, 1084:1–5, 1099:1–5, 1107:1–5, 1115:1–5, 1136:1–5

0.1.0. dabin šà-g[al] nam-ra-ak ki ^{d}*ma-lik-ba-ni*-ta ***a-da-làl*** šu ba-a[n-t]i, "*Adallal* received 60 liters of semolina, provisions of the booty, from *Malik-bani*," 1085:1–5

n dabin ki ^{d}*ma-lik-ba-ni*-ta ***a-da-làl*** (muḫaldim) šu ba-an-ti, "*Adallal*, (the cook), received n liter(s) of semolina from *Malik-bani*," 1137:1–4, 1151:1–4

3.1.13 Sesame from *Adad-tillati*

[n s]ìla ĝeš-ì [x]-ga_6? a[ka x? k]i ^{d}*adad-tillati*-ta ***a-da-làl*** šu ba-ti, "*Adallal* received [n] liter(s) of (?) sesame from *Adad-tillati*," 1181:1–5

3.1.14 Wages for Female Millers from *Adad-tillati*

1.0.0. še gur á géme kíkken-šè ki ^{d}*adad-tillati*-ta ***a-d[a-l]àl*** šu ba-ti, "*Adallal* received 1 bushel of barley from *Adad-tillati* for wages of female millers," 538:1–5

3.1.15 Workwomen from *Aštaqqar*

390 géme u_4-1-šè ⌜ki⌝ *aš-tá-qar*-ta [***a***]***-da-làl*** [ì]-dab_5, "*Adallal* took in charge 390 workwomen for 1 day from *Aštaqqar*," 812:1–5

3.1.16 Commodity Broken or Uncertain

40 x-x 3-kam-ús 44 gu_4?-tur [n] ku_6 al-dar-ra [. . .]-x-gen ki ^{d}*adad-tillati*-ta ***a-da-làl* šu ba-an-ti, "*Adallal* received 40 (liters?) of 3rd-quality x-x, 44 (liters?) of peas, [n] (liters?) of split (dried) fish (and) [n] ordinary [. . .] from *Adad-tillati*," 1070:1–7

4 gú-ús-sa sullim ki ^{d}*adad-tillati*-ta ***a-da-làl* muḫaldim šu ba-ti, "*Adallal*, the cook, received 4 (?) from *Adad-tillati*," 1143:1–4

[. . .] ki [^{d}*ma-lik-ba-ni*-ta] ***a-da-làl*** šu ba-ti, "*Adallal* received [. . .] from [*Malik-bani*]," 1191:1–5

[. . .ki] *ì-lí-aš-r*[*a-ni*]-ta [***a***]***-da-làl*** [šu ba-ti], "*Adallal* received [. . .] from *Ili-ašranni*," 1213:1–4

3.2 As a Witness

igi ***a-da-làl*** muḫaldim, "witnessed by *Adallal*, the cook," 1046:11, 1065:8

4. *Adallal,* the Gardener and Son of *Si'um*

4.1 Deliveries: Wood

(. . .) ì-⌜DU⌝ ***a-da-làl*** dumu *si-um* um-mi-a šà zabala$_4^{ki}$(. . .) [n] sar gíd-da [níĝ]-šid-da $^{[d]}$*adad-tillati* šabra [ì]-dab$_5$ [zi-ga *sí*]*mat-*^{d}*ištaran* [ĝìri *a-ḫ*]*u-ma* dub-sar, "{parcels of land; in it: date palm, pine boards of boats, seedlings and planks}, the delivery of *Adallal*, the son of *Si'um*, the craftsman, in Zabala, (and) {2 other deliveries of similar commodities}. (In total:) [n] sar (of land) was surveyed. *Adad-tillati*, the majordomo, took in charge the account. (It was) [the expenditure] of *Simat-Ištaran* [under the authority of] *Aḫuma*, the scribe," 1362:'49–'51, '73–'78

4.2 Receipts

4.2.1 Dates and Palm Products

14.3.[n.] zú-lum gur 2.1.0. u$_4$-ḫi-in gur 600½ 4 gín ^{ĝeš}zé-na 820 peš-múrgu 4⅔ 8 gín peš-ga 1500 á-an-zú-lum ká[b d]u$_{11}$-ga ^{ĝeš}kiri$_6$ ***a-da-làl*** dumu *si-um* šu ba-ti, "*Adallal*, the son of *Si'um*, received 14 bushels (and) 180[+n] liters of dates, 2 bushels (and) 60 liters of fresh dates, 600½ (minas and) 4 shekels of date palm frond midribs, 820 date palm spines, 4⅔ (minas and) 8 shekels of date palm hearts (and) 1500 date clusters; commodities of the garden measured for accounting," 1237:1–9

4.2.2 Seed from *Adad-tillati*

6 sìla numun ga ki ^{d}*adad-tillati*-ta ***a-da-làl*** dumu *še-um* šu ba-an-ti, "*Adallal*, the son of *Si'um*, received 6 liters of leek(?) seed from *Adad-tillati*," 1129:1–6

4.3 Garden Products in his Possession

lá-ìa 40 ma-na 10⅔ gín ^{ú}sullim-a 132 gín ^{ĝeš}zé-na 192 peš-múrgu lá-ìa-àm ***a-da-***[***là***]***l*** dumu *si-um* [in]-da-ĝál, "The remainder of 40 minas (and) 10⅔ shekels of fenugreek, 132 shekels of date palm frond midribs (and) 192 date palm spines are with *Adallal*, the son of *Si'um*," 1350:1–6

[lá-ì]a 1.2.4.4 sìla zú-lum gu[r] 5⅚<ma-na> 3 gín peš-ga 565 á-an-zú-lum lá-ìa ***a-da-làl*** nu-^{ĝeš}kiri$_6$ in-da-ĝál, "The remainder of 1 bushel (and) 164 liters of dates, 5⅚ minas (and) 3 shekels of date palm hearts (and) 565 date clusters are with *Adallal*, the gardener," 1066:1–5

5. *Adallal,* the Fish-sauce Manufacturer

5.1 Receipts

5.1.1 Asssorted Commodities for Fish-sauce

0.0.1. Ú.KUR 0.0.4. gazi 40 ma-na ki-lá šeg$_{12}$-mun-[sig$_5$] mu ku$_6$ al-[ús-sa-šè] ***a-da-làl*** šu ba-ti iti u$_5$-bí-gu$_7$ (. . .) úgu a ĝá-ĝá ga-ga-ra-a ki ^{d}*adad-tillati*-ta ⌜ba⌝-zi, "In month 4, *Adallal* received 10 liters Ú.KUR, 40 liters gazi (and) a brick of [fine] salt weighing 40 minas [for] fish-sauce from *Adad-tillati*, (and) {other disbursals}, the total placed in the account," 1162:'44–'50, '66–'70[20]

---

20 Although *Adallal*'s title is not specified, the context suggests that it is *Adallal* the fish-sauce manufacturer and not some other *Adallal*.

5.1.2 Chaff for Burning[21]

1.0.4.2. sìla tuḫ-duru$_5$-sig$_5$ bíl-šè ***a-da-làl*** šu ba-ti (. . .) iti ki-siki-^{d}nin-[a-zu] úgu-a g̃á-g̃á ga-ga-ra-a ki ^{d}*adad-tillati*-ta ⸢ba⸣-zi, "In month 5, *Adallal* received 1 bushel (and) 42 liters of fine fresh chaff for burning from *Adad-tillati*, (and) {other disbursals}; the total placed in the account," 1162:'51–'54, '64–'70

1.3.1. tuḫ-duru$_5$-sig$_5$ bíl-šè ***a-da-làl*** lú-ùr-ra šu ba-ti ki ^{d}*adad-tillati*-ta ba-zi, "*Adallal*, the fish-sauce manufacturer, received 1 bushel (and) 190 liters of fine fresh chaff for burning from *Adad-tillati*," 1218:1–6

1.3.2. tuḫ-duru$_5$-gen gur bíl-šè ***a-da-làl*** šu ba-ti ki ^{d}*adad-tillati*-ta ba-zi, "*Adallal* received 1 bushel (and) 200 liters of ordinary fresh chaff for burning from *Adad-tillati*," 1219:1–6

6. *Adallal*, Title Unspecified

6.1 Deliveries

6.1.1 Female Millers

6 géme kíkken u$_4$-10-šè še ù-dag-ga^{ki}-ta gar-ša-an-na^{ki}-šè de$_6$-a 6 géme kíkken u$_4$-[n-šè] še [GN-ta GN-šè de$_6$-a g̃ìri ^{d}*adad-tillati*] šabra ki ***a-da-làl***-ta ba-zi, "[Under the authority of *Adad-tillati*], the majordomo, *Adallal* disbursed 6 female millers for 10 days having brought barley from Udaga to Garšana (and) 6 female millers [for n] day(s) [having brought] barley [from GN to GN]," 289:1–10

10 géme kíkken u$_4$-1-šè a-rá-1-kam 10 géme kíkken u$_4$-1-šè a-rá-2-kam 10 géme kíkken u$_4$-1-šè a-rá-3-kam še an-za-qar-*da-da*-ta gar-ša-an-na^{ki}-šè de$_6$-a g̃ìri ^{d}*adad-tillati* šabra ki ***a-da-làl***-ta ba-zi, "Under the authority of *Adad-tillati*, the majordomo, *Adallal* disbursed 10 female millers for 1 day for the 1st time, 10 female millers for 1 day for the 2nd time (and) 10 female millers for 1 day for the 3rd time having brought barley from the fortified tower of *Dada* to Garšana," 296:1–12

4 géme kíkken u$_4$-20-šè še é-duru$_5$-kab-bi^{ki}-ta gar-ša-an-na^{ki}-šè de$_6$-a g̃ìri ^{d}*adad-tillati* šabra [ki ***a***]***-da-làl***-ta [ba]-zi, "Under the authority of *Adad-tillati*, the majordomo, *Adallal* disbursed 4 female millers for 20 days having brought barley from the Kabbi village to Garšana," 301:1–6

6.1.2 Flour, Receipt of *Aštaqqar*

2 sìla zì-gu-ús ki ***a-da-làl***-ta *aš-tá-qar* šu ba-ti, "*Aštaqqar* received 2 liters of 2nd-quality gu-flour from *Adallal*," 816:1–4

6.1.3 Pine Trees, Receipt of *A'allu*

1800 ^{geš}ù-⸢suḫ$_5$⸣-tur-tur ki ***a-da-làl***-[ta] *a-al-lu-ú* šu ba-an-ti, "*A'allu* received 1800 small pine trees from *Adallal*," 1056 :1–4

6.1.4 Semolina, Receipt of *Anaḫ-ili*

5 sìla dabin kuš-udu-niga ki ***a-da-làl***<-ta> *a-na-aḫ-ì-lí* šu ba-ti, "*Anaḫ-ili* received 5 liters of semolina (for processing) skins of fattened sheep from *Adallal*," 957:1–5

---

21 Although *Adallal*'s title is not specified in nos. 1162 and 1219, these texts have been included here to highlight their parallels with no. 1218.

6.2 Receipts

6.2.1 Barley from *Adad-tillati*, Seal of *Šubultum*, Wife of *Adallal*

2.0.0 še gur sahar zi-ga-šè ki ^{d}*adad-tillati*-ta ***a-da-làl*** šu ba-ti kišib *šu-bu-ul-tum* dam-ni íb-ra, "*Adallal* received 2 bushels of barley for having moved dirt from *Adad-tillati*. *Šubultum*, his wife, rolled (her) seal," 1201:1–6

6.2.2 Semolina

6.2.2.1 From the Account of *Ili-bilani*, the Cook

0.2.0. dabin ***a-da-làl*** iti 6-kam šu ba-ti (. . .) [níĝ-kas$_7$]-aka [*ì-lí*]-*bi-la-ni* muhaldim, "In the 6th month, *Adallal* received 120 (liters) of semolina, (and) {other allotments}; the balanced account of *Ili-bilani*, the cook," 1527:31–34, 48–49

6.2.2.2 From *Ili-andul*

1.0.0. dabin ⸢gur⸣ 0.0.3. [. . . x]-ús ki *ì-lí-an-dùl*-ta ***a-da-làl*** šu ba-ti, "*Adallal* received 1 bushel of semolina (and) 30 liters 2nd-quality [. . .] from *Ili-andul*," 1186:1–5

6.2.2.3 From *Malik-bani*

2.0.0. dabin gur ki ^{d}*ma-lik-ba-ni*-ta ***a-da-làl*** šu ba-an-ti, "*Adallal* received 2 bushels of semolina from *Malik-bani*," 1082:1–4

6.2.3 Workers Assigned to Crush Malt, Supervised by *Simat-Ea*

n ĝuruš n géme ugula *simat-é-a* munu$_4$ naĝ$_4$-ĝá-dè ***a-da-làl*** ì-dab$_5$ kurum$_7$ aka, "Inspection (of the work) of n workmen (and) n workwomen, supervised by *Simat-Ea*. *Adallal* took (the workers) in charge to crush malt," 164:1–6, 165:1–7, 168:1–6

10 ĝuruš [n] géme ugula *simat*-[*é*]-*a* munu$_4$ naĝ$_4$-⸢ĝa⸣-dè ***a-da-làl*** ì-dab$_5$, "*Adallal* took in charge 10 workmen and [n] workwomen, supervised by *Simat-Ea*, to crush malt," 166:1–5

6.2.4 Contents Lost

a-da-làl ì-dab$_5$ kurum$_7$ aka, "Inspection (of the work of workers), whom *Adallal* took in charge," 218:'1–'3

6.3 Barley in his Possession

41.2.0. še gur še apin-lá ki ***a-da-làl*** in-da-ĝál ĝìri *nu-úr*-^{d}*adad* šà du$_6$-sahar-ra^{ki}, "Under the authority of *Nur-Adad* in Du-sahara, 41 bushels (and) 120 liters of barley, barley of the cultivator, are with *Adallal* at his place" 1158:1–6

6.4 *Adallal* in Worker-Inspection Texts

6.4.1 *Adallal*, the Runaway from the Gang of *Abiati*, the Ox-Herder

zàh ***a-da-làl*** *a-bí-a-ti* nu-bànda-gu$_4$ (. . .) ugula *ba-ba-ni* šabra, "*Adallal*, the runaway (from the gang of) *Abiati*, the ox-herder, (and) {other runaways}, supervised by *Babani*, the majordomo," 192:'22,'26, 195:'30, '34, 196:'33, '37, 197:42, 46

6.4.2 Inspection of his Workmen

17 g̃uruš ***a-da-làl*** (. . .) kurum$_7$ aka saḫar ⸢zi⸣-ga $^{\text{g̃eš}}$kiri$_6$ gar-ša-an-na^{ki}, "Inspection (of the work) of 17 workmen of *Adallal*, (and) {other workers}, having moved dirt at the Garšana garden," 179:5, 17–18

a-ga-ti

Agati, Sister of *Šu-Kabta*

1. Provisions: Fresh Apples

0.0.3. $^{\text{g̃eš}}$hašḫur-duru$_5$ ***a-ga-ti*** nin$_9$ *šu-kab-tá* zi-ga g̃iri *šu-kab-tá*, "30 liters of fresh apples (for) *Agati*, the sister of *Šu-Kabta*. (It was) the expenditure of *Šu-Kabta* under his authority," 415:1–4

a-gu-a

é-***a-gu-a***, "house of *Agua*" > *Household Index*

Agua, Overseer of 60

1. Under the Authority of *Agua*: Delivery of Wool and Baskets

(. . .) 28 ^{gi}gúrdub siki ka<-tab> sè-ga ki *a-wi-lum-ma*-ta ^{d}*adad-tillati* šu ba-an-ti g̃iri ***a-gu-a*** ugula-g̃éš-da, "Under the authority of *Agua*, overseer of 60, *Adad-tillati* received {assorted wool} (and) 28 reed baskets of wool fitted with a cover from *Awilumma*," 623:4–8

a-ḫa-ni-šu

1. Requisitions

$^{\text{[d]}}$*adad-tillati* ù-na-a-du$_{11}$ 5.0.0. še gur 0.0.1.2 sìla ì-g̃eš [n] ma-na siki [níg̃]-dab$_5$ zà-mu-k[a]-ni ***a-ḫa-ni-šu*** ḫé-na-ab-sum-mu, "Say to *Adad-tillati* that '5 bushels of barley, 12 liters of sesame oil (and) [n] mina(s) of wool, the requisitions at the beginning of the year, should be given to *Aḫanišu*,'" 1042:1–8

a-ḫu-a

1. *Aḫu'a*, Spouse of *Gasusu*

1 géme-^{d}en-ki géme uš-bar sag̃-ba *ga-su-su* dam ***a-ḫu-a*** *a-na-a* maškim zi-ga *tá-ki-il-ì-lí-ís-sú* ki ^{d}*adad-tillati*-ta ba-zi, "*Adad-tillati* disbursed Geme-Enki, the female weaver, the servant of *Gasusu*, the wife of *Aḫu'a*. (It was) the expenditure of *Takil-ilissu*. *Ana'a* was the deputy," 270:1–7

2. *Aḫu'a*, Title Unspecified

2.1 As a Deputy: Offerings for Lamentation Singers

(. . .) gala-e-ne a-rá-5-kam ér iri ni$_{10}$-ni$_{10}$ ***a-ḫu-a*** maškim zi-ga *simat*-^{d}*ištaran* [ki ^{d}]*adad-tillati*-ta ba-zi, "*Adad-tillati* disbursed {assorted comestibles} of the lamentation singers (for the performance of) a *takribtum* (involving) circling around the city for the 5th time (and on) {4 other occasions}. (It was) the expenditure of *Simat-Ištaran*. *Aḫu'a* was the deputy," 1030:36–41

2.2 Receipts: Sheep and Sheep Products

[6]9 ádda-udu 69 kuš-udu 2 ma-na 18 gín sa ⌈udu⌉ ***a-ḫu-a*** mu-na-b[a?] ki *á-wi-lum-ma*-ta ^{d}*adad-tillati* šu ba-[ti], "*Adad-tillati* received from *Awilumma* [6]9 sheep carcasses, 69 sheep skins, (and) 2 minas (and) 18 shekels of sheep sinews alloted for *Aḫu'a*," 459:1–7

1 udu-niga ***a-ḫu-a*** zi-ga *tá-ki-il-ì-lí-ís-sú* ki ^{d}*adad-tillati*-ta ba-zi, "*Adad-tillati* disbursed 1 fattened sheep (for) *Aḫu'a*. (It was) the expenditure of *Takil-ilissu*," 519:1–6

3. The Personal Gods of *Aḫu'a*

3.1 Nana

12 udu sá-du$_{11}$-^{d}na?-na ***a-ḫu-a***, "(In total:) 12 sheep, regular offerings of Nana, (the personal deity of) *Aḫu'a*," 984:'44–'45

3.2 Nin-Siana

kaš-dé-a ^{d}nin-^{d}si$_{4}$-an-na ***a-ḫu-a***, "the banquet of Nin-Siana, (the personal deity of) *Aḫu'a*" > **kaš-dé-a**

[n] udu [s]á-du$_{11}$-^{d}nin-$^{[d]}$si$_{4}$-an-na ***a-ḫu-a***, "[n] sheep, regular offerings of Nin-Siana, (the personal deity of) *Aḫu'a*," 982:1–2

a-ḫu-ba-qar

Aḫu-baqar, Man from Karkar

[1] ***a-ḫu-ba-qar*** (. . .) ugula *á-ni*-x-x (. . .) lú-karkar^{ki}-me, "*Aḫu-baqar*, supervised by *á-ni*-x-x, (and) {other workers}, men from Karkar," 559:19, 25, 28

a-ḫu-DU$_{10}$

1. *Aḫu-ṭabu*, the Reed Craftsman

1.1 Assorted Commodities, in his Possession

lá-ìa 0.3.2.9⅓ sìla 6 gín ésir-é-a 1 ma-na 18 gín níğ-U.NU-a siki-ud$_{5}$ 1 ma-na im-bábbar 34⅔ ma-na BÚR [n] gú 6½ ma-na 5 gín šu-sar peš 331⅔ ⅓ gín ğuruš u$_{4}$-1-šè lá-ìa-àm ***a-ḫu*-DU$_{10}$** ad-kub$_{4}$ in-da-ğál, "The remainder of 209⅓ liters (and) 6 shekels of house bitumen, 1 mina (and) 18 shekels of goat hair thread, 1 mina of gypsum, 34⅔ minas of BÚR, [n] talent(s), 6½ minas (and) 5 shekels of palmleaf cord (and) 331⅔ ⅓ workmen days are with *Aḫu-ṭabu*, the reed craftsman," 1343:1–8

[60?+]60 ^{gi}ku-ni-na [n ^{gi}m]a-sá-a[b n]-sìla-ta ***a-ḫu*-DU$_{10}$** ⌈ad⌉-kub$_{4}$ in-da-ğál, "[60?+]60 drinking straws (and) [n] ma-sab basket(s) of [n]-liter(s) each are with *Aḫu-ṭabu*, the reed craftsman," 1345:1–4

2. *Aḫu-ṭabu*, Title Unspecified

2.1 Receipts from *Adad-tillati*

2.1.1 Assorted Commodities

[n dug] kaš 0.0.3.-ta 6 gi-ma-s[ab] 30 ^{gi}ku-ni-n[a . . .] 26 gú ì[(-x?) n.n.n.]-ta ⌈ki⌉ ^{d}*adad-tillati*-[ta ***a***]***-ḫu*-DU$_{10}$** šu ba-ti, "*Aḫu-ṭabu* received [n] 30 liter [jug(s)] of beer, 6 ma-sab baskets, 30 [. . .] drinking straws (and) 26 talents [(x?)] oil (jugs?) of [n]-liter(s) each from *Adad-tillati*," 1312:1–7

2.1.2 Reeds

30 sa gi-šid ki ^{d}*adad-tillati*-ta ***a-ḫu*-DU$_{10}$** šu ba-ti, "*Aḫu-ṭabu* received 30 bundles of dry reeds from *Adad-tillati*," 1348:1–4

2.2 Under his Authority: Delivery of Reeds

[7]80 sa gi-zi gu-níĝin 11-sa-ta ki *šu-ì-lí*-ta ^{d}*adad-tillati* šu ba-ti ĝìri ***a-ḫu*-DU$_{10}$**, "Under the authority of *Aḫu-ṭabu*, *Adad-tillati* received [7]80 bundles of fresh reeds, bales of 11 bundles each, from *Šu-ili*," 1335:1–6

a-ḫu-ma

Aḫuma, the Scribe

1. Under his Authority: Land Surveyed in Zabala and Garšana and the Wood Produced on It

(. . .) ì-DU *a-da-làl* dumu *šu*-ma-ma um-mi-a (. . .) ì-⌜DU⌝ *a-da-làl* dumu *si-um* um-mi-a šà zabala$_{4}^{ki}$ (. . .) [ì]-DU [x-x?]-ti-en um-mi-a [šà gar]-ša-an-na^{ki} [n] sar gíd-da [níĝ]-šid-da $^{[d]}$*adad-tillati* šabra [ì]-dab$_{5}$ [zi-ga *si*]*mat*-^{d}*ištaran* [ĝìri ***a-ḫ*]*u-ma*** dub-sar, "{parcels of land; in it: date palm, pine boards of boats, seedlings}, the delivery of *Adallal*, the son of *Šu-*Mama, the craftsman; {parcels of land; in it: date palm, pine boards of boats, seedlings and planks}, the delivery of *Adallal*, the son of *Si'um*, the craftsman in Zabala; (and) {parcels of land; in it: date palm, pine boards of boats and seedlings}, the delivery of [PN], the craftsman, in Garšana. (In total:) [n] sar (of land) was surveyed. *Adad-tillati*, the majordomo, took in charge the account. (It was) [the expenditure] of *Simat-Ištaran* [under the authority of] *Aḫuma*, the scribe," 1362:'23–'24, '49–'51, '69–'78

a-ḫu-ni

1. As a Deputy: Barley Wages

[n+]5.0.0. še gur á 5-sìla-ta [šeg$_{12}$ d]u$_{8}$-a-šè [ki ^{d}]*adad-tillati*-[ta] *simat-é*-[*a* ugula lú]-ḫuĝ-[ĝá] ***a-ḫu-ni*** maškim šu ba-an-ti, "*Simat-Ea*, [overseer] of hired workers, received from *Adad-tillati* [n+]5 bushels of barley, wages of 5 liters each for (workers) having molded bricks. *Aḫuni* was the deputy," 447:1–7

a-ḫu-wa-qar

1. *Aḫu-waqar*, the Gardener

1.1 Receipts

1 ^{urudu}gu$_{4}$-zi-bi-ir ½ ma-na 1 gín ki ^{d}*adad-tillati*-ta ***a-ḫu-wa-qar*** nu-^{ĝeš}kiri$_{6}$ šu ba-an-ti, "*Aḫu-waqar*, the gardener, received 1 stepladder (weighing) ½ mina (and) 1 shekel from *Adad-tillati*," 1269:1–4

2. *Aḫu-waqar*, Man from Du-lugal-pa'e

2.1 A Message Brought to *Aḫu-waqar*

1 *šu*-^{d}*belum* á-áĝ ki ***a-ḫu-wa-qar*** lú-du$_{6}$-lugal-pa-è^{ki} de$_{6}$-a, "*Šu-Belum* having brought a message to the place of *Aḫu-waqar*, the man from Du-lugal-pa'e," 45:28–29, 46:'44, 47:56, 48:62–63

3. *Aḫu-waqar*, Man from *Izin-Erra*

3.1 As a Runaway

zàḫ ***a-ḫu-wa-qar*** zàḫ *u-bar-um* [lú]-*i-zi-in-èr-ra*^{ki}-éš, "*Aḫu-waqar* (and) *Ubarum*, runaways from *Izin-Erra*," 378:6–8

3.2 Provisions

[2 sìla] ninda-ta (. . .) 1 ***a-ḫu-wa-qar*** 1 *u-bar-um* lú-*i-zi-in-èr-ra*^{ki} (. . .) šà-gal ši[dim-e-n]e ⌜u$_4$⌝ [bàd egir] é-a dù-dè, "[2 liters] of bread each for *Aḫu-waqar* (and) *Ubarum*, men from *Izin-Erra*, (and for) {other workers}, food (for) builders when they were constructing [the (enclosure) wall behind] the house," 386:1, 7–9, 29–30

4. *Aḫu-waqar*, the Scribe: Transactions Under his Authority

4.1 Assignments for Craftsmen

4.1.1 Bringing Barley to Garšana

1 g̃uruš ašgab 1 g̃uruš ad-kub$_4$ 1 géme kíkken u$_4$-[2]7-šè še ^{d}*šu*-^{d}*suen*-<am->ma-ra$^{[ki]}$ ù bàd-ga-zi^{ki}-⌜ta⌝ gar-ša-an-na^{ki}-šè de$_6$-a g̃ìri ***a-ḫu-wa-qar*** dub-sar ù g̃iri-né-ì-dab$_5$ ra-gaba ki ^{d}*adad-tillati*-ta ba-zi, "Under the authority of *Aḫu-waqar*, the scribe, and G̃irine-idab, the courier, *Adad-tillati* disbursed 1 leather worker, 1 reed craftsman (and) 1 female miller for [2]7 days having brought barley from *Šu-suen*-ammara and Bad-gazi to Garšana" 259:1–10

4.1.2 Moving Dirt

1 g̃uruš túg-du$_8$ [u$_4$]-21-šè saḫar zi-ga i$_7$-sur du$_6$-ba-an-du$_8$-du$_8$ a-⌜šà⌝ sum-túl-túl g̃ìri ***a-ḫu-wa-qar*** dub-sar, "Under the authority of *Aḫu-waqar*, the scribe, 1 braider for 21 [days] having moved dirt at the Sur canal of Du-bandudu (and?/in?) the Sum-tultul field," 268:1–6

4.1.3 Reaping Barley at the Field of *Dimbun*-Ašgi

1 g̃uruš ašgab u$_4$-1-šè še gur$_{10}$-gur$_{10}$-dè a-šà-*dì-im-bu-na*-àš-gi$_5$ gub-ba ur-^{d}nin-^{d}si$_4$-an-na maškim ki ^{d}*adad-tillati*-ta ba-zi g̃ìri ***a-ḫu-wa-qar*** dub-sar, "Under the authority of *Aḫu-waqar*, the scribe, *Adad-tillati* disbursed 1 leather worker employed for 1 day to reap barley at the *Dimbun*-Ašgi field. Ur-Nin-Siana was the deputy," 282:1–6

4.2 Receipts of *Adad-tillati*

4.2.1 Barley Rations at the Field of *Dimbun*-Ašgi

3.3.1.5 sìla še še-ba géme-árad ki *i-mé-èr-ra*-ta ^{d}*adad-tillati* šu ba-ti ⌜g̃ìri⌝ ***a-ḫu-wa-[qar]*** dub-[sar] a-šà-*dì-im-bu-[na]*-^{aš}aš$_7$-gi$_4$^{ki}, "Under the authority of *Aḫu-waqar*, the scribe, *Adad-tillati* received from *Im-Erra* 3 bushels (and) 195 liters of barley, barley rations of female and male servants at the *Dimbun*-Ašgi field," 527:1–7

4.2.2 Dates

[n].4.2. zú-[lum] gur ki *za-la-a*-ta ^{d}*adad-tillati* šu ba-ti ⌜g̃ìri⌝ ***a-ḫu-wa-qar*** dub-sar, "Under the authority of *Aḫu-waqar*, the scribe, *Adad-tillati* received [n] bushel(s) (and) 260 liters of dates from *Zala'a*," 1205:5

4.2.3 Reeds

1470 sa gi-zi gu-níg̃in 10-sa-ta gu-níg̃in-bi 147-àm ^{d}*adad-tillati* šu ba-ti ki *puzur$_4$*-^{d}en-líl-ta ba-zi g̃ìri ***a-ḫu-wa-qar*** dub-sar kišib ***a-ḫu-wa-qar****-ra*! u$_4$-um-de$_6$ kišib *puzur$_4$*-^{d}en-líl zi-re-dam, "Under the authority of *Aḫu-waqar*, the scribe, *Adad-*

tillati received from *Puzur*-Enlil 1470 bundles of fresh reeds, bales of 10 bunches each, its bales are 147. When the sealed tablet of *Aḫu-waqar* is brought, *Puzur*-Enlil's sealed tablet will be canceled," 1361:1–12

5. *Aḫu-waqar*, Title Unspecified

5.1 Deliveries: Offerings for the (Enclosure) Wall

1 sìla dabin ½ sìla eša sízkur bàd-šè ki ***a-ḫu-wa-qar*** ba-zi g̃ìri ^{d}*adad-tillati ù puzur*$_4$-^{d}nin-kar-ak dub-sar, "Under the authority of *Adad-tillati* and *Puzur*-Ninkarak, the scribe, *Aḫu-waqar* disbursed 1 liter of semolina (and) ½ liter of fine flour, (ceremonial) offerings for the (enclosure) wall," 992:1–7, 993:1–7, 995:1–7

5.2 Orders Received

a-ḫu-wa-qar ù-na-a-⌜du$_{11}$⌝ 1 sila$_4$-máš [ḫi-a] 5 gú ⌜sar⌝ ḫi-a *a-na-*[*a*?] ḫé-na-ab-sum-mu, "Say to *Aḫu-waqar* that '[various] lambs (and) goats (and) 5 talents of various vegetables(?) should be given to *Ana'a*,'" 1041:1–6

ur-^{d}dumu-zi ù ***a-ḫu-wa-qar*** ù-na-a-⌜du$_{11}$⌝ 0.0.2. ku-[x] *šu*-^{d}nisaba ḫé-na-ab-sum-mu 1 g̃uruš šà-gu$_4$ iri^{ki}-ta iri^{ki}-šè ḫé-eb-sá-e nam-mi-gur-re, "Say to Ur-Dumuzi and *Aḫu-waqar* that '20 liters of (?) should be given to *Šu*-Nisaba. 1 ox-driver from the city should arrive at the city. They should not argue!'" 1045:1–11

a-ku$_8$-a-nu-ri

1. Provisions: a Textile

1 túg-^{d}*al-la-tum*-gùn-a ù zi-in-bi ki-lá-bi 9 ma-[na] 12 gín ***a-ku$_8$-a-nu-ri* *nu-úr-*^{d}*adad* maškim zi-ga g̃ìri *šu-kab-ta* ki *aš-tá-qar*-ta ba-zi, "*Aštaqqar* disbursed 1 colored textile of *Allatum* and its zi-in weighing 9 minas (and) 12 shekels (for) *Akua-nuri*. (It was) the expenditure of *Šu-Kabta* under his authority. *Nur-Adad* was the deputy," 584:1–7

a-la-tum

1. Sheep for his Funerary Libation Place

1 udu-ú ki-a-nag-árad-^{d}nana ù ***a-la-tum*** ki *ì-lí-aš-ra-ni*-ta ba-zi, "*Ili-ašranni* disbursed 1 range-fed sheep (for) the funerary libation place of *Arad*-Nanna and *Allatum*," 971:1–5

a-lí-a-bi

é-ki-ba-g̃ar-ra ***a-lí-a-bi***, "the replacement house of *Aliabi*" > *Household Index*

1. Provisions: Barley

[n+]2.4.0. gur ***a-lí-a-bi*** [gur] (. . .) [šu+níg̃in n+]5.4.1.8 sìla še gur lugal-ú-šim-e árad!-me-éš, "[n+]160 liters of barley (for) *Aliabi*, (and barley for) {others}, [in total: n+]5 bushels and 258 liters of barley (for) the servants (supervised by) Lugal-ušime," 504:3, 7–10

0.0.4. ***a-⌜lí⌝-a-bi*** (. . .) mu dabin-šè šu ba-ti, "*Aliabi* received 40 liters of barley (and barley for) {9 other individuals}, (barley) in place of semolina," 560:7, 12–13

a-lí-aḫ

Ali-aḫ, the Household Servant from the Gang of *Irib*

1. **Bringing Barley from G̃irsu**

1 ***a-lí-aḫ*** še è(-dè) g̃ír-su^ki^-šè g̃en-na, "*Ali-aḫ* having gone to G̃irsu to bring out barley," 37:34–35, 38:40–41, 43:'45–'46, 44:44–45, 45:26–27, 47:57, 48:64–65

1 *ta-tù-ri* ù ***a-lí-aḫ*** še è-dè g̃ír-su^ki^-šè g̃en-na g̃ìri *ṣa-al-lum* ^lú^kíg̃-gi$_4$-a-lugal, "*Tatturi* and *Ali-aḫ* having gone to G̃irsu to bring out barley under the authority of *Ṣallum*, the royal messenger," 31:37–38, 32:37, 33:40–41, 35:44–45, 36:39

2. **Guarding Barley in G̃irsu**

1 ***a-lí-aḫ*** 1 *ta-tù-ri* še šà g̃ír-su^ki^ en-nu ke$_4$-dè gub-ba, "*Ali-aḫ* (and) *Tatturi* employed to guard barley in G̃irsu," 51:'19–'21, 52:56–58, 53:58–60

[1 ***a***]***-lí-a***[***ḫ*** 1 *ta-tù*]-⌜*ri*⌝ še šà [g̃ír]-su^ki^ en-nu k[e$_4$-dè] tuš-[a], "*Ali-aḫ* (and) *Tatturi* having sat [in order to] guard barley in G̃irsu," 56:'29–'31

3. **Broken Context**

1 ***a-lí-***[***aḫ***] 1 *ta-*[*tù-ri*] š[e . . .], 54:'35–'37

a-lim-ma

1. **Deliveries: Wool and Baskets, Receipt of *Adad-tillati***

(. . .) 14 ^gi^gúrdub siki ka-tab sè-ga ki ***a-lim-ma***-ta ^d^*adad-tillati* šu ba-⌜ti⌝ g̃ìri ^d^*puzur$_4$-a-gu$_5$-um*, "Under the authority of *Puzur-agum*, *Adad-tillati* received {assorted wool and textiles} (and) 14 reed baskets of wool fitted with a cover from *Alima*," 667:18–22

a-ma-a

1. **Deliveries: Ordinary Linen, Receipt of *Puzur-agum***

1 gada-gen ki ***a-ma-a***-ta *puzur$_4$-a-gu$_5$-um* šu ba-ti, "*Puzur-agum* received 1 ordinary linen from *Ama'a*," 688:1–5, 707:1–4

1.1 **Under the Authority of *Adad-tillati***

1 gada-gen ki ***a-ma-a***-ta *puzur$_4$-a-gu$_5$-um* šu ba-ti g̃ìri ^d^*adad-tillati* šabra, "Under the authority of *Adad-tillati*, the majordomo, *Puzur-agum* received 1 ordinary linen from *Ama'a*," 659:1–6

1.2 **Under the Authority of *Adad-tillati* and *Malik-bani***

1 gada-gen ki ***a-ma-a***-ta *puzur$_4$-a-gu$_5$-um* šu ba-ti g̃ìri ^d^*adad-tillati* ù ^d^*ma-lik-ba-ni*, "Under the authority of *Adad-tillati* and *Malik-bani*, *Puzur-agum* received 1 ordinary linen from *Ama'a*," 664:1–6

a-na-a

1. ***Ana'a*, the Female Miller**

1.1 **Provisions**

[1] *za-a-za* [1] ***a-na-a*** [1] *lu$_5$-zi-lá* {indent} 8 [géme é]-kíkken-me-éš, "(Provisions for) *Zaza*, *Ana'a*, (and) *Luzila*, 8 [workwomen] of the mill," 562:'1–'5

2. ***Ana'a*, Title Unspecified**

2.1 **As a Deputy: Expenditures of *Takil-ilissu***

1 géme-^d^en-ki géme uš-bar sag̃-ba *ga-su-su* dam *a-ḫu-a* ***a-na-a*** maškim zi-ga *tá-ki-il-ì-lí-ís-sú* ki ^d^*adad-tillati*-ta ba-zi, "*Adad-tillati* disbursed Geme-Enki, the female weaver, the

servant of *Gasusu*, the wife of *Aḫu'a*. (It was) the expenditure of *Takil-ilissu*. *Ana'a* was the deputy," 270:1–7

(. . .) ba-na-ḫa-[la ***a*]-*na-a*** PA.[KAŠ$_4$ s]a$_{10}$-bi g̃eš 1 [x x]-na-[x] *tu-ra-am-ì-lí* d[ub-sar] PA.A[L z]i-ga [*t*]*á-ki-il-ì-lí-ís-sú* [ki] ^{d}*adad-tillati*-ta ⌜ba⌝-zi, "*Adad-tillati* disbursed {assorted commodities}. They were divided for {female weavers, sesame pressers, and millers}. *Ana'a* was the deputy. (?). *Turam-ili*, the scribe, was the majordomo. (These were) the expenditures of *Takil-ilissu*," 536:22–31

2.2 Provisions

a-ḫu-wa-qar ù-na-a-⌜du$_{11}$⌝ 1 sila$_4$-máš [ḫi-a] 5 gú ⌜sar⌝ ḫi-a ***a-na-*[*a*?]** ḫé-na-ab-sum-mu, "Say to *Aḫu-waqar* that '[various] lambs (and) goats (and) 5 talents of various vegetables(?) should be given to *Ana'a*,'" 1041:1–6

2.3 As a Witness

i[gi ***a*?-*n*]*a-a-a***, "witnessed by *Ana'a*," 1062:13

a-na-aḫ-ì-lí

Anaḫ-ili, the Leather Worker[22]

1. Deliveries

1.1 Delivery of Finished Leather Goods

1.1.1 Placed in Various Accounts

★★(. . .) $^{g̃eš}$gu-za-níta $^{g̃eš}$ku!-ku! ba-a-g̃ar x x ezem-da-šè ba-a-g̃ar ^{gi}x $^{g̃eš}$gu-za-šè ba-a-g̃ar (. . .) *bí-du-lu-um*-šè ba-a-g̃ar (. . .) *ḫu-im*-šè ba-a-g̃ar (. . .) *ib-du-um*-šè ba-a-g̃ar ki ***a-na-aḫ-ì-lí***-ta ba-zi, "*Anaḫ-ili* disbursed {finished leather products}. They were (used to) cover the man's chair (and?) the loom. (?) was placed for the festival. {Assorted commodities} were placed for *Bidulum*, for *Ḫu'im*, (and) for *Ibdum*," 1517:6, 10, 12, 15, 18, 20–21

1.1.2 Receipt of *Ili-ašranni*

5 ^{kuš}súḫub-gen é-ba-an 15 ^{kuš}súḫub-tur-gen é-ba-an 1 ^{gi}bisag̃ túg-aš *ì-lí-aš-ra-ni* šu ba-ti ki ***a-na-aḫ-ì-lí***-ta ba-zi, "*Ili-ašranni* received 5 pairs of ordinary shoes, 15 pairs of small ordinary shoes (and) 1 single textile basket from *Anaḫ-ili*," 913:1–7

1.1.3 Unspecified Recipient, Seal of *Adad-tillati*

(. . .) ki ***a-na-aḫ-ì-lí***-ta (ba-zi), "*Anaḫ-ili* disbursed {assorted leather products}," 838:3–4, 839:3–4, 853:5, 871:2–3, 892:6–7, 897:3–4, 900:3–4, 906:6, 925:'16, 933:4–5, 964:'3, 965:5–6, 966:5–6

1.1.3.1 Completed Work for the Warehouse

32 ^{kuš}*maš-lí-um*-udu-niga 17 ^{kuš}ummu$_x$ 4 ^{kuš}du$_{10}$-gan-ti-bal 2 ^{kuš}súḫub-e-sír-munus-babbar é-ba-an 2 ^{kuš}súḫub-munus-babbar é-[ba-an] 3 ^{kuš}súḫub-munus-e-[sír] é-ba-[an] kíg̃-til-[la] mu-⌜DU⌝ é-kišib-ba-⌜šè⌝ ki ***a-na-aḫ-ì-lí***-ta ba-zi, "*Anaḫ-ili* disbursed 32 leather buckets of skin of fattened sheep, 17 waterskins, 4 leather bags with markings?, 2 pairs of a woman's white

22 Although *Anaḫ-ili*'s title is not specified in every account, context dictates that there was only one person by this name operating at Garšana.

sandals, 2 pairs of a woman's white shoes, (and) 3 pairs of a woman's sandals; delivery of completed work for the warehouse," 932:1–12

1.1.3.2 (Completed) Work

7 ^{kuš}du$_{10}$-⸢gan⸣-ti-bal-⸢babbar⸣ ki ***a-na-ḫi-lí***-⸢ta⸣ mu-DU g̃iri ^{d}*adad-tillati*, "Under the authority of *Adad-tillati*, *Anaḫ-ili* disbursed 7 white leather bags with markings?; delivery (of completed work)," 849:1–4

28 ^{kuš}*maš-lí-um* 5 ^{kuš}a-g̃á-lá-[bad] á mu-DU ki ***a-na-aḫ-ì-lí***-ta ba-zi, "*Anaḫ-ili* disbursed 28 leather buckets (and) 5 [open] leather sacks; delivery of (completed) work," 930:1–6

[1?] ^{kuš}ùmmu á mu-DU ***a-na-aḫ-ì-lí***, "[1?] waterskin, delivery of (completed) work by *Anaḫ-ili*," 938:1–3

⅔ kuš-máš-g[al-ni]ga 4 ^{túg}íb-lá-su$_{4}$-a-gíd 4 kùš 2 šu-dù 1-šè ba-a-g̃ar á mu-DU ***a-na-aḫ-ì-lí***, "⅔ of a skin of a fattened billy-goat was (used for) covering 4 long red/brown belts of 4 kùš and 2 šu-dù in length; delivery of (completed) work by *Anaḫ-ili*," 939:1–4

2 kuš-udu-babbar á mu-DU ***a-na-aḫ-ì-lí***, "2 white sheep skins, delivery of (completed) work by *Anaḫ-ili*," 942:1–4

1 kuš-udu e-rí-na á mu-DU ***a-na-aḫ-ì-lí***, "1 root-tanned sheep skin; delivery of (completed) work by *Anaḫ-ili*," 945:1–3

10 ^{kuš}maš-NI-x-x-gal-še 60 ^{kuš}a-gá-lá 40 kuš-udu ka-tab e-rí-na á mu-DU ki ***a-na-aḫ-ì-lí***-ta ba-zi, "*Anaḫ-ili* disbursed 10 (?) skins, 60 leather sacks, (and) 40 root-tanned sheep skin covers; delivery of (completed) work," 1525:1–6

1.1.3.3 Requisitions of the Gendarmes

12 ^{kuš}[e-sí]r-gen é-ba-an níg̃-dab$_{5}$ àga-ús-e-ne ki ***a-na-aḫ-ì-lí***-ta ba-zi, "*Anaḫ-ili* disbursed 12 pairs of regular sandals, requisitions of the gendarmes," 858:1–3

1.2 Delivery of Leather: For Manufacture of Assorted Leather Products

1⅔ [kuš-g]u$_{4}$ 10 gín še-gín 10 gín sa-udu g̃eš-rín-⸢na⸣? gú 2 ù 30 ma-na 7 gín kuš-gu$_{4}$ ⅓ kuš-máš e-rí-na 1 gín sa-udu ^{kuš}⸢*na*⸣-*aḫ-ba*-⸢*tum*⸣ 1 kuš-[udu?]-babbar ^{gi}kid $^{g̃eš}$gu-za 1 ^{kuš}⸢súḫub⸣-gen [é]-ba-an *ba-zi* ⸢ugula⸣ lú-[ḫug̃]-g̃á 1½ [kuš-udu] e-rí-na ^{gi}kid $^{g̃eš}$gu-za-šè 1½ kuš-udu e-rí-na $^{g̃eš}$*ḫu-pu-um* 14-kam 1 kuš e-rí-na ka-la 10 gín kuš-gu$_{4}$ 5 gín sa-udu 5 gín še-gín $^{g̃eš}$gu-za kéše-da-šè 1 ^{kuš}e-sír é-ba-an 1 ^{kuš}súḫub-gen é-ba-an ^{d}*adad-tillati* ki ***a-na-aḫ-ì-lí***-ta ba-zi, "*Anaḫ-ili* disbursed 1⅔ ox [skins], 10 shekels of glue (and) 10 shekels of sheep sinew for a scale of 2 talents and 30 minas; 7 shekels of ox skin, ⅓ of a root-tanned goat skin (and) 1 shekel of sheep sinew (for) a leather carrying case; 1 white [sheep?] skin (for) a chair mat; 1 pair of ordinary shoes (for) *Bazi*, overseer of hired workers; 1½ root-tanned [sheep skins] for a chair mat; 1½ root-tanned sheep skins (for) 14 wheel rims; 1 root-tanned ka-la skin, 10 shekels of ox skin, 5 shekels of sheep sinew (and) 5 shekels of glue for binding the chair; (and) 1 pair of sandals (and) 1 pair of ordinary shoes (for) *Adad-tillati*," 855:1–26

3 kuš-udu-babbar $^{g̃eš}$šudul-gu$_{4}$-šè ba-a-g̃ar 2 kuš-udu e-rí-na a?-g̃eš-šè ba-a-g̃ar 2 ^{kuš}du$_{10}$-gan-ti-bal-babbar ⅔ 9 gín kuš-gu$_{4}$ x-x-KA×X? ka-gur-tur? x? ⸢KU⸣?-ta?? ki ***a-na-aḫ-ì-lí***-ta, "*Anaḫ-ili* disbursed 3 white sheep skins—they were (used for) covering an ox yoke—2 root-tanned sheep skins—they were (used for) covering (a wooden object?)—

2 white leather bags with markings(?) (and) ⅔ mina (and) 9 shekels of ox skin (?)," 864:1–9

5 kuš-udu e-rí-na ma-an-ḫara$_4$–3-šè ba-a-g̃ar 3 kuš-udu-babbar $^{<\text{g̃eš}>}$šudul-gu$_4$-šè ba-a-g̃ar 1 kuš-máš ⌜*mul*⌝-*tum*-šè ba-a-g̃ar [10?+]5 gín k[uš-g]u$_4$-ú-ḫáb $^{\text{g̃eš}}$gu-za kéš[e-da-š]è ⌜*šu*⌝?-*kab*?-⌜*ta*⌝? ki ***a-na-aḫ-ì-lí***-ta ba-[zi], "*Anaḫ-ili* disbursed 5 root-tanned sheep skins—they were (used for) covering 3 manhara containers—3 white sheep skins—they were (used for) covering an ox yoke—1 goat skin—it was (used for) covering a comb—(and) 15 shekels of madder-tanned ox skins for binding the chair of *Šu-Kabta*," 923:1–10

1.3 Delivery of Leather Workers and Other Workmen: Unspecified Recipient, Seal of *Adad-tillati*

(. . .) 3 g̃uruš ašgab u$_4$-2-šè gub-ba mu-DU ***a-na-<aḫ->ì-lí***, "*Anaḫ-ili* delivered {assorted leather products} (and) 3 leather workers employed for 2 days," 912:11–12

[n] kuš-udu e-r[í-na] ka-tab [n?+]1 g̃uruš u$_4$-1-šè [ki] ***a-na-aḫ-ì-lí***-ta ba-zi, "*Anaḫ-ili* disbursed [n] root-tanned sheep skin cover(s) (and) [n?+]1 workmen for 1 day," 969:'1–'3

1.3.1 Workmen to Beat their Breasts and Employed at the Storehouse

(. . .) 3 g̃uruš u$_4$-9½-šè gaba sàg-dè gub-ba 3 g̃uruš u$_4$-2-šè é-šu-sum-ma gub-ba ki ***a-na-aḫ-ì-lí***-[ta ba-zi], "*Anaḫ-ili* [disbursed] {assorted leather products} (and) 3 workmen employed to beat (their) breasts for 9½ days (and) 3 workmen employed for 2 days at the storehouse," 968:18–23

1.3.2 Workmen to Tow Boats and Transport Barley

1 kuš-udu-babbar *la-lum* 7 g̃uruš ašgab u$_4$-1-šè é-da-na^{ki}-šè má gíd-da 1 g̃uruš u$_4$-1-šè še ga$_6$-⌜g̃a⌝ 3 g̃uruš u$_4$-1-šè še é-da-[na^{ki}] karkar^{ki}-[ta] gar-ša-an-na^{ki}[-šè] íb-ga$_6$ ki ***a-na-aḫ-ì-lí***-ta ba-zi, "*Anaḫ-ili* disbursed 1 white sheep skin (for) *Lalum*, 7 leather workers for 1 day having towed a boat to Edana, 1 workman for 1 day having carried barley (and) 3 workmen for 1 day. They carried barley [from] Edana (and) Karkar [to] Garšana," 884:1–12

5 ^{kuš}e-sír-g̃en é-ba-an 3 g̃uruš u$_4$-11-šè dabin ninda túg ù ì ḫi-a gar-ša-an-na^{ki}-ta nibru^{ki}-šè má gíd-da ki ***a-na-aḫ-ì-lí***-ta ba-zi, "*Anaḫ-ili* disbursed 5 pairs of ordinary sandals (and) 3 workmen for 11 days having towed a boat (with) various (amounts of) semolina, bread, textiles (and) oil from Garšana to Nippur," 931:1–8

1.4 Delivery of Leather Workers

1.4.1 Taken in Charge by *Bala'a*

9 g̃uruš ašgab u$_4$-1-šè *ba-la-a* ì-dab$_5$ ki ***a-na-aḫ-ì-lí***-ta ba-zi, "*Bala'a* took in charge 9 leather workers for 1 day from *Anaḫ-ili*," 962:1–5

1.4.2 To Bring Barley to Garšana

1⅔ g̃uruš ⌜ašgab⌝ u$_4$-4-⌜šè⌝ še [GN]^{ki}-ta gar-[ša-an-na^{ki}]-šè de$_6$-a 1⅔ g̃uruš ašgab u$_4$-3-šè kar-ta gur$_7$-šè še íb-ga$_6$ ki ***a-na-aḫ-ì-lí***-ta ba-zi, "*Anaḫ-ili* disbursed 1⅔ leather workers for 4 days having brought barley from [GN] to Garšana (and) 1⅔ leather workers for 3 days. They carried barley from the quay to the granary," 229:1–9

2 g̃uruš [ašgab] u$_4$-[1-šè] a-rá-1-[kam] 2 g̃uruš ašgab [u$_4$-1-šè] a-rá-2-kam 2 g̃uruš ašgab u$_4$-1-šè a-rá-3-kam 2 g̃uruš ašgab u$_4$-1-šè a-rá-4-kam 2 g̃uruš ašgab u$_4$-1-šè a-rá-5-kam še an-za-qar-*da-da*-[ta] gar-ša-an-na^{ki}-šè de$_6$-a g̃iri ^{d}*adad-tillati* šabra ki ***a-na-aḫ-ì-lí***-ta ba-zi, "Under the authority of *Adad-tillati*, the majordomo, *Anaḫ-ili*

disbursed 2 [leather] workers [for 1] day (on) {5 different occasions} having brought barley [from] the fortified tower of *Dada* to Garšana," 297:1–17

[n g̃uru]š ašgab [u$_4$]-20-šè [še] é-duru$_5$-kab-bi-ta^{ki} [gar-ša]-an-na^{ki}-šè de$_6$-a [g̃iri] ^{d}*adad-tillati* šabra [ki ***a-n***]***a-aḫ-ì-lí***-ta ba-zi, "[Under the authority] of *Adad-tillati*, the majordomo, *Anaḫ-ili* disbursed [n] leather worker(s) for 20 [days] having brought [barley] from the Kabbi village to Garšana," 305:1–7

1.4.3 To Bring Wool

1⅔ g̃uruš ašgab u$_4$-6-šè siki é-^{d}*šu*-^{d}*suen*^{ki}-ka-ta mu-un-LI-sa-a ki ***a-na-aḫ-ì-lí*-ta ba-zi, "*Anaḫ-ili* disbursed 1⅔ leather workers for 6 days who brought wool from *Bit-Šu-Suen*," 228:1–7

1.4.4 To Irrigate the Garšana Garden

1⅔ guruš ašgab u$_4$-2-šè a bala-e-dè gub-ba ^{geš}kiri$_6$ šà gar-ša-an-na^{ki} ki ***a-na-aḫ-ì-lí***-ta ba-zi, "*Anaḫ-ili* disbursed 1⅔ leather workers for 2 days employed to irrigate the garden in Garšana," 1523:1–6

1.4.5 To Move Dirt

1 g̃uruš ⸢ašgab⸣ u$_4$-14-[šè] iti ezem-an-⸢na⸣ 1 g̃uruš ⸢ašgab⸣ ⸢u$_4$⸣-[n-šè n g̃uruš] ašgab i[ti ezem]-m[e-ki-g̃]ál ⸢saḫar⸣ zi-⸢ga⸣ i$_7$-ma-ma-*šar-ra-at* g̃iri *ba-ba-ni* dub-sar ki ***a-na-aḫ-ì-lí***-ta ba-zi, "Under the authority of *Babani*, the scribe, *Anaḫ-ili* disbursed 1 leather worker [for] 14 days in month 11, 1 leather worker [for n] day(s) (and) [n] leather worker(s) in month 12 having moved dirt at the Mama-*šarrat* canal," 281:1–11

1.4.6 To Pull out a Door

1 g̃uruš ašgab u$_4$-3-šè ^{geš}ig šà é-a bu-ra ki ***a-na-aḫ-ì-lí***-ta ba-zi, "*Anaḫ-ili* disbursed 1 leather worker for 3 days having pulled out a door in the house," 239:1–4

1.4.7 To Tow Boats

1 g̃uruš u$_4$-7-šè má gíd má-40-gur-ta 2-àm gar-ša-an-na^{ki}-ta nibru^{ki}-šè in-gíd-sa-a ki ***a-na-aḫ-ì-lí***-ta ba-zi, "*Anaḫ-ili* disbursed 1 workman for 7 days who towed 2 40-bushel boats from Garšana to Nippur," 255:1–7

1.4.8 Various Tasks

3 g̃uruš ašgab u$_4$-1-šè u$_4$ siki ba-a-ka šu bar-ra 2 g̃uruš ⸢u$_4$⸣-[1-š]è níg̃-gú-na é-d[a-na^{ki}-šè d]e$_6$-a 3 g̃uruš u$_4$-1-šè gaba sàg-dè gub-ba u$_4$ ^{d}šul-gi-*r*[*a-ma* ba-uš-a] 2 g̃uruš u$_4$-1-[šè] gi zabala$_4$$^{[ki]}$-[šè] de$_6$-[a] ki ***a-na-aḫ-ì-lí***-ta ba-zi, "*Anaḫ-ili* disbursed 3 leathers workers, released for 1 day on the day of the wool rations, 2 workmen for 1 day having brought the commodity tax to Edana, 3 workmen employed for 1 day to beat (their) breasts when Šulgi-*rama* [died] (and) 2 workmen [for] 1 day having brought reeds [to] Zabala," 246:1–11

2. Receipts

2.1 Animal Skins

2.1.1 From *Adad-tillati*

2.1.1.1 Assorted Skins

[12]6 kuš-⸢udu⸣ 20 kuš-sila$_4$ a-g̃ar gu$_7$ 7½ ma-na sa-udu ki ^{d}*adad-tillati*-ta ***an-na-ḫi-li***(sic!) šu ba-an-ti, "*Anaḫ-ili* received [12]6 sheep skins, 20 de-haired lamb skins (and) 7½ minas of sheep sinews from *Adad-tillati*," 840:1–7

14 kuš-udu 3 kuš-sila$_4$ 2 kuš-máš-gal 1 kuš-máš kuš-udu ba-úš ki ^{d}*adad-tillati*-ta ***a-na-aḫ-ì-lí*** šu ba-an-ti, "*Anaḫ-ili* received 14 sheep skins, 3 lamb skins, 2 billy-goat skins, (and) 1 goat skin, skins from dead (caprids), from *Adad-tillati*," 844:1–8

21 kuš-udu-ú 3 kuš-sila$_4$ 1 kuš-máš-gal 7 kuš-máš ki ^{d}*adad-tillati*-ta ***a-na-ḫi-li*** ašgab ⸢šu⸣ ba-an-ti, "*Anaḫ-ili*, the leather worker, received 21 skins of range-fed sheep, 3 lamb skins, 1 billy-goat skin, (and) 7 goat skins from *Adad-tillati*," 847:1–7

[4]2 kuš-udu 5 kuš-sila$_4$ 2 kuš-máš-gal 6 ⸢kuš⸣-[x] ki ^{d}*adad-till*[*ati*-ta] ***a-na-*** [***aḫ-ì-lí***] šu ba-[ti], "*Anaḫ-ili* received [4]2 sheep skins, 5 lamb skins, 2 billy-goat skins, (and) 6 [x] skins from *Adad-tillati*," 887:1–7

[n] kuš-udu 1 kuš-sila$_4$ 7 kuš-máš ki ^{d}*adad-tillati*-ta ***a-na-aḫ-ì-lí*** šu ba-ti, "*Anaḫ-ili* received [n] sheep skin(s), 1 lamb skin (and) 7 goat skins from *Adad-tillati*," 888:1–6

10 kuš-gu$_4$ 50 kuš-udu 10 kuš-máš ki ^{d}*adad-tillati*-ta ***a-na-aḫ-ì-lí*** šu ba-ti, "*Anaḫ-ili* received 10 ox skins, 50 sheep skins (and) 10 goat skins from *Adad-tillati*," 915:1–6

4 kuš-⸢udu⸣ 1 kuš-sila$_4$ 6 gín sa-udu ki ^{d}*adad-tillati*-ta ***an-na-ḫi-li***(sic!) ašgab [šu] ba-ti, "*Anaḫ-ili*, the leather worker, received 4 sheep skins, 1 lamb skin (and) 6 shekels of sheep sinews from *Adad-tillati*," 926:1–6

10 kuš-⸢udu⸣ 8 kuš-amar-gu$_4$ 2 kuš-anše 15 kuš-amar-anše [n kuš-am]ar?-[x n] si-gu$_4$ ki ^{d}*adad-tillati*-ta ***a-na-aḫ-ì-lí*** šu ba-ti, "*Anaḫ-ili* received 10 sheep skins, 8 calf skins, 2 donkey skins, 15 donkey-foal skins, [n] young? [x skin(s)] (and) [n] ox horn(s) from *Adad-tillati*," 927:1–9

2.1.1.2 Assorted Skins from Regular Offerings

1 kuš-máš-gal-niga sá-du$_{11}$-^{d}nin-^{d}si$_4$-an-na ki ^{d}*adad-tillati*-ta [***a-na***]-***aḫ-ì-lí*** [šu ba]-ti, "*Anaḫ-ili* received 1 skin of a fattened billy-goat, regular offerings of Nin-Siana, from *Adad-tillati*," 842:1–5

1 kuš-udu-niga 1 kuš-máš-niga kuš-udu sá-du$_{11}$ ki ^{d}*adad-tillati*-ta ***a-na-aḫ-ì-lí*** šu ba-an-ti, "*Anaḫ-ili* received 1 skin of a fattened sheep (and) 1 skin of a fattened billy-goat, caprid skins of regular offerings, from *Adad-tillati*," 851:1–6

1 kuš-udu sá-du$_{11}$-^{d}inana-zabala$_4^{ki}$ 1 kuš-máš sá-du$_{11}$-^{d}šára-ĜEŠ.KÚŠU^{ki} ki ^{d}*adad-tillati*-ta ***a-na-aḫ-ì-lí*** šu ba-ti, "*Anaḫ-ili* received 1 sheep skin, regular offerings of Inana of Zabala, (and) 1 goat skin, regular offerings of Šara of ĜEŠ.KÚŠU, from *Adad-tillati*," 860:1–7

1 kuš-sila$_4$-niga 1 kuš-máš-gal-niga kuš-udu sá-du$_{11}$ ki ^{d}*adad-tillati*-ta ***a-na-aḫ-ì-***[***lí***] šu ba-an-ti, "*Anaḫ-ili* received 1 skin of a fattened lamb (and) 1 skin of a fattened billy-goat, caprid skins of regular offerings, from *Adad-tillati*," 861:1–6

1 kuš-[x] 1 kuš-⸢udu⸣ 2 kuš-[x] kuš-udu zi-[ga] 2 kuš-udu kuš-udu sá-du$_{11}$ ki ^{d}*adad-tillati*-ta ***a-na-aḫ-ì-lí*** šu ba-an-ti, "*Anaḫ-ili* received an expenditure of sheep skins (consisting) of 1 [x] skin, 1 sheep skin, (and) 2 [x] skins, (and) 2 sheep skins, sheep skins of regular offerings, from *Adad-tillati*," 867:1–9

2 kuš-udu-niga sá-du$_{11}$-^{d}nin-^{d}si$_{4}$-an-na ki ^{d}*adad-tillati*-ta ***a-na-aḫ-ì-lí***, "*Anaḫ-ili* received 2 skins of fattened sheep, regular offerings of Nin-Siana, from *Adad-tillati*," 874:1–4

1 kuš-udu 1 kuš-máš-gal kuš-udu sá-du$_{11}$ ki ^{d}*adad-tillati*-ta ***a-[na-aḫ]-ì-lí*** šu ba-an-ti, "*Anaḫ-ili* received 1 sheep skin (and) 1 billy-goat skin, caprid skins of regular offerings, from *Adad-tillati*," 877:1–6

51 kuš-udu-niga 10 kuš-máš-gal 1 kuš-máš-niga 1 kuš-sila$_{4}$-niga [kuš]-udu zi-ga [n kuš]-udu-niga [kuš]-udu sá-du$_{11}$ 2 kuš-udu-niga kuš-udu ba-úš ki ^{d}*adad-tillati*-ta ***a-na-aḫ-ì-lí*** šu ba-ti, "*Anaḫ-ili* received 51 skins of fattened sheep, 10 billy-goat skins, 1 skin of a fattened goat, (and) 1 skin of a fattened lamb, expended caprid skins, [n skin(s) of (a) fattened sheep], sheep skins of regular offerings, (and) 2 skins of fattened sheep, skins of dead sheep, from *Adad-tillati*," 922:1–11

2 kuš-udu-niga kuš-udu sá-du$_{11}$ ki ^{d}*adad-tillati*-ta ***a-na-aḫ-ì-lí*** šu ba-an-ti, "*Anaḫ-ili* received 2 skins of fattened sheep, sheep skins of regular offerings, from *Adad-tillati*," 1516:1–5

2.1.1.3 Billy-goat Skins

n kuš-máš-gal-niga ki ^{d}*adad-tillati*-ta ***a-na-aḫ-ì-lí*** šu ba(-an)-ti, "*Anaḫ-ili* received n skin(s) of (a) fattened billy-goat(s) from *Adad-tillati*," 841:1–4, 909:1–5, 914:1–4, 918:1–4

2.1.1.4 Goat Skins

1 kuš-ud$_{5}$ ki ^{d}*adad-tillati*-ta ***a-na-aḫ-ì-[lí]*** šu ba-ti, "*Anaḫ-ili* received 1 female goat skin from *Adad-tillati*," 921:1–4

1 kuš-máš ki ^{d}*adad-tillati*-ta ***[a]-na-aḫ-ì-lí*** [šu] ba-ti, "*Anaḫ-ili* received 1 goat skin from *Adad-tillati*," 936:1–4

2.1.1.5 Lamb Skins

1 kuš-sila$_{4}$ kuš-udu <ba->úš ki ^{d}*adad-tillati*-ta ***a-na-aḫ-ì-lí*** ašgab šu ba-an-ti, "*Anaḫ-ili*, the leather worker, received 1 lamb skin of a dead caprid from *Adad-tillati*," 843:1–5

1 kuš-sila$_{4}$ ki ^{d}*adad-tillati*-ta ***a-na-aḫ-ì-lí*** šu ba-ti, "*Anaḫ-ili* received 1 lamb skin from *Adad-tillati*," 941:1–4

2.1.1.6 Ox Horns, Skins, and Tails

1 kuš-kun-gu$_{4}$ ki ^{d}*adad-tillati*-ta ***a-na-aḫ-ì-lí*** šu ba-an-ti, "*Anaḫ-ili* received 1 ox tail from *Adad-tillati*," 846:1–4

1 kuš-gu$_{4}$ 2 si-gu$_{4}$ 1 kuš-kun!-gu$_{4}$ ki ^{d}*adad-tillati*-ta ***a-na-aḫ-ì-lí*** šu ba-an-ti, "*Anaḫ-ili* received 1 ox skin, 2 ox horns (and) 1 ox tail from *Adad-tillati*," 881:1–6

1 kuš-gu$_{4}$ 1 kuš-amar-gu$_{4}$ ki ^{d}*adad-tillati*-⌈ta⌉ ***a-na-aḫ-ì-[lí]*** šu ba-[ti], "*Anaḫ-ili* received 1 ox skin (and) 1 calf skin from *Adad-tillati*," 910:1–5

2.1.1.7 Pig Skins

1 kuš-šáḫ ki ^{d}*adad-tillati*-ta ***a-na-aḫ-ì-lí*** šu [ba-an-ti], "*Anaḫ-ili* received 1 pig skin from *Adad-tillati*," 901:1–4

1 kuš-šáḫ-niga ki ^{d}*adad-tillati*-ta ***a-na-aḫ-ì-lí*** šu ba-ti, "*Anaḫ-ili* received 1 skin of a fattened pig from *Adad-tillati*," 953:1–4

2.1.1.8 Sheep Skins

n kuš-udu ki ^{d}*adad-tillati*-ta ***a-na-aḫ-ì-lí*** (ašgab) šu ba(-an)-ti, "*Anaḫ-ili*, (the leather worker), received n sheep skin(s) from *Adad-tillati*," 859:1–4, 862:1–4, 872:1–4, 882:1–4, 886:1–4, 905:1–4, 919:1–4, 928:1–4, 929:1–5

1 kuš-udu ba-úš ki ^{d}*adad-tillati*-ta ***a-na-aḫ-ì-lí*** šu ba-an-ti, "*Anaḫ-ili* received 1 skin of a dead sheep from *Adad-tillati*," 894:1–5

2.1.1.8.1 Hairless-Sheep Skins

4 kuš-udu a-ĝar gu_7-a ki ^{d}*adad-tillati*-ta ***a-na-aḫ-ì-lí*** šu ba-ti, "*Anaḫ-ili* received 4 de-haired sheep skins from *Adad-tillati*," 868:1–4

73 kuš-udu a-ĝar gu_7-a [n+]⅔ ma-na sa-udu ki ^{d}*adad-tillati*-ta ***a-na-aḫ-ì-lí*** šu ba-ti, "*Anaḫ-ili* received 73 de-haired sheep skins (and) [n+]⅔ minas of sheep sinews from *Adad-tillati*," 958:1–5

2.1.1.8.2 Skins of Fattened Sheep

n kuš-udu-niga ki ^{d}*adad-tillati*-ta ***a-na-aḫ-ì-lí*** (ašgab) šu ba(-an)-ti, "*Anaḫ-ili*, (the leatherworker), received n skin(s) of (a) fattened sheep from *Adad-tillati*," 845:1–4, 856:1–4, 865:1–4, 866:1–4, 889:1–5, 904:1–4, 907:1–4, 937:1–4

n kuš-udu-niga ba-úš ki ^{d}*adad-tillati*-ta ***a-na-aḫ-ì-lí*** šu ba(-an)-ti, "*Anaḫ-ili* received n skin(s) of (a) dead fattened sheep from *Adad-tillati*," 850:1–4, 854:1–4, 896:1–5

1 kuš-udu-niga kuš-udu zi-ga ki ^{d}*adad-tillati*-ta ***a-na-aḫ-ì-lí*** šu ba-an-ti, "*Anaḫ-ili* received 1 skin of a fattened sheep, expenditure of sheep skin from *Adad-tillati*," 863:1–5

2.1.1.9 Sheep and Goat Skins

3 kuš-udu 1 kuš-máš ki ^{d}*adad-tillati*-ta ***a-na-aḫ-ì-lí*** šu ba-ti, "*Anaḫ-ili* received 3 sheep skins (and) 1 goat skin from *Adad-tillati*," 908:1–6

2 kuš-udu-niga 1 kuš-máš-niga ki ^{d}*a[dad-tilla]ti*-ta [***a-na***]***-aḫ-ì-lí*** [šu ba]-ti, "*Anaḫ-ili* received 2 skins of fattened sheep (and) 1 skin of a fattened goat from *Adad-tillati*," 944:1–5

2.1.1.10 Sheep and Billy-goat Skins

n kuš-udu-niga n kuš-máš-gal ki ^{d}*adad-tillati*-ta ***a-na-aḫ-ì-lí*** šu ba-ti, "*Anaḫ-ili* received n skin(s) of (a) fattened sheep (and) n billy-goat skin(s) from *Adad-tillati*," 902:1–5, 934:1–5

2 kuš-udu-niga 1 kuš-máš-gal-niga kuš-udu ba-úš ki ^{d}*adad-tillati*-ta [***a-na-aḫ-ì-lí***] šu ba-a[n-ti], "[*Anaḫ-ili*] received 2 skins of fattened sheep (and) 1 skin of a fattened billy-goat, skins of dead caprids, from *Adad-tillati*," 852:1–6

n kuš-udu-niga n kuš-máš-gal-niga ki ^{d}*adad-tillati*-ta ***a-na-aḫ-ì-lí*** šu ba-an-ti, "*Anaḫ-ili* received n skin(s) of (a) fattened sheep (and) n skin(s) of (a) fattened billy-goat(s) from *Adad-tillati*," 870:1–5, 875:1–6, 890:1–6

1 kuš-udu 1 kuš-máš-gal ki ^{d}*adad-tillati*-ta ***a-na-aḫ-ì-lí*** šu ba-ti, "*Anaḫ-ili* received 1 sheep skin (and) 1 billy-goat skin from *Adad-tillati*," 1524:1–5

2.1.1.11 Sheep and Lamb Skins

9 kuš-udu-[niga] 1 kuš-sila$_4$-niga ki ^{d}*adad-tillati*-ta [***a-na-aḫ-ì-lí*** šu ba-ti], "[*Anaḫ-ili* received] 9 skins of [fattened] sheep (and) 1 skin of a fattened lamb from *Adad-tillati*," 949:1–5

1 kuš-udu 1 [kuš-sil]a$_4$ ki ^{d}*a*[*dad-ti*]*llati*-ta ***a-na-aḫ-ì-lí*** šu ba-ti, "*Anaḫ-ili* received 1 sheep skin (and) 1 lamb skin from *Adad-tillati*," 951:1–5

11 kuš-udu-[niga] 10 kuš-sila$_4$ [ki] ^{d}*adad-tillati*-ta [***a***]***-na-aḫ-ì-lí*** šu ba-[t]i, "*Anaḫ-ili* received 11 skins of [fattened] sheep (and) 10 lamb skins from *Adad-tillati*," 959:1–5

2.1.1.12 Sheep and Ox Skins

1 k[uš-gu$_4$] 11? [kuš-udu] ki ^{d}*adad-till*[*ati*-ta] ***a-na-aḫ-ì-lí*** [šu ba]-an-[ti], "*Anaḫ-ili* received 1 [ox] skin (and) 11? [sheep skins] from *Adad-tillati*," 911:1–5

2.1.1.13 Waterskins

1 ^{kuš}ùmmu ki ^{d}*adad-tillati*-ta ***a-na-aḫ-ì-lí*** šu ba-ti, "*Anaḫ-ili* received 1 waterskin from *Adad-tillati*," 940:1–4

2.1.1.14 Contents Lost

8 kuš-udu 7? [kuš-x ki ^{d}*adad-tillati*-ta ***a-na-aḫ-ì-lí*** šu] ba-[ti], "*Anaḫ-ili* received 8 sheep skins (and) 7? [x skins from *Adad-tillati*]," 960:1–5

2.1.2 From *Ili-bilanni*: Lamb and Goat Skins

2 kuš-sila$_4$ 2 kuš-máš ki *ì-lí-bi-la-ni*-ta ***a-na-ḫi-li***(sic!) šu ba-ti, "*Anaḫ-ili* received 2 lamb skins (and) 2 goat skins from *Ili-bilani*," 903:1–5

2.1.3 From *Simu*

2.1.3.1 Fattened-Sheep and Goat Skins

1 kuš-udu-niga 1 kuš-máš ki *si-mu* kurušda-ta ***a-na-aḫ-ì-lí*** šu ba-ti, "*Anaḫ-ili* received 1 skin of a fattened sheep (and) 1 goat skin from *Simu*, the animal fattener," 935:1–5

2.1.3.2 Sheep Skins

5 kuš-udu ba-úš ki *si-mu*-ta ***a-na-aḫ-ì-lí*** šu ba-ti, "*Anaḫ-ili* received 5 sheep skins of dead (sheep) from *Simu*," 956:1–4

2.2 Receipt of Materials for Tanning

2.2.1 From *Adad-tillati*

2.2.1.1 *Alluḫarum*, Lard, Madder (Dye) and Sheep Sinews

[n sìl]a ì-šáḫ 5 ma-na *al-lu-ḫa-ru-um*-sig$_5$ [n ma-na *a*]*l-lu*-[*ḫa-ru-um*] 3 ma-na sa-udu 15 ma-na ú-ḫáb ki ^{d}*adad-tillati*-ta ***a-na-aḫ-ì-lí*** šu ba-ti, "*Anaḫ-ili* received [n] liter(s) of lard, 5 minas of fine *alluḫarum*, [n mina(s)] of (ordinary) *alluḫarum*, 3 minas of sheep sinews (and) 15 minas of madder (dye) from *Adad-tillati*," 898:1–8

2.2.1.2 Lard

2 sìla ì-šáḫ mu kuš-šè ki ^{d}*adad-tillati*-ta ***a-na-aḫ-ì-lí*** šu ba-an-ti, "*Anaḫ-ili* received 2 liters of lard for (processing) skins from *Adad-tillati*," 878:1–5, 899:1–5

3 sì[la ì-š]aḫ ki ^{d}⸢*adad*⸣*-tillati*-ta [***a-na***]***-aḫ-ì-lí*** šu ba-ti, "*Anaḫ-ili* received 3 liters of lard from *Adad-tillati*," 946:1–4

2.2.1.3 Lard and Glue

3 sìla ì-šáḫ ½ ma-na še-gín ki ^{d}*adad-tillati*-ta ***a-na-aḫ-ì-lí*** šu ba-ti, "*Anaḫ-ili* received 3 liters of lard (and) ½ mina of glue from *Adad-tillati*," 1520:1–5

2.2.1.4 Lard, Red Clay and Mud-brick

5 sìla ì-šáḫ 2 sìla im-kù-sig$_{17}$ 20 ma-na ki-lá šeg$_{12}$ [ki ^{d}]*adad-tillati*-ta ***a-na-aḫ-ì-lí*** šu ba-ti, "*Anaḫ-ili* received 5 liters of lard, 2 liters of red clay (and) 20 minas of bricks from *Adad-tillati*," 891:1–5

2.2.1.5 Mutton Fat

1⁵⁄₆ ma-na ì-udu ki ^{d}*adad-tillati*-ta ***a-na-aḫ-ì-lí*** ⸢šu⸣ ba-an-ti, "*Anaḫ-ili* received 1⁵⁄₆ minas of mutton fat from *Adad-tillati*," 876:1–4

2.2.1.6 Semolina

0.0.1. dabin kuš a-ĝar gu$_{7}$-a-šè ki ^{d}*adad-tillati*-ta ***a-na-aḫ-ì-lí*** šu ba-an-ti, "*Anaḫ-ili* received 10 liters of semolina for (processing) de-haired skins," 837:1–5, 895:1–5

0.0.1. dabin mu kuš-udu-niga-šè ki ^{d}*adad-tillati*-ta ***a-na-aḫ-ì-lí*** šu ba-ti, "*Anaḫ-ili* received 10 liters of semolina for (processing) skins of fattened sheep from *Adad-tillati*," 954:1–5

0.0.2. dabin ⸢mu⸣ kuš-šè ki ^{d}*adad-tillati*-ta [***a-na-a***]***ḫ-ì-***[***lí*** šu ba-ti], "*Anaḫ-ili* received 20 liters of semolina for (processing) skins from *Adad-tillati*," 961:1–5

2.2.2 From *Adallal*: Semolina

5 sìla dabin kuš-udu-niga ki *a-da-làl*<-ta> ***a-na-aḫ-ì-lí*** šu ba-ti, "*Anaḫ-ili* received 5 liters of semolina (for processing) skins of fattened sheep from *Adallal*," 957:1–5

2.2.3 From *Ḫali*

2.2.3.1 *Alluḫarum*, Lard and Madder (Dye)

3 sìla ì-šáḫ ⅔ ma-na ú-ḫáb 5 ma-na *al-lu-ḫa-ru-um* ***a-na-aḫ-ì-lí*** šu ba-ti ki *ḫa-lí*-ta ba-zi, "*Anaḫ-ili* received 2 liters of lard, ⅔ mina of madder (dye) (and) 5 minas of *alluḫarum* from *Ḫali*," 947:1–6

2.2.3.2 *Alluḫarum* and Wool Meshworks

1⅓ ma-na *al-lu-ḫa-ru-um*-sig$_{5}$ 4 ma-na *al-lu*<*-ḫa*>*-ru-um* 2 túg-du$_{8}$-a [siki]-ĝír-gul ki *ḫa-lí*-ta *a-na-aḫ-ì-lí* šu ba-ti, "*Anaḫ-ili* received 1⅓ minas of fine *alluḫarum*, 4 minas of ordinary *alluḫarum* (and) 2 meshworks of ĝír-gul [wool] from *Ḫali*," 924:1–6

2.2.3.3 Wool Meshworks

6 túg-du$_{8}$-a siki ^{ĝeš}garig aka 1 túg-du$_{8}$-a siki-ĝír-gul [ki-lá-bi n ma]-na 5 gín [igi]-12-ĝál ki *ḫa-lí*-ta ***a-na-aḫ-ì-lí*** šu ba-an-ti, "*Anaḫ-ili* received 6 meshworks of combed wool (and) 1 meshwork of ĝír-gul wool from *Ḫali*. [Their weight is n] mina(s) (and) 5¹⁄₁₂ shekels," 883:1–7

2.2.4 From *Ili-andul*: Semolina

0.0.1. dabin [ki] *ì-lí-an-d*[*ùl*]-ta ***a-na-aḫ-ì-*[*lí*]** šu ba-ti, "*Anaḫ-ili* received 10 liters of semolina from *Ili-andul*," 950:1–4

0.0.1. dabin mu kuš-šè ki *ì-lí-an-dùl*-ta ***a-na-aḫ-ì-lí*** šu ba-ti, "*Anaḫ-ili* received 10 liters of semolina for (processing) skins from *Ili-andul*," 952:1–5

2.2.5 From *Malik-bani*: Semolina

0.0.1. dabin ki ^{d}*ma-lik-ba-ni*-ta ***a-na-aḫ-ì-lí*** [šu b]a-an-ti, "*Anaḫ-ili* received 10 liters of semolina from *Malik-bani*," 879:1–4

2.3 Receipt of Hired Workmen from *Adad-tillati*

16 ĝuruš [ḫuĝ]-ĝá u$_4$-1-šè ki ^{d}*adad-tillati*-ta ***a-na-a*[*ḫ-ì*]*-lí*** ì-dab$_5$, "*Anaḫ-ili* took in charge 16 [hired] workmen for 1 day from *Adad-tillati*," 873:1–5

2.4 Receipt of Leather Products from *Adad-tillati*

95 ^{kuš}*maš-lí-um* ^{kuš}a-ĝá-lá ḫi-a é-kišib-ba-ta ki ^{d}*adad-tillati*-ta ***a-na-aḫ-ì-lí*** šu ba-ti, "*Anaḫ-ili* received 95 various leather buckets (and) leather sacks from the warehouse from *Adad-tillati*," 963:1–5

3. In Legal Texts

3.1 As a Witness

[igi ***a-na-aḫ***]***-ì-lí***, "[witnessed by] *Anaḫ-ili*," 1062:12

igi ***a-na-aḫ-ì-lí*** ašgab, "witnessed by *Anaḫ-ili*, the leather worker," 1065:9

3.2 Testifying

3.2.1 That Oil was Brought from Garšana to Nippur

★★0.0.1.1 sìla ì-ĝeš ⸢lá⸣-ìa šà ì-ĝeš 2.0.0. gur-kam gar-ša-an-na^{ki}-ta nibru^{ki}-šè in-de$_9$-ša-a *ì-⸢lí⸣-an-dùl* dub-sar ***[a]-na-⸢aḫ⸣-ì-lí*** ašgab [x-*r*]*a?-ra-am* ú ga$_6$-[ĝá . . .] ka-ga-na-ne-ne ba-ge-en, "*Ili-andul*, the scribe, (and) *Anaḫ-ili*, the leather worker, confirmed 11 liters of oil, the remainder of 2 bushels, which they brought from Garšana to Nippur (?) and (?)," 1062:1–9

3.2.2 Regarding Stolen Commodities

1 kuš-udu-niga a-ĝar gu$_7$ *nu-úr-^{d}adad* ašgab ba-an-zuḫ ***a-na-aḫ-ì-lí*** ašgab in-ge-en, "*Nur-Adad*, the leather-worker, stole 1 de-haired skin of a fattened-sheep. *Anaḫ-ili*, the leather-worker, confirmed it," 1061:1–4

0.2.0. še zuḫ-a ***a-na-aḫ-ì-*[*lí*]** ašgab šà ka i$_7$-nar-e-⸢ne⸣ ka-ga-na ba-ge-en, "*Anaḫ-ili*, the leather worker, confirmed at the opening of the singers' canal that there were 120 liters of stolen barley," 1063:1–4

a-ta-li-ku

Ataliku, the Bird Warden

1 ir$_7^{mušen}$ *li-bur-i-du-ni* in-gu$_7$-a ka-ga-na ba-a-ge-en *na-na* géme kíkken ***a-ta-li-ku*** sipa-mušen-na in-ge-né-eš "*Libur-iduni* confirmed that he ate 1 pigeon. *Nana*, the female miller (and) *Ataliku*, the bird warden, verified it," 1055:1–7

a-wi-lí

1. As a Witness

igi ***a-wi-lí***, "witnessed by *Awili*," 1058:9

a-wi-lum-ma

1. ***Awilumma***, the Scribe: Sailors under his Authority

2 g̃uruš má-lah̬$_5$ u$_4$-30-šè má sah̬ar ég a-ab-ba se-gé-dè gub-ba g̃ìri ***a-wi-lum-ma*** dub-sar ki ^{d}*adad-tillati*-ta ba-zi šà *maš-kán-šar-ru-um*^{ki}, "Under the authority of *Awilumma*, the scribe, *Adad-tillati* disbursed 2 sailors employed for 30 days to tamp dirt (delivered by) boat at the sea dike in *Maškan-šarrum*," 274:1–7, 275:1–7

2. ***Awilumma***, Title Unspecified

2.1 Deliveries

2.1.1 Assorted Textiles, Receipt of ***Puzur-agum***

(. . .) ki ***á-w[i-lum-ma***-ta] *puzur*$_4$*-a-[gu*$_5$*-um]* šu ba-ti, "*Puzur-agum* received {assorted textiles} from *Awilumma*," 701:13–15

2.1.2 Skins, Receipt of ***Adad-tillati***

[6]9 ádda-udu 69 kuš-udu 2 ma-na 18 gín sa ⸢udu⸣ *a-h̬u-a* mu-na-⸢ba⸣? ki ***á-wi-lum-ma***-ta ^{d}*adad-tillati* šu ba-[ti], "*Adad-tillati* received from *Awilumma* [6]9 sheep carcasses, 69 sheep skins, 2 minas (and) 18 shekels of sheep sinews, alloted for *Ah̬u'a*," 459:1–7

[n] kuš-udu ki ***á-wi-lu[m-ma***-ta] ^{d}*adad-tillati* ⸢šu⸣ ba-ti [egir bu]ru$_{14}$ gi$_4$-gi$_4$-[dè], "*Adad-tillati* received from *Awilumma* [n] sheep skin(s) [to] be paid back after the harvest," 893:1–5

2.1.3 Wool, Baskets and Skins, Receipt of ***Adad-tillati***

2 gú siki 2 ^{gi}gúrdub ⸢siki⸣-gi ki ***a-wi-lum-ma***-ta ^{d}*adad-tillati* šu ba-an-ti, "*Adad-tillati* received 2 talents of wool (and) 2 reed baskets of wool of an eme-GI sheep from *Awilumma*," 616:1–5

(. . .) 28 ^{gi}gúrdub siki ka<-tab> sè-ga ki ***a-wi-lum-ma***-ta ^{d}*adad-tillati* šu ba-an-ti g̃ìri *a-gu-a* ugula-g̃éš-da, "Under the authority *Agua*, overseer of 60, *Adad-tillati* received {assorted wool} (and) 28 reed baskets of wool fitted with a cover from *Awilumma*," 623:4–8

20 gú siki-[gen] 20 ^{gi}gúrdub ka-[tab] sè-ga 180 kuš-udu-ú ki ***á-wi-lum-ma***-ta ^{d}*adad-tillati* šu ba-ti g̃ìri *za-ak-ì-lí* ^{lú}kaš$_4$, "Under the authority of *Zakili*, the runner, *Adad-tillati* received 20 talents of [ordinary] wool, 20 reed-baskets of wool fitted with covers, (and) 180 skins of range-fed sheep from *Awilumma*," 1285:1–7

2.2 Receipts

2.2.1 Dead Animals from ***Ili-bilani***

★★4 ⸢máš⸣ 4 u$_8$ [n] ud$_5$ [n] máš-gal ba-úš bi+šu-ab-ta? ^{d}inana-zabala$_4^{ki}$ u$_4$-1-šè é-šu-^{d}E[N.Z]U 32 udu 1 ud$_5$ b[a-úš] é-kišib-ba-šè ***[a-w]i-lum-ma*** ⸢šu⸣ ba-[an-t]i [ki] *ì-lí-[bi]-la-ni*-ta [ba]-zi, "*Awilumma* received from *Ili-bilani* 4 goats, 4 ewes, [n] female goat(s), [n] billy-goat(s), slaughtered (?) (for) Inana of Zabala for one day (in) *Bit-Šu-Suen*, (and) 32 sheep (and) 1 female goat, slaughtered for the warehouse," 1019:1–14

2.2.2 Lard for Boat Towers from *Adad-tillati*

[n.n.n.n (sìla n gín)] ì-šáh̬ [ì-ba] má gíd-e-ne [***a-w***]***i-lum-ma*** ⌜šu⌝ ba-an-ti ki ^{d}*ad*[*ad-tillati*-ta] ba-zi, "*Awilumma* received [n liter(s) (and) n shekel(s)] of lard, [oil rations] of boat towers from *Adad-tillati*," 419:1–6

á-g̃eš-u

1. Provisions: Barley

1.0.0. gur **á-g̃eš-u**? (. . .) [šu+níg̃in n+]7.0.0. gur še-ba *ba-zi-tum* šu+níg̃in 47.1.[n.] še-ba é, "1 bushel of (barley) (for) Ag̃ešu (and barley for) {other individuals}; [in total: n+]7 bushels of the barley rations of *Bazitum*; in total: 47 bushels (and) 60[+n] liters of barley rations of the household," 555:8, 24–25

á-ni-á

Ani'a, the Son of *ur*?-[x]

1. Provisions: Equid Fodder

0.0.1. še šà-gal ^{anše}kúnga ***á-ni-á*** dumu *ùr*?-[x] 1 udu *ru-ba-ti-a* 0.0.3. ésir-é-a *al-la* gudu$_4$ ^{d}*adad-tillati* šabra maškim z[i-g]a [*tá*]-*ki*-⌜*il*⌝-*ì-lí-ís-sú* ki ^{d}*adad-tillati*-ta ba-zi, "*Adad-tillati* disbursed 10 liters of barley, fodder of equids (for) *Ani'a*, the son of *Ur*?-[x], 1 sheep (for) *Rubati'a*, and 30 liters of dried bitumen for *Alla*, the gudu-priest. (It was) the expenditure of *Takil-ilissu*. *Adad-tillati*, the majordomo, was the deputy," 534:1–12

á-pil-la-núm

Apillanum, Man from Karkar

[1] ***á-pil-la-núm*** (. . .) ugula [*šu*]-*la-núm* (. . .) lú-karkar^{ki}-me, "*Apillanum*, supervised by *Šulanum*, (and) {other workers}, men from Karkar," 559:3, 12, 28

á-pil-lí-a

Apillia, Man from Karkar

1 [***á***]***-pil-lí-a*** (. . .) ugula *á-ni*-x-x (. . .) lú-karkar^{ki}-me, "*Apilli'a*, supervised by *á-ni*-x-x, (and) {other workers}, men from Karkar," 559:18, 25, 28

(. . .) lú-karkar^{ki}-me [1 *w*]*a-qar-dan* 1 ***á-pil-lí-a*** ninda-ta nu-tuku, "{workers}, men from Karkar (received bread). *Waqar-dan* (and) *Apilli'a*, they each did not get bread," 559:28–32

ad-da-kal-la

1. Provisions

1.1 For Ada-kala, Workman of the Mill

[n g]ín ì-g̃eš-ta 1 ma-na tuh̬-g̃eš-ì-h̬ád-ta 0.0.1. ádda-udu-ta [½] sìla mun-ta [n] gín luh̬-lá-ta [1 **a**]**d-da-kal-la** [1] ur-^{d}šul-pa-è [1] *h̬a-la-ša* {indent} 3 [g̃uruš? é]-kíkken é-^{d}nin-^{d}si$_4$-an-na-me-éš, "[n] shekel(s) of sesame oil each, 1 mina of dried sesame chaff each, 10 sheep carcasses each, [½] liter of salt each (and) [n] shekel(s) of luh̬-lá each,

(provisions for) Ada-kala, Ur-Šulpa'e (and) *Ḫalaša*, 3 [workmen?] of the mill of Nin-Siana," 562:'6–'15

1.2 For Ada-kala, Title Unspecified

1.0.0. ninda gur še-ba **ad-da-kal-la** (. . .) [níĝ-kas$_7$]-aka [*ì-lí*]-*bi-la-ni* muḫaldim, "1 bushel of bread, barley rations of Ada-kala (and) {other allotments}, the balanced account of *Ili-bilani*, the cook," 1527:21–22, 48–49

ad-da-ni

1. Provisions

[. . .] ⅓ sìla mu[n-ta] 6 gín luḫ-lá-[ta] ĝìri *ì-lí*-[. . .] 1 ***ad-da-ni*** 1 *bi-za-tum* 1 *i-din-*^{d}*šamaš* 1 *in-ga-la* 1 *be-lí-a-sú* níta-me-éš, "[. . .], ⅓ liter of salt [each], (and) 6 shekels of luḫ-lá [each] under the authority of *Ili*-[. . .], (provisions for) *Adani*, *Bizatum*, *Iddin-Šamaš*, *Ingala* (and) *Beli-asu*, the men," 562:'31–'39

^{d}*adad*-SIG$_5$

1. Deliveries of Animals, Receipt of *Adad-tillati*

16 udu 1 sila$_4$ 7 máš-gal 6 máš sá-du$_{11}$-šè ki ^{d}***adad***-⌜SIG$_5$⌝-ta ^{d}*adad-tillati* ì-dab$_5$, "*Adad-tillati* took in charge 16 sheep, 1 lamb, 7 billy-goats, (and) 2 goats for regular offerings from *Adad-damiq*," 448:1–7

[1]4 udu-niga [n?+]4 udu-ú iti-u$_4$-12-ba-zal [ki] ^{d}***adad***-SIG$_5$-ta ^{d}*adad-tillati* ì-⌜dab$_5$⌝, "At the end of the 12th day of the month, *Adad-tillati* took in charge [1]4 fattened sheep (and) [n?+]4 range-fed sheep from *Adad-damiq*," 1067:1–6

2. Receipt of Animal Skins from *Adad-tillati*

2 kuš-gu$_4$ 2 kuš-kun-gu$_4$ 4 si gu$_4$ 18 kuš-udu 8 kuš-sila$_4$ 14 kuš-máš-gal 9 kuš-máš [ki ^{d}]***adad***-SIG$_5$-ta $^{[d]}$*adad-tillati* [šu] ba-ti, "*Adad-damiq* received 2 ox skins, 2 ox-tails, 4 ox horns, 18 sheep skins, 8 lamb skins, 14 billy-goat skins (and) 9 goat skins from *Adad-tillati*," 857:1–10

2 kuš-⌜udu⌝ 2 ku[š-m]áš ki [^{d}*ad*]*ad-tillati*-ta ^{d}***adad***-SIG$_5$ šu ba-ti, "*Adad-damiq* received 2 sheep skins (and) 2 goat skins from *Adad-tillati*," 916:1–5

aḫ-dam-ì-lí

1. *Aḫdam-ili*, Overseer of Hired Workers

10 géme ugula ***aḫ-dam-*[*ì*]*-lí***, "10 workwomen supervised by *Ahdam-ili*," 148:'8

2. *Aḫdam-ili*, Title Unspecified: Provisions

1.0.0. ninda gur še-ba ***aḫ-dam-ì-lí*** (. . .) [níĝ-kas$_7$]-aka [*ì-lí*]-*bi-la-ni* muḫaldim, "1 bushel of bread, barley rations of *Aḫdam-ili* (and) {other allotments}, the balanced account of *Ili-bilani*, the cook," 1527:23–24, 48–49

ak-ba-zum

1. *Akbazum*, the Gardener

[***ak-b***]***a-zum*** nu-^{ĝeš}kiri$_6$-⌜ke$_4$⌝ má-lugal-na saḫar tùm-dè zabala$_4^{ki}$-šè in-la-aḫ saḫar mu-un-de$_9$ ^{ĝeš}kiri$_6$-lugal-na-šè nu-un-ni-ku$_4$ é-ni-šè ba-an-dé ka-ga-na ba-ge-en, "*Akbazum*, the gardener, confirmed that they took a boat of his master to Zabala in order to bring dirt, that he brought the dirt, that it did not enter the garden of his master but was brought for his (own) house," 1049:1–10

2. *Akbazum*, the Master Craftsman

2.1 Deliveries: Pomegranate Planks

4 ^{ĝeš}nu-úr-ma-sig$_5$ 7 ^{ĝeš}nu-úr-ma-ús mu-DU ***ak-ba-zum*** um-mi-a ^{d}*adad-tillati* šu ba-an-ti ĝìri ^{d}*ma-lik-ba-ni* ù *puzur*$_4$-^{d}nin-kar-ak, "Under the authority of *Malik-bani* and *Puzur-*Ninkarak, *Adad-tillati* received 4 fine pomegranate planks (and) 7 lesser-quality pomegranate planks. (It was) the delivery of *Akbazum*, the master craftsman," 1298:1–6

2.2 Receipts: Wood

ĝeš é-⸢^{ĝeš}kiri$_6$⸣-a gub-ba šu-sum-ma ^{ĝeš}kiri$_6$ igi-érim-iri^{ki} ki ^{d}*ma-lik-ba-ni* santana-ta ***ak-ba-zum*** um-mi-a ì-dab$_5$ šà gar-ša-an-na^{ki} ⸢ĝìri⸣ *tu-ra-am-ì-lí* dub-sar, "From *Malik-bani*, the date orchard administrator, *Akbazum*, the master craftsman, took in charge wood stored in the garden house, the inventory of the Igi-erim-iri garden. (Transaction) in Garšana under the authority of *Turam-ili*, the scribe," 1375:45–51

3. *Akbazum*, Title Unspecified: Receipts

3.1 Onion Sprouts from *Adad-tillati*

18 ḫar sum-sikil-mar-ḫa-ši ki ^{d}*adad-tillati*-ta ***ak-ba-zum*** [šu b]a-ti, "*Azbazum* received 18 Marḫaši onion sprouts? from *Adad-tillati*," 1168:1–4

3.2 Wood Products from *Malik-bani*

(. . .) [ki ^{d}]*ma-lik-ba-ni*-ta ***ak-ba-zum*** šu ba-an-ti, "*Akbazum* received {wood products} from *Malik-bani*," 1255:10–12

3.3 Wood and Reeds from *Adad-tillati*

4 ^{ĝeš}é-da-ásal 30 sa gi-⸢izi⸣ 1 ^{gi}dur daĝal a-[rá]-3-tab-ba gíd 5 nindan ⸢ti⸣?-gu ^{ĝeš}kiri$_6$ gar-ša-[an-n]a^{ki} ba-a-ĝar [ki ^{d}*adad*]-*tillati*-ta [***ak***]-***ba-zum*** šu ba-an-ti, "*Akbazum* received from *Adad-tillati* 4 poplar joists, 30 bundles of fuel reeds (and) 1 30-meter 3-ply wide rope. They were placed at the Garšana garden," 1273:1–7

al-la

Alla, the Gudu-priest

1. Provisions: House Bitumen

0.0.1. še šà-gal ^{anše}kúnga á-ni-á dumu *ùr*?-[x] 1 udu ru-ba-ti-a 0.0.3. ésir-é-a ***al-la*** gudu$_4$ ^{d}*adad-tillati* šabra maškim z[i-g]a [*tá*]-*ki-*⸢*il*⸣-*ì-lí-ís-sú* ki ^{d}*adad-tillati*-ta ba-zi, "*Adad-tillati* disbursed 10 liters of barley, fodder of equids (for) Ani'a, the son of *Ur*?-[x], 1 sheep (for) *Rubati'a*, (and) 30 liters of house bitumen (for) Alla, the gudu-priest. (It was) the expenditure of *Takil-ilissu*. *Adad-tillati*, the majordomo, was the deputy," 534:1–12

al-la-ša-ru-um

1. Provisions: Flour and Semolina

0.0.1. zì-KAL 2 sìla dabin 1 sìla eša ⸢***al***⸣***-la-ša-ru-um*** *š*[*u*-^{d}E]N.ZU-*ba-ni* šu-i maškim, "10 liters of KAL-flour, 2 liters of semolina (and) 1 liter of fine flour (for) *Alla-šarrum*. *Šu-Suen-bani*, the barber, was the deputy," 1016:9–12

am-ri-ni

1. Deliveries: Textiles, Receipt of *Šu*-Nininsi

1 ⌈túg⌉níĝ-lám 3-kam-ús 1 túgníĝ-lám 3-kam-ús *a-gi₄-um* 1 túg ba-tab *tuḫ-ḫu-um* tab-ba-gen ĝešgu-za *šu-kab-tá* [ki] ***am-ri-ni***-ta [*šu*]-dnin-in<-si> šu ba-ti, "*Šu*-Nininsi received from *Amrini* 1 3rd-quality níĝ-lám textile, 1 3rd-quality *a-gi₄-um* níĝ-lám textile (and) 1 ordinary double ba-tab *tuḫ-ḫu-um* textile of the chair of *Šu-Kabta*," 737:1–6

2. Receipts: Textiles from *Adad-tillati*

(. . .) 21 ***am-ri-ni*** šu ba-ti (. . .)[ki d*adad-tilla*]*ti*-ta [ba-z]i, "*Amrini* received 21 {textiles} from *Adad-tillati*," 511:'124–'126, '135–'136

1 túgníĝ-lám-PI-ús-NI 2 túgníĝ-lám-ús-NI ***am-ri-ni*** šu ba-an-ti ki d*adad-tillati*-ta ba-zi, "*Amrini* received 1 níĝ-lám-PI-ús-NI textile (and) 2 túgníĝ-lám-ús-NI textiles from *Adad-tillati*," 711:1–6

(. . .) 21 túg-sa-gi₄-àm ⌈***am***⌉***-ri-ni*** šu ba-ti ki d*adad-tillati*-ta ba-zi, "*Amrini* received 21 {assorted} finished textiles from *Adad-tillati*," 746:10–15

ama-kal-la

Ama-kala, Wife of *A'alli*

1. Receipts: Sprouted Malt

0.2.0. munu₄-si-è **ama-kal-la** dam *a-al-lí* šu ba-ti, "Ama-kala, the wife of *A'alli*, received 120 liters of sprouted malt," 1250:1–4

amar-dda-mu

1. Seal of Amar-Damu: Delivery of Woven Textiles

5 túgníĝ-lám 3-kam-ús ki-lá-bi 9⅓ ma-na [n gín] túg ki-lá tag-a ki *šu-ì-lí-su*-ta mu-DU kišib **amar-dda-mu**, "5 3rd-quality níĝ-lám textiles, their weight is 9⅓ minas [(and) n shekel(s)], delivery of weighed textiles having been woven from *Šu-ilissu*, seal of Amar-Damu," 582:1–6

AN.ŠUM.TAG.KAL

1. AN.ŠUM.TAG.KAL, the Runaway from the Gang of *Im-Erra*, the Ox-Herder

zàḫ **AN.ŠUM.TAG.KAL** (nu-bànda-gu₄) zàḫ *puzur₄-šu-ba* (nu-bànda-gu₄) *i-me-èr-ra* nu-bànda-gu₄ ugula *ba-ba-ni* šabra, "AN.ŠUM.TAG.KAL, (the ox-herder), (and) *Puzur-Šuba*, (the ox-herder), runaways (from the gang of) *Im-Erra*, the ox-herder, (ox-drivers) supervised by *Babani*, the majordomo," 185:31–34, 191:35–38, 192:'23–'26, 194:64–67, 196:'34–'37, 197:43–46

2. AN.TAG.KAL,[23] from the Gang of *Malik-tillati*, the Ox-Herder

[1 ĝuruš] dú-ra 1 *ú-bar*-⌈*um*⌉ 1 *bí-za*-⌈*tum*⌉ 1 *šu*-d⌈*adad*⌉ 1 **AN.TAG.⌈KAL⌉** d*ma-lik-tillati* [nu-bànda]-gu₄ ugula *nu-úr*-d*adad* šabra, "[1] sick [workman], *Ubarum*, *Bizatum*, *Šu-Adad* (and) AN.TAG.KAL, (workers from the gang of) *Malik-tillati*, the ox-herder, supervised by *Nur-Adad*, the majordomo," 198:'32–'38

---

23 Given that AN.TAG.KAL is part of a different work gang than is AN.ŠUM.TAG.KAL, the former name might not be a variant spelling of the latter but instead might designate a second individual.

an-ta-lú

Antalu, the Steward

1. As a Deputy: Disbursals of *Adad-tillati*

1.1 Additional Provisions for *Antalu*'s House

(. . .) dirig sá-du$_{11}$-é-agrig-šè ***an-ta-lú*** agrig maškim zi-ga *šu-kab-tá* ki ^{d}*adad-tillati*-ta ba-zi, "*Adad-tillati* disbursed {assorted comestibles on the nth and nth days}, surplus of the regular offerings for the house of the steward. (It was) the expenditure of *Šu-Kabta*. *Antalu*, the steward, was the deputy," 493:19–23, 494:17–21

1.2 Animals for the Ox-Driver of Nin-Siana and the Funerary Libation Place of Dada

1 udu-niga gu$_{4}$-e-ús-[sa] ^{d}nin-^{d}si$_{4}$-an-na šà [é]-⸢gal⸣ iti u$_{4}$-6-ba-zal 1 šáḫ-zé-da-ga ki-a-nag-*da-da*-šè ***an-ta-lú*** agrig maškim (. . .) ki ^{d}*adad-tillati*-ta ba-zi, "*Adad-tillati* disbursed 1 fattened sheep '(fed) following the oxen' (for) Nin-Siana in the palace at the end of the 6th day of the month (and) 1 suckling piglet for the funerary libation place of *Dada*. *Antalu*, the steward, was the deputy," 970:7–12, 23

1.3 Bread and Beer for *Abu-ṭabu*

{erased number} kaš-gen 0.0.1. ninda [. . .] ki? [. . .] 0.0.1. ninda-šu-ra-gen *a-bu*-DU$_{10}$ nu-bànda ***an-ta-lú*** agrig maškim (. . .) zi-ga *simat*-^{d}K[A.DI] ki ^{d}[*adad*]-*tillati*-ta ba-zi, "*Adad-tillati* disbursed ordinary beer, 1 liter [. . .] bread (and) 1 liter of ordinary half (loaf) bread (for) *Abu-ṭabu*, the overseer. *Antalu*, the steward, was the deputy. {Other disbursals under different authority.} (It was) the expenditure of *Simat-Ištaran*," 507:7–11, 16–18

1.4 Ducklings for the Warehouse

1 uz-⸢tur⸣ iti u$_{4}$-11-ba-zal 1 uz-tur iti u$_{4}$-13?-ba-zal 1 uz-tur iti u$_{4}$-20-ba-zal 1 uz-tur [iti u$_{4}$-2]8-ba-zal [ba-úš é]-kišib-ba-[šè x] ***an-ta-lú*** agrig <maškim> ki ^{d}*adad-tillati*-[ta] ba-zi, "*Adad-tillati* disbursed 1 duckling at the end of the 11th day of the month, 1 duckling at the end of the 13th? day of the month, 1 duckling at the end of the 20th day of the month (and) 1 duckling at the end of the 28th [day of the month]. (The birds) [were slaughtered for] the warehouse. *Antalu*, the steward, was the <deputy>," 1176:1–12

1.5 Flour for Bread

0.0.2. zì-KAL 0.0.1. zì-gu-ús ninda-gur$_{4}$-ra-šè ^{d}inana-zabala$_{4}^{ki}$ ama *tá-ḫi-iš-a-tal* ***an-ta-lú*** agrig maškim [zi]-ga *šu-kab-tá* ki ^{d}*adad-tillati*-ta ba-zi (šà zabala$_{4}^{ki}$), "*Adad-tillati* disbursed 20 liters of KAL-flour (and) 10 liters of ordinary gu-flour for thick bread (for) Inana of Zabala (and) the mother of *Taḫiš-atal*. (It was) the expenditure of *Šu-Kabta* (in Zabala). *Antalu*, the steward, was the deputy," 1015:1–8, 1018:1–11

1.6 Food for Soldiers

0.0.4. ⅔ sìla [. . . àga]-ús é-gal-la gub-ba [íb]-gu$_{7}$ ⸢u$_{4}$ má⸣ *ra-ba-tum* nibru^{ki}-ta gar-ša-an-na^{ki}-šè i[n-g]íd-sa-a ***an-ta-lú*** agrig [ma]škim (. . .) ⸢zi⸣-ga *simat*-[^{d}KA].DI [ki ^{d}*adad*]-*tillati*-ta ba-zi, "*Adad-tillati* disbursed 4⅔ [. . .]. The gendarme employed at the palace ate it when they towed the boat of *Rabatum* from Nippur to Garšana. *Antalu*, the steward, was the deputy. {Other disbursals under different authority.} (It was) the expenditure of *Simat-Ištaran*," 506:22–27, 29–30

1.7 Grains for the Tureen

(. . .) ^{dug}útul-šè u$_{4}$-2-kam (. . .) ^{dug}útul-šè u$_{4}$-3-kam {erasure}-šè ***an-ta-lú*** agrig maškim zi-ga *šu-kab-tá* ki ^{d}*adad-tillati*-ta ba-zi, "*Adad-tillati* disbursed {flour and other grains} for the tureen on the 2nd (and) 3rd days. (It was) the expenditure of *Šu-Kabta*. *Antalu*, the steward, was the deputy," 1167:8–9, 17–21

1.8 Reeds for Baking Bread and Cooking Soup

n sa gi-izi ninda ba-ra-du$_8$ ù tu$_7$ ba-ra-šeg̃$_6$ n ^{dug}sìla-bur-zi tu$_7$ ba-a-si ***an-ta-lú*** agrig maškim (. . .) ki ^{d}*adad-tillati*-ta ba-zi, "*Adad-tillati* disbursed n bundle(s) of fuel reeds with which bread was baked and soup was cooked (and) n 1-liter offering bowl(s) into which the soup was filled. *Antalu*, the steward, was the deputy (and) {other disbursals under different authority}," 1013:15–19, 24–25, 1014:'9–'12, '18–'19

1.9 Broken Contents

[. . .]-x $^{g̃eš}$gi-[x? . . . ***a[n-ta-l]ú*** agrig [maškim] (. . .) zi-ga *simat-*^{d}*ištaran* ki ^{d}*adad-tillati*-ta [ba]-zi, "*Adad-tillati* disbursed [. . .]. *Antalu*, the steward, [was the deputy]. {Other disbursals under different authority.} (It was) the expenditure of *Simat-Ištaran*," 505:8–10, 14–16

ar-ri-az

Arriaz, the Sick Worker

1. Supervised by *Beli-ili*

1 ***ar-ri-az*** dú-ra ugula *be-lí-ì-lí*, "*Arriaz,* the sick (workman) supervised by *Beli-ili*," 37:45–46

2. Supervised by *Irib*

1 *ta-tù-ri* dú-ra 1 ***ar-ri-az*** dú-ra ugula *i-ri-ib*, "*Tatturi* (and) *Arriaz*, sick (workmen) supervised by *Irib*," 38:45–47

árad-g̃u$_{10}$

Arad-g̃u, the sugal-maḫ

1. Provisions during his Travels

2 udu-⌜niga⌝ iti u$_4$-27-ba-zal 0.1.0. še-kaš 3 ^{dug}epig kaš ba-an-dé 0.0.3. ninda-*u$_4$-tuḫ-ḫu-um* 0.0.3. ninda-šu-ra-sig$_5$ 0.2.0. ninda-šu-ra-gen **árad-g̃u$_{10}$** sugal$_7$-maḫ g̃ír-su^{ki}-šè du-ni zi-ga *šu-kab-tá* ki ^{d}*adad-tillati*-ta, "*Adad-tillati* disbursed 2 fattened sheep at the end of the 27th day of the month, 60 liters of barley (for) beer, 3 drinking vessels (into which) he poured beer, 30 liters of *utuḫḫum* bread, 30 liters of fine half (loaf) bread (and) 20 liters of ordinary half (loaf) bread, (when) Arad-g̃u, the sugal-maḫ, came to G̃irsu. (It was) the expenditure of *Šu-Kabta*," 449:1–12

árad-^{d}nana

1. Sheep for his Funerary Libation Place

1 udu-ú ki-a-nag-**árad-^{d}nana** ù *a-la-tum* ki *ì-lí-aš-ra-ni*-ta ba-zi, "*Ili-ašranni* disbursed 1 range-fed sheep for the funerary libation place of Arad-Nanna and *Allatum*," 971:1–5

aš-tá-qar

Aštaqqar, Overseer of Weavers

1. Deliveries

1.1 Assorted textiles: Receipt of *Puzur-agum*

(. . .) túg ki-lá tà(g) ki ***aš-tá-qar***-ta *puzur$_4$-a-gu$_5$-um* šu ba-(an-)ti, "*Puzur-agum* received {assorted textiles}, weighed textiles having been woven, from *Aštaqqar*," 594:5–8,

608:10–13, 685:5–8, 686:4–7, 687:3–6, 690:8–11, 708:11–15, 724:3–7, 738:18–20, 744:14–16, 765:8–11, 778:11–13, 803:5–8, 804:6–9, 821:11–14, 832:2–5

(. . .) ki ***aš-tá-qar***-ta *puzur$_4$-a-gu$_5$-um* šu ba-(an-)ti, "*Puzur-agum* received {assorted textiles} from *Aštaqqar*," 610:2–4, 631:7–9, 660:2–4, 669:11–14, 674:11–13, 676:6–8, 677:3–5, 683:2–4, 684:2–4, 692:9–11, 697:3–5, 700:4–6, 713:2–4, 715:2–4, 720:3–5, 722:2–4, 731:7–9, 732:5–7, 736:4–6, 739:8–9, 742:12–13, 743:'8–'10, 745:9–11, 753:16–18, 757:2–4, 758:17–19, 760:9–11, 764:13–15, 766:7–9, 771:8–10, 775:3–5, 780:2–4, 787:7–10, 789:3–5, 793:13–14, 794:3–5, 799:6–8, 800:8–10, 801:8–10, 802:4–6, 806:9–11, 810:5–7, 811:16–17, 814:13–15, 817:1–4

(. . .) ⸢ki⸣ ***aš-tá-qar***-ta ⸢*puzur$_4$*⸣*-a-gu$_5$-um* ^{lú}ázlag [šu b]a-ti, "*Puzur-agum*, the fuller, received {assorted textiles} from *Aštaqqar*," 827:11–13

1.1.1 Under the Authority of *Adad-tillati*

(. . .) ki ***aš-tá-qar***-ta *puzur$_4$-a-gu$_5$-um* šu ba-ti g̃ìri ^{d}*adad-tillati*, "Under the authority of *Adad-tillati*, *Puzur-agum* received {assorted textiles} from *Aštaqqar*," 654:10–12, 658:9–13, 691:6–9, 696:2–5, 725:7–11, 786:16–19

(. . .) túg ki-lá tà-ga *puzur$_4$-a-gu$_5$-um* šu ba-ti ki ***aš-tá-qar***-ta ba-zi g̃ìri ^{d}*adad-tillati* (šabra), "Under the authority of *Adad-tillati*, (the majordomo), *Puzur-agum* received {assorted textiles}, weighed textiles having been woven, from *Aštaqqar*," 730:6–10, 747:18–22

(. . .) *puzur$_4$-a-gu$_5$-um* šu ba-ti ki ***aš-tá-qar***-ta ba-zi g̃ìri ^{d}*adad-tillati* šabra, "Under the authority of *Adad-tillati*, the majordomo, *Puzur-agum* received {assorted textiles} from *Aštaqqar*," 796:14–18

1.1.2 Under the Authority of *Adad-tillati* and *Malik-bani*

(. . .) túg ki-lá tà-ga ki ***aš-tá-qar***-ta *puzur$_4$-a-gu$_5$-um* šu ba-an-ti g̃ìri ^{d}*adad-tillati* (šabra) ù ^{d}*ma-lik-ba-ni*, "Under the authority of *Adad-tillati*, (the majordomo), and *Malik-bani*, *Puzur-agum* received {assorted textiles}, weighed textiles having been woven from *Aštaqqar*," 617:11–15, 618:13–17

(. . .) ki ***aš-tá-qar***-ta *puzur$_4$-a-gu$_5$-um* šu ba-(an-)ti g̃ìri ^{d}*adad-tillati* (šabra) ù ^{d}*ma-lik-ba-ni*, "Under the authority of *Adad-tillati*, (the majordomo), and *Malik-bani*, *Puzur-agum* received {assorted textiles} from *Aštaqqar*," 626:4–8, 636:8–11, 637:5–9, 639:6–9, 643:2–6, 645:'5–'9, 646:7–10, 647:7–10, 649:11–13, 662:11–15, 663:9–13, 673:9–13, 680:6–9, 694:10–13, 748:16–19, 829:'9–'13

1 túg-guz-za-gen ki ***aš-tá-qar***-ta *puzur$_4$-a-gum*! šu ba-an-ti kìšib *tu-ra-a* íb-ra g̃ìri ^{d}*adad-tillati* ù ^{d}*ma-lik-ba-ni*, "Under the authority of *Adad-tillati* and *Malik-bani*, *Puzur-agum* received 1 ordinary tufted textile from *Aštaqqar*. *Tura'a* rolled (his) seal," 644:1–7

1.1.3 (Under the Authority of) *Puzur*-Ninkarak

(. . .) 30-lá-1 [túg] ki-lá tag [ki] ***aš-tá-qar***-ta [*puzur$_4$-a-gu$_5$-um* šu ba-ti . . . *pù-zu*]*r$_8$*-^{d}nin-kar-ak dub-sar, "[*Puzur-agum* received] 29 textiles, weighed [textiles] having been woven, from *Aštaqqar*. [. . .] Puzur-Ninkarak was the scribe," 835:'16–'22

1.2 Delivery of Textiles: Other Recipients

1.2.1 For *Akua-nuri*: Authority of *Šu-Kabta*

1 túg-^{d}*al-la-tum*-gùn-a ù zi-in-bi ki-lá-bi 9 ma-[na] 12 gín *a-ku$_8$-a-nu-ri nu-úr-*^{d}*adad* maškim zi-ga g̃ìri *šu-kab-ta* ki ***aš-tá-qar*-ta ba-zi, "*Aštaqqar* disbursed 1 colored textile of *Allatum* and its zi-in weighing 9 minas (and) 12 shekels (for) *Akua-nuri*. (It was) the expenditure of *Šu-Kabta* under his authority. *Nur-Adad* was the deputy," 584:1–7

1.2.2 Receipt of *Ili-andul*

546 túg-⌜gen⌝[124] *ì-lí-an-dùl* ì-dab$_5$ [ki] ***aš-tá-qar***-ta ba-zi, "*Ili-andul* took in charge 546 ordinary textiles from *Aštaqqar*," 1187:1–5

1.3 Delivery of Weavers and Workwomen

1.3.1 To Bring Barley

16⅓ géme uš-bar u$_4$-10-šè še ù-dag-ga^{ki}-ta gar-ša-an-na^{ki}-šè de$_6$-a 5 géme uš-bar u$_4$-1-šè še *dì-im-bu-na*-^{d}àš-gi$_5$-ta [é]-duru$_5$-kab-bí<ki>-šè de$_6$-a g̃iri ^{d}*adad-tillati* šabra ki ***aš-tá-qar***-ta ba-zi, "Under the authority of *Adad-tillati*, the majordomo, *Aštaqqar* disbursed 16⅓ female weavers for 10 days having brought barley from Udaga to Garšana (and) 5 female weavers for 1 day having brought barley from *Dimbun*-Ašgi to the Kabbi village," 290:1–11

3 géme uš-bar u$_4$-20-šè še é-duru$_5$-ka[b-bí]-ta gar-š[a-an]-n[a^{k}]^{i}-šè [de$_6$]-a <g̃iri> ^{d}*adad-tillati* šabra ki ***aš-tá-qar***-ta ba-zi, "<Under the authority of> *Adad-tillati*, the majordomo, *Aštaqqar* disbursed 3 female weavers for 20 days having [brought] barley from the Kabbi village to Garšana," 303:1–7

1.3.2 To Bring Reeds and the Commodity Tax

5 géme u$_4$-1-[šè] gi da-*si-ḫu-um*-ta de$_6$-a 4 géme u$_4$-1-šè níg̃-gú-na zabala$_4$$^{[ki]}$-šè d[e$_6$-a] ki ***aš-tá-qar***-ta [ba-zi], "*Aštaqqar* [disbursed] 5 workwomen [for] 1 day having brought reeds from Da-*siḫum* (and) 4 workwomen for 1 day having brought the commodity tax to Zabala," 258:1–6

1.3.3 To Crush Malt

66 géme uš-bar u$_4$-1-šè munu$_4$ nag̃$_4$-g̃á-dè gub-ba *èr-ra-ba-ni* maškim zi-[ga *šu-k*]*ab-tá* k[i ***aš-tá-qar***-t]a [ba]-zi, "*Aštaqqar* disbursed 66 female weavers employed for 1 day to crush malt. (It was) the expenditure of *Šu-Kabta*. *Erra-bani* was the deputy," 245:1–6

1.3.4 To Mourn for the King and *Šu-Kabta*

97 géme sag̃-dub 15 géme á-⅓-ta géme uš-bar-me-éš [n] géme gu [u$_4$]-9½-šè [gaba] sìg-dè gub-[ba] u$_4$ *šu-kab-tá* ba-úš<-a> *é-a-šar* maškim ki ^{d}*adad*-[*tillati*-ta] (so tablet!) [ki ***aš***]***-tá-qar***-ta (so envelope!) ba-[zi], "*Adad-tillati* / *Aštaqqar* disbursed 97 full-time female weavers (and) 15 female weavers at ⅓ wages (and) [n] female spinners employed for 9½ days to beat (their) breasts when *Šu-Kabta* died. *Ea-šar* was the deputy," 252:1–10

85 géme-⌜sag̃⌝-dub 16-géme á-⅓-⌜ta⌝ u$_4$-1-šè géme uš-bar-me-éš gaba sàg-dè gub-ba u$_4$ lugal-e ba-úš-[a] ki ***aš-tá-q***[***ar***-ta] ba-⌜zi⌝, "*Aštaqqar* disbursed 85 full-time female weavers (and) 16 female weavers at ⅓ wages employed for 1 day to beat (their) breasts when the king died," 257:1–9

---

[124] A reading udu-⌜níta⌝ is also possible here. Neither restoration conforms to the expected pattern.

1.3.5 Delivery of Workwomen, Receipt of *Adallal*

390 géme u_4-1-šè ⸢ki⸣ ***aš-tá-qar***-ta [*a*]-*da-làl* [ì]-dab_5, "*Adallal* took in charge 390 workwomen for 1 day from *Aštaqqar*," 812:1–5

1.3.6 Delivery of Workwomen, Receipt of *Puzur-agum*

[n gé]me á-diri-ta nam-^{lú}ázlag-šè ki ***aš-tá-qar***-ta *puzur*$_4$-*a-gu*$_5$-*um* ì-⸢dab_5⸣, "*Puzur-agum* took in charge [n] workwomen at additional wages for fulling from *Aštaqqar*," 714:1–5

1.3.7 Delivery of Workwomen and Textiles

70 géme uš-bar u_4-1-šè [n] ^{túg}[níĝ-lá]m-ús [n-ka]m [n] túg-guz-za-ús [n]-kam t[úg?-ba]r?-r[a-n]i? *ḫa-um na-wi-ir-ilum* zi-ga *šu-kab-tá* ki ***aš-tá-qar***-ta ba-zi, "*Aštaqqar* disbursed 70 female weavers for 1 day (and) [n n^{th}]-quality níĝ-lam textile(s) (and) [n n^{th}]-quality tufted textile(s), *ha'um* textiles of *Nawir-ilum*. (It was) the expenditure of *Šu-Kabta*," 650:1–8

1.4 Delivery of Wool, Receipt of *Tadina*

12 gín siki ^{geš}garig aka 4-kam-ús ⅔ ma-na siki ^{geš}garig aka gen [ki ***aš***]-***tá-qar***-ta [*tá-di-na*] túg-[du_8 šu b]a-⸢ti⸣, "[*Tadina*], the braider, received 12 shekels of 4th-quality combed wool (and) ⅔ mina of ordinary combed wool from *Aštaqqar*," 710:1–5

2. Receipts

2.1 From *Adad-tillati*

2.1.1 Assorted Commodities

1 gum-ésir 2 ĝeš-íb 1 ^{gi}bunin-bunin 1 ^{gi}ma-sim dabin ki ^{d}*adad-tillati*-ta ***aš-tá-qar*** šu ba-an-ti, "*Aštaqqar* received 1 pestle (for crushing) bitumen, 2 (wooden products?), 1 bucket, (and) 1 semolina sieve from *Adad-tillati*," 592:1–7

2.1.2 *Alluḫarum* Remnants

2 ma-na *al-lu-ḫa-ru-um li-iq-tum* ki ^{d}*adad-tillati*-ta ***aš-tá-qar*** šu ba-ti, "*Aštaqqar* received 2 minas of *alluḫarum* remnants from *Adad-tillati*," 668:1–4

2.1.3 Beer

11 dug $dida_x$-gen 0.0.3.-ta še-bi 2.1.0. gur ki ^{d}*adad-tillati*-ta ***aš-tá-qar*** šu ba-an-ti egir $buru_{14}$ g[i_4-gi_4-dè], "*Aštaqqar* received from *Adad-tillati* 11 jugs of 30 liters each of ordinary dida beer—their barley (equivalent) is 2 bushels (and) 60 liters—[to] be paid back after the harvest," 629:1–6

2.1.4 Combs

29½ ^{geš}garig šà-kal é-ba-an ki ^{d}*adad-tillati*-ta ***aš-tá-qar*** ugula uš-bar šu ba-ti, "*Aštaqqar*, overseer of weavers, received 29½ pairs of wooden combs from *Adad-tillati*," 598:1–4

2.1.5 Loom Parts

(. . .) ki ^{d}*adad-tillati*-ta ***aš-tá-qar*** ugula uš-bar šu ba-an-ti, "*Aštaqqar*, overseer of weavers, received {wooden loom parts} from *Adad-tillati*," 635:11–13, 1290:5–7

2.1.6 Millstones

1 ^{na4}kinkin-zi-[bí] šu sè-[ga] ki ^{d}*adad-tillati*-[ta] ***aš-tá-q***[***ar*** ugula uš-bar] šu ba-an-ti, "*Aštaqqar*, overseer of weavers, received 1 'hand-held' zi-bí millstone from *Adad-tillati*," 615:1–4

2.1.7 Wool and Cloth

(. . .) ki ^{d}*adad-tillati*-ta ***aš-tá-qar*** (ugula uš-bar) šu ba-an-ti, "*Aštaqqar*, (overseer of weavers), received {assorted wool and cloth} from *Adad-tillati*," 585:17–18, 596:9–11, 605:2–4, 619:4–6, 625:15–16, 628:4–6, 632:2–4, 640:2–4, 657:2–4, 703:2–4, 728:3–5, 752:2–4, 777:2–4, 813:2–4

2.1.8 Wool, Cloth and Baskets of Wool

(. . .) n ^{gi}gúrdub siki ka-tab sè-ga ki ^{d}*adad-tillati*-ta ***aš-tá-qar*** (ugula uš-bar) šu ba(-an)-ti, "*Aštaqqar*, (overseer of weavers), received {assorted wool and cloth} (and) n reed basket(s) of wool fitted with a cover from *Adad-tillati*," 600:1–4, 603:2–5, 613:2–5, 614:2–5, 620:9–11, 624:2–5, 633:6–8, 641:2–5, 648:3–7, 666:6–9, 670:2–5, 672:2–5, 675:2–6, 719:6–10, 750:2–5, 763:3–6, 784:4–7, 826:8–10

(. . .) 4 ^{gi}gúrdub siki ka-tab sè-ga 60 gi ka-tab gúrdub ki ^{d}*adad-tillati*-ta ***aš-tá-qar*** šu ba-ti, "*Aštaqqar* received {assorted wool and cloth}, 4 reed-baskets of wool fitted with a cover (and) 60 reed covers of reed baskets from *Adad-tillati*," 815:8–11

2.1.9 Workwomen

n géme u_4-n-šè ki ^{d}*adad-tillati*-ta ***aš-tá-qar*** (ugula uš-bar) ì-dab_5, "*Aštaqqar*, (overseer of weavers), took in charge n workwomen for n day(s) from *Adad-tillati*," 599:1–4, 612:1–4, 656:1–4, 729:1–4, 735:1–4

n géme sağ-dub(-ba) ki ^{d}*adad-tillati*-ta ***aš-tá-qar*** ì-dab_5, "*Aštaqqar* took in charge n full-time workwomen from *Adad-tillati*," 611:1–4, 622:1–4

2.2 From *Adallal*: Flour

2 sìla zì-gu-ús ki *a-da-làl*-ta ***aš-tá-qar*** šu ba-ti, "*Aštaqqar* received 2 liters of 2nd-quality gu-flour from *Adallal*," 816:1–4

2.3 From *Ḫali:* Wool

25 ma-na siki-ğír-gul ***aš-tá-qar*** šu ba-ti ki *ḫa-lí*-ta [ba]-zi, "*Aštaqqar* received 25 minas of ğír-gul wool from *Ḫali*," 805:1–5

2.4 From *Ili-andul*: Beer

5 sìla kaš-sig_5 ki *ì-lí-an-dùl*-ta ***aš-tá-qar*** šu ba-ti, "*Aštaqqar* received 5 liters of fine-quality beer from *Ili-andul*," 661:1–4

2.5 From *Malik-bani*

368 [. . .] ki ^{d}*ma-lik-ba-ni*-ta ***aš-tá-qar*** ì-dab_5, "*Aštaqqar* took in charge 368 [. . .] from *Malik-bani*," 652:1–4

2.6 From *Ummi-Kabta*: Assorted Wool

(. . .) ki *um-mi-*⌜*kab*⌝*-ta*-ta ***aš-tá-qar*** šu ba-an-ti, "*Aštaqqar* received {assorted wool} from *Ummi-Kabta*," 671:5–6

2.7 Receipt of *Aštaqqar*: Broken Context

[. . .] ***aš-tá-qar*** šu ba-ti, "*Aštaqqar* received [. . .]," 769:7–8

3. Provisions: Barley

0.1.0. še ***aš-tá-qar*** 0.0.3. še ér-kal-la šu ba-an-ti, "*Aštaqqar* received 60 liters of barley, Erkala received 30 liters of barley," 653:1–5

– B –

ba-aḫ-zi-gi

Baḫ-zigi, Man from Karkar

[1] ***ba-aḫ-zi-gi*** (. . .) ugula [*šu*]-*la-núm* (. . .) lú-karkar^{ki}-me, "*Baḫ-zigi*, supervised by *Šulanum*, (and) {other workers}, men from Karkar," 559:1, 12, 28

ba-ba-ni

1. *Babani*, the Majordomo

1.1 Overseer of Ox-drivers

1.1.1 Ox-drivers from the Gang of *Abiati*

2 g̃uruš šà-gu$_4$ *a-bí-a-ti* nu-bànda-gu$_4$ ugula ***ba-ba-ni*** PA.[AL] árad-é-a-me-[éš], "2 ox-drivers (from the gang of) *Abiati*, the ox-herder, household servants supervised by *Babani*, the majordomo," 183:4–7

1.1.2 Ox-drivers from the Gangs of *Abiati*, *Puzur-abi* and *Im-Erra*

n g̃uruš (ugula) *a-bí-a-ti* nu-bànda-gu$_4$ n g̃uruš (ugula) *puzur$_4$-a-bi* nu-bànda-gu$_4$ n g̃uruš (ugula) *i-mé-èr-ra* nu-bànda-gu$_4$ (šà-gu$_4$-me-éš ugula) ***ba-ba-ni*** šabra, "n workmen (from the gang of) *Abiati*, the ox-herder, n workmen (from the gang of) *Puzur-abi*, the ox-herder, n workmen (from the gang of) *Im-Erra*, the ox-herder, (ox-drivers supervised by) *Babani*, the majordomo," 184:1–6, 185:1–5, 186:1–5, 187:1–4

1.1.3 Ox-drivers from the Gangs of *Abiati*, *Puzur-abi*, *Im-Erra* and *Puzur*-Enlil

[3] g̃uruš *a-bí-a-*[*ti* nu-bànda-gu$_4$] 1 g̃uruš *puzur$_4$-a-*[*bi* nu-bànda-gu$_4$] 3 g̃uruš *i-me-èr-r*[*a* nu-bànda-gu$_4$ 3] g̃uruš *puzur$_4$*-^{d}en-⌜líl⌝ nu-[bànda-gu$_4$] ugula ***ba-ba-ni*** PA.A[L], "[3] workmen (from the gang of) *Abiati*, [the ox-herder], 1 workman (from the gang of) *Puzur-abi*, [the ox-herder], 3 workmen (from the gang of) *Im-Erra*, [the ox-herder], (and) [3] workmen (from the gang of) *Puzur*-Enlil, the ox-herder, (ox-drivers) supervised by *Babani*, the majordomo," 189:1–5

1.1.4 Ox-drivers from the Gangs of *Abiati*, *Puzur-abi*, *Im-Erra*, *Puzur*-Enlil, Lu-Inana and *Zabula*

[n g̃uruš *a-bí-a-ti* nu-bànda-gu$_4$ n g̃uruš *pù*]-*zur$_8$*-[*a-bi* nu-bànda-gu$_4$ n g̃uruš] *i-me-èr-ra* nu-bànda-gu$_4$ [1 g̃uruš] *puzur$_4$*-^{d}en-líl nu-[bànda-gu$_4$] 1 g̃uruš lú-^{d}inana nu-bànda-gu$_4$ 1 g̃uruš *za-bu-la* nu-bànda-gu$_4$ ugula ***ba-ba-ni*** šabra, "[n workmen (from the gang of) *Abiati*, the ox-herder, n workmen] (from the gang of) *Puzur-abi*, [the ox-herder, n workmen] (from the gang of) *Im-Erra*, the ox-herder, [1 workmen] (from the gang of) *Puzur*-Enlil, the ox-herder, 1 workman (from the gang of) Lu-Inana, the ox-herder, (and) 1 workman (from the gang of) *Zabula*, the ox-herder, (ox-drivers) supervised by *Babani*, the majordomo," 190:1–7

1.1.5 Ox-drivers from the Gangs of *Abiati*, *Puzur-abi*, *Im-Erra*, *Puzur*-Enlil, Lu-Inana, *Zabula*, and *Munanum*

[n g̃uruš *a-bí-a-ti* nu-bànda-gu$_4$ n g̃uruš] *puzur$_4$*-a-bi nu-bànda-[gu$_4$ n g̃uruš] *i-me-èr-ra* nu-bànda-g[u$_4$ n g̃uruš] *puzur$_4$*-^{d}en-líl nu-bànda-gu$_4$ [n] g̃uruš lú-^{d}inana nu-bànda-gu$_4$ [n] g̃uruš *za-bu-la* nu-bànda-gu$_4$ 2 g̃uruš *mu-na-núm* nu-bànda-gu$_4$ {indent} 15 ugula ***ba-ba-ni*** PA.[AL], "[n workmen (from the gang of) *Abiati*, the ox-herder, n workmen] (from the gang of) *Puzur-abi*, the ox-herder, [n workmen] (from the gang of) *Im-Erra*, the ox-herder, [n workmen] (from the gang of) *Puzur*-Enlil, the ox-herder, [n] workmen (from the gang of) Lu-Inana, the ox-herder, [n] workmen (from the gang of) *Zabula*, the ox-herder, (and) 2 workmen (from the gang of) *Munanum*, the ox-herder; 15 (ox-drivers) supervised by *Babani*, the majordomo," 191:1–10

1.2 Overseer of Ox-Drivers and Hired Workers

1.2.1 From the Gangs of *Abiati*, *Puzur-abi*, *Im-Erra*, *Puzur*-Enlil, Lu-Inana, *Zabula* and *Puzur-abi*, the Equerry

[2 g̃uruš *a-b*]*í-a-ti* n[u-bànda-gu$_4$] 1 g̃uruš *p*[*ù-zu*]*r*$_8$*-a-bi* nu-bànda-[gu$_4$] 2 g̃uruš *i-me-èr-ra* nu-bànda-gu$_4$ 2 g̃uruš *puzur*$_4$-^{d}en-líl [nu]-bànda-gu$_4$ 2 g̃uruš lú-^{d}inana nu-bànda-gu$_4$ 1 g̃uruš *za-bu-la* nu-bànda-gu$_4$ šà-gu$_4$-me-éš 20-lá-1 g̃uruš ḫug̃-g̃á *pù-*[*zur*$_8$]*-a-bi* ⸢kuš$_7$⸣ ugula ⸢***ba***⸣***-ba-ni*** P[A.AL], "[2 workmen] (from the gang of) *Abiati*, the ox-herder, 1 workman (from the gang of) *Puzur-abi*, the ox-herder, 2 workmen (from the gang of) *Im-Erra*, the ox-herder, 2 workmen (from the gang of) *Puzur*-Enlil, the ox-herder, 2 workmen (from the gang of) Lu-Inana, the ox-herder, 1 workman (from the gang of) *Zabula*, the ox-herder; ox-drivers (and) 19 hired workers (from the gang of) *Puzur-abi*, the equerry, supervised by *Babani*, the majordomo," 193:1–9

1.2.2 From the Gangs of *Abiati*, *Puzur-abi*, *Im-Erra*, *Puzur*-Enlil, Lu-Inana, *Zabula*, *Munanum* and *Puzur-abi*, the Equerry

n g̃uruš *a-bí-a-ti* nu-bànda-gu$_4$ n g̃uruš *puzur*$_4$*-a-bi* nu-bànda-gu$_4$ n g̃uruš *i-me-èr-ra* nu-bànda-gu$_4$ n g̃uruš *puzur*$_4$-^{d}en-líl nu-bànda-gu$_4$ n g̃uruš lú-^{d}inana nu-bànda-gu$_4$ n g̃uruš *za-bu-la* nu-bànda-gu$_4$ šà-gu$_4$-me-éš (árad-é-a-me-éš) n g̃uruš ḫug̃-g̃á *mu-na-núm* nu-bànda-gu$_4$ n g̃uruš ḫug̃-g̃á *puzur*$_4$*-a-bi* kuš$_7$ lú-ḫug̃-g̃á-me-éš {indent} n ugula ***ba-ba-ni*** šabra, "n workmen (from the gang of) *Abiati*, the ox-herder, n workmen (from the gang of) *Puzur-abi*, the ox-herder, n workmen (from the gang of) *Im-Erra*, the ox-herder, n workmen (from the gang of) *Puzur*-Enlil, the ox-herder, n workmen (from the gang of) Lu-Inana, the ox-herder, n workmen (from the gang of) *Zabula*, the ox-herder; ox-drivers—(household servants)—(and) n hired workmen (from the gang of) *Munanum*, the ox-herder, (and) n hired workmen (from the gang of) *Puzur-abi*, the equerry; n (ox-drivers) supervised by *Babani*, the majordomo," 194:1–15, 197:1–11

1.3 Supervision of Workers Assigned to Specific Tasks

9 g̃uruš u$_4$-1-šè še 6 sìla-ta ba-ḫug̃ im si-li ⸢gub⸣-ba *mu-na-núm* ⸢ugula⸣ ***ba-ba-ni*** <šabra>, "9 workmen (from the gang of) *Munanum*, (ox-drivers) supervised by *Babani*, <the majordomo>, were hired for 1 day (for) 6 liters of barley each, (workers) employed to break up earth," 474:1–5

1.4 Runaway and Sick Workers from Gangs Supervised by *Babani*

[. . . zàḫ AN.ŠUM.TAG.KAL zàḫ *puzur*$_4$*-šu-ba i-me-èr-ra*] nu-bànda-[gu$_4$] ugula [***ba-ba***]***-ni*** šabra, "[. . . AN.ŠUM.TAG.KAL (and) *Puzur-šuba*, runaways, (from the gang of) *Im-Erra*], the ox-herder, (ox-drivers) supervised by *Babani*, the majordomo," 191:34–38, 195:31–34

⸢zàḫ⸣ *a-da-làl a-*[*bí-a-ti* nu-bànda-gu$_4$] ⸢zàḫ⸣ AN.[ŠUM.TAG.KAL nu-bànda-g]u$_4$ [zàḫ *puzur*$_4$*-šu-ba* nu-bànda-gu$_4$ *i-me*]*-èr-*[*ra* nu-bànda-g]u$_4$ [ugula ***ba***]***-ba-ni*** šabra, "*Adallal*, the runaway (from the gang of) *Abiati* [the ox-herder], AN.ŠUM.TAG.KAL (and) [*Puzur-*

šuba, runaway ox-herders] (from the gang of) *Im-Erra*, the ox-herder, (ox-drivers) [supervised by] *Babani*, the majordomo," 192:'22–'26, 196:'33–'37

[z]àḫ *a-bu*-D[U$_{10}$ *p*]*ù-zur*$_8$*-a-bi* nu-bànda-[gu$_4$ zà]ḫ AN.TAG.KA[L zàḫ] *puzur*$_4$*-šu-*⸢*ba*⸣ *i-me-èr-ra* nu-bà[nda-gu$_4$] ugula ***ba-ba-ni*** P[A.AL], "*Abu-ṭabu*, the runaway (from the gang of) *Puzur-abi*, the ox-herder (and) AN.TAG.KAL (and) *Puzur-šuba*, runaways (from the gang of) *Im-Erra*, the ox-herder, (ox-drivers) supervised by *Babani*, the majordomo," 194:62–67

[zàḫ *a*]*-da-làl a-b*[*í-a-t*]*i* nu-[bànda-gu$_4$ zàḫ] AN.ŠUM.TAG.[KAL nu-bànda-gu$_4$ [zàḫ *pù-zu*]*r*$_8$*-šu-ba* [i-me-èr-ra] nu-bànda-gu$_4$ [ugula ***ba-ba-ni***] šabra, "*Adallal*, [the runaway], (from the gang of) *Abiati*, the ox-herder, AN.ŠUM.TAG.KAL (and) *Puzur-šuba*, [runaway] ox-herders (from the gang of) [*Im-Erra*], the ox-herder, (ox-drivers) [supervised by *Babani*], the majordomo," 197:42–46

1 ĝuruš dú-ra *a-bí-a-ti* nu-bànda-gu$_4$ zàḫ *a-bu*-DU$_{10}$ *puzur*$_4$*-a-bi* nu-bànda-gu$_4$ zàḫ [*šu*?]-^{d}*i-šum* zàḫ *p*[*ù-zu*]*r*$_8$*-šu-ba* [*i-me-èr-ra*] nu-bànda-gu$_4$ [ugula ***ba-ba-ni***] šabra, "1 sick workman (from the gang of) *Abiati*, the ox-herder, *Abu-ṭabu*, the runaway (from the gang of) *Puzur-abi*, the ox-herder, [*Šu*?]*-išum* (and) *Puzur-šuba*, runaways (from the gang of) [*Im-Erra*], the ox-herder, [(ox-drivers) supervised by *Babani*,] the majordomo," 198:'39–'44

1.5 Broken Context

[. . .n] ĝuruš x-x [. . .] ugula ***ba-ba-n***[***i*** šabra], 196:'1–'4

[. . . ugula ***ba-ba-ni*** šabra], 198:'1

2. *Babani*, the Scribe: Transactions under his Authority

2.1 Craftsmen to Remove Dirt at the Mama-*šarrat* Canal

1 ĝuruš ⸢ašgab⸣ u$_4$-14-[šè] iti ezem-an-⸢na⸣ 1 ĝuruš ⸢ašgab⸣ ⸢u$_4$⸣-[n-šè n ĝuruš] ašgab i[ti ezem]-m[e-ki-ĝ]ál ⸢saḫar⸣ zi-⸢ga⸣ i$_7$-ma-ma-*šar-ra-at* ĝìri ***ba-ba-ni*** dub-sar ki *a-na-aḫ-ì-lí-ta* ba-zi, "Under the authority of *Babani*, the scribe, *Anaḫ-ili* disbursed 1 leather worker [for] 14 days in month 11, 1 leather worker [for n] day(s) (and) [n] leather worker(s) in month 12 having moved dirt at the Mama-*šarrat* canal," 281:1–11

1 ĝuruš túg-[du$_8$] u$_4$-13-šè saḫar zi-ga i$_7$-ma-ma-*šar-ra-at* ĝìri ***ba-ba-ni*** dub-sar (. . .) ki *ḫa-lí*-ta ba-zi, "Under the authority of *Babani*, the scribe, *Ḫali* disbursed 1 braider for 13 days having moved dirt at the Mama-*šarrat* canal (and) {other craftsmen}," 283:1–4, 10–11

[1] ĝuruš ad-kub$_4$ [u$_4$]-13-šè saḫar zi-ga i$_7$-ma-ma-šar-*ra-at* ĝìri ***ba-ba-ni*** dub-sar (. . .) ki *ud-du-ur*-ta ba-zi, "Under the authority of *Babani*, the scribe, *Uddur* disbursed [1] reed craftsman for 13 [days] having moved dirt at the Mama-*šarrat* canal (and) {other craftsmen}," 284:1–4, 12

2.2 Baskets from *Adad-tillati*

30 ^{gi}gúrdub siki ka-tab sè-ga zú-si ĝír-su^{ki}-šè ĝìri ***ba-ba-ni*** dub-⸢sar⸣ ki ^{d}*adad-tillati*-ta ba-zi, "Under the authority of *Babani*, the scribe, *Adad-tillati* disbursed 30 baskets fitted with covers to Ĝirsu (to pack) plucked (wool)," 502:1–5

ba-ba-ti-a

1. *Babati'a*, Overseer of Hired Workers

[n ĝuruš/géme ugula ***ba-ba*]*-ti-a*** (. . .) lú-ḫuĝ-ĝá-me-éš, "[n] hired [workmen/workwomen supervised by] *Babati'a*," 135:17

1 ĝuruš ugula ***ba-ba-ti-a*** (. . .) lú-ḫuĝ-ĝá-me-éš, "1 hired workman supervised by *Babati'a*," 136:15, 151:14

n ĝuruš n géme ugula ***ba-ba-ti-a*** (. . .) lú-ḫuĝ-ĝá-me-éš "n hired workmen (and) n hired workwomen supervised by *Babati'a*," 138:17, 140:15, 143:16, 145:19, 146:'11, 147:17, 150:18, 153:'9, 154:14, 155:12

2. *Babati*, Title Unspecified

2.1 Under his Authority: Distance Measurements

šu+níĝin 3 ⸢da⸣-n[a 240+]120 nindan ús gú i_7-me-kal-kal *simat-é-a* a-da-ga-ta ká-^{d}*šu*-^{d}*suen*-šè ĝìri ***ba-ba-ti***, "In total: 3 da-na (and) 360 nindan, the length from the bank of the Mekalkal canal of *Simat-Ea* (and its) irrigation ditch to the *Šu-Suen* gate. (Distance measured) under the authority of *Babati*," 1382:14–16

ba-da-a

Bada'a, the Caretaker

1. Provisions: Barley, Wool, Oil, and Baskets

0.1.0. [še] 4 ma-na siki-[gen] 1 sìla ì-ĝeš 2 ^{gi}bisaĝ-gíd-da-tur sa-ḫa ***ba-da****?*-{erasure}-***a*** (. . .) mu udug kislaḫ saḫar zi-zi-dè-šè, "60 liters of [barley], 4 minas of [ordinary] wool, 1 liter of sesame oil (and) 2 small, long, canvas-lined baskets (for) *Bada'a* (and) {others}, (provisions) for caretakers to move dirt (to/from) the lot,'" 1011:1–5, 15

ba-la-a

1. *Bala'a*, the Majordomo

1.1 Deliveries

1.1.1 Animals

5 udu-máš ḫi-a ki ***ba-la-a*** šabra-ta (. . .) níĝ-kas_7-aka ^{d}*adad-tillati* šabra, "(In total:) 5 various sheep (and) goats from *Bala'a*, the majordomo, (and) {other deliveries}, the balanced account of *Adad-tillati*, the majordomo," 984:'26–'27, '75–'76

1.1.2 Beer Poured as an Offering

0.0.1. kaš-sig_5 0.0.1. kaš-gen 0.4.0. kaš-ninda 5 sìla-ta kaš ba-an-dé *ri-im-ilum* $sugal_7$ gaba-ri-a $unug^{ki}$-ta du-ni ***ba-la-a*** šabra zi-ga *simat*-^{d}*ištaran* ki ***ba-la-a***-ta ba-zi šà é-^{d}*šu*-^{d}*suen*, "*Bala'a*, the majordomo, disbursed 10 liters of fine beer, 10 liters of ordinary beer (and) 240 liters of beer (and) bread, 5 liters each; he poured the beer when *Rim-ilum*, the sugal, came from Uruk (for) a meeting. (It was) the expenditure of *Simat-Ištaran* in Bit-*Šu-Suen*," 517:1–10

2. *Bala'a*, Overseer of Builders

2 ĝuruš šidim ⸢ugula⸣ ***ba-la-a***, "2 builders supervised by *Bala'a*," 202:5–6, 203:5–6

3. *Bala'a*, Title Unspecified

3.1 Deliveries: Barley, Receipt of *Adad-tillati*

1.0.0. še gur ki ***ba-la-a***-ta ^{d}*adad-tillati* šu ba-ti, "*Adad-tillati* received 1 bushel of barley from *Bala'a*," 1093:1–4

3.2 Receipts

3.2.1 From *Adad-tillati*

3.2.1.1 Assorted Commodities for Regular Offerings

(. . .) sá-du$_{11}$-[šè] ***ba-la-a*** šu ba-⸢ti⸣ ki ^{d}*adad-tillati*-ta ⸢ba⸣-zi, "*Bala'a* received {assorted commodities} [for] regular offerings from *Adad-tillati*," 1033:15–17

3.2.1.2 Ox and Sheep Carcasses

1 ádda-gu$_{4}$ 60 ádda-udu 10 gú ^{ĝeš}ma-nu šu aka ki ***ba-la-a***-ta ^{d}*adad-tillati* šu ba-ti, "*Bala'a* received 1 ox carcass, 60 sheep carcasses (and) 10 talents of processed manu wood from *Adad-tillati*," 1223:1–6

3.2.1.3 Wood of a Boat

(. . .) má-40-gur 1-kam [? ***ba***]-***la-a*** ugula [. . .] šu ba-ti [ki ^{d}]*adad-tillati*-ta [ba]-zi, "*Bala'a*, the overseer [. . .], received {assorted wood} of 1 40-bushel boat from *Adad-tillati*," 1368:7–10

3.2.2 From *Anaḫ-ili*: Leather Workers

9 ĝuruš ašgab u$_{4}$-1-šè ***ba-la-a*** ì-dab$_{5}$ ki *a-na-aḫ-ì-lí*-ta ba-zi, "*Bala'a* took in charge 9 leather workers for 1 day from *Anaḫ-ili*," 962:1–5

^{d}ba-ú-da

^{ĝeš}kiri$_{6}$ **^{d}ba-ú-da**, "the garden of Ba'uda" > *Garden Index*

1. Ba'uda, the Gardener

^{d}ba-ú-da [nu]-^{ĝeš}kiri$_{6}$-ke$_{4}$ má-lugal-na saḫar tùm-dè zabala$_{4}$^{ki}-šè in-la-aḫ saḫar mu-un-de$_{9}$ ^{ĝeš}kiri$_{6}$-lugal-na nu-un-ni-ku$_{4}$ é-ni-šè ba-an-dé ka-ga-na ba-ge-en, "Ba'uda, the gardener, confirmed that they took a boat of his master to Zabala in order to bring dirt, that he brought the dirt, that it did not enter the garden of his master but was brought for his (own) house," 1050:1–10

2. Ba'uda, Title Unspecified

2.1 Expenditure: Fresh Apples

[n.n.n.n sìl]a ḫašḫur-duru$_{5}$ gur ⸢*ilum*⸣-*ra-pi*$_{5}$ dam-gàr šu ba-ti níĝ-kas$_{7}$-aka-ta **^{d}ba-ú-da** ba-⸢na⸣-zi kišib *ilum-ra-pi*$_{5}$ u$_{4}$-um-de$_{6}$ kišib **^{d}ba-ú-da** zi-re-dam, "*Ilum-rapi*, the merchant, received [n] bushel(s) (and) [n] liter(s) of fresh apples. Ba'uda expended (them) from the account for him. When the sealed tablet of *Ilum-rapi* is brought, Ba'uda's sealed tablet will be canceled," 1173:1–10

2.2 Receipts: Wood of the Garden House from *Malik-bani*

(. . .) é-^{ĝeš}kiri$_{6}$-a gub-ba ⸢ki⸣ ^{d}*ma-lik-*[*ba-n*]*i*-ta [**^{d}ba-ú**]-**da** šu ba-an-ti, "Ba'uda received {wood} stored in the garden house from *Malik-bani*," 1256:39–41

ba-zi

Bazi, Overseer of Hired Workers

1. Supervision of Hired Workers

1 ĝuruš šidim n ĝuruš n géme ugula ***ba-zi*** (. . .) lú-ḫuĝ-ĝá-me-éš, "1 hired builder, n hired workmen (and) n hired workwomen supervised by *Bazi*," 140:10, 145:11–12, 147:11–12, 150:10–11, 154:9–10

5 ĝuruš ḫuĝ-ĝá 2 géme ḫuĝ-ĝá ugula ***ba-zi***, "5 hired workmen (and) 2 hired workwomen supervised by *Bazi*," 7:12–14, 8:12–14

n ĝuruš n géme ugula ***ba-zi*** (. . .) lú-ḫuĝ-ĝá-me-éš, "n hired workmen (and) n hired workwomen supervised by *Bazi*," 10:8, 14:7–8, 15:7–8, 16:7, 17:7, 18:7, 20:9, 21:8, 22:9, 23:8, 24:9, 29:'6, 30:9, 31:9, 32:9, 33:9, 35:9, 36:9, 37:8, 38:8, 39:8, 42:8, 43:8–9, 44:8, 46:3, 47:8, 48:8, 51:7, 52:7–8, 53:7–8, 54:2, 56:7, 57:7, 58:7–8, 59:7–8, 60:7–8, 71:7, 72:3–4, 73:7, 75:6, 77:3–4, 86:3, 94:6, 98:'3, 99:4, 101:4, 102:7, 103:6, 104:10, 105:10, 106:12, 107:14, 108:11, 109:11, 110:12, 111:13, 114:13, 115:'4, 116:10, 117:11, 118:10, 119:10, 120:10, 123:14, 125:10, 126:10, 127:10, 128:9, 129:10, 130:10, 131:'4, 132:10, 133:10, 134:10, 135:10, 136:10, 137:10, 138:10, 143:10, 146:'6, 151:9, 155:8, 156:8, 157:9, 158:9, 159:7, 161:'1, 162:8, 163:8, 173:7, 174:7, 175:7, 199:1–2, 212:'5, 213:4–5

n ĝuruš ugula ***ba-zi*** (. . .) lú-ḫuĝ-ĝá-me-éš, "n hired workmen supervised by *Bazi*," 9:8, 34:9, 84:3, 93:'6, 121:10, 141:10–11, 142:10

n géme ugula ***ba-zi*** (. . .) lú-ḫuĝ-ĝá-me-éš, "n hired workwomen supervised by *Bazi*," 40:9, 41:9, 49:8, 208:1, 209:8, 211:3–4

[n ĝuruš/géme] ugula ***ba-[zi]*** (. . .) lú-ḫuĝ-ĝá-me-éš, "[n] hired [workmen/workwomen] supervised by *Bazi*," 177:8

2. Supervision of Brick Carriers and Delivery of Bricks and Earth

2.1 Delivery of Bricks

2.1.1 For the Craftsmen's House

é-gašam-e-ne mu-DU ***ba-zi***, "delivery (of bricks for) the craftsmen's house by *Bazi*," 334:65–66

2.1.2 For Replacement Houses

mu-DU é-ki-ba-ĝar-ra en-^{d}inana-gal ***ba-zi*** ugula, "delivery (of bricks for) the replacement house of the senior priest of Inana by *Bazi*, the overseer," 337:30–33

[mu-DU é]-ki-ba-ĝar-ra *z[u-zu-t]um* ***ba-zi*** [ugula l]ú-ḫuĝ-ĝá, "[delivery] (of bricks for) the replacement house of *Zuzutum* by *Bazi*, [overseer] of hired workers," 342:83–85

é-ki-ba-ĝar-ra *puzur*$_4$*-ra-bí* mu-DU ***ba-zi*** ugula ⸢lú⸣-ḫuĝ-ĝá, "delivery (of bricks for) the replacement house of *Puzur-rabi* by *Bazi*, overseer of hired workers," 344:'25–'27

2.1.3 For the Textile Mill

é-uš-bar(-šè) mu-DU ***ba-zi*** ugula, "delivery (of bricks for) the textile mill by *Bazi*, the overseer," 323:124–126, 327:82–84

2.1.4 For the Textile Mill and Craftsmen's House

[é]-uš-bar [ù é]-gašam-e-ne mu-DU ***ba-zi*** ugula lú-ḫuĝ-ĝá, "delivery (of bricks) for the textile mill [and] craftsmen's house by *Bazi,* overseer of hired workers," 368:'60–'63

2.1.5 For the (Enclosure) Wall

bàd-šè ⌜mu⌝-DU ***ba-zi*** ugula lú-ḫuĝ-ĝá, "delivery (of bricks) for the (enclosure) wall by *Bazi*, overseer of hired workers," 309:74–76

ù-ru-a bàd-šè mu-DU ***ba-zi*** ugula lú-ḫuĝ-ĝá, "delivery (of bricks) for the urua wall by *Bazi*, overseer of hired workers," 318:'50–'52

mu-DU bàd-šè ***ba-zi*** ugula lú-ḫuĝ-ĝá, "delivery (of bricks) for the (enclosure) wall by *Bazi*, overseer of hired workers," 340:33–34, 345:'15–'17

2.2 Delivery of Dirt for the Side of the (Enclosure) Wall

saḫar zi-ga tùn-lá da bàd [sè-ga m]u-DU ***ba-zi*** ugula l[ú-ḫuĝ-ĝá], "Dirt removed via a tùn-lá device, [tamped] at the side of the (enclosure) wall. Delivery (of dirt) by *Bazi*, overseer of hired workers," 329:13–15

saḫar zi-ga tùn-lá da bàd sè-ga á ^{tumu}mer mu-DU ***ba-zi*** ugula lú-ḫuĝ-ĝá, "Dirt removed via a tùn-lá device, tamped at the north side of the (enclosure) wall. Delivery (of dirt) by *Bazi*, overseer of hired workers," 331:34–36, 333:21–24

3. Supervision of Workers Assigned to Specific Tasks

3.1 Crushing Malt

2 géme ugula ***ba-zi*** lú-ḫuĝ-ĝá-me-[éš] $munu_4$ $naĝ_4$-ĝá $kurum_7$ aka, "Inspection (of the work) of 2 hired workwomen, supervised by *Bazi*, having crushed malt," 172:5–8

n ĝuruš n géme ugula ***ba-zi*** $munu_4$ al-$naĝ_4$-ĝá-dè gub-ba $kurum_7$ aka ĝìri ^{d}*adad-tillati* (šabra) ù *puzur*$_4$-^{d}nin-kar-ak dub-sar, "Under the authority of *Adad-tillati*, the (majordomo), and *Puzur*-Ninkarak, the scribe, inspection (of the work) of n workmen (and) n workwomen, supervised by *Bazi*, employed to crush malt," 67:1–8, 68:1–7, 69:1–8

[n] ĝuruš [n] géme [ugula] ***ba-zi*** [$munu_4$ a]l-$naĝ_4$-[ĝá-d]è gub-ba [ĝìri ^{d}*adad*]-*tillati* [ù] *puzur*$_4$-^{d}nin-[kar]-ak dub-sar, "[Under the authority of] *Adad-tillati* [and] *Puzur*-Ninkarak, the scribe, [n] workmen (and) [n] workwomen, supervised by *Bazi*, employed to crush malt," 70:'1–'7

3.2 Garden Work

14 ĝ[uruš n géme] ugula [***ba-zi***] (. . .) $kurum_7$ aka saḫar zi-ga [^{ĝeš}kiri$_6$ gar-ša-an-na^{ki}], "Inspection (of the work) of 14 workmen [(and) n workwomen], supervised by [*Bazi*], (and) {other workers} having moved dirt [at the Garšana garden]," 176:5–6, 16–17

3.3 Pouring Water

[n ĝuruš ugula] ***ba-zi*** (. . .) [a] bal-a (. . .) [$kurum_7$ aka], "[Inspection (of the work) of n workmen, supervised by] *Bazi*, (and) {other workers} having poured [water]," 181:3, 5, 8

3.4 Towing Boats

52 ĝuruš ugula ***ba-zi*** (. . .) 4 má-10-gur-ta gar-ša-an-na^{ki}-ta karkar^{ki}-šè gíd-da, "52 workmen, supervised by *Bazi* (and) {other workers} having towed 4 10-bushel boats from Garšana to Karkar," 236:1, 7–9

3.5 The Volume of Earth Used to Build the Adobe Wall under the Supervision of *Bazi*

8 nindan gíd 4 kùš dağal 2 kùš sukud saḫar-bi 5⅓ sar 8 nindan gíd 3 kùš dağal 2 kùš gi_4-bi 4 kùš sukud saḫar-bi 6⅔ [sar] 7½ nindan gíd 3 kùš [dağal] 2 kùš gi_4-bi 5 kùš sukud saḫar-bi 8⅚ sar ⌜igi⌝-4-⌜ğal⌝ 6½ nindan 4 kùš gíd 2½ kùš dağal 2 kùš ba-an-gi_4-bi 4 kùš sukud saḫar-bi 5 sar 7½ gín [erased sign] 25⅚ sar 8⅔ gín 15 še im-du_8-a ugula ***ba-zi***, "8 nindan long, 4 kùš wide, 2 kùš high, its dirt is 5⅓ sar; 8 nindan long, 3 kùš wide, 2 kùš tapered from 4 kùš high, its earth is 6⅔ [sar]; 7½ nindan long, 3 kùš [wide], 2 kùš tapered from 5 kùš high, its earth is 8⅚ sar and ¼; 6½ nindan and 4 kùš long, 2½ kùš wide, 2 kùš tapered from 4 kùš high, its earth is 5 sar and 7½ gín; (the total volume) of the adobe wall is 25⅚ sar, 8⅔ gín (and) 15 še, (built) under the supervision of *Bazi*," 366:'5–'13

3.6 Wages for Workers Assigned to Pile Earth

[. . .] á [ğuruš]-a 10 gín-ta ğuruš-bi 4 u_4-1-šè še 6-sìla-ta ba-ḫuğ saḫar zi-ga kar-ki-mu-ra si-ga mu-DU *ìl-su-dan* ugula ***ba-zi***, "[. . . workmen] wages of 10 shekels each; its workmen (equal) 4 workerdays, (workers) hired for 6 liters of barley each, having piled up excavated dirt at the quay of the textile depository. Delivery of *Ilsu-dan*, supervised by *Bazi*," 354:1–7

4. Receipts: Barley

70.0.0. še gur šà gar-ša-an-na^{ki} 90-lá-1.0.0. gur šà karkar^{ki} šu+níğin 160.0.0.-lá-1.0.0. gur ***ba-zi-tum*** šu ba-ti, "*Bazitum* received 70 bushels of barley in Garšana (and) 89 bushels of barley in Karkar, 159 bushels in total," 1252:1–7[25]

5. Provisions

5.1 Barley

(. . .) [šu+níğin n+]7.0.0. gur še-ba ***ba-zi-tum*** šu+níğin 47.1.[n.] še-ba é [šu+níğin 60+]31.1.5. ⌜gur⌝, "{barley for individuals}; [in total: n+]7 bushels of the barley rations of *Bazitum*. In total: 47 bushels (and) 60[+n] liters of barley rations of the household, [in total: 60+]31 bushels (and) 110 liters," 555:24–28

0.0.2. [***ba***]-***zi*** (. . .) mu dabin-šè šu ba-ti, "*Bazi* received 20 liters of barley (and barley for) {9 other individuals}, (barley) in place of semolina," 560:5, 12–13

5.2 Shoes

1 kuš-⌜súḫub⌝-gen [é]-ba-an ***ba-zi*** ⌜ugula⌝ lú-[ḫuğ]-ğá (. . .) ki *a-na-aḫ-ì-lí*-ta ***ba-zi***, "*Anaḫ-ili* disbursed 1 pair of ordinary shoes (for) *Bazi*, overseer of hired workers, (and) {other leather products}," 855:11–12, 25–26

5.3 Wages for Molding Bricks

921½ [. . .] ***ba***-[***zi***] (. . .) $šeg_{12}$ du_8-[a], "921½ [(units of bricks from)] *Bazi* (and bricks from) {other workers}, {wages for workers} having molded bricks," 350:1–2, '23

6. Under the Authority of *Bazi*: Delivery of Bricks

73⅓ sar $šeg_{12}$ NE-gu_7-bi íb-ta-zi mu-DU *i-din-é-a* ugula lú-ḫuğ-ğá ğìri ***ba-zi***, "73⅓ sar of bricks, the damaged bricks were deducted. Delivery of *Iddin-Ea*, overseer of hired workers, under the authority of *Bazi*," 315:1–5

---

[25] It is assumed here and in no. 555 that *Bazitum* is the full form of *Bazi*.

7. As a Witness

⸢igi⸣ ***ba-zi*** ugula lú-ḫug̃-g̃á, "witnessed by *Bazi*, overseer of hired workers," 1046 :9

be-lí-a-ri-ik

1. Receipts

2 udu ***be-lí-a-ri-ik*** u_4 iri-ni-šè ì-g̃en-na-a 1 udu ki *ì-lí-bi-la-ni*-ta ba-zi, "*Ili-bilani* disbursed 2 sheep (for) *Beli-arik* when he went to his city (and) 1 (additional) sheep," 410:1–7

be-lí-a-sú

1. *Beli-asu*, the Builder from Isin: Provisions

1.1 Bread

2 sìla ninda-ta *en-nim-ma* 1 ***be-lí-a-sú*** lú-ì-si-in^{ki}-me-éš (. . .) šà-gal šidim-e-ne, "2 liters of bread each (for) *Enima* (and) *Beli-asu*, men from Isin, (and for) {other workers}, food (for) builders," 381:1–4, 21

[2 sìla] ninda-ta 1 *en-nim-ma* 1 ***be-lí-a-sú*** lú-ì-si-in^{ki} (. . .) šà-gal ši[dim-e-n]e ⸢u_4⸣ [bàd egir] é-a dù-dè, "[2 liters] of bread each (for) *Enima* (and) *Beli-asu*, men from Isin, (and for) {other workers}, food (for) builders when they were constructing [the (enclosure) wall behind] the house," 386:1, 10–12, 29–30

[1 *en-ni-ma* 1 ***be-lí*]*-a-sú*** [lú-ì]-si-in^{ki} (. . .) šà-gal šidim-e-ne ⸢u_4⸣ bàd eger é-a dù-dè, "[(bread)] (for) [*Enima*] (and) *Beli-asu*, men from Isin, (and for) {other workers}, food (for) builders when they were constructing the (enclosure) wall behind the house," 387:1–3, 20–21

1.2 Ordinary Beer

2 sìla kaš-gen-ta *en-ni-ma* 1 ***be-lí-a-sú*** lú-ì-si-in^{ki}(-me-éš) (. . .) šidim-e-ne íb-nag̃, "2 liters of ordinary beer each (for) *Enima* (and) *Beli-asu*, men from Isin, (and for) {other builders}; the builders drank (the beer)," 378:9–12, 16, 380:1–4, 8, 389:1–4, 8

2 sìla kaš-gen-ta *en-ni-ma* 1 ***be-lí-a-sú*** (. . .) [šidim-e-ne] íb-nag̃, "2 liters of ordinary beer each (for) *Enima* (and) *Beli-asu*, (and for) {other builders}; [the builders] drank (the beer)," 384:1–3, 7

1.3 Semolina

2 sìla dabin-ta *en-nim-ma* 1 ***be-lí-a-sú*** lú-ì-si-in^{ki} šidim (. . .) šà-gal šidim-e-ne u_4 bàd in-dù-sa-a, "2 liters of semolina each (for) *Enima* (and) *Beli-asu*, builders of Isin, (and for) {other builders}, food (for) builders when they constructed the (enclosure) wall," 396:1–4, 19–20, 397:1–4, 19–20

1.4 Sheep and Grains

(. . .) 1 *en-ni-ma* 1 ***be-lí-a-sú*** lú-ì-si-in^{ki}-me-éš (. . .) [šà-gal šidim] ù dub-sar-e-ne, "{sheep carcasses, semolina, and barley} (for) *Enima* (and) *Beli-asu*, men from Isin, (and for) {other workers}, [food (for) builders] and scribes," 399:10–12, 24

2. *Beli-asu*, the Sick Workman from the Gang of *Irib*

2.1 Supervised by *Beli-ili*

1 ***be-lí-a-sú*** dú-ra ugula *be-lí-ì-lí*, "*Beli-asu*, the sick (workman) supervised by *Beli-ili*," 33:46

2.2 Supervised by *Irib*

1 ***be-lí-a-sú*** dú-ra ugula *i-ri-ib*, "*Beli-asu*, the sick (workman) supervised by *Irib*," 27:'20, 28:'31, 29:'36, 31:40, 32:41, 34:'20, 35:50

1 ***be-[lí]-a-sú*** 1 *e-pe-eš* ^{na}nam!<-dú?-ra?> ugula *i-[ri]-ib*, "*Beli-asu*, satisfying the allowance of sick leave, supervised by *Irib*," 36:44–45

3. *Beli-asu*, Title Unspecified: Provisions

[. . .] ⅓ sìla mu[n-ta] 6 gín luḫ-lá-[ta] g̃ìri *ì-lí-*[. . .] 1 *ad-da-ni* 1 *bi-za-tum* 1 *i-din-*^{d}*šamaš* 1 *in-ga-la* 1 ***be-lí-a-sú*** níta-me-éš, "[. . .], ⅓ liter of salt [each], (and) 6 shekels of luḫ-lá [each] under the authority of *Ili-*[. . .], (provisions for) *Adani*, *Bizatum*, *Iddin-Šamaš*, *Ingala* (and) *Beli-asu*, the men," 562:'31–'39

be-lí-ì-lí

1. *Beli-ili*, Overseer of Household Servants

n g̃uruš ugula ***be-lí-ì-lí*** árad-é-a-me-éš, "n workmen, household servants supervised by *Beli-ili*," 20:5–6, 21:50–6, 22:5–6, 23:4–5, 24:5–6, 30:5, 31:5–6, 32:5, 33:5, 34:5, 35:5–6, 36:4, 37:4, 38:4, 6, 39:4, 40:4, 41:4, 42:4, 43:4, 44:4, 45:4, 47:4, 48:5, 49:4, 51:4, 52:4, 6, 53:4, 55:5–6, 56:5–6, 57:5–6, 58:5–6, 59:5–6, 60:5–6, 61:5–6, 63:5–6, 71:5, 73:4, 6, 75:4–5, 92:3, 93:'3, 98:'2, 99:3, 101:3, 157:1–6, 159:5–6, 212:'3–'4

n g̃uruš gub-ba ugula ***be-lí-ì-lí*** árad-é-a-me-éš, "n present workmen, household servants supervised by *Beli-ili*," 155:5–7, 156:5–6, 158:5–7, 162:5–7, 163:5–7, 173:5–6, 174:5–6, 175:5–6, 177:5–7, 180:5–7

2. Present Workers and the Explained Absence of Others Supervised by *Beli-ili*

2.1 Guarding Bricks

17 g̃uruš gub-ba 2 g̃uruš šeg$_{12}$ en-nu aka ugula ***be-lí-ì-lí*** árad-é-a-me-éš, "17 workmen present (and) 2 workmen having guarded bricks, household servants supervised by *Beli-ili*," 151:5–8, 154:5–8

2.2 Guarding Bricks and Running Errands

17 g̃uruš gub-ba 2 g̃uruš šeg$_{12}$ en-nu aka 1 é-[ì-gára] á-ág̃-g̃á k[i *š*]*u-kab-tá*-šè de$_6$-a ugula ***be-lí-ì-lí***, "17 workmen present, 2 workmen having guarded bricks, (and) E'igara having brought a message to the place of *Šu-Kabta*, (workers) supervised by *Beli-ili*," 102:3–6

2.3 Guarding Bricks and Being Sick

n g̃uruš gub-ba 2 g̃uruš šeg$_{12}$ en-nu aka 1 *e-pe-eš* na-am-dú-ra ugula ***be-lí-ì-lí*** árad-é-a-me-éš, "n workmen present, 2 workmen having guarded bricks, (and) 1 (workman) satisfying the allowance of sick leave, household servants supervised by *Beli-ili*," 116:5–9, 117:5–10, 118:5–9, 119:5–9, 120:5–9, 121:5–9, 133:5–9, 134:5–9, 135:5–9, 136:5–9, 137:5–9, 138:5–9, 139:5–9, 140:5–9, 141:5–9, 142:5–9, 143:5–9, 145:5–9, 147:5–9, 149:1–9, 150:1–9

2.4 Guarding Bricks, Running Errands and Being Sick

n g̃uruš gub-ba 2 g̃uruš šeg$_{12}$ en-nu aka 1 é-ì-gára 1 *šu-*^{d}*belum* á-ág̃-g̃á ki *šu-kab-ta*-šè de$_6$-a 1 *e-pe-eš* na-am-dú-ra ugula ***be-lí-ì-lí*** árad-é-a-me-éš, "n workmen present, 2 workmen having guarded bricks, E'igara (and) *Šu-Belum* having brought a message to the place of *Šu-Kabta*, (and) 1 (workman) satisfying the allowance of sick leave, household servants supervised by *Beli-ili*," 110:5–11, 111:4–12

15 g̃uruš gub-ba 2 g̃uruš šeg$_{12}$ en-nu [aka] 1 *šu-*^{d}*belum* á-ág̃-g̃á ki *šu-kab-ta*-šè de$_6$-a 1 *e-pe-eš* na-am-dú-ra 2! é-ì-gára ugula ***be-lí-ì-lí*** árad-é-a-me-éš, "15 workmen present, 2 workmen having guarded bricks, *Šu-Belum* having brought a message to the place of *Šu-Kabta*, 1 (workman) satisfying the allowance of sick leave (and) E'igara (having gone with *Šu-Belum*), household servants supervised by *Beli-ili*," 114:5–12

9 g̃uruš gub-ba 6 g̃uruš siki é-^{d}*šu-*^{d}*suen*-ka-šè g̃en-[na] 2 g̃uruš šeg$_{12}$ en-nu aka 1 ***be-lí-ì-lí*** 1 é-ì-gára á-ág̃-g̃á ki *šu-kab-ta*-šè de$_6$-a 1 *e-pe-eš* na-am-dú-ra ugula ***be-lí-ì-lí*** árad-é-a-me-éš, "9 workmen present, 6 workmen having gone to *Bit-Šu-Suen* (for) wool, 2 workmen having guarded bricks, *Beli-ili* and E'igara having brought a message to the place of *Šu-Kabta*, (and) 1 (workman) satisfying the allowance of sick leave, household servants supervised by *Beli-ili*," 123:5–13

2.5 Guarding Bricks, Keeping the Door, Running Errands and Being Sick

12 g̃uruš gu[b-ba 3] g̃uruš šeg$_{12}$ en-[nu aka] 1 g̃uruš ì-⸢du$_8$⸣ 1 é-ì-[gára] 1 *šu-*^{d}nin-k[ar-ak] á-á[g̃-g̃]á [ki *šu-kab-t*]*a*-[šè de$_6$-a] 1 *e-pe-eš* na-am-dú-ra ugula ***be-lí-ì-***[***lí***] árad-é-[a-me-éš], "12 workmen present, [3] workmen having guarded bricks, 1 doorkeeper, E'igara (and) *Šu*-Ninkarak [having brought] a message [to the place of *Šu-Kabta*], (and) 1 (workman) satisfying the allowance of sick leave, household servants supervised by *Beli-ili*," 106:3–11

n g̃uruš gub-ba n g̃uruš šeg$_{12}$ en-nu aka 1 g̃uruš ì-du$_8$ 1 é-ì-gára á-ág̃ ki *šu-kab-ta*-šè de$_6$-a 1 *šu-*^{d}nin-kar-ak á-ág̃-g̃á ù-dag-ga^{ki}-šè de$_6$-a 1 *e-pe-eš* na-am-dú-ra ugula ***be-lí-ì-lí*** árad-é-a-me-éš, "n workmen present, n workmen having guarded bricks, 1 doorkeeper, E'igara having brought a message to the place of *Šu-Kabta*, *Šu*-Ninkarak having brought a message to Udaga (and) 1 (workman) satisfying the allowance of sick leave, household servants supervised by *Beli-ili*," 107:6–13, 108:3–10, 109:3–10

2.6 Explained Absences of all his Workers

17 g̃uruš níg̃-gú-na g̃á-g̃á é-da-na^{ki}-šè g̃en-na 2 g̃uruš šeg$_{12}$ en-nu aka 1 *e-pe-eš* na-am-dú-ra ugula ***be-lí-ì-lí*** árad-é-a-me-éš, "17 workmen having gone to Edana to deposit the commodity tax, 2 workmen having guarded bricks, (and) 1 (workman) satisfying the allowance of sick leave, household servants supervised by *Beli-ili*," 125:1–9, 126:5–9, 127:5–9, 128:5–8

17 g̃uruš níg̃-gú-na kar-ta é-kìšib(-ba-šè) ga$_6$-g̃á 2 g̃uruš šeg$_{12}$ en-nu aka 1 *e-pe-eš* na-am-dú-ra ugula ***be-lí-ì-lí*** árad-é-a-me-éš, "17 workmen having carried the commodity tax from the quay to the warehouse, 2 workmen having guarded bricks, (and) 1 (workman) satisfying the allowance of sick leave, household servants supervised by *Beli-ili*," 129:5–9, 130:5–9, 132:5–9,

2.7 Broken Context

1 g̃uruš [. . .] ugula ***be-lí-ì-lí*** árad-é-a-me-éš, "1 workman [. . .], household servants supervised by *Beli-ili*," 115:'1–'3

[. . . 2] g̃uruš [šeg$_{12}$ en-nu aka 1] *e-pe-eš* na-am-dú-ra [ugula] ***be-lí-ì-lí*** [árad]-é-a-me-éš, "[. . . 2] workmen [having guarded bricks], (and) [1] (workman) satisfying the allowance of sick leave, household servants supervised by *Beli-ili*," 146:'1–'4

3. Errands for Individual Workers Supervised by *Beli-ili*

3.1 Gone to Gu'abba to Purchase Flying Fish

1 *ša-lim-be-lí* ku$_6$-sim sa$_{10}$-sa$_{10}$-dè gú-ab-ba^{ki}-šè g̃en-na 1 *ar-ri-az* dú-ra ugula ***be-lí-ì-lí***, "*Šalim-beli* having gone to Gu'abba to purchase flying fish (and) *Arriaz* having been sick, (workmen) supervised by *Beli-ili*," 37:41–46

1 *ša-lim-be-lí* ku$_6$-sim sa$_{10}$-sa$_{10}$-dè gú-ab-ba^{ki}-šè g̃en-na ugula ***be-lí-ì-lí***, "*Šalim-beli* having gone to Gu'abba to purchase flying fish, supervised by *Beli-ili*," 38:48–50, 49:65–67

1 *ša-lim-be-lí* ⌜ku$_6$⌝-sim sa$_{10}$-dè gú-ab-ba^{ki}-šè g̃en-na zàḫ *ir-du-du* ugula ***be-lí-ì-lí***, "*Šalim-beli* having gone to Gu'abba to purchase flying fish (and) *Irdudu*, the runaway, (workmen) supervised by *Beli-ili*," 47:64–68, 48:71–74

3.2 Gone to Bring a Message to *Šu-Kabta*

1 é-ì-gára á-ág̃-g̃á ki *šu-kab-ta*-šè de$_6$-a ugula ***be-lí-ì-lí***, "E'igara having brought a message to the place of *Šu-Kabta*, supervised by *Beli-ili*," 50:'16–'18, 59:52–53, 60:48–50

1 é-ì[-gára] 1 *šu*-^{d}[*belum*] á-ág̃ ki *šu-k*[*ab-ta*-šè de$_6$-a] ugula ***be-lí-ì-***[***lí***], "E'igara (and) *Šu-Belum* [having brought] a message [to] the place of *Šu-Kabta*," 71:32–35

3.3 Various Tasks

1 *ta-tù-ri* á-ág̃ ki *šu-kab-ta*-šè nibru^{ki}-šè de$_6$-a 1 *ḫi-lu-a* á-ág̃ g̃ír-su^{ki}-šè de$_6$-a 1 *lu-kà-du-um* ninda du$_8$-dè gub-ba 1 *en-nim-ma* šidim 1 *šál-maḫ* šidim dú-ra-me-éš 1 *e-pe-eš* na-am-dú-ra ugula ***be-lí-ì-lí***, "*Tatturi* having brought a message to Nippur to the place of *Šu-Kabta*, *Ḫilua* having brought a message to G̃irsu, *Lukadum* employed to bake bread, *Enima* and *Šal-maḫ*, the builders, having been sick, (and) 1 (workman) satisfying the allowance of sick leave, (workmen) supervised by *Beli-ili*," 24:'25–'31

1 é-ì-gára á-ág̃ nibru^{ki}-šè ki *šu-kab-ta*-šè de$_6$-a 1 *ḫi-lu-a* dub *i-din*-^{d}*adad* nibru^{ki}-šè de$_6$-a 1 *lu-kà-dum* ninda du$_8$-dè gub-ba 1 *be-lí-a-sú* dú-ra ugula ***be-lí-ì-lí***, "E'igara having brought a message to the place of *Šu-Kabta* in Nippur, *Ḫilua* having brought the tablet of *Iddin-Adad* to Nippur, *Lukadum* employed to bake bread (and) *Beli-asu* having been sick, (workmen) supervised by *Beli-ili*," 33:43–46

1 *i-ṭib-ší-na-at* 1 é-ì-gára á-ág̃ ki *šu-kab-ta*-šè de$_6$-a 1 *ḫi-lu-a* á-ág̃ *šu-eš$_4$-tár* ù-dag-ga^{ki}-šè de$_6$-a 1 *šu*-^{d}*belum* á-ág̃ ki *a-ḫu-wa-qar* lú-du$_6$-lugal-pa-è^{ki} de$_6$-a 1 *lu-kà-dum* [1] šeš-kal-la [ku$_6$-sim] sa$_{10}$-sa$_{10}$-dè [gú-ab-ba]^{ki}-šè g̃en-na [. . .] gú-áb(sic!)-[ba^{ki}. . .] zàḫ *ir-*[*du-du*] ugula ***b*[*e*]*-lí-ì-lí***, "*Iṭibšinat* (and) E'igara having brought a message to the place of *Šu-Kabta*, *Ḫilua* having brought a message to *Šu-Eštar* in Udaga, *Šu-Belum* having brought a message to the place of *Aḫu-waqar*, the man from Du-lugal-pa'e, *Lukadum* (and) Šeš-kala having gone to [Gu'abba] to purchase [flying fish . . .] Gu'abba [. . .] (and) *Irdudu* the runaway, (workmen) supervised by *Beli-ili*," 46:'39–'50

[1 *a*]*-lí-a*[*ḫ* 1 *ta-tù*]-⌜*ri*⌝ še šà [g̃ír]-su^{ki} *en-nu-um* ke$_4$-d[è gub-ba] 1 ***be-lí-ì-lí*** 1 *šu*-^{d}nin-kar-[ak] dub ^{d}*ma-lik-ba-*[*ni* é]-da-na^{ki}-šè [de$_6$-a 1 *š*]*u*-^{d}*belum* [á-ág̃ ki] *šu-kab-t*[*a*-š]è šu?-x-[x?]-x G̃EŠ.KÚŠU[^{ki}-šè?] de$_6$-[a] ugula [***be-lí***]***-ì-***[***lí***], "*Aliaḫ* (and) *Tatturi* [employed] to guard barley in G̃irsu, *Beli-ili* (and) *Šu*-Ninkarak [having brought] the tablet of *Malik-bani* to Edana, *Šu-Belum* having brought [a message] to [the place of] *Šu-Kabta* (?) [in?] G̃EŠ.KÚŠU, (workmen) supervised by *Beli-ili*," 56:'29–'39

6 [g̃uruš . . .] a-šà pa$_4$-lu[gal-g̃]u$_{10}$-⌜ka⌝ gi tùm-⌜dè⌝ g̃en-[na] 1 g̃uruš šeg$_{12}$ en-nu ke$_4$-[dè] gub-⌜ba⌝ 1 g̃uruš g̃á-nun-na [tuš-a] ugula ***be-lí-ì-lí***, "6 [workmen. . .], having gone to the Palugalg̃u field to bring reeds, 1 workman employed to guard bricks, 1 workman [having sat (idle)] at the storehouse, (workmen) supervised by *Beli-ili*," 57:'22–'26

[n g̃uru]š gi-zi tùm-dè [a-š]à *ši-⌜ḫu⌝-um*-šè g̃en-na [n] g̃uruš zi-ga didli gub-ba [1] g̃uruš g̃á-nu[n-na tuš-a n] g̃uruš ká é-gašam tuš-a [ugula] ***be-lí-ì-lí***, "[n] workmen having gone to the *Šiḫum* field to bring fresh reeds, [n] employed workmen having removed additional (dirt), [1] workman [having sat (idle)] at the storehouse (and) [n] workmen having sat (idle) at the gate of the craftsmen's house, (workmen) [supervised] by *Beli-ili*," 75:26–31

3.4 Broken Context

[. . .] ugula ***be-lí-ì-⌜lí⌝***, 58:64–65

4. Sick Workmen Supervised by *Beli-ili*

1 g̃uruš dú-ra ugula ***be-lí-ì-lí***, "1 sick workman supervised by *Beli-ili*," 21:'29

[1 *e-pe-eš* na-am-dú-ra ugula ***be-lí-ì-lí*** ára]d-é-[a]-me-éš, "[1 (workman) satisfying the allowance of sick leave], household servants [supervised by *Beli-ili*]," 131:'1–'3

5. Workers Assigned to Specific Tasks Supervised by *Beli-ili*

5.1 Crushing Malt

n g̃uruš ugula ***be-lí-ì-lí*** árad-é-a-me-éš munu$_4$ nag̃$_4$-g̃á-dè kurum$_7$ aka, "Inspection (of the work) of n workmen, household servants supervised by *Beli-ili*, to crush malt," 170:4–8, 171:4–7, 172:1–3, 7–8

6 [géme] ugula ***be-lí-ì-[lí]*** árad-é-a-me-éš (. . .) munu$_4$ al-nag̃$_4$-g̃á [erased sign]-dè ⌜gub⌝-ba, "6 [workwomen], household servants supervised by *Beli-ili*, (and) {other workers} employed to crush malt," 217:'1–'3, '7–'8

5.2 Gatekeepers

3 g̃uruš ì-[du$_8$] ugula ***be-lí-ì-[lí]***, "3 gatekeepers supervised by *Beli-ili*," 40:49

6. Receipt of Provisions

6.1 Barley in Place of Semolina

0.1.1. ***[be-l]í-ì-lí*** (. . .) mu dabin-šè šu ba-ti, "*Beli-ili* received 70 liters of barley, (and barley for) {9 other individuals}, (barley) in place of semolina," 560:6, 12–13

6.2 Bread and Dates for his Workers

1 g̃uruš ugula 2 sìla ninda-dabin 2 sìla zú-lum 18 g̃uruš 1 sìla ninda 2 sìla zú-lum-[ta] ugula ***be-lí-ì-lí*** (. . .) ḫa-la-a g̃uruš árad-é-a-e-[ne], "(For) 1 overseer: 2 liters of semolina bread (and) 2 liters of dates; (for) 18 workmen: 1 liter of bread (and) 2 liters of dates each, (workers) supervised by *Beli-ili*, (and) {provisions for other workers} divided for household servants," 402:4–6, 17

7. *Beli-ili*, the Errand Runner

7.1 With *Šu*-Ninkarak: Bringing the Tablet of *Malik-bani* to Edana

1 ***be-lí-ì-lí*** 1 *šu*-^{d}nin-kar-ak dub ^{d}*ma-lik-ba-ni* é-[da]-na^{ki}-šè de$_6$-a, "*Beli-ili* and *Šu*-Ninkarak having brought the tablet of *Malik-bani* to Edana," 51:'22–'24, 52:59–62, 53:61–63, 56:'32–'35

7.2 With E'igara: Bringing a Message to *Šu-Kabta*

1 ***be-lí-ì-lí*** 1 é-ì-gára á-ág̃-g̃á ki *šu-kab-ta*-šè de$_6$-a, "*Beli-ili* and E'igara having brought a message to the place of *Šu-Kabta*," 123:8–10

7.3 Broken Context

[. . . 1] ***be-lí-ì-[lí]***, 39:'50

8. *Beli-ili*, Overseer of Boat-Towers

8.1 As a Witness

1 ***be-lí-ì-lí*** ugula má gíd, "(witnessed by) *Beli-ili*, overseer of boat towers," 1048:12, 1057:10

igi ***be-lí-ì-lí***, "witnessed by *Beli-ili*," 1051:10[26]

8.2 Transactions under his Authority

8.2.1 Distribution of Barley: Delivery of *Puzur*-Enlil, Receipt of *Adad-tillati*

60.0.0. ⸢sìla⸣ še gur ki *puzur*$_4$-^{d}en-líl-ta ^{d}*adad-tillati* šu ba-ti ĝiri ***be-lí-ì-lí***, "Under the authority of *Beli-ili*, *Adad-tillati* received 60 bushels of barley from *Puzur*-Enlil," 1195:1–5[27]

448.4.0. še gur ^{d}*adad-tillati* šabra šu ba-ti ki *puzur*$_4$-^{d}en-líl nu-bànda-gu$_4$-ta ba-zi ĝiri ***be-lí-ì-lí*** ugula má-gíd, "Under the authority of *Beli-ili*, overseer of boat towers, *Adad-tillati*, the majordomo, received 448 bushels (and) 240 liters of barley from *Puzur*-Enlil, the ox-herder," 1212, 1–6

8.2.2 Distribution of Reeds: Delivery of *Pušu-kin*, Receipt of *Adad-tillati*

n sa gi-izi gu-níĝin 15-sa-ta n sa gi-zi gu-níĝin (10/20)-sa-ta ki *pu-šu-ki-in*-ta ^{d}*adad-tillati* šu ba-an-ti ĝìri ***be-lí-ì-lí*** ugula má gíd, "Under the authority of *Beli-ili*, overseer of boat towers, *Adad-tillati* received from *Pušu-kin* n bundle(s) of fuel reeds, bales of 15 bunches each, (and) n bundle(s) of fresh reed(s), bales of (10 or 20) bunches each," 1276:1–8, 1277:1–8

3540 sa gi-izi gu-níĝin 15-sa-ta 600 sa gi-šid gu-níĝin 20-sa-ta ki *pu-š*[*u-k*]*i-in*-ta ^{d}*a*[*dad*]-*tillati* šu [ba-a]n-ti ĝìri ***be-lí-ì-lí*** ugula má gíd, "Under the authority of *Beli-ili*, overseer of boat towers, *Adad-tillati* received from *Pušu-kin* 3540 bundles of fuel reeds, bales of 15 bunches each, (and) 600 bundles of dry reeds, bales of 20 bunches each," 1278:1–8

8.2.3 Craftsmen to Bring Reeds

1⅔ ĝuruš ašgab 1 ĝuruš túg-du$_8$ 1 ĝuruš simug u$_4$-1-šè ⸢gi⸣ ù gi-zi é-^{d}šára-ta gar-ša-an-na^{ki}-šè [de$_6$]-a ĝìri ***be-lí-ì-lí*** ki ^{d}*adad-tillati*-ta ba-zi, "Under the authority of *Beli-ili*, *Adad-tillati* disbursed 1 leather worker, 1 braider (and) 1 smith for 1 day having brought reeds and fresh reeds from the Šara temple to Garšana," 232:1–11[28]

8.3 Under the Authority of *Adad-tillati* and *Beli-ili*: Craftsmen to Bring Reeds to Garšana

(. . .) u$_4$-10-še gi-izi ù-dag^{ki}-ga-ta gar-ša-an-na^{ki}-šè [de$_6$]-a ⸢ĝìri⸣ ^{d}⸢*adad*⸣-*tillati* 2? ù ***be-lí-ì-***[***lí*** ugula má gíd] zi-ga ĝìri *šu-kab-ta*<<-ta>> ki ^{d}*adad-tillati*-ta ba-zi, "*Adad-tillati* disbursed {craftsmen} for 10 days having [brought] fuel reeds from Udaga to Garšana.

---

26 Although *Beli-ili*'s title is not specified, this text is included here on the assumption that there was only one person by this name operating at Garšana (Heimpel, personal communication).

27 Although *Beli-ili's* title is not specified, this text is included here in light of the parallel transaction, no. 1212.

28 Although *Beli-ili*'s title is not specified, this text is included here in light of similar transactions, nos. 1276, 1277, 1278.

(It was) the expenditure of *Šu-Kabta*, under his own authority, (and) the authority of *Adad-tillati* and *Beli-ili*, overseer of boat towers," 230:6–14

3 ĝuruš saĝ-tag 1 ĝuruš á-⅔ lú-ašláĝ-me-éš u_4-10-šè gi-izi ù-dag[ki]-ga-ta [gar-š]a-an-na[ki]-šè de_6-a ĝìri [d]*adad-tillati* šabra ù ***be-lí-ì-lí*** ugula má gíd zi-ga ĝìri *šu-kab-ta* ki *puzur$_4$-a-gu$_5$-um*-ta ba-zi, "*Puzur-agum* disbursed 3 full-time fullers (and) 1 fuller at ⅔ wages for 10 days having brought fuel reeds from Udaga to Garšana. (It was) the expenditure of *Šu-Kabta* under his authority (and) the authority of *Adad-tillati*, the majordomo, and *Beli-ili*, overseer of boat towers," 231:1–11

8.3.1 Wages for Sailors

[1.1.4.] še gur [á má-ḫuĝ]-ĝá má 50-gur-ta 2-kam ù má-$la\underset{\smile}{h}_5$-bi [0].1.2.5 sìla-ta [á] 0.0.2.5 sìla-ta á má-ḫuĝ-ĝá má 40-gur-ta 2-kam ù má-$la\underset{\smile}{h}_5$-bi á 0.0.2.-ta [u_4]-8-šè ⸢še⸣ ù-dag-ga[ki]-ta [gar-ša]-an-na[ki]-šè de_6-a [ĝìri] [d]*adad-tillati* šabra [ù?] ***be-lí-ì-lí*** ugula-má gíd [zi-g]a ĝìri *šu-kab-tá* [ki [d]]*adad-tillati*-ta [ba]-zi, "[1] bushel (and) 100 liter(s) of barley, [wages] (for) each of 2 hired 50-bushel boats and their sailors, 85 liters each; [wages] of 25 liters each, wages (for) each of 2 hired 40-bushel boats and their sailors, 20 liters each; (wages for sailors) for 8 days having brought barley from Udaga to Garšana. (It was) the expenditure of *Šu-Kabta*, under his authority (and) that of *Adad-tillati*, the majordomo, [and?] *Beli-ili*, overseer of boat towers," 414:1–16

8.4 As a Deputy: Oil for *Ḫili*

½ sìla ì-ĝeš *ḫi-li* má gíd u_4 ḫi-bar-ra-ni in-na-gig-ga ***be-lí-ì-lí*** maškim, "½ liter of sesame oil for *Ḫili*, the boat tower, when his 'outer knee' was hurting him. *Beli-ili* was the deputy," 444:4–6[29]

bi-da-sa_6-sa_6

Bidasasa, Man from Karkar

[1 b]i?-**da-sa_6-sa_6** (. . .) ugula *á-ni*-x-x (. . .) lú-karkar[ki]-me, "Bidasasa, supervised by *á-ni*-x-x, (and) {other workers}, men from Karkar," 559:21, 25, 28

bí-du-lu-um

1. Provisions

2 kuš-udu 2 kuš-šáḫ-babbar ***bí-du-lu-um***-šè ba-a-ĝar, "2 sheep skins (and) 2 white pig skins were placed for *Bidulum*," 1517:13–15

bí-za-a

é-ki-ba-ĝar-ra ***bí-za-a***, "the replacement house of *Biza'a*" > *Household Index*

---

[29] Although *Beli-ili*'s title is not specified, this text is included here based on the profession of the recipient of this transaction.

bí-za-tum[30]

1. **Bizatum, the ox-herder(?) from the Gang of *Malik-tillati***

[n] ***bí-za-tum*** [. . .*eš*$_4$]-*tár* [. . .i]m [. . .]-lu ^{d}*ma-li*[*k-tillati* nu-bànda-g]u$_4$ [. . .], "Bizatum, [. . .], (workers from the gang of) *Malik-tillati*, the ox-herder, [. . .]," 194:70–73

[1 g̃uruš] dú-ra 1 *ú-bar-*⌜*um*⌝ 1 ***bí-za-***⌜***tum***⌝ 1 *šu-*^{d}⌜*adad*⌝ 1 AN.TAG.⌜KAL⌝ ^{d}*ma-lik-tillati* [nu-bànda]-gu$_4$ ugula *nu-úr-*^{d}*adad* šabra, "[1] sick [workman], *Ubarum*, *Bizatum*, *Šu-Adad*, (and) AN.TAG.KAL, (workers from the gang of) *Malik-tillati*, the ox-herder, supervised by *Nur-Adad*, the majordomo," 198:'32–'38

2. **Bizatum, the Servant: Provisions**

[. . .] ⅓ sìla mu[n-ta] 6 gín luḫ-lá-[ta] g̃ìri *ì-lí-*[. . .] 1 *ad-da-ni* 1 ***bi-za-tum*** 1 *i-din-*^{d}*šamaš* 1 *in-ga-la* 1 *be-lí-a-sú* níta-me-éš, "[. . .], ⅓ liter of salt [each], (and) 6 shekels of luḫ-lá [each] under the authority of *Ili-*[. . .], (provisions for) *Adani*, *Bizatum*, *Iddin-Šamaš*, *Ingala* (and) *Beli-asu*, the men," 562:'31–'39

bu-lu-za

Buluza, the Fuller

1. **As a Witness**

igi ***bu-lu-za*** ^{lú}ázlag, "witnessed by *Buluza*, the fuller," 1064:10

bu-za-du-a

Buzadua, the Female Miller

1. **Provisions: Oil When She was Sick**

10 gín ì-g̃eš-ta ^{d}šára-sá-g̃u$_{10}$ 1 ***bu-za-du-a*** géme kíkken-me-éš u$_4$ dú-ra i-me é-gal!-šè, "10 shekels of sesame oil each (for) Šara-sag̃u (and) *Buzadua*, female millers, when they were sick at the palace," 466:3–7

– D –

da-a-a

Da'a, the Cook

1. **Bread**

1.1 **In his Account**

[šu+níg̃in n.]1.0.6 sìla ninda gur [zi-ga]-àm [šu+níg̃in] 9½ sìla [zi-ga]-àm níg̃-kas$_7$-aka ***da-a-a*** muḫaldim, "[In total: n] bushel(s) (and) 66 liters of bread were expended; [in total:] 9½ liters were expended; the balanced account of *Da'a,* the cook," 1031:20–26

1.2 **In his Possession**

lá-ìa 1.3.1.2⅚ sìla ninda gur lá-ìa-àm ***da-a-a*** muḫaldim in-da-g̃ál, "the remainder of 1 bushel (and) 192⅚ liters of bread are with *Da'a*, the cook," 1243:1–4

---

30 While it is possible that *Bizatum* is the full form of the name *Biza'a*, the context of the texts in which each name occurs does not suggest identification at this time.

2. Receipts

2.1 Containers

2.1.1 From *Adad-tillati*

1 ^{gi}bisağ-BÚR-tab-ba ğeš-tab-ba ki ^{d}*adad-tillati*-ta ***da-a-a*** šu ba-ti, "*Da'a* received 1 (?) basket from *Adad-tillati*," 1336:1–4

2 ^{dug}útul 0.0.1.-ta 1 ^{dug}útul 5-sila ki ^{d}*adad-tillati*-ta ***da-a-a*** muḫaldim šu ba-ti, "*Da'a*, the cook, received 2 10-liter tureens (and) 1 5-liter tureen from *Adad-tillati*," 1344:1–5

1 ^{gi}gur-^{dug}útul ésir šub-ba ki ^{d}*adad-tillati*-ta ***da-a-a*** muḫaldim šu ba-ti, "*Da'a*, the cook, received 1 reed basket shaped like a tureen coated with bitumen from *Adad-tillati*," 1370:1–4

2.1.2 From *Malik-bani*

120 [sa? g]i?-izi 1 ^{gi}bisağ? é-ĞAR kuš ğar-ra ki ^{d}*ma-lik-ba-ni*-ta ***da-a-a*** šu ba-ti, "*Da'a* received 120 [bundles? of] fuel [reeds?] (and) 1 (?) basket covered with leather from *Malik-bani*," 1332:1–5

2.2 Broken Context

2? ^{ğeš}maš DI-d[a?. . .] 2? udu *šu-ka*-[. . .] 2 ^{ğeš}maš DI-[. . .] ka-ba UD.K[A.BAR. . .] ⸢ki⸣ ^{d}*adad*-[*tillati*-ta ***da***]***-a-***[***a*** muḫaldim šu] ba-[ti], "*Da'a*, [the cook], [received] (?) from *Adad-tillati*," 1342:1–7

da-da

é-***da-da***, "the house of *Dada*" > *Household Index*

é-ki-ba-ğar-ra ***da-da***, "the replacement house of *Dada*" > *Household Index*

1. The Funerary Libation Place of *Dada*: Offering of a Piglet

1 šáḫ-zé-da-ga ki-a-nağ-***da-da***-šè *an-ta-lú*, "1 suckling piglet for the funerary libation place of *Dada*," 970:10–11

2. The Fortified Tower of *Dada*

2.1 Barley Brought from the Tower

10 géme kíkken u_4-1-šè a-rá-1-kam 10 géme kíkken u_4-1-šè a-rá-2-kam 10 géme kíkken u_4-1-šè a-rá-3-kam še an-za-qar-***da-da***-ta gar-ša-an-na^{ki}-šè de_6-a, "10 female millers for 1 day for the 1st time, 10 female millers for 1 day for the 2nd time (and) 10 female millers for 1 day for the 3rd time having brought barley from the fortified tower of *Dada* to Garšana," 296:1–9

2 ğuruš [ašgab] u_4-[1-šè] a-rá-1-[kam] 2 ğuruš ašgab [u_4-1-šè] a-rá-2-kam 2 ğuruš ašgab u_4-1-šè a-rá-3-kam 2 ğuruš ašgab u_4-1-šè a-rá-4-kam 2 ğuruš ašgab u_4-1-šè a-rá-5-kam še an-za-qar-***da-da***-[ta] gar-ša-an-na^{ki}-šè de_6-a, "2 leather workers for 1 day having brought barley [from] the fortified tower of *Dada* to Garšana {on 5 different occasions}," 297:1–14

2.2 A Boat Towed to the Tower and Barley Unloaded There

1 ğuruš túg-du_8 u_4-[1-kam] gú-saḫar^{har}.DU^{ki}-ta a[n-za-qar]-***da-da***-šè má gíd-da ù [še ba-al], "1 braider for 1 day having towed a boat from Gu-saḫar.DU to the fortified tower of *Dada* and [having unloaded barley]," 298:11–12

2 g̃uruš ašgab u_4-1-šè gú-sah̬ar[har].DU[ki]-ta an-za-qar-***da-da***-šè má gíd-da ù še ba-al, "2 leather workers for 1 day having towed a boat from Gu-sah̬ar.DU to the fortified tower of *Dada* and having unloaded barley," 299:11–12

da-da-a

1. *Dada'a*, the Bird Warden

1.1 Lost Birds and Mice

5 $tu-gur_4$[mušen] 31 péš-igi-gùn úgu dé-a ***da-da-a*** sipa-mušen-⌜na⌝ íb-su-su, "*Dada'a*, the bird warden will replace 5 lost doves (and) 31 lost striped-eyed mice," 1138:1–4

23 péš-i[gi-gùn] úgu dé-a ***da-da-a*** sipa-mušen-na íb-su-su, "*Dada'a*, the bird warden, will replace 23 lost striped-eyed mice," 1152:1–3

3 uz-tur 7 tum_{12}[mušen] 4 $tu-gur_4$[mušen] 15 péš-g̃eš-gi 23 péš-igi-gùn úgu d[é-a] ***da-da-a*** sipa-mušen-na, "3 ducklings, 7 wild doves, 4 doves, 15 mice (and) 23 striped-eyed mice—lost (animals) of *Dada'a*, the bird warden," 1172:1–7

1.2 In Legal Texts

1.2.1 Slaughtered Birds

1 tum_{12}[mušen] 2 $tu-gur_4$[mušen] ba-úš mušen-bi ki záh̬ ì-g̃ál [d]*ma-lik-ba-ni* ì-dab_5 sim-da ***da-da-a*** sipa-mušen-na, "*Malik-bani* took in charge 1 wild dove (and) 2 doves, slaughtered birds that had (previously) escaped; branding mark of *Dada'a*, the bird warden," 1058:1–8

1.2.2 Stolen Birds and Mice

4 tum_{12}[mušen] 1 péš-g̃eš-gi 1 péš-igi-gùn [níg̃-z]uh̬-a [***da-d***]***a-a*** sipa-⌜mušen-na⌝, "4 wild doves, 1 mouse (and) 1 striped-eyed mouse; stolen [goods] of *Dada'a*, the bird warden," 1059:2–5

[n] ⌜ir_7⌝[mušen]-niga [n] tum_{12}[mušen]-niga 47 $tu-gur_4$[mušen]-niga 21 péš-igi-gùn-niga níg̃-zuh̬-a ***da-da-a*** sipa-mušen-na, "[n] fattened pigeon(s), [n] fattened wild dove(s), 47 fattened doves (and) 21 fattened striped-eyed mice; stolen goods of *Dada'a*, the bird warden," 1060:1–6

1.2.3 Testifying

2 uz-tur-niga 1 kur-gi[mušen]-niga 6 ir_7[mušen]-niga 10 $tu-gur_4$[mušen]-niga 5 péš-g̃eš-gi-niga 30-lá-1 péš-igi-gùn-niga ***da-da-a*** sipa-mušen-na in-KA-[x] ù ba-an-d[u_{11}-ga] ka-ga-[na ba-gen_7], "*Dada*, the bird warden, confirmed that he (?) and (?) 2 fattened ducklings, 1 fattened goose, 6 fattened pigeons, 10 fattened doves, 5 fattened mice, (and) 29 fattened, striped-eyed mice," 1053:1–9

1.2.4 Translation Uncertain

[. . .] še mušen-[na . . .] šu bala-dè [. . .] 6 ir_7[mušen]-niga 30 $tu-gur_4$[mušen]-niga ***da-da-a* sipa-mušen-na é-[a . . .] *šu*-[d]na-zi sipa-mušen-na é-[a . . .], 1253:'1–'7

2. *Dada'a*, Father of *H̬ululu*

2.1 Reciept of *H̬ululu*: House Bitumen from *Iddin-Adad*

0.1.0. ésir-é-a ki *i-din-*[d]*adad*-ta *h̬u-lu-lu* dumu ***da-d***[***a-a***] šu ba-a[n-ti], "*H̬ululu*, the son of *Dada'a*, received 60 liters of house bitumen from *Iddin-Adad*," 1257:1–5

3. ***Dada'a*, Father of *Šu-Eštar***

3.1 **Provisions for *Šu-Eštar*, the Caretaker**

0.1.0. še 3 ma-na siki-gen 1 sìla ì-g̃eš 2 ^{gi} bisag̃-gíd-da-tur sa-ḫa *šu-eš$_4$-tár* dumu ***da-da-a*** (. . .) mu udug kislaḫ saḫar zi-zi-dè-šè, "60 liters of barley, 3 minas of ordinary wool, 1 liter of sesame oil (and) 2 small, long canvas-lined baskets (for) *Šu-Eštar*, the son of *Dada'a*, (and) {others}, (provisions) for caretakers to move dirt (to/from) the lot," 1011:6–10, 15

4. ***Dada'a*, the Porter**

4.1 **Receipts: Oil When He was Injured**

10 gín ì-g̃eš ***da-da-a*** un-ga$_6$ u$_4$ dùb bar-ra-ni in-na-gig-ga, "10 shekels of sesame oil (for) *Dada'a*, the porter, when his 'outer knee' was hurting him," 466:1–2

da-da-AN

1. **Nergal, the Personal Deity of *Dada*-AN's Son**

1 udu-ú ^{d}nergal$_x^{eri_{11}\text{-gal}}$ dumu ***da-da*-AN** ki *ì-lí-bi-la-ni*-ta ba-zi, "*Ili-bilani* disbursed 1 range-fed sheep (for) Nergal, (the personal deity of) the son of *Dada*-AN," 422:1–4

120 ^{dug}sìla-bu[r-zi] tu$_7$ ba-a[ka] kaš-dé-a ^{d}nergal$_x^{[eri_{11}\text{-gal}]}$ dumu ***da-d*[*a*-AN]**, "120 1-liter offering bowls of soup were served at the banquet of Nergal, (the personal deity of) the son of *Dada*-AN," 1025:54–56

dan-ḫi-li

Danḫili, the Brewer

1. **Grains in his Possession**

0.4.4.5 sìla [še?] 0.0.3. zíz 0.0.1. kib$_x$ ***dan-ḫi-li*** ^{lú}[^{ú}lùn]ga in-⌜da⌝-g̃ál še é-^{d}*šu*-^{d}*suen*^{ki}-ta de$_6$-a, "285 liters of [barley?], 30 liters of emmer wheat (and) 10 liters of wheat are with *Danḫili*, the brewer, who brought barley from *Bit-Šu-Suen*," 1065:1–6

du-du-gu

Dudugu, Builder from Nig̃-Ba'u

1. **Receipts: Provisions**

1.1 **Semolina and Barley**

2 sìla dabin-ta 2 sìla še-ta ur-te-me-na 1 ur-^{d}asar-lu-ḫi 1 ***du-du-gu*** 1 ^{d}utu-sá-bí [1] lú-me-lám lú-níg̃-^{d}ba-ú šidim-me-éš (. . .) šà-gal šidim-e-ne, "2 liters of semolina each (and) 2 liters of barley each (for) Ur-temena, Ur-Asarluḫi, *Dudugu*, Utu-sabi (and) Lu-melam, builders from Nig̃-Ba'u, (and for) {other workers}, food (for) builders," 381:5–12, 21

2 sìla dabin-ta 2 sìla še-ta ur-te-me-na 1 ur-^{d}asar-lu-ḫi 1 ***du-du-gu*** 1 ^{d}utu-sá-bí 1 lú-me-lám lú-níg̃-^{d}ba-ú šidim (. . .) šà-gal šidim-e-ne u$_4$ bàd egir é-a dù-dè, "2 liters of semolina each (and) 2 liters of barley each (for) Ur-temena, Ur-Asarluḫi, *Dudugu*, Utu-sabi (and) Lu-melam, builders from Nig̃-Ba'u, (and for) {other workers}, food (for) builders when they were constructing the (enclosure) wall behind the house," 386:13–20, 29–30, 387:5–11, 20–21

2 sìla dabin-ta 2 sìla še-ta ur-te-me-na 1 ur-^{d}asar-lu-ḫi 1 ***du-du-gu*** 1 ^{d}utu-sá-bí 1 lú-me-lám lú-níĝ-^{d}ba-ú šidim (. . .) šà-gal šidim-e-ne u_4 bàd in-dù-sa-a, "2 liters of semolina each (and) 2 liters of barley each (for) Ur-temena, Ur-Asarluḫi, *Dudugu*, Utu-sabi (and) Lu-melam, builders from Niĝ-Bau, (and for) {other workers}, food (for) builders when they constructed the (enclosure) wall," 396:5–12, 19–20, 397:5–13, 19–20

1.2 Sheep and Grains

[0.1.0 še-ta 0.1.0 dabin-ta 3 údda]-udu-ta [ur-te]-me-na [1 ur-^{d}a]sar-lu-ḫi [1] ***du-du-gu*** [1] lú-me-lám [1] ^{d}utu-sá-ti(!) lú-níĝ-^{d}ba-ú-me-éš (. . .) [šà-gal šidim] ù dub-sar-e-ne, "[60 liters of barley, 60 liters of semolina (and) 3] sheep [carcasses] each (for) Ur-temena, Ur-Asarluḫi, *Dudugu*, Lu-melam (and) Utu-sabi, men from Niĝ-Ba'u, (and for) {other workers}, [food (for) builders] and scribes," 399:1–9, 24

dub-si-ga

Dub-siga, the Carpenter

1. As a Witness

igi **dub-si-ga** naĝar, "witnessed by Dub-siga, the carpenter," 1059:8

– E –

$e_{(2)}$-é-zi

1. Nergal, the Personal Deity of E'ezi's Son

[n.n.n.n sìl]a zì gu[r ^{d}PIRI]G.UNU-gal dumu **e-é-zi**, "[n] bushel(s) (and) [n] liter(s) of flour (for) Nergal, (the personal deity of) the son of E'ezi," 484:4–5

120 ^{dug}sìla-bur-zi tu_7 ba-aka kaš-dé-a ^{d}nergal$_x^{eri11-[gal]}$ dumu **é-é-⸢zi⸣**, "120 1-liter (offering) bowls of soup were served at the banquet of Nergal, (the personal deity of) the son of E'ezi," 1025:89–91

e-ri-ib-bu-um

Eribum, Man from Karkar

1 ***[e-r]i-ib-b[u-u]m*** (. . .) ugula *á-ni*-x-x (. . .) lú-karkar^{ki}-me, "*Eribum*, supervised by *á-ni*-x-x, (and) {other workers}, men from Karkar," 559:13, 25, 28

e-ṣí-dum

1. His Geese, Ducklings, and Mice

2 ⸢kur⸣-gi^{mušen} 3 uz-tur 6 péš-ĝeš-gi ***e-ṣí-dum*** 15 péš-igi-gùn ⸢*lú*⸣-*ša-lim* iti u_4-13-ba-zal mu-DU *šu-kab-tá* ^{d}*adad-tillati* ì-dab_5, "At the end of the 13th day of the month *Adad-tillati* took in charge 2 geese, 3 ducklings (and) 6 mice of *Eṣidum* (and) 15 striped-eyed mice of *Lušallim*, the delivery of *Šu-Kabta*," 1127:1–10

é-a-bu

Ea-abu, the Scribe

1. Under his Authority: Animals Slaughtered for the Warehouse

1 mušen-tur u_4-14-kam 5 mušen-tur u_4-28-kam 4 tu-gur_4 mušen 2 péš-g̃eš-gi 2 péš-igi-gùn u_4-30-kam ba-úš é-kišib-ba-šè g̃iri ***é-a-bu*** dub-sar zi-ga-àm, "Under the authority of *Ea-abu*, the scribe, expenditure of 1 young bird on the 14th day, 5 young birds on the 28th day, 4 doves, 2 mice (and) 2 striped-eyed mice on the 30th day. They were slaughtered for the warehouse," 1254:'27–'35

é-a-dan

1. *Ea-dan*, the Scribe

1.1 Receipts: Provisions for Scribes

(. . .) 0.0.4.5 sìla ***é-a-dan*** (. . .) [še]-ba dub-sar-e-ne, "45 liters (of barley for) *Ea-dan*, (and for) {other workers}, [barley] rations of the scribes," 394:4, 7

0.1.3. še 3 ádda-udu-ta *puzur₄*-^{d}nin-kar-ak 1 *la-qì-ip* 1 ***é-a-dan*** dub-sar-me-éš (. . .) [šà-gal šidim] ù dub-sar-e-ne, "90 liters of barley (and) 3 sheep carcasses each (for) *Puzur*-Ninkarak, *Laqip* (and) *Ea-dan*, the scribes, (and for) {other workers}, [food (for) builders] and scribes," 399:16–20, 24

0.1.3. še-ta [n s]ìla ì-g̃eš-ta [n] ádda-udu-ta [*pù*]-*zur₈*-^{d}nin-kar-ak [***é***]-***a-dan*** 3 g̃uruš du[b-s]ar-me-éš, "13 liters of barley each, [n] liter(s) of sesame oil each (and) [n] sheep carcass(es) each (for) *Puzur*-Ninkarak (and) *Ea-dan*, the scribes," 406:1–6

2. *Ea-dan*, Title Unspecified

2.1 Deliveries: Semolina and Fine Flour as (Ceremonial) Offerings

1 sìla ⌜dabin⌝ ½ sìla eša sízkur bàd-šè [ki ***é***]-***a-dan***-ta ba-zi, "*Ea-dan* disbursed 1 liter of semolina (and) ½ liter of fine flour, (ceremonial) offerings for the (enclosure) wall," 987:1–5, 988:1–5, 989:1–5

1 sìla dabin ½ sìla eša sízkur bàd-šè ki ***é-a-dan***-ta ba-zi g̃iri ^{d}*adad-tillati ù puzur₄*-^{d}nin-kar-ak dub-sar, "Under the authority of *Adad-tillati* and *Puzur*-Ninkarak, the scribe, *Ea-dan* disbursed 1 liter of semolina (and) ½ liter of fine flour, (ceremonial) offerings for the (enclosure) wall," 990:1–7

1 sìla dabin ½ sìla eša sízkur bàd ù é-uš-bar-šè ⌜ki⌝ ***é-a-dan***-ta ba-zi, "*Ea-dan* disbursed 1 liter of semolina (and) ½ liter of fine flour, (ceremonial) offerings for the (enclosure) wall and the textile mill," 991:1–5, 994:1–5

é-a-ra-bí

1. Receipts: Semolina

21.1.0. dabin gur zì-ba má gíd-e-ne ***é-a-ra-bí*** šu ba-an-ti ki ^{d}*adad-tillati*-[ta] ba-zi, "*Ea-rabi* received 21 bushels (and) 60 liters of semolina, flour rations of boat towers, from *Adad-tillati*," 426:1–6

é-a-šar

1. *Ea-šar*, the Majordomo: Transactions under his Authority

1.1 Grains, Receipt of Ur-Dumuzi, the Ox-Herder[31]

21.4.3 še gur ì-dub še-ba iti-3-kam g̃ìri ***é-a-šar*** ur-^{d}dumu-zi nu-bànda-gu$_4$, "Under the authority of *Ea-šar*, Ur-Dumuzi, the ox-herder, (received) 21 bushels (and) 270 liters of barley of the granary (for) barley rations (for) 3 months," 542:1–6

33.4.1. še gur numun-šè 0.1.0. še-ba lú-^{d}*suena* má-laḫ$_5$ ba-zi g̃ìri ***é-a-šar*** ur-^{d}dumu-zi [nu]-bànda-gu$_4$, "Ur-Dumuzi, the ox-herder, (received) 33 bushels (and) 250 liters of barley for seed (and) 60 liters (for) the barley ration of Lu-*Suena*, the sailor, disbursed under the authority of *Ea-šar*," 543:1–6

5.0.0. zíz gur 0.3.3. kib$_x$ ì-dub a-šà mí-mí 15.2.0. zíz gur 0.1.3. kib$_x$ ì-dub šà *dì-im-bu-bu*(sic!)<-aš>-gi$_5$ 20.2.0. ziz gur 1.0.0. kib$_x$ gur ki *i-dì-èr-ra*-ta ur-^{d}dumu-zi šu ba-ti g̃ìri ***é-a-šar*** šabra, "Under the authority of *Ea-šar*, the majordomo, Ur-Dumuzi received from *Iddi-Erra* 5 bushels of emmer wheat (and) 210 liters of wheat of the granary of the Mimi field, 15 bushels (and) 120 liters of emmer wheat (and) 90 liters of wheat of the granary in *Dimbun*-Ašgi, (and) 20 bushels (and) 120 liters of emmer wheat (and) 1 bushel of wheat," 1232:1–12

[šu+níg̃in] 242.2.4.5 sìla še gur šu+níg̃in 25.0.0. zíz gur šu+níg̃in 4.1.4. kib$_x$ gur u[r-^{d}dumu-z]i nu-bànda-gu$_4$ [šu] ⸢ba⸣-ti g̃ìri ***é-a-ša*[*r*** šabra], "Under the authority of *Ea-šar*, [the majordomo], Ur-Dumuzi, the ox-herder, received a total of 242 bushels (and) 165 liters of barley, 25 bushels of emmer wheat (and) 4 bushels (and) 100 liters of wheat," 1233:20–26

27.1.4. še gur mur-gud-šè ba-zi g̃ìri ***é-a-šar*** ur-^{d}dumu-zi nu-bànda-gu$_4$, "Ur-Dumuzi, the ox-herder, (received) 27 bushels (and) 100 liters of barley for ox fodder, disbursed under the authority of *Ea-šar*," 1236:1–5

1.2 Work Assignments for Craftsmen

1 g̃uruš túg-du$_8$ u$_4$-4-šè *dì-im-bu-na*-àš-gi$_5$-ta a-šà *ṣe-ru-um*-šè g̃ìri ***é-a-šar*** šabra ki *ḫa-lí*-ta ba-zi, "Under the authority of *Ea-šar*, the majordomo, *Ḫali* disbursed 1 braider for 4 days (having gone) from *Dimbun*-Ašgi to the *Ṣerum* field," 283:5–11

1 g̃uruš ad-kub$_4$ u$_4$-4-šè *dì-im-bu-na*-àš-gi$_5$-ta a-šà *ṣe-r*[*u-u*]*m*-šè še gur$_{10}$-gur$_{10}$-[dè] gub-ba g̃ìri ***é-a-*⸢*šar*⸣** šabra ki *ud-du-ur*-ta ba-zi, "Under the authority of *Ea-šar*, the majordomo, *Uddur* disbursed 1 reed craftsman (having gone) from *Dimbuna*-Ašgi to the *Ṣerum* field, employed for 4 days [to] reap barley," 284:5–12

2. *Ea-šar*, the Scribe

2.1 As a Deputy

2.1.1 Offerings for Inana of Zabala

1 udu-niga gu$_4$-e-ú[s-sa] 0.0.1. zì-⸢KAL⸣ 3 sìla zì-[x] 2 sìla eš[a] ^{d}inana-zabala$_4$[ki] ***é-a-šar*** dub-sar ⸢maškim⸣ (. . .) zi-ga [*šu-kab*]-*tá* ki ^{d}*adad-tillati*-ta ba-zi, "*Adad-tillati* disbursed 1 fattened sheep '(fed) following the oxen', 10 liters of KAL-flour, 3 liters of [x] flour (and) 2 liters of fine flour (for) Inana of Zabala. *Ea-šar*, the scribe,

[31] Although *Ea-šar*'s title is not specified in nos. 543 and 1236, these texts are included here in light of the similar texts nos. 542, 1232, and 1233.

was the deputy. {Other offerings}. (They were) the expenditures of *Šu-Kabta*," 970:1–6, 22–23

2.1.2 Provisions and Rations

2.1.2.1 Assorted Commodities for Builders and Hired Workers

(. . .) mu šidim-e-ne-šè (. . .) mu lú-[ḫu]g̃-g̃á-e-ne-šè u_4 igi *šu-kab-tá* ninda in-gu_7-ša-a ***é-a-šar*** dub-sar maškim zi-ga *šu-kab-tá* ki ^d^*adad-tillati*-ta ba-zi, "*Adad-tillati* disbursed {assorted comestibles} for the builders (and) {flour, groats and reeds with which bread was baked and soup was cooked} for the hired workers when they ate bread before *Šu-Kabta*. (It was) the expenditure of *Šu-Kabta*. *Ea-šar*, the scribe, was the deputy," 479:9, 14–20

(. . .) mu šidim ù lú-ḫug̃-g̃[á-šè] ***é-a-šar*** maškim d[ub-sar] zi-ga *šu-kab*-[*ta*] ki ^d^*adad-tillati*-ta [ba-zi], "*Adad-tillati* disbursed {assorted comestibles} [for] the builders and hired workers. (It was) the expenditure of *Šu-Kabta*. *Ea-šar*, the scribe, was the deputy," 483:24–27

2.1.2.2 Assorted Grains for Hired Workers

0.4.0. ninda-dabin ù zì-šà-gen íb-ta-ḫi 0.1.3.2 sìla ninda-gur_4-ra zì-KAL 0.0.1. níg̃-àr-ra-sig_5 ^uruduᵘ^šen-šè lú-ḫug̃-g̃á iri^ki^-didli-ke_4-ne íb-gu_7 ***é-a-šar*** dub-sar m[aškim z]i-ga *šu-kab-tá* [ki] ^d^*adad-tillati*-ta ⌜ba⌝-zi, "*Adad-tillati* disbursed 240 liters of bread—(the bread) was mixed from semolina and ordinary šà-flour—92 liters of thick bread of KAL-flour (and) 10 liters of fine groats for the (soup) cauldron. The hired workers of various cities ate (the soup). (It was) the expenditure of *Šu-Kabta*. *Ea-šar*, the scribe, was the deputy," 490:1–8

2.1.2.3 Barley Groats for the Workers

0.0.2.5 sìla níg̃-àr-ra-s[ig_5 su]m-mu-da-éš ⌜mu⌝ éren-na-šè [***é***]***-a-šar*** dub-sar maškim, "25 liters of fine barley groats to be given to the workers. *Ea-šar*, the scribe, was the deputy," 1016:5–8

2.1.2.4 Bread

2.1.2.4.1 For Boat Towers

(. . .) [má . . . gar-ša-an-na^ki^-ta] nibru^ki^-[šè] in-gíd-s[a-a] ***é-a-šar*** d[ub-sar PA].$KAŠ_4$ šà nibru^[ki]^ zi-ga *šu-kab-tá* ki ^d^*adad-tillati*-ta ba-zi, "*Adad-tillati* disbursed {bread for the men of various cities} who towed [a boat (. . .) from Garšana to] Nippur. (It was) the expenditure of *Šu-Kabta* in Nippur. *Ea-šar*, the scribe, was the deputy," 463:5–13

2.1.2.4.2 For the Man of the Replacement House, the Builder and the Overseer of Hired Workers

(. . .) lú-é-ki-ba-g̃ar-ra šidim ugula lú-ḫug̃-[g̃á . . .]-ka é-ka gub-ba [. . .]-e-ne ***é-a-šar*** dub-sar maškim zi-ga *šu-kab-tá* ki ^d^*adad-tillati*-ta ba-zi, "*Adad-tillati* disbursed {assorted breads} for the man of the replacement house, the builder, the overseer of the hired workers, employed in the [. . .] of the house. [. . .] (It was) the expenditure of *Šu-Kabta*. *Ea-šar*, the scribe, was the deputy," 485:5–9

2.1.2.5 Fattened Sheep

2.1.2.5.1 For *Lušallim*, the Overseer

1 udu-niga iti u$_4$-5-ba-zal *lú-ša-lim* nu-bànda ***é-a-šar*** dub-sar maškim zi-ga *šu-kab-tá* ki ^{d}*adad*-[*tillati*-t]a ba-zi, "*Adad-tillati* disbursed 1 fattened sheep at the end of the 5th day of the month (for) *Lušallim*, the overseer. (It was) the expenditure of *Šu-Kabta*. *Ea-šar*, the scribe, was the deputy," 1159:1–7

2.1.2.5.2 For the Builder from Nig̃-Ba'u

1 udu-[niga] iti u$_4$-10-ba-zal [lú-níg̃-^{d}]ba-ú šidim ***é-a-šar*** maškim zi-ga *šu-kab-tá* ki ^{d}*adad-tillati*-ta ba-zi, "*Adad-tillati* disbursed 1 [fattened] sheep at the end of the 10th day of the month (for) the builder from Nig̃-Ba'u. (It was) the expenditure of *Šu-Kabta*. *Ea-šar* was the deputy," 420:1–6

2.1.2.6 Regular Offerings of the Steward

0.0.2. [. . .] 0.1.0. ninda dabin dirig sá-du$_{11}$-é-agrig-[šè] ***é-a-šar*** dub-[sar] PA.K[AŠ$_4$ šà gar]-ša-an-na^{ki} ⸢zi⸣-ga *šu-kab-tá* ⸢ki⸣ ^{d}*adad-tillati*-ta ba-zi, "*Adad-tillati* disbursed 20 liters [. . .] (and) 60 liters of semolina bread, surplus of the regular offerings [for] the house of the steward. (It was) the expenditure of *Šu-Kabta*. *Ea-šar*, the scribe, was the deputy [in] Garšana," 501:1–9

2.1.3 Work Assignments

2.1.3.1 The Man from *Izin-Erra* to Bake Bread

60 ninda-gúg-zì-KAL 3 sìla ni[nda-š]u-ra-gen lú-*i-zi-in-èr-ra*^{ki} ke$_4$-dè u$_4$ dabin *i-zi-in-*[*èr-ra*] ^{ki}-ta gar-ša-an-na^{ki}-šè de$_6$-a ***é-a-šar*** dub-sar PA.[KAŠ$_4$] zi-ga *šu-kab-*⸢*tá*⸣ ki ^{d}*adad-tillati*-⸢ta⸣ ba-zi, "*Adad-tillati* disbursed the man from *Izin-Erra* to make 60 cakes of KAL-flour (and) 3 liters of ordinary half (loaf) bread when semolina was brought from *Izin-Erra* to Garšana. (It was) the expenditure of *Šu-Kabta*. *Ea-šar*, the scribe, was the deputy," 495:1–9

2.1.3.2 Craftsmen to Mourn

(. . .) ⸢u$_4$⸣-1-šè gaba sìg-dè gub-ba u$_4$ dig̃ir-re gaba *na-wi-ir-ilum* ba-a-g̃ar-ra ***é-a-šar*** dub-sar maškim zi-ga *šu-kab-tá* [ki] ^{d}*adad-tillati*-ta ba-zi, "*Adad-tillati* disbursed {craftsmen} for 1 day employed to beat (their) breasts when the god made the breast of *Nawir-ilum* subside (i.e. when he died). (It was) the expenditure of *Šu-Kabta*. *Ea-šar*, the scribe, was the deputy," 251:8–13

2.2 Under the Authority of *Ea-šar*, the Scribe

2.2.1 Assorted Transactions

2.2.1.1 Animals

1 udu 1 sila$_4$ ba-úš g̃ìri ***é-a-šar*** dub-sar ki *ì-lí-bi-la-ni*-ta ba-zi "Under the authority of *Ea-šar*, the scribe, *Ili-bilani* disbursed 1 dead sheep (and) 1 dead lamb," 1095:1–5

1 uz-tur 1 péš-g̃eš-gi iti u$_4$-28-ba-zal ba-úš é-kišib-ba-šè g̃ìri ***é-a-šar*** dub-sar [ki ^{d}*adad-tillati*-ta ba-zi], "Under the authority of *Ea-šar*, the scribe, [*Adad-tillati* disbursed] 1 duckling (and) 1 mouse slaughtered at the end of the 28th day of the month for the warehouse," 1104:1–7

1 uz-tur niga iti u$_4$-22-ba-zal ba-úš é kišib-ba-šè g̃ìri ***é-a-šar*** dub-sar ki ^{d}*adad-tillati*-ta ba-zi, "Under the authority of *Ea-šar*, the scribe, *Adad-tillati*

disbursed 1 fattened duckling slaughtered at the end of the 22nd day of the month for the warehouse," 1112:1–6

1 uz-tur u$_4$-14-kam 5 uz-tur u$_4$-27-kam 4 tu-gur$_4$^{mušen} 2 péš-g̃eš-gi 2 péš-igi-gùn u$_4$-30-kam ba-úš é-kišib-ba-šè g̃iri ***é-a-šar*** dub-sar zi-ga-àm, "1 duckling on the 14th day, 5 ducklings on the 27th day, 4 doves, 2 mice (and) 2 striped-eyed mice on the 30th day were slaughtered for the warehouse. The expenditure was under the authority of *Ea-šar*, the scribe," 1254:'27–'35

2.2.1.2 Assorted Commodities

(. . .) ba-úš iti-u$_4$-8-ba-zal šà-gal šidim-e-ne ⅓ sìla ì-⌜šáḫ⌝ di$_4$-di$_4$-la àga-ús *simat-^{d}ištaran* ba-ab-šeš$_4$ [n] gín še-gín mu x-šè [. . . n ma]-na šu-sar m[angaga? ^{geš}?]ig ^{geš}kug̃$_5$-šè ⌜u$_4$⌝ é-e im sumur ba-aka ⌜g̃iri⌝ ***é-a-šar*** dub-sar ki *^{d}adad-tillati*-ta ba-zi, "Under the authority of *Ea-šar*, the scribe, *Adad-tillati* disbursed {assorted dead animals} at the end of the 8th day of the month (as) food (for) builders, ⅓ liter of lard (used by) *Simat-Ištaran* (when) she anointed the small child(ren) of the gendarme, [n] shekel(s) of glue for [x], [. . .] (and) [n mina(s)] of cord (made from) date palm fibers for the door (and) ladder when the house was plastered," 472:6–17

[n.n.n] še [. . . n.n.n.] siki-gen [n.n.]3?. gu[r? . . .] gi-šid 3255 sa sa$_{10}$ gi-zi 0.0.1. še gi 13 sa-ta ki *^{d}adad-tillati*-ta ba-zi g̃iri ***é-a-šar*** dub-sar, "Under the aurthority of *Ea-šar*, the scribe, *Adad-tillati* disbursed [n] liter(s) of barley, [n] liter(s) of ordinary wool, [. . .] (and) 3255 bundles of dry reeds, the price of fresh reeds is 10 liters of barley for reeds of 13 bundles each," 1320:1–8

2.2.1.3 Barley for Baking Bread

[n.n.n.] še gur sa$_{10}$ saḫar 48-kam *tá-din-eš$_4$-tár* 0.4.0. še sa$_{10}$ saḫar 12-kam *ša-at-èr-ra* ninda du$_8$-dè-š[è x]-da g̃iri ***é-a-šar*** dub-sar [ki] *^{d}adad-tillati*-ta ba-zi, "Under the authority *Ea-šar*, the scribe, *Adad-tillati* disbursed [n] bushel(s) (and) [n liter(s)] of barley, the price of 48 units of dirt for *Tadin-Eštar* (and) 240 liters of barley, the price of 12 units of dirt for *Šat-Erra* to bake bread, (?)," 1169:1–10

2.2.1.4 Baskets for Tablets

1 ^{gi}bisag̃-im-sar-ra [sa-ḫ]a ⅔ kùš íb-sá im-sar g̃á-g̃á-dè u$_4$ é-[e] im sumur ba-aka g̃i[ri ***é]-a-šar*** dub-sar [ki] *^{d}adad-tillati*-ta ba-zi, "Under the authority of *Ea*-šar, the scribe, *Adad-tillati*, disbursed 1 canvas-lined clay tablet coffer—it is ⅔ kùš square—(in which) to deposit clay tablets, when the house was plastered," 1318:1–5

2.2.1.5 Bricks[32]

2.2.1.5.1 Deliveries of *Adad-tillati*

37⅔ sar 4-gín igi–4-g̃ál šeg$_{12}$ u$_4$-1-kam 37 sar 1 gín šeg$_{12}$ u$_4$-2-kam ⌜NE⌝-gu$_7$-bi nu-ub-ta-zi šeg$_{12}$ šid-da g̃á-šub-ba g̃á-g̃ál mu-DU *simat-é*-a ugula lú-ḫug̃-g̃á g̃iri ***é-a-šar*** dub-sar, "37⅔ sar (and) 4¼ shekels of bricks for 1 day, 37 sar

32 Although *Ea-šar*'s title is not specified in nos. 359 and 360, these texts are included here in light of parallels with no. 357.

(and) 1 shekel of bricks for 2 days, the damaged bricks were not deducted; the count of bricks took place in the brickyard. The delivery of *Simat-Ea*, overseer of hired workers, was under the authority of *Ea-šar*, the scribe," 357:1–10

188 sar 10 gín šeg$_{12}$ NE-gu$_7$-bi nu-zi šid-da šà g̃á-šub-ba g̃ìri ***é-a-šar*** ús-sa i$_7$-*a-ga-mu-um* mu-DU *simat-é-a* ugula lú-[ḫug̃-g̃]á, "188 sar (and) 10 shekels of bricks along the *Agamum* canal, damaged bricks not deducted; the count (of bricks) in the brickyard. The delivery of *Simat-Ea*, the overseer of hired workers, was under the authority of *Ea-šar*," 359:1–7

113 sar 16 gín šeg$_{12}$ NE-gu$_7$-bi nu-zi [. . .]-IR?–2-kam [x]-da g̃ìri ***é-a-šar***, "Under the authority of *Ea-šar*, 113 sar (and) 16 shekels of bricks, damaged bricks not deducted (?)," 360:1–5

203 šeg$_{12}$-al-ur$_x$-ra GÍN-bal ^{geš}kiri$_6$ g̃á-nun-na-šè ba-a-g̃ar g̃ìri ***é-a-šar*** dub-sar ki ^{d}*adad-tillati*-ta ba-zi, "Under the authority of *Ea-šar*, the scribe, *Adad-tillati* disbursed 203 bricks placed for the GÍN-bal of the garden of the storehouse," 1326:1–5

2.2.1.6 Building Supplies[33]

½ sìla ì-udu dúr ^{geš}ig-[x] ba-ab-šeš$_4$ u$_4$ é-e im sumur ba-aka g̃ìri ***é-a-šar*** dub-sar ⌜ki⌝ ^{d}*adad-tillati*-ta ba-zi, "Under the authority of *Ea-šar*, the scribe, *Adad-tillati* disbursed ½ liter of mutton fat (with which) the back of the [x] door was oiled when the house was plastered," 1319:1–7

480 sa gi-⌜izi⌝ gu-níg̃in 12-sa-ta gi-sal$_4$-la-an-za-qar-^{geš}kiri$_6$-zabala$_4^{\text{ki}}$-šè ba-a-g̃ar ⌜g̃ìri⌝ ***é-a-šar*** [dub-s]ar ⌜ki⌝ ^{d}*adad-tillati*-[ta] ba-zi, "Under the authority of *Ea-šar*, the scribe, *Adad-tillati* disbursed 480 bundles of fuel reeds, bales of 12 bundles each. The thin reeds were placed for the tower of the Zabala garden," 1323:1–7

300 [sa] gi-izi gu-níg̃in-[bi n] sa-ta gi-sal$_4$-la [é]-*gi-na-tum* ká-dedal-[lí]-a-šè ba-a-g̃ar 210 sa [gi]-izi gu-níg̃in 12 s[a-t]a *dì-um* é-ki-mu-ra-šè ba-a-g̃ar 63 ^{dug}ù-lu-lu 2-kùš-ta *a-za-bu-um* šà é-a-šè ba-a-g̃ar [n sìl]a mun [šà-ga]l šidim-e-ne [n.n.n.] ésir-ḫád gur [0.n.n.n] sìla ésir-é-a [0.0.]1 zì 1 sìla 10 gín ì-udu du$_{10}$-ús ésir du$_8$-dè g̃ìri ***é-a-šar*** dub-sar ki ^{d}*adad-tillati*-ta ba-zi, "Under the authority of *Ea-šar*, the scribe, *Adad-tillati* disbursed 300 [bundles] of fuel reeds, bales of [n] bundle(s) each—the thin reeds were placed for the barracks of the Dedali'a gate—210 bundles of fuel reeds, bales of 12 bunches each—they were placed for wattle and daub of the textile depository, 63 pipes of 2 cubits each—they were placed for the cistern in the house, [n] liter(s) of salt, food (for) builders, (and) [n] bushel(s) (and) [n liter(s)?] of dry bitumen, [n] liter(s) of house bitumen, 10 liters of flour (and) 1 liter (and) 10 shekels of mutton fat to seal the bath with bitumen," 1325:1–18

190 sa gi-izi 60 ^{gi}kid-maḫ 30 ^{gi}dur-gazi a-rá-2-tab-ba gíd-1½ nindan-ta 7 gi-guru$_5$ a-rá-3-tab-ba é-*gi-na-tum*-šè ba-a-g̃ar x-éš-x-[. . .] g̃ìri ***é-a-šar*** dub-sar ki ^{d}*adad-tillati*-ta ba-zi, "Under the authority of *Ea-šar*, the scribe, *Adad-tillati* disbursed 190 bundles of fuel reeds, 60 large reed mats, 30 9-meter 2-

---

33 See also 2.2.2.4.3 below.

ply gazi ropes (and) 7 triple reed work panels. They were placed for the barracks (?)," 1328:1–'9

0.0.1.6 sìla ésir-é-a 7½ ma-na im-bábbar ^{ĝeš}ig mi-rí-za ba-ab-sù-ub 1⅓ ĝuruš ad-kub$_4$ u$_4$-1-[šè] ésir-é-a ù im-bábbar ^{ĝeš}ig bí-ib-sù-ub ĝìri ***é-a-šar*** dub-sar ki ^{d}*adad-tillati*-ta ba-zi, "Under the authority of *Ea-šar*, the scribe, *Adad-tillati* disbursed 16 liters of house bitumen, 7½ minas of gypsum (with which) the door plank was coated (and) 1⅓ reed craftsmen for 1 day. They coated the door with house bitumen and gypsum," 1329:1–10

(. . .) GÍN-bal [*a*]-*za-bu-um* šà é-a-šè ba-a-⌜ĝar⌝ ĝìri ***é-a-šar*** dub-sar ki ^{d}*adad-tillati*-ta ba-zi, "Under the authority of *Ea-šar*, the scribe, *Adad-tillati* disbursed {assorted wood products, reeds, and ropes}. They were placed for the GÍN-bal of the cistern in the house," 1380:9–12

2.2.1.7 Garden Products

4.3.0. zú-lum gur 0.0.5. u$_4$-ḫi-in n+3 gín peš-ga 5? sìla á-an-zú-lum [káb d]u$_{11}$-ga ^{ĝeš}kiri$_6$ *eš*$_4$*-tár-*<um->*mi* dumu-munus *šu-kab-tá* ^{d}*adad-tillati* šu ba-an-ti šà gar-ša-an-na^{ki} ĝìri ***é-a-šar*** dub-sar, "Under the authority of *Ea-šar*, the scribe, *Adad-tillati* received 4 bushels (and) 180 liters of dates, 50 liters of fresh dates, [n+]3 shekels of date palm hearts (and) 5? liters of date clusters, commodities of the garden of *Eštar-ummi*, the daughter of *Šu-Kabta*, measured for accounting in Garšana," 1102:1–8

2.2.2 Provisions and Rations

2.2.2.1 For Builders

2 uz-tur 1 ir$_7^{mušen}$ ba-úš šà-gal šidim-e-ne ĝìri ***é-a-šar*** dub-sar ki ^{d}*adad-tillati*-ta ba-zi, "Under the authority of *Ea-šar*, the scribe, *Adad-tillati* disbursed 2 slaughtered ducklings (and) 1 slaughtered pigeon, food (for) builders," 470:1–7

[n.n].1[+n].6½ [sìla ì-ĝeš gur] 4? sìla 5 gín [ì-šáḫ] ì-ba šidim-e-[ne] u$_4$ é-e im sumur ba-aka ĝìri ***é-a-šar*** dub-sar ki ^{d}*adad-tillati*-ta ba-zi, "Under the authority of *Ea-šar*, the scribe, *Adad-tillati* disbursed [n bushel(s) (and) n liter(s) of sesame oil] (and) 4? liters (and) 5 shekels [of lard], oil rations of the builders when the house was plastered," 482:1–7

30 ku$_6$ al-dar-ra šà-gal šidim-e-ne ĝìri ***é-[a-š]ar*** dub-sar ki ^{d}*ad*[*ad-til*]*lati*-ta ba-zi, "Under the authority of *Ea-šar*, the scribe, *Adad-tillati* disbursed 30 split (dried) fish, food (for) builders," 489:1–5

2.2.2.2 For Ox-Drivers

0.3.0. še šà-gu$_4$-me-éš dirig še-ba-ne-ne mu zì nu-ĝál-la-šè ba-na-ḫa-la *šu-kab-tá* bí-in-dug$_4$ ⌜ĝìri⌝-né-ì-dab$_5$ ra-gaba maškim u$_4$ é-e i[m sumur ba-aka] ĝìri ***é-a-šar*** dub-sar ki ^{d}*adad-tillati*-ta ba-zi, "Under the authority of *Ea-šar*, the scribe, *Adad-tillati* disbursed 180 liters of barley for the ox-drivers when the house was plastered. *Šu-Kabta* had ordered that additional barley rations were to be divided for them because there was no flour. Ĝirine-idab, the courier, was the deputy," 481:1–9

2.2.2.3 For Servants and Other Workers

(. . .) ⌜ĝuruš⌝ árad-é-a ù lú-ḫuĝ-ĝá-e-ne ba-na-ḫa-la u$_4$ é<-e> im sumur <ba->aka ki ^{d}*adad-tillati*-ta ba-zi ĝìri ***é-a-šar*** dub-sar, "Under the authority of *Ea-šar*, the scribe, *Adad-tillati* disbursed {bread, beer and dates}. They were divided for the household servants and hired workers when the house was plastered," 471:4–8

0.0.2.6 sìla ninda ^{kuš}a-g̃á-lá kéše-rá g̃uruš nam–60 *a-⸢bu⸣*-DU$_{10}$ u$_{4}$ é-^{d}*šu*-^{d}*suen*^{ki}-šè i-⸢re⸣-ša-a u$_{4}$ é-e im sumur ba-aka g̃ìri ***é-a-šar*** dub-sar ki ^{d}*adad-tillati*-ta ba-zi, "Under the authority of *Ea-šar*, the scribe, *Adad-tillati* disbursed 26 liters of bread in bound leather sacks (for) *Abu-ṭabu*, the overseer of 60 workmen, when (his workers) went to *Bit-Šu-Suen* when the house was plastered," 480:1–6

1½ ma-na siki-gen siki-ba árad *šu-eš*$_{4}$*-tár* g̃ìri ***é-a-šar*** dub-sar ki ^{d}*adad-tillati*-ta ba-zi, "Under the authority of *Ea-šar*, the scribe, *Adad-tillati* disbursed 1½ minas of ordinary wool, wool rations of the servant of *Šu-Eštar*," 627:1–4

8 gú 1½ ma-na siki-gen ⸢siki⸣-ba géme-árad [ki ^{d}]*adad-tillati*-ta [ba-z]i g̃ìri ***é-a-šar*** dub-sar, "Under the authority of *Ea-šar*, the scribe, *Adad-tillati* disbursed 8 talents (and) 1½ minas of ordinary wool, wool rations of female and male servants," 721:1–5

2.2.2.4 Other

2.2.2.4.1 For the Man who Brought Fish

3 sìla ninda lú ku$_{6}$ du$_{6}$-lugal-pa-è^{ki}-ta de$_{6}$-a u$_{4}$ é-e im sumur ba-aka [g̃ìri] ***é-a-šar*** dub-[sar] ki ^{d}*adad-tillati*-ta ba-zi, "[Under the authority of] *Ea-šar*, the scribe, *Adad-tillati* disbursed 3 liters of bread (for) the man who brought fish from Du-lugalpa'e when the house was plastered," 476:1–7

2.2.2.4.2 For Homeowners

0.0.1.2 sìla [. . .] 5 sìla ninda-sal-la-dabin lú é-ne-ne <é->⸢ki⸣-ba-gar-ra sa$_{10}$-a 0.0.1. A.[TIR] x x AD ^{d}x [. . .] 2 sìla [. . .] g̃ìri ***é-a-šar*** [dub-sar] ki ^{d}⸢*adad-tillati*⸣-[ta] ba-[zi], "Under the authority of *Ea-šar,* [the scribe], *Adad-tillati* disbursed 12 liters [. . .], (and) 5 liters of semolina (for) thin bread, (for) men having bought their houses as replacements, 10 liters of fine flour (?) (and) 2 liters [. . .]," 487:1–11

0.0.1.2? sìla ninda-gal-gen 1 sìla du$_{8}$ [u$_{4}$ l]ú **é-ne-ne** ba-an-ši-sa$_{10}$-a íb-gu$_{7}$ ki ^{d}*adad-tillati*-ta ba-zi g̃ìri ***é-a-šar*** dub-sar, "Under the authority of *Ea-šar*, the scribe, *Adad-tillati* disbursed 12? liters of ordinary large bread baked (in) 1 liter (loaves); the men who bought their houses ate (the bread)," 491:1–6

2.2.2.4.3 For the Messenger of the Governor of Nippur (and Building Supplies for the Barracks)

45 sa gi-izi gi-ka-du-šè é-*gi-na-tum* ká-dedal-lí-a-⸢šè⸣ ba-a-⸢g̃ar⸣ 5 sìla [kaš?] ninda ^{lú}kíg̃-gi$_{4}$-a-énsi-nibru$^{[ki]}$ g̃ìri [***é***]***-a-šar*** dub-⸢sar⸣ ki ^{d}*adad-tillati*-ta ba-zi, "Under the authority of *Ea-šar*, the scribe, *Adad-tillati* disbursed 45 bundles of fuel reeds—they were placed for a reed shelter for the barracks of the Dedali'a gate—(and) 5 liters of [beer?] (and) bread (for) the messenger of the governor of Nippur," 1324:1–8

2.2.2.5 Unspecified Recipient: when the House was Plastered

24 sa gi-[izi] ninda ba-ra-⸢du$_{8}$⸣ 10 sa gi-[izi] tu$_{7}$ [ba]-ra-⸢šeg̃$_{6}$⸣ u$_{4}$ é-e im sumur ⸢ba⸣-aka g̃ìri ***é-a-šar*** dub-sar ki ^{d}*adad-tillati*-[ta] ba-zi, "Under the authority of *Ea-šar*, the scribe, *Adad-tillati* disbursed 24 bundles of [fuel]

reeds, with which bread was baked, (and) 10 bundles of [fuel] reeds, with which soup was cooked, when the house was plastered," 473:1–10

2.2.3 Work Assignments

2.2.3.1 Builders Going to Edana

1 g̃uruš šidim é-da-na[ki]-šè g̃en-na g̃iri ***é-a-šar*** dub-sar, "1 builder having gone to Edana under the authority of *Ea-šar,* the scribe," 195:'26–'27, 196:'29–'30

2.2.3.2 Leather Workers Binding the Crossbar of a Door

4 kuš-gu$_4$ kuš a-g̃ar nu-gu$_7$-a bar-da [geš]ig-g̃e$_6$ 1-àm ba-a-kéše 3 g̃uruš ašgab u$_4$-2-⸢šè⸣ bar-da [geš]ig-⸢g̃e$_6$⸣ kéše-⸢rá⸣ g̃iri ***é-a-šar*** dub-⸢sar⸣ ki [d]*adad-tillati*-⸢ta⸣ ba-zi, "Under the authority of *Ea-šar,* the scribe, *Adad-tillati* disbursed 4 ox skins, skins whose hair has not been removed—they were (used) to bind the crossbar of 1 black door—and 3 leather workers for 2 days having bound the crossbar of the black door," 247:1–8

2.2.3.3 Workmen

5 g̃uruš im lu-a 3 g̃uruš ka-al-la-ka 2 g̃uruš bisag̃ im sar-ra im ga$_6$-g̃á g̃iri ***é-a-šar*** dub-sar, "Under the authority of *Ea-šar,* the scribe, 5 workmen having mixed earth, 3 workmen at the dirt quarry (and) 2 workmen having carried earth in the clay tablet coffer," 103:28–31

11 g̃uruš sag̃-[tag] 2 g̃uruš á-⅔-ta 2 g̃uruš á-½-ta u$_4$-2-šè iz-zi sumun ku-bu-gu gul-dè gub-ba ⸢g̃iri⸣ ***é-a-šar*** dub-sar ki *puzur$_4$-a-gu$_5$-um*-ta ba-zi, "Under the authority of *Ea-šar,* the scribe, *Puzur-agum* disbursed 11 full-time workers, 2 workers at ⅔ wages (and) 2 workers at ½ wages employed for 2 days to demolish the old ku-bu-gu wall," 244:1–8

3. *Ea-šar,* Title Unspecified

3.1 As a Deputy

3.1.1 Assorted Transactions: Delivery of Textiles

(. . .) ***é-a-šar*** maškim ki *puzur$_4$-a-gu$_5$-um*-ta ba-zi, "*Puzur-agum* disbursed {assorted textiles}. *Ea-šar* was the deputy," 565:4–5

3.1.2 Work Assignments for Craftsmen

3.1.2.1 Fullers

1 g̃uruš [lú]ázlag nibru[ki]-ta [d]*šu*-[d]*suen*-DU$_{10}$[ki]-šè [urudu]šim-da gu$_4$-udu de$_6$-a kaskal šu+níg̃in-na-bi u$_4$-11-kam u$_4$ *šu-kab-tá* é-dam-*zé-ra-ra* šu sum-mu-dè ì-g̃en-na-a ***é-a-šar*** maškim zi-ga g̃iri *šu-kab-tá* ki *puzur$_4$-a-gu$_5$-um*-ta ba-zi, "*Puzur-agum* disbursed 1 fuller having brought a sheep and cattle brand from Nippur to *Šu-Suen-ṭabu,* a trip of 11 days in total, when *Šu-Kabta* went to the house of the wife of *Zerara* in order to take inventory. This was the expenditure of *Šu-Kabta* under his authority. *Ea-šar* was the deputy," 219:1–14

8 g̃uruš [lú]ázlag u$_4$-1-šè siki é-[d]*šu*-[d]*suen*-ta gar-ša-an-n[a[ki]]-šè mu-un-de$_9$-sa-a ***é-a-šar*** ⸢maškim⸣ ki *puzur$_4$-a-gu$_5$-um*-ta ba-zi, "*Puzur-agum* disbursed 8 fullers for 1 day who brought wool from *Bit-Šu-Suen* to Garšana. *Ea-šar* was the deputy," 243:1–7

11 g̃uruš sa[g̃-tag] 2 g̃uruš á-⅔-ta 4 g̃uruš á-½-ta 1 g̃uruš á-⅓<-ta> lúázlag-me-éš u_4-1-šè gaba sàg-gé-dè [gub-ba] u_4 *na-wi-ir-[ilum* ba-úš-a] ***é-a-šar*** maškim zi-ga *šu-kab-⌜tá⌝* ki *puzur₄-a-gu₅-um-*⌜ta⌝ ba-zi, "*Puzur-agum* disbursed 11 full-time fullers, 2 fullers at ⅔ wages, 4 fullers at ½ wages (and) 1 fuller at ⅓ wages [employed] for 1 day to beat (their) breasts when *Nawir-ilum* [died]. (It was) the expenditure of *Šu-Kabta*. *Ea-šar* was the deputy," 250:1–12

3.1.2.2 **Spinners**

2 géme sag̃-dub-ba 1 géme á-⅔ géme gu-me-éš u_4-1-šè u_4 siki-ba-ka [šu bar]-ra ***é-a-šar*** maškim zi-ga g̃ìri *šu-kab-ta* ki d*adad-tillati*-ta ba-zi, "*Adad-tillati* disbursed 2 full-time female spinners (and) 1 female spinner at ⅔ wages released for 1 day on the day of the wool rations. It was the expenditure of *Šu-Kabta* under his authority. *Ea-šar* was the deputy," 234:1–9

3.1.2.3 **Weavers and Spinners**

97 géme sag̃-dub 15 géme á-⅓-ta géme uš-bar-me-éš [n] géme gu [u_4]-9½-šè [gaba] sìg-dè gub-[ba] u_4 *šu-kab-tá* ba-úš<-a> ***é-a-šar*** maškim ki d*adad-[tillati*-ta] (so tablet!) [ki *aš*]-*tá-qar*-ta (so envelope!) ba-[zi], "*Adad-tillati* (tablet) / *Aštaqqar* (envelope) disbursed 97 full-time female weavers (and) 15 female weavers at ⅓ wages (and) [n] female spinner(s) employed for 9½ days to beat (their) breasts when *Šu-Kabta* died. *Ea-šar* was the deputy," 252:1–10

3.2 **Deliveries of *Ea-šar*: Barley**

n.0.0. še gur ki ***é-a-šar***-ta d*adad-tillati* šu ba-ti, "*Adad-tillati* received n bushel(s) of barley from *Ea-šar*," 1200:1–4, 1202:1–4

3.3 **Under the Authority of *Ea-šar***

3.3.1 **Grain in the Granary**

10.0.0. zíz gur ì-dub g̃ìri ***é-a-šar***, "10 bushels of emmer wheat of the granary under the authority of *Ea-šar*," 1234:1–4

3.3.2 **Orchard Products Measured for Accounting**

d*adad-tillati* ù-na-a-du₁₁ káb-du₁₁-ga g̃ìri ***é-a-šar*** g̃ešzé-na ù peš-[múrgu] nu-g̃eškiri₆-ke₄-ne na-ba-ab-sum-mu-⌜dè⌝ šà dub-za ḫa-ba-tur-re, "Say to *Adad-tillati* that 'the gardeners should not give date palm frond midrib(s) and date palm spine(s), commodities (that were) measured for accounting under the authority of *Ea-šar*. Let it be subtracted in your tablet,'" 1037:1–9

3.3.3 **Provisions: Beer for Builders**

0.0.1.6 sìla kaš-gen sá-du₁₁ šidim-e-ne u_4 bàd ba-dù-a g̃ìri ***é-a-šar*** ki *èr-ra-ba-ni*-ta ba-zi, "Under the authority of *Ea-šar*, *Erra-bani* disbursed 16 liters of ordinary beer, regular provisions of the builders, when the (enclosure) wall was constructed," 478:1–6

é-ì-gára

E'igara, the Household Servant from the Gang of *Irib*

1. Bringing a Message to *Šu-Kabta*

1 **é-ì-gára** á-ãg̃(-g̃á) nibru[ki]-šè ki *šu-kab-ta*-šè de_6-a, "E'igara having brought a message to *Šu-Kabta* in Nippur," 31:40, 32:39, 33:43, 34:'17, 35:46

1 **é-ì-gára** á-ãg̃(-g̃á) ki *šu-kab-tá*-šè de_6-a, "E'igara having brought a message to the place of *Šu-Kabta*," 36:41, 47:53–54, 48:58–59, 49:57, 50:'16–'17, 59:52, 60:48–49, 102:5, 103:5, 107:9, 108:6, 108:40, 109:6

1.1 With *Beli-ili*

1 *be-lí-ì-lí* 1 **é-ì-gára** á-ãg̃-g̃á ki *šu-kab-ta*-šè de_6-a, "*Beli-ili* (and) E'igara having brought a message to the place of *Šu-Kabta*," 123:8–10

1.2 With *Iṭibšinat*

1 *i-ṭib-ši-na-at* 1 **é-ì-gára** á-ãg̃ ki *šu-kab-tá*-šè de_6-a, "*Iṭibšinat* (and) E'igara having brought a message to the place of *Šu-Kabta*," 43:'43–'44, 44:41–43, 46:'39–'41

1 *i-ṭib-ši-na-at* 1 **é-ì-gára** á-ãg̃ [ki] *šu-kab-tá*-ta [d]e_6-a, "*Iṭibšinat* (and) E'igara having brought a message from the place of *Šu-Kabta*," 45:22–23

1.3 With *Šu-belum*

1 **é-ì-gára** 1 *šu-*[d]*belum* á-ãg̃(-g̃á) ki *šu-kab-ta*-šè de_6-a, "E'igara (and) *Šu-Belum* having brought a message to the place of *Šu-Kabta*," 65:'26–'27, 71:32–34, 110:7–8, 111:7–9

2! **é-ì-gára**, "E'igara, (having brought a message with *Šu-Belum* to the place of *Šu-Kabta*)," 114:10

1.4 With *Šu*-Ninkarak

1 **é-ì-gára** 1 *šu-*[d]nin-kar-ak á-ãg̃ ki *šu-kab-ta*-šè de_6-a, "E'igara (and) *Šu*-Ninkarak having brought a message to the place of *Šu-Kabta*," 106:6–8, 106:45–47

2. Bringing a Message to *Šu-Eštar*. With *Ḫilua*

1 *ḫi-lu-a* 1 **é-ì-gára** á-ãg̃ ki *šu-e*[*$š_4$-tár*-šè] ⌜de_6⌝-[a], "*Ḫilua* (and) E'igara having brought a message [to] the place of *Šu-Eštar*," 37:31–33

[1] **é-ì-gára** 1 *ḫi-lu-a* 1 á-ãg̃ ki *šu-e$š_4$-tár*-[šè] de_6-a, "E'igara (and) *Ḫilua* having brought a message [to] the place of *Šu-Eštar*," 38:37–39

3. Bringing Roof Beams

1 **é-ì-gára** g̃eš ùr tùm-dè g̃en-na, "E'igara having gone to bring roof beams," 51:'18, 52:54–55, 53:56, 54:33–34

4. Bringing Wool from *Bit-Šu-Suen*

1 **é-ì-gára** siki tùm-dè é-[d]*šu-*[d]*suen*[ki]-[ta] g̃en-a, "E'igara having gone to bring wool [from] *Bit-Šu-Suen*," 39:46

1 **é-ì-gára** é-[d]*šu-*[d]*suen*[ki]-ta siki tùm-dè g̃en-na, "E'igara having gone to bring wool from *Bit-Šu-Suen*," 40:40–41

5. Broken Context

[1 **é-ì-gára**. . .], 49:57

el-pa-dan

Elpadan, the Reed Carrier

1. **Provisions**

[. . . n m]a-na tuḫ-g̃eš-ì-ḫád-ta [n.n.n.] ádda-udu-ta [n gín] mun-ta [n gí]n luḫ-lá-ta [1 *e*]*l*?-***pa-dan*** [1] *tu-ra-am-ì-lí* 2 [gi-g]a$_6$-me-éš, "[. . ., n] mina(s) dried sesame chaff each, [n] sheep carcass(es) each, [n shekel(s)] of salt each, (and) [n shekel(s)] of luḫ-lá each, (provisions for) *Elpadan* (and) *Turam-ili*, 2 [reed] carriers," 562:'62–'69

ᵈen-líl-*ba-za-du*

Enlil-*bazadu*, the Scribe

1. **Under his Authority: Workwomen**

8 géme u$_4$-1-šè [siki] igi sag̃-g̃á šà é-ᵈ*šu*-ᵈ*suen*[ki]-ka de$_6$-a g̃ìri **ᵈen-lîl-*ba-za-du*** ù *ù-ṣí-na-wi-ir* dub-sar-me ki ᵈ*adad-tillati*-ta ba-zi, "Under the authority of Enlil-*bazadu* and *Uṣi-nawir*, the scribes, *Adad-tillati* disbursed 8 workwomen for 1 day having brought [wool] sorted in *Bit-Šu-Suen*," 279:1–7

en-nam-ᵈma-lik

Ennam-Malik, the Barber

1. **Under his Authority: Craftsmen Carrying Barley**

8 g̃uruš sag̃-tag 2 g̃uruš á-⅔-ta 4 g̃uruš á-½-ta [lú]ázlag-me-éš [u$_4$]-1-šè ⌜še⌝ ᵈ*šu*-ᵈ*suen*-am-ma-ar-[ki]-ta de$_6$-a íb-[ga$_6$] g̃ìri ***en-nam-ᵈm*[*a-lik*** z]i-ga *š*[*u-kab-ta*] ki *puzur$_4$-a-*[*gu$_5$-um*-ta ba]-zi, "Under the authority of *Ennam-Malik*, *Puzur-agum* disbursed 8 full-time fullers, 2 fullers at ⅔ wages, (and) 4 fullers at ½ wages for 1 [day]. They [carried] barley brought from *Šu-Suen*-ammara. (It was) the expenditure of *Šu-Kabta*," 248:1–10[34]

3 géme g̃eš-ì-sur-sur u$_4$-1-šè še ᵈ*šu*-ᵈ*suen*-am-ma-ar[ki]-ta de$_6$-a íb-ga$_6$ g̃ìri ***en-nam-***[d]***ma-lik*** šu-i zi-ga *šu-kab-tá* ki ᵈ*adad-tillati*-ta ba-zi, "Under the authority of *Ennam-Malik*, the barber, *Adad-tillati* disbursed 3 female sesame pressers for 1 day. They carried barley brought from *Šu-Suen*-ammara. (It was) the expenditure of *Šu-Kabta*," 249:1–7

en-nim-ma

1. ***Enima*, the Builder from Isin: Provisions**

1.1 **Bread**

2 sìla ninda-ta ***en-nim-ma*** 1 *be-lí-a-sú* lú-ì-si-in[ki]-me-éš (. . .) šà-gal šidim-e-ne, "2 liters of bread each (for) *Enima* (and) *Beli-asu*, men from Isin, (and for) {other workers}, food (for) builders," 381:1–4, 21

[2 sìla] ninda-ta 1 ***en-nim-ma*** 1 *be-lí-a-sú* lú-ì-si-in[ki] (. . .) šà-gal ši[dim-e-n]e ⌜u$_4$⌝ [bàd egir] é-a dù-dè, "[2 liters] of bread each (for) *Enima* (and) *Beli-asu*, men from Isin, (and for) {other workers}, food (for) builders when they were constructing [the (enclosure) wall behind] the house," 386:1, 10–12, 29–30

[1 ***en-ni-ma*** 1 *be-lí*]*-a-sú* [lú-ì]-si-in[ki] (. . .) šà-gal šidim-e-ne ⌜u$_4$⌝ bàd eger é-a dù-dè, "[(bread)] (for) [*Enima*] (and) *Beli-asu*, men from Isin, (and for) {other workers}, food

[34] Although *Ennam-Malik*'s title is not specified, this text is included here in light of the parallel transaction no. 249.

(for) builders when they were constructing the (enclosure) wall behind the house," 387:1–3, 20–21

1.2 Ordinary Beer

2 sìla kaš-gen-ta ***en-ni-ma*** 1 *be-lí-a-sú* lú-ì-si-in^{ki}(-me-éš) (. . .) šidim-e-ne íb-naĝ, "2 liters of ordinary beer each (for) *Enima* (and) *Beli-asu*, men from Isin, (and for) {other builders}; the builders drank (the beer)," 378:9–12, 16, 380:1–4, 8, 389:1–4, 8

2 sìla kaš-gen-ta ***en-ni-ma*** 1 *be-lí-a-sú* (. . .) [šidim-e-ne] íb-naĝ, "2 liters of ordinary beer each (for) *Enima* (and) *Beli-asu*, (and for) {other builders}; [the builders] drank (the beer)," 384:1–3, 7

1.3 Semolina

[2] sìla dab[in-ta] ***en-nim-[ma]*** 1 *be-lí-a-[sú]* lú-[ì]-si-in[^{ki} ši]dim (. . .) šà-gal šidim-e-ne u_4 bàd in-dù-sa-a, "[2] liters of semolina [each] (for) *Enima* (and) *Beli-asu*, builders from Isin, (and for) {other workers}, food (for) builders when they constructed the (enclosure) wall," 396:1–4, 19–20, 397:1–4, 19–20

1.4 Sheep and Grains

(. . .) 1 ***en-ni-ma*** 1 *be-lí-a-sú* lú-ì-si-in^{ki}-me-éš (. . .) [šà-gal šidim] ù dub-sar-e-ne, "{sheep carcasses, semolina, and barley} (for) *Enima* (and) *Beli-asu*, men from Isin, (and for) {other workers}, [food (for) builders] and scribes," 399:10–12, 24

2. *Enima*, the Sick Builder

1 ***en-nim-ma*** šidim 1 *šál-maḫ* šidim dú-ra-me-éš, "*Enima* (and) *Šal-maḫ*, sick builders," 24:'28–'30

(1) ***en-nim-ma*** šidim dú-ra, "*Enima*, the sick builder," 39:48, 40:52, 41:'30

en-um-ì-li

1. Under his Authority: Workwomen Sorting Wool

4 géme uš-bar u_4-1-šè siki-igi-sağ-ğá šà é-^{d}*šu*-^{d}*suen*^{ki} ĝìri *ù-ṣí-na-wi-ir* ù ***en-um-ì-lí*** ki ^{d}*adad-tillati*-ta ba-zi, "Under the authority of *Uṣi-nawir* and *Enum-ili*, *Adad-tillati* disbursed 4 female weavers for 1 day having sorted wool in *Bit-Šu-Suen*," 264:1–6

ér-kal-la

1. Receipt of Barley

0.1.0. še *aš-tá-qar* 0.0.3. še **ér-kal-la** šu ba-an-ti, "*Aštaqqar* received 60 liters of barley, Erkala received 30 liters of barley," 653:1–5

èr-ra-ba-ni

1. *Erra-bani*, the Brewer

1.1 As a Deputy: Weavers to Crush Malt

66 géme uš-bar u_4-1-šè munu$_4$ naĝ$_4$-ĝá-dè gub-ba ***èr-ra-ba-ni*** maškim zi-[ga *šu-k*]*ab-tá* k[i *aš-tá-qar*-t]a [ba]-zi, "*Aštaqqar* disbursed 66 female weavers employed for 1 day to crush malt. (It was) the expenditure of *Šu-Kabta*. *Erra-bani* was the deputy," 245:1–6[35]

---

[35] Although *Erra-bani*'s title is not specified, this text is included here in light of the parallel transaction no. 277.

15 géme uš-bar u_4-1-šè $munu_4$ $nag̃_4$-g̃á-dè gub-ba ***èr-ra-ba-ni*** lùnga maškim zi-ga *simat-*^{d}*ištaran* [ki ^{d}*adad-till*]*ati*-ta ba-zi, "*Adad-tillati* disbursed 15 female weavers for 1 day employed to crush malt. (It was) the expenditure of *Simat-Ištaran*. *Erra-bani*, the brewer, was the deputy," 277:1–6

2. *Erra-bani*, the Majordomo: As a Witness

igi ***èr-ra-ba-ni*** šabra, "witnessed by *Erra-bani*, the majordomo," 1055:10

3. *Erra-bani*, the Scribe: As a Witness

igi ***èr-ra-ba-ni*** dub-sar, "witnessed by *Erra-bani*, the scribe," 1060:7

4. *Erra-bani*, Title Unspecified

4.1 Deliveries

4.1.1 Barley: Receipt of *Adad-tillati*

48.0.0. še gur ki ***èr-ra-ba-ni***-ta ^{d}*adad-tillati* šu ba-an-ti, "*Adad-tillati* received 48 bushels of barley from *Erra-bani*," 1101:1–4

4.1.2 Gazi: Receipt of *Adallal*, the Cook

1.2.[n. g]azi gur ki ***èr-ra-ba-ni***-ta *a-da-làl* muḫaldim šu ba-ti, "*Adallal*, the cook, received 1 bushel and 120[+n] liters of gazi from *Erra-bani*," 1204:1–4

4.1.3 Ordinary Beer: Provisions of the Builders

0.0.1.6 sìla kaš-gen $sá-du_{11}$ šidim-e-ne u_4 bàd ba-dù-a g̃ìri *é-a-šar* ki ***èr-ra-ba-ni***-ta ba-zi, "Under the authority of *Ea-šar*, *Erra-bani* disbursed 16 liters of ordinary beer, regular provisions of the builders, when the (enclosure) wall was constructed," 478:1–6

4.2 Receipts: From *Adad-tillati*

4.2.1 Beer Bread

1 gú 10 ma-na báppir-sig_5 ki ^{d}*adad-tillati*-ta ***èr-ra-ba-ni*** [šu] ba-⸢ti⸣, "*Erra-bani* received 1 talent (and) 10 minas of fine beer bread from *Adad-tillati*," 1230:1–4

1 gú báppir-gen kaš dirig-šè ki ^{d}*adad-tillati*-ta ***èr-ra-ba-ni*** šu ba-ti, "*Erra-bani* received 1 talent of ordinary beer bread for additional beer from *Adad-tillati*," 1244:1–5

1 gú [. . .] 7 gú 25 m[a-n]a báppir-gen [n g]ú ku?-[. . .]-zì [ki ^{d}]*adad-tillati*-[ta] ***èr-ra-ba-ni*** šu ba-ti, "*Erra-bani* received 1 talent [. . .], 7 talents (and) 25 minas of ordinary beer (and) [n] talent(s) [. . .] from *Adad-tillati*," 1247:1–6

4.2.2 A Millstone

1 ^{na_4}kinkin-GI-bí šu sè-ga ki ^{d}*adad-tillati*-[ta] ***èr-ra-ba-ni*** šu ba-ti, "*Erra-bani* received 1 'hand-held' GI-bí millstone from *Adad-tillati*," 1341:1–4

4.2.3 Sprouted Malt for (Brewing) Additional Beer

5.0.0. $munu_4$-si-è gur kaš dirig-šè ki ^{d}*adad-tillati*-ta ***èr-ra-ba-ni*** šu ba-⸢ti⸣, "*Erra-bani* received 5 bushels of sprouted malt for additional beer from *Adad-tillati*," 1227:1–5

4.3 Provisions: Wages for Molding Bricks

25⅓ sar 8⅓ gín [. . .] ***èr-ra-ba-⸢ni⸣*** (. . .) $šeg_{12}$ du_8-[a], "25⅓ sar (and) 8⅓ gín [(of bricks from)] *Erra-bani* (and bricks from) {other workers}, {wages for workers} having molded bricks," 350:10–11, '23

4.4 As a Witness

igi ***èr-ra-ba-ni***, "witnessed by *Erra-bani*," 1049:11, 1050:11, 1058:10

eš$_4$-tár-im-dì

1. Provisions: Barley

0.0.2. ***eš$_4$-tár-[im]-dì*** (. . .) mu dabin-šè šu ba-ti, "*Eštar-imdi* received 20 liters of barley (and barley for) {9 other individuals}, (barley) in place of semolina," 560:3, 12–13

eš$_4$-tár-um-mi

1. *Eštar-ummi*, Daughter of *Šu-Kabta*

^{ĝeš}kiri$_6$ ***eš$_4$-tár-um-mi*** dumu-munus *šu-kab-tá*, "the garden of *Eštar-ummi*, daughter of *Šu-Kabta*" > *Garden Index*

2. *Eštar-ummi*, Title Unspecified: Provisions

0.2.0. ***eš$_4$-tár-um-mi*** (. . .) šu+níĝin 27.1.1.3 sìla še gur ki ugula-nam–10-ka ⌜ĝal⌝-la ugula *simat-é-a* lú-ḫuĝ-ĝá, "180 liters (of barley) (for) *Eštar-ummi*, (and barley for) {others}, in total: there are 27 bushels (and) 73 liters of barley at the place of the overseer of 10; *Simat-Ea*, the overseer of hired workers," 504:17, 20–23

– G –

ga-su-su

Gasusu, Wife of *Aḫu'a*

1. Disbursal of her Servant, Geme-Enki

1 géme-^{d}en-ki géme uš-bar saĝ-ba ***ga-su-su*** dam *a-ḫu-a a-na-a* deputy zi-ga *tá-ki-il-ì-lí-ís-sú* ki ^{d}*adad-tillati*-ta ba-zi, "*Adad-tillati* disbursed Geme-Enki, the female weaver, the servant of *Gasusu*, the wife of *Aḫu'a*. (It was) the expenditure of *Takil-ilissu*. *Ana'a* was the deputy," 270:1–7

géme-^{d}en-ki

Geme-Enki, Female Weaver and Servant of *Gasusu*

1. Disbursed by *Adad-tillati*

1 **géme-^{d}en-ki** géme uš-bar saĝ-ba *ga-su-su* dam *a-ḫu-a a-na-a* deputy zi-ga *tá-ki-il-ì-lí-ís-sú* ki ^{d}*adad-tillati*-ta ba-zi, "*Adad-tillati* disbursed Geme-Enki, the female weaver, the servant of *Gasusu*, the wife of *Aḫu'a*. (It was) the expenditure of *Takil-ilissu*. *Ana'a* was the deputy," 270:1–7

géme-tur

é-**géme-tur**, "the house of Geme-tur" > *Household Index*

1. Provisions

0.0.1.1 sìla zú-lum eša b[a-ḫ]i ½ x **géme-tur** ba-na-ḫa-la *išdum-ki-in* ⌜sagi⌝ maškim šà zabala$_4^{ki}$, "11 liters of dates were mixed (with) fine flour, ½ x. They were portioned out to Geme-tur in Zabala. *Išdum-kin*, the cupbearer, was the deputy," 506:16–19, 21

gù-zi-dé-a

Guzidea, the Man of *Adad-tillati*

1. Under his Authority: Comestibles for the Sugal-maḫ

1 udu-niga 2.0.0. ninda-gal-gen gur 0.1.0. zì-gu-ús sugal$_{7}$-maḫ g̃ìri **gù-zi-dé-a** lú-na zi-ga *simat-*^{d}*ištaran* ⸢ki⸣ ^{d}*adad-tillati*-[ta] ba-zi, "Under the authority of Guzidea, his man, *Adad-tillati* disbursed 1 fattened sheep, 2 bushels of large ordinary bread (and) 60 liters of 2nd-quality gu-flour (for) the sugal-maḫ. (It was) the expenditure of *Simat-Ištaran*," 1184:1–8

– G̃ –

G̃AR-*šà-ti*

1. G̃AR-*šati*, the Craftsman

1.1 Receipts: Shadufs, Measuring Containers, and Wooden Boards

4 ^{geš}*zi-ri-qum*-ásal 7 ^{gi}gur a bala ésir šub-ba 4 ^{geš}ba-an-la ki ^{d}*adad-tillati*-ta [**G̃AR-*š*]*à-ti*** um-mi-a [šu ba]-ti, "G̃AR-*šati*, the craftsman, received 4 poplar shadufs, 7 measuring containers coated with bitumen for pouring water (and) 4 wooden boards from *Adad-tillati*," 1349:1–6

2. G̃AR-*šati*, the Gardener

2.1 Garden Products in his Possession

lá-ìa 0.0.3.3 sìla zú-lum 0.0.5.4 sìla ^{geš}ḫašḫur-duru$_{5}$ 0.0.3. gazi 5 sìla *ḫu-ri-um* 2 sìla zà-ḫi-li 120⅔ 6 gín ^{geš}zé-na 4 gín gir-ga 16 peš-múrgu ⸢lá⸣-ìa-àm **G̃AR-*šà-ti*** nu-^{geš}kiri$_{6}$ in-da-g̃ál, "the remainder of 33 liters of dates, 54 liters of fresh apples, 30 liters of gazi, 5 liters of *ḫu-ri-um* spice, 2 liters of zà-ḫi-li seeds, 120⅔ (and) 6 shekels of date palm frond midribs, 4 shekels of gir-ga (and) 16 date palm spines are with G̃AR-*šati*, the gardener," 1190:1–12

g̃ìri-^{d}ba-ú-ì-dab$_{5}$

1. G̃iri-Ba'u-idab, the Barber

1.1 As a Deputy: Flour and Potash

[0.n.n.] zì [n n]ag̃a [. . .]-šè **g̃ìri-^{d}ba-ú-ì-dab$_{5}$** šu-i maškim, "[n] liter(s) of flour (and) [n liter(s)] of potash for [. . .]. G̃iri-Ba'u-idab, the barber, was the deputy," 1013:3–5

2. G̃iri-Ba'u-idab, Title Unspecified

2.1 As a Deputy: Supplies for the House of the Barbers

2 sìla x-x nag̃a? é-šu-i-e-ne-šè **g̃ìri-^{d}ba-ú-ì-dab$_{5}$** maškim [ki] ^{d}*adad-tillati*-ta ba-zi "*Adad-tillati* disbursed 2 liters of x-x potash? for the house of the barbers. G̃iri-Ba'u-idab was the deputy," 492:1–4

2.2 Under the Authority of G̃iri-Ba'u-idab: Fullers to Tow the Boat of *Nawir-ilum*

3 g̃uruš ^{lú}ázlag u$_{4}$-2½-šè nibru^{ki}-ta é-^{d}*šu*-^{d}*suen*-šè má *na-wi-ir-ilum* íb-gíd g̃ìri **g̃ìri-^{d}ba-ú-ì-dab$_{5}$** zi-ga g̃ìri *šu-kab-tá* ki *puzur$_{4}$-a-gu$_{5}$-um*-ta ba-zi, "*Puzur-agum* disbursed 3 fullers for 2½ days. They towed the boat of *Nawir-ilum* from Nippur to *Bit-Šu-Suen*. (It was) the expenditure of *Šu-Kabta*, under his authority (and) that of G̃iri-Ba'u-idab," 220:1–11

g̃ìri-né-ì-dab$_5$

1. G̃irine-idab, the Courier

1.1 As a Deputy: Provisions for Ox-Drivers

0.3.0. še šà-gu$_4$-me-éš dirig še-ba-ne-ne mu zì nu-g̃ál-la-šè ba-na-ḫa-la *šu-kab-tá* bí-in-dug$_4$ **⸢g̃ìri⸣-né-ì-dab$_5$** ra-gaba maškim u$_4$ é-e i[m sumur ba-aka] g̃ìri *é-a-šar* dub-sar ki ^{d}*adad-tillati*-ta ba-zi, "Under the authority of *Ea-šar*, the scribe, *Adad-tillati* disbursed 180 liters of barley for the ox-drivers when the house was plastered. *Šu-Kabta* had ordered that additional barley rations were to be divided for them because there was no flour. G̃irine-idab, the courier, was the deputy," 481:1–9

1.2 Under the Authority of G̃irine-idab: Work Assignments for Craftsmen

1.2.1 Bringing Barley

1 g̃uruš ašgab 1 g̃uruš ad-kub$_4$ 1 géme kíkken u$_4$-[2]7-šè še ^{d}*šu*-^{d}*suen*-<am->ma-ra$^{[ki]}$ ù bàd-ga-zi^{ki}-⸢ta⸣ gar-ša-an-na^{ki}-šè de$_6$-a g̃ìri *a-ḫu-wa-qar* dub-sar ù **g̃ìri-né-ì-dab$_5$** ra-gaba ki ^{d}*adad-tillati*-ta ba-zi, "Under the authority of *Aḫu-waqar*, the scribe, and G̃irine-idab, the courier, *Adad-tillati* disbursed 1 leather worker, 1 reed craftsman (and) 1 female miller for [2]7 days having brought barley from *Šu-suen*-ammara and Bad-gazi to Garšana," 259:1–10

1.2.2 Harvesting

(. . .) še gur$_{10}$-gur$_{10}$-dè zàr tab-ba-dè ù g̃eš ra-ra-dè a-šà *ṣe-ru-um* gub-ba g̃ìri **g̃ìri-né-ì-dab$_5$** ra-gaba zi-ga *simat*-^{d}*ištaran* ki ^{d}*adad-tillati*-ta ba-zi, "*Adad-tillati* disbursed {craftsmen} employed at the *Ṣerum* field to reap barley, stack (its) sheaves (for drying) and flail (them). (It was) the expenditure of *Simat-Ištaran* under the authority of G̃irine-idab, the courier," 262:19–26

2. G̃irine-idab, Title Unspecified

2.1 As a Witness

igi **g̃ìri-né-ì-dab$_5$**, "witnessed by G̃irine-idab," 1059:9

– Ḫ –

ḫa-la-ša

Ḫalaša, Workman of the Mill

1. Provisions

[n g]ín ì-g̃eš-ta 1 ma-na tuḫ-g̃eš-ì-ḫád-ta 0.0.1. ádda-udu-ta [½] sìla mun-ta [n] gín luḫ-lá-ta [1 a]d-da-kal-la [1] ur-^{d}šul-pa-è [1] ***ḫa-la-ša*** {indent} 3 [g̃uruš? é]-kíkken é-^{d}nin-^{d}si$_4$-an-na-me-éš, "[n] shekel(s) of sesame oil each, 1 mina of dried sesame chaff each, 10 sheep carcasses each, [½] liter of salt each (and) [n] shekel(s) of luḫ-lá each, (provisions for) Ada-kala, Ur-Šulpa'e (and) *Ḫalaša*, 3 [workmen?] of the mill of Nin-Siana," 562:'6–'15

1.1.0. ninda gur še-ba ***ḫa-la-ša*** é?-[kíkken?] gub-ba (. . .) [níg̃-kas$_7$]-aka [*ì-lí*]-*bi-la-ni* muḫaldim, "1 bushel (and) 60 liters of bread, barley rations of *Ḫalaša*, employed in the [mill?] (and) {other allotments}, the balanced account of *Ili-bilani*, the cook," 1527:19–20, 48–49

ḫa-lí

Ḫali, the Braider[36]

1. Deliveries

1.1 Braiders

1.1.1 Bringing Barley

1 ĝuruš túg-du$_{8}$ u$_{4}$-1-šè še *dì-im-bu-na-*^{d}*àš-gi*$_{5}$-ta é-duru$_{5}$-˹kab˺-bí-[šè] ĝìri ^{d}*adad-*[*tillati*] ˹šabra˺ ki ***ḫa-lí***-˹ta˺ ba-zi, "Under the authority of *Adad-tillati*, *Ḫali* disbursed 1 braider for 1 day (having brought) barley from *Dimbun*-Ašgi [to] the Kabbi village," 256:1–7

[n] ĝuruš tú[g-d]u$_{8}$ u$_{4}$-9-šè še ù-dag-ga^{ki}-ta gar-ša-an-na^{ki}-šè de$_{6}$-a ù kar-[ta] ĝá-nun-šè íb-˹ga$_{6}$˺ ki ***ḫa-lí***-ta ba-zi, "*Ḫali* disbursed [n] braider(s) for 9 days having brought barley from Udaga to Garšana and carried it [from] the quay to the storehouse," 261:1–8

1 ĝuruš túg-du$_{8}$ u$_{4}$-12-šè du$_{6}$-saḫar-ra^{ki}-ta en-zu-bábbar^{ki}-šè [še] íb-ga$_{6}$ [ús-b]i 1500 éš kaskal š[u+níĝin]-na-bi ki ***ḫa-lí***-ta ba-zi, "*Ḫali* disbursed 1 braider for 12 days. He carried [barley] from Du-saḫara to Enzu-babbar. Its distance: 1500 ropes is the entire trip," 263:1–7

[n ĝuruš] túg-d[u$_{8}$ u$_{4}$]-20-[šè še é]-duru$_{5}$-kab-bi[^{ki}-ta gar]-ša-an-na^{ki}-[šè] de$_{6}$-a ĝìri ^{d}*adad-*˹*tillati*˺ šabra ki ***ḫ*[*a-l*]*í***-ta ba-zi, "Under the authority of *Adad-tillati*, the majordomo, *Ḫali* disbursed [n] braider(s) [for] 20 [days] having brought [barley from] the Kabbi village [to] Garšana," 302:1–6

1.1.2 Bringing the Commodity Tax

1 ĝuruš túg-du$_{8}$ u$_{4}$-6-šè še! en-zu-bábbar$^{<ki>}$-ta [de$_{6}$]-a 1 ĝuruš túg-du$_{8}$ u$_{4}$-6-šè níĝ-gú-na tum-ma-al^{ki}-šè de$_{6}$-a 1 ĝuruš túg-du$_{8}$ u$_{4}$-11-šè níĝ-gú-na é-da-na^{ki}-šè de$_{6}$-a 1 ĝuruš túg-du$_{8}$ u$_{4}$-6-šè níĝ-gú-na nag-su^{ki}-ta de$_{6}$-a ki ***ḫa-lí***-ta ba-zi, "*Ḫali* disbursed 1 braider for 6 days having [brought] barley from Enzu-babbar, 1 braider for 6 days having brought the commodity tax to Tumal, 1 braider for 11 days having brought the commodity tax to Edana (and) 1 braider for 6 days having brought the commodity tax from Nagsu," 267:1–12

1.1.3 Demolishing a Boat and Bringing Assorted Commodities

1 ĝuruš túg-du$_{8}$ u$_{4}$-3-˹šè˺ má gul-dè gub<-ba> 1 ĝuruš u$_{4}$-2-šè ĝeš ùr ga$_{6}$-ĝá 1 ĝuruš u$_{4}$-11-šè má ú-sa unug^{ki}-ta gar-ša-an-na$^{<ki>}$-šè má gíd-da 1 ĝuruš u$_{4}$-1-šè gi-zi ĜEŠ.KÚŠU^{ki}-[ta] de$_{6}$-[a n] ĝuruš u$_{4}$-[n-šè] ḫar lam ^{ĝeš}ù-suḫ$_{5}$ ke$_{4}$-[dè] ^{d}gu$_{4}$-an-na-˹ta˺ gar-ša-an-na^{ki}-šè de[$_{6}$-a] ki ***ḫa-lí***-ta ba-zi, "*Ḫali* disbursed 1 braider employed for 3 days to demolish a boat, 1 workman for 2 days having brought roof beams, 1 workman for 11 days having towed a processed boat from Uruk to Garšana, 1 worker for 1 day having brought fresh reeds [from] ĜEŠ.KÚŠU, (and) [n] workmen for [n] day(s) having brought a seedling container of pine trees from from Guanna to Garšana," 272:1–15

---

36 Although *Ḫali*'s title is not specified in every passage cited here, the nature of these transactions suggests that all references are to the same person.

1.1.4 During the *Abum* Festival

1 g̃uruš túg-du$_8$ u$_4$-12-šè gaba sàg̃-dè ⌜gub⌝-ba u$_4$ ezem-*a-bu-um-ma* g̃iri ᵈ*suen-a-bu-šu* ki ***ḫa-lí***-ta ba-zi, "Under the authority of *Suen-abušu*, *Ḫali* disbursed 1 braider, employed for 12 days to beat (his) breast during the *Abum* festival," 278:1–7

1.1.5 Released on the Day of the Wool Rations

1 g̃uruš [túg-du$_8$] u$_4$-1-šè u$_4$ siki ba-a-ka šu bar-ra ki ***ḫa-lí***-ta ba-zi, "*Ḫali* disbursed 1 [braider] released for 1 day on the day of the wool rations," 265:1–5

1.1.6 Removing Dirt at the Mama-*šarrat* Canal

1 g̃uruš túg-[du$_8$] u$_4$-13-šè saḫar zi-ga i$_7$-ma-ma-*šar-ra-at* g̃iri *ba-ba-ni* dub-sar 1 g̃uruš túg-du$_8$ u$_4$-4-šè *dì-im-bu-na*-àš-gi$_5$-ta a-šà *ṣe-ru-um*-šè g̃iri *é-a-šar* šabra ki ***ḫa-lí***-ta ba-zi, "*Ḫali* disbursed 1 braider for 13 days who moved dirt at the Mama-*šarrat* canal under the authority of *Babani*, the scribe, (and) 1 braider for 4 days (having gone) from *Dimbun*-Ašgi to the *Ṣerum* field, under the authority of *Ea-šar*, the majordomo," 283:1–11

1.2 Materials for Tanning: Receipt of *Anaḫ-ili*

⅔ sìla ì-šáḫ ⅔ ma-na ú-ḫáb 5 ma-na *al-lu-ḫa-ru-um a-na-aḫ-ì-lí* šu ba-ti ki ***ḫa-lí***-ta ba-zi, "*Anaḫ-ili* received ⅔ liter of lard, ⅔ mina of madder (dye) (and) 5 minas of *alluḫarum* from *Ḫali*," 947:1–6

1⅓ ma-na *al-lu-ḫa-ru-um*-sig$_5$ 4 ma-na *al-lu*<-*ḫa*>-*ru-um* 2 túg-du$_8$-a [siki]-g̃ír-gul ki ***ḫa-lí***-ta *a-na-aḫ-ì-lí* šu ba-ti, "*Anaḫ-ili* received 1⅓ minas of fine *alluḫarum*, 4 minas of (ordinary) *alluḫarum* (and) 2 meshworks of g̃ír-gul [wool] from *Ḫali*," 924:1–6

1.3 Wool and Hair

1.3.1 Goat Hair

10 gín siki-ud$_5$ 1 ma-na níg̃-U.NU-a siki-ud$_5$ ki ***ḫa-lí***-ta ba-zi, "*Ḫali* disbursed 10 shekels of goat hair (and) 1 mina of goat hair thread," 716:1–4

3⅚ ma-na siki-ud$_5$ ki ***ḫa-lí***-ta ba-zi, "*Ḫali* disbursed 3⅚ minas of goat hair," 772:1–3

1.3.1.1 Goat Hair Mattresses

1 šà-tuku$_5$-siki-ud$_5$ ki-lá-bi 5 ma-na 10 gín ***ḫa-lí*** túg-du$_8$ ì-lá, "*Ḫali*, the braider, weighed out 1 goat hair mattress—its weight is 5 minas (and) 10 shekels," 706:1–3

5 éš-siki-ud$_5$ ki-lá-bi 15⅔ ma-na 1 bar-si siki-ud$_5$ šà-tuku$_5$ é-ba-an ki-lá-bi 2 ma-na 1 [. . .] ki-lá-b[i . . .] 10 [. . .] ki-lá-bi [. . .] ***ḫa-lí*** ì-[lá], "*Ḫali* weighed out 5 goat hair ropes—their weight is 15⅔ minas—1 pair of goat hair bands (for) a mattress—their weight is 2 minas—1 [. . .]—its weight is [. . .]—(and) 10 [. . .]—their weight is [. . .]," 740:1–9

1.3.1.2 Goat-Hair Sacks and Rope

6 barag-siki-ud$_5$ ki-lá-bi 18 ma-na 1⅚ ma-na éš-siki-ud$_5$ ***ḫa-lí*** in-lá, "*Ḫali* weighed out 6 sacks of goat hair—their weight is 18 minas—(and) 1⅚ minas of goat hair ropes," 717:1–4

1.3.2 Combed Wool

1.3.2.1 Combed Wool for Belts, Shoes, and Caps

[1] túg-íb-[lá]-kaskal ⌜siki⌝-bi ⅓ ma-⌜na⌝ 1 gín [1] ^{túg}sagšu siki ^{ĝeš}garig aka 4-kam-ús ⌜siki⌝-bi ⅓ ma-na [x-*t*]*um*?? ANŠE+BAR+MUL [^{ĝeš}ga]rig aka gen [siki-bi] ⅔ ma-[na] 4 gín [***ḫa-l***]***í*** túg-du$_8$ ì-lá, "*Ḫali*, the braider, weighed out ⅓ mina (and) 1 shekel of wool (for) [1] traveling belt, 4th-quality combed wool (weighing) ⅓ mina (for) 1 cap (and) ⅔ mina (and) 4 shekels of ordinary combed wool (for) (?)," 702:1–8

2 ^{túg}sagšu siki ^{ĝeš}garig aka 4-kam-ús ki-lá-bi 13 gín ***ḫa-l***[***í*** túg-d]u$_8$ ì-[lá], "*Ḫali*, the braider, weighed out 4th-quality combed wool—its weight is 13 shekels (for) 2 caps," 741:1–5

4 ^{túg}sagšu siki ^{ĝeš}garig a[ka . . .] ⅔ [. . .níĝ]-U.NU-a [. . .túg-*ḫa*]-*bu-um*-šè [. . .***ḫa-lí*** túg-d]u$_8$ [ì]-lá, "*Ḫali*, the braider, weighed out combed wool (for) 4 caps, ⅔ [. . . (for)] thread, [. . .] for *ḫa-bu-um* [textiles, (and) . . .]," 755:1–11

1 $^{\text{<kuš>}}$súḫub-túg-du$_8$-a-⌜babbar⌝? siki ^{ĝeš}garig aka 3-kam-ús ki-lá-bi ½ ma-na 2 gín 2 túg-sagšu-ĝe$_6$ siki ^{ĝeš}garig aka 4-kam-ús ki-lá-bi 13 gín 1 ^{túg}íb-lá siki-a-[gíd] siki ^{ĝeš}garig aka ĝen ki-lá-bi 16 gín ***ḫa-lí*** túg-du$_8$ ì-lá, "*Ḫali*, the braider, weighed out 3rd-quality combed wool—its weight is ½ mina (and) 2 shekels—(for) 1 (pair) of white? meshwork shoes, 4th-quality combed wool—its weight is 13 shekels—(for) 2 black caps (and) ordinary combed wool—its weight is 16 shekels—(for) 1 belt of a-[gíd] wool," 756:1–11

[. . .]x-ka-ĝe$_6$-sig$_5$ [. . .siki] ^{ĝeš}garig aka 4-kam-ús [n] ^{túg}íb-lá-su$_4$-a siki ^{ĝeš}ZUM.[SI aka 4-kam-ús k]i ***ḫa-lí***-ta [. . .], "*Ḫali* [disbursed] 4th-quality combed wool (for) a fine black [. . .] (and) [4th-quality combed wool] (for) [n] red/brown belt(s)," 833:1–5

1.3.2.2 Meshworks of Combed Wool

1 túg-d[u$_8$-a . . .] siki ^{ĝeš}⌜garig⌝ [aka] 4-kam-ús ki-lá-bi ½ ma-na 1 túg-du$_8$-a-babbar é-ba-an ^{ĝeš}garig aka gen ki-l[á-bi n] ma-na [n gín] 1 túg-du$_8$-a-babbar túg-tur siki ^{ĝeš}garig aka 3-kam-ús ki-lá-bi 7 gín ki ***ḫa-lí***-ta ba-zi, "*Ḫali* disbursed 1 [. . .] meshwork of 4th-quality combed wool—its weight is ½ mina—1 pair of white meshworks of ordinary combed wool—their weight is [n] mina(s) (and) [n shekel(s)]—(and) 1 white meshwork (for) a small textile of 3rd-quality combed wool—its weight is 7 shekels," 583:1–11

[. . .] 1 túg-du$_8$-a ⌜siki⌝ ^{ĝeš}NÍĜIN-garig aka 4-kam-ús ki-lá-bi ½ ma-na ***ḫa-lí*** ì-lá, "*Ḫali* weighed out [. . .] (and) 1 meshwork of 4th-quality combed wool—its weight is ½ mina," 767:1–5

1.3.3 Combed Wool and Goat Hair

4 túg-*bu-ti-um*? ^{ĝeš}*be-rum* siki ^{ĝeš}garig aka gen ki-lá-bi ⅔ ma-na [n] ma-na 15 gín siki-ud$_5$ ki ***ḫa-lí***-ta ba-zi, "*Ḫali* disbursed ordinary combed wool—its weight is ⅔ mina—for 4 *bu-ti-um* textiles (and) [n] mina(s) (and) 15 shekels of goat hair," 807:1–6

1.3.4 ĝír-gul Wool

5 ^{túg}sagšu-babbar siki-⌜ĝír⌝-gul ki-lá-bi ⅔ ma-na ***ḫa-lí*** túg-du$_8$ ì-lá ĝìri ^{d}*adad-till*[*ati*] ù ^{d}*ma-lik-ba-*[*ni*], "Under the authority of *Adad-tillati* and *Malik-bani*, *Ḫali*, the

braider, weighed out ĝír-gul wool—its weight is ⅔ mina—(for) 5 white caps," 679:1–5

25 ma-na siki-ĝír-gul *aš-tá-qar* šu ba-ti ki ***ḫa-lí***-ta [ba]-zi, "*Aštaqqar* received 25 minas of ĝír-gul wool from *Ḫali*," 805:1–5

1.3.4.1 Meshworks of ĝír-gul wool

5 túg-du$_8$-a siki-ĝír-gul ^{ĝeš}gu-za-munus šà!-kal ki-lá-bi 3⅔ ma-na ***ḫa-lí*** túg-du$_8$ [ì]-lá, "*Ḫali*, the braider, weighed out 5 meshworks of ĝír-gul wool—their weight is 3⅔ minas—(for) a wooden woman's chair," 761:1–4

1 túg-du$_8$-a siki-ĝír-gul ki-lá-bi ⅓ ma-na 3 gín ***ḫa-lí*** ì-lá, "*Ḫali* weighed out 1 meshwork of ĝír-gul wool—its weight is ⅓ mina (and) 3 shekels," 776:1–4

6 túg-du$_8$-a siki ^{ĝeš}garig aka 1 túg-du$_8$-a siki-ĝír-gul [ki-lá-bi n ma]-na 5 gín [igi]-12-ĝál ki ***ḫa-lí***-ta *a-na-aḫ-ì-lí* šu ba-an-ti, "*Anaḫ-ili* received 6 meshworks of combed wool (and) 1 meshwork of ĝír-gul wool from *Ḫali*. [Their weight is n] mina(s) (and) 5$^{1}/_{12}$ shekels," 883:1–7

1.4 Workmen

30 ĝuruš u$_4$-1-šè nam-ša-ra-ab<-du> a-šà pa$_4$-lugal-ĝu$_{10}$-ka gub-ba ki ***ḫa-lí***-ta ba-zi, "*Ḫali* expended 30 workmen for 1 day employed for the administration of the Palugalĝu field," 276:1–5

1.5 Other

1.5.1 Assorted Commodities

12 gín siki-ĝír-gul šà-tuku$_5$ kala-kala-gé-dè 5½ naĝa-si-è 2 ma-na im-bábbar šà-tuku$_5$ lu-luḫ-dè 1 ĝuruš túg-du$_8$ u$_4$-6-šè má gíd-da ĝìri *šar-ru-sú*-DU$_{10}$ ⅓ ma-na siki-ud$_5$ 1 ĝuruš túg-du$_8$ u$_4$-5-šè ĝìri *u-bar-tum* 1 ^{túg}sagšu-ĝe$_6$-sig$_5$ ki ***ḫa-lí***-ta ba-zi, "*Ḫali* disbursed 12 shekels of ĝír-gul wool in order to reinforce a mattress, 5½ (liters) of sprouted naĝa (and) 2 minas of gypsum in order to clean a mattress (and) 1 braider for 6 days having towed a boat under the authority of *Šarrussu-ṭabu*; ⅓ mina of goat hair (and) 1 braider for 5 days under the authority of *Ubartum*; (and) 1 fine black cap," 783:1–13

1.5.2 Potash

1⅔ ma-na ki-lá šeg$_{12}$ naĝa ki ***ḫa-lí***-ta ba-zi, "*Ḫali* disbursed a brick of potash weighing 1⅔ minas," 788:1–5

2. In the Possession of *Ḫali*

[n+]6½ [. . .11]$^5/_6$ ma-na 7$^5/_6$ [gín] *al-lu-ḫa-ru-um* 10 ma-na 2$^5/_6$ gín 10 še ú-ḫáb 15 gín sa$_{10}$+didli 10 še ì-šáḫ lá-ìa-àm ***ḫa-lí*** túg-du$_8$ in-da-ĝál, "The remainder of [. . .], [11]$^5/_6$ minas (and) 7$^5/_6$ [shekels] of *alluḫarum*, 10 minas (and) 2$^5/_6$ shekels (and) 10 barley corn of madder (dye), (and) 15 shekels of lard, worth 10 barley corn, are with *Ḫali*, the braider," 828:1–7

ḫal-lí-a

1. *Ḫallia*, Overseer of Hired Workers

1.1 Workmen

n ĝuruš ugula ***ḫal-lí-a*** (. . .) lú-ḫuĝ-ĝá-me-éš, "n hired workmen supervised by *Ḫalli'a*," 10:10, 15:12, 16:9, 17:9, 18:11, 20:11, 21:11, 24:12, 27:'5, 28:'2, 29:'9, 33:13, 34:12, 35:13, 36:13, 39:10, 40:11, 43:14, 44:12, 47:12, 48:12

1.2 Belongings of *Ḫallia*

1 ^{dug}útul-0.0.2. 1 ^{dug}útul-0.0.1. 1 ^{ĝeš}zé-na 2 ^{gi}ma-sab ugula ***ḫal-lí-a*** ki ^{d}*adad-tillati*-ta *a-da-làl* muḫaldim šu ba-an-ti, "*Adallal*, the cook, received from *Adad-tillati* 1 20-liter tureen, 1 10-liter tureen, 1 date palm frond midrib (and) 2 ma-sab baskets of the overseer, *Ḫallia*," 1265:1–7

2. *Ḫallia*, the Fuller

2.1 Testifying to the Delivery of Wool to the Palace

★★(. . .) [. . .] kišib íb-ra é-kìšib-ba-ta dub-bi in-du$_8$ siki bala-dè in-kéše é-gal-šè mu-DU ***ḫal-lí-a*** ^{lú}ázlag ka-ga-na ba-gi-in, "{assorted textiles} [. . .]. The seal was rolled, he baked its tablet (in) the warehouse, (and) bound the wool to be baled (for) delivery for the palace. *Ḫallia*, the fuller, confirmed it," 609:11–16

3. *Ḫallia*, Title Unspecified

3.1 Provisions: Semolina

0.4.1 dabin ***ḫal-li-[a]*** mu-DU *šu-kab-t[á* ^{d}*ma-lik-ba-ni*] šu ba-an-ti, "[*Malik-bani*] received 250 liters of semolina (for) *Ḫalli'a*, delivery of *Šu-Kabta*," 464:1–6

ḫi-li

Ḫili, the Boat Tower

1. Provisions: Oil when He was Injured

½ sìla ì-ĝeš ***ḫi-li*** má gíd u$_4$ dùb bar-ra-ni in-na-gig-ga, "½ liter of sesame oil (for) *Ḫili*, the boat tower, when his 'outer knee' was hurting him," 444:4–5

ḫi-lu-a

Ḫilua, the Household Servant from the Gang of *Irib*

1. Bringing Messages

1.1 To Ĝirsu

1 ***ḫi-lu-a*** á-áĝ ĝír-su^{ki}-šè de$_6$-a, "*Ḫilua* having brought a message to Ĝirsu," 24:'26, 25:'3, 26:'22, 27:'18, 28:'29, 29:'34

1.2 To *Šu-Eštar*

1 ***ḫi-lu-a*** 1 é-ì-gára á-áĝ ki *šu-e*[*š$_4$-tár*-šè] de[$_6$-a], "*Ḫilua* (and) E'igara having brought a message [to] the place of *Šu-Eštar*," 37:31–33

[1] é-ì-gára 1 ***ḫi-lu-a*** 1 á-áĝ ki *šu-eš$_4$-tár*-[šè] de$_6$-a, "E'igara (and) *Ḫilua* having brought a message [to] the place of *Šu-Eštar*," 38:37–39

1 ***ḫi-lu-a*** á-áĝ *šu-eš$_4$-tár* ù-dag-ga^{ki}-šè de$_6$-a, "*Ḫilua* having brought a message to *Šu-Eštar* in Udaga," 43:'47, 45:24–25, 46:'42–'43, 47:55, 48:60–61

1 ***ḫi-lu-a*** á-ãĝ ki *šu-eš$_4$-tár*-šè de$_6$-a, "*Ḫilua* having brought a message to the place of *Šu-Eštar*," 52:52–53, 53:55

1.3 To Udaga

1 ***ḫi-lu-a*** á-ãĝ-[ĝá] ù-dag-ga$^{\langle ki \rangle}$-šè de$_6$-a, "*Ḫilua* having brought a message to Udaga," 44:46

1.4 GN Lost

1 [PN] 1 ***ḫi-lu-[a]*** 1 *šu-^{d}b[elum]* á-ãĝ-ĝá ki [. . . –šè de$_6$-a], "[PN], *Ḫilua* (and) *Šu-Belum* [having brought] a message to [. . .]," 54:'27–'30

2. Bringing the Tablet of *Iddin-Adad* to Nippur

1 ***ḫi-lu-a*** dub *i-din-^{d}adad* nibru^{ki}-šè de$_6$-a, "*Ḫilua* having brought the tablet of *Iddin-Adad* to Nippur," 33:44, 34:'18, 35:47, 36:42, 39:44, 40:42

ḫu-im

1. Provisions: Leather and Flour

½ kuš-udu-babbar ½ gín eša ***ḫu-im***-šè ba-a-ĝar, "½ of a white sheep skin (and) ½ shekel of fine flour were placed for *Ḫu'im*," 1517:16–18

ḫu-lu-lu

é-***ḫu-lu-lu***, "the house of *Ḫululu*" > *Household Index*

Ḫululu, the Son of *Dada'a*

1. Receipts: House Bitumen from *Iddin-Adad*

0.1.0. ésir-é-a ki *i-din-^{d}adad*-ta ***ḫu-lu-lu*** dumu *da-d[a-a]* šu ba-a[n-ti], "*Ḫululu*, the son of *Dada'a*, received 60 liters of house bitumen from *Iddin-Adad*," 1257:1–5

– I –

i-ba-a-a

Iba'a, Man from Karkar

1 ***i-ba-a-a*** (. . .) ugula *á-ni*-x-x (. . .) lú-karkar^{ki}-me, "*Iba'a*, supervised by *á-ni*-x-x, (and) {other workers}, men from Karkar," 559:16, 25, 28

i-dì-èr-ra

1. Deliveries: Grains

5.0.0. zíz gur 0.3.3. kib$_x$ ì-dub a-šà mí-mí ki ***i-dì-èr-ra***-ta ur-^{d}dumu-zi šu ba-ti, "Ur-Dumuzi received 5 bushels of emmer wheat (and) 210 liters of wheat of the granary of the Mimi field from *Iddi-Erra*," 1235:1–6

i-din-a-bu-um

1. *Iddin-abum*, Man from Karkar

[1] ***i-din-a-bu-um*** (. . .) ugula *[šu]-la-núm* (. . .) lú-karkar^{ki}-me, "*Iddin-abum*, supervised by *Šulanum*, (and) {other workers}, men from Karkar," 559:4, 12, 28

2. ***Iddin-abum***, **Title Unspecified**

2.1 **Receipts: From *Adad-tilllati***

2.1.1 **Jugs**

2? ^{dug}*ku-kur-rú* ki ^{d}*adad-tillati*-[ta] ***i-din-a-bu-um*** šu ba-an-ti, "*Iddin-abum* received 2? *kukurru* jugs from *Adad-tillati*," 1267:1–4

2.1.2 **Ordinary Beer Bread**

2 gú báppir-gen ki ^{d}*adad-tillati*-ta ***i-din-a-bu-um*** šu ba-ti, "*Iddin-abum* received 2 talents of ordinary beer bread from *Adad-tillati*," 1210:1–4

3. ***Šu-Adad***, **the Man of *Iddin-abum***

3.1 **Receipts of *Šu-Adad*: Pots from *Adad-tillati***

3 ^{dug}ḪI?-x-[. . .] ki ^{d}*adad-tillati*-ta *šu*-^{d}*adad* lú-***i-din-a-bu-um*** [šu] ba-an-ti, "*Šu-Adad*, the man of *Iddin-abum*, received 3 [. . .] pots from *Adad-tillati*," 1268:1–4

i-din-^{d}adad

1. **Deliveries: House Bitumen**

0.1.0 ésir-é-a ki ***i-din-^{d}adad***-ta *ḫu-lu-lu* dumu *da-d*[*a-a*] šu ba-a[n-ti], "*Ḫululu*, the son of *Dada'a*, received 60 liters of house bitumen from *Iddin-Adad*," 1257:1–5

2. **Possessions of *Iddin-Adad***

é-du$_6$-gur$_4$-***i-din-^{d}adad***, "the round-hill-house of *Iddin-Adad*" > *Household Index*

2.1 **His Tablet**

1 *ḫi-lu-a* dub ***i-din-^{d}adad*** nibru^{ki}-šè de$_6$-a, "*Ḫilua* having brought the tablet of *Iddin-Adad* to Nippur," 33:44, 34:'18, 35:47, 36:42, 39:44, 40:42

i-din-é-a

Iddin-Ea, Overseer of Hired Workers

1. **Deliveries: Bricks, under the Authority of *Bazi***

73⅓ sar šeg$_{12}$ NE-gu$_7$-bi íb-ta-zi mu-DU ***i-din-é-a*** ugula lú-ḫuĝ-ĝá ĝìri *ba-zi*, "73⅓ sar of bricks, the damaged bricks were deducted. Delivery of *Iddin-Ea*, overseer of hired workers, under the authority of *Bazi*," 315:1–5

i-din-èr-ra

1. **Translation Uncertain**

še-gán-bi 36.1.0. še gur 11.1.0. zíz gur lá-ìa su-ga še gu$_4$ e-na-am-DU ur-^{d}dumu-zi ù ***i-din-èr-ra*, "Their barley of the field: 36 bushels (and) 60 liters of barley (and) 11 bushels (and) 60 liters of emmer wheat; the remainder was replaced. Ur-Dumuzi and *Iddin-Erra* (?) barley and oxen," 1233:8–11

i-din-^{d}*šamaš*

1. *Iddin-Šamaš*, the Fish-sauce Manufacturer

1.1 Receipts: Ingredients for Fish-sauce

0.0.4. Ú.KUR 0.2.0. gazi 2 gú ki-lá šeg$_{12}$-mun-sig$_{5}$ mu ku$_{6}$ al-ús-sa-šè 10 ^{gi}ḫal-^{geš}ḫašḫur ***i-din-***^{d}***šamaš*** lú-ùr-ra šu ba-ti (. . .) iti u$_{5}$-bí-gu$_{7}$ (. . .) úgu-a g̃á-g̃á ga-ga-ra-a ki ^{d}*adad-tillati*-ta ⸢ba⸣-zi "In month 4, *Iddin-Šamaš*, the fish-sauce manufacturer, received from *Adad-tillati* 40 liters of Ú.KUR, 120 liters of gazi (and) a brick of fine salt weighing 2 talents for fish-sauce (and) 10 apple wood baskets, (and) {other disbursals}, the total placed in the account," 1162:'37–'43, '50, '66–'70

0.0.3. gín [. . .] 0.1.0. [. . .] 2 sìla ^{ú}gámun [. . .] 6 gú ki-lá mun-sig$_{5}$ mu ku$_{6}$ al-ús-sa-šè ***i-din-***^{d}***šamaš*** lú-ùr-ra [šu ba(-an)-ti] ki ^{d}*adad-tillati*-ta ba-zi, "*Iddin-Šamaš*, the fish-sauce manufacturer, received 30 shekels [. . .], 60 [. . .], 2 liters of cumin [. . .] (and) fine salt weighing 6 talents for fish-sauce from *Adad-tillati*," 1178:1–9

2. *Iddin-Šamaš*, Title Unspecified

2.1 Provisions

⅓ sìla mu[n-ta] 6 gín luḫ-lá-[ta] g̃ìri *ì-lí*-[. . .] 1 *ad-da-ni* 1 *bi-za-tum* 1 ***i-din-***^{d}***šamaš*** 1 *in-ga-la* 1 *be-lí-a-sú* níta-me-éš, "⅓ liter of salt [each] (and) 6 shekels of luḫ-lá [each] under the authority of *Ili*-[. . .], (provisions for) *Adani*, *Bizatum*, *Iddin-Šamaš*, *Ingala* (and) *Beli-asu*, the men," 562:'31–'39

i-gi-zu-tum

1. Under his Authority: Reeds for the (Enclosure) Wall

660 sa gi-[izi] gu-níg̃in [n sa-ta] gi-sal-[x] bàd-šè g̃ìri ***i-gi-zu-tum*** ki ^{d}*adad-tillati*-⸢ta⸣ ba-zi, "Under the authority of *Igizutum*, *Adad-tillati* disbursed 660 bundles of [fuel] reeds, bales of [n bundle(s) each], [x] thin reeds for the (enclosure) wall," 1316:1–6

i-ku-nu-um

1. Under his Authority: Delivery of *Išdum-kin*, Receipt of *Adad-tillati*

1.1 Date Palm Spines and a Rope

3 peš-[múrgu] 1 éš má g[íd. . .] ki *išdum-ki-*[*in*-ta] ^{d}*adad-tillati* šu ba-an-ti u$_{4}$ g̃eš ùr i-im-de$_{6}$-a [g̃ìri] ***i-ku-nu-um***, "[Under the authority of] *Ikunum*, *Adad-tillati* received 3 date palm spines, (and) 1 rope (for?) towing a boat from *Išdum-kin* when the roof beams were brought," 1306:1–7

1.2 Wood

180 g̃eš ùr ásal 180 ^{geš}é-da ásal 130 ^{geš}eme-sig al-dúb-ba [ki *iš*]*dum-ki-in*-ta $^{[d]}$*adad-tillati* šu ba-an-ti ⸢g̃ìri⸣ ***i-ku-nu-um***, "Under the authority of *Ikunum*, *Adad-tillati* received 180 poplar roof beams, 180 poplar joists (and) 130 extracted planks from *Išdum-kin*," 1303:1–7

i-la-ak-nu-id

1. *Ilak-nu''id*, Man from *Tulium*

1.1 As an Runaway

zàḫ ***i-la-ak-*[*nu-id*]** zàḫ *šu-kà-*[*kà*] lú-*tu-lí-um*[^{ki}-me-éš], "*Ilak-*[*nu''id*] (and) *Šu-kaka*, runaways from *Tulium*," 378:1–3

1.2 Provisions

[2 sìla] ninda-ta [1 ***i*]*-la-ak-nu-id*** 1 *šu-kà-kà* lú-*tu-lí-um*^{ki} (. . .) šà-gal ši[dim-e-n]e ⌜u$_4$⌝ [bàd egir] é-a dù-dè, "[2 liters] of bread each (for) *Ilak-nu''id* (and) *Šu-kaka*, men from *Tulium*, (and for) {other workers}, food (for) builders when they were constructing [the (enclosure) wall behind] the house," 386:1–4, 29–30

2. *Ilak-nu''id*, Title Unspecified

2.1 Ordered to Give Barley to the Workers

i-la-ak-nu-id ù-na-a-du$_{11}$ 5.1.4. še gur še-ba éren-na *šu-*^{d}nin-in-[si ḫé-na]-ab-[sum-m]u, "Say to *Ilak-nu''id* that '5 bushels (and) 100 liters of barley, barley rations of the workers, should be given to *Šu*-Nininsi,'" 1043:1–6

i-me-èr-ra

1. *Im-Erra*, the Ox-Herder, Supervised by *Babani*, the Majordomo

1.1 Ox-drivers from his Gang

n g̃uruš (ugula) ***i-me-èr-ra*** nu-bànda-gu$_4$ (. . .) (šà-gu$_4$-me-éš ugula) *ba-ba-ni* šabra, "n workmen (from the gang of) *Im-Erra*, the ox-herder, (and) {other gangs}, (ox-drivers supervised by) *Babani*, the majordomo," 184:4–6, 185:3–5, 186:3–5, 187:3–4, 189:3, 5, 190:3, 7, 191:4, 10

2 g̃uruš ***i-me-èr-ra*** nu-bànda-gu$_4$ (. . .) šà-gu$_4$-me-éš (. . .) ugula *ba-ba-ni* šabra, "2 workmen (from the gang of) *Im-Erra*, the ox-herder, (and) {other gangs}, ox-drivers (and) {hired workers} supervised by *Babani*, the majordomo," 193:3, 7, 9, 197:3, 8, 11

2 g̃uruš ***i-me-èr-ra*** nu-bànda-gu$_4$ (. . .) [šà-gu$_4$]-me-éš [árad-é]-a-me-éš (. . .) ugula *ba-ba-ni* šabra, "2 workmen (from the gang of) *Im-Erra*, the ox-herder, (and) {other gangs}, ox-drivers—household servants—(and) {hired workers} supervised by *Babani*, the majordomo," 194:3, 7–8, 15

1.2 Runaways from his Gang

zàḫ AN.ŠUM.TAG.KAL (nu-bànda-gu$_4$) zàḫ *puzur$_4$-šu-ba* (nu-bànda-gu$_4$) ***i-me-èr-ra*** nu-bànda-gu$_4$ ugula *ba-ba-ni* šabra, "AN.ŠUM.TAG.KAL, (the ox-herder), (and) *Puzur-Šuba*, (the ox-herder), runaways (from the gang of) *Im-Erra*, the ox-herder, (ox-drivers) supervised by *Babani*, the majordomo," 185:31–34, 191:35–38, 192:'23–'26, 194:64–67, 196:'34–'37, 197:43–46

zàḫ [*šu*?]-^{d}*i-šum* zàḫ [*p*]*ù-*[*zu*]*r$_8$-šu-ba* [***i-me-èr-ra***] nu-bànda-gu$_4$ [ugula *ba-ba-ni*] šabra, "[*Šu*?]-*Išum* (and) *Puzur-šuba*, runaways (from the gang of) [*Im-Erra*], the ox-herder, (ox-drivers) [supervised by *Babani*], the majordomo," 198:'41–'44

2. *Im-Erra*, Title Unspecified

2.1 Deliveries: Barley Rations for Servants

3.3.1.5 sìla še še-ba géme-árad ki ***i-mé-èr-ra***-ta ^{d}*adad-tillati* šu ba-ti ⌜g̃iri⌝ *a-ḫu-wa-*[*qar*] dub-[sar] a-šà *dì-im-bu-*[*na*]-^{aš}aš$_7$-gi$_4$^{ki}, "Under the authority of *Aḫu-waqar*, the scribe,

Adad-tillati received from *Im-Erra* 3 bushels (and) 195 liters of barley, barley rations of female and male servants at the *Dimbun*-Ašgi field," 527:1–7

i-mi-iq-^{d}šul-gi

1. Receipts: Workmen in G̃irsu and Requisitions

^{d}*a*[*dad-till*]*ati* ù-n[a-a]-du$_{11}$ 3 g̃uruš ḫi-a sag̃-dub g̃ír-su^{ki}-šè ù níg̃-dab$_{5}$ zà-mu-bi ***i-mi-iq-***^{d}**šul-gi** [ḫé]-na-ab-sum-mu, "Say to *Adad-tillati* that '3 various full-time workmen in G̃irsu and the requisitions at the beginning of its year should be given to *Imiq*-Šulgi,'" 1038:1–7

i-ri-ib

Irib, Overseer of Household Servants

1. Overseer of Builders

[3] g̃uruš šidim [ugula] ***i-ri-ib*** (. . .) [árad-é-a-me-éš], "[3] builders, [household servants supervised by] *Irib*," 55:4, 6

2. Overseer of Household Servants

n g̃uruš ugula ***i-ri-ib*** árad-é-a-me-éš, "n workmen, household servants supervised by *Irib*," 13:8–9, 14:4–5, 15:4–5, 16:3–5, 17:4–5, 18:4–5, 19:6–8, 20:3–4, 6, 21:4, 6, 22:4, 6, 23:3, 5, 24:4, 6, 30:4, 6, 31:4, 6, 32:4, 6, 33:4, 6, 34:4, 6, 35:4, 6, 36:5–6, 37:5–6, 38:5–6, 39:5–6, 40:5–6, 41:5–6, 42:5–6, 43:5–6, 44:5–6, 45:5–6, 47:5–6, 48:6–7, 49:5–6, 51:5–6, 52:5–6, 53:5–6, 56:4, 6, 57:4, 6, 58:4, 6, 59:4, 6, 60:4, 6, 61:4, 6, 63:4, 6, 71:4, 6, 73:4–5

3. The Explained Absence of Workers Supervised by *Irib*

3.1 Baking Bread and Being Sick

1 *lu-kà-dum* ninda du$_{8}$-dè gub-ba 1 *ta-tù-ri* dú-ra ugula ***i-ri-ib***, "*Lukadum* employed to bake bread (and) *Tatturi* having been sick, (workmen) supervised by *Irib*," 41:'27–'29

1 šeš-kal-la dú-[ra] 1 *lu-kà-dum* ninda du$_{8}$-dè gub-⌜ba⌝ ugula ***i-ri-ib***, "Šeš-kala having been sick (and) *Lukadum* employed to bake bread, (workmen) supervised by *Irib*," 57:'27–'30

1 *lu-kà-dum* ninda du$_{8}$-dè gub-ba 1 šeš-kal-la dú-ra ugula ***i-ri-ib***, "*Lukadum* employed to bake bread (and) Šeš-kala having been sick, (workmen) supervised by *Irib*," 58:66–68, 59:54–57, 60:50–53, 62:'12–'15, 71:36–38, 73:'17–'19

3.2 Bringing Messages, Baking Bread, and Being Sick

1 *ḫi-lu-a* á-ág̃ g̃ír-su^{ki}-šè de$_{6}$-a 1 *lu-kà-du-um* ninda du$_{8}$-dè gub-ba 1 *be-lí-a-sú* dú-ra ugula ***i-ri-ib***, "*Ḫilua* having brought a message to G̃irsu, *Lukadum* employed to bake bread, (and) *Beli-asu* having been sick, (workmen) supervised by *Irib*," 27:'18–'20, 28:'29–'31, 29:'34–'36

1 é-ì-gára á-ág̃(-g̃á) nibru^{ki}-šè ki *šu-kab-ta*-šè de$_{6}$-a 1 *lu-kà-dum* ninda du$_{8}$-dè gub-ba 1 *be-lí-a-sú* dú-ra ugula ***i-ri-ib***, "E'igara having brought a message to *Šu-Kabta* in Nippur, *Lukadum* employed to bake bread (and) *Beli-asu* having been sick, (workmen) supervised by *Irib*," 31:40–42, 32:39–41

3.2.1 And Transporting Barley

1 *ḫi-lu-a* 1 é-ì-gára á-ág̃ ki *šu-e*[*š*$_{4}$*-tár*-šè] de[$_{6}$-a] 1 *a-lí-aḫ* še è-dè g̃ír-su^{ki}-šè g̃en-na 1 šeš-kal-la 1 *lu-kà-dum* ku$_{6}$-sim sa$_{10}$-sa$_{10}$-dè gú-ab-ba^{ki}-šè g̃en-na 1 *ta-tù-ri* dú-ra

ugula ***i-ri-ib***, "*Ḫilua* (and) E'igara having brought a message to the place of *Šu-Eštar*, *Ali-aḫ* having gone to G̃irsu to bring out barley, Šeš-kala (and) *Lukadum* having gone to Gu'abba to purchase flying fish (and) *Tatturi* having been sick, (workmen) supervised by *Irib*," 37:31–41

[1] é-ì-gára 1 *ḫi-lu-a* 1 á-ág̃ ki *šu-eš$_{4}$-tár*-[šè] de$_{6}$-a 1 *a-lí-*⌜*aḫ*⌝ še è-dè [g̃ír-su^{ki}]-šè g̃en-[na] 1 šeš-kal-la 1 *lu-kà-dum* ku$_{6}$-sim sa$_{10}$-sa$_{10}$-dè gú-ab-ba^{ki}-šè de$_{6}$-a 1 *ta-tù-ri* dú-ra 1 *ar-ri-az* dú-ra ugula ***i-ri-ib***, "E'igara (and) *Ḫilua* having brought a message to the place of *Šu-Eštar*, *Ali-aḫ* having gone to [G̃irsu] to bring out barley, Šeš-kala (and) *Lukadum* having gone to Gu'abba to purchase flying fish (and) *Tatturi* (and) *Arriaz* having been sick, (workmen) supervised by *Irib*," 38:37–47

3.2.2 And Transporting Tablets

[1 é-ì-gára á-ág̃ nibru]^{ki}-šè [ki *šu-kab*]-*ta*-šè de$_{6}$-[a 1 *ḫi-lu-a* dub *i*]-*din-*^{d}*adad* EN.[LÍL^{ki}]-šè de$_{6}$-[a 1 *lu*]-*kà-dum* ninda du$_{8}$-dè g[ub-ba 1 *be*]-*lí-a-sú* dú-ra ugula ***i-***[***ri-ib***], "[E'igara] having brought [a message] to *Šu-Kabta* in [Nippur, *Ḫilua*] having brought [the tablet] of *Iddin-Adad* to Nippur, *Lukadum* employed to bake bread (and) *Beli-asu* having been sick, (workmen) supervised by *Irib*," 34:'17–'20

1 é-ì-gára á-ág̃ ki *šu-kab-ta*-šè de$_{6}$-a 1 *ḫi-lu-a* dub *i-din-*^{d}*adad* nibru^{ki}-šè de$_{6}$-a 1 *lu-k*[*à-d*]*um* ninda du$_{8}$-dè gub-ba 1 *be*-[*lí*]-*a-zu* 1 *e-pe-eš* ^{na}nam!?<-dú?-ra?> ugula ***i-***[***ri***]***-ib***, "E'igara having brought a message to the place of *Šu-Kabta*, *Ḫilua* having brought the tablet of *Iddin-Adad* to Nippur, *Lukadum* employed to bake bread (and) *Beli-asu*, satisfying the allowance of sick leave, (workmen) supervised by *Irib*," 36:41–45

3.3 Purchasing Flying Fish and Being Sick

1 šeš-kal-la 1 *lu-kà-dum* [ku$_{6}$-si]m sa$_{10}$-sa$_{10}$-dè gú-ab-ba^{ki}-š[è g̃]en-na 1 *ta-tù-ri* dú-ra ugula ***i-ri-ib***, "Šeš-kala (and) *Lukadum* having gone to Gu'abba to purchase flying fish, (and) *Tatturi* having been sick, (workmen) supervised by *Irib*," 49:60–64

3.4 Sick and Runaway Workmen from his Gang

1 g̃uru[š zà]ḫ ugula ***i-ri-ib***, "1 runaway workman supervised by *Irib*," 19:17

[n] g̃uruš šidim dú-[ra n] g̃uruš zàḫ ugula ***i-ri-***[***ib***], "[n] sick builder(s) (and) [n] runaway workmen supervised by *Irib*," 20:35–36

1 *be-lí-a-sú* dú-ra ugula ***i-ri-ib***, "*Beli-asu*, the sick workman, supervised by *Irib*," 27:'20, 28:'31, 31:40, 32:41, 34:'20, 35:50

1 *be-*[*lí*]*-a-zu* 1 *e-pe-eš* ^{na}nam!?<-dú?-ra?> ugula ***i-***[***ri***]***-ib***, "*Beli-asu*, 1 (workman) satisfying the allowance of sick leave, supervised by *Irib*," 36:44–45

[. . . 1 šeš]-kal-l[a dú-ra ugu]la ***i-ri-***[***ib***], "[. . . (and)] Šeš-kala, the sick workman, (workers) supervised by *Irib*," 61:'13–'14

3.5 Various Tasks

1 *šu-*^{d}*belum* á-ág̃ ki *šu-kab-ta*-šè g̃en-na 1 é-ì-gára é-^{d}*šu-*^{d}*suen*^{ki}-ta siki tùm-dè g̃en-na 1 *ḫi-lu-a* [dub *i-din-*^{d}*adad*] nibru^{ki}-š[è de$_{6}$-a] zàḫ lugal-[ḫa-ma-ti] 1 *lu-kà-d*[*um* ninda du$_{8}$-dè gub-ba] 1 *t*[*a-tù-ri* dú-ra] ⌜ugula⌝ ***i-r***[***i-ib***], "*Šu-Belum* having brought a message to the place of *Šu-Kabta*, E'igara having gone to bring wool from *Bit-Šu-Suen*, *Ḫilua* [having brought the tablet of *Iddin-Adad*] to Nippur, Lugal-ḫamati, the runaway, *Lukadum* [employed to bake bread] (and) *Tatturi* [having been sick], (workmen) supervised by *Irib*," 40:38–47

1 *i-ṭib-ší-na-at* 1 é-ì-gára á-áĝ [ki] *šu-kab-tá*-ta [d]e$_6$-a [1 *ḫi*]-*lu-a* á-áĝ *šu-eš$_4$-tár* [ù-d]ag-ga^{ki}-šè de$_6$-a [1] *a-lí-aḫ* še [UD].DU [ĝír]-su^{ki}-šè ĝen-[na 1] *šu-^{d}belum* á-áĝ [ki] *a-ḫu-wa-qar* lú-du$_6$-lugal-[pa-UD].DU^{ki}-šè de$_6$-[a 1 ur-ša]-lu-ḫi šidim [dú-ra . . .-d]è [1 *ta-tù*]-*ri* d[ú-ra 1 *šu*]-*eš$_4$-tár* ugula ***i-r*[*i-ib*]**, "*Iṭibšinat* (and) E'igara having brought a message from the place of *Šu-Kabta, Ḫilua* having brought a message to *Šu-Eštar* in Udaga, *Ali-aḫ* having gone to Ĝirsu to bring out barley, *Šu-Belum* having brought a message to the place of *Aḫu-waqar*, the man from Du-lugal-pa'e, Ur-šaluḫi, the builder, [having been sick, . . .], *Tatturi* having been sick, (and) *Šu-Eštar*, (workmen) supervised by *Irib*," 45:22–33

1 é-ì-gára á-áĝ ki *šu-kab-ta*-šè de$_6$-a 1 *ḫi-lu-a* á-áĝ *šu-eš$_4$-tár* ù-dag-ga^{ki}-šè de$_6$-a 1 *šu-^{d}belum* á-áĝ ki *a-ḫu-wa-qar* lú-du$_6$-lugal-pa-è^{ki} de$_6$-a 1 *a-lí-aḫ* še è ĝír-su^{ki}-šè ĝen-na 1 šeš-kal-la 1 *lu-kà-dum* ku$_6$-sim sa$_{10}$-sa$_{10}$-dè gú-ab-ba^{ki}-šè ĝen-na 1 *ta-tù-ri* dú-ra ugula ***i-ri-ib***, "E'igara having brought a message to the place of *Šu-Kabta, Ḫilua* having brought a message to *Šu-Eštar* in Udaga, *Šu-Belum* having brought a message to the place of *Aḫu-waqar*, the man from Du-lugal-pa'e, *Ali-aḫ* having gone to Ĝirsu to bring out barley, Šeš-kala (and) *Lukadum* having gone to Gu'abba to purchase flying fish, (and) *Tatturi* having been sick, (workmen) supervised by *Irib*," 47:53–63, 48:58–70

1 [*šu*]-^{d}nin-kar-ak dub [^{d}*m*]*a-lik-ba-ni* é-[da]-na^{ki}-šè de$_6$-a zàḫ [PN 1 x]-ga?-x ⌜dú⌝-ra [1 *lu*]-*kà*-⌜*dum*⌝ ninda du$_8$-⌜dè⌝ gub-ba 1 lug[al-ḫ]a-ma-ti á-á[ĝ ši]dim-e-ne ĝír-su$^{[ki]}$-šè de$_6$-a ugula ***i-ri-ib***, "*Šu*-Ninkarak having brought the tablet of *Malik-bani* to Edana, [PN] the runaway, [PN] having been sick, Lukadum employed to bake bread, (and) Lugal-ḫamati having brought a message concerning builders to Ĝirsu, (workmen) supervised by *Irib*," 52:60–70

3.6 Broken Context

[. . . ugula ***i-r*]*i-ib***, 210:'39

4. Provisions for Workmen Supervised by *Irib*

4.1 Bread, Beer, and Soup

14 ĝuruš 1 sìla kaš ½ sìla ninda ⅓ sìla tu$_7$-ta ugula ***i-ri-ib*** (. . .) kaš-ninda ḫa-la-a? al-⌜tar⌝ gub-ba, "(For) 14 workmen: 1 liter of beer, ½ liter of bread (and) ⅓ liter of soup each, (workmen) supervised by *Irib*, (and) {provisions for other workers}, beer and bread rations divided (for workers) employed (for) construction," 379:2–3, 20

4.2 Semolina, Bread, and Dates

[1 ĝuru]š ugula 2 sìla ninda-dabin 2 sìla zú-lum 10 ĝuruš 1 sìla ninda 2-sìla zú-lum-ta ugula ***i-ri-ib*** (. . .) ḫa-la-a ĝuruš árad-é-a-e-[ne], "(For) [1] overseer: 2 liters of semolina bread (and) 2 liters of dates; (for) 10 workmen: 1 liter of bread (and) 2 liters of dates each, (workmen) supervised by *Irib*, (and) {provisions for other workers} divided (for) household servants," 402:1–3, 17

5. As a Witness

igi ***i-ri-bu-um***,[37] "witnessed by *Iribum*," 1049:14, 1050:14

[37] Possibly a fuller writing of the name *Irib*.

i-sú-a-ri-iq

1. ***Isu-ariq*, the Cupbearer**

1.1 **As a Witness**

igi ***i-sú-a-ri-iq***, "witnessed by *Isu-ariq*," 1062:11[38]

igi ***i-sú-a-ri-iq*** sagi, "witnessed by *Isu-ariq*, the cupbearer," 1063:7, 1064:8

1.2 **Receipts**

1.2.1 **Bronze from *Adad-tillati***

(. . .) ki-a-n[ag *š*]*u-kab-ta* ki ^{d}*adad-tillati*-ta ***i-sú-a-ri-iq*** šu ba-ti, "*Isu-ariq* received {bronze vessels} of the funerary libation place of *Šu-Kabta* from *Adad-tillati*," 977:'8–'10

(. . .) ki ^{d}*adad-tillati*-ta ***i-sú-a-ri-iq*** sagi šu ba-ti g̃ìri ^{d}*ma-lik-ba-ni*, "*Isu-ariq*, the cupbearer, received {bronze vessels} from *Adad-tillati* under the authority of *Malik-bani*," 1337:8–11

1.2.2 **Copper and Silver from *Šu-Adad***

3 ^{urudu}ḫa-zi-in 2 ma-na-ta ki *šu-*^{d}*adad-*[ta ***i***]***-s***[***ú-a-ri-iq***] š[u b]a-⸢ti⸣, "*Isu-ariq* received 3 copper axes of 2 minas each from *Šu-Adad*," 1283:1–4

1 gal kù-babbar ½ ma-na 5½ gín 1 gal ka-balag-a-bar?? kù-babbar 19 gín $^{g̃eš}$gu-za *šu-*[*kab*]*-tá-*šè ki *šu-*^{d}*adad*-ta ***i-sú-a-rí-iq*** šu ba-ti, "*Isu-ariq* received 1 large silver cup (weighing) ½ mina (and) 5½ shekels (and) 1 large silver ka-balag-a-bar cup (weighing) 19 shekels for the chair of *Šu-Kabta* from *Šu-Adad*," 1339:1–6

2. ***Isu-ariq*, Man from Karkar**

1 [***i-sú***]***-a-rí-íq*** (. . .) ugula *á-ni*-x-x (. . .) lú-karkar^{ki}-me, "*Isu-ariq*, supervised by *á-ni*-x-x, (and) {other workers}, men from Karkar," 559:17, 25, 28

i-ṣur-^{d}***suen***

1. ***Iṣur-Suen*, the Scribe**

1.1 **As a Deputy: Basket for Tablets**

1 ^{gi}bisag̃-im-sar-ra sa-ḫa ⅔ kùš íb-sá im-sar g̃á-g̃á-dè ***i-ṣur-***^{d}***suen*** dub-sar maškim ⸢zi⸣-ga ⸢*šu*⸣?-*x-ki?-ra?-ta?-ni?* [ki] ^{d}*adad-tillati*-ta ⸢ba⸣-zi, "*Adad-tillati* disbursed 1 canvas-lined clay tablet coffer—it is ⅔ kùš square—(in which) to deposit clay tablets. (It was) the expenditure of [PN]. *Iṣur-Suen*, the scribe, was the deputy," 1365:1–7

1.2 **Under his Authority: Textile and Wool Rations**

(. . .) túg-ba siki-ba géme-árad *simat-*^{d}K[A.DI] ki ^{d}*adad-tillati*-ta ba-zi g̃ìri ***i-ṣur-***^{d}***suen*** dub-sar, "Under the authority of *Iṣur-Suen*, the scribe, *Adad-tillati* disbursed {assorted textiles and wool}, the textile and wool rations of the female and male servants of *Simat-Ištaran*," 795:5–9

---

[38] Title implied from parallel texts.

2. *Iṣur-Suen*, Title Unspecified

2.1 Deliveries: Assorted Grains and Containers, Receipt of *Malik-bani*

(. . .) ki ***i-ṣur-^{d}suen***-ta ^{d}*ma-lik-ba-ni* šu ba-an-ti, "*Malik-bani* received {assorted grains and containers} from *Iṣur-Suen*," 1068:7–9, 1074:9–11, 1075:7–9

0.0.5.7 sìla zì-gu-sig$_5$ 0.2.5.4 sìla zì-gu 6 dug 0.0.3.-ta ki ***i-ṣur-^{d}suen***-ta ^{d}*ma-lik-ba-ni* šu ba-an-ti g̃iri *la-ma-súm*, "Under the authority of *Lamasum*, *Malik-bani* received 57 liters of fine gu-flour, 174 liters of gu-flour (and) 6 jugs of 30-liters each from *Iṣur-Suen*," 1069:1–7

(. . .) ki ***i-ṣur-^{d}suen***-ta ^{d}*ma-lik-ba-ni* <šu ba-ti> g̃iri *šu*-^{d}nisaba maškim, "Under the authority of *Šu*-Nisaba, the deputy, *Malik-bani* <received> {assorted grains and containers} from *Iṣur-Suen*," 1072:9–11

2.2 Under his Authority: Craftsmen Released on the Day of the Wool Rations

(. . .) [u$_4$-1-šè] ⸢u$_4$⸣ siki-ba-ka šu bar-⸢ra⸣ g̃iri ***i-ṣur-^{d}suen*** zi-ga *tá-ki-il-ì-lí-ís*-[*sú* ki ^{d}]*adad-tillati*-[ta ba]-⸢zi⸣, "Under the authority of *Iṣur-Suen*, *Adad-tillati* disbursed {craftsmen} released [for 1 day] on the day of the wool rations. (It was) the expenditure of *Takil-ilissu*," 280:17–23

i-ṭib-ší-na-at

Iṭibšinat, the Household Servant from the Gang of *Irib*

1. Errands: Bringing a Message to *Šu-Kabta*

1 ***i-ṭib-ší-na-at*** 1 é-ì-gára á-ág̃ ki *šu-kab-tá*-šè de$_6$-a, "*Iṭibšinat* (and) E'igara having brought a message to the place of *Šu-Kabta*," 43:'43–'44, 44:41–43, 46:'39–'41

1 ***i-ṭib-ší-na-at*** 1 é-ì-gára á-ág̃ [ki] *šu-kab-tá*-ta ⸢de$_6$⸣-a, "*Iṭibšinat* (and) E'igara having brought a message from the place of *Šu-Kabta*," 45:22–23

ì-lí-a-núm

1. Deliveries: Ropes, Receipt of *Adad-tillati*

200 ^{gi}dur-dag̃al a-rá-3-tab-ba gíd 5 nindan-ta 300 ^{gi}dur-gazi a-rá-3-tab-ba gíd 1½ nindan-ta 1800 ^{gi}dur-gazi a-rá-2-tab-ba gíd 1½ nindan-ta ki ***ì-lí-a-núm***-ta ^{d}*adad-tillati* šu ba-an-ti g̃iri *ìl-su-ba-ni* ^{lú}kaš$_4$, "Under the authority of *Ilsu-bani*, the runner, *Adad-tillati* received from *Ili-Anum* 200 30-meter 3-ply wide ropes, 300 9-meter 3-ply gazi ropes, (and) 1800 9-meter 2-ply gazi ropes," 1291:1–7

ì-lí-an-dul

1. *Ili-andul*, the Scribe

1.1 Testifying

★★0.0.1.1 sìla ì-g̃eš ⸢lá⸣-ìa šà ì-g̃eš 2.0.0. gur-kam gar-ša-an-na^{ki}-ta nibru^{ki}-šè in-de$_9$-ša-a ***ì-⸢lí⸣-an-dùl*** dub-sar [*a*]-*na*-⸢*aḫ*⸣-*ì-lí* ašgab [x-*r*]*a*?-*ra-am* ú ga$_6$-[g̃á . . .] ka-ga-na-ne-ne ba-ge-en, "*Ili-andul*, the scribe, (and) *Anaḫ-ili*, the leather worker, confirmed they brought 11 liters of sesame oil, the remainder of 2 bushels from Garšana to Nippur, (?) and (?)," 1062:1–9

2. *Ili-andul*, Title Unspecified

2.1 Deliveries

2.1.1 Beer: Reciept of *Aštaqqar*

5 sìla kaš-sig$_5$ ki ***ì-lí-an-dùl***-ta *aš-tá-qar* šu ba-ti, "*Aštaqqar* received 5 liters of fine beer from *Ili-andul*," 661:1–4

2.1.2 Grains: Receipt of *Adallal*

(. . .) ki ***ì-lí-an-dùl***-ta *a-da-làl* muḫaldim šu ba-ti, "*Adallal,* the cook, received {assorted grains} from *Ili-andul*," 1182:9–11

1.0.0 dabin ⸢gur⸣ 0.0.3. [. . . x]-ús ki ***ì-lí-an-dùl***-ta *a-da-làl* šu ba-ti, "*Adallal* received 1 bushel of semolina and 30 liters of 2nd-quality [. . .] from *Ili-andul*," 1186:1–5

2.1.3 Semolina: Receipt of *Anaḫ-ili*

0.0.1 dabin [ki] ***ì-lí-an-⸢dùl⸣***-ta *a-na-aḫ-ì-*[*lí*] šu ba-ti, "*Anaḫ-ili* received 10 liters of semolina from *Ili-andul*," 950:1–4

0.0.1 dabin mu kuš-šè ki ***ì-lí-an-dùl***-ta *a-na-aḫ-ì-lí* šu ba-ti, "*Anaḫ-ili* received 10 liters of semolina for (processing) skins from *Ili-andul*," 952:1–5

2.2 Receipts

2.2.1 Textiles from *Aštaqqar*

546 túg-⸢gen⸣[139] ***ì-lí-an-dùl*** ì-dab$_5$ [ki] *aš-tá-qar*-ta ba-zi, "*Ili-andul* took in charge 546 ordinary textiles from *Aštaqqar*," 1187:1–5

2.2.2 Broken Context

0.2.1.3⅓ sìla [. . . -g]en sa$_{10}$ ki-siki ½ [. . .]-kam ù é-^{d}[. . .] ***ì-lí-an-dùl* šu ba-ti ki ^{d}*adad-tillati*-ta [ba-z]i, "*Ili-andul* received from *Adad-tillati* 133⅓ liters of ordinary [. . .] the (?) price of ½ [. . .] and the [DN] temple," 1391:1–6

2.3 In the Possession of *Ili-andul*: Sesame and Peas

0.1.1 4½ sìla g̃eš-ì 6 sìla gú-tur *ì-lí-an-dùl* in-da-g̃ál, "74½ liters of sesame (and) 6 liters of peas are with *Ili-andul*," 1192:1–4

2.4 In Legal Texts

2.4.1 As a Witness

igi ***ì-lí-an-dùl***, "witnessed by *Ili-andul*," 1479:9

2.4.2 Testifying

0.3.1. [. . .] é-kišib-ba é-udu-[. . .] ***ì-lí-an-dùl* [. . .] ba-an-z[uḫ(-a)] ka-ga-na ba-a-[ge-en], "[. . .] in the storehouse, the sheep pen [. . .] *Ili-andul* [. . .] he stole it. He confirmed it," 1064:1–5

2.4.3 Broken Context

*****ì-lí-an-*[*dùl*]** gaba-ri dub [. . .] um-ma [. . .] 0.3.0. ⸢še⸣ 6 ma-na siki-⸢gen⸣ u$_4$ *ša-lim-a-ḫu-um* [. . .] nu-un-na-an-[. . .] in-na-RU-[. . .] ka-ga-na [ba-a]-[gen$_7$] x [. . .] ***ì-lí-an-*[*dùl*** . . .], 1052:1–10

---

139 A reading udu-⸢níta⸣ is also possible here. Neither restoration conforms to the expected pattern.

2.5. Other

2.5.1 Bringing a Tablet

1 (bùr) GÁNA zàr tab-ba nu-de$_5$-de$_5$-ga dub *šar-ru-um-ì-lí* ***ì-lí-an-dùl*** tùm-dam, "*Ili-andul* will bring *Šarrum-ili's* tablet (saying) that the sheaves stacked on 1 bur of acreage are not to be collected," 1398:1–6

2.5.2 Listed in Worker Inspection Accounts

[1 ***ì-lí***]***-an-dùl***, 36:50

2.6 Broken Context

ì-lí-an-d[***ùl*** . . .], 1393:1–2

ì-lí-aš-ra-ni

1. ***Ili-ašranni*, the Majordomo**

1.1 Deliveries: Flour and Semolina

1.0.0. [zì g]ur 0.2.0. dabin ki ***ì-lí-aš-ra-ni*** šabra-ta ^{d}*adad-tillati* šu ba-ti, "*Adad-tillati* received 1 bushel of [flour] (and) 120 liters of semolina from *Ili-ašranni*, the majordomo," 1144:1–5

2. ***Ili-ašranni*, the Porter**

2.1 Under the Authority of *Ili-ašranni*: Barley Wages

3.0.0. š[e gur] á lú-ḫuĝ-[ĝá] mu saḫar-šè ki *za-bu-la*-ta ^{d}*adad-tillati* šabra [šu b]a-ti ⌜ĝìri⌝ ***ì-lí-aš-ra-ni*** un-ga$_6$ [a-š]à sum-túl-túl, "Under the authority of *Ili-ašranni*, the porter, *Adad-tillati*, the majordomo, received 3 bushels of barley from *Zabula*, wages of hired workers for (moving?) dirt at the Sum-tultul field," 545:1–8

3. ***Ili-ašranni*, Overseer of Builders**

n ĝuruš šidim ugula ***ì-lí-aš-ra-ni***, "n builder(s) supervised by *Ili-ašranni*," 202:2–3, 203:3–4

4. ***Ili-ašranni*, Title Unspecified**

4.1 Deliveries

4.1.1 Receipt of *Adad-tillati*

4.1.1.1 Bread and Bread Baskets

0.4.3. ninda-šu-ra-ĝen 20-lá-1 ^{gi}ma-sá-ab ninda ki ***ì-lí-aš-ra-ni***-ta ^{d}*adad-tillati* šu ba-ti, "*Adad-tillati* received 270 liters of ordinary half (loaf) bread (and) 19 ma-sá-ab bread baskets from *Ili-ašranni*," 1135:1–5

4.1.1.2 Fattened Oxen

2 gu$_4$-niga iti u$_4$-5-ba-zal ki ***ì-lí-aš-ra-ni***-ta ^{d}*adad-tillati* ì-dab$_5$, "At the end of the 5th day of the month *Adad-tillati* took in charge 2 fattened oxen from *Ili-ašranni*," 1125:1–5

4.1.1.3 Grains

3.0.0. zíz [gur] 2.0.0. kib$_x$ [gur ki] ***ì-lí-aš-ra***-[***ni***-ta^{d}*adad*]*-tillati* [šu ba]-ti, "*Adad-tillati* received 3 bushels of emmer wheat (and) 2 bushels of wheat from *Ili-ašranni*," 1197:1–5

2.2.1. še gur ki [***ì-lí-aš***]***-ra-ni***-ta ^{d}*adad-tillati* šu ba-an-ti, "*Adad-tillati* received 2 bushels (and) 130 liters of barley from *Ili-ašrani*," 1222:1–4

4.1.1.4 Ordered to Give Barley and Emmer

ì-lí-aš-ra-ni ù-na-a-du$_{11}$ 30.0.0. še gur 30.0.0. zíz gur ^{d}*adad-tillati* ḫé-na-ab-sum-mu kišib-ba-a-ni [šu] ḫa-ba-ab-ti-g̃e$_{26}$ [nam-m]i-gur-re, "Say to *Ili-ašranni* that '30 bushels of barley (and) 30 bushels of emmer wheat should be given to *Adad-tillati*. He should take his seal(ed tablet). He should not argue!'" 1039:1–9

4.1.2 Receipt of *Adallal*

[. . . ki] ***ì-lí-aš-r[a-ni]***-ta [*a*]-*da-làl* [šu ba-ti], "*Adallal* [received . . .] from *Ili-ašranni*," 1213:1–4

4.1.3 For Funerary Libations: A Sheep

1 udu-ú ki-a-nag-árad-^{d}nana ù *a-la-tum* ki ***ì-lí-aš-ra-ni***-ta ba-zi, "*Ili-ašranni* disbursed 1 range-fed sheep for the funerary libation place of *Arad*-Nanna and *Allatum*," 971:1–5

4.2. Receipts

4.2.1 From *Adad-tillati*

4.2.1.1 Assorted Commodities

[n.n].2.5? [sìla] še [gur n.n].4. [ZÌ].ŠE gur [n] sìla ì-šáḫ* [n] tuḫ-g̃eš-ì-ḫád [***ì***]-***lí-aš-ra-***[***ni***] šu ba-ti ki ^{d}*adad-tillati*-[ta b]a-⌜zi⌝, "*Ili-ašranni* received [n bushel(s)] and [n+]25? liters of barley, [n+]40 liters of semolina, [n] liter(s) of lard (and) [n liter(s)] of dry sesame chaff from *Adad-tillati*," 1196:1–8

3.4.2. dabin [gur] 0.4.5.5. sìla zì-[KAL] 2 dug 0.3.0-⌜ta⌝ ***ì-lí-aš-ra-ni*** šu ba-ti [ki] ^{d}[*adad-tillati*] ba-zi, "*Ili-ašranni* received 3 bushels (and) 260 liters of semolina, 295 liters of [KAL]-flour (and) 2 pots of 30-liters each from *Adad-tillati*," 1203:1–7

4.2.1.2 For Regular Offerings

(. . .) sá-du$_{11}$-šè ***ì-lí-aš-ra-ni*** šu ba-ti ki ^{d}*adad-tillati*-ta ba-zi, "*Ili-ašranni* received {assorted comestibles and other commodities} for regular offerings from *Adad-tillati*," 523:16–18

3 gú $^{g̃eš}$ma-nu šu aka sá-du$_{11}$-šè ***ì-lí-aš-ra-ni*** šu ba-ti ki ^{d}*adad*-[*tillati*-ta], "*Ili-ašranni* received 3 talents of processed manu wood for regular offerings from *Adad-tillati*," 1351:1–5

4.2.1.3 Workwomen and Sailors

1 [géme] sag̃-dub [***ì***]-***lí-aš-ra-ni*** ì-dab$_{5}$ ki ^{d}*adad-tillati*-ta ba-zi, "*Ili-ašranni* took in charge 1 full-time [workwoman] from *Adad-tillati*," 254:1–5

30 g̃uruš má-laḫ$_{5}$ u$_{4}$-1-šè ***ì-lí-aš-ra-ni*** ì-dab$_{5}$ ki ^{d}*adad-tillati*-ta ba-zi, "*Ili-ašranni* took in charge 30 sailors for 1 day from *Adad-tillati*," 269:1–6

4.2.2 From *Anaḫ-ili*: Shoes and a Textile Basket

5 ^{kuš}súḫub-gen é-ba-an 15 ^{kuš}súḫub-tur-gen é-ba-an 1 ^{gi}bisag̃ túg-aš ***ì-lí-aš-ra-ni*** šu ba-ti ki *a-na-aḫ-ì-lí*-ta ba-zi, "*Ili-ašranni* received 5 pairs of ordinary shoes, 15 pairs of ordinary small shoes (and) 1 single textile basket from *Anaḫ-ili*," 913:1–7

4.2.3 Provisions

0.0.2.5 <sìla> ***ì-lí-aš-ra-ni***, "25 <liters> (for) *Ili-ašranni*," 558:'3

ì-lí-bi-la-ni

1. *Ili-bilani*, the Animal Fattener

1.1 Animals in his Possession

lá-ìa 18 udu 8 u$_8$ 3 máš lá-ìa-àm ***ì-lí-bi-la-ni*** kurušda in-da-g̃ál, "The remainder of 18 sheep, 8 ewes (and) 3 goats are with *Ili-bilani*, the animal fattener," 1217:1–6

2. *Ili-bilani*, the Cook: His Balanced Account

(. . .) sá-du$_{11}$ ku$_5$-rá iti-6-kam [šu+níg̃in 10+]1.3.3.5 sìla še ninda gur [sag-níg̃]-gur$_{11}$-ra-kam [šà-b]i-ta (. . .) šu+nígin 15.0.3.4 sìla še ninda gur zi-ga-[àm] diri 3.1.5.[9 sìla gur gur] diri-[ga-àm . . . níg̃-kas$_7$]-aka [***ì-lí***]-***bi-la-ni*** muḫaldim, "{regular offerings of the gods}, deducted regular offerings of the 6th month—[in total:] 11 bushels (and) 215 liters of barley (for) bread—are the available assets. From among it: {barley rations and requisitions for various individuals}. In total: 15 bushels (and) 34 liters of barley (for) bread was expended. There are an additional 3 bushels (and) 109 liters. [. . .] The balanced account of *Ili-bilani*, the cook," 1527:8–13, 41–48

3. *Ili-bilani*, Title Unspecified

3.1 Deliveries

3.1.1 Assorted Animals

3.1.1.1 For Regular Offerings

1 udu abzu-šè 1 máš ká kù-^{d}inana-zabala$_4^{ki}$ u$_4$ ezem-gur-buru$_{14}$ g̃ìri nin-zi-šà-g̃ál 1 u$_8$ sá-du$_{11}$-^{d}inana-zabala$_4^{ki}$ 1 udu sá-du$_{11}$-^{d}šára sá-du$_{11}$-dig̃ir-re-ne ki ***ì-lí-bi-la-ni***-ta ba-zi, "*Ili-bilani* disbursed regular offerings of the gods: 1 sheep for the abzu, 1 goat for the gate of bright Inana of Zabala during the bushel harvest festival under the authority of Nin-zišag̃al, 1 ewe, regular offerings of Inana of Zabala (and) 1 sheep, regular offerings of Šara," 996:1–9

[1] ⸢udu⸣ sá-du$_{11}$-^{d}[. . .] 1 [udu] sá-du$_{11}$-^{d}en-[líl?] 1 udu sá-[du$_{11}$-^{d} . . .] 1 máš ^{d}nin-ḫur-sag̃-g̃á 1 máš ^{d}nin-^{d}si$_4$-an-na 1 sila$_4$ ^{d}inana-zabala$_4^{[ki]}$ ki ***ì-lí-bi-la-ni***-ta ba-zi, "*Ili-bilani* disbursed [1] sheep, regular offerings of [DN], 1 [sheep], regular offerings of Enlil, 1 sheep, regular offerings of [DN], 1 goat, regular offerings of Nin-ḫursag̃, 1 goat, regular offerings of Nin-siana (and) 1 lamb, regular offerings of Inana of Zabala," 1003:1–14

1 udu sá-du$_{11}$-^{d}inana-zabala$_4^{ki}$ 1 udu sá-du$_{11}$-^{d}šára-G̃EŠ.KÚŠU$^{[ki]}$ 1 máš alam-lugal 1 udu ⸢*ma*⸣-*la-ti* 3 udu nin-zi-šà-⸢g̃ál⸣ ki ***ì-lí-bi-la-ni***-ta ba-zi, "*Ili-bilani* disbursed 1 sheep, regular offerings of Inana of Zabala, 1 sheep, regular offerings of Šara of G̃EŠ.KÚŠU, 1 goat (for) the royal statue, 1 sheep (for) *Malati* (and) 3 sheep (for) Nin-zišagal," 1012:1–7

3.1.1.2 For *Tadin-Eštar*

1 udu *tá-din-eš$_4$-tár* 1 máš *š*[*a-at*?-x?]-ab-[x] ki ***ì-lí-bi-la-***[***ni***-ta] ba-zi, "*Ili-bilani* disbursed 1 sheep (for) *Tadin-Eštar* (and) 1 goat (for) *Šat*-[x]," 497:1–4

3.1.1.3 For *Ummi-Kabta*

3 udu 1 máš-ga šáḫ-g̃e$_6$ TAG$_4$.ALAM 2 udu-ú *um-mi-kab-tá* dumu-munus é-a ⸢ki⸣ ***ì-lí-bi-la-ni***-ta ba-zi, "*Ili-bilani* disbursed 3 sheep, 1 suckling goat, (1?) TAG$_4$.ALAM black pig (and) 2 range-fed sheep (for) *Ummi-Kabta*, daughter of the house," 421:1–5

3.1.1.4 For the Zabar-dab Official in ĜEŠ.KÚŠU

★★[n] máš-gal [UD.K]A.BAR-dab$_5$ 1? udu?-x-x-x šà ĜEŠ.KÚŠU^{ki} ki ***ì-lí-bi-la-ni***-ta ba-zi, "*Ili-bilani* disbursed [n] billy-goat(s) (for) the zabar-dab$_5$ official (and) 1? (?) sheep? in ĜEŠ.KÚŠU," 469:1–6

3.1.1.5 Receipt of *Adad-tillati*

10 ud$_5$ 1 ^{munus}áš-gàr 3 máš-gal 1 máš k[i ***ì-lí-b***]***í-la-***[***ni***]-ta ^{d}*adad-tillati* ì-dab$_5$, "*Adad-tillati* took in charge 10 female goats, 1 female kid, 3 billy-goats, (and) 1 male goat from *Ili-bilani*," 1519:1–7

3.1.1.6 Receipt of *Simu*

2 udu 5 máš-gal *si-mu* ì-dab$_5$ ki ***ì-lí-bi-la-ni***-ta ba-zi, "*Simu* took in charge 2 sheep (and) 5 billy-goats from *Ili-bilani*," 1175:1–5

3.1.1.7 Unspecified Recipient

[1] u$_8$ 1 sila$_4$-ga ki ***ì-lí-bi-la-ni***-ta ba-zi, "*Ili-bilani* disbursed [1] ewe (and) 1 suckling lamb," 1083:1–4

1 udu 1 máš ki ***ì-lí-bi-la-ni***-ta ba-zi, "*Ili-bilani* disbursed 1 sheep (and) 1 goat," 1518:1–4

4 udu-ú 1 [gukkal?] 2 ku[š-. . .]-šè [. . .]-x-šè ki [***ì-lí-bí***]-***la-ni***-ta ba-zi, "*Ili-bilani* disbursed 4 range-fed sheep, 1 [fat-tailed sheep?] for 2 [. . .] skins for [. . .]," 1521:1–6

3.1.2 Dead Animals

3.1.2.1 Receipt of *Awilumma*

★★4 ⸢máš⸣ 4 u$_8$ [n] ud$_5$ [n] máš-gal ba-úš bi+šu-ab-ta? ^{d}inana-zabala$_4^{ki}$ u$_4$-1-šè é-šu-^{d}E[N.Z]U 32 udu 1 ud$_5$ b[a-úš] é-kišib-ba-šè [*a-w*]*i-lum-ma* ⸢šu⸣ ba-[an-t]i [ki] ***ì-lí-***[***bi***]***-la-ni***-ta [ba]-zi, "*Awilumma* received from *Ili-bilani* 4 goats, 4 ewes, [n] female goat(s), [n] billy-goat(s), slaughtered (?) (for) Inana of Zabala for 1 day (in) *Bit-Šu-Suen*, (and) 32 sheep (and) 1 female goat, slaughtered for the warehouse," 1019:1–14

3.1.2.2 Unspecified Recipient

1 udu 1 sila$_4$ ba-úš ĝìri *é-a-šar* dub-sar ki ***ì-lí-bi-la-ni***-ta ba-zi, "*Ili-bilani* disbursed 1 dead sheep (and) 1 dead lamb under the authority of *Ea-šar*, the scribe," 1095:1–5

16 udu ba-úš ki ***ì-lí-bi-la-ni***-ta ba-zi, "*Ili-bilani* disbursed 16 dead sheep," 1142:1–4

3.1.3 Lambs

1 sila$_4$ ki ***ì-l***[***í-b***]***i-la-ni***-⸢ta⸣ ba-zi, "*Ili-bilani* disbursed 1 lamb," 1160:1–3

3.1.4 Sheep

3.1.4.1 For *Beli-arik*

2 udu *be-lí-a-ri-ik* u$_4$ iri-ni-šè ì-ĝen-na-a 1 udu ki ***ì-lí-bi-la-ni***-ta ba-zi, "*Ili-bilani* disbursed 2 sheep (for) *Beli-arik* when he went to his city (and) 1 (additional) sheep," 410:1–7

3.1.4.2 For Nergal

1 udu-ú ^{d}nergal$_{x}^{eri_{11}\text{-}gal}$ dumu *da-da*-AN ki ***ì-lí-bi-la-ni***-ta ba-zi, "*Ili-bilani* disbursed 1 range-fed sheep (for) Nergal, (the personal deity of) the son of *Dada*-AN," 422:1–4

[1] udu [^{d}ne]rgal$_{x}^{eri_{11}\text{-}gal}$ u$_4$ *e-lu-núm-ma* ki ***ì-lí-bi-la-ni***-ta ba-zi, "*Ili-bilani* disbursed [1] sheep (for) Nergal during the *Elunum* (festival)," 1032:1–5

3.1.4.3 For *Puzur-Ninkarak*

1 ⌜udu⌝ *puzur*$_4$-^{d}⌜nin⌝-kar-ak ki ***ì-lí-[bi-l]a-n[i***-ta] ba-zi, "*Ili-bilani* disbursed 1 sheep (for) *Puzur*-Ninkarak," 450:1–4

3.1.4.4 For *Šu-Suen-dan*

[1] udu-ú ^{d}*šu*-^{d}*suen-dan* [1] udu-ú-niga ⌜ki⌝ ***ì-lí-bi-l[a-ni]***-ta ba-zi, "*Ili-bilani* disbursed [1] range-fed sheep (for) *Šu-Suen-dan* (and) [1] fattened range-fed sheep," 411:1–5

3.1.4.5 Receipt of *Simu*

20 udu *si-mu* ì-dab$_5$ [ki ***ì]-lí-bi-la-ni***-ta ba-zi, "*Simu* took in charge 20 sheep from *Ili-bilani*," 1155:1–4

3.1.4.6 Regular Offerings of the Gods

1 udu sá-du$_{11}$-^{d}inana-zabala$_4^{ki}$ 1 udu sá-du$_{11}$-^{d}šára-ĞEŠ.KÚŠU^{ki} ki ***ì-lí-bi-la-ni***-ta ba-zi, "*Ili-bilani* disbursed 1 sheep, regular offerings of Inana of Zabala (and) 1 sheep, regular offerings of Šara of ĞEŠ.KÚŠU," 1000:1–6, 1010:1–6, 1021:1–5

3.1.4.7 Unspecified Recipient

2 udu ki ***ì-lí-bi-la-ni***-ta ba-zi, "*Ili-bilani* disbursed 2 sheep," 1146:1–3, 1177:1–3

4 udu-ú 1 gukkal ki ***ì-lí-bi-la-ni***-ta ba-zi, "*Ili-bilani* disbursed 4 range-fed sheep (and) 1 fat-tailed sheep," 1522:1–5

3.1.5 Skins: Receipt of *Anaḫ-ili*

2 kuš-sila$_4$ 2 kuš-máš ki ***ì-lí-bi-la-ni***-ta *a-na-ḫi-li*(sic!) šu ba-ti, "*Anaḫ-ili* received 2 lamb skins (and) 2 goat skins from *Ili-bilani*," 903 :1–5

3.1.6 Contents Lost

15 [. . .] ki ***ì-lí-bi-[la]-ni***-ta ba-⌜zi⌝, "*Ili-bilani* disbursed 15 [. . .]," 1156:1–3

3.2 Receipts: Assorted Animals from *Adad-tillati*

1 gukkal 3 u$_8$-gukkal 4 sila$_4$-gukkal 2 kir$_{11}$-gukkal 2 máš-gal 3 ud$_5$ iti-u$_4$-15-ba-zal ki ^{d}*adad-tillati*-ta ***ì-lí-bi-la-ni*** ì-dab$_5$, "At the end of the 15th day of the month *Ili-bilani* took in charge 1 fat-tailed sheep, 3 fat-tailed ewes, 4 fat-tailed lambs, 2 fat-tailed female lambs, 2 billy-goats (and) 3 goats from *Adad-tillati*," 1154:1–10

1 udu 9 u$_8$ 4 sila$_4$ 2 máš ki ^{d}*adad-tillati*-ta ***ì-lí-bi-la-ni*** ì-dab$_5$, "*Ili-bilani* took in charge 1 sheep, 9 ewes, 4 lambs (and) 2 goats from *Adad-tillati*," 1165:1–6

1 u$_8$ 20 udu 5 sila$_4$ 3 ud$_5$ 4 máš ki ^{d}*adad-tillati*-ta ***ì-lí<-bi>-la-ni*** ì-dab$_5$, "*Ili-bilani* took in charge 1 ewe, 20 sheep, 5 lambs, 3 female goats (and) 4 goats from *Adad-tillati*," 1171:1–8

3.3. **As a Witness**

igi ***ì-lí-bi-la-ni***, "witnessed by *Ili-bilani*," 1053:13

ì-lí-ra-bí

1. As a Deputy: Ducklings and a Piglet

★★[n] uz-tur šu-ur$_4$-ra [x?] šu tag-a ki *na-bu-tum*-šè [1] šáh-zé-da é-muhaldim mu *simat-*^{d}*ištaran*<-šè> ***ì-lí-ra-bí*** maškim zi-ga *simat-*^{d}*ištaran*, "[n] duckling wing(s)?, (?) to the place of *Nabutum*, (and) [1] piglet (for) the kitchen for *Simat-Ištaran*. (It was) the expenditure of *Simat-Ištaran*. *Ili-rabi* was the deputy," 529:20–26

ì-lí-si-na-at

1. Receipts: Fine Flour and Processed Peas

0.0.1. eša 5 sìla gú-tur al-ús-sa ki ^{d}*adad-tillati*-ta ***ì-lí-si-na-at*** [šu b]a-ti, "*Ili-sinat* received 10 liters of fine flour (and) 5 liters of processed peas from *Adad-tillati*," 1193:1–5

ì-lí-uṣ-ra-ni

1. Disbursals

1.1 Beer: Under the Authority of *Adad-tillati* and *Puzur*-Ninkarak

1.1.1 For the Builders

2 sìla kaš-gen-ta *en-ni-ma* 1 *be-lí-a-sú* (lú-ì-si-in^{ki}) 1 sìla *ma-šum* árad-é-a kaš-gen-bi 5-sìla šidim-e-ne íb-nağ ki ***ì-lí-uṣ-ra-ni***-ta ba-zi ĝìri ^{d}*adad-tillati* šabra ù *puzur*$_4$-^{d}nin-kar-ak dub-sar, "Under the authority of *Adad-tillati*, the majordomo, and *Puzur*-Ninkarak, the scribe, *Ili-uṣranni* disbursed 2 liters of ordinary beer each (for) *Enima* (and) *Beli-asu*, (men from Isin and) 1 liter (for) *Mašum*, the household servant. (In total:) their ordinary beer is 5 liters. The builders drank (the beer)," 378:9–19, 380:1–1, 384:1–11, 389:1–11

n sìla kaš-gen šidim-e-ne íb-nağ ki ***ì-lí-uṣ-ra-ni***-ta ba-zi ĝìri ^{d}*adad-tillati* (šabra) *ù puzur*$_4$-^{d}nin-kar-ak dub-sar, "Under the authority of *Adad-tillati*, (the majordomo), and *Puzur*-Ninkarak, the scribe, *Ili-uṣranni* disbursed n liter(s) of ordinary beer. The builders drank (the beer)," 398:1–6, 401:1–7

1.1.2 For the Builders and the Overseer

7 sìla kaš-gen dirig sá-du$_{11}$ šidim ù ugula lú-huğ-ğá-e-ne íb-nağ ki ***ì-lí-uṣ-ra-ni***-ta ba-zi [ĝìri] ^{d}*adad-tillati* [ù] *puzur*$_4$-^{d}nin-kar-ak dub-sar, "[Under the authority] of *Adad-tillati* [and] *Puzur*-Ninkarak, the scribe, *Ili-uṣranni* disbursed 7 liters of ordinary beer, surplus of the regular offerings. The builders and overseer of hired workers drank (the beer)," 400:1–6

1.1.3 For the Cultic Place

0.0.1. kaš-gen níĝ ki-zàh-šè sízkur ⸢bàd⸣-šè ki ***ì-[lí]-uṣ-ra-ni***-ta ba-zi ĝìri ^{d}*adad-tillati* šabra [ù *pù*]-*zur*$_8$-^{d}nin-ka[r-a]k, "Under the authority of *Adad-tillati*, the majordomo, [and] *Puzur*-Ninkarak, *Ili-uṣranni* disbursed 10 liters of ordinary beer, provisions for the cultic place, (ceremonial) offerings for the (enclosure) wall," 986:1–6

1.1.4 For the Household Servants and Hired Workers

[n] sìla 10 gín [kaš?] árad-é-a ù lú-ḫuĝ-ĝá-e-ne ib-gu_7(sic!) u_4 al-tar bàd gub-ba ki ***ì-lí-uṣ-ra-ni***-[ta ba]-zi ĝìri *^{d}adad-tillati* šabra ù *$puzur_4$*-^{d}nin-kar-ak dub-sar, "Under the authority of *Adad-tillati*, the majordomo, and *Puzur*-Ninkarak, the scribe, *Ili-uṣranni* disbursed [n] liter(s) (and) 10 shekels of [beer?]. The household servants and hired workers consumed (the beer) when they were employed (for) construction of the (enclosure) wall," 392:1–7

0.0.5.4 sìla kaš árad-é-a ù lú-ḫuĝ-ĝá-e-ne u_4 al-tar bàd gub-ba ki ***ì-lí-uṣ-ra-ni***-ta ba-zi ĝìri *^{d}adad-tillati* šabra ù *$puzur_4$*-^{d}nin-kar-ak dub-sar, "Under the authority of *Adad-tillati*, the majordomo, and *Puzur*-Ninkarak, the scribe, *Ili-uṣranni* disbursed 54 liters of beer (for) the household servants and hired workers when they were employed (for) construction of the (enclosure) wall," 395:1–6

1.1.5 For the Overseer of Hired Workers

1 dug $dida_x$-gen sízkur uš bàd 5 sìla kaš-gen ugula lú-ḫuĝ-ĝá-e-ne íb-naĝ [ki] ***ì-lí-uṣ-ra-ni***-ta ba-zi ĝìri *^{d}adad-tillati* šabra ù *$puzur_4$*-^{d}nin-kar-ak dub-sar, "Under the authority of *Adad-tillati*, the majordomo, and *Puzur*-Ninkarak, the scribe, *Ili-uṣranni* disbursed 1 jug of ordinary dida beer, an offering for the foundation of the (enclosure) wall (and) 5 liters of ordinary beer. The overseer of hired workers drank (the beer)," 377:1–8

5 sìla kaš-gen ugula lú-ḫuĝ-ĝá-e-ne íb-naĝ ki ***ì-lí-uṣ-ra-ni***-ta ba-⌜zi⌝ ĝìri *^{d}adad-[tillati]* šabra, "Under the authority of *Adad-tillati*, the majordomo, *Ili-uṣranni* disbursed 5 liters of ordinary beer. The overseer of hired workers drank (the beer)," 393:1–4

1.2 Ropes

[n] éš-maḫ *[ḫa]-bu-u[m* k]i-lá-bi ½ ⌜gú⌝ 15⅓ ma-⌜na⌝ ì-lá-1-a-ni ki ***ì-lí-[uṣ-ra-ni***-t]a [PN šu ba(-an)-ti ĝì]ri *ì-lí*-NI-x, "Under the authority of *Ili*-X, [PN received n] large *ḫabum*-fabric rope(s)—their weight is ½ talents and 15⅓ minas—from *Ili-[uṣranni]*, which he had weighed out," 831:1–7

ì-sum-a-bí

1. In Worker Assignment Texts: Broken Context

[n] ⌜ĝuruš⌝ ***ì-sum-a-bí*** [. . .] gi-zi [. . .], 213:'10–'12

ib-du-um

1. Provisions: Ox Hide

5 gín [kuš]-gu_4 ú-ḫáb ***ib-du-um***-šè ba-a-ĝar, "5 shekels of madder-tanned oxhide were placed for *Ibdum*," 1517:19–20

ib-ni-^{d}adad

Ibni-Adad, the Scribe

1. Under his Authority

1.1 Assorted (Damaged?) Commodities

(. . .) [. . .]-gaz-a-ḫi? [x]-gaz-gaz [. . .]-zi-ra é-tab-tab-ba [?]x-šè ba-an-ku_4 [g̃ìri] ***ib-ni-^{d}adad*** dub-sar [ki] ^{d}*adad-tillati*-ta [ba]-zi, "[Under the authority of] *Ibni-Adad*, the scribe, *Adad-tillati* disbursed {baskets and other reed products, ropes, palm products, leather products, pots and other containers}; [. . .] broken(? vessels?) entered the double house for [x?]," 1376:87–93

1.2 A Demolished Boat

1 má 60.0.0. gur ba-gul ésir-bi zuḫ-a ba-g̃ar ^{geš}éš-bi <<BI>> nu-g̃ál ki ^{d}*adad-tillati*-⸢ta⸣ ba-zi g̃ìri ***ib-ni-^{d}adad*** dub-sar, "1 60-bushel boat was dismantled. Its bitumen was replaced (but) its rope is (still) missing. (It was) the disbursal of *Adad-tillati* under the authority of *Ibni-Adad*, the scribe," 1369:1–7

1.3 Fodder Counted in the House

(. . .) é-a šid-da ^{d}*adad-tillati* šabra é-*simat*-^{d}*ištaran* g̃ìri ***ib-ni-^{d}adad*** dub-sar, "{assorted grains, fodder for sheep and pigs}, counted in the house under the authority of *Ibni-Adad*, the scribe; *Adad-tillati*, the majordomo of the house of *Simat-Ištaran*," 1189:17–20

1.4 Stones and Woods, the Account of *Adad-tillati*

(. . .) šu-sum-ma g̃ìri ***ib-ni-^{d}adad*** d[ub-sar] iti ezem-me-ki-g̃ál ba-zal mu en-^{d}inana-unu^{ki}-ga máš-e ì-pàd (. . .) ⸢diri⸣ g̃ál-la níg̃-kas_7-aka ^{d}*adad-tillati* šabra, "{millstones, diorite stones, woods, yokes, and wooden containers}, the consignment under the authority of *Ibni-Adad*, the scribe, the 12th month of *Ibbi-Suen* Year 2 having passed. There are additional {millstones, diorite stones, woods, yokes, and wooden containers}; the account of *Adad-tillati*, the majordomo," 1372:46–49, 103–106

ib-ni-ilum

Ibni-ilum, Overseer of Hired Workers

1. Supervision of Hired Workers

n g̃uruš šidim ugula ***ib-ni-ilum*** (. . .) lú-ḫug̃-g̃á-me-éš, "n hired builder(s) supervised by *Ibni-ilum*," 140:13, 19, 145:16, 21, 146:'10, '14, 147:16, 21, 150:15, 21, 151:12, 16

n g̃uruš n géme ugula ***ib-ni-ilum*** lú-ḫug̃-g̃á-me-éš, "n hired workmen (and) n hired workwomen supervised by *Ibni-ilum*," 125:14–15, 130:13

n g̃uruš ugula ***ib-ni-ilum*** (. . .) lú-ḫug̃-g̃á-me-éš, "n hired workmen supervised by *Ibni-ilum*," 118:14, 119:14, 120:14, 121:14, 122:'4, 123:18, 126:13, 127:13, 128:12, 129:13, 131:'7, 132:13, 133:13, 134:13, 135:13, 136:13, 137:13, 138:13, 141:16, 142:13, 143:13, 154:17, 155:11, 158:14, 159:10, 161:'4, 162:11, 163:12, 173:11, 174:11, 175:12

2. Supervision of Workers Assigned to Garden Work

4 g̃uruš ***ib-[ni-ilum]*** (. . .) $kurum_7$ aka saḫar zi-ga [$^{geš}kiri_6$ gar-ša-an-na^{ki}], "Inspection (of the work) of 4 workmen, supervised by *Ibni-ilum* (and) {other workers} having moved dirt [at the Garšana garden]," 176:14, 16–17

(. . .) 171½ g̃uruš ugula ***ib-ni-ilum*** saḫar zi-ga in-lá tùn-lá $^{geš}kiri_6$ $zabala_4^{ki}$ $kurum_7$ [aka], "Inspection (of the work) of 171½ workmen, supervised by *Ibni-ilum*, (and) {other workers} having transported dirt removed via a tùn-lá device at the Zabala garden," 178:4–8

3. Deliveries: Earth for the Adobe Wall of the Zabala Garden

im-du$_8$-a ^{geš}[kiri$_6$] zabala$_4$$^{[ki]}$ mu-[DU] ***ib-ni-ilum*** ugula [lú-ḫuĝ-ĝá], "Delivery (of earth) for the adobe wall of the Zabala [garden] by *Ibni-ilum*, overseer [of hired workers]," 356:5–7

ìl-su-ba-ni

1. *Ilsu-bani*, the Runner

1.1 Under his Authority: Ropes

200 ^{gi}dur-daĝal a-rá-3-tab-ba gíd 5 nindan-ta 300 ^{gi}dur-gazi a-rá-3-tab-ba gíd 1½ nindan-ta 1800 ^{gi}dur-gazi a-rá-2-tab-ba gíd 1½ nindan-ta ki *ì-lí-a-núm*-ta ^{d}*adad-tillati* šu ba-an-ti ĝìri ***ìl-su-ba-ni*** ^{lú}kaš$_4$, "Under the authority of *Ilsu-bani*, the runner, *Adad-tillati* received from *Ili-Anum* 200 30-meter 3-ply wide ropes, 300 9-meter 3-ply gazi ropes, (and) 1800 9-meter 2-ply gazi ropes," 1291:1–7

2. *Ilsu-bani*, Title Unspecified

2.1 As a Witness

igi ***ìl-su-ba-ni***, "witnessed by *Ilsu-bani*," 1049:13, 1050:13, 1051:9

ìl-su-dan

1. Deliveries

[. . .] á [ĝuruš]-a 10 gín-ta ĝuruš-bi 4 u$_4$-1-šè še 6-sìla-ta ba-ḫuĝ saḫar zi-ga kar-ki-mu-ra si-ga mu-DU ***ìl-su-dan*** ugula *ba-zi*, "[. . . workmen] wages of 10 shekels each, its workmen (equal) 4 workerdays, (workers) hired for 6 liters of barley each, having piled up excavated dirt at the quay of the textile depository. Delivery of *Ilsu-dan*, supervised by *Bazi*," 354:1–7

ilam-šu-qir$_x$

Ilam-šuqir, Man from *Dimat-kalbum*

1. As an Runaway

zàḫ ***ilam-šu-qir***$_x$ lú-*dì-ma-at-kál*-[*bu*]-*um*$^{[ki]}$, "*Ilam-šuqir*, the runaway from *Dimat-kalbum*," 378:4–5

2. Receipts: Bread for Builders when the Wall was Built

[2 sìla] ninda-ta (. . .) 1 ***ilam-šu-qir***$_x$ lú-*dì-ma-at-kál-bu-um*^{ki} (. . .) šà-gal ši[dim-e-n]e ⸢u$_4$⸣ [bàd egir] é-a dù-dè, "[2 liters] of bread each for *Ilam-šuqir*, the man from *Dimat-kalbum*, (and for) {other workers}, food (for) builders when they were constructing [the (enclosure) wall behind] the house," 386:1, 5–6, 29–30

ilum-ba-ni

1. *Ilum-bani*, the Ox-Herder, Supervised by *Nur-Adad*, the Majordomo

1.1 Hired Workers from his Gang

n ĝuruš ḫuĝ-ĝá ***ilum-ba-ni*** nu-bànda-gu$_4$ (. . .) ugula *nu-úr*-^{d}*adad* (šabra), "n hired workmen (from the gang of) *Ilum-bani*, the ox-herder, (and) {other gangs}, supervised by *Nur-Adad*, (the majordomo)," 194:23–24, 26, 195:'4, '6, 196:'11, '13, 197:18, 20

1.2 Wages: Barley for Hired Workmen

5.0.0. [še] gur á lú-ḫuḡ-ḡá-šè ki ^{d}*adad-tillati*-ta ***ilum-ba-ni*** ugula lú-ḫuḡ-ḡá šu ba-ti, "*Ilum-bani*, overseer of hired workers, received 5 bushels of [barley] for the wages of hired workers from *Adad-tillati*," 544:1–5[40]

2. *Ilum-bani*, the Servant

2.1 Receipts: Barley

0.2.3. ***ilum-ba-ni*** (. . .) [šu+níḡin n+]5.4.1.8 sìla še gur lugal-ú-šim-e árad!-me-éš, "150 liters of barley (for) *Ilum-bani*, (and barley for) {others}, [in total: n+]5 bushels and 258 liters of barley (for) the servants (supervised by) Lugal-ušime," 504:5, 7–10

ilum-dan

Ilum-dan, Overseer of Hired Workers

1. Supervision of Hired Workers

17 ḡuruš šidim ugula ***ilum-dan***, "17 builders supervised by *Ilum-dan*," 32:7, 13

n ḡuruš ugula ***ilum-dan***, "n workmen supervised by *Ilum-dan*," 5:10, 6:10, 7:9, 8:11, 9:6, 10:6, 14:6, 15:6, 16:6, 17:6, 18:6, 19:9, 20:7, 21:7, 22:7, 23:6, 24:7, 29:'4, 30:7, 31:7, 33:7, 34:7, 35:7, 36:7

2. Runaways and Sick Workmen from his Gang

n ḡuruš zàḫ ugula ***ilum-dan***, "n runaway workmen supervised by *Ilum-dan*," 7:'37, 8:42, 16:29

1 ḡur[uš dú]-ra 2 ḡur[uš zàḫ ugula ***ilum***]***-dan***, "1 sick workman (and) 2 [runaway] workmen [supervised by] *Ilum-dan*," 17:30–31

1 *ku-ru-ub-*^{d}*adad* zàḫ ugula ***ilum-dan***, "*Kurub-Adad*, the runaway, supervised by *Ilum-dan*," 31:44, 32:43, 33:47, 34:'21, 35:51

3. Supervision of Workmen Removing Earth at the Dirt Quarry

n ḡuruš ugula ***ilum-dan*** saḫar zi-ga ka-la$_{(2)}$-ka gub-ba, "n workmen, supervised by *Ilum-dan*, employed at the dirt quarry having removed dirt," 7:'36, 8:41

4. Provisions for Workmen Supervised by *Ilum-dan*

10-lá-1 ḡuruš 1 sìla kaš ½ sìla ninda ⅓ sìla tu$_7$-ta ugula ***ilum-dan*** (. . .) kaš-ninda ḫa-la-a? al-⌜tar⌝ gub-ba, "(For) 10 workmen: 1 liter of beer, ½ liter of bread (and) ⅓ liter of soup each, (workmen) supervised by *Ilum-dan* (and) {other workers}, bread, (and) beer divided (for workers) employed (for) construction," 379:4–5, 20

[n ḡuru]š 1 sì[la kaš-ninda n sìla tu$_7$-ta ugula] ***ilum-***[***dan***], "[(For) n] workmen: 1 liter [of beer (and) bread (and) n liter(s) of soup each, (workmen) [supervised by] *Ilum-dan*," 556:'1–'2

---

[40] For reasons unclear, this text uses ugula instead of nu-bànda.

ilum-ma-zi

1. Provisions: a Textile

1 túg-gùn-a ***ilum-ma-⌜zi⌝*** ki-lá-bi 11½ ma-na, "1 multi-colored textile (for) *Ilum-mazi*, its weight is 11½ minas," 747:16–17

ilum-mu-tá-bíl

1. Receipts

1.1 A Goat from *Adad-tillati*

1 máš ki ᵈ*adad-tillati*-ta ***ilum-mu-tá-bíl*** ì-dab$_5$, "*Ilum-mutabil* took in charge 1 goat from *Adad-tillati*," 1216:1–4

1.2 Semolina from *Malik-bani*

0.1.0. ⌜ZÌ⌝?.ŠE [ki] ᵈ*ma-lik-ba-ni*-ta ***ilum-mu-tá-bìl*** šu ba-an-ti, "*Ilum-Mutabil* received 10 liters of semolina from *Malik-bani*," 1088:1–4

ilum-ra-pi$_5$

Ilum-rapi, the Merchant

1. Receipts: Fresh Apples

[n.n.n.n sìl]a hašhur-duru$_5$ gur ***⌜ilum⌝-ra-pi$_5$*** dam-gàr šu ba-ti níĝ-kas$_7$-aka-ta ᵈba-ú-da ba-⌜na⌝-zi kìšib ***ilum-ra-pi$_5$*** u$_4$-um-de$_6$ kìšib ᵈba-ú-da zi-re-dam, "*Ilum-rapi*, the merchant, received [n] bushel(s) (and) [n] liter(s) of fresh apples. Ba'uda expended (them) from the account for him. When the sealed tablet of *Ilum-rapi* is brought, Ba'uda's sealed tablet will be canceled," 1173:1–10

in-ga-la

1. Provisions

0.0.2.5 <sìla> ***in-ga-⌜la⌝***, "25 <liters> (for) *Ingala*," 558:'5

[. . .] ⅓ sìla mu[n-ta] 6 gín luh-lá-[ta] ĝìri *ì-lí*-[. . .] 1 *ad-da-ni* 1 *bi-za-tum* 1 *i-din*-ᵈ*šamaš* 1 ***in-ga-la*** 1 *be-lí-a-sú* níta-me-éš, "[. . .], ⅓ liter of salt [each], (and) 6 shekels of luh-lá [each] under the authority of *Ili*-[. . .], (provisions for) *Adani*, *Bizatum*, *Iddin-Šamaš*, *Ingala* (and) *Beli-asu*, the men," 562:'31–'39

1.1.0. dabin gur še-ba ***in-ga-⌜la⌝*** (. . .) [níĝ-kas$_7$]-aka [*ì-lí*]-*bi-la-ni* muhaldim, "1 bushel (and) 60 liters of semolina, barley rations of *Ingala*, (and) {other allotments}, the balanced account of *Ili-bilani*, the cook," 1527:29–30, 48–49

ip-qú-ša

1. Receipts: Barley and Beer Bread

0.2.0. še 1 gú báppir-gen ki ᵈ*adad-tillati*-ta ***ip-qú-ša*** šu ba-ti, "*Ipquša* received 120 liters of barley (and) 1 talent of ordinary beer bread from *Adad-tillati*," 1206:1–5

ir-du-du

Irdudu, the Runaway from the Gang of *Beli-ili*

zàḫ ***ir-du-du*** ugula *be-lí-ì-lí*, "*Irdudu*, the runaway, supervised by *Beli-ili*," 46:'49–'50, 47:67–68, 48:74

ir₁₁-dam

Irdam, Overseer of the Men from Karkar

1 ni-x ugula ***ir₁₁-dam*** lú-karkar[ki]-me, "Ni-x, supervised by *Irdam*, (and) {other workers}, men from Karkar," 559:26–28

iš̆dum-ki-in

1. *Išdum-kin*, the Cupbearer

1.1 As a Deputy: Disbursal of Offerings and Provisions

1.1.1 Assorted Commodities in Zabala

0.0.1.1 sìla zú-lum eša b[a-ḫ]i ½ x géme-tur ba-na-ḫa-la ***išdum-ki-in*** ⌜sagi⌝ maškim šà zabala₄[ki], "11 liters of dates were mixed with (fine) flour, ½ x. They were portioned out to Geme-tur in Zabala. *Išdum-kin*, the cupbearer, was the deputy," 506:16–19, 21

(. . .) zì-dub-dub-šè (. . .) [sá-du₁₁-[d]ina]na-zabala₄[ki] [. . .]-na [***išdum-ki***]-***in*** sagi maškim ⌜zi⌝-ga [*tá*]-*ki-il-ì-lí-ís-sú* [ki] [d]*adad-tillati*-ta ba-zi šà zabala₄[ki], "*Adad-tillati* disbursed {assorted comestibles} for the small flour heap (and) [the regular offerings] of Inana of Zabala [. . .]. (It was) the expenditure of *Takil-ilissu* in Zabala. *Išdum-kin*, the cupbearer, was the deputy," 1027:6, 12–19

(. . .) ninda ba-ra-du₈ uzu ù tu₇ ba-ra-šeg̃₆ é-kù-ga (. . .) a-níg̃in-šè (. . .) zì-dub-dub-šè (. . .) 60 [dug]sìla-bur-zi tu₇-šè šà kisal-lá [d]inana-zabala₄[ki] (. . .) a-níg̃in-šè gaba-ri-a ki na-rú-a ***išdum-ki-in*** sagi maškim zi-ga *tá-ki-il-ì-lí-ís-sú* ki [d]*adad-tillati*-ta ba-zi šà zabala₄[ki] u₄-2-kam, "*Adad-tillati* disbursed {assorted commodities} with which bread was baked (and) meat and soup were cooked for the bright temple, {bread and beer} for the a-níg̃in ceremony, {grain} for the small flour heap, {assorted commodities} for 60 one-liter offering bowls of soup in the courtyard of Inana of Zabala, (and) {assorted commodities} for the a-níg̃in ceremony at the meeting at the place of the stele. (It was) the expenditure of *Takil-ilissu* in Zabala on the 2nd day. *Išdum-kin*, the cupbearer, was the deputy," 1028:10–11, 17, 30, 35–37, 40–45

1.1.2 Semolina, Fine Flour, and Dates

8 sìla dabin 4 sìla eša 1 sìla zú-lum eša ḫi-dè *tak-ri-ib-tum* iri[ki] ne-ne-de₄ ***išdum-ki-in*** sagi maškim, "8 liters of semolina, 4 liters of fine flour (and) 1 liter of dates to mix (with) fine flour, (for the performance of) a *takribtum* (involving) circling around the city. *Išdum-kin*, the cupbearer, was the deputy," 1016:18–22

2. *Išdum-kin*, Title Unspecified

2.1 Deliveries: Receipt of *Adad-tillati*, Authority of *Ikunum*

2.1.1 Assorted Woods

180 g̃eš ùr ásal 180 [g̃eš]é-da ásal 130 [g̃eš]eme-sig al-dúb-ba [ki ***iš***]***dum-ki-in***-ta [d]*adad-tillati* šu ba-an-ti ⌜g̃ìri⌝ *i-ku-nu-um*, "Under the authority of *Ikunum*, *Adad-tillati* received 180 poplar roof beams, 180 poplar joists (and) 130 extracted boat planks from *Išdum-kin*," 1303:1–7

2.1.2 Date Palm Spines and Rope

3 peš-[múrgu] 1 éš má g[íd. . .] ki ***išdum-ki-[in***-ta] ^{d}*adad-tillati* šu ba-an-ti u_4 g̃eš ùr i-im-de_6-a [g̃iri] *i-ku-nu-um*, "[Under the authority of] *Ikunum*, *Adad-tillati* received 3 date palm spines, (and) 1 rope (for?) towing a boat from *Išdum-kin* when the roof beams were brought," 1306:1–7

– K –

kà-al-ma-ti

1. Provisions: Wages for Molding Bricks

10[+n] sar ***kà-al-ma-ti*** (. . .) $šeg_{12}$ du_8-[a], "10[+n] sar (of bricks from) *Kalmati* (and bricks from) {other workers}, {wages for workers} having molded bricks," 350:13, '23

ki-ùr-en-mur

1. Deliveries: Barley, Receipt of *Adad-tillati*

30.0.0. še gur ki ***ki-ùr-re-en***-ta [^{d}*adad*]-*tillati* [šu ba]-ti, "*Adad-tillati* received 30 bushels of barley from *Ki'ur-en*," 1238:1–4[41]

2. Receipts: Bran, Delivery of *Adad-tillati*

2.0.0. tuḫ-ḫád ⌜gur⌝ ki ^{d}*adad-tillati*-ta ***ki-ùr-en-mur*** šu ba-an-ti, "*Ki'ur-enmur* received 2 bushels of dry bran from *Adad-tillati*," 1116:1–4

ku-du-du-ú

Kududu, the Runaway from Du-lugal-pa'e

zàḫ ***ku-du-du-ú*** lú-du_6-lugal-pa-è^{ki}, "*Kududu*, the runaway from Du-lugal-pa'e," 43:'50–'51

1. With a Sick Workwoman

zàḫ ***ku-du-d[u-ú***] 1 géme dú-[ra] lú-du_6-lugal-[pa-è^{ki}]-me-⌜éš⌝, "*Kududu*, the runaway, (and) 1 workwoman having been sick, (workers) from Du-lugal-pa'e," 40:53–55

1 géme dú-ra zàḫ ***ku-du-du-ú*** lú-du_6-lugal-pa-è^{ki}, "1 workwoman having been sick (and) *Kududu*, the runaway, (workers) from Du-lugal-pa'e," 41:'33–'35

2. With a Workwoman Milling Flour

1 géme zì-da àra-⌜dè⌝ gub-ba zàḫ ***ku-du-du-ú*** lú-du_6-lugal-pa-è^{ki}, "1 workwoman employed to mill flour (and) *Kududu*, the runaway, (workers) from Du-lugal-pa'e," 45:34–36, 46:'51–'53, 47:69–71, 48:75–77

ku-ru-ub-^{d}*adad*

Kurub-Adad, the Runaway

1 ***ku-ru-ub-***^{d}***adad*** zàḫ ugula *ilum-dan*, "*Kurub-Adad*, the runaway, supervised by *Ilum-dan*," 31:44, 32:43, 33:47, 34:'21, 35:51

---

41 While it is not certain that *ki-ùr-re-en* is a shortened form of *ki-ùr-en-mur*, the occurrence of the two names in similar transactions is suggestive.

ku-un-si-ma-at

Kun-simat, the Weaver

1. In her Possession

lá-ìa 3⅔ [ma-n]a 6⅔ gín siki-g̃ír-gul peš$_5$-a 6 ma-na ⅔ gín mug ½ $^{g̃eš}$zúm nu-úr-ma é-ba-an 207½ 2 gín igi–6-g̃ál géme u$_4$-1-šè lá-ìa-àm ***ku-un-si-ma-at*** ugula uš-bar in-da-g̃ál, "the remainder of 3⅔ minas (and) 6⅔ shekels of plucked g̃ír-gul wool, 6 minas (and) ⅔ shekel of wool combings, ½ pair of zúm nu-úr-ma, (and) 207½ (and) 2$^1/_6$ shekels of workwomen days are with *Kun-simat*, overseer of weavers," 593:1–7

– L –

la-la-a

1. Provisions: Wages for Molding Bricks

7⅓ sar ***la-la-[a]*** (. . .) šeg$_{12}$ du$_8$-[a], "7⅓ sar (of bricks from) *Lala'a* (and bricks from) {other workers}, {wages for workers} having molded bricks," 350:9, '23

la-lum

1. Possessions

1 kuš-udu-babbar ***la-lum*** (. . .) ki *a-na-aḫ-ì-lí*-ta ba-zi, "*Anaḫ-ili* disbursed 1 white sheep skin (for) *Lalum* (and) {leather workers to transport barley}," 884:1–2, 11–12

la-ma-gir$_{11}$

1. As a Witness

igi ***la-ma-gir$_{11}$***, "witnessed by *Lamagir*," 1051:8

la-ma-sà-tum

1. As a Deputy: Piglets and Mice

1 šáḫ-zé-da 1 péš-igi-gùn u$_4$-26-kam 1 šáḫ-zé-da 1 péš-igi-gùn u$_4$-27-kam [GN]^{ki}-šè ***la-ma-sà-tum*** maškim (. . .) zi-ga *simat-^{d}ištaran* ki *^{d}adad-tillati*-ta ba-zi, "*Adad-tillati* disbursed 1 piglet (and) 1 striped-eyed mouse on the 26th day (and) 1 piglet (and) 1 striped-eyed mouse on the 27th day for [GN]. *Lamasatum* was the deputy. {Other disbursals}. (These were) the expenditures of *Simat-Ištaran*," 541:6–13, 27–28

2. Receipts: Barley for (Milling) Semolina

0.1.0. ***la-[ma]-sà-tum*** (. . .) mu dabin-šè šu ba-ti, "*Lamasatum* received 60 liters of barley (and barley for) {9 other individuals}, (barley) in place of semolina," 560:4, 12–13

la-ma-súm

1. Under his Authority: Flour and Jugs

0.0.5.7 sìla zì-gu-sig$_5$ 0.2.5.4 sìla zì-gu 6 dug 0.0.3.-ta ki *i-ṣur-^{d}suen*-ta *^{d}ma-lik-ba-ni* šu ba-an-ti g̃iri ***la-ma-súm***, "Under the authority of *Lamasum*, *Malik-bani* received 57 liters of fine gu-flour, 174 liters of gu-flour (and) 6 jugs of 30 liters each from *Iṣur-Suen*," 1069:1–7

la-qì-ip

1. *Laqip*, the Fuller

1.1 Provisions: Barley

0.1.0. ***la-qì-ip*** lúázlag (. . .) [šu+níĝin n+]7.0.0. gur še-ba *ba-zi-tum* šu+níĝin 47.1.[n.] še-ba é, "60 liters of (barley) (for) *Laqip*, the fuller, (and barley for) {other individuals}; [in total: n+]7 bushels of the barley rations of *Bazitum*; in total: 47 bushels (and) 60[+n] liters of barley rations of the household," 555:9, 24–25

2. *Laqip*, the Royal Gendarme

2.1 Receipts: Wages for Molding Bricks

0.2.3.0 še 5 ma-na siki še 0.0.3.-ta $šeg_{12}$ du_8-dè ki ᵈ*adad-tillati*-ta ***la-qì-ip*** šu ba-an-ti, "*Laqip* received from *Adad-tillati* 170 liters of barley (and) 5 minas of wool, the equivalent of 30 liters of barley each, (for workers) to mold bricks," 431:1–6[42]

[n.n.n.] še gur $šeg_{12}$ du_8-dè á-5-sìla-ta ki ᵈ*adad-tillati*-ta ***la-qì-pu-um*** àga-ús-lugal [šu b]a-[t]i, "*Laqipum*, the royal gendarme, received from *Adad-tillati* [n] bushel(s) (and) [n liter(s)] of barley, wages of 5 liters each (for workers) to mold bricks," 451:1–6

3. *Laqip*, the Scribe

3.1 Receipts: Provisions

[0.1.3.] še ***la-qì-pu-um*** (. . .) [še]-ba dub-sar-e-ne, "[90] liters of barley (for) *Laqipum* (and for) {other workers}, [barley] rations of the scribes," 394:1–2, 7

0.1.3. še 3 ádda-udu-ta $puzur_4$-ᵈnin-kar-ak 1 ***la-qì-ip*** 1 *é-a-dan* dub-sar-me-éš (. . .) [šà-gal šidim] ù dub-sar-e-ne, "90 liters of barley (and) 3 sheep carcasses each (for) *Puzur-Ninkarak*, *Laqip* (and) *Ea-dan*, the scribes, (and for) {other workers}, [food (for) builders] and scribes," 399:16–20, 24

la-te-ni-si

La-tenneši, Overseer of Hired Workers

2 ĝuruš 15 géme <ugula> ***la-te-ni-si*** lú-ḫuĝ-ĝá-me-éš, "2 hired workmen (and) 15 hired workwomen <supervised> by *La-tenneši*," 140:18–19

2 ĝuruš ugula ***la-te-ni-si*** (. . .) lú-ḫuĝ-ĝá-me-éš, "2 hired workmen supervised by *La-tenneši*," 136:16, 19

n géme ugula ***la-te-ni-si*** (. . .) lú-ḫuĝ-ĝá-me-éš, "n hired workwomen supervised by *La-tenneši*," 145:18, 146:'12, 147:18

[n ĝuruš/géme ugula] ***la-te-ni-si*** lú-ḫuĝ-ĝá-me-éš, "[n] hired [workmen/workwomen] supervised by *La-tenneši*," 135:18–19

làl-la

Lala, the Carpenter

[42] Although *Laqip*'s title is not specified, this text is included here in light of the parallel transaction no. 451.

1. **Receipts: A Bronze Plow and a Saw**

1 apin!(GÍN) UD.K[A.B]AR ki-lá-bi 1 ma-[na] 3 gín 1 ^{urudu}šum ki-lá-bi ½ ma-na ki ^{d}*adad-tillati*-ta **làl-la** nagar šu ba-an-ti, "Lala, the carpenter, received from *Adad-tillati* 1 bronze plow, its weight is 1 mina (and) 3 shekels, (and) 1 saw, its weight is ½ mina," 1310:1–7

2. **As a Witness**

igi **làl-la** nağar, "witnessed by Lala, the carpenter," 1065:10

li-bur

Libur, the Gudu-priest

1. **In his Possession: Remainder of the Regular Offerings from Nin-Siana**

[lá-ì]a 2.1.1.5 sìla [x lá]-ìa šà sá-du$_{11}$-^{d}nin-[^{d}si$_{4}$]-an-na-ta lá-ìa-àm ***li-bur*** gudu$_{4}$ in-[da]-ğál, "The remainder of 2 bushels (and) 75 liters of [x], the remainder of the regular offerings from Nin-Siana, are with *Libur*, the gudu-priest," 998:1–5

2. **Under his Authority: Grains**

2 sìla níğ-àr-ra-sig$_{5}$ 4 sìla eša 4 sìla ba-ba-munu$_{4}$ šà-bi-ta 0.0.1. 2½ sìla kaš-ğe$_{6}$ 2-ta 0.0.1.5 ⌜sìla⌝ tuḫ-duru$_{5}$-sig$_{5}$-ğe$_{6}$ káb du$_{11}$-ga ğìri ***li-bur*** gudu$_{4}$, "2 liters of fine groats, 4 liters of fine flour (and) 4 liters of malt porridge. From among it: 12½ liters of black beer, 2 liters each, (and) 15 liters of fine fresh dark bran, commodities measured for accounting under the authority of *Libur*, the gudu-priest," 1046:1–8

3. **As a Witness**

igi ***li-bur*** gudu$_{4}$, "witnessed by *Libur*, the gudu-priest," 1064:11

li-bur-be-lí

Libur-beli, the Gardener

1. **As a Witness**

igi ***li-bur-be-lí*** nu-^{ğeš}kiri$_{6}$, "witnessed by *Libur-beli*, the gardener," 1053:14

li-bur-i-du-ni

1. **Testifying**

1 ir$_{7}$^{mušen} ***li-bur-i-du-ni*** in-gu$_{7}$-a ka-ga-na ba-a-ge-en *na-na* géme kíkken *a-ta-li-ku* sipa-mušen-na in-ge-né-eš "*Libur-iduni* confirmed that he ate 1 pigeon. *Nana*, the female miller, (and) *Ataliku*, the bird warden, verified it," 1055:1–7

li-bur-ni-rum

1. ***Libur-nirum*, the Fattener**

1.1 **As a Deputy: Assignments for Craftsmen**

[n] ğuruš ^{lú}ázlag á-½ ⌜u$_{4}$⌝-8-šè kurušda ***li-bur-ni-rum*** [PA].KAŠ$_{4}$ še apin-lá-a ⌜káb⌝ dì-de$_{4}$ ì-im-ğen-na-a [ki] ^{d}*adad-tillati*-ta [ba]-zi, "*Adad-tillati* disbursed [n] fuller(s) at ½ wages for 8 days who went to check on the grain of the leased fields. *Libur-nirum*, the fattener, was the deputy," 271:1–9

6 ğuruš ašgab 8 ğuruš ^{lú}ázlag 24 géme uš-bar u$_{4}$-1-šè al-tar é-*a-bí-a-ti* gul-dè gub-ba 30 géme uš-bar u$_{4}$-1-šè gi ğá-udu-ta kun-zi-id!(Á)-šè íb-ga$_{6}$ a-šà du$_{6}$-ba-an-du$_{8}$-du$_{8}$ ***li-bur-***

ni-rum maškim ki ^{d}*adad-tillati*-ta ba-zi, "*Adad-tillati* disbursed 6 leather workers, 8 fullers (and) 24 female weavers employed for 1 day for construction in order to demolish the house of *Abiati* (and) 30 female weavers for 1 day. They brought reeds from the sheep-shearing shed to the weir (in?) the Du-bandudu field. *Libur-nirum* was the deputy," 273:1–13[43]

2. *Libur-nirum*, Title Unspecified

2.1 Deliveries

★★[n ^{ĝeš}]ig mi-r[í-za x?] gu_4 du_{11}-⸢ga⸣ [x] gu_4-ta 1 ^{ĝeš}ig mi-rí-za-gal ésir šub-ba 3 ^{ĝeš}nu-kú[š k]i ***li-bur-ni-rum***-ta ^{d}*adad-tillati* šu ba-an-ti, "*Adad-tillati* received [n] door plank(s) decorated? with (?) from an ox, 1 large door plank coated with bitumen (and) 3 pivots from *Libur-nirum*," 1307:1–7

li-la-a

Lila'a, Overseer of Hired Workers

1. Supervision of Hired Workers

n ĝuruš n géme ugula ***li-la-a*** (. . .) lú-ḫuĝ-ĝá-me-éš, "n hired workmen (and) n hired workwomen supervised by *Lila'a*," 132:14, 136:17, 138:15, 140:17, 143:18, 145:20, 146:'13, 147:20, 148:'6, 150:17, 153:'10, 163:14

n ĝuruš ugula ***li-la-a*** (. . .) lú-ḫuĝ-ĝá-me-éš, "n hired workmen supervised by *Lila'a*," 151:15, 154:15, 155:13, 156:12, 158:12, 175:13, 207:8

n géme ugula ***li-la-á*** (. . .) lú-ḫuĝ-ĝá-me-éš, "n hired workwomen supervised by *Lila'a*," 126:14, 127:14, 128:13, 129:14, 131:'8, 133:14, 134:14, 135:14, 199:6, 208:4, 209:9

2. Supervision of Workers Assigned to Specific Tasks

2.1 Garden Work: Moving Dirt at the Garšana Garden

4 ĝuruš 1 [géme] ugula ***li-l[a-a]*** (. . .) $kurum_7$ aka saḫar zi-ga [$^{ĝeš}kiri_6$ gar-ša-an-na^{ki}], "Inspection (of the work) of 4 workmen (and) 1 [workwoman], supervised by *Lila'a*, (and) {other workers} having moved dirt [at the Garšana garden]," 176:11–12, 16–17

[n+]2 ĝuruš ugula ***li-la-a*** (. . .) $kurum_7$ aka saḫar ⸢zi⸣-ga $^{ĝeš}kiri_6$ gar-ša-an-na^{ki}, "Inspection (of the work) of [n+]2 workmen, supervised by *Lila'a*, (and) {other workers} having moved dirt at the Garšana garden," 179:9, 17–18

2.2 Milling

7 géme u_4-1-šè še 3-sìla-ta ba-ḫuĝ ⸢níĝ⸣-àr-ra àr-ra-⸢dè⸣ ⸢gub⸣-ba [ugula] ***li-la-á***, "7 workwomen, [supervised] by *Lila'a*, hired for 1 day (for) 3 liters of barley each, employed to grind groats," 423:4

3. The Account of *Lila'a*

6.4.[0. še gur] 10 ma-na siki [1 ma-na še 0.0.3.-ta] še-bi 1.0.0. [še gur] šu+níĝin 7.4.0. š[e gur] šà-bi-⸢ta⸣ 124⅔ sar [$šeg_{12}$] NE-gu_7-bi í[b-ta-zi] á ĝuruš-a ⅓ sa[r-ta] ĝuruš-bi 360+14 [u_4-1-šè] še 5 sìla-ta [ba-ḫuĝ še-bi] 6.1.1. [gur š]eg_{12}-bi 124⅔ [sar 1].2.5. še gur [*sí*]-*ì-tum* níĝ-kas_7-a[ka] ***li-⸢la⸣-á*** ugu[la lú-ḫuĝ-ĝá], "6 bushels (and) 240 liters [of barley], 10 minas of wool, [1 mina (is the equivalent of) 30 liters of barley each], their barley is 1 bushel [of

[43] Although *Libur-nirum*'s title is not specified, this text is included here in light of the parallel transaction no. 271.

barley]; in total: 7 bushels (and) 240 liters of barley. From among it 124⅔ sar damaged [bricks] were deducted. Workmen wages at ⅓ sar [each], its workmen (equal) 374 workerdays, (workers) [hired (for)] 5 liters of barley each, their barley (rations equal) 6 bushels (and) 70 liters. Their bricks are 124⅔ sar. 1 bushel and 170 liters is the remainder. The account of *Lila'a*, overseer [of hired workers]," 496:1–19

4. Deliveries

4.1 Dirt

saḫar zi-ga [ki-s]á-a é-l[ùnga ù é-kíkken] mu-⸢DU⸣ ***li-la-a*** ugula lú-ḫuĝ-ĝá, "Delivery of dirt removed at the foundation terrace of the brewery and mill, delivery of *Lila'a*, overseer of hired workers," 355:6–8

4.2 Grains: Receipt of *Malik-bani*

0.2.4.9 sìla dabin mu-DU ***li-la-a*** ^{d}*ma-lik-ba-*[*ni*] šu ba-an-⸢ti⸣, "*Malik-bani* received 169 liters of semolina, delivery of *Lila'a*," 1141:1–5

0.4.0. zíz [. . .] mu-[DU] ugula ***li-*[*la-a*]** ^{d}*ma-*[*lik-ba-ni*] šu ba-an-[ti], "*Malik-bani* received 240 liters of [. . .] emmer wheat, delivery of *Lila'a*, the overseer," 1147:1–5

5. In *Lila'a*'s Possession: Barley, Remainder of Wages for Brick Carriers

0.3.2.4 sìla 16⅔ gín še *si-ì-tum* á šeg$_{12}$ ga$_{6}$-ĝá ù al-tar-ra ***li-la-a***(!) ugula lú-ḫuĝ-ĝá in-da-ĝál, "204 liters (and) 16⅔ shekels of barley, the remainder of wages of (workers) having carried bricks and (employed) for construction, are with *Lila'a*, overseer of hired workers," 498:1–6

1.2.5. še gur *si-ì-tum* á šeg$_{12}$ [ga$_{6}$-ĝá] á 5 sìla-⸢ta⸣ ***li-l*[*a-á*]** i[n]-d[a-ĝál], "1 bushel (and) 170 liters of barley, the remainder of wages for (workers) [having carried] bricks—wages of 5 liters each—are with *Lila'a*," 499:1–6

lu-ba

1. Receipts: Textiles to Repair

1 ^{túg}níĝ-lám-gen 1 túg-guz-za *šu-*⸢*kab*⸣*-ta* 1 ^{túg}bar-dul$_{5}$-⸢ús⸣ *šu-kab-ta* 3 ^{túg}uš-bar ⸢siki⸣-ĝír-⸢gul⸣ kala-kala-gé-dè ki *la-ša?-*[x]-ta ***lu-ba*** šu ba-an-ti, "*Luba* received 1 ordinary níĝ-lám textile, 1 tufted textile of *Šu-Kabta*, 1 2nd-quality bar-dul$_{5}$ textile of *Šu-Kabta*, (and) 3 uš-bar textiles of ĝír-gul wool from *La-ša-*[x] in order to repair (them)," 588:1–8

lu-kà-dum

Lukadum, the Household Servant from the Gang of *Irib*

1. Baking Bread

1 ***lu-kà-dum***[44] ninda du$_{8}$-dè gub-ba, "*Lukadum* employed to bake bread," 24:'27, 25:'4, 26:'23, 27:'19, 28:'30, 29:'35, 31:41, 32:40, 33:45, 34:'19, 35:48, 36:43, 39:47, 40:45, 41:'27, 52:66, 53:64, 57:'28–'29, 58:66, 59:54–55, 60:51, 62:'12–'13, 71:36, 73:'17

---

44 Var: *-du-um.*

2. Purchasing Flying Fish

1 šeš-kal-la 1 ***lu-kà-dum*** ku_6-sim sa_{10}(-sa_{10})-dè gú-ab-ba[ki]-šè g̃en-na, "Šeš-kala (and) *Lukadum* having gone to Gu'abba to purchase flying fish," 37:36–39, 47:58–61, 48:66–69, 49:60–62

1 šeš-kal-la 1 ***lu-kà-dum*** ku_6-sim sa_{10}-sa_{10}-dè gú-ab-ba[ki]-šè g̃en-a, "Šeš-kala (and) *Lukadum* having gone to Gu'abba to purchase flying fish," 38:42–44

1 ***lu-kà-dum*** 1 šeš-kal-la ku_6-sim sa_{10}-sa_{10}-dè gú-ab-ba[ki]-šè g̃en-na, "*Lukadum* (and) Šeš-kala having gone to Gu'abba to purchase flying fish," 46:'45–'47, 50:'9–'10, 50:'19–'20

3. Broken Context

1 š[eš-kal-la] dú-⌜ra⌝ 1 ***lu-[kà]-dum*** [. . .], "Šeš-kal having been sick (and) *Lukadum* [. . .]," 56:'40–'41

lu-lu

1. Receipts: Provisions

5 gín ì-šáh̬-ta 15 gín níg̃-àr-ra-sig_5 1⅓ ma-na tuh̬-g̃eš-ì-[h̬ád-ta] 10 gín ádda-u[du-ta] 10 gín mun-ta 3 gín luh̬-lá-⌜ta⌝ ga-na-⌜na⌝ 1 ***lu-⌜lu⌝***? 1 *ni-a-ma* 1 *ni-a-ma* [min?] 1 *simat-*[d]*ištaran* nu-x 1 *simat-*[d]*ištaran* zi-[x] 1 *simat-*[d]*ištaran* [x]-ti 1 ***lu-⌜lu⌝***? min munus-me-éš {indent}10, "5 shekels of lard each, 15 shekels of fine groats, 1⅓ minas of [dried] sesame chaff [each], 10 shekels of sheep carcasses [each], 10 shekels of salt each, 3 shekels of luh̬-lá each (?), (provisions for) *Lulu, Ni'ama, Ni'ama* [the 2nd?], *Simat-Ištaran* [x], *Simat-Ištaran* [x], (and) *Lulu*, the 2nd, 10 women," 562:'40–'55

lú-[d]h̬a-ìa

1. Silver Placed in his Account

(. . .) [šà]-bi-ta [10] ½ gín 12 še kù-babbar úgu **lú-[d]h̬a-ìa** ba-a-g̃ar níg̃-kas_7-aka mun-gazi nu-[g̃eš]$kiri_6$-a-pí-sal_4[ki]-ke_4-ne, "{silver allotments to workmen}, from among it, 10½ shekels (and) 12 barley corns of silver placed in the account of Lu-H̬a'ia; the balanced account of mun-gazi agricultural products of the gardeners of Apisal," 540:7–12

lú-[d]inana

Lu-Inana, the Ox-Herder, Supervised by *Babani*, the Majordomo

n g̃uruš **lú-[d]inana** nu-bànda-gu_4 (. . .) ugula *ba-ba-ni* šabra, "n workmen (from the gang of) Lu-Inana, the ox-herder, (and) {other gangs}, supervised by *Babani*, the majordomo," 190:5, 7, 191:6, 10

2 g̃uruš **lú-[d]inana** nu-bànda-gu_4 (. . .) šà-gu_4-me-éš (. . .) ugula *ba-ba-ni* šabra, "2 workmen (from the gang of) Lu-Inana, the ox-herder, (and) {other gangs}, ox-drivers (and) {hired workers} supervised by *Babani*, the majordomo," 193:5, 7, 9, 197:5, 8, 11

4 g̃uruš **lú-[d][inana]** nu-[bànda-gu_4] (. . .) [šà-gu_4]-me-éš [árad-é]-a-me-éš (. . .) ugula *ba-ba-ni* šabra, "4 workmen (from the gang of) Lu-Inana, the ox-herder, (and) {other gangs}, ox-drivers—household servant—(and) {hired workers} supervised by *Babani*, the majordomo," 194:5, 7–8, 15

lú-kal-la

1. Under his Authority: Transport of Barley

14 g̃uruš še ki ur-[d]šul-pa-UD.⌜DU⌝-ta de$_6$-a kar-ta gur$_7$-šè íb-[ga$_6$] g̃ìri **lú-kal-⌜la⌝**, "Under the authority of Lu-kala, 14 workmen, having brought barley from Ur-Šulpa'e, [carried] it from the quay to the granary," 192:'18–'20

lú-kìri-zal

1. Seal of Lu-kirizal: Delivery of Linen

4 gada-gen ki-lá-bi 7⅓ ma-na ki-lá tag-a mu-DU kišib **lú-kìri-zal**, "4 ordinary linens, their weight is 7⅓ minas. Delivery of weighed (linen) having been woven, seal of Lu-kirizal," 575:1–5

lú-me-lám

Lu-melam, Builder from Nig̃-Ba'u

1. Provisions

1.1 Semolina and Barley

2 sìla dabin-ta 2 sìla še-ta ur-te-me-na 1 ur-[d]asar-lu-ḫi 1 *du-du-gu* 1 [d]utu-sá-bí [1] **lú-me-lám** lú-níg̃-[d]ba-ú šidim-me-éš (. . .) šà-gal šidim-e-ne, "2 liters of semolina each (and) 2 liters of barley each (for) Ur-temena, Ur-Asarluḫi, *Dudugu*, Utu-sabi, (and) Lu-melam, builders from Nig̃-Ba'u, (and for) {other workers}, food (for) builders," 381:5–12, 21

2 sìla dabin-ta 2 sìla še-ta ur-te-me-na 1 ur-[d]asar-lu-ḫi 1 *du-du-gu* 1 [d]utu-sá-bí 1 **lú-me-lám** lú-níg̃-[d]ba-ú šidim (. . .) šà-gal šidim-e-ne u$_4$ bàd egir é-a dù-dè, "2 liters of semolina (and) 2 liters of barley each (for) Ur-temena, Ur-Asarluḫi, *Dudugu*, Utu-sabi, (and) Lu-melam, builders from Nig̃-Ba'u, (and for) {other workers}, food (for) builders when they were constructing the (enclosure) wall behind the house," 386:13–20, 29–30, 387:5–11, 20–21

2 sìla dabin-ta 2 sìla še-ta ur-te-me-na 1 ur-[d]asar-lu-ḫi 1 *du-du-gu* 1 [d]utu-sá-bí 1 **lú-me-lám** lú-níg̃-[d]ba-ú šidim (. . .) šà-gal šidim-e-ne u$_4$ bàd in-dù-sa-a, "2 liters of semolina each (and) 2 liters of barley each (for) Ur-temena, Ur-Asarluḫi, *Dudugu*, Utu-sabi (and) Lu-melam, builders from Nig̃-Bau, (and for) {other workers}, food (for) builders when they constructed the (enclosure) wall," 396:5–12, 19–20, 397:5–13, 19–20

1.2 Sheep and Grains

[0.1.0 še-ta 0.1.0 dabin-ta 3 ádda]-udu-ta [ur-te]-me-na [1 ur-[d]a]sar-lu-ḫi [1] *du-du-gu* [1] **lú-me-lám** [1] [d]utu-sá-ti(sic!) lú-níg̃-[d]ba-ú-me-éš (. . .) [šà-gal šidim] ù dub-sar-e-ne, "[60 liters of barley, 60 liters of semolina (and) 3] sheep [carcasses] each (for) Ur-temena, Ur-Asarluḫi, *Dudugu*, Lu-melam, (and) Utu-sabi, men from Nig̃-Ba'u, (and for) {other workers}, [food (for) builders] and scribes," 399:1–9, 24

lú-^{d}nana

1. Deliveries: Barley

[n+]1[.n.n.] še gur ki **lú-^{d}nana**-ta ^{d}*adad-tillati* šu ba-ti g̃ìri lugal-ḫa-ma-ti ugula má-gíd, "Under the authority of Lugal-ḫamati, overseer of boat towers, *Adad-tillati* received [n] bushel(s) (and) 60[+n] liters of barley from Lu-Nana," 1225:1–5

lú-^{d}nin-šubur

1. As a Witness

igi **lú-^{d}nin-šubur**, "witnessed by Lu-Ninšubur," 1047:9

lú-^{d}*suena*

Lu-*Suena,* the Sailor

1. Provisions: Barley

33.4.1. še gur numun-šè 0.1.0. še-ba **lú-^{d}*suena*** má-laḫ$_{5}$ ba-zi g̃ìri *é-a-šar* ur-^{d}dumu-zi [nu]-bànda-gu$_{4}$, "Ur-Dumuzi, the ox-herder, (received) 33 bushels (and) 250 liters of barley for seed (and) 60 liters (for) the barley ration of Lu-*Suena*, the sailor, disbursed under the authority of *Ea-šar*," 543:1–6

lú-ša-lim

1. *Lušallim*, the Overseer

1.1 Receipts: A Fattened Sheep

1 udu-niga iti u$_{4}$-5-ba-zal ***lú-ša-lim*** nu-bànda *é-a-šar* dub-sar maškim zi-ga *šu-kab-tá* ki ^{d}*adad-*[*tillati*-t]a ba-zi, "*Adad-tillati* disbursed 1 fattened sheep at the end of the 5th day of the month (for) *Lušallim*, the overseer. It was the expenditure of *Šu-Kabta*. *Ea-šar*, the scribe, was the deputy," 1159:1–7

2. *Lušallim*, Title Unspecified

2.1 Receipts: Regular Offerings

1 *mu-du-lum* udu-niga sag̃ u$_{4}$-sakar 1 *mu-du-lum* udu-niga é-u$_{4}$-15 sá-du$_{11}$ *simat-*^{d}*ištaran* é-gal-ta ***lú-ša-lim*** šu ba-an-ti, "*Lušallim* received 1 salted fattened sheep on the new moon day (and) 1 salted fattened sheep on the full moon day, regular offerings of *Simat-Ištaran* from the palace," 375:1–8

2.2 His Possessions: Mice

2 ⸢kur⸣-gi^{mušen} 3 uz-tur 6 péš-g̃eš-gi *e-ṣí-dum* 15 péš-igi-gùn ***⸢lú⸣-ša-lim*** iti u$_{4}$-13-ba-zal mu-DU *šu-kab-tá* ^{d}*adad-tillati* ì-dab$_{5}$, "At the end of the 13th day of the month *Adad-tillati* took in charge 2 geese, 3 ducklings (and) 6 mice (for) *Eṣidum* (and) 15 striped-eyed mice (for) *Lušallim*, the delivery of *Šu-Kabta*," 1127:1–10

lu$_{5}$-zi-lá

Luzila, the Female Miller

1. Provisions

[1] *za-a-za* [1] *a-na-a* [1] ***lu$_{5}$-zi-lá*** {indent} 8 [géme é]-kíkken-me-éš, "{provisions} (for) *Zaza*, *Ana'a*, (and) *Luzila*, 8 [workwomen] of the mill," 562:'1–'5

lugal-ezem

1. In his Possession: Barley

[9]?.2.0.8 sìla še gur [lá-ìa]-àm [ki] ^{d}*adad-tillati*-ta ⸢**lugal**⸣**-ezem** in-da-g̃ál, "The remainder of [9]? bushels (and) 128 liters of barley from *Adad-tillati* are with Lugal-ezem," 1185:1–5

lugal-ḫa-ma-ti

1. Lugal-ḫamati, Household Servant from the Gang of *Irib*

1.1 As an Runaway

zàḫ **lugal-[ḫa-ma-ti]** (. . .) ⸢ugula⸣ *i-r*[*i-ib*], "Lugal-ḫamati, the runaway, (and) {other workers assigned to various tasks}, supervised by *Irib*," 40:44, 47

zàḫ **lugal-ḫa-ma-ti**, "Lugal-ḫamati, the runaway," 41:'36

1.2 Errands: Bringing a Message to G̃irsu

1 **lug[al-ḫ]a-ma-ti** á-á[g̃ ši]dim-e-ne g̃ír-su$^{[ki]}$-šè de$_{6}$-a, "Lugal-ḫamati having brought a message concerning builders to G̃irsu," 52:67–79

2. Lugal-ḫamati, Overseer of Boat Towers: Under his Authority

[n+]1[.n.n.] še gur ki lú-^{d}nana-ta ^{d}*adad-tillati* šu ba-ti g̃ìri **lugal-ḫa-ma-ti** ugula má-gíd, "Under the authority of Lugal-ḫamati, overseer of boat towers, *Adad-tillati* received [n] bushel(s) (and) 60[+n] liters of barley from Lu-Nana," 1225:1–5

lugal-ú-šim-e

1. (Overseer of) Servants

[šu+níg̃in n+]5.4.1.8 sìla še gur **lugal-ú-šim-e** árad!-me-éš, "[In total: n+]5 bushels and 258 liters of barley (for) the servants (supervised by) Lugal-ušime," 504:7–10

– M –

ma-aš-rum

1. Provisions: Barley

1.0.0. gur ***ma-aš-***⸢***rum***⸣ (. . .) [šu+níg̃in n+]7.0.0. gur še-ba *ba-zi-tum* šu+níg̃in 47.1.[n.] še-ba é, "1 bushel of (barley) (for) *Mašrum* (and barley for) {other individuals}; [in total: n+]7 bushels of the barley rations of *Bazitum*; in total: 47 bushels (and) 60[+n] liters of barley rations of the household," 555:7, 24–25

ma-áš-tum

1. Provisions: Barley

1.4.4.5 sìla <gur> ***ma-áš-tum*** (. . .) šu+níg̃in 27.1.1.3 sìla še gur ki ugula-nam–10-ka ⸢g̃al⸣-la ugula *simat-é-a* lú-ḫug̃-g̃á, "1 bushel (and) 285 liters (of barley) (for) *Maštum*, (and barley for) {others}, in total: there are 27 bushels (and) 73 liters of barley at the place of the overseer of 10; *Simat-Ea*, the overseer of hired workers," 504:14, 20–23

0.0.3. ***ma-áš-tum*** (. . .) mu dabin-šè šu ba-ti, "*Maštum* received 20 liters of barley, (and barley for) {9 other individuals}, (barley) in place of semolina," 560:9, 12–13

ma-at-ì-lí

Mat-ili, the Servant

1. Provisions: Barley

[n.n.n.] še gur ***ma-at-ì-lí*** (. . .) [šu+níĝin n+]5.4.1.8 sìla še gur lugal-ú-šim-e árad!-me-éš, "[n bushel(s) (and) n liter(s)] of barley (for) *Mat-ili*, [in total: n+]5 bushels and 258 liters of barley (for) the servants (supervised by) Lugal-ušime," 504:1, 7–10

ma-la-ti

1. Provisions

1.1 Grains

2 sìla dabin 1 sìla eša *um-mi-kab-tá* 2 sìla dabin 1 sìla eša ***ma-la-ti*** ^{d}*ma-lik-tillat-sú* šu-i maškim, "2 liters of semolina (and) 1 liter of fine flour (for) *Ummi-Kabta* (and) 2 liters of semolina (and) 1 liter of fine flour (for) *Malati*. *Malik-tillassu*, the barber, was the deputy," 1016:13–17

1.2 Sheep

1 udu ⌜***ma***⌝***-la-ti*** (. . .) ki *ì-lí-bi-la-ni*-ta ba-zi, "*Ili-bilanni* disbursed 1 sheep (for) *Malati* (and) {others}," 1012:4, 6–7

^{d}*ma-lik-ba-ni*

1. Deliveries

1.1 Flour

1.1.1 Receipt of *Adallal*

0.1.0 zì-kum-sig$_{5}$ 0.1.0. eša ninda-*u*$_{4}$*-tuḫ-ḫ*[*u-um*-šè] ki ^{d}***ma-lik-ba-ni***-ta *a-da-làl* ⌜muḫaldim⌝ šu ba-an-ti, "*Adallal*, the cook, received 60 liters of fine kum-flour (and) 10 liters of fine flour [for] *utuḫḫum*-bread from *Malik-bani*," 1077:1–6

0.2.0. zì-gu-ús 0.2.0. dabin al-ús-sa ki ^{d}***ma-lik-ba-ni***-ta *a-da-làl* šu ba-an-ti, "*Adallal* received 120 liters of 2nd-quality gu-flour (and) 120 liters of processed semolina from *Malik-bani*," 1086:1–5

[0].1.1. tuḫ [0.n].2. zì-KAL [0].3.2. zì-kum [0].0.1. zì-gu-ús [ki] ^{d}***ma-lik-ba-ni***-ta [*a-d*]*a-làl* ⌜šu⌝ ba-an-ti, "*Adallal* received 70 liters of bran, [n+]20 liters of KAL-flour, 200 liters of kum-flour, (and) 10 liters of gu-flour from *Malik-bani*," 1128:1–7

1.1.2 Receipt of *Ilum-mutabil*

0.1.0. ⌜ZÌ⌝?.ŠE [ki] ^{d}***ma-lik-ba-ni***-ta *ilum-mu-tá-bìl* šu ba-an-ti, "*Ilum-mutabil* received 10 liters of semolina from *Malik-bani*," 1088:1–4

1.2 Provisions for Builders

1.2.1 Building the (Enclosure) Wall of the House

1.2.1.1 Under the Authority of *Adad-tillati* and *Puzur*-Ninkarak

(. . .) šà-gal šidim-e-ne ĝiri ^{d}*adad-tillati* ù *puzur*$_{4}$-^{d}nin-kar-ak ki ^{d}***ma-lik-ba-ni***-ta ba-zi, "Under the authority of *Adad-tillati* and *Puzur*-Ninkarak, *Malik-bani* disbursed {assorted grains}, food (for) builders," 381:21–24

(. . .) šà-gal šidim-e-ne (. . .) árad-é-[a lú-ḫuĝ]-ĝá ù ugula lú-[ḫuĝ-ĝá-e-n]e íb-gu$_7$ [1] sìla dabin ½ sìla eša zì-dub-dub-šè u$_4$ bàd é-a dù-dè ĝìri ^{d}*adad-tillati* ù *puzur$_4$*-[^{d}nin-kar-a]k ki ^{d}***ma-l[ik-b]a-n[i***-ta ba]-zi, "Under the authority of *Adad-tillati* and *Puzur*-Ninkarak, *Malik-bani* disbursed {assorted grains}, food (for) builders, {assorted grains}—the servants, hired workers and overseer of the hired workers ate (the grain)—[1] liter of semolina (and) ½ liter of fine flour for the small flour heap, (provisions of the workers) when they were constructing the (enclosure) wall of the house," 383:5, 8–13

(. . .) šà-gal šidim-e-ne u$_4$ bàd egir é-a dù-dè ĝìri ^{d}*adad-tillati* (šabra) ù *puzur$_4$*-^{d}nin-kar-ak ki ^{d}***ma-lik-ba-ni***-ta ba-zi, "Under the authority of *Adad-tillati*, (the majordomo), and *Puzur*-Ninkarak, *Malik-bani* disbursed {assorted commodities}, food (for) builders, when they were constructing the (enclosure) wall behind the house," 386:29–34, 387:20–24

(. . .) šà-gal šidim-e-ne u$_4$ bàd in-dù-sa!-a ĝìri ^{d}*adad-tillati* ù *puzur$_4$*-^{d}nin-kar-ak šà gar-ša-an-na^{ki} ki ^{d}***ma-lik-ba-ni***-ta ba-zi, "Under the authority of *Adad-tillati* and *Puzur*-Ninkarak in Garšana, *Malik-bani* disbursed {assorted grains}, food (for) builders, when they constructed the (enclosure) wall," 396:19–24, 397:19–24

1.2.1.2 Under the Authority of *Puzur*-Ninkarak

(. . .) šà-gal šidim-e-ne 5 sìla ninda ugula lú-ḫuĝ-ĝá-e-ne íb-gu$_7$ 3 sìla ^{lú}kíĝ-gi$_4$-a *šu-kab-ta* 1 sìla dabin ½ sìla eša dub-dub-ne bà[d egi]r é-a dù-dè ⌜ĝìri⌝-*puzur$_4$*-^{d}nin-kar-ak dub-sar ki ^{d}***ma-lik-ba-ni***-ta ba-zi, "Under the authority of *Puzur*-Ninkarak, the scribe, *Malik-bani* disbursed {assorted grains}, food (for) builders, 5 liters of bread—the overseer of hired workers ate (the bread)—3 liters (of bread for) the messenger of *Šu-Kabta* (and) 1 liter of semolina (and) ½ liter of fine flour for heaping, (provisions of the workers) to construct the (enclosure) wall behind the house," 385:5–11

1.3 Reeds and Baskets: Receipt of *Da'a*

120 [sa? g]i?-izi 1 ^{gi}bisaĝ? é-ĜAR kuš ĝar-ra ki ^{d}***ma-lik-ba-ni***-ta *da-a-a* šu ba-ti, "*Da'a* received 120 [bundles? of] fuel [reeds?] (and) 1 (?) basket covered with leather from *Malik-bani*," 1332:1–5

1.4 Requisitions for the *Abum* Festival: Receipt of *Adallal*

(. . .) níĝ-dab$_5$ ezem-*a-bu-um-ma*-šè u$_4$-10-lá-1-kam ki ^{d}***ma-lik-ba-ni***-ta *a-da-làl* šu ba-an-ti, "*Adallal* received {assorted grains}, requisitions for the *Abum* festival on the 9th day from *Malik-bani*," 999:12–15

1.5 Semolina

1.5.1 Receipt of *Adallal*

n dabin gur níĝ-*na-kab-tum*-šè ki ^{d}***ma-lik-ba-ni***-ta *a-da-làl* muḫaldim šu ba-an-ti, "*Adallal*, the cook, received n bushel(s) of semolina for the *nakabtum* from *Malik-bani*," 1080:1–5, 1084:1–5, 1099:1–5, 1107:1–5, 1115:1–5, 1136:1–5

0.1.0. dabin šà-⌜gal⌝ nam-ra-ak ki ^{d}***ma-lik-ba-ni***-ta *a-da-làl* šu ba-a[n-t]i, "*Adallal* received 60 liters of semolina, provisions of the booty, from *Malik-bani*," 1085:1–5

n dabin ki ^{d}***ma-lik-ba-ni***-ta *a-da-làl* (muḫaldim) šu ba-an-ti, "*Adallal*, (the cook), received n liter(s) of semolina from *Malik-bani*," 1137:1–4, 1151:1–4

1.5.2 Receipt of *Anaḫ-ili*

0.0.1. dabin ki ^{d}***ma-lik-ba-ni***-ta *a-na-aḫ-ì-lí* [šu b]a-an-ti, "*Anaḫ-ili* received 10 liters of semolina from *Malik-bani*," 879:1–4

1.6 Wood

1.6.1 Receipt of *Adad-tillati*

★★4 ^{geš}ḫašḫur éren 6-kùš-[ta] 7 ^{geš}ḫašḫur éren 5-kùš-[ta] 11 ^{geš}ḫašḫur éren 4-kùš-ta 11 ^{geš}ḫašḫur éren 3-kùš-ta šà éren ^{geš}ig-šè ⸢ki⸣ ^{d}***ma-lik-ba-ni***-ta ^{d}*adad-tillati* [šu b]a-⸢ti⸣, 1327:1–8

1.6.2 Receipt of *Akbazum*

(. . .) [ki ^{d}]***ma-lik-ba-ni***-ta *ak-ba-zum* šu ba-an-ti, "*Akbazum* received {wood products} from *Malik-bani*," 1255:10–12

g̃eš é-⸢$^{g̃eš}$kiri$_6$⸣-a gub-ba šu-sum-ma ^{geš}kiri$_6$ igi-érim-iri^{ki} ki ^{d}***ma-lik-ba-ni*** santana-ta *ak-ba-zum* um-mi-a ì-dab$_5$ šà gar-ša-an-na^{ki} ⸢g̃iri⸣ *tu-ra-am-ì-lí* dub-sar, "From *Malik-bani*, the date orchard administrator, *Akbazum*, the master craftsman, took in charge wood stored in the garden house, the inventory of the Igi-erim-iri garden. (Transaction) in Garšana under the authority of *Turam-ili*, the scribe," 1375:45–51[45]

1.6.3 Receipt of Ba'uda

(. . .) é-$^{g̃eš}$kiri$_6$-a gub-ba ⸢ki⸣ ^{d}***ma-lik-[ba-n]i***-ta [^{d}ba-ú]-da šu ba-an-ti, "Ba'uda received {wood} stored in the garden house from *Malik-bani*," 1256:39–41

1.7 Broken Context

1.7.1 Receipt of *Adallal*

[. . .] ki [^{d}***ma-lik-ba-ni***-ta] *a-da-làl* šu ba-ti, "*Adallal* received [. . .] from *Malik-bani*," 1191:1–5

1.7.2 Receipt of *Aštaqqar*

368 [. . .] ki ^{d}***ma-lik-ba-ni***-ta *aš-tá-qar* ì-dab$_5$, "*Aštaqqar* took in charge 368 [. . .] from *Malik-bani*," 652:1–4

2. Receipts

2.1 From *Adad-tillati*

2.1.1 Animals

4 [x] 2 udu [ki] ^{d}*adad-*[*tillati*-t]a ^{d}***ma-lik-ba-ni*** ⸢šu⸣ ba-an-ti, "*Malik-bani* received 4 [x] (and) 2 sheep from *Adad-tillati*," 1076:1–5

2.1.2 Barley

n.0.0. še gur ki ^{d}*adad-tillati*-ta ^{d}***ma-lik-ba-ni*** šu ba-an-ti, "*Malik-bani* received n bushel(s) of barley from *Adad-tillati*," 1094:1–4, 1120:1–4

---

[45] This is the only text in the Garšana archive in which *Malik-bani* bears a title. Based on *Malik-bani*'s activities mentioned here, it is clear that there is only one *Malik-bani* at Garšana.

2.1.2.1 Barley and a Field

5.4.0. še gur á al aka ù gu$_{4}$-ḫuĝ-ĝá a-šà 1 (bùr) 2 (iku) gána ki ^{d}*adad-tillati*-ta ^{d}***ma-lik-ba-ni*** šu [ba]-an-ti, "*Malik-bani* received from *Adad-tillati* 5 bushels (and) 240 liters of barley, wages (for) hoeing and the hired oxen (and) a field of 1 bur (and) 2 iku of acreage," 1051:1–6

2.1.2.2 Barley and Reed Mats

20.0.0. še gur 60 ^{gi}kid-maḫ-sun ki ^{d}*adad-tillati*-ta ^{d}***ma-lik-ba-ni*** šu ba-an-ti, "*Malik-bani* received 20 bushels of barley (and) 60 large sun-mats from *Adad-tillati*," 1119:1–5

2.1.3 Baskets

10 ^{gi}gur še ki ^{d}*adad-tillati*-ta ^{d}***ma-lik-ba-ni*** šu ba-an-ti, "*Malik-bani* received 10 reed baskets of barley from *Adad-tillati*," 1087:1–4

4 ^{gi}gur a bala ésir šub-⸢ba⸣ 3 ^{ĝeš}*zi-ri-qum* ki ^{d}*adad-tillati*-ta ^{d}***ma-lik-ba-ni*** šu ba-an-ti, "*Malik-bani* received 4 reed baskets coated with bitumen for pouring water (and) 3 (pieces) of *ziriqum* wood from *Adad-tillati*," 1271:1–6

3 ^{gi}gu[rdub siki] k[a-tab sè-g]a [. . .] dabin ki ^{d}*adad-tillati*-ta ^{d}***ma-lik-*[*ba-ni*]** šu ba-an-[ti], "*Malik-bani* received 3 reed baskets [of wool] fitted with a cover (and) [. . .] semolina from *Adad-tillati*," 1279:1–5

10 ^{gi}gur še ésir šub-ba ⸢ki⸣ [^{d}*adad-tillati*]-ta [^{d}***ma-li*]*k-ba-ni*** [šu] ba-an-ti, "*Malik-bani* received 10 reed baskets (containing) barley coated with bitumen from [*Adad-tillati*]," 1301:1–4

2.1.4 Beer Bread

10 ma-na báppir-sig$_{5}$ ki ^{d}*adad-tillati*-ta $^{[d]}$***ma-lik-ba-ni*** šu ba-ti, "*Malik-bani* received 10 minas of fine beer bread from *Adad-tillati*," 1131:1–4

2.1.5 Dates

0.0.1 zú-lum ki ^{d}*adad-tillati*-ta ^{d}***ma-lik-ba-ni*** šu ba-an-ti šà zabala$_{4}^{ki}$, "*Malik-bani* received 10 liters of dates from *Adad-tillati* in Zabala," 1071:1–5

2.1.6 Emmer

2.0.0. imĝaĝa$_{3}$ gur ki [^{d}*adad-tillati*]-ta [^{d}***ma-lik-b*]*a-ni*** šu ba-ti, "*Malik-bani* received 2 bushels of emmer from [*Adad-tillati*]," 1174:1–4

2.1.7 Grains and Seasonings

2.0.0. imĝaĝa$_{3}$ gur 0.0.2. gazi 0.0.2. še-lú 30 ma-na ki-lá š[eg$_{12}$ mun-s]ig$_{5}$ [ki ^{d}*adad*]-*tillati*-[ta] ^{d}***ma-lik-ba-ni*** šu ba-an-ti, "*Malik-bani* received from *Adad-tillati* 2 bushels of emmer, 20 liters of gazi, 20 liters of coriander, (and) a 30 mina brick of fine [salt]," 1130:1–7

2.1.8 Leather Sacks

15 barag 20 ^{kuš}a-ĝá-lá barag-bi udu 40 ^{kuš}a-ĝá-lá barag-bi maš-dù ki ^{d}*adad-tillati*-ta ^{d}***ma-lik-ba-ni*** šu ba-an-ti, "*Malik-bani* received from *Adad-tillati* 15 sacks, 20 leather sacks, their barag of sheep skin, (and) 40 leather sacks, their barag of goat skin," 848:1–6

2.1.9 Pots

10 dug 0.0.3.-ta ki ^{d}*adad-tillati*-ta ^{d}***ma-lik-ba-ni*** šu ba-an-ti, "*Malik-bani* received 10 pots of 30-liters each from *Adad-tillati*," 1300:1–4, 1304:1–4

2.1.10 Raw Grains for Processing

13.2.5. [zíz gur] zíz-ba-na 5-sìla-[ta ì-ĝál] 2.0.0. imĝaĝa$_3$ gur ki ^{d}*adad-tillati*-ta ^{d}***ma-lik-ba-ni*** šu ba-an-ti, "*Malik-bani* received from *Adad-tillati* 13 bushels (and) 170 liters of [emmer wheat], in [each] ban (=10 liters) [of it there are] 5 liters, (and) 2 bushels of emmer," 1110:1–5

2.1.10.1 Labor of Female Millers

6.0.0. še gur á géme àr-ra ki ^{d}*adad-tillati*-ta ^{d}***ma-lik-ba-ni*** šu ba-an-ti, "*Malik-bani* received 6 bushels of barley, labor of female grinders, from *Adad-tillati*," 405:1–5

n še gur á géme kíkken-šè ki ^{d}*adad-tillati*-ta ^{d}***ma-lik-ba-ni*** šu ba-an-ti, "*Malik-bani* received n bushel(s) of barley for labor of female millers, from *Adad-tillati*," 376:1–5, 404:1–5, 407:1–5, 417:1–5

4.0.0. zíz gur zíz-ba-na zì-KAL 4½ sìla 5 gín-ta ì-ĝál 7.4.0. kib$_x$ gur ⌜saĝ⌝? ĝál-la nu-ub-tuku á géme kíkken-šè ⌜ki⌝ ^{d}*adad-tillati*-ta ^{d}***ma-lik-ba-ni*** šu ba-an-ti, "*Malik-bani* received from *Adad-tillati* 4 bushels of emmer wheat, in each ban (=10 liters) of the emmer wheat there are 4½ liters and 5 shekels of KAL-flour (and) 7 bushels (and) 240 liters of wheat, which did not have (?), for labor of female millers," 412:1–7

10.0.0. še gur 10.0.0. zíz gur ba-na zì-KAL 5 sìla-ta ì-ĝál á géme kíkken ki ^{d}*adad-tillati*-ta ^{d}***ma-lik-ba-ni*** šu ba-an-ti, "*Malik-bani* received from *Adad-tillati* 10 bushels (of) barley (and) 10 bushels of emmer wheat, in each ban (=10 liters) of it there are 5 liters of KAL-flour, labor of female millers," 433:1–6

5.0.0. še gur 0.1.0. imĝaĝa$_3$ á géme kíkken-šè ki ^{d}*adad-tillati*-ta ^{d}***ma-lik-ba-ni*** šu ba-an-ti, "*Malik-bani* received 5 bushels of barley (and) 60 liters of emmer for labor of female millers from *Adad-tillati*," 455:1–6

14.2.0. zíz gibil gur zíz ba-na imĝaĝa$_3$ 5 sìla 7-gín-ta ì-ĝál 5.3.0 zíz sumun gur zíz ba-na imĝaĝa$_3$ 4-sìla-ta ì-ĝál á géme kíkken-šè [ki ^{d}*adad-tillati*-ta ^{d}***ma-lik***]***-ba-ni*** [šu ba]-an-⌜ti⌝, "*Malik-bani* received [from *Adad-tillati*] 14 bushels (and) 120 liters of new emmer wheat, in each ban (=10 liters) of the emmer wheat there are 5 liters (and) 7 shekels of emmer, (and) 5 bushels (and) 180 liters of old emmer wheat, in each ban (=10 liters) of emmer wheat there are 4 liters of emmer, for labor of female millers," 461:1–8

20.0.0. še gur 0.0.1 zíz gur ba-na zì-KAL-ta á géme kíkken-šè ki ^{d}*adad-tillati*-ta [^{d}***ma-lik-ba-ni*** šu ba-(an-)ti], "[*Malik-bani* received] from *Adad-tillati* 20 bushels of barley and 10 liters of emmer wheat in each ban (=10 liters) (of it there is) KAL-flour, for labor of female millers," 467:1–6

2.1.11 Semolina

n.n.n. dabin gur ki ^{d}*adad-tillati*-ta ^{d}***ma-lik-ba-ni*** šu ba-an-ti, "*Malik-bani* received n bushel(s) (and) n liter(s) of semolina from *Adad-tillati*," 1108:1–4, 1114:1–4

2.1.12 Sieves

3 ^{gi}ma-an-sim dabin ki ^{d}*adad-tillati*-[ta] ^{d}***ma-lik-ba-ni*** šu ba-an-ti, "*Malik-bani* received 3 semolina sieves from *Adad-tillati*," 1270:1–4

2.1.13 Wool and Goat Hair

25 ma-na siki g̃ír-gul 13 ma-na siki-ud$_5$ ki ^{d}*adad-tillati*-ta ^{d}***m[a-lik-ba]-ni*** šu ba-ti, "*Malik-bani* received 25 minas of g̃ír-gul wool (and) 13 minas of goat hair from *Adad-tillati*," 704:1–5

2.1.14 Workwomen

90-lá-1 géme še 3 sìla-ta ba-[ḫug̃] á níg̃-àr-ra-ra ki ^{d}*adad-tillati*-ta ^{d}***ma-lik-ba-ni*** ì-dab$_5$, "*Malik-bani* took in charge 89 workwomen, hired (for) 3 liters of barley each as wages for (milling) groats, from *Adad-tillati*," 432:1–6

2.2 Receipts from Others

2.2.1 Assorted Commodities from *Iṣur-Suen*

(. . .) ki *i-ṣur*-^{d}*suen*-ta ^{d}***ma-lik-ba-ni*** šu ba-an-ti, "*Malik-bani* received {assorted grains and containers} from *Iṣur-Suen*," 1068:7–9, 1074:9–11, 1075:7–9

(. . .) ki *i-ṣur*-^{d}*suen*-ta ^{d}***ma-lik-ba-ni*** <šu ba-ti> g̃iri *šu*-^{d}nisaba maškim, "Under the authority of *Šu*-Nisaba, the deputy, *Malik-bani* <received> {assorted grains and containers} from *Iṣur-Suen*," 1072:9–11

2.2.2 Emmer Wheat from *Lila'a*

0.4.0. zíz [. . .] mu-[DU] ugula *li-*[*la-a*] ^{d}***ma-*[*lik-ba-ni*]** šu ba-an-[ti], "*Malik-bani* received 240 [liters] of [. . .] emmer wheat, delivery of *Lila'a,* the overseer," 1147:1–5

2.2.3 Flour

0.2.3.7⅓ sìla zì mu-DU *simat-é-a* ^{d}***ma-lik-ba-ni*** šu ba-an-ti, "*Malik-bani* received 157⅓ liters of flour, delivery of *Simat-Ea*," 1140:1–5

0.0.3. zì-gu-gen ki *šu*-^{d}nin-girim$_x$-⌜ta⌝ ^{d}***ma-lik-ba-ni*** šu ba-ti, "*Malik-bani* received 30 liters of ordinary gu-flour from *Šu*-Ningirim," 1153:1–4

2.2.4 Flour and Pots from *Iṣur-Suen*

0.0.5.7 sìla zì-gu-sig$_5$ 0.2.5.4 sìla zì-gu 6 dug 0.0.3.-ta ki *i-ṣur*-^{d}*suen*-ta ^{d}***ma-lik-ba-ni*** šu ba-an-ti g̃iri *la-ma-súm*, "Under the authority of *Lamasum*, *Malik-bani* received from *Iṣur-Suen* 57 liters of fine gu-flour, 174 liters of gu-flour (and) 6 pots of 30-liters each," 1069:1–7

2.2.5 Groats

14.2.2.[n gur] níg̃-àr-ra 2.3.0.5 [sìla x gur . . .] ^{d}***ma-*[*lik-ba-ni*]** šu ba-[an-ti], "*Malik-bani* received 14 bushels (and) 140[+n] liters of groats, 2 bushels (and) 185 liters of [. . .]," 1073:1–6

1.1.3. níg̃-àr-ra 0.0.2. kaš-níg̃-àr-ra-gen ^{d}***ma-lik-ba-ni*** [šu] ba-an-ti, "*Malik-bani* received 1 bushel (and) 90 liters of groats (and) 20 liters of ordinary groat beer," 1103:1–5

2.2.6 Semolina

2.2.6.1 From Overseers of Hired Workers

0.2.2. dabin mu-DU *simat-é-*[*a*] $^{d!}$***ma-lik-ba-*[*ni*]** šu ba-an!-ti, "*Malik-bani* received 140 liters of semolina, delivery of *Simat-Ea*," 1118:1–4

0.4.1.8 sìla dabin mu-DU *ša-at-bi-zi-il* ^{d}***ma-lik-ba-ni*** šu ba-an-ti, "*Malik-bani* received 258 liters of semolina, delivery of *Šat-bizil*," 1121:1–5

1.4.1.8 [sìla] dabin gur mu-DU ugula *zi-ti-a* ^{d}***ma-lik-ba-ni*** šu ba-an-ti, "*Malik-bani* received 1 bushel and 258 [liters] of semolina, delivery of *Zitia,* the overseer," 1122:1–5

n sìla dabin mu-DU *za-la-a* ^{d}***ma-lik-ba-ni*** šu ba-an-ti, "*Malik-bani* received n liter(s) of semolina, delivery of *Zala'a,*" 1124:1–5, 1132:1–5

0.2.4.9 sìla dabin mu-DU *li-la-a* ^{d}***ma-lik-ba-***[***ni***] šu ba-an-⸢ti⸣, "*Malik-bani* received 169 liters of semolina, delivery of *Lila'a,*" 1141:1–5

2.2.6.2 Semolina for Bird Fodder

0.0.2. dabin šà-gal mušen-na ^{d}***ma-lik-ba-ni*** šu ba-ti, "*Malik-bani* received 20 liters of semolina, fodder of birds," 1161:1–4

2.2.6.3 Semolina for *Ḫalli'a,* Delivery of *Šu-Kabta*

0.4.1 dabin *ḫal-li-*[*a*] mu-DU *šu-kab-t*[*á* ^{d}***ma-lik-ba-ni***] šu ba-an-ti, "[*Malik-bani*] received 250 liters of semolina (for) *Ḫalli'a*, delivery of *Šu-Kabta,*" 464:1–6

2.3 Broken Context

^{d}***ma-lik-ba-***[***ni*** šu] ba-ti [. . .], "*Malik-bani* received [. . .]," 1400:'1–'2

3. As a Deputy

3.1 Barley Wages

0.4.0. še á lú-ḫuĝ-ĝá a bala-e-dè gub-ba ^{ĝeš}kiri$_{6}$ šà gar-š[a-an-na]^{ki} ù ^{ĝeš}kiri$_{6}$ šà zabala$_{4}^{ki}$ ^{d}***ma-lik-ba-ni*** maškim zi-ga ⸢ĝìri⸣ *šu-kab-tá* ki ^{d}*adad-tillati*-ta ba-zi, "*Adad-tillati* disbursed 240 liters of barley, wages of hired workers employed to irrigate the gardens in Garšana and Zabala. (It was) the expenditure of *Šu-Kabta* under his authority. *Malik-bani* was the deputy," 390:1–8

3.2 Oil for *Tukulli,* the Sick Builder

½ sìla ì-[ĝeš] *tu-ku-lí* šidim u$_{4}$ dú-ra i-[me-a] ^{d}***ma-lik-ba-ni*** ⸢maškim⸣, "½ liter of sesame oil for *Tukulli* the builder when he was sick. *Malik-bani* was the deputy," 444:1–3

4. Under the Authority of *Malik-bani*

4.1 Assorted Bronzes: Receipt of *Isu-ariq*

(. . .) ki ^{d}*adad-tillati*-ta *i-sú-a-ri-iq* sagi šu ba-ti ĝìri ^{d}***ma-lik-ba-ni***, "Under the authority of *Malik-bani*, *Isu-ariq*, the cupbearer, received {assorted bronze products} from *Adad-tillati,*" 1337:8–11

4.2 Under the Authority of *Adad-tillati* and *Malik-bani*

4.2.1 Textiles

4.2.1.1 Weighed by *Ḫali*

5 ^{túg}sagšu-babbar siki-⸢ĝír⸣-gul ki-lá-bi ⅔ ma-na *ḫa-lí* túg-du$_{8}$ ì-lá ĝìri ^{d}*adad-till*[*ati*] ù ^{d}***ma-lik-ba-***[***ni***], "Under the authority of *Adad-tillati* and *Malik-bani*, *Ḫali,* the braider, weighed out ĝír-gul wool weighing ⅔ mina (for making) 5 white caps," 679:1–5

4.2.1.2 Receipt of *Puzur-agum*

(. . .) túg ki-lá tà-ga ki *aš-tá-qar*-ta *puzur$_{4}$-a-gu$_{5}$-um* šu ba-an-ti ĝìri ^{d}*adad-tillati* (šabra) ù ^{d}***ma-lik-ba-ni***, "Under the authority of *Adad-tillati*, (the majordomo), and *Malik-bani*, *Puzur-agum* received {assorted textiles}, weighed textiles having been woven, from *Aštaqqar*," 617:11–15, 618:13–17

(. . .) ki *aš-tá-qar*-ta *puzur*$_4$*-a-gu*$_5$*-um* šu ba-(an-)ti g̃ìri ^{d}*adad-tillati* (šabra) ù ^{d}***ma-lik-ba-ni***, "Under the authority of *Adad-tillati*, (the majordomo), and *Malik-bani*, *Puzur-agum* received {assorted textiles} from *Aštaqqar*," 626:4–8, 636:8–11, 637:5–9, 639:6–9, 643:2–6, 645:'5–'9, 646:7–10, 647:7–10, 649:11–13, 662:11–15, 663:9–13, 673:9–13, 680:6–9, 694:10–13, 748:16–19, 829:'9–'13

1 túg-guz-za-gen ki *aš-tá-qar*-ta *puzur*$_4$*-a-gum*! šu ba-an-ti kìšib *tu-ra-a* íb-ra g̃ìri ^{d}*adad-tillati ù* ^{d}***ma-lik-ba-ni***, "Under the authority of *Adad-tillati* and *Malik-bani*, *Puzur-agum* received 1 ordinary tufted textile from *Aštaqqar*. *Tura'a* rolled (his) seal," 644:1–7

1 gada-gen ki *a-ma-a*-ta *puzur*$_4$*-a-gu*$_5$*-um* šu ba-ti g̃ìri ^{d}*adad-tillati* ù ^{d}***ma-lik-ba-ni***, "Under the authority of *Adad-tillati* and *Malik-bani*, *Puzur-agum* received 1 ordinary linen cloth from *Ama'a*," 664:1–6

4.3 Under the Authority of *Malik-bani* and *Puzur*-Ninkarak: Pomegranate Planks

4 $^{g̃eš}$nu-úr-ma-sig$_5$ 7 $^{g̃eš}$nu-úr-ma-ús mu-DU *ak-ba-zum* um-mi-a ^{d}*adad-tillati* šu ba-an-ti g̃ìri ^{d}***ma-lik-ba-ni*** ù *puzur*$_4$-^{d}nin-kar-ak, "Under the authority of *Malik-bani* and *Puzur*-Ninkarak, *Adad-tillati* received 4 fine pomegranate planks (and) 7 lesser-quality pomegranate planks, the delivery of *Akbazum*, the craftsman," 1298:1–8

5. Legal Texts

5.1 As a Witness

igi ^{d}***ma-lik-ba-ni***, "witnessed by *Malik-bani*," 609:18, 1047:8, 1049:12, 1050:12, 1053:11, 1059:7

5.2 Receipt of Dead Birds

1 tum$_{12}$^{mušen} 2 tu-gur$_4$^{mušen} ba-úš mušen-bi ki záḫ ì-g̃ál ^{d}***ma-lik-ba-ni*** ì-dab$_5$ sim-da *da-da-a* sipa-mušen-na, "*Malik-bani* took in charge 1 wild dove (and) 2 doves, dead birds that had (previously) escaped; branding mark of *Dada'a*, the bird warden," 1058:1–8

5.3 Testifying

iti u$_4$-29-ba-zal še nu-g̃ál bí-in-gi$_4$ u$_4$-1-àm mu-[un-g̃ál] še šabra in-na-an-sum šu te-g̃e$_6$-dè nu-un-dab$_5$? ^{d}***ma-lik-ba-ni*** ka-ga-na ba-a-gen$_7$, "At the end of the 29th day of the month there was no barley. (Someone) returned it. On the 1st day, it was there. (Then) the barley was given to the majordomo. In order for him to receive it, it will not (first) be taken (by someone else). *Malik-bani* confirmed this," 1057:1–9

5.4 Translation Uncertain

1 (bùr) GÁNA [. . .] apin-l[á-šè] ^{d}*ma-lik-ba-ni*** ì-dab$_5$ gú-ba kíg̃ bí-na egir-ra-ka in-sù-ub a-šà-bi nu-ub-ta-gi$_4$-gi$_4$-da-éš, "*Malik-bani* took in charge 1 bur of acreage [. . .] for plowing. He did work on its side (?)," 1048:1–8

^{d}*ma-lik-ba-ni*** rá-gaba u$_4$-5-àm ki šà-ga-na-ka mu-un-til-la-⸢šè⸣ é-agrig i[n-x] ka-ga-na ba-a-[gen$_7$], 1054:1–6

6. The Tablet of *Malik-bani*: Brought to Edana

1 *be-lí-ì-lí* 1 *šu*-^{d}nin-kar-ak dub ^{d}***ma-lik-ba-ni*** é-[da]-na^{ki}-šè de$_6$-a, "*Beli-ili* and *Šu*-Ninkarak having brought the tablet of *Malik-bani* to Edana," 51:'22–'24, 52:59–62, 53:61–63, 56:'32–'35

^{d}*ma-lik-tillati*

Malik-tillati, the Ox-Herder, Supervised by *Nur-Adad*, the Majordomo

1. Ox-Drivers from his Gang

n g̃uruš ^{d}***ma-lik-tillati*** nu-bànda-gu$_4$ (. . .) ugula *nu-úr-*^{d}*adad* šabra šà-gu$_4$-me-éš, "n workmen (from the gang of) *Malik-tillati*, the ox-herder, (and) {other gangs}, ox-drivers supervised by *Nur-Adad*, the majordomo," 188:'1, '3–'4, 189:8–10, 190:10, 12–13, 191:13, 17–18, 193:12, 14–15, 198:'4, '7, '9

[n] g̃uruš ^{d}***ma-lik-tillati*** nu-bànda-gu$_4$ (. . .) šà-g[u$_4$-me-éš ára]d-é-a-[me-eš] (. . .) ugula *nu-úr-*^{d}*a*[*dad*], "[n] workmen (from the gang of) *Malik-tillati*, the ox-herder (and) {other gangs}, ox-drivers—household servants—(and) {hired workers} supervised by *Nur-Adad*," 194:18, 21–22, 26

n g̃uruš ^{d}***ma-lik-tillati*** nu-bànda-gu$_4$ (. . .) šà-gu$_4$-me-éš (. . .) ugula *nu-úr-*^{d}*adad* šabra, "n workmen (from the gang of) *Malik-tillati*, the ox-herder, (and) {other gangs}, ox-drivers (and) {hired workers} supervised by *Nur-Adad*, the majordomo," 196:'7, '10, '13, 197:14, 17, 20

2. Overseer of Sick Workers

[n] g̃uruš dú<-ra> ^{d}***ma-***[***lik-tillati***] nu-bànda-g[u$_4$ ugula] *nu-úr-*^{d}*adad* [šabra], "[n] sick workmen (from the gang of) *Malik-tillati*, the ox-herder, (ox-drivers) [supervised by] *Nur-Adad*, [the majordomo]," 195:'28–'29

1 g̃uruš dú-ra ^{d}***ma-li***[***k-til***]***lati*** nu-bànda-gu$_4$ [ugula] *nu-úr-*^{d}*adad* šabra, "1 sick workman (from the gang of) *Malik-tillati*, the ox-herder, (ox-drivers) [supervised by] *Nur-Adad*, the majordomo," 196:'31–'32, 197:40–41

[1 g̃uruš] dú-ra 1 *ú-bar-*⸢*um*⸣ 1 *bí-za-*⸢*tum*⸣ 1 *šu-*^{d}⸢*adad*⸣ 1 AN.TAG.⸢KAL⸣ ^{d}***ma-lik-tillati*** [nu-bànda]-gu$_4$ ugula *nu-úr-*^{d}*adad* šabra, "[1] sick [workman], *Ubarum*, *Bizatum*, *Šu-Adad* (and) AN.TAG.KAL, (workers from the gang of) *Malik-tillati*, the ox-herder, supervised by *Nur-Adad*, the majordomo," 198:'32–'38

3. Broken Context

★★[n] *bí-za-tum* [. . .*eš*$_4$]-*tár* [. . .i]m [. . .]-lu ^{d}***ma-li***[***k-tillati*** nu-bànda-g]u$_4$ [. . .], 194:70–73

^{d}*ma-lik-tillat-sú*

Malik-tillassu, the Barber

1. As a Deputy

1.1 Distribution of Barley

[0.n.n. š]e ensi-šè [PN] ^{lú}kíg̃-gi$_4$-a-lugal [x].GA.URU ⸢níg̃⸣-šu-taka$_4$-lugal [mu]-un-de$_9$-a [x? š]e? *nu-úr-ma-ti-šu* rá-gaba ^{d}***ma-lik-tillat-sú*** [šu-i] ⸢maškim⸣ u$_4$-7-kam, "[n liter(s)] of barley for the dream interpreter; [PN], the royal messenger, who brought the (?), the royal consignment. (?) *Nur-matišu* was the courier. *Malik-tillassu*, [the barber], was the deputy on the 7th day," 484:10–16

0.0.2. še ^{lú}kíg̃-gi$_4$-a-lugal ⸢u$_4$⸣-3-kam 4 sìla še ^{d}*šu-*^{d}*suen-na-ra-am-*^{d}en-líl u$_4$-4-kam ^{d}***ma-lik-tillat-sú*** šu-i maškim, "20 liters of barley (for) the royal messenger on the 3rd day (and) 4 liters of barley (for) *Šu-Suen-naram*-Enlil on the 4th day. *Malik-tillassu*, the barber, was the deputy," 488:1–7

5 sìla še ^{d}*šu*-^{d}*suen-na-ra-am*-^{d}en-líl ^{d}***ma-lik-tillat-sú*** maškim, "5 liters of barley (for) *Šu-Suen-naram*-Enlil. *Malik-tillassu*, was the deputy," 554:1–3

1.2 Distribution of Semolina and Emmer

2 sìla dabin 1 sìla eša *um-mi-kab-tá* 2 sìla dabin 1 sìla eša *ma-la-ti* ^{d}***ma-lik-tillat-sú*** šu-i maškim, "2 liters of semolina (and) 1 liter of fine flour (for) *Ummi-Kabta* (and) 2 liters of semolina (and) 1 liter of fine flour (for) *Malati*. *Malik-tillassu*, the barber, was the deputy," 1016:13–17

ma-ma-*ri-be*

1. Receipt of Barley and Oil

^{d}*adad-tillati* ù-na-a-du$_{11}$ 10.0.0. še gur 0.0.1. ì-g̃eš **ma-ma-*ri-be*** ḫé-na-ab-sum-mu, "Say to *Adad-tillati* that '10 bushels of barley (and) 10 liters of sesame oil should be given to Mama-*ribe*,'" 1044:1–6

ma-nu-um-ki-^{d}šul-gi

1. Receipts

[. . .] *mu-du-lum* ***ma-nu-um-ki*-^{d}šul-gi** šu ba-ti ki ^{d}*adad-tillati*-[ta] ba-[zi], "*Manum-ki*-Šulgi received salted [. . .] from *Adad-tillati*," 1188:1–6

ma-šum

1. *Mašum*, the Builder and Household Servant[46]

1.1 As a Witness

igi ***ma-šum*** ár[ad-é-a], "witnessed by *Mašum*, the household servant," 1052:14

igi ***ma-šum*** šidim, "witnessed by *Mašum*, the builder," 1057:12, 1061:7

1.2 Errands: Sent to *Šu-Kabta*

1 ***ma-šum*** šidim ki *šu-kab-ta*-šè g̃en-na, "*Mašum*, the builder, having gone to the place of *Šu-Kabta*," 59:58–59, 60:54–55, 61:15, 62:'16

1.3 Receipts: Provisions for Builders

(. . .) 1 sìla ***ma-šum*** árad-é-a kaš-gen-bi 5-sìla šidim-e-ne íb-nag̃, "{4 liters of ordinary beer for other workers} (and) 1 liter (of beer for) *Mašum*, the household servant. (In total:) their ordinary beer is 5 liters. The builders drank (the beer)," 378:13–16, 380:5–8, 384:1–7, 389:5–8

1 sìla ninda ***ma-šum*** árad-é-a (. . .) šà-gal šidim-e-ne u$_{4}$ bàd egir é-a dù-dè, "1 liter of bread (for) *Mašum*, the household servant, (and for) {other workers}, food (for) builders when they were constructing the (enclosure) wall behind the house," 386:21, 39–30, 387:12, 20–21

---

46 That these two individuals are the same person is suggested by the fact that *Mašum*, the builder, runs errands normally assigned to household servants.

1 sìla dabin ***ma-šum*** árad-é-a (. . .) šà-gal šidim-e-ne u_4 bàd in-dù-sa-a, "1 liter of semolina (for) *Mašum*, the household servant, (and for) {other workers}, food (for) builders, when they constructed the (enclosure) wall," 396:13, 19–20, 397:13, 19–20

⅓ sìla níĝ-àr-ra-sig_5 1 sìla še níĝ-àr-ra 1 sìla ninda ***ma-šum*** ár[ad-é-a] (. . .) šà-gal šidim-e-ne, "⅓ liter of fine groats, 1 liter of barley groats (and) 1 liter of bread (for) *Mašum*, the household servant, (and for) {other workers}, food (for) builders," 381:13–15, 21

2. *Mašum*, the Craftsman

2.1 Receipts: Provisions for Builders and Scribes

0.0.3. še níĝ-àr-ra-sig_5 ^{dug}útul [0.n.n.] dabin 3 ádda-[udu ***ma***]***-šum*** um-mi-[a] (. . .) [šà-gal šidim] ù dub-sar-e-ne, "30 liters of fine barley groats (for) the tureen, [n liter(s)] of semolina, (and) 3 [sheep] carcasses (for) *Mašum*, the craftsman, (and for) {other workers}, [food (for) builders] and scribes," 399:13–15, 24

mu-na-núm

Munanum, the Ox-Herder, Supervised by *Babani*, the Majordomo

1. Ox-Drivers from his Gang

2 ĝuruš ***mu-na-núm*** nu-bànda-gu_4 (. . .) ugula *ba-ba-ni* PA.[AL], "2 workmen (from the gang of) *Munanum*, the ox-herder, (and) {other gangs}, supervised by *Babani*, the majordomo," 191:8, 10

5? ⸢ĝuruš⸣ ḫuĝ-ĝá ***mu-na-núm*** nu-bànda-gu_4 (. . .) lú-ḫuĝ-ĝá-me-éš ugula *ba-ba-ni* šabra, "5? hired workmen (from the gang of) *Munanum*, (and) {other gangs}, hired workers supervised by *Babani*, the majordomo," 194:9–10, 13–15

2 ĝuruš ***mu-na-núm*** n[u-bànda-gu_4] šà-⸢gu_4⸣-me-éš (. . .) ugula [*ba-b*]*a-ni* šabra, "2 ox-driver (from the gang of) *Munanum*, the ox-herder, ox-drivers (and) {hired workers} supervised by *Babani*, the majordomo," 197:7–8, 11

2. Workers from his Gang Hired to Break up Earth

9 ĝuruš u_4-1-šè še 6 sìla-ta ba-ḫuĝ im si-le ⸢gub⸣-ba ***mu-na-núm*** ⸢ugula⸣ *ba-ba-ni*, "9 workmen (from the gang of) *Munanum*, supervised by *Babani*, hired for 1 day (for) 6 liters of barley each, (workers) employed to break up earth," 474:1–5

– N –

na-bu-tum

1. Birds Sent to his Place

[n] uz-tur šu-ur_4-ra [x?] šu tag-a ki ***na-bu-tum*-šè [1] šáḫ-zé-da é-muḫaldim mu *simat-*^{d}*ištaran*<-šè> *ì-lí-ra-bí* maškim zi-ga *simat-*^{d}*ištaran*, "[n] duckling wing(s)?, (?) to the place of *Nabutum*, (and) 1 piglet (for) the kitchen for *Simat-Ištaran*. (It was) the expenditure of *Simat-Ištaran*. *Ili-rabi* was the deputy," 529:20–26

na-na

Nana, the Female Miller

1. **Verifying *Libur-iduni*'s Dinner**

1 ir_7[mušen] *li-bur-i-du-ni* in-gu_7-a ka-ga-na ba-a-ge-en ***na-na*** géme kíkken *a-ta-li-ku* sipa-mušen-na in-ge-né-eš "*Libur-iduni* confirmed that he ate 1 pigeon. *Nana* the female miller (and) *Ataliku* (the bird warden) verified it," 1055:1–7

na-sìm

1. ***Nasim*, Father of *Dada***

0.1.0. še 4 ma-na siki-gen ½ sìla ì-šáh̬ 5 sìla zì-kum 5 sìla zú-lum udug é-*da-da* dumu ***na-sìm***, "60 liters of barley, 4 minas of ordinary wool, ½ liter of lard, 5 liters of kum-flour (and) 5 liters of dates (for) the caretaker at the house of *Dada*, son of *Nasim*," 438:1–6

2. ***Nasim*, the Royal Messenger**

1 g̃uruš [lú]ázlag u_4-25-šè ***na-sìm*** [lú]kíg̃-gi_4<-a>-lugal-ta lú te-te-dè in-da-$g̃e_{26}$-en zi-ga g̃ìri *šu-kab-tá* ki [PN]-ta [ba-z]i?, "[PN] disbursed 1 fuller for 25 days. *Nasim*, the royal messenger, went to bring the man (i.e., the fuller) from the king. It was the expenditure of *Šu-Kabta* under his authority" 222:1–8

na-wi-ir-ilum

1. **His Possessions: Expended by *Šu-Kabta***

1.1 **His Boat**

3 g̃uruš [lú]ázlag u_4-2½-šè nibru[ki]-ta é-[d]*šu*-[d]*suen*-šè má ***na-wi-ir-ilum*** íb-gíd g̃ìri g̃ìri-[d]ba-ú-ì-dab_5 zi-ga g̃ìri *šu-kab-tá* ki *puzur₄-a-gu₅-um*-ta ba-zi, "*Puzur-agum* disbursed 3 fullers for 2½ days. They towed the boat of *Nawir-ilum* from Nippur to *Bit-Šu-Suen*. (It was) the expenditure of *Šu-Kabta* under his authority (and) that of G̃iri-Ba'u-idab," 220:1–11

1.2 **Textiles for his Chair Covering**

[n] [túg][níg̃-lá]m-ús [n-ka]m [n] túg-guz-za-ús [n]-kam t[úg?-ba]r?-r[a-n]i? *h̬a-um* ***na-wi-ir-ilum*** zi-ga *šu-kab-tá* ki *aš-tá-qar*-ta ba-zi, "*Aštaqqar* disbursed [n n[th]]-quality níg̃-lám textile(s), [n n[th]]-quality tufted textile(s), (and) *h̬a-um* textiles of *Nawir-ilum*. (It was) the expenditure of *Šu-Kabta*," 650:2–8

2. **Under his Authority: Freed Workmen**

[n g̃ur]uš du_8-h̬a-me-éš ⌜gìri⌝ ***na-wi-ir-ilum***, "[n] workmen released under the authority of *Nawir-ilum*," 65:'22–'23

3. **After his Death**

3.1 **Possessions**

3.1.1 **Assorted Textiles**

(. . .) níg̃-gur_{11} ***na-wi-ir-ilum***-ma ba-úš! *nu-úr-*[d]*adad* maškim šà nibru[ki] ki *puzur₄-a-gu₅-um*-ta ba-zi, "In Nippur, *Puzur-agum* disbursed {assorted textiles}, the property of *Nawir-ilum*, who had died. *Nur-adad* was the deputy," 574:3–7

3.1.2 **Sheep for Regular (Funerary) Offerings**

12 udu sá-du_{11}-ki-a-nag-***na-wi-ir-ilum*** ki [d]*adad-tillati*-ta ba-zi, "*Adad-tillati* disbursed 12 sheep, regular offerings of the funerary libation place of *Nawir-ilum*," 982:3–6

3.2. Workers to Mourn *Nawir-ilum*

11 ĝuruš sa[ĝ-tag] 2 ĝuruš á-⅔-ta 4 ĝuruš á-½-ta 1 ĝuruš á-⅓<-ta> ^{lú}ázlag-me-éš u_4-1-šè gaba sàg-gé-dè [gub-ba] u_4 ***na-wi-ir-*[*ilum*** ba-úš-a] *é-a-šar* maškim zi-ga *šu-kab-*⌜*tá*⌝ ki *puzur*$_4$*-a-gu*$_5$*-um-*⌜ta⌝ ba-zi, "*Puzur-agum* disbursed 11 full-time fullers, 2 fullers at ⅔ wages, 4 fullers at ½ wages (and) 1 fuller at ⅓ wages employed for 1 day to beat (their) breasts when *Nawir-ilum* [died]. (It was) the expenditure of *Šu-Kabta*. *Ea-šar* was the deputy," 250:1–12

(. . .) ⌜u_4⌝-1-šè gaba sàg-dè gub-ba u_4 diĝir-re gaba ***na-wi-ir-ilum*** ba-a-ĝar-ra *é-a-šar* dub-sar maškim zi-ga *šu-kab-tá* [ki] ^{d}*adad-tillati*-ta ba-zi, "*Adad-tillati* disbursed {craftsmen} employed for 1 day to beat (their) breasts when the god made the breast of *Nawir-ilum* subside (i.e. when he died). (It was) the expenditure of *Šu-Kabta*. *Ea-šar*, the scribe, was the deputy," 251:8–13

nar-^{d}inana[47]

1. Provisions

[. . .] **nar?-^{d}inana** (. . .) [šu+níĝin n+]7.0.0. gur še-ba *ba-zi-tum* šu+níĝin 47.1.[n.] še-ba é, "[barley? (for)] Nar-Inana (and barley for) {other individuals}; [in total: n+]7 bushels of the barley rations of *Bazitum*; in total: 47 bushels (and) 60[+n] liters of barley rations of the household," 555:17, 24–25

ni-a-ma

1. Provisions

5 gín ì-šáḫ-ta 15 gín níĝ-àr-ra-sig$_5$ 1⅓ ma-na tuḫ-ĝeš-ì-[ḫád-ta] 10 gín ádda-u[du-ta] 10 gín mun-ta 3 gín luḫ-lá-⌜ta⌝ ga-na-⌜na⌝ 1 *lu-*⌜*lu*⌝? 1 ***ni-a-ma*** 1 ***ni-a-ma*** [min?] 1 *simat-*^{d}*ištaran* nu-x 1 *simat-*^{d}*ištaran* zi-[x] 1 *simat-*^{d}*ištaran* [x]-ti 1 *lu-*⌜*lu*⌝? min munus-me-éš {indent}10, "5 shekels of lard each, 15 shekels of fine groats, 1⅓ minas of [dried] sesame chaff [each], 10 shekels of sheep carcasses [each], 10 shekels of salt each, 3 shekels of luḫ-lá each (?), (provisions for) *Lulu*, *Ni'ama*, *Ni'ama* [the 2nd], *Simat-Ištaran* [x], *Simat-Ištaran* [x] (and) *Lulu*, the 2nd, 10? women," 562:'40–'55

nin-lu-lu

1. Provisions: Barley

0.0.1. še **nin-lu-lu** a-bu-DU$_{10}$ maškim ba-[zi], "10 liters of barley were disbursed (for) Ninlulu. *Abu-ṭabu* was the deputy," 486:1–4

nin-zi-šà-ĝál

1. Possessions: His Boat, Towed from Garšana to ĜEŠ.KÚŠU

[. . . n] ĝuruš á-[n-ta] ^{lú}ázlag-me-[éš] u_4-1-[šè] má-**nin-zi-šà-ĝál** gar-ša-an-na^{ki}-ta ĜEŠ.KÚŠU^{ki}-šè in-gíd-ša-a, "[. . .] (and) [n] fuller(s) at [n] wages [for] 1 day. They towed the boat of Nin-zišaĝal from Garšana to ĜEŠ.KÚŠU," 238:1–7

---

47 That this is a personal name and not a title is suggested by context.

2. Provisions: Sheep

3 udu **nin-zi-šà-⌜g̃ál⌝** ki *ì-lí-bi-la-ni*-ta ba-zi, "*Ili-bilani* disbursed 3 sheep (for) Nin-zišag̃al," 1012:5–7

3. Under his Authority: Animals

1 udu abzu-šè 1 máš ká kù-^{d}inana-zabala$_{4}$^{ki} u$_{4}$ ezem-gur-buru$_{14}$ g̃ìri **nin-zi-šà-g̃ál** (. . .) ki *ì-lí-bi-la-ni*-ta ba-zi, "Under the authority of Nin-zišag̃al, *Ili-bilanni* disbursed 1 sheep for the abzu (and) 1 goat for the gate of bright Inana of Zabala during the bushel harvest festival (and) {other disbursements}," 996:1–5, 9–10

nu-ru-uš-e-lí

1. As a Deputy: Linen for the House of the Women

3 gín šudum-gada é-munus-šè ***nu-ru-uš-e-lí*** maškim šà gar-ša-an-na^{ki} u$_{4}$-25-kam (. . .) zi-ga *simat-*^{d}*ištaran* ki ^{d}*adad-tillati*-ta ba-zi, "In Garšana on the 25th day, *Adad-tillati* disbursed 3 shekels of linen warp-thread for the house of the women. *Nuruš-eli* was the deputy. {Other disbursals}. (These were) the expenditures of *Simat-Ištaran*," 541:1–5, 27–28

2. Receipts: Assorted Textiles

[n ^{túg}]bar-dul$_{5}$ *šu-kab-tá a-ši-um* ***nu-ru-uš-e-li*** šu ba-ti ki *šu*-^{d}nin-in-si-ta ba-zi, "*Nuruš-eli* received [n] *a-si-um* bar-dul$_{5}$ textile(s) of *Šu-Kabta* from *Šu*-Nininsi," 762:1–5

(. . .) túg-sa-gi$_{4}$-àm ***nu-ru-uš-e-lí*** šu ba-ti ki ^{d}*adad-tillati*-ta ba-zi, "*Nuruš-eli* received {assorted} finished textiles from *Adad-tillati*," 773:12–16, 790:3–6

2 ^{túg}gú-è *tá-ki-ru-um* bar-s[i g̃ar-r]a tur lugal ***nu-ru-uš-[e]-lí*** šu ba-ti [ki] ^{d}*adad-tillati*-ta ba-zi, "*Nuruš-eli* received 2 small royal *takkirum* capes [fashioned] with bands from *Adad-tillati*," 824:1–5

(. . .) ki ^{d}*adad-tillati*-ta ***nu-ru-uš-e-lí*** šu ba-ti, "*Nuruš-eli* received {assorted textiles} from *Adad-tillati*," 825:4–6

nu-úr-^{d}adad

1. *Nur-Adad*, the Leather Worker and Thief

1 kuš-udu-niga a-g̃ar gu$_{7}$ ***nu-úr-^{d}adad*** ašgab ba-an-zuḫ *a-na-aḫ-ì-lí* ašgab in-ge-en, "*Nur-Adad*, the leather-worker, stole 1 de-haired skin of a fattened sheep. *Anaḫ-ili*, the leather-worker, confirmed it," 1061:1–4

2. *Nur-Adad*, the Majordomo

2.1 Supervision of Ox-drivers

[n] g̃uruš šà-gu$_{4}$ ugula ***nu-úr-^{d}adad*** šabra, "[n] ox-driver(s) supervised by *Nur-Adad*, the majordomo," 190:31

2.1.1 Ox-drivers from the Gangs of *Sukkalia* and *Malik-tillati*

1 g̃uruš *su-kà-lí-a* nu-bànda-gu$_{4}$ 2 g̃uruš nu-bànda-gu$_{4}$ 2 g̃uruš ^{d}*ma-lik-tillati* nu-bànda-gu$_{4}$ ugula ***nu-úr-^{d}adad*** šabra šà-gu$_{4}$-me-éš, "1 workman (from the gang of) *Sukkalia*, the ox-herder, 2 workmen (from the gang of) an ox-herder, (and) 2 workmen (from the gang of) *Malik-tillati*, the ox-herder, ox-drivers supervised by *Nur-Adad*, the majordomo," 189:6–10

2.1.2 Ox-drivers from the Gangs of *Sukkalia* and *Tigan*

2 g̃uruš ugula *ti-ga-an* nu-bànda-[gu_4] 1 g̃uruš ugula *su-kà-lí-a* nu-bànda-[gu_4] 3 g̃uruš ugula ⸢***nu***⸣***-úr-***^{d}***adad*** nu-bànda-gu_4, "2 workmen supervised by *Tigan*, the ox-herder, 1 workman supervised by *Sukkalia*, the ox-herder, 3 workmen supervised by *Nur-Adad*, the ox-herder," 187:5–8

2.1.3 Ox-drivers from the Gangs of *Sukkalia, Malik-tillati,* and Ur-Dumuzi

n g̃uruš *su-kà-lí-a* nu-bànda-gu_4 n g̃uruš nu-bànda-gu_4 n g̃uruš ^{d}*ma-lik-tillati* nu-bànda-gu_4 n g̃uruš ur-^{d}dumu-zi nu-bànda-gu_4 ugula ***nu-úr-***^{d}***adad*** (šabra / nu-bànda-gu_4) šà-gu_4-me-éš, "n workmen (from the gang of) *Sukkalia*, n workmen (from the gang of) an ox-herder, n workmen (from the gang of) *Malik-tillati*, (and) n workmen (from the gang of) Ur-Dumuzi, the ox-herder, ox-drivers supervised by *Nur-Adad*, (the majordomo / the ox-herder)," 190:8–13, 193:10–15

2.1.4 Ox-drivers from the Gangs of *Sukkalia, Malik-tillati*, Ur-Dumuzi, and *Tigan*

n g̃uruš *su-kà-lí-a* nu-bànda-gu_4 n g̃uruš nu-bànda-gu_4 2 g̃uruš ^{d}*ma-lik-tillati* nu-bànda-gu_4 n g̃uruš ur-^{d}dumu-zi nu-bànda-gu_4 n g̃uruš *ti-ga-an* nu-bànda-gu_4 {indent} n ugula ***nu-úr-***^{d}***adad*** šabra šà-gu_4-me-éš, "n workmen (from the gang of) *Sukkalia*, the ox-herder, n workmen (from the gang of) an ox-herder, 2 workmen (from the gang of) *Malik-tillati*, the ox-herder, n workmen (from the gang of) Ur-Dumuzi, the ox-herder, (and) n workmen (from the gang of) *Tigan*, the ox-herder; (in total:) n ox-drivers supervised by *Nur-Adad*, the majordomo," 191:11–18, 198:'1–'9

2.2 Supervision of Ox-Drivers and Hired Workers

2.2.1 From the Gangs of *Sukkalia, Malik-tillati*, Ur-Dumuzi, *Tigan*, and *Ilum-bani*

n g̃uruš *su-kà-lí-a* nu-bànda-gu_4 n g̃uruš nu-bànda-gu_4 n g̃uruš ^{d}*ma-lik-tillati* nu-bànda-gu_4 n g̃uruš ur-^{d}dumu-zi nu-bànda-gu_4 n g̃uruš *ti-ga-an* nu-bànda-gu_4 šà-gu_4-me-éš árad-é-a-me-éš n g̃uruš ḫug̃-g̃á *ilum-ba-ni* nu-bànda-gu_4 {indent} n ugula ***nu-úr-***^{d}***adad*** (šabra), "n workmen (from the gang of) *Sukkalia*, the ox-herder, n workmen (from the gang of) an ox-herder, n workmen (from the gang of) *Malik-tillati*, the ox-herder, n workmen (from the gang of) Ur-Dumuzi, the ox-herder, (and) n workmen (from the gang of) *Tigan*, the ox-herder—ox-drivers (and) household servants—(and) n hired workmen (from the gang of) *Ilum-bani*, the ox-herder; (in total:) n workmen supervised by *Nur-Adad*, (the majordomo)," 194:16–26, 196:'5–'13, 197:12–20

2.2.2 Team Members Broken

[. . . n g̃uruš ^{d}*ma-lik-tillati*] nu-bànda-gu_4 [n g̃uruš ur]-^{d}dumu-zi nu-bànda-gu_4 [ugula ***n***]***u-úr-***^{d}***adad*** šabra [šà]-gu_4-me-éš, "[. . . n workmen (from the gang of) *Malik-tillati*], the ox-herder, (and) [n workmen (from the gang of)] Ur-Dumuzi, the ox-herder, ox-drivers [supervised by] *Nur-Adad*, the majordomo," 188:'1–'4

2.3 Sick Workers from Gangs Supervised by *Nur-Adad*

1 g̃uruš dú-ra ^{d}*ma-li*[*k-til*]*lati* nu-bànda-gu_4 [ugula] ***nu-úr-***^{d}***adad*** šabra, "1 sick workman (from the gang of) *Malik-tillati*, the ox-herder, (workers) supervised by *Nur-Adad*, the majordomo," 185:'29, 196:'31–'32, 197:40–41

[1 g̃uruš] dú-ra 1 *ú-bar-*⸢*um*⸣ 1 *bí-za-*⸢*tum*⸣ 1 *šu-*^{d}⸢*adad*⸣ 1 AN.TAG.⸢KAL⸣ ^{d}*ma-lik-tillati* [nu-bànda]-gu_4 ugula ***nu-úr-***^{d}***adad*** šabra, "[1] sick [workman], *Ubarum*, *Bizatum*, *Šu-*

Adad (and) AN.TAG.KAL, (workers from the gang of) *Malik-tillati*, the ox-herder, supervised by *Nur-Adad*, the majordomo," 198:'32–'38

3. *Nur-Adad*, Overseer of 60

n g̃uruš sag̃-tag n g̃uruš á-½-ta nam–60 ***nu-úr-^{d}adad***, "n full-time workmen (and) n workmen at ½ wages (supervised by) *Nur-Adad*, overseer of 60," 202:7–9, 203:7–9, 205:2–4, 206:2–4, 207:2–4, 209:2–4

4. *Nur-Adad*, Title Unspecified

4.1 As a Deputy

4.1.1 Textiles

4.1.1.1 Delivery of *Aštaqqar*

1 túg-^{d}*al-la-tum*-gùn-a ù zi-in-bi ki-lá-bi 9 ma-[na] 12 gín *a-ku$_{8}$-a-nu-ri* ***nu-úr-^{d}adad* maškim zi-ga g̃ìri *šu-kab-ta* ki *aš-tá-qar*-ta ba-zi, "*Aštaqqar* disbursed 1 colored textile of *Allatum* and its zi-in weighing 9 minas (and) 12 shekels (for) *Akua-nuri*. (It was) the expenditure of *Šu-Kabta* under his authority. *Nur-Adad* was the deputy," 584:1–7

4.1.1.2 Delivery of *Puzur-agum*

(. . .) níg̃-gur$_{11}$ *na-wi-ir-ilum-ma* ba-úš! ***nu-úr-^{d}adad*** maškim šà nibru^{ki} ki *puzur$_{4}$-a-gu$_{5}$-um*-ta ba-zi, "In Nippur, *Puzur-agum* disbursed {assorted textiles}, the property of *Nawir-ilum*, who had died. *Nur-adad* was the deputy," 574:3–7

1 túg-guz-za-tur 4-kam-ús ^{d}*ištaran* ***nu-úr-^{d}adad*** maškim šà nibru^{ki} zi-ga g̃ìri *simat-^{d}ištaran* ki *puzur$_{4}$-a-gum*-ta ba-zi, "*Puzur-agum* disbursed 1 small 4th-quality tufted textile of *Ištaran*. (It was) the expenditure of *Simat-Ištaran* under her authority in Nippur. *Nur-Adad* was the deputy," 576:1–6

4.1.2 Work Assignments for Fullers

4.1.2.1 Bringing Wool to Nippur

1 g̃uruš ^{lú}ázlag sag̃-tag u$_{4}$-2-šè 2 g̃uruš sag̃-tag 2 g̃uruš á-½-ta u$_{4}$-2-šè siki é-^{d}*šu-^{d}suen*^{ki}-ta nibru^{ki}-šè DU(sic!) de$_{6}$-a ***nu-úr-^{d}adad*** maškim ki *puzur$_{4}$-a-gu$_{5}$-um*-ta ba-zi, "*Puzur-agum* disbursed 1 full-time fuller for 2 days, 2 full-time workmen (and) 2 half-time workmen for 2 days having brought wool from *Bit-Šu-Suen* to Nippur. *Nur-Adad* was the deputy," 226:1–10

4.1.2.2 For the Royal Banquet

2 g̃uruš ^{lú}ázlag u$_{4}$-1-šè zi-ga kaš-dé-a lugal šà á-<ki->ti gub-ba ***nu-úr-^{d}adad*** maškim zi-ga g̃ìri *šu-kab-ta* ki *puzur$_{4}$-a-gu$_{5}$-um*-ta ba-zi, "*Puzur-agum* disbursed 2 fullers employed for 1 day, expended (for) the royal banquet of the Akiti festival. (It was) the expenditure of *Šu-Kabta* under his authority. *Nur-Adad* was the deputy," 221:1–7

4.2 Under his Authority in Du-saḫara: Barley in the Possession of *Adallal*

41.2.0. še gur še apin-lá ki *a-da-làl* in-da-g̃ál g̃ìri ***nu-úr-^{d}adad*** šà du$_{6}$-saḫar-ra^{ki}, "Under the authority of *Nur-Adad* in Du-saḫara, 41 bushels (and) 120 liters of barley, barley of the cultivator, are with *Adallal* at his place," 1158:1–6

nu-úr-ì-lí

Nur-ili, the Šarabdu Official

1. Under his Authority: Barley

10.2.4.5 sìla še gur še apin-lá-a ^{d}*adad-tillati* [PA].AL šu ba-an-ti ĝìri ***nu-úr-ì-lí*** ša-ra-ab-du, "Under the authority of *Nur-ili*, the šarabdu-official, *Adad-tillati*, the majordomo, received 10 bushels (and) 165 liters of barley, barley of the cultivator," 1089:1–5

nu-úr-ma-ti-šu

1. *Nur-matišu*, the Courier: Distribution of Barley

[0.n.n. š]e ensi-šè [PN] ^{lú}kíĝ-gi$_4$-a-lugal [x].GA.URU ⸢níĝ⸣-šu-taka$_4$-lugal [mu]-un-de$_9$-a [x? š]e? ***nu-úr-ma-ti-šu*** rá-gaba ^{d}*ma-lik-tillat-sú* [šu-i] ⸢maškim⸣ u$_4$-7-kam, "[n liter(s)] of barley for the dream interpreter; [PN], the royal messenger, who brought (?), the royal consignment. (?) *Nur-matišu* was the courier. *Malik-tillassu*, [the barber], was the deputy on the 7th day," 484:10–16

2. *Nur-matišu*, Title Unspecified

2.1 As a Deputy: Provisions for the Cult

0.0.3. ninda-šu-ra-gen ½ sìla du$_8$ gala ù kur-ĝá-ra-a-ne ***nu-úr-ma-ti-šu*** maškim (. . .) zi-ga *simat*-^{d}*ištaran* ki ^{d}*adad-tillati*-ta ba-zi, "*Adad-tillati* disbursed 30 liters of ordinary half (loaf) bread baked (in) ½ liter (loaves) for the lamentation singers and the cultic performers. *Nur-matišu* was the deputy. {Other disbursals}. (These were) the expenditures of *Simat-Ištaran*," 541:14–16, 27–28

nu-úr-zu

Nurzu, the Doorkeeper

1. As a Witness

igi ***nu-úr-zu*** ì-du$_8$, "witnessed by *Nurzu*, the doorkeeper," 1054:9

– P –

pa-da-^{d}šul-gi

Pada-Šulgi, the Courier

1. Distrbution of Beer

0.1.0. kaš-gen 0.0.2.1½ [sìl]a ⸢kaš⸣ lú gaba sàg-dè íb-naĝ **pa?-da-^{d}šul-gi** rá-⸢gaba⸣ (. . .) zi-ga *simat*-^{d}K[A.DI] ki ^{d}[*adad*]-*tillati*-ta ba-zi, "*Adad-tillati* disbursed 60 liters of ordinary beer (and) 21½ liters of beer. The men who beat (their) breasts drank (the beer). Pada-Šulgi was the courier. {Other disbursals under different authority.} (It was) the expenditure of *Simat-Ištaran*," 507:12–14, 16–18

pe-ṣe-ti

1. Provisions: Wages for Molding Bricks

15½ sar 4 gín ***pe-ṣe-ti*** (. . .) šeg$_{12}$ du$_8$-[a], "15½ sar (and) 4 shekels (of bricks from) *Peṣeti* (and bricks from) {other workers}, {wages for workers} having molded bricks," 350:14, '23

2. **Translation Uncertain**

[. . .] 1 gíd-[. . .] 12 sar 18 gín ⌜apin⌝? šà é-g̃ar 16½ sar 5 gín **[*pe*]-*ṣe-ti* NE-gu$_7$-bi g̃ìri ^{d}*adad-*[*till*]*ati*, 1397:'1–'9

pi$_5$-ša-aḫ-ilum

é-***pi$_5$-ša-aḫ-ilum***, "the house of *Pišaḫ-ilum*" > *Household Index*

pu-šu-ki-in

1. ***Pušu-kin*, Man from Karkar**

pu-šu-ki-in (. . .) ugula [*šu*]-*la-núm* (. . .) lú-karkar^{ki}-me, "*Pušukin*, supervised by *Šulanum*, (and) {other workers}, men from Karkar," 559:2, 12, 28

2. ***Pušu-kin*, Title Unspecified**

2.1 **Deliveries: Reed Bundles**

n sa gi-izi gu-níg̃in 15-sa-ta n sa gi-zi gu-níg̃in (10 / 20)-sa-ta ki ***pu-šu-ki-in***-ta ^{d}*adad-tillati* šu ba-an-ti g̃ìri *be-lí-ì-lí* ugula má gíd, "Under the authority of *Beli-ili*, overseer of boat towers, *Adad-tillati* received from *Pušu-kin* n bundle(s) of fuel reeds, bales of 15 bunches each, (and) n bundle(s) of fresh reeds, bales of (10 or 20) bunches each," 1276:1–8, 1277:1–8

3540 sa gi-izi gu-níg̃in 15-sa-ta 600 sa gi-šid gu-níg̃in 20-sa-ta ki ***pu-š*[*u-k*]*i-in***-ta ^{d}⌜*adad*⌝-*tillati* šu [ba-a]n-ti g̃ìri *be-lí-ì-lí* ugula má gíd, "Under the authority of *Beli-ili*, overseer of boat towers, *Adad-tillati* received from *Pušu-kin* 3540 bundles of fuel reeds, bales of 15 bunches each, (and) 600 bundles of dry reeds, bales of 20 bunches each," 1278:1–8

pu-ta-nu-um

é-***pu-ta-nu-um***, "the house of *Putanum*" > *Household Index*

1. **His Wool**

5 ma-na siki-gen dirig sa$_{10}$ siki-a-šè ***pu-ta-nu-um*** ki ^{d}*adad-tillati*-ta ba-zi, "*Adad-tillati* disbursed 5 minas of supplementary ordinary wool for the purchase of (more) wool of *Putanum*," 1005:7–11

puzur$_4$-a-bi

1. ***Puzur-abi*, the Equerry, Supervised by *Babani*, the Majordomo**

1.1 **Overseer of Hired Workmen**

n g̃uruš ḫug̃-g̃á ***puzur$_4$-a-bi*** šùš (. . .) ugula *ba-ba-ni* šabra, "n hired workmen (from the gang of) *Puzur-abi*, the equerry, (and) {ox-drivers} supervised by *Babani*, the majordomo," 193:8–9, 194:12, 15, 197:9, 11

2. ***Puzur-abi*, the Ox-Herder, Supervised by *Babani*, the Majordomo**

2.1 **Ox-Drivers from his Gang**

n g̃uruš (ugula) ***puzur$_4$-a-bi*** nu-bànda-gu$_4$ (. . .) (šà-gu$_4$-me-éš ugula) *ba-ba-ni* šabra, "n workmen (from the gang of) *Puzur-abi*, the ox-herder, (and) {other gangs}, (ox-drivers supervised by) *Babani*, the majordomo," 184:3, 5–6, 185:2, 4–5, 186:2, 4–5, 187:2, 4, 189:2, 10, 190:2, 7, 191:3, 10

1 g̃uruš ***puzur$_4$-a-bi*** nu-bànda-gu$_4$ (. . .) šà-gu$_4$-me-éš (. . .) ugula *ba-ba-ni* šabra, "1 workman (from the gang of) *Puzur-abi*, the ox-herder, (and) {other gangs}, ox-drivers (and) {hired workers} supervised by *Babani*, the majordomo," 193:2, 7, 9, 197:2, 8, 11

[n] g̃ur[uš ***pù]-zur$_8$-a-b[i*** n]u-bàn[da-g]u$_4$ (. . .) [šà-gu$_4$]-me-éš [árad-é]-a-me-éš (. . .) ugula *ba-ba-ni* šabra, "[n] workmen (from the gang of) *Puzur-abi*, the ox-herder, (and) {other gangs}, ox-drivers—household servants—(and) {hired workers} supervised by *Babani*, the majordomo," 194:2, 7–8, 15

2.2 Overseer of *Abu-ṭabu*, the Runaway

zàḫ *a-bu*-DU$_{10}$ ***puzur$_4$-a-bi*** nu-bànda-gu$_4$, "*Abu-ṭabu*, the runaway (from the gang of) *Puzur-abi*, the ox-herder," 194:62–63, 198:'40

puzur$_4$-a-gu$_5$-um

Puzur-agum, the Fuller

1. Deliveries

1.1 Assorted Textiles

1.1.1 Delivery of Completed Work

7 ^{túg}uš-bar *a-gi$_4$-um* túg-ma-dur$_7$-ra *še-lí-a-núm* dub-sar maškim á mu-DU ki ***puzur$_4$-a-gu$_5$-um***-ta ba-zi, "*Puzur-agum* disbursed 7 *a-gi$_4$-um* uš-bar textiles, mourning textiles, delivery of (completed) work. *Šelianum*, the scribe, was the deputy," 566:1–8

[n+]4 gada-⸢gen⸣ *a-gi$_4$-um* túg-ma-dur$_7$-ra á mu-DU ki ***puzur$_4$-a-gu$_5$-um*** ^{lú}ázlag-ta ba-zi, "*Puzur-agum*, the fuller, disbursed [n]+4 ordinary *a-gi$_4$-um* linen textiles, mourning textiles, delivery of (completed) work," 573:1–5

4 ^{túg}bar-si níg̃-lá 3-kam-ús 4 ^{túg}bar-si níg̃-lá 4-kam-ús túg-ma-dur$_7$-ra-àm á mu-DU [ki ***p]ù-zur$_8$-a-gu$_5$-um*** ^{lú}ázlag-ta [ba]-zi, "*Puzur-agum*, the fuller, disbursed 4 3rd-quality níg̃-lá bands (and) 4 4th-quality níg̃-lá bands, mourning textiles, delivery of (completed) work," 580:1–6

1 ^{túg}*ḫa-um a-gi$_4$-um simat-^{d}ištaran* túg-ma-dur$_7$-ra-àm á mu-DU-⸢ra⸣? ki ***puzur$_4$-a-gu$_5$-um***-ta ba-zi, "*Puzur-agum* disbursed 1 *a-gi$_4$-um ḫa'um* textile of *Simat-Ištaran*, a mourning textile, delivery of (completed) work," 581:1–5

1.1.2 Of *Ištaran* in Nippur

1 túg-guz-za-tur 4-kam-ús ^{d}*ištaran nu-úr-^{d}adad* maškim šà nibru^{ki} zi-ga g̃iri *simat-^{d}ištaran* ki ***puzur$_4$-a-gum***-ta ba-zi, "*Puzur-agum* disbursed 1 small 4th-quality tufted textile of *Ištaran*. (It was) the expenditure of *Simat-Ištaran* under her authority in Nippur. *Nur-Adad* was the deputy," 576:1–6

1.1.3 Property of Individuals

1.1.3.1 *Nawir-ilum*

(. . .) níg̃-gur$_{11}$ *na-wi-ir-ilum-ma* ba-úš! *nu-úr-^{d}adad* maškim šà nibru^{ki} ki ***puzur$_4$-a-gu$_5$-um***-ta ba-zi, "In Nippur, *Puzur-agum* disbursed {assorted textiles}, the property of *Nawir-ilum*, who had died. *Nur-adad* was the deputy," 574:3–7

1.1.3.2 *Šu-Eštar*

(. . .) túg-sa-gi$_4$-a ⌜mu⌝-DU ***puzur$_4$-a-gu$_5$-um*** ^{lú}ázlag túg-*šu-eš$_4$-tár*, "{assorted} finished textiles, the delivery of *Puzur-agum*, the fuller, are the textiles of *Šu-Eštar*," 823:4–7

1.1.4 Receipt of Individuals

1.1.4.1 Receipt of *Ṣumid-ilum*

1 ^{túg}bar-si-abzu *a-ši-um* 1 túg-guz-za 3-kam-ús 8 g̃uruš ^{lú}ázlag á-bi u$_4$-1-še *ṣú-mi-id-ilum* ki ***puzur$_4$-a-gu$_5$-um***-ta ba-zi, "*Puzur-agum* disbursed 1 abzu *a-ši-um* band (and) 1 3rd-quality tufted textile, labor of 8 fullers for 1 day, (for) *Ṣumid-ilum*," 571:1–6

1.1.4.2 Receipt of *Šu-Adad*

(. . .) *šu-^{d}adad* šu ba-(an-)ti ki ***puzur$_4$-a-gu$_5$-um***-ta ba-zi, "*Šu-Adad* received {assorted textiles} from *Puzur-agum*," 563:3–5, 564:3–6, 572:6–8

(. . .) ki ***puzur$_4$-a-gum***-ta *šu-^{d}adad* šu ba-ti, "*Šu-Adad* received {assorted textiles} from *Puzur-agum*," 569:21–22

(. . .) túg-sa-gi$_4$-àm ki ***puzur$_4$-a-gu$_5$-um***-ta *šu-^{d}adad* šu ba-(an-)ti, "*Šu-Adad* received {assorted} finished textiles from *Puzur-agum*," 567:2–5, 570:4–8, 578:19–22, 579:20–24, 586:4–7, 587:4–7, 590:4–7

(. . .) túg-sa-gi$_4$-a mu-DU *šu-^{d}adad* šu ba-an-ti ki ***puzur$_4$-a-gu$_5$-um***-ta ba-zi, "*Šu-Adad* received a delivery of {assorted} finished textiles from *Puzur-agum*," 568:4–9

(. . .) túg-sa-gi$_4$-a mu-DU ki ***puzur$_4$-a-gu$_5$-um***-ta *šu-^{d}adad* šu ba-ti, "*Šu-Adad* received a delivery of {assorted} finished textiles from *Puzur-agum*," 577:5–9

(. . .) túg-sa-gi$_4$-[àm] ki ***puzur$_4$-a-gu$_5$-um***-[ta] *šu-^{d}adad* šu ba-an-ti šà tum-ma-al^{ki}, "*Šu-Adad* received {assorted} finished textiles from *Puzur-agum* in Tumal," 591:'12–'15

1.1.5 Unspecified Recipient

(. . .) *é-a-šar* maškim ki ***puzur$_4$-a-gu$_5$-um***-ta ba-zi, "*Puzur-agum* disbursed {assorted textiles}. *Ea-šar* was the deputy," 565:4–5

1.2 Workmen

1.2.1 Fullers

1.2.1.1 Bringing Textiles to Garšana

1 g̃uruš ^{lú}ázlag nibru^{ki}-ta gar-ša-an-na^{ki}-šè túg de$_6$-a kaskal šu+níg̃in-na-bi u$_4$-4-àm ki ***puzur$_4$-a-gum***(!)-ta ba-zi, "*Puzur-agum* disbursed 1 fuller having brought textiles from Nippur to Garšana, a trip of 4 days in total," 224 :1–7

1.2.1.2 Bringing Reeds to Garšana

3 g̃uruš sag̃-tag 1 g̃uruš á-⅔ ^{lú}ázlag-me-éš u$_4$-10-šè gi-izi ù-dag^{ki}-ga-ta [gar-š]a-an-na^{ki}-šè de$_6$-a g̃iri *^{d}adad-tillati* šabra ù *be-lí-ì-lí* ugula má gíd zi-ga g̃iri *šu-kab-ta* ki ***puzur$_4$-a-gu$_5$-um***-ta ba-zi, "*Puzur-agum* disbursed 3 full-time fullers (and) 1 fuller at ⅔ wages for 10 days having brought fuel reeds from Udaga to Garšana. (It was) the expenditure of *Šu-Kabta* under his authority

(and) the authority of *Adad-tillati*, the majordomo, and *Beli-ili*, overseer of boat towers," 231:1–11

1.2.1.3 Bringing a Sheep and Cattle Brand

1 ĝuruš ^{lú}ázlag nibru^{ki}-ta ^{d}*šu*-^{d}*suen*-DU$_{10}$^{ki}-šè ^{urudu}šim-da gu$_4$-udu de$_6$-a kaskal šu+níĝin-na-bi u$_4$-11-kam u$_4$ *šu-kab-tá* é-dam-*zé-ra-ra* šu sum-mu-dè ì-ĝen-na-a *é-a-šar* maškim zi-ga ĝìri *šu-kab-tá* ki ***puzur$_4$-a-gu$_5$-um***-ta ba-zi, "*Puzur-agum* disbursed 1 fuller having brought a sheep and cattle brand from Nippur to *Šu-Suen-ṭabu*, a trip of 11 days in total, when *Šu-Kabta* went to the house of *Zerara*'s wife in order to take inventory. (It was) the expenditure of *Šu-Kabta* under his authority. *Ea-šar* was the deputy," 219:1–14

1.2.1.4 Bringing Wool

1.2.1.4.1 From *Bit-Šu-Suen*

1 ĝuruš ^{lú}ázlag saĝ-tag u$_4$-2-šè 2 ĝuruš saĝ-tag 2 ĝuruš á-½-ta u$_4$-2-šè siki é-^{d}*šu*-^{d}*suen*^{ki}-ta nibru^{ki}-šè DU(sic!) de$_6$-a *nu-úr-*^{d}*adad* maškim ki ***puzur$_4$-a-gu$_5$-um***-ta ba-zi, "*Puzur-agum* disbursed 1 full-time fuller for 2 days (and) 2 full-time workmen (and) 2 half-time workmen for 2 days having brought wool from *Bit-Šu-Suen* to Nippur. *Nur-Adad* was the deputy," 226:1–10

8 ĝuruš ^{lú}ázlag u$_4$-1-šè siki é-^{d}*šu*-^{d}*suen*-ta gar-ša-an-n[a^{ki}]-šè mu-un-de$_9$-sa-a *é-a-šar* ⌜maškim⌝ ki ***puzur$_4$-a-gu$_5$-um***-ta ba-zi, "*Puzur-agum* disbursed 8 fullers for 1 day who brought wool from *Bit-Šu-Suen* to Garšana. *Ea-šar* was the deputy," 243:1–7

3 ĝuruš ^{lú}ázlag siki é-^{d}*šu*-^{d}*suen*^{ki}-ka-ta nibru^{ki}-šè de$_6$-a kaskal šu+níĝin-na-bi u$_4$-10!-kam u$_4$-2 kaš-dé-[a] á-⌜ki⌝-ti šu-numun ki ***puzur$_4$-a-[gu$_5$-um]***-ta ba-⌜zi⌝, "*Puzur-agum* disbursed 3 fullers having brought wool from *Bit-Šu-Suen* to Nippur, a trip of 10 days in total, on day 2 of the banquet of the Akiti festival of month 4," 240:1–7

1.2.1.4.2 From *Šu-Suen*-ammara

8 ĝuruš saĝ-tag 2 ĝuruš á-⅔-ta 4 ĝuruš á-½-ta ^{lú}ázlag-me-éš [u$_4$]-1-šè ⌜še⌝ ^{d}*šu*-^{d}*suen*-am-ma-ar-^{ki}-ta de$_6$-a íb-[ga$_6$] ĝìri *en-nam-*^{d}*m*[*a-lik* z]i-ga *š*[*u-kab-ta*] ki ***puzur$_4$-a-[gu$_5$-um***-ta ba]-zi, "Under the authority of *Ennam-Malik*, *Puzur-agum* disbursed 8 full-time fullers, 2 fullers at ⅔ wages, (and) 4 fullers at ½ wages for 1 [day]. They [carried] barley brought from *Šu-Suen*-ammara. (It was) the expenditure of *Šu-Kabta*," 248:1–10

1.2.1.5 Construction of the Textile Depository

8 ĝuruš saĝ-tag 2 ĝuruš á-⅔-ta ^{lú}ázlag-me-éš u$_4$-[1-šè] šeg$_{12}$ šu dím sum-mu-dè gub-ba al-tar é-[ki-m]u-ra ki ***puzur$_4$-a-gu$_5$-um***-ta ba-zi, "*Puzur-agum* disbursed 8 full-time fullers (and) 2 fullers at ⅔ wages employed [for 1] day to hand (up) bricks for building (for) construction of the textile depository," 242:1–6

1.2.1.6 Expended for the Royal Banquet

2 ĝuruš ^{lú}ázlag u$_4$-1-šè zi-ga kaš-dé-a lugal šà á-<ki->ti gub-ba *nu-úr-*^{d}*adad* maškim zi-ga ĝìri *šu-kab-ta* ki ***puzur$_4$-a-gu$_5$-um***-ta ba-zi, "*Puzur-agum* disbursed 2 fullers employed for 1 day, expended (for) the royal banquet of

the Akiti festival. (It was) the expenditure of *Šu-Kabta* under his authority. *Nur-Adad* was the deputy," 221:1–7

1.2.1.7 Mourning for *Nawir-ilum*

11 g̃uruš sa[g̃-tag] 2 g̃uruš á-⅔-ta 4 g̃uruš á-½-ta 1 g̃uruš á-⅓<-ta> ^{lú}ázlag-me-éš u$_4$-1-šè gaba sàg-gé-dè [gub-ba] u$_4$ *na-wi-ir-[ilum* ba-úš-a] *é-a-šar* maškim zi-ga *šu-kab-⸢tá⸣* ki ***puzur$_4$-a-gu$_5$-um***-⸢ta⸣ ba-zi, "*Puzur-agum* disbursed 11 full-time fullers, 2 fullers at ⅔ wages, 4 fullers at ½ wages (and) 1 fuller at ⅓ wages employed for 1 day to beat (their) breasts when *Nawir-ilum* [died]. (It was) the expenditure of *Šu-Kabta*. *Ea-šar* was the deputy," 250:1–12

1.2.1.8 Towing Boats: from Nippur to *Bit-Šu-Suen*

3 g̃uruš ^{lú}ázlag u$_4$-2½-šè nibru^{ki}-ta é-^{d}*šu*-^{d}*suen*-šè má *na-wi-ir-ilum* íb-gíd g̃ìri g̃ìri-^{d}ba-ú-ì-dab$_5$ zi-ga g̃ìri *šu-kab-tá* ki ***puzur$_4$-a-gu$_5$-um***-ta ba-zi, "*Puzur-agum* disbursed 3 fullers for 2½ days. They towed the boat of *Nawir-ilum* from Nippur to *Bit-Šu-Suen*. (It was) the expenditure of *Šu-Kabta* under his authority (and) that of G̃iri-Ba'u-idab," 220:1–11

1.2.2 Unspecified Workers

1.2.2.1 Construction

11 g̃uruš sag̃-[tag] 2 g̃uruš á-⅔-ta 2 g̃uruš á-½-ta u$_4$-2-šè iz-zi sumun ku-bu-gu gul-dè gub-ba ⸢g̃ìri⸣ *é-a-šar* dub-sar ki ***puzur$_4$-a-gu$_5$-um***-ta ba-zi, "Under the authority of *Ea-šar*, the scribe, *Puzur-agum* disbursed 11 full-time workers, 2 workers at ⅔ wages (and) 2 workers at ½ wages employed for 2 days to demolish the old ku-bu-gu wall," 244:1–8

1.2.2.2 Traveling between Garšana and Nippur

2 g̃uruš s[ag̃-tag] 1 g̃uruš á-[⅔] u$_4$-1½-[šè] gar-ša-an-[na^{ki}-ta] nibru^{ki}-šè g̃[en-na] 2 g̃uruš [sag̃-tag] 1 [g̃uruš á-⅔] u$_4$-[n-šè] nibru^{ki}-[ta GN-šè g̃en-na] 2 g̃uruš sag̃-[tag] 1 g̃uruš á-⅔ u$_4$-1-šè gar-ša-an-na^{ki}-šè? [?] zi-ga [*šu-kab-tá*] ki ***puzur$_4$-a-gu$_5$-um***-[ta ba-zi], "*Puzur-agum* disbursed 2 full-time workmen (and) 1 workman at [⅔] wages [for] 1½ days having gone from Garšana to Nippur, 2 [full-time] workmen (and) 1 [workman at ⅔ wages for n] day(s) [having gone from] Nippur [to GN], (and) 2 full-time workmen (and) 1 workman at ⅔ wages for 1 day (having gone?) to Garšana. (It was) the expenditure of [*Šu-Kabta*]," 223:1–17

2. Receipts

2.1 From *Adad-tillati*

2.1.1 Assorted Textiles

(. . .) túg ki-lá tà-ga ki ^{d}*adad-tillati*-t[a ***puzur$_4$***]***-a-gu$_5$-um*** [šu b]a-ti, "*Puzur-agum* received {assorted textiles}, weighed textiles having been woven, from *Adad-tillati*," 597:3–6

(. . .) ki ^{d}*adad-tillati*-ta ***puzur$_4$-a-gu$_5$-[um]*** šu ba-ti, "*Puzur-agum* received {assorted textiles} from *Adad-tillati*," 606:2–4, 651:8–10, 655:2–4, 678:3–5, 693:9–11

(. . .) túg-sumun-àm 53 túg-ma-dur$_7$-ra ki ^{d}*adad-tillati*-ta ***puzur$_4$-a-gu$_5$-[um]*** šu ba-an-ti, "*Puzur-agum* received {assorted} old textiles—53 mourning textiles—from *Adad-tillati*," 698:28–33

2.1.2 Supplies for Fulling

2.1.2.1 Assorted

0.0.0.5 sìla ì-ĝeš 0.0.3. ì-šáh̬ 1.0.0. naĝa-si-è gur 2 gú 1 ma-na im-bábbar 2 ^{gi}gur-dub 1 dug 0.0.3. kéše-rá 1 ^{dug}epig ki ^{d}*adad-tillati*-ta ***puzur$_4$-a-gu$_5$-um*** šu ba-ti, "*Puzur-agum* received from *Adad-tillati* 5 liters of sesame oil, 30 liters of lard, 1 bushel of sprouted naĝa, 2 talents (and) 1 mina of gypsum, 2 reed baskets, 1 bound 30-liter jug (and) 1 sprinkling vessel," 595:1–10

1 gú 10 ma-na im-bábbar 5 sìla ì-ĝeš ki ^{d}*adad-tillati*-ta ⌜***pù***⌝***-zur$_8$-***[***a-gu$_5$-um*** šu] ba-ti, "*Puzur-agum* received 1 talent (and) 10 minas of gypsum (and) 5 liters of sesame oil from *Adad-tillati*," 695:1–5

1 ma-na 15 gín siki-gen 3⅓ sìla 5 gín ì-ĝeš 0.0.3.½ sìla naĝa-si-è 23 ma-na im-bábbar mu túg-ga-šè ki ^{d}*adad-tillati*-ta ***puzur$_4$-a-gu$_5$-um*** šu ba-ti, "*Puzur-agum* received from *Adad-tillati* 1 mina (and) 15 shekels of ordinary wool, 3⅓ liters (and) 5 shekels of sesame oil, 3½ liters of sprouted naĝa (and) 23 minas of gypsum for textiles," 699:1–8

1 sìla 11 gín ì-ĝeš 0.0.5.2 sìla 15 gín naĝa-si-è 9 ma-na im-bábbar 7½ gín siki-gen mu túg-ga-šè ki ^{d}*adad-tillati*-ta ***puzur$_4$-a-gu$_5$-um*** šu ba-ti, "*Puzur-agum* received from *Adad-tillati* 1 liter (and) 11 shekels of sesame oil, 52 liters (and) 15 shekels of sprouted naĝa, 9 minas of gypsum (and) 7½ shekels of ordinary wool for textiles," 705:1–8

4.0.0. naĝa-si-è gur 2 gú im-bábbar ki ^{d}*adad-tillati*-ta [***puzur$_4$-a-gu$_5$-um*** šu ba-ti], "[*Puzur-agum* received] 4 bushels of sprouted naĝa (and) 2 talents of gypsum from *Adad-tillati*," 768:1–5

1.0.0. ì-ĝeš <gur> 1 gú ki-lá šeg$_{12}$ naĝa 1.0.0. naĝa-si-è gur ki ^{d}*adad-tillati*-ta ***puzur$_4$-a-gu$_5$-um*** šu ba-ti, "*Puzur-agum* received 1 bushel of sesame oil, 1 talent of potash weighed in bricks, (and) 1 bushel of sprouted naĝa from *Adad-tillati*," 774:1–6

0.3.0. naĝa 2 gú im-bábbar ki ^{d}*adad-tillati*-ta ***puzur$_4$-a-gu$_5$-um*** šu ba-ti, "*Puzur-agum* received 180 liters of potash (and) 2 talents of gypsum from *Adad-tillati*," 791:1–5

2.1.2.2 Gypsum

n gú im-bábbar mu túg-ga-šè ki ^{d}*adad-tillati*-ta ***puzur$_4$-a-gu$_5$-um*** šu ba(-an)-ti, "*Puzur-agum* received n talent(s) of gypsum for textiles from *Adad-tillati*," 642:1–4, 689:1–5

1 gú im-bábbar ki ^{d}*adad-tillati*-ta ***puzur$_4$-a-gu$_5$-um*** [šu ba]-ti, "*Puzur-agum* received 1 talent of gypsum from *Adad-tillati*," 785:1–4

2.1.2.3 Millstone

1 ^{na4}kinkin-zi-bí šu sè-ga ki ^{d}*adad-tillati*-ta ***puzur$_4$-a-gu$_5$-um*** šu ba-an-ti, "*Puzur-agum* received 1 'hand-held' zi-bí millstone from *Adad-tillati*," 601:1–4

2.1.2.4 Oil and Lard

0.0.1. ì-ĝeš 0.0.1. ì-šáh̬ mu túg-ga-šè ki ^{d}*adad-tillati*-ta ***puzur$_4$-a-gu$_5$-um*** šu ba-ti, "*Puzur-agum* received 10 liters of sesame oil (and) 10 liters of lard for textiles from *Adad-tillati*," 712:1–6

0.0.1. ì-g̃eš [mu túg]-ga-šè [ki ^{d}]*adad-tillati*-ta ***[puzur$_4$]-a-gu$_5$-um*** [šu ba]-ti, "*Puzur-agum* received 10 liters of sesame oil for textiles from *Adad-tillati*," 770:1–5

0.0.1. ì-šáḫ ki ^{d}*adad-tillati*-ta ***puzur$_4$-a-gu$_5$-um*** šu [ba-ti], "*Puzur-agum* received 10 liters of lard from *Adad-tillati*," 822:1–4

2.1.2.5 Potash

0.1.0. nag̃a ki ^{d}*adad-tillati*-ta ***puzur$_4$-a-[gu$_5$-um]*** šu ba-an-ti, "*Puzur-agum* received 60 liters of potash from *Adad-tillati*," 630:1–4

2.1.2.6 Sprouted nag̃a

[n].2.0. nag̃a-si-è gur ki ^{d}*adad-tillati*-ta ***puzur$_4$-a-gu$_5$-um*** šu ba-an-ti, "*Puzur-agum* received [n] bushel(s) (and) 120 liters of sprouted nag̃a from *Adad-tillati*," 621:1–4

2.1.2.7 Wool and Containers

2 dug [. . .] 2 ^{gi}bisag̃-gíd-da [túg]-ga sa-ḫa ki ^{d}*adad-tillati*-ta ***puzur$_4$-a-gu$_5$-um*** šu [ba-ti], "*Puzur-agum* received 2 [. . .] pots (and) 2 long canvas-lined baskets (for) textiles from *Adad-tillati*," 602:1–5

★★20 ma-na siki túg-guz-za-gen mu siki-gu kéše-šè 1 ^{gi}gúrdub ka-tab sè-ga ki ^{d}*adad-tillati*-ta ***puzur$_4$-a-gu$_5$-um*** šu ba-an-ti, "*Puzur-agum* received from *Adad-tillati* 20 minas of wool (for manufacturing) an ordinary tufted textile (to be used) for wool cord bindings (and) 1 reed-basket fitted (with) a cover," 665:1–6

1 ^{gi}bisag̃-gíd-da túg-ga-tur ésir šub-ba ka-bi kuš-g̃ar-ra ki ^{d}*adad-tillati*-ta ***puzur$_4$-a-gu$_5$-um*** šu ba-ti, "*Puzur-agum* received from *Adad-tillati* 1 long basket coated with bitumen, its opening covered with leather, (for) small textiles," 798:1–6

103 ⸢túg⸣-sa-gi$_4$-àm 2 ^{gi}bisag̃-gíd-da túg-ga 2 ^{gi}kid-uzu ki ^{d}*adad-tillati*-ta ***puzur$_4$-a-gu$_5$-[um]*** šu [ba-ti], "*Puzur-agum* received 103 finished textiles, 2 long baskets (for) textiles (and) 2 reed uzu-mats from *Adad-tillati*," 834:17–23

2.1.2.8 Wood Products

120 ^{geš}zé-na 10 ^{geš}dal-ásal 2 kùš-ta 5 ^{geš}ú-bíl-lá 10 ^{geš}ù-suḫ$_5$ mi-rí-za mu dal é-túg-ga-šè ki ^{d}*adad-tillati*-ta ***puzur$_4$-a-gu$_5$-um*** šu ba-ti, "*Puzur-agum* received from *Adad-tillati* 120 date palm frond midribs, 10 poplar beams of 2 kùš in length each, 5 (units) of charcoal wood (and) 10 pine boards, for the shelves? of a textile container," 779:1–8

1 ^{geš}kug̃$_5$ ga-lam-8 ki ^{d}*adad-tillati*-ta ***puzur$_4$-a-gu$_5$-um*** šu ba-ti, "*Puzur-agum* received 1 ladder of 8 steps from *Adad-tillati*," 808:1–4

2.1.3 Wages

2.1.3.1 Barley for Hired Fullers

1.0.0. še gur á ^{lú}ázlag ḫug̃-g̃á ki ^{d}*adad-tillati*-ta ***puzur$_4$-a-gu$_5$-um*** šu ba-ti, "*Puzur-agum* received 1 bushel of barley, wages of hired fullers, from *Adad-tillati*," 820:1–5

2.1.3.2 Barley and Wool to Carry Bricks

2.2.3. še-gur 15 ma-na siki šeg$_{12}$ ga$_{6}$-g̃á-[dè] ki ^{d}*adad-tillati*-ta [***puzur$_{4}$-a-gu$_{5}$***]-***um*** šu ba-ti, "*Puzur-agum* received 2 bushels (and) 150 liters of barley (and) 15 minas of wool, (for workers) [to] carry bricks, from *Adad-tillati*," 638:1–6

2.1.4 Workers

2.1.4.1 Hired Workmen

n g̃uruš ḫug̃-g̃á u$_{4}$-1-šè ki ^{d}*adad-tillati*-ta ***puzur$_{4}$-a-gu$_{5}$-um*** ì-dab$_{5}$, "*Puzur-agum* took in charge n hired workmen for 1 day from *Adad-tillati*," 792:1–4, 797:1–4

2.1.4.2 Fullers

1⅓ g̃uruš ^{lú}ázlag ki ^{d}*adad-tillati*-ta ***puzur$_{4}$-a-gu$_{5}$-um*** ^{lú}ázlag [ì-dab$_{5}$], "*Puzur-agum* [took in charge] 1⅓ fullers from *Adad-tillati*," 604:1–4

2.2 From *Ama'a*: Ordinary Linen

1 gada-gen ki *a-ma-a*-ta ***puzur$_{4}$-a-gu$_{5}$-um*** šu ba-ti g̃ìri ^{d}*adad-tillati* šabra, "Under the authority of *Adad-tillati*, the majordomo, *Puzur-agum* received 1 ordinary linen from *Ama'a*," 659:1–6

1 gada-gen ki *a-ma-a*-ta ***puzur$_{4}$-a-gu$_{5}$-um*** šu ba-ti g̃ìri ^{d}*adad-tillati* ù ^{d}*ma-lik-ba-ni*, "Under the authority of *Adad-tillati* and *Malik-bani*, *Puzur-agum* received 1 ordinary linen from *Ama'a*," 664:1–6

1 gada-gen ki *a-ma-a*-ta ***puzur$_{4}$-a-gu$_{5}$-um*** šu ba-ti, "*Puzur-agum* received 1 ordinary linen from *Ama'a*," 688:1–5, 707:1–4

2.3 From *Aštaqqar*

2.3.1 Assorted textiles

(. . .) túg ki-lá tà(g)-ga ki *aš-tá-qar*-ta ***puzur$_{4}$-a-gu$_{5}$-um*** šu ba-(an-)ti, "*Puzur-agum* received {assorted textiles}, weighed textiles having been woven, from *Aštaqqar*," 594:5–8, 608:10–13, 685:5–8, 686:4–7, 687:3–6, 690:8–11, 708:11–15, 724:3–7, 738:18–20, 744:14–16, 765:8–11, 778:11–13, 803:5–8, 804:6–9, 821:11–14, 832:2–5

(. . .) ki *aš-tá-qar*-ta ***puzur$_{4}$-a-gu$_{5}$-um*** šu ba-(an-)ti, "*Puzur-agum* received {assorted textiles} from *Aštaqqar*," 610:2–4, 631:7–9, 660:2–4, 669:11–14, 674:11–13, 676:6–8, 677:3–5, 683:2–4, 684:2–4, 692:9–11, 697:3–5, 700:4–6, 713:2–4, 715:2–4, 720:3–5, 722:2–4, 731:7–9, 732:5–7, 736:4–6, 739:8–9, 742:12–13, 743:'8–'10, 745:9–11, 753:16–18, 757:2–4, 758:17–19, 760:9–11, 764:13–15, 766:7–9, 771:8–10, 775:3–5, 780:2–4, 787:7–10, 789:3–5, 793:13–14, 794:3–5, 799:6–8, 800:8–10, 801:8–10, 802:4–6, 806:9–11, 810:5–7, 811:16–17, 814:13–15

1 túg 1⅓ <ma->na siki-gen ki *aš-tá-qar*-ta ***puzur$_{4}$-a-gu$_{5}$-um*** šu ba-ti, "*Puzur-agum* received 1 textile of ⅓ mina of ordinary wool from *Aštaqqar*," 817:1–4

(. . .) ⌜ki⌝ *aš-tá-qar*-ta ⌜***puzur$_{4}$***⌝***-a-gum*** ^{lú}ázlag [šu b]a-ti, "*Puzur-agum*, the fuller, received {assorted textiles} from *Aštaqqar*," 827:11–13

2.3.1.1 Under the Authority of *Adad-tillati*

(. . .) ki *aš-tá-qar*-ta ***puzur$_{4}$-a-gu$_{5}$-um*** šu ba-ti g̃ìri ^{d}*adad-tillati*, "Under the authority of *Adad-tillati*, *Puzur-agum* received {assorted textiles} from *Aštaqqar*," 654:10–12, 658:9–13, 691:6–9, 696:2–5, 725:7–11, 786:16–19

(. . .) túg ki-lá tà-ga ***puzur$_4$-a-gu$_5$-um*** šu ba-ti ki *aš-tá-qar*-ta ba-zi g̃iri ^{d}*adad-tillati* (šabra), "Under the authority of *Adad-tillati,* (the majordomo), *Puzur-agum* received from *Aštaqqar* {assorted textiles}, weighed textiles having been woven," 730:6–10, 747:18–22

(. . .) ***puzur$_4$-a-gu$_5$-um*** šu ba-ti ki *aš-tá-qar*-ta ba-zi g̃iri ^{d}*adad-tillati* šabra, "Under the authority of *Adad-tillati,* the majordomo, *Puzur-agum* received {assorted textiles} from *Aštaqqar,*" 796:14–18

2.3.1.2 Under the Authority of *Adad-tillati* and *Malik-bani*

(. . .) túg ki-lá tà-ga ki *aš-tá-qar*-ta ***puzur$_4$-a-gu$_5$-um*** šu ba-an-ti g̃iri ^{d}*adad-tillati* (šabra) ù ^{d}*ma-lik-ba-ni,* "Under the authority of *Adad-tillati* (the majordomo), and *Malik-bani, Puzur-agum* received from *Aštaqqar* {assorted textiles}, weighed textiles having been woven," 617:11–15, 618:13–17

(. . .) ki *aš-tá-qar*-ta ***puzur$_4$-a-gu$_5$-um*** šu ba-(an-)ti g̃iri ^{d}*adad-tillati* (šabra) ù ^{d}*ma-lik-ba-ni,* "Under the authority of *Adad-tillati,* (the majordomo) and *Malik-bani, Puzur-agum* received {assorted textiles} from *Aštaqqar,*" 626:4–8, 636:8–11, 637:5–9, 639:6–9, 643:2–6, 645:'5–'9, 646:7–10, 647:7–10, 649:11–13, 662:11–15, 663:9–13, 673:9–13, 680:6–9, 694:10–13, 748:16–19, 829:'9–'13

1 túg-guz-za-gen ki *aš-tá-qar*-ta *puzur$_4$-a-gum*! šu ba-an-ti kišib *tu-ra-a* íb-ra g̃iri ^{d}*adad-tillati ù* ^{d}*ma-lik-ba-ni,* "Under the authority of *Adad-tillati* and *Malik-bani, Puzur-agum* received 1 ordinary tufted textile from *Aštaqqar. Tura'a* rolled (his) seal," 644:1–7

2.3.1.3 Under the Authority of *Puzur*-Ninkarak

(. . .) 30-lá-1 [túg] ki-lá tag [ki] *aš-tá-qar*-ta [***puzur$_4$-a-gu$_5$-um*** šu ba-ti [. . .] *pù-zu*]*r$_8$*-^{d}nin-kar-ak dub-sar, "[*Puzur-agum* received] from *Aštaqqar* 29 {textiles}, weighed [textiles] having been woven. [. . .] *Puzur*-Ninkarak was the scribe," 835:'16–'22

2.3.2 Workwomen for Fulling

[n gé]me á-diri-ta nam-^{lú}ázlag-šè ki *aš-tá-qar*-ta ***puzur$_4$-a-gu$_5$-um*** ì-⌜dab$_5$⌝, "*Puzur-agum* took in charge [n] workwomen at additional wages for fulling from *Aštaqqar,*" 714:1–5

2.4 From *Awilumma*: Assorted Textiles

(. . .) ki *á-w*[*i-lum-ma*-ta] ***puzur$_4$*-a-[*gu$_5$-um*]** šu ba-ti, "*Puzur-agum* received {assorted textiles} from *Awilumma,*" 701:13–15

2.5 Broken Context: Assorted Textiles

[. . . ***puzur$_4$***]***-a-gu$_5$-um*** [šu] ba-ti, "*Puzur-agum* received [. . .]," 709:'7–'8

3. Under the Authority of *Puzur-agum*

(. . .) 14 ^{gi}gúrdub siki ka-tab sè-ga ki *a-lim-ma*-ta ^{d}*adad-tillati* šu ba-⌜ti⌝ g̃iri ^{d}***puzur$_4$-a-gu$_5$-um,*** "Under the authority of *Puzur-agum, Adad-tillati* received {assorted wool and textiles} (and) 14 reed baskets of wool fitted with a cover from *Alimma,*" 667:18–22

4. As a Witness

igi ***puzur$_4$-a-gu$_5$-um,*** "witnessed by *Puzur-agum,*" 609:20, 1060:9, 1063:8, 1064:9

igi ***puzur$_4$-a-gu$_5$-um*** [^{lú}ázlag], "witnessed by *Puzur-agum,* [the fuller]," 1052:13

puzur$_4$-é-a

1. As a Witness

igi [***pù-z***]***ur$_8$-é-a***, "witnessed by *Puzur-Ea*," 1056:5

puzur$_4$-^{d}en-líl

1. *Puzur*-Enlil, the ox-herder, Supervised by *Babani*, the Majordomo

1.1 Ox-Drivers from his Gang

n g̃uruš ***puzur$_4$*-^{d}en-líl** nu-bànda-gu$_4$ (. . .) ugula *ba-ba-ni* šabra, "n workmen (from the gang of) *Puzur*-Enlil, the ox-herder, (and) {other gangs}, supervised by *Babani*, the majordomo," 190:4, 7, 191:5, 10

2 g̃uruš ***puzur$_4$*-^{d}en-líl** nu-bànda-gu$_4$ (. . .) šà-gu$_4$-me-éš (. . .) ugula *ba-ba-ni* šabra, "2 workmen (from the gang of) *Puzur*-Enlil, the ox-herder, (and) {other gangs}, ox-drivers (and) {hired workers} supervised by *Babani*, the majordomo," 193:4, 7, 9, 197:4, 8, 11

[4?] g̃uruš ***puzur$_4$*-[^{d}en-l]íl** nu-bànda-gu$_4$ (. . .) [šà-gu$_4$]-me-éš [árad-é]-a-me-éš (. . .) ugula *ba-ba-ni* šabra, "[4?] workmen (from the gang of) *Puzur*-Enlil, (and) {other gangs}, ox-drivers—household servants—(and) {hired workers} supervised by *Babani*, the majordomo," 194:4, 7–8, 15

1.2 Deliveries: Receipt of *Adad-tillati*

1.2.1 Barley under *Beli-ili's* Authority

60.0.0. ⸢sìla⸣ še gur ki ***puzur$_4$*-^{d}en-líl**-ta ^{d}*adad-tillati* šu ba-ti g̃ìri *be-lí-ì-lí*, "Under the authority of *Beli-ili*, *Adad-tillati* received 60 bushels of barley from *Puzur*-Enlil," 1195:1–5[48]

448.4.0. še gur ^{d}*adad-tillati* šabra šu ba-ti ki ***puzur$_4$*-^{d}en-líl** nu-bànda-gu$_4$-ta ba-zi g̃ìri *be-lí-ì-lí* ugula má-gíd, "Under the authority of *Beli-ili*, overseer of boat towers, *Adad-tillati*, the majordomo, received 448 bushels (and) 240 liters of barley from *Puzur*-Enlil, the ox-herder," 1212:1–6

1.2.2 Oxen

1 gu$_4$-ú ki ***puzur$_4$*-^{d}en-líl**-ta ^{d}*adad-tillati* ì-⸢dab$_5$⸣, "*Adad-tillati* took in charge 1 range-fed ox from *Puzur*-Enlil," 1214:1–4[49]

1.2.3 Ox Skins, Horns, and Tails

1 kuš-[gu$_4$] 2 si-[gu$_4$] 1 kuš-kun-gu$_4$ ki ***puzur$_4$*-^{d}en-líl** nu-bànda-gu$_4$-ta ^{d}*adad-tillati* šu ba-ti, "*Adad-tillati* received 1 [ox] hide, 2 [ox] horns (and) 1 ox-tail from *Puzur*-Enlil, the ox-herder," 880:1–6

---

48 Although *Puzur*-Enlil's title is not specified, this text is included here in light of the parallel transaction no. 1212.

49 In light of the object of the transaction, this is likely *Puzur*-Enlil, the ox-herder.

2. *Puzur*-Enlil, Title Unspecified

2.1 Deliveries

2.1.1 Reeds

1470 sa gi-zi gu-níĝin 10-sa-ta gu-níĝin-bi 147-àm ^{d}*adad-tillati* šu ba-ti ki ***puzur$_4$*-^{d}en-líl**-ta ba-zi ĝiri *a-ḫu-wa-qar* dub-sar kìšib *a-ḫu-wa-qar-ra*! u$_4$-um-de$_6$ kìšib ***puzur$_4$*-^{d}en-líl** zi-re-dam, "Under the authority of *Aḫu-waqar*, the scribe, *Adad-tillati* received from *Puzur*-Enlil 1470 bundles of fresh reeds, bales of 10 bunches each, its bales are 147. When the sealed tablet of *Aḫu-waqar* is brought, *Puzur*-Enlil's sealed tablet will be canceled," 1361:1–12

2.1.2 Women

[1] géme sağ-dub 1 dumu-munus ki ***puzur$_4$*-^{d}en-líl**-ta ^{d}*adad-tillati* ì-dab$_5$, "*Adad-tillati* took in charge [1] full-time workwoman and 1 daughter from *Puzur*-Enlil," 1515:1–5

puzur$_4$-èr-ra

1. Receipts: Wool to Purchase Land

[n+]⅓ ma-na 9 gín siki-gen sa$_{10}$ ⸢kislaḫ⸣ 1 sar 9? gín-kam ***puzur$_4$-èr-ra*** šu ba-ti [ki ^{d}*adad*]-*tillati*-ta [ba-zi], "*Puzur-Erra* received [n+]⅓ minas (and) 9 shekels of ordinary wool, the price of 1 sar and 9? gín of uncultivated land, from *Adad-tillati*," 681:1–6

puzur$_4$-^{d}nin-kar-ak

***Puzur*-Ninkarak**, the Scribe[50]

1. As a Deputy

1.1 Craftsmen Bringing Barley to Garšana

9 ĝuruš sağ-tag 1 ĝuruš á-⅔ 1 ĝuruš á-⅓ ^{lú}ázlag-me-éš u$_4$-1-šè še é-kab-ba^{ki} ⸢karkar⸣^{ki}-ta ⸢gar-ša-an-na^{ki}⸣-šè de$_6$-a ***puzur$_4$*-^{d}[nin-kar-ak]** dub-sar maškim zi-ga *šu-kab-tá* ki ^{d}*adad-tillati*-ta ba-zi, "*Adad-tillati* disbursed 9 full-time fullers, 1 fuller at ⅔ wages, (and) 1 fuller at ⅓ wages for 1 day having brought barley from the Kabbi village (and) Karkar to Garšana. (It was) the expenditure of *Šu-Kabta*. *Puzur*-[Ninkarak], the scribe, was the deputy," 237:1–12

1.2 Oil for Sick Workers

10 gín ì-ĝeš *da-da-a* un-ga$_6$ u$_4$ dùb bar-ra-ni in-na-gig-ga [n] gín ì-ĝeš-ta ^{d}šára-sá-ĝu$_{10}$ DIŠ *bu-za-du-a* géme kíkken-me-éš u$_4$ dú-ra i-me é-gal!-šè ***puzur$_4$*-^{d}nin-kar-ak** dub-sar maškim zi-ga *šu-kab-tá* ki ^{d}*adad-tillati*-ta ⸢ba⸣-zi, "*Adad-tillati* disbursed 10 shekels of sesame oil (for) *Dada'a*, the porter, when his 'outer knee' was hurting him, (and) [n] shekel(s) of sesame oil each (for) Šara-sağu (and) for *Buzadua*, female workers at the mill, when they were sick at the palace. (It was) the expenditure of *Šu-Kabta*. *Puzur*-Ninkarak, the scribe, was the deputy," 466:1–10

---

[50] Although *Puzur*-Ninkarrak's title is not specified in every passage cited here, the nature of these transactions suggests that all references are to the same person.

2. Under his Authority

2.1 Disbursals of *Adad-tillati*

2.1.1 Assorted Commodities

0.1.0. še 4 ma-na siki-gen ½ sìla ì-šáḫ 5 sìla zì-kum 5 sìla zú-lum udug é-*da-da* dumu *na-sìm* 5 sìla ninda 0.0.2. zú-lum 10 ma-na tuḫ-g̃eš-ì-ḫád lú-$^{g̃eš}$tir ki ^{d}*adad-tillati*-ta ba-zi g̃ìri ***puzur$_4$***-**^{d}nin-kar-ak** dub-sar, "Under the authority of *Puzur*-Ninkarak, the scribe, *Adad-tillati* disbursed 60 liters of barley, 4 minas of ordinary wool, ½ liter of lard, 5 liters of kum-flour (and) 5 liters of dates (for) the caretaker at the house of *Dada*, son of *Nasim*, (and) 5 liters of bread, 20 liters of dates (and) 10 minas of dried sesame chaff (for) the forester," 438:1–11

[n sìla] še [n sìla] dabin [n] dug dida$_x$-gen [n] sìla Ú.KUR [n] $^{g̃eš}$nimbar [ki ^{d}*adad*]-*tillati*-ta ba-zi [g̃ìri ***pù-z*]*ur$_8$***-**^{d}nin-[kar]-ak** dub-sar, "[Under the authority of] *Puzur*-Ninkarak, the scribe, *Adad-tillati* disbursed [n liter(s)] of barley, [n liter(s)] of semolina, [n] jug(s) of ordinary dida beer, [n] liter(s) of Ú.KUR (and) [n] date palm(s)," 1117:1–7

(. . .) *šit-tum* é-lùnga é-kíkken ù *ma-aZ-ḫa-ru-um* é-muḫaldim-šè ba-a-g̃ar (. . .) níg̃ al-⸢zi⸣-ra 70 ⸢sa⸣ gi-izi gi-izi-lá-šè 31 ^{gi}kid-ka-ḫa-ra gir-ra ba-ab-gu$_7$ ki ^{d}*adad-tillati*-ta ba-⸢zi⸣ g̃ìri ***puzur$_4$***-**^{d}⸢nin-kar⸣-ak** dub-sar, "Under the authority of *Puzur*-Ninkarak, the scribe, *Adad-tillati* disbursed {bitumen and lard}, the balance (of the settled account)—(they) were placed for the brewery, the mill and the *maZḫarum* of the kitchen—(and) {assorted baskets}—used goods—70 bundles of fuel reeds for torches (and) 31 reed mats—fire consumed (the used goods)," 1299:5, 23–29

2.1.2 Baskets for the Caretaker

4 ^{gi}bisag̃-gíd-da-tur sa-ḫa gíd-2-kùš dag̃al-1-kùš udug é-ki-ba-g̃ar-ra-a *al-lu-a*-šè ba-a-g̃ar ki ^{d}*adad-tillati*-ta ba-zi g̃ìri ***puzur$_4$***-**^{d}nin-kar-ak** dub-sar, "Under the authority of *Puzur*-Ninkarak, the scribe, *Adad-tillati* disbursed 4 small, long, canvas-lined baskets, 2 kùš in length, 1 kùš in width. They were placed for the caretaker of the replacement house of *Allua*," 1006:1–5

2.1.3 Building Supplies

2.1.3.1 Assorted Commodities

0.1.0. ⸢še⸣ 2 ma-na siki-gen 2 sìla ì-g̃eš luḫ 60.0.0. gur-kam mu ésir šeg$_{12}$-al-ur$_x$-ra-šè ki ^{d}*adad-tillati*-ta ba-zi g̃ìri ***puzur$_4$***-**^{d}nin-kar-ak** dub-sar, "Under the authority of *Puzur*-Ninkarak, the scribe, *Adad-tillati* disbursed 60 liters of barley, 2 minas of ordinary wool, (and) 2 liters of sesame oil—cleaning? of 60 bushels—for the bitumen of the bricks," 1296:1–8

2.1.3.2 Baskets and Bitumen for the GÍN-bal of the Garšana Garden

(. . .) [GÍN]-bal $^{g̃eš}$ki[ri$_6$ gar-ša-an-na^{ki} dù-a g̃ìri ***pù*]-*zur$_8$***-**^{d}[nin-kar]-ak** d[ub-sar ki ^{d}*adad*]-*tillati*-ta [ba]-zi, "[Under the authority] of *Puzur*-Ninkarak, the scribe, *Adad-tillati* disbursed {assorted baskets} [(used by workers) having constructed] the [GÍN-bal] of the [Garšana] garden," 1292:'25–'28

21.0.0. ésir-ḫád ⸢gur⸣ 2.1.3. ésir-é-a gur GÍN-bal $^{g̃eš}$kiri$_6$ gar-[ša-an-na ^{ki} dù-a ki ^{d}*adad-tillati*-ta] ba-zi g̃ìri ***puzur$_4$***-**^{d}[nin]-kar-ak** dub-⸢sar⸣, "Under the authority of *Puzur*-Ninkarak, the scribe, [*Adad-tillati*], disbursed 21 bushels of dry bitumen (and) 2 bushels (and) 90 liters of house bitumen, [(used by workers) having constructed] the GÍN-bal of the Garšana garden," 1302:1–6

2.1.3.3 Bitumen and Oil for Repair of the Bathroom

7.4.0. ésir-ḫád gur 0.0.4.6 sìla ésir-é-a 0.0.0.7 sìla ì-ḫur-sag̃-g̃á ⸢*šít-tum*⸣ é-lùnga ⸢*šít-tum*⸣ é-kišib-ba ugula kíkken [?] du$_{10}$-ús é-didli *ták-si-*[*ru-um*]-šè ba-a-g̃ar [g̃iri] ***puzur$_4$-^{d}nin-kar-ak*** dub-sar [ki] ^{d}*adad-tillati*-ta ba-zi, "[Under the authority] of *Puzur*-Ninkarak, the scribe, *Adad-tillati* disbursed 7 bushels (and) 240 liters of dried bitumen, 46 liters of house bitumen (and) 7 liters of mountain fat, the balance (of the settled account) of the brewery (and) of the warehouse. They were placed (in the account of) the overseer of the mill for repair of the bathroom of various houses," 1260:1–7

2.1.3.4 Reeds, Roof Beams, and Ropes

2.1.3.4.1 For the Brewery-Kitchen-Mill Complex

[n] g̃eš ùr šinig 31 ^{geš}é-da-ásal 56 ^{geš}ká 260 ^{gi}dur-gazi a-rá-3-tab-ba gíd 1½ nindan-⸢ta⸣ g̃eš-ká kéše-dè é-lùnga é-muḫaldim ù é-kíkken ki ^{d}*adad-tillati*-ta ba-zi g̃iri ***puzur$_4$-^{d}nin-kar-ak*** dub-sar, "Under the authority of *Puzur*-Ninkarak, the scribe, *Adad-tillati* disbursed [n] tamarisk roof beam(s), 31 poplar joists, 56 gate timbers (and) 260 9-meter 3-ply gazi ropes in order to bind the gate timbers of the brewery-kitchen-mill complex," 1293:1–11

2980 sa g[i-iz]i a-rá-1-kam 2970 sa g[i-iz]i a-rá-2-kam 1078 sa gi-izi a-rá-3-kam gi-sal é-lùnga é-muḫaldim ù é-kíkken ba-a-g̃ar ki ^{d}*adad-tillati*-ta ba-zi g̃iri ***puzur$_4$-^{d}nin-kar-ak***, "Under the authority of *Puzur*-Ninkarak, *Adad-tillati* disbursed 2980 bundles of fuel reeds for the 1st time, 2970 bundles of fuel reeds for the 2nd time (and) 1078 bundles of fuel reeds for the 3rd time. The thin reeds were placed (for) the brewery-kitchen-mill complex," 1294:1–12

8 ^{gi}dur-gazi a-rá-2-tab-ba gíd 1½ nindan-ta g̃eš ùr kéše gíd-da 3 $^{g̃eš}$ù-suḫ$_5$ 3-kam-ús 15 $^{g̃eš}$é-da ásal ká-suḫur é-lùnga-šè ba-a-g̃ar 60 $^{g̃eš}$ù-bil-lá *ZA-ḫa-LUM*-šè 300 sa gi-izi 40 sa a-ZI/ZI gi-guru$_5$-šè 1 sìla dabin!(ZI.ŠE) ½ sìla eša zì-dub-dub-šè é-lùnga é-muḫaldim ù é-kíkken 240 sa gi-izi 420 gu-níg̃in $^{g̃eš}$kišig gir$_4$–2-kam 12 sa gi-izi níg̃-sù-a ^{urudu}šen-šè ki ^{d}*adad-tillati*-ta ba-zi g̃iri ***puzur$_4$-^{d}nin-kar-ak***, "Under the authority of *Puzur*-Ninkarak, the scribe, *Adad-tillati* disbursed 8 9-meter 2-ply gazi ropes having tightened bound roof beams, 3 3rd-quality pine planks (and) 15 poplar side-house planks—they were placed for the tree-top gate of the brewery—60 cabinet planks for *ZA-ḫa-lum*, 300 bundles of fuel reeds, 40 bundles of rushes for trimming, 1 liter of semolina (and) ½ liter of fine flour for the small flour heap of the brewery-kitchen-mill complex, 240 bundles of fuel reeds (and) 420 bales of shok (for) the 2nd oven (and) 12 bundles of fuel reeds for the níg̃-sù-a (soup) cauldron," 1297:1–20

2.1.3.4.2 For Bricks

120 sa gi-[x] 240 gu-níg̃in $^{g̃eš}$[ásal?] šeg$_{12}$-al-ur$_x$-ra šé-g̃e$_6$-dè ki ^{d}*adad-tillati* ba-zi g̃iri ***puzur$_4$-^{d}nin-kar-ak*** [dub-sar], "Under the authority of *Puzur*-Ninkarak, [the scribe], *Adad-tillati* disbursed 120 bundles of [x] reeds (and) 240 bales of [poplar?] wood in order to bake bricks," 1313:1–6

2.1.3.4.3 For the Foundation Terrace of the Textile Mill

445 sa gi-izi gu-níĝin 13-sa-ta gi-sal uš ki-sá-a é-uš-bar-šè ba-[a-ĝa]r ĝìri **puzur$_4$-^{d}[nin-k]ar-ak** dub-[sar ki ^{d}*a*]*dad-tillati*-ta [ba]-zi, "Under the authority of *Puzur*-Ninkarak, the scribe, *Adad-tillati* disbursed 445 bundles of fuel reeds, bales of 13 bundles each. The thin reeds were placed for the foundation of the foundation terrace of the textile mill," 1261:1–6

2.1.3.4.4 For the Gate

10 ^{ĝeš}ká 3 ^{gi}dur-gazi a-rá-2-tab-ba gíd-1½ ⌜nindan⌝-ta ká-*ḫu-lu-lu* im šeg$_{12}$ ku$_4$-ra-šè ba-a-[ĝar] ki ^{d}*adad-tillati*-ta ba-zi ĝìri **puzur$_4$-$^{[d]}$nin-kar-ak** dub-sar, "Under the authority of *Puzur*-Ninkarak, the scribe, *Adad-tillati* disbursed 10 gate timbers (and) 3 9-meter 2-ply gazi ropes. They were placed at the *Ḫululu* gate for the 'service entrance'," 1287:1–7

2.1.3.4.5 For the Quay of the Textile Depository

[n+]13 ^{ĝeš}ú-[bíl-lá] 120 ^{gi}dur daĝal [a-r]á-3-tab-ba gíd 5 nindan-ta 40 gu-níĝin ZI/ZI.ÉŠ kar-ki-mu-ra-šè ba-a-ĝar ki ^{d}*adad-tillati*-ta ba-zi ĝìri **puzur$_4$-^{d}[nin]-kar-ak** dub-sar, "Under the authority of *Puzur*-Ninkarak, *Adad-tillati* disbursed [n+]13 (units) of charcoal, 120 30-meter 3-ply wide ropes, (and) 40 bales of rushes. They were placed for the quay of the textile depository," 1305:1–7

20 ⌜^{ĝeš}⌝ú-b[íl-lá] 130 sa gi-izi 360 $^{[gi]}$dur-ga[zi a-rá]-3-tab-ba gíd 5 nindan-⌜ta⌝ 260 gu-níĝin ^{ú}ZI/ZI.ÉŠ kar-ki-mu-ra-šè ba-a-ĝar ki ^{d}*adad-tillati*-ta ba-zi ĝìri **puzur$_4$-^{d}nin-ka[r-ak]** dub-sar, "Under the authority of *Puzur*-Ninkarak, the scribe, *Adad-tillati* disbursed 20 (units) of charcoal, 130 bundles of fuel reeds, 360 30-meter 3-ply wide ropes (and) 260 bales of rushes. They were placed for the quay of the textile depository," 1308:1–8

2.1.3.4.6 For Replacement Houses

(. . .) ĝeš ùr kéše-rá (. . .) ĝeš ká-šè ba-gul (. . .) gi-sal-šè ba-gul (. . .) é-ki-ba-ĝar-ra é-*u-bar-ri-a*-šè ba-a-ĝar ĝìri **puzur$_4$-^{d}nin-kar-ak** dub-sar ki ^{d}*adad-tillati*-ta ba-zi, "Under the authority of *Puzur*-Ninkarak, the scribe, *Adad-tillati* disbursed {assorted woods}, bound roof beams, {assorted woods}—the wood was cut for gate timber—(and) {reeds}—they were trimmed for thin reeds. {Building supplies} were placed for the replacement house of *Ubarria*," 1286:5, 7, 8, 12–14, 1289:5, 7, 8, 12–14

[6]0 ^{gi}dur-gazi a-⌜rá⌝-2-tab-ba gíd 1½-nindan-ta 80 sa gi-izi é-ki-ba-ĝar-ra *da-da*-šè ba-a-ĝar ĝìri **puzur$_4$-^{d}nin-kar-ra-ak** dub-sar [ki ^{d}]*adad-tillati*-ta ba-zi, "Under the authority of *Puzur*-Ninkarak, the scribe, *Adad-tillati* disbursed [6]0 9-meter 2-ply gazi ropes (and) 80 bundles of fuel reeds. They were placed for the replacement house of *Dada*," 1378:'1–'6

2.1.3.4.7 For the Textile Mill and Craftsmen's House

n sa gi-izi gu-níĝin 36-sa-ta gi-sal é-uš-bar ù é-gašam-e-ne-šè ba-a-ĝar ĝìri **puzur$_4$-^{d}nin-kar-ak** dub-sar ki ^{d}*adad-tillati*-ta ba-zi, "Under the authority of *Puzur*-Ninkarak, the scribe, *Adad-tillati* disbursed n bundle(s) of fuel reeds, bales of 36 bundles each. The thin reeds were placed for the textile mill and craftsmen's house," 1262:1–6, 1264:1–6

2.1.3.4.8 For Various Houses

[n] ĝeš ùr ásal 140 sa gi-izi é-*ḫu-lu-lu* 120 ĝeš ùr ásal 170 sa gi-izi é-*pu-ta-nu-um* 240 ĝeš ùr ásal 30 sa gi-izi é-*šu-eš$_4$-tár* é-ki-ba-ĝar-ra-šè ⸢ba⸣-a-ĝar 60 sa gi-izi ^{ĝeš}lam ku-bu-dè ki ^{d}*adad-tillati*-ta ba-zi ĝìri ***puzur$_4$*-^{d}nin-kar-ak** dub-sar "Under the authority of *Puzur*-Ninkarak, the scribe, *Adad-tillati* disbursed [n] poplar roof beam(s) (and) 140 bundles of fuel reeds (for) the house of *Ḫululu*, 120 poplar roof beams (and) 170 bundles of fuel reeds (for) the house of *Putanum*, 240 poplar roof beams (and) 30 bundles of fuel reeds—they were placed for the replacement house of *Šu-Eštar*—(and) 60 bundles of fuel reeds to prop up (young) trees," 1309:1–14

2.1.3.4.9 For the (Enclosure) Wall

n sa gi-izi gu-níĝin n-sa-ta gi-sal bàd-šè ba-ĝar ĝìri ***puzur$_4$*-^{d}nin-kar-ak** dub-sar ki ^{d}*adad-tillati*-ta ba-zi, "Under the authority of *Puzur*-Ninkarak, the scribe, *Adad-tillati* disbursed n bundle(s) of fuel reeds, bales of n bundle(s) each. The thin reeds were placed for the (enclosure) wall," 1259:1–6, 1288:1–6

2.1.3.5 Shok for the Brick Stack

[600?+12]0+27 g[u-níĝin] ^{ĝeš}kišig dúr SIG$_4$.ANŠE-šè ba-a-ĝar ĝìri ***puzur$_4$*-^{d}nin-kar-ak** dub-sar ki ^{d}*adad-tillati*-ta ba-zi, "Under the authority of *Puzur*-Ninkarak, the scribe, *Adad-tillati* disbursed [74]7 bales of shok. They were placed for (use as) the bottom of a brick stack," 1295:1–5

2.1.4 Rations, Wages, and Allotments

2.0.4. še gur 1.2.3. dabin gur 3⅔ sìla ì-ĝeš 7 ádda-udu 35 ku$_6$ al-dár-ra ½ sìla 5 gín [. . .] 2⅔ sìla [. . .] 1 sìla 10 gín [. . .] še-ba ì-b[a ù níĝ-dab$_5$] ki ^{d}*adad-tillati*-ta b[a-zi] ĝìri ***puzur$_4$*-^{d}nin-kar-ak** dub-sar, "Under the authority of *Puzur*-Ninkarak, the scribe, *Adad-tillati* disbursed 2 bushels (and) 40 liters of barley, 1 bushel (and) 150 liters of semolina, 3⅔ liters of sesame oil, 7 sheep carcasses, 35 split (dried) fish, [. . .], barley (and) oil rations [and requisitions]," 446 1–11

2.1.4.1 For the Flour Heap

1 dug dida$_x$-gen 1 sìla dabin 0.0.1 eša zì-dub-dub-šè u$_4$ ĝeš ùr ba-kéše-rá é-lùnga é-muḫaldim ù é-kíkken ki ^{d}*adad-tillati*-ta ba-zi ĝìri ***puzur$_4$*-[^{d}nin-kar-ak** dub-sar], "Under the authority of *Puzur*-Ninkarak, [the scribe], *Adad-tillati* disbursed 1 jug of ordinary dida beer, 1 liter of semolina (and) 10 liters of fine flour for the small flour heap when the roof beams of the brewery-kitchen-mill complex were bound," 1251:9–15

2.1.4.2 (Ceremonial) Offerings

1 dug dida$_x$-gen 0.0.3?-[ta] 1 sìla dabin [1 sìl]a eša ⸢sízkur⸣-šè u$_4$ ká é-lùnga é-muḫaldim ù é kíkken kéše-⸢rá⸣ 1 ⸢sìla⸣ dabin 1 sìla eša sízkur gir$_4$? ki ^{d}*adad-*[*tillati*]-ta ba-zi ĝìri ***puzur$_4$*-^{d}nin-kar-ak** dub-sar, "Under the authority of *Puzur*-Ninkarak, the scribe, *Adad-tillati* disbursed 1 jug of ordinary dida beer, 30? liters [each], 1 liter of semolina, (and) [1] liter of fine flour for (ceremonial) offerings when the gate of the brewery-kitchen-mill complex was bound (and) 1 liter of semolina (and) 1 liter of fine flour, (ceremonial) offerings of the oven?," 1007:1–11

[n] sìla ⸢eša⸣ a-rá-1-[kam] 1 dug dida$_x$-⸢gen⸣ 2 sìla dabin 1 sìla eša ½ sìla zú-lum a-rá-2-kam 3 sìla dabin 2 sìla eša 1 sìla zú-lum zì-dub-dub-didli-šè sízkur má a-a-ba [ki] ^{d}*adad-tillati*-[ta ba-zi g̃ir]ì ***puzur$_4$*-[^{d}nin-kar-ak** dub-sar], "Under the authority of *Puzur*-[Ninkarak, the scribe], *Adad-tillati* [disbursed n] liter(s) of fine flour for the 1st time, 1 pot of ordinary dida beer, 2 liters of semolina, 1 liter of fine flour (and) ½ liter of dates for the 2nd time, (and) 3 liters of semolina, 2 liters of fine flour (and) 1 liter of dates for various small flour heaps, (ceremonial) offerings of the sea(-going) boat," 1034:'1–'14

2.1.4.3 Provisions

2.1.4.3.1 For Builders

2.1.4.3.1.1 Assorted Commodities during Construction of the Brewery-Kitchen-Mill-Complex and its Components

0.0.1.5 sìla kaš-gen šidim-e-ne íb-nag̃ u$_4$ al-tar ki-sá-a é-lùnga ù é-[kíkken] ^{d}*adad-*[*tillati*] ba-zi g̃iri ***puzur$_4$*-[^{d}nin]-kar-ak** [dub-sar], "Under the authority of *Puzur*-Ninkarak, [the scribe], *Adad-tillati* disbursed 15 liters of ordinary beer. The builders drank (the beer) during construction of the foundation terrace of the brewery and [mill]," 428:1–7

1.2.2.5 sìla zú-lum <gur> šidim ù lú-ḫug̃-g̃á- e-ne ba-na-ḫa-la u$_4$ al-tar é-lùnga é-muḫaldim ù é-kíkken g̃iri ***puzur$_4$*-^{d}nin-kar-ak** dub-sar ki ^{d}*adad-tillati*-ta ba-zi, "Under the authority of *Puzur*-Ninkarak, the scribe, *Adad-tillati* disbursed 1 bushel (and) 145 liters of dates. They were divided for the builders and hired workers during construction of the brewery-kitchen-mill complex," 429:1–7

5 sìla ninda 0.0.2. kaš-gen šidim-e-ne íb-gu$_7$ ù íb-nag̃ [u$_4$] al-tar é-lùnga é-muḫaldim ù é-kíkken gub-ba ki ^{d}*adad-tillati*-ta ba-zi g̃iri ***puzur$_4$*-^{d}nin-kar-ak** dub-sar, "Under the authority of *Puzur*-Ninkarak, the scribe, *Adad-tillati* disbursed 5 liters of bread (and) 20 liters of ordinary beer. The builders ate and drank it [when] they were employed (for) construction of the brewery-kitchen-mill complex," 430:1–7

1 sìla dabin ½ sìla eša sízkur-šè 0.0.n. kaš-gen šidim-e-ne íb-nag̃ u$_4$ al-tar é-lùnga é-muḫaldim ù é-kíkken ki ^{d}*adad-tillati*-[ta] ba-zi g̃iri ***puzur$_4$*-^{d}nin-kar-ak** dub-sar, "Under the authority of *Puzur*-Ninkarak, the scribe, *Adad-tillati* disbursed 1 liter of semolina (and) ½ liter of fine flour for regular offerings (and) n liter(s) of ordinary beer. The builders drank (the beer) during construction of the brewery-kitchen-mill complex," 435:1–9, 439:1–9, 441:1–9

2.1.4.3.1.2 Assorted Commodities during Construction of the Brick Stack

[n.n.n.n sìla] zú-lum ⸢gur⸣ šidim ù lú-ḫug̃-g̃á-e-ne ba-na-ḫa-la u$_4$ al-tar SIG$_4$.⸢ANŠE⸣ g̃iri ***pù-zu*[*r$_8$*-^{d}nin-kar]-ak** [dub-sar] ki ^{d}*adad-*⸢*tillati*⸣-ta ba-zi, "Under the authority of *Puzur*-Ninkarak, [the scribe], *Adad-tillati* disbursed [n bushel(s) and liter(s)] of dates. They were divided for the builders and hired workers during construction of the brick stack," 424:1–6

2.1.4.3.1.3 Beer

5 sìla kaš-gen šidim-[e-n]e íb-nag̃ ki ^{d}*adad-tillati*-ta ⸢ba⸣-zi ⸢g̃iri⸣ ***puzur$_4$*-^{d}[nin-ka]r-ak** dub-sar, "Under the authority of *Puzur*-Ninkarak, the scribe,

Adad-tillati disbursed 5 liters of ordinary beer. The builders drank (the beer)," 418:1–6, 425:1–6

2.1.4.3.1.4 Fish

[10+]10 ku$_6$ al-dar-ra níĝ-gu$_7$ šidim-e-ne ki ^{d}*adad-tillati*-ta ba-zi ĝìri ***puzur$_4$*-^{d}nin-kar-ak** dub-sar, "Under the authority of *Puzur*-Ninkarak, the scribe, *Adad-tillati* disbursed 20 split (dried) fish, food of the builders," 427:1–5

2.1.4.3.2 For Caretakers

(. . .) *ba-da?*-[erasure]-*a* (. . .) *šu-eš$_4$-tár* dumu *da-da-a* (. . .) ur-me-[da?]-ni mu udug kislaḫ saḫar zi-zi-dè-šè ki ^{d}*adad-tillati*-ta ba-zi ĝìri ***puzur$_4$*-^{d}nin-kar-ak**, "Under the authority of *Puzur*-Ninkarak, *Adad-tillati* disbursed {barley, ordinary wool, oil, and baskets} to *Bada'a*, *Šu-Eštar*, son of *Dada'a* (and) Ur-medani, (provisions) for caretakers to move dirt (to/from) the lot," 1011:5, 10, 14–18

2.1.4.3.3 For Household Servants

(. . .) ḫa-la-a ĝuruš árad-é-a-e-[ne] ĝìri ***puzur$_4$*-^{d}nin-kar-ak** dub-sar [ki ^{d}*adad*]-*tillati*-ta ba-zi, "Under the authority of *Puzur*-Ninkarak, the scribe, *Adad-tillati* disbursed {bread and dates}, divided (provisions) of household servants," 402:17–19

131 túg ⸢ḫi⸣-a [n] ma-na ⸢siki-gen⸣ túg-⸢ba⸣ siki-bá géme-⸢árad⸣ [*simat*-^{d}K]A.⸢DI⸣ ⸢ĝìri⸣ [***pù-zu*]*r$_8$*-^{d}[nin-kar-ak** k]i ^{d}*adad-tillati*-[ta ba-zi], "Under the authority of *Puzur*-Ninkarak, *Adad-tillati* [disbursed] 131 assorted textiles (and) [n] mina(s) of ordinary wool, the textile and wool rations of the female and male servants of *Simat-Ištaran*," 734:6–12

2.1.4.3.4 For Workers when the (Enclosure) Wall was Built

2 ádda-udu ^{urudu}šen-šè éren al-tar bàd gub-ba íb-gu$_7$ ĝìri ***puzur$_4$*-^{d}nin-kar-ak** dub-sar ki ^{d}*adad-tillati*-ta ba-zi, "Under the authority of *Puzur*-Ninkarak, the scribe, *Adad-tillati* disbursed 2 sheep carcasses for the (soup) cauldron. The workers, employed (for) construction of the (enclosure) wall, ate (the soup)," 382:1–7, 388:1–7

2.1.5 Disbursals for Various Purposes

1 sìla dabin ½ sìla eša zì-dub-dub-šè é-lùnga é-muḫaldim ù é-kíkken 0.0.2. še 5 sìla5 ninda lú-^{ĝeš}tir-ra 0.0.1.5 sìla kaš-gen šidim-e-ne íb-naĝ 0.0.4. tuḫ-duru$_5$-sig$_5$ gibil lú-ḫuĝ-ĝá-e-ne ba-na-ḫa-[la] 2 sa gi-izi 2 gu-níĝin A.ZI/ZI(.ÉŠ) gir$_4$ 1-kam ki ^{d}*adad-tillati*-ta ba-zi ĝìri ***puzur$_4$*-^{d}nin-kar-ak**, "Under the authority of *Puzur*-Ninkarak, *Adad-tillati* disbursed 1 liter of semolina (and) ½ liter of fine flour for the small flour heap of the brewery-kitchen-mill complex, 20 liters of barley (and) 5 liters of bread for the forester, 15 liters of ordinary beer—the builders drank (the beer)—40 liters of fine fresh new bran—(the bran) was divided for the hired workers—(and) 2 bundles of fuel reeds (and) 2 bales of rushes (for) the oven," 436:1–15

2? dida$_x$-gen a-níĝin-[šè] 5 sìla dabin 3 sìla eša 1 sìla zú-lum zì-dub-dub-šè 0.0.1. dabin ninda ne-mur-šè sízkur-šè šidim-e-ne íb-gu$_7$ 0.0.1.2 sìla ninda 0.0.1. kaš-gen ½ sìla níĝ-àr-ra-sig$_5$ 1 ku$_6$ al-dar-ra ^{dug}útul-šè gala-e-ne *tak-ri-ib-tum* é-⸢lùnga⸣ é-muḫaldim ù é-kíkken 0.0.1.3 sìla kaš-gen ugula lú-ḫuĝ-ĝá-e-ne íb-naĝ ki ^{d}*adad-tillati*-⸢ta⸣ ba-zi ĝìri ***puzur$_4$*-^{d}nin-kar-ak** dub-sar, "Under the authority of

Puzur-Ninkarak, the scribe, *Adad-tillati* disbursed 2? liters of ordinary dida beer [for] the a-níĝin ceremony, 5 liters of semolina, 3 liters of fine flour, (and) 1 liter of dates for the small flour heap, 10 liters of semolina for bread (baked in) ash for offerings—the builders ate (the bread)—12 liters of bread, 10 liters of ordinary beer, ½ liter of fine groats (and) 1 dried (split) fish for the tureen of the lamentation singers (for their performance of) a *takribtum*—(delivery from) the brewery-kitchen-mill complex—(and) 13 liters of ordinary beer. The overseer of hired workers drank (the beer)," 437:1–17

(. . .) udug é-ki-ba-ĝar-ra *u-bar-ri-a* 5 ma-na siki-gen dirig sa_{10} siki-a-šè pu-*ta-nu-um* ki ^{d}*adad-tillati*-ta ba-zi ĝìri **puzur$_4$-^{d}nin-kar-ak**, "Under the authority of *Puzur*-Ninkarak, *Adad-tillati* disbursed {barley, ordinary wool, lard, flour and dates} (for) the caretaker of the replacement house of *Ubarria* (and) 5 minas of supplementary ordinary wool for the purchase of (more) wool of *Putanum*," 1005:6–12

(. . .) ĝeš ùr kéše-dè (. . .) zì-dub-dub-[šè] é-lùnga é-muḫaldim ù [é-kíkken] (. . .) peš-šè mu GÍN-bal ^{ĝeš}kiri$_6$-[šè] (. . .) ⌜udug⌝ é-ki-ba-ĝar-ra (. . .) [šidim-e-n]e íb-gu$_7$ [ki ^{d}*ad*]*ad-tillati*-t[a ba]-zi [ĝìri] **puzur$_4$-^{d}nin-kar-ak** dub-sar, "[Under the authority] of *Puzur*-Ninkarak, the scribe, *Adad-tillati* disbursed {ropes} to bind roof beams, {grains} [for] the small flour heap of the brewery-kitchen-mill complex, {house bitumen} for palmleaflet (mats) [for] the GÍN-bal of the garden, {barley and oil} (for) the caretaker of the replacement house, (and) {oil}. The [builders] consumed (the oil)," 1008:3, 5–6, 11, 14–17

2.2 Disbursals of Other Individuals

2.2.1 Provisions for Workers

(. . .) šà-gal šidim-e-ne 5 sìla ninda ugula lú-ḫuĝ-ĝá-e-ne íb-gu$_7$ 3 sìla ^{lú}kíĝ-gi$_4$-a *šu-kab-ta* 1 sìla dabin ½ sìla eša dub-dub-ne bà[d egi]r é-a dù-dè ⌜ĝìri⌝ **puzur$_4$-^{d}nin-kar-ak** dub-sar ki ^{d}*ma-lik-ba-ni*-ta ba-zi, "Under the authority of *Puzur*-Ninkarak, the scribe, *Malik-bani* disbursed {assorted grains}, food (for) builders, 5 liters of bread—the overseer of hired workers ate (the bread)—3 liters (of bread for) the messenger of *Šu-Kabta* (and) 1 liter of semolina (and) ½ liter of fine flour for heaping, (provisions of the workers) to construct the (enclosure) wall behind the house," 385:5–11

2.2.2 Textiles

(. . .) 30-lá-1 [túg] ki-lá tag [ki] *aš-tá-qar*-ta [*puzur$_4$-a-gu$_5$-um* šu ba-ti **pù-zu**]**r$_8$-^{d}nin-kar-ak** dub-sar, "(Under the authority of) *Puzur*-Ninkarak, the scribe, [*Puzur-agum* received] 29 {textiles}, weighed [textiles] having been woven, from *Aštaqqar*," 835:'16–'22

2.2.3 Broken Context

[n] sìla dabin ½ sìla eša zì-[dub]-d[ub-šè] é-lùnga é muḫaldim ù é-kíkken 240 ^{gi}kid-[. . . x]-e ba-ab-[. . . x] ésir-é-a [. . .] gar-š[a-an-na^{ki}-šè? . . .] ĝìri **puzur$_4$-**[**^{d}nin-kar**]**-ak** dub-[sar], "Under the authority of *Puzur*-Ninkarak, the scribe, [n] liter(s) of semolina (and) ½ liter of fine flour [for] the small flour heap of the brewery-kitchen-mill complex, 240 [. . .] reed mats were [. . .], [x] house bitumen [. . . for?] Garšana [. . .]," 1249:1–12

2.3 Inspection of Labor

2.3.1 A Basket of Inspection Accounts

bisaĝ-dub-ba gaba-ri kurum$_7$ aka éren al-tar-ra gub-ba ĝìri ***puzur$_4$*-^{d}nin-kar-ak** dub-sar, "A tablet basket of copies of inspection (of the work) of the workers employed for construction under the authority of *Puzur*-Ninkarak, the scribe," 1314:1–5

2.3.2 Dirt Moved at the Garšana Garden

kurum$_7$ aka saḫar ⸢zi⸣-ga ^{ĝeš}kiri$_6$ gar-ša-an-na^{ki} ĝìri ***puzur$_4$*-^{d}nin-kar-ak** dub-sar, "Inspection of dirt moved at the Garšana garden under the authority of *Puzur*-Ninkarak, the scribe," 176:16–18, 179:17–19

2.3.3 Pouring Water and Moving Dirt

5 ĝuruš *šu-kab-tá* 5 ĝuruš *a-a-ni* [n ĝuruš ugula] *ba-zi* [n ĝu]ruš ugula *simat-é-a* [a] bal-a 15 ĝuruš ugula *za-la-a* saḫar zi-⸢ga⸣ [kurum$_7$ aka ĝìri ***puzur$_4$*-^{d}nin-kar-ak** dub-sar], "[Under the authority of *Puzur*-Ninkarak, the scribe, inspection (of the work)] of 5 workmen of *Šu-Kabta*, 5 workmen of *A'ani*, [n workmen supervised by] *Bazi*, (and) [n] workmen supervised by *Simat-Ea* having poured water (and) 15 workmen, supervised by *Zala'a* having moved dirt," 181:1–9

2.4 Receipt of *Adad-tillati*

19 ma-na siki-gen ⅓ ma-na siki-ĝe$_6$ bar-udu 32-kam ^{d}*adad-tillati* šu ba-ti ĝìri ***puzur$_4$*-^{d}[nin]-kar-ra(!)-ak**, "Under the authority of *Puzur*-Ninkarak, *Adad-tillati* received 19 minas of ordinary wool (and) ⅓ mina of black wool of 32 sheep fleeces," 634:1–6

3. Under the Authority of *Malik-bani* and *Puzur*-Ninkarak

4 ^{ĝeš}nu-úr-ma-sig$_5$ 7 ^{ĝeš}nu-úr-ma-ús mu-DU *ak-ba-zum* um-mi-a ^{d}*adad-tillati* šu ba-an-ti ĝìri ^{d}*ma-lik-ba-ni* ù ***puzur$_4$*-^{d}nin-kar-ak**, "Under the authority of *Malik-bani* and *Puzur*-Ninkarak, *Adad-tillati* received 4 fine pomegranate planks (and) 7 lesser-quality pomegranate planks, the delivery of *Akbazum*, the craftsman," 1298:1–8

4. Under the Authority of *Puzur*-Ninkarak and *Adad-tillati*

4.1 Delivery of Bricks

4.1.1 For the Craftsmen's House

é-NUN.ME.TA[G-e-ne-šè] mu-[DU] *šál-maḫ* [ugula lú-ḫuĝ-ĝá] ĝìri ^{d}*adad-ti*[*llati* šabra] ù ***puzur$_4$*-^{d}nin-kar-ak**, "delivery (of bricks) [for] the craftsmen's house by *Šal-maḫ*, [overseer of hired workers,] under the authority of *Adad-tillati*, [the majordomo], and *Puzur*-Ninkarak," 325:18–22

é-gašam-e-ne mu-DU *za-la-a* ugula lú-ḫuĝ-ĝá ĝìri ^{d}*adad-tillati* ù ***puzur$_4$*-^{d}nin-kar-ak**, "delivery (of bricks for) the craftsmen's house by *Zala'a*, overseer of hired workers, under the authority of *Adad-tillati* and *Puzur*-Ninkarak," 330:27–31

é-gašam-e-ne mu-DU *ba-zi* ⸢ĝìri⸣ ^{d}*adad-tillati* ù ***puzur$_4$*-^{d}nin-kar-ak** dub-sar, "delivery (of bricks for) the craftsmen's house by *Bazi*, under the authority of *Adad-tillati* and *Puzur*-Ninkarak, the scribe," 334:65–68

4.1.2 For the Foundation Terrace

4.1.2.1 Of the Kitchen and Mill

ki-sá-a é-lùnga [ù é-kíkken?] mu-DU *simat*-^{d}[nanna ugula] ĝìri ***puzur$_4$*-^{d}[nin-kar-ak** ú] ^{d}*adad-tillati* [šabra], "delivery (of bricks for) the foundation terrace of the brewery [and mill?] by *Simat*-Nanna, [the overseer], under the authority of *Puzur*-Ninkarak [and] *Adad-tillati*, [the majordomo]," 353:17–20

4.1.2.2 Of the Textile Mill

ki-sá-a é-uš-bar-šè mu-DU *za-la-a* ugula lú-ḫ[ug̃-g̃á] g̃iri [d]*adad-tillati* [ù] ***pù-zur₈***-**[d]nin-kar-ak** du[b-sar], "delivery (of bricks) for the foundation terrace of the textile mill by *Zala'a*, overseer of hired workers, under the authority of *Adad-tillati* [and] *Puzur*-Ninkarak, the scribe," 311:21–24, 362:'20–'25

[ki]-sá-a é-uš-bar-šè mu-DU árad-é-a ugula g̃iri [d]*adad-tillati* ù ***puzur₄***-**[d]nin-kar-ak** dub-sar, "delivery (of bricks) for the foundation terrace of the textile mill by the overseer of the household servants under the authority of *Adad-tillati* and *Puzur*-Ninkarak, the scribe," 322:'83–'86

[ki-sá-a] é-uš-bar-šè [mu-DU] *simat-é-a* ugula lú-ḫug̃-g̃á ⸢g̃iri⸣ [d]*ad[ad-till]ati* šabra [ù] ***puzur₄***-**[d][nin-k]ar-ak** du[b-sa]r, "[delivery] (of bricks) for the [foundation terrace] of the textile mill by *Simat-Ea*, overseer of hired workers, under the authority of *Adad-tillati*, the majordomo, [and] *Puzur*-Ninkarak, the scribe," 324:94–97

4.1.2.3 Of the Textile Mill and Craftsmen's House

mu-DU ki-sá-a [é-uš-bar] ù é-NUN.[ME.TAG-e]-ne [PN ugula] lú-ḫug̃-g̃á [g̃iri [d]*ada*]*d-tillati* [ù ***puzu***]***r₄***-**[d]nin-[kar-ak]** dub-sar, "delivery (of bricks) for the foundation terrace of the [textile mill] and craftsmen's house by [PN, overseer] of hired workers, under the authority of *Adad-tillati* [and] *Puzur*-Ninkarak, the scribe," 321:'33–'37

4.1.3 For the House of the Barbers

é-šu-i-[e-ne-šè] *simat-é-a* ugula lú-ḫug̃-g̃á g̃iri [[d]*adad-tillati*] šabra ù [***puzur₄***-**[d]nin-kar-ak** dub-sar], "(delivery of bricks) [for] the house of the barbers by *Simat-Ea*, overseer of hired workers, under the authority of [*Adad-tillati*], the majordomo, and [*Puzur*-Ninkarak, the scribe]," 352:39–42

4.1.4 For Replacement Houses

mu-DU é-ki-ba-g̃ar-ra en-[d]inana-gal *ba-zi* ugula g̃iri [d]*adad-tillati* ù ***puzur₄***-**[d]nin-kar-ak**, "delivery (of bricks for) the replacement house of the senior priest of Inana by *Bazi*, the overseer, under the authority of *Adad-tillati* and *Puzur*-Ninkarak," 337:31–35

[mu-DU é]-ki-ba-g̃ar-ra *z[u-zu-t]um ba-zi* [ugula l]ú-ḫug̃-g̃á g̃iri [d]*adad-tillati* šabra ù ***puzur₄***-**[d]nin-kar-[ak** dub]-sar, "[delivery] (of bricks for) the replacement house of *Zuzutum* by *Bazi*, [overseer] of hired workers, under the authority of *Adad-tillati*, the majordomo, and *Puzur*-Ninkarak, the scribe," 342:83–87

mu-DU é-ki-ba-g̃ar-ra *u-bar-um za-la-a* ugula lú-ḫug̃-g̃á g̃iri ***puzur₄***-**[d]nin-kar-ak** dub-sar, "delivery (of bricks for) the replacement house of *Ubarum* by *Zala'a*, overseer of hired workers, under the authority of *Puzur*-Ninkarak, the scribe," 343:11–15[51]

---

[51] Although *Puzur*-Ninkarak does not act in conjunction with *Adad-tillati*, this text is included here in light of parallel texts, nos. 337 and 342.

4.1.5 For the Textile Depository

mu-⸢DU⸣ ki-mur-ra-šè *simat-é-a* [ugula] lú-[ḫug̃]-g̃á g̃ìri ^{d}*adad-*[*tillati* PA.A]L ù ***puzur*$_4$-[^{d}nin-kar-ak]** dub-sar, "delivery (of bricks) for the textile depository by *Simat-Ea*, [overseer] of hired workers, under the authority of *Adad-tillati*, the majordomo, and *Puzur*-Ninkarak, the scribe," 335:41–44

ki-mu-ra-šè mu-DU *za-la-a* ugula lú-ḫug̃-g̃á g̃ìri ^{d}*adad-tillati* ù ***puzur*$_4$-^{d}nin-kar-ak**, "delivery (of bricks) for the textile depository by *Zala'a*, overseer of hired workers, under the authority of *Adad-tillati* and *Puzur*-Ninkarak," 338:21–24

4.1.6 For the Textile Mill

é-uš-bar-šè mu-DU *simat-é-a* ugula g̃ìri ^{d}*adad-tillati* ù ***puzur*$_4$-^{d}nin-kar-ak** dub-sar, "delivery (of bricks) for the textile mill by *Simat-Ea*, the overseer, under the authority of *Adad-tillati* and *Puzur*-Ninkarak, the scribe," 316:72–76

é-uš-bar-[šè mu-DU] *šál-maḫ* [ugula lú-ḫug̃-g̃á] g̃ìri ^{d}*adad-*[*tillati* šabra] ù ***puzur*$_4$-[^{d}nin-kar-ak** dub-sar], "[delivery] (of bricks) [for] the textile mill by *Šal-maḫ*, [overseer of hired workers], under the authority of *Adad-tillati*, [the majordomo], and *Puzur*-[Ninkarak, the scribe]," 320:11–14

é-uš-bar(-šè) mu-DU *ba-zi* ugula g̃ìri ^{d}*adad-tillati* ù ***puzur*$_4$-^{d}nin-kar-ak** dub-sar, "delivery of bricks (for) the textile mill by *Bazi*, the overseer, under the authority of *Adad-tillati* and *Puzur*-Ninkarak, the scribe," 323:124–128, 327:82–86

4.1.7 For the Textile Mill and Craftsmen's House

é-uš-bar ù [é-NUN].ME.⸢TAG⸣-e-⸢ne⸣ mu-[DU] *simat-é-a* ugula [lú-ḫug̃-g̃á g̃ìri ^{d}*adad-tillati*] ù [***puzur*$_4$-^{d}n]in-kar-[ak** dub-sar], "delivery (of bricks for) the textile mill and craftsmen's [house] by *Simat-Ea*, overseer [of hired workers, under the authority of *Adad-tillati*] and *Puzur*-Ninkarak, [the scribe]," 328:14–18

[é]-uš-bar [ù é]-gašam-e-ne mu-DU *ba-zi* ugula lú-ḫug̃-g̃á g̃ìri ^{d}*adad-tillati* šabra [ù ***puzur*$_4$-^{d}]nin-[kar-ak** dub-sa]r, "delivery (of bricks) for the textile [mill and] craftsmen's [house] by *Bazi*, overseer of hired workers, under the authority of *Adad-tillati*, the majordomo, [and] *Puzur*-Ninkarak, the scribe," 368:'60–'65

4.1.8 For the (Enclosure) Wall

mu-DU bàd-šè *simat-é-a* ugula lú-ḫug̃-g̃á g̃ìri ^{d}*adad-tillati* šabra ù ***puzur*$_4$-^{d}nin-kar-ak** dub-sar, "delivery (of bricks) for the (enclosure) wall by *Simat-Ea*, overseer of hired workers, under the authority of *Adad-tillati*, the majordomo, and *Puzur*-Ninkarak, the scribe," 308:47–51

mu-DU bàd-šè *ba-zi* ugula lú-ḫug̃-g̃á g̃ìri ^{d}*adad-tillati* šabra ù ***puzur*$_4$-^{d}nin-kar-ak** dub-sar, "delivery (of bricks) for the (enclosure) wall by *Bazi*, overseer of hired workers, under the authority of *Adad-tillati*, the majordomo, and *Puzur*-Ninkarak, the scribe," 309:74–78, 340:33–36, 345:'15–'18

bàd-šè mu-⸢DU⸣ *za-la-a* ugula lú-ḫug̃-g̃á g̃ìri ^{d}*adad-tillati* šabra ù ***puzur*$_4$-^{d}nin-kar-ak** dub-sar, "delivery (of bricks) for the (enclosure) wall by *Zala'a*, overseer of hired workers, under the authority of *Adad-tillati*, the majordomo, and *Puzur*-Ninkarak, the scribe," 313:23–26

[mu]-DU bàd-šè [*za*]-*la-a* ugula lú-ḫug̃-g̃á ⸢g̃ìri⸣ ^{d}*adad-tillati* šabra ù ***puzur*$_4$-^{d}nin-kar-ak** dub-sar, "delivery (of bricks) for the (enclosure) wall by *Zala'a*, overseer

of hired workers, under the authority of *Adad-tillati*, the majordomo, and *Puzur*-Ninkarak, the scribe," 361:'13–'16

4.1.9 Bricks for the urua wall

ù-ru-a bàd-šè mu-DU *za-la-a* ugula lú-ḫug̃-g̃á g̃iri ^{d}*adad-tillati* šabra ù ***puzur$_{4}$*-^{d}nin-kar-ak** dub-sar, "delivery (of bricks) for the urua wall by *Zala'a*, overseer of hired workers, under the authority of *Adad-tillati*, the majordomo, and *Puzur*-Ninkarak, the scribe," 312:35–38, 317:30–34

ù-ru a bàd-šè mu-DU *ba-zi* ugula lú-ḫug̃-g̃á g̃iri ^{d}*adad-tillati* šabra ù ***puzur$_{4}$*-^{d}nin-kar-ra-ak** dub-sar, "delivery (of bricks) for the urua wall by *Bazi*, overseer of hired workers, under the authority of *Adad-tillati*, the majordomo, and *Puzur*-Ninkarak, the scribe," 318:'51–'53

4.1.10 Count of Bricks

73⅓ sar šeg$_{12}$ NE-gu$_{7}$-bi íb-ta-zi mu-DU *i-din-é-a* ugula lú-ḫug̃-g̃á g̃iri *ba-zi* šid-da g̃iri ^{d}*adad-tillati* ù ***puzur$_{4}$*-^{d}nin-kar-a[k** dub-sar], "73⅓ sar of bricks, the damaged bricks were deducted. Delivery of *Iddin-Ea*, overseer of hired workers. The count (of bricks) was under the authority of *Bazi*. (Transaction) under the authority of *Adad-tillati* and *Puzur*-Ninkarak, [the scribe]," 315:1–8

4.2 Delivery of Dirt

saḫar zi-ga tùn-lá da bàd [sè-ga m]u-DU *ba-zi* ugula l[ú-ḫug̃-g̃á g̃i]ri ^{d}*adad-tillati* [šabra ù ***pù***]-***zur$_{8}$***-^{d}**n[in-kar-ak]** dub-[sar], "dirt removed via a tùn-lá device, [tamped] at the side of the (enclosure) wall. Delivery (of dirt) by *Bazi*, overseer of [hired] workers, under the authority of *Adad-tillati*, the majordomo, [and] *Puzur*-Ninkarak, the scribe," 329:13–17

saḫar zi-ga tùn-lá da bàd sè-ga á ^{tumu}mer mu-DU *ba-zi* ugula lú-ḫug̃-g̃á g̃iri ^{d}*adad-tillati* šabra ù ***puzur$_{4}$*-^{d}nin-kar-ak** dub-sar, "dirt removed via a tùn-lá device, tamped at the north side of the (enclosure) wall. Delivery (of dirt) by *Bazi*, overseer of hired workers, under the authority of *Adad-tillati*, the majordomo, and *Puzur*-Ninkarak, the scribe," 331:34–38, 333:21–25

saḫar zi-ga [ki-s]á-a é-l[ùnga ù é-kíkken] mu-⌜DU⌝ *li-la-a* ugula lú-ḫug̃-g̃á g̃iri ***puzur$_{4}$*-^{d}nin-kar-ak** dub-sar ù ^{d}*adad-tillati* šabra, "delivery of dirt removed at the foundation terrace of the b[rewery and mill] by *Lila'a*, overseer of hired workers, under the authority of *Puzur*-Ninkarak, the scribe, and *Adad-tillati*, the majordomo," 355:6–10

im-du$_{8}$-a $^{g̃eš}$[kiri$_{6}$] zabala$_{4}$$^{[ki]}$ mu-[DU] *ib-ni-ilum* ugula [lú-ḫug̃-g̃á] g̃iri ***puzur$_{4}$*-^{d}ni[n-kar]-ak** dub-[sar] ù ^{d}*adad-tillati* P[A.AL], "delivery (of dirt) for the adobe wall of the Zabala [garden] by *Ibni-ilum*, overseer [of hired workers], under the authority of *Puzur*-Ninkarak, the scribe, and *Adad-tillati*, the majordomo," 356:5–9

4.3 Disbursal of Various Commodities as Rations, Wages, and Allotments

4.3.1 (Ceremonial) Offerings for the (Enclosure) Wall

4.3.1.1 Beer

0.0.1. kaš-gen níg̃ ki-zàḫ-šè sízkur ⌜bàd⌝-šè ki *ì-[lí]-uṣ-ra-ni*-ta ba-zi g̃iri ^{d}*adad-tillati* šabra [ù ***pù***]-***zur$_{8}$***-^{d}**nin-ka[r-a]k**, "Under the authority of *Adad-tillati*, the majordomo, [and] *Puzur*-Ninkarak, *Ili-uṣranni* disbursed 10 liters of ordinary beer, provisions for the cultic place, (ceremonial) offerings for the (enclosure) wall," 986:1–6

4.3.1.2 Semolina and Fine Flour

1 sìla dabin ½ sìla eša sízkur bàd-šè ki *é-a-dan*-ta ba-zi g̃ìri ^{d}*adad-tillati* ù ***puzur$_4$*-^{d}nin-kar-ak** dub-sar, "Under the authority of *Adad-tillati* and *Puzur*-Ninkarak, the scribe, *Ea-dan* disbursed 1 liter of semolina (and) ½ liter of fine flour, (ceremonial) offerings for the (enclosure) wall," 987:1–7, 988:1–7, 989:1–7

1 sìla dabin ½ sìla eša sízkur bàd-šè ki *é-a-šar*-ta ba-zi g̃ìri ^{d}*adad-tillati* ù ***puzur$_4$*-^{d}nin-kar-ak** dub-sar, "Under the authority of *Adad-tillati* and *Puzur*-Ninkarak, the scribe, *Ea-šar* disbursed 1 liter of semolina (and) ½ liter of fine flour, (ceremonial) offerings for the (enclosure) wall," 990:1–7

1 sìla dabin ½ sìla eša sízkur bàd-šè ki *a-ḫu-wa-qar* ⌜ba⌝-zi g̃ìri ^{d}*adad-tillati* ù ***puzur$_4$*-^{d}nin-kar-ak** dub-sar, "Under the authority of *Adad-tillati* and *Puzur*-Ninkarak, the scribe, *Aḫu-waqar* disbursed 1 liter of semolina (and) ½ liter of fine flour, (ceremonial) offerings for the (enclosure) wall," 993:1–7, 995:1–7

4.3.1.3 Semolina, Fine Flour, and an Ox

[o.n.n.] dabin [o.n.n.] eša [1] gu$_4$-gaz bàd-šè ⌜ki⌝ *a-ḫu-wa-qar*-ta ba-zi g̃ìri ^{d}*adad-tillati* ù ***[pù]-zur$_8$*-^{d}nin-⌜kar⌝-ak** dub-sar, "Under the authority of *Adad-tillati* and *Puzur*-Ninkarak, the scribe, *Aḫu-waqar* disbursed [n] liter(s) of semolina, [n] liter(s) of fine flour (and) [1] slaughtered ox for the (enclosure) wall," 992:1–7

4.3.2 (Ceremonial) Offerings for the (Enclosure) Wall and the Overseer

1 dug dida$_x$-gen sízkur uš bàd 5 sìla kaš-gen ugula lú-ḫug̃-g̃á-e-ne íb-nag̃ [ki] *ì-lí-uṣ-ra-ni*-ta ba-zi g̃ìri ^{d}*adad-tillati* šabra ù ***puzur$_4$*-^{d}nin-kar-ak** dub-sar, "Under the authority of *Adad-tillati*, the majordomo, and *Puzur*-Ninkarak, the scribe, *Ili-uṣranni* disbursed 1 jug of ordinary dida beer, (ceremonial) offerings for the foundation of the (enclosure) wall (and) 5 liters of ordinary beer. The overseer of hired workers drank (the beer)," 377:1–8

4.3.3 (Ceremonial) Offerings for the (Enclosure) Wall and the Textile Mill

1 sìla dabin ½ sìla eša sízkur bàd ù é-uš-bar ki *é-a-dan*-ta ba-zi g̃ìri ^{d}*adad-tillati* ù ***puzur$_4$*-^{d}nin-kar-ak** dub-sar, "Under the authority of *Adad-tillati* and *Puzur*-Ninkarak, the scribe, *Ea-dan* disbursed 1 liter of semolina (and) ½ liter of fine flour, (ceremonial) offerings of the (enclosure) wall and the textile mill," 991:1–7, 994:1–7

4.3.4 Provisions for Builders

4.3.4.1 Assorted Grains

(. . .) šà-gal šidim-e-ne g̃ìri ^{d}*adad-tillati* ù ***puzur$_4$*-^{d}nin-kar-ak** ki ^{d}*ma-lik-ba-ni*-ta ba-zi, "Under the authority of *Adad-tillati* and *Puzur*-Ninkarak, *Malik-bani* disbursed {assorted grains}, food (for) builders," 381:21–24

4.3.4.2 Beer

2 sìla kaš-gen-ta *en-ni-ma* 1 *be-lí-a-sú* (lú-ì-si-in^{ki}) 1 sìla *ma-šum* árad-é-a kaš-gen-bi 5-sìla šidim-e-ne íb-nag̃ ki *ì-lí-uṣ-ra-ni*-ta ba-zi g̃ìri ^{d}*adad-tillati* šabra ù ***puzur$_4$*-^{d}nin-kar-ak** dub-sar, "Under the authority of *Adad-tillati*, the majordomo, and *Puzur*-Ninkarak, the scribe, *Ili-uṣranni* disbursed 2 liters of ordinary beer each (for) *Enima* (and) *Beli-asu*, men from Isin (and) 1 liter

(for) *Mašum*, the household servant. (In total:) their ordinary beer is 5 liters. The builders drank (the beer)," 378:9–19, 380:1–1, 384:1–11, 389:1–11

n sìla kaš-gen šidim-e-ne íb-nag̃ ki *ì-lí-uṣ-ra-ni*-ta ba-zi g̃ìri ^{d}*adad-tillati* (šabra) ù ***puzur***$_4$**-^{d}nin-kar-ak** dub-sar, "Under the authority of *Adad-tillati*, the majordomo, and *Puzur*-Ninkarak, the scribe, *Ili-uṣranni* disbursed n liter(s) of ordinary beer. The builders drank (the beer)," 398:1–6, 401:1–7

7 sìla kaš-gen dirig sá-du$_{11}$ šidim ù ugula lú-ḫug̃-g̃á-e-ne íb-nag̃ ki *ì-lí-uṣ-ra-ni*-ta ba-zi [g̃ìri] ^{d}*adad-tillati* [ù] ***puzur***$_4$**-^{d}nin-kar-ak** dub-sar, "[Under the authority] of *Adad-tillati* [and] *Puzur*-Ninkarak, the scribe, *Ili-uṣranni* disbursed 7 liters of ordinary beer, surplus of the regular offerings. The builders and overseer of hired workers drank (the beer)," 400:1–6

4.3.5 Provisions for Workers Employed for Construction

šu+níg̃in 0.1.0.3 sìla 10 gín kaš-gen šu+níg̃in 0.0.5.3⅔ sìla ninda šu+níg̃in 0.0.3. 8 sìla tu$_7$ kaš-ninda ḫa-la-a? al-⌜tar⌝ gub-ba g̃ìri ^{d}*adad-tillati* šabra ù ***puzur***$_4$**-^{d}nin-kar-ak** [dub-sar], "In total: 63 liters (and) 10 shekels of ordinary beer, 53⅔ liters of bread (and) 38 liters of soup; beer (and) bread divided (for workers) employed (for) construction, under the authority of *Adad-tillati*, the majordomo, and *Puzur*-Ninkarak, [the scribe]," 379:17–21

4.3.6 Provisions when the (Enclosure) Wall was Built

4.3.6.1 For Builders

(. . .) šà-gal šidim-e-ne (. . .) árad-é-[a lú-ḫug̃]-g̃á ù ugula lú-[ḫug̃-g̃á-e-n]e íb-gu$_7$ [1] sìla dabin ½ sìla eša zì-dub-dub-šè u$_4$ bàd é-a dù-dè g̃ìri ^{d}*adad-tillati* ù ***puzur***$_4$**-[^{d}nin-kar-a]k** ki ^{d}*ma-l[ik-b]a-n[i*-ta ba]-zi, "Under the authority of *Adad-tillati* and *Puzur*-Ninkarak, *Malik-bani* disbursed {assorted grains}, food (for) builders—the servants, hired workers, and overseer of the hired workers ate (the grains)—(and) 1 liter of semolina (and) ½ liter of fine flour for the small flour heap, (provisions of the workers) when they were constructing the (enclosure) wall of the house," 383:5, 8–13

(. . .) šà-gal šidim-e-ne u$_4$ bàd egir é-a dù-dè g̃ìri ^{d}*adad-tillati* (šabra) ù ***puzur***$_4$**-^{d}nin-kar-ak** ki ^{d}*ma-lik-ba-ni*-ta ba-zi, "Under the authority of *Adad-tillati*, (the majordomo), and *Puzur*-Ninkarak, *Malik-bani* disbursed {assorted commodities}, food (for) builders when they were constructing the (enclosure) wall behind the house," 386:29–34, 387:20–24

(. . .) šà-gal šidim-e-ne u$_4$ bàd in-dù-sa-a g̃ìri ^{d}*adad-tillati* ù ***puzur***$_4$**-^{d}nin-kar-ak** šà gar-ša-an-na^{ki} ki ^{d}*ma-lik-ba-ni*-ta ba-zi, "Under the authority of *Adad-tillati* and *Puzur*-Ninkarak in Garšana, *Malik-bani* disbursed {assorted grains}, food (for) builders when they constructed the (enclosure) wall," 396:19–24, 397:19–24

4.3.6.2 For Household Servants and Hired Workers

[n] sìla 10 gín [kaš?] árad-é-a ù lú-ḫug̃-g̃á-e-ne ib-gu$_7$(sic!) u$_4$ al-tar bàd gub-ba ki *ì-lí-uṣ-ra-ni*-[ta ba]-zi g̃ìri ^{d}*adad-tillati* šabra ù ***puzur***$_4$**-^{d}nin-kar-ak** dub-sar, "Under the authority of *Adad-tillati*, the majordomo, and *Puzur*-Ninkarak, the scribe, *Ili-uṣranni* disbursed [n] liter(s) (and) 10 shekels of [beer?]. The household servants and hired workers consumed (the beer)

when they were employed (for) construction of the (enclosure) wall," 392:1–7

0.0.5.4 sìla kaš árad-é-a ù lú-ḫuĝ-ĝá-e-ne u_4 al-tar bàd gub-ba ki *ì-lí-uṣ-ra-ni*-ta ba-zi ĝìri [d]*adad-tillati* šabra ù ***puzur*$_4$-[d]nin-kar-ak** dub-sar, "Under the authority of *Adad-tillati*, the majordomo, and *Puzur*-Ninkarak, the scribe, *Ili-uṣranni* disbursed 54 liters of beer (for) the household servants and hired workers when they were employed (for) construction of the (enclosure) wall," 395:1–6

4.3.7 Wages for Construction: the Balanced Account of *Šu*-Dumuzi

níĝ-kas$_7$-aka *šu*-[d]dumu-zi ugula lú-ḫuĝ-ĝá ĝìri [d]*adad-tillati* šabra ù ***puzur*$_4$-[d]nin-kar-ak** dub-sar, "{barley, wages for workers employed for construction}, the balanced account of *Šu*-Dumuzi, overseer of hired workers, under the authority of *Adad-tillati*, the majordomo, and *Puzur*-Ninkarak, the scribe," 336:55–58

4.4 Inspection of Workers Assigned to Various Tasks

kurum$_7$ aka ĝìri [d]*adad-tillati* ù ***puzur*$_4$-[d]nin-kar-ak** dub-sar, "Inspection under the authority of *Adad-tillati* and *Puzur*-Ninkarak, the scribe," 34:'29, 38:58–60, 40:62–64, 41:'42–'43, 51:'29–'31, 52:79–81, 57:'36–'38, 58:74–76, 59:66–68, 60:61–63, 71:45–47, 78:18, 79:18–19, 213:'20–'22

kurum$_7$ aka ĝìri [d]*adad-tillati* dub-sar ù ***puzur*$_4$-[d]nin-kar-ak** dub-sar, "Inspection under the authority of *Adad-tillati*, the scribe, and *Puzur*-Ninkarak, the scribe,"10:'29–'30

kurum$_7$ aka ĝìri [d]*adad-tillati* šabra ù ***puzur*$_4$-[d]nin-kar-ak** dub-sar, "Inspection under the authority of *Adad-tillati*, the majordomo, and *Puzur*-Ninkarak, the scribe," 7:'40–'42, 13:'28–'29, 18:'4–'5, 19:19–21, 36:56–57, 37:53–55, 39:'56–'58, 42:'13–'15, 43:'57–'59, 44:53–55, 45:42–44, 47:77–79, 48:83–85, 49:74–76, 53:73–75, 54:46–48, 56:'45–'47, 61:22–24, 75:37–39, 93:'38–'40, 99:36–38, 100:'38–'39, 101:40–41

kurum$_7$ aka ĝìri ***puzur*$_4$-[d]nin-kar-ak** dub-sar ù [d]*adad-tillati* šabra, "Inspection under the authority of *Puzur*-Ninkarak, the scribe, and *Adad-tillati*, the majordomo," 106:54–56, 108:48–49, 109:43–45, 110:44–46, 114:55–57, 120:'43–'45, 121:43–45, 126:41–43, 127:'26–'28, 128:43–45, 129:46–48, 135:44–46, 136:49–51, 137:22–23, 138:49–50, 142:42–44, 147:55–57, 149:'14–'16, 159:41–43, 174:37–39, 182:7–8

4.4.1 Inspection Accounts: *Puzur*-Ninkarak, Title Unspecified

kurum$_7$ aka ĝìri [d]*adad-tillati* šabra ù ***puzur*$_4$-[d]nin-kar-ak**, "Inspection under the authority of *Adad-tillati*, the majordomo, and *Puzur*-Ninkarak," 94:39–41, 102:41–43

kurum$_7$ aka ĝìri ***puzur*$_4$-[d]nin-kar-ak** ù [d]*adad-tillati*, "Inspection under the authority of *Puzur*-Ninkarak and *Adad-tillati*," 103:45–47, 111:52–54, 118:33–35, 125:45–47, 130:'26–'27, 132:45–47, 133:44–46, 140:50–52, 151:46–48, 155:43–45, 157:30–32, 158:49–51, 159:41–43, 162:38–40, 173:39–41, 175:36–37, 180:25–27

kurum$_7$ aka ĝìri ***puzur*$_4$-[d]nin-kar-ak** ù [d]*adad-tillati* šabra, "Inspection under the authority of *Puzur*-Ninkarak and *Adad-tillati*, the majordomo," 107:'24–'25, 116:'16–'18, 117:41–43, 119:31–33, 123:53–55, 124:7–9, 134:25–27, 139:'16–'18, 141:47–49, 145:50–52, 150:51–53, 154:49–51, 156:43–45, 161:'30–'32, 163:42–44

[kurum$_7$ aka ĝì]ri [d]*adad*-KASKAL.[KUR ù ***pù*]-*zur*$_8$-[d]nin-[kar-ak]**, "[Inspection] under the authority of *Adad-tillati* [and] *Puzur*-Ninkarak," 212:'13–'14

4.4.2 Construction of the Textile Depository

kurum$_7$ aka al-tar ki-mur-ra gub-ba g̃iri [d]*adad-tillati* šabra ù ***puzur$_4$*-[d]nin-kar-ak** dub-sar, "Inspection of (the work of workers) employed (for) construction of the textile depository, under the authority of *Adad-tillati*, the majordomo, and *Puzur*-Ninkarak, the scribe," 72:28–30, 76:19–21, 77:10–12

4.4.3 Construction of the (Enclosure) Wall

kurum$_7$ aka al-tar bàd gub-ba g̃iri [d]*adad-tillati* šabra ù ***puzur$_4$*-[d]nin-kar-ak** dub-sar, "Inspection (of the work) of (workers) employed (for) construction of the (enclosure) wall, under the authority of *Adad-tillati*, the majordomo, and *Puzur*-Ninkarak, the scribe," 14:40–42, 15:41–43, 17:37–39, 20:42–44, 21:'36–'38

kurum$_7$ aka éren al-tar bàd gub-ba g̃iri [d]*adad-tillati* šabra ù ***puzur$_4$*-[d]nin-kar-ak** dub-sar, "Inspection (of the work) of workers employed (for) construction of the (enclosure) wall, under the authority of *Adad-tillati*, the majordomo, and *Puzur*-Ninkarak, the scribe," 16:35–37, 24:'38–'40

kurum$_7$ aka éren šu dím bàd gub-ba g̃iri [d]*adad-tillati* šabra ù ***puzur$_4$*-[d]nin-kar-ak** dub-sar, "Inspection (of the work) of workers employed to build the (enclosure) wall, under the authority of *Adad-tillati*, the majordomo, and *Puzur*-Ninkarak, the scribe," 30:'20–'22

4.4.4 Construction of the (Enclosure) Wall and the Textile Mill

kurum$_7$ aka al-tar bàd ù ki-sá é-uš-bar g̃iri [d]*adad-tillati* šabra ù ***puzur$_4$*-[d]nin-kar-ak** dub-sar, "Inspection (of the work) of (workers) employed (for) construction of the (enclosure) wall and the foundation terrace of the textile mill, under the authority of *Adad-tillati*, the majordomo, and *Puzur*-Ninkarak, the scribe,"31:51–52, 35:57–59

kurum$_7$ aka al-tar bàd ù é-uš-bar g[ub-ba] g̃iri [d]*adad-tillati* ⌜šabra⌝ ù ***puzur$_4$*-[d]nin-k[ar-ak** dub-sar], "Inspection (of the work) of (workers) employed (for) construction of the (enclosure) wall and textile mill, under the authority of *Adad-tillati*, the majordomo, and *Puzur*-Ninkarak, [the scribe]," 32:50–52

kurum$_7$ aka éren al-tar bàd ù é-uš-bar g̃iri [d]*adad-tillati* šabra ù ***puzur$_4$*-[d]nin-kar-ak** dub-sar, "Inspection (of the work) of workers employed (for) construction of the (enclosure) wall and textile mill, under the authority of *Adad-tillati*, the majordomo, and *Puzur*-Ninkarak, the scribe," 33:54–56

4.4.5 Crushing Malt

4.4.5.1 Supervised by *Bazi*

n g̃uruš n géme ugula *ba-zi* munu$_4$ al-nag̃$_4$-g̃á-dè gub-ba kurum$_7$ aka g̃iri [d]*adad-tillati* (šabra) ù ***puzur$_4$*-[d]nin-kar-ak** dub-sar, "Under the authority of *Adad-tillati*, the (majordomo), and *Puzur*-Ninkarak, the scribe, inspection (of the work) of n workmen (and) n workwomen, supervised by *Bazi*, employed to crush malt," 67:1–8, 68:1–7, 69:1–8

[n] g̃uruš [n] géme [ugula] *ba-zi* [munu$_4$ a]l-nag̃$_4$-[g̃á-d]è gub-ba [g̃iri [d]*adad*]-*tillati* [ù] ***puzur$_4$*-[d]nin-[kar]-ak** dub-sar, "[Under the authority of] *Adad-tillati* [and] *Puzur*-Ninkarak, the scribe, [n] workmen (and) [n] workwomen, supervised by *Bazi*, employed to crush [malt]," 70:'1–'7

4.4.5.2 **Supervised by *Simat-Ea***

6 g̃uruš [n géme] ugula *simat-é-[a]* munu$_4$ nag̃$_4$-[g̃á-dè] g[ub-ba] kurum$_7$ aka g̃ìri ^{d}*adad-[tillati* šabra] ù ***puzur$_4$*-[^{d}nin]-kar-ak** dub-[sar], "Under the authority of *Adad-tillati*, [the majordomo], and *Puzur*-Ninkarak, the scribe, inspection (of the work) of 6 workmen and [n workwomen], supervised by *Simat-Ea*, employed [to] crush malt," 216:2–7

4.4.5.3 **Broken Context**

kurum$_7$ aka al-t[ar . . .] g̃ìri ^{d}*adad-tillati* [šabra] ù ***puzur$_4$*-^{d}nin-kar-ak** d[ub-sar], 22:'16–'18, 23:'13–'15

[. . .] x [g̃ìri ^{d}*adad-till*]*ati* [ù ***puzur$_4$*-^{d}]nin-[kar-ak** dub]-sar, 50:'24–'25

[. . . ù ***puzur$_4$*-^{d}nin-kar]-ak** dub-[sar], 64:'5

kurum$_7$ [aka . . .] g̃ìri ^{d}[*adad-tillati* šabra] ù ***puzur$_4$*-[^{d}nin-kar-ak** dub-sar], 73:'25–'27

[. . . g̃ìri ^{d}]adad-*tillati* [ù ***puzur$_4$*]-^{d}nin-kar-ak** dub-[sar], 211:10–11

[. . .] g̃ìri ^{d}[*adad*]-*tillati* šabra ù ***puzur$_4$*-[^{d}nin-k]ar-ak** dub-[sar], 307:'9–'11, 332:'16–'17

5. **Provisions for *Puzur*-Ninkarak**

5.1 **Rations for Scribes**

(. . .) 0.0.4.5 sìla ***puzur$_4$*-^{d}nin-kar-ak** (. . .) [še]-ba dub-sar-e-ne, "45 liters (of barley for) *Puzur*-Ninkarak, (and for) {other workers}, [barley] rations of the scribes," 394:3, 7

0.1.3. še 3 ádda-udu-ta ***puzur$_4$*-^{d}nin-kar-ak** 1 *la-qì-ip* 1 *é-a-dan* dub-sar-me-éš (. . .) [šà-gal šidim] ù dub-sar-e-ne, "90 liters of barley (and) 3 sheep carcasses each (for) *Puzur*-Ninkarak, *Laqip*, (and) *Ea-dan*, the scribes, (and for) {other workers}, [food (for) builders] and scribes," 399:16–20, 24

0.1.3. še-ta [n s]ìla ì-g̃eš-ta [n] ádda-udu-ta **[*pù*]-*zur$_8$*-^{d}nin-kar-ak** [*é*]-*a-dan* du[b-s]ar-me-éš, "13 liters of barley each, [n] liter(s) sesame oil each (and) [n] sheep carcass(es) each (for) *Puzur*-Ninkarak (and) *Ea-dan*, the scribes," 406:1–6

5.2 **A Sheep**

1 ⌜udu⌝ ***puzur$_4$*-^{d}⌜nin⌝-kar-ak** ki *ì-lí-[bi-l]a-n[i-*ta] ba-zi, "*Ili-bilani* disbursed 1 sheep (for) *Puzur*-Ninkarak," 450:1–4

6. **As a Witness**

igi ***puzur$_4$*-^{d}nin-kar-ak** dub-sar, "witnessed by *Puzur*-Ninkarak, the scribe," 609:19, 1052:12, 1055:9

igi ***puzur$_4$*-^{d}nin-kar-ak**, "witnessed by *Puzur*-Ninkarak," 1051:7

puzur$_4$-ra-bi

é-ki-ba-g̃ar-ra ***puzur$_4$-ra-bi***, "the replacement house of *Puzur-rabi*" > *Household Index*

puzur$_4$-šu-ba

Puzur-šuba, the Runaway

1. From the Gang of *Im-Erra*, the Ox-Herder

zàḫ AN.ŠUM.TAG.KAL (nu-bànda-gu$_4$) zàḫ ***puzur$_4$-šu-ba*** (nu-bànda-gu$_4$) *i-me-èr-ra* nu-bànda-gu$_4$ ugula *ba-ba-ni* šabra, "AN.ŠUM.TAG.KAL, (the ox-herder, and) *Puzur-Šuba*, (the ox-herder), runaways (from the gang of) *Im-Erra*, the ox-herder, (ox-drivers) supervised by *Babani*, the majordomo," 185:31–34, 191:35–38, 192:'23–'26, 194:64–67, 196:'34–'37, 197:43–46

zàḫ [*šu*?]-^{d}*i-šum* zàḫ ⌜***pù-zur$_8$***⌝***-šu-ba*** [*i-me-èr-ra*] nu-bànda-gu$_4$ [ugula *ba-ba-ni*] šabra, "[*Šu*?]-*Išum* (and) *Puzur-šuba*, runaways (from the gang of) [*Im-Erra*], the ox-herder, (ox-drivers) [supervised by *Babani*], the majordomo," 198:'41–'44

– R –

ra-ba-tum

1. Possessions: his Boat

0.0.4. ⅔ sìla [. . . àga]-ús é-gal-la gub-ba [íb]-gu$_7$ ⌜u$_4$ má⌝ ***ra-ba-tum*** nibru^{ki}-ta gar-ša-an-na^{ki}-šè i[n-g]íd-sa-a, "The gendarme employed at the palace ate 4⅔ liters [. . .] when they towed the boat of *Rabatum* from Nippur to Garšana," 506:22–26

2. Receipts: Regular Offerings

0.0.2. kaš-sig$_5$ 0.0.4. kaš-gen sá-du$_{11}$-***ra-ba-tum***, "20 liters of fine beer (and) 40 liters of ordinary beer, regular offerings of *Rabatum*," 505:1–3, 507:1–3, 508:1–3

(. . .) dirig sá-du$_{11}$-u$_4$-[n-šè] ***ra-ba-tum*** ù ^{d}*šu*-^{d}E[N.ZU]-[*e*]-*te-el-pi$_5$*-^{d}en-líl[l sugal$_7$] ⌜u$_4$⌝ ezem-*a-bu-um* ⌜g̃iri⌝ ^{d}[*suen-a-bu-šu*], "{assorted commodities}, surplus of the regular offerings on the [nth] day of *Rabatum* and *Šu-Suen-etelpi*-Enlil, [the sugal], during the *Abum* festival under the authority of [*Suen-abušu*]," 509:'12–'14

ra-qa-šu-bu-um

Raqašubum, Man from Karkar

[1] ⌜***ra***⌝***?-qa?-šu-bu-um*** (. . .) ugula [*šu*]-*la-núm* (. . .) lú-karkar^{ki}-me, "*Raqašubum*, supervised by *Šulanum*, (and) {other workers}, men from Karkar," 559:5, 12, 28

ri-im-ilum

1. *Rim-ilum*, the Gendarme

1.1 Provisions along his Journeys

0.0.1. kaš-gen ugula àga-ús-e-ne á-u$_4$-te-na u$_4$-2-kam àga-ús ***ri-im-ilum*** íb-nag̃ ù *ṣú-mi-id-ilum* dub-sar P[A.KAŠ$_4$] u$_4$ má-*simat*-^{d}*ištaran puzur$_4$-iš*-^{d}*da-gan*^{ki}-ta gar-ša-an-na^{ki}-šè mu-un-gíd-š[a-a] zi-ga *simat*-^{d}*ištaran* ki ^{d}*adad-tillati*-ta ba-zi, "*Adad-tillati* disbursed 10 liters of ordinary beer, in the evening of the 2nd day. The overseer of the gendarmes—the gendarme, *Rim-ilum*—drank (the beer) when they towed the boat of *Simat-Ištaran* from *Puzriš-Dagan* to Garšana. (It was) the expenditure of *Simat-Ištaran*. *Ṣumid-ilum*, the scribe, was the deputy," 550:'22–'30

0.0.5. ninda-kaš á-u$_4$-[te-na] 2 sìla níg̃-àr-[ra-sig$_5$] šà zabala$_4$$^{[ki]}$ u$_4$-1-[kam] 4 sìla níg̃-àr-ra-[sig$_5$] u$_4$-2-[kam] á-gú-zi-⌜ga⌝ 4 sìla níg̃-àr-ra-⌜sig$_5$⌝ á-u$_4$-te-na u$_4$-3-kam šà kaskal^{ki} àga-ús [***ri-im***]***-ilum*** íb-gu$_7$ u$_4$ má-*simat*-^{d}*ištaran* gar-ša-an-na^{ki}-ta *puzur$_4$-iš*-^{d}*da-gan*[^{ki}-šè] in-gíd-sa-a *ṣú-ú-mi-id-ilum* maškim zi-ga *simat*-^{d}KA.[DI] ki ^{d}*adad-tillati*-ta [ba-zi], "*Adad-*

tillati disbursed 50 liters of bread (and) beer [in] the evening (and) 2 liters of [fine] barley groats in Zabala on the 1st day, 4 liters of [fine] groats at dawn of the 2nd day, (and) 4 liters of fine groats in the evening of the 3rd day of the journey. The gendarme *Rim-ilum* consumed (the food) when they towed the boat of *Simat-Ištaran* from Garšana to *Puzriš-Dagan*. (It was) the expenditure of *Simat-Ištaran*. *Ṣumid-ilum* was the deputy," 551:1–18

2. *Rim-ilum*, the Sugal

2.1 A Beer Offering when He Came to *Bit-Šu-Suen*

0.0.1. kaš-sig$_5$ 0.0.1. kaš-gen 0.4.0. kaš-ninda 5 sìla-ta kaš ba-an-dé ***ri-im-ilum*** sugal$_7$ gaba-ri-a unug^{ki}-ta du-ni *ba-la-a* šabra zi-ga *simat-*^{d}*ištaran* ki *ba-la-a*-ta ba-zi šà é-^{d}*šu*-^{d}*suen*, "*Bala'a*, the majordomo, disbursed 10 liters of fine beer, 10 liters of ordinary beer, (and) 240 liters of beer (and) bread, 5 liters each. He poured the beer when *Rim-ilum*, the sugal, came from Uruk (for) a meeting. (It was) the expenditure of *Simat-Ištaran* in *Bit-Šu-Suen*," 517:1–10

ru-ba-ti-a

1. Provisions: a Sheep

0.0.1. še šà-gal ^{anše}kúnga *á-ni-á* dumu ùr?-[x] 1 udu ***ru-ba-ti-a*** 0.0.3. ésir-é-a *al-la* gudu$_4$ ^{d}*adad-tillati* šabra maškim z[i-g]a [*tá*]-*ki-*⌜*il*⌝-*ì-lí-ís-sú* ki ^{d}*adad-tillati*-ta ba-zi, "*Adad-tillati* disbursed 10 liters of barley, fodder of equids (for) *Ani'a*, the son of Ur?-[x], 1 sheep (for) *Rubatia*, 30 liters of dried bitumen (for) *Alla*, the gudu-priest. (It was) the expenditure of *Takil-ilissu*. *Adad-tillati*, the majordomo, was the deputy," 534:1–12

– S –

sa$_{10}$-é-ama-tu

1. Provisions: Barley

[n.n.n.] gur **sa$_{10}$-é-ama-tu** (. . .) [šu+níĝin n+]7.0.0. gur še-ba *ba-zi-tum* šu+níĝin 47.1.[n.] še-ba é, "[n] bushel(s) of (barley) (for) Sa-e'amatu (and barley for) {other individuals}; [in total: n+]7 bushels of the barley rations of *Bazitum*; in total: 47 bushels (and) 60[+n] liters of barley rations of the household," 555:16, 24–25

si-mu

Simu, the Animal Fattener

1. Deliveries: Skins, Receipt of *Anaḫ-ili*

1 kuš-udu-niga 1 kuš-máš ki ***si-mu*** kurušda-ta *a-na-aḫ-ì-lí* šu ba-ti, "*Anaḫ-ili* received 1 skin of a fattened sheep and 1 goat skin from *Simu*, the animal fattener," 935:1–5

5 kuš-udu ba-úš ki ***si-mu***-ta *a-na-aḫ-ì-lí* šu ba-ti, "*Anaḫ-ili* received 5 sheep skins of dead (sheep) from *Simu*," 956:1–4

2. Receipts

2.1 Assorted Animals from *Ili-bilani*

2 udu 5 máš-gal ***si-mu*** ì-dab$_5$ ki *ì-lí-bi-la-ni*-ta ba-zi, "*Simu* took in charge 2 sheep and 5 billy-goats from *Ili-bilani*," 1175:1–5

2.2 Sheep

2.2.1 From *Adad-tillati*

8 udu-niga 1 udu-[. . .] 16 [udu-. . .] ki ^{d}[*adad-tillati*-t]a ***si-mu*** kurušda ì-dab$_5$, "*Simu*, the animal fattener, took in charge 8 fattened sheep, 1 [. . .] sheep (and) 16 [. . . sheep] from *Adad-tillati*," 1245:1–6

2.2.2 From *Ili-bilani*

20 udu ***si-mu*** ì-dab$_5$ [ki *ì*]-*lí-bi-la-ni*-ta ba-zi, "*Simu* took in charge 20 sheep from *Ili-bilani*," 1155:1–4

3. As a Witness

igi ***si-mu*** kurušda, "witnessed by *Simu*, the animal fattener," 1055:11, 1057:13, 1059:10

si-na-ti

1. As a Witness

igi ***si?-na-ti***, "witnessed by *Sinati*," 1056:7

si-um

Si'um, the Craftsman and Father of *Adallal*

a-da-làl dumu ***si-um*** um-mi-a, "*Adallal*, the son of *Si'um*, the craftsman" > *Adallal*

a-da-làl dumu ***še-um***, "*Adallal*, the son of *Si'um*" > *Adallal*

simat-é-a

Simat-Ea, Overseer of Hired Workers

1. Supervision of Hired Workers

1 ĝuruš šidim n ĝuruš n géme ugula ***simat-é-a*** (. . .) lú-ḫuĝ-ĝá-me-éš, "1 builder, n workmen (and) n workwomen, hired workers supervised by *Simat-Ea*," 145:13–14, 146:7'–8', 147:13–14, 150:12–13

3 ĝuruš ḫuĝ-ĝá 7 géme ḫuĝ-ĝá ugula ***simat-é-a***, "3 hired workmen and 7 hired workwomen supervised by *Simat-Ea*," 7:13–15, 8:15–16

n ĝuruš n géme ugula ***simat-é-a*** (. . .) lú-ḫuĝ-ĝá-me-éš, "n hired workmen (and) n hired workwomen supervised by *Simat-Ea*," 9:10, 10:11, 14:9–10, 15:9–10, 16:8, 17:8, 18:8, 20:8, 21:9, 22:10, 23:9, 24:10, 29:'7, 30:10, 31:10, 32:10, 33:10, 34:10, 35:10, 36:10, 37:9, 38:9, 39:9, 42:9, 43:10–11, 44:9, 46:'4, 47:9, 48:9, 49:9, 51:8, 53:9–10, 54:3, 56:8, 57:8, 58:9–10, 59:9–10, 60:9–10, 71:8, 72:5–6, 73:8, 75:7, 93:'4, 94:4, 98:'4, 99:5, 101:5, 102:8, 103:7, 104:11, 105:11, 106:13, 107:15, 108:12, 109:12, 110:13, 111:14, 114:14, 115:'5, 116:11, 117:12, 118:11, 119:11, 120:11, 121:11, 122:'1, 123:15, 125:11, 126:11, 127:11, 128:10, 129:11, 130:11, 131:'5, 132:11, 133:11, 134:11, 135:11, 136:11, 137:11, 138:11, 140:11, 141:12–13, 142:11, 143:11, 151:10, 154:11, 156:9, 158:10, 161:'2, 162:9, 163:9, 173:8, 174:8, 175:8, 205:5–6, 208:7–8, 212:'6, 213:7

n ĝuruš ugula ***simat-é-a*** (. . .) lú-ḫuĝ-ĝá-me-éš, "n hired workmen supervised by *Simat-Ea*," 157:7, 182:3, 207:6, 211:1–2

n géme ugula ***simat-é-a*** (. . .) lú-ḫuĝ-ĝá-me-éš, "n hired workwomen supervised by *Simat-Ea*," 40:10, 41:10, 77:5–6, 84:4, 86:4, 159:8, 199:5, 209:7

[. . . ugula] ***simat-é-[a]*** (. . .) lú-ḫuĝ-ĝá-me-éš, "[. . .], hired workers [supervised by] *Simat-Ea*," 52:10, 210:'1

2. Supervision of Brick Carriers and Delivery of Bricks and Earth

2.1 For the House of Barbers

é-šu-i-[e-n]e-[šè] ***simat-é-a*** ugula lú-ḫuĝ-ĝá, "(delivery of bricks) [for] the house of the barbers by *Simat-Ea*, overseer of hired workers," 352:39–40

2.2 For the Textile Depository

mu-⌜DU⌝ ki-mur-ra-šè ***simat-é-a*** [ugula] lú-[ḫuĝ]-ĝá, "delivery (of bricks) for the textile depository by *Simat-Ea*, [overseer] of hired workers," 335:41–42

2.3 For the Textile Mill

é-uš-bar-šè mu-DU ***simat-é-a*** ugula, "delivery (of bricks) for the textile mill by *Simat-Ea*, the overseer," 316:72–74

[ki-sá-a] é-uš-bar-šè [mu-DU] ***simat-é-a*** ugula lú-ḫuĝ-ĝá, "[delivery] (of bricks) for the [foundation terrace] of the textile mill by *Simat-Ea*, overseer of hired workers," 324:94–95

2.4 For the Textile Mill and the Craftsmen House

é-uš-bar ù [é-NUN].ME.⌜TAG⌝-e-⌜ne⌝ mu-[DU] ***simat-é-a*** ugula [lú-ḫuĝ-ĝá], "delivery (of bricks for) the textile mill and craftsmen's [house] by *Simat-Ea*, overseer [of hired workers]," 328:14–16

2.5 For the (Enclosure) Wall

mu-DU bàd-šè ***simat-é-a*** ugula lú-ḫuĝ-ĝá, "delivery (of bricks) for the (enclosure) wall by *Simat-Ea*, overseer of hired workers," 308:47–49

2.6 Volumes of Bricks Delivered

37⅔ sar 4-gín igi–4-ĝál $šeg_{12}$ u_4-1-kam 37 sar 1 gín $šeg_{12}$ u_4-2-kam ⌜NE⌝-gu_7-bi nu-ub-ta-zi $šeg_{12}$ šid-da ĝá-šub-ba ĝá-ĝál mu-DU ***simat-é-a*** ugula lú-ḫuĝ-ĝá ĝìri *é-a-šar* dub-sar, "37⅔ sar (and) 4¼ shekels of bricks for 1 day, 37 sar (and) 1 shekel of bricks for 2 days, the damaged bricks were not deducted; the count of bricks took place in the brickyard. The delivery of *Simat-Ea*, overseer of hired workers, was under the authority of *Ea-šar*, the scribe," 357:1–10

270 sar 13 gín $šeg_{12}$ ús-⌜sa⌝ i_7-*a*-⌜*ga*⌝-*mu-um* 60 sar 13 gín $šeg_{12}$ é-[d][x]-SAḪAR [NE?]-gu_7-bi ù PA [NE-gu_7]-bi nu-zi [šid-d]a šà ĝá-šub-ba mu-DU ***simat-é-a*** ĝìri [d]*adad-tillati*, "270 sar (and) 13 shekels of bricks along the *Agamum* canal, 60 sar (and) 13 shekels of bricks of the temple of [DN], damaged bricks and damaged (?) not deducted; the count (of bricks) in the brickyard. The delivery of *Simat-Ea* was under the authority of *Adad-tillati*," 358:1–10

188 sar 10 gín $šeg_{12}$ NE-gu_7-bi nu-zi šid-da šà ĝá-šub-ba ĝìri *é-a-šar* ús-sa i_7-*a-ga-mu-um* mu-DU ***simat-é-a*** ugula lú-[ḫuĝ-ĝ]á, "188 sar (and) 10 shekels of bricks along the *Agamum* canal, damaged bricks not deducted; the count (of bricks) in the brickyard. The delivery of *Simat-Ea*, overseer of hired workers, was under the authority of *Ea-šar*," 359:1–7

3. Supervision of Workers Assigned to Specific Tasks

3.1 Crushing Malt

3.1.1 Receipt of *Adallal*

n ĝuruš n géme ugula ***simat-é-a*** $munu_4$ $nag̃_4$-ĝá-dè *a-da-làl* (lùnga) ì-dab_5 $kurum_7$ aka, "Inspection (of the work) of n workmen (and) n workwomen, supervised by *Simat-Ea*. *Adallal*, (the brewer), took (the workers) in charge to crush malt," 164:1–6, 167:1–6, 168:1–6

10 ĝuru[š u_4-n-šè] ugula ***simat-é-[a*** $munu_4$ n]ag_4-ĝá-[dè *a*]-*da-*⌜*làl*⌝ ì-d[ab_5 $kurum_7$] aka, "Inspection (of the work) of 10 workmen, supervised by *Simat-Ea*. *Adallal* took (the workers) in charge [for n day(s)] to crush [malt]," 165:1–7

10 ĝuruš [n] géme ugula ***simat-[é]-a*** $munu_4$ $nag̃_4$-⌜ĝa⌝-dè *a-da-làl* ì-dab_5, "*Adallal* took in charge 10 workmen and [n] workwomen, supervised by *Simat-Ea*, to crush malt," 166:1–5

3.1.2 Employed at the Place of the Brewer

4 ĝuruš ugula ***simat-é-a*** ki [lú]lùnga! gub-ba $kurum_7$ aka, "Inspection (of the work) of 4 workmen, supervised by *Simat-Ea*, employed at the place of the brewer," 169:3–7

3.1.3 Under the Authority of *Adad-tillati* and *Puzur*-Ninkarak

6 ĝuruš [n géme] ugula ***simat-é-[a]*** $munu_4$ $nag̃_4$-[ĝá-dè] g[ub-ba] $kurum_7$ aka ĝìri [d]*adad*-[*tillati* šabra] ù *puzur*$_4$-[[d]nin]-kar-ak dub-[sar], "Inspection (of the work) of 6 workmen and [n workwomen], supervised by *Simat-Ea*, employed [to] crush malt, under the authority of *Adad-tillati*, [the majordomo,] and *Puzur*-Ninkarak, the scribe," 216:1–7

3.2 Garden Work

n ĝuruš 1 géme ugula ***simat-é-a*** (. . .) $kurum_7$ aka saḫar zi-ga [ĝeš]$kiri_6$ gar-ša-an-na[ki], "Inspection (of the work) of n workmen (and) 1 workwoman, supervised by *Simat-Ea*, (and) {other workers} having moved dirt at the Garšana garden," 176:7–8, 16–17, 179:7, 17–18

1 ĝuruš ***simat-[é-a]*** (. . .) saḫar zi-ga in-lá tùn-lá [ĝeš]$kiri_6$ $zabala_4$[ki] $kurum_7$ [aka], "Inspection (of the work) of 1 workman, supervised by *Simat-Ea*, (and) {other workers} having transported dirt removed via a tùn-lá device at the Zabala garden,"178:2, 6–8

3.3 Pouring Water

(. . .) [n ĝu]ruš ugula ***simat-é-a*** [a] bal-a (. . .) [$kurum_7$ aka], "[Inspection (of the work) of n] workmen, supervised by *Simat-Ea*, (and) {other workers} having poured water," 181:4–5, 8

3.4 Volume of Earth Used to Build the Adobe Wall

1½ nindan 3 kùš gíd 4 kùš dag̃al 2 kùš sukud saḫar-bi 1 sar 10 gín 5½ nindan gíd 2 kùš dag̃al 2 kùš ba-an-gi_4-bi 5 kùš sukud saḫar-bi 5⅔ sar 3⅔ gín 15 še 6⅚ sar 3⅔ gín 13 še i[m-du_8-a] ugula ***simat-[é-a]***, "1½ nindan 3 kùš long, 4 kùš wide, 2 kùš long, its dirt is 1 sar (and) 10 gín; 5½ nindan long, 2 kùš wide, 2 kùš tapered from 5 kùš in height, its earth is 5⅔ sar 3⅔ gín (and) 15 še; (the total volume) of the adobe wall is 6⅚ sar, 3⅔ gín (and) 13 še, (built) under the supervision of *Simat-Ea*," 366:'15–'20

4. Deliveries: Receipt of *Malik-bani*

4.1 Flour

0.2.3.7⅓ sìla zì mu-DU ***simat-é-a*** ^{d}*ma-lik-ba-ni* šu ba-an-ti, "*Malik-bani* received 157⅓ liters of flour, delivery of *Simat-Ea*," 1140:3

4.2 Semolina

0.2.2. dabin mu-DU ***simat-é-*[*a*]** $^{d!}$*ma-lik-ba-*[*ni*] šu ba-an!-ti, "*Malik-bani* received 140 liters of semolina, delivery of *Simat-Ea*," 1118:1–4

5. Receipts from *Adad-tillati*

5.1 Building Supplies

3 ^{ĝeš}ù-šub šeg$_{12}$-⌜BÁḪAR⌝-ra 3 ^{ĝeš}ù-šub šeg$_{12}$ 2 ^{ĝeš}al [n] ^{ĝeš}dusu 1 ^{gi}gur i[n-u-da] 1 dug 0.0.3.-[ta] 1 ^{gi}gur gazi? ki ^{d}*adad-tillati*-ta ***simat-é-a*** šu ba-ti, "*Simat-Ea* received from *Adad-tillati* 3 brick molds (for baked) brick, 3 brick molds, 2 hoes, [n] brick carrying frame(s), 1 basket (for the transport of) straw, 1 30-liter pot (and) 1 basket (for the transport of) gazi?," 1340:1–9

5.2 Barley

5.2.1 For Baking Bread

1?.2.3. še gur mu ninda du$_8$-dè ki ^{d}*adad-tillati*-ta ***simat-é-a*** šu ba-an-ti, "*Simat-Ea* received 1? bushel (and) 150 liters of barley to bake bread from *Adad-tillati*," 1163:1–5

5.2.2 Provisions: In Place of Semolina

0.0.2. ***simat-é-a*** (. . .) mu dabin-šè šu ba-ti, "*Simat-Ea* received 20 liters of barley, (and barley for) {9 other individuals}, (barley) in place of semolina," 560:10, 12–13

5.3 Commodities (to Distribute as) Wages

šu+níĝin 27.1.1.3 sìla še gur ki ugula-nam–10-ka ⌜ĝal⌝-la ugula ***simat-é-a*** lú-ḫuĝ-ĝá, "{barley for individuals}; in total: there are 27 bushels (and) 73 liters of barley at the place of the overseer of 10, *Simat-Ea*, overseer of hired workers," 504:20–23

5.3.1 For Workers Molding Bricks

[n+]5.0.0. še gur á 5-sìla-ta [šeg$_{12}$ d]u$_8$-a-šè [ki ^{d}]*adad-tillati*-[ta] ***simat-é-*[*a*** ugula lú]-ḫuĝ-[ĝá] *a-ḫu-ni* maškim šu ba-an-ti, "*Simat-Ea*, the overseer of hired workers, received from *Adad-tillati* [n+]5 bushels of barley, (to pay) wages of 5 liters each for (workers) having molded [bricks]. *Aḫuni* was the deputy," 447:1–7

[n.n.n.] še gur ⌜šeg$_{12}$⌝ du$_8$-dè á 5-sìla-ta ba-ḫuĝ ki ^{d}*adad-tillati*-ta ***simat-é-a*** ugula lú-ḫuĝ-ĝá šu ba-an-ti, "*Simat-Ea*, the overseer of hired workers, received from *Adad-tillati* [n] bushel(s) of barley (used to) hire (workers) to mold bricks at wages of 5 liters each," 454:1–6

12.0.0. še gur šeg$_{12}$ du$_8$-dè á 5-sìla-ta ki ^{d}*adad-tillati*-ta ***simat-é-a*** šu ba-ti, "*Simat-Ea* received from *Adad-tillati* 12 bushels of barley, (to pay) wages of 5 liters each (for workers) to mold bricks," 456:1–6

0.4.3. eša 12 ma-na siki še-0.0.3!.-[ta] 2 sìla ì-ĝeš še-0.0.4.-ta šeg$_{12}$ du$_8$-dè á 5-sìla-ta ki ^{d}*adad-tillati*-ta ***simat-é-a*** šu ba-an-ti, "*Simat-Ea* received from *Adad-tillati* 270 liters of fine flour, 12 minas of wool, the equivalent of 30! liters of barley [each], (and) 2 liters of sesame oil the equivalent of 40 liters of barley each, (to pay) wages of 5 liters each (for workers) to mold bricks," 457:1–8

6. In the Possession of *Simat-Ea*: Barley Wages for Brick Carriers

23.3.4. 5/6 sìla še gur á 6-sìla-ta 12.4.2. ⅔ sìla-⌜ta⌝ še gur á 5-sìla-⌜ta⌝ á šeg$_{12}$ g[a$_6$-g̃á] ù al-[tar-ra] ***simat-é-a*** ugula lú-ḫug̃-g̃á in-da-g̃ál, "23 bushels (and) 224 5/6 liters of barley, wages of 6 liters each, (and) 12 bushels (and) 260⅔ liters of barley, wages of 5 liters each, wages of (workers) having carried bricks and (employed) [for] construction, are with *Simat-Ea*, overseer of hired workers," 503:1–9

7. Distance Measurements

šu+níg̃in 3 ⌜da⌝-n[a 240+]120 nindan ús gú i$_7$-me-kal-kal ***simat-é-a*** a-da-ga-ta ká-^{d}*šu*-^{d}*suen*-šè, "In total: 3 da-na (and) 360 nindan, the length from the bank of the Mekalkal canal of *Simat-Ea* (and its) irrigation ditch to the *Šu-Suen* gate," 1382:14–16

simat-^{d}*ištaran*

1. Expenditures

1.1 Expenditure of Craftsmen

1.1.1 Bringing Barley to Garšana

(. . .) u$_4$-20-šè še é-duru$_5$-kab-bi-ta gar-ša-an-na^{ki}-šè mu-un-de$_9$-sa-a g̃iri ^{d}*adad-tillati* šabra zi-ga ***simat-***^{d}***ištaran*** ki ^{d}*adad-tillati*-ta ba-zi, "Under his own authority, *Adad-tillati*, the majordomo, disbursed {craftsmen} for 20 days who brought barley from the Kabbi village to Garšana. (It was) the expenditure of *Simat-Ištaran*," 304:7–14

1.1.2 Bringing Reeds to Garšana

(. . .) gi-zi a-gàr G̃EŠ.KÚŠU^{ki}-ta gar-ša-an-na^{ki}-⌜šè⌝ zi-ga ***simat-***^{d}***ištaran*** ki ^{d}*adad-tillati*-ta ba-zi "*Adad-tillati* disbursed {female millers} (having brought) fresh reeds from the G̃EŠ.KÚŠU meadow to Garšana. (It was) the expenditure of *Simat-Ištaran*," 295:10–14

1.1.3 Bringing Straw, Oil, and Wood to Garšana

(. . .) é-^{d}*šu*-^{d}*suen*^{ki}-ta gar-ša-an-na^{ki}-šè (g̃en-a) g̃iri ^{d}*adad-tillati* šabra zi-ga ***simat-***^{d}***ištaran*** ki ^{d}*adad-tillati*-ta ba-zi, "Under his own authority, *Adad-tillati*, the majordomo, disbursed {craftsmen} (having gone) from *Bit-Šu-Suen* to Garšana {to transport straw from various meadows, and bring oil and wool}. (It was) the expenditure of *Simat-Ištaran*," 285:7–13, 286:12–17, 306:12–17

1.1.4 Crushing Malt

15 géme uš-bar u$_4$-1-šè munu$_4$ nag̃$_4$-g̃á-dè gub-ba *èr-ra-ba-ni* lùnga maškim zi-ga ***simat-***^{d}***ištaran*** [ki ^{d}*adad-till*]*ati*-ta ba-zi, "*Adad-tillati* disbursed 15 female weavers for 1 day employed to crush malt. (It was) the expenditure of *Simat-Ištaran*. *Erra-bani*, the brewer, was the deputy," 277:1–6

1.1.5 Harvesting Barley

(. . .) še gur$_{10}$-gur$_{10}$-dè zàr tab-ba-dè ù g̃eš ra-ra-dè a-šà *ṣe-ru-um* gub-ba g̃iri g̃iri-né-ì-dab$_5$ ra-gaba zi-ga ***simat-***^{d}***ištaran*** ki ^{d}*adad-tillati*-ta ba-zi, "Under the authority of G̃irine-idab, the courier, *Adad-tillati* disbursed {craftsmen} employed at the *Ṣerum* field to reap barley, stack (its) sheaves (for drying), and flail (them). (It was) the expenditure of *Simat-Ištaran*," 262:19–26

1.1.6 Towing and Unloading Boats

2 g̃uruš ašgab 1 g̃uruš $ad-kub_4$ u_4-4-[šè] má ^{geš}šim ḫi-a gar-ša-an-na^{ki}-ta nibru^{ki}-šè in-gíd-sa-a g̃iri *šu-*^{d}*adad* dub-sar zi-ga ***simat-***^{d}***ištaran*** ki ^{d}*adad-tillati*-ta ba-zi, "Under the authority of *Šu-Adad*, the scribe, *Adad-tillati* disbursed 2 leather workers (and) 1 reed craftsman [for] 4 days who towed a boat (with) various resinous woods from Garšana to Nippur. (It was) the expenditure of *Simat-Ištaran*," 253:1–11

(. . .) g̃iri ^{d}[*adad-tillati* šabra] zi-ga [***simat-***^{d}**KA**].**DI** ki ^{d}[*adad-tillati*-ta] ba-[zi], "Under his own authority, *Adad-tillati*, the majordomo, disbursed {braiders for towing and unloading boats}. (It was) the expenditure of *Simat-Ištaran*," 298:13–16

1.1.7 Traveling to the Ulluḫ-Urim Village for Barley

(. . .) u_4-2-šè še é-duru$_5$-ul-luḫ-uri$_5$^{ki}-ma-šè g̃en-na mu še-ba-ne-ne-šè g̃iri ^{d}*adad-tillati* šabra zi-ga ***simat-***^{d}***ištaran*** ki ^{d}*adad-tillati*-ta ba-zi, "Under his own authority, *Adad-tillati*, the majordomo, disbursed {craftsmen} for 2 days having gone to the Ulluḫ-Urim village for barley for barley rations. (It was) the expenditure of *Simat-Ištaran*," 291:12–18, 292:12–18, 293:2–8, 294:2–8

1.1.8 Various Tasks

(. . .) [mu] lugal-bi in-IGI.[RU] zi-ga [***simat***]-^{d}**KA**.[**DI**] ki ^{d}*adad*-[*tillati*]-ta ba-[zi], "*Adad-tillati* disbursed {craftsmen for various tasks in different cities}. (It was) the expenditure of *Simat-Ištaran*. *Adad-tillati* swore by the name of the king," 260:35–37

(. . .) g̃iri ^{d}*adad-tillati* PA.AL zi-ga ***simat-***^{d}***ištaran*** ki ^{d}*adad-tillati*-ta ba-zi "Under his own authority, *Adad-tillati*, the majordomo, disbursed {leather workers for various tasks}. (It was) the expenditure of *Simat-Ištaran*," 299:13–16

1.1.9 Task Unspecified

[n] g̃uruš [. . .n+]20 g̃uruš $ad-kub_4$ [n+]15 g̃uruš má-laḫ$_5$ u_4-1-šè zi-ga ***simat-***^{d}***ištaran***, "[n . . .] workmen, [n+]20 reed craftsmen (and) [n+]15 sailors for 1 day. (It was) the expenditure of *Simat-Ištaran*," 511:15–20

1.2 Expenditure of Offerings and Provisions

1.2.1 Assorted Commodities

1.2.1.1 For the Banquet of the Gods

(. . .) šu+níg̃in 680 ^{dug}sìla-bur-zi kaš-dé-a dig̃ir-re-e-ne zi-ga ***simat-***^{d}***ištaran*** ki ^{d}*adad-tillati*-ta ba-zi, "*Adad-tillati* disbursed a total of 680 1-liter offering bowls of {soup} (for) the beer banquet of the gods. (It was) the expenditure of *Simat-Ištaran*," 1025:113–119

1.2.1.2 For Household Servants

(. . .) géme árad-é-a ba-na-ḫa-la g̃iri *tu-ra-am-ì-lí* dub-sar zi-ga ***simat-***^{d}***ištaran*** ki ^{d}*adad-tillati*-ta ba-zi, "Under the authority of *Turam-ili*, the scribe, *Adad-tillati* disbursed {assorted commodities}. They were divided for the female and male household servants. (It was) the expenditure of *Simat-Ištaran*," 528:12–16, 548:15–20

1.2.1.3 For Priests and Cultic Performers

(. . .) zi-ga ***simat-***^{d}***ištaran*** ki ^{d}*adad-tillati*-ta ba-zi, "*Adad-tillati* disbursed {linen to the house of the women, piglets and mice, and bread for the gala-priests and cultic performers and the *muškenu*, the worker at the gate of the palace, and beer for the cupboard}. (These were) the expenditures of *Simat-Ištaran* {in Garšana and Zabala}," 541:27–28

(. . .) gala-e-ne a-rá-5-kam ér iri ni$_{10}$-ni$_{10}$ *a-ḫu-a* maškim zi-ga ***simat-^{d}ištaran*** [ki ^{d}]*adad-tillati*-ta ba-zi, "*Adad-tillati* disbursed {assorted comestibles} of the lamentation singers (for the performance of) a *takribtum* (involving) circling around the city for the 5th time (and on) {4 other occasions}. (It was) the expenditure of *Simat-Ištaran*. *Aḫu'a* was the deputy," 1030:36–41

1.2.1.4 For the Workmen She Stationed

(. . .) maš-en-gag ^{lú}kaš$_{4}$ ká-é-gal-ka gub-ba ⌈***simat***⌉***-^{d}ištaran*** íb-gu$_{7}$ u$_{4}$ má-***simat-^{d}ištaran*** é-^{d}šára-ta gar-ša-an-na^{ki}-šè mu-un-gíd-ša-a *ṣu-mi-id-ilum* maškim (. . .) zi-ga ***simat-^{d}ištaran***, "The *muškenu* (and?) the runner, stationed by *Simat-Ištaran* at the gate of the palace, ate {soup} when they towed the boat of *Simat-Ištaran* from the Šara temple to Garšana. (It was) the expenditure of *Simat-Ištaran*. *Ṣumid-ilum* was the deputy," 529:13–19, 26

1.2.1.5 For Workmen on the Road

[n.n.n sìla] ninda-šu-ra-gen ^{kuš}a-g̃á-lá kéše-rá g̃uruš 7-kam u$_{4}$ kaskal-šè i-re-sa-a *ta-ḫu-lam* maškim (. . .) zi-ga ***simat-^{d}ištaran***, "[n liter(s)] of ordinary half (loaf) bread in bound leather sacks (for) 7 workmen when they went on a journey (and) {provisions for other workers}. (It was) the expenditure of *Simat-Ištaran*. *Taḫulam* was the deputy," 529:1–4, 26

1.2.1.6 In Zabala and for the Gendarme Employed at the Palace

(. . .) šà kisal-lá-^{d}inana-za[bala$_{4}^{ki}$] (. . .) *išdum-ki-in* ⌈sagi⌉ maškim šà zabala$_{4}^{ki}$ 0.0.4. ⅔ sìla [. . .àga]-ús é-gal-la gub-ba [íb]-gu$_{7}$ ⌈u$_{4}$ má⌉ *ra-ba-tum* nibru^{ki}-ta gar-ša-an-na^{ki}-šè i[n-g]íd-sa-a *an-ta-lú* agrig [ma]škim [. . .]-x-zu-⌈sa⌉?-šè [. . . zi]-ga ***simat-***[^{d}**KA**].**DI** [ki ^{d}*adad*]*-tillati*-ta ba-zi, "*Adad-tillati* disbursed {assorted commodities} in the courtyard of Inana of Zabala, {other offerings to deities, and other commodities}. *Išdum-kin*, the cupbearer, was the deputy in Zabala. The gendarme employed at the palace ate 4⅔ liters [. . .] when they towed the boat of *Rabatum* from Nippur to Garšana. *Antalu*, the steward, was the deputy. [. . .] (These were) the expenditures of *Simat-Ištaran*," 506:9, 20–30

1.2.2 Beer: Regular Offerings of Individuals

0.0.1. kaš-sig$_{5}$ 0.0.4. kaš-gen sá-du$_{11}$*-ra-ba-tum* 5 sìla kaš-sig$_{5}$ 0.0.1. kaš-[gen sá]-du$_{11}$-^{d}*šu*-^{d}[*suen*]*-e-te-íl-pi$_{4}$*-^{d}en-líl ur-^{d}nin-^{d}si$_{4}$-an-na sagi maškim [. . .]-x ^{ĝeš}gi-[x? . . . x] ⌈*an-ta-lú*⌉ agrig [maškim x]-ru [. . .ma-n]a ki-lá šeg$_{12}$ ⌈nag̃a⌉ [. . .]-šè [. . . *n*]*a?-ì-lí* zi-ga ***simat-^{d}ištaran*** ki ^{d}*adad-tillati*-ta [ba]-zi, "*Adad-tillati* disbursed 10 liters of fine beer (and) 40 liters of ordinary beer, regular offerings of *Rabatum* (and) 5 liters of fine beer (and) 10 liters of [ordinary] beer, regular offerings of *Šu-Suen-etelpi-Enlil*. Ur-Nin-Siana, the cupbearer, was the deputy. [. . .], *Antalu*, the steward, was the [deputy]. [. . .] (These were) the expenditures of *Simat-Ištaran*," 505:1–16

0.0.2. kaš-[sig$_{5}$] 0.0.4. kaš-[gen] sá-du$_{11}$*-ra-ba-*⌈*tum*⌉ 0.0.5 sìla kaš-sig$_{5}$ 0.0.1 kaš-gen sá-du$_{11}$-^{d}*šu*-^{d}*suen-e-te-èl-pi$_{4}$*-^{d}en-líl sugal$_{7}$ [erased number] kaš-gen 0.0.1. ninda [. . .] ki? [. . .] 0.0.1. ninda-šu-ra-gen *a-bu*-DU$_{10}$ nu-bànda *an-ta-lú* agrig maškim 0.1.0. kaš-gen 0.0.2.1½ ⌈sìla kaš⌉ lú gaba sàg-dè íb-nag̃ pa?-da-^{d}šul-gi rá-⌈gaba⌉ 1 šáḫ-zé-da é-muḫaldim-⌈šè⌉ zi-ga ***simat-^{d}K***[**A.DI**] ki ^{d}[*adad*]*-tillati*-ta ba-zi, "*Adad-tillati* disbursed 20 liters of [fine] beer (and) 40 liters of [ordinary] beer, regular offerings of *Rabatum*, 50 liters of fine beer (and) 10 liters of ordinary beer, regular offerings of *Šu-Suen-etelpi*-Enlil, the sugal, ordinary beer, 1 liter of [. . .] bread (and) 1 liter of ordinary half-(loaf) bread (for) *Abu-ṭabu*, the captain—*Antalu*, the steward, was the deputy—60 liters of ordinary beer (and) 21½ liters of beer—the men who beat (their) breasts drank (the beer)—Pada-Šulgi was the courier—(and) 1 piglet for the kitchen. (These were) the expenditures of *Simat-Ištaran*," 507:1–18

0.0.2. kaš-sig$_5$ 0.0.4. kaš-gen sá-du$_{11}$-*ra-ba-tum* 5 sìla kaš-sig$_5$ 0.0.1. kaš-gen sá-du$_{11}$-^{d}*šu*-^{d}*suen-e-te-íl-pi*$_5$-^{d}en-líl ur-^{d}nin-^{d}si$_4$-an-⌜na⌝ sagi PA.⌜KAŠ$_4$⌝ zi-ga ***simat-***^{d}***ištaran*** ki ^{d}*adad-tillati*-ta ba-zi, "*Adad-tillati* disbursed 20 liters of fine beer (and) 40 liters of ordinary beer, regular offerings of *Rabatum* (and) 5 liters of fine beer (and) 10 liters of ordinary beer, regular offerings of *Šu-Suen-etelpi*-Enlil. (It was) the expenditure of *Simat-Ištaran*. Ur-Nin-Siana, the cupbearer, was the deputy," 508:8

0.0.1. kaš-sig$_5$ 0.0.1. kaš-gen 0.4.0. kaš-ninda 5 sìla-ta kaš ba-an-dé *ri-im-ilum* sugal$_7$ gaba-ri-a unug^{ki}-ta du-ni *ba-la-a* šabra zi-ga ***simat-***^{d}***ištaran*** ki *ba-la-a*-ta ba-zi šà é-^{d}*šu*-^{d}*suen*, "*Bala'a*, the majordomo, disbursed 10 liters of fine beer, 10 liters of ordinary beer, (and) 240 liters of beer (and) bread, 5 liters each. He poured the beer (when) *Rim-ilum*, the sugal, came from Uruk (for) a meeting. (It was) the expenditure of *Simat-Ištaran* in *Bit-Šu-Suen*," 517:1–10

1.2.3 Beer and Fine Groats: Traveling Provisions for Gendarmes

0.0.1. kaš-gen ugula àga-ús-e-ne á-u$_4$-te-na u$_4$-2-kam àga-ús *ri-im-ilum* íb-nağ ù *ṣú-mi-id-ilum* dub-sar P[A.KAŠ$_4$] u$_4$ má-***simat-***^{d}***ištaran*** *puzur*$_4$*-iš*-^{d}*da-gan*^{ki}-ta gar-ša-an-na^{ki}-šè mu-un-gíd-š[a-a] zi-ga ***simat-***^{d}***ištaran*** ki ^{d}*adad-tillati*-ta ba-zi, "*Adad-tillati* disbursed 10 liters of ordinary beer, in the evening of the 2nd day. The overseer of the gendarmes—the gendarme, *Rim-ilum*—drank (the beer) when they towed the boat of *Simat-Ištaran* from *Puzriš-Dagan* to Garšana. (It was) the expenditure of *Simat-Ištaran*. *Ṣumid-ilum*, the scribe, was the deputy," 550:'22–'30

0.0.5. ninda-kaš á-u$_4$-[te-na] 2 sìla níğ-àr-[ra-sig$_5$] šà zabala$_4$$^{[ki]}$ u$_4$-1-[kam] 4 sìla níğ-àr-ra-[sig$_5$] u$_4$-2-[kam] á-gú-zi-⌜ga⌝ 4 sìla níğ-àr-ra-⌜sig$_5$⌝ á-u$_4$-te-na u$_4$-3-kam šà kaskal^{ki} àga-ús [*ri-im*]-*ilum* íb-gu$_7$ u$_4$ má-***simat-***^{d}***ištaran*** gar-ša-an-na^{ki}-ta *puzur*$_4$*-iš*-^{d}*da-gan*[^{ki}-šè] in-gíd-sa-a *ṣú ú-mi-id-ilum* maškim zi-ga ***simat-***^{d}**KA.[DI]** ki ^{d}*adad-tillati*-ta [ba-zi], "*Adad-tillati* disbursed 50 liters of bread (and) beer [in] the evening (and) 2 liters of [fine] barley groats in Zabala on the 1st day, 4 liters of [fine] groats at dawn of the 2nd day (and) 4 liters of fine groats, in the evening of the 3rd day of the journey. The gendarme *Rim-ilum* consumed (the food) when they towed the boat of *Simat-Ištaran* from Garšana to *Puzriš-Dagan*. (It was) the expenditure of *Simat-Ištaran*. *Ṣumid-ilum* was the deputy," 551:1–18

1.2.4 Bread and Flour for the sugal-maḫ

1 udu-niga 2.0.0. ninda-gal-gen gur 0.1.0. zì-gu-ús sugal$_7$-maḫ ğìri gù-zi-dé-a lú-na zi-ga ***simat-***^{d}***ištaran*** ⌜ki⌝ ^{d}*adad-tillati*-[ta] ba-zi, "Under the authority of Guzidea, his man, *Adad-tillati* disbursed 1 fattened sheep, 2 bushels of ordinary large (loaves of) bread (and) 60 liters of 2nd-quality gu-flour (for) the sugal-maḫ. (It was) the expenditure of *Simat-Ištaran*," 1184:1–8

1.2.5 Textiles for Ištaran in Nippur

1 túg-guz-za-tur 4-kam-ús ^{d}*ištaran nu-úr*-^{d}*adad* maškim šà nibru^{ki} zi-ga ğìri ***simat-***^{d}***ištaran*** ki *puzur*$_4$*-a-gum*-ta ba-zi, "*Puzur-agum* disbursed 1 small 4th-quality tufted

textile of *Ištaran*. (It was) the expenditure of *Simat-Ištaran*, under her authority in Nippur. *Nur-Adad* was the deputy," 576:1–6

1.3 Expenditure of Workmen: Traveling from Tumal to Garšana

(. . .) [tum-ma]-al^{ki}-ta [gar-š]a-an-na^{ki}-šè g̃en-na u$_{4}$-2-šè ⌜zi⌝-ga [***simat***]-^{d}**ištaran** [ki] ^{d}*adad-tillati*-ta ba-zi, "*Adad-tillati* disbursed {workmen} for 2 days having gone from Tumal to Garšana. (It was) the expenditure of *Simat-Ištaran*," 266:17–19

1.4 Expenditure of Land Surveyed in Garšana and Zabala and its Wood Production

(. . .) ì-DU *a-da-làl* dumu *šu*-ma-ma um-mi-a (. . .) ì-⌜DU⌝ *a-da-làl* dumu *si-um* um-mi-a šà zabala$_{4}^{ki}$ (. . .) [ì]-DU [x-x?]-ti-en um-mi-a [šà gar]-ša-an-na^{ki} [n] sar gíd-da [níg̃]-šid-da $^{[d]}$*adad-tillati* šabra [ì]-dab$_{5}$ [zi-ga ***si***]***mat-***^{d}***ištaran*** [g̃iri *a-ḫ*]*u-ma* dub-sar, "{parcels of land; in it: date palm, pine boards of boats, and seedlings}, the delivery of *Adallal*, the son of *Šu*-Mama, the craftsman; {parcels of land; in it: date palm, pine boards of boats, and seedlings and planks}, the delivery of *Adallal*, the son of *Si'um*, the craftsman in Zabala; (and) {parcels of land; in it: date palm, pine boards of boats and seedlings}, the delivery of [PN], the craftsman, in Garšana. (In total:) [n] sar (of land) surveyed. *Adad-tillati*, the majordomo, took in charge the account. (It was) [the expenditure] of *Simat-Ištaran* [under the authority of] *Aḫuma*, the scribe," 1362:'23–'24, '49–'51, '69–'78

2. Offerings and Allotments for *Simat-Ištaran*

2.1 A Fattened Sheep

1 mu-du-lum udu-niga sag̃ u$_{4}$-sakar 1 mu-du-lum udu-niga é-u$_{4}$-15 sá-du$_{11}$ ***simat-***^{d}***ištaran*** é-gal-ta *lú-ša-lim* šu ba-an-ti, "*Lušallim* received 1 salted fattened sheep on the new moon day (and) 1 salted fattened sheep on the full moon day, regular offerings of *Simat-Ištaran* from the palace," 375:1–8

2.2 A Piglet

★★[n] uz-tur šu-ur$_{4}$-ra [x?] šu tag-a ki *na-bu-tum*-šè [1] šáḫ-zé-da é-muḫaldim mu ***simat-***^{d}***ištaran***<-šè> *ì-lí-ra-bí* maškim zi-ga ***simat-***^{d}***ištaran***, "[n] duckling wing(s)?, (?) to the place of *Nabutum*, (and) 1 piglet (for) the kitchen for *Simat-Ištaran*. (It was) the expenditure of *Simat-Ištaran*. *Ili-rabi* was the deputy," 529:20–26

3. Her Installations and Other Possessions

é-duru$_{5}$-***simat-***^{d}***ištaran***, "the village of *Simat-Ištaran*" > *Toponym Index*

é-***simat-***^{d}***ištaran***, "the house of *Simat-Ištaran*" > *Household Index*

kiri$_{6}$ ***simat-***^{d}***ištaran*** gar-ša-an-na^{ki}, "the garden of *Simat-Ištaran* at Garšana" > *Garden Index*

má-***simat-***^{d}***ištaran***, "the boat of *Simat-Ištaran*" > Sec. 1.2.1.4 and 1.2.3 above

3.1 Textiles

n ^{túg}sagšu *tá-ki-ru-um* ***simat-***^{d}***ištaran***, "n *takkirum* cap(s) of *Simat-Ištaran*," 563:2, 569:16, 579:17, 617:2, 636:2, 669:2, 753:2, 764:2, 789:2, 793:1, 796:1, 814:3, 1162:'14

[. . .] ***simat-***^{d}***ištaran***, 578:15

1 ^{túg}*ḫa-um a-gi*$_{4}$*-um* ***simat-***^{d}***ištaran***, "1 *a-gi*$_{4}$*-um ḫa-um* textile of *Simat-Ištaran*," 581:1

1 ^{túg}níg̃-lám-tur ***simat-***^{d}***ištaran***, "1 small níg̃-lám textile of *Simat-Ištaran*," 591:4

1 túg ba-tab *tuḫ-ḫu-um*-PI ***simat-***^{d}***ištaran***, "1 ba-tab *tuḫ-ḫu-um*-PI textile of *Simat-Ištaran*," 608:1

1 túg ba-tab *tuḫ*-[*ḫu-um*]-PI-ús-tur ***simat-***[^{d}***ištaran***], "1 small 2nd-quality ba-tab *tuḫ-ḫu-um*-PI textile of *Simat-Ištaran*," 610:1

1 túg ba-tab *tuḫ-ḫu-um* ***simat-^{d}ištaran***, "1 ba-tab *tuḫ-ḫu-um* textile of *Simat-Ištaran*," 618:1, 801:1, 823:1

1 ^{túg}níĝ-lám-AB ***simat-^{d}ištaran***, "1 níĝ-lám-AB textile of *Simat-Ištaran*," 720:1, 811:1, 814:1

1 ^{túg}ĝeštu$_{x}$(PI.TÚG) ***simat-^{d}ištaran*** é-ba-an, "1 pair of ĝeštu textiles of *Simat-Ištaran*," 720:2

1 ^{túg}níĝ-lám ***simat-^{d}ištaran***, "1 níĝ-lám textile of *Simat-Ištaran*," 753:1

$2\frac{5}{6}$ ma-na 3 gín siki ^{túg}níĝ-lám ***simat-^{d}ištaran***, "$2\frac{5}{6}$ minas (and) 3 shekels of wool (for) a níĝ-lám textile of *Simat-Ištaran*," 815:1

[1] ma-na 15 gín siki túg ba-tab *tuḫ-ḫu-um* ***simat-^{d}ištaran***, "[1] mina (and) 15 shekels of wool (for) a ba-tab *tuḫ-ḫu-um* textile of *Simat-Ištaran*," 826:2

1 ma-na siki-za-rí-in túg-lugal-gen ***simat-^{d}ištaran*** *šu-kab-tá* mug-bi ⅓ ma-na 4 gín-ta NE-gu$_{7}$-bi 6 gín-ta,"1 mina of coarsely cleaned wool material (for) textiles of royal to ordinary quality of *Simat-Ištaran* (and) *Šu-Kabta*; its wool combings are ⅓ of a mina (and) 4 shekels each, its wastage is 6 shekels each," 836:1–3

3.2 Her Servants

n sìla še n sìla dabin n sìla ninda še-ba géme-árad ***simat-^{d}ištaran*** ki ^{d}*adad-tillati*-ta ba-zi, "*Adad-tillati* disbursed n liter(s) of barley, n liter(s) of semolina (and) n liter(s) of bread, barley rations of the female and male servants of *Simat-Ištaran*," 533:4–6, 537:4–7, 539:4–7, 552:4–7

131 túg ⸢ḫi⸣-a [n] ma-na ⸢siki-gen⸣ túg-⸢ba⸣ siki-bá géme-á[rad ***simat-^{d}*K]A.D[I** gì]ri [*pù-zu*]*r*$_{8}$-^{d}[nin-kar-ak k]i ^{d}*adad-tillati*-[ta ba-zi], "Under the authority of *Puzur*-Ninkarak, *Adad-tillati* disbursed 131 assorted textiles (and) [n] mina(s) of ordinary wool, textile and wool rations of the female and male servants of *Simat-Ištaran*," 734:6–12

(. . .) túg-ba siki-ba géme-árad ***simat-^{d}*K[A.DI]** ki ^{d}*adad-tillati*-ta ba-zi ĝìri *i-ṣur-^{d}suen* dub-sar, "Under the authority of *Iṣur-Suen*, the scribe, *Adad-tillati* disbursed {assorted textiles and wool}, textile and wool rations of the female and male servants of *Simat-Ištaran*," 795:5–9

(. . .) tú[g-ba] siki-ba géme-árad ***simat-$^{[d]}$ištaran*** ki ^{d}*adad-tillati*-ta ba-zi ĝìri [*puzur*$_{4}$]-^{d}ni[n-kar-ak] dub-sar, "Under the authority of *Puzur*-Ninkarak, the scribe, *Adad-tillati* disbursed {assorted textiles and wool}, textile and wool rations of the female and male servants of *Simat-Ištaran*," 818:7–1

4. Other

4.1 Anointing the Gendarme

(. . .) ⅓ sìla ì-⸢šáḫ⸣ di$_{4}$-di$_{4}$-la àga-ús ***simat-^{d}ištaran*** ba-ab-šeš$_{4}$ (. . .) ⸢u$_{4}$⸣ é-e im sumur ba-aka ⸢ĝìri⸣ *é-a-šar* dub-sar ki ^{d}*adad-tillati*-ta ba-zi, "Under the authority of *Ea-šar*, the scribe, *Adad-tillati* disbursed {assorted dead animals, food for builders}, ⅓ liter of lard (used by) *Simat-Ištaran* (when) she anointed the small child(ren) of the gendarme, (and) {building supplies} when the house was plastered," 472:8–9, 14–17

4.2 Context Uncertain: Provisions for Women

5 gín ì-šáḫ-ta 15 gín níĝ-àr-ra-sig$_{5}$ 1⅓ ma-na tuḫ-ĝeš-ì-[ḫád-ta] 10 gín ádda-u[du-ta] 10 gín mun-ta 3 gín luḫ-lá-⸢ta⸣ ga-na-⸢na⸣ 1 *lu-⸢lu⸣*? 1 *ni-a-ma* 1 *ni-a-ma* [min?] 1 ***simat-^{d}ištaran*** nu-x 1 ***simat-^{d}ištaran*** zi-[x] 1 ***simat-^{d}ištaran*** [x]-ti 1 *lu-⸢lu⸣*? min munus-me-éš {indent}10, "5 shekels of lard each, 15 shekels of fine groats, 1⅓ minas of [dried] sesame chaff [each], 10 shekels of sheep carcasses [each], 10 shekels of salt each, 3

shekels of luḫ-lá each (?), (provisions for) *Lulu*, *Ni'ama*, *Ni'ama* [the 2nd], *Simat-Ištaran* [x], *Simat-Ištaran* [x], (and) *Lulu*, the 2nd, 10? women," 562:'40–'55

simat-ᵈnana

***Simat*-Nana**, Overseer of Hired Workers

1. Supervision of Hired Workers

n ĝuruš n géme ugula ***simat*-ᵈnana** (. . .) lú-ḫug̃-g̃á-me-éš, "n hired workmen (and) n hired workwomen supervised by *Simat*-Nana," 108:14, 109:14, 110:15, 111:16, 114:16, 115:'7, 117:14, 118:13, 119:13, 123:17, 125:13

n ĝuruš ugula ***simat*-ᵈnana** (. . .) lú-ḫug̃-g̃á-me-éš, "n hired workmen supervised by *Simat*-Nana," 120:13, 121:13, 122:'3

2. Supervision of Brick Carriers and Delivery of Bricks

ki-sá-a é-lùnga [ù é-kíkken?] mu-DU ***simat*-ᵈ[nana** ugula], "delivery (of bricks) for the foundation terrace of the brewery [and mill?] by *Simat*-Nana, [the overseer]," 353:17–18

simat-ᵈnin-šubur

1. Provisions: Barley

2.0.5. gur ***simat*-ᵈnin-šubur** (. . .) šu+níĝin 27.1.1.3 sìla še gur ki ugula-nam–10-ka ⌜g̃al⌝-la ugula *simat-é-a* lú-ḫug̃-g̃á, "2 bushels (and) 50 liters (of barley) (for) *Simat*-Ninšubur, (and barley for) {others}, in total: there are 27 bushels (and) 73 liters of barley at the place of the overseer of 10, *Simat-Ea*, the overseer of hired workers," 504:16, 20–23

su-kà-lí-a

1. *Sukkalia*, the Ox-Herder, Supervised by *Nur-Adad*, the Majordomo

1.1 Ox-Drivers from his Gang

1 ĝuruš ugula ***su-kà-lí-a*** nu-bànda-[gu$_4$] (. . .) [ugula *n*]*u-úr*-ᵈ*adad* nu-bànda-gu$_4$, "1 workman supervised by *Sukkalia*, the ox-herder, (and) {other gangs}, supervised by *Nur-Adad*, the ox-herder," 187:6, 8

n ĝuruš ***su-kà-lí-a*** nu-bànda-gu$_4$ (. . .) ugula *nu-úr*-ᵈ*adad* šabra šà-gu$_4$-me-éš, "n workmen (from the gang of) *Sukkalia*, the ox-herder, (and) {other gangs}, ox-drivers supervised by *Nur-Adad*, the majordomo," 189:6, 9–10, 190:8, 12–13, 191:11, 17–18, 198:'2, '7, '9

2 ĝuruš ***su-kà-lí-a*** nu-bànda-gu$_4$ (. . .) šà-gu$_4$-me-éš (. . .) ugula *nu-úr*-ᵈ*adad* šabra, "2 workmen (from the gang of) *Sukkalia*, the ox-herder, (and) {other gangs}, ox-drivers (and) {hired workers} supervised by *Nur-Adad*, the majordomo," 193:10, 14–15, 17, 196:'5, '10, '13, 197:12, 17, 20

2 ĝuruš ***su-kà-lí-a*** nu-bànda-gu$_4$ (. . .) šà-g[u$_4$-me-éš ára]d-é-a-[me-éš] (. . .) ugula *nu-úr*-ᵈ⌜*adad*⌝, "2 workmen (from the gang of) *Sukkalia*, the ox-herder, (and) {other gangs}, ox-drivers—household servants—(and) {hired workers} supervised by *Nur-Adad*," 194:16, 21–2, 26

2. ***Sukkali*, Title Unspecified**

2.1 **Under his Authority: Delivery of a Sheep**

1 udu ki ur-mes-[ta] ^{d}*adad-tillati* ì-dab$_5$ g̃iri ***sú-kà-lí***, "Under the authority of *Sukkali*, *Adad-tillati* took in charge 1 sheep from Ur-mes," 1149:1–5[52]

^{d}*suen-a-bu-šu*

1. **Under his Authority: Transactions during the *Abum* Festival**

1.1 **A Braider to Beat (his) Breast**

1 g̃uruš túg-du$_8$ u$_4$-12-šè gaba sàg-d[è gu]b-ba u$_4$ ezem-*a-bu-um-ma* g̃iri ^{d}***suen-a-bu-šu*** ki *ḫa-lí*-ta ba-zi, "Under the authority of *Suen-abušu*, *Ḫali* disbursed 1 braider, employed for 12 days to beat (his) breast during the *Abum* festival," 278:1–7

1.2 **Regular Offerings**

(. . .) dirig sá-du$_{11}$ u$_4$-[n-šè] *ra-ba-tum* ù ^{d}*šu*-^{d}E[N.ZU-*e*]-*te-íl-pi*$_4$-^{d}en-lí[l sugal$_7$] ⌜u$_4$⌝ ezem-*a-bu-um* ⌜g̃iri⌝ ^{d}[***suen-a-bu-šu***], "{assorted commodities}, surplus of the regular offerings on the [nth] day of *Rabatum* and *Šu-Suen-etelpi*-Enlil, [the sugal], during the *Abum* festival under the authority of [*Suen-abušu*]," 509:'12–'14

– Ṣ –

ṣa-al-lum

Ṣalum, the Royal Messenger

1. **His Workmen: Bringing Flour to Karkar**

[2 g̃uruš] ***ṣa-a-l*[*um*** ^{lú}kíg̃-gi$_4$-a-lugal zì] karkar^{ki}-šè i[n-tùm-uš], "[2 workmen] of *Ṣallum*, [the royal messenger, brought flour] to Karkar," 27:'16

2 g̃uruš ***ṣa-al-*[*lum*** ^{lú}kíg̃-gi$_4$-a-lu]gal zì g̃á-g̃á-dè karkar^{ki}-šè in-tùm-uš, "2 workmen of *Ṣallum*, the royal [messenger], brought flour to Karkar in order to deposit it," 28:'27

2. **Under his Authority: *Tatturi* and *Ali-aḫ* Bringing Barley from G̃irsu**

1 *ta-tù-ri* ù *a-lí-aḫ* še è-dè g̃ír-su^{ki}-šè g̃en-na g̃iri ***ṣa-al-lum*** ^{lú}kíg̃-gi$_4$-a-lugal, "Under the authority of *Ṣallum*, the royal messenger, *Tatturi* and *Ali-aḫ* having gone to G̃irsu to bring out barley," 31:37–38, 32:37, 33:40–41, 35:44–45, 36:39

ṣú-mi-id-ilum

1. ***Ṣumid-ilum*, the Scribe**

1.1 **As a Deputy: Provisions**

1.1.1 **For the *Muškenu* and the Runner**[53]

(. . .) maš-en-gag ^{lú}kaš$_4$ ká-é-gal-ka gub-ba ⌜*simat*⌝-^{d}*ištaran* íb-gu$_7$ u$_4$ má-*simat*-^{d}*ištaran* é-^{d}šára-ta gar-ša-an-na^{ki}-šè mu-un-gíd-ša-a ***ṣú-mi-id-ilum*** maškim (. . .) zi-

---

52 Although *sú-kà-lí* is likely a shortened form of *sú-kà-lí-a*, the identification is not certain.

53 Although *Ṣumid-ilum* is not called a scribe, nos. 529 and 541 are included here in light of *Ṣumid-ilum*'s activities as a deputy similar to transaction no. 550.

ga *simat-*^{d}*ištaran*, "The *muškenu* (and?) the runner, stationed by *Simat-Ištaran* at the gate of the palace, ate {soup} when they towed the boat of *Simat-Ištaran* from the Šara temple to Garšana. (It was) the expenditure of *Simat-Ištaran*. *Ṣumid-ilum* was the deputy," 529:13–19, 26

0.0.2.6 sìla <ninda->šu-ra-gen ½ sìla du$_8$ maš-en-gag ká-é-gal-ka gub-ba íb-gu$_7$ ***ṣú-mi-id-ilum*** maškim (. . .) zi-ga *simat-*^{d}*ištaran* ki ^{d}*adad-tillati*-ta ba-zi, "*Adad-tillati* disbursed 26 liters of ordinary half (loaf) <bread> baked (in) ½ liter (loaves). The *muškenu* employed at the gate of the palace ate (the bread). *Ṣumid-ilum* was the deputy. {Other disbursals}. (These were) the expenditures of *Simat-Ištaran*," 541:17–19, 27–28

1.1.2 Travel Provisions

0.0.1. kaš-gen ugula àga-ús-e-ne á-u$_4$-te-na u$_4$-2-kam àga-ús *ri-im-ilum* íb-nağ ù ***ṣú-mi-id-ilum*** dub-sar P[A.KAŠ$_4$] u$_4$ má-*simat-*^{d}*ištaran puzur$_4$-iš-*^{d}*da-gan*^{ki}-ta gar-ša-an-na^{ki}-šè mu-un-gíd-š[a-a] zi-ga *simat-*^{d}*ištaran* ki ^{d}*adad-tillati*-ta ba-zi, "*Adad-tillati* disbursed 10 liters of ordinary beer, in the evening of the 2nd day. The overseer of the gendarmes—the gendarme *Rim-ilum*—drank (the beer) when they towed the boat of *Simat-Ištaran* from *Puzriš-Dagan* to Garšana. (It was) the expenditure of *Simat-Ištaran*. *Ṣumid-ilum*, the scribe, was the deputy," 550:'22–'30

0.0.5. ninda-kaš á-u$_4$-[te-na] 2 sìla níĝ-àr-[ra-sig$_5$] šà zabala$_4$$^{[ki]}$ u$_4$-1-[kam] 4 sìla níĝ-àr-ra-[sig$_5$] u$_4$-2-[kam] á-gú-zi-⌜ga⌝ 4 sìla níĝ-àr-ra-⌜sig$_5$⌝ á-u$_4$-te-na u$_4$-3-kam šà kaskal^{ki} àga-ús [*ri-im*]-*ilum* íb-gu$_7$ u$_4$ má-*simat-*^{d}*ištaran* gar-ša-an-na^{ki}-ta *puzur$_4$-iš-*^{d}*da-gan*[^{ki}-šè] in-gíd-sa-a ***ṣú-mi-id-ilum*** maškim zi-ga *simat-*^{d}KA.[DI] ki ^{d}*adad-tillati*-ta [ba-zi], "*Adad-tillati* disbursed 50 liters of bread (and) beer [in] the evening (and) 2 liters of [fine] barley groats in Zabala on the 1st day, 4 liters of [fine] groats at dawn of the 2nd day, (and) 4 liters of fine groats in the evening of the 3rd day of the journey. The gendarme *Rim-ilum* consumed (the food) when they towed the boat of *Simat-Ištaran* from Garšana to *Puzriš-Dagan*. (It was) the expenditure of *Simat-Ištaran*. *Ṣumid-ilum* was the deputy," 551:1–18[54]

2. *Ṣumid-ilum*, Title Unspecified

2.1 Provisions: Textiles

1 ^{túg}bar-si-abzu *a-ši-um* 1 túg-guz-za 3-kam-ús 8 ĝuruš ^{lú}ázlag á-bi u$_4$-1-še ***ṣú-mi-id-ilum*** ki *puzur$_4$-a-gu$_5$-um*-ta ba-zi, "*Puzur-agum* disbursed 1 abzu *a-ši-um* band (and) 1 3rd-quality tufted textile, labor of 8 fullers for 1 day, (for) *Ṣumid-ilum*," 571:1–6

[54] Although *Ṣumid-ilum*'s title is not specified, this text is included here in light of the parallel transaction no. 550.

– Š –

ša-at-bi-zi-il

1. Deliveries: Semolina, Receipt of *Malik-bani*

0.4.1.8 sìla dabin mu-DU ***ša-at-bi-zi-il*** ^{d}*ma-lik-ba-ni* šu ba-an-ti, "*Malik-bani* received 258 liters of semolina, delivery of *Šat-Bizil*," 1121:1–5

2. Provisions: Barley

1.0.5. gur ***ša-at-bi-zi-il!*** (. . .) šu+níĝin 27.1.1.3 sìla še gur ki ugula-nam–10-ka ⸢ĝal⸣-la ugula *simat-é-a* lú-ḫug̃-ĝá, "1 bushel (and) 50 liters (of barley) (for) *Šat-Bizil*, (and barley for) {others}, in total: there are 27 bushels (and) 73 liters of barley at the place of the overseer of 10, *Simat-Ea*, the overseer of hired workers," 504:12, 20–23

0.1.4. ***ša-at-bi-zi-il*** (. . .) mu dabin-šè šu ba-ti, "*Šat-Bizil* received 64 liters of barley, (and barley for) {9 other individuals}, (barley) in place of semolina," 560:2, 12–13

ša-at-èr-ra

Šat-Erra, Overseer of Hired Workers

1. Supervision of Hired Workers

n ĝuruš n géme ugula ***ša-at-èr-ra*** (. . .) lú-ḫug̃-ĝá-me-éš, "n hired workmen (and) n hired workwomen supervised by *Šat-Erra*," 140:16, 143:15, 148:'7, 153:'11

1 ĝuruš ugula ***ša-at-èr-ra*** (. . .) lú-ḫug̃-ĝá-me-éš, "1 hired workman supervised by *Šat-Erra*," 136:18–19, 138:16, 18

2 géme ugula ***ša-at-èr-ra*** (. . .) lú-ḫug̃-ĝá-me-éš, "2 hired workwomen supervised by *Šat-Erra*," 128:14, 129:15, 131:'9, 132:15, 133:15, 135:15, 145:17, 147:19, 150:19, 154:16

2. Provisions: Barley for Baking Bread

0.4.0. še sa$_{10}$ saḫar 12-kam ***ša-at-èr-ra*** ninda du$_{8}$-dè-⸢šè⸣, "240 liters of barley, the price of 12 units of dirt for *Šat-Erra* to bake bread," 1169:4–6

3. In *Šat-Erra*'s Possession: Wages for Brick Carriers

0.0.1.8 sìla [še] *si-ì-[tum]* á šeg$_{12}$ g[a$_{6}$-ĝá] ù al-tar-ra ⸢***ša***⸣***-at-èr-ra*** [in]-da-ĝál, "18 liters of [barley], the remainder of wages of (workers) having carried bricks and (employed) for construction, are with *Šat-Erra*," 452:1–6

ša-at-ì-lí

1. Provisions: Barley

3.0.3.5 sìla <gur> ***ša-at-ì-lí*** (. . .) šu+níĝin 27.1.1.3 sìla še gur ki ugula-nam–10-ka ⸢ĝal⸣-la ugula *simat-é-a* lú-ḫug̃-ĝá, "3 bushels (and) 35 liters (of barley) (for) *Šat-ili*, (and barley for) {others}, in total: there are 27 bushels (and) 73 liters of barley at the place of the overseer of 10, *Simat-Ea*, the overseer of hired workers," 504:11, 20–23

ša-at-kab-tá

1. Receipts

0.3.2.4 sìla [x] sa$_{10}$ kù-babbar 1⅓ šar kam(?) ***ša-at-kab-tá*** šu ba-ti ki ^{d}*adad-tillati*-ta ba-zi, "*Šat-Kabta* received from *Adad-tillati* 204 liters [x], the silver price is 1⅓," 1139:1–6

ša-bar-zi-na-at

Šabarzinat, Man from Karkar

[1] ***ša-bar-zi-na-at*** (. . .) ugula *á-ni*-x-x (. . .) lú-karkar^{ki}-me, "*Šabarzinat*, supervised by *á-ni*-x-x, (and) {other workers}, men from Karkar," 559:20, 25, 28

ša-lim-a-ḫu-um

1. *Šalim-aḫum*, Overseer of Hired Workers

1 [g̃uruš ugula ***ša*]*-lim-a-ḫu-*⸢*um*⸣** (. . .) lú-[ḫug̃-g̃]á-me-éš, "1 hired [workman, supervised by] *Šalim-aḫum*," 9:9

2. *Šalim-aḫum*, Title Unspecified

ì-lí-an-*[*dùl*] gaba-ri dub [. . .] um-ma [. . .] 0.3.0. ⸢še⸣ 6 ma-na siki-⸢gen⸣ u_4 ***ša-lim-a-ḫu-um [. . .] nu-un-na-an-[. . .] in-na-RU-[. . .] ka-ga-na [ba-a-gen_7], 1052:1–8

ša-lim-be-lí

Šalim-beli, Hired Worker from the Gang of *Beli-ili*

1. Purchasing Flying Fish in Gu'abba

1 ***ša-lim-be-lí*** ku_6-sim sa_{10}(-sa_{10})-dè gú-ab-ba^{ki}-šè g̃en-na, "*Šalim-beli* having gone to Gu'abba to purchase flying fish," 37:41–44, 38:48–50, 47:64–65, 48:71–73, 49:65–67

šà-gu_4

Šagu, Man from Karkar

1 **šà-gu_4**? (. . .) ugula *á-ni*-x-x (. . .) lú-karkar^{ki}-me, "Šagu, supervised by *á-ni*-x-x, (and) {other workers}, men from Karkar," 559:24, 25, 28

šál-maḫ

1. *Šál-maḫ*, the Builder

1.1 In his Possession: A Copper Axe

[n ma-n]a 5 gín ^{urudu} ḫa-zi-in lá-ìa-àm ***šál-maḫ*** šidim in-da-g̃ál, "The remainder (of the value) of a copper axe, weighing [n mina(s)] (and) 5 shekels, are with *Šal-maḫ*, the builder," 1258:1–4

1.2 *Šal-maḫ*, the Sick Builder

1 *en-nim-ma* šidim 1 ***šál-maḫ*** šidim dú-ra-me-éš, "*Enima* (and) *Šal-maḫ*, sick builders," 24:'28–'30

1 ***šál-maḫ*** šidim dú-ra, "*Šal-maḫ*, the sick builder," 25:'5, 26:'24

2. *Šal-maḫ*, Overseer of Hired Workers

2.1.Supervision of Hired Workers

1 g̃uruš šidim ugula ***šál-maḫ*** (. . .) lú-ḫug̃-g̃á-me-éš, "1 hired builder, supervised by *Šal-maḫ*," 140:14, 19

n g̃uruš n géme ugula ***šál-maḫ*** (. . .) lú-ḫug̃-g̃á-me-éš, "n workmen (and) n workwomen, hired workers supervised by *Šal-maḫ*," 21:12, 24:13, 31:12, 32:12, 33:12,

35:12, 43:13, 44:11, 46:'6, 94:7, 95:5, 98:'6, 99:7, 101:7, 102:10, 103:9, 104:13, 105:13, 106:15

1 ĝuruš ḫuĝ-ĝá ugula ***šál-maḫ***, "1 hired workman supervised by *Šal-maḫ*," 7:16–17, 8:17

n ĝuruš ugula ***šál-maḫ*** (. . .) lú-ḫuĝ-ĝá-me-éš, "n hired workman supervised by *Šal-maḫ*," 10:9, 14:11, 15:11, 17:10, 18:9, 20:10, 27:'4, 28:'3, 29:'10, 36:12, 14, 38:11, 47:11, 48:11, 93:'7, 133:16, 136:14, 19, 135:16, 137:14, 138:14, 18, 141:17, 143:14, 163:13, 173:12, 174:12, 175:11

n géme ugula ***šál-maḫ*** (lú-ḫuĝ-ĝá-me-éš), "n (hired) workwomen supervised by *Šal-maḫ*," 56:10–11, 78:3, 150:20–21

[n ĝuruš/géme] ugula ***šál-maḫ*** (. . .) lú-ḫuĝ-ĝá-me-éš, "[n] hired [workmen/women] supervised by *Šal-maḫ*," 52:12, 14

2.2 Supervision of Brick Carriers and Delivery of Bricks

2.2.1 For the Craftsmen's House

é-NUN.ME.TA[G-e-ne-šè] mu-[DU] ***šál-maḫ*** [ugula lú-ḫuĝ-ĝá], "delivery (of bricks) [for] the craftsmen's house by *Šal-maḫ*, [overseer of hired workers]," 325:18–20

2.2.2 For the Textile Mill

é-uš-bar-[šè mu-DU] ***šál-maḫ*** [ugula lú-ḫuĝ-ĝá], "[delivery] (of bricks) [for] the textile mill by *Šal-maḫ*, [overseer of hired workers]," 320:11–12

2.2.3 Broken Context

[. . . ugula ***šál***]***-maḫ***, 351:139

ᵈšamaš-a-bi

1. Provisions: Barley

0.4.0. ***ᵈšamaš-a-bí*** (. . .) šu+níĝin 27.1.1.3 sìla še gur ki ugula-nam–10-ka ⸢ĝal⸣-la ugula *simat-é-a* lú-ḫuĝ-ĝá, "240 liters (of barley) (for) *Šamaš-abi*, (and barley for) {others}, in total: there are 27 bushels (and) 73 liters of barley at the place of the overseer of 10, *Simat-Ea*, the overseer of hired workers," 504:13, 20–23

0.0.2. ***ᵈšamaš-a-bi*** (. . .) mu dabin-šè šu ba-ti, "*Šamaš-abi* received 20 liters of barley, (and barley for) {9 other individuals}, (barley) in place of semolina," 560:8, 12–13

ᵈšamaš-di-in

Šamaš-din, the Sick Builder

1 ***ᵈšamaš-di-in*** šidim dú-ra, "*Šamaš-din*, the sick builder," 43:'49, 44:48

šar-ru-sú-ṭa-ba-at

1. Receipts from *Adad-tillati*

1.1. Oil

0.1.5.5⅚ sìla ì-ĝeš ***šar-ru-sú-ṭa-ba-at*** šu ba-ti ki ᵈ*ad*[*ad-tillati*-t]a ba-zi, "*Šarrussu-ṭabat* received 115⅚ liters of sesame oil from *Adad-tillati*," 1246:1–5

1.2 Dates, for the House of the Women

0.1.2. zú-lum é-munus-šè ***šar-ru-sú-ṭa-ba-at*** šu ba-ti úgu(!)-a nu-um-g̃ar ki ^{d}*adad-tillati*-ta ba-zi, "*Šarrussu-ṭabat* received 80 liters of dates for the house of the women from *Adad-tillati*. It was not placed on the account," 515:1–7

2. Under his Authority: Commodities for Mattresses and a Braider to Tow a Boat

12 gín siki-g̃ír-gul šà-tuku$_5$ kala-kala-gé-dè 5½ nag̃a-si-è 2 ma-na im-bábbar šà-tuku$_5$ lu-luḫ-dè 1 g̃uruš túg-du$_8$ u$_4$-6-šè má gíd-da g̃iri ***šar-ru-sú***-DU$_{10}$ (. . .) ki *ḫa-lí*-ta ba-zi, "Under the authority of *Šarrussu-ṭab*, *Ḫali* disbursed 12 shekels of g̃ír-gul wool in order to reinforce a mattress, 5½ (units) of sprouted nag̃a (and) 2 minas of gypsum in order to clean a mattress (and) 1 braider for 6 days having towed a boat (and) {other commodities under different authority}," 783:1–8

šar-ru-um-ba-ni

Šarrum-bani, the Animal Fattener

1. Delivery of Sheep and Goats

80 udu-máš ḫi-a ki ***šar-ru-um-ba-ni*** kurušda-ta (. . .) níg̃-kas$_7$-aka ^{d}*adad-tillati* šabra, "(In total:) 80 various sheep (and) goats from *Šarrum-bani*, the animal fattener, (and) {other commodities}, the balanced account of *Adad-tillati*, the majordomo," 984:'21–'22, '75–'76

šar-ru-um-ì-lí

1. His Tablet

1 (bùr) gána zàr tab-ba nu-de$_5$-de$_5$-ga dub ***šar-ru-um-ì-lí*** *ì-lí-an-dùl* tùm-dam, "*Ili-andul* will bring *Šarrum-ili*'s tablet (saying) that the sheaves stacked in 1 bur of acreage are not to be collected," 1398:1–6

2. Instructions for *Šarrum-ili*

šar-ru-um-ì-lí ù-na-a-du$_{11}$ [x]-g̃ál-la [x] é-za ì-g̃ál é-ki-ba-g̃ar-ra du$_8$-dè ^{d}*adad-tillati* ḫé-na-ab-sum-mu a-ba šeš-g̃u$_{10}$-gin$_7$, "Say to *Šarrum-ili* that '(?) that is in your house should be given to *Adad-tillati* in order to caulk the replacement house. Who is like my brother?'" 1526:1–7

^{d}šára-ì-ša$_6$

1. As a Witness

igi **^{d}šára-ì-ša$_6$**, "witnessed by Šara-iša," 1061:8

2. Under his Authority: Wood from Demolished Boats

8.1.0. ésir-ḫád [gur] 4 g̃eš-íb-ra má-[20?-g]ur 28 ^{geš}ù-má má-20-gur má gul-la-ta ^{d}*adad-tillati* šu ba-ti g̃iri **^{d}šára-ì-ša$_6$**, "Under the authority of Šara-iša, *Adad-tillati* received 8 bushels (and) 60 liters of dry bitumen, 4 íb-ra planks of a [20?]-bushel boat (and) 28 boat planks of a 20-bushel boat, (wood) from demolished boats," 1359:1–7

^{d}**šára-kam**

1. **Šara-kam, the Scribe**

1.1 **As a Witness**

igi ^{d}**šára-kam** dub-sar, "witnessed by Šara-kam, the scribe," 1064:12

2. **Šara-kam, Title Unspecified**

2.1 **Receipts: From *Adad-tillati***

2.1.1 **Grains**

0.1.0. zì-gu-[x?] ki ^{d}*adad-tillati*-[ta] ^{d}**šára-kam** šu ba-ti, "Šara-kam received 60 liters of [x?] gu-flour from *Adad-tillati*," 1221:1–4

6.0.0. še gur ki ^{d}*adad-tillati*-ta ^{d}**šára-kam** šu ba-ti, "Šara-kam received 6 bushels of barley from *Adad-tillati*," 1239:1–4

2.1.2 **Grains and Workwomen**

4 sìla zì-KAL 8 géme u_4-1-šè ki ^{d}*adad-tillati*-ta ^{d}**šára-kam** šu ba-ti, "Šara-kam received 4 liters of KAL-flour (and) 8 workwomen for 1 day from *Adad-tillati*," 1395:1–5

2.1.3 **Pigs**

2 šáḫ-munus-ama-gan 1 šáḫ-níta ki ^{d}*adad-tillati*-ta ^{d}**šára-kam** ì-dab_5, "Šara-kam took in charge 2 female breeding pigs (and) 1 male pig from *Adad-tillati*," 1211:1

2.1.4 **Reeds and Reeds Baskets**

40 sa gi-šid ki ^{d}*adad-tillati*-ta ^{d}**šára-kam** šu ba-ti, "Šara-kam received 40 bundles of dry reeds from *Adad-tillati*," 1366:1–4

[n+]4 ^{gi}gur-sal-la 0.0.1.-ta 6 ^{gi}gur-sal-la 3-sìla-ta [ki ^{d}*adad-tillati*]-ta ^{d}**šára-kam** šu ba-ti, "Šara-kam received [n+]4 thin baskets of 10 liters each (and) 6 thin baskets of 3 liters each from [*Adad-tillati*]," 1367:1–5

[120?+]5 ^{gi}m[a-sá]-ab ½-[sìla-ta] 120 ^{gi}ku-[. . .] 5-sìla-ta 11 ^{gi}ma!-sá-ab 5-s[ìla-t]a AŠ.AŠ NE-ku-nu šu aka ki ^{d}*adad-tillati*-ta $^{[d]}$šára-kam [šu] ba-ti, "Šara-kam received from *Adad-tillati* [120?+]5 ma-sab baskets of ½ liter [each], 120 [. . .] of 5 liters each, 11 ma-sab baskets of 5 liters each (and) processed (?)," 1371:1–7

^{d}**šára-sá-g̃u$_{10}$**

Šara-sag̃u, the Female Miller

1. **Provisions: Oil, When She was Sick**

10 gín ì-g̃eš-ta ^{d}**šára-sá-g̃u$_{10}$** 1 *bu-za-du-a* géme kíkken-me-éš u_4 dú-ra i-me é-gal!-šè, "10 shekels of sesame oil each (for) Šara-sag̃u (and) *Buzadua*, female millers, when they were sick at the palace," 466:3–7

še-da

Šeda, the Cupbearer

1. **As a Deputy: Animals and Grains for Šara**

(. . .) ^{d}šára ezem-níg̃-ab-è ***še-da*** sagi maškim zi-ga g̃iri *šu-kab-tá* ki ^{d}*adad-tillati*-ta ba-zi, "*Adad-tillati* disbursed {sheep and assorted grains} (for) Šara (during) the níg̃-ab-e festival.

(It was) the expenditure of *Šu-Kabta* under his authority. *Šeda*, the cupbearer, was the deputy," 1001:6–12

2. As a Witness

igi ***še-da*** sagi, "witnessed by *Šeda*, the cupbearer," 1061:9

še-lí-a-núm

Šelianum, the Scribe

1. As a Deputy: Disbursal of Textiles

7 ^{túg}uš-bar *a-gi$_4$-um* túg-ma-dur$_7$-ra ***še-lí-a-núm*** dub-sar maškim á mu-DU ki *puzur$_4$-a-gu$_5$-um*-ta ba-zi, "*Puzur-agum* disbursed 7 *a-gi$_4$-um* uš-bar textiles, mourning textiles, delivery of (completed) work. *Šelianum*, the scribe, was the deputy," 566:1–8

šeš-kal-la

Šeš-kala, the Household Servant from the Gang of *Irib*

1. Purchasing Flying Fish: With *Lukadum*

1 **šeš-kal-la** 1 *lu-kà-dum* ku$_6$-sim sa$_{10}$(-sa$_{10}$)-dè gú-ab-ba^{ki}-šè ĝen-na, "Šeš-kala (and) *Lukadum* having gone to Gu'abba to purchase flying fish," 37:36–39, 47:58–61, 48:66–69, 49:60–62

1 **šeš-kal-la** 1 *lu-kà-dum* ku$_6$-sim sa$_{10}$-sa$_{10}$-dè gú-ab-ba^{ki}-šè ĝen-a, "Šeš-kala (and) *Lukadum* having gone to Gu'abba to purchase flying fish," 38:42–44

1 *lu-kà-dum* 1 **šeš-kal-la** ku$_6$-sim sa$_{10}$-sa$_{10}$-dè gú-ab-ba^{ki}-šè ĝen-na, "*Lukadum* (and) Šeš-kala having gone to Gu'abba to purchase flying fish," 46:'45–'47, 50:'9–'10, 50:'19–'20

2. Šeš-kala, the Sick Workman

1 **š[eš-kal-la]** dú-⌜ra⌝, "Šeš-kala, the sick (workman)," 56:'40

1 **šeš-kal-la** dú-ra ugula *i-ri-ib*, "Šeš-kala, the sick (workman) supervised by *Irib*," 57:'27–'30, 58:67–68, 59:56–57, 60:52–53, 61:13–14, 62:'14–'15, 71:37, 73:'18–'19

šu-a-ku

Šu-aku, Man from Karkar

1 ***šu-a-ku*** (. . .) ugula *á-ni*-x-x (. . .) lú-karkar^{ki}-me, "*Šu-aku*, supervised by *á-ni*-x-x, (and) {other workers}, men from Karkar," 559:15, 25, 28

šu-^{d}adad

1. *Šu-Adad*, the Man of *Iddin-abum*

1.1 Receipts: Pots from *Adad-tillati*

3 ^{dug}HI?-x-[. . .] ki ^{d}*adad-tillati*-ta ***šu-^{d}adad*** lú-*i-din-a-bu-um* [šu] ba-an-ti, "*Šu-Adad*, the man of *Iddin-abum*, received 3 [. . .] pots from *Adad-tillati*," 1268:1–4

2. *Šu-Adad*, the Ox-Herder (from the Gang of) *Malik-tillati*

[1 ĝuruš] dú-ra 1 *ú-bar-⌜um⌝* 1 *bí-za-⌜tum⌝* 1 *šu-^{d}⌜adad⌝* 1 AN.TAG.⌜KAL⌝ ^{d}*ma-lik-tillati* [nu-bànda]-gu$_4$ ugula *nu-úr-^{d}adad* šabra, "[1] sick [workman], *Ubarum*, *Bizatum*, *Šu-Adad* (and) AN.TAG.KAL, (workers from the gang of) *Malik-tillati*, the ox-herder, supervised by *Nur-Adad*, the majordomo," 198:'32–'38

3. *Šu-Adad*, the Scribe

3.1 Under his Authority: Craftsmen to Tow a Boat

2 g̃uruš ašgab 1 g̃uruš ad-kub$_4$ u$_4$-4-[šè] má ^{ĝeš}šim ḫi-a gar-ša-an-na^{ki}-ta nibru^{ki}-šè in-gíd-sa-a g̃ìri ***šu-^{d}adad*** dub-sar zi-ga *simat-^{d}ištaran* ki ^{d}*adad-tillati*-ta ba-zi, "Under the authority of *Šu-Adad*, the scribe, *Adad-tillati* disbursed 2 leather workers (and) 1 reed craftsman [for] 4 days who towed a boat (with) various resinous woods from Garšana to Nippur. (It was) the expenditure of *Simat-Ištaran*," 253:1–11

4. *Šu-Adad*, Title Unspecified

4.1 Deliveries

4.1.1 Textiles: Rations for Servants in Nippur

780 ^{túg}uš-bar 12 ^{túg}uš-bar x [(. . .)] túg-ba géme-árad šà nibru^{ki} ki ***šu-^{d}adad***-ta ba-zi, "In Nippur, *Šu-Adad* disbursed 780 uš-bar textiles (and) 12 [. . .] uš-bar textiles, textile rations of female and male servants," 589:1–6

4.1.2 Metals and Metal Objects

4.1.2.1 Receipt of *Adad-tillati*

[n] gú UD.KA.B[AR x?] urudu g̃ar-⸢ra⸣ [ki ***šu***]-^{d}***adad***-ta ^{d}*adad-tillati* [šu ba-ti], "*Adad-tillati* received [n] talent(s) of bronze [(and) x] covered (with) copper from *Šu-Adad*," 1377:1–5

4.1.2.2 Receipt of *Isu-ariq*

3 ^{urudu}ḫa-zi-in 2 ma-na-ta ki ***šu-^{d}adad***-[ta *i*]-⸢*sú*⸣-[*a-ri-iq*] š[u b]a-⸢ti⸣, "*Isu-ariq* received 3 copper axes of 2 minas each from *Šu-Adad*," 1283:1–4

1 gal kù-babbar ½ ma-na 5½ gín 1 gal ka-balag-a-bar?? kù-babbar 19 gín ^{ĝeš}gu-za *šu-*[*kab*]-*tá*-šè ki ***šu-^{d}adad***-ta *i-sú-a-rí-iq* šu ba-ti, "*Isu-ariq* received 1 large silver cup (weighing) ½ mina (and) 5½ shekels (and) 1 large silver ka-balag-a-bar cup (weighing) 19 shekels for the chair of *Šu-Kabta* from *Šu-Adad*," 1339:1–6

4.1.3 Oil: Receipt of *Adad-tillati*

(. . .) mu dig̃ir-re-e-ne-šè ki ***šu-^{d}adad***-ta ^{d}*adad-tillati* šu ba-an-ti, "*Adad-tillati* received {assorted oils} for the gods from *Šu-Adad*," 1004:4–7

4.1.4 Contents Lost

[. . . ki] ***šu-^{d}⸢adad⸣***-⸢ta⸣ zì ⸢^{lú}⸣lùnga [x?] kurum$_7$ [aka g̃ìri ^{d}*adad-tillati* šabra], "Inspection of [. . .], flour (for?) the brewer from *Šu-Adad*, [under the authority of *Adad-tillati*, the majordomo]," 1145:1–6

4.2 Receipts

4.2.1 Oil Vessels from *Adad-tillati*

1 ^{dug}dal 0.1.0. 1 ^{dug}dal [0.n.n.] 8 [. . .] 0.0.1. [. . .] 1 [. . .]-x-KA-x 1 [. . .] ki ^{d}*adad-tillati*-ta ***šu-^{d}adad*** šu ba-an-ti, "*Šu-Adad* received 1 60-liter oil vessel, 1 [n]-liter oil vessel, 8 10-liter [(vessels)], 1 [. . .], (and) 1 [. . .] from *Adad-tillati*," 1266:1–9

4.2.2 Textiles

4.2.2.1 From *Adad-tillati*

(. . .) túg-sa-gi$_4$-àm ***šu-^{d}adad*** šu ba-ti (. . .) iti u$_5$-bí-gu$_7$ (. . .) úgu a g̃á-g̃á ga-ga-ra-a ki ^{d}*adad-tillati*-ta ⸢ba⸣-zi, "In month 4, *Šu-Adad* received from *Adad-*

tillati {assorted} finished textiles, (and) {other disbursals}, the total placed in the account," 1162:'34–'36, '50, '66–'70

(. . .) [túg]-sa-gi$_4$-a [***šu***]-^{d}***adad*** [šu] ba-an-ti ⌜úgu⌝ a g̃á-[g̃á ga]-ga-ra-a [ki ^{d}]*adad-tillati*-[ta ba-zi], "*Šu-Adad* received [from] *Adad-tillati* {assorted} finished [textiles], the total placed in the account," 1254:'44–'51

4.2.2.2 From *Puzur-agum*

(. . .) ***šu-^{d}adad*** šu ba-(an-)ti ki *puzur$_4$-a-gu$_5$-um*-ta ba-zi, "*Šu-Adad* received {assorted textiles} from *Puzur-agum*," 563:3–5, 564:3–6, 572:6–8

(. . .) ki *puzur$_4$-a-gum*-ta ***šu-^{d}adad*** šu ba-ti, "*Šu-Adad* received {assorted textiles} from *Puzur-agum*," 569:21–22

(. . .) túg-sa-gi$_4$-àm ki *puzur$_4$-a-gu$_5$-um*-ta ***šu-^{d}adad*** šu ba-(an-)ti, "*Šu-Adad* received {assorted} finished textiles from *Puzur-agum*," 567:2–5, 570:4–8, 578:19–22, 579:20–24, 586:4–7, 587:4–7, 590:4–7

(. . .) túg-sa-gi$_4$-a mu-DU ki *puzur$_4$-a-gu$_5$-um*-ta ***šu-^{d}adad*** šu ba-ti, "*Šu-Adad* received a delivery of {assorted} finished textiles from *Puzur-agum*," 577:5–9

(. . .) túg-sa-gi$_4$-a mu-DU ***šu-^{d}adad*** šu ba-an-ti ki *puzur$_4$-a-gu$_5$-um*-ta ba-zi, "*Šu-Adad* received a delivery of {assorted} finished textiles from *Puzur-agum*," 568:4–9

(. . .) túg-sa-gi$_4$-[àm] ki *puzur$_4$-a-gu$_5$-um*-[ta] ***šu-^{d}adad*** šu ba-an-ti šà tum-ma-al^{ki}, "*Šu-Adad* received {assorted} finished textiles from *Puzur-agum* in Tumal," 591:'12–'15

4.2.2.3 Source Unspecified

(. . .) túg-sa-gi$_4$-àm ***šu-^{d}adad*** šu ba-(an-)ti, "*Šu-Adad* received {assorted} finished textiles," 1254:'44–'46

4.3 Listed in Worker Inspection Accounts

1 [***šu***]-^{d}***adad***, 36:48

šu-ba-ra-ni

Šubarani, the Fisherman

1. Receipts

20 ma-na gu-$^{g̃eš}$ba *zi-ba-tum* mu sa-par$_4$-šè ***šu-ba-ra-ni*** šu-ku$_6$ (. . .) iti ki-siki-^{d}nin-[a-zu] úgu a g̃á-g̃á ga-ga-ra-a ki ^{d}*adad-tillati*-ta ⌜ba⌝-zi, "In month 5, *Šubarani*, the fisherman, received from *Adad-tillati* 20 minas of (?) cord for a net, (and) {other disbursals} the total placed in the account," 1162:'55–'57, '64–'70

šu-^{d}belum

Šu-Belum, the Household Servant from the Gang of *Irib*

1. Bringing Messages

1.1 To *Aḫu-waqar*

1 ***šu-^{d}belum*** á-ág̃ ki *a-ḫu-wa-qar* lú-du$_6$-lugal-pa-è^{ki} de$_6$-a, "*Šu-Belum* having brought a message to the place of *Aḫu-waqar*, the man from Du-lugal-pa'e," 45:28–29, 46:'44, 47:56, 48:62–63

1.2 To *Šu-Kabta*

1 ***šu-^{d}belum*** á-ág̃-g̃á ki *šu-kab-ta*-šè de$_6$-a, "*Šu-Belum* having brought a message to the place of *Šu-Kabta*," 39:45, 114:7–8

1 ***šu-^{d}belum*** á-ág̃ ki *šu-kab-ta*-šè g̃en-na "*Šu-Belum* having gone to the place of *Šu-Kabta* (to bring) a message," 40:38–39

[1 ***š*]***u-^{d}belum*** [á-ág̃ ki] *šu-kab-t*[*a*-š]è šu?-x-[x?]-x G̃EŠ.KÚŠU[ki-šè?] de$_6$-[a], "*Šu-Belum* having brought [a message] to [the place of] *Šu-Kabta* (?) [in?] G̃EŠ.KÚŠU," 56:'36–'38

1 é-ì-gára 1 ***šu-^{d}belum*** á-ág̃(-g̃á) ki *šu-kab-ta*-šè de$_6$-a, "E'igara (and) *Šu-Belum* having brought a message to the place of *Šu-Kabta*," 65:'26–'27, 71:32–34, 110:7–8, 111:7–9

1.3 Recipient Broken

1 [PN] 1 *ḫi-lu-*[*a*] 1 ***šu-$^{d⌜}$belum***] á-ág̃-g̃á ki [. . . –šè de$_6$-a], "[PN], *Ḫilua* (and) *Šu-Belum* [having brought] a message [to . . .]," 54:'27–'30

2. Broken Context

[. . .] ***šu-^{d}***[***belum*** . . .], 71:26

šu-bu-ul-tum

Šubultum, Wife of *Adallal*

1. Her Seal

2.0.0 še gur saḫar zi-ga-šè ki ^{d}*adad-tillati*-ta *a-da-làl* šu ba-ti kìšib ***šu-bu-ul-tum*** dam-ni íb-ra, "*Adallal* received 2 bushels of barley for having moved dirt from *Adad-tillati*. *Šubultum*, his wife, rolled (her) seal," 1201:1–6

Šu-^{d}Dumu-zi

1. *Šu*-Dumuzi, Overseer of Hired Workers

1.1 Supervision of Hired Workers

1 g̃uruš šidim ugula ***šu-^{d}*dumu-zi** (. . .) lú-ḫug̃-g̃á-me-éš, "1 hired builder supervised by *Šu*-Dumuzi," 150:16, 151:13, 153:'8

1 g̃ur[uš ši]dim 11 g̃uruš 3 géme ugula ***šu-^{d}*dumu-zi** (. . .) lú-ḫug̃-g̃á-me-éš, "1 builder, 11 workmen (and) 3 workwomen, hired workers supervised by *Šu*-Dumuzi," 154:13

1 g̃uruš 2 géme [ugula ***šu-^{d}*dumu-zi**] (. . .) lú-ḫug̃-g̃á-[me-éš], "1 workman (and) 2 workwomen, hired workers [supervised by *Šu*-Dumuzi]," 163:1

n g̃uruš ugula ***šu-^{d}*dumu-zi** (. . .) (lú-ḫug̃-g̃á-me-éš), "n (hired) workmen supervised by *Šu*-Dumuzi," 38:12, 39:11, 40:12, 41:11–12, 43:15, 44:13, 46:'7, 53:11, 78:2, 81:2, 82:2, 83:5, 84:2, 156:11, 158:13, 159:11, 161:'5, 162:12, 173:10, 174:10, 175:10, 180:8, 10

[n g̃uruš/géme ugula] ***šu-^{d}*dumu-zi** lú-ḫug̃-g̃á-me-éš, "[n] hired [workmen/women supervised by] *Šu*-Dumuzi," 52:13

1.2 Supervision of Brick Carriers and Delivery of Bricks

1.2.1 For the Cistern in the Palace

a-*ZA-BU-um* šà é-gal mu-DU ***šu-^{d}*dumu-zi**, "delivery (of bricks for) the cistern in the palace by *Šu*-Dumuzi," 339:13–15[55]

1.2.2 For the Replacement House

<é->⸢ki⸣-ba-g̃ar-ra é-*p*[*i*$_5$*-š*]*a-aḫ-*⸢*ilum*⸣ mu-⸢DU⸣ ***šu***-^{d}**dumu-zi** ugula l[ú-ḫug̃-g̃á], "delivery (of bricks for) the replacement house of *Pišaḫ-ilum* by *Šu*-Dumuzi, overseer of hired workers," 341:13–15

1.3 Supervision of Workmen Assigned to Specific Tasks

1.3.1 Bringing Straw

40 g̃uruš u$_4$-1-šè še 6 sìla-ta ba-ḫug̃ a-šà a-gi-li-⸢ta⸣ gar-⸢ša⸣-an-na^{ki}-šè in-u de$_6$-a ugula ***šu***-^{d}**dumu-zi**, "40 workmen, supervised by *Šu*-Dumuzi, were hired for 1 day (for) 6 liters of barley each, (workers) having brought straw from the Agili field to Garšana," 443:1–6

1.3.2 Crushing Malt

3 g̃uruš ugula ***šu***-^{d}**dumu-zi** (. . .) lú-ḫug̃-g̃á-me-éš munu$_4$ nag̃$_4$-g̃á-⸢dè⸣ kurum$_7$ aka, "Inspection (of the work) of 3 hired workmen, supervised by *Šu*-Dumuzi, (and) {other workers} to crush malt," 170:2, 6–8, 171:1, 6–7

3 g̃uruš ugula ***šu***-^{d}**dumu-zi** (. . .) lú-ḫug̃-g̃á-me-[éš] munu$_4$ nag̃$_4$-g̃á kurum$_7$ aka, "Inspection (of the work) of 3 hired workmen, supervised by *Šu*-Dumuzi, (and) {other workers} having crushed malt," 172:4, 6–8

1.3.3 Employed at the Place of the Brewer

10-lá-1 g̃uruš ugula ***šu***-^{d}**dumu-zi** (. . .) ki ^{lú}lùnga! gub-ba kurum$_7$ aka, "Inspection (of the work) of 9 workmen, supervised by *Šu*-Dumuzi, (and) {other workers}, employed at the place of the brewer," 169:1–2, 5–7

1.3.4 Towing Boats with Shok to Garšana

10 gu-níg̃in ^{geš}kišig á g̃uruš-a 4 gu-níg̃in-ta á-bi 2½ u$_4$-1-šè a-šà-karkar^{ki}-šè ^{geš}kišig ku$_5$-rá 4 g̃uruš u$_4$-1-šè gar-ša-an-na^{ki}-ta karkar^{ki}-šè má gíd-da 4 g̃uruš u$_4$-1-šè m[á g̃a]r-ra 4 g̃uruš u$_4$-1-šè kar[kar^{ki}-ta] gar-ša-an-na^{ki}-šè 4 g̃uruš u$_4$-1-šè kar-ta g̃á-nun-šè ga$_6$-⸢g̃a⸣ ugula ***šu***-^{d}**dumu-zi**, "(In total:) 10 bales of shok. The workmen wages were for 4 bales each. Their wages were for 2½ days (for workers) having cut shok at the Karkar field. 4 workmen for 1 day having towed a boat from Garšana to Karkar (and then) 4 workmen for 1 day having placed the boat (i.e. loaded it with shok). 4 workmen for 1 day (having towed the boat back) [from] Karkar to Garšana (and) 4 workmen for 1 day having carried (shok) from the quay to the storehouse, (workmen) supervised by *Šu*-Dumuzi," 235:1–13

1.4 The Account of *Šu*-Dumuzi: Wages for Construction Work

[21 ma]-na siki-gen siki 1 [ma-n]a še 0.0.3.-ta še-bi [2.0].3. gur 0.0.4. še šu+níg̃in 2.1.1. še gur sag̃-níg̃-gur$_{11}$-ra-kam šà-[bi]-ta (. . .) šu+níg̃in+ba 2.0.3.7½ sìla še gur zi-ga-àm 0.0.3.2½ sìla še ⸢*si*⸣*-ì-tum* níg̃-kas$_7$-aka ***šu***-^{d}**dumu-zi** ugula lú-ḫug̃-g̃á g̃iri ^{d}*adad-tillati* šabra ù *puzur4*-^{d}nin-kar-ak dub-sar, "[21] minas of ordinary wool, 1 mina of wool (is the equivalent of) 30 liters of barley; (therefore) their barley is [2] bushels (and) 30 liters (plus an additional) 40 liters of barley (is) in total: 2 bushels (and) 70 liters of barley. These are the available assets. From among it: {workmen employed for construction of

---

55 Although *Šu*-Dumuzi's title is not specified, this text is included here in light of the similar transaction no. 341.

the enclosure wall, workwomen having carried bricks, and workers for other construction projects; calculation of their wages}. In total: 2 bushels and 37½ liters of barley was expended. 32½ liters of barley is the remainder. The balanced account of *Šu*-Dumuzi, overseer of hired workers, under the authority of *Adad-tillati*, the majordomo, and *Puzur*-Ninkarak, the scribe," 336:1–7, 50–58

1.4.1 **Colophon of the Account**

[***šu***]-^{d}**dumu-zi** ugula lú-ḫuĝ-ĝá, "*Šu*-Dumuzi, overseer of hired workers," 336:62

2. ***Šu*-Dumuzi, the Ox-Herder**

2.1 **A Sick Worker from his Gang**

1 ĝuruš dú-ra ***šu***-^{d}**dumu-zi** nu-bànda-gu$_{4}$, "1 sick workman, (from the gang of) *Šu*-Dumuzi, the ox-herder," 198:'31

3. ***Šu*-Dumuzi, Title Unspecified**

3.1 **As a Witness**

1 ***šu***-^{d}**dumu-zi**, "(witnessed by) *Šu*-Dumuzi," 1048:13

šu-^{d}en-líl

1. **His Seal**

(. . .) ki ^{d}*adad-tillati*-ta *šu*-^{d}nin-girim$_{x}$ šu ba-ti kišib ***šu***-^{d}**en-líl**, "*Šu*-Ningirim received {assorted leather, woods, mats and vessels} from *Adad-tillati*, seal of *Šu*-Enlil," 1334:13–16

2. **Under his Authority: Receipt of Bitumen**

0.0.2. ésir-é-a ki ^{d}*adad-tillati*-ta *šu*-^{d}nin-girim$_{x}$ šu ba-ti ĝìri ***šu***-^{d}**en-líl**, "Under the authority of *Šu*-Enlil, *Šu*-Ningirim received 20 liters of house bitumen from *Adad-tillati*," 1338:1–5

šu-èr-ra

Šu-Erra, the Scribe

1. **As a Deputy: Fuel Reeds to Cook Fish**

80 sa gi-izi ku$_{6}$ šé-ĝe$_{6}$-dè ***šu-èr-ra*** dub-sar maškim (. . .) [ki ^{d}*a*]*dad-tillati*-ta [ba]-zi, "*Adad-tillati* disbursed 80 bundles of fuel reeds to cook fish. *Šu-Erra*, the scribe, was the deputy, (and) {other disbursals under different authority}," 1013:20–22, 24–25, 1014:'13–'15, '18–'19

80 sa gi-izi ku$_{6}$ šé-ĝe$_{6}$-dè ***šu-èr-ra*** maškim šà ĜEŠ.KÚŠU^{ki} zi-ga *šu-kab*!(DA)-*tá* ki ^{d}*adad-tillati*-ta ba-zi, "*Adad-tillati* disbursed 80 bundles of fuel reeds to cook fish, the expenditure of *Šu-Kabta* in ĜEŠ.KÚŠU. *Šu-Erra* was the deputy," 1321:1–8[56]

2. **Deliveries: Fish**

60 ku$_{6}$ al-dar-ra ki ***šu-èr-ra***-ta ^{d}*adad-tillati* šabra šu ba-ti, "*Adad-tillati*, the majordomo, received 60 split (dried) fish from *Šu-Erra*," 1198:1–4[57]

---

[56] Although *Šu-Erra*'s title is not specified, this text is included here in light of similar transactions nos. 1014 and 1013.

[57] Although *Šu-Erra*'s title is not specified, this text is included here in light of parallels to his activities in nos. 1014 and 1013.

šu-eš$_4$-tár

1. *Šu-Eštar*, the Fisherman

1.1 As a Witness

igi ***šu-eš$_4$-tár*** šu-ku$_6$, "witnessed by *Šu-Eštar*, the fisherman," 1058:11

igi ***šu-eš$_4$-tár*** šu-ku$_6$ min, "witnessed by *Šu-Eštar*, the 2nd fisherman," 1058:12

2. *Šu-Eštar*, the Household Servant from the Gang of *Irib*

[1 ***šu***]***-eš$_4$-tár*** ugula *i-r*[*i-ib*], "*Šu-Eštar*, supervised by *Irib*," 45:33

2.1 *Šu-Eštar* to Bring a Message to Udaga

1 ***šu-eš$_4$-***[***tár***] á-áĝ-ĝá ú-[dag-ga]^{ki}-[šè de$_6$-a], "*Šu-Eštar* [having brought] a message [to] U[dagà]," 54:31–32

2.2 Broken Context

1 ***šu-eš$_4$-tár*** [x-x-x]^{ki}-šè [x]-šè? de$_6$-a, "*Šu-Eštar* having brought (a message) to [GN] for? [x]," 53:57

3. *Šu-Eštar*, the Royal Messenger

3.1 Pruning *Simat-Ištaran*'s Garden

2 pa ^{ĝeš}kíĝ ^{ĝeš}kiri$_6$ *simat-^{d}ištaran* gar-ša-an-na^{ki} ***šu-eš$_4$-tár*** ^{lú}kíĝ-gi$_4$-[a-lugal] in-ku$_5$, "*Šu-Eštar*, the [royal] messenger, pruned 2 kíĝ trees (in) the garden of *Simat-Ištaran* at Garšana," 1354:1–6

4. *Šu-Eštar*, the Servant

4.1 Provisions: Barley

[n+]1.1.4.5 sìla ***šu-eš$_4$-tár*** [gur] (. . .) [šu+níĝin n+]5.4.1.8 sìla še gur lugal-ú-šim-e árad!-me-éš, "[n+]1 bushels (and) 105 liters of barley (for) *Šu-Eštar*, (and barley for) {others}, [in total: n+]5 bushels and 258 liters of barley (for) the servants; (supervised by) Lugal-ušime," 504:4, 7–10

5. *Šu-Eštar*, the Son of *Dada'a* and the Caretaker

5.1 Provisions and Caretaker

0.1.0. še 3 ma-na siki-gen 1 sìla ì-ĝeš 2 ^{gi}bisaĝ-gíd-da-tur sa-ḫa ***šu-eš$_4$-tár*** dumu *da-da-a* (. . .) mu udug kislaḫ saḫar zi-zi-dè-šè, "60 liters of barley, 3 minas of ordinary wool, 1 liter of sesame oil (and) 2 small, long canvas-lined baskets (for) *Šu-Eštar*, the son of *Dada'a*, (and) {others}, (provisions) for caretakers to move dirt (to/from) the lot," 1011:6–10, 15

6. *Šu-Eštar*, Title Unspecified

6.1 His Possessions

é-ki-ba-ĝar-ra *za-ki-ti* ù ***šu-eš$_4$-tár***, "the replacement house of *Zakiti* and *Šu-Eštar*" > *Household Index*

é-***šu-eš$_4$-tár***, "the house of *Šu-Eštar*" > *Household Index*

^{ĝeš}kiri$_6$ ***šu-eš$_4$-tár***, "the garden of *Šu-Eštar*" > *Garden Index*

6.1.1 Rations for his Servant

(. . .) še-ba árad ***šu-eš$_4$-tár*** [ki ^{d}]*adad-tillati*-ta ba-zi, "*Adad-tillati* disbursed {assorted commodities}, barley rations of the servant(s) of *Šu-Eštar*," 557:18–19

1½ ma-na siki-gen siki-ba árad ***šu-eš$_4$-tár*** g̃ìri *é-a-šar* dub-sar ki ^{d}*adad-tillati*-ta ba-zi, "Under the authority of *Ea-šar*, the scribe, *Adad-tillati* disbursed 1½ minas of ordinary wool, wool rations of the servant(s) of *Šu-Eštar*," 627:1–4

6.1.2 His Seal

1 udu-níta mu kù-^{d}⌜šára⌝-šè iti dirig sum-mu-dam kìšib ***šu-^{d}eš$_4$-tár***, "1 ram for bright Šara, to be provided in month 13, seal of *Šu-Eštar*," 1078:1–5

6.1.3 His Textiles

(. . .) túg-sa-gi$_4$-a ⌜mu⌝-DU *puzur$_4$-a-gu$_5$-um* ^{lú}ázlag túg-***šu-eš$_4$-tár***, "{assorted} finished textiles, the delivery of *Puzur-agum*, the fuller, are the textiles of *Šu-Eštar*," 823:4–7

6.2 A Message Brought to *Šu-Eštar*

1 *ḫi-lu-a* 1 é-ì-gára á-ág̃ ki ***šu-e[š$_4$-tár***-šè] d[e$_6$-a], "*Ḫilua* (and) E'igara having brought a message [to] the place of *Šu-Eštar*," 37:31–33

[1] é-ì-gára 1 *ḫi-lu-a* 1 á-ág̃ ki ***šu-eš$_4$-tár***-[šè] de$_6$-a, "E'igara (and) *Ḫilua* having brought a message [to] the place of *Šu-Eštar*," 38:37–39

1 *ḫi-lu-a* á-ág̃ ***šu-eš$_4$-tár*** ù-dag-ga^{ki}-šè de$_6$-a, "*Ḫilua* having brought a message to *Šu-Eštar* in Udaga," 43:'47, 45:24–25, 46:'42–'43, 47:55, 48:60–61

1 *ḫi-lu-a* á-ág̃ ki ***šu-eš$_4$-tár***-šè de$_6$-a, "*Ḫilua* having brought a message to the place of *Šu-Eštar*," 52:52–53, 53:55

šu-^{d}i-šum

Šu-Išum, the Runaway from the Gang of *Im-Erra*, the Ox-Herder

zàḫ [***šu***?]-***^{d}i-šum*** zàḫ ⌜*pù-zur$_8$*⌝-*šu-ba* [*i-me-èr-ra*] nu-bànda-gu$_4$ [ugula *ba-ba-ní*] šabra, "[*Šu*?]-*Išum* (and) *Puzur-šuba*, runaways (from the gang of) [*Im-Erra*], the ox-herder, (ox-drivers) [supervised by *Babani*], the majordomo," 198:'41–'44

šu-ì-lí-su

1. Deliveries

1.1 Reeds

[7]80 sa gi-zi gu-níg̃in 11-sa-ta ki ***šu-ì-lí***-ta ^{d}*adad-tillati* šu ba-ti g̃ìri *a-ḫu*-DU$_{10}$, "Under the authority of *Aḫu-ṭabu*, *Adad-tillati* received [7]80 bundles of fresh reeds, bales of 11 bundles each, from *Šu-ili*," 1335:1–6[58]

1.2 Textiles

5 ^{túg}níg̃-lám 3-kam-ús ki-lá-bi 9⅓ ma-na [n gín] túg ki-lá tag-a ki ***šu-ì-lí-su***-ta mu-DU kìšib amar-^{d}da-mu, "5 3rd-quality níg̃-lám textiles, their weight is 9⅓ minas [(and) n shekel(s)], delivery of weighed textiles having been woven from *Šu-ilissu*, seal of Amar-Damu," 582:1–6

[58] Although *šu-ì-lí* is likely a shortened form of *šu-ì-lí-su*, the identification is not certain.

šu-kà-kà

Šu-Kaka, Man from *Tulium*

1. As a Runaway

zàḫ *i-la-ak-*[*nu-id*] zàḫ ***šu-kà-***[***kà***] lú-*tu-lí-um*[ki-me-éš], "*Ilak-*[*nu''id*] (and) *Šu-Kaka*, runaways from *Tulium*," 378:1–3

2. Provisions: Bread when the House was Built

[2 sìla] ninda-ta [1 *i*]*-la-ak-nu-id* 1 ***šu-kà-kà*** lú-*tu-lí-um*ki (. . .) šà-gal ši[dim-e-n]e ⌜u$_4$⌝ [bàd egir] é-a dù-dè, "[2 liters] of bread each (for) *Ilak-nu''id* (and) *Šu-Kaka*, men from *Tulium*, (and for) {other workers}, food (for) builders when they were constructing [the (enclosure) wall behind] the house," 386:1–4, 29–30

šu-kab-tá

1. Deliveries

1.1 Mice and Birds, Receipt of *Adad-tillati*

2 ⌜kur⌝-gimušen 3 uz-tur 6 péš-g̃eš-gi *e-sí-tum* 15 péš-igi-gùn ⌜*lú*⌝*-ša-lim* iti u$_4$-13-ba-zal mu-DU ***šu-kab-tá*** d*adad-tillati* ì-dab$_5$, "At the end of the 13th day of the month *Adad-tillati* took in charge 2 geese, 3 ducklings (and) 6 mice (for) *Esitum* (and) 15 striped-eyed mice (for) *Lušallim*, the delivery of *Šu-Kabta*," 1127:1–10

4? péš-g̃eš-gi iti u$_4$-22-ba-zal mu-DU ***šu-kab-tá*** d*adad-tillati* ì-[dab$_5$ šà] G̃EŠ.KÚŠU⌜ki⌝, "*Adad-tillati* took in charge 4? mice at the end of the 22nd day of the month, the delivery of *Šu-Kabta* [in] G̃EŠ.KÚŠU," 1170:1–7

1.2 Semolina, Receipt of *Malik-bani*

0.4.1 dabin *ḫal-li-*[*a*] mu-DU ***šu-kab-t***[***á*** d*ma-lik-ba-ni*] šu ba-an-ti, "[*Malik-bani*] received 250 liters of semolina (for) *Ḫalli'a*, the delivery of *Šu-Kabta*," 464:1–6

1.3 Broken Context, Receipt of *Adad-tillati*

[. . .] mu-DU ***šu-kab-tá*** d*adad-tillati* ì-dab$_5$, "*Adad-tillati* took in charge [. . .], the delivery of *Šu-Kabta*," 1384:1–11

2. Expenditures under the Authority of *Šu-Kabta*

2.1 Expenditure of Craftsmen

2.1.1 Bringing Reeds to Garšana

(. . .) u$_4$-10-še gi-izi ù-dagki-ga-ta gar-ša-an-naki-šè [de$_6$]-a ⌜g̃iri⌝ d⌜*adad*⌝*-tillati* 2? ù *be-lí-ì-lí* zi-ga g̃iri ***šu-kab-ta***<<***-ta***>> ki d*adad-tillati*-ta ba-zi, "*Adad-tillati* disbursed {craftsmen} for 10 days having brought fuel reeds from Udaga to Garšana. (It was) the expenditure of *Šu-Kabta* under his authority (and) that of *Adad-tillati* and *Beli-ili*," 230:6–14

3 g̃uruš sag̃-tag 1 g̃uruš á-⅔ lúázlag-me-éš u$_4$-10-šè gi-izi ù-dagki-ga-ta [gar-š]a-an-naki-šè de$_6$-a g̃iri d*adad-tillati* šabra ù *be-lí-ì-lí* ugula má gíd zi-ga g̃iri ***šu-kab-ta*** ki *puzur$_4$-a-gu$_5$-um*-ta ba-zi, "*Puzur-agum* disbursed 3 full-time fullers (and) 1 fuller at ⅔ wages for 10 days having brought fuel reeds from Udaga to Garšana. (It was) the expenditure of *Šu-Kabta* under his authority (and) that of *Adad-tillati*, the majordomo, and *Beli-ili*, overseer of boat towers," 231:1–11

2.1.2 Bringing the Royal Messenger

1 g̃uruš ^{lú}ázlag u$_4$-25-šè *na-sìm* ^{lú}kíg̃-gi$_4$<-a>-lugal-ta lú te-te-dè in-da-g̃e$_{26}$-en zi-ga g̃ìri ***šu-kab-tá*** ki [PN]-ta [ba-z]i?, "[PN] disbursed 1 fuller for 25 days. *Nasim*, the royal messenger, went to bring the man (i.e. the fuller) from the king. (It was) the expenditure of *Šu-Kabta* under his authority," 222:1–8

2.1.3 Bringing a Sheep and Cattle Brand

1 g̃uruš ^{lú}ázlag nibru^{ki}-ta ^{d}*šu*-^{d}*suen*-DU$_{10}$^{ki}-šè ^{urudu}šim-da gu$_4$-udu de$_6$-a kaskal šu+níg̃in-na-bi u$_4$-11-kam u$_4$ ***šu-kab-tá*** é-dam-*zé-ra-ra* šu sum-mu-dè ì-g̃en-na-a *é-a-šar* maškim zi-ga g̃ìri ***šu-kab-tá*** ki *puzur$_4$-a-gu$_5$-um*-ta ba-zi, "*Puzur-agum* disbursed 1 fuller having brought a sheep and cattle brand from Nippur to *Šu-Suen-ṭabu*, a trip of 11 days in total, when *Šu-Kabta* went to the house of the wife of *Zerara* in order to take inventory. (It was) the expenditure of *Šu-Kabta* under his authority. *Ea-šar* was the deputy," 219:1–14

2.1.4 Canal Work

13 g̃uruš sag̃-tag 3 g̃uruš á-⅔-ta ^{lú}ázlag-me-éš u$_4$-2-šè i$_7$-mi-me-er gub-ba ba-al-la ^{d}šul-gi-*wa-qar* maškim šà nibru^{ki} zi-ga g̃ìri ***šu-kab-tá*** ki ^{d}šul-gi-*wa-qar*-ta ba-zi, "Šulgi-*waqar* disbursed 13 full-time fullers and 3 fullers at ⅔ wages employed for 2 days having dug the Mimer canal in Nippur. (It was) the expenditure of *Šu-Kabta* under his authority. Šulgi-*waqar* was the deputy," 227:1–10

2.1.5 For the Royal Banquet

2 g̃uruš ^{lú}ázlag u$_4$-1-šè zi-ga kaš-dé-a lugal šà á-<ki->ti gub-ba *nu-úr*-^{d}*adad* maškim zi-ga g̃ìri ***šu-kab-ta*** ki *puzur$_4$-a-gu$_5$-um*-ta ba-zi, "*Puzur-agum* disbursed 2 fullers employed for 1 day, expended (for) the royal banquet of the Akiti-festival. (It was) the expenditure of *Šu-Kabta* under his authority. *Nur-Adad* was the deputy," 221:1–7

2.1.6 Towing Boats

3 g̃uruš ^{lú}ázlag u$_4$-2½-šè nibru^{ki}-ta é-^{d}*šu*-^{d}*suen*-šè má *na-wi-ir-ilum* íb-gíd g̃ìri g̃ìri-^{d}ba-ú-ì-dab$_5$ zi-ga g̃ìri ***šu-kab-tá*** ki *puzur$_4$-a-gu$_5$-um*-ta ba-zi, "*Puzur-agum* disbursed 3 fullers for 2½ days. They towed the boat of *Nawir-ilum* from Nippur to *Bit-Šu-Suen*. (It was) the expenditure of *Šu-Kabta* under his authority (and) that of G̃iri-Ba'u-idab," 220:1–11

2.1.7 Released on the Day of the Wool Rations

2 géme sag̃-dub-ba 1 géme á-⅔ géme gu-me-éš u$_4$-1-šè u$_4$ siki-ba-ka [šu bar]-ra *é-a-šar* maškim zi-ga g̃ìri ***šu-kab-ta*** ki ^{d}*adad-tillati*-ta ba-zi, "*Adad-tillati* disbursed 2 full-time female spinners (and) 1 female spinner at ⅔ wages released for 1 day on the day of the wool rations. (It was) the expenditure of *Šu-Kabta* under his authority. *Ea-šar* was the deputy," 234:1–9

2.2 Expenditure of Offerings and Provisions

2.2.1 For *Agati*, his Sister

0.0.3. ^{geš}ḫašḫur-duru$_5$ *a-ga-ti* nin$_9$ *šu-kab-tá* zi-ga g̃ìri ***šu-kab-tá***, "30 liters of fresh apples (for) *Agati*, the sister of *Šu-Kabta*. (It was) the expenditure of *Šu-Kabta* under his authority," 415:1–4

2.2.2 For Šara

(. . .) ^{d}šára ezem-níĝ-ab-e *še-da* sagi maškim zi-ga ĝìri ***šu-kab-tá*** ki ^{d}*adad-tillati*-ta ba-zi, "*Adad-tillati* disbursed {sheep and assorted grains} (for) Šara (during) the níĝ-ab-e festival. (It was) the expenditure of *Šu-Kabta* under his authority. *Šeda*, the cupbearer, was the deputy," 1001:6–12

2.3 Expenditures of Rations, Wages, and Allotments

2.3.1 For Hired Workers

0.4.0. še á lú-ḫuĝ-ĝá a bala-e-dè gub-ba ^{ĝeš}kiri$_6$ šà gar-š[a-an-na]^{ki} ù ^{ĝeš}kiri$_6$ šà zabala$_4$^{ki} ^{d}*ma-lik-ba-ni* maškim zi-ga ⸢ĝìri⸣ ***šu-kab-tá*** ki ^{d}*adad-tillati*-ta ba-zi, "*Adad-tillati* disbursed 240 liters of barley, wages of hired workers employed to irrigate the gardens in Garšana and Zabala. (It was) the expenditure of *Šu-Kabta* under his authority. *Malik-bani* was the deputy," 390:1–8

2.3.2 For Sailors

2.3.2.1 Bringing Barley to Garšana

0.2.3. ⸢še⸣ á má ḫuĝ-ĝá 4[0]-gur-kam ù má-laḫ$_5$-bi á 0.0.3.-ta 2 ĝuruš ad-kub$_4$ 1½ ĝuruš báḫar u$_4$-5-šè [še] du$_6$-saḫar-ra^{ki}-ta gar-ša-an-na^{ki}-šè de$_6$-a zi-ga ĝìri ***šu-kab-ta*** ki ^{d}*adad-tillati*-ta ba-zi, "*Adad-tillati* disbursed 150 liters of barley, wages of the hired 40-bushel boat and its sailors, wages of 30 liters each, (and) 2 reed craftsmen (and) 1½ potters (for) 5 days having brought [barley] from Du-saḫara to Garšana. (It was) the expenditure of *Šu-Kabta* under his authority," 233:1–10

[1.1.4.] še gur [á má-ḫuĝ]-ĝá má 50-gur-ta 2-kam ù má-laḫ$_5$-bi [0].1.2.5 sìla-ta [á] 0.0.2.5 sìla-ta á má-ḫuĝ-ĝá má 40-gur-ta 2-kam ù má-laḫ$_5$-bi á 0.0.2.-ta [u$_4$]-8-šè ⸢še⸣ ù-dag-ga^{ki}-ta [gar-ša]-an-na^{ki}-šè de$_6$-a [ĝìri] ^{d}*adad-tillati* šabra [ù?] *be-lí-ì-lí* ugula-má gíd [zi-g]a ĝìri ***šu-kab-tá*** [ki ^{d}]*adad-tillati*-ta [ba]-zi, "[1] bushel (and) [100 liters] of barley, [wages] (for) each of 2 hired 50-bushel boats and their sailors, 85 liters each; [wages] of 25 liters each, wages (for) each of 2 hired 40-bushel boats and their sailors, 20 liters each; (wages for sailors) for 8 days having brought barley from Udaga to Garšana. (It was) the expenditure of *Šu-Kabta* under his authority (and) that of *Adad-tillati*, the majordomo, [and] *Beli-ili*, overseer of boat towers," 414:1–16

0.4.0. še á má ḫuĝ-ĝá [40-gur-kam] ù má-la[ḫ$_5$-bi] á 0.1.2.-ta u$_4$-3-šè še *dar-ra-um*^{ki}-⸢ta⸣ gar-ša-an-na^{ki}-[šè] de$_6$-[a] zi-ga ĝìri ***šu-*[*kab-ta*]** ki ^{d}*adad-tilla*[*ti*-ta] ba-[zi], "*Adad-tillati* disbursed 40 liters of barley, wages of the hired [40-bushel] boat and [its] sailors, wages of 80 liters each for 3 days (for sailors) having brought barley from *Darra'um* [to] Garšana. (It was) the expenditure of *Šu-Kabta* under his authority," 462:1–8

2.3.2.2 Bringing Straw to the Bank of the Canal

2.2.0. še gur á má ḫuĝ-ĝá má-90-gur-kam á 0.0.4-ta ù má-laḫ$_5$-bi u$_4$-18-šè in-u é-ù-ri-a<ki>-ta gú i$_7$-da lá-a zi-ga ĝìri ***šu-kab-ta*** ki ^{d}*adad-tillati*-ta ba-zi, "*Adad-tillati* disbursed 2 bushels (and) 120 liters of barley, wages of the hired 90-bushel boats and its sailors, wages of 40 liters each for 18 days (for sailors) having transported straw from E-uria to the bank of the canal. (It was) the expenditure of *Šu-Kabta* under his authority," 413:1–9

2.4 Expenditure of Textiles

1 ^{túg}*ḫa-bu-um* 4-kam-ús *šu-^{d}ma-mi-tum* ì-du$_8$ zi-ga g̃ìri ***šu-kab-ta*** [ki *^{d}adad-til*]*lati*-[ta ba-zi], "*Adad-tillati* [disbursed] 1 4th-quality *ḫabum* textile (for) *Šu-Mamitum*, the gate-keeper. (It was) the expenditure of *Šu-Kabta* under his authority," 607:1–5

1 túg-^{d}*al-la-tum*-gùn-a ù zi-in-bi ki-lá-bi 9 ma-[na] 12 gín *a-ku$_8$-a-nu-ri nu-úr-^{d}adad* maškim zi-ga g̃ìri ***šu-kab-ta* ki *aš-tá-qar*-ta ba-zi, "*Aštaqqar* disbursed 1 colored textile of *Allatum* and its zi-in weighing 9 minas (and) 12 shekels (for) *Akua-nuri*. (It was) the expenditure of *Šu-Kabta* under his authority. *Nur-Adad* was the deputy," 584:1–7

3. Expenditures of *Šu-Kabta* under Other Authority

3.1 Expenditure of Craftsmen

3.1.1 Bringing Barley

9 g̃uruš sag̃-tag 1 g̃uruš á-⅔ 1 g̃uruš á-⅓ ^{lú}ázlag-me-éš u$_4$-1-šè še é-kab-ba^{ki} ⸢karkar⸣^{ki}-ta ⸢gar-ša-an⸣-n[a^{ki}]-šè de$_6$-a *puzur$_4$-^{d}*[nin-kar-ak] dub-sar maškim zi-ga ***šu-kab-tá*** ki *^{d}adad-tillati*-ta ba-zi, "*Adad-tillati* disbursed 9 full-time fullers, 1 fuller at ⅔ wages, (and) 1 fuller at ⅓ wages for 1 day having brought barley from E-kabba (and) Karkar to Garšana. (It was) the expenditure of *Šu-Kabta*. *Puzur*-Ninkarak, the scribe, was the deputy," 237:1–12

8 g̃uruš sag̃-tag 2 g̃uruš á-⅔-ta 4 g̃uruš á-½-ta ^{lú}ázlag-me-éš [u$_4$]-1-šè ⸢še⸣ ^{d}*šu-^{d}suen*-am-ma-ar^{ki}-ta de$_6$-a íb-[ga$_6$] g̃ìri *en-nam-^{d}m*[*a-lik* z]i-ga ***š*[*u-kab-tá*]** ki *puzur$_4$-a-*[*gu$_5$*-*um*-ta ba]-zi, "Under the authority of *Ennam-Malik*, *Puzur-agum* disbursed 8 full-time fullers, 2 fullers at ⅔ wages, (and) 4 fullers at ½ wages for 1 day. They [carried] barley brought from *Šu-Suen*-ammara. (It was) the expenditure of *Šu-Kabta*," 248:1–10

3 géme g̃eš-ì-sur-sur u$_4$-1-šè še ^{d}*šu-^{d}suen*-am-ma-ar^{ki}-ta de$_6$-a íb-ga$_6$ g̃ìri *en-nam-*$^{[d]}$*ma-lik* šu-i zi-ga ***šu-kab-tá*** ki *^{d}adad-tillati*-ta ba-zi, "Under the authority of *Ennam-Malik*, the barber, *Adad-tillati* disbursed 3 female sesame pressers for 1 day. They carried barley brought from *Šu-Suen*-ammara. (It was) the expenditure of *Šu-Kabta*," 249:1–7

3.1.2 Crushing Malt

66 géme uš-bar u$_4$-1-šè munu$_4$ nag̃$_4$-g̃á-dè gub-ba *èr-ra-ba-ni* maškim zi-[ga ***šu-k*]*ab-tá*** k[i *aš-tá-qar*-t]a [ba]-zi, "*Aštaqqar* disbursed 66 female weavers employed for 1 day to crush malt. (It was) the expenditure of *Šu-Kabta*. *Erra-bani* was the deputy," 245:1–6

3.1.3 Female Weavers and Textiles

70 géme uš-bar u$_4$-1-šè [n] ^{túg}[níg̃-lá]m-ús [n-ka]m [n] túg-guz-za-ús [n]-kam t[úg?-ba]r?-r[a-n]i? *ḫa-um na-wi-ir-ilum* zi-ga ***šu-kab-tá* ki *aš-tá-qar*-ta ba-zi, "*Aštaqqar* disbursed 70 female weavers for 1 day (and) [n nth]-quality níg̃-lam textile(s) (and) [n] nth-quality tufted textile(s), *ḫa'um* textiles of *Nawir-ilum*. (It was) the expenditure of *Šu-Kabta*," 650:1–8

3.1.4 Making Bread

60 ninda-gúg-zì-KAL 3 sìla ni[nda-š]u-ra-gen lú-*i-zi-in-èr-ra*^{ki} ke$_4$-dè u$_4$ dabin *i-zi-in-*[*èr-ra*]^{ki}-ta gar-ša-an-na^{ki}-šè de$_6$-a *é-a-šar* dub-sar PA.[KAŠ$_4$] zi-ga ***šu-kab-*⸢*tá*⸣** ki *^{d}adad-tillati*-⸢ta⸣ ba-zi, "*Adad-tillati* disbursed the man from *Izin-Erra* to make 60 cakes of KAL-flour (and) 3 liters of ordinary half-(loaf) bread, when semolina was

being brought from *Izin-Erra* to Garšana. (It was) the expenditure of *Šu-Kabta. Ea-šar*, the scribe, was the deputy," 495:1–9

3.1.5 Mourning *Nawir-ilum*

11 g̃uruš sa[g̃-tag] 2 g̃uruš á-⅔-ta 4 g̃uruš á-½-ta 1 g̃uruš á-⅓<-ta> ^{lú}ázlag-me-éš u$_4$-1-šè gaba sàg-gé-dè [gub-ba] u$_4$ *na-wi-ir-[ilum* ba-úš-a] *é-a-šar* maškim zi-ga ***šu-kab-⸢tá⸣*** ki *puzur$_4$-a-gu$_5$-um-*⸢ta⸣ ba-zi, "*Puzur-agum* disbursed 11 full-time fullers, 2 fullers at ⅔ wages, 4 fullers at ½ wages (and) 1 fuller at ⅓ wages [employed] for 1 day to beat (their) breasts when *Nawir-ilum* [died]. (It was) the expenditure of *Šu-Kabta. Ea-šar* was the deputy," 250:1–12

(. . .) ⸢u$_4$⸣-1-šè gaba sàg-dè gub-ba u$_4$ dig̃ir-re gaba *na-wi-ir-ilum* ba-a-g̃ar-ra *é-a-šar* dub-sar maškim zi-ga ***šu-kab-tá*** [ki] ^{d}*adad-tillati*-ta ba-zi, "*Adad-tillati* disbursed {craftsmen} for 1 day employed to beat (their) breasts when the god made the breast of *Nawir-ilum* subside (i.e. when he died). (It was) the expenditure of *Šu-Kabta. Ea-šar*, the scribe, was the deputy," 251:8–13

3.1.6 Released for the Priest

(. . .) u$_4$-15-šè ⸢ki⸣ en-šè šu bar-ra zi-ga [***šu***]***-kab-tá*** ki ^{d}*adad-tillati*-ta ba-zi, "*Adad-tillati* disbursed {craftsmen}, released for 15 days for the priest. (It was) the expenditure of *Šu-Kabta*," 225:6–11

3.1.7 Towing Boats

[. . . x] g̃uruš á-[n-ta] ^{lú}ázlag-me-[éš] u$_4$-1-[šè] má-nin-zi-šà-g̃ál gar-ša-an-na^{ki}-ta G̃EŠ.KÚŠU^{ki}-šè in-gíd-ša-a zi-ga ***šu-kab-tá*** ki ^{d}*adad-tillati*-[ta] ba-zi, "*Adad-tillati* disbursed [. . .] (and) [n] fuller(s) at [n] wages [for] 1 day. They towed the boat of Nin-zišag̃al from Garšana to G̃EŠ.KÚŠU. (It was) the expenditure of *Šu-Kabta*," 238:1–10

3.1.8 Traveling: between Garšana and Nippur

2 g̃uruš s[ag̃-tag] 1 g̃uruš á-[⅔] u$_4$-1½-[šè] gar-ša-an-[na^{ki}-ta] nibru^{ki}-šè g̃[en-na] 2 g̃uruš [sag̃-tag] 1 [g̃uruš á-⅔] u$_4$-[n-šè] nibru^{ki}-[ta GN-šè g̃en-na] 2 g̃uruš sag̃-[tag] 1 g̃uruš á-⅔ u$_4$-1-šè gar-ša-an-na^{ki}-šè? [?] zi-ga [***šu-kab-tá***] ki *puzur$_4$-a-gu$_5$-um-*[ta ba-zi], "*Puzur-agum* disbursed 2 full-time workmen (and) 1 workman at [⅔] wages [for] 1½ days having gone [from] Garšana to Nippur, 2 [full-time] workmen (and) 1 [workman at ⅔ wages for n] day(s) [having gone from] Nippur [to GN] (and) 2 full-time workmen (and) 1 workman at ⅔ wages for 1 day (having gone?) to? Garšana. (It was) the expenditure of [*Šu-Kabta*]," 223:1–17

3.2 Expenditure of Offerings

3.2.1 Surplus of the Regular Offerings of the House of the Steward

(. . .) dirig sá-du$_{11}$-é-agrig-šè *an-ta-lú* agrig maškim zi-ga ***šu-kab-tá*** ki ^{d}*adad-tillati*-ta ba-zi, "*Adad-tillati* disbursed {assorted comestibles}, surplus of the regular offerings for the house of the steward. (It was) the expenditure of *Šu-Kabta. Antalu*, the steward, was the deputy," 493:19–23, 494:17–21

0.0.2. [. . .] 0.1.0. ninda dabin dirig sá-du$_{11}$-é-agrig-[šè] *é-a-šar* dub-[sar] PA.K[AŠ$_4$ šà gar]-ša-an-na^{ki} ⸢zi⸣-ga ***šu-kab-tá*** ⸢ki⸣ ^{d}*adad-tillati*-ta ba-zi, "*Adad-tillati* disbursed 20 liters [. . .] (and) 60 liters of semolina bread, surplus of the regular offerings [for] the house of the steward. (It was) the expenditure of *Šu-Kabta. Ea-šar*, the scribe, was the deputy [in] Garšana," 501:1–9

3.2.2 (Ceremonial) Offerings

(. . .) 12 ^{dug}b[a-x] ˹mu˺ diĝir-re-e-ne-šè gaz-dè (. . .) 0.0.1. zú-lum eša ba-ḫi ˹sízkur˺-didli-šè (. . .) zi-ga ***šu-kab-tá*** ki ^{d}*adad-tillati*-ta ba-zi, "*Adad-tillati* disbursed {assorted commodities}, 12 [x]-vessels to be broken for the gods, 10 liters of dates mixed (with) fine flour for various (ceremonial) offerings, (and) {reeds for baking bread, cooking soup and fish}. (It was) the expenditure of *Šu-Kabta*," 1013:6–7, 9–10, 23–25

(. . .) ˹sízkur˺-didli-šè (. . .) zi-ga ***šu-kab-˹tá˺*** [ki ^{d}*a*]*dad-tillati*-ta [ba]-zi, "*Adad-tillati* disbursed {assorted commodities} for various (ceremonial) offerings, (and) {reeds for baking bread, cooking soup and fish}. (It was) the expenditure of *Šu-Kabta*," 1014:'2–'3, '16–'19

★★(. . .) sízkur diĝir-re-[e?]-ne [. . . x N]IM?^{ki} ur-é-an-na dub-sar maškim zi-ga ***šu-kab-tá*** ki ^{d}*adad-tillati*-ta ba-zi, "*Adad-tillati* disbursed {assorted grains and dates}, (ceremonial) offerings of the gods, [. . .El]am? (It was) the expenditure of *Šu-Kabta*. Ur-Eana, the scribe, was the deputy," 1017:6–10

3.2.3 For the Gods

★★(. . .) ^{d}inana-zabala$_4$$^{[ki]}$ (. . .) ^{d}nin-^{d}si$_4$-an-na šà [é]-˹gal˺ iti u$_4$-6-ba-zal (. . .) ki-a-nag-*da-da*-šè (. . .) [ĝuruš?] SI ^{ĝeš}sìg-ga pad-dirig [?] ĝír-su^{ki} a-a-ba-[šè? . . .] níĝ-^{d}b[a-ú-šè?] (. . .) al-[. . .] ma-x [. . .] x(?) [. . . mašk]im zi-ga [***šu-kab***]-***tá*** ki ^{d}*adad-tillati*-ta ba-zi, "*Adad-tillati* disbursed {assorted commodities} (for) Inana of Zabala, (for) Nin-Siana in the palace at the end of the 6th day of the month, for the funerary libation of *Dada*, [for?] the (?) [workmen?], (?) [. . . for?] Niĝ-Ba'u (and) (?) [for?] (?). (It was) the expenditure of *Šu-Kabta*. [PN] was the deputy," 970:5, 8–9, 11, 15–16, 19–23

0.0.2. zì-KAL 0.0.1. zì-gu-ús ninda-gur$_4$-ra-šè ^{d}inana-zabala$_4$^{ki} ama *tá-ḫi-iš-a-tal an-ta-lú* agrig maškim zi-ga ***šu-kab-tá*** ki ^{d}*adad-tillati*-ta ba-zi (šà zabala$_4$^{ki}), "*Adad-tillati* disbursed 20 liters of KAL-flour (and) 10 liters of 2nd-quality gu-flour for thick bread (for) Inana of Zabala (and) the mother of *Taḫis-atal*. (It was) the expenditure of *Šu-Kabta* (in Zabala). *Antalu*, the steward, was the deputy," 1015:1–8, 1018:1–11

3.2.4 For Flour Heaps

3.2.4.1 When *Šu-Kabta* Traveled to and from ĜEŠ.KÚŠU

0.0.4.4 sìla dabin 0.0.2.8 sìla eša 0.0.1. zú-lum eša {erased} ba-ḫi zì-dub-dub-didli-šè u$_4$ ***šu-kab-ta*** ĜEŠ.KÚŠU^{ki}-šè du-ni u$_4$ ***šu-kab-ta*** ĜEŠ.KÚŠU^{ki}-ta du-ni ur-^{d}nin-si$_4$-an-na sagi maškim zi-ga ***šu-kab-ta*** ki ^{d}*adad-tillati* ba-zi, "*Adad-tillati* disbursed 44 liters of semolina, 28 liters of fine flour and 10 liters of dates. They were mixed (with) fine flour for various small flour heaps when *Šu-Kabta* went to ĜEŠ.KÚŠU (and) when *Šu-Kabta* came from ĜEŠ.KÚŠU. (It was) the expenditure of *Šu-Kabta*. Ur-Nin-Siana, the cupbearer, was the deputy," 488:8–26

3.2.4.2 For Flour Heaps and the Dream Interpreter

(. . .) ˹zi˺-ga ***šu-kab-˹tá˺*** ki ^{d}*adad-tillati*-ta ba-zi, "*Adad-tillati* disbursed {assorted comestibles for various small heaps of flour (and) for the dream interpreters on the 7th and 8th days}. (It was) the expenditure of *Šu-Kabta*," 484:20–22

3.3 Rations, Wages, and Allotments

3.3.1 For Boat Towers

(. . .) níĝ-dab$_5$ ĝuruš má gíd-e-ne u$_4$ al-tar-ra gub-ba šà gar-ša-an-na[ki] zi-ga ***šu-kab-ta*** ki [d]*adad-tillati*-ta ba-⸢zi⸣, "*Adad-tillati* disbursed {assorted commodities}, requisitions of the boat towers when they were employed for construction in Garšana. (It was) the expenditure of *Šu-Kabta*," 442:19–22

(. . .) [má . . . gar-ša-an-na[ki]-ta] nibru[ki]-[šè] in-gíd-s[a-a] *é-a-šar* d[ub-sar PA].KAŠ$_4$ šà nibru[[ki]] zi-ga ***šu-kab-tá*** ki [d]*adad-tillati*-ta ba-zi, "*Adad-tillati* disbursed {bread for men from various cities} who towed [a boat . . . from Garšana to] Nippur. (It was) the expenditure of *Šu-Kabta* in Nippur. *Ea-šar*, the scribe, was the deputy," 463:5–13

3.3.2 For Builders

1 udu-[niga] iti u$_4$-10-ba-zal [lú-níĝ-[d]]ba-ú šidim *é-a-šar* maškim zi-ga ***šu-kab-tá*** ki [d]*adad-tillati*-ta ba-zi, "*Adad-tillati* disbursed 1 [fattened] sheep at the end of the 10th day of the month (for) the builder from Niĝ-Ba'u. (It was) the expenditure of *Šu-Kabta*. *Ea-šar* was the deputy," 420:1–6

3.3.3 For Builders and Hired Workers

(. . .) mu šidim-e-ne-šè (. . .) mu lú-[ḫu]ĝ-ĝá-e-ne-šè u$_4$ igi ***šu-kab-tá*** ninda in-gu$_7$-ša-a *é-a-šar* dub-sar maškim zi-ga ***šu-kab-tá*** ki [d]*adad-tillati*-ta ba-zi, "*Adad-tillati* disbursed {assorted comestibles} for the builders (and) {flour, groats and reeds with which bread was baked and soup was cooked} for the hired laborers when they ate bread before *Šu-Kabta*. (It was) the expenditure of *Šu-Kabta*. *Ea-šar*, the scribe, was the deputy," 479:9, 14–20

(. . .) mu šidim ù lú-ḫuĝ-ĝ[á-šè] *é-a-šar* maškim d[ub-sar] zi-ga ***šu-kab-[ta]*** ki [d]*adad-tillati*-ta [ba-zi], "*Adad-tillati* disbursed {assorted comestibles} [for] the builders and hired workers. (It was) the expenditure of *Šu-Kabta*. *Ea-šar*, the scribe, was the deputy," 483:24–27

(. . .) lú-é-ki-ba-ĝar-ra šidim ugula lú-ḫuĝ-[ĝá . . .]-ka é-ka gub-ba [. . .]-e-ne *é-a-šar* dub-sar maškim zi-ga ***šu-kab-tá*** ki [d]*adad-tillati*-ta ba-zi, "*Adad-tillati* disbursed {assorted breads} for the man of the replacement house, the builder, the overseer of the hired workers, employed in the [. . .] of the house. [. . .] (It was) the expenditure of *Šu-Kabta*. *Ea-šar*, the scribe, was the deputy," 485:5–9

3.3.4 For Household Servants

5.0.1. [še gur] ninda-ba géme-⸢árad⸣ é-[a] zi-ga ***šu-[kab-ta]*** ki [d]*adad-[tillati*-ta] b[a-zi], "*Adad-tillati* disbursed 5 bushels (and) 10 liters of [barley], bread rations of the female and male household servants. (It was) the expenditure of *Šu-Kabta*," 468:1–5

3.3.5 For Hired Workers

0.4.0. ninda-dabin ù zì-šà-gen íb-ta-ḫi 0.1.3.2 sìla ninda-gur$_4$-ra zì-KAL 0.0.1. níĝ-àr-ra-sig$_5$ [uru]^{du}šen-šè lú-ḫuĝ-ĝá iri[ki]-didli-ke$_4$-ne íb-gu$_7$ *é-a-šar* dub-sar m[aškim z]i-ga ***šu-kab-tá*** [ki] [d]*adad-tillati*-ta ⸢ba⸣-zi, "*Adad-tillati* disbursed 240 liters of bread—(the bread) was mixed from semolina and ordinary šà-flour—92 liters of thick bread of KAL-flour (and) 10 liters of fine groats for the (soup) cauldron. The hired workers from various cities ate (the food). (It was) the expenditure of *Šu-Kabta*. *Ea-šar*, the scribe, was the deputy," 490:1–8

3.3.6 For *Lušallim*

1 udu-niga iti u_4-5-ba-zal *lú-ša-lim* nu-bànda *é-a-šar* dub-sar maškim zi-ga ***šu-kab-tá*** ki ^{d}*adad-*[*tillati*-t]a ba-zi, "*Adad-tillati* disbursed 1 fattened sheep at the end of the 5th day of the month (for) *Lušallim*, the overseer. (It was) the expenditure of *Šu-Kabta*. *Ea-šar*, the scribe, was the deputy," 1159:1–7

3.3.7 For the Servants of the Sugal-maḫ

(. . .) árad-géme $sugal_7$-maḫ g̃ír-su^{ki}-šè du-ni zi-ga ***šu-kab-tá*** ki ^{d}*adad-tillati*-ta, "*Adad-tillati* disbursed {sheep, bread, and beer} when the male and female servants of the sugal-maḫ came to G̃irsu. (It was) the expenditure of *Šu-Kabta*," 449:9–12

3.3.8 For Sick Workers

½ sìla ì-[g̃eš] *tu-ku-lí* šidim u_4 dú-ra i-[me-a] ^{d}*ma-lik-ba-ni* ⌜maškim⌝ ½ sìla ì-g̃eš *ḫi-li* má gíd u_4 du_{10} bar-ra-ni in-na-gig-ga *be-lí-ì-lí* maškim šà gar-ša-an-na^{ki} zi-ga ***šu-kab-tá*** ki ^{d}*adad-tillati*-ta ba-zi, "*Adad-tillati* disbursed ½ liter of sesame oil (for) *Tukulli*, the builder, when he was sick. *Malik-bani* was the deputy. He (also) disbursed ½ liter of sesame oil for *Ḫili*, the boat tower, when his 'outer knee' was hurting him. *Beli-ili* was the deputy. (These were) the expenditures of *Šu-Kabta* in Garšana," 444:1–10

10 gín ì-g̃eš *da-da-a* $un-ga_6$ u_4 du_{10} bar-ra-ni in-na-gig-ga 10 gín ì-g̃eš-ta ^{d}šára-sá-$g̃u_{10}$ 1 *bu-za-du-a* géme kíkken-me-éš u_4 dú-ra i-me é-gal!-šè *puzur*$_4$-^{d}nin-kar-ak dub-sar maškim zi-ga ***šu-kab-tá*** ki ^{d}*adad-tillati*-ta ⌜ba⌝-zi, "*Adad-tillati* disbursed 10 shekels of sesame oil (for) *Dada'a*, the porter, when his 'outer knee' was hurting him, (and) 10 shekels of sesame oil each (for) Šara-sag̃u (and) *Buzadua*, female millers, when they were sick at the palace. (It was) the expenditure of *Šu-Kabta*. *Puzur*-Ninkarak, the scribe, was the deputy," 466:1–10

3.3.9 For Various Recipients

(. . .) ^{d}gu-la (. . .) ⌜sum⌝-mu-da-éš ⌜mu⌝ éren-na-šè (. . .) ⌜*al*⌝*-la-ša-ru-um* (. . .) *um-mi-kab-tá* (. . .) *ma-la-ti* (. . .) *tak-ri-ib-tum* iri^{ki} ne-ne-de_4 (. . .) zi-ga ***šu-kab-tá*** ki ^{d}*adad-tillati*-ta ba-zi šà G̃EŠ.KÚŠU^{ki}, "*Adad-tillati* disbursed {assorted commodities} (for) Gula, to be given to the workers, (for) *Allašarrum*, *Ummi-Kabta*, (and) *Malati* (and) for the (performance of) a *takribtum* (involving) circling around the city. (It was) the expenditure of *Šu-Kabta* in G̃EŠ.KUŠU," 1016:3, 6–7, 11, 14, 16, 21, 23–26

3.4 Other Expenditures

3.4.1 Textiles

[. . .^{túg} . . .]-PI-[. . .] zi-ga ***šu-ka*[*b-tá*]** ki ^{d}*adad-tillati*-ta ba-zi, "*Adad-tillati* disbursed [textile(s)]. (It was) the expenditure of *Šu-Kabta*," 682:1–5

3.4.2 Groats for the Tureen

(. . .) ^{dug}útul-šè u_4-2-kam (. . .) ^{dug}útul-šè u_4-3-kam {erasure}-šè *an-ta-lú* agrig maškim zi-ga ***šu-kab-tá*** ki ^{d}*adad-tillati*-ta ba-zi, "*Adad-tillati* disbursed {flour and other grains} for the tureen on the 2nd and 3rd days. (It was) the expenditure of *Šu-Kabta*. *Antalu*, the steward, was the deputy," 1167:8–9, 17–21

3.4.3 Reeds for Cooking Fish

80 sa gi-izi ku$_6$ šé-g̃e$_6$-dè *šu-èr-ra* maškim šà G̃EŠ.KÚŠU^{ki} zi-ga ***šu-kab***!(DA)***-tá*** ki ^{d}*adad-tillati*-ta ba-zi, "*Adad-tillati* disbursed 80 bundles of fuel reeds to cook fish. It was the expenditure of *Šu-Kabta* in G̃EŠ.KÚŠU. *Šu-erra* was the deputy," 1321:1–8

4. Activities of *Šu-Kabta*

4.1 Order of Additional Rations

0.3.0. še šà-gu$_4$-me-éš dirig še-ba-ne-ne mu zì nu-g̃ál-la-šè ba-na-ḫa-la ***šu-kab-tá*** bí-in-dug$_4$ ⸢g̃iri⸣-né-ì-dab$_5$ ra-gaba maškim u$_4$ é-e i[m sumur ba-aka] ⸢g̃iri⸣-né-ì-dab$_5$ dub-sar ki ^{d}*adad-tillati*-ta ba-zi, "Under the authority of *Ea-šar*, the scribe, *Adad-tillati* disbursed 180 liters of barley for the ox-drivers when the house was plastered. *Šu-Kabta* had ordered that additional barley rations were to be divided for them because there was no flour. G̃irine-idab, the courier, was the deputy," 481:1–9

5. Allotments for *Šu-Kabta*

5.1 Textiles

n ^{túg}níg̃-lám-AB ***šu-kab-ta***, "n níg̃-lám-AB textile(s) of *Šu-Kabta*," 569:4, 578:5, 579:5, 676:1, 827:2

n ^{túg}šà-ga-dù-níg̃-lám ***šu-kab-ta***$_{(2)}$, "n níg̃-lám belt(s) of *Šu-Kabta*," 579:13, 590:3, 591:7, 608:3, 636:3, 647:1, 658:1, 676:2, 690:1, 827:3, 829:'2

1 túg-guz-za ***šu-kab-tá***, "1 tufted textile of *Šu-Kabta*," 586:1, 587:1, 588:2, 723:1

1 ^{túg}bar-dul$_5$-⸢ús⸣ ***šu-kab-ta***, "1 2nd-quality bar-dul$_5$ textile of *Šu-Kabta*," 588:3

1 ^{túg}bar-dul$_5$-AB ***šu-kab-tá***, "1 bar-dul$_5$-AB textile of *Šu-Kabta*," 591:5, 677:1

1 ^{túg}níg̃-lám ***šu-kab-tá***, "1 níg̃-lám textile of *Šu-Kabta*," 591:6

1 ^{túg}bar-dul$_5$ ***šu-kab-ta***, "1 bar-dul$_5$ textile of *Šu-Kabta*," 608:2, 654:1

5.2 Regular Offerings

šu+níg̃in 1 udu-⸢niga⸣ šu+níg̃in 1 udu-ú šu+níg̃in 1 máš-gal-niga šu+níg̃in 2 [. . .] šu+níg̃in 3 lulim?-dar?-[x] šu+níg̃in 1 šáḫ-zé-da sá-du$_{11}$-ta?-***šu-kab-tá*** ki ^{d}*adad-tillati*-ta ba-zi, "*Adad-tillati* disbursed a total of 1 fattened sheep, 1 range-fed sheep, 1 fattened billy-goat, 2 [. . .], 3 speckled stags? (and) 1 piglet from? the regular offerings of *Šu-Kabta*," 983:18–26

5.3 A Sheep

[n+]1 udu-sag̃ ***šu-kab-tá***, "[n+]1 lead sheep of *Šu-Kabta*," 484:8

5.4 Wool

½ ma-[na] 5 gín siki ^{túg}bar-dul$_5$ ***šu-kab-ta***, "½ mina (and) 5 shekels of wool (for) a bar-dul$_5$ textile of *Šu-Kabta*," 585:5

n ma-na siki ^{túg}níg̃-lám ***šu-kab-tá***, "n mina(s) of wool (for) a níg̃-lám textile of *Šu-Kabta*," 585:6, 619:2, 620:4, 625:6, 667:6

n ma-na siki túg-guz-za ***šu-kab-tá***, "n mina(s) of wool (for) a tufted textile of *Šu-Kabta*," 585:7, 625:7, 667:7

1 ma-na siki-za-rí-in túg-lugal-gen *simat-*^{d}*ištaran* ***šu-kab-tá*** mug-bi ⅓ ma-na 4 gín-ta NE-gu$_7$-bi 6 gín-ta, "1 mina of coarsely cleaned wool material (for) textiles of royal to ordinary quality of *Simat-Ištaran* (and) *Šu-Kabta*; its wool combings are ⅓ mina (and) 4 shekels each, its wastage is 6 shekels each," 836:1–3

6. The Family of *Šu-Kabta*

a-ga-ti nin$_9$ ***šu-kab-tá***, "*Agati*, sister of *Šu-Kabta*" > *Agati*

eš$_4$-tár-um-mi dumu-munus ***šu-kab-tá***, "*Eštar-ummi*, daughter of *Šu-Kabta*" > *Eštar-ummi*

7. The Messenger of *Šu-Kabta*

7.1 Provisions

3 sìla ^{lú}kíĝ-gi$_4$-a ***šu-kab-ta***, "3 liters (of bread for) the messenger of *Šu-Kabta*," 385:7

7.2 Work Assignments

2 ĝuruš ^{lú}kíĝ-gi$_4$-a ***šu-kab-ta*** še karkar^{ki}-ta nibru^{ki}-šè ba-an-tùm, "2 messengers of *Šu-Kabta* brought barley from Karkar to Nippur," 20:33, 21:'27

8. The Workmen of *Šu-Kabta*

8.1 Meeting the Boat

12 ĝuruš má gaba ri-a igi ***šu-kab-tá***-šè ĝen-⸢na⸣, "12 workmen having gone before *Šu-Kabta* to meet the boat," 163:37

8.2 Pouring Water

5 ĝuruš ***šu-kab-tá*** (. . .) [a] bal-a (. . .) [kurum$_7$ aka], "[Inspection (of the work)] of 5 workmen of *Šu-Kabta* (and) {other workers} having poured water," 181:1, 5, 8

8.3 Moving Dirt at the Garšana Garden

12 ĝuruš 1 géme ***šu-kab-[tá]*** (. . .) kurum$_7$ aka saḫar zi-ga [^{ĝeš}kiri$_6$ gar-ša-an-na^{ki}], "Inspection (of the work) of 12 workmen and 1 workwoman of *Šu-Kabta* (and) {other workers} having moved dirt [at the Garšana garden]," 176:1, 16–17

[n ĝuru]š ***šu-ka[b-tá]*** (. . .) kurum$_7$ aka saḫar-⸢zi⸣-ga ^{ĝeš}kiri$_6$ gar-ša-an-na^{ki}, "Inspection (of the work) of [n] workmen of *Šu-Kabta* (and) {other workers} having moved dirt at the Garšana garden," 179:1, 17–18

9. Workmen Bringing a Message to *Šu-Kabta*

9.1 Builders and Workmen

1 ĝuruš šidim á-áĝ(-ĝá) ki ***šu-kab-ta***$_{(2)}$-šè de$_6$-a, "1 builder having brought a message to the place of *Šu-Kabta*," 2:19, 3:15, 4:20

n ĝuruš á-áĝ ki ***šu-kab-ta***-šè de$_6$-a, "n workmen having brought a message to the place of *Šu-Kabta*," 21:'28, 153:'36

9.2 Specific Individuals

9.2.1 *Beli-ili* and E'igara

1 *be-lí-ì-lí* 1 é-ì-gára á-áĝ-ĝá ki ***šu-kab-ta***-šè de$_6$-a, "*Beli-ili* and E'igara having brought a message to the place of *Šu-Kabta*," 123:8–10

9.2.2 E'igara

1 é-ì-gára á-áĝ(-ĝá) nibru^{ki}-šè ki ***šu-kab-ta***-šè de$_6$-a, "E'igara having brought a message to *Šu-Kabta* in Nippur," 32:39, 33:43, 34:'17, 35:46

1 é-ì-gára á-áĝ(-ĝá) ki ***šu-kab-tá***-šè de$_6$-a, "E'igara having brought a message to the place of *Šu-Kabta*," 36:41, 47:53–54, 48:58–59, 49:57, 50:'16–'17, 59:52, 60:48–49, 102:5, 103:5, 107:9, 108:6, 108:40, 109:6

9.2.3 E'igara and *Šu-Belum*

1 é-ì-gára 1 *šu*-^{d}*belum* á-áĝ(-ĝá) ki ***šu-kab-ta***-šè de$_{6}$-a, "E'igara (and) *Šu-Belum* having brought a message to the place of *Šu-Kabta*," 65:'26–'27, 71:32–34, 110:7–8, 111:7–9

9.2.4 E'igara and *Šu*-Ninkarak

1 é-ì-gára 1 *šu*-^{d}nin-kar-ak á-áĝ ki ***šu-kab-ta***-šè de$_{6}$-a, "E'igara (and) *Šu*-Ninkarak having brought a message to the place of *Šu-Kabta*," 106:6–8, 106:45–47

9.2.5 *Iṭibšinat* and E'igara

1 *i-ṭib-ší-na-at* 1 é-ì-gára á-áĝ ki ***šu-kab-tá***-šè de$_{6}$-a, "*Iṭibšinat* (and) E'igara having brought a message to the place of *Šu-Kabta*," 43:'43–'44, 44:41–43, 45:22–23, 46:'39–'41

9.2.6 *Mašum*, the Builder

1 *ma-šum* šidim ki ***šu-kab-ta***-šè ĝen-na, "*Mašum*, the builder, having gone to the place of *Šu-Kabta*," 59:58–59, 60:54–55, 61:15, 62:'16

9.2.7 *Šu-Belum*

1 *šu*-^{d}*belum á*-áĝ-ĝá ki ***šu-kab-ta***-šè de$_{6}$-a, "*Šu-Belum* having brought a message to the place of *Šu-Kabta*," 39:45, 114:7–8

1 *šu*-^{d}*belum* á-áĝ ki ***šu-kab-ta***-šè ĝen-na "*Šu-Belum* gone (to bring) a message to the place of *Šu-Kabta*," 40:38–39

[1 *š*]*u*-^{d}*belum* [á-áĝ ki] ***šu-kab-t*[*a*-š]è šu?-x-[x?]-x ĜEŠ.KÚŠU[^{ki}-šè?] de$_{6}$-[a], "*Šu-Belum* having brought [a message] to [the place of] *Šu-Kabta* (?) [in?] ĜEŠ.KÚŠU," 56:'36–'38

9.2.8 *Šu*-Ninkarak

1 *šu*-^{d}nin-kar-ak á-áĝ ki ***šu-kab-ta***-šè de$_{6}$-a, "*Šu*-Ninkarak having brought a message to the place of *Šu-Kabta*," 104:7, 104:47, 105:7, 105:45

9.2.9 *Tatturi*

1 *ta-tù-ri* á-áĝ ki ***šu-kab-ta***-šè nibru^{ki}-šè de$_{6}$-a, "*Tatturi* having brought a message to the place of *Šu-Kabta* in Nippur," 24:'25

9.2.10 Personal Name Broken

[1 PN á]-áĝ ki ***šu-kab-ta***-šè de$_{6}$-a, "[PN] having brought a message to the place of *Šu-Kabta*," 162:30

10. Transactions after the Death of *Šu-Kabta* (in ŠS 8 XI)[59]

10.1 Belongings of *Šu-Kabta* Disbursed after his Death

10.1.1 Chairs

1 túg ba-tab *tuh-hu-um* tab-ba-gen ^{ĝeš}gu-za ***šu-kab-tá*** [ki] *am-ri-ni*-ta [*šu*]-^{d}nin-in<-si> šu ba-ti, "*Šu*-Nininsi received 1 ordinary double ba-tab *tuh-hu-um* textile of the chair of *Šu-Kabta* from *Amrini*," 737:3–6

[59] See no. 252.

10.1.2 Textiles

10.1.2.1 Receipt of *Aštaqqar* from *Puzur-agum*

1 ^{túg}níĝ-lám-AB ***šu-kab-tá*** 1 ^{túg}šà-ga-dù-níĝ-lám ***šu-kab-tá*** ki ^{d}*puzur$_4$-a-gu$_5$-um*-ta *aš-tá-qar* šu ba-an-ti, "*Aštaqqar* received 1 níĝ-lám-AB textile of *Šu-Kabta* (and) 1 níĝ-lám belt of *Šu-Kabta* from *Puzur-agum*," 736:1–6

10.1.2.2 Receipt of *Nuruš-eli* from *Šu*-Nininsi

[n ^{túg}]bar-dul$_5$ ***šu-kab-tá*** *a-ši-um nu-ru-uš-e-li* šu ba-ti ki *šu*-^{d}nin-in-si-ta ba-zi, "*Nuruš-eli* received [n] *a-ši-um* bar-dul$_5$ textile(s) of *Šu-Kabta* from *Šu*-Nininsi," 762:1–5

10.1.2.3 Receipt of *Puzur-agum* from *Adad-tillati* and *Aštaqqar*

1 túg-guz-za-ús [***šu-kab-tá***], "1 2nd-quality tufted textile of [*Šu-Kabta*]," 698:1

1 ^{túg}bar-dul$_5$-AB ***šu-kab-tá***, "1 bar-dul$_5$-AB textile of *Šu-Kabta*," 698:2, 794:3

1 ^{túg}níĝ-lám ***šu-kab-[tá]***, "1 níĝ-lám textile of *Šu-Kabta*," 698:3

n ^{túg}šà-ga-dù níĝ-lám ***šu-kab-tá***, "n níĝ-lám belt(s) of *Šu-Kabta*," 698:4, 698:14

n ^{túg}níĝ-lám ***šu-kab-tá***, "n níĝ-lám textile(s) of *Šu-Kabta*," 698:13, 789:1

[n túg-]guz-za 4-kam-ús [***šu***]***-kab-tá***, "[n] 4th-quality tufted textile(s) of *Šu-Kabta*," 698:21

[n] ^{gada}aktum 3-kam-ús [***šu-kab-t***]***á***, "[n] 3rd-quality aktum textile(s) of Šu-*Kabta*," 698:23

[n ^{túg}š]à-ga-dù-níĝ-lám ***šu-kab-tá*** [ki-lá-b]i ⅓ ma-na 2 gín (. . .) [túg] ki-lá tà-ga, "[n] níĝ-lám belt(s) of *Šu-Kabta*, their weight is ⅓ mina and 2 shekels, (and) {other textiles}, weighed textiles having been woven," 738:1–2, 18

10.1.2.4 Receipt of *Šu*-Nininsi from *Adad-tillati*

1 túg-guz-za ***šu-kab-tá***, "1 tufted textile of *Šu-Kabta*," 723:1

1 ^{túg}šà-ga-dù [. . .] ***šu-kab-[tá]***, "1 [. . .] belt of *Šu-Kabta*," 759:4

1 ^{túg}níĝ-lám [?] ***šu-kab-⌜ta⌝***, "1 [?] níĝ-lám textile of *Šu-Kabta*," 781:1

2 ^{kuš}súḫub-túg-du$_8$-a-su$_4$-a ***šu-kab-tá*** é-ba-an 1 ^{kuš}e-sír du$_8$-ši-[a] túg-du$_8$-a-su$_4$-a ***šu-kab-[ta*** é]-ba-an 1 ^{kuš}e-sír túg-[du$_8$-a] ***šu-kab-tá*** é-[ba-an], "2 pairs of red meshwork shoes of *Šu-Kabta*, 1 pair of turquoise sandals lined with red meshwork of *Šu-Kabta*, (and) 1 pair of meshwork-lined sandals of *Šu-Kabta*," 782:2–5

10.1.2.5 Unspecified Recipient from *Puzur-agum*

1 túg ba-tab *tuḫ-ḫu-um simat-*^{d}*ištaran* 1 ^{túg}níĝ-lám-AB ***šu-kab-ta*** 1 ^{túg}níĝ-lám 3-kam-ús túg-sa-gi$_4$-a ⌜mu⌝-DU *puzur$_4$-a-gu$_5$-um* ^{lú}ázlag túg-*šu-eš$_4$-tár*, "*Puzur-agum*, the fuller, delivered 1 ba-tab *tuḫ-ḫu-um* textile of *Simat-Ištaran*, 1 níĝ-lám-AB textile of *Šu-Kabta*, (and) 1 3rd-quality níĝ-lám textile, finished textiles of *Šu-Eštar*," 823:1–7

10.2 Craftswomen to Mourn for *Šu-Kabta*

97 géme saĝ-dub 15 géme á-⅓-ta géme uš-bar-me-éš [n] géme gu [u$_4$]-9½-šè [gaba] sìg-dè gub-[ba u$_4$ ***šu***]***-kab-tá*** ba-⌜úš⌝-a *é-a-šar* maškim ki ^{d}*adad-*[*tillati*-ta] (so tablet!) [ki

aš]-*tá-qar*-ta (so envelope !) ba-[zi], "*Adad-tillati / Aštaqqar* disbursed 97 full-time female weavers (and) 15 female weavers at ⅓ wages (and) [n] female spinner(s) employed for 9½ [days] to beat (their) [breasts] when *Šu-Kabta* died. *Ea-šar* was the deputy," 252:1–10

10.3 Regular Offerings of the Funerary Libations of *Šu-Kabta*

10.3.1 Assorted Animals

1 šáḫ-zé-da iti u$_4$-1-ba-zal 1 máš-gal-niga iti u$_4$-10-ba-zal 1 šáḫ-zé-da iti u$_4$-15-ba-zal 1 udu-aslum$_x$-niga-babbar iti u$_4$-20-ba-zal 1 udu-niga-babbar iti u$_4$-28-ba-zal sá-du$_{11}$-ki-a-nag-***šu-*[*kab*]*-tá*** ki ^{d}*adad-tillati*-ta ⌜ba⌝-zi, "*Adad-tillati* disbursed 1 piglet at the end of the 1st day of the month, 1 fattened billy-goat at the end of the 10th day of the month, 1 piglet at the end of the 15th day of the month, 1 fattened white long-fleeced sheep at the end of the 20th day of the month (and) 1 fattened white sheep at the end of the 28th day of the month, regular offerings of the funerary libation place of *Šu-Kabta*," 973:1–10

1 šáḫ-zé-[da] u$_4$-1-[kam] 1 udu-niga u$_4$-10-kam 1 tum$_{12}^{mušen}$ u$_4$-15-kam 1 udu-niga u$_4$-20-kam 1 udu-niga 1 tum$_{12}^{mušen}$ u$_4$-28-kam sá-du$_{11}$-ki-a-nag-***šu-kab-tá*** ki ^{d}*adad-tillati*-ta ba-zi, "*Adad-tillati* disbursed 1 piglet on the 1st day, 1 fattened sheep on the 10th day, 1 wild dove on the 15th day, 1 fattened sheep on the 20th day (and) 1 fattened sheep (and) 1 wild dove on the 28th day, regular offerings of the funerary libation place of *Šu-Kabta*," 976:1–11

[1] udu-niga u$_4$-10-kam 1 šáḫ-zé-da 1 tu-gur$_4^{mušen}$ u$_4$-15-kam 1 udu-niga u$_4$-20-[kam] 1 udu-[niga 1] šáḫ-zé-[da 1] tu-gur$_4^{⌜mušen⌝}$ [u$_4$-n-kam] sá-du$_{11}$-ki-[a-nag-***šu-kab-tá***] ki ^{d}[*adad*]-*tillati*-ta ba-zi, "*Adad-tillati* disbursed [1] fattened sheep on the 10th day, 1 piglet (and) 1 dove on the 15th day, 1 fattened sheep on the 20th day (and) 1 [fattened] sheep, [1] piglet (and) [1] dove [on the nth day], regular offerings of the [funerary libation] place of [*Šu-Kabta*]," 978:1–13

1 péš-g̃eš-gi u$_4$-1-kam 1 udu-niga u$_4$-10-kam 1 péš-g̃eš-gi u$_4$-15-[kam] 1 ^{munus}áš-[gàr] ⌜u$_4$⌝-20-[kam] 1 udu-[niga] 1 [. . .] u$_4$-[n-kam] sá-du$_{11}$-ki-[a-nag]-***š*[*u-kab-tá*]** ki ^{d}*adad-tillati*-⌜ta⌝ ba-zi, "1 large mouse on the 1st day, 1 fattened sheep on the 10th day, 1 mouse on the 15th day, 1 female goat on the 20th day, 1 [fattened] sheep (and) 1 [. . . on the nth] day, regular offerings of the funerary libation place of *Šu-Kabta*," 979:1–14

10.3.2 Assorted Commestibles

(. . .) sá-du$_{11}$-ki-a-nag-***šu-kab-tá*** ki ^{d}*adad-tillati*-ta ba-zi, "*Adad-tillati* disbursed {assorted comestibles} regular offerings of the funerary libation place of *Šu-Kabta*," 972:107–109, 975:108–110, 981:33–35

10.3.3 Bronze Vessels

(. . .) ki-a-n[ag ***š*]*u-kab-ta*** ki ^{d}*adad-tillati*-ta *i-sú-a-ri-iq* šu ba-ti, "*Isu-ariq* received {bronze vessels} of the funerary libation place of *Šu-Kabta* from *Adad-tillati*," 977:'8–'10

10.3.4 Leather

[n kuš- . . .] 3 kuš-udu-niga sá-du$_{11}$-ki-a-nag-***šu-kab-ta***-ta(sic!?) [ki ^{d}*adad*]-*tillati*-[ta ba-zi], "*Adad-tillati* disbursed [n . . . skin(s)] (and) 3 skins of fattened sheep, regular offerings of the funerary libation place of *Šu-Kabta*," 974:1–6

10.3.5 **Offerings Returned from the Sanctuary**

[n] sìla ninda [n] kuš-u[du-nig]a ki-a-nag-***šu-kab-⸢tá⸣*** èš-ta-gur-ra ^{d}*adad-tillati* šu ba-ti u_4 ezem-*e-lu-núm*-^{d}nergal$_x^{eri11-gal}$, "*Adad-tillati* received [n] liter(s) of bread (and) [n] skin(s) of fattened sheep of the funerary libation of place of *Šu-Kabta*, offerings returned from the sanctuary during the *Elunum* festival of Nergal," 980:4–11

10.4 **Items Disbursed on Behalf of *Šu-Kabta* in the Month of his Death (ŠS 8 XI)**

10.4.1 **Leather for his Chair**

[10?+]5 gín k[uš-g]u_4 ú-ḫáb ^{geš}gu-za kéš[e-da-š]è ⸢***šu***⸣?-***kab***?-⸢***ta***⸣? ki *a-na-aḫ-ì-lí*-ta ba-[zi], "*Anaḫ-ili* disbursed [10?+]5 shekels of madder-tanned ox-hide for binding the chair of *Šu-Kabta*?," 923:7–10

10.4.2 **Silver for his Chair**

(. . .) ^{geš}gu-za ***šu-[kab]-tá***-šè ki *šu*-^{d}*adad*-ta *i-sú-a-rí-iq* šu ba-ti, "*Isu-ariq* received {silver} for the chair of *Šu-Kabta* from *Šu-Adad*," 1339:3–6

11. **Possessions of *Šu-Kabta* in Undated texts**

11.1 **His Chair House**

[. . . zi]-ga é-^{geš}gu-za ***šu-kab-tá***-me-šè, "{assorted commodities} expended for the house of the chair of *Šu-Kabta*," 562:'76

11.2 **Sandals**

1 ^{kuš}e-sír du_8-ši-a ⸢***šu***⸣***-kab-tá*** é-ba-an 1 ^{kuš}e-sír ***šu-kab-tá*** é-ba-[an], "1 pair of turquoise sandals of *Šu-Kabta* (and) 1 pair of sandals of *Šu-Kabta*," 1376:57–58

11.3 **Textiles**

1 ^{túg}níĝ-lám-AB ***šu-ka[b-tá***. . .]-za ⸢***šu***⸣***-kab-tá*** (. . .) [túg]-sa-gi_4-a [*šu*]-^{d}*adad* [šu] ba-an-ti, "*Šu-Adad* received finished textiles (including) 1 níĝ-lám-AB textile of *Šu-Kabta* (and) [. . .] of *Šu-Kabta*," 1254:'38–'39, '44–'46

11.4 **Broken Context**

[. . .] ⸢***šu***⸣***-kab-tá*** [?] ^{d}*adad*-[*tillati* šu] ba-ti, 1396:'1–'4

šu-ku-bu-um

é-***šu-ku-bu-um***, "the house of *Šukubum*" > *Household Index*

Šukubum, the Scribe

1. **As a Witness**

igi ***šu-ku-bu-um*** dub-[sar], "witnessed by *Šukubum*, the scribe," 1063:9

šu-la-núm

1. ***Šulanum*, the Malster**

1.1 **Grain in his Possession**

0.1.1.7$^{5}/_{6}$ sìla še 9 sìla tuḫ-$duru_5$-sig_5 0.0.4.2 sìla tuḫ-$duru_5$-gen lá-ìa kaš zi-ga ezem-*a-bu-um* ***šu-la-núm*** $munu_4$-mú in-da-ĝál, "77$^{5}/_{6}$ liters of barley, 9 liters of fine fresh bran (and) 42 liters of ordinary fresh bran, the remainder from the beer expended (for) the *Abum* festival, are with *Šulanum*, the maltster," 1047:1–7

1.2 Receipts from *Adad-tillati*

1.2.1 Barley for Malt

n.n.n. še gur mu munu$_4$-šè ki ^{d}*adad-tillati*-ta ***šu-la-núm*** šu ba-an-ti, "*Šulanum* received n bushel(s) (and) n liter(s) of barley for malt from *Adad-tillati*," 1123:1–5, 1133:1–5[60]

1.2.2 Baskets

2 ^{gi}bisağ-gí[d-d]a 3 ^{gi}ma-sab ki ^{d}*adad-tillati*-ta ***šu-la-*[*núm*]** šu ba-ti, "*Šulanum* received 2 long baskets (and) 3 ma-sab baskets from *Adad-tillati*," 1311:1–5[61]

2. *Šulanum*, the Overseer of the Men from Karkar

(. . .) ugula [***šu***]***-la-núm*** (. . .) lú-karkar^{ki}-me, "{workmen} from Karkar, supervised by *Šulanum*," 559:12, 28

3. *Šulanum*, the Servant

3.1 Provisions: Barley

[n+]1.0.3. gur ***šu-la-núm*** (. . .) [šu+níğin n+]5.4.1.8 sìla še gur lugal-ú-šim-e árad!-me-éš, "[n bushel(s)] (and) 63 liters of barley (for) *Šulanum*, (and barley for) {others}, [in total: n+]5 bushels and 258 liters of barley (for) the servants (supervised by) Lugal-ušime," 504:6, 7–10

4. *Šulanum*, Title Unspecified

4.1 Provisions: Wages for Molding Bricks

7⅓ sar ***šu-la-*[*núm*]** (. . .) šeg$_{12}$ du$_8$-[a], "7⅓ sar [(of bricks from)] *Šulanum* (and bricks from) {other workers}, {wages for workers} having molded bricks," 350:9, '23

šu-ma-ma

1. *Šu*-Mama, Father of *Adallal* the Craftsman

a-da-làl dumu ***šu*-ma-ma** um-mi-a, "*Adallal*, the son of *Šu*-Mama, the craftsman" > *Adallal*

2. *Šu*-Mama, the Sick Builder

1 ***šu*-ma-ma** šidim dú-ra, "*Šu*-Mama, the sick builder," 25:'6, 26:'25, 32:42, 37:47, 49:68

šu-^{d}*ma-mi-tum*

é-***šu-***^{d}***ma-mi-tum***, "the house of *Šu-Mamitum*" > *Household Index*

1. *Šu-Mamitum*, the Gatekeeper

1.1 Provisions: Textiles

1 ^{túg}*ḫa-bu-um* 4-kam-ús *šu-*^{d}*ma-mi-tum* ì-du$_8$ zi-ga ğìri *šu-kab-ta* [ki ^{d}*adad-til*]*lati*-[ta ba-zi], "*Adad-tillati* [disbursed] 1 4th-quality *ḫabum* textile (for) *Šu-Mamitum*, the gate-keeper. (It was) the expenditure of *Šu-Kabta* under his authority," 607:1–5

---

60 In light of his activities here, these two transactions surely are receipts of *Šulanum*, the maltster.

61 Although his title is not specified here, the seal on the tablet indicates that *Šulanum*'s father was a maltster. It is likely that this *Šulanum* is the same maltster known from no. 1047.

2. **Šu-Mamitum**, Title Unspecified

2.1 As a Witness

igi ***šu-ma-mi-tum***, "witnessed by *Šu-Mamitum*," 1064:13

šu-^{d}na-zi

1. ***Šu***-Nazi, the Bird Warden

★★[. . .] še mušen-[na . . .] šu bala-dè [. . .] 6 $ir_{7}^{mušen}$-niga 30 $tu\text{-}gur_{4}^{mušen}$-niga *da-da-a* sipa-mušen-na é-[a . . .] ***šu***-^{d}**na-zi** sipa-mušen-na é-[a . . .], 1253:'1–'7

šu-^{d}nin-$girim_{x}$

1. Deliveries

1.1. Flour: Receipt of ***Malik-bani***

0.0.3. zì-gu-gen ki ***šu***-^{d}**nin-**$\mathbf{girim_{x}}$-⌜ta⌝ ^{d}*ma-lik-ba-ni* šu ba-ti, "*Malik-bani* received 30 liters of ordinary gu-flour from *Šu*-Ningirim," 1153:2

2. Receipts: from ***Adad-tillati***

2.1 Assorted Commodities: Seal of ***Šu***-Enlil

(. . .) ki ^{d}*adad-tillati*-ta ***šu***-^{d}**nin-**$\mathbf{girim_{x}}$ šu ba-ti kišib *šu*-^{d}en-líl, "*Šu*-Ningirim received {assorted leather, woods, mats and vessels} from *Adad-tillati*, seal of *Šu*-Enlil," 1334:13–16

2.2 Beer Bread: Regular Offerings of Nin-Siana

1 gú [n ma-na] báppir-sig_{5} sá-du_{11}-^{d}nin-$^{d}si_{4}$-an-na ki ^{d}*adad-tillati*-ta ***šu***-^{d}**nin-**$\mathbf{girim_{x}}$ šu ba-ti, "*Šu*-Ningirim received 1 talent of fine beer bread, regular offerings of Nin-Siana, from *Adad-tillati*," 1020:1–5

2.3 Bitumen: Under the Authority of ***Šu***-Enlil

0.0.2. ésir-é-a ki ^{d}*adad-tillati*-ta ***šu***-^{d}**nin-**$\mathbf{girim_{x}}$ šu ba-ti g̃ìri *šu*-^{d}en-líl, "Under the authority of *Šu*-Enlil, *Šu*-Ningirim received 20 liters of house bitumen from *Adad-tillati*," 1338:1–5

2.4 Door Parts

1 $^{g̃eš}$apin-ig-ù-$suḫ_{5}$ 1 $^{g̃eš}$ù-šar-ig-ù-$suḫ_{5}$ 3 $^{g̃eš}$suḫuš-ig-ù-$suḫ_{5}$ ki ^{d}*adad-tillati*-ta ***šu***-^{d}**nin-**$\mathbf{girim_{x}}$ šu ba-ti, "*Šu*-Ningirim received 1 frame of a pine door, 1 point/crescent of a pine door (and) 1 foundation of a pine door from *Adad-tillati*," 1333:1–7

2.5 Broken Context

[. . .] ki ^{d}*adad-tillati*-ta ***šu***-^{d}**nin-**$\mathbf{girim_{x}}$ šu ba-ti, "*Šu*-Ningirim received [. . .] from *Adad-tillati*," 1392:1–4

3. As a Witness

igi ***šu***-^{d}**nin-**$\mathbf{girim_{x}}$, "witnessed by *Šu*-Ningirim," 1054:8

šu-^{d}nin-in-si

1. *Šu*-Nininsi, the Barber

1.1 As Deputy: Pots

12 ^{dug}b[a-x] ⌜mu⌝ diğir-re-e-ne-šè gaz-dè ⌜***šu***⌝-^{d}**nin-in-si** šu-i maškim, "12 [x]-vessels to be broken for the gods. *Šu*-Nininsi, the barber, was the deputy," 1013:6–8

[. . . ***šu***-^{d}**nin-in-si** šu-i] maškim, 1014:'1[62]

1.2 Receipts: Shoes and Textiles

2 ^{túg}sagšu-ğe$_6$-⌜sig$_5$⌝ 2 ^{kuš}súḫub-túg-du$_8$-a-su$_4$-a *šu-kab-tá* é-ba-an 1 ^{kuš}e-sír du$_8$-ši-[a] túg-du$_8$-a-su$_4$-a *šu-kab*-[*ta* é]-ba-an 1 ^{kuš}e-sír túg-[. . .] *šu-kab-tá* é-[ba-an] 1 ^{kuš}e-sí[r. . .] é-ba-an 2 ^{túg}íb-lá-su$_4$-a KWU–809-ba du$_8$-ši-a ğar-ra ki ^{d}*adad-tillati*-ta ***šu***-^{d}**nin-in**<**-si**> šu-i šu ba-ti, "*Šu*-Nininsi, the barber, received from *Adad-tillati* 2 fine black caps, 2 pairs of red/brown meshwork shoes of *Šu-Kabta*, 1 pair of turquoise sandals lined with red/brown meshwork of *Šu-Kabta*, 1 pair of [. . .] sandals of *Šu-Kabta*, 1 pair of [. . .] sandals, (and) 2 red/brown belts covered with turquoise (?)," 782:1–11

2. *Šu*-Nininsi, Title Unspecified

2.1 Deliveries: Textiles of *Šu-Kabta*, Receipt of *Nuruš-eli*

[n ^{túg}]bar-dul$_5$ *šu-kab-tá a-ši-um nu-ru-uš-e-li* šu ba-ti ki ***šu***-^{d}**nin-in-si**-ta ba-zi, "*Nuruš-eli* received [n] *a-ši-um* bar-dul$_5$ textile(s) of *Šu-Kabta* from *Šu*-Nininsi," 762:1–5

2.2 Receipts from *Adad-tillati*

2.2.1 Baskets

1 ^{gi}bisağ-gíd-da-tur sa-ḫa ki ^{d}*adad-tillati*-ta ***šu***-^{d}**nin-in-[si]** šu ba-ti, "*Šu*-Nininsi received 1 small, long canvas-lined basket from *Adad-tillati*," 1347:1–4

1 ^{gi}bisağ túg-aš ki ^{d}*adad-tillati*-ta ***šu***-^{d}**nin-in-si** šu ba-ti, "*Šu*-Nininsi received 1 single textile basket from *Adad-tillati*," 1352:1–4

2.2.2 Raw Materials

0.0.2. ì-ğeš 1.0.0. nağa-si-è gur ki ^{d}*adad-tillati*-ta ***šu***-^{d}**nin-in-si** šu ba-ti, "*Šu*-Nininsi received 20 liters of sesame oil (and) 1 bushel of sprouted nağa from *Adad-tillati*," 809:1–5

2.2.3 Textiles

1 ^{túg}bar-si-ús ki ^{d}*adad-tillati*-ta ***šu***-^{d}**nin-in-si** šu ba-ti, "*Šu*-Nininsi received 1 2nd-quality band from *Adad-tillati*," 718:1–4, 726:1–4

1 ^{túg}bar-dul$_5$-túg-⌜sig$_5$⌝?-t[ur] ki ^{d}*adad*-[*tillati*-ta] ***šu***-[^{d}**n]in-in-si** šu [ba-t]i, "*Šu*-Nininsi received 1 small fine? bar-dul$_5$ textile from *Adad-tillati*," 727:3

1 ^{túg}níğ-lám-PI-ús-ni 1 ^{túg}níğ-lám 4-kam-ús-ni 1 ^{gi}bisağ túg-aš ki ^{d}*adad-tillati*-ta ***šu***-^{d}**nin-in-si** šu ba-ti, "*Šu*-Nininsi received 1 2nd-quality níğ-lám-PI textile, 1 4th-quality níğ-lám textile (and) 1 single textile basket from *Adad-tillati*," 749:1–6, 751:1–6

---

[62] Although the beginning of the tablet is broken, the remainder parallels no. 1013 suggesting a similar restoration.

1 ^{túg}níg̃-lám 4-kam-ús-ni ki ^{d}*adad-tillati*-ti ***šu*-^{d}nin-in-⌜si⌝** šu ba-ti g̃ìri *šu*-^{d}nisaba, "Under the authority of *Šu*-Nisaba, *Šu*-Nininsi received 1 4th-quality níg̃-lám textile from *Adad-tillati*," 754:1–5

1 ^{túg}níg̃-lám tab-ba ús x-ḪI? ki ^{d}*adad-tillati*-ta ***šu*-^{d}nin-in-si** šu ba-ti, "*Šu*-Nininsi received 1 double (?) níg̃-lám textile from *Adad-tillati*," 819:1–4

2.2.4 Textiles of *Šu-Kabta*

1 túg-guz-za *šu-kab-tá* ki ^{d}*adad-tillati*-ta ***šu*-^{d}nin-in-si** šu ba-ti, "*Šu*-Nininsi received 1 tufted textile of *Šu-Kabta* from *Adad-tillati*," 723:1–4

1 ^{túg}níg̃-lám [?] *šu-kab-*⌜*ta*⌝ ki ^{d}*adad-tillati*-⌜ta⌝ ***šu*-^{d}nin-in-si** šu ba-ti, "*Šu*-Nininsi received 1 [?] níg̃-lám textile of *Šu-Kabta* from *Adad-tillati*," 781:1–4

1 ^{túg}*á-[gu$_4$-ḫu-um]*-ús 3-[kam-ús] 1 ^{túg}níg̃-[lám. . .] 1 ^{túg}níg̃-⌜lám⌝-[. . .] ni-[. . .] 1 ^{túg}šà-ga-dù [. . .] *šu-kab-[tá* ki ^{d}*adad-tillati*-ta ***šu*]-^{d}nin-in-[si]** šu ba-ti, "*Šu*-Nininsi received 1 3rd-[quality] belt, 1 [. . .] níg̃-lám textile, 1 [. . .] níg̃-lám textile, (and) 1 [. . .] belt of *Šu-Kabta* from *Adad-tillati*," 759:1–7

2.3 Receipts from Others

2.3.1 Barley for Distribution to the Workers

i-la-ak-nu-id ù-na-a-du$_{11}$ 5.1.4. še gur še-ba éren-na ***šu*-^{d}nin-in-[si** ḫé-na]-ab-[sum-m]u, "Say to *Ilak-nu'id* that '5 bushels (and) 100 liters of barley, barley rations of the workers, should be given to *Šu*-Nininsi,'" 1043:1–6

2.3.2 Textiles from *Amrini*

1 ⌜túg⌝níg̃-lám 3-kam-ús 1 ^{túg}níg̃-lám 3-kam-ús *a-gi$_4$-um* 1 túg ba-tab *tuḫ-ḫu-um* tab-ba-gen $^{g̃eš}$gu-za *šu-kab-tá* [ki] *am-ri-ni*-ta **[*šu*]-^{d}nin-in<-si>** šu ba-ti, "*Šu*-Nininsi received 1 3rd-quality níg̃-lám textile, 1 3rd-quality *a-gi$_4$-um* níg̃-lám textile (and) 1 ba-tab *tuḫ-ḫu-um* textile of the chair of *Šu-Kabta* from *Amrini*," 737:1–6

2.4 As a Witness

[igi] ***šu*-^{d}*ni*[n-i]n-si**, "[witnessed by] *Šu*-Nininsi," 1065:7

šu-^{d}nin-kar-ak

***Šu*-Ninkarak**, the Household Servant from the Gang of *Irib*

1. Bringing Messages

1.1 To *Šu-Kabta*

1 ***šu*-^{d}nin-kar-ak** á-ág̃ ki [*šu-k*]*ab-ta*-šè de$_6$-[a], "*Šu*-Ninkarak having brought a message to the place of *Šu-Kabta*," 104:7, 104:47, 105:7, 105:45

1 é-ì-gára 1 ***šu*-^{d}nin-kar-ak** á-ág̃ ki *šu-kab-ta*-šè de$_6$-a, "E'igara (and) *Šu*-Ninkarak having brought a message to the place of *Šu-Kabta*," 106:6–8, 106:45–47

1.2 To Udaga

1 ***šu*-^{d}nin-kar-ak** á-ág̃-g̃á ù-dag-ga^{ki}-šè de$_6$-a, "*Šu*-Ninkarak having brought a message to Udaga," 107:10, 107:'17, 108:7, 108:42, 109:7

2. Bringing the Tablet of *Malik-bani* to Edana

1 *be-lí-ì-lí* 1 ***šu-*^{d}nin-kar-ak** dub ^{d}*ma-lik-ba-ni* é-[da]-na^{ki}-šè de$_{6}$-a, "*Beli-ili* and *Šu*-Ninkarak having brought the tablet of *Malik-bani* to Edana," 51:'22–'24, 52:59–62, 53:61–63, 56:'32–'35

šu-^{d}nin-súmun

1. Provisions: Bread

0.1.3. ninda šuku ***šu-*^{d}nin-súmun** iti 4-kam (. . .) níĝ-kas$_{7}$-aka *da-a-a* muḫaldim, "63 liters of bread are the food allocation of *Šu*-Ninsumun in the 4th month (and) {other expenditures}; the balanced account of *Da'a*, the cook," 1031:16, 26

šu-^{d}nin-šubur

***Šu*-Ninšubur**, Man from Karkar

[1 ***šu***]-^{d}**nin-šubur** (. . .) ugula [*šu*]-*la-núm* (. . .) lú-karkar^{ki}-me, "*Šu*-Ninšubur, supervised by *Šulanum*, (and) {other workers}, men from Karkar," 559:9, 12, 28

šu-^{d}nisaba

1. *Šu*-Nisaba, Overseer of Hired Workers

n ĝuruš n géme ugula ***šu-*^{d}nisaba** (. . .) (lú-ḫuĝ-ĝá-me-éš), "n (hired) workmen (and) n (hired) workwomen supervised by *Šu*-Nisaba," 145:10, 146:'5, 147:10, 208:2–3, 209:5

2 ĝuruš ugula ***šu-*^{d}nisaba** (. . .) lú-ḫuĝ-ĝá-me-éš, "2 hired workmen supervised by *Šu*-Nisaba," 132:16, 143:17, 158:8, 207:5

1.1 Receipts: Barley Wages[63]

1.1.1 For Brick Molders

1.0.0. še gur šeg$_{12}$ du$_{8}$-dè á [n sìla-t]a [ki] ^{d}*adad-tillati*-ta [***šu-*^{d}]nisaba** [šu ba]-ti, "*Šu*-Nisaba received 1 bushel of barley, wages of [n liter(s)] each (for workers) to mold bricks, from *Adad-tillati*," 458:1–6

1.1.2 For Hoeing the Garden

4.4.0. še gur al aka ^{ĝeš}kiri$_{6}$ ki ^{d}*adad-tillati*-ta ***šu-*^{d}nisaba** šu ba-ti, "*Šu*-Nisaba received from *Adad-tillati* 4 bushels (and) 240 liters of barley (for workers) having hoed the garden," 500:1–5

2. *Šu*-Nisaba, Title Unspecified

2.1 Receipts

ur-^{d}dumu-zi ù *a-ḫu-wa-qar* ù-na-a-⌜du$_{11}$⌝ 0.0.2. ku-[x] ***šu-*^{d}nisaba** ḫé-na-ab-sum-mu 1 ĝuruš šà-gu$_{4}$ iri^{ki}-ta iri^{ki}-šè ḫé-eb-sá-e nam-mi-gur-re, "Say to Ur-Dumuzi and *Aḫu-waqar* that '20 liters of [x] should be given to *Šu*-Nisaba. 1 ox-driver from the city should arrive at the city. They should not argue!'" 1045:1–11

---

63 Although *Šu*-Nisaba's title is not specified here, the context of these receipts imply that the overseer *Šu*-Nisaba is intended.

2.2 Under his Authority

2.2.1 As a Requistioner: Grains and Containers

(. . .) ki *i-ṣur-*^{d}*suen*-ta ^{d}*ma-lik-ba-ni* <šu ba-ti> g̃iri ***šu***-^{d}**nisaba** maškim, "Under the authority of *Šu*-Nisaba, the deputy, *Malik-bani* <received> {assorted grains and containers} from *Iṣur-Suen*," 1072:9–11

2.2.2 Textiles

1 ^{túg}níg̃-lám 4-kam-ús-ni ki ^{d}*adad-tillati*-ta *šu*-^{d}nin-in-⌜si⌝ šu ba-ti g̃iri ***šu***-^{d}**nisaba**, "Under the authority of *Šu*-Nisaba, *Adad-tillati* received 1 4th-quality níg̃-lám textile from *Šu*-Nininsi," 754:1–5

šu-^{d}*suen-ba-ni*

Šu-Suen-bani, the Barber

1. As a Deputy

0.0.1. zì-KAL 2 sìla dabin 1 sìla eša ⌜*al*⌝*-la-ša-ru-um* ***š***[***u***-^{d}**E**]**N.ZU-*ba-ni*** šu-i maškim, "10 liters of KAL-flour, 2 liters of semolina (and) 1 liter of fine flour (for) *Alla-šarrum*. *Šu-Suen-bani*, the barber, was the deputy," 1016:9–12

^{d}*šu*-^{d}*suen-dan*

1. Provisions: A Sheep

[1] udu-ú ^{d}***šu***-^{d}***suen-dan*** [1] udu-ú-niga ⌜ki⌝ *ì-lí-bi-l*[*a-ni*]*-ta* ba-zi, "*Ili-bilani* disbursed [1] range-fed sheep (for) *Šu-Suen-dan* (and) [1] fattened range-fed sheep," 411:1–5

^{d}*šu*-^{d}*suen-e-te-íl-pi*$_{4}$-^{d}en-líl

1. Regular Offerings

5 sìla kaš-sig$_{5}$ 0.0.1. kaš-gen sá-du$_{11}$-^{d}***šu***-^{d}***suen*-e-te-íl-pi**$_{4}$-^{d}**en-líl**, "5 liters of fine beer (and) 10 liters of regular beer, regular offerings of *Šu-Suen-etelpi*-Enlil," 505:4–6, 507:4–6, 508:4–6

(. . .) dirig sá-du$_{11}$-u$_{4}$-[n-šè] *ra-ba-tum* ù ^{d}***šu***-^{d}**E**[**N.ZU**]-[***e***]***-te-íl-pi***$_{4}$-^{d}**en-lí**[**l** sugal$_{7}$] ⌜u$_{4}$⌝ ezem-*a-bu-um* ⌜g̃iri⌝ ^{d}[*suen-a-bu-šu*], "{assorted commodities}, surplus of the regular offerings on the [nth] day of *Rabatum* and *Šu-Suen-etelpi*-Enlil, [the sugal], during the *Abum* festival under the authority of [*Suen-abušu*]," 509:'12–'14

2. Under the Authority of *Šu-Suen-etelpi*-Enlil: Slaughtered Birds

1 [mu]šen-tur u$_{4}$-24-kam 1 [muš]en-tur u$_{4}$-30-kam ba-úš é-kišib-ba-šè g̃iri ^{d}***šu***-^{d}***suen-e-te-íl-pi***$_{4}$-^{d}**en-líl** ki ^{d}*adad-tillati*-ta ba-zi, "Under the authority of *Šu-Suen-etelpi*-Enlil, *Adad-tillati* disbursed 1 young bird on the 24th day (and) 1 young bird on the 30th day. (The birds) were slaughtered for the warehouse," 1183:1–7

^{d}*šu*-^{d}*suen*-ḫa-ma-ti

1. Receipts: Bread and Date Palm Hearts

1.0.0. ninda-gal zì-gen gur 1.0.0. ninda-gal zì-kum gur 16.0.0. peš gur IB?-g̃ar ^{d}***šu***-^{d}***suen*-ḫa-ma-ti** šu ba-ti, "*Šu-Suen*-ḫamati received 1 bushel of large (loaves of) bread of ordinary flour, 1 bushel of large (loaves of) bread of kum-flour (and) 16 bushels of (?) date palm hearts," 1248:1–4

^{d}***šu***-^{d}***suen-na-ra-am***-^{d}**en-líl**

1. Provisions: Barley

0.0.2. še ^{lú}kíĝ-gi$_4$-a-lugal ⌜u$_4$⌝-3-kam 4 sìla še ^{d}***šu***-^{d}***suen-na-ra-am***-^{d}**en-líl** u$_4$-4-kam ^{d}*ma-lik-tillat-sú* šu-i maškim, "20 liters of barley (for) the (royal) messenger on the 3rd day (and) 4 liters of barley (for) *Šu-Suen-naram*-Enlil on the 4th day. *Malik-tillassu*, the barber, was the deputy," 488:1–7

5 sìla še ^{d}***šu***-^{d}***suen-na-ra-am***-^{d}**en-líl** ^{d}*ma-lik-tillat-sú* maškim, "5 liters of barley (for) *Šu-Suen-naram*-Enlil. *Malik-tillassu* was the deputy," 554:1–3

šu-^{d}***šamaš***

Šu-Šamaš, the Bird Warden

1. Deliveries: Pigeons, Receipt of *Adad-tillati*

2 ir$_7$^{mušen} iti u$_4$-7-ba-zal ki ***šu***-^{d}***šamaš*** mušen-dù-ta ^{d}*adad-tillati* ì-dab$_5$, "At the end of the 7th day of the month, *Adad-tillati* took in charge 2 pigeons from *Šu-Šamaš*, the bird warden," 1126:1–5

^{d}**šul-gi-*ra-ma***

1. Workers to Mourn his Death

3 ĝuruš u$_4$-1-šè gaba sàg-dè gub-ba u$_4$ ^{d}**šul-gi-*r*[*a-ma*** ba-uš-a], "3 workmen for 1 day to beat (their) breasts when Šulgi-*rama* [died]," 246:5–7

^{d}**šul-gi-*wa-qar***

1. Deliveries

1.1 As a Deputy: Fullers for Canal Work

13 ĝuruš saĝ-tag 3 ĝuruš á-⅔-ta ^{lú}ázlag-me-éš u$_4$-2-šè i$_7$-mi-me-er gub-ba ba-al-la ^{d}**šul-gi-*wa-qar*** maškim šà nibru^{ki} zi-ga ĝìri *šu-kab-tá* ki ^{d}**šul-gi-*wa-qar-ta*** ba-zi, "Šulgi-*waqar* disbursed 13 full-time fullers and 3 fullers at ⅔ wages employed for 2 days having dug the Mimer canal in Nippur. (It was) the expenditure of *Šu-Kabta* under his authority. Šulgi-*waqar* was the deputy," 227:1–10

1.2 Receipt of *Adad-tillati*

1.2.1 Flour

5 sìla zì-kum *mu-du-lum* ku-úr gu-ru-dè ki ^{d}**šul-gi-*wa-qar***-ta ^{d}*adad-tillati* [šu] ba-ti, "*Adad-tillati* received from Šulgi-*waqar* 5 liters of salted kum-flour to be returned in the future," 1090:1–6

1.2.2 Reeds and Reed Products

30 sa gi-izi 2 ^{gi}dur-kisal-lá ki ^{d}**šul-gi-*wa-qar***-ta ^{d}*adad-tillati* šu! ba-ti, "*Adad-tillati* received 30 bundles of fuel reeds and 2 kisal-lá ropes from Šulgi-*waqar*," 1282:1–5

2 ^{gi}kid-uzu ki ^{d}**šul-gi-*wa*!-*qar***-ta ^{d}*adad-tillati* šu ba-ti, "*Adad-tillati* received 2 uzu-mats from Šulgi-*waqar*," 1284:1–4

2. Receipts: Flour, Grains, Baskets, and Jugs

(. . .) 27 ^{gi}gur-dub 0.1.0.-ta 8 dug 0.0.3.-ta **^{d}šul-gi-*wa-qar*** šu ba-ti ki ^{d}*adad-tillati*-ta ba-zi, "Šulgi-*waqar* received {assorted flours and grains}, 27 reed baskets of 60 liters each (and) 8 jugs of 30 liters each from *Adad-tillati*," 1134:8–13

– T –

ta-ḫu-lam

1. As a Deputy

1.1 Bread Bound in Sacks

[n.n.n sìla] ninda-šu-ra-gen ^{kuš}a-g̃á-lá kéše-rá g̃uruš 7-kam u_4 kaskal-šè i-re-sa-a ***ta-ḫu-lam*** maškim (. . .) zi-ga *simat-^{d}ištaran*, "[n liter(s)] ordinary half-(loaf) bread in bound leather sacks (for) 7 workmen when they went on a journey. (It was) the expenditure of *Simat-Ištaran*. *Taḫulam* was the deputy," 529:1–4, 26

1.2 Disbursal of Beer

(. . .) 0.0.1. kaš-sig_5 u_4-28-kam 0.0.1. kaš-sig_5 u_4-29-kam gú-ne-sag̃-g̃á-šè ***ta-ḫu-la-am*** maškim šà $zabala_4^{ki}$ zi-ga *simat-^{d}ištaran* ki ^{d}*adad-tillati*-ta ba-zi, "*Adad-tillati* disbursed {assorted commodities} (and) 10 liters of fine beer on the 28th day (and) 10 liters of fine beer on the 29th day for the cupboard in Zabala. *Taḫulam* was the deputy. (These were) the expenditures of *Simat-Ištaran*," 541:20–28

[n] ^{dug}níg̃ 2-sìla-ta kaš-[x?]-šè ***ta-ḫu-lam*** maškim ba-zi, "[n] jug(s) of 2 liters each were disbursed for [x?] beer. *Taḫulam* was the deputy," 1330:1–5

ta-tù-ri

Tatturi, the Household Servant from the Gang of *Irib*

1. Errands

1.1 Bringing Barley from G̃irsu

1 ***ta-tù-ri*** ù *a-lí-aḫ* še è-dè g̃ír-su^{ki}-šè g̃en-na g̃iri *ṣa-al-lum* ^{lú}kíg̃-gi_4-a-lugal, "*Tatturi* and *Ali-aḫ* having gone to G̃irsu to bring out barley under the authority of *Ṣallum*, the royal messenger," 31:37–38, 32:37, 33:40–41, 35:44–45, 36:39

1 *a-lí-*[*aḫ*] 1 ***ta-*[*tù-ri*]** š[e . . .], 54:'35–'37

1.2 Bringing a Message to ***Šu-Kabta*** in Nippur

1 ***ta-tù-ri*** á-ág̃ ki *šu-kab-ta*-šè $nibru^{ki}$-šè de_6-a, "*Tatturi* having brought a message to *Šu-Kabta* in Nippur," 24:'25

1.3 Guarding Grain in G̃irsu

1 *a-lí-aḫ* 1 ***ta-tù-ri*** še šà g̃ír-su^{ki} en-nu ke_4-dè gub-ba, "*Ali-aḫ* (and) *Tatturi* employed to guard grain in G̃irsu," 51:'19–'21, 52:56–58, 53:58–60

[1 *a*]-*lí-a*[*ḫ* 1 ***ta-tù***]-⌜***ri***⌝ še šà [g̃ír]-su^{ki} en-nu k[e_4-dè] tuš-[a], "*Ali-aḫ* (and) *Tatturi* having sat in order to guard grain in G̃irsu," 56:'29–'31

2. ***Tatturi***, the Sick Worker

1 ***ta-tù-ri*** dú-ra ugula ***i-ri-ib***, "*Tatturi*, the sick (workman), supervised by *Irib*," 37:40–41, 40:46–47, 41:'27–'29, 47:62–63, 48:70, 49:63–64

1 ***ta-tù-ri*** dú-ra 1 *ar-ri-az* dú-ra ugula *i-ri-ib*, "*Tatturi* and *Arriaz*, sick (workmen) supervised by *Irib*," 38:45–47

[1 ***ta-tù***]***-ri*** d[ú-ra 1 *šu*]*-eš$_4$-tár* ugula *i-r*[*i-ib*], "*Tatturi*, the sick (workman), (and) *Šu-Eštar*, (workers) supervised by *Irib*," 45:32–33

tá-di-na

Tadina, the Braider

1. Receipts: Wool from *Aštaqqar*

12 gín siki ^{geš}garig aka 4-kam-ús ⅔ ma-na siki ^{geš}garig aka gen [ki *aš*]*-tá-qar*-ta [***tá-di-na***][64] túg-[du$_8$ šu b]a-⌜ti⌝, "[*Tadina*], the braider, received 12 shekels of 4th-quality combed wool (and) ⅔ mina of ordinary combed wool from *Aštaqqar*," 710:1–5

tá-din-eš$_4$-tár

1. Provisions

1.1 From *Adad-tillati*

1.1.1 Barley

[n.n.n.] še gur sa$_{10}$ saḫar 48-kam ***tá-din-eš$_4$-tár*** 0.4.0. še sa$_{10}$ saḫar 12-kam *ša-at-èr-ra* ninda du$_8$-dè-⌜šè⌝, "[n] bushel(s) (and) [n] liter(s) of barley, the price of 48 units of dirt for *Tadin-Eštar* (and) 240 liters of barley, the price of 12 units of dirt for *Šat-Erra* to bake bread," 1169:1–6

1.1.2 Regular offerings

1 [. . .] sá-du$_{11}$ ***tá-***⌜***din***⌝***-eš$_4$-tár*** [ki ^{d}]*adad-tillati*-ta ba-zi, "*Adad-tillati* disbursed 1 [. . .], regular offerings of *Tadin-Eštar*," 513:1–5

300 sa gi-izi sá-du$_{11}$-***tá-din-eš$_4$-tár*** ki ^{d}*adad-tillati*-ta ba-zi, "*Adad-tillati* disbursed 300 bundles of fuel reeds, regular offerings of *Tadin-Eštar*," 516:1–5

1.2. A Sheep From *Ili-bilani*

1 udu ***tá-din-eš$_4$-tár*** 1 máš *š*[*a-at*?-x?]*-ab-*[x] ki *ì-lí-bi-la-*[*ni*-ta] ba-zi, "*Ili-bilani* disbursed 1 sheep (for) *Tadin-Eštar* (and) 1 goat (for) *Šat-*[x]," 497:1–4

tá-ḫi-iš-a-tal

1. The Mother of *Taḫiš-atal*

1.1 Provisions: Flour for Bread

0.0.2. zì-KAL 0.0.1. zì-gu-ús ninda-gur$_4$-ra-šè ^{d}inana-zabala$_4^{ki}$ ama ***tá-ḫi-iš-a-tal*** *an-ta-lú* agrig maškim [zi]-ga *šu-kab-tá* ki ^{d}*adad-tillati*-ta ba-zi (šà zabala$_4^{ki}$), "*Adad-tillati* disbursed 20 liters of KAL-flour (and) 10 liters of 2nd-quality gu-flour for thick bread (for) Inana of Zabala (and) the mother of *Taḫiš-atal*. (It was) the expenditure of *Šu-Kabta* in Zabala. *Antalu*, the steward, was the deputy," 1015:1–8, 1018:1–11

---

[64] Restored from seal.

tá-ki-il-ì-lí-ís-sú

1. Expenditures

1.1 Craftsmen and Servants

1 géme-^{d}en-ki géme uš-bar sağ-ba *ga-ṣu-su* dam *a-ḫu-a a-na-a* maškim zi-ga ***tá-ki-il-ì-lí-ís-sú*** ki ^{d}*adad-tillati*-ta ba-zi, "*Adad-tillati* disbursed Geme-Enki, the female weaver, the servant of *Gasusu*, the wife of *Aḫu'a*. (It was) the expenditure of *Takil-ilissu*. *Ana'a* was the deputy," 270:1–7

(. . .) [u$_{4}$-1-šè] ⸢u$_{4}$⸣ siki-ba-ka šu bar-⸢ra⸣ ĝìri *i-ṣur-*^{d}*suen* zi-ga ***tá-ki-il-ì-lí-ís-***[***sú*** ki ^{d}]*adad-tillati*-[ta ba]-⸢zi⸣, "*Adad-tillati* disbursed {craftsmen} released [for 1 day] on the day of the wool rations. (It was) the expenditure of *Takil-ilissu* under the authority of *Iṣur-Suen*," 280:17–23

1.2 Offerings

(. . .) zì-dub-dub-šè (. . .) [sá-du$_{11}$-^{d}ina]na-zabala$_{4}^{ki}$ [. . .]-na [*išdum-ki*]-*in* sagi maškim ⸢zi⸣-ga [***tá***]***-ki-il-ì-lí-ís-sú*** [ki] ^{d}*adad-tillati*-ta ba-zi šà zabala$_{4}^{ki}$, "*Adad-tillati* disbursed {assorted comestibles} for the small flour heap (and) [the regular offerings] of Inana of Zabala [. . .]. (It was) the expenditure of *Takil-ilissu* in Zabala. *Išdum-kin*, the cupbearer, was the deputy," 1027:6, 12–19

(. . .) ninda ba-ra-du$_{8}$ uzu ù tu$_{7}$ ba-ra-šeğ$_{6}$ é-kù-ga (. . .) a-níĝin-šè (. . .) zì-dub-dub-šè (. . .) 60 ^{dug}sìla-bur-zi tu$_{7}$-šè šà kisal-lá ^{d}inana-zabala$_{4}^{ki}$ (. . .) a-níĝin-šè gaba-ri-a ki na-rú-a *išdum-ki-in* sagi maškim zi-ga ***tá-ki-il-ì-lí-ís-sú*** ki ^{d}*adad-tillati*-ta ba-zi šà zabala$_{4}^{ki}$ u$_{4}$-2-kam, "*Adad-tillati* disbursed {assorted commodities} with which bread was baked (and) meat and soup were cooked for the bright temple, {bread and beer} for the a-níĝin ceremony, {grain} for the small flour heap, {assorted commodities} for 60 1-liter offering bowls of soup in the courtyard of Inana of Zabala, (and) {assorted commodities} for the a-níĝin ceremony at the meeting at the place of the stele. (It was) the expenditure of *Takil-ilissu* in Zabala on the 2nd day. *Išdum-kin*, the cupbearer, was the deputy," 1028:10–11, 17, 30, 35–37, 40–45

1.3 Rations, Wages, and Allotments

1.3.1 Equid Fodder for *Ani'a*, a Sheep for *Rubatia*, and Bitumen for *Alla*

0.0.1. še šà-gal ^{anše}kúnga *á-ni-á* dumu ùr?-[x] 1 udu *ru-ba-ti-a* 0.0.3. ésir-é-a *al-la* gudu$_{4}$ ^{d}*adad-tillati* šabra maškim z[i-g]a [***tá***]***-ki-***⸢***il***⸣***-ì-lí-ís-sú*** ki ^{d}*adad-tillati*-ta ba-zi, "*Adad-tillati* disbursed 10 liters of barley, fodder of equids (for) *Ani'a*, the son of Ur?-[x], 1 sheep (for) *Rubatia*, 30 liters of house bitumen (for) *Alla*, the gudu-priest. (It was) the expenditure of *Takil-ilissu*. *Adad-tillati*, the majordomo, was the deputy," 534:1–12

1.3.2 A Sheep for *Aḫu'a*

1 udu-niga *a-ḫu-a* zi-ga ***tá-ki-il-ì-lí-ís-sú*** ki ^{d}*adad-tillati*-ta ba-zi, "*Adad-tillati* disbursed 1 fattened sheep (for) *Aḫu'a*. (It was) the expenditure of *Takil-ilissu*," 519:1–6

1.3.3 Provisions for Craftswomen

(. . .) ba-na-ḫa-[la *a*]-*na-a* PA.[KAŠ$_{4}$ s]a$_{10}$-bi ĝeš 1 [x x]-na-[x] *tu-ra-am-ì-lí* d[ub-sar] PA.A[L z]i-ga ⸢***tá***⸣***-ki-il-ì-lí-ís-sú*** [ki] ^{d}*adad-tillati*-ta ⸢ba⸣-zi, "*Adad-tillati* disbursed {assorted commodities}. They were divided for {female weavers, sesame pressers, and millers}. *Ana'a* was the deputy. (?). *Turam-ili*, the scribe, was the majordomo. (These were) the expenditures of *Takil-ilissu*," 536:22–31

ti-ga-an

Tigan, the Ox-Herder, Supervised by *Nur-Adad*, the Majordomo

1. **Ox-drivers from his Gang**

2 g̃uruš ugula ***ti-ga-an*** nu-bànda-[gu_4] (. . .) ⸢*nu*⸣-*úr*-^{d}*adad* nu-bànda-gu_4, "2 workmen supervised by *Tigan*, the ox-herder, (and) {other gangs}, supervised by *Nur-Adad*, the ox-herder," 187:5, 8, 10

n g̃uruš ***ti-ga-an*** nu-bànda-gu_4 (. . .) ugula *nu-úr-*^{d}*adad* šabra šà-gu_4-me-éš, "n workmen (from the gang of) *Tigan* (and) {other gangs}, ox-drivers supervised by *Nur-Adad*, the majordomo," 191:15, 17–18, 198:'6–'7, '9

[n g̃uru]š ***ti-ga-an*** nu-bànda-gu_4 (. . .) šà-g[u_4-me-éš ára]d-é-a-[me-éš] (. . .) ugula *nu-úr-*^{d}⸢*adad*⸣, "[n] workmen (from the gang of) *Tigan*, the ox-herder, (and) {other gangs}, ox-drivers—household servants—(and) {hired workers} supervised by *Nur-Adad*," 194: 20–22, 26

n g̃uruš ***ti-ga-an*** nu-bànda-gu_4 šà-gu_4-me-éš (. . .) ugula *nu-úr-*^{d}*adad* šabra, "n workmen (from the gang of) *Tigan*, the ox-herder, (and) {other gangs}, ox-drivers (and) {hired workers} supervised by *Nur-Adad*, the majordomo," 196:'9–'10, '13, 197:16–17, 20

tu-ku-lí

Tukulli, the Sick Builder

1. **Provisions: Oil**

½ sìla ì-[g̃eš] ***tu-ku-lí*** šidim u_4 dú-ra i-[me-a], "½ liter of sesame oil (for) *Tukulli*, the builder, when he was sick," 444:1–2

tu-ra-a

1. **Seal of *Tura'a*: Delivery of a Textile**

1 túg-guz-za-gen ki *aš-tá-qar*-ta *puzur*$_4$*-a-gum*! šu ba-an-ti kišib ***tu-ra-a*** íb-ra g̃iri ^{d}*adad-tillati* ù ^{d}*ma-lik-ba-ni*, "Under the authority of *Adad-tillati* and *Malik-bani*, *Puzur-agum* received 1 ordinary tufted textile from *Aštaqqar*. *Tura'a* rolled (his) seal," 644:1–7

tu-ra-am-ì-lí

1. ***Turam-ili*, the Scribe and Majordomo**

(. . .) ba-na-ḫa-[la *a*]-*na-a* PA.[$KAŠ_4$ s]a_{10}-bi g̃eš 1 [x x]-na-[x] ***tu-ra-am-ì-lí*** d[ub-sar] PA.A[L z]i-ga ⸢*tá*⸣-*ki-il-ì-lí-ís-sú* [ki] ^{d}*adad-tillati*-ta ⸢ba⸣-zi, "*Adad-tillati* disbursed {assorted commodities}. They were divided for {female weavers, sesame pressers and millers}. *Ana'a* was the deputy. (?). *Turam-ili*, the scribe, was the majordomo. (These were) the expenditures of *Takil-ilissu*," 536:22–31

2. ***Turam-ili*, Man from Karkar**

1 ***tu-ra-am-ì-lí*** (. . .) ugula *á-ni*-x-x (. . .) lú-karkar^{ki}-me, "*Turam-ili*, supervised by *á-ni*-x-x, (and) {other workers}, men from Karkar," 559:14, 25, 28, 559:22, 25, 28

3. ***Turam-ili***, **the Reed Carrier: Provisions**

[. . . n m]a-na tuḫ-ĝeš-ì-ḫád-ta [n.n.n.] ádda-udu-ta [n gín] mun-ta [n gí]n luḫ-lá-ta [1 *e*]*l?-pa-dan* [1] ***tu-ra-am-ì-lí*** 2 [gi-g]a$_6$-me-éš, "[. . ., n] mina(s) of dried sesame chaff each, [n] sheep carcass(es) each, [n shekel(s)] of salt each, (and) [n shekel(s)] of luḫ-lá each, (provisions for) *Elpadan* (and) *Turam-ili*, 2 [reed] carriers," 562:'62–'69

4. ***Turam-ili***, **the Scribe**

4.1 Under his Authority

4.1.1 Rations, Wages, and Allotments

4.1.1.1 For Household Servants

(. . .) géme árad-é-a ba-na-ḫa-la ĝìri ***tu-ra-am-ì-lí*** dub-sar zi-ga *simat-*^{d}*ištaran* ki ^{d}*adad-tillati*-ta ba-zi, "Under the authority of *Turam-ili*, the scribe, *Adad-tillati* disbursed {assorted commodities}. They were divided for the female and male household servants. (It was) the expenditure of *Simat-Ištaran*," 528:12–16, 548:15–20

4.1.1.2 Slaughtered Birds for the House of the Steward

(. . .) ba-úš é-agrig$_5$-šè ĝìri ***tu-ra-am-ì-lí*** dub-sar ki ^{d}*adad-tillati*-ta ba-zi, "*Adad-tillati* disbursed {assorted birds on the 20th, 25th and 28th of the month}. They were slaughtered for the house of the steward under the authority of *Turam-ili*, the scribe," 526:12–15

4.1.2 Wood Stored in the Garden House

ĝeš é-⸢^{ĝeš}kiri$_6$⸣-a gub-ba šu-sum-ma ^{ĝeš}kiri$_6$ igi-érim-iri^{ki} ki ^{d}*ma-lik-ba-ni* santana-ta *ak-ba-zum* um-mi-a ì-dab$_5$ šà gar-ša-an-na^{ki} ⸢ĝìri⸣ ***tu-ra-am-ì-lí*** dub-sar, "From *Malik-bani*, the date orchard administrator, *Akbazum*, the master craftsman, took in charge wood stored in the garden house, the inventory of the Igi-erim-iri garden. (Transaction) in Garšana under the authority of *Turam-ili*, the scribe," 1375:45–51

5. ***Turam-ili***, **Title Unspecified**

5.1 Ordered to Deliver the Accounts of *Adad-tillati*

tu-ra-am-ì-lí ù-na-a-du$_{11}$ níĝ-kas$_7$ ^{d}*adad-tillati* šabra mu na-rú-a-maḫ-ta mu si-mu-ru-um^{ki} ba-ḫulu-šè ḫé-en-ĝá-ĝá ú-lá-bi, "Say to *Turam-ili* that 'the account of *Adad-tillati*, the majordomo, for the year *Šu-Suen* 6 to *Šu-Suen* 7, should be brought forth quickly,'" 1040:1–7

5.2 Provisions

0.0.2.5 <sìla> ***tu-ra-am-ì-lí***, "23 <liters> (for) *Turam-ili*," 558:'4

– U –

u-bar-ri-a

é-ki-ba-g̃ar-ra ***u-bar-ri-a***, "the replacement house of *Ubarria*" > *Household Index*

é-***u-bar-ri-a***, "the house of *Ubarria*" > *Household Index*

u-bar-tum

1. Deliveries: Grains

4.0.0. dabin gur ⸢bisag̃⸣-dub-ba-ka g̃ál-la 17.3.4.5 sìla še gur 3.4.0. zíz gur ki ***u-bar-tum***-ta, "From *Ubartum* there are 4 bushels of semolina in the tablet basket (and) 17 bushels (and) 225 liters of barley (and) 3 bushels (and) 240 liters of emmer wheat," 1233:12–16

2. Under her Authority: Goat Hair and a Braider

⅓ ma-na siki-ud$_5$ 1 g̃uruš túg-du$_8$ u$_4$-5-šè g̃iri ***u-bar-tum*** (. . .) ki *ḫa-lí*-ta ba-zi, "Under the authority of *Ubartum*, *Ḫali* disbursed ⅓ mina of goat hair (and) 1 braider for 5 days (and) {other commodities under different authority}," 783:9–11, 13

u-bar-um

é-ki-ba-g̃ar-ra ***u-bar-um***, "the replacement house of *Ubarum*" > *Household Index*

1. *Ubarum*, Man from *Izin-Erra*

1.1 As a Runaway

zàḫ *a-ḫu-wa-qar* zàḫ ***u-bar-um*** [lú]-*i-zi-in-èr-ra*^{ki}-éš, "*Aḫu-waqar* (and) *Ubarum*, runaways from *Izin-Erra*," 378:6–8

1.2 Provisions

[2 sìla] ninda-ta (. . .) 1 *a-ḫu-wa-qar* 1 ***u-bar-um*** lú-*i-zi-in-èr-ra*^{ki} (. . .) šà-gal ši[dim-e-n]e ⸢u$_4$⸣ [bàd egir] é-a dù-dè, "[2 liters] of bread each for *Aḫu-waqar* (and) *Ubarum*, men from *Izin-Erra*, (and for) {other workers}, food (for) builders when they were constructing [the (enclosure) wall behind] the house," 386:1, 7–9, 29–30

2. *Ubarum*, from the Gang of *Malik-tillati*, the Ox-Herder

[1 g̃uruš] dú-ra 1 ***ú-bar-⸢um⸣*** 1 *bí-za-⸢tum⸣* 1 *šu-*^{d}*⸢adad⸣* 1 AN.TAG.⸢KAL⸣ ^{d}*ma-lik-tillati* [nu-bànda]-gu$_4$ ugula *nu-úr-*^{d}*adad* šabra, "[1] sick [workman], *Ubarum*, *Bizatum*, *Šu-Adad* (and) AN.TAG.KAL, (workers from the gang of) *Malik-tillati*, the ox-herder, supervised by *Nur-Adad*, the majordomo," 198:'32–'38

3. *Ubarum*, Title Unspecified

[. . .]-3-[. . . ***ú***]***-bar-um***, 1254:1–3

ù-ṣí-na-wi-ir

Uṣi-nawir, the Scribe

1. Under his Authority: Garden Products

9.1.1.5 sìla zú-lum gur 1.0.1. u$_4$-ḫi-in gur 10⅚ 6 gín ^{geš}zé-na 656 peš-múrgu 3½ 3 gín peš-ga 1065 á-an-zú-lum káb du$_{11}$-ga ^{geš}⸢kiri$_6$⸣ ki ^{d}*adad-tillati*-ta *a-da-làl* um-mi-a dumu *šu*-ma-ma šu ba-ti g̃iri ***ù-ṣí-na-wi-ir*** dub-sar, "Under the authority of *Uṣi-nawir*, the scribe, *Adallal*, the craftsman, the son of *Šu*-Mama, received from *Adad-tillati* 9 bushels (and) 75 liters of dates, 1 bushel and 10 liters of fresh dates, 10⁵/₆ (minas and) 6 shekels of date palm frond midribs, 656 date palm spines, 3½ (minas and) 3 shekels of date palm hearts (and) 1065 date clusters; commodities of the garden measured for accounting," 1215:1–11

2. Under his Authority: Workwomen Sorting Wool

4 géme uš-bar u_4-1-šè siki igi sağ-ğá šà é-^{d}*šu*-^{d}*suen*^{ki} ğìri ***ù-ṣí-na-wi-ir*** ù *en-um-ì-lí* ki ^{d}*adad-tillati*-ta ba-zi, "Under the authority of *Uṣi-nawir* and *Enum-ili*, *Adad-tillati* disbursed 4 female weavers for 1 day having sorted wool in *Bit-Šu-Suen*," 264:1–6[65]

8 géme u_4-1-šè [siki] igi sağ-ğá šà é-^{d}*šu*-^{d}*suen*^{ki}-ka de_6-a ğìri ^{d}en-líl-*ba-za-du* ù ***ù-ṣí-na-wi-ir*** dub-sar-me ki ^{d}*adad-tillati*-ta ba-zi, "Under the authority of Enlil-*bazadu* and *Uṣi-nawir*, the scribes, *Adad-tillati* disbursed 8 workwomen for 1 day having brought [wool] sorted in *Bit-Šu-Suen*," 279:1–7

ud-du-ur

1. Delivieries: Reed Craftsmen

1.1 To Bring Barley

2 ğuruš [ad-kub_4 u_4]-10-šè ⌜še⌝ ù-dag-ga^{ki}-t[a gar-ša]-an-na^{ki}-šè de_6-a 2 ğuruš ad-kub_4 u_4-1-šè ⌜še⌝ *dì-im-bu-*⌜*na*⌝-^{d}àš-gi_5-[ta é]-$duru_5$-kab-bi^{ki}-[šè] ğìri ^{d}*adad-tillati* šabra [ki ***ud***]-***du-ur***-ta ba-zi, "Under the authority of *Adad-tillati*, the majordomo, *Uddur* disbursed 2 [reed craftsmen] for 10 [days] having brought barley from Udaga to Garšana (and) 2 reed craftsmen for 1 day (having brought) barley [from] *Dimbun*-Ašgi [to] the Kabbi village," 288:1–11

2 ğuruš ad-kub_4 u_4-20-šè še é-$duru_5$-kab-bí-ta gar-ša-an-na^{ki}-šè de_6-a ğìri [^{d}*adad*]-*tillati* [šabra] ki ***ud-*[*du*]*-ur***-⌜ta⌝ ba-zi, "Under the authority of *Adad-tillati*, [the majordomo], *Uddur* disbursed 2 reed craftsmen for 20 days having brought barley from the Kabbi village to Garšana," 300:1–7

1.2 To Remove Dirt and Harvest Barley

[1] ğuruš ad-kub_4 [u_4]-13-šè saḫar zi-ga i_7-ma-ma-*šar-ra-at* ğìri *ba-ba-ni* dub-sar 1 ğuruš ad-kub_4 u_4-4-šè *dì-im-bu-na*-àš-gi_5-ta a-šà *ṣe-r*[*u-u*]*m*-šè še gur_{10}-gur_{10}-[dè] gub-ba ğìri *é-a-*⌜*šar*⌝ šabra ki ***ud-du-ur***-ta ba-zi, "*Uddur* disbursed [1] reed craftsman for 13 [days] having moved dirt at the Mama-*šarrat* canal under the authority of *Babani*, the scribe, (and) 1 reed craftsman (having gone) from *Dimbun*-Ašgi to the *Ṣerum* field, employed for 4 days [to] reap barley under the authority of *Ea-šar*, the majordomo," 284:1–12

2. Receipts from *Adad-tillati*

2.1 Barley: Wages of Reed Craftsmen

0.2.0. še á ad-kub_4 ḫuğ-ğá-šè ki ^{d}*adad-tillati*-ta ***ud-du-ur*** šu ba-ti, "*Uddur* received 120 liters of barley for wages of hired reed craftsmen from *Adad-tillati*," 518:1–5

0.n.0. še á ad-kub_4-šè ki ^{d}*adad-tillati*-ta ***ud-du-ur*** šu ba-ti, "*Uddur* received n liter(s) of barley for wages of reed craftsmen from *Adad-tillati*," 546:1–5, 547:1–5

[65] Although *Uṣi-nawir's* title is not specified, this text is included here in light of no. 279.

2.2 House Bitumen

n sìla ésir-é-a ki ᵈ*adad-tillati*-ta ***ud-du-ur*** šu ba-ti, "*Uddur* received n liter(s) of house bitumen from *Adad-tillati*," 1353:1–4, 1355:1–4

2.3 House Bitumen and Reeds

0.0.n.n ésir-é-a n sa gi-šid ki ᵈ*adad-tillati*-ta ***ud-du-ur*** šu ba-ti, "*Uddur* received n liter(s) of house bitumen (and) n bundle(s) of dry reeds from *Adad-tillati*," 1357:1–5, 1358:1–5, 1363:1–5, 1373:1–5, 1374:1–5

2.4 Reeds

37 sa gi ki ᵈ*adad-tillati*-ta ***ud-du-ur*** [šu ba]-ti, "*Uddur* received 37 bundles of reeds from *Adad-tillati*," 1356:1–4

n sa gi-šid ki ᵈ*adad-tillati*-ta ***ud-du-ur*** šu ba-ti, "*Uddur* received n bundle(s) of dry reeds from *Adad-tillati*," 1360:1–4, 1364:1–4

um-mi-kab-tá

1. *Ummi-Kabta*, Daughter of the House

1.1 Provisions

1.1.1 Animals

3 udu 1 máš-ga šáḫ-ĝe$_6$ TAG$_4$.ALAM 2 udu-ú ***um-mi-kab-tá*** dumu-munus é-a ⌜ki⌝ *ì-lí-bi-la-ni*-ta ba-zi, "*Ili-bilani* disbursed 3 sheep, 1 suckling goat, (1?) TAG$_4$.ALAM black pig (and) 2 range-fed sheep (for) *Ummi-Kabta*, daughter of the house," 421:1–5

1.1.2 Barley Groats, Grits, Processed Peas, and Reeds

3⅓ sìla níĝ-àr-r[a-si]g$_5$ 3⅓ sìla ar-za-[na] 3⅓ sìla gú-tur al-ús-sa 60 sa gi-izi ⌜níĝ⌝-dab$_5$ ***um-mi-kab-tá*** dumu-munus šà é-a [ki] ᵈ*adad-tillati*-ta, "*Adad-tillati* disbursed 3⅓ liters of fine groats, 3⅓ liters of barley-grits, 3⅓ liters of processed peas (and) 60 bundles of fuel reeds, requisitions of *Ummi-Kabta*, daughter of the house," 409:1–6

3⅓ sìla níĝ-àr-ra 3⅓ sìla ar-za-na [3?]⅓ sìla gú-tur al-ús-sa 60 sa gi-izi ⌜sá⌝-du$_{11}$-***um-mi-kab-ta*** dumu-[munus] é-a [ki ᵈ*a*]*dad-tillati*-ta [ba]-zi, "*Adad-tillati* disbursed 3⅓ liters of groats, 3⅓ liters of barley-grits, [3?]⅓ liters of processed peas (and) 60 bundles of fuel reeds, regular offerings of *Ummi-Kabta*, daughter of the house," 416:1–7

2. *Ummi-Kabta*, Title Unspecified

2.1 Deliveries: Assorted Wool, Receipt of *Aštaqqar*

(. . .) ki ***um-mi-⌜kab⌝-ta***-ta *aš-tá-qar* šu ba-an-ti, "*Aštaqqar* received {assorted wool} from *Ummi-Kabta*," 671:5–6

2.2 Provisions: Semolina and Fine Flour

2 sìla dabin 1 sìla eša ***um-mi-kab-tá*** 2 sìla dabin 1 sìla eša *ma-la-ti* ᵈ*ma-lik-tillat-sú* šu-i maškim, "2 liters of semolina (and) 1 liter of fine flour (for) *Ummi-Kabta* (and) 2 liters of semolina (and) 1 liter of fine flour (for) *Malati*. *Malik-tillassu*, the barber, was the deputy," 1016:13–17

2.3 Requisitions

0.4.0. ninda níĝ-dab$_5$ ***um-mi-kab-tá*** (. . .) [níĝ-kas$_7$]-aka [*ì-lí*]-*bi-la-ni* muḫaldim, "240 liters of bread, requisitions of *Ummi-Kabta*, (and) {other allotments} the balanced account of *Ili-bilani*, the cook," 1527:25–26

ur-^{d}asar-lu-ḫi

Ur-Asarluḫi, Builder from Niĝ-Ba'u

1. Provisions

1.1 Semolina and Barley

2 sìla dabin-ta 2 sìla še-ta ur-te-me-na 1 **ur-^{d}asar-lu-ḫi** 1 *du-du-gu* 1 ^{d}utu-sá-bí [1] lú-me-lám lú-níĝ-^{d}ba-ú šidim-me-éš (. . .) šà-gal šidim-e-ne, "2 liters of semolina each (and) 2 liters of barley each (for) Ur-temena, Ur-Asarluḫi, *Dudugu*, Utu-sabi (and) Lu-melam, builders from Niĝ-Ba'u, (and for) {other workers}, food (for) builders," 381:5–12, 21

2 sìla dabin-ta 2 sìla še-ta ur-te-me-na 1 **ur-^{d}asar-lu-ḫi** 1 *du-du-gu* 1 ^{d}utu-sá-bí 1 lú-me-lám lú-níĝ-^{d}ba-ú šidim (. . .) šà-gal šidim-e-ne u$_4$ bàd egir é-a dù-dè, "2 liters of semolina (and) 2 liters of barley each (for) Ur-temena, Ur-Asarluḫi, *Dudugu*, Utu-sabi (and) Lu-melam, builders from Niĝ-Ba'u, (and for) {other workers}, food (for) builders when they were constructing the (enclosure) wall behind the house," 386:13–20, 29–30, 387:5–11, 20–21

2 sìla dabin-ta 2 sìla še-ta ur-te-me-na 1 **ur-^{d}asar-lu-ḫi** 1 *du-du-gu* 1 ^{d}utu-sá-bí 1 lú-me-lám lú-níĝ-^{d}ba-ú šidim (. . .) šà-gal šidim-e-ne u$_4$ bàd in-dù-sa-a, "2 liters of semolina each (and) 2 liters of barley each (for) Ur-temena, Ur-Asarluḫi, *Dudugu*, Utu-sabi (and) Lu-melam, builders from Niĝ-Bau, (and for) {other workers}, food (for) builders when they constructed the (enclosure) wall," 396:5–12, 19–20, 397:5–13, 19–20

1.2 Sheep and Grains

[0.1.0 še-ta 0.1.0 dabin-ta 3 ádda]-udu-ta [ur-te]-me-na [1 **ur-^{d}a]sar-lu-ḫi** [1] *du-du-gu* [1] lú-me-lám [1] ^{d}utu-sá-ti(!) lú-níĝ-^{d}ba-ú-me-éš (. . .) [šà-gal šidim] ù dub-sar-e-ne, "[60 liters of barley, 60 of liters of semolina (and) 3] sheep [carcasses] each (for) Ur-temena, Ur-Asarluḫi, *Dudugu*, Lu-melam, (and) Utu-sabi, men from Niĝ-Ba'u, (and for) {other workers}, [food (for) builders] and scribes," 399:1–9, 24

ur-^{d}dumu-zi

1. Ur-Dumuzi, the Ox-Herder, Supervised by *Nur-Adad*, the Majordomo

1.1 Ox-drivers from his Gang

n ĝuruš **ur-^{d}dumu-zi** nu-bànda-gu$_4$ (. . .) ugula *nu-úr-^{d}adad* šabra šà-gu$_4$-me-éš, "n workmen (from the gang of) Ur-Dumuzi, the ox-herder, (and) {other gangs}, ox-drivers supervised by *Nur-Adad*, the majordomo," 188:'2–'4, 190:11–13, 191:14, 17–18, 198:'5, '7, '9

n ĝuruš **ur-^{d}dumu-zi** nu-bànda-gu$_4$ (. . .) šà-gu$_4$-me-éš (. . .) ugula *nu-úr-^{d}adad* (šabra), "n workmen (from the gang of) Ur-Dumuzi, the ox-herder, (and) {other gangs}, ox-drivers (and) {hired workers} supervised by *Nur-Adad*, (the majordomo)," 193:13–15, 196:'8, '10, '13, 197:15, 17, 20 [n g̃uruš] **ur-^{d}dumu-zi** nu-bànda-gu$_4$ (. . .) šà-g[u$_4$-me-éš ára]d-é-a-[me-éš] (. . .) ugula *nu-úr-*^{d}⌜*adad*⌝, "[n workmen] (from the gang of) Ur-Dumuzi, the ox-herder, (and) {other gangs}, ox-drivers—household servants—(and) {hired workers} supervised by *Nur-Adad*," 194:19, 21–22, 26

1.2 Sick Workmen from his Gang

[n] g̃uruš dú-ra-éš [**ur-^{d}]dumu-zi** nu-bànda-gu$_4$ ù ugula-é, "[n] sick workmen (from the gang of) Ur-Dumuzi, the ox-herder and overseer of the house," 194:68–69

1.3 Receipts: Grains

[šu+níg̃in] 242.2.4.5 sìla še gur šu+níg̃in 25.0.0. zíz gur šu+níg̃in 4.1.4. kib$_x$ gur **u[r-^{d}dumu-z]i** nu-bànda-gu$_4$ [šu] ⌜ba⌝-ti g̃ìri *é-a-ša*[*r* šabra], "Under the authority of *Ea-šar*, [the majordomo], Ur-Dumuzi, the ox-herder, received a total of 242 bushels (and) 165 liters of barley, 25 bushels of emmer wheat (and) 4 bushels (and) 100 liters of wheat," 1233:20–26

1.3.1 For Fodder

27.1.4. še gur mur-gud-šè ba-zi g̃ìri *é-a-šar* **ur-^{d}dumu-zi** nu-bànda-gu$_4$, "Under the authority of *Ea-šar*, Ur-Dumuzi, the ox-herder, (received) 27 bushels (and) 100 liters of barley for ox fodder disbursed," 1236:1–5

1.3.2 For Seed and Rations

33.4.1. še gur numun-šè 0.1.0. še-ba lú-^{d}*suen* má-laḫ$_5$ ba-zi g̃ìri *é-a-šar* **ur-^{d}dumu-zi** [nu]-bànda-gu$_4$, "Ur-Dumuzi, the ox-herder, (received) 33 bushels (and) 250 liters of barley for seed (and) 60 liters (for) the barley ration of Lu-*Suena*, the sailor, disbursed under the authority of *Ea-šar*," 543:1–6

1.3.3 From the Granary

21.4.3. še gur ì-dub še-ba iti-3-kam g̃ìri *é-a-šar* **ur-^{d}dumu-zi** nu-bànda-gu$_4$, "Under the authority of *Ea-šar*, Ur-Dumuzi, the ox-herder, (received) 21 bushels (and) 270 liters of barley of the granary (for) barley rations (for) 3 months," 542:1–6

5.0.0. zíz gur 0.3.3. kib$_x$ ì-dub a-šà mí-mí 15.2.0. zíz gur 0.1.3. kib$_x$ ì-dub šà *dì-im-bu*-bu(sic!)<-aš>-gi$_5$ 20.2.0. ziz gur 1.0.0. kib$_x$ gur ki *i-dì-èr-ra*-ta **ur-^{d}dumu-zi** šu ba-ti g̃ìri *é-a-šar* šabra, "Under the authority of *Ea-šar*, the majordomo, Ur-Dumuzi received from *Iddi-Erra* 5 bushels of emmer wheat (and) 210 liters of wheat of the granary of the Mimi field, 15 bushels (and) 120 liters of emmer (and) 90 liters of wheat of the granary in *Dimbun*-Ašgi, (and) 20 bushels (and) 120 liters of emmer wheat (and) 1 bushel of wheat," 1232:1–12[66]

5.0.0. zíz gur 0.3.3. kib$_x$ ì-dub a-šà mí-mí ki *i-dì-èr-ra*-ta **ur-^{d}dumu-zi** šu ba-ti, "Ur-Dumuzi received 5 bushels of emmer wheat (and) 210 liters of wheat of the granary of the Mimi field from *Iddi-Erra*," 1235:1–6

---

[66] Although Ur-Dumuzi's title is not specified in nos. 1232 and 1235, these texts are included here in light of the similar transaction no. 542.

2. Ur-Dumuzi, Title Unspecified

2.1 Orders for Ur-Dumuzi and *Aḫu-waqar*

ur-^{d}dumu-zi ù *a-ḫu-wa-qar* ù-na-a-⸢du$_{11}$⸣ 0.0.2. ku-[x] *šu*-^{d}nisaba ḫé-na-ab-sum-mu 1 g̃uruš šà-gu$_{4}$ iri^{ki}-ta iri^{ki}-šè ḫé-eb-sá-e nam-mi-gur-re, "Say to Ur-Dumuzi and *Aḫu-waqar* that '20 liters of (?) should be given to *Šu*-Nisaba. 1 ox-driver from the city should arrive at the city. They should not argue!'" 1045:1–11

2.2 Translation Uncertain

še-gán-bi 36.1.0. še gur 11.1.0. zíz gur lá-ìa su-ga še gu$_{4}$ e-na-am-DU **ur-^{d}dumu-zi ù *i-din-èr-ra*, "Their barley of the field: 36 bushels (and) 60 liters of barley (and) 11 bushels (and) 60 liters of emmer wheat; the remainder was replaced. Ur-Dumuzi and *Iddin-Erra* (?) barley and oxen," 1233:8–11

ur-é-an-na

Ur-Eana, the Scribe

1. As a Deputy: Deliveries of *Adad-tillati*

1.1 A Basket for Tablets

[1] ^{gi}bisag̃-im-sar-ra [sa-ḫ]a ⅔ kùš íb-sá im-sar-ra g̃[á-g̃á-dè **u**]**r-é-an-na** [dub]-sar maškim [ki] ^{d}*adad-tillati*-ta ba-zi, "*Adad-tillati* disbursed [1] canvas-lined clay tablet coffer —it is ⅔ kùš square—(in which) to deposit clay tablets. Ur-Eana, the scribe, was the deputy," 1331:1–5

1.2 Leather

1 kuš-[udu] ú-ḫáb 4 kuš-udu e-rí-na ⸢ka⸣-tab-šè [n ^{kuš}du$_{10}$]-gan-ti-bal [**ur-é-an**]**-na** dub-sar maškim [ki] ^{d}[*adad-til*]*lati*-ta ba-zi, "*Adad-tillati* disbursed 1 madder-tanned [sheep] skin (and) 4 root-tanned sheep skins for covers (and) [n leather] bag(s) with a marking?. Ur-Eana, the scribe, was the deputy," 917:1–7

1.3 Offerings

(. . .) sízkur dig̃ir-re-[e?]-ne [. . . x N]IM?^{ki} **ur-é-an-na** dub-sar maškim zi-ga *šu-kab-tá* ki ^{d}*adad-tillati*-ta ba-zi, "*Adad-tillati* disbursed {assorted grains and dates}, (ceremonial) offerings of the gods, [. . . El]am? (It was) the expenditure of *Šu-Kabta*. Ur-Eana, the scribe, was the deputy," 1017:6–10

1.3 Broken Context

[. . .**u**]**r-é-an-na** dub-sar maškim, "[. . .], Ur-Eana, the scribe, was the deputy," 1013:1–3

2. Under his Authority

2.1 Dead Birds for the Steward's House: Delivery of *Adad-tillati*

2 ir$_{7}^{mušen}$ u$_{4}$-20-kam 2 ir$_{7}^{mušen}$ u$_{4}$-10-kam [ba]-úš é-⸢agrig⸣-šè g̃ìri **ur-é-an-na** dub-sar [ki ^{d}]*ada*[*d-tillati*]-ta ba-zi, "Under the authority of Ur-Eana, the scribe, *Adad-tillati* disbursed 2 pigeons on the 20th day (and) 2 pigeons on the 10th day. They were slaughtered for the house of the steward," 522:1–8

ur-^{d}en-líl-lá

1. Provisions: Barley

17.3.2. gur **ur-^{d}en-líl-lá** (. . .) [šu+níĝin n+]7.0.0. gur še-ba *ba-zi-tum* šu+níĝin 47.1.[n.] še-ba é, "17 bushels (and) 200 liters of (barley) (for) Ur-Enlila (and barley for) {other individuals}; [in total: n+]7 bushels of the barley rations of *Bazitum*. In total: 47 bushels (and) 60[+n] liters of barley rations of the household," 555:14–15, 24–25

2. As a Witness

igi **ur-^{d}en-líl-lá**, "witnessed by Ur-Enlila," 1060:8

ur-gi-a-zu

Ur-giazu, the Servant

1. Provisions: Barley

[0.n].3. **ur?-gi-a-zu** [gur] (. . .) [šu+níĝin n+]5.4.1.8 sìla še gur lugal-ú-šim-e árad!-me-éš, "[n+]30 liters of barley (for) Ur-giazu, (and barley for) {others}, [in total: n+]5 bushels (and) 258 liters of barley (for) the servants (supervised by) Lugal-ušime," 504:2, 7–10

ur-me

Ur-me, the Date Orchard Administrator

1. Provisions: Wool and Oil

0.0.2. še 2 ma-na siki-gen 1 [sìla ì-ĝeš] **ur-me** ⸢santana⸣ mu udug kislaḫ saḫar zi-zi-dè-šè, "20 liters of barley, 2 minas of ordinary wool, (and) 1 [liter of sesame oil] (for) Ur-me, the date orchard administrator, (provisions) for caretakers to move dirt (to/from) the lot," 1011:11–15

ur-mes

1. Ur-mes, the Builder

1.1 Provisions: Dried Fish

10 ku_6 al-dar-ra **ur-mes** šidim (. . .) ⸢u_4⸣ é-e im sumur ba-aka, "10 (split) dried fish for Ur-mes, the builder (and) {other allotments} when the house was plastered," 472:1–2, 14

2. Ur-mes, Title Unspecified

2.1 Deliveries: A Sheep

1 udu ki **ur-mes**-[ta] ^{d}*adad-tillati* ì-dab_5 ĝìri *sú-kà-lí*, "Under the authority of *Sukkali*, *Adad-tillati* took in charge 1 sheep from Ur-mes," 1149:1–5

ur-^{d}nanše

1. Ur-^{d}Nanše, the Builder

1 **ur-^{d}nanše** šidim l[ú-GN], "Ur-Nanše, the builder from [GN]," 111:45

ur-ni$_9$-g̃ar

1. Deliveries: Sheep and Goats

★★(. . .) 60 udu-máš ḫi-a [x]-*qar* [x-x]-dig̃ir?-a [. . .] 140 [?] ki **ur-ni$_9$-g̃ar**-[ta] (. . .) níg̃-kas$_7$-aka ^{d}*adad-tillati* šabra, "(In total:) 60 various sheep (and) goats (?) [. . .] (and) 140 (?), from Ur-nig̃ar, (and) {other commodities}, the balanced account of *Adad-tillati*, the majordomo," 984:12–15, '75–'76

1 udu-níta é-udu-niga-šè ki **ur-ni$_9$-g̃ar**-[ta] ^{d}*adad-tillati* ì-dab$_5$, "*Adad-tillati* took in charge 1 fattened sheep for the fattening pen from Ur-nig̃ar," 1207:1–5

ur-^{d}nin-^{d}si$_4$-an-na

1. Ur-Nin-Siana, the Cupbearer: As a Deputy

1.1 Craftsmen to Harvest Barley

1 g̃uruš ašgab u$_4$-1-šè še gur$_{10}$-gur$_{10}$-dè a-šà *dì-im-bu-na*-àš-gi$_5$ gub-ba **ur-^{d}nin-^{d}si$_4$-an-na** maškim ki ^{d}*adad-tillati*-ta ba-zi g̃ìri *a-ḫu-wa-qar* dub-sar, "Under the authority of *Aḫu-waqar*, the scribe, *Adad-tillati* disbursed 1 leather worker employed for 1 day to reap barley at the *Dimbun*-Ašgi field. Ur-Nin-Siana was the deputy,"[67] 282:1–6

1.2 Offerings and Provisions

1.2.1 Assorted Commodities

1.2.1.1 For the Additional Flour Heap and Nergal

[. . . n.n.n. A.TI]R zú-lu[m ba-ḫi zì-dub]-dub-didli-[šè n.n.n.n sìl]a zì gu[r ^{d}PIRI]G.UNU-gal dumu e-é-zi [**ur**]-**^{d}nin-^{d}si$_4$-an-na** sagi ⌜maškim⌝, "[. . . (and) n liter(s)] of fine flour [were mixed (with)] dates [for] various small [flour] heaps (and) [n] bushel(s) (and) [n] liter(s) of flour (for) Nergal, (the personal deity of) the son of E'ezi. Ur-Nin-Siana, the cupbearer, was the deputy," 484:1–6

1.2.1.2 When *Šu-Kabta* Went to and from G̃EŠ.KÚŠU

0.0.4.4 sìla dabin 0.0.2.8 sìla eša 0.0.1. zú-lum eša {erased} ba-ḫi zì-dub-dub-didli-šè u$_4$ *šu-kab-ta* G̃EŠ.KÚŠU^{ki}-šè du-ni {erased} u$_4$ *šu-kab-ta* G̃EŠ.KÚŠU^{ki}-ta du-ni **ur-^{d}nin-si$_4$-an-na** sagi maškim zi-ga *šu-kab-ta* ki ^{d}*adad-tillati* ba-zi, "*Adad-tillati* disbursed 44 liters of semolina, 28 liters of fine flour and 10 liters of dates. They were mixed (with) fine flour for various small flour heaps when *Šu-Kabta* went to G̃EŠ.KÚŠU (and) when *Šu-Kabta* came from G̃EŠ.KÚŠU. It was the expenditure of *Šu-Kabta*. Ur-Nin-Siana, the cup-bearer, was the deputy," 488:8–26

1.2.2 Beer

0.0.1. kaš-sig$_5$ 0.0.4. kaš-gen sá-du$_{11}$-*ra-ba-tum* 5 sìla kaš-sig$_5$ 0.0.1. kaš-gen sá-du$_{11}$-^{d}*šu*-^{d}*suen-e-te-íl-pi$_4$*-^{d}en-líl **ur-^{d}nin-^{d}si$_4$-an-na** sagi maškim (. . .) zi-ga *simat-^{d}ištaran* ki ^{d}*adad-tillati*-ta [ba]-zi, "*Adad-tillati* disbursed 10 liters of fine beer (and) 40 liters of ordinary beer, regular offerings of *Rabatum* (and) 5 liters of fine beer (and) 10 liters of ordinary beer, regular offerings of *Šu-Suen-etelpi*-Enlil. (It was)

---

67 Although Ur-Nin-Siana's title is not specified, this text is included here in light of his activities as a deputy.

the expenditure of *Simat-Ištaran*. Ur-Nin-Siana, the cupbearer, was the deputy," 505:1–7, 14–16, 508:1–10

1.2.3 Flour Mixed with Dates

0.0.1. zú-lum eša ba-ḫi sízkur-didli-šè n ^{dug}níĝ 5-sìla-ta n ^{dug}níĝ 2-sìla-ta [x]-šè **ur-^{d}nin-^{d}si$_4$-an-na** sagi maškim, "10 liters of dates—they were mixed (with) fine flour for various (ceremonial) offerings—[n+]4 5-liter pots (and) [n] 2-liter pots for [x]. Ur-Nin-Sianna, the cupbearer, was the deputy," 1013:9–14, 1014:'2–'7

0.0.3. ZÌ.[ŠE] 0.0.2. eša zú-lum eša ḫi-dè **ur-^{d}nin-^{d}si$_4$-an-na** maškim, "30 liters of semolina (and) 20 liters of fine flour to mix dates (and) fine flour. Ur-Nin-Siana was the deputy," 1166:1–5[68]

1.2.4 Semolina and Fine Flour

[1] sìla dabin 1 sìla eša ^{d}gu-la **⌜ur⌝-^{d}nin-^{d}si$_4$-an-na** sagi maškim, "[1] liter of semolina (and) 1 liter of fine flour (for) Gula. Ur-Nin-Siana, the cupbearer, was the deputy," 1016:1–4

1.2.5 Broken Context

[. . .]-x-gal [n sìl]a dabin [n] sìla eša [. . .] gar-ša-[an-na^{ki}] **ur-[^{d}n]in-[^{d}si$_4$-an]-na** maškim, "[. . . n] liter(s) of semolina (and?) [n] liter(s) of fine flour [. . .] (in?) Garšana. Ur-Nin-Siana was the deputy," 1164:1–7[69]

2. Ur-Nin-Siana, the Singer

2.1 Requisitions: Bread

0.1.0. ninda níĝ-dab$_5$ **ur-^{d}nin-^{d}si$_4$-an-na** nar (. . .) [níĝ-kas$_7$]-aka [*ì-lí*]-*bi-la-ni* muḫaldim, "10 liters of bread, requisitions of Ur-Nin-Siana, the singer, (and) {other allotments} the balanced account of *Ili-bilani*, the cook, "1527:27–28, 48–49

ur-^{d}*suena*

1. Ur-*Suena*, the Merchant

1.1 In his Possession: Silver, Emmer, and Bran

3⅓ gín 3 še kù-babbar 1.0.0. zíz gur 3.0.0. tuḫ-ḫád-gen gur *si-ì-tum* [**ur-**^{d}]***suena*** dam-[gàr] i[n-d]a-ĝál, "The remainder of 3⅓ shekels (and) 3 barley-corns of silver, 1 bushel of emmer wheat (and) 3 bushels of ordinary dried bran are with Ur-*Suena*, the merchant," 1224:1–6

2. Ur-*Suena*, Title Unspecified

2.1 His Workmen: Moving Dirt at the Garšana Garden

[n] ĝuruš **ur-^{d}EN**.[**ZU**] (. . .) kurum$_7$ aka saḫar ⌜zi⌝-ga ^{ĝeš}kiri$_6$ gar-ša-an-na^{ki}, "Inspection (of the work) of [n] workmen of Ur-*Suena*, (and) {other workers} having moved dirt at the Garšana garden," 179:6, 17–18

---

[68] Although Ur-Nin-Siana's title is not specified, this text is included here in light of similar transactions nos. 1013 and 1014.

[69] Although Ur-Nin-Siana's title is not mentioned, this text is included here in light of his activities as a deputy.

ur-ša-lu-ḫi

Ur-šaluḫi, the (Sick) Builder

1 **ur-ša-lu-ḫi** šidim dú-ra, "Ur-šaluḫi, the sick builder," 43:'48, 44:47, 45:30

ur-^{d}šul-pa-è

1. Ur-Šul-pa'e, Workman of the Mill

1.1 Provisions

[n g]ín ì-g̃eš-ta 1 ma-na tuḫ-g̃eš-ì-ḫád-ta 0.0.1. ádda-udu-ta [½] sìla mun-ta [n] gín luḫ-lá-ta [1 a]d-da-kal-la [1] **ur-^{d}šul-pa-è** [1] *ḫa-la-ša* {indent} 3 [g̃uruš? é]-kíkken é-^{d}nin-^{d}si$_4$-an-na-me-éš, "[n] shekel(s) of sesame oil each, 1 mina of dried sesame chaff each, 10 sheep carcasses each, [½] liter of salt each (and) [n] shekel(s) of luḫ-lá each, (provisions for) Ada-kala, Ur-Šulpa'e, (and) *Ḫalaša*, 3 [workmen?] of the mill of Nin-Siana," 562:'6–'15

2. Ur-Šul-pa'e, Title Unspecified

2.1 As a Witness

igi **ur-^{d}šul-pa-è**, "witnessed by Ur-Šulpa'e," 1053:12

ur-te-me-na

Ur-temena, Builder from Nig̃-Ba'u

1. Provisions

1.1 Semolina and Barley

2 sìla dabin-ta 2 sìla še-ta **ur-te-me-na** 1 ur-^{d}asar-lu-ḫi 1 *du-du-gu* 1 ^{d}utu-sá-bí [1] lú-me-lám lú-níg̃-^{d}ba-ú šidim-me-éš (. . .) šà-gal šidim-e-ne, "2 liters of semolina each (and) 2 liters of barley each (for) Ur-temena, Ur-Asarluḫi, *Dudugu*, Utu-sabi (and) Lu-melam, builders from Nig̃-Ba'u, (and for) {other workers}, food (for) builders," 381:5–12, 21

2 sìla dabin-ta 2 sìla še-ta **ur-te-me-na** 1 ur-^{d}asar-lu-ḫi 1 *du-du-gu* 1 ^{d}utu-sá-bí 1 lú-me-lám lú-níg̃-^{d}ba-ú šidim (. . .) šà-gal šidim-e-ne u$_4$ bàd egir é-a dù-dè, "2 liters of semolina (and) 2 liters of barley each (for) Ur-temena, Ur-Asarluḫi, *Dudugu*, Utu-sabi (and) Lu-melam, builders from Nig̃-Ba'u, (and for) {other workers}, food (for) builders when they were constructing the (enclosure) wall behind the house," 386:13–20, 29–30, 387:5–11, 20–21

2 sìla dabin-ta 2 sìla še-ta **ur-te-me-na** 1 ur-^{d}asar-lu-ḫi 1 *du-du-gu* 1 ^{d}utu-sá-bí 1 lú-me-lám lú-níg̃-^{d}ba-ú šidim (. . .) šà-gal šidim-e-ne u$_4$ bàd in-dù-sa-a, "2 liters of semolina each (and) 2 liters of barley each (for) Ur-temena, Ur-Asarluḫi, *Dudugu*, Utu-sabi (and) Lu-melam, builders from Nig̃-Bau, (and for) {other workers}, food (for) builders when they constructed the (enclosure) wall," 396:5–12, 19–20, 397:5–13, 19–20

1.2 Sheep and Grains

[0.1.0 še-ta 0.1.0 dabin-ta 3 ádda]-udu-ta **[ur-te]-me-na** [1 ur-^{d}a]sar-lu-ḫi [1] *du-du-gu* [1] lú-me-lám [1] ^{d}utu-sá-bí!(TI) lú-níg̃-^{d}ba-ú-me-éš (. . .) [šà-gal šidim] ù dub-sar-e-ne, "[60 liters of barley, 60 liters of semolina (and) 3] sheep [carcasses] each (for) Ur-temena, Ur-Asarluḫi, *Dudugu*, Lu-melam (and) Utu-sabi, men from Nig̃-Ba'u, (and for) {other workers}, [food (for) builders] and scribes," 399:1–9, 24

ur-zikum-ma

1. **As a Witness**

igi **ur-zikum-ma**, "witnessed by Ur-zikuma," 1054:10

^{d}utu-sá-bí

Utu-sabi, Builder from Niĝ-Ba'u

1. **Provisions**

1.1 **Semolina and Barley**

2 sìla dabin-ta 2 sìla še-ta ur-te-me-na 1 ur-^{d}asar-lu-ḫi 1 *du-du-gu* 1 **^{d}utu-sá-bí** [1] lú-me-lám lú-níĝ-^{d}ba-ú šidim-me-éš (. . .) šà-gal šidim-e-ne, "2 liters of semolina each (and) 2 liters of barley each (for) Ur-temena, Ur-Asarluḫi, *Dudugu*, Utu-sabi (and) Lu-melam, builders from Niĝ-Ba'u, (and for) {other workers}, food (for) builders," 381:5–12, 21

2 sìla dabin-ta 2 sìla še-ta ur-te-me-na 1 ur-^{d}asar-lu-ḫi 1 *du-du-gu* 1 **^{d}utu-sá-bí** 1 lú-me-lám lú-níĝ-^{d}ba-ú šidim (. . .) šà-gal šidim-e-ne u_4 bàd egir é-a dù-dè, "2 liters of semolina (and) 2 liters of barley each (for) Ur-temena, Ur-Asarluḫi, *Dudugu*, Utu-sabi (and) Lu-melam, builders from Niĝ-Ba'u, (and for) {other workers}, food (for) builders when they were constructing the (enclosure) wall behind the house," 386:13–20, 29–30, 387:5–11, 20–21

2 sìla dabin-ta 2 sìla še-ta ur-te-me-na 1 ur-^{d}asar-lu-ḫi 1 *du-du-gu* 1 **^{d}utu-sá-bí** 1 lú-me-lám lú-níĝ-^{d}ba-ú šidim (. . .) šà-gal šidim-e-ne u_4 bàd in-dù-sa-a, "2 liters of semolina each (and) 2 liters of barley each (for) Ur-temena, Ur-Asarluḫi, *Dudugu*, Utu-sabi (and) Lu-melam, builders from Niĝ-Bau, (and for) {other workers}, food (for) builders when they constructed the (enclosure) wall," 396:5–12, 19–20, 397:5–13, 19–20

1.2 **Sheep and Grains**

[0.1.0 še-ta 0.1.0 dabin-ta 3 ádda]-udu-ta [ur-te]-me-na [1 ur-^{d}a]sar-lu-ḫi [1] *du-du-gu* [1] lú-me-lám [1] **^{d}utu-sá-bí**!(TI) lú-níĝ-^{d}ba-ú-me-éš (. . .) [šà-gal šidim] ù dub-sar-e-ne, "[60 liters of barley, 60 liters of semolina (and) 3] sheep [carcasses] each (for) Ur-temena, Ur-Asarluḫi, *Dudugu*, Lu-melam (and) Utu-sabi, men from Niĝ-Ba'u, (and for) {other workers}, [food (for) builders] and scribes," 399:1–9, 24

– W –

wa-qar-dan

Waqar-dan, Man from Karkar

(. . .) lú-karkar^{ki}-me [1 ***w***]***a-qar-dan*** 1 *á-pil-lí-a* ninda-ta nu-tuku, "{workers}, men from Karkar (received bread). *Waqar-dan* (and) *Apillia*, they each did not get bread," 559:28–32

– Z –

za-a-za

Zaza, the Female Miller

1. Provisions

[1] ***za-a-za*** [1] *a-na-a* [1] lu_5-zi-lá {indent} 8 [géme é]-kíkken-me-éš, "(provisions for) *Zaza*, *Ana'a*, (and) Luzila, 8 [workwomen] of the mill," 562:'1–'5

za-ak-ì-lí

Zakili, the Courier

1. Under his Authority: Delivery of Wool, Baskets, and Skins

20 gú siki-[gen] 20 ^{gi}gúrdub ka-[tab] sè-ga 180 kuš-udu-ú ki *á-wi-lum-ma*-ta ^{d}*adad-tillati* šu ba-ti g̃ìri ***za-ak-ì-lí*** lú-$kaš_4$, "Under the authority of *Zakili*, the courier, *Adad-tillati* received 20 talents of [ordinary] wool, 20 reed-baskets of wool fitted with covers, (and) 180 skins of range-fed sheep from *Awilumma*," 1285:1–7

za-bu-la

1. *Zabula*, the Ox-Herder, Supervised by *Babani*, the Majordomo

1.1 Ox-Drivers from his Gang

n g̃uruš ***za-bu-la*** nu-bànda-gu_4 (. . .) ugula *ba-ba-ni* šabra, "n workmen (from the gang of) *Zabula*, the ox-herder, (and) {other gangs}, supervised by *Babani*, the majordomo," 190:6–7, 191:7, 10

1 g̃uruš ***za-bu-la*** nu-bànda-gu_4 (. . .) šà-⸢gu_4⸣-me-éš (. . .) ugula *ba-ba-ni* šabra, "1 workman (from the gang of) *Zabula*, the ox-herder, (and) {other gangs}, ox-drivers (and) {hired workers} supervised by *Babani*, the majordomo," 193:6–7, 9, 197:6, 8, 11

[n g̃u]ruš ***za-[bu-la*** n]u-bànda-gu_4 [šà-gu_4]-me-éš [árad-é]-a-me-éš (. . .) ugula *ba-ba-ni* šabra, "[n] workmen (from the gang of) *Zabula*, (and) {other gangs}, ox-drivers—household servants—(and) {hired workers} supervised by *Babani*, the majordomo," 194:6–8, 13, 15

2. *Zabula*, Title Unspecified

2.1 Deliveries: Barley

.0.0. š[e gur] á lú-ḫug̃-[g̃á] mu saḫar-šè ki ***za-bu-la***-ta ^{d}*adad-tillati* šabra [šu b]a-ti ⸢g̃ìri⸣ *ì-lí-aš-ra-ni* un-ga_6 [a-š]à sum-túl-túl, "Under the authority of *Ili-ašranni*, the porter, *Adad-tillati*, the majordomo, received 3 bushels of barley from *Zabula*, wages of hired workers for (moving?) dirt at the Sum-tultul field," 545:1–8

za-ki-ti

é-ki-ba-g̃ar-ra ***za-ki-ti*** ù *šu-eš*$_4$*-tár*, "the replacement house of *Zakiti* and *Šu-Eštar*" > *Household Index*

é-*šu-eš*$_4$*-tár* ù ***za-ki-ti***, "the house of *Šu-Eštar* and *Zakiti*" > *Household Index*

za-ki-tum

1. Provisions: Barley

0.2.4. ***za-ki-tum*** (. . .) šu+níĝin 27.1.1.3 sìla še gur ki ugula-nam–10-ka ⌜ĝal⌝-la ugula *simat-é-a* lú-ḫuĝ-ĝá, "160 liters (of barley) (for) *Zakitum*, (and barley for) {others}, in total: there are 27 bushels (and) 73 liters of barley at the place of the overseer of 10, *Simat-Ea*, the overseer of hired workers," 504:15, 20–23

za-la-a

Zala'a, Overseer of Hired Workers

1. Supervision of Hired Workers

n ĝuruš n géme ugula ***za-la-a*** (. . .) lú-ḫuĝ-ĝá-me-éš, "n hired workman (and) n hired workwomen supervised by *Zala'a*," 24:11, 30:11, 31:11, 32:11, 33:11, 35:11, 38:10, 39:12, 42:10, 43:12, 44:10, 46:'5, 47:10, 48:10, 54:4, 56:9, 57:9, 58:11–12, 73:9, 93:'5, 94:5, 98:'5, 99:6, 101:6, 102:9, 103:8, 104:12, 105:12, 106:14, 107:16, 108:13, 109:13, 110:14, 111:15, 114:15, 115:'6, 117:13, 118:12, 119:12, 120:12, 121:12, 122:'2, 123:16, 125:12, 126:12, 127:12, 128:11, 129:12, 130:12 131:'6, 132:12, 133:12, 134:12, 135:12, 136:12, 137:12, 138:12, 140:12, 141:14–15, 142:12, 143:12, 146:'9, 147:15, 150:14, 151:11, 154:12, 156:10, 158:11, 159:9, 161:'3, 162:10, 163:10 173:9, 174:9, 175:9, 199:3–4, 208:5–6, 209:6, 210:'2–'3, 212:'7

n ĝuruš ugula ***za-la-a*** (. . .) lú-ḫuĝ-ĝá-me-éš, "n hired workmen supervised by *Zala'a*," 20:12, 21:10, 22:11, 27:'3, 29:'8, 34:11, 36:11, 72:7, 75:8, 76:3, 145:15, 155:10, 157:8, 182:4, 206:5–6, 207:7

n géme ugula ***za-la-a*** (. . .) (lú-ḫuĝ-ĝá-me-éš), "n (hired) workwomen supervised by *Zala'a*," 18:10, 37:10, 49:10, 53:12, 78:4, 84:5

n ĝuruš má-laḫ$_5$ n ĝuruš n géme ugula ***za-la-a*** (. . .) lú-ḫuĝ-ĝá-me-éš, "n hired sailor(s), n hired workmen (and) n hired workwomen supervised by *Zala'a*," 59:11–13, 60:11–13

1 ĝuruš má-laḫ$_5$ 1 géme ugula ***za-la-a*** lú-ḫuĝ-ĝá-me-éš, "1 hired sailor (and) 1 hired workwoman supervised by *Zala'a*," 71:9–11

[n ĝuruš/géme] ugula ***za-la-a*** (. . .) lú-ḫuĝ-ĝá-me-éš, "[n] hired [workmen/women] supervised by *Zala'a*," 51:9, 52:11

2. Supervision of Brick Carriers and Delivery of Bricks

2.1 Delivery of Bricks

2.1.1 For the Craftsmen's House

é-gašam-e-ne mu-DU ***za-la-a*** ugula lú-ḫuĝ-ĝá, "delivery (of bricks for) the craftsmen's house by *Zala'a*, overseer of hired workers," 330:27–29

2.1.2 For the Foundation Terrace of the Textile Mill

ki-sá-a é-uš-bar-šè mu-DU ***za-la-a*** ugula lú-ḫ[uĝ-ĝá], "delivery (of bricks) for the foundation terrace of the textile mill by *Zala'a*, overseer of hired workers," 311:21–23, 362:'20–'23

2.1.3 For the Replacement House of *Ubarum*

mu-DU é-ki-ba-ĝar-ra *u-bar-um* ***za-la-a*** ugula lú-ḫuĝ-ĝá, "delivery (of bricks for) replacement house of *Ubarum* by *Zala'a*, overseer of hired workers," 343:11–14

2.1.4 For the Textile Depository

ki-mu-ra-šè mu-DU ***za-la-a*** ugula lú-ḫuĝ-ĝá, "delivery (of bricks) for the textile depository by *Zala'a*, overseer of hired workers," 338:21–22

2.1.5 For the (Enclosure) Wall

mu-DU bàd-šè ***za-la-a*** ugula lú-ḫuĝ-ĝá, "delivery (of bricks) for the (enclosure) wall by *Zala'a*, overseer of hired workers," 310:'18–'19, 361:'13–'15

bàd-šè mu-⸢DU⸣ ***za-la-a*** ugula lú-ḫuĝ-ĝá, "delivery (of bricks) for the (enclosure) wall by *Zala'a*, overseer of hired workers," 313:23–24

ù-ru-a bàd-šè mu-DU ***za-la-a*** ugula lú-ḫuĝ-ĝá, "delivery (of bricks) for the urua wall by *Zala'a*, overseer of hired workers," 312:35–36, 317:30–32

3. Supervision of Workers Assigned to Specific Tasks

3.1 Garden Work

16 ĝuruš [n géme] ugula ***za-la-[a]*** (. . .) kurum$_7$ aka saḫar zi-ga [^{ĝeš}kiri$_6$ gar-ša-an-na^{ki}], "Inspection (of the work) of 16 workmen [(and) n workwomen], supervised by *Zala'a* (and) {other workers} having moved dirt [at the Garšana garden]," 176:9–10, 16–17

52 ĝuruš ugula ***za-la-[a]*** (. . .) saḫar zi-ga in-lá tùn-lá ^{ĝeš}kiri$_6$ zabala$_4^{ki}$ kurum$_7$ [aka], "Inspection (of the work) of 52 workmen, supervised by *Zala'a*, (and) {other workers} having transported dirt removed via a tùn-lá device at the Zabala garden," 178:3, 6–8

[n+]23 ĝuruš ugula ***za-la-a*** (. . .) kurum$_7$ aka saḫar ⸢zi⸣-ga ^{ĝeš}kiri$_6$ gar-ša-an-na^{ki}, "Inspection (of the work) of [n+]23 workmen, supervised by *Zala'a*, (and) {other workers} having moved dirt at the Garšana garden," 179:8, 17–18

3.2 Crushing Malt

3 ĝuruš ugula ***za-l[a-a]*** (. . .) munu$_4$ naĝ$_4$-ĝá-dè ⸢kurum$_7$ aka⸣, "Inspection (of the work) of 3 workmen, supervised by *Zala'a*, (and) {other workers} to crush malt," 170:1, 6–8

3 géme ugula ⸢***za-la***⸣***-a*** (. . .) munu$_4$ naĝ$_4$-ĝá-⸢dè⸣ kurum$_7$ aka, "Inspection (of the work) of 3 workwomen, supervised by *Zala'a*, (and) {other workers} to crush malt," 171:2, 6–7

3.3 Moving Dirt

15 ĝuruš ugula ***za-la-a*** saḫar zi-g[a kurum$_7$ aka], "[inspection (of the work) of] 15 workmen, supervised by *Zala'a*, having moved dirt," 181:6–8

3.4 Towing Boats

24 ĝuruš ugula ***za-la-a*** (. . .) 4 má-10-gur-ta gar-ša-an-na^{ki}-ta karkar^{ki}-šè gíd-da, "24 workmen, supervised by *Zala'a* (and) {other workers} having towed 4 10-bushel boats from Garšana to Karkar," 236:2, 7–9

3.5 The Volume of Earth Used to Build the Adobe Wall under the Supervision of *Zala'a*

[n nindan gíd n kùš daĝal n kùš g]i$_4$-bi 4 kù[š sukud saḫar]-bi 4 sar 10 ⸢gín⸣ 7½ sar im-du$_8$-a ugula ***za-la-a***, "[n nindan long, n kùš in wide, n kùš] tapered from 2 kùš [high], its dirt is 4 sar and 10 gin, (the total volume) of the adobe wall is 7½ sar, (built) under the supervision of *Zala'a*," 366:'1–'4

4. Deliveries

4.1 Dates: Receipt of *Adad-tillati*

[n].4.2. zú-[lum] gur ki ***za-la-a***-ta ^{d}*adad-tillati* šu ba-ti ˹g̃iri˺ *a-ḫu-wa-qar* dub-sar, "Under the authority of *Aḫu-waqar*, the scribe, *Adad-tillati* received [n] bushel(s) (and) 260 liters of dates from *Zala'a*," 1205:5

4.2 Semolina: Receipt of *Malik-bani*

0.n.n.n sìla dabin mu-DU ***za-la-a*** ^{d}*ma-lik-ba-ni* šu ba-an-ti, "*Malik-bani* received n liter(s) of semolina, delivery of *Zala'a*," 1124:1–5, 1132:1–5

5. Receipts: Barley Wages for Molding Bricks

5.0.0. še gur á 5-sìla-ta šeg$_{12}$ du$_{8}$-dè ki ^{d}*adad-tillati*-ta ***za-la-a*** šu ba-ti, "*Zala'a* received 5 bushels of barley, wages of 5 liters each (for workers) to mold bricks from *Adad-tillati*," 530:1–6

5.0.0. še gur šeg$_{12}$ du$_{8}$-dè á 5-sìla-ta ki ^{d}*adad-tillati*-ta ***za-la-a*** šu ba-ti, "*Zala'a* received 5 bushels of barley, wages of 5 liters each (for workers) to mold bricks from *Adad-tillati*," 531:1–6

6. Provisions: Barley in Place of Semolina

0.1.4. še ugula ***za-la-a*** (. . .) mu dabin-šè šu ba-ti, "*Zala'a*, the overseer, received 14 liters of barley, (and barley for) {9 other individuals}, (barley) in place of semolina," 560:1, 12–13

za-la-tum

1. Broken Context

[. . .]-ta? ***za-la-tum***, 260:10

zé-ra-ra

é-dam-***zé-ra-ra***, "the house of the wife of *Zerara*" > *Household Index*

zi-ti-a

Zitia, the Overseer

1. Deliveries: Semolina, Receipt of *Malik-bani*

1.4.1.8 [sìla] dabin gur mu-DU ugula ***zi-ti-a*** ^{d}*ma-lik-ba-ni* šu ba-an-ti, "*Malik-bani* received 1 bushel and 258 [liters] of semolina, delivery of *Zitia*, the overseer," 1122:1–5

2. Receipts: Barley

2?.0.3. še gur á dabin-šè ki ^{d}*adad-tillati*-ta ***zi-ti-a*** šu ba-ti, "*Zitia* received 2? bushels (and) 30 liters of barley, wages for (milling) semolina from *Adad-tillati*," 475:1–4[70]

---

[70] Although *Zitia*'s title is not specified, in light of the similar text no. 453 it is likely that *Zitia*, the overseer, is intended here.

3. Supervision of Workwomen for Milling

2 géme u_4-1-šè še 3-sìla ⸢ús⸣-sa-šè ⸢níg̃⸣-àr-ra àr-ra-dè ús-sa ugula ***zi-ti-a***!, "2 workwomen for 1 day, supervised by *Zitia*, 3 liters of barley for processing, (the women) having processed (the barley) in order to grind groats," 434:1–3

4. In Her[71] Possession: Remainder of Wages (for processing) Semolina

0.3.4.5 sìla ⸢še⸣ si-ì-tum á dabin ***zi-ti*!*-a*** ugula in-da-g̃ál, "225 liters of barley, the remainder of the wages (for processing) semolina are with *Zitia*, the overseer," 453:1–5

zu-zu-tum

é-ki-ba-g̃ar-ra ***zu-zu-tum***, "the replacement house of *Zuzutum*" > *Household Index*

é-***zu-zu-tum***, "the house of *Zuzutum*" > *Household Index*

[71] Gender confirmed from seal.

Broken Personal Names

1. Deliveries

1.1 Textiles

1 ^{túg}níĝ-lám-gen 1 túg-guz-za *šu-*⌜*kab*⌝*-ta* 1 ^{túg}bar-dul$_5$-⌜ús⌝ *šu-kab-ta* 3 ^{túg}uš-bar ⌜siki⌝-ĝír-[gu]l kal-kal-gé-dè ki **la-ša**?-[x]-ta lu-ba šu ba-an-ti, "Luba received 1 ordinary níĝ-lám textile, 1 tufted textile of *Šu-Kabta*, 1 2nd-quality bar-dul$_5$ textile of *Šu-Kabta*, (and) 3 uš-bar textiles of ĝír-gul wool from [PN] in order to repair (them)," 588:1–8

1.2 Woods

(. . .) [ì]-DU [x-x?]-**ti-en** um-mi-a [šà gar]-ša-an-na^{ki} [n] sar gíd-da [níĝ]-kas$_7$-da $^{[d]}$*adad-tillati* šabra [ì]-dab$_5$ [zi-ga *si*]*mat-*^{d}*ištaran* [ĝìri *a-h*]*u-ma* dub-sar, "{parcels of land; in it: {date palm, pine boards of boats, seedlings, and planks}, the delivery of [PN], the craftsman, in Garšana (and) {2 other deliveries of similar commodities}. (In total:) [n] sar (of land) was surveyed. *Adad-tillati*, the majordomo, took in charge the account. (It was) [the expenditure] of *Simat-Ištaran* [under the authority of] *Ahuma*, the scribe," 1362:'69–'78

2. Expenditures

1 ^{gi}bisaĝ-im-sar-ra sa-ḫa ⅔-kùš íb-sá im-sar ĝá-ĝá-dè *i-ṣur-*^{d}*suen* dub-sar maškim ⌜zi⌝-ga ⌜***šu***⌝?-x-***ki***?-***ra***?-***ta***?-***ni***? [ki] ^{d}*adad-tillati*-ta ⌜ba⌝-zi, "*Adad-tillati* disbursed 1 canvas-lined clay tablet coffer—it is ⅔ kùš square—(in which) to deposit) clay tablets. (It was) the expenditure of [PN]. *Iṣur-Suen*, the scribe, was the deputy," 1365:1–7

3. The Father of *Ani'a*

á-ni-á dumu **ùr**?-[x], "*Ani'a*, the son of [PN]" > *Ani'a*

4. Overseers

(. . .) ugula ***á-ni***-x-x (. . .) lú-karkar^{ki}-me, "{workmen} from Karkar, supervised by [PN]," 559:25, 28

5. Personnel List: Context Broken or Unspecified

[1 . . .]-**DU**$_{10}$ (. . .) ugula [*šu*]*-la-núm* (. . .) lú-karkar^{ki}-me, "[PN], supervised by *Šulanum*, (and) {other workers}, men from Karkar," 559:6, 12, 28

[1 . . .]-***um*** (. . .) ugula [*šu*]*-la-núm* (. . .) lú-karkar^{ki}-me, "[PN], supervised by *Šulanum*, (and) {other workers} men from Karkar," 559:7, 12, 28

[1 . . .]-**a-ku**?-**lá** (. . .) ugula [*šu*]*-la-núm* (. . .) lú-karkar^{ki}-me, "[PN], supervised by *Šulanum*, (and) {other workers}, men from Karkar," 559:8, 12, 28

[1 . . .]-***ì-lí*** (. . .) ugula [*šu*]*-la-núm* (. . .) lú-karkar^{ki}-me, "[PN], supervised by *Šulanum*, (and) {other workers}, men from Karkar," 559:10, 12, 28

(. . .) 1 [. . .]-***bí-tum*** ugula [*šu*]*-la-núm* (. . .) lú-karkar^{ki}-me, "[PN] supervised by *Šulanum*, (and) {other workers}, men from Karkar," 559:11–12, 28

1 **ni**-x ugula *ir*$_{11}$*-dam* lú-karkar^{ki}-me, "[PN], supervised by *Irdam*, (and) {other workers}, men from Karkar," 559:26–28

6. Provisions

6.1 Animals

1 udu *tá-din-eš*$_4$*-tár* 1 máš ***š***[***a-at***?-x?]-***ab***-[x] ki *ì-lí-bi-la-*[*ni*-ta] ba-zi, "*Ili-bilani* disbursed 1 sheep (for) *Tadin-Eštar* (and) 1 goat (for) [PN]," 497:1–4

6.2 Barley

2.0.0. gur **bà[d-. . .]** (. . .) [šu+níĝin n+]7.0.0. gur še-ba *ba-zi-tum* šu+níĝin 47.1.[n.] še-ba é, "2 bushels (of barley for) [PN] (and barley for) {other individuals}; [in total: n+]7 bushels of the barley rations of *Bazitum*; in total: 47 bushels (and) 60[+n] liters of barley rations of the household," 555:3, 24–25

4.3.0. gur **á-[. . .]** (. . .) [šu+níĝin n+]7.0.0. gur še-ba *ba-zi-tum* šu+níĝin 47.1.[n.] še-ba é, "4 bushels (and) 180 liters (of barley for) [PN] (and barley for) {other individuals}; [in total: n+]7 bushels of the barley rations of *Bazitum*; in total: 47 bushels (and) 60[+n] liters of barley rations of the household," 555:5, 24–25

1.0.0. gur **lugal-k[a?-. . .]** (. . .) [šu+níĝin n+]7.0.0. gur še-ba *ba-zi-tum* šu+níĝin 47.1.[n.] še-ba é, "1 bushel (of barley for) [PN] (and barley for) {other individuals}; [in total: n+]7 bushels of the barley rations of *Bazitum*; in total: 47 bushels (and) 60[+n] liters of barley rations of the household," 555:6, 24–25

[. . .^{d} **PI]RIG.UNU.GAL** (. . .) [šu+níĝin n+]7.0.0. gur še-ba *ba-zi-tum* šu+níĝin 47.1.[n.] še-ba é, "[barley? (for) PN] (and barley for) {other individuals}; [in total: n+]7 bushels of the barley rations of *Bazitum*; in total: 47 bushels (and) 60[+n] liters of barley rations of the household," 555:17, 24–25

6.3 Wages for Molding Bricks

12 sar 18 gín **u[r-. . .]** (. . .) šeg$_{12}$ du$_{8}$-[a], "12 sar (and) 18 shekels (of bricks from) [PN] (and bricks from) {other workers}, {wages for workers} having molded bricks," 350:7, '23

9 ⌜sar⌝ 10 gín **ur-[. . .]** (. . .) šeg$_{12}$ du$_{8}$-[a], "9 sar (and) 10 shekels (of bricks from) [PN] (and bricks from) {other workers}, {wages for workers} having molded bricks," 350:8, '23

11[+n] sar 6½ gín **zu-[. . .]** (. . .) šeg$_{12}$ du$_{8}$-[a], "11[+n] sar (of bricks from) [PN] (and bricks from) {other workers}, {wages for workers} having molded bricks," 350:12, '23

[n] sar ***puzur$_{4}$*-[. . .]** (. . .) šeg$_{12}$ du$_{8}$-[a], "[n] sar (of bricks from) [PN] (and bricks from) {other workers}, {wages for workers} having molded bricks," 350:17, '23

6.4 Broken Context

0.0.2.5 sìla **a-[x?-]ši-[. . .]**, "25 liters (for) [PN]," 558:'2

0.0.2.5 <sìla> **ga-[x-. . .]**, 558:'6

0.0.2.5 <sìla> ***simat-za*-[. . .]**, 558:'7

0.0.2.5 <sìla> **ì-[. . .]**, 558:'8

7. Receipts: Pots

30 kaš-UD+gunu-gi 2 kaš-sig$_{5}$ ^{dug}níĝ 5-sìla-ta 4 ^{dug}[níĝ] 2 sìla-ta [ki] ^{d}*adad-tillati*-ta [. . .]***-ì-lí*** šu [ba]-ti, "[PN] received 30 (liters?) of (?) beer, 2 5-liter pots of fine beer (and) 4 2-liter jugs from *Adad-tillati*," 1180:1–6

8. Under the Authority of PN

8.1 Animals in the Storehouse, the Account of *Adad-tillati*

5[0 ud]u-máš ḫi-a gub-ba [é-š]u-sum-ma ĝìri ***a-ḫu*-[x]** dub-sar iti dirig ezem-me-ki-ĝál ba-zal mu ^{d}*i-bí-*^{d}*suen* lugal, "(In total:) 50 various sheep (and) goats present in the storehouse under the authority of [PN], the scribe, at the end of the 13th month of *Ibbi-Suen* Year 1," 984:5–9

8.2 Textiles

(. . .) tú[g-ba] siki-ba géme-árad *simat-*[d]*ištaran* ki [d]*adad-tillati*-ta ba-zi g̃ìri **i[m**-. . .] dub-sar, "Under the authority of [PN], the scribe, *Adad-tillati* disbursed {wool and assorted textiles}, the textile and wool rations of the female and male servants of *Simat-Ištaran*," 818:7–11

8.3 Provisions

⅓ sìla mu[n-ta] 6 gín luḫ-lá-[ta] g̃ìri ***ì-lí***-[. . .] 1 *ad-da-ni* 1 *bi-za-tum* 1 *i-din-*[d]*šamaš* 1 *in-ga-la* 1 *be-lí-a-sú* níta-me-éš, "⅓ liter of salt [each], (and) 6 shekels of luḫ-lá [each] under the authority of [PN], (provisions for) *Adani, Bizatum, Iddin-Šamaš, Ingala,* (and) *Beli-asu*, the men," 562:'31–'39

9. Witnesses

igi **NE**-[. . .], "witnessed by [PN]," 609:21

igi **a**[**b**?-. . .], 609:22

[igi] ***a***?-⌜***al***⌝-***la***-[x?], 1056:6

[igi . . .]-**na**-x, 1059:6

10. Workmen

[1 x]-**ga**?-x ⌜dú⌝-ra (. . .) ugula *i-ri-ib*, "[PN], the sick (workman) (and) {other workers} supervised by *Irib*," 52:65, 70

11. Context Uncertain

[. . . ***n***]***a***?-***ì-lí***, 505:13

Index of Brick-Hauler Personal Names[1]

nam–10 *a-a-lí*, 327:19

a-a-lí-⌜*tum*⌝, 323:103([n])

nam–10 *a-a-ni*, 367:11, 372:'17

a-bi-ma-a, 365:'4([n])

[*a*]*-bi-nu-ri*, 367:16(240)

[*a*]*-bí-ì-lí*, 346:108(1420)

a-bi$_{(2)}$*-sí-im-ti*, 321:'19(1020), 351:77(720), 351:124([n+]40)

a-bí-ṭabu(DU$_{10}$), 323:14([n]), 367:26(720)

a-bu-ṭabu(DU$_{10}$), 325:9(840), 327:28(260), 367:'49(360)

a-bu-um-ilum, 323:51(360), 327:42(240), 337:14(360), 342:4(240[+n]), 342:15(90), 367:'107(600+[n])

a-da-làl, 316:59(360), 318:'30([n]), 322:25(120), 322:'60(300), 323:50(240), 324:35([n]), 324:64([n]), 325:8(240), 327:46(120), 330:4(240), 372:'12([n])

a-da-làl min, 322:'68(480), 330:11(300)

a-du-tum, 338:3([n])

a-ga-ma-a, 323:94(180), 334:46(120), 367:'51(240)

a-ga-ti, 318:'26(120), 323:56(240), 323:69(360), 323:97(120), 327:49(240), 343:1(360), 346:106(1860), 362:'10(120)

a-ga-ti-a, 311:9(240), 363:'14(360), 367:13(390), 367:'64(240), 367:'94([n])

a-ga-tum, 346:62(1180), 346:73(760)

a-ḫa-am-ar-ši, 327:44(280), 367:'105(240)

a-ḫa-ni-šu, 309:20([n]), 340:18(120), 351:7([n+]30), 351:31([n]), 367:'86(360)

a-ḫa-sú-um, 309:40([n]), 346:95(1600)

a-ḫa-ti-á, 352:7([630])

a-ḫi-ba-aš$_{(2)}$*-ti*, 309:43(300), 318:'39(120), 323:2([n]), 334:33(300), 346:92(800)

a-ḫi-ba-ša-at, 346:12(930), 367:'35([n])

a-ḫi-ma, 322:'62(300), 324:43(1320), 352:8([180+]30)

a-ḫi-[. . .], 310:9([n+]30)

nam–10 *a-ḫu-ni*, 322:'75, 324:49, 335:12

a-ḫu-ni, 322:'61(360), 323:10(180), 324:39(840), 326:4(240), 335:20(520), 338:7(720), 367:34(720)

a-ḫu-wa-qar$_{(4)}$, 316:9(240), 324:2([n]), 324:45(480), 327:14(120), 334:24(120), 335:22(270)

[*a*]*-la-ḫi*, 351:101(160)

a-la-ni-tum, 307:7([n]), 310:2(300), 317:17(360), 330:14(240), 348.1:'10([n])

a-la-ni-tum min, 310:7(510)

nam–10 *a-lí-a-bi*, 308:26, 316:57, 322:12, 324:79, 335:30, 352:27

a-lí-a-bi$_{(2)}$, 308:18([n]), 311:8(240), 313:7(750), 316:52(360), 322:8([n]), 322:23(120), 323:22(240), 323:104([n]), 324:70([n]), 342:63(90), 346:17(1600), 348:'2([n]), 351:44(240), 351:64(480), 351:112(1020), 352:19(690), 363:'15(360), 364:'6(300), 367:'44(420), 370:21(600), 370:35([n])

a-lí-a-ḫa-ti, 308:21(420), 352:24([n])

a-lí-a-ḫi, 309:47(300), 317:13(240), 321:'7(360), 321:'17(720), 322:11([n]), 324:10([n]), 324:28(120), 324:69([n]), 327:4([n]), 330:3(240), 335:26(270), 337:7(450), 340:17(120), 342:30([n]), 342:37(90),

[1] The numbers in parentheses specify the quantity of bricks carried.

344:'5(140), 346:7(900), 367:12(240), 367:31(720), 367:'46(360), 367:'84(480), 351:25(1020), 370:8([n]), 370:40([n])

a-lí-a-ḫi min, 324:74(480), 330:12(480), 346:11(1260), 346:99(600)

a-lí-a-ḫi ù *ku-bu-ul-tum*, 370:20(840)

a-lí-tum, 309:41([n]), 323:18(340), 338:4([n]), 363:'18(360), 364:'8(450), 367:'71(360), 368:'36(300)

a-lí-um-mi, 316:35(120), 322:43(120), 327:22(240), 352:18(360), 372:'20([n])

a-lí-[. . .], 309:10(900)

a-lu-zi-na, 367:24(360)

a-ma-a-a, 364:'7(750)

a-mur-ì-[*lí*], 372:'23([n])

a-na-ḫe-pá-at, 323:96(120), 337:9(300)

a-na-ḫi-lí-bi, 323:85([n]), 372:'21([n])

a-na-ti-a, 312:7(120)

a-na-tum, 352:23([n]), 367:'101(240)

a-na-ṭa-ba-at, 367:'65(360)

a-NI-da, 344:'3(140)

a-SI-[x], 353:2(570)

a-sí-núm, 308:16([n]), 321:'3([n]), 324:23(240)

a-wi-lí, 327:23(240)

[*a*]-*wi-lum*, 334:18(240)

a-z[*a*-. . .], 345:'5(390)

a-[x]-*a*, 327:30(120)

a-x-x, 323:81([n])

a-x-[. . .], 323:80(120)

a-[. . .], 323:106([n]), 323:107([n]), 346:31(700), 363:'8(150)

á-bí?-[. . .], 317:16(60)

nam–10 ^{d}*adad-nu-ri*, 308:33, 316:45, 322:51, 324:61, 352:30

^{d}*adad-nu-ri*, 308:24(300), 308:29(450), 316:40([n]), 316:55(120), 322:7([n]), 322:40([n]), 323:20(360), 323:47(120), 323:67(120), 324:24(240), 324:55(360), 324:71([n]), 327:60(120), 342:28(45), 342:35(90), 344:'4(210), 351:5([n]), 351:35(640), 367:21(240)

^{d}*adad-nu-ri* min, 316:42(240), 322:41([n])

^{d}*adad-ra-bí*, 323:89(240), 323:100(480), 327:27([n]), 367:'53(480), 372:'19(360)

^{d}*adad*-[x-x], 334:23(120)

ag-ma-a, 372:'26([n])

nam–10 *al-du-ru-um*, 344:'16, 346:67

ar-ša-ti, 313:3(300)

ar-ša-tum, 312:14([n]), 317:15(150), 348:'7([n])

ar-wa-tum, 322:48(120), 351:78(600[+n?]), 351:119(1200[+n])

árad-é-a, 318:'23(120), 323:65(360), 367:'112(480)

awil-é-a, 346:27(1080), 346:90(800)

ba-a-ti-a, 318:'25(120), 323:70(420), 367:'110(240)

ba-al-ba-la, 335:2(1560)

ba-ba-da, 351:49(330), 351:60(480), 351:96(180)

ba-za-za, 318:4(360), 323:68(240), 367:'91(240), 367:'115([n])

be-lí-nu-ri, 367:'72(240)

bi-ku-ku, 342:59(120), 342:62(90)

bi-ku-um, 340:14(300)

bi-la-la, 325:4(480)

bi-zi-za-á, 334:29(240)

bi-[. . .], 314':5(360)

bí-ba-a, 330:18(720)

bí-za-a, 309:16(900[+n?]), 323:5(360), 367:30(720)

bí-za-ni, 327:21(240), 367:'43(420)

bi$_{(2)}$-*za-tum*, 308:5(300), 367:'52(240), 372:'24([n])

bi$_{(2)}$-*zu-a*, 323:95(120), 327:29([n]), 367:'54(240)

bí-⸢*zu*⸣-*zu*, 324:42(360)

bíl-lum, 323:17([n]), 327:8(240), 334:11(300), 337:4(240), 351:8([n+]20), 351:36(1290), 367:'77(480), 370:31([n])

bu-ru-[*uq*]-*tum*, 323:64(240)

bu-ru-qum, 330:10(240)

da-da-á, 316:32(360)

diĝir(?)-é, 325:5(600)

du-ku-[x], 346:43(120), 346:49(180)

du-šu-pu-um, 324:17(240), 335:17(675)

e-bu-ri-tum, 330:9(240), 337:15(240[+n?]), 340:6(120), 347:'4(270)

e-le/lí-en, 327:61(120), 367:14(360)

nam–10 *im-ti-dam*, 308:14, 316:62, 322:18, 324:33, 335:32(270)
im-ti-dam, 309:52([n]), 316:10(240), 316:60(240), 322:15([n]), 324:3([n]), 324:22(600), 324:38(360), 335:9(120), 364:'3(450), 369:'8(240)
in-nu-[. . .], 323:46(360)
ip-qú-ša, 367:18(330), 369:'9(120)
iz-[*bu-um?*], 339:1([n])

kà-al-ma-ti, 312:4(180)
KI-ID-ma-ti, 330:8(480)
ki-na-na, 309:23(240), 318:2(210), 351:71(80), 351:120(600[+n])
ku-bu-lum, 308:28(450)
nam–10 *ku-ku-za-n*[*u-um*], 328:6
ku-ku-za-nu-um, 335:8(270), 363:'23([n])
ku-ub-ḫa-zi, 367:'87(360)
ku-zu-NI, 368:'49(60), 370:47([n])
ku-[. . .], 369:'11(240)

nam–10 *la-al-ku-da*, 308:38, 310:11, 316:34, 321:'24, 322:37, 335:31(140), 352:16, 363:'21
la-al-ku-da, 310:8([n+]10), 321:'21(540), 322:19(240)
la-ḫu-tum, 309:4([n]), 327:6([n]), 351:27(600[+n]), 351:97(540), 367:'68(240)
˹*la*˺*-ḫu-*[*x*], 309:2([n])
la-la-a, 307:3(300), 312:1([n]), 317:9(300), 330:5(120), 335:6(300), 348:'5([n]), 348:'16([n])
la-la-ti, 327:9([n]), 334:10(360), 342:44(180), 342:50(90)
la-lí-a, 323:92(240)
nam–10 *la-ma-sà-tum*, 309:22, 323:40, 327:16, 334:17, 337:6, 340:16, 342:58, 344:'13, 351:20, 351:42, 351:104, 365:'1, 367:'90
la-ma-sà-tum, 316:6(120), 316:53([n]), 321:'4([n+]300), 322:9([n]), 324:8([n]), 324:75(480), 327:11(240), 334:13(360), 337:2(150), 340:11(240), 342:46(50[+n?]), 342:52(90), 346:4(600[+n]), 346:87(960), 351:28(1680), 367:'76(480), 370:36(540)
la-˹*qí*˺*-ip*, 322:'65(360)
la-[. . .], 313:10(930)
lá-en-ni-si-im, 323:23(360)
[*li?*]*-la-tum*, 330:13(360)
lu-lu-ti, 367:'55(240)
lu-ud-lu-ul, 322:44(60?)
lú-ba-lí-iṭ, 365:'7(240)
˹lú˺-^{d}nin-šubur, 322:46(120)
lú-^{d}nin-[x], 369:'17([n])
lú-ša-lim, 318:'41(120), 323:4(360), 327:35(180), 334:38(120), 335:5(540)
lugal-inim-gi-na, 322:'64(720)

ma-aq-ra-ni-tum, 342:9(500), 342:20(90), 346:60(1640), 346:76(1540), 368:'18(1440)
ma-as-ḫa-ti, 324:51(360)
ma-áš-tum, 352:9(210)
ma-at-ì-li, 346:3([n])
ma-ma-*šar-ra-at*, 324:27(120), 346:97(1200)
˹*ma*˺?*-ma-*˹*tum*˺, 308:19(240)
ma?-x-[. . .]*-gi*, 313:5(600)
me-li$_{(2)}$*-tum*, 323:86([n]), 367:'48(360)
ME-NE?-mu, 367:'97(360)
ME-x-[x], 316:3([n])
mi-na-á, 327:41(120)
mi-˹*na*˺?*-ni*, 362:'7(120)
mi-na-ti-a, 322:24(120)
mi-na-ú, 312:12(120), 351:15([n+]40), 351:30([n+]20), 351:98(320), 367:'81(240)
mu-tum-ilum, 351:51(200), 351:66(480), 351:106(1110)
mur-tum, 324:1([n])

na-a-a, 319:5([n]), 323:24(360), 324:12([n]), 325:3(480), 342:1(170), 342:12(90), 346:65(1300), 346:79(660), 367:'99(120), 368:'21(960)
na-a(-a)-ti, 327:13(140), 346:107(200)
na-a(-a)-tum, 308:9(510), 346:45(120), 367:'75(480), 370:16(240), 370:24(480)
nam–10 *na-ab-ri-tum*, 309:33, 318:12, 351:80, 351:127
na-ab-ri-tum, 309:15(900[+n?]), 309:27([n]), 310:3(880), 311:2(360), 312:5(180),

313:1(630), 317:2(120), 324:52(240), 330:2(60), 351:18([n]), 351:32([n]), 351:46(300), 351:100(220), 351:115(1300), 352:22([n]), 352:28(420), 362:'8(120)

simat-^{d}nin-šubur min, 317:11(210)

simat-su-kál, 323:91(120), 367:'41(300)

simat-^{d}*šamaš*, 367:29(360), 370:41([n])

simat-^{d}[. . .], 312:9(120), 312:11(240), 351:58(610), 361:'1([n])

simat-[. . .], 312:24([n])

ṣa-bu-ri-tum, 342:5(150), 342:16([90])

ṣíl-lí-ší-it, 316:54(120), 322:5(120), 324:66([n]), 352:20([n])

ṣú-mi-id-ìl, 340:12(240), 347:'1(540)

ša-at-a-a, 346:20(1600), 367:27(1200), 367:'62(240)

nam–10 *ša-at-bi-zi-il*, 309:58, 318:'37, 323:99, 327:32, 334:28, 337:11, 340:24, 342:67, 346:34, 367:'67, 368:'45

nam–10 [*ša-at-b*]*i-zi-la*, 346:104

ša-at-$bi_{(2)}$*-zi-il*, 307:6(1020), 311:11(360), 312:20([n]), 313:6(1800[+n]), 317:14(420), 323:90(480), 327:30(360), 334:22(120), 340:21(120), 344:'10(140), 346:16(947), 347:'3(180), 352:21([n+]20), 361:'3(960), 362:'11(660), 367:'60(240), 368:'33(600), 368:'42([n]), 370:7([n])

ša-at-é-a, 309:48(450), 318:'38(120), 323:9(360), 323:12(360), 323:53(480), 327:54(360), 334:34(240), 342:29(240), 342:36(90), 346:15(990), 346:37(960), 351:47(330), 351:114(1320), 367:'36(600)

ša-at-èr-ra, 309:18(600[+n?]), 309:56(390), 316:46(240), 322:52(240), 323:29(1080), 324:21(600), 324:68(600), 327:40(240), 342:7(250), 342:18(90), 346:52(720), 346:64(740), 346:101(800), 346:109(1160), 351:4([n+]20), 351:34(960), 352:13(180), 367:'69(360), 367:'104(240), 368:'19([n]), 368:'47(180)

ša-at-$e\check{s}_4$*-tár*, 309:51([n]), 330:1(120), 330:15(360), 338:5([n]), 364:'4(450)

nam–10 *ša-at-ì-lí*, 308:11, 316:15, 322:'59, 335:25, 352:6, 363'11

ša-at-ì-lí, 308:6(450), 308:12(660), 308:34(630), 309:53([n]), 316:8(240), 316:49(240), 318:8(240), 318:'32(120), 322:3(300), 322:16([n]), 322:26(120), 323:21(240), 323:82([n]), 324:15(720), 324:26(720), 330:17(240), 334:50(360), 340:13(240), 346:77(480), 352:4(510), 352:11(420), 362:'59(120), 363:'9(150), 363:'19(480), 364:'15(450), 365:'11(60), 367:'57(240), 367:'85(720), 371:'5(240)

ša-at-kab-ta, 312:8(120), 361:'2(180?)

ša-at-ki/kin_7*-ti*, 307:2(600), 317:3(300)

ša-at-ma-mi, 309:63(300), 318:'24(120), 321:'6(420), 324:25(240), 334:35(240), 335:23(390), 342:45(150), 342:51(90), 346:105(800), 352:2(360[+n]), 367:'40(360), 367:'78(480), 370:18(480), 372:'8(36)

ša-at-ri-tum, 346:117(400), 351:26(960)

ša-at-^{d}*suen*, 352:10(210), 367:32(240), 370:42([n])

ša-at-^{d}*šamaš*, 367:'39(120)

ša-at-we-er, 340:4(120)

ša-a[*t*-x-x], 351:57(610)

nam–10 *ša-a*[*t* . . .], 369:'14

ša-at-[. . .], 309:9(1200), 310:1(1260), 310:4(660), 312:26([n]), 322:33(120), 323:73(480), 345:'7(390), 346:41([n]), 346:93(980)

ša-ḫi-ti, 316:47(240), 322:4(240), 324:77(720)

ša-lim-a-bi, 363:'12(480)

ša-lim-$du_{(2)}$*-ri*, 308:3(450), 322:53(120), 324:13(720)

ša-lim-mi, 309:24(600), 318:3(120), 322:13([n+]30), 323:3([n]), 324:31(720), 327:68(240), 334:25(120), 344:'2([n]), 351:73(1155), 351:121(1120), 364:'5(750), 367:20(240), 367:'45(600), 367:'93([n])

ša-lim-mi min, 309:26([n]), 318:7(240), 351:76(720[+n?])

ša-lim-[. . .], 365:'12(720)

ša-[. . .], 314:'4(480)

$ša_6$-ga, 327:69(120), 367:15([n])

šál-maḫ, 323:28(240), 324:47(120), 327:5([n]), 353:4(390), 367:'82(840)

^{d}*šamaš-a-bi*, 316:11(360), 316:37([n]), 322:28(120), 322:45(120), 324:56(360), 324:81(600), 363:'13(360), 363:'17(360)

⸢*šar*⸣*-ru-um-ba-ni*, 326:2(240)

ur-me-lám, 322:49(360), 324:54(240)
u[r-^{d}]nin-zadim, 334:6(120)
ù/ur-ri-tum, 323:7(120), 346:55(790), 368:'46([180]), 370:48([n]), 372:'6(120)
ur-sugal$_{7}$, 371:'3(360)
ur-^{d}šul-pa-è, 351:2([n])
ur-^{d}utu, 328:4(180)
ús-⌜*si*⌝*-im-eš$_{4}$-tár*, 308:17([n])

wa-qar-tum, 367:'80(360)

za-⌜*bu*⌝*-ku-a*, 319:2(660)
za-ki-ti, 327:38(120), 337:13(600), 340:2(240), 340:20(120)
za?-ku?-[. . .], 321:'20(520)
za-la-a, 338:13([n+]20)
za-[. . .], 346:83(800)
zi-ib-ni-tum, 324:14(450)
zi-na-ma, 309:61(240), 312:2([n]), 318:'19(120), 327:56([n]), 346:39(1120), 346:47(320), 367:'114([n])
nam–10 *zi-ti-a*, 323:49
zi-ti-a, 309:25([n+]30), 318:6(240), 323:45(300), 351:74(940), 351:125(660), 364:'22(450), 367:17(480)
zi-ti-a min, 318:9(120)
nam–10 *zi-ti-ma*, 318:'17, 334:54, 367:23
zi-ti-ma, 323:62([n]), 327:64(360), 334:43(120), 334:52(240), 367:'47(240)
zi-ti-[*ma* min], 327:66(360)
zi-[. . .], 372:'2(240)
zu-zu-tum, 346:14(990), 346:91([800?]), 351:107([n])

x-*a-m*[*u?*], 341:4([12]24)
x-*ḫi-a*, 346:2([n+]90)
x-*it*, 334:21(240)
[x]-*me-lu*, 321:'11([n])
[x]-*na-a*, 316:4(360)
[x]-NE-[x], 351:12([n+]20)
x-NI-x, 323:19(240)
x-*ta*-x-x, 346:42(780)
[x]-*u*-[x], 312:21([n])
x-*zu-*[*a*], 351:43(260)
x-[x-*b*]*i-a*, 335:7(420)
[x?]-x-*ig-tum*, 309:30([n])
[x-x-*m*]*u*, 367:'88
x-[x]-*qar-ba-at*, 353:6(400)
[x-x]-*šar-tum*, 353:5(390)
[x(-x)]-x-*šu*, 339:3([n])
[x-x]-*te*-[x], 339:4([n])
x-x-x, 323:55(120), 372:'13
x-[. . .], 324:83(480), 372:'10([n]), 372:'18(120)
^{d}[. . .], 364:'13(600)
[. . .]-*a*, 368:'28([n]), 368:'30([n])
[. . .]-*a-a*, 351:9([n])
[. . .]-^{d}*adad*, 309:35([n]), 348:'14([n])
[. . .]-*bi*, 323:32([n])
[. . .]-*èr-ra*, 316:18([n])
[. . .]-*gi*, 368:'29([n])
[. . .]-*ḫu?-ru-um*, 309:34([n])
[. . .]-*ì-lí*, 348.1:'13([n])
[. . .]-*im*-x, 370:43([n])
[. . .]-*ku*, 368:'10([n])
[. . .]-*la*, 309:36([n])
[. . .]-*ma-ti*, 362:'3(360[+n])
[. . .]-*mi* min, 370:5([n])
[. . .]-NI, 316:17([n])
[. . .]-*na*, 346:40([n])
[. . .]-*nu-ri*, 339:2([n])
[. . .]-*ra*, 316:24([n]), 367:'116([n])
[. . .]-*ri*, 370:45([n])
[. . .-^{d}šul-pa]-è, 351:24(960)
[. . .]-*ti*, 362:'4(480), 368:'32([n])
[. . .*t*]*i-ú-ku?*, 348:'15([n])
[. . .]-*ti*-[. . .], 316:2([n])
[. . .]-*tum*, 316:23([n]), 323:30([n]), 323:31([n]), 348:'18([n]), 362:'2([n]), 368:'9([n]), 368:'15(600), 368:'26([n]), 368:'27([n]), 368:'31([n])
[. . .]-*ú*, 316:26([n])
[. . .]-*um*, 368:'12([n]), 370:6([n])
[. . .]-*um-mi*, 370:9([n])
[. . .]-*za*-[. . .], 323:74([n])
[. . .]-*zi-tum*, 345:'4(390)
[. . .*z*]*i?*-x, 368:'16(600)
[. . .]-x, 346:116(400), 348:'19([n]), 368:'11([n]), 370:11([n])

Analytical Index of Toponyms

1 We follow Lambert, 1990, 75–80 and Frayne 2008, 357–58 in their interpretation of the reading of the city name, which, in all likelihood, was pronounced Ĝiša in the Ur III period.

2 Civil 1985, 29 and 32; Owen 1997, 369 (Nesbit A:10 [AS 8/iii/13]) and 380–81 (ref. W. Heimpel).

3 The name can be read zabalam$_4$^{ki} (MÙŠ. UNUG.KI) according to P. Steinkeller 1985, 195–96. The shorter reading, zabala$_4$^{ki}, was established by M. Powell 1976, 100, n. 5.

adab^{ki}

1. A Boat Towed from Garšana

9 g̃uruš gar-ša-an-na^{ki}-ta **adab**^{ki}-šè má gíd-da é-du$_{6}$-gur$_{4}$-*i-din-*^{d}*adad*-šè, "9 workmen having towed a boat from Garšana to Adab, to the round-hill-house of *Iddin-Adad*," 207:23–25

a-pi$_{4}$-sal-la^{ki}

1. Boats Towed to and from the Weir of Apisal

(. . .) u$_{4}$-2-[šè] **a-pi$_{4}$-sal$_{4}$-[la^{ki}**-ta] ù-dag-[ga^{ki}-šè] má sù [gíd-da] še má-[a si-ga] ù-dag-[ga^{ki}-ta] kun-zi-[da] **a-pi$_{4}$-[sal$_{4}$-la^{ki}**-šè] má-[a si-ga], "{workmen and boats} [for] 2 days, (the workers) [having towed] the sunken boats [from] Apisal [to] Udaga, [having loaded] the boats with barley (and then having towed) [the loaded] boats from Udaga [(back) to] the weir of Apisal," 553:29–38

(. . .) u$_{4}$-[n-šè] še má-a [si-ga] kun-zi-⌜da⌝ **a-pi$_{4}$-sal$_{4}$-la^{ki}**-[ta] gar-ša-an-na^{ki}-[šè] má še ⌜gíd⌝-da, "{workmen and boats} [for n] day(s), (the workers) having towed boats [loaded] with barley [from] the weir of Apisal [to] Garšana," 553:45–52

2. The Gardeners of Apisal

níg̃-kas$_{7}$-aka mun-gazi nu-$^{g̃eš}$kiri$_{6}$ **a-pí-sal$_{4}$^{ki}**-ke$_{4}$-ne, "the balanced account of mun-gazi agricultural products of the gardeners of Apisal," 540:11–12

ba-la-nu^{ki}

1. Traveling from *Balanu* to Iri-sag̃rig

[n g̃uruš . . .] ***ba?-la-nu***^{ki}-ta [. . . iri-sag̃]-rig$_{7}$$^{[ki]}$-šè g̃en-na, "[n workmen ...] having gone from *Balanu* [. . .] to Iri-sag̃rig," 193:34–35

bàd-ga-zi^{ki}

1. Barley Brought from Bad-gazi to Garšana

1 g̃uruš ašgab 1 g̃uruš ad-kub$_{4}$ 1 géme kíkken u$_{4}$-[2]7-šè še ^{d}*šu*-^{d}*suen*-<am->ma-ra$^{[ki]}$ ù **bàd-ga-zi^{ki}**-⌜ta⌝ gar-ša-an-na^{ki}-šè de$_{6}$-a, "1 leather worker, 1 reed craftsman, (and) 1 female miller for [2]7 days having brought barley from *Šu-Suen*-ammara and Bad-gazi to Garšana," 259:1–7

bàd-^{d}šul-gi

1. Distance Measurements

gú i$_{7}$-me-kal-kal-ta 1 da-na 1200 nindan ús **bàd-^{d}šul-gi**-šè, "1 da-na (and) 1200 nindan, the length from the bank of the Mekalkal canal to Bad-Šulgi," 1382:1–3

bàd-^{d}šul-gi-ta 1200 nindan ús é-lugal-eden-na-šè, "1200 nindan, the distance from Bad-Šulgi to E-lugal-edena," 1382:4–6

dar-ra-um^{ki}

1. Barley from *Darra'um*

13.1.5. dabin gur še ***dar-ra-um***^{ki} ki ^{d}*adad-tillati*-ta *a-da-làl* muḫaldim [šu] ba-an-ti, "*Adallal*, the cook, received 13 bushels (and) 110 liters of semolina, grain from *Darra'um*, from *Adad-tillati*," 1097:1–5

2. Barley Brought from *Darra'um* to Garšana

0.4.0. še á má ḫuĝ-ĝá [40-gur-kam] ù má-la[ḫ$_{5}$-bi] á 0.1.2.-ta u$_{4}$-3-šè še *dar-ra-um*^{ki}-⸢ta⸣ gar-ša-an-na^{ki}-[šè] de$_{6}$-[a], "240 liters of barley, wages of the hired [40-bushel] boat and [its] sailors, wages of 80 liters each for 3 days (for sailors) having brought barley from *Darra'um* [to] Garšana," 462:1–6

dì-ma-at-kál-bu-um^{ki}

ilum-šu-mur lú-***dì-ma-at-kál-bu-um***^{ki}, "*Ilum-šumur*, the man from *Dimat-kalbum*" > *Personal Name Index*

1. Builders from *Dimat-kalbum*

1 ĝuruš šidim lú-***dì-ma-at-kál-bu-um***^{ki}, "1 builder from *Dimat-kalbum*," 1:3–4, 2:3–4, 3:2, 4:3–4, 5:3–4, 6:3–4, 9:2, 10:2, 11:3

2 ĝuruš šidim lú-***dì-ma-at-kál-bu-um***^{ki}, "2 builders from *Dimat-kalbum*," 111:2, 114:2, 116:2, 117:2, 118:2, 119:2, 120:2, 121:2, 123:2, 124:2, 125:2, 126:2, 127:2, 128:2, 129:2, 130:2, 132:2, 133:2, 134:2, 135:2, 136:2, 137:2, 138:2, 139:2, 140:2, 141:2, 142:2, 143:2, 147:2, 149:2, 150:2, 151:2, 154:2, 155:2, 156:2, 157:2, 158:2, 159:2, 162:2, 163:2, 173:2, 174:2, 175:2, 177:2, 180:2, 214:2

3 ĝuruš šidim lú-***dì-ma-at-kál-bu-um***^{ki}, "3 builders from *Dimat-kalbum*," 52:2, 109:2, 145:2

[n] ĝuruš šidim lú-***dì-ma-at-kál-bu-um***^{ki}, "[n] builder(s) from *Dimat-kalbum*," 7:1–2, 8:3–4

1 ĝuruš šidim zàḫ lú-***dì-ma-at-kál-bu-um***^{ki}, "1 runaway builder from *Dimat-kalbum*," 13:3

1.1 Provisions for Men from *Dimat-kalbum*

3.4.5. ninda šu-r[a gur lú]-é-^{d}šu-^{d}EN.[ZU^{ki} l]ú-***dì-ma-a***[***t-kál-bu***]***-um***$^{⸢ki⸣}$ lú-^{d}*šu*-^{d}EN.Z[U-am-ma]-ar-[ra^{ki} má . . . gar-ša-an-na^{ki}-ta] nibru^{ki}-[šè] in-gíd-s[a-a], "3 bushels (and) 290 liters of half (loaf) bread (for) the [men] from *Bit-Šu-Suen*, the men from *Dimat-kalbum* (and) the men from *Šu-Suen*-ammara who towed [a . . . boat from Garšana] to Nippur," 463:1–8

dì-im-bu-na-^{d}***àš-gi***$_{5}$

a-šà ***dì-im-bu-na-àš-gi***$_{5}$, "the *Dimbun*-Ašgi field" > *Field Index*

1. Grain Brought from *Dimbun*-Ašgi to the Kabbi Village

1 ĝuruš túg-du$_{8}$ u$_{4}$-1-šè še ***dì-im-bu-na-***^{d}***àš-gi***$_{5}$-ta é-duru$_{5}$-⸢kab⸣-bí-[šè], "1 braider for 1 day (having brought) barley from *Dimbun*-Ašgi [to] the Kabbi village," 256:1–4

(. . .) u$_{4}$-1-[šè] še ***dì-im-bu-na-***^{d}***àš-gi***$_{5}$-ta é-duru$_{5}$-kab-bi-šè <de$_{6}$->a, "{craftsmen} [for] 1 day having <brought> barley from *Dimbun*-Ašgi to the Kabbi village," 287:16–18

2 ĝuruš ad-kub$_{4}$ u$_{4}$-1-šè ⸢še⸣ ***dì-im-bu-***⸢***na***⸣***-***^{d}***àš-gi***$_{5}$-[ta é]-duru$_{5}$-kab-bi^{ki}-[šè], "2 reed craftsmen for 1 day (having brought) barley [from] *Dimbun*-Ašgi [to] the Kabbi village," 288:5–8

5 géme uš-bar u$_{4}$-1-šè še ***dì-im-bu-na-***^{d}**aš-gi**$_{5}$-ta [é]-duru$_{5}$-kab-bí-šè de$_{6}$-a, "5 female weavers for 1 day having brought barley from *Dimbun*-Ašgi to the Kabbi village," 290:5–8

iti u$_{5}$-bí-[gu$_{7}$] ù iti ki-siki-^{d}n[in-a-zu x?] še-zíz ḫi-a 720 g[ur (. . .)] ***dì-im-bu-na-á[š-gi***$_{5}$-ta] é-duru$_{5}$-kab-bí-šè lá-[a], "(In) month 4 and month 5 720 bushels of various barley (and) emmer wheat were transported from *Dimbun*-Ašgi to the Kabbi village," 1029:'1-'5

2. Grain in *Dimbun*-Ašgi

15.2.0. zíz gur 0.1.3. kib$_{x}$ ì-dub šà **dì-im-bu-bu**(sic!)<**-aš**>**-gi**$_{5}$, "15 bushels (and) 120 liters of emmer wheat (and) 90 liters of wheat of the granary in *Dimbun*-Ašgi," 1232:4–7

3. Traveling from *Dimbun*-Ašgi to the *Ṣerum* Field

1 g̃uruš túg-du$_{8}$ u$_{4}$-4-šè ***dì-im-bu-na-àš-gi***$_{5}$-ta a-šà *ṣe-ru-um*-šè, "1 braider for 4 days (having gone) from *Dimbun*-Ašgi to the *Ṣerum* field," 283:5–8

1 g̃uruš ad-kub$_{4}$ u$_{4}$-4-šè ***dì-im-bu-na-àš-gi***$_{5}$-ta a-šà *ṣe-r[u-u]m*-šè še gur$_{10}$-gur$_{10}$-[dè] gub-ba, "1 reed craftsmen (having gone) from *Dimbun*-Ašgi to the *Ṣerum* field, employed for 4 days [to] reap barley," 284:5–10

du$_{6}$-lugal-pa-è^{ki}

a-ḫu-wa-qar lú-**du$_{6}$-lugal-pa-è^{ki}**, "*Aḫu-waqar*, the man from Du-lugal-pa'e" > *Personal Name Index*

ku-du-du-ú lú-**du$_{6}$-lugal-pa-è^{ki}**, "*Kududu*, the man from Du-lugal-pa'e" > *Personal Name Index*

1. Workmen from Du-lugal-pa'e

4 g̃uruš lú-**du$_{6}$-lugal-pa-è^{ki}**, "4 workmen from Du-lugal-pa'e," 38:7, 49:7

[n g̃ur]uš lú-**du$_{6}$-lugal-pa-è^{ki}**, "[n] workmen from Du-lugal-pa'e," 31:8, 37:7

2. Workmen and Women from Du-lugal-pa'e

5 g̃uruš 1 géme lú-**du$_{6}$-lugal-pa-è^{ki}**(-me), "5 workmen (and) 1 workwoman from Du-lugal-pa'e," 22:8, 23:7, 24:8, 29:'5, 30:8, 32:8, 33:8, 34:8, 35:8, 36:8, 39:7, 40:7–8, 42:7, 43:7, 44:7, 45:7, 46:'2, 47:7, 48:8

2.1 A Sick Workwoman

1 géme dú-ra lú-**du$_{6}$-lugal-pa-è^{ki}**, "1 sick workwoman from Du-lugal-pa'e," 24:'32, 25:'7, 27:'21, 28:'32, 29:'37, 31:45, 32:44, 33:48, 34:'23, 35:52, 40:54–55, 41:'33, '35

1 *be-[lí]-a-sú* 1 *e-pe-eš̌* ^{na}nam!?<-dú?-ra?> ugula *i-[ri]-ib* 1 géme lú-**du$_{6}$-lugal-pa-è**<^{ki}> ⌜dú⌝-ra-m[e-é]š, "*Beli-asu*, satisfying the allowance of sick leave, supervised by *Irib*, (and) 1 workwoman from of Du-lugal-pa'e, sick (workers)," 36:44–47

2.2 A Woman to Mill Flour

1 géme zì-da àra-dè gub-ba zàḫ *ku-du-du-ú* lú-**du$_{6}$-lugal-pa-è^{ki}**(-me-éš), "1 workwoman employed to mill flour (and) *Kududu*, the runaway, persons from Du-lugal-pa'e," 45:34–36, 46:'51-'53, 47:69–71, 48:76–78

3. Fish Brought from Du-lugal-pa'e

3 sìla ninda lú ku$_6$ **du$_6$-lugal-pa-è^{ki}**-ta de$_6$-a u$_4$ é-e im sumur ba-aka, "3 liters of bread (for) the man who brought fish from Du-lugalpa'e when the house was plastered," 476:1–4

du$_6$-saḫar-ra^{ki}

1. Barley Brought from Du-saḫara to Garšana

2 g̃uruš ad-kub$_4$ 1½ g̃uruš báḫar u$_4$-5-šè [še] **du$_6$-saḫar-ra^{ki}**-ta gar-ša-an-na^{ki}-šè de$_6$-a, "2 reed craftsmen (and) 1½ potters for 5 days having brought [barley] from Du-saḫara to Garšana," 233:4–8

2. Barley Carried from Du-Saḫar to Enzu-Babbar

1 g̃uruš túg-du$_8$ u$_4$-12-šè **du$_6$-saḫar-ra^{ki}**-ta en-zu-bábbar^{ki}-šè [še] íb-ga$_6$ [ús-b]i 1500 éš kaskal š[u+níg̃in]-na-bi, "1 braider for 12 days carried [barley] from Du-saḫara to Enzu-babbar. Its distance: 1500 ropes is the entire trip," 263:1–6

3. Barley: Transaction in Du-saḫara

41.2.0 še gur še apin-lá ki *a-da-làl* in-da-g̃ál g̃ìri *nu-úr-^{d}Adad* šà **du$_6$-saḫar-ra^{ki}**, "Under the authority of *Nur-Adad* in Du-saḫara, 41 bushels (and) 120 liters of barley, barley of the cultivator, are with *Adallal* at his place," 1158: 1–6

é-da-na^{ki}

1. A Builder Gone to Edana

1 g̃uruš šidim **é-da-na^{ki}**-šè g̃en-na, "1 builder having gone to Edana," 190:30, 195:'26-'27, 196:'29-'30, 197:39

2. A Boat Towed to Edana

7 g̃uruš ašgab u$_4$-1-šè **é-da-na^{ki}**-šè má gíd-da, "7 leather workers for 1 day having towed a boat to Edana," 884:3–4

3. The Commodity Tax Brought to Edana

17 g̃uruš níg̃-gú-na g̃á-g̃á **é-da-na^{ki}**-šè g̃en-na, "17 workmen having gone to Edana to deposit the commodity tax," 125:5, 125:37, 126:5, 126:33, 127:5, 128:5, 128:35

1 g̃uruš túg-du$_8$ u$_4$-11-šè níg̃-gú-na **é-da-na^{ki}**-šè de$_6$-a, "1 braider for 11 days having brought the commodity tax to Edana," 267:6–8

2 g̃uruš ⌜u$_4$-1-šè⌝ níg̃-gú-na **é-d[a-na^{ki}**-šè d]e$_6$-a, "2 workmen for 1 day having brought the commodity tax [to] Edana," 246:3–4

4. The Tablet of *Malik-bani* Brought to Edana

1 *be-lí-ì-lí* 1 *šu-*^{d}nin-kar-ak dub ^{d}*ma-lik-ba-ni* **é-da-na^{ki}**-šè de$_6$-a, "*Beli-ili* and *Šu*-Ninkarak having brought the tablet of *Malik-bani* to Edana," 51:'22-'24, 52:59–62, 53:61–63, 56:'32-'35

é-duru$_5$-^{d}ba-ú

1. Broken Context

[. . .] NE-x[. . . n] dida$_x$-g[en . . . x]-ki-ri?-šè šà **é-duru$_5$-^{d}b[a?-ú? (x)] tuḫ-bi ba-zi, "[. . . n (liters?) . . .] ordinary dida beer for (?) in the B[a'u?] village, its bran was disbursed," 1009:18–21

é-duru$_5$-kab-bi

1. Barley Brought from the Kabbi Village to Garšana

2 ĝuruš ad-kub$_4$ u$_4$-20-šè še **é-duru$_5$-kab-bí**-ta gar-ša-an-na^{ki}-šè de$_6$-a, "2 reed craftsmen for 20 days having brought barley from the Kabbi village to Garšana," 300:1–4

4 géme kíkken u$_4$-20-šè še **é-duru$_5$-kab-bi^{ki}**-ta gar-ša-an-na^{ki}-šè de$_6$-a, "4 female millers for 20 days having brought barley from the Kabbi village to Garšana," 301:1–3

[n ĝuruš] túg-d[u$_8$ u$_4$]-20-[šè še **é]-duru$_5$-kab-bi[^{ki}**-ta ĝar]-ša-an-na^{ki}-[šè] de$_6$-a, "[n] braider(s) [for] 20 [days] having brought [barley from] the Kabbi village [to] Garšana," 302:1–3

3 géme uš-bar u$_4$-20-šè še **é-duru$_5$-ka[b-bí]**-ta gar-š[a-an]-n[a^{k}]^{i}-šè [de$_6$]-a, "3 female weavers for 20 days having [brought] barley from the Kabbi village to Garšana," 303:1–4

(. . .) u$_4$-20-šè še **é-duru$_5$-kab-bi**-ta gar-ša-an-na^{ki}-šè mu-un-de$_9$-sa-a, "{craftsmen} for 20 days who brought barley from the Kabbi village to Garšana," 304:7–10

[n ĝuru]š ašgab [u$_4$]-20-šè [še **é]-duru$_5$-kab-bi**-ta^{ki} [gar-ša]-an-na^{ki}<-šè> de$_6$-a, "[n] leather worker(s) for 20 [days] having brought [barley] from the Kabbi village <to> Garšana," 305:1–4

2. Grain Brought to the Kabbi Village from *Dimbun*-Ašgi

1 ĝuruš túg-du$_8$ u$_4$-1-šè še *dì-im-bu-na*-^{d}àš-gi$_5$-ta **é-duru$_5$-⸢kab⸣-bí**-[šè], "1 braider for 1 day (having brought) barley from *Dimbun*-Ašgi [to] the Kabbi village," 256:1–4

u$_4$-1-[šè] še *dì-im-bu-na*-^{d}àš-gi$_5$-ta **é-duru$_5$-kab-bi**-šè(!) <de$_6$->a, "{craftsmen} [for] 1 day having <brought> barley from *Dimbun*-Ašgi to the Kabbi village," 287:16–18

2 ĝuruš ad-kub$_4$ u$_4$-1-šè ⸢še⸣ *dì-im-bu-*⸢*na*⸣-^{d}àš-gi$_5$-[ta **é]-duru$_5$-kab-bi^{ki}**-[šè], "2 reed craftsmen for 1 day (having brought) barley [from] *Dimbun*-Ašgi [to] the Kabbi village," 288:5–8

5 géme uš-bar u$_4$-1-šè še *dì-im-bu-na*-^{d}àš-gi$_5$-ta **[é]-duru$_5$-kab-bí**-šè de$_6$-a, "5 female weavers for 1 day having brought barley from *Dimbun*-Ašgi to the Kabbi village," 290:5–8

iti u$_5$-bí-[gu$_7$] ù iti ki-siki-^{d}n[in-a-zu x?] še-zíz-ḫi-a 720 g[ur (. . .)] *dì-im-bu-na*-á[š-gi$_5$-ta] **é-duru$_5$-kab-bí**-šè lá-[a], "(In) month 4 and month 5 720 bushels of various barley (and) emmer wheat were transported from *Dimbun*-Ašgi to the Kabbi village," 1029:'1-'5

3. Boats Towed from the Kabbi Village

3.1 To the Bank of the *Maništišu* Canal

0.2.3. á má-ḫuĝ-ĝá 0.2.0. á ĝuruš ḫuĝ-ĝá 0.0.1.6 sìla šà-gal má-laḫ$_5$ 0.0.1.6 sìla < še->b[i s]a$_{10}$ má-[la]ḫ$_5$ u$_4$-1-šè **é-duru$_5$-ka[b-bí**-ta] gú i$_7$-[*ma-an-iš-ti-šu*-šè] má gí[d-da], "150 liters, wages of the hired boat (and) 120 liters, wages of hired workmen; 16 liters, food (for) sailors, 16 liters <of barley> is the (hiring) price of the sailors for 1 day having towed boats [from] the Kabbi Village [to] the bank of the [*Maništišu*] canal," 561:'28-'32

3.2 To the *Simat-Ištaran* Village

[. . .] á-ĝuruš-[a . . .] 0.0.1.6 sìla še-bi sa$_{10}$ má-laḫ$_5$-e-ne u$_4$-1-[šè] **é-duru$_5$-kab-⸢bí⸣**-ta é-duru$_5$-*simat*-^{d}*ištaran*-šè má diri-ga, "[. . .] wages of [. . .] workmen, 16 liters of barley is the (hiring) price of the sailors [for] 1 day having floated boats from the Kabbi village to the *Simat-Ištaran* village," 561:'1-'5

é-duru$_5$-*simat*-^{d}*ištaran*

1. Boats Towed to and from the Village

[. . .] á-g̃uruš-[a . . .] 0.0.1.6 sìla še-bi sa$_{10}$ má-laḫ$_5$-e-ne u$_4$-1-[šè] é-duru$_5$-kab-⸢bí⸣-ta **é-duru$_5$-*simat*-^{d}*ištaran***-šè má diri-ga, "[. . .] wages of [. . .] workmen, 16 liters of barley is the (hiring) price of the sailors [for] 1 day having floated boats from the Kabbi village to the *Simat-Ištaran* village," 561:'1-'5

[. . . u]$_4$-1-[šè] **é-duru$_5$-*simat*-^{d}[*ištaran***-ta] ka i$_7$-^{d}[nin-ḫur-sag̃-g̃á-šè] má gíd-da, "[(wages of sailors) for] 1 day having towed boats [from] the *Simat-Ištaran* village [to] the mouth of the [Ninḫursag̃] canal," 561:'11-'14

é-duru$_5$-ul-luḫ-uri$_5$^{ki}

1. Barley Rations Distributed in the Ulluḫ-Urim Village

(. . .) u$_4$-2-šè še **é-duru$_5$-ul-luḫ-ŠEŠ.[AB]^{ki}**-ma-šè g̃en-⸢na⸣ mu še-ba-ne-ne-šè, "{craftsmen} for 2 days having gone to the Ulluḫ-Urim village for barley for barley rations," 291:12–14, 292:12–14

1 g̃uruš báḫar u$_4$-2-šè še **é-duru$_5$-ul-luḫ-uri$_5$^{ki}**-ma-šè g̃en-na mu še-ba-ne-ne-šè, "1 potter for 2 days having gone to the Ulluḫ-Urim village for barley for barley rations," 293:1–2

g̃uruš ad-kub$_4$ u$_4$-2-šè še **é-duru$_5$-ul-luḫ-uri$_5$^{ki}**-ma-šè g̃en-na mu še-ba-ne-ne-šè, "2 reed craftsmen for 2 days having gone to the Ulluḫ-Urim village for barley for barley rations," 294:1–4

iti ezem-maḫ še tùm-dè **é-duru$_5$-ul-luḫ-uri$_5$^{ki}**-[ma-šè g̃en-na], "(workers) [having gone to] the Ulluḫ-Urim village to bring barley (in) month 10," 1029:'18-'19

é-kab-ba^{ki}

1. Barley Brought from E-kabba and Karkar to Garšana

9 g̃uruš sag̃-tag 1 g̃uruš á-⅔ 1 g̃uruš á-⅓ ^{lú}ázlag-me-éš u$_4$-1-šè še **é-kab-ba^{ki}** ⸢karkar⸣^{ki}-ta [ga]r-š[a-a]n-⸢na⸣$^{⸢ki⸣}$-šè de$_6$-a, "9 full-time fullers, 1 fuller at ⅔ wages, (and) 1 fuller at ⅓ wages for 1 day having brought barley from E-kabba (and) Karkar to Garšana," 237:1–8

3 g̃uruš u$_4$-1-šè še **é-kab-[ba^{ki}]** karkar^{ki}-[ta] gar-ša-an-na^{ki}-[šè] íb-ga$_6$, "3 workmen for 1 day carried barley [from] E-kabba (and) Karkar [to] Garšana," 884:6–10

é-lugal-eden-na

1. Distance Measurements

bàd-^{d}šul-gi-ta 1200 nindan ús **é-lugal-eden-na**-šè, "1200 nindan, the distance from Bad-Šulgi to E-lugal-edena," 1382:4–6

é-lugal-eden-na-ta 1200 nindan ús gú i$_7$-*ì-diš$_x$-tum*-šè, "1200 nindan, the distance from E-lugal-edena to the bank of the *Idištum* canal," 1382:7–9

é-^{d}*šu*-^{d}*suen*^{ki}

1. Men from *Bit-Šu-Suen*

1.1 Builders

3 g̃uruš šidim lú-**é-^{d}*šu*-^{d}*suen*^{ki}**-me-éš, "3 builders from *Bit-Šu-Suen*," 183:1–2, 184:9–10, 185:7, 186:8

3 [g̃ur]uš šidim l[ú-**é-^{d}š**]**u-^{d}suen**-me-éš ugula *a-bu*-DU$_{10}$, "3 builders from *Bit-Šu-Suen*, supervised by *Abu-ṭabu*," 187:11–12

3 g̃uruš šidim lú-**é-^{d}š**[**u-^{d}suen**]^{ki}-me-éš *a-bu*-DU$_{10}$ nu-bà[nda], "3 builders from *Bit-Šu-Suen* (from the gang of) *Abu-ṭabu*, the ox-ḫerder," 188:'7-'8, 189:13–15

1.2 Provisions for Men from *Bit-Šu-Suen*

[n sìl]a níg̃-àr-r[a-sig$_5$ t]u$_7$-šè lú-**é-^{d}šu-^{d}**E[N.ZU]^{ki}-ke$_4$-ne ba-na-ḫa-la u$_4$ [é]-e [im sumur ba-aka], "[n] liter(s) of [fine] barley groats for soup were divided among the men from *Bit-Šu-Suen* when [the house was plastered]," 391:1–5

3.4.5. ninda šu-r[a gur lú]-**é-^{d}šu-^{d}EN.**[**ZU**^{ki} l]ú-*dì-ma-a*[*t-kál-bu*]-*um*$^{⌜ki⌝}$ lú-^{d}*šu*-^{d}EN.Z[U-am-ma]-ar-[ra^{ki} má . . . gar-ša-an-na^{ki}-ta] nibru^{ki}-[šè] in-gíd-s[a-a], "3 bushels (and) 290 liters of half (loaf) bread (for) the [men] from *Bit-Šu-Suen*, the men from *Dimat-kalbum* (and) the men from *Šu-Suen*-ammara who towed [a . . . boat from Garšana] to Nippur," 463:1-8

2. Errands from *Bit-Šu-Suen*

2.1 Barley Brought from *Bit-Šu-Suen*

0.4.4.5 sìla [še?] 0.0.3. zíz 0.0.1. kib$_x$ *dan-ḫi-li* ^{l}[^{ú}lùn]ga in-⌜da⌝-g̃ál še **é-^{d}šu-^{d}suen**^{ki}-ta de$_6$-a, "285 liters of [barley?], 30 liters of emmer wheat (and) 10 liters of wheat are with *Danḫili*, the brewer, who brought barley from *Bit-Šu-Suen*," 1065:1–6

2.2 Oil and Wool Brought from *Bit-Šu-Suen*

2 g̃uruš ad-kub$_4$ u$_4$-1-šè a-rá–2-kam 2 g̃uruš ad-kub$_4$ u$_4$-1-šè a-rá–3-kam siki de$_6$-a **é-^{d}šu-^{d}suen**^{ki}-ta gar-ša-an-na^{ki}-šè (g̃en-a), "2 reed craftsmen for 1 day for the 2nd time (and) 2 reed craftsmen for 1 day for the 3rd time having brought wool, (reed craftsmen having gone) from *Bit-Šu-Suen* to Garšana," 285:7–13, 286:7–13

2 g̃uruš túg-du$_8$ u$_4$-1-šè ⌜siki⌝ de$_6$-a a-rá–2-kam **é-^{d}šu-^{d}suen**^{ki}-ta gar-ša-an-na^{ki}-šè g̃en-a, "2 braiders for 1 day having brought wool for the 2nd time, (braiders) having gone from *Bit-Šu-Suen* to Garšana," 306:9–13

2.3 Wool Brought from *Bit-Šu-Suen*

2.3.1 To Garšana

8 g̃uruš ^{lú}ázlag u$_4$-1-šè siki **é-^{d}šu-^{d}suen**-ta gar-ša-an-n[a^{ki}]-šè mu-un-de$_9$-sa-a, "8 fullers for 1 day who brought wool from *Bit-Šu-Suen* to Garšana," 243:1–4

2.3.2 To Nippur

1 g̃uruš ^{lú}ázlag sag̃-tag u$_4$-2-šè 2 g̃uruš sag̃-tag 2 g̃uruš á–½-ta u$_4$-2-šè siki **é-^{d}šu-^{d}suen**^{ki}-ta nibru^{ki}-šè DU(sic!) de$_6$-a, "1 full-time fuller for 2 days, (and) 2 full-time workmen (and) 2 workmen at ½ wages for 2 days having brought wool from *Bit-Šu-Suen* to Nippur," 226:1–8

3 g̃uruš ^{lú}ázlag siki **é-^{d}šu-^{d}suen**^{ki}-ka-ta nibru^{ki}-šè de$_6$-a kaskal šu+níg̃in-na-bi u$_4$-10!-kam u$_4$-2 kaš-dé-[a] á-⌜ki⌝-ti šu-numun, "3 fullers having brought wool from *Bit-Šu-Suen* to Nippur, a trip of 10 days in total, on day 2 of the banquet of the Akiti festival of month 4," 240:1–6

2.3.3 Destination Unspecified

1⅔ g̃uruš ašgab u$_4$-6-šè siki **é-^{d}šu-^{d}suen^{ki}-ka-ta mu-un-li-sa-a, "1⅔ leather workers for 6 days who brought wool from *Bit-Šu-Suen*," 228:1–4

4 g̃uruš sag̃-tag 1 g̃uruš á-⅔ ^{lú}ázlag-me-éš u$_4$-2-šè siki **é-^{d}šu-^{d}suen^{ki}**-ta de$_6$-a, "4 full-time fullers (and) 1 fuller at ⅔ wages for 2 days having brought wool from *Bit-Šu-Suen*," 241:1–4

2.4 Boats Towed from *Bit-Šu-Suen* to Gu-saḫar.DU

1 g̃uruš túg-du$_8$ u$_4$-[1-šè] **é-^{d}šu-^{d}suen$^{⌜ki⌝}$**-[ta] gú-saḫar^{ḫar}.DU^{ki}-šè m[á gíd-da], "1 braider [for 1] day [having towed] a boat [from] *Bit-Šu-Suen* to Gu-saḫar.DU," 298:6–8

3 g̃uruš ašgab u$_4$-1-šè **é-^{d}šu-[^{d}EN].ZU^{ki}**-ta gú-saḫar^{ḫar}.DU^{ki}-šè má gíd-da, "3 leather workers for 1 day having towed a boat from *Bit-Šu-Suen* to Gu-saḫar.DU," 299:6–8

3. Errands to *Bit-Šu-Suen*

3.1 Delivering a Message

[n] g̃uruš á-àg̃-g̃á še túl-tur **é-^{d}šu-^{d}suen^{ki}**-šè de$_6$<-a>, "[n] workmen having brought a message to *Bit-Šu-Suen* concerning barley (and?) the small well," 175:28

3.2 Sorting Wool in *Bit-Šu-Suen*

4 géme uš-bar u$_4$-1-šè siki igi sag̃-g̃á šà **é-^{d}šu-^{d}suen^{ki}**, "4 female weavers for 1 day having sorted wool in *Bit-Šu-Suen*," 264:1–3

8 géme u$_4$-1-šè [siki] igi sag̃-g̃á šà **é-^{d}šu-^{d}suen^{ki}**-ka de$_6$-a, "8 workwomen for 1 day having brought [wool] sorted in *Bit-Šu-Suen*," 279:1–3

3.3 Traveling to *Bit-Šu-Suen*

3.3.1 Traveling for Wool

1 é-ì-gára siki tùm-dè **é-^{d}šu-^{d}suen^{ki}**-[ta] g̃en-a, "E'igara having gone to bring wool [from] *Bit-Šu-Suen*," 39:46

1 é-ì-gára **é-^{d}šu-^{d}suen^{ki}**-ta siki tùm-dè g̃en-na, "E'igara having gone to bring wool from *Bit-Šu-Suen*," 40:40–41

6 g̃uruš siki **é-^{d}šu-^{d}suen^{ki}**-ka-šè g̃en-na, "6 workmen having gone for *Bit-Šu-Suen* wool," 122:'30, 123:6, 123:42

3.3.2 Traveling from Garšana

1 g̃uruš [túg-du$_8$ u$_4$-1-šè] gar-ša-an-na^{ki}-ta **é-^{d}šu-^{d}suen**[^{ki}-a] g̃en-[na], "1 [braider for 1 day] having gone from Garšana [into] *Bit-Šu-Suen*," 298:1–3

3 g̃uruš ašgab u$_4$-1-šè gar-ša-an-na^{ki}-ta **é-^{d}šu-^{d}suen^{ki}**-a g̃en-a, "3 leather workers for 1 day having gone from Garšana into *Bit-Šu-Suen*," 299:1–3

3.3.3 Traveling when the House was Plastered

0.0.2.6 sìla ninda ^{kuš}a-g̃á-lá kéše-rá g̃uruš nam–60 *a-⌜bu⌝*-DU$_{10}$ u$_4$ **é-^{d}šu-^{d}suen^{ki}**-šè i-⌜re⌝-ša-a u$_4$ é-e im sumur ba-aka, "36 liters of bread in bound leather sacks (for) *Abu-ṭabu*, the overseer of 60 workmen, when (his workers) went to *Bit-Šu-Suen* when the house was plastered," 480:1–3

3.4 Boats Towed to *Bit-Šu-Suen*

3 g̃uruš ^{lú}ázlag u$_4$-2½-šè nibru^{ki}-ta **é-^{d}šu-^{d}suen**-šè má *na-wi-ir-ilum* íb-gíd, "3 fullers for 2½ days towed the boat of *Nawir-ilum* from Nippur to *Bit-Šu-Suen*," 220:1–6

4. Transactions in *Bit-Šu-Suen*

4.1 A Beer Offering, the Expenditure of *Simat-Ištaran*

(. . .) kaš ba-an-dé *ri-im-ilum* sugal$_7$ gaba-ri-a unug^{ki}-ta du-ni (. . .) šà **é-^{d}*šu*-^{d}*suen***, "{assorted beer}; he poured the beer when *Rim-ilum*, the sugal, came from Uruk (for) a meeting. {Transaction} in *Bit-Šu-Suen*," 517:4–6, 10

4.2 Animals Slaughtered for Inana of Zabala

★★4 ⸢máš⸣ 4 u$_8$ [n] ud$_5$ [n] máš-gal ba-úš bi+šu-ab-ta? ^{d}inana-zabala$_4$^{ki} u$_4$-1-šè **é-*šu*-^{d}E[N.Z]U**, "4 goats, 4 ewes, [n] female goat(s), [n] billy-goat(s), slaughtered (?) (for) Inana of Zabala for one day (in) *Bit-Šu-Suen*," 1019:1–7

é-ù-ri-a^{ki}

1. Straw Brought from E-uri'a to the Canal

[n g̃uruš] gi-zi [é-^{d}]šára-ta [gar-ša-an]-na^{ki}-šè de$_6$-a [in-u] **é-ù-ri-a^{ki}**-ta [ka i$_7$ UD].DU-šè de$_6$-a, "[n workmen] having brought fresh reeds from the Šara [temple] to Garšana (and) having brought straw from E-uri'a to the mouth of the 'Outgoing' canal," 193:29–32

2.2.0. še gur á má ḫug̃-g̃á má–90-gur-kam á 0.0.4-ta ù má-laḫ$_5$-bi u$_4$-18-šè in-u **é-ù-ri-a**<ki>-ta gú i$_7$-da lá-a, "2 bushels (and) 120 liters of barley, wages of the hired 90-bushel boat and its sailors, wages of 40 liters each for 18 days (for sailors) having transported straw from E-uri'a to the bank of the canal," 413:1–7

2. Traveling from E-uri'a to the Canal

7 g̃uruš **é-ù-ri-a**[^{ki}-ta] ka i$_7$-è g̃[en-na], "7 workmen having gone [from] E-uri'a (to) the opening of the 'Outgoing' canal," 192:'21

Elam(NIM)^{ki}

1. Broken Context

★★0.0.5. zì-KAL 0.0.2. zì-gu-ús 0.0.4.3 sìla dabin 0.0.2.4 sìla eša 7⅓ sìla zú-lum eša ḫi-dè sízkur dig̃ir-re-[e?]-ne [. . . x **N]IM?^{ki}**, "50 liters of KAL-flour, 20 liters of 2nd-quality gu-flour, 43 liters of semolina, 24 liters of fine flour (and) 7⅓ liters of dates to mix (with) fine flour, (ceremonial) offerings of the gods, [. . . El]am?," 1017:1–7

en-zu-bábbar^{ki}

1. Barley Brought from Enzu-babbar

1 g̃uruš túg-du$_8$ u$_4$-6-šè še(40)! **en-zu-bábbar**<ki>-ta [de$_6$]-a, "1 braider for 6 days having [brought] barley from Enzu-babbar," 267:1–2

2. Barley Carried from Enzu-babbar to Du-saḫara

1 g̃uruš túg-du$_8$ u$_4$-12-šè du$_6$-saḫar-ra^{ki}-ta **en-zu-bábbar^{ki}**-šè [še] íb-ga$_6$ [ús-b]i 1500 éš kaskal š[u+níg̃in]-na-bi, "1 braider for 12 days carried [barley] from Du-saḫara to Enzu-babbar. Its distance: 1500 ropes is the entire trip," 263:1–6

gar-ša-an-na^{ki}

šà **gar-ša-an-na^{ki}**, "in Garšana," *passim*

1. Commodities Brought to Garšana

1.1 Barley

1.1.1 From *Darra'um*

0.4.0. še á má ḫuĝ-ĝá [40-gur-kam] ù má-la[h$_5$-bi] á 0.1.2.-ta u$_4$-3-šè še dar-ra-um^{ki}-⸢ta⸣ **gar-ša-an-na^{ki}**-[šè] de$_6$-[a], "40 liters of barley, wages of the hired [40-bushel] boat and [its] sailors, wages of 80 liters each for 3 days (for sailors) having brought barley from *Darra'um* [to] Garšana," 462:1–6

1.1.2 From Du-saḫara

2 ĝuruš ad-kub$_4$ 1½ ĝuruš báḫar u$_4$-5-šè [še] du$_6$-saḫar-ra^{ki}-ta **gar-ša-an-na^{ki}**-šè de$_6$-a, "2 reed craftsmen (and) 1½ potters (for) 5 days having brought [barley] from Du-saḫara to Garšana," 233:4–8

1.1.3 From the Kabbi Village

2 ĝuruš ad-kub$_4$ u$_4$-20-šè še é-duru$_5$-kab-bí-ta **gar-ša-an-na^{ki}**-šè de$_6$-a, "2 reed craftsmen for 20 days having brought barley from the Kabbi village to Garšana," 300:1–4

4 géme kíkken u$_4$-20-šè še é-duru$_5$-kab-bi^{ki}-ta **gar-ša-an-na^{ki}**-šè de$_6$-a, "4 female millers for 20 days having brought barley from the Kabbi village to Garšana," 301:1–3

[n ĝuruš] túg-d[u$_8$ u$_4$]-20-[šè še é]-duru$_5$-kab-bi[^{ki}-ta **gar**]-**ša-an-na^{ki}**-[šè] de$_6$-a, "[n] braider(s) [for] 20 [days] having brought [barley from] the Kabbi village [to] Garšana," 302:1–3

3 géme uš-bar u$_4$-20-šè še é-duru$_5$-ka[b-bí]-ta **gar-š[a-an]-n[a^{k}]^{i}**-šè [de$_6$]-a, "3 female weavers for 20 days having [brought] barley from the Kabbi village to Garšana," 303:1–4

(. . .) u$_4$-20-šè še é-duru$_5$-kab-bi-ta **gar-ša-an-na^{ki}**-šè mu-un-de$_9$-sa-a, "{craftsmen} for 20 days who brought barley from the Kabbi village to Garšana," 304:7–10

[n ĝuru]š ašgab [u$_4$]-20-šè [še é]-duru$_5$-kab-bi-ta^{ki} **[gar-ša]-an-na^{ki}**<-šè> de$_6$-a, "[n] leather worker(s) for 20 [days] having brought [barley] from the Kabbi village <to> Garšana," 305:1–4

1.1.4 From E-kabba and Karkar

9 ĝuruš saĝ-tag 1 ĝuruš á-⅔ 1 ĝuruš á-⅓ ^{lú}ázlag-me-éš u$_4$-1-šè še é-kab-ba^{ki} ⸢karkar⸣^{ki}-ta ⸢**gar**⸣**-š[a-a]n-n[a]**$^{⸢ki⸣}$-šè de$_6$-a, "9 full-time fullers, 1 fuller at ⅔ wages, (and) 1 fuller at ⅓ wages for 1 day having brought barley from E-kabba (and) Karkar to Garšana," 237:1–8

3 ĝuruš u$_4$-1-šè še é-kab-[ba^{ki}] karkar^{ki}-[ta] **gar-ša-an-na^{ki}**-[šè] íb-ga$_6$, "3 workmen for 1 day carried barley [from] E-kabba (and) Karkar [to] Garšana," 884:6–10

1.1.5 From the Fortified Tower of *Dada*

10 géme kíkken u$_4$-1-šè a-rá–1-kam 10 géme kíkken u$_4$-1-šè a-rá–2-kam 10 géme kíkken u$_4$-1-šè a-rá–3-kam še an-za-qar-*da-da*-ta **gar-ša-an-na^{ki}**-šè de$_6$-a, "10 female millers for 1 day for the 1st time, 10 female millers for 1 day for the 2nd

time (and) 10 female millers for 1 day for the 3rd time having brought barley from the fortified tower of *Dada* to Garšana," 296:1–9

2 g̃uruš [ašgab] u$_4$-[1-šè] a-rá–1-[kam] 2 g̃uruš ašgab [u$_4$-1-šè] a-rá–2-kam 2 g̃uruš ašgab u$_4$-1-šè a-rá–3-kam 2 g̃uruš ašgab u$_4$-1-šè a-rá–4-kam 2 g̃uruš ašgab u$_4$-1-šè a-rá–5-kam še an-za-qar-*da-da*-[ta] **gar-ša-an-na**^{ki}-šè de$_6$-a, "2 leather workers for 1 day having brought barley from the fortified tower of *Dada* to Garšana (on) {5 different occasions}," 297:1–14

1.1.6 From *Šu-Suen*-ammara and Bad-gazi

1 g̃uruš ašgab 1 g̃uruš ad-kub$_4$ 1 géme kíkken u$_4$-[2]7-šè še ^{d}*šu*-^{d}*suen*-<am->ma-ra$^{[ki]}$ ù bàd-ga-zi^{ki}-⸢ta⸣ **gar-ša-an-na**^{ki}-šè de$_6$-a, "1 leather worker, 1 reed craftsman (and) 1 female miller for [2]7 days having brought barley from *Šu-Suen*-ammara and Bad-gazi to Garšana," 259:1–7

1.1.7 From Udaga

[n] g̃uruš tú[g-d]u$_8$ u$_4$-9-šè še ù-dag-ga^{ki}-ta **gar-ša-an-na**^{ki}-šè de$_6$-a ù kar-[ta] g̃á-nun-šè íb-[g]a$_6$, "[n] braider(s) for 9 days having brought barley from Udaga to Garšana and carried it [from] the quay to the storehouse," 261:1–6

(. . .) u$_4$-10-šè še ù-dag-ga^{ki}-ta **gar-ša-an-na**^{ki}-šè de$_6$-a, "{craftsmen} for 10 days having brought barley from Udaga to Garšana," 287:7–9

2 g̃uruš [ad-kub$_4$ u$_4$]-10-šè ⸢še⸣ ù-dag-ga^{ki}-t[a **gar-ša**]**-an-na**^{ki}-šè de$_6$-a, "2 [reed craftsmen] for 10 [days] having brought barley from Udaga to Garšana," 288:1–4

6 géme kíkken u$_4$-10-šè še ù-dag-ga^{ki}-ta **gar-ša-an-na**^{ki}-šè de$_6$-a, "6 female millers for 10 days having brought barely from Udaga to Garšana," 289:1–4

16⅓ géme uš-bar u$_4$-10-šè še ù-dag-ga^{ki}-ta **gar-ša-an-na**^{ki}-šè de$_6$-a, "16⅓ female weavers for 10 days having brought barley from Udaga to Garšana," 290:1–4

1.1.8 City of Origin Lost

1⅔ g̃uruš ašg[ab] u$_4$-4-⸢šè⸣ še [GN]^{ki}-ta **gar-[ša-an-na**^{ki}]-šè de$_6$-a, "1⅔ leather workers for 4 days having brought barley from [GN] to Garšana," 229:1–4

1.1.9 Boats with Barley Towed to Garšana

1.1.9.1 From Apisal

(. . .) u$_4$-[n-šè] še má-a [si-ga] kun-zi-⸢da⸣ a-pi$_4$-sal$_4$-la^{ki}-[ta] **gar-ša-an-na**^{ki}-[šè] má še ⸢gíd⸣-da, "{workmen and boats} [for n] day(s), (the workers) having towed boats [loaded] with barley [from] the weir of Apisal [to] Garšana," 553:45–52

1.1.9.2 From the Canals

0.2.3. á má-ḫug̃-g̃á 0.2.0. á g̃uruš ḫug̃-g̃á 0.0.1.6 šà-gal má-laḫ$_5$ 0.0.1.6 <še->bi sa$_{10}$ má-laḫ$_5$ u$_4$-1-šè gú i$_7$-^{d}nin-ḫur-sag̃-g̃á-ta [**gar-ša-an-na**^{ki}-šè má] gíd-da, "150 liters, wages of the hired boat (and) 120 liters, wages of hired workmen; 16 liters, food (for) sailors, 16 liters <of barley> is the (hiring) price of the sailors [for] 1 day having towed [boats] from the bank of the Ninḫursag̃a canal [to Garšana]," 561:'19-'23

(. . .) [gú] i$_7$-⸢*ma*⸣-*an-iš-ti-šu*-ta **gar-ša-an-na**^{ki}-⸢šè⸣ má diri-ga da-na-bi 9-àm, "{barley in boats} having floated from the [bank] of the *Maništišu* canal to Garšana, (a distance of) 9 double-miles," 561:'41-'44

1.1.9.3 From Udaga

6 g̃uruš gub-ba še ù-da[g-ga][ki]-ta **gar-ša-a[n-na][ki]**-šè má gíd-da, "6 employed workmen having towed a boat (with) barley from Udaga to Garšana," 185:16–19

[1.1.4.] še gur [á má-ḫug̃]-g̃á má 50-gur-ta 2-kam ù má-laḫ$_5$-bi [0].1.2.5 sìla-ta [á] 0.0.2.5 sìla-ta á má-ḫug̃-g̃á má 40-gur-ta 2-kam ù má-laḫ$_5$-bi á 0.0.2.-ta [u$_4$]-8-šè ⸢še⸣ ù-dag-ga[ki]-ta **[gar-ša]-an-na[ki]**-šè de$_6$-a, "[1] bushel (and) [100 liters] of barley, [wages] (for) each of 2 hired 50-bushel boats and their sailors, 85 liters each; [wages] of 25 liters each, wages (for) each of 2 hired 40-bushel boats and their sailors, 20 liters each; (wages for sailors) for 8 days having brought barley from Udaga to Garšana," 414:1–11

[. . .] 0.1.0.8 s[ìla š]e-bi sa$_{10}$ má-laḫ$_5$-e-ne 6.1.1.4 sìla še gur še ù-dag-ga[[ki]-ta **gar]-ša-an-na[[ki]**-šè] de$_6$-[a], "[. . . (and)] 68 liters of barley is the (hiring) price of the sailors. (In total:) 6 bushels (and) 74 liters of barley having been brought [from] Udaga [to] Garšana," 553:54–59

1.1.9.4 From *Uṣar*-E'ura

6 g̃uruš še *ù-ṣa-ar*-é-ú-ra-ta **gar-ša-an-na[ki]**-šè má gíd-da, "6 workmen having towed a boat with barley from *Uṣar*-E'ura to Garšana," 6:25

1.2 Textiles Brought to Garšana from Nippur

1 g̃uruš [lú]ázlag nibru[ki]-ta **gar-ša-an-na[ki]**-šè túg de$_6$-a kaskal šu+níg̃in-na-bi u$_4$-4-àm, "1 fuller having brought textiles from Nippur to Garšana, a trip of 4 days in total," 224:1–6

1.3 Reeds Brought to Garšana

1.3.1 From G̃EŠ.KÚŠU

10 géme ⸢kíkken⸣ u$_4$-1-šè a-rá-1-kam 10 géme kíkken u$_4$-1-šè a-rá-2-kam 12 géme kíkken u$_4$-1-šè a-rá-3-kam gi-zi a-gàr-G̃EŠ.KÚŠU[ki]-ta **gar-ša-an-na[ki]**-⸢šè⸣, "10 female millers for 1 day for the 1st time, 10 female millers for 1 day for the 2nd time (and) 12 female millers for 1 day for the 3rd time (having brought) fresh reeds from the meadow of G̃EŠ.KÚŠU to Garšana," 295:1–11

1.3.2 From the Šara Temple

[n g̃uruš] gi-zi [é-[d]]šára-ta **[gar-ša-an]-na[ki]**-šè de$_6$-a, "[n workmen] having brought fresh reeds from the Šara [temple] to Garšana," 193:29–31

1⅔ g̃uruš ašgab 1 g̃uruš túg-du$_8$ 1 g̃uruš simug u$_4$-1-šè ⸢gi⸣ ù gi-zi é-[d]šára-ta **gar-ša-an-na[ki]**-šè [de$_6$]-a {erasure} de$_6$-a (sic!) "1⅔ leather workers, 1 braider, (and) 1 smith for 1 day having brought reeds and fresh reeds from the Šara temple to Garšana," 232:1–8

1.3.3 From Udaga

6 g̃uruš gi má-⸢lá⸣-a ù-dag-⸢ga⸣[⸢ki⸣]-ta **gar-ša-an-na[ki]**-⸢šè⸣ gíd-[da], "6 workmen having towed reeds in a freight boat from Udaga to Garšana," 189:25–28

(. . .) u$_4$-10-še gi-izi ù-dag[ki]-ga-ta **gar-ša-an-na[ki]**-šè [de$_6$]-a, "{craftsmen} for 10 days having [brought] fuel reeds from Udaga to Garšana," 230:6–9

3 g̃uruš sag̃-tag 1 g̃uruš á-⅔ lú-ašlág̃-me-éš u$_4$-10-šè gi-izi ù-dag[ki]-ga-ta **[gar-š]a-an-na[ki]**-šè de$_6$-a, "3 full-time fullers (and) 1 fuller at ⅔ wages for 10 days having brought fuel reeds from Udaga to Garšana," 231:1–6

1.4 Semolina Brought to Garšana from Izin-Erra

60 ninda-gúg-zì-KAL 3 sìla ni[nda-š]u-ra-gen lú-*i-zi-in-èr-ra*^{ki} ke$_4$-dè u$_4$ dabin *i-zi-in-*[*èr-ra*]^{ki}-ta **gar-ša-an-na^{ki}**-šè de$_6$-a, "The man from *Izin-Erra* (was assigned) to make 60 cakes of KAL-flour (and) 3 liters of ordinary half (loaf) bread, when semolina was brought from *Izin-Erra* to Garšana," 495:1–5

1.5 Straw Brought to Garšana

1.5.1 From the Agili Field

40 g̃uruš u$_4$-1-šè še 6 sìla-ta ba-ḫug̃ a-šà a-gi-li-⸢ta⸣ **gar-⸢ša⸣-an-na^{ki}**-šè in-u de$_6$-a, "40 workmen were hired for 1 day for 6 liters of barley each having brought straw (from) the Agili field to Garšana," 443:1–5

1.5.2 From Various Meadows

2 g̃uruš ad-kub$_4$ u$_4$-1-šè in-u a-gàr-didli-ta **gar-ša-an-na^{ki}**-šè lá-a, "2 reed craftsmen for 1 day having transported straw from various meadows to Garšana," 285:1–3, 286:1–3

10 g̃uruš túg-du$_8$ u$_4$-1-šè in-u a-gàr-didli-ta **gar-ša-an-na^{ki}**-šè lá-a, "10 braiders for 1 day having transported straw from various meadows to Garšana," 306:3–5

1.5.3 City of Origin Lost

6 g̃uruš [GN-ta] **gar-ša-a[n-na]^{ki}**-[šè] in-u l[á-a], "6 workmen having transported straw [from GN to] Garšana," 194:46–48

1.6 Wool and Oil Brought to Garšana from *Bit-Šu-Suen*

8 g̃uruš ^{lú}ázlag u$_4$-1-šè siki é-^{d}*šu*-^{d}*suen*- ta **gar-ša-an-n[a^{ki}]**-šè mu-un-de$_9$-sa-a, "8 fullers for 1 day who brought wool from *Bit-Šu-Suen* to Garšana," 243:1–4

2 g̃uruš ad-kub$_4$ u$_4$-1-šè a-rá-2-kam 2 g̃uruš ad-kub$_4$ u$_4$-1-šè a-rá-3-kam siki de$_6$-a é-^{d}*šu*-^{d}*suen*^{ki}-ta **gar-ša-an-na^{ki}**-šè (g̃en-a), "2 reed craftsmen for 1 day for the 2nd time, (and) 2 reed craftsmen for 1 day for the 3rd time having brought wool, (reed craftsmen having gone) from *Bit-Šu-Suen* to Garšana," 285:7–13, 286:7–13

2 g̃uruš túg-du$_8$ u$_4$-1-šè [s]iki de$_6$-a a-rá-2-kam é-^{d}*šu*-^{d}*suen*^{ki}-ta **gar-ša-an-na^{ki}**-šè g̃en-a, "2 braiders for 1 day having brought wool for the 2nd time, (braiders) having gone from *Bit-Šu-Suen* to Garšana," 306:9–13

1.7 Other

1 g̃uruš u$_4$-11-šè má ú-sa unug^{ki}-ta **gar-ša-an-na**$^{\langle ki \rangle}$-šè má gíd-da 1 g̃uruš u$_4$-1-šè gi-zi G̃EŠ.KÚŠU^{ki}-[ta] de$_6$-[a n] g̃uruš u$_4$-[n-šè] ḫar lam $^{g̃eš}$ù-suḫ$_5$ ke$_4$-[dè] ^{d}gu$_4$-an-na-⸢ta⸣ **gar-ša-an-na^{ki}**-šè d[e$_6$-a], "1 workman for 11 days who, having processed a boat, towed it from Uruk to Garšana, 1 worker for 1 day having brought fresh reeds [from] G̃EŠ.KÚŠU, (and) [n] workmen [for n] day(s) having brought a seedling container of pine trees from Guanna to Garšana," 272:5–15

2. Commodities Transported from Garšana

2.1 A Fattened Ox Brought to Nippur

1 g̃uruš gu$_4$-niga **gar-ša-an-na^{ki}**-ta nibru^{ki}-šè ba-an-tùm, "1 workman brought a fattened ox from Garšana to Nippur," 17:29, 20:32

2.2 Oil Brought to Nippur

0.0.1.1 sìla ì-ĝeš ⌜lá⌝-ìa šà ì-ĝeš 2.0.0. gur-kam **gar-ša-an-na^{ki}**-ta nibru^{ki}-šè in-de$_9$-ša-a, "11 liters of sesame oil, the remainder of 2 bushels, which they brought from Garšana to Nippur," 1062:1–4

2.3 Straw Brought to the Canal

2 ĝuruš **gar-ša-an-na^{ki}**-ta ka i$_7$-è-šè in-u lá-a, "2 workmen having transported straw from Garšana to the mouth of the 'Outgoing' canal," 194:52–55

3. Boats Towed from Garšana

3.1 To Adab

9 ĝuruš **gar-ša-an-na^{ki}**-ta adab^{ki}-šè má gíd-da é-du$_6$-gur$_4$-*i-din-^{d}adad*-šè, "9 workmen having towed a boat from Garšana to Adab, to the round-hill-house of *Iddin-Adad*," 207:23–25

3.2 To ĜEŠ.KÚŠU

[. . . x] ĝuruš á-[n-ta] ^{lú}ázlag-me-[éš] u$_4$-1-[šè] má-nin-zi-šà-ĝál **gar-ša-an-na^{ki}**-ta ĜEŠ.KÚŠU^{ki}-šè in-gíd-ša-a, "[. . .] (and) [n] fuller(s) [at n] wages [for] 1 day who towed the boat of Nin-zišaĝal from Garšana to ĜEŠ.KÚŠU," 238:1–7

3.3 To Karkar

9 ĝuruš **gar-ša-an-na^{ki}**-ta karkar^{ki}-šè má gíd-⌜da⌝, "9 workmen having towed a boat from Garšana to Karkar," 209:33–34

76 ĝuruš 4 má–10-gur-ta **gar-ša-an-na^{ki}**-ta karkar^{ki}-šè gíd-da, "76 workmen having towed 4 10-bushel boats from Garšana to Karkar," 236:6–9

3.4 To Nippur

2 ĝuruš ašgab 1 ĝuruš ad-kub$_4$ u$_4$-4-[šè] má ^{ĝeš}šim ḫi-a **gar-ša-an-na^{ki}**-ta nibru^{ki}-šè in-gíd-sa-a, "2 leather workers (and) 1 reed craftsman [for] 4 days who towed a boat (with) various resinous woods from Garšana to Nippur," 253:1–7

1 ĝuruš u$_4$-7-šè má gíd má–40-gur-ta 2-àm **gar-ša-an-na^{ki}**-ta nibru^{ki}-šè in-gíd-sa-a(sic!), "1 workman for 7 days who towed 2 40-bushel boats from Garšana to Nippur," 255:1–5

(. . .) [má . . . **gar-ša-an-na^{ki}**-ta] nibru^{ki}-[šè] in-gíd-s[a-a], "{provisions for men} who towed [a . . . boat from Garšana to] Nippur," 463:5–8

3 ĝuruš u$_4$-11-šè dabin ninda túg ù ì ḫi-a **gar-ša-an-na^{ki}**-ta nibru^{ki}-šè má gíd-da "3 workmen for 11 days having towed a boat (with) various (amounts of) semolina, bread, textiles (and) oil from Garšana to Nippur," 931:2–6

3.5 To the Opening of the Canal

2 [ĝuruš **gar-ša**]-**an-na^{ki}**-ta ka ⌜i$_7$⌝-šè má gíd-da, "2 [workmen] having towed a boat from Garšana to the opening of the canal," 198:'26-'27

3.6 To Puzriš-Dagan

(. . .) u$_4$ má *simat-^{d}ištaran puzur$_4$-iš-^{d}da-gan*^{ki}-ta **gar-ša-an-na^{ki}**-šè mu-un-gíd-š[a-a], "{assorted commodities for the gendarmes} when they towed the boat of *Simat-Ištaran* from *Puzriš-Dagan* to Garšana," 550: '27-'29

0.0.5. ninda-kaš á-u$_4$-[te-na] 2 sìla níĝ-àr-[ra-sig$_5$] šà zabala$_4$$^{[ki]}$ u$_4$-1-[kam] 4 sìla níĝ-àr-ra-[sig$_5$] u$_4$-2-[kam] á-gú-zi-⌜ga⌝ 4 sìla níĝ-àr-ra-⌜sig$_5$⌝ á-u$_4$-te-na u$_4$-3-kam šà kaskal^{ki} àga-ús [*ri-im*]-*ilum* íb-gu$_7$ u$_4$ má-*simat-^{d}ištaran* **gar-ša-an-na^{ki}**-ta *puzur$_4$-iš-^{d}da-gan*[^{ki}-šè] in-gíd-sa-a, "The gendarme *Rim-ilum* consumed 50 liters of bread (and) beer [in] the evening (and) 2 liters of [fine] barley groats in Zabala on the 1st day, 4 liters of [fine] groats at dawn on the 2nd day (and) 4 liters of fine groats as in the evening on the 3rd day of the journey when they towed the boat of *Simat-Ištaran* from Garšana to *Puzriš-Dagan*," 551:1–15

4. Boats Towed to Garšana

4.1 From Nippur

0.0.4. ⅔ sìla [. . . àga]-ús é-gal-la gub-ba [íb]-gu$_7$ u[$_4$ m]á *ra-ba-tum* nibru^{ki}-ta **gar-ša-an-na^{ki}**-šè i[n-g]íd-sa-a, "The gendarme employed at the palace ate 4⅔ liters [. . .] when they towed the boat of *Rabatum* from Nippur to Garšana," 506:22–26

4.2 From the Šara Temple

(. . .) maš-en-gag ^{lú}kaš$_4$ ká-é-gal-ka gub-ba ⸢*simat*⸣-^{d}*ištaran* íb-gu$_7$ u$_4$ má-*simat*-^{d}*ištaran* é-^{d}šára-ta **gar-ša-an-na^{ki}**-šè mu-un-gíd-ša-a, "The *muškenu* (and?) the runner, stationed by *Simat-Ištaran* at the gate of the palace, ate {soup} when they towed the boat of *Simat-Ištaran* from the Šara temple to Garšana," 529:13–18

4.3 City of Origin Lost

[6?] g̃uruš má níg̃-gú-na [GN-ta] **gar-ša-an-na**$^{<ki>}$-šè má gíd-⸢da⸣, "[6?] workmen having towed a boat (with) the commodity tax [from GN] to Garšana," 206:26–27

5. Towing Boats: Round Trip

1 [g̃uruš . . .] má–20-gur-bi 2-à[m **gar-š]a-an-na^{ki}**-ta [. . . ka] i$_7$-è-šè gíd-⸢da⸣ ⸢ka⸣ i$_7$-è-ta [**gar-ša-an]-na^{ki}**-šè má di[ri-ga], "1 [. . . workman] having towed 2 20-bushel boats from Garšana to the 'Outgoing' canal (and) the boats having floated from the mouth of the 'Outgoing' canal to Garšana," 195:'17-'22

10 gu-níg̃in ^{geš}kišig á-g̃uruš-a 4 gu-níg̃in-ta á-bi 2½ u$_4$-1-šè a-šà-karkar^{ki}-šè ^{geš}kišig ku$_5$-rá 4 g̃uruš u$_4$-1-šè **gar-ša-an-na^{ki}**-ta karkar^{ki}-šè má gíd-da 4 g̃uruš u$_4$-1-šè m[á g̃a]r-ra 4 g̃uruš u$_4$-1-šè kar[kar^{ki}-ta] **gar-ša-an-na^{ki}**-šè 4 g̃uruš u$_4$-1-šè kar-ta g̃á-nun-šè ga$_6$-⸢g̃a⸣, "(In total:) 10 bales of shok. The workmen wages (were) for 4 bales each. Their wages were for 2½ days (for workers) having cut shok (at) the field of Karkar. 4 workmen for 1 day having towed a boat from Garšana to Karkar (and then) 4 workmen for 1 day having placed the boat (i.e. loaded it with shok). 4 workmen for 1 day (having towed the boat back) from Karkar to Garšana (and) 4 workmen for 1 day having carried (shok) from the quay to the storehouse," 235:1–12

6. Traveling

6.1 To Garšana

6.1.1 From Tumal

5 g̃uruš sag̃-t[ag 1+]1 g̃uruš á-⅔ 1 g̃uruš á–½ 1 g̃uruš á–⅓ u$_4$-2-šè **gar-ša-an-na^{ki}**-ta tum-ma-al^{ki}-šè x x? a 140-àm de$_6$-a, "5 full-time workmen, 2 workmen at ⅔ wages, 1 workman at ½ wages (and) 1 workman at ⅓ wages for 2 days having brought 140 (?) from Garšana to Tumal," 266:1–7

[n] g̃uruš sag̃-tag [n] g̃uruš á-⅔ [n] g̃uruš á–½ [n] g̃uruš á–⅓ [tum-ma]-al^{ki}-ta [**gar-š]a-an-na^{ki}**-šè g̃en-na u$_4$-2-šè, "[n] full-time workmen, [n] workmen at ⅔ wages, [n] workmen at ½ wages (and) [n] workmen at ⅓ wages for 2 days having gone from Tumal to Garšana for 2 days," 266:13–17

6.1.2 City of Origin Broken or Unspecified

[n] g̃uruš [GN][ki]-ta **[gar-ša]-an-⌜na⌝**[ki]-[šè g̃en-na], "[n] workmen [having gone] from [GN to] Garšana," 184:17–19

2 g̃uruš sag̃-[tag] 1 g̃uruš á-⅔ u_4-1-šè **gar-ša-an-na**[ki]-šè? [?], "2 full-time workmen (and) 1 workman at ⅔ wages for 1 day (having gone?) to? Garšana," 223:11–14

6.1.3 Broken Context

3 g̃uruš má-[d]*šu*-[d]E[N.ZU . . .] é-[d]nin?-si_4-in-[na . . . t]a[ki]-ta **gar-ša-[an-na[ki]-šè] D[U-x], 206:24–25

6.2 Traveling from Garšana

6.2.1 To *Bit-Šu-Suen*

1 g̃uruš [túg-du_8 u_4-1-šè] **gar-ša-an-na**[ki]-ta é-[d]*šu*-[d]*suen*[[ki]-a] g̃en-[na], "1 [braider for 1 day] having gone from Garšana [into] *Bit-Šu-Suen*," 298:1–3

3 g̃uruš ašgab u_4-1-šè **gar-ša-an-na**[ki]-ta é-[d]*šu*-[d]*suen*[ki]-a g̃en-a, "3 leather workers for 1 day having gone from Garšana into *Bit-Šu-Suen*," 299:1–3

6.2.2 To Nippur

2 g̃uruš s[ag̃-tag] 1 g̃uruš á-[⅔] u_4-1½-[šè] **gar-ša-an-[na**[ki]-ta] nibru[ki]-šè d[e_6-a], "2 full-time workmen (and) 1 workman at [⅔] wages [for] 1½ days having gone [from] Garšana to Nippur," 223:1–5

6.2.3 To Udaga

n g̃uruš u_4-1-šè **gar-ša-an-na**[ki]-ta ù-dag-ga[ki]-šè g̃en-na, "n workmen for 1 day having gone from Garšana to Udaga," 553:3–5, 553:23–25

7. Installations in Garšana

a-šà **gar-ša-an-na**[ki], "the Garšana field" > *Field Index*

[g̃eš]kiri$_6$ **gar-ša-an-na**[ki], "the Garšana garden" > *Garden Index*

[g̃eš]kiri$_6$ *simat-*[d]*ištaran* **gar-ša-an-na**[ki], "the garden of *Simat-Ištaran* at Garšana" > *Garden Index*

1 g̃uruš šidim im-du_8-a **gar-ša-an-na**⌜ki⌝ [gub-ba], "1 builder [employed] at the adobe wall of Garšana," 80:6

8. Transactions in Garšana, as Specified in the Body of the Account

8.1 Garden Products Measured for Accounting

4.3.0. zú-lum gur 0.0.5. u_4-ḫi-in [n+]3 gín peš-ga 5? sìla á-an-zú-lum [káb d]u_{11}-ga [g̃eš]kiri$_6$ *eš*$_4$*-tár-<um->mi* dumu-munus *šu-kab-tá* (. . .) šà **gar-ša-an-na**[ki] (. . .), "4 bushels (and) 180 liters of dates, 50 liters of fresh dates, [n+]3 shekels of date palm hearts (and) 5? liters of date clusters, commodities of the garden of *Eštar-ummi*, the daughter of *Šu-Kabta*, measured for accounting. {Transaction} in Garšana," 1102:1–6, 8

8.2 Inventory of the Garden

g̃eš é-⌜[g̃eš]⌝⌜kiri$_6$⌝-a gub-ba šu-sum-ma [g̃eš]kiri$_6$ igi-érim-iri[ki] (. . .) šà **gar-ša-an-na**[ki] (. . .), "Wood stored in the garden house, the inventory of the Igi-erim-iri garden. {Transaction} in Garšana," 1375:45–46, 50

8.3 Linen for the House of the Women

3 gín šudum gada é-munus-šè (. . .) šà **gar-ša-an-na**[ki] u_4-25-kam, "3 shekels of warp-thread (for) linen for the house of the women, {authorizing official}, in Garšana on the 25th day," 541:1–2, 4–5

8.4 Receipts

8.4.1 Barley for *Bazitum*

70.0.0. še gur šà **gar-ša-an-na^{ki}** 90-lá–1.0.0. gur šà karkar^{ki} šu+níĝin 160.0.0.-lá–1.0.0. gur *ba-zi-tum* šu ba-ti, "*Bazitum* received 70 bushels of barley in Garšana (and) 89 bushels of barley in Karkar, 159 bushels in total," 1252:1–7

8.4.2 Surplus of the Offerings for the House of the Steward

0.0.2. [. . .] 0.1.0. ninda-dabin dirig sá-du$_{11}$-é-agrig-[šè] (. . .) [šà **gar**]-**ša-an-na^{ki}** (. . .), "20 liters [. . .] (and) 60 liters of semolina bread, surplus of the regular offerings [for] the house of the steward. {Expenditure} [in] Garšana," 501:1–4, 6

8.5 Regular Offerings

[. . .] sá-[du$_{11}$-^{d}. . .] saĝ-x-[. . .] šà **gar-ša-[an-na^{ki}]** (. . .) sá-du$_{11}$-diĝir-re-e-ne, "[. . .], regular offerings [of DN ...] in Garšana, (and) {other comestibles}, regular offerings of the gods," 1036:'42-'44, '78

8.6 Workmen Employed in Garšana

(. . .) níĝ-dab$_{5}$ ĝuruš má gíd-e-ne u$_{4}$ al-tar-ra gub-ba šà **gar-ša-an-na^{ki}**, "{assorted commodities}, requisitions of the boat towers when they were employed for construction in Garšana," 442:19–20

9. Broken Context

★★[n ĝuruš . . .]-bi? bala um-[. . .] **gar-š[a-an-na]^{ki}**-šè in-u lá-[a], "[. . . workmen?] having transported straw [from GN?] to Garšana," 198:'22-'23

★★[... x? iti ez]em-^{d}šul-g[i x? . . . im] sumur aka **[gar]-ša-an-na$^{[ki]}$** ù ĝír-[su]^{ki}-⌜šè⌝ D[U-x?], 1029:'11-'14

★★[. . .]-x-gal [n sìl]a dabin [n] sìla eša [. . .] **gar-ša-[an-na^{ki}]**, "[. . .n] liter(s) semolina, [n] liter(s) fine flour [. . .] Garšana," 1164:1–6

★★240 ^{gi}kid-[. . . x]-e ba-ab-[. . . x] ésir-é-a [. . .] **gar-š[a-an-na^{ki}-šè?]**, "240 [. . .] reed mats were [. . ., x] house bitumen [. . . to?] Garšana," 1249:5–9

gú-ab-ba^{ki}

1. Flying Fish Purchased in Gu'abba

1 šeš-kal-la 1 *lu-kà-dum* ku$_{6}$-sim sa$_{10}$(-sa$_{10}$)-dè **gú-ab-ba^{ki}**-šè ĝen-na, "Šeš-kala (and) *Lukadum* having gone to Gu'abba to purchase flying fish," 37:36–39, 47:58–61, 48:66–69, 49:60–62

1 *ša-lim-be-lí* ku$_{6}$-sim sa$_{10}$(-sa$_{10}$)-dè **gú-ab-ba^{ki}**-šè ĝen-na, "*Šalim-Beli* having gone to Gu'abba to purchase flying fish," 37:41–44, 38:48–49, 47:64–65, 48:72–75, 49:65–66

1 šeš-kal-la 1 *lu-kà-dum* ku$_{6}$-sim sa$_{10}$-sa$_{10}$-dè **gú-ab-ba^{ki}**-šè ĝen-a, "Šeš-kala (and) *Lukadum* having gone to Gu'abba to purchase flying fish," 38:42–44

1 *lu-kà-dum* 1 šeš-kal-la ku$_{6}$-sim sa$_{10}$-sa$_{10}$-dè **gú-ab-ba^{ki}**-šè ĝen-na, "*Lukadum* (and) Šeš-kala having gone to Gu'abba to purchase flying fish," 46:'45-'47, 50:'9-'10, 50:'19-'20

2. Broken Context

gú-áb(sic!)-**[ba^{ki}**. . .], 46:'48

gú-saḫar^{ḫar}.DU^{ki}

1. Towed Boats

1.1 From Gu-saḫar.DU to the Fortified Tower of *Dada*

1 g̃uruš túg-du$_8$ u$_4$-[1-šè] **gú-saḫar^{ḫar}.DU^{ki}**-ta a[n-za-qar]-*da-da*-šè má gíd-da ù [še ba-al], "1 braider [for 1] day having towed a boat from Gu-saḫar.DU to the fortified tower of *Dada* and [having unloaded barley]," 298:11–12

2 g̃uruš ašgab u$_4$-1-šè **gú-saḫar^{ḫar}.DU^{ki}**-ta an-za-qar-*da-da*-šè má gíd-da ù še ba-al, "2 leather workers for 1 day having towed a boat from Gu-saḫar.DU to the fortified tower of *Dada* and having unloaded barley," 299:11–12

1.2 To Gu-saḫar.DU from *Bit-Šu-Suen*

1 g̃uruš túg-du$_8$ u$_4$-[1-šè] é-^{d}*šu*-^{d}*suen*$^{⌜ki⌝}$-[ta] **gú-saḫar^{ḫar}.DU^{ki}**-šè m[á gíd-da], "1 braider [for 1] day [having towed] a boat [from] *Bit-Šu-Suen* to Gu-saḫar.DU," 298:6–8

3 g̃uruš ašgab u$_4$-1-šè é-^{d}*šu*-[^{d}EN].ZU^{ki}-ta **gú-saḫar^{ḫar}.DU^{ki}**-šè má gíd-da, "3 leather workers for 1 day having towed a boat from *Bit-Šu-Suen* to Gu-saḫar.DU," 299:6–8

2. Idling in Gu-saḫar.DU

1 g̃uruš túg-d[u$_8$ u$_4$-1-šè] šà [**gú-saḫar^{ḫa}**]^{r}.**DU^{ki}** tuš-[a šà] a im še-⌜g̃á⌝, "1 braider [for 1 day] having sat (idle) in Gu-saḫar.DU [because of] rain," 298:9–10

3 g̃uruš ašgab u$_4$-2-šè šà **gú-saḫar^{ḫar}.DU^{ki}** tuš-a šà a im še-g̃á, "3 leather workers for 2 days having sat (idle) in Gu-saḫar.DU because of rain," 299:9–10

^{d}gu$_4$-an-na

1. Pine Seedlings Brought to Garšana

[n] g̃uruš u$_4$-[n-šè] ḫar lam $^{g̃eš}$ù-suḫ$_5$ ke$_4$-[dè] **^{d}gu$_4$-an-na-⌜ta⌝ gar-ša-an-na^{ki}-šè de[$_6$-a], "[n] workmen for [n] day(s) having brought a seedling container of pine trees from Guanna to Garšana," 272:10–15

G̃EŠ.KÚŠU^{ki}

a-gàr **G̃EŠ.KÚŠU^{ki}**, "G̃EŠ.KÚŠU meadow" > **a-gàr**

^{d}šára-**G̃EŠ.KÚŠU^{ki}**, "Šara of G̃EŠ.KÚŠU" > *Deities Index*

1. Boats Towed to G̃EŠ.KÚŠU from Garšana

[. . . x] g̃uruš á-[n-ta] ^{lú}ázlag-me-[éš] u$_4$-1-[šè] má-nin-zi-šà-g̃ál gar-ša-an-na^{ki}-ta **G̃EŠ.KÚŠU^{ki}**-šè in-gíd-ša-a, "[. . .] (and) [n] fuller(s) [at n] wages for 1 day towed the boat of Nin-zišag̃al from Garšana to G̃EŠ.KÚŠU," 238:1–7

2. Reeds Brought from G̃EŠ.KÚŠU

1 g̃uruš u$_4$-1-šè gi-zi **G̃EŠ.KÚŠU^{ki}**-[ta] de$_6$-[a], "1 workman for 1 day having brought fresh reeds [from] G̃EŠ.KÚŠU," 272:8–9

3. Transactions in G̃EŠ.KÚŠU

3.1 Disbursal of Assorted Commodities

0.0.4.4 sìla dabin 0.0.2.8 sìla eša 0.0.1. zú-lum eša {erasure} ba-ḫi zì-dub-dub-didli-šè u$_4$ *šu-kab-ta* **G̃EŠ.KÚŠU^{ki}**-šè du-ni {erasure} u$_4$ *šu-kab-ta* **G̃EŠ.KÚŠU^{ki}**-ta du-ni, "44 liters of semolina, 28 liters of fine flour, (and) 10 liters of dates were mixed (with) fine flour for various small flour heaps when *Šu-Kabta* went to G̃EŠ.KÚŠU (and) when *Šu-Kabta* came from G̃EŠ.KÚŠU," 488:8–23

(. . .) ^{d}gu-la (. . .) ˹sum˺-mu-da-éš ˹mu˺ éren-na-šè (. . .) ˹*al*˺*-la-ša-ru-um* (. . .) *um-mi-kab-tá* (. . .) *ma-la-ti* (. . .) *tak-ri-ib-tum* iri^{ki} ne-ne-de$_4$ (. . .) šà **G̃EŠ.KÚŠU^{ki}**, "{assorted comestibles} (for) Gula, to be given to the workers, *Allašarrum*, *Ummi-Kabta*, (and) *Malati* (and) for (the performance of) a *takribtum* (involving) circling around the city. {Expenditure} in G̃EŠ.KÚŠU," 1016:3, 6–7, 11, 14, 16, 21, 26

3.2 Billy Goats for the Zabar-dab$_5$ Official

★★[n] máš-gal [UD.K]A.BAR-dab$_5$ 1? udu?-x-x-x šà **G̃EŠ.KÚŠU^{ki}**, "[n] billy-goat(s) (for) the zabar-dab$_5$ official (and) 1? (?) sheep? in G̃EŠ.KÚŠU," 469:1–4

3.3 Mice

4? péš-g̃eš-gi iti u$_4$-22-ba-zal (. .) [šà] **G̃EŠ.KÚŠU**$^{˹ki˺}$, "4? mice at the end of the 22nd day of the month, {delivery} [in] G̃EŠ.KÚŠU," 1170:1–2, 7

3.4 Reeds for Cooking Fish

80 sa gi-izi ku$_6$ šé-g̃e$_6$-dè (. . .) šà **G̃EŠ.KÚŠU^{ki}**, "80 bundles of fuel reeds to cook fish. {Expenditure} in G̃EŠ.KÚŠU," 1321:1–2, 5

4. Traveling to G̃EŠ.KÚŠU

4.1 To Bring a Message to *Šu-Kabta*

★★[1 *š*]*u*-^{d}*belum* [á-ág̃ ki] *šu-kab-t*[*a*-š]è šu?-x-[x?]-x **G̃EŠ.KÚŠU**[^{ki}-šè?] de$_6$-[a], "*Šu-Belum* having brought [a message] to [the place of] *Šu-Kabta* (?) [in?] G̃EŠ.KÚŠU," 56:'36-'38

5. Broken Context

★★6 g̃uruš má g̃ar-r[a . . .] **G̃EŠ.˹KUŠU˺^{ki}**-[. . .], 193:36–37

g̃ír-su^{ki}

1. Barley Guarded in G̃irsu

1 *a-lí-aḫ* 1 *ta-tù-ri* še šà **g̃ír-su^{ki}** en-nu ke$_4$-dè gub-ba, "*Ali-aḫ* (and) *Tatturi* employed to guard barley in G̃irsu," 51:'19-'21, 52:56–58, 53:58–60

[1 *a*]*-lí-a*[*ḫ* 1 *ta-tù*]-˹*ri*˺ še šà [**g̃ír**]**-su^{ki}** en-nu k[e$_4$-dè] tuš-[a], "*Ali-aḫ* (and) *Tatturi* having sat [in order to] guard barley in G̃irsu," 56:'29-'31

2. Traveling to G̃irsu

2.1 To Bring out Barley

1 *ta-tù-ri* ù *a-lí-aḫ* še è-dè **g̃ír-su^{ki}**-šè g̃en-na g̃ìri *ṣa-al-lum* ^{lú}kíg̃-gi$_4$-a-lugal, "*Tatturi* and *Ali-aḫ* having gone to G̃irsu to bring out barley under the authority of *Ṣallum*, the royal messenger," 31:37–38, 32:37, 33:40–41, 35:44–45, 36:39

1 *a-lí-aḫ* še è(-dè) **g̃ír-su^{ki}**-šè g̃en-na, "*Ali-aḫ* having gone to G̃irsu to bring out barley," 37:34–35, 38:40–41, 43:'45-'46, 44:44–45, 45:26–27, 47:57, 48:64–65

2.2 To Bring Builders

2 g̃uruš šidim šidim la-ḫa-dè **g̃ír-su^{ki}**-šè g̃en-na, "2 builders having gone to G̃irsu in order to bring builders," 40:50–51, 41:'31-'32

2.3 To Bring Messages

1 g̃uruš šidim á-ág̃ **g̃ír-su**[ki]-šè de$_6$-a, "1 builder having brought a message to G̃irsu," 20:34, 148:'22, 150:44

1 *ḫi-lu-a* á-ág̃ **g̃ír-su**[ki]-šè de$_6$-a, "*Ḫilua* having brought a message to G̃irsu," 24:'26, 25:'3, 26:'22, 27:'18, 28:'29, 29:'34

1 lug[al-ḫ]a-ma-ti á-á[g̃ ši]dim-e-ne **g̃ír-su**[[ki]]-šè de$_6$-a, "Lugal-ḫamati having brought a message concerning builders to G̃irsu," 52:67–69

1 g̃uruš šidim lú-níg̃-[d]ba-ú á-ág̃ šidim-e-ne **g̃ír-su**[ki]-šè de$_6$-a, "1 builder from Níg̃-Ba'u, having brought a message concering builders to G̃irsu," 52:71–73

3. Other

3.1 Baskets Sent to G̃irsu

30 [gi]gúrdub siki ka-tab sè-ga zú-si **g̃ír-su**[ki]-šè, "30 baskets fitted with a cover (were sent) to G̃irsu (to pack) plucked (wool)," 502:1–2

3.2 G̃irsu Textile

siki túg-**g̃ír-su**[ki], "wool (for) a G̃irsu textile" > **siki**

3.3 Orders Regarding Workmen in G̃irsu

[d]*a*[*dad-till*]*ati* ù-n[a-a]-du$_{11}$ 3 g̃uruš ḫi-a sag̃-dub **g̃ír-su**[ki]-šè ù níg̃-dab$_5$ zà-mu-bi *i-mi-iq-*[d]šul-gi [ḫé]-na-ab-sum-mu, "Say to *Adad-tillati* that '3 various full-time workmen in G̃irsu and the requisitions (at) the beginning of the year should be given to *Imiq-Šulgi*,'" 1038:1–7

3.4 Provisions for the Sugal-maḫ in G̃irsu

0.0.3. ninda-*u$_4$-tuḫ-ḫu-um* 0.0.3. ninda-šu-ra-sig$_5$ 0.2.0. ninda-šu-ra-gen árad-g̃u$_{10}$ sugal$_7$-maḫ **g̃ír-su**[ki]-šè du-ni, "30 liters of *utuḫḫum* bread, 30 liters of fine half (loaf) bread (and) 120 liters of fine half (loaf) bread (for) Arad-g̃u, the sugal-maḫ, who came to G̃irsu," 449:6–10

4. Broken Context

[o.n.n.] še [n sì]la ì-g̃eš [g̃uruš?] SI [g̃eš]sìg-ga pad-dirig [?] **g̃ír-su[ki] a-a-ba-[šè? . . .] níg̃-[d]b[a-ú-šè?], 970:13–16

[... x? iti ez]em-[d]šul-g[i x? . . . im] sumur aka [gar]-ša-an-na[[ki]] ù **g̃ír-[su][ki]-⌜šè⌝ D[U-x?], 1029:'11-'14

i-zi-in-èr-ra[ki]

1. Builders of *Izin-Erra*

2 g̃uruš šidim lú-***i-zi-in-èr-ra***[ki], "2 builders from *Izin-Erra*," 2:5–6, 3:3, 5:5–6, 6:5–6, 9:3, 10:3, 11:4

[n] g̃uruš šidim lú-***i-zi-in-èr-ra***[ki](-me), "[n] builder(s) from *Izin-Erra*," 7:3–4, 8:5–6

2 g̃uruš šidim zàḫ lú-***i-zi-in-èr-ra***[ki]-me-éš, "2 runaway builders from *Izin-Erra*," 13:4

2. Men from *Izin-Erra*

1 *a-ḫu-wa-qar* 1 *u-bar-um* lú-***i-zi-in-èr-ra***[ki], "*Aḫu-waqar* and *Ubarum*, men from *Izin-Erra*" > *Personal Name Index*

60 ninda-gúg-zì-KAL 3 sìla ni[nda-š]u-ra-gen lú-***i-zi-in-èr-ra***[ki] ke$_4$-dè u$_4$ dabin ***i-zi-in-***[***èr-ra***][ki]-ta gar-ša-an-na[ki]-šè de$_6$-a, "The man from *Izin-Erra* (was assigned) to make 60 cakes

of KAL-flour (and) 3 liters of ordinary half (loaf) bread, when semolina was brought from *Izin-Erra* to Garšana," 495:1–5

ì-si-in^{ki}

1 *en-nim-ma* 1 *be-lí-a-sú* lú-**ì-si-in^{ki}**, "*Enima* (and) *Beli-asu*, men from Isin" > *Personal Name Index*

1. Builders from Isin

2 ĝuruš šidim lú-**ì-si-in^{ki}**(-me-éš), "2 builders from Isin," 2:7–8, 3:4, 4:7–8, 5:7–8, 6:7–8, 7:5–6, 8:7–8, 9:4, 10:4, 12:1, 13:5, 14:1, 15:1, 16:1, 17:1, 18:1, 19:1–2, 20:1, 21:1, 22:1, 23:1, 24:1, 30:1, 31:1, 32:1, 33:1, 34:1, 35:1, 36:1, 37:1, 38:1, 39:1, 40:1, 41:1, 42:1, 43:1, 44:1, 45:1, 47:1, 48:1, 49:1, 51:1, 53:1, 55:1, 56:1, 57:1, 58:1, 59:1, 60:1, 61:1, 63:1, 71:1, 73:1, 75:1

igi-érim-iri^{ki}

^{ĝeš}kiri$_6$ **igi-érim-iri^{ki}**, "the Igi-erim-iri garden" > *Garden Index*

iri-ki-gíd-da

1. Traveling to Irikigida for Shok

n ĝuruš ^{ĝeš}kišig **iri-ki-gíd-da**-šè ĝen-na, "n workmen having gone to Irikigida for shok," 128:34, 129:36, 130:'16, 131:'29, 132:36, 133:35, 134:'16

1.1. To Bring Shok

n ĝuruš ^{ĝeš}kišig **iri-ki-gíd-da** tùm-dè ĝen-na, "n workmen having gone to Irikigida to bring shok," 145:41, 146:'43

1.2 To Transport Shok

n ĝuruš $^{ú/ĝeš}$kíšig **iri-ki-gíd-da**-šè lá-e-dè ĝen-na, "n workmen having gone to Irikigida to transport shok," 133:36, 134:17, 135:36, 143:4

iri-saĝ-rig$_7$^{ki}

1. Traveling to Iri-saĝrig

[n ĝuruš . . .] *ba?-la-nu^{ki}*-ta [. . . **iri-saĝ**]-**rig$_7$**$^{[ki]}$-šè ĝen-na, "[n workmen . . .] having gone from *Balanu* [. . .] to Iri-saĝrig," 193:34–35

1 ĝuruš ad-kub$_4$ udu la-ḫe-dè **iri-saĝ-ri[g$_7$]**^{ki}-šè [ĝe]n-⌜na⌝, "1 reed craftsman having gone to Iri-saĝrig in order to bring a sheep," 260:1–2

ka-saḫar-ra^{ki}

1. Reeds Brought from Ka-saḫara

15 ĝuruš **ka-saḫar-ra^{ki}**-šè gi tùm-dè ĝen-na, "15 workmen having gone to Ka-saḫara to bring reeds," 136:41, 138:39–40,[4] 140:43, 141:38, 143:40

---

[4] No. 138:40 has ka-saḫar-ra^{ki}-TA, but this is almost certainly a mistake for -šè.

kab-šu^{ki}

a-bu-um-ilum lú-**kab-šu^{ki}**, "*Abum-ilum*, the man from Kabšu" > *Personal Name Index*

kàr-da-ḫi

1. Traveling to Kardaḫi for Straw

n g̃uruš in-u **kàr-da-ḫi**-šè g̃en-na(-me-éš), "n workmen having gone to Kardaḫi (for) straw," 26:'18, 29:'29, 31:33, 32:33, 36:34

karkar^{ki}

a-šà **karkar^{ki}**, "the Karkar field" > *Field Index*

1. Errands from Karkar: Bringing Barley

1.1 From Karkar to Garšana

9 g̃uruš sag̃-tag 1 g̃uruš á-⅔ 1 g̃uruš á–⅓ ^{lú}ázlag-me-éš u$_4$-1-šè še é-kab-ba^{ki} ⸢**karkar**⸣^{ki}-ta [ga]r-š[a-a]n-⸢na⸣$^{⸢ki⸣}$-šè de$_6$-a, "9 full-time fullers, 1 fuller at ⅔ wages, (and) 1 fuller at ⅓ wages for 1 day having brought barley from E-kabba (and) Karkar to Garšana," 237:1–8

3 g̃uruš u$_4$-1-šè še é-kab-[ba^{ki}] **karkar^{ki}**-[ta] gar-ša-an-na^{ki}-[šè] íb-ga$_6$, "3 workmen for 1 day carried barley [from] E-kabba (and) Karkar [to] Garšana," 884:6–10

1.2 From Karkar to Nippur

2 g̃uruš ^{lú}kíg̃-gi$_4$-a *šu-kab-ta* še **karkar^{ki}**-ta nibru^{ki}-šè ba-an-tùm, "2 messengers of *Šu-Kabta* brought barley from Karkar to Nippur," 20:33, 21:'27

2. Errands to Karkar: Bringing Flour

[2 g̃uruš] *ṣa-a-l[um* ^{lú}kíg̃-gi$_4$-a-lugal zì] **karkar^{ki}**-šè i[n-tùm-uš], "[2 workmen] of *Ṣallum*, [the royal messenger], brought [flour] to Karkar," 27:'16

2 g̃uruš *ṣa-al-[lum* ^{lú}kíg̃-gi$_4$-a-lu]gal zì g̃á-g̃á-dè **karkar^{ki}**-šè in-tùm-uš, "2 workmen from *Ṣallum*, the royal [messenger], brought flour to Karkar in order to deposit it," 28:'27

3. Boats Towed between Garšana to Karkar

9 g̃uruš gar-ša-an-na^{ki}-ta **karkar^{ki}**-šè má gíd-⸢da⸣, "9 workmen having towed a boat from Garšana to Karkar," 209:33–34

10 gu-níg̃in $^{g̃eš}$kišig á-g̃uruš-a 4 gu-níg̃in-ta á-bi 2½ u$_4$-1-šè a-šà-**karkar^{ki}**-šè $^{g̃eš}$kišig ku$_5$-rá 4 g̃uruš u$_4$-1-šè gar-ša-an-na^{ki}-ta **karkar^{ki}**-šè má gíd-da 4 g̃uruš u$_4$-1-šè m[á g̃a]r-ra 4 g̃uruš u$_4$-1-šè **kar[kar^{ki}**-ta] gar-ša-an-na^{ki}-šè 4 g̃uruš u$_4$-1-šè kar-ta g̃á-nun-šè ga$_6$-⸢g̃a⸣, "(In total:) 10 bales of shok. The workmen wages (were) for 4 bales each. Their wages were for 2½ days (for workers) having cut shok at the Karkar field. 4 workmen for 1 day having towed a boat from Garšana to Karkar (and then) 4 workmen for 1 day having placed the boat (i.e. loaded it with shok). 4 workmen for 1 day (having towed the boat back) from Karkar to Garšana (and) 4 workmen for 1 day having carried (shok) from the quay to the storehouse," 235:1–12

76 g̃uruš 4 má–10-gur-ta gar-ša-an-na^{ki}-ta **karkar^{ki}**-šè gíd-da, "76 workmen having towed 4 10-bushel boats from Garšana to Karkar," 236:6–9

4. The Men from Karkar

(. . .) ugula [*šu*]-*la-núm* (. . .) ugula *á-ni*-x-x (. . .) ugula ir_{11}-dam lú-**karkar**[ki]-me, "{workers} supervised by *Šulanum*, *á-ni*-x-x (and) Irdam, men from Karkar," 559:12, 25, 27–28

5. Transactions in Karkar

70.0.0. še gur šà gar-ša-an-na[ki] 90-lá–1.0.0. gur šà **karkar**[ki] šu+níĝin 160.0.0.-lá–1.0.0. gur *ba-zi-tum* šu ba-ti, "*Bazitum* received 70 bushels of barley in Garšana (and) 89 bushels of barley in Karkar, 159 bushels in total," 1252:1–7

mar-ḫa-ši[ki]

1. Marḫaši Onions

15 sum-sikil!-**mar-ḫa-ši**[ki] mu-DU, "delivery of 15 Marḫaši onions," 1113:1–2

18 ḫar sum-sikil-**mar-ḫa-ši**, "18 Marḫaši onion sprouts?," 1168:1

marad[ki]

1. Builders of the Governor of Marad

n ĝuruš šidim lú-énsi-**marad**[ki](-me-éš), "n builder(s), men of the governor of Marad," 194:30, 198:'12

maš-kán[ki]

1. Boats Towed to *Maškan*

★★[n] ĝuruš [lú][ázlag n] ĝuruš ašgab [n] ĝuruš ad-kub_4 [n] ĝ[uruš tú]g-du_8 [. . .]-x-šè [x]-zi-[x]-x ***maš-kán***[ki]-⸢šè⸣ má gíd-⸢da⸣, "[n] fuller(s), [n] leather worker(s), [n] reed craftsmen (and) [n] braider(s) having towed a boat [. . .] to *Maškan*," 260:11–17

maš-kán-šar-ru-um[ki]

1. The Sea Dike in *Maškan-šarrum*

2 ĝuruš má-$laḫ_5$ u_4-30-šè má saḫar ég a-ab-ba se-gé-dè gub-ba (. . .) šà ***maš-kán-šar-ru-um***[ki], "2 sailors employed for 30 days to tamp dirt (delivered by) boat at the sea dike, {authorizing officials}, in *Maškan-šarrum*," 274:1–3, 7, 275:1–3, 7

naĝ-su[ki]

1. The Commodity Tax to Brought to Naĝsu

1 ĝuruš túg-du_8 u_4-6-šè níĝ-gú-na **naĝ-su**[ki]-ta de_6-a, "1 braider for 6 days having brought the commodity tax to Naĝsu," 267:9–11

2. Traveling to Naĝsu for Wages

1 ĝuruš á-ne **naĝ-su**⸢ki⸣-šè ĝen-a, "1 workman having gone to Naĝsu for his wages," 96:'9

2 ĝuruš še á-ne **naĝ-su**[ki]-šè ĝen, "2 workmen having gone to Naĝsu for their barley wages," 189:30

nibru^{ki}

1. Assorted Commodities Brought from Nippur

1 g̃uruš ^{lú}ázlag **nibru^{ki}**-ta ^{d}*šu*-^{d}*suen*-DU$_{10}$^{ki}-šè ^{urudu}šim-da gu$_4$-udu de$_6$-a kaskal šu+níg̃in-na-bi u$_4$-11-kam u$_4$ šu-kab-tá é-dam-zé-ra-ra šu sum-mu-dè ì-g̃en-na-a "1 fuller having brought a sheep and cattle brand from Nippur to *Šu-Suen-ṭabu*, a trip of 11 days in total, when *Šu-Kabta* went to the house of the wife of *Zerara* in order to take inventory," 219:1–10

2. Assorted Commodities Brought to Nippur

2.1 Barley Brought from Karkar

2 g̃uruš ^{lú}kíg̃-gi$_4$-a *šu-kab-ta* še karkar^{ki}-ta **nibru^{ki}**-šè ba-an-tùm, "2 messengers of *Šu-Kabta* brought barley from Karkar to Nippur," 20:33, 21:'27

2.2. Brought from Garšana

2.2.1 A Fattened Ox

1 g̃uruš gu$_4$-niga gar-ša-an-na^{ki}-ta **nibru^{ki}**-šè ba-an-tùm, "1 workman brought a fattened ox from Garšana to Nippur," 17:29, 20:32

2.2.2 Textiles

1 g̃uruš ^{lú}ázlag **nibru^{ki}**-ta gar-ša-an-na^{ki}-šè túg de$_6$-a kaskal šu+níg̃in-na-bi u$_4$-4-àm, "1 fuller having brought textiles from Nippur to Garšana, a trip of 4 days in total," 224:1–6

2.2.3 Oil

0.0.1.1 sìla ì-g̃eš ⌜lá⌝-ìa šà ì-g̃eš 2.0.0. gur-kam gar-ša-an-na^{ki}-ta **nibru^{ki}**-šè in-de$_9$-ša-a, "11 liters of sesame oil, the remainder of 2 bushels, which they brought from Garšana to Nippur," 1062:1–4

2.3 Wool Brought from *Bit-Šu-Suen*

3 g̃uruš ^{lú}ázlag siki é-^{d}*šu*-^{d}*suen*^{ki}-ka-ta **nibru^{ki}**-šè de$_6$-a kaskal šu+níg̃in-na-bi u$_4$-10!-kam u$_4$-2 kaš-dé-[a] á-⌜ki⌝-ti šu-numun, "3 fullers having brought wool from *Bit-Šu-Suen* to Nippur, a trip of 10 days in total, on day 2 of the banquet of the Akiti festival of month 4," 240:1–6

1 g̃uruš ^{lú}ázlag sag̃-tag u$_4$-2-šè 2 g̃uruš sag̃-tag 2 g̃uruš á-½-ta u$_4$-2-šè siki é-^{d}*šu*-^{d}*suen*^{ki}-ta **nibru^{ki}**-šè DU(sic!) de$_6$-a, "1 full-time fuller for 2 days (and) 2 full-time workmen (and) 2 workmen at ½ wages for 2 days having brought wool from *Bit-Šu-Suen* to Nippur," 226:1–8

2.4 City of Origin Unspecified

2.4.1 Textiles

3 g̃uruš túg **nibru^{ki}**-šè de$_6$-a, "3 workmen having brought textiles to Nippur," 148:'20

2.4.2 The Tablet of *Iddin-Adad*

1 *ḫi-lu-a* dub *i-din-*^{d}*adad* **nibru^{ki}**-šè de$_6$-a, "*Ḫilua* having brought the tablet of *Iddin-Adad* to Nippur," 33:44, 34:'18, 35:47, 36:42, 39:44, 40:42

3. Boats Towed from Nippur

3.1 The Boat of *Nawir-ilum* to *Bit-Šu-Suen*

3 g̃uruš ^{lú}ázlag u_4-2½-šè **nibru**^{ki}-ta é-^{d}*šu*-^{d}*suen*-šè má *na-wi-ir-ilum* íb-gíd, "3 fullers for 2½ days towed the boat of *Nawir-ilum* from Nippur to *Bit-Šu-Suen*," 220:1–6

3.2 The Boat of *Rabatum* to Garšana

0.0.4. ⅔ sìla [. . . àga]-ús é-gal-la gub-ba [íb]-gu_7 ⌜u_4 má⌝ *ra-ba-tum* **nibru**^{ki}-ta gar-ša-an-na^{ki}-šè i[n-g]íd-sa-a, "The gendarme employed at the palace ate 4⅔ liters [. . .] when they towed the boat of *Rabatum* from Nippur to Garšana," 506:22–26

4. Boats Towed to Nippur from Garšana

2 g̃uruš ašgab 1 g̃uruš ad-kub_4 u_4-4-[šè] má ^{geš}šim ḫi-a gar-ša-an-na^{ki}-ta **nibru**^{ki}-šè in-gíd-sa-a, "2 leather workers (and) 1 reed craftsman [for] 4 days who towed a boat (with) various resinous woods from Garšana to Nippur," 253:1–7

1 g̃uruš u_4-7-šè má gíd má–40-gur-ta 2-àm gar-ša-an-na^{ki}-ta **nibru**^{ki}-šè in-gíd-sa-a(sic!), "1 workman for 7 days who towed 2 40-bushel boats from Garšana to Nippur," 255:1–5

3 g̃uruš u_4-11-šè dabin ninda túg ù ì ḫi-a gar-ša-an-na^{ki}-ta **nibru**^{ki}-šè má gíd-da, "3 workmen for 11 days having towed a boat (with) various (amounts of) semolina, bread, textiles (and) oil from Garšana to Nippur," 931:2–6

5. Transactions in Nippur

5.1 Bread for Boat Towers

3.4.5. ninda šu-r[a gur lú]-é-^{d}*šu*-^{d}EN.[ZU^{ki} l]ú-*dì-ma-a*[*t-kál-bu*]-*um*$^{⌜\text{ki}⌝}$ lú-^{d}*šu*-^{d}EN.Z[U-am-ma]-ar-[ra^{ki} má . . . gar-ša-an-na^{ki}-ta] **nibru**^{ki}-[šè] in-gíd-s[a-a] (. . .) šà **nibru**$^{[\text{ki}]}$, "3 [bushels] (and) 290 liters of half (loaf) bread (for) the [men] from *Bit-Šu-Suen*, the men from *Dimat-kalbum* (and) the men from *Šu-Suen*-ammara who towed [a . . . boat from Garšana to] Nippur. {Expenditure} in Nippur," 463:1–8, 10

5.2 The Property of *Nawir-ilum*

(. . .) níg̃-gur_{11} *na-wi-ir-ilum-ma* ba-úš! (. . .) šà **nibru**^{ki}, "{assorted textiles}, the property of *Nawir-ilum*, who died. {Expenditure} in Nippur," 574:3–4, 6

5.3 A Textile of *Ištaran*

1 túg-guz-za-tur 4-kam-ús ^{d}*ištaran* (. . .) šà **nibru**^{ki}, "1 small 4th-quality tufted textile of *Ištaran*. {Expenditure} in Nippur," 576:1–2, 4

5.4 Textile Rations

780 ^{túg}uš-bar 12 ^{túg}uš-bar x [(. . .)] túg-ba géme-árad šà **nibru**^{ki}, "780 uš-bar textile (and) 12 [. . .] uš-bar textiles, textile rations of female and male servants in Nippur," 589:1–4

6. Traveling to Nippur

6.1 To Bring a Message

n g̃uruš á-ág̃-(g̃á) **nibru**^{ki}-[šè de_6-a], "n workmen having brought a message to Nippur," 150:41, 151:39, 152:'23, 154:43 160:'14, 161:'20

6.1.1 A Message for *Šu-Kabta* in Nippur

1 *ta-tù-ri* á-ág̃ ki *šu-kab-ta*-šè **nibru**^{ki}-šè de_6-a, "*Tatturi* having brought a message to *Su-Kabta* in Nippur," 24:'25

1 é-ì-gára á-ág̃ **nibru**^{ki}-šè ki *šu-kab-ta*-šè de_6-a, "E'igara having brought a message to *Šu-Kabta* in Nippur," 31:40, 32:39, 33:43, 34:'17, 35:46

6.2 Traveling from Garšana, Purpose Unspecified

2 g̃uruš s[ag̃-tag] 1 g̃uruš á-[⅔] u$_4$-1½-[šè] gar-ša-an-[na^{ki}-ta] **nibru^{ki}**-šè g̃[en-na], "2 full-time workmen (and) 1 workman at [⅔] wages having gone from Garšana to Nippur [for] 1½ days," 223:1–5

2 g̃uruš [sag̃-tag] 1 [g̃uruš á-⅔] u$_4$-[n-šè] **nibru^{ki}**-[ta GN-šè g̃en-na], "2 [full-time] workmen (and) 1 [workman at ⅔] wages [for n] day(s) [having gone from] Nippur [to GN]," 223:6–9

6.3 Broken Context

[. . .]-da **nibru^{ki}**-šè ⌜ba⌝-tùm, "[. . .] brought [. . .] to Nippur," 24:'24

7. Work Assignments in Nippur: Digging the Canal

13 g̃uruš sag̃-tag 3 g̃uruš á-⅔-ta ^{lú}ázlag-me-éš u$_4$-2-šè i$_7$-mi-me-er gub-ba ba-al-la (. . .) šà **nibru^{ki}**, "13 full-time fullers and 3 fullers at ⅔ wages employed for 2 days having dug the Mimer canal. {Expenditure} in Nippur," 227:1–5, 7

8. The Governor of Nippur: Bread for his Messenger (in Garšana)

5 sìla [kaš?] ninda ^{lú}kíg̃-gi$_4$-a-énsi-**nibru$^{[ki]}$** (. . .) šà gar-ša-an-na^{ki}, "5 liters of [beer?] (and) bread (for) the messenger of the governor of Nippur. {Expenditure} in Garšana," 1324:4–5, 9

níg̃-^{d}ba-ú[5]

1. Builders from Nig̃-Ba'u

ur-te-me-na 1 ur-^{d}asar-lu-ḫi 1 *du-du-gu* 1 ^{d}utu-sá-bí 1 lú-me-lám lú-**níg̃-^{d}ba-ú** šidim-me-éš, "Ur-Temena, Ur-Asarluḫi, *Dudugu*, Utu-sabi, (and) Lu-melam, builders from Nig̃-Bau" > *Personal Name Index*

[2] g̃uruš šidim [lú-**níg̃**]-**^{d}ba-ú**(-me-éš), "[2] builders from Nig̃-Ba'u," 83:3, 84:2

3 g̃uruš šidim lú-**níg̃-^{d}ba-ú**-(me-éš), "3 builders from Nig̃-Ba'u," 41:2, 85:1–2, 86:1, 87:1, 88:1–2, 90:1–2, 91:1–2, 92:1, 94:1, 99:1, 101:1, 102:1, 103:1, 104:1, 105:1, 106:1, 108:1, 109:1, 111:1, 114:1, 116:1, 117:1, 118:1, 119:1, 120:1, 121:1, 123:1, 124:1, 125:1, 126:1, 127:1, 128:1, 129:1, 130:1, 132:1, 133:1, 134:1, 135:1, 136:1, 137:1, 138:1, 139:1, 140:1, 141:1, 142:1, 143:1, 145:1, 147:1, 149:1, 150:1, 151:1, 154:1, 155:1, 156:1, 157:1, 158:1, 159:1, 162:1, 163:1, 173:1, 174:1, 175:1, 177:1, 180:1, 214:1

3 g̃uruš šidim lú-**níg̃-^{d}ba-ú** šidim, "3 builders from Nig̃-Ba'u," 89:1–2

5 g̃uruš šidim lú-**níg̃-^{d}ba-ú**-(me-éš), "5 builders from Nig̃-Ba'u," 5:9, 6:9, 7:7–8, 8:9–10, 9:5, 10:5, 13:6, 14:2, 15:2, 16:2, 17:2, 18:2, 19:3–4, 20:2, 21:2, 22:2, 23:2, 24:2, 30:2, 31:2, 32:2, 33:2, 34:2, 35:2, 36:2, 37:2, 38:2, 39:2, 40:2, 42:2, 43:2, 44:2, 45:2, 47:2, 48:2, 49:2, 51:2, 52:1, 53:2, 55:2, 56:2, 57:2, 58:2, 59:2, 60:2, 61:2, 63:2, 71:2, 73:2, 75:2

[n g̃uruš šidim lú-**ní**]**g̃-^{d}ba-ú**, "[n builder(s)] from Nig̃-Ba'u," 213:1

1.1 Bringing a Message to G̃irsu

1 g̃uruš šidim lú-**níg̃-^{d}ba-ú** á-ág̃ šidim-e-ne g̃ír-su^{ki}-šè de$_6$-a, "1 builder from Níg̃-Ba'u having brought a message to G̃irsu concerning builders," 52:71–73

---

5 See Heimpel 2008, §2.2.1 for Nig̃-Ba'u as the name of a settlement and not the well-attested personal name.

1.2 Provisions

1 udu-[niga] iti u$_4$-10-ba-zal [lú-**níĝ-^{d}**]**ba-ú** šidim, "1 fattened sheep at the end of the 10th day of the month (for) the builder from Niĝ-Ba'u," 420:1–3

2. Broken Context

[o.n.n.] še [n sì]la ì-ĝeš [ĝuruš?] SI ^{ĝeš}sìg-ga pad-dirig [?] ĝír-su^{ki} a-a-ba-[šè? . . .] **níĝ-^{d}b[**a-ú**-šè?], 970:13–16

puzur$_4$-iš-^{d}da-gan^{ki}

1. A Boat Towed from Garšana to Puzriš-Dagan

(. . .) u$_4$ má *simat-^{d}ištaran* ***puzur$_4$-iš-^{d}da-gan^{ki}***-ta gar-ša-an-na^{ki}-šè mu-un-gíd-š[a-a], "{assorted commodities for the gendarmes} when they towed the boat of *Simat-Ištaran* from *Puzriš-Dagan* to Garšana," 550:'22-'25, '27-'29

0.0.5. ninda-kaš á-u$_4$-[te-na] 2 sìla níĝ-àr-[ra-sig$_5$] šà zabala$_4$$^{[ki]}$ u$_4$-1-[kam] 4 sìla níĝ-àr-ra-[sig$_5$] u$_4$-2-[kam] á-gú-zi-⸢ga⸣ 4 sìla níĝ-àr-ra-⸢sig$_5$⸣ á-u$_4$-te-na u$_4$-3-kam šà kaskal^{ki} àga-ús [*ri-im*]-*ilum* íb-gu$_7$ u$_4$ má-*simat-^{d}ištaran* gar-ša-an-na^{ki}-ta ***puzur$_4$-iš-^{d}da-gan***[^{ki}-šè] in-gíd-sa-a, "The gendarme *Rim-ilum* consumed 50 liters of bread (and) beer [in] the evening (and) 2 liters of [fine] barley groats in Zabala on the 1st day, 4 liters of [fine] groats at dawn on the 2nd day (and) 4 liters of fine groats as in the evening on the 3rd day of the journey when they towed the boat of *Simat-Ištaran* from Garšana to *Puzriš-Dagan*," 551:1–15

^{d}*šu*-^{d}*suen*-am-ma-ar^{ki}

1. Assorted Commodities Brought from *Šu-Suen*-ammara

1.1 Barley

8 ĝuruš saĝ-tag 2 ĝuruš á-⅔-ta 4 ĝuruš á-½-ta ^{lú}ázlag-me-éš [u$_4$]-1-šè ⸢še⸣ **^{d}*šu*-^{d}*suen*-am-ma-ar^{ki}**-ta de$_6$-a íb-[ga$_6$], "8 full-time fullers, 2 fullers at ⅔ wages, (and) 4 fullers at ½ wages for 1 [day carried] barley brought from *Šu-Suen*-ammara," 248:1–6

3 géme ĝeš-ì-sur-sur u$_4$-1-šè še **^{d}*šu*-^{d}*suen*-am-ma-ar^{ki}**-ta de$_6$-a íb-ga$_6$, "3 female oil pressers for 1 day carried barley brought from *Šu-Suen*-ammara," 249:1–3

1 ĝuruš ašgab 1 ĝuruš ad-kub$_4$ 1 géme kíkken u$_4$-[2]7-šè še **^{d}*šu*-^{d}*suen*-<am->ma-ra$^{[ki]}$** ù bàd-ga-zi^{ki}-⸢ta⸣ gar-ša-an-na^{ki}-šè de$_6$-a, "1 leather worker, 1 reed craftsman (and) 1 female miller for [2]7 days having brought barley from *Šu-Suen*-ammara and Bad-gazi to Garšana," 259:1–7

1.2 Straw

37 ĝuruš in-u tùm-dè **^{d}*šu*-^{d}*suen*-am-ma-ar-ra^{ki}**-šè ĝen-na, "37 workmen having gone to *Šu-Suen*-ammara to bring straw," 196:'25-'26, 197:36–37

6 ĝuruš in-u [**^{d}*šu*]-^{d}*suen*-am-ma-ar-ra^{ki}**-ta de$_6$-a kar-ta ĝá-nun-šè íb-ga$_6$, "6 workmen, having brought straw from *Šu-Suen*-ammara, carried it from the quay to the storehouse," 198:'28

2. Men from *Šu-Suen*-ammara: Provisions

3.4.5. ninda šu-r[a gur lú]-é-^{d}*šu*-^{d}EN.[ZU^{ki} l]ú-*dì-ma-a*[*t-kál-bu*]-*um*$^{⸢ki⸣}$ lú-**^{d}*šu*-^{d}EN.Z[U-am-ma]-ar-[ra^{ki}** má . . . gar-ša-an-na^{ki}-ta] nibru^{ki}-[šè] in-gíd-s[a-a], "3 bushels (and) 290 liters of half (loaf) bread (for) the [men] from *Bit-Šu-Suen*, the men from *Dimat-kalbum* (and) the men from *Šu-Suen*-ammara who towed [a . . . boat from Garšana] to Nippur," 463:1–8

^{d}***šu*-**^{d}***suen*-DU**$_{10}$^{ki}

1. A Sheep and Cattle Brand Brought from Nippur to *Šu-Suen-ṭabu*

1 g̃uruš ^{lú}ázlag nibru^{ki}-ta ^{d}***šu*-**^{d}***suen*-DU**$_{10}$^{ki}-šè ^{urudu}šim-da gu$_4$-udu de$_6$-a kaskal šu+níg̃in-na-bi u$_4$-11-kam u$_4$ *šu-kab-tá* é-dam-*zé-ra-ra* šu sum-mu-dè ì-g̃en-na-a "1 fuller having brought a sheep and cattle brand from Nippur to *Šu-Suen-ṭabu*, a trip of 11 days in total, when *Šu-Kabta* went to the house of the wife of *Zerara* in order to take inventory," 219:1–10

tu-lí-um^{ki}

i-la-ak-nu-id šu-kà-kà lú-***tu-lí-um***^{ki}-me-éš, "*Ilak-nu''id* (and) *Šu-kaka*, men from *Tulium*" > *Personal Name Index*

1. Builders from *Tulium*

2 g̃uruš šidim lú-***tu-lí-um***^{ki}(-me), "2 builders from *Tulium*," 9:1, 10:1, 11:1–2

3 g̃uruš šidim lú-***tu-lí-um***^{ki}, "3 builders from *Tulium*," 1:1–2, 2:1–2, 3:1, 4:1–2, 5:1–2, 6:1–2, 8:1–2

2 g̃uruš šidim zàḫ lú-***tu-lí-um***^{ki}-me-éš, "2 runaway builders from *Tulium*," 13:1–2

tum-ma-al^{ki}

1. Assorted Commodities Brought to Tumal

1.1 The Commodity Tax

1 g̃uruš túg-du$_8$ u$_4$-6-šè níg̃-gú-na **tum-ma-al**^{ki}-šè de$_6$-a, "1 braider for 6 days having brought the commodity tax to Tumal," 267:3–5

1.2 Commodity Uncertain

5 g̃uruš sag̃-t[ag 1+]1 g̃uruš á-⅔ 1 g̃uruš á-½ 1 g̃uruš á-⅓ u$_4$-2-šè gar-ša-an-na^{ki}-ta **tum-ma-al**^{ki}-šè x x? a 140-àm de$_6$-a, "5 full-time workmen, 2 workmen at ⅔ wages, 1 workman at ½ wages (and) 1 workman at ⅓ wages for 2 days having brought 140 (?) from Garšana to Tumal," 266:1–7

5 g̃uruš sag̃-tag 2 g̃uruš á-[⅔ 1] g̃uruš [á]-½ [1 g̃uruš á-⅓ u$_4$]-5-šè **tum-ma-al**$^{[ki]}$ de$_6$-a, "5 full-time workmen, 2 workmen at [⅔] wages, [1] workman at ½ [wages] (and) [1 workman at ⅓ wages] for 5 [days] having brought (items) [to/from?] Tumal," 266:8–12

2. Traveling: from Tumal to Garšana

[n] g̃uruš sag̃-tag [n] g̃uruš á-⅔ [n] g̃uruš á-½ [n] g̃uruš á-⅓ [**tum-ma**]-**al**^{ki}-ta [gar-š]a-an-na^{ki}-šè g̃en-na u$_4$-2-šè, "[n] full-time workmen, [n] workmen at ⅔ wages, [n] workmen at ½ wages (and) [n] workmen at ⅓ wages having gone from Tumal to Garšana for 2 days," 266:13–17

3. Transactions in Tumal

(. . .) túg-sa-gi$_4$-[àm] ki *puzur$_4$-a-gu$_5$-um*-[ta] *šu*-^{d}*adad* šu ba-an-ti šà **tum-ma-al**^{ki}, "*Šu-Adad* received {assorted} finished textiles from *Puzur-agum* in Tumal," 591:'12-'15

ù-dag-ga^{ki}

1. Assorted Commodities Brought from Udaga to Garšana

1.1 Barley

[n] g̃uruš tú[g-d]u$_{8}$ u$_{4}$-9-šè še **ù-dag-ga^{ki}**-ta gar-ša-an-na^{ki}-šè de$_{6}$-a ù kar-[ta] g̃á-nun-šè íb-[g]a$_{6}$, "[n] braider(s) for 9 days having brought barley from Udaga to Garšana and carried it [from] the quay to the storehouse," 261:1–6

(. . .) u$_{4}$-10-šè še **ù-dag-ga^{ki}**-ta gar-ša-an-na^{ki}-šè de$_{6}$-a, "{craftsmen} for 10 days having brought barley from Udaga to Garšana," 287:7–9

2 g̃uruš [ad-kub$_{4}$ u$_{4}$]-10-šè ⸢še⸣ **ù-dag-ga^{ki}**-t[a gar-ša]-an-na^{ki}-šè de$_{6}$-a, "2 [reed craftsmen] for 10 [days] having brought barley from Udaga to Garšana," 288:1–4

6 géme kíkken u$_{4}$-10-šè še **ù-dag-ga^{ki}**-ta gar-ša-an-na^{ki}-šè de$_{6}$-a, "6 female millers for 10 days having brought barley from Udaga to Garšana," 289:1–4

16⅓ géme uš-bar u$_{4}$-10-šè še **ù-dag-ga^{ki}**-ta gar-ša-an-na^{ki}-šè de$_{6}$-a, "16⅓ female weavers for 10 days having brought barley from Udaga to Garšana," 290:1–4

1.2 Reeds

1 g̃uruš ašgab 1 g̃uruš ad-kub$_{4}$ 1½ g̃uruš báḫar 1 g̃uruš simug 1 g̃uruš túg-du$_{8}$ u$_{4}$-10-še gi-izi **ù-dag^{ki}-ga**-ta gar-ša-an-na^{ki}-šè [de$_{6}$]-a, "1 leather workman, 1 reed craftsman, 1½ potters, 1 smith (and) 1 braider for 10 days having [brought] fuel reeds from Udaga to Garšana," 230:1–9

3 g̃uruš sag̃-tag 1 g̃uruš á-⅔ ^{lú}ázlag-me-éš u$_{4}$-10-šè gi-izi **ù-dag^{ki}-ga**-ta [gar-š]a-an-na^{ki}-šè de$_{6}$-a, "3 full-time fullers (and) 1 fuller at ⅔ wages for 10 days having brought fuel reeds from Udaga to Garšana," 231:1–6

2. Barley Brought to Udaga

[1 g̃uruš u$_{4}$-n]-šè še **ù-dag-ga^{ki}**-šè de$_{6}$-a, "[1 workman] for [n day(s)] having brought barley to Udaga," 162:31

3. Boats Towed from Udaga to Garšana

3.1 Transporting Barley

6 g̃uruš gub-ba še **ù-da[g-ga]^{ki}**-ta gar-ša-a[n-na]^{ki}-šè má gíd-da, "6 workmen employed to tow a boat (with) barley from Udaga to Garšana," 185:16–19

[1.1.4.] še gur [á má-ḫug̃]-g̃á má 50-gur-ta 2-kam ù má-laḫ$_{5}$-bi [0].1.2.5 sìla-ta [á] 0.0.2.5 sìla-ta á má-ḫug̃-g̃á má 40-gur-ta 2-kam ù má-laḫ$_{5}$-bi á 0.0.2.-ta [u$_{4}$]-8-šè ⸢še⸣ **ù-dag-ga^{ki}**-ta [gar-ša]-an-na^{ki}-šè de$_{6}$-a, "[1] bushel (and) [100 liters] of barley, [wages] (for) each of 2 hired 50-bushel boats and their sailors, 85 liters each; [wages] of 25 liters each, wages (for) each of 2 hired 40-bushel boats and their sailors, 20 liters each; (wages for sailors) for 8 days having brought barley from Udaga to Garšana," 414:1–11

[. . .] 0.1.0.8 s[ìla š]e-bi sa$_{10}$ má-laḫ$_{5}$-e-ne 6.1.1.4 sìla še gur še **ù-dag-ga**[^{ki}-ta gar]-ša-an-na[^{ki}-šè] de$_{6}$-[a], "[. . . (and)] 68 liters of barley is the (hiring) price of the sailors. (In total:) 6 bushels (and) 74 liters of barley having been brought [from] Udaga [to] Garšana," 553:54–59

3.2 Transporting Reeds

6 g̃uruš gi má-⸢lá⸣-a **ù-dag-⸢ga⸣$^{⸢ki⸣}$**-ta gar-ša-an-na^{ki}-⸢šè⸣ gíd-[da], "6 workmen having towed reeds in a freight boat from Udaga to Garšana," 189:25–28

6 g̃uruš má-lá-a gi **ù-da[g-ga**^{ki}-ta] tùm-dè g̃e[n-na], "6 workmen having gone in order to bring a freight boat (with) reeds [from] Udaga," 205:26–27

4. Boats Towed between Apisal and Udaga

(. . .) u_4-2-[šè] a-pi_4-sal_4-[la^{ki}-ta] **ù-dag-[ga**^{ki}-šè] má sù [gíd-da] še má-[a si-ga] **ù-dag-[ga**^{ki}-ta] kun-zi-[da] a-pi_4-[sal_4-la^{ki}-šè] má-[a si-ga], "{workmen and boats} for 2 days, (the workers) [having towed] the sunken boats [from] Apisal [to] Udaga, [having loaded] the boats with barley (and then having towed) [the loaded] boats from Udaga [(back) to] the weir of Apisal," 553:29–38

5. Traveling to Udaga

5.1 To Bring a Message

1 *ḫi-lu-a* á-ág̃-[g̃á] **ù-dag-ga**<ki>-šè de_6-a, "*Ḫilua* having brought a message to Udaga," 44:46

1 *ḫi-lu-a* á-ág̃ šu-$eš_4$-tár **ù-dag-ga**^{ki}-šè de_6-a, "*Ḫilua* having brought a message to Šu-Eštar in Udaga," 43:'47, 45:24–25, 46:'42-'43, 47:55, 48:60–61

1 *šu-eš*$_4$-[*tár*] á-ág̃-g̃á **ù-dag-ga]**^{ki}-[šè de_6-a], "*Šu-Eštar* [having brought a message to] U[daga]," 54:31–32

1 *šu*-^{d}nin-kar-ak á-ág̃-g̃á **ù-dag-ga**^{ki}-šè de_6-a, "*Šu*-Ninkarak having brought a message to Udaga," 107:10, 107:'17, 108:7, 108:41, 109:7

1 g̃uruš á-ág̃(-g̃á) **ù-dag-ga**^{ki}-šè de_6-a, "1 workman having brought a message to Udaga," 148:'21, 150:43, 156:34, 157:21, 159:32

5.2 Traveling to Udaga from Garšana

n g̃uruš u_4-1-šè gar-ša-an-na^{ki}-ta **ù-dag-ga**^{ki}-šè g̃en-na, "n workmen for 1 day having gone from Garšana to Udaga," 553:3–5, 553:23–25

ù-ṣa-ar-é-ú-ra

1. Boats Towed with Barley to Garšana

6 g̃uruš še ***ù-ṣa-ar*-é-ú-ra**-ta gar-ša-an-na^{ki}-šè má gíd-da, "6 workmen having towed a boat with barley from *Uṣar*-E'ura to Garšana," 6:25

ur-^{d}šul-pa-è

1. Builders of Ur-Šul-pa'e

2 g̃uruš šidim lú-ur-^{d}šul-pa-è, "2 builders from Ur-Šul-pa'e," 52:3, 111:3, 114:3, 116:3, 117:3, 118:3, 119:3, 120:3, 121:3, 123:3, 124:3, 125:3, 126:3, 127:3, 128:3, 129:3, 130:3, 132:3, 133:3, 134:3, 135:3, 136:3, 137:3, 138:3, 139:3, 140:3, 141:3, 142:3, 143:3, 145:3, 147:3, 149:3, 150:3, 151:3, 154:3, 155:3, 156:3, 157:3, 158:3, 159:3, 162:3, 163:3, 173:3, 174:3, 175:3, 177:3, 180:3

[n] g̃uruš šidim lú-ur-^{d}šul-pa-è, "[n] builder(s) from Ur-Šulpa'e, 213:2, 214:3

2. Barley from Ur-Šulpa'e

14 g̃uruš še ki **ur-^{d}šul-pa-UD.**⌜DU⌝-ta de_6-a kar-ta gur_7-šè íb-[ga_6], "14 workmen, having brought barley from Ur-Šulpa'e, [carried] it from the quay to the granary," 192:'18-'19

uri_5^{ki}

1. Fabrics for the Throne of Ur

1 ^{túg}*ḫa-um* ^{ĝeš}g[u-za] **uri_5^{ki}** 3-k[am-ús], "1 3rd-quality *ḫa'um* fabric of the throne of Ur," 631:3

1 ^{túg}*ḫa-bu-um* 3-kam-ús ^{ĝeš}gu-za **uri_5^{ki}-ma**, "1 3rd-quality *ḫabum* fabric of the throne of Ur," 821:5

2. Broken Context

2.0.0. gur bà[d-. . .] **uri_5^{ki}-[. . .], "2 bushels (of barley for) [PN . . .] Ur [. . .]," 555:3–4

$unug^{ki}$

^{d}**inana-unu^{ki}-ga**, "Inana of Uruk" > *Deities Index*

1. Boats Towed from Uruk to Garšana

1 ĝuruš u_4-11-šè má ú-sa **$unug^{ki}$**-ta gar-ša-an-na$^{<ki>}$-šè má gíd-da, "1 workmen for 11 days having towed a processed boat from Uruk to Garšana," 272:5–7

2. Traveling from Uruk

(. . .) kaš ba-an-dé *ri-im-ilum* $sugal_7$ gaba-ri-a **$unug^{ki}$**-ta du-ni, "{assorted beer}; he poured the beer when *Rim-ilum*, the sugal, came from Uruk (for) a meeting," 517:4–6

$zabala_4^{ki}$

^{d}inana-**$zabala_4^{ki}$**, "Inana of Zabala" > *Deities Index*

$^{ĝeš}kiri_6$ **$zabala_4^{ki}$**, "the Zabala garden" > *Garden Index*

1. Assorted Commodities Brought to Zabala

1.1 The Commodity Tax

4 géme u_4-1-šè níĝ-gú-na **$zabala_4^{[ki]}$**-šè d[e_6-a], "4 workwomen for 1 day having brought the commodity tax to Zabala," 258:3–4

1.2 Dirt

[*ak-b*]*a-zum* nu-$^{ĝeš}kiri_6$-⌜ke_4⌝ má-lugal-na saḫar tùm-dè **$zabala_4^{ki}$**-šè in-la-aḫ saḫar mu-un-de_9 $^{ĝeš}kiri_6$-lugal-na-šè nu-un-ni-ku_4 é-ni-šè ba-an-dé ka-ga-na ba-ge-en, "*Akbazum*, the gardener, confirmed that they took a boat of his master to Zabala in order to bring dirt, that he brought the dirt, that it did not enter the garden of his master but was brought for his (own) house," 1049:1–10

^{d}ba-ú-da [nu]-$^{ĝeš}kiri_6$-ke_4 má-lugal-na saḫar tùm-dè **$zabala_4^{ki}$**-šè in-la-aḫ saḫar mu-un-de_9 $^{ĝeš}kiri_6$-lugal-na nu-un-ni-ku_4 é-ni-šè ba-an-dé ka-ga-na ba-ge-en, "Ba'uda, the gardener, confirmed that they took a boat of his master to Zabala in order to bring dirt, that he brought the dirt, that it did not enter the garden of the his master but was brought for his (own) house," 1050:1–10

1.3 Reeds

2 ĝuruš u_4-1-[šè] gi **$zabala_4^{[ki]}$**-[šè] de_6-[a], "2 workmen [for] 1 day having brought reeds [to] Zabala," 246:8–9

2. Construction in Zabala

2.1 Builders Employed in Zabala

1 ĝuruš um-mi-a 1 ĝuruš šidim šà **$zabala_4^{ki}$** gu[b-ba], "1 master builder (and) 1 builder employed in Zabala," 117:21–22

2.2 Work on the Brick Stack of Zabala

1 g̃uruš šidim SIG$_4$.ANŠE **zabala$_4$^{ki}**, "1 builder at the brick stack of Zabala," 110:23, 111:32, 114:24

[1 g̃uruš šidim u]m-mi-a [1 g̃uruš š]idim SIG$_4$.ANŠE šà **zabala$_4$^{ki}** g̃ar-ra, "[1] master builder (and) [1] builder having placed the brick stack in Zabala," 113:'1-'2

3. Transactions in Zabala

3.1 Beer for the Cupboard

0.0.1. kaš-sig$_5$ u$_4$-28-kam 0.0.1. kaš-sig$_5$ u$_4$-29-kam gú-ne-sag̃-g̃á-šè (. . .) šà **zabala$_4$^{ki}**, "10 liters of fine beer on the 28th day (and) 10 liters of fine beer on the 29th day for the cupboard. {Expenditure} in Zabala," 541:20–24, 26

3.2 Dates

0.0.1.1 sìla zú-lum eša b[a-ḫ]i ½ x géme-tur ba-na-ḫa-la (. . .) šà **zabala$_4$^{ki}**, "11 liters of dates were mixed (with) fine flour, ½ x. They were portioned out to Geme-tur. {Expenditure} in Zabala," 506:16–19, 21

0.0.1 zú-lum (. . .) šà **zabala$_4$^{ki}**, "10 liters of dates. {Expenditure} in Zabala," 1071:1, 5

3.3 Grains for the Gendarme in Zabala

0.0.5. ninda-kaš á-u$_4$-[te-na] 2 sìla níg̃-àr-[ra-sig$_5$] šà **zabala$_4$$^{[ki]}$** u$_4$-1-[kam] (. . .) àga-ús [*ri-im*]-*ilum* íb-gu$_7$ u$_4$ má-*simat*-^{d}*ištaran* gar-ša-an-na^{ki}-ta *puzur$_4$-iš-^{d}da-gan*[^{ki}-šè] in-gíd-sa-a, "The gendarme *Rim-ilum* consumed 50 liters of bread (and) beer [in] the evening (and) 2 liters of fine barley groats in Zabala on the 1st day (and) {other provisions throughout the journey}, when they towed the boat of *Simat-Ištaran* from Garšana to *Puzriš-Dagan*," 551:1–3, 12–15

3.4 Offerings

(. . .) ninda ba-ra-du$_8$ uzu ù tu$_7$ ba-ra-šeg̃$_6$ é-kù-ga (. . .) a-níg̃in-šè (. . .) zì-dub-dub-šè (. . .) 60 ^{dug}sìla-bur-zi tu$_7$-šè šà kisal-lá ^{d}inana-**zabala$_4$^{ki}** (. . .) a-níg̃in-šè gaba-ri-a ki na-rú-a (. . .) šà **zabala$_4$^{ki}** u$_4$-2-kam, "{assorted commodities} with which bread was baked (and) meat and soup were cooked for the bright temple, {bread and beer} for the a-níg̃in ceremony, {grain} for the small flour heap, {assorted commodities} for 60 1-liter offering bowls of soup in the courtyard of Inana of Zabala (and) {assorted commodities} for the a-níg̃in ceremony at the meeting at the place of the stele. {Expenditure} in Zabala on the 2nd day," 1028:10–11, 17, 30, 35–37, 40, 45

3⅓ [sìla . . .] 0.0.1. ninda [. . .] 0.0.1. níg̃-[àr-ra-x] 0.0.1. munu$_4$-[si-è] sá-du$_{11}$-^{d}[. . .] šà **MÙŠ.ZA.[UNUG^{ki}** . . .] (. . .) sá-du$_{11}$-dig̃ir-re-e-ne, "3⅓ [liter(s) of x], 10 liters of [. . .] bread, 10 liters of [x] groats (and) 10 liters of sprouted malt, regular offerings of [DN] in Zabala, (and) {other comestibles}, regular offerings of the gods," 1036:'51-'56, '78

3.5 Wood

(. . .) ì-⌜DU⌝ *a-da-làl* dumu *si-um* um-mi-a šà **zabala$_4$^{ki}**, "{assorted woods} delivered (by) *Adallal*, the son of *Si'um*, the master craftsman, in Zabala," 1362:'49-'51

Analytical Index of Canals

i$_7$-*a-ga-mu-um*
i$_7$-a-gàr-ús-sa
i$_7$-^{d}amar-^{d}*suena*
i$_7$-è
i$_7$-gu$_4$
i$_7$-*ì-diš$_x$-tum*
i$_7$-ir-ni-na
i$_7$-kar$_4$-na
i$_7$-*ma-an-iš-ti-šu*
i$_7$-ma-ma-*šar-ra-at*
i$_7$-me-kal-kal
i$_7$-mi-me-er
i$_7$-nar-e-ne
i$_7$-nin-ḫur-sağ-ğá
i$_7$-sur
i$_7$-*šu*-^{d}*suen*-ḫe-ğál

i$_7$, "canal"

1. Commodities Brought from the Canal: Straw

20? ğuruš gú **i$_7$-da**-ta ğá-nun-sè in-u ga$_6$-ğá, "20? workmen having carried straw from the bank of the canal to the storehouse," 16:25

2. Commodities Brought to the Canal

2.1 Bricks from the Oven

20 géme šeg$_{12}$-al-ur$_x$-ra gir$_4$-ta **i$_7$**-šè ga$_6$-ğá, "20 workwomen having carried bricks from the oven to the canal," 113:'16

n ğuruš šeg$_{12}$-al-ur$_x$-ra gir$_4$-ta **i$_7$**-šè ga$_6$-ğá, "n workmen having carried bricks from the oven to the canal," 143:35, 145:37

[n] ğuruš 17 géme šeg$_{12}$-al-ur$_x$-r[a gir$_4$-ta] **i$_7$**-šè ga$_6$-[ğá], "[n] workmen (and) 17 workwomen having carried bricks [from the oven] to the canal," 146:'38

2.2 Straw from E-uri'a

2.2.0. še gur á má ḫuğ-ğá má-90-gur-kam á 0.0.4-ta ù má-laḫ$_5$-bi u$_4$-18-šè in-u é-ù-ri-a<ki>-ta gú **i$_7$-da** lá-a, "2 bushels (and) 120 liters of barley, wages of the hired 90-bushel boat and its sailors, wages of 40 liters each for 18 days (for sailors) having transported straw from E-uri'a to the bank of the canal," 413:1–7

3. Land on the Bank of the Canal

½ ¼ iku 3 sar gú **i$_7$**, "½ +? ¼ iku (and) 3 sar (of land) on the bank of the canal," 1362:4, 1362:'27

4. The Opening of the Canal

4.1 A Boat Towed through the Opening

[n] ĝuruš ka **i$_7$-da** ka-gal kuš má gíd, "[n] workmen having towed a boat (with?) leather through the large opening of the canal," 175:27

2 [ĝuruš gar-ša]-an-na^{ki}-ta ka ⌜**i$_7$**⌝-šè má gíd-da, "2 [workmen] having towed a boat from Garšana to the opening of the canal," 198:'26-'27

4.2 Straw Guarded at the Opening

1 ĝuruš in-u ka **i$_7$**-[ta] gub-ba en-n[u aka] ĝen-[na], "1 employed workman having gone, having guarded straw [at] the opening of the canal," 196:'27-'28

1 ĝuruš in-u ka **i$_7$**-ta UD.[DU]-šè en-nu-ĝá ak-a [gub-ba], "1 workman employed to guard straw betwen the opening of the canal (and) the 'entrance,'" 198:'30

5. Broken Context

[. . .]-ša **i$_7$ dù-a, 1383:1–2

i$_7$-*a-ga-mu-um*

1. Location of a Brick Yard with Respect to the Canal

270 sar 13 gín šeg$_{12}$ ús-⌜sa⌝ **i$_7$-*a-*⌜*ga*⌝*-mu-um*** 60 sar 13 gín šeg$_{12}$ é-^{d}[x]-SAḪAR [NE?]-gu$_7$-bi ù PA [NE-gu$_7$]-bi nu-zi [šid-d]a šà ĝá šub-ba, "270 sar (and) 13 gín of bricks along the *Agamum* canal, 60 sar (and) 13 gín of bricks of the [DN] temple, damaged bricks and damaged (?) not deducted; the count (of bricks) in the brickyard," 358:1–7

188 sar 10 gín šeg$_{12}$ NE-gu$_7$-bi nu-zi šid-da šà ĝá šub-ba (. . .) ús-sa **i$_7$-*a-ga-mu-um***, "188 sar (and) 10 gín of bricks along the *Agamum* canal, damaged bricks not deducted; the count (of bricks) in the brickyard, {authorizing official}," 359:1–3, 5

[n sar n gín šeg$_{12}$ ús-sa **i$_7$-*a-ga*]*-mu-um*** [. . .] x x, "[n sar (and) n gín of bricks along] the *Agamum* [canal . . .]," 339:1–3

2. Earth Carried from the Bank

[n] ĝuruš 21 géme [SIG$_4$].ANŠE ĝá-ĝá [1]8 géme im ⌜ga$_6$⌝-ĝá ⌜gú⌝-**i$_7$-[*a*]*-ga-mu-um***-ta é-*gi-na-tum* ká-bil-[lí]-a-šè, "[n] workmen (and) 21 workwomen having placed the brick stack (and) 18 workwomen having carried earth from the bank of the *Agamum* canal to the barracks of the Billi'a gate," 208:13–19

i$_7$-a-gàr-ús-sa

1. Boats Towed to the Weir of the Canal

(. . .) [u$_4$]-3-šè [še x] x x x an-za-qar-ta kun-zi-da **i$_7$-a-gàr-ús-sa** a-šà lú-maḫ-šè íb-ga$_6$ ù má-a si-ga, "{workers and boats} for 3 [days]; (the boats) carried [barley . . .] from the fortified tower to the weir of the Agar-usa Canal of the Lu-maḫ field and (the workers) having loaded the boats," 553:11–15

i$_7$-^{d}amar-^{d}*suena*

1. Straw Carried from the Canal

3 ĝuruš [in]-u gú **i$_7$-^{d}amar-^{d}E[N.ZU]**-ta im lu-a-šè íb-ga$_6$, "3 workmen carried straw from the bank of the Amar-*Suena* canal for mixing (with) earth," 194:49–51

i_7-**è**, "the 'Outgoing' Canal"

1. **ka** i_7-**è**, "the opening of the 'Outgoing' Canal"

1.1 Boats Towed to and from the Opening

1 [g̃uruš . . .] má–20-gur-bi 2-à[m gar-š]a-an-na[ki]-ta [. . . ka] **i_7-è**-šè gíd-⌜da⌝ ⌜**ka**⌝ **i_7-è**-ta [gar-ša-an]-na[ki]-šè má di[ri-ga] **ka i_7 ⌜UD⌝.DU**-[šè . . .] "1 [workman. . .] having towed 2 20-bushel boats from Garšana to the [opening] of the 'Outgoing' canal (and) the boats having floated from the opening of the 'Outgoing' canal to Garšana [. . .] to the opening of the 'Outgoing' canal," 195:'17-'23

1.2 Straw Brought to the Opening of the Canal

[n g̃uruš] gi-zi [é-[d]]šára-ta [gar-ša-an]-na[ki]-šè de_6-a [in-u] é-ù-ri-a[ki]-ta [**ka i_7-UD**].**DU**-šè de_6-a, "[n workmen] having brought fresh reeds from the Šara [temple] to Garšana (and) having brought [straw] from E-uri'a to the opening of the 'Outgoing' canal," 193:29–32

2 g̃uruš gar-ša-an-na[ki]-ta **ka i_7-è**-šè in-u lá-a, "2 workmen having transported straw from Garšana to the opening of the 'Outgoing' canal," 194:52–55

1.3 Straw Guarded at the Opening

1 g̃uruš in-u [**ka**] **i_7-è**-šè e[n-n]u aka tuš-a, "1 workman having sat at [the opening of] the 'Outgoing' canal having guarded straw," 194:56–57

1.4 Traveling

7 g̃uruš é-ù-ri-a[[ki]-ta] **ka i_7-è** g̃[en-na], "7 workmen having gone [from] E-uri'a (to) the opening of the 'Outgoing' canal," 192:'21

i_7-**gu_4**

★★3.0.0. še gur-⌜ta⌝? **i_7-gu_4** sila-a g̃ál-la, 1233:17–18

i_7-***ì-$diš_x$-tum***

1. Distance Measurements

é-lugal-eden-na-ta 1200 nindan ús gú **i_7-*ì-$diš_x$-tum***-šè, "1200 nindan, the distance from E-lugal-edena to the bank of the *Idištum* canal," 1382:7–9

i_7-*ì-$diš_x$-tum*-ta 360 [nindan ú]s ká-[d]*šu*-[d]*suen*-šè, "360 nindan, the distance from the *Idištum* canal to the *Šu-Suen* gate," 1382:12–10

i_7-**ir-ni-na**

1. Straw (Brought) to the Mouth of the Canal

6 g̃uruš in-[u (x x)] ka **i_7-ir-ni-na**-š[è lá-a / ga_6-g̃á], "6 workmen [having transported / carried] straw to the mouth of the Irnina canal," 40:32–33

i_7-**kar-na_4**

1. Straw Carried from the Canal

[10]-lá–1 g̃uruš ⌜in⌝-u ⌜**i_7-kar**⌝-na_4-t[a g]a_6-g̃á-dè gub-ba, "9 workmen employed to carry straw from the Karna canal," 83:14–16

2. Broken Context

6 ĝuruš in-u [**i$_7$**]-**kar-na$_4$**-ta in-[. . .], "6 workmen [. . .] straw from the Karna [canal]," 81:9

i$_7$-*ma-an-iš-ti-šu*

1. Boats Towed to its Bank

0.2.3. á má-ḫuĝ-ĝá 0.2.0. á ĝuruš ḫuĝ-ĝá 0.0.1.6 sìla šà-gal má-laḫ$_5$ 0.0.1.6 sìla < še->b[i s]a$_{10}$ má-⸢laḫ$_5$⸣ u$_4$-1-šè é-duru$_5$-ka[b-bí-ta] gú **i$_7$-[*ma-an-iš-ti-šu*-**šè] má gí[d-da], "150 liters, wages of the hired boat (and) 120 liters, wages of hired workmen; 16 liters, food (for) sailors, 16 liters is the (hiring) price of the sailors for 1 day having towed boats [from] the Kabbi village [to] the bank of the [*Maništišu*] canal," 561:'28-'32

2. Boats Floated from its Bank

(. . .) [gú] **i$_7$-⸢*ma*⸣-*an-iš-ti-šu***-ta gar-ša-an-na^{ki}-⸢šè⸣ má diri-ga da-na-bi 9-àm, "{barley in boats} having floated from the [bank] of the *Maništišu* canal to Garšana, (a distance of) 9 double-miles," 561:'41-'44

i$_7$-ma-ma-*šar-ra-at*

1. Dirt Removed at the Canal

1 ĝuruš ⸢ašgab⸣ u$_4$-14-[šè] iti ezem-an-⸢na⸣ 1 ĝuruš ⸢ašgab⸣ u[$_4$-n-šè n ĝuruš] ašgab i[ti ezem]-m[e-ki-ĝ]ál [s]ahar zi-⸢ga⸣ **i$_7$-ma-ma-*šar-ra-at***, "1 leather worker [for] 14 days in month 11 (and) 1 leather worker for [n] day(s) (and) [n] leather worker(s) in month 12 having moved dirt at the Mama-*šarrat* canal," 281:1–8

1 ĝuruš túg-[du$_8$] u$_4$-13-šè saḫar zi-ga **i$_7$-ma-ma-*šar-ra-at***, "1 braider for 13 days having moved dirt at the Mama-*šarrat* canal," 283:1–3

[1] ĝuruš ad-kub$_4$ [u$_4$]-13-šè saḫar zi-ga **i$_7$-ma-ma-*šar-ra-at***, "[1] reed craftsman for 13 [days] having moved dirt at the Mama-*šarrat* canal," 284:1–3

i$_7$-me-kal-kal

1. Distance Measurements

gú **i$_7$-me-kal-kal**-ta 1 da-na 1200 nindan ús bàd-^{d}šul-gi-šè, "1 da-na (and) 1200 nindan measured from the bank of the Mekalkal canal to Bad-Šulgi," 1382:1–3

šu+níĝin 3 ⸢da⸣-n[a 240+]120 nindan ús gú **i$_7$-me-kal-kal** *simat-é-a* a-da-ga-ta ká-^{d}*šu*-^{d}*suen*-šè, "In total: 3 da-na (and) 360 nindan measured from the bank of the Mekalkal canal of *Simat-Ea* (and its) irrigation ditch to the *Šu-Suen* gate," 1382:14–16

i$_7$-mi-me-er

1. Dug in Nippur

13 ĝuruš saĝ-tag 3 ĝuruš á-⅔-ta lú-ašláĝ-me-éš u$_4$-2-šè **i$_7$-mi-me-er** gub-ba ba-al-la (. . .) šà nibru^{ki}, "13 full-time fullers and 3 fullers at ⅔ wages employed for 2 days having dug the Mimer canal. {Expenditure} in Nippur," 227:1–5, 7

i$_7$-nar-e-ne

1. Barley Stolen at Its Opening

0.2.0.še še zuḫ-a *a-na-aḫ-ì-*[*lí*] ašgab šà ka **i$_7$-nar-e-⸢ne⸣** ka-ga-na ba-ge-en, "*Anaḫ-ili*, the leather worker, confirmed that 120 liters of barley were stolen at the opening of the Singers' canal," 1063:1–4

i$_7$-^{d}nin-ḫur-sağ-ğá

1. Wages for Sailors Towing Boats to and from the Canal

[. . . u]$_4$-1-[šè] é-duru$_5$-*simat*-^{d}[*ištaran*-ta] ka **i$_7$-^{d}[nin-ḫur-sağ-ğá**-šè] má gíd-da, "[(wages of sailors) for] 1 [day] having towed boats [from] the *Simat-Ištaran* village [to the] opening of the [Ninḫursağ] canal," 561:'11-'14

0.2.3. á má-ḫuğ-ğá 0.2.0. á ğuruš ḫuğ-ğá 0.0.1.6 šà-gal má-laḫ$_5$ 0.0.1.6 <še->bi sa$_{10}$ má-laḫ$_5$ u$_4$-1-šè gú **i$_7$-^{d}nin-ḫur-sağ-ğá**-ta [gar-ša-an-na^{ki}-šè má] gíd-da, "150 liters (of barley), wages of the hired boat (and) 120 liters, wages of hired workmen; 16 liters, food (for) sailors, 16 liters <of barley> is the (hiring) price of the sailors [for] 1 day having towed [boats] from the bank of the Ninḫursağa canal [to Garšana]," 561:'19-'23

i$_7$-sur

1. Dirt Removed from the Canal

1 ğuruš túg-du$_8$ [u$_4$]-21-šè saḫar zi-ga **i$_7$-sur** du$_6$-ba-an-du$_8$-du$_8$ a-⸢šà⸣ sum-túl-túl, "1 braider for 21 [days] having moved dirt at the Sur canal of Du-bandudu (and?/in?) the Sum-tultul field," 268:1–5

i$_7$-^{d}*šu*-^{d}*suen*-ḫé-ğál

1. Straw Carried from the Canal

3 ğuruš in-[u] **i$_7$-^{d}*šu*-^{d}*suen*-⸢ḫé⸣-ğál**-ta im lu-a-šè íb-ga$_6$, "3 workmen carried straw from the *Šu-Suen* Canal of Abundance for mixing (with) earth," 198:'24-'25

Analytical Index of Gardens

^{ğeš}kiri$_{6}$ ba-ga-a, "the garden of Baga'a"
^{ğeš}kiri$_{6}$ ^{d}ba-ú-da, "the garden of Ba'uda"
^{ğeš}kiri$_{6}$ *eš$_{4}$-tár-um-mi*, "the garden of *Eštar-ummi*"
^{ğeš}kiri$_{6}$ ĝá-nun-na, "the garden of the storehouse"
^{ğeš}kiri$_{6}$ gar-ša-an-na^{ki}, "the Garšana garden"
^{ğeš}kiri$_{6}$ igi-érim-iri^{ki}, "the Igi-erim-iri garden"
^{ğeš}kiri$_{6}$ lugal, "the master's garden"
^{ğeš}kiri$_{6}$ *simat-^{d}ištaran*, "the garden of *Simat-Ištaran*"
^{ğeš}kiri$_{6}$ *šu-eš$_{4}$-tár*, "the garden of *Šu-Eštar*"
^{ğeš}kiri$_{6}$ zabala$_{4}^{\text{ki}}$, "the Zabala garden"

^{ğeš}**kiri$_{6}$**, "the garden"

é-*gi-na-tum* ^{ğeš}**kiri$_{6}$**, "the garden barracks" > *Household Index*

é-^{ğeš}**kiri$_{6}$**, "the garden house" > *Household Index*

1. Construction of Garden Structures

1.1 The GÍN-bal

n ĝuruš šidim n guruš n géme GÍN-bal ^{ğeš}**kiri$_{6}$** dù-a, "n builder(s), n workmen (and) n workwomen having constructed the GÍN-bal of the garden," 151:36–37, 154:39–40, 159:27–28

13 ĝuruš 10 géme GÍN-bal ^{ğeš}**kiri$_{6}$** dù-a, "13 workmen (and) 10 workwomen having constructed the GÍN-bal of the garden," 155:32

20 ĝuruš GÍN-bal ^{ğeš}**kiri$_{6}$** dù-a, "20 workmen having constructed the GÍN-bal of the garden," 158:41

1.2 Building Supplies for Construction of the GÍN-bal

5 sìla ésir-é-a peš-šè mu GÍN-bal ^{ğeš}**kiri$_{6}$**-[šè], "5 liters of house bitumen for palmleaflet mats [for] the GÍN-bal of the garden," 1008:7–8

2. Garden Products

2.1 Assorted Commodities Measured for Accounting

9.1.1.5 sìla zú-lum gur 1.0.1. u$_{4}$-ḫi-in gur 10⅚ 6 gín ^{ğeš}zé-na 656 peš-múrgu 3½ 3 gín peš-ga 1065 á-an-zú-lum káb du$_{11}$-ga ^{ğeš}⌜**kiri$_{6}$**⌝, "9 bushels (and) 75 liters of dates, 1 bushel (and) 10 liters of fresh dates, 10⅚ (minas and) 6 shekels of date palm frond midribs, 656 date palm spines, 3½ (minas and) 3 shekels of date palm hearts (and) 1065 date clusters, commodities of the garden measured for accounting," 1215:1–7

14.3.[n.] zú-lum gur 2.1.0. u$_{4}$-ḫi-in gur 600½ 4 gín ^{ĝeš}zé-na 820 peš-múrgu 4⅔ 8 gín peš-ga 1500 á-an-zú-lum ká[b du]$_{11}$-ga ^{ĝeš}**kiri$_{6}$**, "14 bushels (and) 180[+n] liters of dates, 2 bushels (and) 60 liters of fresh dates, 600½ (minas and) 4 shekels of date palm frond midribs, 820 date palm spines, 4⅔ (minas and) 8 shekels of date palm hearts (and) 1500 date clusters, commodities of the garden measured for accounting," 1237:1–7

2.2 Seedlings

1 har ^{ĝeš}ásal-UD–2! 6 har ^{ĝeš}ásal-UD 1-⌜ta⌝ ^{ĝeš}**kiri$_{6}$**-ta, "1 poplar seedling of 2 (units) (and) 6 poplar seedlings of 1 (unit) each from the garden," 1315:1–3

3. Garden Work

3.1 Provisions for Hoeing

4.4.0. še gur al aka ^{ĝeš}**kiri$_{6}$**, "4 bushels (and) 240 liters of barley (for workers) having hoed the garden," 500:1–2

3.2 Broken Context

1 ĝuruš šidim 1 géme x ^{ĝeš}**kiri$_{6}$** [u$_{4}$]-1?-šè? x x x, 210:'33-'34

^{ĝeš}**kiri$_{6}$ ba-ga-a**, "the garden of Baga'a"

1. Bricks from the Garden

šu+níĝin [n sar n] gín ⌜šeg$_{12}$⌝ (. . .) ^{ĝeš}**kiri$_{6}$ b[a-ga-a]**, "In total: [n sar (and) n] shekel(s) of bricks, {wages for brick carriers}, (from?) the garden of Baga'a," 351:81, 85

1.1 Delivered for the Craftsmen's House

é-gašam-e-ne mu-DU (. . .) ^{ĝeš}**kiri$_{6}$ ba-ga-a**-ta, "(bricks) delivered (for) the craftsmen's house, {authorizing officials}, from the garden of Baga'a," 325:18–19, 25, 330:27–28, 36

^{ĝeš}**kiri$_{6}$** ^{d}**ba-ú-da**, "the garden of Ba'uda"

n ĝuruš a bal-a ^{ĝeš}**kiri$_{6}$** ^{d}**ba-ú-da**, "n workmen having irrigated the garden of Ba'uda" > **a . . . bal**

^{ĝeš}**kiri$_{6}$** ***eš$_{4}$-tár-um-mi***, "the garden of *Eštar-ummi*"

1. Garden Products

4.3.0. zú-lum gur 0.0.5. u$_{4}$-ḫi-in n+3 gín peš-ga 5? sìla á-an-zú-lum [káb d]u$_{11}$-ga ^{ĝeš}**kiri$_{6}$** ***eš$_{4}$-tár-<um->mi*** dumu-munus *šu-kab-tá*, "4 bushels (and) 180 liters of dates, 50 liters of fresh dates, [n+]3 shekels of date palm hearts (and) 5? liters of date clusters, commodities of the garden of *Eštar-ummi*, the daughter of *Šu-Kabta*, measured for accounting," 1102:1–6

^{ĝeš}**kiri$_{6}$ ĝá-nun-na**, "the garden of the storehouse"

1. Bricks for the GÍN-bal of the Garden

203 šeg$_{12}$-al-ur$_{x}$-ra GÍN-bal ^{ĝeš}**kiri$_{6}$ ĝá-nun-na**-šè ba-a-ĝar, "203 bricks were placed for the GÍN-bal of the garden of the storehouse," 1326:1–2

^{ĝeš}**kiri$_{6}$ gar-ša-an-na^{ki}**, "the Garšana garden"

é-*gi-na-tum* ^{ĝeš}**kiri$_{6}$ gar-ša-an-na^{ki}**, "the Garšana garden barracks" > *Household Index*

1. Building Supplies for the Garden

★★4 ^{ğeš}é-da-ásal 30 sa gi-⸢izi⸣ 1 ^{gi}dur dağal a-[rá]-3-tab-ba gíd 5 nindan ⸢ti⸣?-gu **^{ğeš}kiri$_6$ gar-ša-[an-n]a^{ki}** ba-a-ğar, "4 poplar joists, 30 bundles of fuel reeds (and) 1 30-meter 3-ply wide rope (?) were placed at the Garšana garden," 1273:1–4

2. Construction of Garden Structures

2.1 The Adobe Wall

n ğuruš šidim im-du$_8$-a **^{ğeš}kiri$_6$ gar-ša-an-na^{ki}** gub-ba, "n builder(s) employed at the adobe wall of the Garšana garden," 81:7, 82:8, 84:12

2.2 The GÍN-bal

1 ğuruš šidim [n] ğuruš GÍN-bal šà **^{ğeš}kiri$_6$ gar-ša-a[n-n]a^{ki}** dù-a, "1 builder (and) [n] workmen having constructed the GÍN-bal in the Garšana garden," 129:33–34

1 ğuruš šidim n ğuruš n géme GÍN-bal **^{ğeš}kiri$_6$ gar-ša-an-na^{ki}** dù-a, "1 builder, n workmen (and) n workwomen having constructed the GÍN-bal of the Garšana garden," 131:'24-'25, 133:32–33, 135:31–32, 136:35–36, 146:36–37, 147:41–42

1 ğuruš šidim 6 ğuruš [GÍN]-bal **^{ğeš}kiri$_6$ gar-ša-an-na^{ki}** dù-a, "1 builder (and) 6 workmen having constructed the [GÍN]-bal of the Garšana garden," 132:33–34

2 ğuruš šidim 15 ğuruš 5 géme GÍN-bal **^{ğeš}kiri$_6$ gar-ša-an-na^{ki}**, "2 builders, 15 workmen (and) 5 workwomen at the GÍN-bal of the Garšana garden," 138:32–33

2.2.1 Moving Dirt

14 [ğuruš saḫar] zi-ga GÍN-bal **[^{ğeš}ki]ri$_6$ gar-ša-an-na^{ki}**, "14 [workmen] having moved [dirt] at the GÍN-bal of the Garšana garden," 125:35

1 ğuruš šidim 14 [ğuruš 3 géme] saḫar zi-ga GÍN-bal **^{ğeš}kiri$_6$ gar-ša-an-na^{ki}**-a,"1 builder, 14 [workmen (and) 3 workwomen] having moved dirt at the GÍN-bal of the Garšana garden," 128:31–32

2.2.2 Moving Dirt at the GÍN-bal of the Garden's Field

12 ğuruš saḫar zi-ga GÍN-bal a-šà **^{ğeš}kiri$_6$ gar-ša-an-na^{ki}**, "12 workmen having moved dirt at the GÍN-bal of the field of the Garšana garden," 123:39

2.2.3 Building Supplies for the GÍN-bal

(. . .) [níğ] al-zi-ra [. . . gir-r]a ba-ab-g[u$_7$ GÍN]-bal **^{ğeš}ki[ri$_6$ gar-ša-an-na^{ki}** dù-a], "{assorted baskets and containers}—fire consumed the used goods—[(used by workers) having constructed the GÍN]-bal of the [Garšana] garden," 1292:'23-'25

21.0.0. ésir-ḫád ⸢gur⸣ 2.1.3. ésir-é-a gur GÍN-bal **^{ğeš}kiri$_6$ gar-[ša-an-na^{ki}** dù-a], "21 bushels of dry bitumen (and) 2 bushels (and) 90 liters of house bitumen, [(used by workers) having constructed] the GÍN-bal of the Garšana garden," 1302:1–3

3. Inspection of Garden Work

kurum$_7$ aka saḫar ⸢zi⸣-ga **^{ğeš}kiri$_6$ gar-ša-an-na^{ki}**, "Inspection of dirt moved at the Garšana garden," 176:16–17, 179:17–18

4. Irrigation

0.4.0. še á lú-ḫuĝ-ĝá a bala-e-dè gub-ba ^{ĝeš}**kiri$_6$ šà gar-š[a-an-na]**^{ki} ù ^{ĝeš}kiri$_6$ šà zabala$_4$^{ki}, "240 liters of barley, wages of hired workers employed to irrigate the gardens in Garšana and Zabala," 390:1–3

1⅔ guruš ašgab u$_4$-2-šè a bala-e-dè gub-ba ^{ĝeš}**kiri$_6$ šà gar-ša-an-na**^{ki}, "1⅔ leather workers employed for 2 days to irrigate the garden in Garšana," 1523:1–4

5. Broken Context

[. . .-g]u ^{ĝeš}**kiri$_6$ ⌜gar⌝-ša-an-na**^{ki}, 1251:7–8

^{ĝeš}**kiri$_6$ igi-érim-iri**^{ki}, "the Igi-erim-iri garden"

1. Wood, the Inventory of the Garden

ĝeš é-⌜^{ĝeš}kiri$_6$⌝-a gub-ba šu-sum-ma ^{ĝeš}**kiri$_6$ igi-érim-iri**^{ki}, "wood stored in the garden house, the inventory of the Igi-erim-iri garden," 1375:45–46

^{ĝeš}**kiri$_6$ lugal**, "the master's garden"[1]

1. Earth for the Gardeners' Houses, Not the Master's Garden

[*ak-b*]*a-zum* nu-^{ĝeš}kiri$_6$-⌜ke$_4$⌝ má-lugal-na saḫar tùm-dè zabala$_4$^{ki}-šè in-la-aḫ saḫar mu-un-de$_9$ ^{ĝeš}**kiri$_6$ lugal**-na-šè nu-un-ni-ku$_4$ é-ni-šè ba-an-dé ka-ga-na ba-ge-en, "*Akbazum*, the gardener, confirmed that they took a boat of his master to Zabala in order to bring dirt, that he brought the dirt, that it did not enter the garden of his master but was brought for his (own) house," 1049:1–10

^{d}ba-ú-da [nu]-^{ĝeš}kiri$_6$-ke$_4$ má-lugal-na saḫar tùm-dè zabala$_4$^{ki}-šè in-la-aḫ saḫar mu-un-de$_9$ ^{ĝeš}**kiri$_6$ lugal**-na nu-un-ni-ku$_4$ é-ni-šè ba-an-dé ka-ga-na ba-ge-en, "Ba'uda, the gardener, confirmed that they took a boat of his master to Zabala in order to bring dirt, that he brought the dirt, that it did not enter the garden of his master but was brought for his (own) house," 1050:1–10

^{ĝeš}**kiri$_6$ *simat-^{d}ištaran***, "the garden of *Simat-Ištaran*"

1. Cut from the Garden

2 pa ^{ĝeš}kíĝ ^{ĝeš}**kiri$_6$ *simat-^{d}ištaran*** gar-ša-an-na^{ki} *šu-eš$_4$-tár* ^{lú}kíĝ-gi$_4$-[a-lugal] in-ku$_5$, "*Šu-Eštar*, the [royal] messenger, pruned 2 kíĝ trees in the garden of *Simat-Ištaran* at Garšana," 1354:1–6

^{ĝeš}**kiri$_6$ *šu-eš$_4$-tár***, "the garden of *Šu-Eštar*"

1. Work on the Adobe Wall of the Garden

3 ĝuruš šidim im-⌜du$_8$⌝-a ^{ĝeš}**kiri$_6$ *šu-eš$_4$-tár*** gub-ba, "3 builders employed at the adobe wall of the garden of *Šu-Eštar*," 83:11

[1] Here not "the royal garden," but possibly the garden of *Šu-Kabta* (Heimpel, pesonal communication).

^{ğeš}**kiri**$_6$ **zabala**$_4$^{ki}, “the Zabala garden”

1. Construction of Garden Structures

1.1 The Adobe Wall

1 ĝuruš šidim um-mi-a 1 ĝuruš šidim im-du$_8$-a ^{ğeš}**kiri**$_6$ **zabala**$_4$^{ki} dù-a, “1 master builder (and) 1 builder having constructed the adobe wall of the Zabala garden,” 146:'20-'21

1.1.1 Builders Employed at the Wall

n ĝuruš šidim im-du$_8$-a ^{ğeš}**kiri**$_6$ **zabala**$_4$^{ki} gub-ba, “n builder(s) employed at the adobe wall of the Zabala garden,” 78:14, 79:13, 81:8, 82:7, 83:12–13, 84:11

1 ĝuruš šidim im-du$_8$-a ^{ğeš}**kiri**$_6$ **zabala**$_4$^{ki}, “1 builder at the adobe wall of the Zabala garden,” 148:18

1.1.2 Provisions for Work on the Adobe wall

(. . .) im-du$_8$-a ^{ğeš}[**kiri**$_6$] **zabala**$_4$$^{\text{[ki]}}$ mu-[DU], “delivery (of barley), {wages of workers employed} at the adobe wall of Zabala,” 356:5–6

1.2 The GÍN-bal

1 ĝuruš šidim GÍN-bal ^{ğeš}**kiri**$_6$ **zabala**$_4$^{ki} dù-dè gub-ba, “1 builder employed to construct the GÍN-bal of the Zabala garden,” 1:12, 3:13–14, 4:18–19

1 ĝuruš šidim GÍN-bal ^{ğeš}**kiri**$_6$ **zabala**$_4$^{ki} dù-a, “1 builder having constructed the GÍN-bal of the Zabala garden,” 2:17–18

1.3 The Tower

1 ĝuruš šidim ⸢um-mi⸣-a 1 ĝuruš šidim [1]0 ĝuruš im šu dím-ma sum-mu-dè 11 ĝuruš im ga$_6$-ĝá 3 ĝuruš im lu-a [n] ĝuruš a bal-a-e-dè úgu iz-zi-da a ĝá-ĝá an-za-qar-^{ğeš}**kiri**$_6$ **zabala**$_4$^{ki}, “1 master builder, 1 builder, (and) [1]0 workmen to hand earth for building, 11 workmen having carried earth, 3 workmen having mixed earth (and) [n] workmen to pour water, (workers) having water-proofed the top of the iz-zi wall of the tower of the Zabala garden,” 200:'2-'9

[n] ĝuruš im lu-a [n] ĝuruš a bal-a-e-dè [n ĝuruš i]m sumur aka [4] ĝuruš im dì-um ga$_6$-ĝá [n géme da]-iz-zi-da-šè an-za-qar-^{ğeš}**kiri**$_6$ **zabala**$_4$$^{\text{⸢ki⸣}}$ [gub-ba], “[n] workmen having mixed earth, [n] workmen to pour water, [n workmen] having plastered, [4] workmen having carried the adobe mix (and) [n workwomen] for [the side] of the iz-zi wall, (workers) [employed] at the tower of the Zabala garden,” 201:'1-'6

1.3.1 Plastering the Tower

2 ĝuruš šidim [im] šu dím-ma sum-mu-dè 2 ĝuruš im ga$_6$-ĝá 2 ĝuruš im lu-a 3 ĝuruš a bal-a-e-dè 8 ĝuruš saḫar šà é-a sè-gé-dè im sumur aka an-za-qar-^{ğeš}**kiri**$_6$ **zabala**$_4$^{ki}, “2 builders to hand [earth] for building, 2 workmen having carried earth, 2 workmen having mixed earth, 3 workmen to pour water, 8 workmen to tamp earth in the house, (workers) having plastered the tower of the Zabala garden,” 202:14–21

1 ĝuruš šidim um-mi-a 3 ĝuruš šidim 3 ĝuruš im šu dím-ma [sum]-mu-dè 7 ĝuruš im ga$_6$-ĝá 3 ĝuruš im lu-a 3 ĝuruš a bal-a im sumur aka an-za-qar-^{ğeš}**kiri**$_6$ **za[bala**$_4$^{ki}], “1 master builder, 3 builders (and) 3 workmen to hand earth for building, 7 workmen having carried earth, 3 workmen having mixed earth (and) 3 workmen having poured water, (workers) having plastered the tower of the Zabala garden,” 203:14–21

1.3.2 Building Supplies for the Tower

480 sa gi-⸢izi⸣ gu-níĝin 12-sa-ta gi-sal$_4$(!)-la an-za-qar **^{ğeš}kiri$_6$ zabala$_4$^{ki}**-šè ba-a-ĝar, "480 bundles of fuel reeds of 12 bundles each, thin reeds were placed for the tower of the Zabala garden," 1323:1–4

2. Garden Work

n ĝuruš a bal-a **^{ğeš}kiri$_6$ zabala$_4$^{ki}**, "n workmen having irrigated the Zabala garden" > **a . . . bal**

2.1 Inspection of Garden Work

saḫar zi-ga in-lá tùn-lá **^{ğeš}kiri$_6$ zabala$_4$^{ki}** kurum$_7$ [aka], "inspection (of the work of workers). They transported dirt removed via a tùn-lá device at the Zabala garden," 178:6–8

2.2 Irrigation

0.4.0. še á lú-ḫuĝ-ĝá a bala-e-dè gub-ba ^{ğeš}kiri$_6$ šà gar-š[a-an-na]^{ki} ù **^{ğeš}kiri$_6$ šà zabala$_4$^{ki}**, "240 liters of barley, wages of hired workers employed to irrigate the gardens in Garšana and Zabala," 390:1–3

Analytical Index of Fields

a-šà a-gi-li
a-šà *dì-im-bu-na*-àš-gi$_5$
a-šà du$_6$-ba-an-du$_8$-du$_8$
a-šà gar-ša-an-na^{ki}
a-šà karkar^{ki}
a-šà ^{geš}kiri$_6$ gar-ša-an-na^{ki} > a-šà gar-ša-an-na^{ki}
a-šà lú-maḫ
a-šà mí-mí
a-šà pa$_4$-lugal-g̃u$_{10}$
a-šà sum-túl-túl
a-šà *ṣé-ru-um*[1]
a-šà *ši-ḫu-um*
da-*si-ḫu-um*[2]

a-šà, "field"

1. A Field Allotment

5.4.0. še gur á al aka ù gu$_4$-ḫug̃-g̃á **a-šà** 1 (bùr) 2 (iku) gána ki ^{d}*adad-tillati*-ta ^{d}*ma-lik-ba-ni* šu [ba]-an-ti, "*Malik-bani* received from *Adad-tillati* 5 bushels and 240 liters of barley, wages of hoers and rented oxen (and) a field of 1 bur (and) 2 iku of acreage," 1051:1–6

2. Broken Context: Provisions List

(. . .) [. . . -b]i **a-šà** [šu+níg̃in n+]7.0.0. gur še-ba *ba-zi-tum* šu+níg̃in 47.1.[n.] še-ba é, "{barley for individuals}; [. . .] the field; [in total: n+]7 bushels of the barley rations of *Bazitum*, in total: 47 bushels (and) 60[+n] liters of barley rations of the household," 555:23–25

a-šà a-gi-li

1. Straw Brought from the Field to Garšana

40 g̃uruš u$_4$-1-šè še 6 sìla-ta ba-ḫug̃ **a-šà a-gi-li**-⌜ta⌝ gar-⌜ša⌝-an-na^{ki}-šè in-u de$_6$-a, "40 workmen were hired for 1 day for 6 liters of barley each having brought straw from the Agili field to Garšana," 443:1–5

---

1 The PN *Ṣerum* occurs in only one place and is associated with Adamšaḫ, *ṣe-ru-um* sugal$_7$ a-dam-šáḫ^{ki}-šè du-ni, SAT 1 158, rev. 1.

2 This field occurs twice in Nippur texts *NATN* 798:'17 and TMH NF 1–2 87:10 as a-šà *tá-si-ḫu-um*.

a-šà *dì-im-bu-na*-àš-gi$_5$

1. Barley Reaped at the Field

1 g̃uruš ašgab u$_4$-1-šè še gur$_{10}$-gur$_{10}$-dè **a-šà *dì-im-bu-na*-àš-gi$_5$** gub-ba, "1 leather worker employed for 1 day to reap barley at the *Dimbun*-Ašgi field," 282:1–3

2. Barley Rations Disbursed at the Field

3.3.1.5 sìla še še-ba géme-árad (. . .) **a-šà *dì-im-bu*-[*na*]-^{aš}aš$_7$-gi$_4^{\text{ki}}$**, "3 bushels (and) 195 liters of barley, barley rations of female and male servants, {expenditure} at the field of *Dimbun*-Ašgi," 527:1–2, 7

(a-šà) du$_6$-ba-an-du$_8$-du$_8$

1. Dirt Removed at its Canal

1 g̃uruš túg-du$_8$ [u$_4$]-21-šè sahar zi-ga i$_7$-sur **du$_6$-ba-an-du$_8$-du$_8$ a-⌜šà⌝ sum-túl-túl, "1 braider for 21 [days] having moved dirt at the Sur canal of Du-bandudu (and?/in?) the Sum-tultul field," 268:1–5

2. Reeds Brought to its Weir

30 géme uš-bar u$_4$-1-šè gi g̃á-udu-ta kun-zi-id(Á)-šè íb-ga$_6$ **a-šà du$_6$-ba-an-du$_8$-du$_8$**, "30 female weavers for 1 day brought reeds from the sheep-shearing shed to the weir of the Du-bandudu field," 273:7–10

a-šà gar-ša-an-na^{ki}

1. The GÍN-bal of the Field

12 g̃uruš sahar zi-ga GÍN-bal **a-šà** $^{\text{g̃eš}}$kiri$_6$ **gar-ša-an-na^{ki}**, "12 workmen having moved dirt at the GÍN-bal of the field of the Garšana garden," 123:39

[n g̃uruš sahar] zi-ga GÍN-ba[l **a**]**-šà gar-ša-an-n**[**a^{ki}**], "[n workmen] having moved [dirt] at the GÍN-bal of the Garšana field," 126:30

a-šà karkar^{ki}

1. Wages for Cutting Shok at the Field

10 gu-níg̃in $^{\text{g̃eš}}$kišig á-g̃uruš-a 4 gu-níg̃in-ta á-bi 2½ u$_4$-1-šè **a-šà karkar^{ki}**-šè $^{\text{g̃eš}}$kišig ku$_5$-rá, "(In total:) 10 bales of shok. The workmen wages were for 4 bales each. Their wages were for 2½ days (for workers) having cut shok at the Karkar field," 235:1–4

a-šà lú-mah

1. Barley Brought from the Field

(. . .) [u$_4$]-3-šè [še x] x x x an-za-qar-ta kun-zi-da i$_7$-a-gàr-ús-sa **a-šà lú-mah**-šè íb-ga$_6$ ù má-a si-ga, "{workers and boats} for 3 [days]; (the boats) carried [barley . . .] from the fortified tower to the weir of the Agar-usa Canal of the Lu-mah field and (the workers) having loaded the boats," 553:11–15

a-šà mí-mí

1. Grain from the Field's Granary

5.0.0. zíz gur 0.3.3. kib$_x$ ì-dub **a-šà mí-mí**, "5 bushels of emmer wheat (and) 210 liters of wheat of the granary of the Mimi field," 1232:1–3, 1235:1–4

a-šà pa$_4$-lugal-g̃u$_{10}$

1. Field Administration

30 g̃uruš u$_4$-1-šè nam-ša-ra-ab<-du> **a-šà pa$_4$-lugal-g̃u$_{10}$**-ka gub-ba, "30 workmen for 1 day employed for the administration of the Palugalg̃u field," 276:1–3

30 g̃uruš túg-du$_8$ u$_4$-1-[šè] nam-ša-ra-ab-du **a-šà pa$_4$-lugal-g̃u$_{10}$**-ka gub-ba, "30 braiders [for] 1 day employed for the administration of the Palugalg̃u field," 306:1–2

2. Reeds Brought from the Field

6 [g̃uruš . . .] **a-šà pa$_4$-lu[gal-g̃]u$_{10}$**-k[a-ta] gi tùm-⸢dè⸣ g̃en-[na], "6 [workmen...] having gone to bring reeds [from] the Palugalg̃u field," 57:'22-'23

30 g̃uruš gi-zi **a-šà pa$_5$-lugal-g̃u$_{10}$** tùm-dè g̃en-na, "30 workmen having gone to bring fresh reeds of the Palugalg̃u field," 148:'19

(a-šà) sum-túl-túl

1. Dirt Removed

1 g̃uruš túg-du$_8$ [u$_4$]-21-šè saḫar zi-ga i$_7$-sur du$_6$-ba-an-du$_8$-du$_8$ **a-⸢šà⸣ sum-túl-túl, "1 braider for 21 [days] having moved dirt at the Sur canal of Du-bandudu (and?/in?) the Sum-tultul field," 268:1–5

3.0.0. š[e gur] á lú-ḫug̃-[g̃á] mu saḫar-šè (. . .) **[a-š]à sum-túl-túl**, "3 bushels of barley, wages of hired workers for (moving?) dirt, {expenditure} at the Sum-tultul field," 545:1–3, 8

2. Broken Context

iti ezem-maḫ še tùm-dè é-duru$_5$-ul-luḫ-uri$_5$^{ki}-[ma-šè g̃en-na] é-bu?-ne **sum-túl-tú[l x?], "(In) month 10 (workers) [having gone to] the Ulluḫ-Urim village to bring barley, (?) Sum-tultul," 1029:'18-'20

a-šà *ṣe-ru-um*

1. The Harvest at the Field

(. . .) še gur$_{10}$-gur$_{10}$-dè zàr tab-ba-dè ù g̃eš ra-ra-dè **a-šà *ṣe-ru-um*** gub-ba, "{craftsmen} employed at the *Ṣerum* field to reap barley, stack (its) sheaves (for drying) and reap (them)," 262:19–22

1 g̃uruš ad-kub$_4$ u$_4$-4-šè *dì-im-bu-na*-àš-gi$_5$-ta **a-šà *ṣe-r[u-u]m***-šè še gur$_{10}$-gur$_{10}$-[dè] gub-ba, "1 reed craftsmen (having gone) from *Dimbun*-Ašgi to the *Ṣerum* field, employed for 4 days [to] reap barley," 284:5–10

2. Traveling to the Field

1 g̃uruš túg-du$_8$ u$_4$-4-šè *dì-im-bu-na*-àš-gi$_5$-ta **a-šà *ṣe-ru-um***-šè, "1 braider for 4 days (having gone) from *Dimbun*-Ašgi to the *Ṣerum* field," 283:5–8

a-šà *ši-ḫu-um*

1. Reeds Brought from the Field

n ĝuruš gi-zi tùm(-dè) **a-šà *ši-ḫu-um***-šè ĝen-na(-me), "n workmen having gone to the *Šiḫum* field to bring fresh reeds," 74:'8, 75:26–27

da-*si-ḫu-um*

1. Reeds from the Field

5 géme u_4-1-[šè] gi **da-*si-ḫu-um***-ta de_6-a, "5 workwomen [for] 1 day having brought reeds from Da-*siḫum*," 258:1–2

Analytical Index of Households and Installations

é, *bītu*, "house" [1]

1. Construction of the House

1.1 Construction of its Well

[n] ğuruš šidim [n ğuru]š šu dím gub-ba 5 géme im ga$_6$-ğá-dè gub-ba túl šà **é**-a dù-a, "[n] builder(s), [n] workmen employed to build (and) 5 workwomen employed to carry earth, (workers) having constructed the well in the house," 210:'25-'28

1.2 Carrying Plaster

2 ğuruš im sumur šà **é**-a-šè ga$_6$-ğá, "2 workmen having carried plaster for the interior of the house," 5:22

1.3 Construction with Bitumen(-Soaked) Palmleaflet Mats

1 [ğuruš n gém]e peš-ésir **é** dù-a, "1 [workman (and) n] workwomen having constructed a house with bitumen(-soaked) palmleaflet (mats)," 125:34

1.4 Plastering Reeds

[4] ğuruš šidim 4 ğuruš [4] géme gi-sal šà **é**-a im sumur ke$_4$-dè gub-ba, "[4] builders, 4 workmen (and) [4] workwomen employed to plaster thin reeds in the house," 14:18–19

1.5 Repair

1 ğuruš šidim um-mi-a 7 ğuruš šidim 10-lá-1 ğuruš šu dím gub-⸢ba⸣ *ták-si-ru-um* šà **é**-a, "1 master builder, 7 builders (and) 9 workmen employed to build (for) repair in the house," 45:13–16

1.6 Trimming Reeds

5 ğuruš šidim gi-sal šà **é**-a ⸢gul⸣-dè gub-ba, "5 builders employed to trim thin reeds in the house," 7:'35

[n ğuruš] gi-sal šà **é**-a [gul]-dè [gub-ba], "[n workmen employed] to [trim] thin reeds in the house," 8:40

1.7 Various Tasks

1 ğuruš šidim 8 ğuruš gi-sal ⸢bàd⸣ gul-dè gub-ba 3 géme gi-sal ga$_6$-ğá-d[è gub-ba] 3 ğuruš šidim 1 ğuruš 3 [géme] ^{ğeš}ig šà **é**-a [bu-ra], "1 builder (and) 8 workmen employed to trim thin reeds at the (enclosure) wall, 3 workwomen [employed] to carry thin reeds (and) 3 builders, 1 workman (and) 3 [workwomen having pulled out] a door in the house," 15:19–22

2. (De-)Construction

2.1 Pulling out a Door

1 ğuruš ašgab u$_4$-3-šè ^{ğeš}ig šà **é**-a bu-ra, "1 leather worker for 3 days having pulled out a door in the house," 239:1–3

2.2 Extracting Dirt

n ğuruš saḫar šà **é**-a è-dè, "n workmen to extract dirt (from) inside the house," 192:'16, 193:26–27, 1376:6

---

1 When a house is not immediately qualified or identified later in the text it usually designates the house of *Šu-Kabta*.

3. Household Structures

3.1 The Cistern: Building Supplies

63 ^{dug}ù-lu-lu 2-kùš-ta *a-za-bu-um* šà **é**-a-šè ba-a-ĝar, "63 pipes of 2 cubits each were placed for the cistern in the house," 1325:8

3.2 The GÍN-bal

3.2.1 Building Supplies: Wood and Reed

(. . .) GÍN-bal [*a*]-*za-bu-um* šà **é**-a-šè ba-a-ĝ[ar], "{assorted wood products, reeds and ropes} were placed for the GÍN-bal of the cistern in the house," 1380:9

3.2.2 Manufacturing Reed Screens

1 ĝuruš šidim 2 ĝuruš ḫu-ur-da GÍN-bal šà **é**-a ke$_4$-dè, "1 builder (and) 2 workmen to make a reed screen for the GÍN-bal in the house," 58:57–59

3.3 The iz-zi Wall

3.3.1 (De-)Construction: Leveling the Wall

6 ĝuruš šidim iz-zi šà **é**-a ù-[ru-dè], "6 builders [to] level the iz-zi wall in the house," 184:15–16

n ĝuruš šidim n ĝuruš (sumur) iz-zi šà **é**-a ù-ru-dè gub-ba, "n builder(s) (and) n workmen employed to level the (plastered) iz-zi wall in the house," 183:12–14, 189:20–22

n ĝuruš šidim n ĝuruš sumur iz-zi šà **é**-a ù-ru-dè, "n builder(s) (and) n workmen to level the plastered iz-zi wall in the house," 187:17–19, 188:'14-'16, 193:23–25

3.3.2 Workers Employed at the Wall

5 [ĝuruš šidim] iz-zi š[à **é**-a gub-ba], "5 [builders employed] at the iz-zi wall in [the house]," 185:12–13

3.4 The Sanctuary of Nin-Siana in the House

0.2.0. še-[ninda . . .] 0.1.0. tuḫ-duru$_5$-gen sá-du$_{11}$-zag-gú-lá-^{d}nin-^{d}si$_4$-an-na šà **é**-a (. . .) èš-ta-gur-ra, "120 liters of barley [(for) bread. . .] (and) 60 liters of ordinary fresh bran, regular offerings of the sanctuary of Nin-Siana in the house (and) {offerings of other deities}, offerings returned from the sanctuary," 997:5–7, 12

0.2.0. še-[ninda . . .] sá-du$_{11}$-z[ag-g]ú-lá-^{d}[nin-si$_4$]-an-na š[à **é**-a] (. . .) èš-ta-gur-ra, "20 liters of barley [(for) bread . . .], regular offerings of the sanctuary of Nin-Siana in [the house] (and) {offerings of other deities}, offerings returned from the sanctuary," 1022:6–7, 15

4. Provisions (and Other Supplies) Disbursed during Construction of the House

4.1 Provisions when the House was Plastered

4.1.1 Assorted Commodities

(. . .) šà-gal šidim-e-ne ⅓ sìla ì-⸢šáḫ⸣ di$_4$-di$_4$-la àga-ús *simat-^{d}ištaran* ba-ab-šeš$_4$ [n] gín še-gín mu x-šè [. . . n ma]-na šu-sar m[angaga? $^{ĝeš?}$]ig ^{ĝeš}kuĝ$_5$-šè ⸢u$_4$⸣ **é**-e im sumur ba-aka, "{assorted dead animals}, food (for) builders, ⅓ liter of lard (used by) *Simat-Ištaran* (when) she anointed the small child(ren) of the gendarme(s), [n] shekels of glue for [x] [. . .] (and) [n mina(s)] of cord (made from) date palm fibers for the door (and) ladder when the house was plastered," 472:7–14

4.1.2 For Anointing the Doors

½ sìla ì-udu dúr ^{ĝeš}ig-[x] ba-ab-šeš$_4$ u$_4$ **é**-e im sumur ba-aka, "½ liter of mutton fat (with which) the back of the [x] door was oiled when the house was plastered," 1319:1–4

4.1.3 For Baking Bread and Cooking Soup

24 sa gi-[izi] ninda ba-ra-⸢du$_8$⸣ 10 sa gi-[izi] tu$_7$ [ba]-ra-⸢šeĝ$_6$⸣ u$_4$ **é**-e im sumur ⸢ba⸣-aka, "24 bundles of [fuel] reeds, with which bread was baked, (and) 10 bundles of [fuel] reeds, with which soup was cooked, when the house was plastered," 473:1–5

4.1.4 For Builders

[n.n].1[+n].6½ [sìla ì-ĝeš gur] 4? sìla 5 gín [ì-šaḫ] ì-ba šidim-e-[ne] u$_4$ **é**-e im sumur ba-aka, "[n bushel(s) (and) n]+16½ [liters of sesame oil] (and) 4? liters (and) 5 shekels [of lard], oil rations of the builders when the house was plastered," 482:1–4

4.1.5 For Household Servants and Hired Workers

0.1.0.8 sìla ninda-g[al-gen] 1 sìla [du$_8$] 0.0.5.4 sìla kaš-gen 0.0.5.4 sìla zú-lum ⸢ĝuruš⸣ árad-é-a ù lú-ḫuĝ-ĝá-e-ne ba-na-ḫa-la u$_4$ **é**<-e> im sumur <ba->aka, "68 liters of [ordinary] large bread [baked] (in) 1 liter (loaves), 54 liters of ordinary beer (and) 54 liters of dates were divided for the household servants and hired workers when the house was plastered," 471:1–5

4.1.6 For the Man who Brought Fish from Du-lugal-pa'e

3 sìla ninda lú ku$_6$ du$_6$-lugal-pa-è^{ki}-ta de$_6$-a u$_4$ **é**-e im sumur ba-aka, "3 liters of bread (for) the man who brought fish from Du-lugalpa'e when the house was plastered," 476:1–4

4.1.7 For the Men from *Bit-Šu-Suen*

[n sìl]a níĝ-àr-r[a-sig$_5$ t]u$_7$-šè lú-é-^{d}*šu*-^{d}E[N.ZU]^{ki}-ke$_4$-ne ba-na-ḫa-la u$_4$ [**é**]-e [im sumur ba-aka], "[n] liter(s) of [fine] barley groats for soup were divided among the men from *Bit-Šu-Suen* when [the house was plastered]," 391:1–5

4.1.8 For Ox-Drivers

0.3.0. še šà-gu$_4$-me-éš dirig še-ba-ne-ne mu zì nu-ĝál-la-šè ba-na-ḫa-la *šu-kab-tá* bí-in-dug$_4$ (. . .) u$_4$ **é**-e i[m sumur ba-aka], "180 liters of barley for the ox-drivers when the house was plastered. *Šu-Kabta* had ordered that additional barley rations were to be divided for them because there was no flour. {Authorizing official}," 481:1–4, 6

4.1.9 A Tablet Coffer

1 ^{gi}bisaĝ-im-sar-ra [sa-ḫ]a ⅔ kùš íb-sá im-sar ĝá-ĝá-dè u$_4$ **é**-[e] im sumur ba-aka, "1 canvas-lined clay tablet coffer—it is ⅔ kùš square—(in which) to deposit clay tablets when the house was plastered," 1318:1–3

4.1.10 Workers Traveling to *Bit-Šu-Suen*

0.0.2.6 sìla ninda ^{kuš}a-ĝá-lá kéše-rá ĝuruš nam–60 *a*-⸢*bu*⸣-DU$_{10}$ u$_4$ é-^{d}*šu*-^{d}*suen*^{ki}-šè i-⸢re⸣-ša-a u$_4$ **é**-e im sumur ba-aka, "26 liters of bread in bound leather sacks (for) *Abu-ṭabu*, the overseer of 60 workmen, when (his workers) went to *Bit-Šu-Suen* when the house was plastered," 480:1–3

4.2 Provisions when the (Enclosure) Wall Behind the House was Constructed

4.2.1 For Builders

(. . .) šà-gal šidim-e-ne ⸢u$_4$⸣ bàd eger **é**-a dù-dè, "{assorted comestibles}, food (for) builders when they were constructing the (enclosure) wall behind the house," 386:29–30, 387:20–21

4.2.2 For Builders, the Overseer of Hired Workers (and) the Messenger of *Šu-Kabta*

(. . .) šà-gal šidim-e-ne 5 sìla ninda ugula lú-ḫuĝ-ĝá-e-ne íb-gu$_7$ 3 sìla ^{lú}kíĝ-gi$_4$-a *šu-kab-ta* 1 sìla dabin ½ sìla eša dub-dub-dè bà[d egi]r **é**-a dù-dè, "{assorted grains}, food (for) builders; the overseer of hired workers ate 5 liters of bread, 3 liters (of bread for) the messenger of *Šu-Kabta* (and) 1 liter of semolina (and) ½ liter of fine flour for heaping, (provisions of workers) to construct the (enclosure) wall behind the house," 385:5–9

4.2.3 For Builders, Servants, Hired Workers, and their Overseer

(. . .) šà-gal šidim-e-ne (. . .) árad-é-[a lú-ḫuĝ]-ĝá ù ugula lú-[ḫuĝ-ĝá-e-n]e íb-gu$_7$ [1] sìla dabin ½ sìla eša zì-dub-dub-šè u$_4$ bàd **é**-a dù-dè, "{assorted grains} food (for) builders; the servants, hired workers and overseer of the hired workers ate {assorted grains} (and) 1 liter of semolina (and) ½ liter of fine flour for the small heap of flour, (provisions of workers) when they were constructing the (enclosure) wall of the house," 383:5, 8–11

5. Other

5.1 Fodder for Pigs, Counted in the House

[šà-ga]l šáḫ-[ú] **é**-a šid-da, "fodder of [range-fed] pigs, counted in the house," 1189:'14-'16

5.2 The Houses of the Gardeners

[*ak-b*]*a-zum* nu-^{ĝeš}kiri$_6$-⸢ke$_4$⸣ má-lugal-na saḫar tùm-dè zabala$_4$^{ki}-šè in-la-aḫ saḫar mu-un-de$_9$ ^{ĝeš}kiri$_6$-lugal-na-šè nu-un-ni-ku$_4$ **é**-ni-šè ba-an-dé ka-ga-na ba-ge-en, "*Akbazum*, the gardener, confirmed that they took a boat of his master to Zabala in order to bring dirt, that he brought the dirt, that it did not enter the royal garden but was brought for his (own) house," 1049:1–10

^{d}ba-ú-da [nu]-^{ĝeš}kiri$_6$-ke$_4$ má-lugal-na saḫar tùm-dè zabala$_4$^{ki}-šè in-la-aḫ saḫar mu-un-de$_9$ ^{ĝeš}kiri$_6$-lugal-na nu-un-ni-ku$_4$ **é**-ni-šè ba-an-dé ka-ga-na ba-ge-en, "Ba'uda, the gardener, confirmed that they took a boat of his master to Zabala in order to bring dirt, that he brought the dirt, that it did not enter the royal garden but was brought for his (own) house," 1050:1–10

5.3 New Home Owners

0.0.1.2? sìla ninda-gal-gen 1 sìla du$_8$ [u$_4$ l]ú **é**-ne-ne ba-an-ši-sa$_{10}$-a íb-gu$_7$, "The men who bought their houses ate 12? liters of ordinary large bread baked (in) 1-liter (loaves)," 491:1–3

5.4 Persons Associated with the House

5.4.1 Bird Wardens

da-da-a sipa-mušen-na **é**-[a . . .] *šu*-^{d}na-zi sipa-mušen-na **é**-[a . . .], "*Dada*, the bird warden of the house, [. . .] *Šu*-Nazi, the bird warden of the house, [. . .]," 1253:'6-'7

5.4.2 Daughters of the House

a-ga-ti dumu-munus **é**-a, "*Agati*, daughter of the house" > *Personal Name Index*

um-mi-kab-tá dumu-munus **é**-a, "*Ummi-Kabta*, daughter of the house" > *Personal Name Index*

5.4.3 Household Servants

árad-**é**-a, "household servant," *passim*

géme-árad-**é**-a, "female and male household servants" > *passim*

g̃uruš šidim árad-**é**-a, "household builder" > **árad**

ugula árad-**é**-a, "overseer of household servants" > **árad**

5.4.3.1 Rations for Household Servants

5.0.1. [še gur] ninda-ba géme-⸢árad⸣ **é**-[a], "5 bushels (and) 10 liters of [barley], bread rations of female and male household servants," 468:1–2

(. . .) [šu+níg̃in n+]7.0.0. gur še-ba *ba-zi-tum* šu+níg̃in 47.1.[n.] še-ba **é** [šu+níg̃in 60+]31.1.5. gu[r], "{barley for individuals}; [in total: n+]7 bushels of the barley rations of *Bazitum*, in total: 47 bushels (and) 60[+n] liters of barley rations of the household; [in total 60+]31 bushels (and) 110 liters," 555:24–28

5.5 In Reference to the Tower of the Zabala Garden

2 g̃uruš šidim [im] šu dím-ma sum-mu-dè 2 g̃uruš im ga_6-g̃á 2 g̃uruš im lu-a 3 g̃uruš a bal-a-e-dè 8 g̃uruš saḫar šà **é**-a sè-gé-dè im sumur aka an-za-qar-[g̃eš]$kiri_6$-$zabala_4$[ki], "2 builders to hand [earth] for building, 2 workmen having carried earth, 2 workmen having mixed earth, 3 workmen to pour water, 8 workmen to tamp dirt in the house, (workers) having plastered the tower of the Zabala garden," 202:14–21

5.6 Supplies Brought from the House

šar-ru-um-ì-lí ù-na-a-du_{11} [x]-g̃ál-la [x?] **é**-za ì-g̃ál é-ki-ba-g̃ar-ra du_8-dè [d]*adad-tillati* ḫé-na-ab-sum-mu a-ba šeš-$g̃u_{10}$-gin_7, "Say to *Šarrum-ili* that '(?) that is in your house should be given to *Adad-tillati* in order to caulk the replacement house. Who is like my brother?'" 1526:1–7

6. Broken Context

4 [g̃uruš] 4 [géme] gi-sal-la? **é**-[. . . gul-dè gub-ba], "4 [workmen] (and) 4 [workwomen employed to trim] thin reeds at the house [of. . .]," 49:46–48

[n g̃u]ruš šidim 1 g̃uruš **é**?-šè 5 x-[. . .], "[n] builder(s) (and) 1 workman [. . .] for the house?," 97:'8

**[n] g̃uruš [. . .] é?-a im-[. . .] ⸢x⸣ ba-al-dè, 106:36

1 g̃uruš šidim gi-sal šà **é**-a gul-la [1] g̃uruš šidim $šeg_{12}$ ma šub-[ba] gub-ba [n+]5 g̃uruš [s]ahar šà **é**-a è-d[è n] g̃uruš [é-PN] dù-a, "1 builder having trimmed thin reeds in the house, [1] builder employed at the brick yard, [n+]5 workmen to extract dirt (from) inside the house (and) [n] workmen having constructed [the house of PN]," 191:26–33

4 g̃uruš ⸢šidim⸣ 5 g̃uruš ⸢dub⸣?-lá? šà **é-[a] lá-[a] x, 194:39–41

1 x?-e?-da **é-[. . .] 15 [x], 1220:3–4

7. Broken Temple Names

7.1 é-^{d}x-SAḪAR

270 sar 13 gín šeg$_{12}$ ús-˹sa˺ i$_{7}$-*a*-˹*ga*˺-*mu-um* 60 sar 13 gín šeg$_{12}$ **é-^{d}[x]-SAḪAR** [NE?]-gu$_{7}$-bi ù PA [NE-gu$_{7}$]-bi nu-zi [šid-d]a šà ĝá šub-ba, "270 sar (and) 13 gín of bricks following the *Agamum* canal, 60 sar (and) 13 gín of bricks of the temple [DN], damaged bricks and damaged (?) not deducted; the count (of bricks) in the lot," 358:1–7

7.2 é-^{d}[. . .]

0.2.1.3⅓ sìla [. . . -g]en sa$_{10}$ ki-siki ½ [. . .]-kam ù **é-^{d}**[. . .], "133⅓ liters of ordinary [. . .] the (?) price of ½ [. . .] and the [DN] temple," 1391:1–2

é-a-(al-)lu-a

é-ki-ba-ĝar-ra ***al-lu-a***, "the replacement house of *Alu'a*" > **é-ki-ba-ĝar-ra**

1. Construction

[n ĝuruš šidim n] ĝuruš šu [dím n ĝuruš] in-u ga$_{6}$-[ĝá-dè n] géme šeg$_{12}$ šà é-a [. . .] ***é-a-*** **[*lu*]-*a***, "[n builders (and) n] workmen having built, [n workmen to] carry straw (and) [n] workwomen [. . .] bricks in the house, (work for) the house of *Alu'a*, 101:22–25

1 ĝuruš šidim 2 ĝuruš šu dím 10 géme im ga$_{6}$-ĝá ***é-a-al-lu-*[*a*]** dù-a, "1 builder (and) 2 workmen having built, 10 workwomen having carried earth, (workers) having constructed the house of *Alu'a*," 111:37–39

1.1 Mixing Earth

6 ĝuruš im lu-a 1 ĝuruš šidim 2 ĝuruš 6 géme ***é-a-lu-a*** gub-ba, "6 workmen having mixed earth (and) 1 builder, 2 workmen (and) 6 workwomen employed at the house of *Alu'a*," 102:24–26

1.2 Mixing Earth and Trimming Reeds

10 ĝuruš im *a-ĝá-ri-*[*na*] lu-dè [gub-ba] 3 ˹ĝuruš˺ 3 ˹géme˺ gi-sal-[la] ***é-al*<*-lu*>*-a*** g[ul-dè gub-ba], "10 workmen [employed] to mix earth in the *agarinnum* (and) 3 workmen (and) 3 workwomen [employed to] trim thin reeds, (work for) the house of *Alu'a*," 38:28–32

1.3 Plastering the Brick Stack

[2] ĝuruš šidim 10 ĝuruš 20 géme SIG$_{4}$.ANŠE im sumur aka 1 ĝuruš šidim 2 ĝuruš 10 géme ***é-a-lu-a***, "[2] builders, 10 workmen (and) 20 workwomen having plastered the brick stack (and) 1 builder, 2 workmen (and) 10 workwomen at the house of *Alu'a*," 110:26–29

1.4 Workers Employed at the House

1 ĝur[uš šidim n ĝur]uš 4 gém[e . . .] ***é-a-lu-a*** gub-ba, "1 builder, [n] workmen (and) 4 workwomen employed [. . .] at the house of *Alu'a*," 94:21–23

3 ĝuruš 10 géme ***é-a-lu-a*** gub-ba, "3 workmen (and) 10 workwomen employed at the house of *Alu'a*," 104:30–31, 105:29

1 ĝuruš ˹šidim˺ um-[mi-a] 2 ĝuruš [šidim . . .] ***é-a-*[*lu-a*** gub-ba], "1 master builder, 2 builders [. . .employed at] the house of *Alu'a*," 108:21–23

2. (De-)Construction

2.1 Demolishing the iz-zi Wall

5 g̃uruš 10 géme iz-zi šà é-a gul-la 1 g̃uruš 8 géme ***é-a-al-lu-a***, "5 workmen (and) 10 workwomen having demolished the iz-zi wall in the house (and) 1 workman (and) 8 workwomen at the house of *Alu'a*," 103:24–27

n guruš iz-zi ***é-a-lu-a*** gul-la, "n workmen having demolished the iz-zi wall of the house of *Alu'a*," 120:'32, 129:32

é-a-bí-a-ti

1. (De-)Construction

6 g̃uruš ašgab 8 g̃uruš [lú]ázlag 24 géme uš-bar u_4-1-šè al-tar ***é-a-bí-a-ti*** gul-dè gub-ba, "6 leather workers, 8 fullers (and) 24 female weavers employed for 1 day of construction to demolish the house of *Abi-ati*," 273:1–6

é-a-gu-a

1. Construction

1 g̃uruš šidim 16 g̃uruš 12 géme ***é-a-gu-a*** dù-a, "1 builder, 16 workmen (and) 12 workwomen having constructed the house of *Agua*," 163:26–27

[1] g̃uruš šidim um-mi-a [n g̃uruš šid]im 2 g̃uruš 12 géme **[é]**-***a-gu-a*** dù-a, "[1] master builder, [n] builder(s), 2 workmen (and) 12 workwomen having constructed the [house] of *Agua*," 175:20–22

é-a-lí-a-bi

é-ki-ba-g̃ar-ra ***a-lí-a-bi***, "the replacement house of *Ali-abi*" > **é-ki-ba-g̃ar-ra**

1. Construction

2 g̃uruš šu dí[m-ma] 1 g̃uruš šidim 2 g̃uruš 4 géme ***é-a-lí-a-bi*** dù-a, "2 workmen having built, 1 builder, 2 workmen (and) 4 workwomen having constructed the house of *Ali-abi*," 156:26–28

[n g̃uruš] šidim [n g̃uruš] 4 géme **[*é-a-lí*]*-a-bi*** dù-a, "[n] builder(s), [n workmen] (and) 4 workwomen having constructed the house of *Ali-abi*," 159:25–26

é-agrig, "the house of the steward"

1. Provisions for the Household

1.1 Dead Birds

2 $ir_7^{mušen}$ u_4-20-kam 2 $ir_7^{mušen}$ u_4-10-kam [ba]-úš **é-⌜agrig⌝**-šè, "2 pigeons on the 20th day (and) 2 pigeons on the 10th day were slaughtered for the house of the steward," 522:1–5

1 [$x^{mušen}$] 1 $ir_7^{mušen}$ u_4-20-kam 2 $ir_7^{mušen}$ 5 $tu\text{-}gur_4^{mušen}$ u_4-25-kam 1 $ir_7^{mušen}$ 1 $tum_{12}^{mušen}$ 5 $tu\text{-}gur_4^{mušen}$ [2 péš]-g̃eš-⌜gi⌝ u_4-28-kam ba-úš **é-agrig**-šè, "1 [bird] (and) 1 pigeon on the 20th day, 2 pigeons (and) 5 doves on the 25th day (and) 1 pigeon, 1 wild dove, 5 doves (and) [2] mice on the 28th day were slaughtered for the house of the steward," 526:1–12

1.2 Surplus of Regular Offerings

(. . .) dirig sá-du$_{11}$-**é-agrig**-šè, "{assorted comestibles}, surplus of the regular offerings for the house of the steward," 493:19, 494:17, 501:1–4

2. Translation Uncertain

★★^{d}*ma-lik-ba-ni* rá-gaba u$_{4}$-5-àm ki šà-ga-na-ka mu-un-til-la-⸢šè⸣ **é-agrig** i[n-x] ka-ga-na ba-a-[gen$_{7}$], 1054:1–6

é-*ba-ḫa-a*

1. Construction

[n] g̃uruš šidim 3 g̃uruš 10 géme **é-*ba-ḫa-a*** dù-a, "[n] builder(s), 3 workmen (and) 10 workwomen having constructed the house of *Baḫa'a*," 129:31

1.1 Construction of the Foundation

1 g̃uruš šidim 3 g̃uruš 3 géme ⸢uš⸣ **é-*ba-ḫa-a*** dù-a, "1 builder, 3 workmen (and) 3 workwomen having constructed the foundation of the house of *Baḫa'a*," 113:'8-'9

1.2 Mixing Adobe

2 g̃uruš 4 géme *dì-um* lu-dè gub-ba **é-*ba-ḫa-a*** gub-ba, "2 workmen (and) 4 workwomen employed to mix adobe, (workers) employed at the house of *Baḫa'a*," 84:19

1.3 Various Tasks

2 g̃uruš [šidim] 8 g̃uruš [šu dím] 1 géme *du-ú-um* [aka] 2 géme im gíd 17 géme im [ga$_{6}$-g̃á] **é-*ba-ḫa-a*** dù-[a], "2 [builders] (and) 8 workmen [having built], 1 workwoman [having made] a *du-ú-um*, 2 workwomen having hauled earth, 17 workwomen [having carried] earth, (workers) having constructed the house of *Baḫa'a*," 114:31–36

3 g̃uruš šidim 15 g̃uruš 30 [géme] SIG$_{4}$.ANŠE im sum[ur aka] 3 g̃uruš šidim 16 g̃uruš šu dím 34 géme im ga$_{6}$-g̃á al<-tar> **é-*ba-ḫa-a***, "3 builders, 15 workmen (and) 30 [workwomen] having plastered the brick stack, 3 builders (and) 16 workmen having built (and) 34 workwomen having carried earth, (for) construction of the house of *Baḫa'a*," 117:24–28

1.4 Workers Employed at the House

n g̃uruš **é-*ba-ḫa-a*** gub-ba, "n workmen employed at the house of *Baḫa'a*," 100:'15-'16, 101:33

é-báḫar, "potter's house"

1. Construction

3 [g̃uruš šidim] sumur iz-zi šà [é-a ù-ru-dè] 14 [g̃uruš] saḫar šà é-a è-[dè] 1 g̃uruš šidim 3 ⸢g̃uruš⸣ **é-báḫar** dù-a, "3 builders [to level] the plastered wall in [the house], 14 [workmen to] extract dirt (from) inside the house (and) 1 builder (and) 3 workmen having constructed the potter's house," 190:22–27

é-*bí-za-a*

é-ki-ba-g̃ar-ra ***bí-za-a***, "the replacement house of *Biza'a*" > **é-ki-ba-g̃ar-ra**

1. (De-)Construction

2 ⸢g̃uruš⸣ **é-*bí-za-a*** iz-zi gul-la, "2 workmen having demolished the iz-zi wall of the house of *Biza'a*," 108:34–35

é-*da-da*

é-ki-ba-g̃ar-ra ***da-da***, "the replacement house of *Dada*" > **é-ki-ba-g̃ar-ra**

1. Provisions for the Caretaker of the House

0.1.0. še 4 ma-na siki-gen ½ sìla ì-šáḫ 5 sìla zì-kum 5 sìla zú-lum udug **é-*da-da*** dumu *na-sìm*, "60 liters of barley, 4 minas of ordinary wool, ½ liter of lard, 5 liters of kum-flour (and) 5 liters of dates (for) the caretaker of the house of *Dada*, son of *Nasim*," 438:1–6

é-dam-*zé-ra-ra*

1. The Visit of *Šu-Kabta* for the Inventory

1 g̃uruš ^{lú}ázlag nibru^{ki}-ta ^{d}*šu*-^{d}*suen*-DU$_{10}$^{ki}-šè ^{uruduš}im-da gu$_4$-udu de$_6$-a kaskal šu+níg̃in-na-bi u$_4$-11-kam u$_4$ *šu-kab-tá* **é-dam-*zé-ra-ra*** šu sum-mu-dè ì-g̃en-na-a "1 fuller having brought a sheep and cattle brand from Nippur to *Šu-Suen-ṭabu*, a trip of 11 days in total, when *Šu-Kabta* went to the house of the wife of *Zerara* in order to take inventory," 219:1–10

é-didli, "various houses"

1. Construction of the Bathroom

1.1 Digging the Bathrooms

6 g̃uruš du$_{10}$-ús ⸢**é?-didli**⸣? kíg̃-til ba-al, "6 workmen having completed the work of digging the bathrooms of various? houses?" 158:40

1.2 Repair of the Bathrooms

7.4.0. ésir-ḫád gur 0.0.4.6 sìla ésir-é-a 0.0.0.7 sìla ì-ḫur-sag̃-g̃á ⸢*šit*⸣-*tum* é-lùnga ⸢*šit*⸣-*tum* é-kìšib-ba ugula kíkken [?] du$_{10}$-ús **é-didli** *ták-si-*[*ru-um*]-šè ba-a-g̃ar, "7 bushels (and) 240 liters of dried bitumen, 46 liters of house bitumen (and) 7 liters of mountain fat, the balance (of the settled account) of the brewery (and) of the warehouse, placed (in the account of) the overseer of the mill for repair of the bathrooms of various houses," 1260:1–4

é-*du-gu-a*

1. Construction

1 g̃uruš šidim 1 g̃uruš šu dím 3 géme *dì-um* [g̃á]-g̃á-dè [gub-ba] **é-*du-gu-a*** [. . .] é-g̃ar-r[a x?], "1 builder (and) 1 workman having built (and) 3 workwomen [employed] to place wattle and daub, (work for) the house of *Dugu'a* [. . .], 210:'29-'32

2. (De-)Construction

10-lá-1 g̃uruš iz-zi **é-*du-gu*-[*a*?]** gul-dè gub-ba, "9 workmen employed to demolish the iz-zi wall of the house of *Dugu'a*," 58:54–55

é-du$_6$-gur$_4$-*i-din*-^{d}*adad*, "round-hill-house of *Iddin-Adad*"

1. A Boat Towed from Garšana to the House

9 ĝuruš gar-ša-an-na^{ki}-ta adab^{ki}-šè má gíd-da **é-du$_6$-gur$_4$-*i-din*-^{d}*adad***-šè, "9 workmen having towed a boat from Garšana to Adab, to the round-hill-house of *Iddin-Adad*," 207:23–25

é-en-^{d}inana-gal, "house of the senior priest of Inana"

é-ki-ba-ĝar-ra **é-en-^{d}inana-gal**, "the replacement house of the senior priest of Inana" > **é-ki-ba-ĝar-ra**

é-gal, *ekallum*, "palace"

1. Construction

1.1 Repair

3 ĝuruš šidim 6 ĝuruš *ták-si-ru-um* šà **é-gal** gub-ba, "3 builders (and) 6 workmen employed (for) repair in the palace," 35:33

1 ĝuruš šidim 1 ĝuruš n géme *ták-ši-ru-um* šà **é-gal**-ka gub-ba, "1 builder, 1 workman (and) n workwomen employed (for) repair in the palace," 49:43–45, 120:'30-'31, 150:38–39

1 ĝuruš šidim um-mi-a n ĝuruš šidim n ĝuruš n géme *ták-si-ru-um* šà **é-gal** gub-ba, "1 master builder, n builder(s), n workmen (and) n workwomen employed (for) repair in the palace," 59:21–24, 65:'7-'9, 66:'1-'3, 71:18–20

2 ĝuruš [šidim] 2 ĝuruš [. . .] *ták-ši-ru-u*[*m* šà **é-gal** gub-ba], "2 [builders] (and) 2 workmen [. . . employed] (for) repair [in the palace]," 60:21–23

1 ĝuruš šidim *ták-si-ru-um* šà **é-gal** gub-⌜ba⌝, "1 builder employed (for) repair in the palace," 92:17, 209:22–23

1 ĝuruš šidim um̩-mi-a 1 ĝuruš šidim *ták-si-ru-um* šà **é-gal**-ka, "1 master builder (and) 1 builder (for) repair in the palace," 151:22–23, 152:'5-'6, 154:24–25

1 ĝuruš šidim um-mi-a 1 ĝuruš šidim *ták-si-ru-um* šà **é-gal**-k[a gub]-⌜ba⌝, "1 master builder (and) 1 builder employed (for) repair in the palace," 153:'18-'19

n ĝuruš šidim *ták-si-ru-um* šà **é-gal**, "n builder(s) (for) repair in the palace," 155:22, 156:31, 163:30, 174:27, 175:25, 200:'10, 201:'7-'8, 202:22–23, 203:22–23

1 ĝuruš šidim um-mi-a 10 ĝuruš *ták-si-ru-um* šà **é-gal**, "1 master builder (and) 10 workmen (for) repair in the palace," 161:'11-'12

1.2 Construction of Structures in the Palace

1.2.1 The Barracks

1 ĝuruš ⌜šidim⌝ 8 ĝuruš é-*gi-na-tum* šà **é-[gal]**, "1 builder (and) 8 workmen at the barracks in the palace," 205:18–20

1.2.2 The Double Dike

2 ĝuruš šà **é-gal**-la ke$_4$-dè gub-ba, "2 workmen employed to make (a double dike?) in the palace," 21:'26

1 ĝuruš šidim 3 ĝuruš ég-tab šà **é-gal**-la ke$_4$-dè gub-ba, "1 builder (and) 3 workmen employed to make a double dike in the palace," 28:'14

[n g̃uruš] šidim ég-tab šà **é-gal**-la ke$_4$-dè gub-ba, "[n] builder(s) employed to make a double dike in the palace," 29:'22

1.2.3 The Roof

2 g̃uruš šidim ùr **é-gal** a g̃á-g̃á, "2 builders having waterproofed the roof of the palace," 110:'30, 111:29, 112:'10, 113:'7, 114:41–42, 117:23, 121:33

[n g̃u]ruš šidim 2 g̃uruš 10 géme ùr **é-[gal** a] g̃[á-g̃á], "[n] builder(s), 2 workmen (and) 10 workwomen [having waterproofed] the roof [of the palace]," 146:'41

1.2.4 The Roof of the New Palace

[. . . n g̃ur]uš [. . . n+]4 g̃uruš šidim [n] g̃uruš im ì-li-de$_9$ gub-ba [n] g̃uruš 25 géme im ga$_6$ [ùr **é-gal** gib]il a g̃á-g̃á, "[. . . n] workmen [. . .], [n+]4 builders (and) [n] workmen employed to lift earth (and) [n] workmen (and) 25 workwomen having carried earth, (workers) having waterproofed [the roof of the] new [palace]," 74:'1-'6

[1 g̃uruš šidi]m um-[mi]-a [1 g̃uru]š šidim 1 g̃uruš šu d[ím gub-ba] 23 g̃uruš 20-lá–1 géme im sumur ga$_6$-g̃á-⌜dè⌝ [gub-ba] 7 g̃uruš im sumur lu-dè gub-ba ùr **é-gal** gibil a g̃á-g̃[á-d]è gub-⌜ba⌝, "[1] master builder, [1] builder (and) 1 workman [employed] to build, 23 workmen (and) 19 workwomen [employed] to carry earth (and) 7 workmen employed to mix earth, (workers) employed to waterproof the roof of the new palace," 75:15–21

1.2.5 Broken Context

[n g̃uruš] 1 géme SIG$_4$.ANŠE [im sumur] ke$_4$-dè gub-ba [n g̃uruš] má-laḫ$_5$ 1 g̃uruš [im] ga$_6$-g̃á-dè [n g̃uruš x] x šà? **é?-gal** ke$_4$-dè, "[n workmen] (and) 1 workwoman employed to plaster the brick stack, [n] sailor(s) (and) 1 workman to carry [earth] (and) [n workmen] having made [x] in? the palace," 66:'10-'12

2. Deliveries to and from the Palace

2.1 Building Supplies: Bricks for its Cistern

a-za-bu-um šà **é-gal** mu-DU *šu*-^{d}dumu-zi, "delivery (of bricks for) the cistern in the palace by *Šu*-Dumuzi," 339:13–15

2.2 Offerings for Nin-Siana in the Palace

1 udu-niga gu$_4$-e-ús-[sa] ^{d}nin-^{d}si$_4$-an-na šà [**é**]-⌜**gal**⌝ iti u$_4$-6-ba-zal, "1 fattened sheep '(fed) following the oxen' (for) Nin-Siana in the palace at the end of the 6th day of the month," 970:7–9

2.3 Regular Offerings of *Simat-Ištaran* from the Palace

1 *mu-du-lum* udu-niga sag̃ u$_4$-sakar 1 *mu-du-lum* udu-niga é-u$_4$-15 sá-du$_{11}$ *simat*-^{d}*ištaran* **é-gal**-ta, "1 salted fattened sheep on the new moon day (and) 1 salted fattened sheep on the full moon day, regular offerings of *Simat-Ištaran* from the palace," 375:1–6

2.4 Wool Delivered for the Palace

★★(. . .) [. . .] kišib íb-ra é-kišib-ba-ta dub-bi in-du$_8$ siki bala-dè in-kéše **é-gal**-šè, "{assorted textiles}; he rolled the seal, baked its tablet in the warehouse, (and) bound up the wool to be baled (for) delivery for the palace," 609:11–14

3. Palace Employees: Provisions

0.0.4. ⅔ sìla [. . .àga]-ús **é-gal**-la gub-ba [íb]-gu$_7$ u[$_4$ m]á *ra-ba-tum* nibru^{ki}-ta gar-ša-an-na^{ki}-šè i[n-g]íd-sa-a, "The gendarme employed at the palace ate 4⅔ liters [. . .] when they towed the boat of *Rabatum* from Nippur to Garšana," 506:22–26

3.1 Employed at the Palace Gate

(. . .) maš-en-gag ^{lú}kaš$_4$ ká-**é-gal**-ka gub-ba ⌜*simat*⌝-^{d}*ištaran* íb-gu$_7$ u$_4$ má-*simat*-^{d}*ištaran* é-^{d}šára-ta gar-ša-an-na^{ki}-šè mu-un-gíd-ša-a, "The *muškenu* (and?) the runner, stationed by *Simat-Ištaran* at the gate of the palace, ate {soup} when they towed the boat of *Simat-Ištaran* from the Šara temple to Garšana," 529:13–18

0.0.2.6 sìla <ninda->šu-ra-gen ½ sìla du$_8$ maš-en-gag ká-**é-gal**-ka gub-ba íb-gu$_7$, "The *muškenu* employed at the gate of the palace ate 26 liters of ordinary half(-loaf) <bread> baked (in) ½ liter (loaves)," 541:17–18

3.2 Millers, Sick at the Palace

10 gín ì-ĝeš-ta ^{d}šára-sá-ĝu$_{10}$ 1 bu-za-du-a géme kíkken-me-éš u$_4$ dú-ra i-me **é-gal**!-šè, "10 shekels of sesame oil each (for) Šara-saĝu (and) Buzadua, female millers, when they were sick at the palace," 466:3–7

é-gašam(-e-ne), "craftsmen's house"

é-uš-bar ù **é-gašam-e-ne**, "textile mill and craftsmen's house" > **é-uš-bar ù é-gašam-e-ne**

1. Construction Work

2 ĝuruš šidim 3 ĝuruš šu dím-ma gub-ba 10-lá-1 géme im ga$_6$-ĝá-dè gub-ba 2 ĝuruš im ì-li-dè gub-ba iz-zi im sumur ke$_4$-dè **é-gašam-e-ne**-šè, "2 builders (and) 3 workmen employed to build, 9 workwomen employed to carry earth (and) 2 workmen employed to lift earth, (workers) to plaster the iz-zi wall for the craftsmen's house," 53:30–33

[n] ĝuruš šidim [n] ĝuruš šu dím-ma gub-ba [n ĝuruš] im ga$_6$-dè gub-ba [n ĝuruš im ì]-li-de$_9$ gub-ba [. . .] ke$_4$-dè [. . . **é]-gašam**, "[n] builder(s) (and) [n] workmen employed to build, [n workmen] employed to carry earth, [n] workmen employed to lift [earth] (and) [. . .] to make [. . .], (work for) the craftsmen's [house]," 66:'4-'9

1.1 Workmen Sitting (Idle) at the Gate

[n] ĝuruš ká **é-gašam** tuš-a, "[n] workmen having sat (idle) at the gate of the craftsmen's house," 71:31, 74:'10, 75:30

1.2 Broken Context

[. . .]-**gašam**, 66:'9

2. Building Supplies: Bricks

é-NUN.ME.TA[G-e-ne-šè] mu-[DU] šál-maḫ [ugula lú-ḫuĝ-ĝá], "delivery (of bricks) [for] the craftsmen's house by Šal-maḫ, [overseer of hired workers]," 325:18–20

é-gašam-e-ne mu-DU *za-la-a* ugula lú-ḫuĝ-ĝá, "delivery (of bricks for) the craftsmen's house by *Zala'a*, overseer of hired workers," 330:27–29

é-gašam-e-ne mu-DU *ba-zi*, "delivery (of bricks) for the craftsmen's house by *Bazi*," 334:65–66

é-géme-tur

1. Construction

n ĝuruš šidim n ĝuruš n géme **é-géme-tur** dù-a, "n builder(s), n workmen (and) n workwomen having constructed the house of Geme-tur," 156:29–30, 159:29–30, 160:'9-'10

é-*gi-na-tum*, *šutummu*, "barracks"

1. The Billi'a Gate Barracks: Erection of a Brick Stack

[n] ĝuruš 21 géme [SIG$_4$].ANŠE ĝá-ĝá [1]8 géme im ⸢ga$_6$⸣-ĝá ⸢gú⸣-i$_7$-[*a*]-*ga-mu-um*-ta **é-*gi-na-tum*** ká-bil-[lí]-a-šè, "[n] workmen (and) 21 workwomen having placed the brick stack (and) [1]8 workwomen having carried earth from the bank of the *Agamum* canal to the Billi'a gate barracks," 208:13–19

2. The Dedali'a Gate Barracks

2.1 Construction: Moving Dirt

n ĝuruš saḫar zi-ga **é-*gi-na-tum*** ká-dedal-i-a, "n workmen having moved dirt at the Dedali'a gate barracks," 206:22–23, 207:22, 209:19–21

2.2 Building Supplies: Reeds

45 sa gi-izi gi-ka-du-šè **é-*gi-na-tum*** ká-dedal-lí-a-⸢šè⸣ ba-a-⸢ĝar⸣, "45 bundles of fuel reeds were placed for a reed shelter for the Dedali'a gate barracks," 1324:1–3

300 [sa] gi-izi gu-níĝin-[bi n] sa-ta gi-sal$_4$(!)-la [**é**]-***gi-na-tum*** ká-dedal-[lí]-a-šè ba-a-ĝar, "300 [bundles] of fuel reeds, bales of [n] bundle(s) each, thin reeds, were placed for the Dedali'a gate barracks," 1325:1–3

3. The Garden Barracks: Repair

1 ĝuruš šidim *ták-ši-ru-um* **é-*gi-na-tum*** šà ^{ĝeš}kiri$_6$ gub-[ba], "1 builder employed (for) repair of the barracks in the garden," 92:18

[n] ĝuruš ši[dim n] ĝuruš ⸢*ták*⸣-*si-ru-um* **é-*gi-na*-⸢*tum*⸣** ⸢^{ĝeš}⸣[kiri$_6$], "[n] builder(s) (and) [n] workmen (for) repair of the garden barracks," 205:30–32

4. The Garšana Garden Barracks: Repair

n ĝuruš šidim n ĝuruš n géme *ták-ši-ru-um* **é-*gi-na-tum*** ^{ĝeš}kiri$_6$ gar-ša-an-na^{ki} gub-ba, "n builder(s), n workmen (and) n workwomen employed (for) repair of the Garšana garden barracks," 50:3–7, 59:25–30, 60:24–26

[1] ĝuruš šidim 1 ĝuruš 4 [géme *ták-si-ru-um*] **é-*gi-na-tum*** ^{ĝeš}kiri$_6$ [gar-š]a-an-na^{ki} a ĝá-[ĝá], "[1] builder, 1 workman (and) 4 [workwomen (for) repair], (workers) having waterproofed the Garšana garden barracks," 65:'10-'11

[n] ĝuruš šidim [n ĝuru]š šu dím-[ma *ták-ši*]-*ru-um* **é-*gi-na-tum*** [^{ĝeš}kiri$_6$] gar-ša-an-na^{ki} gub-ba, "[n] builder(s) (and) [n] workmen having built, (workers) employed (for) repair of the Garšana [garden] barracks," 75:22–25

1 ĝuruš šidim 1 ĝuruš ⸢*ták*⸣-*si-ru-um* **é-[*gi-na-tum*** ^{ĝeš}]kiri$_6$ gar-[ša-an]-na^{ki}, "1 builder (and) 1 workman (for) repair of the Garšana garden barracks," 206:18–20

5. The Palace Barracks

1 ĝuruš ⸢šidim⸣ 8 ĝuruš **é-*gi-na-tum*** šà é-[gal], "1 builder (and) 8 workmen at the barracks in the palace," 205:18–20

6. Barracks, Location Unspecified: Building Supplies

190 sa gi-izi 60 ^{gi}kid-maḫ 30 ^{gi}dur-gazi a-rá–2-tab-ba gíd–1½ nindan-ta 7 gi-guru$_5$ a-rá–3-tab-ba ***é-gi-na-tum***-šè ba-a-ĝar, "190 bundles of fuel reeds, 60 large reed mats, 30 9-meter 2-ply gazi ropes (and) 7 triple reedwork panels were placed for the barracks," 1328:1–5

é-^{ĝeš}gu-za, "chair house"

1. Provisions for *Šu-Kabta*'s Chair House

[. . . zi]-ga **é-^{ĝeš}gu-za** šu-kab-tá-me-šè, "{assorted commodities} expended for *Šu-Kabta*'s chair house," 562:'76

2. A Waterskin

1 [^{kuš}ED]IN.A.LÁ **é-$^{<ĝeš>}$gu-za**-šè, "1 waterskin for the chair house," 925:'15

é-gul, "demolished house"

1. Broken Context

[. . .] **é-gul** ⸢iti⸣-u$_4$-18 ba-zal (. . .) sá-du$_{11}$-diĝir-re-e-ne, "[. . .] the demolished house at the end of the 18th day of the month, {assorted comestibles}, regular offerings of the gods," 1036:'1-'4, '78

é-ḫa-bi-ṣa-nu-um

1. Construction of the House

n ĝuruš šidim n ĝuruš n géme ***é-ḫa-bi-ṣa-nu-um*** (dù-a), "n builder(s), n workmen (and) n workwomen (having constructed) the house of *Ḫabiṣanum*," 159:23–24, 160:'11-'12

2. Construction of its iz-zi Wall

5 [ĝuruš] iz-zi ***é-ḫa-bi-ṣa-nu-um*** dù-a, "5 [workmen] having constructed the iz-zi wall of the house of *Ḫabiṣanum*," 158:30–31

é-ḫa-bu-ra-tum

1. Construction

2 [ĝuruš] šidim 3 ĝuruš ***é-ḫa-bu-ra-tum*** é-mušen-na dù-dè gub-ba, "2 builders (and) 3 workmen employed to construct the house of *Ḫaburatum* (and) the bird house," 9:24–25

é-ḫu-lu-lu

1. Construction

n ĝuruš šidim n ĝuruš n géme ***é-ḫu-lu-lu*** dù-a, "n builder(s), n workmen (and) n workwomen having constructed the house of *Ḫululu*," 163:24–25, 173:25–26, 174:24–25

2. Building Supplies

[n] ĝeš ùr ásal 140 sa gi-izi ***é-ḫu-lu-lu***, "[n] poplar roof beam(s) (and) 140 bundles of fuel reeds (for) the house of *Ḫululu*," 1309:1–3

é-i-ti-rum

1. Construction

n g̃uruš šidim n g̃uruš n géme ***é-i-ti-rum*** dù-a, "n builder(s), n workmen (and) n workwomen having constructed the house of *Itirum*," 158:32–33, 161:'15-'16, 162:22–23

é-ì-lí-bi-šu

1. Construction

1.1 Carrying and Mixing Earth

1 g̃uruš šidim 2 g̃uruš šu dím-ma 3 g̃uruš im ga$_{6}$-g̃á 2 g̃uruš im *a-ga-ri-in-na* tuš-a 1 g̃uruš a bal-a al-tar ***é-ì-lí<-bi>-šu***, "1 builder (and) 2 workmen having built, 3 workmen having carried earth, 2 workmen having sat (idle) at the *agarinnum* (and) 1 workman having poured water, (for) construction of the house of *Ili-bišu*," 202:24–29

1 g̃uruš šidim 2 g̃uruš šu dím-ma 3 g̃uruš im ga$_{6}$-g̃á 2 g̃uruš im lu-a 1 g̃uruš a bal-a-e-⸢dè⸣ al-tar ***é-ì-lí-bi-šu***, "1 builder (and) 2 workmen having built, 3 workmen having carried earth, 2 workmen having mixed earth, 1 workman to pour water, (for) construction of the house of *Ili-bišu*," 203:24–29

7 ⸢g̃uruš⸣ SIG$_{4}$.ANŠE i[m su]mur aka 1 g̃uruš šidim 2 g̃uruš šu dím 6 g̃uruš im ga$_{6}$-g̃á 2 g̃uruš im lu-a 2 g̃uruš a bal-a 1 g̃uruš in-u ga$_{6}$-g̃á im lu-a ***é-ì-lí-bi-šu***, "7 workmen having plastered the brick stack, 1 builder (and) 2 workmen having built, 6 workmen having carried earth, 2 workmen having mixed earth, 2 workmen having poured water (and) 1 workman having carried straw (for) mixing (with) earth, (work for) the house of *Ili-bišu*," 204:'1-'9

1.2 Mixing and Carrying Adobe

1 g̃uruš šidim 6 g̃uruš im *dì-um* lu-a ***é-ì-lí-bi-šu***, "1 builder (and) 6 workmen having mixed adobe, (work for) the house of *Ili-bišu*," 207:15–17

1 g̃uruš šidim 6 g̃uruš im [*dì*]-*um* g[a$_{6}$-g̃]á ***[é]-ì-lí-b[i-š]u*** dù-a, "1 builder (and) 6 workmen having carried the adobe mix, (workers) having constructed the house of *Ili-bišu*," 209:16–18

é-ki-ba-g̃ar-ra, "replacement house"

1. The Replacement House

1.1 Construction

[n g̃u]ruš šidim ma šub-ba šeg$_{12}$-al-ur$_{x}$-ra [n g̃u]ruš šidim ma šub-ba šeg$_{12}$ gub-ba [n g̃u]ruš šidim **é-ki-ba-g̃ar-ra** [dù]-dè gub-ba, "[n] builder(s) (to mold) bricks at the brickyard, [n] builder(s) employed at the brick yard (and) [n] builder(s) employed to [construct] the replacement house," 88:5–7

[. . .] **é-ki-ba-[g̃ar]-ra** dù-a, "[. . .] having constructed the replacement house," 215:'3

1.2 Building Supplies

šar-ru-um-ì-lí ù-na-a-du$_{11}$ [x]-g̃ál-la [x?] é-za ì-g̃ál **é-ki-ba-g̃ar-ra** du$_{8}$-dè ^{d}*adad-tillati* ḫé-na-ab-sum-mu a-ba šeš-g̃u$_{10}$-gin$_{7}$, "Say to *Šarrum-ili* that '(?) that is in your house should be given to *Adad-tillati* in order to caulk the replacement house. Who is like my brother?'" 1526:1–7

1.3 Provisions for Construction Workers and Home Owners

(. . .) lú-**é-ki-ba-g̃ar-ra** šidim ugula lú-ḫug̃-[g̃á . . .]-ka é-ka gub-ba [. . .]-e-ne, "{assorted breads} for the man of the replacement house, the builder, the overseer of the hired workers [. . .] of the house employed [. . .]," 485:5

0.0.1.2 sìla [. . .] 5 sìla ninda-sal-la-dabin lú é-ne-ne <**é-**>⸢**ki**⸣**-ba-gar-ra** sa$_{10}$-a, "12 liters of [. . .] (and) 5 liters of thin semolina bread (for) men having bought their houses as replacements," 487:1–4

2. The Replacement House of *Ali-abi*: Provisions for its Caretaker

0.1.0. še 1 sìla ì-g̃eš ⸢udug⸣ **é-ki-ba-g̃ar-ra** [*a-lí*]*-a-bi*, "60 liters of barley (and) 1 liter of sesame oil (for) the caretaker of the replacement house of *Ali-abi*," 1008:9–11

3. The Replacement House of *Alu'a*

3.1 Construction

1 g̃uruš šidim 4 g̃uruš 10-lá-1 géme **é-ki-ba-g̃ar-ra** *a-al-lu*, "1 builder, 4 workmen (and) 9 workwomen at the replacement house of *Alu'a*," 99:17–18

3.2 Baskets for its Caretaker

4 ^{gi}bisag̃-gíd-da-tur sa-ḫa gíd–2-kùš dag̃al–1-kùš udug **é-ki-ba-g̃ar-ra**-a *al-lu-a*-šè ba-a-g̃ar, "4 small, long, canvas-lined baskets, 2 kùš in length, 1 kùš in width, were placed for the caretaker of the replacement house of *Alu'a*," 1006:1–2

4. The Replacement House of *Biza'a*: Construction

[1] g̃uruš šidim um-m[i-a] 3 g̃uruš šidim 1 g̃uruš im lu-a gub-ba [11 gém]e im ga$_6$-[g̃á]-dè gub-ba [**é-ki-b**]**a-g̃ar-ra** ⸢*bí*⸣*-za-a* gub-ba, "[1] master builder, 3 builders, (and) 1 employed workman having mixed earth (and) [11] workwomen employed to carry earth, (workers) employed at the replacement house of *Biza'a*," 86:10–15

1 g̃uruš šidim um-mi-a 3 g̃uruš šidim **é-ki-ba-g̃ar-ra** *bí-za-a* gub-ba, "1 master builder (and) 3 builders employed at the replacement house of *Biza'a*," 87:7–10

5. The Replacement House of *Dada*: Building Supplies

[6]0 ^{gi}dur-gazi a-⸢rá⸣-2-tab-ba gíd 1½-nindan-ta 80 sa gi-izi **é-ki-ba-g̃ar-ra** *da-da*-šè ba-a-g̃ar, "[6]0 9-meter 2-ply gazi ropes (and) 80 bundles of fuel reeds were placed for the replacement house of *Dada*," 1378:'1-'4

6. The Replacement House of the Senior Priest of Inana

6.1 Construction

1 g̃uruš šidim 2 g̃uruš šu dím-ma gub-ba 5 g̃uruš 2 géme im ga$_6$-dè gub-ba **é-ki-ba-g̃ar-ra** en-^{d}inana-gal, "1 builder (and) 2 workmen employed to build (and) 5 workmen (and) 2 workwomen employed to carry earth, (work for) the replacement house of the senior priest of Inana," 78:10–13

2 g̃uruš šidim 3 g̃uruš šu dím-ma gub-ba 5 g̃uruš 2 géme im ga$_6$-dè gub-ba [**é**]**-ki-ba-g̃ar-ra** en-^{d}inana-gal, "2 builders (and) 3 workmen employed to build (and) 5 workmen (and) 2 workwomen employed to carry earth, (work for) the replacement house of the senior priest of Inana," 79:9–12

6.2 Building Supplies: Bricks

mu-DU **é-ki-ba-g̃ar-ra** en-^{d}inana-gal *ba-zi* ugula, "delivery (of bricks for) the replacement house of the senior priest of Inana by *Bazi*, the overseer," 337:30–33

7. The Replacement House of *Pišaḫ-ilum*: Building Supplies

<**é-**>⌜**ki**⌝**-ba-g̃ar-ra** *é-p[i_5-š]a-aḫ-*⌜*ilum*⌝ mu-⌜DU⌝ šu-^{d}dumu-zi ugula l[ú-ḫug̃-g̃á], "delivery (of bricks) for the replacement <house> of the house of *Pišaḫ-ilum* by *Šu*-Dumuzi, overseer of [hired] workers," 341:13–15

8. The Replacement House of *Puzur-rabi*: Building Supplies

é-ki-ba-g̃ar-ra *puzur$_4$-ra-bí* mu-DU *ba-zi* ugula ⌜lú⌝-ḫug̃-g̃á, "delivery (of bricks for) the replacement house of *Puzur-rabi* by *Bazi*, overseer of hired workers," 344:'25-'27

9. The Replacement House of *Šu-Eštar*: Building Supplies

240 g̃eš ùr ásal 30 sa gi-izi é-*šu-eš$_4$-tár* **é-ki-ba-g̃ar-ra**-šè ⌜ba⌝-a-g̃ar, "240 poplar roof beams (and) 30 bundles of fuel reeds were placed for the replacement house of *Šu-Eštar*," 1309:7–10

10. The Replacement House of *Ubarria*

10.1 Construction

1 g̃uruš šidim [šeg$_{12}$-a]l-ur$_x$-ra gub-ba 1 g̃uruš ma šub-ba še[g$_{12}$ gub-ba] 4 g̃uruš šidim [. . .] **é-ki-ba-g̃ar-ra** *u-bar-ri-a* tà-tà<-dè> gub-ba, "1 builder employed to (mold) bricks, 1 workman [employed] at the brickyard (and) 4 builders [. . .], (workers) employed to apply stucco to the replacement house of *Ubarria*," 89:6–8

10.2 Building Supplies: Wood and Reeds

(. . .) g̃eš ùr kéše-rá (. . .) g̃eš ká-šè ba-gul (. . .) gi-sal-šè ba-gul (. . .) **é-ki-ba-g̃ar-ra** é-*u-bar-ri-a*-šè ba-a-g̃ar, "{assorted woods}, roof beams having been bound, {assorted woods} were cut for gate timber, (and) {reeds} were trimmed for thin reeds, {building supplies} were placed for the replacement house of the house of *Ubarria*," 1286:5, 7, 8, 12, 1289:5, 7, 8, 12

10.3 Provisions for its Caretaker

0.1.0. še 4 ma-na siki-gen 1 sìla ì-šáḫ 5 sìla zì-kum 5 sìla zú-lum udug **é-ki-ba-g̃ar-ra** *u-bar-ri-a*, "60 liters of barley, 4 minas of ordinary wool, 1 liter of lard, 5 liters of kum-flour flour (and) 5 liters of dates (for) the caretaker of the replacement house of *Ubarria*," 1005:1–6

11. The Replacement House of *Ubarum*: Building Supplies

mu-DU **é-ki-ba-g̃ar-ra** *u-bar-um za-la-a* ugula lú-ḫug̃-g̃á, "delivery (of bricks for) the replacement house of *Ubarum* by *Zala'a*, overseer of hired workers," 343:11–14

12. The Replacement House of *Zakiti* and *Šu-Eštar*: Building Supplies

2 [g̃uruš ši]dim **é-ki-b[a-g̃]ar-ra** *za-ki-ti* ù *šu-eš$_4$-tár* dù-dè gub-ba, "2 builders employed to construct the replacement house of *Zakiti* and *Šu-Eštar*," 85:7–8

13. The Replacement House of Zuzutum: Building Supplies

[mu-DU **é]-ki-ba-g̃ar-ra** *z[u-zu-t]um ba-zi* [ugula l]ú-ḫug̃-g̃á, "[delivery] (of bricks) for the replacement [house] of *Zuzutum* by *Bazi*, [overseer] of hired workers," 342:83–85

(é-)ki-mur-ra, "the textile depository"

1. Construction

11 g̃uruš kíg̃ ésir!-ra **ki-**⌜**mu**⌝**-ra** dù-a, "11 workmen (for) bitumen work, (workers) having constructed the textile depository," 158:37

1 g̃uruš šidim šeg$_{12}$ ma šub-ba gub-˹ba˺ 1 g̃uruš šidim **é-ki-mu-ra** d[ù-a], "1 builder employed at the brick yard (and) 1 builder having constructed the textile depository," 194:35–38

8 g̃uruš sag̃-tag 2 g̃uruš á-⅔-ta ^{lú}ázlag-me-éš u$_4$-[1-šè] šeg$_{12}$ šu dím sum-mu-dè gub-ba al-tar **é-[ki-m]u-ra**, "8 full-time fullers (and) 2 fullers at ⅔ wages employed [for 1] day to hand (up) bricks (for) building, (for) construction of the textile depository," 242:1–5

1.1 Construction of the Roof

1 g̃uruš ˹šidim˺ šeg$_{12}$ ma šub-ba gub-ba 3 g̃uruš ˹ùr˺ **é-ki-mu-ra** dù-a, "1 builder employed at the brick yard (and) 3 workmen having constructed the roof of the textile depository," 198:'17-'18

1.2 Inspection of Workers Employed for Construction

kurum$_7$ aka al-tar **ki-mur-ra** gub-ba, "Inspection of (the work of workers) employed (for) construction of the textile depository," 72:28, 76:19, 77:10

2. Construction of its Structures

2.1 The Quay

[n] g̃uruš kar-**ki-mu-ra** dù-a, "[n] workmen having constructed the quay of the textile depository," 173:33, 174:32

6 g̃uruš im lu-a 10 g̃uruš kar-**ki-mu-ra** dù-a, "6 workmen having mixed earth (and) 10 workmen having constructed the quay of the textile depository," 163:31–32

[. . .] á [g̃uruš]-a 10 gín-ta g̃uruš-bi 4 u$_4$-1-šè še 6-sìla-ta ba-ḫug̃ saḫar zi-ga kar-**ki-mu-ra** si-ga, "[. . . workmen] wages of 10 shekels each, its workmen (equal) 4 workerdays, (workers) hired for 6 liters of barley each, having piled up excavated dirt at the quay of the textile depository," 354:1–5

2.2 The Reed Hut

2 g̃uruš šidim gi-sig **ki-mu-ra** im sumur ke$_4$-dè gub-ba, "2 builders employed to plaster the reed hut of the textile depository," 85:9–10

3. Building Supplies

3.1 Bricks

mu-˹DU˺ **ki-mur-ra**-šè *simat-é-a* [ugula] lú-[ḫug̃]-g̃á, "delivery (of bricks) for the textile depository by *Simat-Ea*, [overseer] of hired workers," 335:41–42

ki-mu-ra-šè mu-DU *za-la-a* ugula lú-ḫug̃-g̃á, "delivery (of bricks) for the textile depository by *Zala'a*, overseer of hired workers," 338:21–22

3.2 Wood, Ropes and Rushes for its Quay

[n+]13 ^{geš}ú-[bíl-lá] 120 ^{gi}dur dag̃al [a-r]á–3-tab-ba gíd 5 nindan-ta 40 gu-níg̃in ZI/ZI.ÉŠ kar-**ki-mu-ra**-šè ba-a-g̃ar, "[n+]13 (units) of charcoal wood, 120 30-meter 3-ply wide ropes, (and) 40 bales of rushes were placed for the quay of the textile depository," 1305:1–4

é-kíkken, "mill"

é-lùnga ù **é-kíkken**, "brewery and mill" > **é-lùnga ù é-kíkken**

é-lùnga é-muḫaldim ù **é-kíkken**, "brewery-kitchen-mill complex" > **Triple Complex**

1. **Construction**

[n g̃uruš] im lu-a gub-b[a . . . **é-HAR].HAR**-šè [. . .] gub-[ba], "[n workmen] employed to mix earth [. . .], (workers) employed [. . .] for the mill," 99:21–22

2. **Provisions**

2.1 **For Workwomen of the Mill**

[1] *za-a-za* [1] *a-na-a* [1] lu_5-zi-lá (indent) 8 [géme **é]-kíkken**-me-éš, "(provisions for) *Zaza*, *Ana'a*, (and) Luzila, 8 [workwomen] of the mill," 562:'1-'5

1.1.0. ninda gur še-ba *ḫa-la-ša* **é?-[kíkken?]** gub-ba, "1 bushel (and) 60 liters of bread, barley rations of *Ḫalaša*, employed in the [mill?]," 1527:19–20, 48–49

2.2 **For Workmen of the Mill of the Nin-Siana temple**

[n g]ín ì-g̃eš-ta 1 ma-na tuḫ-g̃eš-ì-ḫád-ta 0.0.1. ádda-udu-ta [½] sìla mun-ta [n] gín luḫ-lá-ta [1 a]d-da-kal-la [1] ur-[d]šul-pa-è [1] *ḫa-la-ša* (indent) 3 [g̃uruš? **é]-kíkken** é-[d]nin-[d]si_4-an-na-me-éš, "[n] shekel(s) of sesame oil each, 1 mina of dried sesame chaff each, 10 sheep carcasses each, [½] liter of salt each (and) [n] shekel(s) of luḫ-lá each, (provisions for) Ada-kala, Ur-Šulpa'e (and) *Ḫalaša*, 3 [workmen?] of the mill of Nin-Siana," 562:'6-'15

3. **The Overseer of the Mill**

20 g̃uruš [g̃eš]nimbar sumun te-[x? gub]-ba 2 g̃uruš šidim 7 g̃uruš $šeg_{12}$ šu dím-ma sum-mu-dè gub-ba 1 g̃uruš im gíd-dè gub-ba 3 g̃uruš 14 géme im ga_6-g̃á-dè gub-ba 1 g̃uruš im lu-dè gub-ba é-kìšib-ba ugula **kíkken**, "20 workmen employed to (?) old date palms, 2 builders (and) 7 workmen employed to hand (up) bricks for building, 1 workman employed to haul earth, 3 workmen (and) 14 workwomen employed to carry earth, 1 workman employed to mix earth, (work for) the warehouse (under the authority of?) the overseer of the mill," 36:20–25

1 g̃uruš šidim 3 g̃uruš 10 géme é-kìšib-ba ugula **kíkken** dù-a, "1 builder, 3 workmen (and) 10 workwomen having constructed the warehouse (under the authority of?) the overseer of the mill," 154:26–27

é-[g̃eš]$kiri_6$, "the garden house"

1. **Wood Stored in the Garden House**

(. . .) **é-[g̃eš]$kiri_6$**-a gub-ba, "{wood} stored in the garden house," 1256:39

g̃eš **é-⌜[g̃eš]$kiri_6$⌝**-a gub-ba šu-sum-ma [g̃eš]$kiri_6$ igi-érim-iri[ki], "wood stored in the garden house, the inventory of the Igi-erim-iri garden," 1375:45–46

é-kìšib-ba, "warehouse"

1. **Construction**

1.1 **Construction of the Roof**

1.1.1 **Binding Roof Beams**

2 [. . .] **é-kìšib-ba** [. . . g̃eš] ùr kéše-⌜rá⌝, "2 [(workers) . . .], (work for) the warehouse, [. . .] (workers) having bound roof beams," 49:51–52

1.1.2 Waterproofing

1 g̃uruš šidim 18 géme im ga_6-[g̃á] ùr **é-kìšib-ba** a g̃á-g̃á, "1 builder (and) 18 workwomen having carried earth, (workers) having waterproofed the roof of the warehouse," 122:'26-'27

1.2 (Under the Authority of) the Milling Overseer

20 g̃uruš ^{geš}nimbar sumun te-[x? gub]-ba 2 g̃uruš šidim 7 g̃uruš $šeg_{12}$ šu dím-ma sum-mu-dè gub-ba 1 g̃uruš im gíd-dè gub-ba 3 g̃uruš 14 géme im ga_6-g̃á-dè gub-ba 1 g̃uruš im lu-dè gub-ba **é-kìšib-ba** ugula kíkken, "20 workmen employed [to (?)] old date palms, 2 builders (and) 7 workmen employed to hand (up) bricks for building, 1 workman employed to haul earth, 3 workmen (and) 14 workwomen employed to carry earth, 1 workman employed to mix earth, (work for) the warehouse (under the authority of?) the overseer of the mill," 36:20–25

1 g̃uruš šidim 3 g̃uruš 10 géme **é-kìšib-ba** ugula kíkken dù-a, "1 builder, 3 workmen (and) 10 workwomen having constructed the warehouse (under the authority of?) the overseer of the mill," 154:26–27

2. Deliveries for the Warehouse

2.1 (Dead) Animals

2.1.1 Birds

1 uz-tur iti u_4-22-ba-zal ba-úš **é-kìšib-ba**-šè, "1 fattened duckling was slaughtered at the end of the 22nd day of the month for the warehouse," 1112:1–3

1 uz-⌜tur⌝ iti u_4-11-ba-zal 1 uz-tur iti u_4-13?-ba-zal 1 uz-tur iti u_4-20-ba-zal 1 uz-tur [iti u_4-2]8-ba-zal [ba-úš é]-**kìšib-ba**-[šè], "1 duckling at the end of the 11th day of the month, 1 duckling at the end of the 13th? day of the month, 1 duckling at the end of the 20th day of the month (and) 1 duckling at the end of the [2]8th [day of the month were slaughtered for] the warehouse," 1176:1–9

1 ⌜mušen⌝-tur u_4-24-kam 1 ⌜mušen⌝-tur u_4-30-kam ba-úš **é-kìšib-ba**-šè, "1 young bird on the 24th day and 1 young bird on the 30th day were slaughtered for the warehouse," 1183:1–5

2.1.2 Bird and Mice

1 uz-tur 1 péš-g̃eš-gi iti u_4-28-ba-zal ba-úš **é-kìšib-ba**-šè, "1 duckling (and) 1 mouse were slaughtered for the warehouse at the end of the 28th day of the month," 1104:1–4

1 uz-tur u_4-14-kam 5 uz-tur u_4-27-kam 4 $tu-gur_4^{mušen}$ 2 péš-g̃eš-gi 2 péš-igi-gùn u_4-30-kam ba-úš **é-kìšib-ba**-šè, "1 duckling on the 14th day, 5 ducklings on the 27th day, 4 doves, 2 mice (and) 2 striped-eyed mice on the 30th day were slaughtered for the warehouse," 1254:'27-'33

2.1.3 Sheep and Goats

32 udu 1 ud_5 b[a-úš] **é-kìšib-ba**-šè, "32 sheep (and) 1 (female) goat were slaughtered for the warehouse," 1019:8–10

2.2 Bread

2.4.3.6 sìla ninda gur [**é**]-**kìšib-ba**-šè ba-an-ku_4 (. . .) níg̃-kas_7-aka *da-a-a* muḫaldim, "2 bushels (and) 276 liters of bread entered the warehouse (and) {other expenditures}, the balanced account of *Da'a*, the cook," 1031:17–18, 26

2.3 Commodity Tax: Carried from the Quay

17 ĝuruš níĝ-gú-na kar-ta **é-kìšib-ba**-šè ga_6-ĝá, "17 workmen having carried the commodity tax from the quay to the warehouse," 129:5, 129:39, 130:5, 130:'19, 131:'30, 132:5, 132:37

2.4 Leather

(. . .) kíĝ-til-[la] mu-D[U **é**]**-kìšib-ba**-⌜šè⌝, "{leather products}, delivery of completed work for the warehouse," 932:7–9

3. Disbursal of Goods from the Warehouse

3.1 Leather Buckets and Sacks

95 [kuš]*maš-lí-um* [kuš]a-ĝá-lá ḫi-a **é-kìšib-ba**-ta, "95 various leather buckets (and) leather sacks from the warehouse," 963:1–2

3.2 The Remainder of Bitumen and Oil

7.4.0. ésir-ḫád gur 0.0.4.6 sìla ésir-é-a 0.0.0.7 sìla ì-ḫur-saĝ-ĝá ⌜*šit*⌝*-tum* é-lùnga ⌜*šit*⌝*-tum* **é-kìšib-ba** ugula kíkken [?] du_{10}-ús é-didli *ták-si-*[*ru-um*]-šè ba-a-ĝar, "7 bushels (and) 240 liters of dried bitumen, 46 liters of house bitumen (and) 7 liters of mountain fat, the balance (of the settled account) of the brewery (and) of the warehouse, were placed (in the account of) the overseer of the mill for repair of the bathrooms of various houses," 1260:1–4

4. Transactions in the Warehouse

4.1 Baking Tablets and Baling Wool

★★(. . .) kìšib íb-ra **é-kìšib-ba**-ta dub-bi in-du_8 siki bala-dè in-kéše é-gal-šè mu-DU ḫal-lí-a [lú]ázlag ka-ga-na ba-gi-in, "{assorted textiles}, he rolled the seal, baked its tablet in the warehouse, (and) bound up the wool to be baled (for) delivery for the palace," 609:11–14

5. é-kìšib-ba ĝá-nun-na sumun, "the warehouse of the old storehouse"

5.1 Construction of the Roof

2 ĝuruš [šidim] 6 ĝuruš šu dím gub-ba 10 géme im ga_6-ĝá gub-ba **é-**⌜**kìšib**⌝-ba **ĝá-nun-na sumun** ĝeš ùr kéše-rá, "2 [builders], 6 workmen employed to build, (and) 10 workwomen employed to carry earth, (workers) having bound roof beams for the warehouse of the old storehouse," 49:35–38

5.2 (De-)Construction of the Roof

5 ĝuruš ùr **é-kìšib-ba ĝá-n**[**un-na**] **sumun** zi-le-dè gu[b-ba], "5 workmen employed to strip the roof of the warehouse of the old storehouse," 47:47–48

6. é-kìšib-ba sumun, "the old warehouse"

6.1 (De-)Construction: Stripping the Roof

n ĝuruš ùr **é-kìšib-ba sumun** zi-le-de_9 gub-ba, "n workmen employed to strip the roof of the old warehouse," 48:52–53, 140:40

n ĝuruš ùr **é-kìšib-ba sumun** zi-$le_{(2/9)}$-dè, "n workmen to strip the roof of the old warehouse," 136:37, 138:34, 141:37

6.2 (Re-)Construction

1 ĝuruš šidim um-mi-a 20 ĝuruš **é-kìšib-ba sumun** dù-a, "1 master builder (and) 20 workmen having (re-)constructed the old warehouse," 155:20–21

7. Broken Context

0.3.1. [. . .] **é-kišib-ba é-udu-[. . .] *ì-lí-an-dùl* [. . .] ba-an-z[uḫ(-a)] ka-ga-na ba-a-[ge-en], "[. . .] in the warehouse, the sheep pen [. . .] *Ili-andul* [. . .] he stole it. He confirmed it," 1064:1–5

é-kù, "the bright temple"

1. Food Preparation in the Temple

1 udu-niga 0.0.1. zì-KAL ninda-[gur$_4$-ra]-šè 1 dug dida$_x$-⌜gen⌝ 5 sìla níĝ-àr-ra-⌜sig$_5$⌝ ⅓ sìla mun-sig$_5$ al-naĝ$_4$-ĝá 10 gín gazi al-naĝ$_4$-ĝá ^{urudu}šen-šè 7 sa+níĝin ^{ĝeš}ásal 5 sa gi-izi ninda ba-ra-du$_8$ uzu ù tu$_7$ ba-ra-šeĝ$_6$ **é-kù-ga** (. . .) šà zabala$_4^{ki}$ u$_4$-2-ka, "1 fattened sheep, 10 liters of KAL-flour for [thick] bread, 1 jug of oridinary dida beer, 5 liters of fine groats, ⅓ liter of fine crushed salt, (and) 10 shekels of crushed gazi for the (soup) cauldron (and) 7 bundles of poplar wood (and) 5 bundles of fuel reeds with which bread was baked and meat and soup were cooked in the bright temple (and) {other meals}. {Expenditure} in Zabala on the 2nd day," 1028:1–11, 45

é-lùnga, "brewery"

é-lùnga ù é-kíkken, "brewery and mill" > **é-lùnga ù é-kíkken**

é-lùnga é-muḫaldim ù é-kíkken, "brewery-kitchen-mill complex" > **Triple Complex**

1. Construction: Binding Roof Beams

1 ĝuruš šidim 2 ĝuruš 10 géme **é-lù[nga** ĝeš] ùr kéše-rá, "1 builder, 2 workmen (and) 10 workwomen having bound roof [beams], (work for) the brewery," 205:'22-'23

2. Building Supplies

2.1 Bitumen and Oil, Remainder of the Brewery and Warehouse

7.4.0. ésir-ḫád gur 0.0.4.6 sìla ésir-é-a 0.0.0.7 sìla ì-ḫur-saĝ-ĝá ⌜*šit*⌝-*tum* **é-lùnga** ⌜*šit*⌝-*tum* é-kišib-ba ugula kíkken [?] du$_{10}$-ús é-didli *ták-si-[ru-um]*-šè ba-a-ĝar, "7 bushels (and) 240 liters of dried bitumen, 46 liters of house bitumen (and) 7 liters of mountain fat, the balance (of the settled account) of the brewery (and) of the warehouse, were placed (in the account of) the overseer of the mill for repair of the bathrooms of various houses," 1260:1–4

2.2 Ropes and Wood for its Tree-top Gate

8 ^{gi}dur-gazi a-rá 2 tab-ba gíd 1½ nindan-ta ĝeš ùr kéše gíd-da 3 ^{ĝeš}ù-suḫ$_5$ 3-kam-ús 15 ^{ĝeš}é-da ásal ká-suḫur **é-lùnga**-šè ba-a-ĝar, "8 9-meter 2-ply gazi ropes having tightened bound roof beams, 3 3rd-quality pine boards (and) 15 poplar joists were placed for the tree-top gate of the brewery," 1297:1–5

3. é-lùnga sumun, "the old brewery"

3.1 Construction of its Reed Hut

[n] ĝuruš gi-sig **é-lùnga sumun** ⌜dù⌝-a, "[n] workmen having constructed the reed hut of the old brewery," 143:38

é-lùnga ù é-kíkken, "brewery and mill"[2]

1. Construction

1.1 Of the Foundation Terrace

2 g̃uruš šidim 20 g̃uruš 70 géme ki-sá-a **é-lùnga ù é-kíkken**, "2 builders, 20 workmen (and) 70 workwomen at the foundation terrace of the brewery and mill," 110:24–25

1.1.1 Mixing Earth

1 g̃uruš šidim um-mi-a 2 g̃uruš šidim 7 g̃uruš 40 géme ki-sá-a im lu-a **é-lùnga ù é-kíkken**, "1 master builder, 2 builders, 7 workmen (and) 40 workwomen having mixed earth at the foundation terrace of the brewery and mill," 109:21–23

1.1.2 Moving Dirt

1 g̃uruš šidim 10 g̃[uruš n géme] saḫar zi-ga ki-sá-a **é-lùn[ga ù é-kíkken]**, "1 builder, 10 workmen [(and) n workwomen] having moved dirt at the foundation terrace of the brewery [and mill]," 108:26–27

(. . .) saḫar zi-ga [ki-s]á-a **é-l[ùnga ù é-kíkken]**, "{volume} of dirt moved at the foundation terrace of the b[rewery and mill]," 355:6

1.1.3 Tamping Dirt

1 g̃uruš šidim 10 g̃uruš 10 géme ki-sá-a **é-lùnga ù é-kíkken** saḫar sè-ga, "1 builder, 10 workmen (and) 10 workwomen having tamped dirt at the foundation terrace of the brewery and mill," 104:32–35, 105:30–33

4 g̃uruš 30 géme ki-sá-a **é-lùnga ù é-kíkken** saḫar sè-ga, "4 workmen (and) 30 workwomen having tamped dirt at the foundation terrace of the brewery and mill," 117:29–30

1.1.4 Various Tasks for Construction

1 g̃uruš šidim um-mi-a 1 g̃uruš šidim 16 g̃uruš šu dím 76 géme im ga_6-g̃á al-tar ki-sá-a **[é-lùnga] ù [é-kíkken]**, "1 master builder, 1 builder (and) 16 workmen having built (and) 76 workwomen having carried earth, (for) construction of the foundation terrace of the [brewery] and [mill]," 111:23–26

1 g̃uruš šidim u[m-mi-a] 1 g̃uruš šidim SIG_4.ANŠE [im sumur aka] 2 g̃[uruš šidim] 16 g̃[uruš n géme . . .] im su[mur aka n g̃uruš n] géme im [ga_6-g̃á al-tar ki]-sá-a **é-[lùnga ù é-kíkken]**, "1 master builder, 1 builder [having plastered] the brick stack, 2 [builders], 16 [workmen (and) n workwomen] having plastered [. . .] (and) [n workmen (and) n] workwomen [having carried] earth, (for) [construction of] the foundation terrace of [the brewery and mill]," 112:'4-'9

3 g̃uruš šidim 10 g̃uruš šu dím 5 géme *du-ú-um* aka 4 géme im gíd 30 géme $šeg_{12}$ da-ki-sá-a ⸢g̃a⸣-g̃á 85 géme ⸢im⸣ ga_6-g̃á al-tar ki-sá-a **é-lùnga ù é-kíkken**, "3 builders (and) 10 workmen having built, 5 workwomen having made a *du-ú-um*, 4 workwomen having hauled earth, 30 workwomen having placed bricks at the side of the foundation terrace (and) 85 workwomen having carried earth, (for) construction of the foundation terrace of the brewery and mill," 113:'10-'15

---

2 For the occurrence of these two terms alone, see their respective entries.

1 g̃uruš šidim um-mi-a 1 g̃uruš šidim SIG$_4$.ANŠE zabala$_4$^{ki} 2 g̃uruš šidim 5 g̃uruš šu dím 36 géme im ga$_6$-g̃á al-tar ki-sá-a **é-lùnga ù é-kíkken**, "1 master builder, 1 builder at the brick stack of Zabala, 2 builders (and) 5 workmen having built (and) 36 workwomen having carried earth, (for) construction of the foundation terrace of the brewery and mill," 114:23–27

n g̃uruš šidim n g̃uruš šu dím n géme *du-ú-um* aka n géme im gíd n géme im ga$_6$-g̃á al-tar ki-sá-a **é-lùnga ù é-kíkken**, "n builder(s) (and) n workmen having built, n workwomen having made a *du-ú-um*, n workwomen having hauled earth (and) n workwomen having carried earth, (for) construction of the foundation terrace of the brewery and mill," 115:'17-'21, 121:27–31

1 g̃uruš šidim um-mi-a 2 g̃uruš šidim n g̃uruš šu dím n géme *du-ú-um* aka n géme im gíd n g̃uruš n géme im ga$_6$-g̃á al-tar ki-sá-a **é-lùnga ù é-kíkken**(!), "1 master builder, 2 builders (and) n workmen having built, n workwomen having made *du-ú-um*, n workwomen having hauled earth, n workmen (and) n workwomen having carried earth, (for) construction of the foundation terrace of the brewery and mill," 122:'11-'16, 123:25–30

2. Building Supplies

2.1 Bricks Placed at the Side of the (Enclosure) Wall

[n] géme [šeg$_{12}$ d]a-bàd g̃á-g̃á [n] g̃uruš [. . .] **é-kíkken ù é-lùnga**, "[n] workwomen having placed [bricks] at the side of the (enclosure) wall (and) [n] workmen [. . .], (work for) the mill and brewery," 98:'12-'15

2.2 Bricks for the Foundation Terrace

ki-sá-a **é-lùnga** [**ù é-kíkken**?] mu-DU *simat-*^{d}[nana ugula], "delivery (of bricks) for the foundation terrace of the brewery [and mill?] by *Simat-*[Nana, the overseer]," 353:17–18

3. Provisions During Construction

0.0.1.5 sìla kaš-gen šidim-e-ne íb-nag̃ u$_4$ al-tar ki-sá-a **é-lùnga ù é-**[**kíkken**], "The builders drank 15 liters of ordinary beer during construction of the foundation terrace of the brewery and [mill]," 428:1–4

é-muḫaldim, "kitchen"

é-lùnga **é-muḫaldim** ù é-kíkken, "brewery-kitchen-mill complex" > **Triple Complex**

1. Bread for the Kitchen

(. . .) é-[muḫaldim-šè?] *a-da-làl* muḫaldim šu ba-an-ti, "*Adallal*, the cook, received {bread} [for the kitchen?]," 1079:5–7

2. Piglets for the Kitchen

1 šáḫ-zé-da **é-muḫaldim**-⌜šè⌝, "1 piglet for the kitchen," 507:15

[n] uz-tur šu-ur$_4$-ra [x?] šu tag-a ki *na-bu-tum*-šè [1] šáḫ-zé-da **é-muḫaldim mu *simat-*^{d}*ištaran*<-šè> ì-lí-ra-bí maškim zi-ga *simat-*^{d}*ištaran*, "[n] duckling wing(s)?, [x] (?) to the place of *Nabutum*, (and) [1] piglet (for) the kitchen for *Simat-Ištaran*," 529:20–23

é-munus, "the house of the women"

1. Provisions

1.1 Dates

0.1.2. zú-lum **é-munus**-šè, "80 liters of dates for the house of the women," 515:1–2

1.2 Thread

3 gín šudum-gada **é-munus**-šè, "3 shekels of linen warp-thread for the house of the women," 541:1–2

é-mušen-na, "the bird house"

1. Construction

2 [ĝuruš] šidim 2 géme ḫuĝ-ĝá **é-mušen-na** dù-dè gub-ba, "2 builders (and) 2 hired workwomen employed to construct the bird house," 8:33–34

2 [ĝuruš] šidim 3 ĝuruš é-*ḫa-bu-ra-tum* **é-mušen-na** dù-dè gub-ba, "2 builders (and) 3 workmen employed to construct the house of *Ḫaburatum* (and) the bird house," 9:24–25

1 ĝuruš šidim 2 ĝuruš 8 géme **é-mušen-na** dù-a, "1 builder, 2 workmen (and) 8 workwomen having constructed the bird house," 122:'24-'25

é-^{d}nin-si$_4$-an-na, "the Nin-Siana temple"

1. The Temple Mill: Provisions for the Millers

[n g]ín ì-ĝeš-ta 1 ma-na tuḫ-ĝeš-ì-ḫád-ta 0.0.1. ádda-udu-ta [½] sìla mun-ta [n] gín luḫ-lá-ta [1 a]d-da-kal-la [1] ur-^{d}šul-pa-è [1] *ḫa-la-ša* (indent) 3 [ĝuruš? é]-kíkken **é-^{d}nin-^{d}si$_4$-an-na**-me-éš, "[n] shekel(s) of sesame oil each, 1 mina of dried sesame chaff each, 10 sheep carcasses each, [½] liter of salt each (and) [n] shekel(s) of luḫ-lá each, (provisions for) Ada-kala, Ur-Šulpa'e (and) *Ḫalaša*, 3 [workmen?] of the mill of the Nin-Siana temple," 562:'6-'15

2. Broken Context

3 ĝuruš má-^{d}šu-^{d}E[N.ZU . . .] **é-^{d}nin?-si$_4$-in-[na . . . t]a^{ki}-ta gar-ša-[an-na^{ki}-šè] D[U-x], 206:24–25

é-pí-ša-aḫ-ilum

é-ki-ba-ĝar-ra ***é-pi$_5$-ša-aḫ-ilum***, "the replacement house of the house of *Pišaḫ-ilum*" > **é-ki-ba-ĝar-ra**

1. Construction

1 ĝuruš šidim ***é-p[i$_5$-ša-aḫ-ilum]*** dù-dè [gub-ba], "1 builder [employed] to construct the house of *Pišaḫ-ilum*," 93:'24

1.1 Various Tasks

[n] ĝuruš šidim [. . .] 6 géme im g[a$_6$-ĝá-dè gub-ba] 3 ĝuruš im lu-a g[ub-ba] ***é-pí-ša-aḫ-ilum*** gub-[ba], "[n] builder(s), [. . .], 6 workwomen [employed to] carry earth (and) 3 workmen employed to mix earth, (workers) employed at the house of *Pišaḫ-ilum*," 84:14–17

1 ĝuruš šidim 11 ĝuruš 2 ⌜géme⌝ ⌜SIG$_4$⌝.ANŠE ĝá-ĝá [n+]5 ĝuruš i[m lu]-a [n g]éme in-[u] ga$_6$-ĝá-dè 2 ĝuruš 1 géme ***é-p[i$_5$-š]a-⌜aḫ⌝-ilum***, "1 builder, 11 workmen, (and) 2

workwomen having placed the brick stack, [n+]5 workmen having mixed earth, [n] workwomen to carry straw (and) 2 workmen (and) 1 workwoman at the house of *Pišaḫ-ilum*," 108:28–33

1.2 Workmen Employed at the House

2 g̃uruš **é-*pi*$_5$*-ša-aḫ-ilum*** gub-ba, "2 workmen employed at the house of *Pišaḫ-ilum*," 94:29

2. (De-)Construction

3 g̃uruš 10 géme iz-zi **é-*pí-ša-aḫ-ilum*** gul-la, "3 workmen (and) 10 workwomen having demolished the iz-zi wall of the house of *Pišaḫ-ilum*," 113:'5-'6

é-*pu-ta-nu-um*

1. Construction

n g̃uruš šidim n g̃uruš n géme **é-*pu-ta-nu-um*** dù-a, "n builder(s), n workmen (and) n workwomen having constructed the house of *Putanum*," 133:30–31, 135:33–34, 162:26–27, 175:23–24

1 g̃uruš šidim um-mi-a n g̃uruš šidim n g̃uruš n géme **é-*pu-ta-nu-um*** dù-a, "1 master builder, n builder(s), n workmen (and) n workwomen having constructed the house of *Putanum*," 158:21–23, 159:18–20, 163:21–23, 173:20–22, 174:19–21

1.1 Building

1 g̃uruš šidim 6 g̃uruš šu dím **é-*pu*-[*ta-nu-um*]**, "1 builder (and) 6 workmen having built the house of *Putanum*," 114:28–30

1.2 Dirt from the Foundation Terrace of the House

saḫar zi-ga [ki-s]á-a **é-*p*[*u-ta-nu-um*]** mu-⌜DU⌝ *li-la-a* ugula lú-ḫug̃-g̃á, "delivery of dirt removed at the foundation terrace of the house of *Putanum* by *Lila'a*, overseer of hired workers," 355:6–8

1.3 Handing (up) Bricks and Carrying Earth

1 g̃uruš šidim u[m-mi-a] 1 g̃uruš <šidim> 5 g̃uruš [šeg$_{12}$ šu dím-ma] sum-m[u-dè gub-ba] 10 géme im ga$_6$-⌜g̃a⌝ **é-*pu-ta-nu-um*** dù-[a], "1 master builder, 1 <builder> (and) 5 workmen [employed to] hand (up) [bricks for building] (and) 10 workwomen having carried earth, (workers) having constructed the house of *Putanum*," 156:19–22

1.4 Hauling and Carrying Earth

[n] g̃uruš šidim [. . .] 2 [géme . . .] 2 géme im gíd 6 géme im ga$_6$-[g̃á] **é-*pu-tá-nu-um*** dù-a, "[n] builder(s) [. . .], 2 [workwomen . . .], 2 workwomen having hauled earth (and) 6 workwomen having carried earth, (workers) having constructed the house of *Putanum*," 120:'25-'29

[n géme] im gíd 3 ⌜géme⌝ im ga$_6$-g̃á **é-*pu-ta-nu-um***, "[n workwomen] having hauled earth (and) 3 workwomen having carried earth, (work for) the house of *Putanum*," 122:'18-'20

1.5 Mixing Earth and Moving Dirt

13 g̃uruš im lu-a 3 g̃uruš 3 géme saḫar zi-ga **é-*pu-ta-nu-um***, "13 workmen having mixed earth (and) 3 workmen (and) 3 workwomen having moved dirt at the house of *Putanum*," 123:37–38

1.6 Moving Dirt

[n g̃uruš saḫ]ar zi-ga **é-*pu-ta-nu-um***, "[n workmen] having moved dirt at the house of *Putanum*," 125:31

1.7 Plastering and Carrying Earth

1 g̃uruš šidim 2 [g̃uruš] 1 géme im [sumur aka] 10-lá–1 géme i[m ga$_6$-g̃á] **é-*pu*-[*ta-nu-um*** dù-a], "1 builder, 2 [workmen] (and) 1 workwoman having plastered (and) 9 workwomen [having carried] earth, (workers) [having constructed] the house of *Putanum*," 112:'14-'17

1 g̃uruš šidim [um]-mi-[a] 3 g̃uruš ⸢šidim⸣ 10 g̃uruš [šu dí]m 2 géme *du-ú-*⸢*um*⸣ aka 2 géme im gíd 6 géme im ga$_6$-g̃á al-tar **é-*pu-ta-nu-um***, "1 master builder, 3 builders (and) 10 workmen having built, 2 workwomen having made a *du-ú-um*, 2 workwomen having hauled earth (and) 6 workwomen having carried earth, (for) construction of the house of *Putanum*," 121:21–26

1.8 Workers (Employed at) the House

[n] g̃uruš [**é**]-***pu-tá-núm***, "[n] workmen (employed at) the [house] of *Putanum*," 100:'17-'18

2. Building Supplies: Reeds and Roof Beams

120 g̃eš ùr ásal 170 sa gi-izi **é-*pu-ta-nu-um***, "120 poplar roof beams (and) 170 bundles of fuel reeds (for) the house of *Putanum*," 1309:4–6

é-*puzur$_4$-ra-bí*

é-ki-ba-g̃ar-ra ***puzur$_4$-ra-bí***, "the replacement house of *Puzur-rabi*" > **é-ki-ba-g̃ar-ra**

é-*simat-^{d}ištaran*

1. *Adad-tillati*, Majordomo of her House

(. . .) é-a šid-da ^{d}*adad-tillati* šabra **é-*simat-^{d}ištaran***, "{assorted grains, fodder for sheep and pigs}, counted in the house by *Adad-tillati*, the majordomo of the house of *Simat-Ištaran*," 1189:17–19

é-šáḫ, "the Piggery"

1. Construction

1 g̃uruš šidim 3 g̃uruš 11 géme **é-šáḫ** dù-a, "1 builder, 3 workmen (and) 11 workwomen having constructed the piggery," 123:35–36

[n] g̃uruš im lu-a [1] g̃uruš šidim [n] g̃uruš 2 géme **é-⸢šáḫ⸣** dù-a, "[n] workmen having mixed earth (and) [1] builder, [n] workmen (and) 2 workwomen having constructed the piggery," 125:27–29

é-^{d}šára, "the Šara temple"

1. A Boat Towed from the Temple to Garšana

(. . .) maš-en-gag ^{lú}kaš$_4$ ká-é-gal-ka gub-ba ⸢*simat*⸣-^{d}*ištaran* íb-gu$_7$ u$_4$ má-*simat-^{d}ištaran* **é-^{d}šára**-ta gar-ša-an-na^{ki}-šè mu-un-gíd-ša-a, "The *muškenu* (and?) the runner, stationed by *Simat-Ištaran* at the gate of the palace, ate {soup} when they towed the boat of *Simat-Ištaran* from the Šara temple to Garšana," 529:13–18

2. Reeds Brought from the Temple to Garšana

[n g̃uruš] gi-zi [**é-**^{d}]**šára**-ta [gar-ša-an]-na^{ki}-šè de$_6$-a, "[n workmen] having brought fresh reeds from the Šara [temple] to Garšana," 193:29–31

1⅔ g̃uruš ašgab 1 g̃uruš túg-du$_8$ 1 g̃uruš simug u$_4$-1-šè ⸢gi⸣ ù gi-zi **é-^{d}šára**-ta gar-ša-an-na^{ki}-šè [de$_6$]-a, "1⅔ leather workers, 1 braider, (and) 1 smith for 1 day having brought reeds and fresh reeds from the Šara temple to Garšana," 232:1–7

3. Broken Context

★★[. . .] x-x [. . . **é**]-^{d}**šára**-G̃EŠ.KUŠ[Ú^{ki} . . . o.n.n.]6⅔ sìla [ninda] iti dirig ezem-^{d}me-ki-g̃ál-šè mu ^{d}*i-bí-*^{d}*suen* ⸢lugal⸣, "[. . .] the Šara [temple] of G̃EŠ.KUŠU, [n+]6⅔ liters of [bread] for month 13, *Ibbi-Suen* Year 1" 1031:1–5

é-šu-bu-la-núm

1. Construction

1 g̃uruš šidim 3 g̃uruš [n gém]e **é-**⸢***šu***⸣?-***bu-la-núm*** dù-a, "1 builder, 3 workmen (and) [n] workwomen having constructed the house of *Šubulanum*, 131:'27-'28

é-šu-eš$_4$-tár

é-ki-ba-g̃ar-ra *za-ki-ti* ù ***šu-eš$_4$-tár***, "the replacement house of *Zakiti* and *Šu-Eštar* > **é-ki-ba-g̃ar-ra**

é-šu-eš$_4$-tár é-ki-ba-g̃ar-ra, "the replacement house of *Šu-Eštar*" > **é-ki-ba-g̃ar-ra**

é-šu-eš$_4$-tár ù za-ki-ti, "the house of *Šu-Eštar* and *Zakiti*" > ***é-šu-eš$_4$-tár*** **ù** ***za-ki-ti***

1. Construction

[n g̃uruš šidim] *a-za-bu-um* a im [še-g̃á] e-sír dal-ba-na ⸢bàd⸣ ù ***é-šu-eš$_4$-tár*** dù-[a], "[n builder(s)] having constructed a cistern for rain (in) the alley-way, a wall and the house of *Šu-Eštar*," 53:46

n g̃uruš u$_4$-n-šè *a-za-bu-um* a im še-g̃á e-sír dal-ba-na bàd ù ***é-šu-eš$_4$-tár*** dù-a, "n workmen for n day(s) having constructed a cistern for rain (in) the alley-way, a wall and the house of *Šu-Eštar*," 58:47–50, 336:36–37

2. Moving Dirt

1 g̃uruš šidim saḫar <**é-**>***šu-eš$_4$-tár*** zi-zi-dè gub-[ba], "1 builder employed to move dirt at the <house> of *Šu-Eštar*," 92:20

é-šu-eš$_4$-tár **ù** ***za-ki-ti***[3]

1. (De-)Construction

30 géme šeg$_{12}$ ga$_6$-g̃á [n] g̃uruš 6 géme iz-zi ***é-šu-eš$_4$-tár*** **ù** ***za-ki-ti*** gul-la, "30 workwomen having carried bricks (and) [n] workmen (and) 6 workwomen having demolished the iz-zi wall of the house of *Šu-Eštar* and *Zakiti*," 104:27–29, 105:26–28

---

[3] For the occurrence of these two households alone, see their respective entries.

é-šu-i-e-ne, "the house of the barbers"

1. Building Supplies

é-šu-i-[e-n]e-[šè] *simat-é-a* ugula lú-ḫuĝ-ĝá, "{delivery of bricks} [for] the house of the barbers by *Simat-Ea*, overseer of hired workers," 352:39–40

2. Potash

2 sìla x-x naĝa? **é-šu-i-e-ne**-šè, "2 liters of x-x potash? for the house of the barbers," 492:1–2

é-*šu-i-ti-rum*

1. Construction

1 ĝuruš šidim 3 ĝuruš 11 géme **é-*šu-i-ti-rum*** dù-[dè gub-ba], "1 builder, 3 workmen (and) 11 workwomen [employed to] construct the house of *Šu-iterum*," 138:35–36

é-*šu-ku-bu-um*

1. Construction

1 ĝuruš 4 géme im lu-a gub-ba **[é]-*šu-ku-bu-um*** gub-ba, "1 employed workman (and) 4 employed workwomen having mixed earth, (workers) employed at the [house] of *Šukubum*," 84:21–22

1 ĝuruš šidim **é-*šu-ku-bu-⸢um⸣*** gub-ba, "1 builder employed at the house of *Šu-kubum*," 94:25

é-*šu-ma-mi-tum*

1. Construction

[n ĝuruš šidim n] ĝuruš 10 [géme **é-*šu-m*]*a-mi-t*[*um*** dù-a], "[n builder(s), n] workmen (and) 10 [workwomen having constructed the house of] *Šu-mamitum*," 173:23–24

[2] ĝuruš šidim 10 géme **é-*šu-ma-mi-tum*** dù-a, "[2] builders (and) 10 workwomen having constructed the house of *Šu-mamitum*," 174:22–23

é-šu-sum-ma, "storehouse"

1. Animals in the Storehouse

5[0 ud]u-máš ḫi-a gub-ba **[é-š]u-sum-ma** ĝìri *a-ḫu*-[x] dub-sar iti dirig ezem-me-ki-ĝál ba-zal mu ^{d}*i-bí-*^{d}*suen* lugal, "(In total:) 50 various sheep (and) goats present in the storehouse under the authority of *Aḫu*-[x], the scribe, at the end of the 13th month of *Ibbi-Suen* Year 1," 984:5–9

2. Workmen Employed at the Storehouse

3 ĝuruš u_4-2-šè **é-šu-sum-ma** gub-ba, "3 workmen employed for 2 days at the storehouse," 968:20–21

é-tab-tab, "double house"

1. Assorted (Damaged?) Commodities

★★ (. . .) [. . .]-gaz-a-ḫi? [x]-gaz-gaz [. . .]-zi-ra **é-tab-tab**-ba [?] x-šè ba-an-ku$_4$, "{baskets and other reed products, ropes, palm products, leather products, pots and other containers}; [. . .] broken(? vessels?) entered the double house for [x?]," 1376:87–90

é-til-la, "finished house"

1. Construction: Trimming Thin Reeds

n ĝuruš šidim gi-sal **é-til-la** gul-dè (gub-ba), "n builder(s) (employed) to trim thin reeds at the finished house," 1:10–11, 2:13–14, 3:9–10, 4:14–15

é-*u-bar-ri-a*

é-ki-ba-ĝar-ra **é-*u-bar-ri-a***, "the replacement house of the house of *Ubarria*" > **é-ki-ba-ĝar-ra**

1. Construction

1 ĝuruš šidim um-mi-a 4 ĝuruš šidim **é-*u-bar-ri-a*** gub-ba 1 ĝuruš šidim iz-zi šà é-a gub-ba, "1 master builder (and) 4 builders employed at the house of *Ubarria*, (and) 1 builder employed at the iz-zi wall in the house," 91:6–9

1 ĝuruš šidim um-mi-a 2 ĝuruš šidim 4 ĝuruš šu dím gub-ba 2 ĝuruš im ⌜lu⌝-dè gub-ba 6 géme im ga$_6$-ĝá<-dè> gub-ba 1 ĝuruš im ì-li-d[e$_9$ gub-ba] **é-*u*-⌜*bar*⌝-*ri-a*** gub-[ba], "1 master builder, 2 builders (and) 4 workmen employed to build, 2 workmen employed to mix earth, 6 workwomen employed <to> carry earth (and) 1 workman [employed to] lift earth, (workers) employed at the house of *Ubarria*," 94:14–20

[n] ĝuruš šidim 10 ĝuruš 13 [géme] SIG$_4$.ANŠE im sumur ⌜aka⌝ 1 ĝuruš šidim SIG$_4$.ANŠE šà zaba[la$_4^{ki}$] 26 ĝuruš im lu-a 1 ĝuruš šidim 2 ĝuruš šu ⌜dím⌝ 5 géme im ga$_6$-ĝá **é-*u-bar*-⌜*ri*⌝-*a*** dù-a, "[n] builder(s), 10 workmen (and) 13 [workwomen] having plastered the brick stack, 1 builder at the brick stack in Zabala, 26 workmen having mixed earth, 1 builder (and) 2 workmen having built (and) 5 workwomen having carried earth, (workers) having constructed the house of *Ubarria*," 111:30–36

2 ĝuruš šidim 1 ĝuruš x-[. . .] 5 géme im [sumur aka] **é-*u-bar-ri*-[*a*** dù-a], "2 builders (and?) 1 workman [. . .] (and) 5 workwomen having plastered, (workers) [having constructed] the house of *Ubarria*," 112:'11-'13

1 ĝuruš šidim [um-mi-a n ĝuruš šidim n+]2 ĝuruš 15 géme [**é-*u***]**-*bar-ri!-a*** dù-a, "1 [master] builder, [n builder(s), n]+2 workmen (and) 15 workwomen having constructed the house of *Ubarria*," 162:19–21

1.1 Construction of its Roof

2 ĝuruš šidim ùr **é-*u-bar-ri-a*** im sumur ke$_4$-dè gub-ba, "2 builders employed to plaster the roof of the house of *Ubarria*," 92:19

2. (De-)Construction

7 ĝuruš 6 géme **é-*u-bar-ri-a*** gul-[dè gub-ba], "7 workmen (and) 6 workwomen [employed to] demolish the house of *Ubarria*," 93:'26

3. Broken Context

1 g̃uruš [šidim . . .] **é-*u-b*[*ar-ri-a*]**, 108:24–25

é-*u-bar-um*

é-ki-ba-g̃ar-ra ***u-bar-ri-a***, "the replacement house of *Ubarrum*" > **é-ki-ba-g̃ar-ra**

é-udu-niga, "the sheep-fattening pen"

1. Construction

1 g̃uruš šidim n g̃uruš n géme **é-udu-niga** dù-a, "1 builder, n workmen (and) n workwomen having constructed the sheep-fattening pen," 151:34–35, 152:'20-'21, 153:'33-'34, 154:37–38, 155:23–24, 204:'10-'11, 205:16–17

1.1 Construction of its Reed Hut

1 g̃uruš [šidim n] g̃ur[uš. . .] 1 g̃uruš im sumur [aka] 1 g̃uruš šidim gi-sig **é-udu-niga** [dù-a], "1 builder, [n] workmen [. . .], 1 workman having plastered (and) 1 builder [having constructed] the reed hut of the sheep-fattening pen," 206:12–17

1 g̃uruš [ši]dim 5 g̃uruš gi-sig **é-udu-niga** dù-a, "1 builder (and) 5 workmen having constructed the reed hut of the sheep-fattening pen," 207:26–28

1.2 Construction of its Roof

1 g̃uruš šidim 5 géme im ga_6-g̃á-dè gub-ba 1 g̃uruš im ì-li-dè gub-ba ùr **é-udu-niga**-šè, "1 builder (and) 5 workwomen employed to carry earth (and) 1 workman employed to lift earth, (work) for the roof for the sheep-fattening pen," 53:37–40

2. A Ram for the Pen

1 udu-níta **é-udu-niga**-šè, "1 ram for the sheep-fattening pen," 1207:1–2

3. Sheep of the Pen

24 udu-niga 1-sìla-[ta] sá-du_{11}-šè 26 udu-niga 1-sìla-ta [x]-šè **é-⸢udu⸣-niga** šu-a-⸢gi⸣-na u_4 iti-da ⸢gíd⸣-gíd-⸢dam⸣, "24 fattened sheep, 1 liter (fodder) [each] for regular offerings (and) 26 fattened sheep, 1 liter (fodder) each for [. . .]; (sheep), of the sheep-fattening pen, to be transferred (for) the offering of the month," 525:1–7

4. Broken Context

★★0.3.1. [. . .] é-kìšib-ba **é-udu-**[. . .] *ì-lí-an-dùl* [. . .] ba-an-z[uḫ(-a)] ka-ga-na ba-a-[ge-en], "[. . .] in the storehouse, the sheep pen [. . .] *Ili-andul* [. . .] he stole it. He confirmed it," 1064:1–5

é-ùr ku_6 al-ús-sa, "fish-sauce roof house"

1. Construction

1 g̃uruš šidim 1 g̃uruš 3 géme **é-ùr ku_6 al-ús-sa** dù-dè gub-[ba], "1 builder, 1 workman (and) 3 workwomen employed to construct the fish-sauce roof house," 14:20–21

2. Construction of its Fence

1 g̃uruš šidim 1 g̃uruš 3 géme gaba-tab **é-ùr-ra ku$_6$ a[l-ús-sa]** dù-dè gu[b-ba], "1 builder, 1 workman (and) 3 workwomen employed to construct the breastwork fence of the fish-sauce roof house," 15:23–24

3. Waterproofing the New Fish-sauce Roof House

1 g̃uruš šidim 1 g̃uruš šu dím 10-lá–1 géme im ga$_6$-g̃á gub-ba **é-gibi[l ù]r ku$_6$ al-ús-sa** a [g̃á]-g̃á-dè gub-ba, "1 builder (and) 1 workman having built (and) 9 employed workwomen having carried earth, (workers) employed to waterproof the new roof of the fish-sauce roof house," 49:39–42

é-uš-bar, "textile mill"

1. Construction of the Textile Mill

1.1 Trimming Thin Reeds

n g̃uruš n géme gi-sal **é-uš-bar** gul-dè gub-ba, "n workmen (and) n workwomen employed to trim thin reeds, (work for) the textile mill," 47:45–46, 48:50–51

1.2 Various Tasks

1 g̃uruš šidim iz-zi bàd tà-tà-dè gub-ba 5 g̃uruš š[idim šeg$_{12}$ bà]d tab-bé-dè gub-ba 20 g̃uruš šeg$_{12}$ šu dím-ma sum-mu-dè gub-ba 2 g̃uruš *du-ú-um* ke$_4$-dè gub-ba 4 g̃uruš im gíd-dè gub-ba 6 g̃uruš im a-g̃á-ri-na ì-li-de$_9$ gub-ba 30 géme im ga$_6$-g̃á-dè [gub-ba] 6 g̃uruš im lu-dè gub-[ba] 1 g̃uruš šidim 11 g[éme s]ag̃ bàd i[m sumur ke$_4$]-d[è g]ub-ba [n g̃ur]uš šidim 6 g̃uruš 50[+n? géme . . .] **é-uš-[bar** . . .], "1 builder employed to apply stucco to the iz-zi wall of the (enclosure) wall, 5 builders employed to line-up [bricks] at the (enclosure) wall, 20 workmen employed to hand (up) bricks for building, 2 workmen employed to make a *du-ú-um*, 4 workmen employed to haul earth, 6 workmen employed to lift earth into the *agarinnum*, 30 workwomen [employed] to carry earth, 6 workmen employed to mix earth, 1 workman, (and) 11 workwomen employed to plaster the head of the (enclosure) wall (and) [n] builder(s), 6 workmen, 50[+n? workwomen . . .], (work for) the textile mill," 33:20–30

1 g̃uruš šidim u[m-m]i-a [. . .] 13 g̃u[ruš. . .] 8 g̃uruš [. . .]-dè [gub-ba] 8 géme *du-ú-um* ke$_4$-dè gub-ba 28 géme im ga$_6$-g̃á-dè gub-ba 10 g̃uruš im a-g̃á-ri-na lu-dè gub-ba 4 g̃uruš im ì-li-⸢de$_9$⸣ gub-ba **é-uš-bar**-šè, "1 master builder [. . .], 13 workmen [. . .], 8 workmen [employed] to [. . .], 8 workwomen employed to make a *du-ú-um*, 28 workwomen employed to carry earth, 10 workmen employed to mix earth in the *agarinnum* (and) 4 workmen employed to lift earth, (work) for the textile mill," 37:17–26

1 g̃uruš šidim um-m[i-a] 8 [g̃uruš šidim] 10-lá–1 g̃[uruš šu dím] 6 géme im [gíd-dè gub-ba] 4 géme *du-ú-[um* ke$_4$]-dè gub-ba 40 ⸢géme⸣ im ga$_6$-g̃á-dè gub-ba 4 g̃uruš ⸢im⸣ a-g̃á-ri-na lu-dè gub-ba 4 g̃uruš im ì-li-de$_9$ gub-ba **é-uš-bar**-⸢šè⸣, "1 master builder, 8 [builders] (and) 9 [workmen having built], 6 workwomen [employed to haul] earth, 4 workwomen employed to make a *du-ú-um*, 40 workwomen employed to carry earth, 4 workmen employed to mix earth in the *agarinnum* (and) 4 workmen employed to lift earth, (work) for the textile mill," 38:19–27

1 g̃uruš šidim [. . . n g̃uruš . . . gub-b]a [n g̃ur]uš *du-ú-um* ke$_4$-d[è] gub-ba 1 g̃uruš im ⸢gíd-dè⸣ gub-ba 4 g̃uruš im ì-[li]-de$_9$ gub-ba 4 géme im g[a$_6$-g̃á-dè] gub-ba al-⸢tar⸣ **é-[uš-bar-ra]**, "1 builder [. . . n workmen] employed [. . .], [n] workmen employed to make a *du-ú-um*, 1 workman employed to haul earth, 4 workmen employed to lift earth

(and) 4 workwomen employed to carry earth, (for) construction of [the textile mill]," 52:27–35

[1] ĝuruš šidim um-m[i-a] 1 ĝuruš [šidim n ĝur]uš [n géme] šu dím [gub-ba n géme] *du-ú-*[*um* aka. . . n] géme im ga_6-ĝá-dè gub-ba [n ĝu]ruš im ì-li-dè gub-ba [erasure]-dè gub-ba al-ta[r **u]š é-bar-ra**,[4] "[1] master builder, 1 [builder (and) n] workmen (and) [n workwomen employed] to build, [n workwomen having made] a *du-ú-um*, [. . . n] workwomen employed to carry earth, [n] workmen employed to lift earth, (workers) employed (for) construction of the textile mill," 53:19–29

1.3 Construction of its Foundation

[1] ĝuruš šidim um-mi-a [4?] ĝuruš šidim [n] ĝuruš šu dím gub-ba [4?] géme im gíd ga_6-dè gub-ba [. . .] 30 géme im ga_6-ĝ[á-dè] gub-ba 6 ĝuruš im ì-li-[de_9] gub-ba ⌜uš⌝ **é-uš-bar-ra**, "[1] master builder, [4?] builders (and) [n] workmen employed to build, [4?] workwomen having hauled earth, employed to carry it, [. . .], 30 workwomen employed [to] carry earth (and) 6 workmen employed [to] lift earth, (work) for the foundation of the textile mill," 47:19–26

1.4 Its Foundation Terrace

1.4.1 Applying Stucco

1 ĝuruš šidim um-mi-a ki-sá-a **é-uš-bar** tà-ga gub-ba, "1 employed master builder having applied stucco to the foundation terrace of the textile mill," 35:20

1.4.2 Lining Up Bricks

3 ĝuruš šidim 10 ĝuruš 28 géme [ki]-sá-a **é-uš-bar** $šeg_{12}$ tab-bé-dè gub-ba, "3 builders, 10 workmen (and) 28 workwomen employed to line up bricks at the foundation terrace of the textile mill," 32:29–30

1 ĝuruš šidim ki-sá-a **é-uš-bar** $šeg_{12}$ tab-bé-dè gub-ba, "1 builder employed to line up bricks at the foundation terrace of the textile mill," 35:21

1.4.3 Moving Dirt

2 ĝuruš šidim 14 ĝuruš uš ki-sá-a **é-uš-bar** saḫar zi-zi-dè gub-ba, "2 builders (and) 14 workmen employed to move dirt at the foundation of the foundation terrace of the textile mill," 28:'15

1 ĝuruš 4 géme saḫar zi-zi-dè ki-[sá-a] **é-uš-bar** gub-ba, "1 workman (and) 4 workwomen employed to move dirt at the foundation terrace of the textile mill," 35:2

1.4.4 Various Tasks

1 ĝuruš $šeg_{12}$ šu dím-ma sum-mu-dè gub-ba 1 ĝuruš *du-ú-um* ke_4-dè gub-ba 1 ĝuruš im gíd-dè gub-ba 1 [ĝuruš] im a-ĝá-ri-na ì-li-de_9 gub-ba 1 [ĝuruš] im ga_6-ĝá-dè gub-ba [1 ĝuruš] im lu-dè gub-ba [17] ĝuruš 40 géme $šeg_{12}$ da-ki-sá-a **é-uš-bar** ĝá-ĝá-dè gub-[ba], "1 workman employed to hand (up) bricks for building, 1 workman employed to make a *du-ú-um*, 1 workman employed to haul earth, 1 [workman] employed to lift earth into the *agarinnum*, 1 [workman] employed to carry earth, [1 workman] employed to mix earth (and) [17] workmen (and) 40

[4] Mistake for é-uš-bar-ra (Heimpel, personal communication).

workwomen employed to place bricks at the side of the foundation terrace of the textile mill," 35:22–28

3 ĝuruš š[idim] 15 ĝuruš šu [dím] 6 ĝuruš *du-ú-um* ⸢ke$_4$⸣-dè gub-ba 2 ĝuruš im gíd-dè gub-ba 18 géme im ga$_6$-ĝá-dè g[ub-b]a 5 ĝuruš im ì-⸢li⸣-de$_9$ gub-ba ki-sá-a **é-uš-bar**-šè, "3 builders (and) 15 workmen to build, 6 workmen employed to make a *du-ú-um*, 2 workmen employed to haul earth, 18 workwomen employed to carry earth (and) 5 workmen employed to lift earth, (work) for the foundation terrace of the textile mill," 43:'26-'32

1 ĝuruš šidim um-mi-a 1 ĝuruš šidim 8 ĝuruš 4 géme šeg$_{12}$ šu dím-[ma sum-mu-dè gub-ba . . .] ke$_4$-dè [gub-ba n] ĝuruš im a-ĝá-ri-⸢na⸣ lu-dè gub-ba 3 ĝuruš im ì-li-de$_9$ gub-ba ki-sá-a **é-uš-bar**-šè, "1 master builder, 1 builder, 8 workmen (and) 4 workwomen [employed to hand (up)] bricks for building, [. . . employed] to make [. . ., n] workmen employed to mix earth in the *agarinnum* (and) 3 workmen employed to lift earth, (work) for the foundation terrace of the textile mill," 46:'14-'21

1.5 Waterproofing its Roof

1 ĝuruš šidim ùr **é-uš-bar** a ĝá-ĝá, "1 builder having waterproofed the roof of the textile mill," 109:24–25, 110:'31

2. Inspection of Work on the Textile Mill

kurum$_7$ aka al-tar bàd ù ki-sá(-a) **é-uš-[bar]**, "Inspection of (the work of workers employed for) construction of the (enclosure) wall and foundation terrace of the textile mill," 31:51, 35:57

kurum$_7$ aka al-tar bàd ù **é-uš-b[ar** gub-ba], "Inspection of (the work of workers) [employed] (for) construction of the (enclosure) wall and textile mill," 32:50

kurum$_7$ aka éren al-tar bàd ù **é-uš-bar**, "Inspection (of the work) of workers (employed for) construction of the (enclosure) wall and textile mill," 33:54

3. Building Supplies

3.1 Bricks for the Textile Mill

é-uš-bar-šè mu-DU *simat-é-a* ugula, "delivery (of bricks) for the textile mill by *Simat-Ea*, the overseer," 316:72–74

é-uš-bar-[šè mu-DU] *šál-maḫ* [ugula lú-ḫuĝ-ĝá], "[delivery] (of bricks) [for] the textile mill by *Šal-maḫ*, [overseer of hired workers]," 320:11–12

é-uš-bar(-šè) mu-DU *ba-zi* ugula, "delivery (of bricks for) the textile mill by *Bazi*, the overseer," 323:124–126, 327:82–84

3.2 Building Supplies for its Foundation Terrace

3.2.1 Bricks

[ki]-sá-a **é-uš-bar**-šè mu-DU árad-é-a ugula, "delivery (of bricks) for the foundation terrace of the textile mill by the overseer of the household servants," 322:'83-'84

[ki-sá-a] **é-uš-bar**-šè [mu-DU] *simat-é-a* ugula lú-ḫuĝ-ĝá, "[delivery] (of bricks) for the [foundation terrace] of the textile mill by *Simat-Ea*, overseer of hired workers," 324:94–95 ki-sá-a **é-uš-bar**-šè mu-DU *za-la-a* ugula lú-ḫ[ug̃-g̃á], "delivery (of bricks) for the foundation terrace of the textile mill by *Zala'a*, overseer of hired workers," 311:21–23, 362:'20-'23

3.2.2 Reeds

445 sa gi-izi gu-níg̃in 13-sa-ta gi-sal uš ki-sá-a **é-uš-bar**-šè ba-[a-g̃a]r, "445 bundles of fuel reeds, bales of 13 bundles each, the thin reeds were placed for the foundation of the foundation terrace of the textile mill," 1261:1–3

4. (Ceremonial) Offerings

[1] sìla dabin ½ sìla eša sízkur bàd ù **é-uš-bar**, "[1] liter of semolina (and) ½ liter of fine flour, (ceremonial) offerings for the (enclosure) wall and the textile mill," 991:1–3, 994:1–3

é-uš-bar ù é-gašam-e-ne, "the textile mill and craftsmen's house"[5]

1. Construction

23 g̃uruš u_4-1-⸢šè⸣ al-tar gub-ba **é-uš-bar ù é-gašam-e-ne**, "23 workmen employed for 1 day of construction of the textile mill and craftsmen's house," 336:28–30

1.1 Carrying Bricks

11⅔ sar 5 gín $šeg_{12}$ ús-bi 90 nindan á-géme–1-a 120-$šeg_{12}$-ta géme-bi [70½ u_4-1-šè] á $šeg_{12}$ g[a_6-g̃á] 23 g̃uruš u_4-1-⸢šè⸣ al-tar gub-ba **é-uš-bar ù é-gašam-e-ne**, "11⅔ sar and 5 gín of bricks, its base is 90 nindan (long), workwomen wages for each 120 bricks, its workwomen (equal) [70½ workerdays], hired to carry bricks (and) 23 workmen for 1 day employed (for) construction of the textile mill and craftsmen's house," 336:23–30

1.2 Plastering Crossbeams

[n g̃uruš šidim] 8 g̃uruš šu dím-[ma? n] géme im ga_6<-g̃á>-dè g[ub-ba 2] g̃uruš im ì-li-de_9 [gub-ba *b*]*í-ni-tum* im sumur ke_4-dè **é-uš-bar ù é-gašam**-[**e-ne**(-šè)], "[n builder(s)] (and) 8 workmen having built, [n] workwomen employed to carry earth (and) [2] workmen [employed] to lift earth, (workers) to plaster crossbeams [(for)] the textile mill and craftsmen's house," 71:21–24

1.3 Tamping Dirt around the Fireplace

1 g̃u[ruš šidim n g̃uruš] 18 [géme] KI.NE [saḫar?] sè-gé-d[è gub-ba] **é-uš-bar** [**ù é**]-**gaša**[**m-e-ne**-šè], "1 builder, [n workmen], and 18 [workwomen employed] to tamp [dirt?] around the fireplace [for] the textile mill [and] craftsmen's [house]," 54:'18-'20

1.4 Waterproofing the Roof

[. . . n g̃uruš i]m ì-li-de_9 [gub-ba n g̃uruš] im sumur tà-tà-dè gub-ba [ùr] a g̃á-g̃á-dè [**é-uš**]-**bar ù é-gašam-e**-[**ne**], "[. . . n workmen employed] to lift earth, [n workmen] employed to apply plaster, (workers) to waterproof [the roof] of the textile mill (and) craftmen's house," 65:'15-'19

1.5 Widening (the Opening of) the Roof Vent

2 ⸢g̃uruš⸣ 3 [géme] ab-ba dag̃[al tà-tà]-dè [gub-ba] **é-uš-bar** [**ù**] **é-gašam**-[šè] "2 workmen (and) 3 [workwomen] employed to [widen] (the opening of) the roof vent, (work) [for] the textile mill [and] craftsmen's house," 62:'21-'24

---

[5] For the occurrence of these two terms alone, see their respective entries.

1.6 Various Tasks

1 ĝuruš šidim 1 ĝuruš šu dím gub-[ba] 3 géme im ga_6-ĝá-dè gub-ba iz-zi im sumur ke_4-dè 10 géme $šeg_{12}$ šà é-a ĝá-ĝá-dè gub-ba **é-uš-bar ù é-gašam-e-ne**-šè, "1 builder (and) 1 workman employed to build, 3 workwomen employed to carry earth to plaster the iz-zi wall (and) 10 workwomen employed to place bricks in the house, (work) for the textile mill and craftsmen's house," 58:34–39

4 ĝuruš ⸢šidim⸣ 3 ĝu[ruš šu dím] gub-ba 30 ⸢géme⸣ 10 ⸢ĝuruš⸣ im ga_6-ĝá-dè gu[b-b]a 7 ĝuruš x im ì-li-de_9 gub-ba ùr a ĝá-ĝá-[dè] g[ub-ba] [n] ĝuru[š šidim] 2 [ĝuruš] 3 ⸢géme⸣ ab-ba daĝal t[à-tà-dè] gub-ba é-uš-bar ù é-gašam-šè, "4 builders (and) 3 workmen employed [to build], 30 workwomen (and) 10 workmen employed to carry earth, 7 builders employed to lift earth—(workers) employed to waterproof the roof—(and) [n] builder(s), 2 [workmen], (and) 3 workwomen employed [to] widen (the opening of) the roof vent, (work) for the textile mill and craftmen's house," 59:31–43

2 ĝuruš ⸢šidim⸣ 2 ĝuruš šu dím-m[a gub-ba] 4 géme im ⸢ga_6⸣-ĝá-dè gub-[ba] ab-ba daĝal t[à-tà-dè gub-ba] **é-uš-bar ù é-[NUN].ME.TAG-[e-ne**-šè], "2 builders (and) 2 workmen [employed] to build (and) 4 workwomen employed to carry earth—(workers) [employed to] widen (the opening of) the roof vent—(work) [for] the textile mill and craftsmen's house," 60:36–40

1.7 Broken Context

4 ĝuruš im [. . .] gub-[ba] **é-⸢uš⸣-bar ù é-gašam-e-ne**-šè, "4 workmen employed [to . . .] earth for the textile mill and the craftsmen's house," 56:'25-'26

2. Building Supplies

2.1 Bricks

mu-DU ki-sá-a [**é-uš-bar**] **ù é-NUN.**[**ME.TAG-e**]**-ne** [PN ugula] lú-ḫuĝ-ĝá, "delivery (of bricks) for the foundation terrace of the [textile mill] and craftsmen's house by [PN, overseer] of hired workers," 321:'33-'37

é-uš-bar ù [**é-NUN**]**.ME.**⸢**TAG**⸣**-e-**⸢**ne**⸣ mu-[DU] *simat-é-a* ugula [lú-ḫuĝ-ĝá], "delivery (of bricks for) the textile mill and craftsmen's house by *Simat-Ea*, overseer [of hired workers]," 328:14–16

[**é**]**-uš-bar** [**ù é**]**-gašam-e-ne** mu-DU *ba-zi* ugula lú-ḫuĝ-ĝá, "delivery (of bricks) for the textile [mill and] the craftsmen's [house] by *Bazi*, overseer of hired workers," 368:'60-'63

2.2 Reeds

n sa gi-izi gu-níĝin 36 sa-ta gi-sal **é-uš-bar ù é-gašam-e-ne**-šè ba-a-ĝar, "n bundles of fuel reeds, bales of 36 bundles each, the thin reeds were placed for the textile mill and craftsmen's house," 1262:1–3, 1264:1–3

é-*zu-zu-tum*

é-ki-ba-ĝar-ra ***zu-zu-tum***, "the replacement house of *Zuzutum*" > **é-ki-ba-ĝar-ra**

1. Construction

2 ĝuruš šidim [7] ĝuruš šu dím 10 géme im ga$_6$-ĝá ***é-zu-zu-tum*** dù-a, "2 builders (and) [7] workmen having built (and) 10 workwomen having carried earth, (workers) having constructed the house of *Zuzutum*," 123:31–33

4 ĝuru[š sa]ḫar zi-ga ***é-zu-zu-tum***, "4 workmen having moved dirt at the house of *Zuzutum*," 125:30

1 ĝuruš šidim 3 ĝuruš 10 [géme] al-tar ***é-zu-[zu-tum]***, "1 builder, 3 workmen (and) 10 [workwomen] (for) construction of the house of *Zuzutum*," 128:29–30

n ĝuruš šidim n ĝuruš n géme ***é-zu-zu-tum*** dù-a, "n builder(s), n workmen (and) n workwomen having constructed the house of *Zuzutum*," 132:31–32, 143:36–37, 158:28–29, 159:21–22, 160:'7-'8, 162:24–25

3 ĝuruš šidim 5 ĝuruš 3 géme šeg$_{12}$ šu dím-ma sum-mu-dè 10 géme im ga$_6$-⸢ĝá⸣ ***é-zu-zu-tum*** dù-[a], "3 builders, 5 workmen (and) 3 workwomen having handed (up) bricks for building (and) 10 workwomen having carried earth, (workers) having constructed the house of *Zuzutum*," 156:23–25

2. (De-)Construction

3 ĝuruš iz-zi ***é-⸢zu-zu-tum⸣*** gul-dè g[ub-ba], "3 workmen employed to demolish the iz-zi wall of the house of *Zuzutum*," 58:53–54

3 ĝuruš iz-⸢zi⸣ ***é-zu-zu-tum*** gul-la, "3 workmen having demolished the iz-zi wall of the house of *Zuzutum*," 122:'21

3 ĝuruš šidim 6 ĝuruš 13 géme ***é-zu-zu-⸢tum*** sumun⸣ <<til>> gul-dè, "3 builders, 6 workmen (and) 13 workwoman to demolish the old house of *Zuzutum*," 161:'13-'14

ĝá-nun(-na), *ganūnu*, "storehouse"

^{ĝeš}kiri$_6$ **ĝá-nun-na**, "the garden of the storehouse" > *Garden Index*

1. Construction: Workmen Sitting Idle

1 ĝuruš **ĝá-nun-na** tuš-a, "1 workman having sat (idle) at the storehouse," 27:'17, 28:'28, 29:'32, 31:35, 32:35, 33:38, 35:42, 36:36, 37:30, 38:35, 39:42, 40:36, 43:'40, 44:39, 45:21, 46:37, 47:51, 48:56, 49:55, 50:'15, 52:51, 57:'25-'26, 58:61, 59:51, 60:47, 65:'25, 74:'11, 75:29

2. Construction of its Structures

2.1 The iz-zi Wall

[n ĝuruš] im ⸢ga$_6$⸣-ĝá šu dím gub-ba [n ĝuruš šid]im 7 ĝuruš 7 géme [. . .] im sumur ke$_4$-dè gub-ba [n ĝuruš] im lu-a SIG$_4$.ANŠE gub-ba [n ĝuruš] šidim iz-zi **ĝá-nun-na** dù-dè gub-ba, "[n workmen] employed to carry earth (for) building, [n] builder(s), 7 workmen (and) 7 workwomen employed to plaster [. . .], [n workmen] employed to mix earth at the brick stack (and) [n] builder(s) employed to construct the iz-zi wall of the storehouse," 29:'23-'27

2.2 The Reed Hut

1 ĝuruš šidim gi-sig **ĝá-nun-na** dù-dè gub-ba, "1 builder employed to construct the reed hut of the storehouse," 6:23

[n] ĝuruš 2 géme [gi?-si]g? **ĝá-nun-na**, "[n] workmen (and) 2 workwomen at the [reed?] hut? of the storehouse," 50:8–9

2 ĝuruš [šidim] gi-sig **ĝ[á-nun-na]** dù-[a], "2 [builders] having constructed the reed hut of the storehouse," 60:27–28

3. Deliveries to the Storehouse

3.1 Transported from the Canal: Straw

20? ĝuruš gú i_7-da-ta **ĝá-nun**-šè in-u ga_6-ĝá, "20? workmen having carried straw from the bank of the canal to the storehouse," 16:25

3.2 Transported from the Quay

3.2.1 Barley

12 ĝuruš še kar?-ta **ĝá-nun**-šè ga_6-ĝá, "12 workmen having carried barley from the quay? to the storehouse," 104:42, 105:40

[n] ĝuruš tú[g-d]u_8 u_4-9-šè še ù-dag-ga^{ki}-ta gar-ša-an-na^{ki}-šè de_6-a ù kar-[ta] **ĝá-nun**-šè íb-⌜ga_6⌝ "[n] braider(s) for 9 days having brought barley from Udaga to Garšana and carried it [from] the quay to the storehouse," 261:1–6

3.2.2 Shok

n ĝuruš ^{geš}kišig kar-ta **ĝá-nun**-šè ga_6-ĝá, "n workmen having carried shok from the quay to the storehouse," 147:46, 155:34

30-lá–1 ĝuruš [4 gém]e ^{geš}kišig kar-ta **ĝá-nun**-šè ga_6-ĝá, "29 workmen (and) [4] workwomen having carried shok from the quay to the storehouse," 154:42

4 ĝuruš u_4-1-šè kar-ta **ĝá-nun**-šè ga_6-⌜ĝá⌝, "4 workmen for 1 day having carried (shok) from the quay to the storehouse," 235:11–12

3.2.3 Straw

11 ĝuruš in-u kar-ta **ĝá-nun**-šè ga_6-ĝá, "11 workmen having carried straw from the quay to the storehouse," 35:39

n ĝuruš in-u kar-ta **ĝá-nun-na**-šè íb-ga_6, "n workmen carried straw from the quay to the storehouse," 28:'23, 39:39, 43:'35-'37, 187:22–24, 188:'18-'20

6 ĝuruš in-u [^{d}*šu*]-^{d}*suen*-am-ma-ar-ra^{ki}-ta de_6-a kar-ta **ĝá-nun**-šè íb-ga_6, "6 workmen, having brought straw from *Šu-Suen*-ammara, carried it from the quay to the storehouse," 198:'28

4. Disbursals from the Storehouse: Straw for the Dirt Quarry

n ĝuruš in-u **ĝá-nun**-ta ka-lá(-ka)-šè íb-ga_6, "n workmen carried straw from the storehouse to the dirt quarry," 185:'15-'16, 196:'24

5. ĝá-nun-na sumun, "the old storehouse"

5.1 Construction of its Warehouse

2 ĝuruš [šidim] 6 ĝuruš šu dím gub-ba 10 géme im ga_6-ĝá gub-ba é-kì[š]ib-ba **ĝá-nun-na sumun** ĝeš ùr kéše-rá, "2 [builders] (and) 6 workmen employed to build, (and) 10 workwomen employed to carry earth, (workers) having bound roof beams for the warehouse of the old storehouse," 49:35–38

5.2 Roof Beams Stripped from its Roof

5 ĝuruš ùr é-kìšib-ba **ĝá-n[un-na] sumun** zi-le-dè gu[b-ba], "5 workmen employed to strip the roof of the warehouse of the old storehouse," 47:47–48

6. Broken Context

1 ğ[uruš] x ga_6-[. . .] **ğá-nun-[na** . . .], 52:40–42

3 [. . .] **ganun**-šè x-[. . .], 56:'23-'24

ğá-udu, "sheep-shearing shed"

1. Reeds Carried from the Shed to the Weir

30 géme uš-bar u_4-1-šè gi **ğá-udu**-ta kun-zi-id!(Á)-šè íb-ga_6, "30 female weavers for 1 day brought reeds from the sheep-shearing shed to the weir," 273:7–9

"The Triple Complex"

é-lùnga é-muḫaldim ù é-kíkken, "the brewery-kitchen-mill complex"[6]

1. Construction

[n] ğuruš 4 géme **[é-lùn]ga é-kíkken ù** [**é-muḫaldim** gub-ba], "[n] workmen (and) 4 workwomen [employed] at the brewery-[kitchen]-mill complex," 99:19–20

1.1 Various Tasks

[1] ğuruš šidim 2 ğuruš šu dím [n ğuru]š im sumur [ke_4-dè n] géme $šeg_{12}$ ga_6-[ğá-dè n ğuruš n] géme saḫar z[i-zi-dè **é-lùn]ga é-kíkken** [**ù é-muḫaldim**], "[1] builder (and) 2 workmen having built, [n] workmen [to] plaster, [n] workwomen [to] carry bricks (and) [n workmen (and) n] workwomen [to] move dirt, (work for) the brewery-[kitchen]-mill complex," 106:29–32

10 géme $šeg_{12}$ da-iz-zi ğá-ğá 11 ğuruš 11 géme im ga_6-ğá **é-lùnga é-muḫaldim ù** [**é**]-**kíkken**, "10 workwomen having placed bricks at the side of the iz-zi wall (and) 11 workmen (and) 11 workwomen having carried earth, (work for) the brewery-kitchen-mill complex," 140:37–39

1 ğuruš šidim 3 géme ká ⸢im⸣ sumur aka 20 ğuruš [*bí-n*]*i-tum* gíd-dè 13 [ğuruš ğeš] ùr kéše gíd-da 12 ⸢ğuruš⸣ gi-$guru_5$ aka [. . . **é-lùnga é-muḫaldim**] **ù é-kíkken**, "1 builder (and) 3 workwomen having plastered the gate, 20 workmen to tighten crossbeams, 13 [workmen] having tightened bound roof [beams] (and) 12 workmen having made reedwork panels [. . ., (work for) the brewery-kitchen]-mill complex," 144:'16-'21

1.2 Various Tasks, Specified for Construction (al-tar)

1 ğuruš šidim um-mi-a 7 ğuruš šidim n ğuruš šu dím n géme *du-ú-um* aka n géme im gíd n géme im ga_6-ğá 7 ğuruš n géme gi-sal gul-la 7 ğuruš gi-sal ga_6-ğá al-tar **é-lùnga é-muḫaldim ù é-kíkken**, "1 master builder, 7 builders (and) n workmen having built, n workwomen having made a *du-ú-um*, n workwomen having hauled earth, n workwomen having carried earth, 7 workmen (and) n workwomen having trimmed thin reeds (and) 7 workmen having carried thin reeds, (for) construction of the brewery-kitchen-mill complex," 128:21–28, 129:22–29

1 ğuruš šidim um-m[i-a] 7 ğuruš šidim 12 ğ[uruš šu dím] 8 géme *du-ú-*[*um* aka] 6 ⸢géme⸣ i[m gíd] 50-lá–1 géme im ga_6-[ğá] 5 ğuruš gi-sal ga_6-ğá 7 ğuruš 7 géme g[i-sal] gul-la al-tar **é-bap[pir é-muḫaldim] ù é-kíkken**, "1 master builder, 7 builders, (and) 12

[6] For the occurrence of these two terms alone, see their respective entries.

workmen [having built], 8 workwomen [having made] a *du-ú-um*, 6 workwomen [having hauled] earth, 49 workwomen having carried earth, 5 workmen having carried thin reeds, 7 workmen (and) 7 workwomen having trimmed [thin] reeds, (for) construction of the brewery-[kitchen]-mill complex," 131:'16–'23

[1] g̃uruš šidim um-mi-a [n] g̃uruš šidim 12 g̃uruš šu dím [n géme *du-ú-um* aka n géme] im g[íd n] ⸢géme⸣ im ga[$_{6}$-g̃á] [n+]2 g̃uruš gi-sal ga$_{6}$-g̃á [n g̃ur]uš 6 géme gi-sal gul-la al-tar **é-lùnga é-muḫaldim ù é-kíkken**, "[1] master builder, [n] builder(s) (and) 12 workmen having built, [n workwomen having made a *du-ú-um*, n workwomen] having hauled earth, [n] workwomen having carried earth, [n+]2 workmen having carried thin reeds (and) [n] workmen (and) 6 workwomen having trimmed thin reeds, (for) construction of the brewery-kitchen-mill complex," 132:23–30

1 g̃uruš šidim um-mi-a 7 g̃uruš šidim n g̃uruš šu dím 6 géme *du-ú-um* aka 7 géme im gíd n géme im ga$_{6}$-g̃á n g̃uruš 4 géme gi-sal gul-la al-tar **é-lùnga é-muḫaldim ù é-kíkken**, "1 master builder, 7 builders (and) n workmen having built, 6 workwomen having made a *du-ú-um*, 7 workwomen having hauled earth, n workwomen having carried earth, (and) n workmen (and) 4 workwomen having trimmed thin reeds, (for) construction of the brewery-kitchen-mill complex," 133:23–29, 135:24–30

1 g̃uruš šidim um-mi-a 4 g̃uruš šidim 20 g̃uruš šu dím [n] géme im ga$_{6}$-g̃á g̃eš ùr kéše-rá 4 g̃uruš šidim 15 g̃uruš šu dím 20 géme im ga$_{6}$-g̃á iz-zi ⸢im⸣ sumur aka 2 g̃uruš 2 géme gi-sal gi-ir ke$_{4}$-dè 10 [g̃uru]š 1 géme šeg$_{12}$ šu dím sum-mu-dè al-tar **é-lùnga é-muḫaldim ù é-kíkken**, "1 master builder, 4 builders (and) 20 workmen having built (and) [n] workwomen having carried earth—(workers) having bound roof beams—4 builders (and) 15 workmen having built (and) 20 workwomen having carried earth—(workers) having plastered the iz-zi wall—2 workmen (and) 2 workwomen to (?) thin reeds (and) 10 workmen (and) 1 workwoman to hand (up) bricks for building, (for) construction of the brewery-kitchen-mill complex," 136:25–34

1 g̃uruš šidim um-mi-a 6 g̃uruš šidim 24 g̃uruš šu dím 5 géme *du-ú-um* aka 3 géme im gíd 90[+n] géme [im ga$_{6}$-g̃á] 4 g̃uruš gi-sal [bàd ga$_{6}$-g̃á] 2 ⸢g̃uruš⸣ g̃eš ùr kéše-[rá] al-tar **é-lùnga é-mu[ḫaldim ù é-kík]ken**, "1 master builder, 6 builders (and) 24 workmen having built, 5 workwomen having made a *du-ú-um*, 3 workwomen having hauled earth, 90[+n] workwomen [having carried earth], 4 workmen [having carried] thin reeds [(for) the (enclosure) wall] (and) 2 workmen having bound roof beams, (for) construction of the brewery-kitchen-mill complex," 138:24–31

1 [g̃uruš šidim u]m-mi-a [7 g̃uruš šidim] 20 g̃uruš 10-lá–1 gé[me . . . 2 g̃uruš šidi]m 20 [g̃uruš 16] géme im ga$_{6}$-g̃[á g̃eš ùr] kéše-rá [8] géme šeg$_{12}$ da-iz-zi [g̃á-g̃á] al-[tar] **é-lùnga é-muḫaldim [ù] é-kíkken**, "1 master [builder, 7 builders], 20 workmen (and) 9 workwomen [having . . ., 2] builders, 20 [workmen (and) 16] workwomen having carried earth—(workers) having bound [roof beams—(and) 8] workwomen [having placed] bricks at the side of the iz-zi wall, (for) construction of the brewery-kitchen-mill complex," 141:25–33

[1] g̃uruš šidim um-mi-a 7 g̃uruš <šidim> 20 g̃uruš 10-lá–1 géme šu dím? 27 géme im ga$_{6}$-g̃á iz-zi im su[mur a]ka 2 g̃uruš šidim 20 ⸢g̃uruš⸣ šu dím 16 géme im ga$_{6}$-g̃á <g̃eš ùr kéše-rá> [8] géme šeg$_{12}$ da-iz-zi g̃á-g̃á ⸢al⸣-tar **é-lùnga é-muḫaldim ù é-kíkken**, "[1] master builder, 7 <builders>, 20 workmen (and) 9 workwomen having built? (and) 27 workwomen having carried earth—(workers) having plastered the iz-zi wall, - (and) 2 builders (and) 20 workmen having built, 16 workwomen having carried earth—(workers) <having bound roof beams,> - (and) [8] workwomen having placed bricks at

the side of the iz-zi wall, (for) construction of the brewery-kitchen-mill complex," 142:21–29

[1 g̃uruš š]idim um-mi-[a n g̃uruš šidim] 16 g̃uruš šu [dím n g̃uruš] šeg$_{12}$ šu dím-ma [n g]éme *du-ú-*[*um* aka n] géme im gí[d n] géme im g[a$_6$-g̃á n g̃uruš] 15 [géme g̃eš ùr] kéše-r[á n] géme gi-sal gul-[la al-tar **é-ba**]**ppir é-muḫaldim** [**ù é-kíkken**], "[1] master builder, [n builder(s)] (and) 16 workmen having built, [n workmen] having built with bricks, [n] workwomen [having made] a *du-ú-um*, [n] workwomen having hauled earth, [n] workwomen having carried clay, [n workmen] (and) 15 [workwomen having] bound [roof beams (and) n] workwomen having trimmed thin reeds, [(for) construction of] the brewery-kitchen-mill complex," 143:25–34

[1 g̃uru]š šidim um-mi-a [. . . n g̃ur]uš g̃eš ùr kéše-[rá] 10 g̃uruš *bí-ni-tum* gíd-[da] 12 g̃uruš 12 géme gi-guru$_5$ ⌜aka⌝ al-tar **é-lùnga é-muḫaldim ù é-**⌜**kíkken**⌝, "[1] master builder [. . ., n] workmen having bound roof beams, 10 workmen having hauled crossbeams (and) 12 workmen (and) 12 workwomen having made reedwork panels, (for) construction of the brewery-kitchen-mill complex," 145:27–36

1 g̃uruš šidim 4 g̃uruš 11 géme al-tar gub-[ba] 3 g̃uruš šidim 12 g̃uruš 12 [géme] *bí-ni-*⌜*tum*⌝ i[m sumur aka] 2 g̃uruš 7 géme g̃eš [ùr kéše gíd-dè] 2 g̃uruš šidim 3 g̃ur[uš n géme?] iz-zi im sum[ur a]ka [n g̃u]ruš šidim 31 g̃uruš šu dím [x] sè-gé-dè [n] g̃uruš šidim 2 g̃uruš 10 géme kun dù-a 1 g̃uruš šidim 3 g̃uruš 10 géme [x] mu-gu dù-a [n] g̃uruš 10 géme gi-guru$_5$ aka ⌜al⌝-tar **é-lùnga é-muḫaldim ù** [**é-kíkken**], "1 master builder, 4 workmen (and) 11 workwomen employed (for) construction, 3 builders, 12 workmen (and) 12 [workwomen having plastered] crossbeams, 2 workmen (and) 7 workwomen [having tightened bound roof] beams, 2 builders, 3 workmen [(and) n workwomen?] having plastered the iz-zi wall, [n] builder(s) (and) 31 workmen having built, (worked) to place [x], [n] builder(s), 2 workmen (and) 10 workwomen having installed a ladder, 1 builder, 3 workmen (and) 10 workwomen having constructed (?) (and) [n] workmen (and) 10 workwomen having made reedwork panels, (for) construction of the brewery-kitchen-mill complex," 146:'22-'35

[1] g̃uruš šidim um-mi-a [n] g̃uruš šidim 8 g̃uruš 20 géme [al]-tar gub-[ba n g̃uruš] šidim 4 g̃uruš 14 g[éme *bí-n*]*i-tum* im sum[ur ke$_4$-dè gub-ba n g̃uruš šidi]m 3 g̃uruš [n géme iz-zi] im [sumur aka n g̃uruš šidi]m 3 g̃ur[uš n géme x mu-g]u d[ù-a] 10 géme g[i-guru$_5$ aka n g̃uruš šidim n] g̃uruš šu [dím. . .] *dì-um* [. . . n] g̃u[ruš . . . **é-lùn**]**ga é-muḫaldim ù é-**[**kíkken**], "[1] master builder, [n] builder(s), 8 workmen (and) 20 workwomen employed (for) construction, [n] builder(s), 4 workmen (and) 14 workwomen [employed] to plaster crossbeams, [n] builder(s), 3 workmen [(and) n workwomen] having plastered [the iz-zi wall], [n] builder(s), 3 workmen [(and) n workwomen] having constructed (?), 10 workwomen [having made] reedwork [panels], (and) [n builder(s), n] workmen [having built . . .] wattle and daub, [n] workmen [having ...], (work for) the brewery-kitchen-[mill] complex," 147:27–40

[n g̃ur]uš šidim 3 g̃uruš 6 géme [*a-za-b*]*u-um* šà é-a ba-a[l-dè n g̃uru]š šidim 5 g̃uruš 3 ⌜géme⌝ al-tar gub-⌜ba⌝ 2 g̃uruš šidim 3 g̃uruš 3 géme ká im sumur aka **é-lùnga é-muḫaldim ù é-kíkken**, "[n] builder(s), 3 workmen (and) 6 workwomen [to] dig the cistern in the house, [n] builder(s), 5 workmen (and) 3 workwomen employed (for) construction (and) 2 builders, 3 workmen (and) 3 workwomen having plastered the gate, (work for) the brewery-kitchen-mill complex," 155:25–31

2. Construction of its Structures

2.1 Its Foundation Terrace

1 g̃uruš šidim um-mi-a [n g̃uru]š šidim 31 g̃uruš šu dím 4? géme *du-ú-um* aka 6 géme im gíd 48 géme im ga_6-g̃á ⸢al⸣-tar ki-sá-a **é-lùnga é-muḫaldim ù é-kíkken**, "1 master builder, [n] builder(s) (and) 31 workmen having built, 4? workwomen having made a *du-ú-um*, 6 workwomen having hauled earth (and) 48 workwomen having carried earth, (for) construction of the foundation terrace of the brewery-kitchen-mill complex," 125:21–26

1 g̃uruš šidim um-mi-a 8 g̃uruš šidim 22 g̃uruš šu dím [n+]3 géme *du-ú-um* aka [n] géme im gíd 38 géme im ga_6-g̃á 5 g̃uruš 4 géme ⸢gi⸣-sal ga_6-g̃á 5 g̃uruš gi-[sal] gul-la ⸢al⸣-tar ki-sá-[a **é-lùnga**] **é-muḫaldim** [**ù é**]-**kíkken**, "1 master builder, 8 builders (and) 22 workmen having built, [n+]3 workwomen having made a *du-ú-um*, [n] workwomen having hauled earth, 38 workwomen having carried earth, 5 workmen (and) 4 workwomen having carried thin reeds (and) 5 workmen having trimmed [thin] reeds, (for) construction of the foundation terrace of the [brewery]-kitchen-mill complex," 126:21–28

2.2 Its Roof, iz-zi Wall, and Floor

1 g̃uruš šidim um-mi-a 4 g̃uruš šidim 4 g̃uruš 60 géme ùr a g̃á-g̃á 1 g̃uruš šidim 3 g̃uruš 3 géme *ra-ṭum*-bi dù-a 5 g̃uruš šidim 5 g̃uruš 16 géme *bí-ni-tum* im sumur aka 1 g̃uruš šidim 1 g̃uruš 4 géme iz-zi im sumur aka 28 g̃uruš 20 géme ki-ba sè-ga **é-lùnga é-muḫaldim ù é-kíkken**, "1 master builder, 4 builders, 4 workmen, (and) 60 workwomen having waterproofed the roof, 1 builder, 3 workmen (and) 3 workwomen having constructed its drains, 5 builders, 5 workmen (and) 16 workwomen having plastered crossbeams, 1 builder, 1 workman (and) 4 workwomen having plastered the iz-zi wall (and) 28 workmen (and) 20 workwomen having tamped the floor, (work for) the brewery-kitchen-mill complex," 150:26–36

2.3 Its Roof and Oven

3 g̃uruš šidim 3 g̃uruš 10-lá-1 géme ⸢*bí*⸣-*ni-tum* [im] sumur aka 2 g̃uruš šidim 6 g̃uruš 20 [géme] gir_4 dù-a 1 g̃uruš šidim 1 g̃uruš 5 [géme a]l-tar ⸢dù⸣-a [n] g̃uruš šidim 10 ⸢géme⸣ ùr a g̃á-g̃á 11 g̃uruš [n] géme ki-ba sè-ga **é-lùnga é-muḫaldim ù é-kíkken**, "3 builders, 3 workmen (and) 9 workwomen having plastered crossbeams, 2 builders, 6 workmen (and) 20 [workwomen] having constructed an oven, 1 builder, 1 workman (and) 5 [workwomen] having done construction work, [n] builder(s) (and) 10 workwomen having waterproofed the roof (and) 11 workmen (and) [n] workwomen having tamped the floor, (work for) the brewery-kitchen-mill complex," 151:24–33

2 g̃uruš šidim 2 g̃uruš 50 géme ùr a g̃á-g̃á 1 g̃uruš šidim 12 g̃uruš 10 géme gir_4 dù-a 1 g̃uruš šidim 12 g̃uruš 3 géme *ra-ṭum*-bi dù-a 1 g̃uruš šidim (1 or 4) g̃uruš 7 géme ká im sumur aka 5 g̃uruš šidim 7 g̃uruš 20 géme *bí-ni-tum* im sumur aka 1 g̃uruš šidim 4 g̃uruš 10 géme al-tar dù-a **é-lùnga é-muḫaldim ù é-kíkken**, "2 builders, 2 workmen (and) 50 workwomen having waterproofed the roof, 1 builder, 12 workmen (and) 10 workwomen having constructed an oven, 1 builder, 12 workmen (and) 3 workwomen having constructed its drains, 1 builder, (1 or 4) workmen (and) 7 workwomen having plastered the gate, 5 builders, 7 workmen (and) 20 workwomen having plastered crossbeams (and) 1 builder, 4 workmen (and) 10 workwomen having done construction work, (work for) the brewery-kitchen-mill complex," 152:'7-'19, 153:'20-'32

1 g̃uruš šidim 2 g̃uruš 10 géme gir$_4$ dù-a 3 g̃uruš šidim 3 g̃uruš 10-lá–1 géme *bí-ni-tum* im sumur aka 1 g̃uruš šidim 1 g̃uruš 10 géme al-tar dù-a 1 g̃uruš šidim 11 g̃uruš [5] géme *dì-um* g̃á-g̃á **é-lùnga é-muḫaldim ù é-kíkken**, "1 builder, 2 workmen (and) 10 workwomen having constructed an oven, 3 builders, 3 workmen (and) 9 workwomen having plastered crossbeams, 1 builder, 1 workman (and) 10 workwomen having done construction work (and) 1 builder, 11 workmen (and) [5] workwomen having placed wattle and daub, (work for) the brewery-kitchen-mill complex," 154:28–36

3. Building Supplies

3.1 Bitumen

26.2.1.5 sìla ésir-ḫád gur 0.2.2.5 ⸢sìla⸣ ésir-é-a 0.0.0.8½ sìla ì-šáḫ 0.0.2. ì-ḫur-sag̃-g̃á *šit-tum* **é-lùnga é-kíkken ù** *ma-aZ-ḫa-ru-um* **é-muḫaldim**-šè ba-a-g̃ar, "26 bushels (and) 135 liters of dried bitumen, 145 liters of house bitumen, 8½ liters of lard (and) 20 liters of mountain fat, the balance (of the settled account), were placed for the brewery, the mill and the *maZḫarum* of the kitchen," 1299:1–5

3.2 Reeds

2980 sa g[i-iz]i a-rá–1-kam 2970 sa g[i-iz]i a-rá–2-kam 1078 sa gi-izi a-rá–3-kam gi-sal **é-lùnga é-muḫaldim ù é-kíkken** ba-a-g̃ar, "2980 bundles of fuel reeds for the 1st time, 2970 bundles of fuel reeds for the 2nd time (and) 1078 bundles of fuel reeds for the 3rd time, the thin reeds were placed (for) the brewery-kitchen-mill complex," 1294:1–9

3.3 Reeds and Roof Beams

[n] g̃eš ùr šinig 31 ^{geš}é-da-ásal 56 ^{geš}ká 260 ^{gi}dur-gazi a-rá–3-tab-ba gíd 1½ nindan-⸢ta⸣ g̃eš-ká kéše-dè **é-lùnga é-muḫaldim ù é-kíkken**, "[n] tamarisk roof beam(s), 31 poplar joists, 56 gate timbers (and) 260 9-meter 3-ply gazi ropes in order to bind the gate timbers of the brewery-kitchen-mill complex," 1293:1–6

4. Rations, Wages and Allotments

4.1 For Builders Employed at the Complex

4.1.1 Beer

0.0.n. kaš-gen šidim-e-ne íb-nag̃ u$_4$ al-tar **é-lùnga é-muḫaldim ù é-kíkken**, "The builders drank n liter(s) of ordinary beer during construction of the brewery-kitchen-mill complex," 435:4–6, 439:4–6, 441:4–6

4.1.2 Bread and Beer

5 sìla ninda 0.0.2. kaš-gen šidim-e-ne íb-gu$_7$ ù íb-nag̃ [u$_4$] al-tar **é-lùnga é-muḫaldim ù é-kíkken** gub-ba, "The builders ate and drank 5 liters of bread (and) 20 liters of ordinary beer [when] they were employed (for) construction of the brewery-kitchen-mill complex," 430:1–4

5 sìla ninda [n] kaš-gen ⸢šidim⸣-e-ne íb-gu$_7$ u$_4$ al-tar **é-lùnga é-muḫaldim é-kíkken**, "The builders consumed 5 liters of bread (and) [n] liter(s) of ordinary beer during construction of the brewery-kitchen-mill-complex," 440:9–12

4.2 For Builders and Hired Workers: Dates

1.2.2.5 sìla zú-lum <gur> šidim ù lú-ḫug̃-g̃á-e-ne ba-na-ḫa-la u$_4$ al-tar **é-lùnga é-muḫaldim ù é-kíkken**, "1 bushel (and) 145 liters of dates were divided for the builders and hired workers during construction of the brewery-kitchen-mill complex," 429:1–4

4.3 For the Small Flour Heap

4.3.1 Beer and Flour

1 dug dida$_x$-gen 1 sìla dabin ½ eša zì-dub-dub-šè u$_4$ g̃eš ùr ba-kéše-rá **é-lùnga é-muḫaldim ù é-kíkken**, "1 jug of ordinary dida beer, 1 liter of semolina (and) ½ liter of fine flour for the small flour heap when the roof beams of the brewery-kitchen-mill complex were bound," 1251:9–14

4.3.2 Semolina and Fine Flour

1 sìla dabin ½ sìla eša zì-dub-dub-šè **é-lùnga é-muḫaldim ù é-kíkken**, "1 liter of semolina (and) ½ liter of fine flour for the small flour heap of the brewery-kitchen-mill complex," 436:1–3, 1008:4–6, 1249:1–4, 1297:11–13

4.4 (Ceremonial) Offerings during Construction

4.4.1 Beer, Semolina and Fine Flour

[2 sìla] dabin 1 sìla eša 0.0.1. kaš-gen sízkur gir-ra 1 sìla [dabin] ½ sìla eša sízkur-**é-⸢lùnga⸣ é-[muḫaldim ú] é-kíkken** (. . .) u$_4$ al-tar **é-lùnga é-muḫaldim é-kíkken**, "[2 liters] of semolina, 1 liter of fine flour (and) 10 liters of ordinary beer—(ceremonial) offerings of the fire—1 liter of [semolina] (and) ½ liter of fine flour—(ceremonial) offerings of the brewery-kitchen-mill complex—{food for builders}, during construction of the brewery-kitchen-mill complex," 440:1–7, 12

1 dug dida$_x$-gen 0.0.3?-[ta] 1 sìla dabin [1 sìl]a eša ⸢sízkur⸣-šè u$_4$ ká **é-lùnga é-muḫaldim ù é kíkken** kéše-⸢rá⸣, "1 jug of ordinary dida beer, 30? liters [each], 1 liter of semolina, (and) [1] liter of fine flour, for (ceremonial) offerings when the gate of the brewery-kitchen-mill complex was bound," 1007:1–5

5. Deliveries of the Complex

0.0.1.2 sìla ninda 0.0.1. kaš-gen ½ sìla níg̃-àr-ra-sig$_5$ 1 ku$_6$ al-dar-ra ^{dug}útul-šè gala-e-ne *ták-ri-ib-tum* **é-⸢lùnga⸣ é-muḫaldim ù é-kíkken**, "12 liters of bread, 10 liters of ordinary beer, ½ liter of fine groats (and) 1 split (dried) fish for the tureen of the lamentation singers (for their performance of) a *takribtum*; (delivery from) the brewery-kitchen-mill complex," 437:7–13

Analytical Index of Deities

^{d}*al-la-tum*
^{d}alim-[. . .]
^{d}*da-mu*
^{d}en-líl
^{d}gu-la
^{d}inana
^{d}*ištaran*
^{d}ki-na
^{d}*kab-ta*
^{d}*ma-mi-tum*
^{d}na-na
^{d}nergal$_{x}^{eri_{11}\text{-}gal}$
^{d}nin-ḫur-saĝ-ĝá
^{d}nin-^{d}si$_{4}$-an-na
^{d}nin-unug^{ki}
^{d}šára
^{d}šu-bu-la
^{d}*tá-ad-muṣ-tum*

diĝir-re-e-ne, "the gods"

1. Activities of the Gods

(. . .) ⸢u$_{4}$⸣-1-šè gaba sìg-dè gub-ba u$_{4}$ **diĝir-re** gaba *na-wi-ir-ilum* ba-a-ĝar-ra, "{craftsmen} for 1 day employed to beat (their) breasts when the god made the breast of *Nawir-ilum* subside (i.e., when he died)," 251:8–10

2. Allotments for the Gods

kaš-dé-a **diĝir-re-e-ne**, "banquet of the gods" > **kaš-dé-a**

2.1 Assorted Oils

1 sìla ì-nun-ĝeš-a-rá-me 1 sìla ì-ĝeš-ĝeš-a-rá-me 10 gín ì-dùg-nun-na mu **diĝir-re-e-ne**-šè, "1 liter of a-rá ghee, 1 liter of a-rá sesame oil, (and) 10 shekels of good-quality ghee for the gods," 1004:1–4

2.2 Broken Pots

12 ^{dug}b[a-x] ⸢mu⸣ **diĝir-re-e-ne**-šè gaz-dè, "12 [x]-vessels to be broken for the gods," 1013:6–7

2.3 Ceremonial Offerings

0.0.5. zì-KAL 0.0.2. zì-gu-ús 0.0.4.3 sìla dabin 0.0.2.4 sìla eša 7⅓ sìla zú-lum eša ḫi-dè sízkur **diĝir-re-[e]-ne** [. . .], "50 liters of KAL-flour, 20 liters of 2nd-quality gu-flour, 43 liters of semolina, 24 liters of fine flour (and) 7⅓ liters of dates to mix (with) fine flour, (ceremonial) offerings of the [. . .] gods," 1017:1–6

2.4 Regular Offerings

1 udu abzu-šè 1 máš ká kù-^{d}inana-zabala$_4^{ki}$ u$_4$ ezem-gur-buru$_{14}$ g̃iri nin-zi-šà-g̃ál 1 u$_8$ sá-du$_{11}$-^{d}inana-zabala$_4^{ki}$ 1 udu sá-du$_{11}$-^{d}šára sá-du$_{11}$-**dig̃ir-re-ne**, "regular offerings of gods: 1 sheep for the abzu, 1 goat for the gate of bright Inana of Zabala during the bushel harvest festival under the authority of Nin-zišag̃al (and) 1 ewe, regular offerings of Inana of Zabala (and) 1 sheep, regular offerings of Šara," 996:1–8

2.5 Textiles

5 túg-guz-za 4-ka[m-ú]s **dig̃ir-re-e-ne**, "5 4th-quality tufted textiles of the gods," 739:4

3. Broken Context

[x]-qar [x-x]-dig̃ir**?-a [. . .], 984:13

^{d}*al-la-tum*

1. Allotments: Textiles

1 túg-^{d}*al-la-tum***-gùn-a ù zi-in-bi ki-lá-bi 9 ma-[na] 12 gín *a-ku$_8$-a-nu-ri*, "1 colored textile of *Allatum* and its zi-in weighing 9 minas (and) 12 shekels (for) *Akua-nuri*," 584:1–3

1 túg-zi-li-ḫi túg-^{d}***al-la-tum***, "1 zi-li-ḫi textile of *Allatum*," 715:1

^{d}alim-[. . .]

1. Allotments: Semolina and Fine Flour

2 sìla dabin 1 sìla A.[TIR] ^{d}**alim-**[. . .], "2 liters of semolina (and) 1 liter of fine flour (for) Alim-[. . .]," 506:10–11

^{d}*da-mu*

1. Allotments: Textiles

[1 túg-*ḫa*]-*bu-um* $^{[d]}$***da-mu***, "[1] soft [textile] of *Damu*," 594:2–3

1 ^{túg}níg̃-lám 4-kam-ús ^{d}***da-mu***, "1 4th-quality níg̃-lám textile of *Damu*," 617:6

^{d}en-líl

1. Regular Offerings

1 [udu] sá-du$_{11}$-^{d}**en-[líl?]**, "1 [sheep], regular offerings of Enlil?," 1003:3–4

^{d}gu-la

1. Allotments: Grains

[1] sìla dabin 1 sìla eša ^{d}**gu-la**, "[1] liter of semolina (and) 1 liter of fine flour (for) Gula," 1016:1–3

2. Allotments: Textiles

1 túg-siki-dù-a 3-kam-ús ^{d}**gu-la**, "1 3rd-quality siki-dù-a textile of Gula," 574:1

^{d}inana

1. Inana of Uruk

1.1 The Builders of her Priest

n ĝuruš šidim lú-en-^{d}**inana-unu^{ki}-ga**, "n builder(s), men of the priest of Inana of Uruk," 194:2, 197:22, 198:'11

1.2 Her Waterskin

1 ^{kuš}[EDIN.A].LÁ-^{d}**inana-unug^{ki}**, "1 waterskin of Inana of Uruk," 925:'13

2. Inana of Zabala

kaš-dé-a ^{d}**inana-zabala$_4^{ki}$**, "banquet of Inana of Zabala" > **kaš-dé-a**

2.1 Allotments

2.1.1 Animals

1 sila$_4$ ^{d}**inana-zabala$_4^{[ki]}$**, "1 lamb (for) Inana of Zabala," 1003:11–12

4 ⌜máš⌝ 4 u$_8$ [n] ud$_5$ [n] máš-gal ba-úš bi+šu-ab-ta? ^{d}inana-zabala$_4^{ki}$** u$_4$-1-šè é-šu-^{d}E[N.Z]U, "4 goats, 4 ewes, [n] (female) goat(s), (and) [n] billy-goat(s) were slaughtered (?) (for) Inana of Zabala for 1 day (in) *Bit-Šu-Suen*," 1019:1–7

2.1.2 Animals and Grains

1 udu-niga gu$_4$-e-ú[s-sa] 0.0.1. zì-⌜KAL⌝ 3 sìla zì-[x] 2 sìla ⌜eša⌝ ^{d}**inana-zabala$_4^{[ki]}$**, "1 fattened sheep '(fed) following the oxen,' 10 liters of KAL-flour, 3 liters of [x] flour (and) 2 liters of fine flour (for) Inana of Zabala," 970:1–5

2.1.3 Assorted Commodities in her Courtyard

[n] dabin [. . . iti] u$_4$-[n-ba-z]al [n] udu-niga gu$_4$-e-ús-[sa] iti u$_4$-17-ba-[zal] 0.0.2. zì-⌜KAL⌝ 3 sìla 0.1.0. dabin 2 sìla eša 1 dug dida$_x$-gen 2 [. . .] 10 sa gi-[izi] šà kisal-lá ^{d}**inana-za[bala$_4^{ki}$]**, "[n] liter(s) of semolina [. . .] at the end of the [nth] day of the [month], [n] fattened sheep '(fed) following the oxen' at the end of the 17th day of the month, 20 liters of KAL-flour, 3 liters (and) 60 (units of) semolina, 2 liters of fine flour, 1 jug of ordinary dida beer, 2 [. . .], (and) 10 bundles of [fuel] reeds in the courtyard of Inana of Zabala," 506:1–9

1 túg ba-tab *tuḫ-ḫu-um* 3-kam-ús ^{d}**inana** 10 sa-níĝin ^{ĝeš}⌜ásal⌝ 30 sa gi-izi ninda ba-ra-du$_8$ uzu ù tu$_7$ ba-ra-šeĝ$_6$ 60 ^{dug}sìla-bur-zi tu$_7$-šè šà kisal-lá ^{d}**inana-zabala$_4^{ki}$** (. . .) šà zabala$_4^{ki}$ u$_4$-2-kam, "1 3rd-quality ba-tab *tuḫ-ḫu-um* textile of Inana, 10 bundles of poplar wood, 30 bundles of fuel reeds with which bread was baked (and) meat and soup were cooked; 60 one-liter offering bowls for soup in the courtyard of Inana of Zabala (and) {other "offerings"} in Zabala on the 2nd day," 1028:31–37, 45

2.1.4 Beer

1 kaš-gen 1 dida$_x$-gen ^{d}**inana-zabala$_4$[^{ki}-šè]**, "1 ordinary beer (and) 1 ordinary dida beer [for] Inana of Zabala," 1009:1–3

2.1.5 Grains

0.0.2. zì-KAL 0.0.1. zì-gu-ús ninda-gur$_4$-ra-šè ^{d}**inana-zabala$_4^{ki}$** ama *tá-ḫi-iš-a-tal*, "20 liters of KAL-flour (and) 10 liters of 2nd-quality gu-flour for thick bread (for) Inana of Zabala (and) the mother of *Taḫiš-atal*," 1015:1–4, 1018:1–5

2.2 Regular Offerings

2.2.1 Animals

1 máš ká kù-^{d}**inana-zabala$_4$^{ki}** u$_4$ ezem-gur-buru$_{14}$ g̃ìri nin-zi-šà-g̃ál 1 u$_8$ sá-du$_{11}$-^{d}**inana-zabala$_4$^{ki}**, "1 goat for the gate of bright Inana of Zabala during the bushel harvest festival under the authority of Nin-zišag̃al (and) 1 ewe, regular offerings of Inana of Zabala," 996:2–6

1 udu sá-du$_{11}$-^{d}**inana-zabala$_4$^{ki}**, "1 sheep, regular offerings of Inana of Zabala," 1000:1–2, 1010:1–2, 1012:1, 1021:1–2

2.2.2 Grains

3 sìla níg̃-àr-ra-sig$_5$ [n sìla] zì [n sìla] dabin [n sìla] eša [. . .]-rú?-maḫ [sá-du$_{11}$-^{d}**ina]na-zabala$_4$^{ki}**, "3 liters of fine groats, [n liter(s)] of flour, [n liter(s)] of semolina (and) [n liter(s)] of fine flour, [. . . regular offerings] of Inana of Zabala," 1027:7–12

2.2.3 Skins

1 kuš-udu sá-du$_{11}$-^{d}**inana-zabala$_4$^{ki}**, "1 sheep skin, regular offerings of Inana of Zabala," 860:1–2

2.3 Regular Offerings Returned from the Shrine

2.3.1 Bread and Skins

9 sìl[a . . .] 8 sìla ninda 1 kuš-máš-gal-niga sá-du$_{11}$-^{d}**inana-zabala$_4$^{ki}** (. . .) èš-ta-gur-⌜ra⌝, "9 liters [. . .], 8 liters of bread, (and) 1 skin of a fattened billy-goat, regular offerings of Inana of Zabala (and) {offerings of other deities}, offerings returned from the shrine" 1022:10–12, 15

6 sìla ninda 1 kuš-udu-niga sá-du$_{11}$-^{d}**inana-zabala$_4$$^{[ki]}$** (. . .) èš-ta-gur-ra, "6 liters of bread (and) 1 skin of a fattened sheep, regular offerings of Inana of Zabala (and) {offerings of other deities}, offerings returned from the shrine," 1023:11–12, 15

5? sìla š[e-ninda] 1 kuš-u[du-niga] sá-du$_{11}$-^{d}**inana-MÙŠ.ZA.[UNUG]^{ki}** (. . .) èš-ta-gur-⌜ra⌝, "5? liters of barley [(for) bread] (and) 1 skin of a [fattened] sheep, regular offerings of Inana of Zabala (and) {offerings of other deities}, offerings returned from the shrine," 1024:11–13, 17

2.3.2 Grains

0.0.1?.7⅔ sìla tuḫ-duru$_5$ sá-du$_{11}$-^{d}**inana-zabala$_4$^{ki}** èš-ta-gur-ra, "17⅔ liters of fresh bran, regular offerings of Inana of Zabala, offerings returned from the shrine," 997:10–12

2.3.3 Skins

2 kuš-udu-niga sá-du$_{11}$-^{d}**inana-zabala$_4$^{ki}** (. . .) èš-ta-gur-ra, "2 sheep skins, regular offerings of Inana of Zabala (and) {offerings of other deities}, offerings returned from the shrine," 1026:9–10, 13

3. Inana of the City

kaš-dé-a ^{d}**inana-iri^{ki}**, "banquet of Inana of the city" > **kaš-dé-a**

3.1 Allotments: Beer

1 kaš-gen 1 dida$_x$-gen ^{d}**inana-šà-iri^{ki}**, "1 ordinary beer (and) 1 ordinary dida beer for Inana of the city," 1009:9–11

4. Inana, City Unspecified

en-^{d}**inana**-gal, "senior priest of Inana" > **en**

^{d}*ištaran*

1. Allotments: Textiles

1 túg-guz-za-tur 4-kam-ús ^{d}***ištaran***, "1 small 4th-quality tufted textile of *Ištaran*," 576:1

^{d}*kab-ta*

1. Allotments: Textiles

1 túg-ḫa-la ú-x-x-tur 3-kam-ús ^{d}***kab-ta***, "1 small 3rd-quality ú-x-x textile of *Kabta*," 690:2

1 ^{túg}gú-lá-PI-tur 3-kam-ús ^{d}***kab-ta***, "1 small 3rd-quality gú-lá-PI textile of *Kabta*," 690:3

[n] túg-*ḫu-la-um* ù zi-lí-ḫi 3-kam-ús ^{d}***kab-tá***, "[n] 3rd-quality *ḫu-la-um* and zi-lí-ḫi textile(s) of *Kabta*," 738:6

n ^{túg}gú-lá-PI 3-kam-ús ^{d}***kab-tá***, "n 3rd-quality gú-lá-PI textile(s) of *Kabta*," 738:7, 811:4

^{d}*ma-mi-tum*

1. Allotments: Textiles

n túg-guz-za 4-kam-ús ^{d}***ma-mi-tum***, "n 4th-quality tufted textile(s) of *Mamitum*," 608:7, 617:4

^{d}Na-na

Nana, (the personal deity of) *Aḫu'a*

1. Regular Offerings

12 udu sá-du$_{11}$-^{d}**na-na** *a-ḫu-a*, "(In total:) 12 sheep, regular offerings of Nana, (the personal deity of) *Aḫu'a*," 984:'44-'45

^{d}nergal$_{x}^{eri11-gal}$

kaš-dé-a ^{d}**nergal**, "banquet of Nergal" > **kaš-dé-a**

1. During the *Elunum* Festival of Nergal

1.1 Offerings

[1] udu [^{d}**ne]rgal**$_{x}^{eri11-gal}$ u$_{4}$ *e-lu-núm-ma*, "[1] sheep (for) Nergal during the *Elunum* (festival)," 1032:1–3

1.2 Offerings Returned from the Shrine

[. . .] ^{d}nin-unu?-g[a? n] sìla ninda [n] kuš-u[du-nig]a ki-a-nag *šu-kab-*⌜*tá*⌝ èš-ta-gur-ra ^{d}*adad-tillati* šu ba-ti u$_{4}$ ezem-*e-lu-núm*-^{d}**nergal**$_{x}^{eri11-gal}$, "*Adad-tillati* received [. . .] (of?) Nin-Unug (and) [n] liter(s) of bread (and) [n] skin(s) of fattened sheep of the funerary libation place of *Šu-Kabta*, offerings returned from the shrine during the *Elunum* festival of Nergal," 980:1–11

1.3 Workers Expended

1 ĝuruš šidim 15 ĝuruš u$_{4}$ *e-lu-núm*-^{d}**n[ergal**$_{x}^{eri11-gal}$] šà iri^{ki} ba-zi, "1 builder (and) 15 workmen disbursed during the *Elunum* festival of Nergal in the city," 19:14–16

6 ğuruš šidim u$_4$ *e-lu-núm*-^{d}**nergal$_x$**$^{[eri_{11}\text{-}g]al}$ du$_8$-[dè], "6 builders [to be] released (for) the *Elunum* festival of Nergal," 90:6–7

2. Offerings of Nergal, (personal deity of) PN

1 udu-ú ^{d}**nergal$_x$**$^{eri_{11}\text{-}gal}$ dumu *da-da*-AN, "1 range fed sheep (for) Nergal, (the personal deity of) the son of *Dada*-AN," 422:1–2

[n.n.n.n sìl]a zì gu[r ^{d}**PIRI]G.UNU-gal** dumu e-é-zi, "[n] bushel(s) (and) [n] liter(s) of flour (for) Nergal, (the personal deity of) the son of E'ezi," 484:4–5

^{d}nin-ḫur-sağ-ğá

1. Allotments of Ninḫursağa

1.1 Animals

1 máš ^{d}**nin-ḫur-sağ-ğá**, "1 goat (for) Ninḫursağ," 1003:7–8

1.2 Beer

1 kaš-gen ^{d}**nin-ḫur-sağ-ğá**-šè "1 ordinary beer for Ninḫursağa," 1009:7–8

1.3 Textiles

1 túg-ğe$_6$ ^{d}**nin-ḫur-sağ-ğá**, "1 black textile of Ninḫursağa," 787:1–2

2. Regular Offerings Returned from the Shrine

2.1 Barley and Bread

9 sìla še-ninda sá-du$_{11}$-^{d}**nin-ḫur-sağ-ğá** (. . .) èš-ta-gur-⸢ra⸣, "9 liters of barley (for) bread, regular offerings of Ninḫursağa, (and) {offerings of other deities}, offerings returned from the shrine," 1023:10, 15, 1024:9–10, 17, 1026:7–8, 13

2.2 Bread

9 sìla ninda [sá-du$_{11}$]-^{d}**nin-ḫur-sağ-ğá** (. . .) èš-ta-gur-ra, "9 liters of bread, [regular offerings] of Ninḫursağa, (and) {offerings of other deities}, offerings returned from the shrine," 997 :8–9, 12

^{d}nin-^{d}si$_4$-an-na

é-^{d}**nin-^{d}si$_4$-an-na**, "Nin-Siana temple" > *Household Index*

1. Nin-Siana, (the personal deity of) *Aḫu'a*

kaš-dé-a ^{d}**nin-^{d}si$_4$-an-na** *a-ḫu-a*, "the banquet of Nin-Siana, (the personal deity of) *Aḫu'a*" > **kaš-dé-a**

1.1 Regular Offerings

[n] udu ⸢sá⸣-du$_{11}$-^{d}**nin-$^{[d]}$si$_4$-an-na** *a-ḫu-a*, "[n] sheep, regular offerings of Nin-Siana, (the personal deity of) *Aḫu'a*," 982:1–2

2. The Sanctuary of Nin-Siana

2.1 Regular Offerings

[2.2.0. sá-du$_{11}$ zà-gu-lá ^{d}**nin-^{d}si$_4$-an-na**], "[2 bushels (and) 120 liters, regular offerings of the sanctuary of Nin-Siana]," 1527:3[1]

---

1 Restoration by W. Heimpel based on no. 1031.

2.2 Regular Offerings Returned from the Shrine

2.2.1 Barley and Bread

0.2.0. še-[ninda . . .] sá-du$_{11}$-z[à-g]ú-lá-^{d}[**nin-si$_4$**]**-an-na** š[à é-a] (. . .) èš-ta-gur-⸢ra⸣, "120 liters of barley [(for) bread . . .], regular offerings of the sanctuary of Nin-Siana in [the house] (and) {offerings of other deities}, offerings returned from the shrine," 1022:6–7, 15

0.2.0. še-ninda sá-du$_{11}$-zà-gú-lá-^{d}**nin-**^{d}⸢**si$_4$-an-na**⸣ (. . .) èš-ta-gur-ra, "120 liters of barley (for) bread, regular offerings of the sanctuary of Nin-Siana (and) {offerings of other deities}, offerings returned from the shrine," 1026:4, 13

2.2.2 Barley, Bread, and Other Grains

0.2.0. še-[ninda . . .] 0.1.0. tuḫ-duru$_5$-gen sá-du$_{11}$-zà-gú-lá-^{d}**nin-**^{d}**si$_4$-an-na** šà é-a (. . .) èš-ta-gur-ra, "120 liters of barley [(for) bread . . .] (and) 60 liters of ordinary fresh bran, regular offerings of the sanctuary of Nin-Siana in the house (and) {offerings of other deities}, offerings returned from the shrine," 997:5–7, 12

0.2.0. še-ninda 0.1.0. tuḫ-duru$_5$-gen sá-du$_{11}$-zà-gú-lá-^{d}**nin-**^{d}**si$_4$-an-na** (. . .) èš-ta-gur-ra, "120 liters of barley (for) bread (and) 60 liters of ordinary fresh bran, regular offerings of the sanctuary of Nin-Siana (and) {offerings of other deities}, offerings returned from the shrine," 1023:6–7, 15, 1024:5–6, 17

3. Nin-Siana, Unqualified

3.1 Allotments of Nin-Siana

3.1.1 Animals

1 máš ^{d}**nin-**^{d}**si$_4$-an-na**, "1 goat (for) Nin-Siana," 1003:9–10

3.1.2 Beer

1 kaš-gen 1 dida$_x$-gen ^{d}**nin-**^{d}**si$_4$-an-na**-šè, "1 ordinary beer (and) 1 ordinary dida beer for Nin-Siana," 1009:4–6

3.1.3 Skins

1 udu-niga gu$_4$-e-ús-[sa] ^{d}**nin-**^{d}**si$_4$-an-na** šà [é]-⸢gal⸣ iti u$_4$-6-ba-zal, "1 fattened sheep '(fed) following the oxen' (for) Nin-Siana in the palace at the end of the 6th day of the month," 970:7–9

3.1.4 Textiles

^{túg}*tá-ki-ru-um*-tur **dnin-dsi$_4$-an-na** 3-kam-ú[s], "small 3rd-quality *takkirum* textile of Nin-Siana," 608:5

^{túg}*tá-ki-ru-um* 3-k[am-ús] ^{d}**nin-**^{d}**si$_4$-an-na**, "3rd-quality *takkirum* textile of Nin-Siana," 739:2

^{túg}*tá-ki-ru-um*-tur ^{d}**nin-**^{d}**si$_4$-an-na**, "small *takkirum* textile of Nin-Siana," 766:1

^{túg}*tá-ki-ru-um*-tur 3-kam-ús ^{d}**nin-**^{d}**si$_4$-an-na**, "small 3rd-quality *takkirum* textile of Nin-Siana," 796:4

3.2 Regular Offerings

3.2.1 Animals

1 udu-niga é-u$_4$-7 iti u$_4$-[7]-ba-zal 1 ⸢udu⸣-niga é-[u$_4$]-10 iti u$_4$-10-⸢ba⸣-zal sá-du$_{11}$-ku$_5$-rá ^{d}**nin-**^{d}**si$_4$-an-na**, "1 fattened sheep at the end of the [7th] day of the

month, i.e. the half-moon day, 1 fattened sheep at the end of the 10th day of the month, i.e. the ¾? moon day, deducted regular offerings of Nin-Siana," 985:1–6

3.2.2 Bread

1 gú [n ma-na] báppir-sig$_5$ sá-du$_{11}$-^{d}**nin-^{d}si$_4$-an-na**, "1 talent (and) [n mina(s)] of fine beer bread, regular offerings of Nin-Siana," 1020:1–2

[6.2.0. ninda gur sá-du$_{11}$-^{d}**nin-^{d}si$_4$-an-na**], "[6 bushels (and) 120 liters of bread, regular offerings of Nin-Siana]," 1527:1–2[2]

3.2.3 Skins

1 kuš-máš-gal-niga sá-du$_{11}$-^{d}**nin-^{d}si$_4$-an-na**, "1 fattened billy-goat-skin, regular offerings of Nin-Siana," 842:1–2

2 kuš-udu-niga sá-du$_{11}$-^{d}**nin-^{d}si$_4$-an-na**, "2 fattened sheep skins, regular offerings of Nin-Siana," 874:1–2

3.2.4 Commodity Broken

[lá-ì]a 2.1.1.5 sìla [x lá]-ìa šà sá-du$_{11}$-^{d}**nin-[^{d}si$_4$]-an-na**-ta, "the remainder of 2 bushels (and) 75 liters of [x] (are) the remainder of the regular offerings from Nin-Siana," 998:1–2

3.3 Regular Offerings Returned from the Shrine

3.3.1 Barley and Bran

[0.n].3. ⸢še⸣ 0.3?.2. tuḫ-duru$_5$-s[ig$_5$] 0.3.2. tuḫ-duru$_5$-⸢sig$_5$⸣-ĝe$_6$ sá-du$_{11}$-^{d}**nin-^{d}[si$_4$]-an-na** (. . .) èš-ta-gur-ra, "[n+]30 liters of barley, 200 liters of fine fresh bran (and) 200 liters of fine fresh dark bran, regular offerings of Nin-Siana, (and) {offerings of other deities}, offerings returned from the shrine," 1002:1–4, 13

3.3.2 Barley, Bread, and Bran

0.4.3. še-ninda [?] 0.3.2. tuḫ-duru$_5$-sig$_5$ [. . .] 0.3.2. tuḫ-duru$_5$-sig$_5$ [. . .] sá-du$_{11}$-^{d}**nin-^{d}[si$_4$-an-na]** èš-ta-gur-ra, "270 liters of [?] barley (and) bread, 200 liters of fine fresh bread [. . .] (and) 200 liters of [. . .] fine fresh bran, regular offerings of Nin-Siana, (and) {offerings of other deities}, offerings returned from the shrine," 997:1–4, 12

3.3.3 Grains and Skins

1.0.2. še-ninda gur 0.3.2. tuḫ-duru$_5$-⸢sig$_5$⸣ 0.4.2. tuḫ-duru$_5$-si[g$_5$-ĝe$_6$] 1 kuš-udu-niga 1 kuš-m[áš . . .] sá-du$_{11}$-^{d}**nin-[^{d}si$_4$-an-na]** (. . .) èš-ta-gur-⸢ra⸣, "1 bushel (and) 20 liters of barley (and) bread, 200 liters of fine fresh bran, 260 liters of fine fresh [dark] bran, 1 skin of a fattened sheep (and) 1 skin of a [. . .] goat, regular offerings of Nin-Siana, (and) {offerings of other deities}, offerings returned from the shrine," 1022:1–5, 15

1.0.2. še-ninda ⸢gur⸣ 0.2.3. tuḫ-duru$_5$-sig$_5$ 0.3.2. tuḫ-duru$_5$-sig$_5$-ĝe$_6$ 2 kuš-udu-niga sá-du$_{11}$-^{d}**nin-^{d}si$_4$-an-na** (. . .) èš-ta-gur-ra, "1 bushel (and) 20 liters of barley (and) bread, 150 liters of fine fresh bran, 200 liters of fine fresh black bran (and) 2 skins of fattened sheep, regular offerings of Nin-Siana, (and) {offerings of other deities}, offerings returned from the shrine," 1023:1–5, 15, 1024:1–4, 17

---

[2] Restoration by W. Heimpel based on text 1031.

1.0.2. še-ninda gur 1 kuš-udu-niga sá-du$_{11}$-**^{d}nin-^{d}si$_{4}$-an-na** (. . .) èš-ta-gur-ra, "1 bushel (and) 120 liters of barley (and) bread (and) 1 skin of a fattened sheep, regular offerings of Nin-Siana, (and) {offerings of other deities}, offerings returned from the shrine," 1026:1–3, 13

^{d}nin-unug^{ki}

1. Offerings Returned from the Shrine

[. . .] **^{d}nin-unu?-g[a?** n] sìla ninda [n] kuš-u[du-nig]a ki-a-nag *šu-kab-*⌜*tá*⌝ èš-ta-gur-ra ^{d}*adad-tillati* šu ba-ti u$_{4}$ ezem-*e-lu-núm*-^{d}nergal$_{x}$$^{eri_{11}\text{-gal}}$, "*Adad-tillati* received [. . .] (of?) Nin-Unug (and) [n] liter(s) of bread (and) [n] skin(s) of fattened sheep of the funerary libation place of *Šu-Kabta*, offerings returned from the shrine during the *Elunum* festival of Nergal," 980:1–11

^{d}šára

é-**^{d}šára**, "Šara temple" > *Household Index*

1. Šara of ĜEŠ.KÚŠU

1.1 Regular Offerings

1.1.1 Animals

1 udu sá-du$_{11}$-**^{d}šára**-ĜEŠ.KÚŠU^{ki}, "1 sheep, regular offerings of Šara of ĜEŠ.KÚŠU," 1000:3–4, 1010:3–4, 1012:2, 1021:3–4

1.1.2 Skins

1 kuš-máš sá-du$_{11}$-**^{d}šára**-ĜEŠ.KÚŠU^{ki}, "1 goat skin, regular offerings of Šara of ĜEŠ.KÚŠU," 860:3–4

1.2 Regular Offerings Returned from the Shrine

1.2.1 Bread and Skins

4 sìla ninda 1 kuš-udu-niga sá-du$_{11}$-**^{d}šára**-ĜEŠ.KU[ŠÚ^{ki}] èš-ta-gur-⌜ra⌝, "4 liters of bread (and) 1 skin of a fattened sheep, regular offerings of Šara of ĜEŠ.KÚŠU, offerings returned from the shrine," 1022:13–15

5 sìla še-ninda 1 kuš-udu-niga sá-du$_{11}$-**^{d}šára**-ĜEŠ.KÚŠU^{ki} èš-ta-gur-ra, "5 liters of barley (for) bread (and) 1 skin of a fattened sheep, regular offerings of Šara of ĜEŠ.KÚŠU, offerings returned from the shrine," 1023:13–15, 1024:14–17

1.2.2 Skins

1 kuš-udu-niga sá-du$_{11}$-**^{d}šára**-ĜEŠ.KÚŠU^{ki} èš-ta-gur-ra, "1 skin of a fattened sheep, regular offerings of Šara of ĜEŠ.KÚŠU, offerings returned from the shrine," 1026:10–13

2. Šara, City Unspecified

2.1 Allotments

2.1.1 During Festivals

1 udu-⌜niga⌝ iti-u$_{4}$-11-ba-zal 0.0.2. zì-KAL 5 sìla dabin 5 sìla eša **^{d}šára** ezem-níĝ-ab-e, "1 fattened sheep at the end of the 11th day of the month, 20 liters of KAL-flour, 5 liters of semolina (and) 5 liters of fine flour (for) Šara (during) the níĝ-ab-e festival," 1001:1–7

1 udu-niga u_4-12-kam 0.0.1 zì-KAL 3 sìla dabin 2 sìla eša ⅔ sìla zú-lum **ᵈšára** u_4 ezem-pa-è, "1 fattened sheep on the 12th day, 10 liters of KAL-flour, 3 liters of semolina, 2 liters of fine flour (and) ⅔ liter of dates (for) Šara during the emergence festival," 1030:1–5

2.1.2 In Month 13

1 udu-níta mu kù-ᵈ⌜**šára**⌝-šè iti dirig sum-mu-dam, "1 ram for bright Šara, to be provided in month 13," 1078:1–4

2.2 Regular Offerings

1 udu sá-du_{11}-**ᵈšára**, "1 sheep, regular offerings of Šara," 996:7

ᵈšu-bu-la

1. Allotments: Textiles

1 ᵗᵘ́ᵍníĝ-lám 4-kam-ús **ᵈšu-bu-la**, "1 4th-quality níĝ-lám textile of Šubula," 834:10

2 ᵗᵘ́ᵍníĝ-lám-tur 4-kam-ús **ᵈšu-bu-**⌜**la**⌝, "2 small 4th-quality níĝ-lám textiles of Šubula," 608:6

ᵈ*tá-ad-muṣ-tum*

1. Allotments: Textiles

2 túg-guz-za 4-kam-ús ***ᵈtá-ad-muṣ-tum***, "2 4th-quality tufted textiles of *Tad-muṣtum*," 617:5

Analytical Index of Craftsmen and Craftswomen

CRAFTSMEN

ĝuruš ad-kub$_4$, "reed craftsman"
ĝuruš ašgab, "leather worker"
ĝuruš ^{lú}ázlag, "fuller"
ĝuruš báḫar, "potter"
ĝuruš dù-a-tar, "a type of orchard workman"
ĝuruš ì-du$_8$, "doorkeeper"
ĝuruš lú-kíkken, "miller"
ĝuruš má-gíd, "boat tower"
ĝuruš má-laḫ$_4$, "sailor"
ĝuruš nagar, "carpenter"
ĝuruš níĝ-ga, "class of worker"
ĝuruš si$_x$(g$_7$)-a, "class of worker"
ĝuruš simug, "smith"
ĝuruš túg-du$_8$, "braider"
ĝuruš um-mi-a, "craftsman"
ĝuruš un-ga$_6$, "porter"

CRAFTSWOMEN

géme àr-ra, "female grinder"
géme gu, "female spinner"
géme ĝeš-ì-sur-sur, "female sesame presser"
géme kíkken, "female miller"
géme kisal-luḫ, "female courtyard sweeper"
géme uš-bar, "female weaver"

CRAFTSMEN

ĝuruš ad-kub$_4$, "reed craftsman"

1. Agricultural Work

1 **ĝuruš ad-kub$_4$** u$_4$-105-šè (. . .) še gur$_{10}$-gur$_{10}$-dè zàr tab-ba-dè ù ĝeš ra-ra-dè a-šà *ṣe-ru-um* gub-ba, "1 reed craftsman for 105 days (and) {other craftsmen} employed at the *Ṣerum* field to reap barley, stack (its) sheaves (for drying) and flail (them)," 262:9–10, 19–22

1 **ĝuruš ad-kub$_4$** u$_4$-4-šè *dì-im-bu-na*-àš-gi$_5$-ta a-šà *ṣe-r*[*u-u*]*m*-šè še gur$_{10}$-gur$_{10}$-[dè] gub-ba, "1 reed craftsman (having gone) from *Dimbun*-Ašgi to the *Ṣerum* field, employed for 4 days [to] reap barley," 284:5–10

2. Canal Work

[1] **ĝuruš ad-kub$_4$** [u$_4$]-13-šè saḫar zi-ga i$_7$-ma-ma-*šar-ra-at*, "[1] reed craftsman for 13 [days] having moved dirt at the Mama-*šarrat* canal," 284:1–3

3. Construction Work

1⅓ **ĝuruš ad-kub$_4$** u$_4$-1-[šè] ésir-é-a ù im-bábbar ^{ĝeš}ig bí-ib-sù-ub, "1⅓ reed craftsmen [for] 1 day coated the door with house bitumen and gypsum," 1329:5–7

4. Transporting Barley

4.1 To the Kabbi Village from *Dimbun*-Ašgi

2 **ĝuruš ad-kub$_4$** (. . .) u$_4$-1-[šè] še *dì-im-bu-na*-^{d}àš-gi$_5$-ta é-duru$_5$-kab-bi-šè(!) <de$_6$->a, "2 reed craftsmen (and) {other craftsmen} for 1 day having <brought> barley from *Dimbun*-Ašgi to the Kabbi village," 287:11, 16–18

2 **ĝuruš ad-kub$_4$** u$_4$-1-šè ⸢še⸣ *dì-im-bu-*⸢*na*⸣-^{d}àš-gi$_5$-[ta é]-duru$_5$-kab-bi^{ki}-[šè], "2 reed craftsmen for 1 day (having brought) barley [from] *Dimbun*-Ašgi [to] the Kabbi village," 288:5–8

4.2 To Garšana

2 **ĝuruš ad-kub$_4$** 1½ ĝuruš báḫar u$_4$-5-šè [še] du$_6$-saḫar-ra^{ki}-ta gar-ša-an-na^{ki}-šè de$_6$-a, "2 reed craftsmen (and) 1½ potters for 5 days having brought [barley] from Du-saḫara to Garšana," 233:4–8

1 ĝuruš ašgab 1 **ĝuruš ad-kub$_4$** 1 géme kíkken u$_4$-[2]7-šè še ^{d}*šu*-^{d}*suen*-<am->ma-ra$^{[ki]}$ ù bàd-ga-zi^{ki}-⸢ta⸣ gar-ša-an-na^{ki}-šè de$_6$-a, "1 leather worker, 1 reed craftsman (and) 1 female miller for [2]7 days having brought barley from *Šu-Suen*-ammara and Bad-gazi to Garšana," 259:1–7

2 **ĝuruš ad-kub$_4$** u$_4$-20-šè še é-duru$_5$-kab-bí-ta gar-ša-an-na^{ki}-šè de$_6$-a, "2 reed craftsmen for 20 days having brought barley from the Kabbi village to Garšana," 300:1–4

2 **ĝuruš ad-kub$_4$** u$_4$-20-šè še é-duru$_5$-kab-bi-ta gar-ša-an-na^{ki}-šè mu-un-de$_9$-sa-a, "{other craftsmen} (and) 2 reed craftsmen for 20 days who brought barley from the Kabbi village to Garšana," 304:6–10

2 **ĝuruš ad-kub$_4$** (. . .) u$_4$-10-šè še ù-dag-ga^{ki}-ta gar-ša-an-na^{ki}-šè de$_6$-a, "2 reed craftsmen (and) {other craftsmen} for 10 days having brought barley from Udaga to Garšana," 287:2, 7–9

2 **ĝuruš [ad-kub$_4$** u$_4$]-10-šè ⸢še⸣ ù-dag-ga^{ki}-t[a gar-ša]-an-na^{ki}-šè de$_6$-a, "2 [reed craftsmen] for 10 [days] having brought barley from Udaga to Garšana," 288:1–4

4.3 Gone to the Ulluḫ-Urim Village for Barley Rations

2 **ĝuruš ad-kub$_4$** (. . .) u$_4$-2-šè še é-duru$_5$-ul-luḫ-uri$_5$^{ki}-ma-šè ĝen-na mu še-ba-ne-ne-šè, "2 reed craftsmen (and) {other craftsmen} for 2 days having gone to the Ulluḫ-Urim village for barley for barley rations," 291:10, 12–14, 292:10, 12–14, 294:1–4

5. Transporting Other Commodities

5.1 Oil

2 **ĝuruš ad-kub$_4$** u$_4$-1-šè ì de$_6$-a a-rá-1-kam, "2 reed craftsmen for 1 day having brought oil for the 1st time," 285:4–6, 286:4–6

5.2 Reeds

1 **g̃uruš ad-kub$_4$** (. . .) u$_4$-10-še gi-izi ù-dag^{ki}-ga-ta gar-ša-an-na^{ki}-šè [de$_6$]-a, "1 reed craftsman (and) {other craftsmen} for 10 days having [brought] fuel reeds from Udaga to Garšana," 230:2, 6–9

5.3 A Sheep

1 **g̃uruš ad-kub$_4$** udu la-ḫe-dè iri-sag̃-⸢rig$_7$⸣^{ki}-šè ⸢g̃en-na⸣, "1 reed craftsman having gone to Iri-sag̃rig in order to bring a sheep," 260:1–2

5.4 Straw

2 **g̃uruš ad-kub$_4$** u$_4$-1-šè in-u a-gàr-didli-ta gar-ša-an-na^{ki}-šè lá-a, "2 reed craftsmen for 1 day having transported straw from various meadows to Garšana," 285:1–3, 286:1–3

5.5 Wool

2 **g̃uruš ad-kub$_4$** u$_4$-1-šè a-rá–2-kam 2 **g̃uruš ad-kub$_4$** u$_4$-1-šè a-rá–3-kam siki de$_6$-a é-^{d}*šu*-^{d}*suen*^{ki}-ta gar-ša-an-na^{ki}-šè (g̃en-a), "2 reed craftsmen for 1 day for the 2nd time, (and) 2 reed craftsmen for 1 day for the 3rd time having brought wool, (reed craftsmen having gone) from *Bit-Šu-Suen* to Garšana," 285:7–13, 286:7–13

6. Other Assignments

6.1 Expended by *Simat-Ištaran*, Assignment Unspecified

[n] g̃uruš [. . . n+]20 **g̃uruš ad-kub$_4$** [n+]15 g̃uruš má-laḫ$_5$ u$_4$-1-šè zi-ga *simat-*^{d}*ištaran*, "[n . . .] workmen, [n+]20 reed craftsmen (and) [n+]15 sailors for 1 day. (It was) the expenditure of *Simat-Ištaran*," 511:15–20

6.2 Mourning

2? **g̃uruš ad-kub$_4$** (. . .) ⸢u$_4$⸣–1-šè gaba sàg-dè gub-ba u$_4$ dig̃ir-re gaba *na-wi-ir-ilum* ba-a-g̃ar-ra, "2? reed craftsmen (and) {other craftsmen} employed for 1 day to beat (their) breasts when the god made the breast of *Nawir-ilum* subside (i.e. when he died)," 251:4, 8–10

6.3 Released for the Priest

[n] **g̃uruš ad-⸢kub$_4$⸣** (. . .) u$_4$-15-šè ⸢ki⸣ en-šè šu bar-ra, "[n] reed craftsmen (and) {other craftsmen} released for 15 days for the priest," 225:3, 6–8

6.4 Towing Boats

2 g̃uruš ašgab 1 **g̃uruš ad-kub$_4$** u$_4$-4-[šè] má $^{g̃eš}$šim ḫi-a gar-ša-an-na^{ki}-ta nibru^{ki}-šè in-gíd-sa-a, "2 leather workers (and) 1 reed craftsman [for] 4 days who towed a boat (with) various resinous woods from Garšana to Nippur," 253:1–7

[n] g̃uruš ^{lú}[ázlag n] g̃uruš ašgab [n] **g̃uruš ad-kub$_4$ [n] g̃[uruš tú]g-du$_8$ [. . .]-x-šè [x]-zi-[x]-x maš-kán^{ki}-⸢šè⸣ má gíd-⸢da⸣, "[n] fuller(s), [n] leather worker(s), [n] reed craftsmen (and) [n] braider(s) having towed a boat [. . .] to Maškan," 260:11–17

7. Broken Context

[. . .] **g̃uruš ad-[kub$_4$** . . .], 260:20

g̃uruš ašgab, "leather worker"

1. Agricultural Work

(. . .) 1 **g̃uruš** á-⅔ **ašgab** u$_4$-114-šè (. . .) 2 **g̃uruš ašgab** u$_4$-125-šè še gur$_{10}$-gur$_{10}$-dè zàr tab-ba-dè ù g̃eš ra-ra-dè a-šà *ṣe-ru-um* gub-ba, "1 leather worker at ⅔ wages for 114 days, 2 leather workers for 125 days (and) {other craftsmen} employed at the *Ṣerum* field to reap barley, stack (its) sheaves (for drying) and flail (them)," 262:11–12, 17–22

1 **ĝuruš ašgab** u$_4$-1-šè še gur$_{10}$-gur$_{10}$-dè a-šà *dì-im-bu-na*-àš-gi$_5$ gub-ba, "1 leather worker employed for 1 day to reap barley at the *Dimbun*-Ašgi field," 282:1–3

2. Canal Work

1 **ĝuruš ⸢ašgab⸣** u$_4$-14-[šè] iti ezem-an-⸢na⸣ 1 ĝuruš ⸢ašgab u$_4$⸣-[n-šè n ĝuruš] ašgab i[ti ezem]-m[e-ki-ĝ]ál ⸢saḫar⸣ zi-⸢ga⸣ i$_7$-ma-ma-*šar-ra-at*, "1 leather worker [for] 14 days in month 11 (and) 1 leather worker for [n] day(s) (and) [n] leather worker(s) in month 12 having moved dirt at the Mama-*šarrat* canal," 281:1–8

3. Construction Work

1 **ĝuruš ašgab** u$_4$-3-šè ^{ĝeš}ig šà é-a bu-ra, "1 leather worker for 3 days having pulled out a door in the house," 239:1–2

3 **ĝuruš ašgab** u$_4$-2-⸢šè⸣ bar-da ^{ĝeš}ig-⸢ge$_6$⸣ kéše-⸢rá⸣, "3 leather workers for two days having bound the crossbar of the black door," 247:4–5

6 **ĝuruš ašgab** 8 ĝuruš ^{lú}ázlag 24 géme uš-bar u$_4$-1-šè al-tar é-*a-bí-a-ti* gul-dè gub-ba, "6 leather workers, 8 fullers (and) 24 female weavers employed for 1 day of construction to demolish the house of *Abiati*," 273:1–6

4. Garden Work

1⅔ **ĝuruš ašgab** u$_4$-2-šè a bala-e-dè gub-ba ^{ĝeš}kiri$_6$ šà gar-ša-an-na^{ki}, "1⅔ leather workers employed for 2 days to irrigate the garden in Garšana," 1523:1–4

5. Transporting Barley

5.1 From Gu-saḫar.DU to the Fortified Tower of *Dada*

2 **ĝuruš ašgab** u$_4$-1-šè gú-saḫar^{har}.DU^{ki}-ta an-za-qar-*da-da*-šè má gíd-da ù še ba-al, "2 leather workers for 1 day having towed a boat from Gu-saḫar.DU to the fortified tower of *Dada* and having unloaded barley," 299:11–12

5.2 From the Quay to the Granary

1⅔ **ĝuruš ašgab** u$_4$-3-šè kar-ta gur$_7$-šè še íb-ga$_6$, "1⅔ leather workers for 3 days carried barley from the quay to the granary," 229:5–7

5.3 To the Kabbi Village from *Dimbun*-Ašgi

3 **ĝuruš ašgab** (. . .) u$_4$-1-[šè] še *dì-im-bu-na*-^{d}àš-gi$_5$-ta é-duru$_5$-kab-bi-šè(!) <de$_6$->a, "3 leather workers (and) {other craftsmen} [for] 1 day having <brought> barley from *Dimbun*-Ašgi to the Kabbi village," 287:10, 16–18

5.4 To Garšana

1⅔ **ĝuruš ⸢ašgab⸣** u$_4$-4-⸢šè⸣ še [GN]^{ki}-ta gar-[ša-an-na^{ki}]-šè de$_6$-a, "1⅔ leather workers for 4 days having brought barley from [GN] to Garšana," 229:1–4

1 **ĝuruš ašgab** 1 ĝuruš ad-kub$_4$ 1 géme kíkken u$_4$-[2]7-šè še ^{d}*šu*-^{d}*suen*-<am->ma-ra$^{\text{[ki]}}$ ù bàd-ga-zi^{ki}-⸢ta⸣ gar-ša-an-na^{ki}-šè de$_6$-a, "1 leather worker, 1 reed craftsman (and) 1 female miller for [2]7 days having brought barley from *Šu-Suen*-ammara and Bad-gazi to Garšana," 259:1–7

3 **ĝuruš ašgab** (. . .) u$_4$-10-šè še ù-dag-ga^{ki}-ta gar-ša-an-na^{ki}-šè de$_6$-a, "3 leather workers (and) {other craftsmen} for 10 days having brought barley from Udaga to Garšana," 287:1, 7–9

2 **ĝuruš** [**ašgab**] u$_4$-[1-šè] a-rá–1-[kam] 2 **ĝuruš ašgab** [u$_4$-1-šè] a-rá–2-kam 2 **ĝuruš ašgab** u$_4$-1-šè a-rá–3-kam 2 **ĝuruš ašgab** u$_4$-1-šè a-rá–4-kam 2 **ĝuruš ašgab** u$_4$-1-šè a-rá–5-kam še an-za-qar-*da-da*-[ta] gar-ša-an-na^{ki}-šè de$_6$-a, "2 leather workers for 1 day having brought barley [from] the fortified tower of *Dada* to Garšana (on) {5 different occasions}," 297:1–14

2 **ĝuruš ašgab** (. . .) u$_4$-20-šè še é-duru$_5$-kab-bi-ta gar-ša-an-na^{ki}-šè mu-un-de$_9$-sa-a, "2 leather workers (and) {other craftsmen} for 20 days who brought barley from the Kabbi village to Garšana," 304:5, 7–10

[n **ĝuru**]**š ašgab** [u$_4$]-20-šè [še é]-duru$_5$-kab-bi-ta^{ki} [gar-ša]-an-na^{ki}<-šè> de$_6$-a, "[n] leather worker(s) for 20 [days] having brought [barley] from the Kabbi village <to> Garšana," 305:1–4

5.5 Gone to the Ulluḫ-Urim Village for Barley Rations

3 **ĝuruš ašgab** (. . .) u$_4$-2-šè še é-duru$_5$-ul-luḫ-uri$_5^{ki}$-ma-šè ĝen-na mu še-ba-ne-ne-šè, "3 leather workers (and) {other craftsmen} for 2 days having gone to the Ulluḫ-Urim village for barley for barley rations," 291:9, 2–14, 292:9, 12–14

6. Other Assignments

6.1 Bringing Reeds to Garšana

1 **ĝuruš ašgab** (. . .) u$_4$-10-še gi-izi ù-dag^{ki}-ga-ta gar-ša-an-na^{ki}-šè [de$_6$]-a, "1 leather worker (and) {other craftsmen} for 10 days having [brought] fuel reeds from Udaga to Garšana," 230:1, 6–9

1⅔ **ĝuruš ašgab** 1 ĝuruš túg-du$_8$ 1 ĝuruš simug u$_4$-1-šè ⸢gi⸣ ù gi-zi é-^{d}šára-ta gar-ša-an-na^{ki}-šè [de$_6$]-a de$_6$-a(sic!), "1⅔ leather workers, 1 braider (and) 1 smith for 1 day having brought reeds and fresh reeds from the Šara temple to Garšana," 232:1–8

6.2 Bringing Wool

1⅔ **ĝuruš ašgab u$_4$-6-šè siki é-^{d}*šu*-^{d}*suen*^{ki}-ka-ta mu-un-li-sa-a, "1⅔ leather workers for 6 days who brought wool from *Bit-Šu-Suen*," 228:1–4

6.3 Loading Boats

3 **ĝuruš ašgab u$_4$-1-šè še 120 gur á-áĝ-dè gub-ba ù má si-ga, "3 leather workers for 1 day, instructions about the 120 bushels of barley followed and the boat was loaded," 299:4–5

6.4 Released on the Day of the Wool Rations

3 **ĝuruš ašgab** u$_4$-1-šè u$_4$ siki ba-a-ka šu bar-ra, "3 leather workers released for 1 day on the day of the wool rations," 246:1–2

(. . .) 3 **ĝuruš ašgab** (. . .) [u$_4$-1-šè] ⸢u$_4$⸣ siki-ba-ka šu bar-⸢ra⸣, "3 leather workers (and) {other craftsmen} released [for 1 day] on the day of the wool rations," 280:13, 17–18

6.5 Released for the Priest

[n] **ĝuruš ašgab** (. . .) u$_4$-15-šè ⸢ki⸣ en-šè šu bar-ra, "[n] leatherworker(s) (and) {other craftsmen} released for 15 days for the priest," 225:1, 6–8

6.6 Sitting Idle

3 **ĝuruš ašgab** u$_4$-2-šè šà gú-saḫar^{har}.DU^{ki} tuš-a šà a im še-ĝá, "3 leather workers for 2 days having sat (idle) in Gu-saḫar.DU because of rain," 299:9–10

6.7 Towing Boats

2 **g̃uruš ašgab** 1 g̃uruš ad-kub$_4$ u$_4$-4-[šè] má ^{geš}šim ḫi-a gar-ša-an-na^{ki}-ta nibru^{ki}-šè in-gíd-sa-a, "2 leather workers (and) 1 reed craftsman [for] 4 days who towed a boat (with) various resinous woods from Garšana to Nippur," 253:1–7

[n] g̃uruš ^{lú}[ázlag n] **g̃uruš ašgab [n] g̃uruš ad-kub$_4$ [n] g̃[uruš tú]g-du$_8$ [. . .]-x-šè [x]-zi-[x]-x maš-kán^{ki}-⌜šè⌝ má gíd-⌜da⌝, "[n] fuller(s), [n] leather worker(s), [n] reed craftsmen (and) [n] braider(s) having towed a boat [. . .] to Maškan," 260:11–17

3 **g̃uruš ašgab** u$_4$-1-šè é-^{d}šu-[^{d}EN].ZU^{ki}-ta gú-saḫar^{har}.DU^{ki}-šè má gíd-da, "3 leather workers for 1 day having towed a boat from *Bit-Šu-Suen* to Gu-saḫar.DU," 299:6–8

7 **g̃uruš ašgab** u$_4$-1-šè é-da-na^{ki}-šè má gíd-da, "7 leather workers for 1 day having towed a boat to Edana," 884:3–4

6.8 Traveling to *Bit-Šu-Suen*

3 **g̃uruš ašgab** u$_4$-1-šè gar-ša-an-na^{ki}-ta é-^{d}*šu*-^{d}*suen*^{ki}-a g̃en-a, "3 leather workers for 1 day having gone from Garšana into *Bit-Šu-Suen*," 299:1–3

6.9 Unspecified

3 **g̃uruš ašgab** u$_4$-2-šè gub-ba, "3 leather workers employed for 2 days," 912:11

9 **g̃uruš ašgab** u$_4$-1-šè *ba-la-a* ì-dab$_5$ ki *a-na-aḫ-ì-lí*-ta ba-zi, "*Bala'a* took in charge 9 leather workers for 1 day from *Anaḫ-ili*," 962:1–5

7. Broken Context

[. . .] **g̃uruš** [**ašgab** . . .], 260:19

g̃uruš ^{lú}ázlag, "fuller"

1. Agricultural Work

(. . .) 1 **g̃uruš** á–½ ^{lú}**ázlag-me-éš** u$_4$-105-šè (. . .) 2 g̃uruš sag̃-tag 1 g̃uruš á-⅔ 1 **g̃uruš** á–½ **ázlag-me-éš** u$_4$-125-šè (. . .) še gur$_{10}$-gur$_{10}$-dè zàr tab-ba-dè ù g̃eš ra-ra-dè a-šà *ṣe-ru-um* gub-ba, "1 fuller at ½ wages for 105 days, 2 full-time fullers, 1 fuller at ⅔ wages, (and) 1 fuller at ½ wages for 125 days {and other craftsmen} employed at the *Ṣerum* field to reap barley, stack (its) sheaves (for drying) and flail (them)," 262:7–8, 10 13–16, 18–22

[n] **g̃uruš** ^{lú}**ázlag** á–½ ⌜u$_4$⌝–8-šè (. . .) še apin-lá-a ⌜káb⌝ dì-de$_4$ ì-im-g̃en-na-a, "[n] fuller(s) at ½ wages for 8 days, {authorizing official}, went to check on the grain of the leased fields," 271:1–2, 5–7

2. Canal Work

13 g̃uruš sag̃-tag 3 **g̃uruš** á-⅔-ta ^{lú}**ázlag-me-éš** u$_4$-2-šè i$_7$-mi-me-er gub-ba ba-al-la (. . .) šà nibru^{ki}, "13 full-time fullers and 3 fullers at ⅔ wages employed for 2 days having dug the Mimer canal. {Expenditure} in Nippur," 227:1–5, 7

3. Construction Work

8 g̃uruš sag̃-tag 2 **g̃uruš** á-⅔-ta ^{lú}**ázlag-me-éš** u$_4$-[1-šè] šeg$_{12}$ šu dím sum-mu-dè gub-ba al-tar é-[ki-m]u-ra, "8 full-time fullers (and) 2 fullers at ⅔ wages employed [for 1] day to hand (up) bricks for building, (for) construction of the textile depository," 242:1–5

6 g̃uruš ašgab 8 **g̃uruš** ^{lú}**ázlag** 24 géme uš-bar u$_4$-1-šè al-tar é-*a-bí-a-ti* gul-dè gub-ba, "6 leather workers, 8 fullers (and) 24 female weavers employed for 1 day of construction to demolish the house of *Abiati*," 273:1–6

4. Transporting Barley

4.1 To Garšana

9 g̃uruš sag̃-tag 1 g̃uruš á-⅔ 1 **g̃uruš** á-⅓ ^{lú}**ázlag-me-éš** u$_4$-1-šè še é-kab-ba^{ki} ⸢karkar⸣^{ki}-ta ⸢gar⸣-š[a-a]n-⸢na^{ki}⸣-šè de$_6$-a, "9 full-time fullers, 1 fuller at ⅔ wages, (and) 1 fuller at ⅓ wages for 1 day having brought barley from Ekabba (and) Karkar to Garšana," 237:1–8

2 **g̃uruš** ^{lú}**ázlag** (. . .) u$_4$-10-šè še ù-dag-ga^{ki}-ta gar-ša-an-na^{ki}-šè de$_6$-a, "2 fullers (and) {other craftsmen} for 10 days having brought barley from Udaga to Garšana," 287:3, 7–9

4.2 Gone to the Ulluḫ-Urim Village for Barley Rations

10 10 gín? **g̃uruš** ^{lú}**ázlag** (. . .) u$_4$-2-šè še é-duru$_5$-ul-luḫ-uri$_5$^{ki}-ma-šè g̃en-na mu še-ba-ne-ne-šè, "10 1/6 fullers (and) {other craftsmen} for 2 days having gone to the Ulluḫ-Urim village for barley for barley rations," 291:7, 12–14, 292:7, 12–14

5. Transporting Other Commodities

5.1 Reeds

3 g̃uruš sag̃-tag 1 **g̃uruš** á-⅔ ^{lú}**ázlag-me-éš** u$_4$-10-šè gi-izi ù-dag^{ki}-ga-ta [gar-š]a-an-na^{ki}-šè de$_6$-a, "3 full-time fullers (and) 1 fuller at ⅔ wages for 10 days having brought fuel reeds from Udaga to Garšana," 231:1–6

5.2 A Sheep and Cattle Brand

1 **g̃uruš** ^{lú}**ázlag** nibru^{ki}-ta ^{d}*šu*-^{d}*suen*-DU$_{10}$ki-šè ^{urudu}šim-da gu$_4$-udu de$_6$-a kaskal šu+níg̃in-na-bi u$_4$-11-kam u$_4$ *šu-kab-tá* é-dam-*zé-ra-ra* šu sum-mu-dè ì-g̃en-na-a "1 fuller having brought a sheep and cattle brand from Nippur to *Šu-Suen-ṭabu*, a trip of 11 days in total, when *Šu-Kabta* came to the house of the wife of *Zerara* in order to take inventory," 219:1–10

5.3 Textiles

1 **g̃uruš** ^{lú}**ázlag** nibru^{ki}-ta gar-ša-an-na^{ki}-šè túg de$_6$-a kaskal šu+níg̃in-na-bi u$_4$-4-àm, "1 fuller having brought textiles from Nippur to Garšana, a trip of 4 days in total," 224:1–6

5.4 Wool

1 **g̃uruš** ^{lú}**ázlag** sag̃-tag u$_4$-2-šè u$_4$-2-šè 2 g̃uruš sag̃-tag 2 g̃uruš á-½-ta u$_4$-2-šè siki é-^{d}*šu*-^{d}*suen*-[DU$_{10}$]^{ki}-ta nibru^{ki}-šè DU(sic!) de$_6$-a, "1 full-time fuller for 2 days (and) 2 full-time workmen (and) 2 half-time workmen for 2 days having brought wool from *Bit-Šu-Suen* to Nippur," 226:1–8

3 **g̃uruš** ^{lú}**ázlag** siki é-^{d}*šu*-^{d}*suen*^{ki}-ka-ta nibru^{ki}-šè de$_6$-a kaskal šu+níg̃in-na-bi u$_4$-10!-kam u$_4$-2 kaš-dé-[a] á-⸢ki⸣-ti šu-numun, "3 fullers having brought wool from *Bit-Šu-Suen* to Nippur, a trip of 10 days in total, on day 2 of the banquet of the Akiti festival of month 4," 240:1–6

4 g̃uruš sag̃-tag 1 **g̃uruš** á-⅔ ^{lú}**ázlag-me-éš** u$_4$-2-šè siki é-^{d}*šu*-^{d}*suen*^{ki}-ta de$_6$-a, "4 full-time fullers (and) 1 fuller at ⅔ wages for 2 days having brought wool from *Bit-Šu-Suen*," 241:1–4

8 **g̃uruš** ^{lú}**ázlag** u$_4$-1-šè siki é-^{d}*šu*-^{d}*suen*- ta gar-ša-an-n[a^{ki}]-šè mu-un-de$_9$-sa-a, "8 fullers for 1 day who brought wool from *Bit-Šu-Suen* to Garšana," 243:1–4

8 g̃uruš sag̃-tag 2 g̃uruš á-⅔-ta 4 **g̃uruš** á-½ ta ^{lú}**ázlag-me-éš** [u$_4$]-1-šè ⸢še⸣ ^{d}*šu*-^{d}*suen*-am-ma-ar^{ki}-ta de$_6$-a íb-[ga$_6$], "8 full-time fullers, 2 fullers at ⅔ wages, (and) 4 fullers at ½ wages for 1 [day carried] barley having been brought from *Šu-Suen*-ammara," 248:1–6

6. Labor of Fullers

1 ^{túg}bar-dul$_5$ abzu? *a-ši-um* 1 túg-guz-za 3-kam-ús 8 **g̃uruš ^{lú}ázlag** á-bi u$_4$-1-še *ṣú-mi-id-ilum*, "1 abzu? *a-ši-um* bar-dul$_5$ textile (and) 1 3rd-quality tufted textile, labor of 8 fullers for 1 day, (for) *Ṣumid-ilum*," 571:1–5

7. Other Assignments

7.1 Expended for the Royal Banquet

2 **g̃uruš ^{lú}ázlag** u$_4$-1-šè zi-ga kaš-dé-a lugal šà á-<ki->ti gub-ba, "2 fullers employed for 1 day, expended (for) the royal banquet during the Akiti festival," 221:1–2

7.2 Mourning

11 g̃uruš sa[g̃-tag] 2 g̃uruš á-⅔-ta 4 g̃uruš á-½-ta 1 **g̃uruš** á-⅓<-ta> **^{lú}ázlag-me-éš** u$_4$-1-šè gaba sàg-gé-dè [gub-ba] u$_4$ *na-wi-ir-*[*ilum* ba-úš-a], "11 full-time fullers, 2 fullers at ⅔ wages, 4 fullers at ½ wages (and) 1 fuller <at> ⅓ wages [employed] for 1 day to beat (their) breasts when *Nawir-ilum* [died]," 250:1–8

7.3 Released On the Day of the Wool Rations

(. . .) [n+]2 g̃uruš sag̃-[tag] 2 g̃uruš á-[⅔] 1 g̃uruš á-½ 1 **g̃uruš** á-⅓ **^{lú}ázlag**-me-éš (. . .) [u$_4$-1-šè] ⸢u$_4$⸣ siki-ba-ka šu bar-⸢ra⸣, "[n+]2 full-time fullers, 2 fullers at [⅔] wages, 1 fuller at ½ wages, 1 fuller at ⅓ wages (and) {other craftsmen} released [for 1 day] on the day of the wool rations," 280:6–10, 17–18

7.4 Towing Boats

3 **g̃uruš ^{lú}ázlag** u$_4$-2½-šè nibru^{ki}-ta é-^{d}*šu*-^{d}*suen*-šè má *na-wi-ir-ilum* íb-gíd, "3 fullers for 2½ days towed the boat of *Nawir-ilum* from Nippur to *Bit-Šu-Suen*," 220:1–6

[. . . n] **g̃uruš** á-[n-ta] **^{lú}ázlag**-me-[éš] u$_4$-1-[šè] má-nin-zi-šà-g̃ál gar-ša-an-na^{ki}-ta G̃EŠ.KÚŠU^{ki}-šè in-gíd-ša-a, "[. . . (and) n] fuller(s) at [n] wages for 1 day towed the boat of Nin-zišag̃al from Garšana to G̃EŠ.KÚŠU," 238:1–7

★★[n] **g̃uruš ^{lú}[ázlag** n] g̃uruš ašgab [n] g̃uruš ad-kub$_4$ [n] g̃[uruš túg]g-du$_8$ [. . .]-x-šè [x]-zi-[x]-x maš-kán^{ki}-⸢šè⸣ má gíd-d[a], "[n] fuller(s), [n] leather worker(s), [n] reed craftsmen (and) [n] braider(s) having towed a boat [. . .] to Maškan," 260:11–17

7.5 Unspecified

1 **g̃uruš ^{lú}ázlag** u$_4$-25-šè *na-sìm* ^{lú}kíg̃-gi$_4$<-a>-lugal-ta lú te-te-dè in-da-g̃e$_{26}$-en, "1 fuller for 25 days. *Nasim*, the royal messenger, went to bring the man (i.e. the fuller) from the king," 222:1–5

1⅓ **g̃uruš ^{lú}ázlag** ki ^{d}*adad-tillati*-ta *puzur$_4$-a-gu$_5$-um* **^{lú}ázlag** [ì-dab$_5$], *"Puzur-agum* [took in charge] 1⅓ fullers from *Adad-tillati*," 604:1–4

8. Provisions

★★[. . .]x-še-en [x] dú-ra-a [. . .] 6 sìla gíd-[. . .] 0.0.2. [á]-bi ḫ[ug̃-g̃]á **^{lú}ázlag-me-éš** ⸢mu⸣-⸢DU⸣ NE-KU, 477:1–7

1.0.0. še gur á **^{lú}ázlag** ḫug̃-g̃á, "1 bushel of barley, wages of hired fullers," 820:1–2

9. Broken Context

3 **g̃uruš** ^{lú}⸢**ázlag**⸣, "3 fullers," 260:18

g̃uruš báḫar, "potter"

1. Transporting Barley

1.1 To Garšana

2 g̃uruš ad-kub$_4$ 1½ **g̃uruš báḫar** u$_4$-5-šè [še] du$_6$-saḫar-ra^{ki}-ta gar-ša-an-na^{ki}-šè de$_6$-a, "2 reed craftsmen (and) 1½ potters for 5 days having brought [barley] from Du-saḫara to Garšana," 233:4–8

1.2 Gone to the Ulluḫ-Urim Village for Barley Rations

(. . .) 1 **g̃uruš báḫar** u$_4$-2-šè še é-duru$_5$-ul-luḫ-uri$_5$^{ki}-ma-šè g̃en-na mu še-ba-ne-ne-šè, "{other craftsmen} (and) 1 potter for 2 days having gone to the Ulluḫ-Urim village for barley for barley rations," 291:11–14, 292:11–14, 293:1–4

2. Other Assignments

2.1 Mourning

1 **g̃uruš báḫar** (. . .) ⌜u$_4$⌝-1-šè gaba sàg-dè gub-ba u$_4$ dig̃ir-re gaba *na-wi-ir-ilum* ba-a-g̃ar-ra, "1 potter (and) {other craftsmen} employed for 1 day to beat (their) breasts when the god made the breast of *Nawir-ilum* subside (i.e. when he died)," 251:5, 8–10

2.2 Released for the Priest

(. . .) 1½ **g̃uruš báḫar** u$_4$-15-šè ⌜ki⌝ en-šè šu bar-ra, "{other craftsmen} (and) 1½ potters released for 15 days for the priest," 225:5–7

2.3 Transporting Reeds to Garšana

1½ **g̃uruš báḫar** (. . .) u$_4$-10-še gi-izi ù-dag^{ki}-ga-ta gar-ša-an-na^{ki}-šè [de$_6$]-a, "1½ potters (and) {other craftsmen} for 10 days, having [brought] fuel reeds from Udaga to Garšana," 230:3, 6–9

g̃uruš dù-a-tar, "a type of orchard workman"[1]

1. Provisions: Silver

23[+3] **g̃uruš** um-mi-a ù **dù-a-tar** [⅓ gí]n 3 še kù-babbar-ta (. . .) níg̃-kas$_7$-aka mun-gazi nu-$^{g̃eš}$kiri$_6$ a-pí-sal$_4$^{ki}-ke$_4$-ne, "26 craftsmen and orchard workmen, [⅓] shekel (and) 3 barley corn of silver each (and) {additional consignments of silver}; the balanced account of mun-gazi agricultural products of the gardeners of Apisal," 540:1–2, 11–12

g̃uruš ì-du$_8$, "doorkeeper"

1. In Worker Inspection Accounts

1 **g̃uruš ì-du$_8$**, "1 doorkeeper," 104:6, 104:45, 105:6, 105:43, 106:5, 106:43, 107:8, 108:5, 108:38, 109:5, 109:35, 155:37

3 **g̃uruš ì-du$_8$**, "3 doorkeepers," 156:35, 157:22, 158:39, 159:33, 160:'15, 162:29, 163:35, 175:29

[n] **g̃uruš ì-du$_8$**, "[n] doorkeeper(s)," 106:43, 161:'21, 174:28

---

[1] Yamamoto 1981, 105–6.

2. Mourning

(. . .) 2 ⸢**ğuruš**⸣ **ì-du$_8$** ⸢u$_4$⸣-1-šè gaba sàg-dè gub-ba u$_4$ diğir-re gaba *na-wi-ir-ilum* ba-a-ğar-ra, "{other craftsmen} (and) 2 doorkeepers employed for 1 day to beat (their) breasts when the god made the breast of *Nawir-ilum* subside (i.e. when he died)," 251:7–10

ğuruš lú-kíkken, "miller"

1. Transporting Barley

1.1 To Garšana

1 **ğuruš lú-kíkken** (. . .) u$_4$-20-šè še é-duru$_5$-kab-bi-ta gar-ša-an-na^{ki}-šè mu-un-de$_9$-sa-a, "1 miller (and) {other craftsmen} for 20 days who brought barley from the Kabbi village to Garšana," 304:3, 7–10

1.2 Gone to the Ulluḫ-Urim Village for Barley Rations

3 **ğuruš lú-kíkken** (. . .) u$_4$-2-šè še é-duru$_5$-ul-luḫ-uri$_5$^{ki}-ma-šè ğen-na mu še-ba-ne-ne-šè, "3 millers (and) {other craftsmen} for 2 days having gone to the Ulluḫ-Urim village for barley for barley rations," 291:5, 12–14, 292:5, 12–14

ğuruš má-gíd, "boat tower"

1. Receipts: Requisitions for Construction

18 **ğuruš [má-gíd]** 3 sìla ninda-dabin ù zì-šà-gen-ta 3 sìla še kaš-ta 3 ma-na tuḫ-ğeš-ì-ḫád 3 sìla zú-lum-ta 3 sìla tuḫ-duru$_5$-sig$_5$-ta (. . .) níğ-dab$_5$ ğuruš má gíd-e-ne u$_4$ al-tar-ra gub-ba, "(For) 18 [boat towers]: 3 liters of bread of semolina and ordinary šà-flour each, 3 liters of barley (for) beer each, 3 minas of dried sesame chaff, 3 liters of dates each (and) 3 liters of fine fresh bran each, (and) {provisions for their overseer}; requisitions of the boat towers when they were employed for construction," 442:1–6, 19–20

1.1 For the Overseer of the Boat Towers

1 **ğuruš** ugula **má gíd** 6 sìla ninda-dabin ù zì-šà-gen 6 sìla še kaš 6 ma-na tuḫ-ğ[eš-ì]-ḫád 6 ⸢sìla⸣ zú-⸢lum⸣ 6 sìla tuḫ-duru$_5$-⸢sig$_5$⸣ 1½ sìla 5 gín ì-šáḫ 6⅓ sìla mun 3 sìla 10 gín *kà-ma-am-⸢tum⸣* 5 sìla níğ-àr-ra-⸢sig$_5$⸣ 3 ádda-udu ^{dug}útul-šè níğ-dab$_5$ ğuruš má-gíd-e-ne u$_4$ al-tar-ra gub-ba, "(For) the overseer of the boat towers: 6 liters of bread of semolina and ordinary šà-flour, 6 liters of barley (for) beer, 6 minas of dried sesame chaff, 6 liters of dates, 6 liters of fine fresh bran, 1½ liters (and) 5 shekels of lard, 6⅓ liters of salt, 3 liters (and) 10 shekels of the *kamamtum* vegetable, 5 liters of fine groats (and) 3 sheep carcasses for the tureen; requisitions of the boat towers when they were employed for construction," 442:7–20

ğuruš má-laḫ$_5$, "sailor"

1. Expended by ***Simat-Ištaran***

[n] ğuruš [. . .n+]20 ğuruš ad-kub$_4$ [n+]15 **ğuruš má-laḫ$_5$** u$_4$-1-šè zi-ga *simat-^{d}ištaran*, "[n . . .] workmen, [n+]20 reed craftsmen (and) [n+]15 sailors for 1 day. (It was) the expenditure of *Simat-Ištaran*," 511:15–20

2. Released on the Day of the Wool Rations

(. . .) [n **ğuruš má]-laḫ$_5$** [u$_4$-1-šè] ⸢u$_4$⸣ siki-ba-ka šu bar-⸢ra⸣, "[n] sailor(s) (and) {other craftsmen} released [for 1 day] on the day of the wool rations," 280:16–18

3. Tamping Dirt at the Sea Dike

2 **g̃uruš má-laḫ$_5$** u$_4$-30-šè má saḫar ég a-ab-ba se-gé-dè gub-ba, "2 sailors employed for 30 days to tamp dirt (delivered by) boat at the sea dike," 274:1–3, 275:1–3

4. Unspecified

30 **g̃uruš má-laḫ$_5$** u$_4$-1-šè, "30 sailors for 1 day," 269:1–2

g̃uruš nagar, "carpenter"

1. Released on the Day of the Wool Rations

(. . .) 1 **g̃uruš nagar** (. . .) [u$_4$-1-šè] ⸢u$_4$⸣ siki-ba-ka šu bar-⸢ra⸣, "1 carpenter (and) {other craftsmen} released [for 1 day] on the day of the wool rations," 280:12, 17–18

g̃uruš níg̃-ga, "class of worker"

1. Mixing Earth and Water for the Brick Stack

[1 **g̃]uruš níg̃-ga** a bal-a im lu-a SIG4.ANŠE-šè gub<-ba>, "[1] employed níg̃-ga workman having poured water (for) mixing (with) earth for the brick stack," 21:'3

g̃uruš si$_{12}$(SIG$_7$)-a, "class of worker"[2]

1. Provisions

1 **g̃uruš si$_{12}$-a** 1 sìla kaš-ninda ⅓ sìla tu$_7$ (. . .) kaš-ninda ḫa-la-a? al-⸢tar⸣-gub-ba, "(For) 1 si$_{12}$-a workman: 1 liter of beer (and) bread (and) ⅓ liter of soup (and) {provisions for other workers}, beer (and) bread divided (for workers) employed (for) construction," 379:14, 20

[8] **g̃uruš si$_{12}$-a** [igi]-6-g̃ál 3 še kù-babbar-ta (. . .) níg̃-kas$_7$-aka mun-gazi nu-$^{g̃eš}$kiri$_6$ a-pí-sal$_4$^{ki}-ke$_4$-ne, "[8] si$_{12}$-a workmen, $^1/_6$ (shekel and) 3 barley corn of silver each (and) {additional consignments of silver}; the balanced account of mun-gazi agricultural products of the gardeners of Apisal," 540:3–4, 11–12

1 **g̃uruš si$_{12}$-a** 1 sìla kaš-ninda ⅓ sìla tu$_7$, "(For) 1 si$_{12}$-a workman: 1 liter of beer (and) bread (and) ⅓ liter of soup," 556:'9

7.1.0. ninda [gur] še-ba **si$_{12}$-a ḪA?.[A?], "7 bushels (and) 60 liters of semolina, barley rations of the si$_{12}$-a (workers)," 1527:17–18

g̃uruš simug, "smith"

1. Mourning

1 **g̃uruš simug** (. . .) ⸢u$_4$⸣–1-šè gaba sàg-dè gub-ba u$_4$ dig̃ir-re gaba *na-wi-ir-ilum* ba-a-g̃ar-ra, "1 smith (and) {other craftsmen} employed for 1 day to beat (their) breasts when the god made the breast of *Nawir-ilum* subside (i.e. when he died)," 251:6, 8–10

2. Released for the Priest

[n] **g̃uruš simug** (. . .) u$_4$-15-šè ⸢ki⸣ en-šè šu bar-ra, "[n] smith(s) (and) {other craftsmen} released for 15 days for the priest," 225:4, 6–7

---

[2] Molina and Such-Gutiérrez 2004, 6f.

3. Transporting Reeds to Garšana

1⅔ g̃uruš ašgab 1 g̃uruš túg-du$_8$ 1 **g̃uruš simug** u$_4$-1-šè ˹gi˺ ù gi-zi é-^{d}šára-ta gar-ša-an-na^{ki}-šè [de$_6$]-a de$_6$-a(sic!), "1⅔ leather workers, 1 braider (and) 1 smith for 1 day having brought reeds and fresh reeds from the Šara temple to Garšana," 232:1–8

1 **g̃uruš simug** (. . .) u$_4$-10-še gi-izi ù-dag^{ki}-ga-ta gar-ša-an-na^{ki}-šè [de$_6$]-a, "1 smith (and) {other craftsmen} for 10 days, having [brought] fuel reeds from Udaga to Garšana," 230:4, 6–9

4. Provisions

1 **g̃uruš simug** 1 [sìla ka]š-ninda ⅓ [sìla] tu$_7$(-ta erased), "(For) 1 smith: 1 [liter] of beer (and) bread (and) ⅓ [liter] of soup," 556:'8

g̃uruš túg-du$_8$, "braider"

1. Canal Work

1 **g̃uruš túg-du$_8$** [u$_4$]-21-šè saḫar zi-ga i$_7$-sur du$_6$-ba-an-du$_8$-du$_8$ a-˹šà˺ sum-túl-túl, "1 braider for 21 [days] having moved dirt at the Sur canal of Du-bandudu (and?/in?) the Sum-tultul field," 268:1–5

1 **g̃uruš túg-[du$_8$]** u$_4$-13-šè saḫar zi-ga i$_7$-ma-ma-*šar-ra-at*, "1 braider for 13 days having moved dirt at the Mama-*šarrat* canal," 283:1–3

2. Transporting Barley

2.1 From Du-saḫara to Enzu-babbar

1 **g̃uruš túg-du$_8$** u$_4$-12-šè du$_6$-saḫar-ra^{ki}-ta en-zu-bábbar^{ki}-šè [še] íb-ga$_6$ [ús-b]i 1500 éš kaskal š[u+níg̃in]-na-bi, "1 braider for 12 days carried [barley] from Du-saḫara to Enzu-babbar. Its distance: 1500 ropes is the entire trip," 263:1–6

2.2 To the Kabbi Village from *Dimbun*-Ašgi

1 **g̃uruš túg-du$_8$** u$_4$-1-šè še *dì-im-bu-na*-^{d}àš-gi$_5$-ta é-duru$_5$-˹kab˺-bí-[šè], "1 braider for 1 day (having brought) barley from *Dimbun*-Ašgi [to] the Kabbi village," 256:1–4

1 **g̃uruš túg-du$_8$** (. . .) u$_4$-1-[šè] še *dì-im-bu-na*-^{d}àš-gi$_5$-ta é-duru$_5$-kab-bi-šè(!) <de$_6$->a, "1 braider (and) {other craftsmen} [for] 1 day having <brought> barley from *Dimbun*-Ašgi to the Kabbi village," 287:12, 16–18

2.3 To Garšana

[n] **g̃uruš tú[g-d]u$_8$** u$_4$-9-šè še ù-dag-ga^{ki}-ta gar-ša-an-na^{ki}-šè de$_6$-a ù kar-[ta] g̃á-nun-šè íb-˹ga$_6$˺, "[n] braider(s) for 9 days having brought barley from Udaga to Garšana and carried it [from] the quay to the storehouse," 261:1–6

[n **g̃uruš]** **túg-d[u$_8$** u$_4$]-20-[šè še é]-duru$_5$-kab-bi[^{ki}-ta gar]-ša-an-na^{ki}-[šè] de$_6$-a, "[n] braider(s) [for] 20 [days] having brought [barley from] the Kabbi village [to] Garšana," 302:1–3

1 **g̃uruš túg-du$_8$** (. . .) u$_4$-20-šè še é-duru$_5$-kab-bi-ta gar-ša-an-na^{ki}-šè mu-un-de$_9$-sa-a, "1 braider (and) {other craftsmen} for 20 days who brought barley from the Kabbi village to Garšana," 304:4, 7–10

2.4 Gone to the Ulluḫ-Urim Village for Barley Rations

1 **g̃uruš túg-du$_8$** (. . .) u$_4$-2-šè še é-duru$_5$-ul-luḫ-uri$_5$^{ki}-ma-šè g̃en-na mu še-ba-ne-ne-šè, "1 braider (and) {other craftsmen} for 2 days having gone to the Ulluḫ-Urim village for barley for barley rations," 291:8, 12–14, 292:8, 12–14

3. Transporting Other Commodities

3.1 Barley and the Commodity Tax

1 **g̃uruš túg-du$_8$** u$_4$-6-šè še(40)! en-zu-bábbar<ki>-ta [de$_6$]-a 1 **g̃uruš túg-du$_8$** u$_4$-6-šè níg̃-gú-na tum-ma-al^{ki}-šè de$_6$-a 1 **g̃uruš túg-du$_8$** u$_4$-11-šè níg̃-gú-na é-da-na^{ki}-šè de$_6$-a 1 **g̃uruš túg-du$_8$** u$_4$-6-šè níg̃-gú-na nag̃-su^{ki}-ta de$_6$-a, "1 braider for 6 days having [brought] barley from Enzu-babbar, 1 braider for 6 days having brought the commodity tax to Tumal, 1 braider for 11 days having brought the commodity tax to Edana (and) 1 braider for 6 days having brought the commodity tax from Nag̃su," 267:1–11

3.2 Oil

2 **g̃uruš túg-du$_8$** u$_4$-1-šè ì de$_6$-a a-rá–1-kam, "2 braiders for 1 day having brought oil for the 1st time," 306:6–8

3.3 Reeds

1⅔ g̃uruš ašgab 1 **g̃uruš túg-du$_8$** 1 g̃uruš simug u$_4$-1-šè ⌜gi⌝ ù gi-zi é-^{d}šára-ta gar-ša-an-na^{ki}-šè [de$_6$]-a de$_6$-a(sic!), "1⅔ leather workers, 1 braider (and) 1 smith for 1 day having brought reeds and fresh reeds from the Šara temple to Garšana," 232:1–8

(. . .) 1 **g̃uruš túg-du$_8$** u$_4$-10-še gi-izi ù-dag^{ki}-ga-ta gar-ša-an-na^{ki}-šè [de$_6$]-a, "{other craftsmen} (and) 1 braider for 10 days, having [brought] fuel reeds from Udaga to Garšana," 230:5–9

3.4 Straw

10 **g̃uruš túg-du$_8$** u$_4$-1-šè in-u a-gàr-didli-ta gar-ša-an-na^{ki}-šè lá-a, "10 braiders for 1 day having transported straw from various meadows to Garšana," 306:3–5

3.5 Wool

2 **g̃uruš túg-du$_8$** u$_4$-1-šè ⌜siki⌝ de$_6$-a a-rá–2-kam é-^{d}*šu*-^{d}*suen*^{ki}-ta gar-ša-an-na^{ki}-šè g̃en-a, "2 braiders for 1 day having brought wool for the 2nd time, (braiders) having gone from *Bit-Šu-Suen* to Garšana," 306:9–13

4. Other Assignments

4.1 Dismantling a Boat

1 **g̃uruš túg-du$_8$** u$_4$-3-⌜šè⌝ má gul-dè gub<-ba>, "1 braider employed for 3 days to dismantle a boat," 272:1–2

4.2 For the *Abum* Festival

1 **g̃uruš túg-du$_8$** u$_4$-12-šè gaba sàg-dè ⌜gub⌝-ba u$_4$ ezem-*a-bu-um*-ma, "1 braider employed for 12 days to beat (his) breast during the *Abum* festival," 278:1–4

4.3 For Field Administration

30 **g̃uruš túg-du$_8$** u$_4$-1-[šè] nam-ša-ra-ab-du a-šà pa$_4$-lugal-g̃u$_{10}$-ka gub-ba, "30 braiders [for] 1 day employed for the administration of the Palugalg̃u field," 306:1–2

4.4 Loading Boats

★★1 **g̃uruš túg-du$_8$** [u$_4$-1-šè] še 120 gur á-á[g̃-d]è gub-b[a ù má si-ga], "1 braider [for 1 day], instructions about the 120 bushels of barley followed [and the boat was loaded]," 298:4–5

4.5 Mourning

1 **g̃uruš túg-du$_8$** ⸢u$_4$⸣–1-šè gaba sàg-dè gub-ba u$_4$ dig̃ir-re gaba *na-wi-ir-ilum* ba-a-g̃ar-ra, "1 braider (and) {other craftsmen} employed for 1 day to beat (their) breasts when the god made the breast of *Nawir-ilum* subside (i.e. when he died)," 251:2, 8–10

4.6 Released on the Day of the Wool Rations

1 **g̃uruš [túg-du$_8$]** u$_4$-1-šè u$_4$ siki ba-a-ka šu bar-ra, "1 [braider] released for 1 day on the day of the wool rations," 265:1–3

(. . .) 1 **g̃uruš túg-du$_8$** (. . .) [u$_4$-1-šè] ⸢u$_4$⸣ siki-ba-ka šu bar-⸢ra⸣, "1 braider (and) {other craftsmen} released [for 1 day] on the day of the wool rations," 280:11, 17–18

4.7 Released for the Priest

[n] **g̃uruš túg-[du$_8$]** (. . .) u$_4$-15-šè ⸢ki⸣ en-šè šu bar-ra, "[n] braider(s) (and) {other craftsmen} released for 15 days for the high priest," 225:2, 6–7

4.8 Sitting Idle

1 **g̃uruš túg-d[u$_8$** u$_4$-1-šè] šà [gú-saḫar]$^{⸢ḫar⸣}$.DU^{ki} tuš-[a šà] a im še-g̃á, "1 braider [for 1 day] having sat (idle) in Gu-saḫar.DU because of rain," 298:9–10

4.9 Towing Boats

★★[n] g̃uruš ^{lú}[ázlag n] g̃uruš ašgab [n] g̃uruš ad-kub$_4$ [n] **g̃[uruš tú]g-du$_8$** [. . .]-x-šè [x]-zi-[x]-x maš-kán^{ki}-⸢šè⸣ má gíd-⸢da⸣, "[n] fuller(s), [n] leather worker(s), [n] reed craftsmen (and) [n] braider(s) having towed a boat [. . .] to Maškan," 260:11–17

1 **g̃uruš túg-du$_8$** u$_4$-[1-šè] é-^{d}*šu*-^{d}*suen*$^{⸢ki⸣}$-[ta] gú-saḫar^{ḫar}.DU^{ki}-šè m[á gíd-da], "1 braider [for 1] day [having towed] a boat [from] *Bit-Šu-Suen* to Gu-saḫar.DU," 298:6–8

1 **g̃uruš túg-du$_8$** u$_4$-[1-šè] gú-saḫar^{ḫar}.DU^{ki}-ta a[n-za-qar]-*da-da*-šè má gíd-da ù [še ba-al], "1 braider [for 1] day having towed a boat from Gu-saḫar.DU to the fortified tower of *Dada* and [having unloaded barley]," 298:11–12

1 **g̃uruš túg-du$_8$** u$_4$-6-šè má gíd-da, "1 braider for 6 days having towed a boat," 783:6–7

4.10 Traveling

1 **g̃uruš [túg-du$_8$** u$_4$-1-šè] gar-ša-an-na^{ki}-ta é-^{d}*šu*-^{d}*suen*[^{ki}-a] g̃en-[na], "1 [braider for 1 day] having gone from Garšana [into] *Bit-Šu-Suen*," 298:1–3

1 **g̃uruš túg-du$_8$** u$_4$-4-šè *dì-im-bu-na*-àš-gi$_5$-ta a-šà *ṣe-ru-um*-šè, "1 braider for 4 days (having gone) from *Dimbun*-Ašgi to the *Ṣerum* field," 283:5–8

4.11 Unspecified

1 **g̃uruš túg-du$_8$** u$_4$-5-še, "1 braider for 5 days," 783:10

g̃uruš um-mi-a, "craftsman"

1. Provisions: Silver

23[+3] **g̃uruš um-mi-a** ù dù-a-tar [⅓ gí]n 3 še kù-babbar-ta (. . .) níg̃-kas$_7$-aka mun-gazi nu-$^{g̃eš}$kiri$_6$ a-pí-sal$_4$^{ki}-ke$_4$-ne, "26 craftsmen and orchard workmen, [⅓] shekel (and) 3 barley corn of silver each (and) {additional consignments of silver}; the balanced account of mun-gazi agricultural products of the gardeners of Apisal," 540:1–2, 11–12

g̃uruš un-ga$_6$, "porter"

1. Provisions

[4] **g̃uruš un-ga$_6$** ⅔ [sìla] kaš-ninda ⅓ sìla t[u$_7$-ta] (. . .) kaš-ninda ḫa-la-a? al-⸢tar⸣ gub-ba, "(For) [4] porter(s): ⅔ [liter] of beer (and) bread (and) ⅓ liter of soup [each] (and) {provisions for other workers}, beer (and) bread divided (for workers) employed (for) construction," 379:10, 20

5 **g̃uruš un-ga$_6$** ⅔ sìla kaš-ninda ⅓ sìla tu$_7$-ta, "(For) 5 porters: ⅔ liter of beer (and) bread (and) ⅓ liter of soup each," 556:'11

CRAFTSWOMEN

géme àr-ra, "female grinder"

1. Wages

6.0.0. še gur á **géme àr-ra**, "6 bushels of barley, wages of female grinders," 405:1–2

géme gu, "female spinner"

1. Mourning *Šu-Kabta*

97 géme sag̃-dub 15 géme á–⅓-ta géme uš-bar-me-éš [n] **géme gu** [u$_4$]-9½-šè [gaba] sìg-dè gub-[ba u$_4$ *šu*]-*kab-tá* ba-⸢úš⸣-a, "97 full-time female weavers (and) 15 female weavers at ⅓ wages (and) [n] female spinner(s) employed for 9½ [days] to beat (their) [breasts] when *Šu-Kabta* died," 252:1–7

2. Released on the Day of the Wool Rations

2 géme sag̃-dub 1 géme á-⅔ **géme gu-me-éš** u$_4$-1-šè u$_4$ siki-ba-ka [šu bar]-ra, "2 full-time female spinners (and) 1 female spinner at ⅔ wages [released] for 1 day on the day of the wool rations," 234:1–5

géme g̃eš-ì-sur-sur, "female sesame presser"

1. Agricultural Work

2 **géme g̃eš-ì-sur-sur** (. . .) u$_4$-105-šè (. . .) še gur$_{10}$-gur$_{10}$-dè zàr tab-ba-dè ù g̃eš ra-ra-dè a-šà *ṣe-ru-um* gub-ba, "2 female sesame pressers for 105 days (and) {other craftsmen} employed at the *Ṣerum* field to reap barley, stack (its) sheaves (for drying) and flail (them)," 262:6, 10, 19–22

2. Transporting Barley

2.1 To the Kabbi Village from *Dimbun*-Ašgi

(. . .) 2 **géme g̃eš-ì-[sur-sur]** u$_4$-1-[šè] še *dì-im-bu-na*-^{d}àš-gi$_5$-ta é-duru$_5$-kab-bi-šè(!) <de$_6$->a, "{other craftsmen} (and) 2 female sesame [pressers for] 1 day having <brought> barley from *Dimbun*-Ašgi to the Kabbi village," 287:15–18

2.2 To Garšana from Udaga

(. . .) 2 **géme g̃eš-ì-sur-sur** u$_4$-10-šè še ù-dag-ga^{ki}-ta gar-ša-an-na^{ki}-šè de$_6$-a, "{other craftsmen} (and) 2 female sesame pressers for 10 days having brought barley from Udaga to Garšana," 287:6–9

2.3 From *Šu-Suen*-ammar

3 **géme g̃eš-ì-sur-sur** u_4-1-šè še ^{d}*šu*-^{d}*suen*-am-ma-ar^{ki}-ta de_6-a íb-ga_6, "3 female sesame pressers for 1 day carried barley having been brought from *Šu-Suen*-ammara," 249:1–3

2.4 Gone to the Ulluḫ-Urim Village for Barley Rations

4 **géme g̃eš-ì-[sur]-sur** (. . .) u_4-2-šè še é-$duru_5$-ul-luḫ-uri_5^{ki}-ma-šè g̃en-na mu še-ba-ne-ne-šè, "4 female sesame pressers (and) {other craftsmen} for 2 days having gone to the Ulluḫ-Urim village for barley for barley rations," 291:6, 12–14, 292:6, 12–14

3. Other Assignments

3.1 Mourning *Nawir-ilum*

3 **géme g̃eš-ì-sur-sur** (. . .) ⌜u_4⌝–1-šè gaba sàg-dè gub-ba u_4 dig̃ir-re gaba *na-wi-ir-ilum* ba-a-g̃ar-ra, "3 female sesame pressers (and) {other craftsmen} employed for 1 day to beat (their) breasts when the god made the breast of *Nawir-ilum* subside (i.e. when he died)," 251:1, 8–10

3.2 Released on the Day of the Wool Rations

(. . .) [n] **géme g̃eš-ì-s[ur-sur]** (. . .) [u_4-1-šè] ⌜u_4⌝ siki-ba-ka šu bar-⌜ra⌝, "[n] female sesame presser(s) (and) {other craftsmen} released [for 1 day] on the day of the wool rations," 280:5, 17–18

4. Provisions

12 géme kíkken 4 **géme g̃eš-ì-sur-sur** [n] sìla ninda zì-milla ù zì-šà-gen-t[a n] sìla kaš-gen-t[a 1] ma-na tuḫ-g̃eš-ì-há[d-ta] 5 sìla zú-lum-[ta], "(For) 12 female millers (and) 4 female sesame pressers: [n] liter(s) of bread of milla and ordinary šà-flour each, [n] liter(s) of ordinary beer each, [1] mina of dried sesame chaff [each] (and) 5 liters of dates [each]," 536:12–17

géme kíkken, "female miller"

1. Labor: (Processing) Grain

4.0.0. zíz gur zíz-ba-na zì-KAL 4½ sìla 5 gín-ta ì-g̃ál 7.4.0. kib_x gur ⌜sag̃⌝? g̃ál-la nu-ub-tuku á **géme kíkken**-šè, "4 bushels of emmer wheat, in each ban (=10 liters) of the emmer wheat there are 4½ liters and 5 shekels of KAL-flour (and) 7 bushels (and) 240 liters of wheat, which did not have (?), for labor of female millers," 412:1–5

10.0.0. še gur 10.0.0. zíz gur ba-na zì-KAL 5 sìla-ta ì-g̃ál á **géme kíkken**, "10 bushels (of) barley (and) 10 bushels of emmer wheat, in each ban (=10 liters) of it there are 5 liters of KAL-flour, labor (for) the female millers," 433:1–3

5.0.0. še gur 0.1.0. $img̃ag̃a_3$ á **géme kíkken**-šè, "5 bushels of barley (and) 60 liters of emmer for labor of female millers," 455:1–3

14.2.0. zíz gibil gur zíz ba-na $img̃ag̃a_3$ 5 sìla 7-gín-ta ì-g̃ál 5.3.0 zíz sumun gur zíz ba-na $img̃ag̃a_3$ 4-sìla-ta ì-g̃ál á **géme kíkken**-šè, "14 bushels (and) 120 liters of new emmer wheat, in each ban (=10 liters) of the emmer wheat there are 5 liters (and) 7 shekels of emmer, (and) 5 bushels (and) 180 liters of old emmer wheat, in each ban (=10 liters) of emmer wheat there are 4 liters of emmer, for labor of female millers," 461:1–5

20.0.0. še gur 0.0.1 zíz gur ba-na zì-KAL-ta á **géme kíkken**-šè, "20 bushels of barley and 10 liters of emmer wheat in each ban (=10 liters) (there is) KAL-flour, for labor of female millers," 467:1–3

10.0.0. še gur 20.0.0. zíz gur zíz ba-na imĝaĝa$_3$ 3⅓ sìla-ta ì-ĝál 9.4.0. zíz gur [zíz b]a-[na] zì-KAL 5 [sìla-t]a 1.4.4. kib$_x$ gur á **géme kíkken**-šè, "10 bushels of barley, 20 bushels of emmer wheat, in each ban (=10 liters) of the emmer wheat there are 3⅓ liters of emmer, 9 bushels (and) 240 liters of emmer wheat, in each ban (=10 liters) of emmer wheat (there are) 5 liters of KAL-flour (and) 1 bushel (and) 280 liters of wheat for labor of female millers," 532:1–7

2. Transporting Barley

2.1 To the Kabbi Village from *Dimbun*-Ašgi

6 **géme** **ḪAR**.[**ḪAR**] (. . .) u$_4$-1-[šè] še *dì-im-bu-na*-^{d}àš-gi$_5$-ta é-duru$_5$-kab-bi-šè(!) <de$_6$->a, "6 female millers (and) {other craftsmen} [for] 1 day having <brought> barley from *Dimbun*-Ašgi to the Kabbi village," 287:14, 16–18

2.2 To Garšana

1 ĝuruš ašgab 1 ĝuruš ad-kub$_4$ 1 **géme kíkken** u$_4$-[2]7-šè še ^{d}*šu*-^{d}*suen*-<am->ma-ra$^{[ki]}$ ù bàd-ga-zi^{ki}-⸢ta⸣ gar-ša-an-na^{ki}-šè de$_6$-a, "1 leather worker, 1 reed craftsman (and) 1 female miller for [2]7 days having brought barley from *Šu-Suen*-ammara and Bad-gazi to Garšana," 259:1–7

6 **géme kíkken** (. . .) u$_4$-10-šè še ù-dag-ga^{ki}-ta gar-ša-an-na^{ki}-šè de$_6$-a, "6 female millers (and) {other craftsmen} for 10 days having brought barley from Udaga to Garšana," 287:5, 7–9

6 **géme kíkken** u$_4$-10-šè še ù-dag-ga^{ki}-ta gar-ša-an-na^{ki}-šè de$_6$-a, "6 female millers for 10 days having brought barley from Udaga to Garšana," 289:1–4

10 géme ⸢kíkken⸣ u$_4$-1-šè a-rá–1-kam 10 **géme kíkken** u$_4$-1-šè a-rá–2-kam 12 **géme kíkken** u$_4$-1-šè a-rá–3-kam gi-zi a-gàr ĜEŠ.KÚŠU^{ki}-ta gar-ša-an-na^{ki}-⸢šè⸣, "10 female millers for 1 day for the 1st time, 10 female millers for 1 day for the 2nd time, 12 female millers for 1 day for the 3rd time (having brought) fresh reeds from the ĜEŠ.KÚŠU meadow to Garšana," 295:1–11

10 **géme kíkken** u$_4$-1-šè a-rá–1-kam 10 **géme kíkken** u$_4$-1-šè a-rá–2-kam 10 **géme kíkken** u$_4$-1-šè a-rá–3-kam še an-za-qar-*da-da*-ta gar-ša-an-na^{ki}-šè de$_6$-a, "10 female millers for 1 day for the 1st time, 10 female millers for 1 day for the 2nd time (and) 10 female millers for 1 day for the 3rd time having brought barley from the fortified tower of *Dada* to Garšana," 296:1–9

4 **géme kíkken** u$_4$-20-šè še é-duru$_5$-kab-bi^{ki}-ta gar-ša-an-na^{ki}-šè de$_6$-a, "4 female millers for 20 days having brought barley from the Kabbi village to Garšana," 301:1–3

3 **géme kíkken** (. . .) u$_4$-20-šè še é-duru$_5$-kab-bi-ta gar-ša-an-na^{ki}-šè mu-un-de$_9$-sa-a, "3 female millers (and) {other craftsmen} for 20 days who brought barley from the Kabbi village to Garšana," 304:2, 7–10

2.3 Gone to the Ulluḫ-Urim Village for Barley Rations

12 **géme kíkken** (. . .) u$_4$-2-šè še é-duru$_5$-ul-luḫ-uri$_5$^{ki}-ma-šè ĝen-na mu še-ba-ne-ne-šè, "12 female millers (and) {other craftsmen} for 2 days having gone to the Ulluḫ-Urim village for barley for barley rations," 291:4, 12–14, 292:4, 12–14

2.4 Broken Context

6 **géme kíkken** u$_4$-[n-šè] še [GN-ta GN-šè de$_6$-a], "6 female millers [for n] day(s) [having brought] barley from [GN to GN]," 289:5–8

3. Other Assignments: Released on the Day of the Wool Rations

(. . .) 12 **géme kíkken** (. . .) [u$_4$-1-šè] ⸢u$_4$⸣ siki-ba-ka šu bar-⸢ra⸣, "12 female millers (and) {other craftsmen} released [for 1 day] on the day of the wool rations," 280:4, 17–18

4. Provisions and Wages

n.o.o. še gur á **géme kíkken**-šè, "n bushel(s) of barley for wages of female millers," 376:1–2, 404:1–2, 407:1–2, 417:1–2, 538:1–2

12 **géme kíkken** 4 géme g̃eš-ì-sur-sur [n] sìla ninda zì-milla ù zì-šà-gen-t[a n] sìla kaš-gen-t[a 1] ma-na tuḫ-g̃eš-ì-ḫá[d-ta] 5 sìla zú-lum-[ta], "(For) 12 female millers (and) 4 female sesame pressers: [n] liter(s) of bread of milla and ordinary šà-flour each, [n] liter(s) of ordinary beer each, [1] mina of dried sesame chaff [each] (and) 5 liters of dates [each]," 536:12–17

4.1 Oil for Sick Millers

10 gín ì-g̃eš-ta ^{d}šára-sá-g̃u$_{10}$ 1 bu-za-du-a **géme kíkken-me-éš** u$_4$ dú-ra i-me é-gal!-šè, "10 shekels of sesame oil each (for) Šara-sag̃u (and) Buzadua, female millers, when they were sick at the palace." 466:3–7

géme kisal-luḫ, "female courtyard sweeper"

1. Provisions

1 **géme kisal-luḫ** ⅔ sìla kaš-ninda $^1/_6$ sìla tu$_7$ (. . .) kaš-ninda ḫa-la-a? al-⸢tar⸣ gub-ba, "1 female courtyard sweeper: ⅔ liter of beer (and) bread (and) $^1/_6$ liter of soup (and) {provisions for other workers}, beer (and) bread divided (for workers) employed (for) construction," 379:15, 20

1 **géme kisal-luḫ** ⅔ sìla kaš-ninda $^1/_6$ sìla tu$_7$, "(For) 1 female courtyard sweeper: ⅔ liter of beer (and) bread (and) $^1/_6$ liter of soup," 556:'10

géme uš-bar, "female weaver"

géme-^{d}en-ki **géme uš-bar**, "Geme-Enki, the female weaver" > *Personal Name Index*

1. Agricultural Work

(. . .) 18 géme sag̃-dub 1 géme á-⅔ **géme uš-bar-me-éš** (. . .) u$_4$-105-šè (. . .) še gur$_{10}$-gur$_{10}$-dè zàr tab-ba-dè ù g̃eš ra-ra-dè a-šà *ṣe-ru-um* gub-ba, "18 full-time female weavers (and) 1 female weaver at ⅔ wages for 105 days (and) {other craftsmen} employed at the *Ṣerum* field to reap barley, stack (its) sheaves (for drying) and flail (them)," 262:3–5, 10, 19–22

2. Construction Work

6 g̃uruš ašgab 8 g̃uruš ^{lú}ázlag 24 **géme uš-bar** u$_4$-1-šè al-tar é-*a-bí-a-ti* gul-dè gub-ba, "6 leather workers, 8 fullers (and) 24 female weavers employed for 1 day of construction to demolish the house of *Abiati*," 273:1–6

3. Transporting Barley

3.1 From *Dimbun*-Ašgi to the Kabbi Village

5 **géme uš-bar** (. . .) u$_4$-1-[šè] še *dì-im-bu-na*-^{d}àš-gi$_5$-ta é-duru$_5$-kab-bi-šè(!) <de$_6$->a, "5 female weavers (and) {other craftsmen} [for] 1 day having <brought> barley from *Dimbun*-Ašgi to the Kabbi village," 287:13, 16–18

5 **géme uš-bar** u$_4$-1-šè še *dì-im-bu-na*-^{d}àš-gi$_5$-ta [é]-duru$_5$-kab-bí$^{\langle ki \rangle}$-šè de$_6$-a, "5 female weavers for 1 day having brought barley from *Dimbun*-Ašgi to the Kabbi village," 290:5–8

3.2 To Garšana

16⅓ **géme uš-bar** (. . .) u$_4$-10-šè še ù-dag-ga^{ki}-ta gar-ša-an-na^{ki}-šè de$_6$-a, "16⅓ female weavers (and) {other workers} for 10 days having brought barley from Udaga to Garšana," 287:4, 7–9

16⅓ **géme uš-bar** u$_4$-10-šè še ù-dag-ga^{ki}-ta gar-ša-an-na^{ki}-šè de$_6$-a, "16⅓ female weavers for 10 days having brought barley from Udaga to Garšana," 290:1–4

3 **géme uš-bar** u$_4$-20-šè še é-duru$_5$-ka[b-bí]-ta gar-š[a-an]-⸢na⸣⸢^{ki}⸣-šè [de$_6$]-a, "3 female weavers for 20 days having [brought] barley from the Kabbi village to Garšana," 303:1–4

3 **géme uš-bar** (. . .) u$_4$-20-šè še é-duru$_5$-kab-bi-ta gar-ša-an-na^{ki}-šè mu-un-de$_9$-sa-a, "3 female weavers (and) {other craftsmen} for 20 days who brought barley from the Kabbi village to Garšana," 304:1, 7–10

3.3 Gone to the Ulluḫ-Urim Village for Barley Rations

80 géme sag̃-dub 17 géme á ⅔-ta **géme uš-bar-me-éš** (. . .) u$_4$-2-šè še é-duru$_5$-ul-luḫ-uri$_5$^{ki}-ma-šè g̃en-na mu še-ba-ne-ne-šè, "80 full-time female weavers, 17 female weavers at ⅔ wages (and) {other craftsmen} for 2 days having gone to the Ulluḫ-Urim village for barley for barley rations," 291:1–3, 12, 14, 292:1–3, 12–14

4. Other Assignments

4.1 Bringing Reeds to the Weir

30 **géme uš-bar** u$_4$-1-šè gi g̃á-udu-ta kun-zi-id(Á)-šè íb-ga$_6$, "30 female weavers for 1 day brought reeds from the sheep-shearing shed to the weir," 273:7–9

4.2 Crushing Malt

n **géme uš-bar** u$_4$-1-šè munu$_4$ nag̃$_4$-g̃á-dè gub-ba, "n female weaver(s) for 1 day employed to crush malt," 245:1–2, 277:1–2

4.3 Mourning

97 géme sag̃-dub 15 géme á–⅓-ta **géme uš-bar-me-éš** [n] géme gu [u$_4$]-9½-šè [gaba] sìg-dè gub-[ba u$_4$ *šu*]-*kab-tá* ba-⸢úš⸣-a, "97 full-time female weavers (and) 15 female weavers at ⅓ wages (and) [n] female spinner(s) employed for 9½ [days] to beat (their) [breasts when] *Šu-Kabta* died," 252:1–7

85 géme-⸢sag̃⸣-dub 16 géme á–⅓-⸢ta⸣ u$_4$-1-šè **géme uš-bar-me-éš** gaba sàg-dè gub-ba u$_4$ lugal-e ba-úš-[a], "85 full-time female weavers (and) 16 female weavers at ⅓ wages employed for 1 day to beat (their) breasts when the king died," 257:1–6

4.4 Released on the Day of the Wool Rations

80 géme sag̃-dub 17 géme á-⅔-ta **géme uš-bar-me-éš** [u$_4$-1-šè] ⸢u$_4$⸣ siki-ba-ka šu bar-⸢ra⸣, "80 full-time female weavers (and) 17 female weavers at ⅔ wages (and) {other craftsmen} released [for 1 day] on the day of the wool rations," 280:1–3

4.5 Sorting Wool in *Bit-Šu-Suen*

4 **géme uš-bar** u$_4$-1-šè siki igi sag̃-g̃á šà é-^{d}*šu*-^{d}*suen*^{ki}, "4 female weavers for 1 day having sorted wool in *Bit-Šu-Suen*," 264:1–3

4.6 Assignment Unspecified

70 **géme uš-bar** u_4-1-šè, "70 female weavers for 1 day," 650:1

5. Provisions

[60+]21 géme sağ-⌜dub⌝ [2] sìla zì-milla ù zì-šà-gen-ta [n] sìla kaš-gen-ta [n] ma-na tuḫ-ğeš-ì-ḫád-ta [1+]4 sìla zú-lum-ta [10+]6 géme á-⅔-ta [n] sìla ninda-zì-milla ù zì-šà-gen-ta [n] sìla kaš-gen-ta [n] ma-na tuḫ-ğeš-ì-ḫád-ta 3 sìla zú-lum-[ta] **géme uš-bar-me-éš**, "(For) [60+]21 full-time female weavers: [2] liters of milla and ordinary šà-flour each, [n] liter(s) ordinary beer each, [n] mina(s) of dried sesame chaff each (and) [1+]4 liters of dates each; (for) [10+]6 female weavers at ⅔ wages: [n] liter(s) of milla-flour and ordinary šà-flour each, [n] liter(s) of ordinary beer each, [n] mina(s) of dried sesame chaff each (and) 3 liters of dates each," 536:1–11

Index of Tablets from Umma, G̃irsu, and of Unknown Provenance

Tablets from Umma and G̃irsu, as well as of unknown provenance, are included here because they mention Garšana, contain Akkadian personal names known from Garšana, display typical Garšana ductus, or contain other data suggesting they may have originated in Garšana. Many of these tablets have been published elsewhere and belong to various archives. As such, the structure of their index differs here from the analytical concordance to the Garšana archive. The glossary offers only translations of basic terms and does not provide the contexts in which the terms occurs. The subsequent indices of personal names, toponyms, and divine names are similarly organized.

– A –

a . . . bal, *dalû*, "to pour water; to irrigate"

a bal-a, 1428:18, 1428:35

a bala, 1496:2

a-g̃ar, "depilation fluid," 1453:1, 1453:2

a-ka-a, 1485:63

a-KIN.KIN, 1478:17

a-na, "to, for," 1497:3, 1497:8, 1497:12

a-rá, *adi*, *alaktu*, "times (with numbers); ways; way"

a-rá–1-kam, "for the 1st time," 1441:10

a-rá–2-kam, "for the 2nd time," 1441:11

a-rá–3-àm, "for the 3rd time," 1424:15

a-šà, *eqlu*, "field"

a-šà-bi n sar (n gín), "its field (measures) n sar (and n gín)," 1513:2, 1513:4, 1513:6, 1513:8, 1513:10, 1513:12, 1513:14, 1513:17, 1513:19, 1513:21, 1513:23, 1513:25

a-šà a-kal-^{d}en-ki, 1428:29

a-šà ama-zi-da, 1428:17

a-šà am-rí-ma, 1428:5

a-šà *da-la-ḫu-um*, 1503:5

a-šà du$_{6}$-nunuz-^{d}nin-sún, 1428:3

a-šà gar-ša-na-ka^{ki}, 1414:22

a-šà ì-ku$_{6}$, 1428:23

a-šà ka-ma-rí^{ki}, 1488:'12

a-šà ká-babbar, 1504:8
a-šà kam-sal$_4$-la, 1412:3
a-šà ki-g̃ír-nun-na, 1478:21
a-šà lá-maḫ, 1488:4
a-šà-maḫ, 1446:2
a-šà ^{d}nergal-gar-ša-na-ka^{ki}, 1428:9
a-šà ^{d}nergal-ḪAR-da-ḫi^{ki}, 1428:19
a-šà nigir-za-ú-tuku, 1428:7
a-šà ^{d}nin-⸢gublaga⸣, 1488:5
a-šà ^{d}⸢nin⸣-ur$_4$-ra, 1488:'8
a-šà saḫar-ú-ú, 1412:20
a-šà šeš-barag, 1428:26
a-šà šeš-barag-^{d}nergal$_x$$^{<eri11->gal}$ gar-ša-na-ka^{ki}, 1434:27
a-šà ^{d}šul-pa-è, 1428:12
a-šà *tab-ba-an*, 1502:5
a-šà-uš-gíd-da, 1412:21
aša$_5$(GÁNA)-kam, 1470:50

a-tu-nir, 1445:25

a-zu, *asû*, "doctor," 1442:4, 1467:2

á, *aḫu*, *idu*, "arm; labor; wage," 1425:12, 1470:2, 1470:37, 1470:40, 1470:43, 1470:51, 1476:'1, 1476:'5, 1488:1, 1488:'11

á . . . dar, *dâṣu*, "to confiscate, seize illegally; sequester; take hold of"
á dar-ra, 1423:36, 1427:46, 1429:11

áb, *arḫu*, *littu*, "cow," 1498:3
áb-amar-ga, "young suckling calf," 1462:5
áb-máḫ, "milk producing cow," 1418:1, 1462:1, 1498:2
áb-mu–2-niga, "fattened 2 year old cow," 1489:3
áb-mu–3, "3 year old cow," 1462:2, 1477:1
gu$_4$-áb-amar ḫi-a, "various calves (and) bull-calves," 1462:7
gu$_4$-áb ḫi-a, "various bulls (and) cows," 1460:1, 1460:4

àga-ús, *rēdû*, "gendarme, soldier," 1447:4, 1453:4, 1459:15, 1470:30
àga-ús-lugal, "royal gendarme," 1440:3, 1490:3

agar$_4$, *ugāru*, "meadow," 1470:38

agrig, *abarakku*, "steward, housekeeper," 1474:8, 1474:12, 1492:17

ak(a), *epēšu*, "to do, to make"
kurum$_7$ ak(a), "to make an inspection," 1450:12, 1451:10
má bala aka, "to unload a boat," 1432:3, 1435:3
al aka, "to perform a type of hoeing," 1470:2, 1470:48, 1470:67

alam, *ṣalmu*, "statue"
alam-lugal, "royal statue," 1478:12

ama, *ummu*, "mother," 1412:6

amar, *atmu*, "young animal"
  áb-amar-ga, "young sulking calf," 1462:5
  gu$_4$-áb-amar ḫi-a, "various calves (and) bull-calves," 1462:7
  gu$_4$-amar-ga, "bull-calf," 1413:1, 1462:6
  kuš-amar, "skin of a young animal," 1441:1

anše, *imēru*, "donkey," 1419:10
  kaskal-anše-lugal, 1478:9

^{ĝeš}apin, *epinnu*, "(seed) plow"
  ^{ĝeš}apin šu-du$_7$-a, "fully functional plow," 1462:13
  gu$_4$-apin 3-kam, "plow team of 3 oxen," 1470:4

apin-lá, *errēšu*, "planter, tiller, cultivator," 1412:23, 1428:36

árad, *wardu*, "servant," 1420:2, 1454:9, 1464:25, 1465:26, 1464:55, 1465:59, 1509:52
  arad-me, "servants," 1478:11
  árad-é-a, "household servant," 1482:4
  árad-géme ḫi-a, "various male and female servants," 1464:57, 1465:61
  géme-árad, "female and male servants," 1470:5
  géme-árad ḫi-[a], "various female and male servants," 1509:54

^{ĝeš}ásal, *ṣarbatu*, "poplar," 1423:2, 1423:15, 1423:22, 1423:33, 1427:2, 1427:16, 1427:23, 1427:34, 1427:45, 1461:1

^{lú}ázlag, *ašlāku*, "fuller," 1459:2, 1459:5

– B –

ba, *qiāšu*, *zâzu*, "to divide into shares, share, halve; to allot"
  saĝ in-ni-ba, 1424:5
  siki-ba, "wool rations," 1443:7

ba-al, *ḫerû*, "to unload (a boat)"
  má bala aka, 1432:3, 1435:5
  má ba-al-la, 1425:9, 1446:6
  má-lá-a ba-al-la, 1448:9

ba-ba, "(a kind of porridge)"
  zì-ba-ba-sig$_5$, "fine-quality flour porridge," 1449:5

babbar, *peṣû*, "(to be) white"
  kuš-máš-gal-babbar, "white billy-goat skin," 1455:3

bàd, *dūru*, "(enclosure) wall," 1478:31

bala, "to rotate, turn over, cross," 1428:27
  bal-a, 1428:27

banšur, *paššūru*, "table," 1485:55

bar, *warkatu*, "outside, (other) side"
  gú-bar-ra, 1470:41

bar, "fleece"

sila$_4$-bar, "lamb fleece," 1437:3

bar-g̃ál, *bargallu*, "a designation of sheep: with fleece"
sila$_4$-bar-g̃ál, "lamb with fleece," 1439:4, 1454:3
u$_8$-bar-g̃ál, "ewe with fleece," 1454:1
udu-níta-bar-g̃ál, "male sheep with fleece," 1454:2
udu-ú-bar-g̃ál, "range fed sheep with fleece," 1439:3

bar-su-ga, "a designation of sheep: without fleece"
udu-niga-bar-su-ga, "fattened sheep without fleece," 1439:2

bisag̃, *pisannu*, "basket, container"
bisag̃-dub-ba, "tablet basket," 1463:1, 1482:1, 1483:1
bisag̃-ninda, "bread basket," 1485:17, 1485:68

$^{g̃eš}$bùlug-ga, "(a tree or wooden object)," 1501:3

bur, *būru*, "a unit of area; a unit of volume," 1513:1, 1513:3, 1513:5, 1513:7, 1513:9, 1513:11, 1513:13, 1513:16, 1513:18, 1513:20, 1513:22, 1513:24

bur-zi, *pursû*, "a bowl," 1423:28, 1427:29, 1427:31, 1427:42

buru$_{14}$, *ebūru*, "harvest," 1486:'5
še-buru$_{14}$, "barley harvest," 1490:14

– D –

da, "to approach?"[1]
in-da-a, 1463:5–7

da-na, *bêru*, "a unit of length, double-hour (distance), double-mile," 1497:2, 1497:7, 1497:10

dab$_5$, *ṣabātu*, "to take in charge"
ì-dab$_5$, 1413:5, 1415:5, 1435:IV 12, 1435:IV 14, 1435:V 3, 1454:12, 1471:5, 1475:8, 1485:56, 1485:59, 1489:14

dabin, *tappinu*, "semolina, barley grits," 1449:10, 1469:1, 1470:10, 1470:18, 1470:26, 1470:29, 1470:62, 1494:2, 1495:1, 1495:4, 1495:7, 1495:10
dabin-lugal, "royal semolina," 1472:1

dag̃al, *rapāšu*, "(to be) wide; width, breadth," 1513:1

dal-ba-na, *birītu*, "property held in common; space between," 1489:1

dam, *aššatu*, *mutu*, "wife, spouse," 1501:4

dam-gàr, *tamkaru*, "merchant," 1503:3

de$_5$(g), *laqātu*, "to pick up, glean, gather"
la-ag de$_5$(g), *laqit kirbāni*, "to pick up clods (of earth)," 1488:4, 1488:5

de$_6$, *babālu*, "to bring, carry"
de$_6$-a, 1505:'6

[1] Gomi 1992, 85–86 no. 314 with reference to Sauren 1970, 14.

di-ku$_5$, *dayyānu*, "judge," 1472:4, 1478:41

di-til-la, *dīnu gamru*, *ditillû*, "completed court case," 1419:13, 1420:8

dida$_x$(Ú.SA), *billatu*, "sweet wort, an ingredient for beer making; beer for transport," 1470:54

didli, *mādūtu*, "several, various"
 èš didli, "various shrines," 1416:31, 1428:36
 mu-DU didli, "various deliveries," 1463:4
 zi-ga didli, "various expenditures," 1470:66

dím, *banû*, "to create, make, manufacture"
 ba-na-dím-ma, 1455:5

diri(g), *atru*, "surplus, additional"
 níg̃-dirig ezem-ma, "surplus goods of the festival," 1416:11, 1416:21
 sá-du$_{11}$-iti-dirig, "regular offerings of month 13," 1416:10, 1416:20

DU
 DU-m[u-(x)]-da, 1424:9
 ì-im-[DU?], 1424:8
 nu-mu-DU, 1424:11
 nu-mu-un-DU, 1424:17
 [n g̃uruš] šu dím DU, 1505:'4

dú, *marāṣu*, "to be sick"
 dú-ra, 1490:13

dù, *banû*, *epēšu*,"to construct"
 ba-dù-a, 1482:5

du$_6$, *tīlu*, "(ruin) mound"
 a-šà du$_6$-nunuz-^{d}nin-sún, 1428:3
 ^{d}g̃eštin?-an?-na?-du$_6$-*ar-ḫa-tum*, 1498:8

du$_{10}$-gal, 1441:19

^{kuš}du$_{10}$-gan, *tu(k)kannu*, "leather bag," 1417:1, 1441:20

du$_{10}$-ús, *narmaku*, "bath (within a house)," 1478:42

dub, *ṭuppu*, "tablet," 1470:19, 1496:2
 bisag̃-dub-ba, "tablet basket," 1463:1, 1482:1, 1483:1

dub-sar, *ṭupšarru*, "scribe," 1423:13, 1427:14, 1428:13, 1466:9, 1470:28, 1470:59, 1481:6, 1482:8, 1485:36

dug, *karpatu*, "clay jug," 1462:23, 1470:55, 1485:51

dug$_4$, *atwû*, *dabābu*, *epēšu*, *qabû*, "to speak, talk, say; to order"
 in-na-an-du$_{11}$, 1493:8
 in-na-an-du$_{11}$-⌈ga⌉?, 1424:10
 ù-na-a-du$_{11}$, 1499:2, 1500:2

dumu, *māru*, "son, child," 1423:26, 1427:27, 1431:3, 1432:13, 1435:13, 1450:4, 1450:7, 1451:2, 1451:5, 1459:8, 1459:11, 1459:13, 1460:8, 1470:31, 1485:40, 1507:'1, 1507:'2, 1507:'3 1507:'4, 1507:'5
 dumu gar-ša-na-ka, "citizen of Garšana," 1419:13, 1420:8
 dumu gar-ša-an-na^{ki}-me, "citizens of Garšana," 1459:15

dumu-munus, *mārtu*, "daughter," 1474:11, 1485:14
dumu-munus-lugal, "royal daughter," 1481:10

–E–

é, *bītu*, "house, household, building, temple," 1457:4, 1478:31, 1497:5
árad-é-a, "household servant," 1482:4
é-a, "the (manor) house," 1423:17, 1427:18, 1432:16, 1435:16, 1474:11
é-*é-a-šar*-ka, "house of *Ea-šar*," 1424:13
é-gal, *ekallu*, "palace" 1443:1–2
é-gašam, "craftsmen's house," 1476:'6
é-gibil, "new house," 1482:5
é-ḫal-bi, "house of Ḫalbi," 1478:47
é-lùnga, "brewery," 1450:3
é-ki, 1498:16
é-lugal, "royal house," 1461:1
é-munus, "house of the women," 1485:74
é-^{d}nergal, "temple of Nergal," 1416:17–18, 1416:26, 1437:6, 1454:8
é-*simat*-^{d}*ištaran*, "house of *Simat-Ištaran*," 1482:6
é-*šu-kab-tá*, "house of *Šu-Kabta*," 1448:12, 1452:6
é-šu-sum-ma, "storehouse," 1462:26, 1492:16

é-ba-an, *tāpalu*, "pair," 1440:1

ég, *īku*, "dike, levee," 1470:38, 1470:41

egi-zi, *igiṣītu*, "a priestess," 1414:21

egir, *arkatu*, "back, rear; after," 1423:8, 1424:3, 1427:9, 1486:'5

eme$_6$, *atānu*, "female donkey"
eme$_6$-máḫ, "mature female donkey," 1419:1

en, *entu*, *enu*, "a priest, a priestess"
šabra en-na, "majordomo of the en-priest," 1489:7

en-nu-g̃á, *maṣṣartu*, "watch, guard; watch (as a division of night time); imprisonment; prison," 1424:14, 1490:14

engar, *ikkaru*, "farmer," 1470:50

énsi, *iššaku*, "governor," 1417:6, 1422:3, 1423:23, 1423:35, 1424:5, 1424:16, 1427:24, 1427:47, 1436:5, 1437:9 1440:2, 1457:5, 1457:8, 1478:58, 1490:8, 1490:11, 1491:4, 1514:6

ere, *alāku*, "perfect plural stem of g̃en[to go]"
u$_4$ (. . .) ba-e-re-ša(-a), 1490:7–8

éren, *ṣabu*, "people; (soldier-)workers (used for corvee labor)," 1438:IV 12, 1438:IV 14, 1440:3, 1458:1, 1458:5, 1458:12, 1458:13, 1458:15, 1458:17, 1458:27, 1458:28, 1503:2

ereš-dig̃ir, *ēntu*, "priestess," 1416:15

èš, *bītu*, *eššu*, "shrine"
èš didli, "various shrines," 1416:31

èš didli ma-da, "various shrines of the land," 1428:36
èš-èš u_4-sakar, "shrines of the new moon," 1489:2

eša, *saskû*, "a fine flour," 1492:10, 1495:2, 1495:5, 1495:8, 1495:10

ezem, *issinu*, "festival," 1416:11, 1416:21, 1478:31

– G –

ga, *šību*, "milk; suckling"
áb-amar-ga, "young suckling calf," 1462:5
gu_4-amar-ga, "bull-calf," 1413:1, 1462:6
$sila_4$-ga, "suckling lamb," 1462:8, 1462:9

ga-àr, *eqīdu*, "cheese," 1485:13, 1485:28, 1485:31, 1485:72, 1492:6

ga_6, *našû*, "to bring; to lift, carry; to haul"
ga_6-g̃á, 1425:3, 1432:8, 1432:11, 1432:13, 1435:8 1448:3, 1476:'5, 1482:4
íb-ga_6?, 1431:6
íb-ga_6-g̃á, 1442:5

gaba, *irtu*, "breast, chest"
máš-gaba-[x], 1475:4

gaba-ri, *miḫru*, "copy," 1475:11, 1488:'14

gada, *kitū*, "flax, linen," 1511:'23, 1511:'41
gada-gen, "ordinary linen," 1511:'14
gada-kaskal, 1511:'14
gada ka-suḫur, 1511:'15
gada ᵈmes-lam-ta-UD.[DU-a], 1511:'5
gada šà-ga-dù-gen, "ordinary linen belt," 1511:'6
[gada š]à-ga-dù-ús, "2nd-quality [linen] belt," 1511:'32
gada šu-nir, 1511:'14
gada uš-[. . .], 1511:'4

gal, *rabû*, "(to be) big, great; large"
i_7-gal-la-ka, 1424:1
níg̃-gal, 1431:6

GÁNA, *eqlu*, "field," 1414:23, 1414:11, 1414:20, 1428:1, 1428:2, 1428:35, 1428:5, 1428:7, 1428:8, 1428:11, 1428:14, 1428:18, 1428:22, 1428:25, 1428:28, 1428:32, 1428:33, 1428:35
GÁNA-gu_4, 1416:4, 1416:31
GÁNA-sù, 1428:2, 1428:35

géme, *amtu*, "female worker," 1462:25, 1464:25, 1465:25, 1476:'1, 1509:38
árad-géme ḫi-a, "various male and female servants," 1464:57, 1465:61
géme-árad, "female and male servants," 1470:5
géme-árad ḫi-[a], "various female and male servants," 1509:54
géme u_4-n-šè, "workwomen for n day(s)," 1431:1, 1432:1, 1432:4, 1432:7, 1432:9, 1432:12, 1432:14, 1435:1, 1435:4, 1435:7, 1435:9, 1435:11, 1435:14, 1511:'2, 1511:'7, 1511:'9, 1511:'11, 1511:'12, 1511:'13, 1511:'15, 1511:'17, 1511:'18, 1511:'19, 1511:'21, 1511:'24,

1511:'26, 1511:'28, 1511:'30, 1511:'33, 1511:'35, 1511:'37, 1511:'39

gen, "medium quality, ordinary quality"
gada-gen, "ordinary linen," 1511:'14
gada šà-ga-dù-gen, "ordinary linen belt," 1511:'6
kaš-gen, "ordinary beer," 1449:4
máš-gen, "ordinary goat," 1462:10, 1462:11
túg-guz-za-gen, "ordinary tufted textile," 1443:9

gen, *kânu*, "(to be) permanent; to confirm, establish (in legal contexts), verify; (to be) true"
gi-né-dam, 1498:17

geštin, *karānu*, "vine; wine," 1466:7, 1492:10
geštin-áḫ, *muzīqu*, "raisin," 1492:5

gi, *qanû*, "reed," 1423:36, 1426:3, 1427:46, 1429:11, 1448:3
gi IM+TAK$_4$-IM+TAK$_4$-šè, 1470:44
sa gi, "bundle of reeds," 1422:1, 1422:2, 1423:1, 1423:4, 1423:6, 1423:7, 1423:9, 1423:10, 1423:12, 1423:13, 1423:15, 1423:19, 1423:24, 1423:25, 1423:27, 1423:31, 1427:1, 1427:4, 1427:6, 1427:8, 1427:10, 1427:11, 1427:13, 1427:14, 1427:20, 1427:25, 1427:26, 1427:28, 1427:32, 1427:36, 1427:37, 1427:38, 1427:39, 1427:43, 1429:1, 1429:3, 1429:5, 1429:9, 1514:1
gi-zi, "fresh reeds," 1446:4
gi-ga$_6$-me-éš, "reed carriers," 1450:10

gi$_4$, *lamû*, *târu*, "to turn, return; to go around; to change status," 1425:11
g[i$_4$-gi$_4$-dè], 1486:'5
in-ši-gi$_4$, 1424:16
nu-ub-gi$_4$-gi$_4$-da, 1477:7

gibil, *edēšu*, "(to be) new"
é-gibil, "new house," 1482:5

gíd, *arāku*, "(to be) long; to tighten; to survey, measure out a field; to tow/pull a boat upstream"
apin-lá gíd-da, "long plow," 1428:36
gi gíd-da, "long reed," 1426:3
ĝeš gíd-da, "long beam," 1426:6, 1426:9
má gíd, "to tow a boat," 1425:8, 1430:4, 1433:4, 1446:5, 1448:7
n nindan gíd, "n nindan in length," 1513:1, 1513:3, 1513:5, 1513:7, 1513:9, 1513:11, 1513:13, 1513:15, 1513:16, 1513:18, 1513:20, 1513:22, 1513:24,

^{ĝeš}gigir, *narkabtu*, "chariot," 1424:6, 1424:7, 1424:12

gil-sa, *šutukku*, "treasure," 1417:3

gín, *šiqlu*, "a unit of weight, shekel; a unit of area; a unit of volume"
a-šà-bi n sar n gín, 1513:12, 1513:19, 1513:25
n gín gu-e-ra ì-U+NU, 1511:'10, 1511:'17, 1511:'25, 1511:'36

gir-ab^{ku_6}, "a fish," 1485:3

gir-gíd, *tappinnu*, "a fish," 1485:1

gu, *qû*, "cord, net; unretted flax stalks"
n ma-na gu ĝeš-ba ì-e-ri, 1511:'8, 1511:'16, 1511:'34

n gín gu-e-ra ì-U+NU, 1511:'10, 1511:'17, 1511:'25, 1511:'36

gu-níĝin, "bundle"

n sa gi gu-níĝin-ba n-ta, "n bundle(s) of reeds, bales of n bundle(s) each," 1422:2, 1514:1–2

n gu-níĝin ĝeš ásal, "n bundle(s) of poplar," 1423:33

n gu-níĝin pa-ku_5 ĝeš ásal, "n bundle(s) of poplar staves," 1427:2, 1427:16, 1427:23, 1427:34, 1427:45

n gu-níĝin ĝeš ma-nu, "n bundle(s) of manu wood," 1423:21, 1423:32, 1427:22, 1427:33, 1427:44

1200 sa ĝeš ma-nu gu-níĝin-ba 17-ta gu-níĝin-bi 600⅔ gu-níĝin 700 níĝin 2.0.0. ku_5 gu-níĝin-ba 4½-ta gu-níĝin-bi 150, 1445:19–24

ĝeš gu-za, *kussû*, "chair, stool, throne," 1462:21

gu-za-lá, *guzalû*, "an official," 1462:31

gú, *aḫu*, *kišādu*, "bank, side"

gú i_7, "bank of a canal," 1462:33, 1470:41, 1470:45

gú-idigna, "bank of the Tigris," 1448:3

gú, "pulse, bean," 1470:52

gú-gal, *ḫallūru*, "beans," 1470:15, 1470:64

gú-tur, *kakkû*, "peas," 1470:16, 1470:47, 1470:65

zì-gú-niga, "fattened pulse flour," 1449:6

gú(n), *biltu*, "load; yield; rent, tax, tribute; a unit of weight"

n gú ĝeš ásal, "n talent(s) of poplar," 1423:2, 1423:15, 1423:22

n gú a-tu-nir, 1445:25

n gú sar ḫi-a, "n talent(s) of various vegetables," 1485:39, 1485:42, 1485:70

gu_4(d), *alpu*, "bull, ox, cattle," 1466:3, 1477:2, 1489:7, 1489:8, 1489:9, 1489:10, 1489:11, 1489:12, 1489:17

gu_4-áb-amar ḫi-a, "various calves (and) bull-calves," 1462:7

gu_4-áb ḫi-a, "various bulls (and) cows," 1460:1, 1460:4

gu_4-amar-ga, "bull-calf," 1413:1, 1462:6

gu_4-apin 3-kam, "plow team of 3 oxen,"1470:4

gu_4-ĝeš "draught ox," 1415:1, 1418:2, 1462:3, 1498:1

gu_4-mu–2, "2 year old ox," 1462:4

gu_4-niga, "fattened ox," 1436:1, 1439:1, 1489:1, 1489:2, 1489:3, 1489:5

GÁNA-gu_4, 1416:4, 1416:31

ma-la-lum gu_4-niga, 1474:1, 1474:13

ugula-gu_4, "overseer of oxen" > ugula

gu_7, *akālu*, "to eat"

a-ĝar gu_7-a, "de-ḫaired (skin)," 1453:1

a-ĝar nu-gu_7-a, "(skin) that has not been de-ḫaired," 1453:2

gub, *izuzzu*, "to stand; (to be) assigned (to a task), (to be) employed (at)"

a-gub-ba, 1428:30

gub-ba, 1450:3

$gudu_4$, *pašīšu*, "a priest," 1428:6, 1428:24, 1485:32, 1485:34

gur, *kurru*, "capacity measure," *passim*
gur-lugal, 1421:1, 1447:2

gur, *saḫāru*, *târu*, "to reject (legal evidence), to turn away; to turn, return"
na-mi-gur-re, 1499:6
má-sud gur-ra, 1448:11

guru$_7$, *karû*, "grain heap, grain store; granary"
guru$_7$-ki-sur-ra, 1430:3, 1433:3

guz, "to be tufted"
túg-guz-za-gen, "ordinary tufted textile," 1443:9

– G̃ –

g̃á-nun(-na), "storehouse," 1425:3, 1425:10, 1450:6

g̃ál, *bašû*, *šakānu*, "to be (there, at hand, available); to exist; to put, place, lay down; to have"
ì-g̃ál, 1483:7

g̃ar, *šakānu*, "to put, place, lay down; to deposit," 1425:4
g̃á-g̃á, 1485:63
g̃á-ra, 1446:4
ba-an-g̃ar, 1418:3, 1441:20

g̃en, *alāku*, "to go, to come"
g̃en-na, 1497:12
u$_4$ . . . ba-g̃en-na-a, 1478:53
u$_4$ . . . im-g̃en-na-a, 1478:20, 1478:50, 1490:11, 1490:14, 1490:17

g̃eš, *iṣu*, "wood," 1419:4, 1424:2, 1426:6, 1511:'8, 1511:'16, 1511:'34

g̃eš-ì, *šamaššammū*, "sesame," 1459:9, 1470:14, 1470:66

g̃eš-saḫar-x, 1455:5

g̃i$_6$-par$_4$, *libāru*, "(a type of fruit tree; fruit)"
g̃i$_6$-par$_4$-ḫád, "dried g̃ipar fruit," 1492:8

g̃ìri, *šēpu*, "via, by means of, under the authority of someone; foot, path," 1422:8, 1423:11, 1423:14, 1423:20, 1423:26, 1423:29, 1427:12, 1427:15, 1427:21, 1427:27, 1427:29, 1428:37, 1436:6, 1437:7, 1439:8, 1440:7, 1441:2, 1441:5, 1441:8, 1441:14, 1441:18, 1454:11, 1455:7, 1457:6, 1466:16, 1467:5, 1470:34, 1470:42, 1470:46, 1474:19, 1482:8, 1485:5, 1485:8, 1485:11, 1485:16, 1485:19, 1485:23, 1485:26, 1485:34, 1485:37, 1485:41, 1485:44, 1488:3, 1488:6

g̃uruš, *eṭlu*, *wardu*, "male worker," 1450:1, 1451:1
g̃uruš u$_4$-n-šè, "workmen for n day(s)," 1425:1, 1426:1, 1426:4, 1426:7, 1430:1, 1433:1, 1442:1, 1446:1, 1448:1, 1452:3
g̃uruš šà-gu$_4$, "ox-driver," 1470:49
g̃uruš šidim, "builder," 1505:'3
g̃uruš šidim um-mi-a, "master builder," 1505:'2
g̃uruš šu dím "workman to build," 1505:'4

– Ḫ –

ḫa-za-núm, *ḫazannu*, "mayor"
lú-ša-lim ḫa-za-núm gar-ša-na(-ka)^{ki}(-ka), "*Lušallim*, mayor of Garšana," 1422:4, 1423:10, 1427:11
šu-eš$_4$-tár ḫa-za-nu-um, "*Šu-Eštar*, the mayor," 1473:5

^{urudu}ḫa-zi-in, *ḫaṣṣinu*, "axe," 1460:9

ḫád, *abālu*, *šābulu*, "(to be) dried (out), dry; to dry"
ĝi$_6$-par$_4$-ḫád, "dried ĝipar fruit," 1492:8
ḫašḫur-ḫád, "dried apple," 1492:7

ḫal, "a basket"
ḫal gir-ab^{ku_6}, 1485:3
ḫal gir-gíd, 1485:1
^{gi}ḫal kíĝ-gi$_4$-a, 1441:3, 1441:6, 1441:9, 1441:11, 1441:15
ḫal ku$_6$-ab-ba, 1485:64
ḫal ku$_6$-gíd, 1485:64

ḫašḫur, *ḫašḫûru*, "apple (tree)," 1492:12
ḫašḫur-ḫád "dried apple," 1492:7

ḫi-a, "various, collective plural"
árad-géme ḫi-a, "various male and female servants," 1464:57, 1465:61
géme-árad ḫi-[a], "various female and male servants," 1509:54
gu$_4$-áb-amar ḫi-a, "various bull-calves and calves," 1462:7
gu$_4$-áb ḫi-a, "various bulls and cows," 1460:1, 1460:4
sar ḫi-a, "various vegetables," 1485:39, 1485:42, 1485:70
udu-máš ḫi-a, "various sheep (and) goats," 1460:2, 1460:5, 1462:12

ḫuĝ, *agāru*, "to hire, rent"
ba-ḫuĝ, 1476:'3
lú-ḫuĝ-ĝá(-e-ne), "hired worker(s)," 1468:2, 1482:4, 1488:1
má-ḫuĝ-ĝá, "hired boat," 1470:51

– I –

ì, *šamnu*, "oil"
ì-dan$_6$-dan$_6$, "pure oil," 1511:'12, 1511:'20, 1511:'29, 1511:'38
ì-ĝeš, "sesame oil," 1472:2
ì-nun, "ghee, clarified butter," 1485:12, 1485:27, 1485:30, 1485:71, 1492:2
ì-šáḫ, "lard," 1492:3

ì-du$_8$, *atû*, "doorkeeper," 1423:29, 1427:29

ì-dub, *našpaku*, "granary, grain bin," 1447:8

ì-U+NU
n gín gu-e-ra ì-U+NU, 1511:'10, 1511:'17, 1511:'25, 1511:'36

i$_7$(d$_2$), *nāru*, "river, watercourse, canal"

i$_7$-da, 1432:2, 1432:15, 1435:2, 1435:15
i$_7$-è, 1462:33
i$_7$-eb-la^{ki}, 1498:2, 1498:12
i$_7$ gal-la-ka, 1424:1
i$_7$-g̃eš-gi-gal^{ki}, 1426:5, 1458:8
i$_7$-idigna, "Tigris canal," 1470:41
i$_7$-lugal, "royal canal," 1470:45, 1513:28

ib-tab-bé, "(a commodity)"
n ma-na ib-tab-bé, 1511:'11, 1511:'18, 1511:'27

idigna, "Tigris,"
i$_7$-idigna, "Tigris canal," 1470:41
gú-idigna, "bank of the Tigris," 1448:3

igi, *šību*, "witness," 1462:28, 1462:29, 1462:30, 1462:31, 1471:9, 1471:10, 1471:11, 1471:12, 1471:13, 1473:5, 1473:6, 1473:7, 1473:8, 1477:9, 1477:10, 1477:11, 1477:12, 1477:13, 1477:14, 1477:15, 1477:16, 1477:17, 1479:7, 1479:8, 1479:9, 1479:10, 1484:8, 1484:9, 1484:10, 1484:11, 1484:12, 1484:13, 1484:14, 1486:'2, 1486:'3, 1486:'4, 1510:8, 1510:9, 1510:10, 1510:11
igi-igi-šè, 1462:32

igi … du$_8$, *naplusu*, *naṭālu*, "to see"
igi bí-in-du$_8$-ša-àm, 1419:8

iku, *ikû*, "a unit of area, a unit of volume," 1444:28

íl, *našû*, "to raise, carry"
íl-la, 1432:13, 1452:7

im, *ṭīdu*, "earth, clay," 1417:3, 1510:1

im-sar, *ṭuppu*, "clay tablet," 1440:20

img̃ag̃a$_3$, *kunāšu*, *dišiptuḫḫu*, "emmer, emmer beer," 1470:13, 1470:63

imin, *sebe*, "seven," 1424:6, 1424:7

inim, *amatu*, "word, matter (of affairs)," 1422:7
inim mu-šu-du$_8$, 1498:17
lú-inim-ma, "witness" > lú-inim-ma

ir$_7$^{mušen}, *uršānu*, "pigeon," 1485:9, 1485:68

iri, *ālu*, "city," 1491:2
níg̃-iri, "possessions of the city," 1499:9

iš-tu, "from, out of, since, after," 1497:1, 1497:4, 1497:11

iti, *arḫu*, "month," 1424:6, 1424:7
iti 1 u$_4$-17-kam, 1482:11
iti 10-lá–1-kam, 1416:24
iti–10-kam, 1416:14, 1470:53
iti-bi 12-àm, 1470:8
sá-du$_{11}$-iti–12-kam, 1416:9
sá-du$_{11}$-iti-dirig, 1416:10, 1416:20

Month names mentioned within texts:
iti ezem-^{d}nin-a-zu, 1482:10
iti ki-siki-^{d}nin-a-zu-ta, 1482:9
iti maš-dù-gu$_{7}$, 1470:6
iti níg̃-^{d}en-líl-lá, 1479:4
iti še-kin-ku$_{5}$, 1470:7
iti šu-numun-na-šè, 1493:3

– K –

ka(g), *pû*, "mouth (of a river or canal), opening (of a box/basket)," 1426:5, 1432:15, 1435:15, 1441:19, 1458:8

KA.SAR, 1457:1–2

ka-suḫur
gada ka-suḫur, 1511:'15

kar, *kâru*, "harbor, quay," 1432:6, 1432:7, 1432:10, 1435:6, 1435:7, 1435:10, 1448:5, 1448:11

kaskal, *ḫarrānu*, "way, road; journey, caravan"
gada-kaskal, 1511:'14
kaskal-anše-lugal, 1478:9

kaš, *šikaru*, "beer," 1490:1, 1490:3, 1490:5, 1490:9, 1490:12, 1490:15
kaš-gen, "ordinary beer," 1449:4
kaš-ninda, "beer (and) bread," 1466:1, 1466:6, 1466:10
kaš-sig$_{5}$, "fine-quality beer," 1449:3

kaš$_{4}$, *šānû*, "runner," 1413:5, 1418:5, 1423:13, 1423:24, 1427:14, 1454:11, 1454:12
^{lú}kaš$_{4}$, "runner," 1502:2

kéše, *rakāsu*, "to bind"
ba-ra-kéše, 1441:19
kéše-rá, 1425:2, 1448:4

ki, *ašru*, *erṣetu*, *mātu*, *qaqqaru*, *šaplû*, "place, ground, earth, land, toward," 1423:35, 1449:11, 1453:3, 1478:58, 1489:10, 1489:11, 1501:4, 1502:2, 1512:16, 1512:22
ki PN-ta, "from PN," 1413:4, 1415:3, 1417:5, 1418:4, 1421:2, 1422:3, 1425:13, 1427:47, 1436:4, 1437:8, 1439:9, 1440:2, 1441:23, 1447:5, 1454:9, 1459:8, 1459:13, 1468:2, 1469:4–5, 1470:69, 1471:3, 1472:3, 1473:2, 1474:20, 1475:6, 1479:2, 1480:3, 1484:3, 1488:2, 1489:4, 1489:6, 1489:7, 1489:8, 1489:9, 1489:13, 1491:4, 1510:2

ki-lá, *šuqultu*, "weight," 1443:10

ki-su$_{7}$, *maškanu*, "threshing floor," 1488:5, 1488:'8, 1488:'9

ki-sur-ra, *kisurû*, "border, territory," 1430:3, 1433:3

^{gi}kid, *kītu*, "a reed mat," 1423:17, 1427:18

^{lú}kíg̃-gi$_{4}$-a, *mār šipri*, "messenger," 1462:29
^{lú}kíg̃-gi$_{4}$-a-lugal, "royal messenger," 1419:12, 1470:31, 1478:2, 1478:4, 1478:6, 1478:8, 1478:14, 1478:19, 1478:22, 1478:24, 1478:52, 1490:6, 1490:10

kíg̃-gi$_{4}$-a
^{gi}ḫal kíg̃-gi$_{4}$-a, 1441:3, 1441:6, 1441:9, 1441:11, 1441:15

^{na_4}kinkin, "(a millstone)"
    ^{na_4}kinkin šu sè-ga, "'hand-held' millstone," 1462:19

^{ĝeš}kiri$_6$, *kirû*, "(fruit) plantation, orchard"
    ^{ĝeš}kiri$_6$-lú-šu-ki-na, 1497:8, 1497:12

kìšib, *kunukku*, "seal, sealed tablet," 1417:6, 1418:5, 1423:3, 1423:5, 1423:6, 1423:8, 1423:10, 1423:16, 1423:18, 1423:23, 1425:14, 1426:11, 1427:3, 1427:5, 1427:7, 1427:9, 1427:11, 1427:17, 1427:19, 1427:24, 1430:6, 1431:8, 1432:18, 1433:6, 1435:18, 1436:5, 1437:9, 1441:24, 1442:7, 1446:8, 1448:14, 1452:9, 1457:7, 1459:11, 1459:16, 1470:11, 1470:21, 1470:31, 1470:17, 1470:19, 1470:21, 1470:25, 1470:28, 1470:31, 1470:56, 1481:6, 1488:'14, 1491:6, 1514:6

^{dug}ku-kur-rú, "(a vessel)," 1470:54

kù-babbar, *kaspu*, "silver," 1420:3, 1468:1, 1477:1

kù-ĝál, *gugallu*, "canal inspector," 1462:28, 1470:31

ku$_5$(d^r), *parāsu*, "to cut, break off, deduct," 1445:22
    ku$_5$-dam, 1459:12
    in-ku$_5$-ru-ús-sa, 1466:15
    pa-ku$_5$, "stave, a trimmed part of a tree," 1472:2, 1472:16, 1472:23, 1472:34, 1472:45
    ù-ku$_5$, 1419:9

ku$_6$, *nûnu*, "fish," 1478:1, 1478:3, 1478:5, 1478:7, 1478:10, 1478:13, 1478:15, 1478:18, 1478:21, 1478:23, 1478:26, 1478:28, 1478:40, 1478:51, 1478:54, 1478:56, 1485:38
    ku$_6$-ab-ba, 1485:64
    ku$_6$-gíd, 1485:64
    ku$_6$-gud?, 1485:60
    ku$_6$-šeĝ$_6$, "cooked fish," 1467:1, 1502:1

kun, *zibbatu*, "canal outlet," 1432:2, 1435:2

kúr, "in the future," 1477:7

kurum$_7$, *piqittu*, "inspection, provisions," 1442:4, 1449:12, 1450:12, 1451:10, 1466:14–15

kurušda, *mārû*, "animal fattener," 1481:12

kuš, *mašku*, "skin, leather"
    kuš-amar, "young animal skin," 1441:1
    kuš ka du$_{10}$-gal na$_4$ ba-ra-kéše, 1441:19
    kuš-máš-gal-babbar, "white billy-goat skin,"1455:3
    kuš-máš-gal ú-ḫáb, "madder-tanned billy-goat skin,"1455:2
    kuš-sila$_4$, "lamb skin," 1417:1
    kuš-udu a-ĝar gu$_7$-a, "de-ḫaired sheep skin," 1453:1
    kuš-udu a-ĝar nu-gu$_7$-a, "sheep skin that has not been de-ḫaired," 1453:2
    kuš<-udu> ú-ḫáb-bi–1, "1 madder-tanned <sheep> skin," 1441:16
    kuš-udu ú-ḫáb-bi–2, "2 madder-tanned sheep skins," 1441:4, 1441:7, 1441:12

kùš, *ammatu*, "a unit of length"
    n kùš bur, 1513:1, 1513:3, 1513:5, 1513:7, 1513:9, 1513:11, 1513:13, 1513:16, 1513:18, 1513:20, 1513:22, 1513:24

– L –

la-ag, *kirbānu*, "clod (of earth), lump," 1488:4, 1488:5

lá, *ḫiāṭu*, *šaqālu*, "to transport, to weigh out, to pay"
ì-lá, 1471:7
in-na-ši-lá-àm, 1419:4
lá-da, 1493:11

lá-ìa, *ribbatu*, "arrears, surplus, remainder," 1416:29, 1443:16, 1458:27

laḫ, "plural stem of de$_6$ [to bring]"
ba-ab-la-ḫa, 1460:12

làl, *dišpu*, "syrup, honey," 1492:4

LAM, 1492:9

lú, *awīlu*, "man," 1424:9, 1424:16, 1427:18, 1428:30
lú-*ba-ba-ti*, "man of *Babati*," 1478:55, 1478:57
lú-énsi, "governor's man," 1427:24
lú-énsi-g̃ír-su^{ki}, "man of the governor of G̃irsu," 1423:23
lú-ḫal-bi, "man from Ḫalbi," 1478:44, 1478:46
lú-ma-rí^{ki}, "man from Mari," 1427:38, 1429:6
lú-mar-sa gú-ab-ba^{ki}, "man from the military depot of Gu'abba," 1459:4

lú-*gi-na-ab-tum*, "guarantor,"[2] 1420:7
ma-at-ì-lí lú-*gi-na-tum*, "*Mat-ili*, the guarantor," 1471:8

lú-ḫug̃-g̃á, *agru*, "hired workman," 1468:2, 1482:4, 1488:1

lú-inim-ma, *šību*, "witness," 1477:19, 1510:12

lú-níg̃-dab$_5$, "requisitioner," 1482:3

lú-sa-gaz, *ḫabbātu*, "brigand," 1490:14

lugal, *šarru*, "king, master; royal," 1427:26
àga-ús-lugal, "royal gendarme," 1440:3, 1490:3
alam-lugal, "royal statue," 1478:12
dabin-lugal, "royal semolina," 1472:1
dumu-munus-lugal, "royal daughter," 1481:10
é-a lugal-šè, 1423:17
gur-lugal, "royal bushel," 1421:1, 1447:2
i$_7$-lugal, "royal canal," 1470:45, 1513:28
kaskal-anše-lugal, "royal travel donkey," 1478:9
ki lugal-šè, "to/for the royal place," 1490:8
^{lú}kíg̃-a-gi$_4$-a lugal, "royal messenger," 1419:12
mu lugal pàd, "to swear by the king's name" > mu lugal . . . pàd
níg̃-ba lugal, "royal gift," 1447:3, 1463:2

---

2 Steinkeller 1989, 80–81.

simat-^{d}ištaran dumu lugal-ka, "*Simat-Ištaran*, daughter of the king," 1431:2–3, 1432:13, 1435:12–13
sízkur-lugal, "royal offering," 1437:5, 1439:6
sugal$_7$-lugal, "royal secretary," 1423:11, 1427:12
še-ĝeš-ì-bi 0.4.0. lugal, 1480:2
tir-é-lugal, "forest of the royal house," 1461:16
zi-ga lugal, "royal expenditure," 1417:4
zì-gu lugal, "royal gu-flour,"1449:8
[. . .] lugal, 1487:'11

^{lú}lùnga, *sīrāšû*, "brewer," 1478:27, 1478:29

– M –

ma-da, *mātu*, "land, country," 1428:36

ma-la-lum, *mālalu*, "a container,"
ma-la-lum gu$_4$-niga, "container of fattened ox," 1474:1, 1474:13
ma-la-lum udu, "container of mutton," 1466:2, 1466:8, 1466:11, 1485:67

ma-na, *manû*, "a unit of weight, mina," *passim*

^{ĝeš}ma-nu, *ēru*, "(a tree, perhaps willow)," 1423:21, 1423:32, 1427:22, 1427:33, 1427:44, 1490:17, 1445:19

má, *eleppu*, "ship, boat," 1425:2, 1425:4, 1425:8, 1425:9, 1425:11, 1426:3, 1426:6, 1426:9, 1430:4, 1432:3, 1433:4, 1435:3, 1446:4, 1446:5, 1446:6, 1448:4, 1448:6, 1448:7, 1448:9
má-ḫuĝ-ĝá, "hired boat," 1470:51
má-lá-a, "freight boat," 1426:3, 1426:6, 1426:9, 1448:6, 1448:9

má-gíd, "boat tower," 1470:19
má-gíd-e-ne, "boat towers," 1470:17

má-laḫ$_5$, *malaḫḫu*, "sailor," 1478:16

má-sù, "sunken or submerged ship," 1448:11

maḫ, *kabtu*, *mādu*, *rabû*, *ṣīru*, "to be great"
sugal$_7$-maḫ, "an official, chief minister" > sugal$_7$-maḫ
túg-maḫ, "large textile," 1459:1

máḫ, "(to be) mature, milk producing (of cows)"
áb-máḫ, "milk producing cow," 1418:1, 1462:1, 1498:2
eme$_6$-máḫ, "mature female donkey," 1419:1

mar-dú, *amurru*, "westerner," 1455:4

mar-sa, "military depot"
lú-mar-sa gú-ab-ba^{ki}, "man from the military depot of Gu'abba," 1459:4

maš-dà, *ṣabītu*, "gazelle," 1474:5, 1474:10, 1488:'10

máš, *urīṣu*, "(male) goat," 1437:4, 1439:5, 1454:5, 1498:5, 1498:6, 1498:7
maš, 1456:1
máš-gaba-[x], 1475:4

máš-gen, "ordinary goat," 1462:10, 1462:11
máš-níta, "male goat," 1462:11
udu-máš ḫi-a "various sheep (and) goats," 1460:2, 1460:5, 1462:12

máš-gal, *mašgallu*, "billy-goat"
kuš-máš-gal-babbar, "white billy-goat skin," 1455:3
kuš-máš-gal-ú-ḫáb, "madder-tanned billy-goat skin," 1455:2

maškim, *rābiṣu*, "an administrative position—secretary, bailiff, deputy," 1422:9, 1474:4, 1474:8, 1474:12, 1474:16, 1495:12

mu, *šattu*, "year"
mu–2-kam, 1427:46
mu [. . .], 1510:7
áb-mu–2-niga, "fattened 2 year old cow," 1489:3
áb-mu–3, "3 year old cow," 1462:2, 1477:1
gu$_4$-mu–2, "2 year old bull," 1462:4
Year names mentioned within texts:
(Š 43) mu en-^{d}nanna máš-e ì-pàd, 1416:3
(AS 5) mu en-unu$_6$-gal-an-na en-^{d}inanna ba-ḫug̃, 1427:35
(AS 6) mu ^{d}amar-^{d}suen lugal-e ša-aš-ru-um mu-ḫulu, 1427:40

mu, *šumu*, "name"
mu-ni, "his name," 1471:2

mu lugal . . . pàd, *nīš šarrim tamû*, "to swear by the king's name"
mu lugal pàd, 1486:'7
mu lugal in-pàd, 1493:12
mu lugal-bi in-pàd, 1477:8, 1479:6, 1484:7

mu . . . šè, "for"
mu àga-ús gar-ša-an-na^{ki}-šè, "for the gendarme of Garšana," 1453:4
mu lú-dig̃ir-ra šabra-šè, "for Lu-dig̃ira, the majordomo," 1421:3
(mu) *simat-^{d}ištaran* dumu lugal-ka-šè, "for *Simat-Ištaran*, daughter of the king," 1431:2–3, 1432:13, 1435:12–13
mu *šu-kab-ta*-šè, "for *Šu-Kabta*," 1481:5

mu-didli
mu-didli-TUM-an, 1459:6

mu-DU, *šūrubtu*, "delivery," 1412:23, 1413:2, 1415:2, 1418:3, 1460:10, 1463:4, 1483:3, 1485:76, 1488:'7, 1489:14

mu-du-lum, *muddulu*, "pickled, salted (meat)"
mu-du-lum maš-dà, "salted gazelle," 1474:5, 1474:10
mu-du-lum udu-niga, "salted, fattened sheep," 1474:9

mu-šu-du$_8$
inim mu-šu-du$_8$, 1498:17

mug, *mukku*, "wool combings, (textile made of) poor-quality wool"
túg-mug, "textile of poor-quality wool,"1459:5

muḫaldim, *nuḫatimmu*, "cook," 1498:17

munu$_4$, *buqlu*, "malt," 1443:14, 1470:57, 1510:5, 1510:6

munus, *sinništu*, "woman," 1462:16
  dumu-munus, "daughter," 1474:11, 1485:14
  dumu-munus-lugal, "royal daughter," 1481:10
  é-munus, "house of the women," 1485:74

mur-gu$_4$, *imrû*, "fodder," 1416:12, 1416:22, 1470:1, 1470:48, 1470:67

– N –

^{ĝeš}ná, *eršu*, "bed," 1462:20

na$_4$, *abnu*, "stone, stone weight," 1441:19

nagar, *nagarum*, "carpenter," 1424:12

naĝa, *uḫūlu*, "potash, soap," 1462:23

nam-érim, *māmītu*, "oath," 1419:9, 1459:12, 1466:14

nam-šà-tam, "administration, administrative office," 1425:14, 1442:7–8

niga, *marû*, "(to be) fattened"
  áb-mu-2-niga, "fattened 2 year old cow," 1489:3
  gu$_4$-niga, "fattened ox," 1436:1, 1439:1, 1474:1, 1474:13 1489:1, 1489:2, 1489:3, 1489:5
  udu-niga, "fattened sheep," 1437:1, 1439:2, 1449:1, 1474:9
  zì-gú-niga, "fattened pulse flour," 1449:6

níĝ, *bušu*, *mimma*, "thing, possession, something"
  níĝ-da-bi n ma-na siki, 1509:38, 1509:52
  níĝ-diri, "surplus goods," 1416:11, 1416:21
  níĝ-gal, "large thing," 1431:6
  níĝ-iri, "possessions of the city,"1499:9
  níĝ-ni-x, 1459:17

níĝ-ba, *qīštu*, "gift," 1447:3, 1463:2, 1463:3, 1509:54

níĝ-bún-na, *šeleppû*, "turtle," 1485:66

níĝ-dab$_5$, "requisitioned items"
  lú-níĝ-dab$_5$, "requisitioner," 1482:3

níĝ-gur$_{11}$, *makkuru*, "property," 1457:4, 1481:10
  saĝ-níĝ-gur$_{11}$, "available assets," 1416:7

níĝ-ĝeš-tà-ga, "a type of offering,"[3] 1436:2

níĝ-ì-dé-a, *pannigu*, "(a dessert, pastry)," 1492:1

níĝ-kas$_7$, *nikkassu*, "account"

---

[3] See Snell 1987, 226; Selz 1992, 265 n. 41; Sallaberger 1993, gloss.

níĝ-kas$_7$-aka, 1416:31, 1481:9

níĝ-sa$_{10}$, "price," 1477:3

níĝ-šu-tak$_4$-a, *šūbultu*, "gift, shipment, consignment," 1474:1, 1474:7, 1474:15

níĝin, *esēru*, *lawû*, "to enclose, confine, to encircle"
gu-níĝin 700 níĝin 2.0.0. ku$_5$, 1445:22

^{ĝeš}nimbar, *gišimmaru*, "date palm," 1501:1

nin, *bēltu*, "lady," 1463:3, 1498:4

nin$_9$, *aḫātu*, "sister," 1474:2, 1474:6, 1485:18

ninda, *akalu*, "bread," 1490:1, 1490:3, 1490:5, 1490:9, 1490:12, 1490:15
bisaĝ-ninda, "bread basket," 1485:17, 1485:68
kaš-ninda, "beer (and) bread," 1466:1, 1466:6, 1466:10

nindan, *nindanu*, "pole, a unit of length," 1497:2, 1497:7, 1497:10
n nindan daĝal n nindan gíd n kùš bur, 1513:1
n nindan gíd n kùš bur, 1513:3, 1513:5, 1513:7, 1513:9, 1513:11, 1513:13, 1513:16, 1513:18, 1513:20, 1513:22, 1513:24,
n nindan gíd nu-tuku, 1513:15

níta, *zikaru*, "male"
máš-níta, "male goat," 1462:11
šáḫ-níta, "male pig," 1481:2
udu-níta, "male sheep," 1454:2, 1462:9

nu-bànda, *laputtû*, "overseer, captain," 1423:25, 1440:5, 1458:2, 1458:3, 1458:4, 1458:10, 1458:14, 1458:16, 1458:18, 1458:20, 1470:31, 1485:7, 1485:10, 1485:40, 1490:2, 1490:4, 1502:4, 1503:6, 1504:7, 1512:22
nu-bànda-e-ne, "overseers," 1466:12

nu-úr-ma, *nurmû*, "pomegranate, pomegranate tree," 1492:13

numun, *zēru*, "seed," 1459:10, 1470:1, 1470:48, 1470:67
še-numun, "seed," 1416:12, 1416:22

– P –

pa-ku$_5$, *pakuttu*, "stave, a trimmed part of a tree," 1427:2, 1427:16, 1427:23, 1427:34, 1427:45

pàd, *atû*, *nabû*, "to find, discover, to name, nominate"
mu lugal pàd, "to swear by the king's name" > mu lugal ... pàd

péš-ĝeš-gi, *ušummu*, "a type of large, edible (field) mouse," 1485:6, 1485:24, 1485:57

– R –

ra, *kanāku*, "to roll (seal)"
kìšib nu-ra?-a, 1457:7
kìšib . . . ra-ra-dam, 1459:16

rá-gaba, *rākibu*, "courier, rider, mounted messenger," 1485:5, 1485:23

ri, *alāku*, "to go, walk along"

u_4 . . . ba-e-re-ša-a, 1478:25, 1490:7

u_4 . . . im-da-e-re-ša-a, 1478:12

(u_4) . . . im-e-re-ša-a, 1478:9, 1478:17, 1478:31, 1478:42, 1478:47, 1478:58

ri, *reḫû*, "to pour out"

n ma-na gu g̃eš-ba ì-e-ri, 1511:'8, 1511:'16, 1511:'34

– S –

sa, *matnu*, "sinew, tendon"

sa-udu, "sheep sinew," 1493:1

sa, *kiššu*, "bundle (of reeds)"

sa gi, "bundle of reeds" > gi

sa ^{gi}kid, "bundle of mats," 1423:17, 1427:18

sa $^{g̃eš}$ma-nu, "bundle of manu wood," 1445:19

sa sum-sikil, "bundle of onions," 1485:35, 1485:69

sá-du_{11}, *sattukku*, "regular offering, provision," 1416:19

sá-du_{11}-iti–12-kam, "regular offerings of the 12th month," 1416:9

sá-du_{11}-iti-dirig, "regular offerings of the 13th month," 1416:10, 1416:20

sa_{10}, *šâmu*, "to buy, purchase," 1470:55

níg̃-sa_{10}, "price" > níg̃-sa_{10}

in-sa_{10}, 1420:5

in-ši-sa_{10}, 1477:6

sa_{10}-a, 1454:6, 1454:10

sàg, *dâku*, *nêru*, *sapāḫu*, "to disperse, to kill, beat"

in-sàg-ga, 1490:14

sagi, *šāqû*, "cup-bearer," 1436:6, 1437:7, 1439:8, 1441:5,14

sag̃, *qaqqadu*, *rēšu*, "head, person, capital," 1424:5, 1479:4, 1482:2

sag̃-níg̃-gur_{11}, "available assets," 1416:7

sag̃-níta, "man," 1462:24, 1471:1

sag̃-rig_7, *nudunnû*, "(marriage) gift," 1474:14

saḫar, *eperu*, "earth, soil," 1470:37, 1470:40, 1470:43, 1513:28

sar, *mūšaru*, "garden, a unit of area, a unit of volume," 1513:27

a-šà-bi n sar (n gín), 1513:2, 1513:4, 1513:6, 1513:8, 1513:10, 1513:12, 1513:14, 1513:17, 1513:19, 1513:21, 1513:23, 1513:25

si(g), "to fill, load up; to pile up"

si-ga, 1432:16, 1435:16

si-ì-tum, *šittu*, "balance (of a settled account), left-over surplus, remainder," 1416:2

sig_5, *damqu*, "good, fine (quality)"

KA.SAR sig_5, 1457:1–2
kaš-sig_5, "fine-quality beer," 1449:3
zì-ba-ba-sig_5, "fine-quality flour porridge,"1449:5
zì-gu-sig_5, "fine-quality gu-flour," 1449:8

siki, *šipātu*, "wool, hair," 1459:14, 1509:1, 1509:38, 1509:52, 1509:54
siki-ba, "wool rations," 1443:7

sìla, *mīšertu*, *qû*, "a unit of capacity (liter), a vessel," *passim*

SÌLA.ŠU.DU_8, *šāqû*, "butler, cup-bearer," 1441:14

$sila_4$, *puḫādu*, "lamb," 1498:4, 1498:9, 1498:10, 1498:11, 1498:12
kuš-$sila_4$, "lamb skin," 1417:1
$sila_4$-bar "lamb fleece," 1437:3
$sila_4$-bar-g̃ál, "designation of a lamb with fleece," 1439:4, 1454:3
$sila_4$-ga, "suckling lamb," 1462:8, 1462:9
$sila_4$-[x], 1475,3

simug, *nappāḫu*, "smith, metalworker," 1471:6

sipad, *rē'û*, "shepherd, herdsman,"
sipa-šáḫ, "pig herdsman," 1481:11

sízkur, *nīqu*, "(ceremonial) offering, sacrifice, libation"
sízkur-lugal, "royal offering," 1437:5, 1439:6

su(g_6), *apālu*, *riābu*, "to repay a loan, to replace"
ga-ra-ab-su, 1499:9
íb-su-su, 1419:11
su-su-dam, 1422:6, 1477:5, 1486:'6

sù, *ṭebû*, "to submerge, to sink"
má-sù, *ṭēbû*, "sunken or submerged ship," 1448:11

$sugal_7$, *sugallu*, "secretary, civil servant," 1422:9, 1423:5, 1423:9, 1423:12, 1423:14, 1423:16, 1423:18, 1423:19, 1423:20, 1423:27, 1427:5, 1427:10, 1427:13, 1427:15 1427:17, 1427:19, 1427:20, 1427:21, 1427:25, 1427:28, 1427:37, 1429:2, 1429:4, 1466:3, 1474:4, 1478:52

$sugal_7$-lugal, "royal secretary," 1423:11, 1427:12

$sugal_7$-maḫ, *sugalmaḫu*, "an official, chief minister," 1422:7, 1423:3, 1423:26, 1427:3, 1427:27, 1429:11, 1458:27–28, 1459:16, 1491:6

^{kuš}súḫub, *šuḫuppatu*, "boots, shoes," 1440:1

sum, *nadānu*, "to give"
ḫé-na-ab-sum-mu, 1499:5, 1500:5
nu-un-na-an-sum, 1493:10
sum-mu-da, 1493:7

sum-sikil, *šamaškilu*, "a type of onion," 1485:35, 1485:69

– Š –

šà, *libbu*, "in, inside of," 1414:12, 1416:17, 1421:6, 1425:10, 1426:2,1428:16, 1440:6, 1443:13,1449:15, 1450:13, 1451:11, 1455:10, 1459:17, 1460:11, 1462:33, 1463:8, 1466:17, 1472:6, 1474:17, 1477:18, 1482:7, 1484:18, 1493:6, 1496:2

  šà-bi-ta, "from among it," 1416:8, 1443:8

šà-ga-dù, *šakattû*, "belt"

  šà-ga-dù-gen, "ordinary textile," 1511:'6

  ⸢šà⸣-ga-dù-ús, "2nd-quality textile," 1511:'32

šà-gu$_4$, *kullizu*, "ox-driver," 1470:49

šabra, *šabrû*, "majordomo, chief administrator of a temple or other household," 1412:2, 1421:3, 1428:4, 1460:3, 1460:6, 1460:7, 1460:8, 1462:27, 1469:4, 1470:25, 1470:56, 1489:7, 1489:8, 1489:9, 1489:11

šáḫ, *šaḫû*, "pig," 1481:10

  ì-šáḫ, "lard," 1492:3

  sipa-šáḫ, "pig herdsman," 1481:11

  šáḫ-ama-gan, "breeding pig," 1481:1

  šáḫ-NE-tur, 1481:3

  šáḫ-NE-tur-LAGAB?.A?, 1481:4

  šáḫ-zé-da, "piglet," 1449:2

šagina, *šakkanakku*, "general" 1423:6, 1424:3, 1423:7, 1424:3, 1427:7, 1427:8, 1460:12

šar

  AN šar-ru?, 1458:28

še, *še'u*, "barley," 1412:19, 1412:23, 1416:1, 1416:4, 1416:6, 1416:15, 1416:31, 1425:11, 1432:6, 1432:8, 1435:6, 1435:8, 1447:1, 1447:9, 1464:1, 1465:1, 1470:1, 1470:12, 1470:36, 1470:55, 1470:61, 1473:1, 1476:'3, 1477:4, 1480:1, 1488:1, 1488:3, 1488:4, 1488:5, 1488:'8, 1488:'9, 1488:'11, 1491:1, 1494:1, 1496:1, 1499:3, 1503:1, 1504:1, 1512:1, 1512:15

  GÁNA še-ba ú-bi 4.0.0. gur, 1428:1

  še-bi, 1414:20, 1428:34, 1428:35, 1454:7, 1464:26, 1464:56, 1464:58, 1465:27, 1465:60, 1465:62, 1470:9, 1476:'4, 1499:9

  še-buru$_{14}$, "barley harvest," 1490:14

  še-ta sa$_{10}$-a, 1454:6, 1454:10

  še-x, 1488:'10

še-ba, "barley rations," 1416:13, 1416:24, 1470:5, 1470:17, 1470:30, 1470:49, 1470:53, 1470:66

še-er-gu, *šerku*, "a string of (dried) fruit," 1492:11

še-ĝeš-ì, *šamaššammū*, "sesame"

  2.0.0. še gur še-ĝeš-ì-bi 0.4.0. lugal, 1480:1–2

še-gín, "glue," 1455:1, 1455:10

še-numun, *zēru*, "seed," 1416:12, 1416:22

šeĝ$_6$, *bašālu*, "to cook"

  ku$_6$-šeĝ$_6$, "cooked fish," 1467:1, 1502:1

šeg$_{12}$, *libittu*, "(mud)brick," 1476:'1, 1476:'5, 1482:4, 1510:1

šeš, *aḫu*, "brother," 1428:20

šidim, *itinnu*, "builder, architect"
ĝuruš šidim, "builder," 1505:'3
ĝuruš šidim um-mi-a, "master builder," 1505:'2

šu ib-kur-re, "(a commodity)"
n ma-na šu ib-kur-re, 1511:'3, 1511:'13, 1511:'22, 1511:'31, 1511:'40

šu+níĝin, *napḫaru*, "total, sum" 1412:19, 1416:6, 1416:28, 1423:31, 1423:32, 1423:33, 1427:31, 1427:33, 1427:34, 1427:42, 1427:44, 1427:45, 1428:32, 1428:33, 1428:34, 1428:35, 1429:9, 1462:7, 1462:12, 1462:24, 1462:25, 1464:25, 1464:26, 1464:55, 1464:56, 1465:25, 1465:58, 1465:59, 1470:61, 1470:62, 1470:63, 1470:64, 1470:65, 1470:66, 1482:2, 1489:17, 1497:10, 1509:38, 1509:52, 1509:54, 1512:15, 1513:27
šu+níĝin-ba, 1464:57, 1464:58, 1465:61, 1465:62

šu . . . dím, *banû*, "to build"
ĝuruš šu-dím, "workman to build," 1505:'4

šu . . . ti, *leqû*, *maḫāru*, "to accept, take, receive"
šu ba-ti, 1421:5, 1422:5, 1423:7, 1423:9, 1423:12, 1423:19, 1423:24, 1423:25, 1423:27, 1427:8, 1427:10, 1427:13, 1427:20, 1427:28, 1427:36, 1427:37, 1429:2, 1429:4, 1447:7, 1453:6, 1472:5, 1473:4, 1485:53, 1485:61, 1492:18, 1494:4, 1514:4
šu ba-ab-ti, 1440:4, 1491:3
šu ba-an-ti, 1468:4, 1469:3, 1480:5, 1484:5
šu ba-an-ti-éš, 1479:3
šu ḫa-ba-ši-ib-ti, 1499:8

šu-du$_7$, *šuklulu*, "fully equipped, in full working order"
^{ĝeš}apin šu-du$_7$-a, "fully functional plow," 1462:13

šu-i, *gallābu*, "barber," 1474:16, 1478:33, 1478:35, 1478:37, 1478:39, 1478:41, 1490:16

šu-ku$_6$, *bā'eru*, "fisherman," 1462:30

šu-nir, *šurinnu*, "emblem," 1511:'14

šu-ra
šu-ra-gen, 1506:'1

šuku, *kurummatu*, "food allocation, ration," 1414:21, 1416:15

– T –

taḫ, *aṣābu*, "to add, increase"
taḫ-ḫu, 1470:53

te(ĝ$_3$), *ṭeḫû*,"to be near, to approach"
in-ti-àm, 1424:14

^{ĝeš}tir, *luḫummû*, *qištu*, "mud, forest, wood," 1424:1, 1438:IV 12, 1438:IV 14
n tir-GN^{ki}, 1438:V 3, 1461:2, 1461:3, 1461:5, 1461:7, 1461:9, 1461:11, 1461:13, 1461:15, 1461,17, 1461:19

^{ĝeš}tir-ma-nu, "(a wood)," 1447:8

tu$_7$, *ummaru*, "soup, broth," 1478:1, 1478:3, 1478:5, 1478:7, 1478:10, 1478:13, 1478:15, 1478:18, 1478:21, 1478:23, 1478:26, 1478:28, 1478:32, 1478:34, 1478:36, 1478:38, 1478:43, 1478:45, 1478:48, 1478:51, 1478:54, 1478:56

túg, *ṣubātu*, "cloth, textile, textile," 1459:4
  túg-gìr-sè-ga x-si, 1459:3
  túg-guz-za-gen, "ordinary tufted textile," 1443:9
  túg-maḫ, "large textile," 1459:1
  túg-mug, "textile of poor-quality wool," 1459:5

tuku, *rašû*, "to acquire, get"
  nu-tuku, 1513:15
  tuku-tuku-dam, 1459:7

tukum-bi, *šumma*, "if," 1493:9

tur, *ṣeḫēru*, "(to be) small, young, to reduce"
  šáḫ-NE-tur, 1481:3
  šáḫ-NE-tur-LAGAB?.A?, 1481:4
  ^{dug}útul-tur, "small tureen" > ^{dug}útul

tuš, *wašābu*, "to sit, to dwell, to be idle"
  tuš-a, 1450:6

– U –

ú, *šammu*, "grass," 1425:3, 1425:4, 1470:2
  udu-ú, "range-fed sheep," 1437:2, 1439:3, 1470:57, 1470:66

ú-gu . . . dé, *ḫalāqu*, "to disappear"
  ú-gu dé-a, 1460:9

ú-ḫáb, *ḫûratu*, "madder (dye)"
  kuš-máš-gal ú-ḫáb, "madder-tanned billy-goat skin," 1455:2
  kuš-udu ú-ḫáb-bi-n, "n madder-tanned sheep skin(s)," 1441:4, 1441:7, 1441:12, 1441:16

^{geš}ù-suḫ$_5$, *ašūḫu*, "pine tree," 1500:4

u$_4$, *ūmu*, "day"
  u$_4$-n-àm, 1424:14
  u$_4$-n-kam, 1425:12, 1449:13, 1450:12, 1451:10, 1475:5, 1482:11
  u$_4$-n-šè, 1425:1, 1425:5, 1425:9, 1425:10, 1426:1, 1426:4, 1426:7, 1430:1, 1431:1, 1432:1, 1432:4, 1432:7, 1432:9, 1432:12, 1432:14, 1433:1, 1435:1, 1435:4, 1435:7, 1435:9, 1435:11, 1435:14, 1442:1, 1446:1, 1448:1, 1448:4, 1448:5 1448:8, 1452:3, 1476:'2, 1482:10, 1511:'2, 1511:'7, 1511:'9, 1511:'11, 1511:'12, 1511:'13, 1511:'15, 1511:'17, 1511:'18, 1511:'19, 1511:'21, 1511:'24, 1511:'26, 1511:'28, 1511:'30, 1511:'33, 1511:'35, 1511:'37, 1511:'39
  u$_4$-6-[. . .]-ta, 1510:4
  u$_4$ imin-na, 1424:6, 1424:7
  Relative Clauses:
   u$_4$ a-KIN.KIN-dè im-e-re-ša-a, 1478:17
   u$_4$ alam-lugal-ta im-da-e-re-ša-a, 1478:12
   u$_4$ BÀD.AN^{ki}-ta ki lugal-šè ba-e-re-ša-a, 1490:7–8

u$_4$ ⸢bu⸣-šè im-ĝen-na-a, 1478:50
u$_4$ du$_{10}$-uš-šè im-e-re-ša-a, 1478:42
u$_4$ é-ḫal-bi-šè im-e-re-ša-a, 1478:47
u$_4$ en-nu-ĝá še-buru$_{14}$-ka-šè im-ĝen-na-a, 1490:12
u$_4$ ĝeš-saḫar-x ba-na-dím-ma, 1455:5
u$_4$ kaskal-anše-lugal-šè im-e-re-ša-a, 1478:9
u$_4$ ki énsi-ka-šè im-ĝen-na-a, 1490:11
u$_4$ ki énsi-šè im-e-re-ša-a, 1478:58
u$_4$ kúr nu-ub-ge$_4$-ge$_4$-da, 1477:7
[u$_4$ ^{ĝeš}]ma-nu-šè im-ĝen-na-a, 1490:17
u$_4$ nam-érim in-tar-ru-ús-sa, 1466:14–15
u$_4$ si-maš-ku-um^{ki}-šè ba-e-re-ša-a, 1478:25
u$_4$ šu-šar-su$_6$-šè im-ĝen-na-a, 1478:20
u$_4$ *simat-*^{d}*ištaran ilum-da-mu* in-da-a, 1463:5–7

u$_4$-sakar, *uskāru*, *warḫu*, "crescent moon, moon," 1489:2
u$_4$-sakar-gu-la, 1493:2

u$_8$, *immertum*, *laḫru*, "ewe," 1462:8
u$_8$-bar-ĝál, "ewe with fleece," 1454:1

ud$_5$, *enzu*, "female goat," 1454:4, 1462:10

udu, *immeru*, "sheep," 1460:7, 1460:8, 1466:2, 1466:8, 1466:11, 1485:67, 1498:8
kuš-udu, "sheep skin," 1453:1, 1453:2, 1441:4, 1441:7, 1441:12, 1441:16
sa-udu, "sheep sinew," 1493:1
udu-máš ḫi-a, "various sheep (and) goats," 1460:2, 1460:5, 1462:12
udu-niga, "fattened sheep," 1437:1, 1449:1, 1474:9
udu-niga-bar-su-ga, "fattened sheep without fleece," 1439:2
udu-níta, "male sheep," 1462:9
udu-níta-bar-ĝál, "male sheep with fleece," 1454:2
udu-ú, "range-fed sheep," 1437:2, 1470:57, 1470:66
udu-ú-bar-ĝál, "range-fed sheep with fleece," 1439:3
udu-[x], 1475:2

ugula, *waklu*, "overseer, foreman," 1426:10, 1430:5, 1431:7, 1432:17, 1433:5, 1435:17, 1442:6, 1446:7, 1448:13, 1450:1, 1450:2, 1450:4, 1450:5, 1450:7, 1450:8, 1450:9, 1451:1, 1451:2, 1451:3, 1451:4, 1451:5, 1451:6, 1451:7, 1451:8, 1452:8, 1458:27, 1461:4, 1461:6, 1461:8, 1461:10, 1461:12, 1461:14, 1461:16, 1461:18, 1461:20, 1481:12, 1503:4, 1504:6, 1514:5
ugula–60, "overseer of 60," 1502:3
ugula-gu$_4$, "overseer of oxen," 1480:4

um-mi-a, *ummānu*, "expert, master craftsman"
ĝuruš šidim um-mi-a, "master builder," 1505:'2

^{ĝeš}URU-x?-KWU405, 1462:22

urudu, *erû*, "copper," 1493:11

ús, "(to be) of a lesser quality"
[gada š]à-ga-dù-ús, 1511:'32

uš, "a unit of length," 1497:2, 1497:10

^{dug}útul, *diqāru*, "tureen,"

^{dug}útul-tur ga-àra, "small tureen of cheese," 1485:13, 1485:28, 1485:31, 1485:72

^{dug}útul-tur ì-nun, "small tureen of ghee," 1485:12, 1485:27, 1485:30, 1485:71

– Z –

zabar, *siparru*, "bronze," 1460:9

zabar-dab$_5$, *zabardabbu*, "an official," 1441:8

zi, *baqāmu*, *barāšu*, *naṭāpu*, *nasāḫu*, "to cut, remove"

zé-a, 1470:2

zi(g), *nasāḫu*, "to expend"

ba-zi, 1469:6, 1470:70, 1474:20, 1491:4–5

ba-zi-ga, 1437:3

zi-ga, 1417:4, 1432:3, 1432:6, 1432:15, 1435:3, 1435:6, 1435:16, 1443:15, 1466:16, 1470:37, 1470:40, 1470:43, 1474:18, 1478:60, 1482:2, 1490:19, 1513:28

zi-ga-àm, 1416:29, 1441:22, 1481:8

zi-ga-didli, 1470:66

zì, *qēmu*, "flour," 1432:3, 1432:15, 1432:16, 1435:3, 1435:16, 1449:8, 1452:7, 1470:57

zì-ba-ba-sig$_5$, "fine-quality flour porridge," 1449:5

zì-gu, "gu-flour," 1432:6, 1432:8, 1432:13, 1435:6, 1435:8, 1435:13

zì-gu-sig$_5$, "fine gu-flour," 1449:8

zì-gú-niga, "fattened pulse flour," 1449:6

zì-kum, "kum-flour," 1449:7

zì-KAL, "KAL-flour," 1432:11, 1435:10, 1449:9

zíz, *kunšu*, "emmer wheat," 1421:1

zú-lum, *suluppû*, "date," 1492:14, 1501:1–2

zú-si, "plucking, plucking time," 1443:2

zuḫ, *šarāqu*, "to steal"

ba-zuḫ, 1424:2

Personal Names

– A –

˹*al*˺-*la-ša-ru-um*, 1495:3

al-lu

igi *al-lu* kù-ĝál, 1462:28

àm-na-[*a*?], 1509:31

AN-a-[. . .]

igi AN-a-[. . .]-šè, 1477:15

an-dùl, 1509:48

an-na-ḫi-li-bi

ki *an-na-ḫi-li-bi*-ta, 1436:4

an-ta-lú

ki *an-ta-lú*-ta, 1474:20

ar-ši lú-ḫal-bi, 1478:44

ar-ší-tam, 1512:12

árad-ĝu$_{10}$, 1512:16

lú-^{d}nin-ĝír-su dumu árad-ĝu$_{10}$, 1459:8

^{d}áš-gi$_{5}$-*tillat-sú*

ki ^{d}áš-gi$_{5}$-*tillat-sú*-ta, 1479:2

– B –

ba-a-ga

ugula *ba-a-ga* kurušda, 1481:12

ba-an-zi

˹ki˺ ba-an-zi-[ta], 1475:6

ba-az-ba-zum, 1504:4

ba-ba-a ^{lú}kíĝ-gi$_{4}$-a-lugal, 1478:2

ba-la-la, 1443:12

ĝìri *ba-la-la*, 1485:8

ba-na-a, 1465:1, 1509:1

ba-na-a-a, 1464:1

ba-sa$_{6}$, 1415:5

ba-sa$_{6}$-ga dub-sar, 1466:9

kìšib ba-sa$_{6}$-ga dub-sar, 1481:6

ba-za-a, 1512:13

ba-zi

ur-ab-ba dumu ba-zi, 1459:13

ba-zi-ĝu$_{10}$, 1512:8

ba-[x-x]

i-din-ilum dumu *ba*-[x-x] nu-[bànda], 1485:40

be-lí-a-ri-iq lú-˹ḫal˺-bi, 1478:46

be-lí-dan

ki *be-lí-dan*-ta, 1471:3

be-lí-DU$_{10}$, 1464:52, 1465:56

bi-zé-[x], 1509:24

bí-˹*tum*˺, 1483:2

bu-ku-li, 1464:14, 1465:15

bu-ku-lum, 1509:12

bur-ma-ma

igi *bur*-ma-ma, 1471:9

– D –

da-a-ga, 1412:1

da-ar-na-ta

ki *da-ar-na-ta*-˹ta˺, 1473:2

da-da

ugula *da-da*, 1461:20

DINGIR-*ḫa-am*-˹*ni*˺, 1464:39, 1465:43

diĝir-sugal$_{7}$, 1419:12

du-bi$_{(2)}$-*na*, 1464:51, 1465:55

du-du, 1493:4

dù-a

ĝìri dù-a, 1441:2

du$_{10}$-ga

ugula lú-^{d}šára dumu du$_{10}$-ga, 1450:4, 1451:2

du$_{11}$-ga-zi-da, 1489:10

DUB-ĝu$_{10}$, 1499:7

– E –

e-lu-da-an

nu-bànda *e-lu-da-an*, 1440:5

e-zé-tum nu-bànda, 1485:10

é-a-ma-lik, 1512:21

i-dì-ilum, 1464:31

i-dì-[*ilum* min], 1464:34

i-dì-ilum ^{lú}kíĝ-gi$_4$-a-lugal, 1478:19

i-dì-^{d}*suen* nu-bànda, 1490:4

i-din-a-bu-um

igi *i-din-a-bu-um*, 1486:'3

i-din-ilum, 1465:35

ĝìri *i-din-ilum* rá-gaba, 1485:5

i-din-ilum dumu *ba*-[*x-x*] nu-[bànda], 1485:40

i-din-ilum min, 1465:38

i-mi-id-a-ḫi

ĝìri *i-mi-id-a-ḫi* nu-bànda, 1470:31

i-na-ḫu ^{lú}kíĝ-gi$_4$-a-lugal, 1478:6

i-pá-lí-is, 1453:5

i-ri-ib

i-ri-ib ^{lú}kaš$_4$, 1502:2

ugula–60 *i-ri-ib*, 1502:3

i-šar-a-ḫi gudu$_4$, 1485:32

i-šar-be-lí, 1509:46

i-šar-li-bur, 1469:2

kìšib *i-šar-li-bur*, 1470:11

i-wi-ir di-ku$_5$ šu-i, 1478:41

i$_{(3)}$*-zu-a*, 1464:28, 1465:29

i-[. . .]

igi *i*-[. . .-šè], 1477:11

ì-lí-a-núm ugula-gu$_4$, 1480:4

ì-lí-an-dùl

igi *ì-lí-an-dùl*, 1479:9

ì-lí-aš-ra-ni

kìšib *ì-lí-aš-ra-ni*, 1470:17

kìšib *ì-lí-aš-ra-ni* šabra, 1470:56

ì-lí-bi-la-ni

igi *ì-lí-bi-*[*la?-ni?*], 1486:'2

ì-lí-sa-tu

[igi] *ì-lí-sa-tu*, 1473:8

ib-ni-ilum

kìšib *ib-ni-ilum* sugal$_7$, 1423:5, 1427:5

id-ni-id šu-i, 1478:33

igi-an-na-ke$_4$-zu

ugula igi-an-na-ke$_4$-zu, 1461:14

ìl-su-⸢*ra*⸣*-*[*bí*], 1509:42

ìl-šu-pa-lu, 1464:43, 1465:47

ilum-ba-ni dub-sar KAŠ$_4$, 1423:13, 1427:14

ilum-da-mu, 1463:6

ilum-i-gur$_8$ simug, 1471:6

im-ti-dam, 1420:4

im-zu-tum, 1464:50, 1465:54

⸢*in*⸣*-RI-RI* PA?.[AL??], 1462:27

išdum-ki-in, 1487:'4

išdum-kí sugal$_7$ maškim, 1422:9

iz-zu-zu-ú, 1465:33

– K –

ka-ka, 1412:12

ku-ba-ba-e, 1466:4

ku-da-⸢*tum*⸣, 1464:40, 1465:44

ku-ku, 1419:2

ku-ra-du, 1464:10, 1465:10

ku-ra-du-tum, 1509:13

ku-ti lú-*ba-ba-ti*, 1478:57

kù-^{d}nanna

kìšib kù-^{d}nanna sugal$_7$, 1423:18, 1427:19

kur-bi-èr-ra

ĝìri *kur-bi-èr-ra*, 1488:3

– L –

la-lum, 1458:23

nu-bànda *la-lum*, 1458:2, 1458:14, 1504:7

la-qì-ip, 1487:'3

igi *la-qì-ip*-šè, 1484:10

la-si?-[. . .], 1509:32

– M –

[4] So envelope. Tablet *la!-lí-a*.

– N –

– P –

kišib *šu-eš*$_4$*-tár* šagina gú-du$_8$-a^{ki}(-ka), 1423:6, 1427:7
šu-eš$_4$*-tár* dub-sar, 1470:59
šu-eš$_4$*-tár* ^{lú}kíĝ-gi$_4$-a-lugal, 1490:6

šu-ì-lí, 1447:6, 1458:25
ĝìri *šu-ì-lí* AŠ, 1422:8
šu-ì-lí sugal$_7$, 1423:9, 1427:10
ĝìri *šu-ì-lí* sugal$_7$ lugal, 1423:11, 1427:12
nu-bànda *šu-ì-lí*, 1458:3, 1503:6

šu-^{d}*iš-ḫa-ra* engar, 1470:50

šu-kab-tá, 1449:12, 1457:2
a-ga-ti nin$_9$ *šu-kab-tá*, 1474:2, 1474:6, 1485:18
é-*šu*!*-kab-tá*-šè, 1448:6, 1452:6
ĝìri *šu-kab-tá*, 1466:16, 1474:19
mu *šu-kab-tá*-šè, 1481:5
šu-kab-ta a-zu, 1467:2

šu-kab-te,[5] 1514:3

šu-ku$_8$*-bu-um*, 1419:6, 1427:36
šu-ku$_8$*-ub* sugal$_7$, 1429:2
šu-ku-bu-um sugal$_7$ maškim, 1474:4

šu-la-núm, 1419:7

šu-^{d}*ma-lí-ik*, 1477:2
dub *šu-*^{d}*ma-lik* má-gíd, 1470:19
kišib *šu-*^{d}*ma-lik* šabra unu^{ki}-ga, 1470:25

šu-^{d}ma-mi dumu šabra *za-ak-ì-lí*, 1460:8

šu-^{d}nin-in-si maškim, 1495:12

šu-^{d}nin-šubur, 1487:'2

šu-nu-mur, 1464:33, 1465:37

šu-^{d}*suen*, 1509:43
šu-^{d}*suen* sugal$_7$, 1427:37, 1429:4

šu-su-ra, 1500:1

šu-^{d}*šamaš*
igi *šu-*^{d}*šamaš* ^{lú}k[íĝ-gi$_4$-a] ur-^{d}ba-ú, 1462:29

šu-ur-gu
igi *šu-ur-gu*, 1479:7

šu-zu, 1464:46, 1465:50

šu-^{d}[. . .]
ĝìri *šu-*^{d}[. . .], 1485:44
igi *šu-*^{d}[. . .], 1510:10

šu-[. . .]
igi *šu-*[. . .-šè], 1477:12, 1477:13

[^{d}šul]-gi-*sí-im-tum*, 1441:1

^{d}šul-gi-*wa-qar*, 1485:58

– T –

ta-ki-ìl, 1473:3

ta-ni-a
ki *ta-ni-a*-ta, 1470:69

ta-ni-mu-um, 1504:5

ta-ri-bu, 1464:8, 1465:8

ta-x-[. . .], 1509:34

ta?-[. . .], 1509:18

tá-at-tu-ri
kišib *tá-at-tu-ri*, 1470:31

ti-im-ma-ma
éren *ti-im*-ma-ma, 1458:12

tu-ra-am-ì-lí
ĝìri *tu-ra-am-ì-lí* dub-sar, 1482:8

– U –

u-bar-gu-la, 1512:9

u-bar-tum a-zu, 1442:4

u-IŠ-é, 1509:6

u-še-er-ḫa-lum
dam *u-še-er-ḫa-lum*, 1501:4

ú-ku-bi, 1509:23

ù-ki-pa$_{(2/4)}$*-šu*, 1464:6, 1465:6

ù-zé-na-pi-ir
kišib *ú-zé-na-pi-ir* dub-sar, 1470:28

---

[5] In this ĜEŠ.KÚŠU text it is unclear if he is the *Šū-Kabta* known from Garšana. However, the name is very rare. The /te/ on the tablet is clear, thus it may be understood as **šu-kab-ta*-e.

– Z –

TOPONYMS

1444:29, 1498:13
^{d}nergal$_{x}^{eri11-gal}$-gar-ša-na-ka^{ki}, 1439:7
^{d}nergal$_{x}^{eri11-gal}$ gar-ša-na-ka^{ki}-šè, 1436:3
^{d}nergal-^{d}èr-ra-nu-nir gar-ša-na-ka^{ki}, 1414:24–25
^{d}nergal-gu-la šà gar-ša-na-ka^{ki}, 1414:12–13
níĝ-šu-tak$_{4}$-a gar-ša-an-na^{ki}-šè, 1474:1
šà gar-ša-na^{ki}(-ka), 1421:6, 1449:15, 1450:13, 1451:11, 1493:6,
šagina-gar-ša-na-ka^{ki}, 1460:12
tir éren gar-ša-na-ka^{ki}, 1438:IV 12, 1438:IV 14
tir-gar-ša-na(-ka)^{ki}, 1438:V 3, 1461:3

^{ĝeš}gi-gal^{ki}
tir-^{ĝeš}gi-gal^{ki}, 1461:2

gir$_{13}$?-ĝeš?^{ki}
tir-gir$_{13}$?-ĝeš?^{ki}, 1461:7

gu-kéše
šà gu-kéše-šè, 1443:13

gú-ab-ba^{ki}
^{lú}ázlag gú-ab-ba^{ki}-me, 1459:5
lú-mar-sa gú-ab-ba^{ki}, 1459:4

gú-du$_{8}$-a^{ki}
kišib *šu-eš$_{4}$-tár* šagina gú-du$_{8}$-a^{ki}(-ka), 1423:6, 1427:7

gú-eden-na
numun gú-eden-na-šè, 1459:10

gú-SAḪAR.DU^{ki}
éren gú-SAḪAR.DU^{ki}, 1458:17

– Ĝ –

ĝar-zíd-da^{ki}
é-^{d}nergal-ĝar-zíd-da^{ki}, 1416:26

ĝeš-gi-gal^{ki}, 1458:9
ka i$_{7}$-ĝeš-gi-gal^{ki}, 1458:8
ka i$_{7}$-ĝeš-gi-gal$^{<ki>}$-ta, 1426:5
<šà> ĝeš-gi-gal$^{<ki>}$, 1460:11

ĜEŠ.KÚŠU^{ki}, 1426:9
ĝeš <<BU>> ĜEŠ.KÚŠU^{ki} gíd-da, 1426:6
ĜEŠ.KÚŠU^{ki}-šè, 1432:3, 1432:8, 1435:3, 1435:8
ĜEŠ.KÚŠU^{ki}-ta, 1432:10, 1432:14, 1435:10, 1435:15, 1442:2, 1452:4
ki énsi- ĜEŠ.KÚŠU^{ki}-ka, 1423:35
ki énsi-ĜEŠ.KÚŠU^{ki}-ta, 1422:3, 1427:47

ĝír-su^{ki}
ĝír-su^{ki}-šè, 1489:5
ki énsi ĝír-su^{ki}-ta, 1440:2
kišib ur-^{d}ab-a lú-énsi-ĝír-su^{ki}, 1423:23

– Ḫ –

ḪAR-da-ḫi^{ki}
a-šà-^{d}nergal-ḪAR-da-ḫi^{ki}, 1428:19
^{d}nergal$_{x}^{eri11-gal}$-[ḪAR]-da-ḫi^{ki}, 1498:3

– I –

iri-saĝ-rig$_{7}^{ki}$
iš-tu iri-saĝ-rig$_{7}^{ki}$, 1497:1, 1497:11

– K –

ka$_{(3)}$-ma-rí^{ki}
a-šà-ka-ma-rí^{ki}, 1488:'12
éren kà-ma-rí^{ki}, 1458:13
ka-ma-rí^{ki}-ta, 1432:5,1435:5

karkar^{ki}, 1458:6

KI.AN^{ki}
šà KI.AN^{ki}-ta, 1426:2

– L –

LÀ[L? ...]
tir-LÀ[L? ...], 1461:5

– M –

ma-rí^{ki}
ĝìri-ag-ga lú-ma-rí^{ki}, 1427:38
ĝìri-aga lú-ma-rí^{ki}, 1429:6

maš-kán^{ki}
[^{d}n]in-ḫur-saĝ-maš-kán^{ki}, 1498:14

Divine Names

^{d}amar-*suen*
ki-sura$_{12}$ [^{d}amar]-^{d}*suen*-ki-áĝ-ta, 1488:'9
an
šabra-an, 1489:9
^{d}en-ki
^{d}en-ki àm-rí-ma-ka^{ki}, 1498:9
^{d}en-líl, 1497:6
mu-DU ^{d}en-líl-lá, 1489:14
^{d}èr-ra-nu-nir
^{d}nergal-^{d}èr-ra-nu-nir gar-ša-na-ka^{ki}, 1414:24–25
^{d}gu-la
é-^{d}nergal-gu-la šà gar-ša-na-ka^{ki}, 1416:17–18
^{d}gu-la-šè, 1441:13
^{d}nergal-gu-la šà gar-ša-na-ka^{ki}, 1414:12–13
u$_{4}$-sakar-gu-la, 1493:2
^{d}ĝeštin?-an?-na?-du$_{6}$-*ar-ḫa-tum*, 1498:8
^{d}kal-kal, 1428:27
^{d}mes-lam-ta-è-a
gada ^{d}mes-lam-ta-UD.[DU-a], 1511:'5
^{d}nergal, 1428:27
a-šà-^{d}nergal-gar-ša-na-ka^{ki}, 1428:9
a-šà-^{d}nergal-ḪAR-da-ḫi^{ki}, 1428:19
a-šà-šeš-barag-^{d}nergal$_{x}$$^{\text{<eri11->gal}}$-gar-ša-na-ka^{ki}, 1434:27
é-^{d}nergal-ĝar-zíd-da^{ki}, 1416:26
é-^{d}nergal-gu-la šà gar-ša-na-ka^{ki}, 1416:17–18
é-^{d}nergal$_{x}$$^{\text{eri11-gal}}$-gar-ša-na^{ki}-ka, 1454:8
é-^{d}nergal$_{x}$$^{\text{eri11-gal}}$-gar-ša-na-ka-šè, 1437:6
mu-DU ^{d}nergal-gar-ša-na-ka^{ki}, 1418:3
mu-DU ^{d}nergal$_{x}$-gar-ša-na-ka$^{(ki)}$, 1413:2–3, 1415:2
^{d}nergal$_{x}$$^{\text{eri11-gal}}$-aratta, 1498:1
nergal-gar-ša-na-ka^{ki}, 1456:1
^{d}nergal-gar-ša-na(-ka)^{ki}, 1412:22, 1444:29
^{d}nergal$_{x}$$^{\text{eri11-gal}}$-gar-ša-na-ka, 1441:17
^{d}nergal$_{x}$$^{\text{eri11-gal}}$-gar-ša-na(-ka)^{ki}, 1439:7, 1498:13
^{d}nergal$_{x}$$^{\text{eri11-gal}}$-gar-ša-na-ka^{ki}-šè, 1436:3
^{d}nergal-^{d}èr-ra-nu-nir gar-ša-na-ka^{ki}, 1414:24–25
^{d}nergal-gu-la šà gar-ša-na-ka^{ki}, 1414:12–13
^{d}nergal$_{x}$$^{\text{eri11-gal}}$-[ḪAR]-da-ḫi^{ki}, 1498:3
^{d}nergal$_{x}$$^{\text{eri11-gal}}$-i$_{7}$-eb-la^{ki}, 1498:2, 1498:12
^{d}nergal$_{x}$$^{\text{eri11-gal}}$-šu-na-mu-gi$_{4}$^{ki}, 1498:10
^{d}nergal$_{x}$$^{\text{eri11-gal}}$-tin-tir^{ki}, 1498:11
šuku egi-zi ^{d}nergal, 1414:21
^{d}nin
gil-sa-^{d}nin-zabala$_{4}$^{ki}-gar-ša-na-ka^{ki}-ka, 1417:3
^{d}nin-[é-MIR]-za, 1498:6
^{d}nin-gal
šabra-^{d}nin-gal, 1489:11
^{d}nin-gublaga
a-šà-^{d}nin-⌜gublaga⌝, 1488:5
šabra-^{d}nin-gublaga, 1489:8
^{d}nin-ḫur-saĝ
^{d}nin-ḫur-saĝ-aratta, 1498:7
^{d}nin-ḫur-saĝ-maš-kán^{ki}, 1498:14
^{d}nin-ḫur-saĝ-zálag?-ga, 1428:15
[^{d}n]in-ḫur-saĝ-zálag-ga, 1498:15
^{d}nin-in-sin-na^{ki},1485:33
^{d}[nin-si-ĝar]-eden-na, 1498:5
^{d}nin-sún
a-šà-du$_{6}$-nunuz-^{d}nin-sún, 1428:3
^{d}nin-ur$_{4}$-ra
a-šà-^{d}⌜nin⌝-ur$_{4}$-ra, 1488:'8
^{d}*suen*
ki ^{d}*suen*, 1489:4
^{d}šára
mu-DU ^{d}šára, 1460:10
[. . . -^{d}š]ára mu-DU [. . .], 1488:'7
^{d}šul-pa-è
a-šà-^{d}šul-pa-è, 1428:12

Cornell University Studies in Assyriology and Sumerology
(CUSAS 3)
THE GARŠANA ARCHIVES
ADDITIONS AND CORRECTIONS

The preparation of the Concordance resulted in a number of improvements over the original publication. As a result, all additions and corrections to CUSAS 3 noted below have been included in the Concordance. This separate list is provided as an additional convenience to the reader so that he or she might enter these notations in the text volume. The additions and corrections include significant changes, such as the two texts inadvertently left out or improved readings, as well as minor changes, such as the addition or deletion of dashes, brackets, etc. The list will be updated periodically on the Cornell University website (http://cuneiform.library.cornell.edu) and further corrections will be provided as they appear in forthcoming studies and reviews.

Universal Changes

a-gù > úgu
da-da-DINGIR > *da-da*-AN
é-kí-na-tum > é-gi-na-tum
é-lùmgi > é-lunga
^{ğeš}gariğ > ^{ğeš}garig
gi-NE > gi-izi
kàr-da-ḫi > qar-da-ḫi
lu-ga-tum > *lu-kà-dum*
si_{x} > si_{12}
ŠID > šudum
taq-ri-ib-tum > *tak-ri-ib-tum*
tár-ra-um > *dar-ra-um*
tu-ni-um^{ki} > *tu-lí-um*^{ki}
zì-sig_{15} > zì-KAL

No. 8 l. 41 read: . . . saḫar z[i-ga . . .
No. 9 l. 7 read: 3 ğ[uruš šidi]m ugula!(É) árad-é-a
No. 21 l. '30: níğ-gur > níğ-GA
No. 25 l. '10 read: [18 ğuruš šeg_{12} š]u . . .
No. 26 l. '16 read: . . . im lu-[dè

No. 34: l. '21 read: [1] *ku-ru-ub-*^{d}*adad* <zàḫ> ugula *ilum-dan*

No. 35 l. 34 read: 2 ĝuruš 2 géme <gi-sal> gi-ir bàd ke$_{4}$-[dè] gub-ba

No. 38 l. 44, No. 39 l. 46, No. 184 l. 19, No. 192 l. '22, No. 223 ll. 5, 10, No. 286 l.13, No. 306 l. 13: de$_{6}$-a > ĝen-a

No. 40 l. 32 read: 6 ĝuruš in-[u (x x)]

No. 40 l. 33 read: ka i$_{7}$-ir-ni-na-š[è x x]

No. 41 l. 7: 4 ĝuruš > 5 ĝuruš

No. 46 l. '17 read: šeg$_{12}$ šu dím-[ma sum-mu-dè gub-ba]

No. 52 l. 36 read: 1 ĝuruš [šidim]

No. 53 l. 29 read: al-ta[r u]š:é-bar-ra

No. 54 l. 18 read: 1 ĝu[ruš šidim n ĝuruš]

No. 54 l. 19 read: 18 [géme]

No. 54 l. 20 read: KI.NE [saḫar?] ~ sì-gé-d[é gub-ba]

No. 56 l. '38: ĜEŠ.KÚŠU[^{ki}-ta] > ĜEŠ.KÚŠU[^{ki}-šè?]

No. 59 l. 22 read: 2 ĝuruš ⸢šidim⸣

No. 59 l. 32 read: 3 ĝu[ruš šu dím] gub-ba

No. 59 l. 36 read: 7 ĝuruš x

No. 74 l. '8: PI-*ḫu-um*-šè > *ši-ḫu-um*-šè

No. 82 l. 11 read: dì-um ⸢ĝár⸣-ra

No. 90 l. 7 and No. 145 l. 44: du$_{8}$-[dè] > du$_{8}$-[ḫa]

No. 92 l. 12 read: [3] ĝuruš saḫar GÍN?-[bal?]

No. 92 l. 20: *šu-eš$_{4}$-tár* > <é->*šu-eš$_{4}$-tár*

No. 95 l. 16 read: 4? géme im ga$_{6}$-ĝá-[dè gub-ba]

No. 98 l. '22 read: [šeg$_{12}$-al-ur$_{x}$-ra] du$_{8}$-⸢dè⸣

No. 106 l. 36 read: ~ [. . .] ⸢x⸣ ba-al-dè

No. 111 l. 45 read: 1 ur-^{d}nanše šidim l[ú-GN]

No. 123 l. 30 read: [al-tar ki-sá-a é]-lunga . . .

No. 131 l. '24-'25 read: 1 ĝuruš šidim 10 ĝuruš
[n géme] GÌN-bal <^{ĝeš}kiri->[gar]-š[a-a]n-na^{ki} dù-[a]

No. 131 l. '26 read: lu-[dè gub-ba]

No. 143 l. 33 read: gul-[la]

No. 146 l. '33 read: [x] *mu-gu* dù-a

No. 146 l. '42 read: ⸢im⸣ lu-[a]

No. 147 l. 35 read: [x *mu-g*]*u* d[ù-a]

No. 148 l. '20: zì > túg

No. 158 l. 37 read: kíĝ ésir!-ra

No. 165 l. 1 read: 10 ĝuru[š n géme]

No. 169 l. 5, No. 206 l. 21, No. 1065 l.4, No. 1145 l. 3: ^{lú}lùmgi > ^{lú}lunga

No. 170 l. 2: *šu*-^{d}[nisaba] > *šu*-^{d}[dumu-zi]

No. 189 l. 30: DU > ĝen

No. 195 l. '13 read: 1 [ĝuruš šidim]

No. 195 l. '14 read: ⸢ka⸣-lá-ka [gub-ba]

No. 196 l. '21 read: 1 ĝuruš šidim ka-l[á-k]a <<ga>> gub-ba

No. 196 l. '28 read: in-u ka i$_{7}$-[ta] gub-ba en-n[u ke$_{4}$-dè] ĝen-[na]

No. 240 l. 4: u$_{4}$-60-kam > u$_{4}$-10!-kam

No. 240 l. 6 read: á-⸢ki⸣-ti šu-numun

No. 246 l. 9: [ta] > [šè]

No. 262 l. 20 and No. 1398 l. 20: zàr-tab-ba > zàr tab-ba

No. 263 l. 6 read: [ús-b]i 1500 ~ éš kaskal š[u+níĝin]-na-bi

No. 298 l. 3, No. 299 l. 3: DU-a > ĝen-a

No. 324 l. 29 read: *tu-lí-id-*^{d}*šamaš*^{ši}

No. 336 l. 34 read: SIG4.ANŠE im [sumur ke$_{4}$-dè] ~ gub-[ba]

No. 357, 358, 359: ĝá-šub-ba > ĝá šub-ba

No. 409 l. 5: ⸢nin$_{9}$⸣ > ⸢níĝ⸣-dab$_{5}$

No. 414 l. 10 read: ⸢še⸣ ù-dag-ga^{ki}-ta

No. 438 l. 6: na-silim> *na-sìm*

No. 444 l. 2: tu-ku-ni > tu-ku-lí

No. 457 l. 2: 0.0.2. > 0.0.3!.

No. 466 l. 7 read: é-gal!-šè

No. 482 l. 1 read: [n.n].1[.n].6½ [sìla ì-ĝeš gur]

No. 484 l. 5: e-eb?-zi > e-é-zi

No. 487 l. 3 read: lú é-ne-ne

No. 487 l. 4 read: sa$_{10}$-a

No. 511 l. '122 read: 4 túg- ĝeštu$_{x}$(PI!.TÚG)-gen! é-ba-an

No. 523 l. 11, No. 975 l. 187, No. 981 l. 181, No. 1182 l. 8: ŠIM > šim

No. 548 l. 8, No. 1025 ll. 22, 80, 101: ninda-du$_{8}$ > ninda-tuḫ

No. 551 l. 7 read: á-gú-zi-⸢ga⸣

No. 551 l. 11, No. 955 l. 5: kaskal^{ki} > kaskal-na

No. 558 l. '5 read: *in-ga-*⸢*la*⸣

No. 562 l. '16 read: [ì]-ĝeš-bi 1½ sìla

No. 562 l. '17 read: ì-šáḫ<-bi> 1⅓ sìla

No. 575 l. 5: -kiri$_4$- > -kìri-

No. 576 l. 11 read: [3 túg ba-tab *tuḫ-ḫu-um* 4-kam-ús ^{lú}k]aš$_4$

No. 588 l. 5: kala-kala-gé-dè

No. 589 l. 2 read: 12 ^{túg}uš-bar x [(. . .)]

No. 592 l. 1 read: 1 gum-ésir

No. 648 l. 2 read: 1 gú 24 ma-na ~ siki túg-g̃e$_6$

No. 650 l. 3: 1-kam > [n]-kam

No. 663 l. 2 read: 2 ^{túg}g̃eštu-lugal é(!)-[ba-an]

No. 675 l. 1 read: 2! gú siki-ús

No. 691 l. 1 read: 2 ^{túg}níg̃-lám 3-k[am-ús]

No. 720 l. 2: ^{túg}g̃eštu-dul$_5$ > ^{túg}g̃eštu$_x$(PI.TÚG)

No. 722 l. 1 read: [n ^{túg}]bar-dul-tur-gen

No. 743 l. 7 read: [n ^{túg}gú-DU].DU guz-za 4-kam-⸢ús⸣

No. 744 envelope l. '1 read: [ki-lá-bi] 57⅓ ma-na ('2.) [1] túg-mug

No. 744 tablet l. 10 read: ki-lá-bi 58! ma!-[na]

No. 747 l. 16: ^{d}ma-z[i-x] > *ilum-ma-⸢zi⸣*

No. 748 l. 12 read: 3 ^{túg}uš-bar-[tur]

No. 755 l. 1 read: 4 ^{túg}sagšu

No. 755 l. 8 read: [. . . níg̃]-U.NU-a

No. 759 l. 1 read: ^{túg}*á-[gu$_4$-ḫu-um]*

No. 761 l. 1: $^{\text{g̃eš}}$gu-za MÍ.U$_4$.KAL > $^{\text{g̃eš}}$gu-za-munus šà!-kal

No. 764 l. 7(tablet): [4] > [3]

No. 764 l. 8 read: 4 ^{túg}uš-b[ar . . .]

No. 773 l. 6 read: 2 ^{túg}sag̃-uš!-[bar]

No. 793 l. 7 read: 6 ^{túg}bar-U.<TÚG>-gen

No. 814 l. 8 read: [2] ^{túg}g̃eštu-túg 3-kam-ús é(!)-ba-[an]

No. 825 l. 1: [a-kam] > [lá-mí]

No. 825 l. 3: til? > sumun

No. 829 l. '6 read: ^{túg}bar<-dul$_5$>-níg̃-lám-x-[. . .]

No. 850 l. 1 read: 1 ku[š-udu]-niga <ba->úš

No. 906 l. 5: ⸢šakan⸣ > ⸢šag̃an⸣

No. 930 l. 2, No. 933 l.2: ^{kuš}a-g̃á-lá-bad > ^{kuš}a-g̃á-lá-sumun

No. 968 l. 19: sàg̃ > sàg

No. 972 ll. 1–6:

(1.[0.3.3. zì-gu-sig$_5$]

(2.[1.0.0.] zì-[gu-ús gur]

(3.0.3.3. dabin
(4.0.0.4.5 sìla zì-KAL
(5.[0.1.0.0 sìla] sìla zì-kum-sig$_5$
(6.[ninda]-šè

No. 972 l. 10 read: [níĝ-ì]-dé-a-šè

No. 972 ll. 30, 46, 81; No. 975 l. 49, No. 1020 l. 1, No. 1024 l. 1, No. 1036 l. 24, No. 1230 l. 1: ŠIM > bappir

No. 972 l. 40: [TÚG-NI-(x?)] úr > [TÚG-NI ku]-úr

No. 972 l. 44 read: ⸢gi⸣-izi-lá-šè

No. 972 l. 86: bá[ppir > š[im

No. 975 ll. 1–6:
(1.) [0.3.3 zì-gu-sig$_5$]
(2.) [1.0.0. zì-gu-ús gur]
(3.) [0.3.3 da]bin
(4.) [0.0.4].5 sìla zì-KAL
(5.) [0.1.0.0 sila$_3$ sìla zì-ku]m-sig$_5$
(6.) [ninda]-šè

No. 975 l. 11 read: [níĝ-ì]-dé-[a]-šè

No. 975 l. 23: báppir > šim

No. 975 l. 42: TÚG-NI-[(x?) ú]r > TÚG-NI [ku-ú]r

No. 975 l. 48: u$_4$ > iti

No. 985 l. 2: [n] > [7]

No. 992 l. 1 read: [1 sìla] dabin, l. 2 read: [½ sìla] eša

No. 1011 l. 15 read: mu udug kislaḫ saḫar ~ zi-zi-dè-šè

No. 1014 l. '11 read: [tu$_7$] ba-a-⸢si⸣

No. 1018 l. 2 read: 0.0.1. zì-gu-ús

No. 1022 l. 7: zag > zà

No. 1022 l. 13 read: 5 sìla <še->ninda

No. 1024 l. 1 read: [n.n.]2. še-ninda ⸢gur⸣

No. 1025 l. 1: šim-sig$_5$ > báppir-sig$_5$

No. 1025 l. 91: é-é-z[i(-?)] > é-é-⸢zi⸣

No. 1029 l. '9: zi-[x?] > zi-[ga?]

No. 1029 l. '17 read: sa gi$_4$-gi$_4$ a[ka? x?]

No. 1029 l. '20: sum túl-túl > sum-túl-túl

No. 1030 l. 5: PA-è > pa-è

No. 1030 l. 39: èr > ér

No. 1031 l. 12 read: ba-ab-taḫ-a

No. 1048 l. 5 read: gú-ba kíĝ bí-na

No. 1116 l. 1 read: tuḫ-ḫád-⌜gen⌝ ⌜gur⌝

No. 1149 l. 5: sù > sú

No. 1162 l. '18: si-bar > bar:si

No. 1178 l. 8 and No. 1361 l. 10 read: u_4-um-de_6

No. 1189 l. 5 read: gi-zi!(GI_4)-bi

No. 1235 l. 5 read: ki *i-dì-èr-ra*-ta

No. 1282 l. 2: ^gi^dur > ^gi^gilim

No. 1287 l. 1, No. 1293 l. 3: ^g̃eš^ká > g̃eš-ká

No. 1300 l. 10 read: 10 dug 0.0.3.-ta

No. 1312 l. 2: gi-ma-⌜sab⌝ > ^gi^ma-⌜sab⌝

No. 1334 l. 4 and No. 1369 l. 4: éše > éš

No. 1342 ll. 1, 4: ^g̃eš^maš DI > ^g̃eš^maš-sá

No. 1354 l. 1 read: 2 pa ^g̃eš^kíg̃

No. 1354 l. 6: in-tar > in-ku_5

No. 1362 l. 19 read: ~ [. . . ^g̃eš^]kíg̃-tur

No. 1374 l. 2: 120 > 150

No. 1382 ll. 2, 5, 6, 11, 14: uš > ús

No. 1382 l. 15: a-da-bi-ta > a-da-ga-ta

No. 1383 l. 2 read: [. . .]-ša i_7 ~ dù-a

No. 1466 ll. 2, 8, 11: *ma-la-núm* > *ma-la-lum*

No. 1466 l. 15: in-tar-ru-ús-sa > in-ku_5-ru-ús-sa

No. 1470 l. 69: ta-ni-a > làl-lì-a

No. 1471 ll. 1, 13: *ma-la-núm* > *ma-la-lum*

No. 1485 l. 67: *ma-la-núm* > *ma-la-lum*

No. 1488 ll. 4, 5: ri-ri-ga > de_5-de_5-ga

No. 1517 l. 6: ^g̃eš^gu-za árad > ^g̃eš^gu-za-níta

No. 1517 l. 6: ^g̃eš^túg-túg > ^g̃eš^ku!(TÚG)-ku!(TÚG)

No. 374 Revised

374. CUNES 52-04-079 date: -- -- --
not sealed; no envelope
tablet (beginning of obv. lost)
('1.) [. . .] x [. . .]
('2.) [á]-bi u_4 2?-[kam]
('3.) [n] ^gi^ig-x(dur??)
('4.) [n+]3 kùš dag̃al 1⅔ kùš [x]
('5.) [gi]-bi 3 sa
('6.) ⌜peš⌝-múrgu-bi x?

('7.) á-bi u$_4$-1-kam
('8.) 1 ^{gi}*ba-ti-um* búr 3-sìla
('9.) gi-bi x x IB?
('10.) búr x x ma-x
('11.) x x [x . . .]
('12.) [á-bi u$_4$]–3-[kam]
(rest of obv. lost)
(beginning of rev. lost)
('13.) [. . .] x x [. . .]
('14.) [. . .]-da-tur x x x
~ nu-ub-kíĝ
('15.) [n+]½ kùš daĝal 1 kùš [x]
('16.) [gi]-bi 3 sa
('17.) [. . .]-bi x? 1
('18.) [á-bi] u$_4$-1½-kam
('19.) [. . .] ^{gi}gur-bi-kam
('20.) [. . .] x [. . .]
(rest of the rev. lost)

No. 555 should be CUNES 49-08-008
Replace with:
CUNES 49-08-008 date: y z -- not sealed; no envelope tablet

(1.) 10.0.0. še gur [. . .]
(2.) 3.3.0.gur [. . .]
(3.) 2.0.0. gur bà[d-. . .]
(4.) uri$_5$^{ki}-[. . .]
(5.) 4.3.0.gur á-[. . .]
(6.) 1.0.0 gur lugal-k[a?-. . .]
(7.) 1.0.0 gur *ma-aš-⌜rum⌝*
(8.) 1.0.0. gur á-ĝeš-u?
(9.) 0.1.0 *la-qì-ip* ^{lú}ázlag
(10.) 0.2.0. má-gín sugal$_7$-maḫ
(11.) 8.0.0 gur iti–4-kam
(12.) *a-bu-um-ilum*
(13.) 12.0.0. gur *a-bu-um-ilum*
~ lú-kab-šu^{ki}
(14.) 17.3.2. gur
(15.) ur-^{d}en-líl-lá
(16.) [n.n.n.] gur sa$_{10}$-é-ama-tu
(17.) [. . .] nar?-^{d}inanna
~[. . . ^{d}PI]RIG.UNU.GAL
(rev. 18.) [. . .]-x
(19.) [. . .]
(20.) [. . .] gur
(21.) [. . .]-ga
(22.) [. . . n]3.2. gur

(23.) [. . .-b]i a-
(24.) [šu+níĝin n+]7.0.0. gur še-ba
~ba-zi-tum
(25.) šu+níĝin 47.1.[n.] še-ba é
(26.) BLANK LINE
(27.) BLANK LINE
(28.) [šu+níĝin 60+]31.1.5 ⸢gur⸣
(29.) BLANK LINE
(30.) šà gar-ša-[an-na^{ki}]
(31.) BLANK LINE
(side 32.) BLANK

No. 1400, CUNES 49-09–148 is a small fragment reading:
(obv. mostly lost)
('1.)^{d}*ma-lik-ba-[ni]*
(rev. '2.) [šu ba]-an-ti
(rest of the rev. lost)

Bibliography

Adams, Robert McC.

2008. "An Interdisciplinary Overview of a Mesopotamian City and its Hinterland." *CDLJ* 2008:1 1–23.

Attinger, Pascal.

1993. *Eléments de linguistique sumérienne. La construction de* du_{11}*/e/di <<dire>>*. Göttingen: Vandenhoeck & Ruprecht.

2005. "A propos de AK 'faire.'" *ZA* 95, 46–64 and 208–275.

Bauer, Josef.

1992. "^{ĝiš}NE.DU.KU." *AoN* 45.

Braun-Holzinger, Eva A.

1989. "REC 447. LÁ = Libationsbecher." *ZA* 79, 1–7.

Brunke, Hagan.

2008. *Essen in Sumer - Metrologie, Herstellung und Terminologie nach Zeugnis der Ur III-zeitlichen Wirtschaftsurkunden*. Ph.D. dissertation, Ludwig-Maximilians-Universität.

Forthcoming. "The *nakabtum*—An Administrative Superstructure for the Storage and Distribution of Agricultural Products." *Kaskal*.

Carroué, François.

1986. "Le 'Cours-d'Eau-Allant-à-NINA^{ki}.'" *ASJ* 8, 13–58.

Civil, Miguel.

1961. "Une nouvelle prescription médicale sumérienne." *RA* 55, 91–94.

1985. "On Some Texts Mentioning Ur-Namma (Tab. VI)." *OrNS* 54, 27–45.

1994. *The Farmer's Instructions. A Sumerian Agricultural Manual*. Sabadell: Editorial Ausa.

Crawford. Vaughn Emerson.

1948. *Terminology of the Leather Industry in Late Sumerian Times*. Ph.D. dissertation, Yale University.

Englund, Robert K.

2003. "Worcester Slaughterhouse Account." *CDLB* 2003:1.

Frayne, Douglas R.

2008. *Presargonic Period* (2700–2350 BC). Toronto: University of Toronto Press.

Gabbay, Uri.

Forthcoming. "*takribtum* in Garšana." In *Garšana Studies.* CUSAS 6. Ed. David I. Owen. Bethesda: CDL Press.

Gomi, T., Y. Hirose and K. Hirose.

1992. *Neo-Sumerian Administrative Texts of the Hirose Collection.* Bethesda: CDL Press.

Heimpel, Wolfgang.

1986. "Review of Sigrist: Textes économiques néo-sumériens de l'université de Syracuse." *JAOS* 106, 565.

1994. "ne-sağ." NABU n. 83, 72.

1998. "A Circumambulation Rite." *ASJ* 20, 13–16.

2003. "gu-nigin$_2$, 'bale'." *CDLN* 2003:003.

2004. "AO 7667 and the Meaning of ba-an-gi$_4$." *CDLJ* 2004:1.

2008. *Workers and Construction Work in Garšana.* CUSAS 5. Bethesda: CDL Press.

Forthcoming. "Trees and Orchards in the Garšana Archives." In *Garšana Studies.* CUSAS 6. Ed. David I. Owen. Bethesda: CDL Press.

Hilgert, Markus.

2003. *Drehem Administrative Documents from the Reign of Amar-Suena.* OIP 121. Chicago: Oriental Institute Publications.

Krebernik, M.

1986. "Die Götterlisten aus Fara." *ZA* 76, 161–204.

Lafont, B.

1992. "La tablette ITT II 944." *NABU* n. 57, 43–44.

Lambert, W.G.

1976–80. "Kabta." *RlA* 5, 284.

1990. "The Names of Umma." *JNES* 49, 75–80.

Mander, P.

1986. *Il Pantheon di Abu-Salabikh, Contributo allo studio del pantheon sumerico arcaico.* Naples: IUO Series Minor.

Marchesi, G.

2002. "On the Divine Name ^{d}BA.Ú." *OrNS* 71, 161–172.

Molina, M. and M. Such-Gutierrez.

2004. "On Terms for Cutting Plants and Noses in Ancient Sumer." *JNES* 63, 1–16.

Owen, David. I.

1997. "Ur III Geographical and Prosopographical Notes." In *Crossing Boundaries and Linking Horizons: Studies in Honor of Michael C. Astour on His 80th Birthday*. Eds. G. Young, M. Chavalas, and R. Averbeck. Bethesda: CDL Press, 367–398.

2006. "Pigs and Pig By-Products at Garšana." In *De la domestication au tabou: le cas des suidés dans le Proche-Orient ancien*. Eds. B. Lion and C. Michel. Paris: Diffusion De Boccard, 75–87.

2009. *Uprovenanced Texts Primarily from Iri-Sag̃rig/Āl-Šarrākī and the History of the Ur III Period* (NISABA 15), Messina: Di.Sc.A.M.

Powell, M.

1976. "Evidence for Local Cults at Presargonic Zabala." *OrNS* 45, 100–104.

Röllig, W. and H. Waetzoldt.

1993–1997. "Möbel." *RlA* 8, 325–330.

Rubio, Gonzalo.

2001. "Inanna and Dumuzi: A Sumerian Love Story." *JAOS* 12, 268–274.

Sallaberger, Walter.

1989. "Zum Schilfrohr als Rohstoff in Babylonien." In *Der orientalische Mensch und seine Beziehungen zur Umwelt*. Ed. B. Scholz. Graz: GrazKult, 311–330.

1993. *Der kultische Kalender der Ur III-Zeit*. Berlin, New York: Walter de Gruyter.

1996. *Der Babylonische Töpfer und seine Gefässe*. Ghent: University of Ghent. (Mesopotamian History and Enviornment Series II Memoirs III).

2003. "Nachrichten an den Palast von Ebla. Eine Deutung von Níg̃-MUL-(AN)." In *Semitic and Assyriological Studies Presented to Pelio Fronzaroli by Pupils and Colleagues*. Ed. P. Marrassini. Wiesdbaden: Harrrassowitz, 600–625.

Salonen, Armas.

1970. *Die Fischerei im Alten Mesopotamien nach sumerisch-akkadischen Quellen*. Helsinki: Suomalaisen Kirjallisuuden Kirjapaino Oy.

Sauren, H.

1969. "Untersuchungen zur Schrift- und Lautlehre der neusumerischen Urkunden aus Nippur." *ZA* 59, 11–64.

1970. "Les fêtes néo-sumériennes et leur périodicité." In *Actes de la XVII Rencontre assyriologique internationale*. Ed. A. Finet. Ham-sur-Heure: Comité belge de recherches en Mésopotamie, 11–29.

Selz, Gerhard J.

1992. "Eine Kultstatue der Herrschergemaḫlin Šaša: ein Beitrag zum Problem der Vergöttlichung." *ASJ* 14, 245–268.

1993. *Altsumerische Wirtschaftsurkunden aus Amerikanischen Sammlungen*. FAOS 15/2. Stuttgart: Franz Steiner Verlag.

1995. *Untersuchungen zum Götterwelt des altsumerischen Stadtstaates von Lagaš*. Philadelphia: Occasional Publications of the Samuel Noah Kramer Fund; 13.

1997. "TÙN = tùn bei Gudea." *NABU* n. 36, 32–34.

Sigrist, Marcel.

1981. "Le Travail des Cuirs et Peaux à ĜEŠ.KÚŠU sous la Dynastie d'Ur III." *JCS* 33, 141–190.

1984. *Neo-Sumerian Account Texts in the Horn Archaeological Museum.* AUCT 1. Berrien Springs, Mich.: Andrews University Press.

1992. *Drehem.* Bethesda: CDL Press.

Snell, Daniel C.

1987. "The Ur III Tablets in the Emory University Museum." *ASJ* 9, 203–276.

Steinkeller, Piotr.

1978. "On the Reading and Meaning of a-ZAR-la." *RA* 72, 73–76.

1980. "Mattresses and Meshwork in Early Mesopotamia." *OA* 19, 79–100.

1982a. "On the Reading and Meaning of igi-kár and gúrum(IGI.ĜAR)." ASJ 4, 149–151.

1982b. "Two Sargonic Sale Documents Concerning Women (tab. XXXI)." *OrNS* 51, 355–368.

1985. "Three Assyriological Notes." *ASJ* 7, 195–196.

1987. "Review of The Sumerian Dictionary of the Unversity of Pennyslvania. Vol. 2 B. Edited by Åke W. Sjöberg with the collaboration of H. Behrens, B.L. Eichler, M. W. Green, E. Leichty and D.M. Loding." *JNES* 46, 55–59.

1989. *Sale Documents of the Ur III Period.* Franz Steiner Verlag: Stuttgart.

1993. "Review of A. Westenholz, Old Sumerian and Old Akkadian Texts in Philadelphia, Part 2: The 'Akkadian' Texts, the Enlilemaba Texts, and the Onion Archive." *JNES* 52, 141–145.

1995. "Sheep and Goat Terminology in Ur III Sources from Drehem." *BSA* 8, 49–70.

2004. "Studies in Third Millennium Paleography, 4: Sign KIŠ." *ZA* 94, 175–185.

Steinkeller, P. and J.N. Postgate.

1992. *Third Millennium Legal and Administrative Texts in the Iraq Museum, Baghdad.* Winona Lake, Ind.: Eisenbrauns.

Stępień, Marek.

1996. *Animal Husbandry in the Ancient Near East: A Prosopographic Study of Third-Millennium Umma.* Bethesda, Md. CDL Press.

Stol, Martin.

1980–83. "Leder(industrie)." *RlA* 6, 527–543.

1991. "Old Babylonian Personal Names." *SEL* 8, 191–212.

van de Mieroop, Marc.

1987. *Crafts in the Early Isin Period.* OLA 24. Leuven: Departement Oriëntalistiek.

Waetzoldt, Hartmut.

1972. *Untersuchungen zur Neusumerischen Textilindustrie.* Roma: Centro per le Antichità e la Storia Dell'Arte del Vicino Oriente.

1992. "'Rohr' und dessen Verwendungsweisen anhand der neusumerischen Texte ĜEŠ.KÚŠU." *BSA* 6, 125–146.

Waetzoldt, H. and M. Sigrist.

1993. "Haftung mit Privatvermögen bein Nicht-Erfüllung von Dienstverpflichtungen." In *The Tablet and the Scroll: Near Eastern Studies in honor of Wiliam W. Hallo*. Ed. M.E. Cohen, D.C. Snell and D.B. Weisberg. Bethesda, Md.: CDL Press, 271–280.

Westenholz, Joan Goodnick.

1997. "Nanaya: Lady of Mystery." In *Sumerian Gods and their Representations*. CM 7. Ed. I.L. Finkel and M.J. Geller. Groningen: STYX Publications.

Yamamoto, S.

1981. "The lú-KUR$_6$-dab$_5$-ba People in the é-mí—é-^{d}Ba-Ú in Pre-Sargonic Lagash." *ASJ* 3, 93–110.

Yoshikawa, M.

1993. "The ĜEŠ.KÚŠU Terminology (II)." *ASJ* 15, 300–302.

Cornell University Studies in Assyriology and Sumerology
(CUSAS)

David I. Owen, Editor-in-chief

CUSAS 1: *The Cornell University Archaic Tablets*
Salvatore Monaco. 2007. Pp. xiv + 370. ISBN 978-1934309-001

CUSAS 2: *Sumerian Proverbs in the Schøyen Collection*
Bendt Alster. 2007. Pp. xvi + 156. ISBN 978-1934309-018

CUSAS 3: *The Garšana Archives*
David I. Owen and Rudolf H. Mayr with the assistance of Alex Kleinerman. 2007. Pp. xii + 528. ISBN 978-1934309-025

CUSAS 4: *Analytical Concordance to the Garšana Archives*
Alexandra Kleinerman and David I. Owen. 2009. Pp. x + 795. ISBN 978-1934309-032

CUSAS 5: *Workers and Construction Work at Garšana*
Wolfgang Heimpel. 2009. Pp. xx + 380. ISBN 978-1934309-049

CUSAS 9: *Babylonian Tablets from the First Sealand Dynasty in the Schøyen Collection*
Stephanie Dalley. 2009. Pp. xviii + 320. Pl. 182. ISBN 978-1934309-087

CUSAS 10: *Babylonian Literary Texts in the Schøyen Collection*
A. R. George. 2009. Pp. xx + 160. Pl. 62. ISBN 978-1934309-094

In Preparation

CUSAS 6: *Garšana Studies*
David I. Owen

CUSAS 7: *Seal Impressions and Sealing Practices in the Garšana Archives*
Rudolf H. Mayr

CUSAS 8: *A Late Old Babylonian Temple Archive from Dūr-Abiešuḫ*
Karel van Lerberghe and Gabriella Voet

CUSAS *Private Enterprise in Babylonia at the End of the Third Millennium B.C.E.*
Steven J. Garfinkle

CUSAS *Cuneiform Texts in the Karl A. Kroch Library, Cornell University*
Marcel Sigrist, with Nicole Brisch, Alhena Gadotti, and David I. Owen

CUSAS *The Columbia University Tablets*
Steven J. Garfinkle and Marc van de Mieroop

CUSAS *Early Dynastic and Early Sargonic Tablets from Adab in the Cornell University Collections*
Giuseppe Visicato and A. Westenholz

CUSAS *Middle Sargonic Tablets in the Cornell University Collections*
M. Elena Milone and F. Pomponio

CUSAS *Classical and Late Sargonic Tablets in the Cornell University Collections*
Massimo Maiocchi

CUSAS *The Late Sargonic "mu-iti" Tablets in the Cornell University Collections*
Amadeo Alberti and P. Notizia